GROUNDWATER IN THE URBAN ENVIRONMENT
VOLUME 1: PROBLEMS, PROCESSES AND MANAGEMENT

PROCEEDINGS OF THE XXVII IAH CONGRESS ON GROUNDWATER IN THE URBAN
ENVIRONMENT / NOTTINGHAM / UK / 21-27 SEPTEMBER 1997

Groundwater in the Urban Environment

Edited by
JOHN CHILTON et al.
British Geological Survey, Wallingford, UK

VOLUME 1: Problems, Processes and Management

A.A.BALKEMA / ROTTERDAM / BROOKFIELD / 1997

The texts of the various papers in this volume were set individually by typists under the supervision of each of the authors concerned.

Authorization to photocopy items for internal or personal use, or the internal or personal use of specific clients, is granted by A.A.Balkema, Rotterdam, provided that the base fee of US$1.50 per copy, plus US$0.10 per page is paid directly to Copyright Clearance Center, 222 Rosewood Drive, Danvers, MA 01923, USA. For those organizations that have been granted a photocopy license by CCC, a separate system of payment has been arranged. The fee code for users of the Transactional Reporting Service is: 90 5410 837 1/97 US$1.50 + US$0.10.

Published by
A.A.Balkema, P.O.Box 1675, 3000 BR Rotterdam, Netherlands (Fax: +31.10.413.5947)
A.A.Balkema Publishers, Old Post Road, Brookfield, VT 05036-9704, USA (Fax: 802.276.3837)

For the complete set of two volumes, ISBN 90 5410 837 1
For Volume 1, ISBN 90 5410 923 8
For Volume 2, ISBN 90 5410 924 6

INTERNATIONAL ASSOCIATION OF HYDROGEOLOGISTS
XXVII CONGRESS

ORGANISERS

International Association of Hydrogeologists (British National Committee)
in association with:

 British Geological Survey
(Hydrogeology Group)

 Golder Associates

 Geological Society of London
(Hydrogeology Group)

SPONSORS

 Overseas Development Administration

 UNESCO – Division of Water Sciences

  WHO/UNEP Global Environment Monitoring System

 Severn Trent Water

Entec Entec Europe Ltd

NIREX NIREX-UK Ltd

 Environment Agency

Table of contents

2 *Geotechnical and construction problems*

3 *Water supply experiences*

5 Groundwater management and urban planning

Preface

This volume represents a major part of the proceedings of the International Association of Hydrogeologists XXVII Congress, to be held at the East Midlands Conference Centre in Nottingham-UK during 22-26 September 1997.

The congress and this volume, focus on the theme 'Groundwater in the Urban Environment'. When the IAH British National Committee presented their bid to stage the IAH 1997 Congress in Oslo-Norway in June 1993, the 'urban crisis' was just emerging on the international environmental agenda into the 21st Century, and the role and behaviour of groundwater in this context was just beginning to be seriously discussed. In the intervening period it has become clear that urban water-related issues have rapidly become a predominant and unprecedented challenge of environmental management, given that by the year 2000 about 50% of the world's population will be urban dwellers.

In the rapidly-developing cities of Asia, Latin America and Africa the urban explosion is being accompanied by uncontrolled groundwater abstraction and by indiscriminate solid and liquid waste disposal to the ground, with the result of increasing scarcity and deteriorating quality of groundwater. These cause escalating water-supply costs and can pose serious threats to human health.

In the developed world, where urban growth is stabilising, the industrial legacy of contaminated land represents a serious groundwater pollution threat and may be a significant contributor to inner-city decline. In addition, the abandonment of groundwater abstraction in the central parts of some cities, as a consequence of deteriorating quality and/or changing demand pattern, is leading to rising groundwater levels which threaten urban infrastructure.

This volume includes 8 keynote presentations highlighting the main issues related to the more sustainable use of the ground for water-supply and waste disposal within the urban environment. A further 110 papers are published in this volume, compiled under the 5 topics addressed by the congress. Some of the key questions under each topic are given below:

1. *Urban Groundwater Processes*. How does groundwater recharge occur? What methods can be used to quantify recharge? What are the key controls over groundwater recharge quality?

2. *Geotechnical and Construction Problems*. To what extent do subsurface structures act as barriers or conduits for groundwater flow? What are the impacts of groundwater on urban buildings and subsurface infrastructure, and how can they be predicted?

3. *Water-Supply Experiences*. What are the main advantages, principal problems and main limitations of groundwater as a resource to meet different types of urban water demand?

4. *Groundwater Pollution Hazards*. What are the impacts of on-site sanitation, drainage soakaways, leaking sewers and wastewater reuse for irrigation? How can the spread of contamination from industrial sites, underground storage facilities and waste disposal landfills be assessed and predicted? What can be done to control and to ameliorate these various impacts?

5. *Groundwater Management and Urban Planning.* What are the dangers of ignoring ground-water in urban environmental management? How can consideration of groundwater be better incorporated into the urban planning process?

The remainder of the papers submitted to, and presented at, the congress will be published in a second volume (appearing in 1998, and dealing exclusively with international city case surveys and studies). This will be entitled: 'Groundwater in the Urban Environment – Selected City Profiles'.

Finally, I must acknowledge the generosity of the financial sponsors of the IAH XXVII Congress, without whose contribution both the event and this publication would not have been possible. They are individually identified on page V.

I also wish to congratulate the editorial team for a very professional effort. Undertaking pre-publication of congress proceedings is always a formidable task, but under the extremely able direction of the principal editor, John Chilton of the British Geological Survey-Hydrogeology Group, they have taken 118 papers submitted to the congress under topics 1-5, from initial submission to final camera-ready copy within four months. It is very much my hope, and theirs, that the congress delegates, IAH members and the reader in general, find this volume useful in addressing the problems posed in managing groundwater in the urban environment.

Prof. Dr Stephen Foster
British Geological Survey, Assistant Director
IAH British National Committee, Chair

Nottingham, June 1997

Foreword

As Chair of the Editorial Sub-Committee of the IAH XXVII Congress, I would like to thank all my colleagues on the editorial programme sub-committees who shared the task of editing. The large overall subject area of 'Groundwater in the Urban Environment' was divided into six topics, of which five are compiled into the present volume. These topic co-editors are listed below and appear at the beginning of each of the five topics in this volume.

Topic 1: Kevin Hiscock, University of East Anglia,
     Paul Younger, University of Newcastle;

Topic 2: Brian Morris, British Geological Survey,
     Shaminder Puri, Scott Wilson Kirkpatrick;

Topic 3: Harriet Nash, Wardell Armstrong,
     Phil Aldous, Thames Water;

Topic 4: John Tellam, University of Birmingham,
     Richard Kimblin, CES;

Topic 5: Sue Hennings, Environment Agency,
     John Chilton, British Geological Survey.

All of the submitted manuscripts were read by at least one of the topic editors, and most were read and commented on by both. Bringing a total of 118 papers to readiness for camera-ready processing to meet the deadline to allow pre-publication has been a tremendous task, and I would like to thank all members of the editorial team for their efforts. I would also like to thank the authors, who made our task easier by taking account of our comments on early drafts of the papers and by doing their best to follow the publishers instructions.

In addition to the formal editorial team, a number of colleagues in the Hydrogeology Group of the British Geological Survey assisted in the final stages of editing by checking camera-ready papers and by reading those on which extensive editorial effort was required. I would like, therefore, to thank Marianne Stuart, Jeff Davies, Brian Adams, Nick Robins, Dave Kinniburgh, Bob Shearer and Richard Marks for their careful and prompt help with this. A relatively small number of papers required substantial editorial work, and my grateful thanks go to Hydrogeology Group colleagues Sam Fairhurst for scanning, editing and layout and Marianne Stuart for additional editing and layout.

John Chilton
British Geological Survey

Wallingford, July 1997

Keynote papers

Perspectives on innovations and solutions for groundwater management

Chris Barber
Centre for Groundwater Studies & CSIRO Land and Water, Perth, W.A., Australia

ABSTRACT: Groundwater management should be based on sound science. The role of the scientist in this paradigm is to address perceived problems and develop solutions for uptake by resource managers. Management can then evolve by incorporating scientific developments into an overall strategy to achieve best-available-practice. Technology uptake is crucial, often not actively pursued during research programs, and consequently this is often not effective. Three Australian examples of varying maturity are presented to illustrate the difficulties, although it is believed that these are illustrative of a worldwide problem. Dryland salinity has long been problematic in southern Australia, and the need for broad guidelines on vulnerability assessment more recently identified. Solutions to both have been formulated, but in both cases managers are struggling with implementation. VOCs are a relatively new problem, and the need for monitoring of even minute quantities of these poses significant problems. New technology may help reduce these, and provide more cost-effective monitoring and clean-up of contamination, but this requires researchers changing significantly the way site investigations and monitoring are carried out. It is argued that resource managers and scientists need to work together to achieve more effective technology transfer and better groundwater management. At least as much time needs to be spent on translation of research outcomes into management tools during research programs, as is spent on research itself.

1 INTRODUCTION

Management of our groundwater systems of necessity should be underpinned by sound science. By nature, management strategies should also be evolutionary and adaptive. In this way, best-available practice is maintained as groundwater resource managers continually take up scientific developments and innovations as these become available and relevant. The plethora of papers dealing with groundwater management and protection in the open literature over the last few decades indicates that significant scientific endeavour has taken place. However, it is less clear whether the rate of uptake of technology has been adequate for resource managers to keep pace with new developments. Clearly in some cases there have been notable successes (eg with information technology, GIS and other computer-based systems). In others, it seems that the pace of change has been less than spectacular, and we could have done much better in identifying problem areas and developing and applying solutions.

Australia, one of the driest continents, has significant water resource and environmental management problems as well as a very able and active research community. Unlike a number of other developed countries, Australia is not overly reliant on groundwater for domestic supplies, with only approximately 18% of water use coming from groundwater resources. Despite low groundwater use in the past, there has been a very strong interest in groundwater in relation to environmental management generally, and more specifically to combat land degradation, for maintenance of healthy ecosystems, as well as for protection and maintenance of potable water resources.

There have been mixed results with transfer or uptake of technological developments, and it seems likely that this experience is more general worldwide. Three examples are given below of scientific and technological advances and innovative solutions to problems in Australia, to illustrate at least some of these mixed results. These are issues which relate to dryland (non-irrigated) salinity which started to emerge in Australia in the last century in response to clearing of native vegetation (Peck et al, 1983). This has had a major impact on water resources supplying cities and rural towns in southern parts of the continent. Decades of research and investigation has been carried out to provide an understanding of the problem and to indicate possible solutions. A second issue deals with the protection of groundwater quality against pollution by inappropriate land use developments, particularly urbanisation. The need for and use of vulnerability assessment procedures and wellhead and capture zone protection will be considered here. Thirdly, the problem of volatile organic compounds (VOCs) will be discussed, and the uptake of new technology which could revolutionise the way we monitor groundwater in future.

2 SCIENCE AND GROUNDWATER MANAGEMENT

2.1 Impact of dryland (non-irrigated) salinity on urban water supplies

Salinisation of land and previously potable streamflow has become a major environmental problem in southern Australia. In a recent review (Anon, 1996) it was reported that more than one third of the potable yield from surface waters in the southwest of the state of Western Australia was already brackish or saline, and a further 16% was only of marginal quality as a result of man-induced dryland salinity. This has severely limited any ability to use these resources for potable supplies for urban and rural populations.

Peck and Williamson (1987) and Williamson et al (1987) report that extensive clearing and replacement of deep rooted, perennial eucalyptus vegetation, woodland and savannah scrubland by shallow rooted annual crops and pasture in agricultural regions in Western Australia, had modified the hydrological balance and increased the rate of groundwater recharge at the expense of evapotranspiration. The combination of increased recharge, saline subsoil profiles and brackish or saline groundwater had given rise to increased discharge of water and salts and consequent land and stream salinisation. Better management of groundwater in these catchments is consequently the key to reducing the overall problem.

Despite very early recognition of a potentially large problem, it was not until the 1960's that the state government in Western Australia became concerned over increased salinity in streams in the southwest, particularly in the Collie River Basin,

which provided potable supplies to a wide area in the southwest of the state. In response to this concern, a research program involving paired catchment studies was set up to help define the causes of the problem and identify possible ways of managing and reducing the impacts, particularly on surface freshwater resources which were actual or potential urban supplies. Parts of this extensive study were reported in Peck and Williamson (1983). They concluded that "the study has been successful in providing a sound basis for future management of salinity in the region".

Early attempts at amelioration of salinity focussed on reducing groundwater discharge, which addressed the symptom of the overall problem rather than the cause - increased groundwater recharge. More recently, and with considerable enthusiasm, communities and agencies have accepted that to manage groundwater and reduce the risk of salinisation, there is a need to reduce groundwater recharge at the catchment scale. Again, relatively simple strategies have been developed to promote planting of commercial, perennial woody plant species. The general trend has been towards developing simplistic management strategies with minimal investigation and evaluation, rather than developing broad-scale methodologies for evaluation of diagnostics of the problem. Consequently, the impact of overly-simplistic schemes for managing salinity has been minimal, and the recommendations of the science community (at least partly) have been ignored.

It is arguable that there is no management panacea for what is a very complex and widespread problem. Clearly, most effort has been put into assessing and understanding the problem and nowhere near enough into translating this into practical solutions which are acceptable to the community generally. The recently published Salinity Action Plan (Government of Western Australia, 1996) summarises the current situation. "If all economically feasible water management practices and integration technologies were extensively adopted, a high degree of salinity control could be confidently achieved only in the high rainfall south-west region".

2.2 Groundwater Quality Protection

Many countries have developed strategies for protection of groundwater, as in Australia. In the latter case, these measures (guidelines) are part of the National Water Quality Management Strategy

4

(ARMCANZ/ANZECC, 1995). The guidelines provide a framework for states and territories to develop policies and strategies tailored to their specific legislative and resource management needs.

Guidelines for protection of groundwater are based on prescribed beneficial uses (raw water for drinking, ecosystem protection, recreation and aesthetics, water for agriculture, water for industry). Various approaches and measures for groundwater protection are described including groundwater management plans, vulnerability assessment, aquifer classification systems, wellhead protection systems and action levels (ARMCANZ/ANZECC, 1995).

The assessment, application and interpretation of groundwater vulnerability, are subjects of considerable debate in current literature. Federal agencies have funded research aimed at evaluating existing approaches and developing alternatives (eg see Barber et al, 1993). Perhaps the most widely used (or misused) technique is the DRASTIC system developed in the US (Aller et al, 1985). Evaluation of this scheme in a rural catchment (the Peel catchment in northern NSW) showed that although the scheme provided a general indication of vulnerability (assessed in relation to known levels of nitrate - a ubiquitous contaminant in the area), there were significant drawbacks to the methodologies for developing vulnerability maps, and particularly for their use by non-specialists. The approach, designed to assess the potential impact of contaminants in general, was inadequate for contaminants which behave conservatively, as is the case with nitrate in the Peel catchment. Here, nitrogen loading on land was a critical factor

determining nitrate in groundwater, and the hydrogeological setting (characterised using DRASTIC) was unimportant. Over 70% of wells adjacent to sites where land-spreading of wastes was carried out from intensive animal rearing, showed groundwater with high nitrate. An additional difficulty with developing a DRASTIC map was the cost (time and money) in obtaining spatial data for all seven parameters used in the scheme, and the subjectivity involved in arriving at DRASTIC scores for any one hydrogeological setting.

Attempts to develop less subjective assessments (the weights-of-evidence approach) have been made (Barber et al, 1993). It is interesting that vulnerability maps produced using this approach in the Peel catchment were generally comparable to those developed using the DRASTIC methodology, at least for the western and central parts of the study area which contained the most important aquifers (see Figure 1). An evaluation of all these techniques (Barber and Bates, in press) concluded that although there are a number of widely different ways of assessing vulnerability, they all devolve to a common set of parameters which govern pollutant transport, and consequently all arrive at broadly similar relative vulnerabilities for a given area. The principal problem is thus with application of these, and particularly with the level of interpretation of vulnerability maps.

Several papers emphasise that vulnerability maps are only guides, and cannot be used prescriptively to replace more detailed impact assessments. In Australia, this advice has been repeatedly given (eg in the above references and in

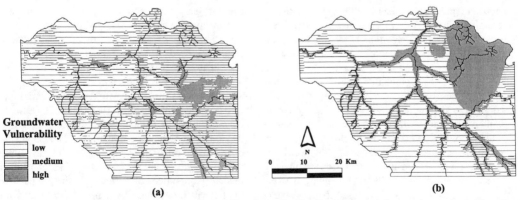

(a)   (b)

Figure 1. Comparison of groundwater vulnerability maps for the Peel River study area in northern New South Wales, Australia (a) produced using the DRASTIC method (b) using the weights-of-evidence method.

5

the National Guidelines by ARMCANZ/ANZECC, 1995). However, as with salinity strategies, there is a need for simple and straightforward guidance for land-use regulation and development. It is inevitable that non-specialist regulators and developers who have been vocal in their support for development of simple tools like vulnerability maps to make their tasks more efficient, will treat these as more definitive than they actually are, rather than as guides, which was the original purpose.

It is apparent from this example that researchers have an educative role, which can only be successfully achieved through a well developed communication plan. In the past, this important aspect of research has not been supported by funding bodies to an extent where it can be fully implemented. However, based on past experience, current research involving vulnerability assessment has adopted a much more proactive stance working closely with collaborators from regulatory agencies to ensure a better appreciation of the appropriate uses and limitations of these methods. It remains to be seen whether this approach will translate into more efficient and effective groundwater management. However, results to date do suggest that vulnerability maps have had a beneficial effect in highlighting the need for groundwater protection.

A different study of land-use impacts on groundwater quality has had more immediate benefits, and again illustrates the benefits of a collaborative approach. This work was a cooperative study between a regulatory authority and funder of research, and a research group, where both groups planned and conducted the work together, to assess impacts of progressive urbanisation on groundwater in a coastal unconfined sand aquifer (Barber et al, 1996). A number of previous studies in this area, the Swan Coastal Plain in Western Australia, had identified the potential for significant degradation of groundwater supplies due to urban development. However, there was still a perception that urban development was compatible with groundwater quality sustainability, as water supply wellfields had been operating apparently successfully for a number of years within this area. The study focussed on the Gwelup wellfield in suburban Perth, where urban development of the wellfield catchment commenced in the late 1950s and was largely completed by the mid 1970s (Figure 2). The time sequence of urban land-use changes were mostly determined from records of water supply and sewer connections. Thus sewered and unsewered (septic tank) residential areas were identified in this way and mapped using a geographic information system (GIS). Additionally, parkland, native bushland, and agricultural and horticultural developments were defined at specific times from aerial photographic records. Well capture zones were determined by modelling (Barber et al, 1996), and these and other coverages were combined using GIS to define the extent and timing of land-use changes within each capture zone. These were compared with available data on trends in groundwater quality in pumping wells (see Figure 2a and 2b).

The study showed that the main threats to potable water supplies were from contamination by volatile organic compounds or VOCs (from spills at fuels storages and from solvents used in light industry primarily) and by nitrate from domestic wastewater disposal through septic tanks and widespread use of fertilisers on parks and gardens.

Water quality data from the Gwelup wellfield was patchy, particularly in the 1980s. The data was also quite noisy due to combined impacts of nitrate stratification in groundwater (high concentrations mostly in the upper part of the aquifer), and variable pumping regimes from production wells screened in the lower part of the aquifer which produce intermittent large drawdowns. Despite this complexity, nitrate concentrations show general trends increasing to above the drinking water standard in the older (southern) area of the wellfield some 20-30 years after completion of urbanisation (Figure 2). This data graphically illustrated the long lead-times required for full development of the nitrate problem. It was also likely that any measures taken to reduce nitrate input to groundwater would also take at least this period before any significant improvement in groundwater quality at the pumping well. This was of more concern to the regulatory authorities, and provided further impetus for the introduction of land-use restrictions in other less urbanised wellfields in this area.

The evidence from earlier studies of potential and actual contamination in urban areas, of nitrate contamination at Gwelup, and more spectacular incidences of VOC contamination and abandonment of three production wells (Barber et al, 1996) provided sufficient evidence for a Parliamentary Select Committee to endorse the need for implementation and strengthening of measures for protection of groundwater source areas in the Perth region (Carew-Hopkins, 1996).

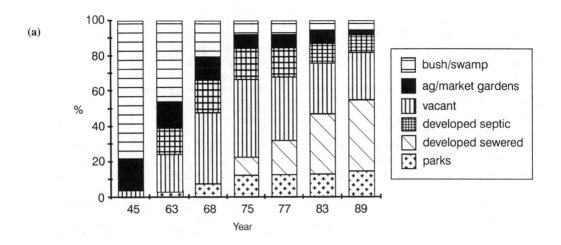

(a)

(b)

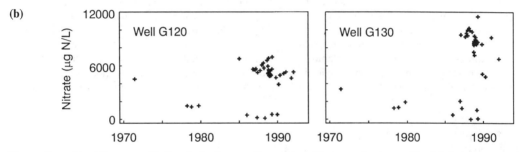

Figures 2a and b. Changes with time in land-use patterns (a) and in groundwater quality (b) during progressive urbanisation of the southern part of the Gwelup wellfield, Western Australia.

The apparent successful outcomes from this and related studies was in part due to the close collaboration between the State Authorities and the researchers at all stages of the work (planning, conducting and reporting research and defining necessary groundwater and land-use management changes). The high degree of "user" input to the research clearly provided a valuable conduit for beneficial change.

2.3 Monitoring of VOCs

Volatile organic compounds (VOCs) such as the BTEX monoaromatics and chlorinated hydro-carbons tri- and perchloroethene (TCE, PCE) are the most prevalent contaminants in groundwater in the US, and probably elsewhere. In most cases, these are derived from leaching of non-aqueous phase liquids (NAPLs) which accumulate in aquifers following leaks and spills of hydrocarbon fuels, solvents and wastes. Pollution plumes from

accumulations of LNAPLs (NAPLs such as oils which are lighter or less dense than water) and denser DNAPLs (solvents like TCE, PCE) can be highly stratified, and in the case of DNAPLs are difficult to identify and monitor. A significant part of the cost of remediation of VOC contamination is for investigation and monitoring.

Monitoring for VOCs in groundwater and soils is not an easy proposition. It is compounded by the need for detection of even low ppb levels of contamination, as drinking water standards for several VOCs are at this level (in Australia the standard for benzene is 1ppb, and for PCE is 30ppb). Groundwater sampling, proper storage, sample preparation and processing and analysis for VOCs is time consuming, labour intensive and costly, and given the analytical sensitivities, false negative and false positive results at these low levels are common.

The above difficulties have prompted development of in situ monitoring devices for

7

VOCs, to help reduce costs and improve overall analytical performance. In the US, fibre-optic chemiluminescence sensors have been developed and commercialised. In Australia, a need for *in situ* monitoring of simple gases and VOCs during remediation was recognised, and devices have been developed for this based on diffusion cell technology (Barber and Briegel, 1987). These are currently being commercialised.

The diffusion cell devices are basically thin-walled hollow-fibre polymer tubes. The tubes are gas filled, and gases and volatiles (in either gaseous, aqueous or NAPL phases) diffuse through the polymer into the internal gas phase, where they can be analysed using various sensors when equilibrium is reached. The diffusion cell concept avoids the problems inherent in conventional sampling/ analysis using monitoring wells (although these devices can be used for *in situ* monitoring in wells). Instead, and for most effective monitoring, several individual probes are buried in boreholes to provide vertical profiles of any subsurface contaminants. Data thus obtained is similar to that provided by multilevel installations which are suited to

investigation of finely stratified plumes typical of VOC contamination. Additionally, remote collection of data and storage on-site in a data logger removes the need for costly, time-consuming site visits.

These devices have been used to obtain daily readings of VOCs in soil and groundwater and determine temporal trends in BTEX plumes, for example during remediation (Figure 3).

Additionally, oxygen has been monitored hourly or less over prolonged periods during bioventing and sparging trials, and to evaluate oxygen utilisation rates which provide essential information for optimising *in situ* remediation (Davis et al, 1995).

It is useful to examine the way the development of these devices has proceeded through to full commercialisation, as these represent new technology which potentially could change significantly the way groundwater monitoring is carried out. As often happens, the technology was developed initially as part of a wider research program investigating volatilisation (of methane) from groundwater (Barber et al, 1990). Some

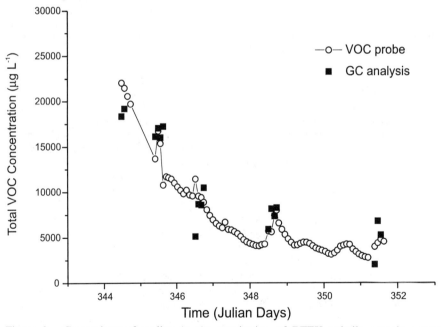

Figure 3. Comparison of on-line *in situ* monitoring of BTEX volatile organic compounds (VOC's) in groundwater using diffusion cell VOC probe with conventional monitoring of samples from the same location followed by gas chromatographic (GC) analysis. Results obtained during an air sparging trial in Western Australia.

further development took place during research on *in situ* remediation, and given the promise of early developments, a research project was set up specifically to help develop the technology further, through the Cooperative Research Centre for Waste Management and Pollution Control Ltd. The latter is one of Australia's new CRCs, which have been set up over the last 5-7 years to help bring research and industry bodies together collaboratively. Following successful early development of the project, the CRC was insistent that commercial partners should be involved in the project, and development through to commercialisation should proceed through direct involvement with commercial partners.

It would seem that the key to the apparent success in developing a commercial product in this case was that almost as much time was spent deliberately on product development and user interaction than on research, once proof-of-concept had been achieved. This was a significant departure from the previous norm, where technology transfer was often an add-on at the end of the project, was often ill-planned and lacked innovation and direction. Proper communication and technology transfer is essential for uptake of this technology which could significantly change the way groundwater monitoring is carried out.

3 SOLUTIONS

The examples above illustrate some of the difficulties encountered with development of innovations which could provide new best-available-practices for groundwater resource management. Although there are clearly some successes, it is abundantly clear that researchers could be less isolationist and allow resource managers to use the results and products of scientific endeavour far more effectively. It is indeed unfortunate that researchers, resource management and consultants (technology users) in the past have been so compartmentalised. Better communication between these groups could only help the development and transfer of ideas, technology and information and provide more focussed research and effective uptake of innovations and advances in our science.

This problem has been identified in federal research funding agencies in Australia, and a number now require to see a plan for technology transfer as part of funding proposals. Although this is clearly a sensible approach, it may need more to

break down the barriers between compartments. By far the most effective way of doing this is by direct involvement of all players in the research process, from planning, through development of a research project to uptake of any advances and possibly beyond.

Attempts have been made in Australia and elsewhere to provide mechanisms to help in this process, through formation of multidisciplinary research centres which provide for direct involvement of researchers, the private sector, resource managers and state agencies. It is arguable whether this limits the scope of research only to "applied" projects at the expense of curiosity-led research, which could lead to starvation of new developments and innovation. However, benefits from this approach are clearly starting to appear.

In the above examples, the most successful projects from the viewpoint of technology uptake, are those where almost as much time and energy is spent on developing innovative ways of achieving uptake during the research program and beyond, than is spent on innovative research.

4 ACKNOWLEDGEMENTS

The helpful discussions with colleagues at CSIRO Land and Water and the Centre for Groundwater Studies in Perth, Western Australia, particularly Margaret Bryant, Lorraine Bates, David Williamson, Greg Davis and Brad Patterson is gratefully acknowledged. Anne McKenzie, Lorraine Bates and Brad Patterson helped with graphics, and Karen Hansen with formatting.

5 REFERENCES

Agriculture and Resource Management Council of Australia and New Zealand and Australian and New Zealand Environment and Conservation Council (ARMCANZ/ANZECC), 1995. National Water Quality Management Strategy - *Guidelines for Groundwater Protection in Australia.* Commonwealth of Australia, September 1995.

Anon, 1996. Salinity - a situation statement for Western Australia. A report to the Ministers for Primary Industry and Minister for the Environment. Prepared by Agriculture WA, Department of Conservation and Land Management, Department of Environmental Protection and Water and Rivers Commission, Western Australia, November 1996.

Barber C, Bates L E, Barron R and Allison H, 1993. Assessment of the relative vulnerability of groundwater to pollution: a review and background paper. *AGSO J. Australian Geol. and Geophys.,* 14 (2/3), 147-154.

Barber C and Bates L E, (in press). Assessing the relative vulnerability of aquifers to pollution: a review of methodologies and recommendations for application of vulnerability mapping in Australia. National Groundwater Committee Special Paper.

Barber C and Briegel, 1987. A method for in situ determination of dissolved methane in groundwater in shallow aquifers. *J. Contam. Hydrol.,* 2, 51-60.

Barber C, Davis G B, Briegel D and Ward J K, 1990. Factors controlling the concentration of methane and other volatiles in groundwater and soil gas around a waste site. *J. Contam. Hydrol.,* 5, 155-169.

Barber C, Otto C J, Bates L E, and Taylor K J, 1996. Evaluation of the relationship between land-use changes and groundwater quality in a water supply catchment, using GIS technology: The Gwelup wellfield, Western Australia. Hydrogeology Journal, 4 (1), 6-19.

Carew-Hopkins, 1996. Findings of the WA Parliamentary Select Committee on Metropolitan Development and Groundwater Supplies. In Proc. Conference on Groundwater and Land-use Planning, 216-227. Australian Centre for Groundwater Studies, September 1996

Davis G B, Johnston C D, Patterson B M, Barber C, Bennett M, Sheehy A, and Dunbavan M, 1995. Monitoring bioremediation of weathered diesel NAPL using oxygen depletion profiles. *Proc. 3rd Intl. Bioreclamation Symposium, San Diego, Calif.,* Battelle, April 1995.

Government of Western Australia, 1996. Western Australia - Salinity Action Plan. Prepared by Agriculture WA, Department of conservation and Land Management, Department of Environmental Protection and the Water and Rivers Commission, Western Australia, November, 1996.

Otto C and Salama R , 1994. Linked enhanced discharge - evaporative disposal systems. In Reeves C and Watts, J (eds), *Groundwater - Drought, Pollution and Management*, Balkema Press, Rotterdam, 1994.

Peck A J, Thomas J F and Williamson D W, 1983. Salinity Issues- effects of man on salinity in Australia. Water 200: Consultants report No. 8, Australian Government Publishing Service, Canberra, 1983.

Peck A J and Williamson D W (eds), 1987. Hydrology and salinity in the Collie River Basin, Western Australia. *J Hydrology, Special Issue, 94* (1/2).

Salama R, Laslett D and Farrington P, 1993. Predictive modelling of management options for the control of dryland salinity in a first-order catchment in the wheatbelt of Western Australia. *J. Hydrol., 145,* 19-40.

Williamson D W, Stokes R A and Ruprecht J K, 1987. Response of input and output of water and chloride to clearing for agriculture. *J Hydrol. Special Issue, 94* (1/2), 1-28.

Groundwater in the Urban Environment: Problems, Processes and Management, Chilton et al. (eds)
© 1997 Balkema, Rotterdam, ISBN 90 5410 837 1

Groundwater quantity and quality changes related to land and water management around urban areas: Blessings and misfortunes

Emilio Custodio

Department of Ground Engineering – CIHS, Polytechnic University of Catalonia, Barcelona, Spain (Presently: Geological and Environmental Institute of Spain, Madrid, Spain)

ABSTRACT: Urban areas affect the behaviour and characteristics of groundwater below and around them. Urbanization produces changes which proceed back and forth. There are no general situations since very diverse local circumstances may play a dominant role, but some common aspects can be drawn together. When aquifer based water supply systems are substituted by surface or imported water to keep pace with urban growth, a period of groundwater level drawdown which lowers the water table is often followed by a period of recovery which may produce water logging of underground spaces and excavations. In some areas this may be balanced by increased recharge due to leakage from water supply networks. Impairment of groundwater quality seems to be the rule but there are exceptions and even improvements, as in coastal aquifers formerly subjected to saline intrusion. Water management decisions such as river regulation, changes in irrigated areas and reuse of treated waste water may affect aquifer water quantity and quality in different ways. Often these aquifers play an essential role for emergency water supply and thus they have to be preserved and carefully operated. Even if these aquifers yield water unsuitable for drinking purposes there are possible uses provided this water is economically acceptable and its abstraction helps to alleviate water logging problems. The case of Barcelona is commented on as an example of a densely populated area.

1 INTRODUCTION

In many urban and peri-urban areas there are cases in which local aquifers are not able to meet the quantity and quality of water needs of the growing population. In other cases the factors which induce unaware water policy makers to discourage groundwater use are the result of poor management, lack of protection and other interests. Thus, large supply waterworks have been developed and local aquifers have been progressively abandoned except for marginal uses, losing or downgrading their large potential, at least as an essential emergency water reserve. This is especially true in the dense conurbations of Southern Europe, in which the steep topography leaves scarce flat land for town development. As a result, towns are placed along major river valleys or coastal strips, through which the major communication pathways run and they themselves become powerful incentives for further urbanization. Often these towns and their surroundings are above relatively important aquifers.

Often management decisions carried out in the area of influence of the town, aimed at correcting and improving water supply problems, are single minded and do not consider how they affect other components of the water system. Aquifer recharge and water quality are affected in many ways. There are both beneficial and detrimental results, depending on the sector and the kind of induced changes, in the short and in the long term. There are blessings and misfortunes. A long series of such actions can be considered, such as well abandonment, river flow modification, canal use changes, treated water reuse and modification of irrigated land.

Most of this paper will consider and discuss some of these actions based on actual situations, mostly from Spain, with especial regard to Barcelona's Metropolitan Area. Written references are scarce and mostly descriptive, or refer to internal reports which generally are not easily available. Then, facts will be mostly commented on without the support of references. Even general reports relevant to the hydrogeology of urban areas are scarce. Lerner (1990) and Carrera (1996) discuss recharge evaluation and Custodio (1995) refers to this type of problem in coastal and island urban areas. Bocanegra and

Custodio (1995) compare Barcelona with Mar del Plata. An interesting recent study on groundwater quality aspects is that of Bruce (1996), although it refers to an extensive, low density urban area (Denver, Colorado), which is quite different to that of the urban areas to which this paper refers.

2 CHANGES RELATED TO GROUNDWATER LEVEL

2.1 Groundwater level drawdown

Water abstraction increases when the urban area grows and produces a progressive groundwater level drawdown. Some common consequences, which depend on local hydrogeology and the pattern and characteristics of wells, are:
 • well yield may decrease and new wells are needed. The old wells may be abandoned or continue to be exploited. Thus the drawdown pattern changes
 • the cost of groundwater abstraction increases. As a consequence, some factories that use large water quantities, both in-town and at the periphery, may decide to relocate and shutdown the wells, or improve their water use efficiency in order to decrease abstraction and reduce the depth to groundwater level. This may be the individual decision of a large water user or the collective decision of a groundwater users' association
 • the relationship with surface water bodies changes and induced infiltration from rivers, lakes or the sea starts or increases. In coastal aquifers saline water penetration increases with the reduction of continental water discharge into the sea
 • in large areas the water table is lowered and some former wetlands and marshy areas progressively dry up. When these areas are used for housing and factory construction, or the subsoil is used to hold entrenched ways, subways, sewers and underground space (car parking, cellars, service chambers) former drainage needs have already disappeared or lessened, and often the former conditions of high water table are not considered or simply forgotten. When bottom sediments below surface water bodies are thick and/or poorly permeable, the water table drawdown gives way to an unsaturated zone between river and aquifer which may be used later to hold tunnels or sewers which were not constructed to cope with later saturated ambient conditions
 • when wooden piles, formerly in the saturated zone, become dewatered, their degradation rate greatly accelerates, with subsequent building damage.

2.2 Groundwater recovery

The above considerations hold while groundwater abstraction is maintained. Its decrease or disappearance, or an eventual increase in recharge, is accompanied by groundwater level recovery that may affect large areas. The main consequences are the progressive inundation of underground spaces and excavations, and the reduction of drainage capacity of systems to deal with storm water. This produces more often and longer lasting inundation periods. Besides drainage problems and uplift on more or less waterproof constructions such as tunnels, cellars, parking lots, sewers, damage to buildings may be produced.

Other related local problems appear when the area with depleted groundwater levels was previously affected by sea water intrusion or by upconing of deep saline water. This is a common cause of well abandonment. The water table recovery brings saline water into contact with concrete and metallic foundations and buried structures, thus increasing the corrosion rate by the saline, often sulphate rich water. The drowned sewers may begin to collect groundwater through discontinuities and cracks; this increases water flow to pumping, treatment and disposal facilities, which may become overloaded. If incoming water is saline, sewage water treatment plants are affected and the possible reuse of treated water is seriously impaired.

2.3 Geotechnical changes

Aside from local effects on buildings and underground structures due to groundwater level changes, large regional groundwater level drawdown may produce compaction of recent sediments, mainly clays and silts. Regionally this subsidence increases the risk of inundation during storms and increases drainage difficulties. In coastal areas this may produce beach retreat that may be mistaken for enhanced coastal erosion. Compaction of relatively shallow formations may affect buildings resting on floating piles and produce differential movements between buildings resting on different foundations. Subsidence is mostly irreversible and then groundwater level recovery has generally a small effect, except for water logging.

3 CHANGES RELATED TO GROUNDWATER RECHARGE

3.1 *Recharge decrease*

Groundwater recharge changes are diverse and refer to very different circumstances. In principle urbanization and the progressive outward displacement of peripheral rural areas leads to a decrease of recharge due to paving and soil compaction. Also point discharges of water into the soil, such as cesspits and disposal wells, are progressively eliminated as the sewerage network extends and improves. A further action that reduces recharge in sloping areas is the sharp reduction of recharge in alluvial fans and creek bottoms when they are urbanized and channelled. The same may happen to influent rivers when they are channelled or its flow is regulated by dams: peak flow greatly decreases and the river bed may be progressively clogged by low permeability sediments.

3.2 *Recharge increase*

Other circumstances lead to recharge increase, which sometimes may exceed the reduction explained above. The most common cause of increase is leakage from the water distribution network. Such water losses are more important the older the town area and the greater the susceptibility of the area to geotechnical disturbance. Leakage may vary from 15-20% in recent, suitably maintained networks to more than 50% in old, poorly surveyed areas. Leakage increases when water pressure is high. Leakage figures are often unclear since in some towns water metering at the household level does not exist or there are unchecked water uses. This leakage may be an important recharge source in true urban areas, whilst recharge in peripheral areas may decrease.

Another source of recharge in urban areas is irrigation of public and private gardens and green areas, applying water from the supply system or sometimes used domestic water. The importance of this depends on town compactness, but in many situations in the town periphery, newcomers are former farmers who try to maintain a small backyard with subsistence crops irrigated with tap water, thus contributing to increase recharge.

3.3 *Geotechnical problems*

In sloping urban areas, which are very common in Mediterranean towns, slope movement is a common process, which is sensitive to loading by new buildings and earth fillings, and to excavations. They may facilitate and trigger land movements, especially after rainy periods. Open joints increase rainwater infiltration, thus backfeeding the process. But one of the most detrimental effects is water leakage from the often unnoticed breakdowns of water supply pipes and sewers. This is not rare in new areas with good water supply and sanitation networks, but also may appear in old quarters of the town, which were quite stable in the past, after water supply and sanitation networks have been improved, but are poorly maintained. In some cases the use of groundwater kept the water table deep enough but the abandonment of wells and galleries facilitates the high water tables which may in turn promote the above mentioned problems.

3.4 *Recharge in peri-urban farmland*

Since many urban areas are near or on alluvial plains, they compete for farmland. This farmland often consists of irrigated plots, generally applying river water distributed by means of canals. Traditional irrigation methods are commonly used since water is easily available and cheap, and consequently irrigation efficiency is low; this means that there are large excess water quantities applied on the land. In well drained lands they may contribute significantly to aquifer recharge. The progressive urbanization and use of these flat areas for peripheral services (roads, motorways, parking and storage lots, factories, new building areas) reduces recharge to aquifers, as do any attempts to increase irrigation efficiency. The role of farmers as unsuspected "artificial rechargers" is rarely recognized but essential. The same can be said when the commonly unlined irrigation canals which may present important losses - are lined. When the sediment loaded river water - which helps to maintain a silt lining on the canal sides - becomes clearer after river regulation by dams, the process is reduced and leakage increases. Aquifer recharge is affected. In coastal low-lying areas losses contribute to maintain a low saltwater wedge position; after being reduced the interface moves upward, water table salinity increases, local wells are salinized and some drains may start to receive brackish water, forcing water use changes and affecting aquifer behaviour.

4 CHANGES RELATED TO GROUNDWATER QUALITY

4.1 *Changes in the recharge source*

Urbanization has a series of effects on groundwater quality, many of which are poorly known and depend on local circumstances. Quality impairment seems to be the rule, but there are exceptions. There are changes in the source of recharge water, produced inside the ground and due to modification of the way groundwater is mixed in the abstraction well.

Quality changes in the recharge water source depend on salinity and chemical content and isotopic composition of leaking supply water, infiltrating river water and excess irrigation water as the main terms, and also on the relative importance of each one and of natural recharge. Infiltration of used water may have a role. This depends on the existence of disposal points, leaking sewers, infiltrating ponding areas, irrigation with used waters, addition of fertilizers and agrochemicals. A common result is an increase of dissolved nitrogen compounds. Exceeding the 50 mg/L NO limit is not a rare circumstance and this leads to the shutdown of supply wells inside the urban area. Also some increase in total dissolved solids is a consequence of additional salts in the infiltrating used water or due to concentration by evapotranspiration in irrigated fields and gardens. This last affect may be important in arid and semiarid climates, especially when irrigation efficiency is high and applied water has relatively high total dissolved solids. It is not uncommon that the infiltrating excess irrigation water becomes brackish.

4.2 *Leaching of wastes and disposal of used waters*

Conspicuous sulphate increase is often observed; in part from urban air pollution deposited on the ground surface, but also from gypsum dissolution when it is a common construction material that easily finds its way into "inert" rubble disposal sites. This may also be the result of the oxidation of ground sulphides due to dewatering; the resulting sulphates are later leached by groundwater after water levels recover.

Groundwater pollution may be serious in certain areas due to washing by rain water of soluble salts, heavy metals and organics (mostly hydrocarbons) deposited on buildings and streets, but point sources are important as well, such as leakages from service areas, workshops, storage tanks and pipes, and leaching of different stored substances, and also from disposal into the ground of contaminated water and solid wastes.

Many of these actions are unknown, made by environmentally unaware persons or carried out clandestinely. Some common results are the presence of hydrocarbons, chlorinated organic solvents and heavy metals in groundwater below urban areas. When pollution is noticed it may often affect a large area and the sources are unknown. Sources may be old factories which are already disappeared, undocumented old disposal sites or substances introduced or leaked into the unsaturated zone that are being slowly leached downwards or intermitently washed when the water table rises. Complex situations may be found when rural areas are taken by industrial settlements and these are later converted into residential areas.

4.3 *Changes in the ground*

Quality changes in the ground are of different types. Oxidation of organic matter in the water and in the soil produces carbon dioxide that is incorporated into the water, enhancing its agressivity; when carbonate materials are present they dissolve, thus increasing water hardness. Also nitrogen compounds are oxidized to nitrate. All this needs aeration of the soil.

When the oxygen supply is limited or impeded and it is consumed, reducing conditions develop. If organic matter is available, nitrate and nitrogen compounds are reduced to nitrogen gas and ammonia. If reducing conditions are strong, some sulphate reduction is possible as well as iron and sometimes manganese solubilization.

The behaviour of dissolved hydrocarbons and halogenated hydrocarbons is variable and not always well understood. There is preferred oxic degradation of some compounds relative to others and thus there is an "ageing" effect. There is also degradation under anoxic conditions, which is slower and with different results. More research is needed if aquifers below and around urban areas must continue to play their role as freshwater sources. It is not rare that what is abstracted from the aquifers by means of wells and drains is a mixture of different groundwater layers. This explains some chemically odd situations such as nitrate rich waters containing ammonia, dissolved organic matter or reduced heavy metal ions.

4.4 *Biological quality*

Biological quality impairing is generally considered characteristic of groundwater abstracted from aquifers in or around urban areas. This may reflect aquifer conditions of shallow water table and where the travel time from pollution sources is relatively short, less than 50 to 200 days. In other cases these aquifers may still contain good quality water from a biological point of view (bacteria and virus free), although not pollution point of view. However, mixing with other biologically polluted water is sometimes frequent due to poor well design, construction, operation and maintenance.

5 INFLUENCE OF WATER MANAGEMENT DECISIONS

Water management decisions may influence aquifers in urban areas. The shift to surface water or imported water is often accompanied by the shutdown of supply and industrial wells. The consequence is the recovery of groundwater levels referred to above and the possibility of creating water logging problems in underground spaces and excavations.

Sewage water has been used for many years in Mediterranean areas for non edible crop and fruit tree irrigation. In peri-urban areas unwritten agreements between factories and farmers for the use of cooling and other sewage water of adequate quality are common. Also waste water is disposed of into irrigation canals to increase the flow and sustain dry period water availability. These are dangerous situations from the health point of view and there are serious efforts to control and eliminate them. Sewage water is now treated in plants and the effluent may be given back to farmers. Groundwater recharge quantity and quality is affected.

When water is scarce a common situation is to try to exchange treated sewage water for good quality groundwater used by farmers for irrigation in nearby areas. Besides other important water quality considerations, this water is often more saline than the water used previously. There is a danger of soil salinization and especially of producing brackish excess irrigation water that sooner or later will reach the aquifer and start a process of groundwater quality deterioration. The consequence is that water from the aquifers - mostly for urban supply - losses its quality and the aquifer has finally to be abandoned for this purpose. Less abstraction means a water table level rise that may water log and increase salinization in some areas. Some extreme situations may happen in coastal towns, when the normal increase of sewage water salinity over original water (0.3 to 0.5 g/L) is greatly enhanced by seawater pollution. Seawater pollution is the consequence of groundwater seepage

into sewers which are maintained at a low level by pumpage, the disposal of cooling saline water - which is cheaper than supply water - and of using brackish water to avoid shortage situations.

In some areas town water supply incorporates desalinated water from the sea or from brackish groundwater sources. The salinity of distilled water before being blended with other water is very low, but reverse osmosis or electrodialysis product water salinity is still noticeable and mostly dominated by sodium chloride. When this water is later used for irrigation, after treatment of sewage water, the high proportion of sodium may reduce soil permeability and produce soil alkalinization and water logging, thus increasing evaporation and further impairing aquifer water quality.

In some cases, as a "provisional" measure, some sewage discharges into rivers used to produce drinking water which continue to be used as such. Provided a good soil exists and the unsaturated zone thickness is enough to provide a long delay and oxidation opportunities, this is not necessarily detrimental to groundwater provided salinity is adequate and nitrate content keeps low. But the increase of oxidisable organic matter in the soil may increase carbon dioxide generation and thus groundwater hardness augments if carbonate materials are available in the ground. Often, the behaviour of microcontaminants is poorly known.

6 THE ROLE OF URBAN AREA AQUIFERS

The water supply of urban areas needs elements to guarantee the availability of water under anomalous circumstances which can be labeled as emergency situations. Aquifers below and around them may play this role quite easily, cheaply and efficiently, besides being a permanent source of water supply. This role is accomplished by the large water storage involved. Emergency situations appear when the normal water supply system is disrupted and water in storage in excess of what is normally available in in-town reservoirs for peak regulation is needed. These emergency situations generally appear in major disruptions of water supply facilities produced by flooding, long lasting pollution events of the water source or severe drought periods. Surface water schemes are especially prone to these failures if large and expensive, close to the town storage facilities are not provided. Local aquifers may easily play the same role in a cheaper and more secure form, provided their water quantity and quality is protected and preserved for this task. In densely populated areas and in coastal areas they are still more valuable since other forms of

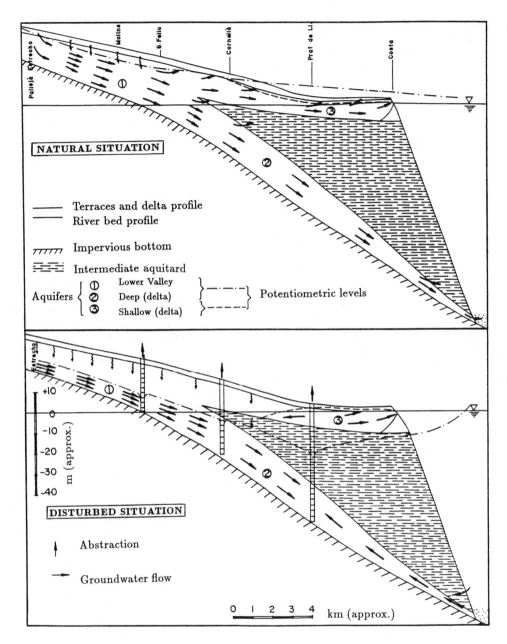

Figure 1 Schematic groundwater flow pattern of the Lower Llobregat aquifer system on the SW boundary of Barcelona.

local water storage are extremely expensive. Coastal aquifers can be used for this purpose if wells are placed to avoid saltwater upconing and away from the temporary saltwater front during the period of abstraction.

In order to keep enough groundwater storage, the recharge rate has to be protected and enhanced by stimulated and artificial means. Groundwater level has to be maintained high enough. As commented earlier, the recovery to high groundwater level in an aquifer which was previously intensively exploited may produce water logging problems in urban areas in which this possibility was not taken into account when expanding them or using underground space. To control these possible inconveniences some abstraction has to be maintained in certain areas, instead of increasing expensive, wasteful and sometimes dangerous drainage. Groundwater modelling greatly helps in proper water management.

When groundwater quality is poor, as happens in some urban areas, local aquifers cannot be used for water supply unless pumped water is adequately treated. This may be a difficult and expensive task under emergency situations, but the available water resources can be put to beneficial use, also alleviating high groundwater level situations. This is something being studied in some large towns. Some possible uses are supplying non potable water for cooling large commercial buildings, factories and industrial establishments, irrigation of streets and public gardens, and providing dilution to some water courses. Separate water distribution networks and adequate rules for operation are needed. This adds to abstraction costs. There are cases in which the solution may be economically unfeasible, but a carefully location of wells may help if this reduces unavoidable pumping expenses to keep drained certain areas and structures. It is important to secure low salinity in order not to impair sewage water treatment plant performance and in some cases to allow for reuse of treated water.

However there are circumstances in which, besides the emergency role of aquifers, the aquifer itself has to be maintained as the main or sole source of drinking water, since there are no other water sources or they are beyond economical possibilities. In this case careful protection and restoration means have to be incorporated into urban and peri-urban soil use and management plans.

7 GROUNDWATER CHANGES IN BARCELONA'S METROPOLITAN AREA

7.1 The water supply system

Barcelona is located on the Mediterranean side of the Iberian Peninsula, in the centre of Catalonia, Spain. It occupies a relatively small, sloping flat area between the coastal range and the sea, and is limited at both sides by two small rivers, the Besos to the NE and the Llobregat to the SW, which is the most important. Both rivers cross the mountain range through deep canyons and develop a coarse alluvium filled valley which ends in a delta area. The deltas are recent formations and contain a two-layer aquifer system which is an extension of the valley alluvium (Figure 1, Custodio 1992). The plain of Barcelona consists of alluvial fans and eolian deposits partly covering a former land surface. Towards the coast there are filled up, old marshes. The lack of space forced a very dense town, with scarce green areas, except for the range land.

Since Roman times the aquifers of the plain have been exploited by means of dug wells and a network of khanat-like water galleries. Now they are not used. In the second half of last century wells were installed in the river valleys. The systems were progressively extended to a capacity of 3 m^3/s by the 1950s. In parallel, during the last century deep flowing wells were drilled in the Llobregat delta for rural and agricultural purposes. Important factories were established in the deltas and valleys to exploit the cheap, good quality groundwater and additional pumping capacity, up to 4 m^3/s, was installed. In the 1940s, the Llobregat river bed started to be carefully scraped to increase infiltration, in the 1950s, a special recharge well facility was installed in the Besos valley and in the early 1970s a line of deep recharge wells to inject treated river water was put into operation in the Llobregat area. All this indicates growing problems due to groundwater level drawdown and the need to secure aquifer recharge.

In the 1950s it was decided to change to surface water. A river water treatment plant for 5.5 m^3/s was put in operation, and later another for 6 m^3/s. Mean river flow is close to 20 m^3/s. Under natural conditions river flow varies between less than 4 m^3/s to more than 50 m^3/s, with flood peaks up to 4000 m^3/s. Regulation storage dams have been contructed. There are also two canals which derive up to 4 m^3/s of water from the river for irrigation of the lower valley and delta areas. This means that most of the river water is currently used.

The Llobregat river water quality is poor due to the large population and the factories existing upstream and also due to the existence of potash mines in the middle basin, which dispose of large quantities of chloride salts. Until the construction of a brine collector about 15 years ago river water was brackish during the dry season, and even with this collector salinity is still relatively high. This high salinity is transferred to the valley and delta aquifers. The Besós river is too polluted to be usable as a source of drinking water.

In the 1960s the water supply of Barcelona's

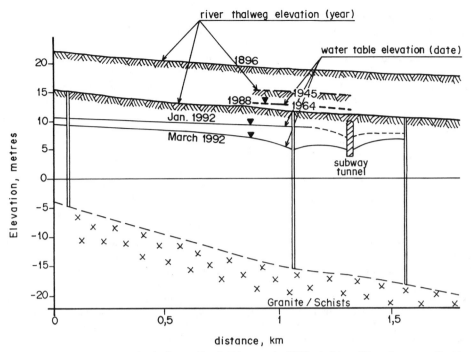

Figure 2. Hydrogeological changes in the Lower Besós River, at the NE boundary of Barcelona, now inside the urban area.

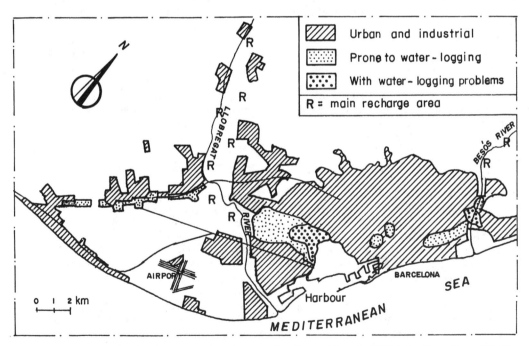

Figure 3. Areas in Barcelona's urban areas presenting waterlogging problems in 1985 (after Custodio and Bayó, 1986) .

Metropolitan Area was supplemented by means of an 80 km long canal transporting good quality water from the Ter river, in Nothern Catalonia. No other new sources of water are currently available. Present and future water needs have to be supplied by means of future good management of what exists.

7.2 Groundwater level changes

Hydrological conditions in the Llobregat delta area are shown in Figure 1. The upper sketch shows the natural situation, before the start of the current century, after about 8000 years of stability. Most groundwater discharges near Cornellà, at the delta apex, but some flow reaches the submarine outcrop of the deep confined aquifer, since the elevation at Cornelà is high enough to produce flow and balance the heavier sea water. The intermediate aquitard still contains connate marine water.

The lower sketch shows the effect of intense groundwater exploitation for urban and industrial water supply, mostly from the valley and the deep delta aquifer. Consequently most of the river length changed from effluent to influent conditions. The river has become perched above the water table in the valley and the main recharge source is excess irrigation water. In the delta deep aquifer piezometric levels and also the water table in some areas dropped below sea level, groundwater flow is reversed, accompanied by progressive sea water intrusion, which progresses faster through the most permeable areas (old river beds and side alluvial fans). Deeper groundwater levels means more expensive water, and partial drainage of former wetlands and shallow water-table areas.

The consequence has been the progressive abandonment of salinized wells or using them only for cooling purposes. The increased cost of groundwater abstraction for factories using large water quantities promoted the organization of a groundwater users' association to protect the aquifer. It was decided to cut costs by increasing in-factory recycling. Now 30% of the former volume of groundwater is used for the same or increased industrial output.

Old factories in the urban areas also decided to shutdown their wells and move to other areas. At the same time, groundwater abstraction for urban supply has been drastically reduced after treated surface water was available for drinking purposes. The result has been groundwater level recovery in many areas, especially in wet years, starting waterlogging problems

(Custodio & Bayo 1986; Vazquez-Suñe & Sánchez Vila 1996a,b).

This situation is illustrated in Figure 2. Gravel mining in the river bed and channelling for flood control produced a conspicuous deepening of the river thalweg. Also the groundwater table was depressed below sea level by supply and industrial abstraction, when most underground space was excavated. Sea water intrusion and contamination produced the progressive abandonment of wells and the recovery of the water table. Several underground car parks are now waterlogged and a subway tunnel constructed when the water table was deep is now suffering from groundwater inflow and under pressure.

Current problems are inundation in subway tunnels, underground parking lots, domestic cellars, and entrenched parts of roads. Some underground spaces have been definitively abandoned due to the cost of pumping and the danger of creating geotechnical problems. In the Barcelona plain leakage from the water distribution network adds to groundwater level recovery. Also subway tunnels and entrenched motorways have probably contributed to the rise of the water table by reducing aquifer transmissivity in some coastal areas.

Figure 3 shows the extent of the waterlogging problems. The areas which were prone to waterlogging in 1985 are now all actually presenting such problems.

7.3 Groundwater quantity changes

The intensive exploitation of alluvial aquifers and deltas means that the current main recharge term of the water balance is river water infiltration. In the Llobregat area river water infiltration is produced both in the river bed and in the irrigated lands, to which large water depths are applied, not only as a tradition but also to control grasses and pests by periodical land innudation, thus reducing the application of agrochemicals. River flow has been progressively regulated by means of dams and the river is channeled to control flood damage. This resuts in every time less frequent and less intense floods, together with increasing water turbidity and pollution, which leads to a decrease of in-bed infiltration rate, only partly compensated for by the recharge activities. The result is the increasing relative importance of recharge through irrigated land. However, the irrigated land surface area is being progressively decreased by new motorways and urban and industrial settlements. Also local recharge from creeks in the delta and valley sides has been drastically reduced after channeling them. Thus aquifer recharge is being impaired.

The mean residence time of groundwater in the Llobregat valley alluvial aquifer, which contains most of the usable storage, is about two years. Thus, groundwater reserves can be used only for a short time and for seasonal regulation. This means that groundwater quantity problems have been solved by chance, since recharge reduction has been more or less compensated by the efforts to reduce groundwater abstraction. The water table recovery mentioned above is mostly due to changes in hydrodynamic pattern and the effect of wet years.

8 GROUNDWATER QUALITY CHANGES

Two main groundwater quality changes have been produced in the alluvial and delta aquifers. One is seawater intrusion, which has penetrated most of the Besos delta and affects a large part of the Llobregat delta. Waters with more than 250 mg/l^{-1} chloride far from the sea correspond to young river recharge water polluted by brine disposal into the river further upstream. Water with less than 150 mg/l^{-1} chloride is old river water which infiltrated before the brine pollution, together with lateral groundwater inflow. Coastal saline water represents the first stages of seawater intrusion in the east of the delta (sodium decreased with respect to chloride). Figure 4 shows the advancement of marine intrusion through more

permeable paths, leaving older, less mobile water in between until this water is gradually consumed by groundwater abstraction.

In the Llobregat delta some industrial wells exploiting saline water are really protecting other wells placed further inland. Some effort is being made to maintain this situation until a groundwater management plan has been adopted. Another main change comes from the poor river water quality; it is heavily polluted in the Besós and in the Llobregat suffers with brine disposal and pollution problems mentioned before.

When river water infiltrates through the river bed there are only small changes in the ionic composition of water, but when recharge is produced in irrigated lands water hardness increases due to the effect of soil carbon dioxide on carbonate sediments (Custodio 1994). Evapotranspiration does not changes significantly water salinity since rainfall compensates for it. Two decades ago, to avoid pollutants being incorporated into the Llobregat river, two highly polluted tributaries upstream from the drinking water treatment plants - waiting for the completion of the sewage water treatment facities - were diverted to one of the irrigation canals. This water has less chloride but higher sulphate content and enough nitrogen compounds to produce a nitrate increase, which can be seen in part of the alluvial water and currently affects part of the supply wells; there is a further hardness increase due to the original water quality water and the enhanced production of carbon

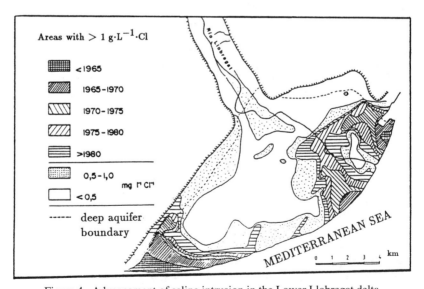

Figure 4. Advancement of saline intrusion in the Lower Llobregat delta.

dioxide in the soil due to the greater organic matter load. Up to now no other pollution effects due to irrigation have been noticed in the carefully monitored supply wells.

In the Barcelona plain groundwater quality mostly reflects the chemical composition of supply water with a variable increase of hardness and nitrate. Areas fed by Llobregat water show chloride pollution and areas fed by the Ter river transfer canal show low chloride content, less than native groundwater.

Groundwater pollution is serious in some areas. Some effects have appeared many years after the activity occurred. Hexavalent chromium is found in some areas in which existed clandestine old disposal wells and pits; also some filled gravel and sand pits received waste material impregnated with soluble chromium or soluble boron compounds. Also during some years urban refuse was used as filling material in sand pits, some penetrating several metres below the water table. Thus chromium, boron, iron, reducing conditions, ammonia and organics are found in groundwater in some areas. Leakages from service stations and oil tanks are not uncommon, but little known. A major gasoline spill by an accidental breakdown of a pipeline in the Llobregat valley needed more than 3 million ECU to control its spreading and protect the use of emergency supply wells. Some of them were shut down and still continue out of use. A naptha leakage from storage tanks produced an extensive floating hydrocarbon layer that moved to the drainage system of a subway tunnel under construction; a large deflagration was produced in it and a large area of aquifer was abandoned. Chlorinated hydrocarbons of different kinds are also creating problems for supply wells. This is the result of clandestine disposal into pits. Ozonisation devices and charcoal filters at the supply well heads have been installed.

Pits filled with contaminants often incorporated into what is euphemistically called "inert" filling materials - slowly leak to the aquifer, especially when they are below irrigated fields or in areas which are periodically flooded. Major contamination episodes appear when groundwater level recovers and part of the filling is placed in the saturated zone. Similar problems appear when residual brines from water softening industrial plants infiltrates the ground in unlined canals or through leaking pipes; after a flood event an episode of high salinity may appear in local wells. When groundwater flows from the valley alluvium to the deep delta aquifer - in which flow is still fast due to the intense pumping downstream - mild reducing conditions appear and nitrate is depleted to low concentration.

Iron and manganese are a problem in upstream alluvial formations and other areas close to urban centres, but not in the area being considered.

9 THE CHANGING ROLE OF AQUIFERS

Aquifers of the Besós river valley are almost abandoned. Aquifers of the Llobregat system continue to be an important source of supply water for some towns and some large industrial settlements. Effort is being made to achieve sustainable use by protecting recharge, controlling seawater intrusion and fighting pollution. Groundwater users have formed an association - now 20 years old and regulatcd by the Water Act - to push action and persuade reluctant policy makers and politicians. Gravel and sand mining and disposal of wastes are now under strict control, sea water intrusion is being monitored and some wells are kept in operation to extract saline water, artificial recharge is continued, and action is being taken to force authorities to consider and correct the impact on groundwater resources of major regional land use plans and structures.

A major role of these aquifers is emergency water supply of the metropolitan area. This requires the aquifer system levels to be lep high which is preserving water quality and operating a well system by means of a central office, already in operation, which also commands the recharge wells. The value of the Llobregat aquifer system has been estimated at 200 million ECU, which is the cost of constructing the cheapest reservoir and water transport pipes giving equivalent service and emergency supply.

Actually emergency supply wells are not idle since the river is very vulnerable to accidental pollution events which enforce the treatment plant to be closed or bypassed rather often. They play a decisive role in summer, when river flow is too low and pollution too high.

The aquifers below the Baracelona plain are much less important but still useful and relatively well recharged. Their use for drinking water ceased a few decades ago but still they are used for cooling purposes at some specific buildings such as large banks and commercial centres downtown. In some areas they are pumped to waste to keep groundwater levels low near subway tunnels and underground spaces. In some areas this water is of reasonable to good mineral quality, even if formerly seawater intruded. Studies are being carried out to know the potential for non potable municipal use (Vazquez-Sune and Sanchez-Vila, 1996a).

10 CONCLUSIONS

Aquifers in and around urban areas are key sources for urban supply and accomplish emergency water supply roles that otherwise would need costly investments. However, the preservation of this role needs good management, technical expertise, cooperation of the public and private sector and political will.

Urbanization affects groundwater levels, aquifer recharge and water quality, both increasing and decreasing them, according to the situation and stage. Monitoring is needed and decisions have to carried out according to actual circumstances.

11 ACKNOWLEDGEMENTS

The author acknowledges the invitation of IAH to prepare the paper, and especially Dr. S.S. Foster and Dr. J. Chilton. Many of the ideas expressed in the paper come from works carried out by the International Centre for Groundwater Hydrology (CIHS) working in cooperation with the Department of Ground Engineering (DITC) of the Polytecnical University of Catalonia, the Water Supply Company of Barcelona (SGAB), the Water Authority of Catalonia (JAC) and the Lower Llobregat Groundwater Users' Association. Typing has been done by J. Sanchez-Vila, of the DITC. The author thanks the unknown reviewers. The ideas expressed in the paper are those of the author and do no necessarily coincide with those of the mentioned organizations, or the Geological and Environmental Institute of Spain, in which the author now is working.

12 REFERENCES

Bocanegra, E.M. & E. Custodio 1995. Utilizaci6n de acuiferos costeros para abastecimiento: dos casos de estudio, Mar del Plata (Prov. de Buenos Aires, GE/ITGE. Madrid (in press). Argentina) y Barcelona (Cataluna, Espana). *Ingeniería del Agua*, Valencia 1(4): 49-78.

Bruce, B.W. & P.B. McMahon 1996. Shallow groundwater quality beneath a major urban center: Denver, Colorado. USA. *J. Hydrol.*, 186(1996): 129-151.

Carrera, J 1996. *Observación, evaluación y medida de la recarga (descarga) a partir de aguas superficiales y conducciones, transferencias y fugas. La Recarga Natural de Acuíferos en la Planificación Hidrológica*. AIH-GE/ITGE. Madrid.

Custodio, E 1992. Progresiva degradación de la cantidad y calidad de los recursos de agua en el sistema acuífero del Bajo Llobregat. *Anais 7° Congresso Brasileiro de Aguas Subterrâneas*. Belo Horizonte: 18-48.

Custodio, E 1994. Endurecimiento del agua del Valle Bajo del Llobregat por cambios en los procesos de recarga. Análisis y Evolución de la Contaminación de Aguas Subterráneas. AIH-GE. *Alcalá de Henares*, II: 123-140.

Custodio, E 1995. Water, tourism and island management. *1ª Reunión Nacional de Geología Ambiental y Ordenación del Territorio: Problemática Geoambiental y Desarrollo Sostenible*. M.P. Cantu (ed.). Univ. Nac. Rio Cuarto, Argentina 515.

Custodio, E. & A. Bayó 1986. Interactions between land-use and aquifer behaviour in the surroundings of Barcelona (Spain). *Integrated Land Use Planning and Groundwater Protection Management in Rural Areas,* Karlovy Vary. IAH: 90-97.

Lerner, D.N 1990. Recharge due to urbanization. Groundwater Recharge. E. Issar & J. Simmers (ed.), IAH, *International Contributions to Hydrogeology*, Heise, 8: 210-214.

Vázquez-Suñé, E. & X. Sanchez-Vila 1996a. Informe sobre l'estudi de les aigües subterrànies del Plà de Barcelona. UPC-CLABSA. Barcelona (internal report): 1-13.

Vázquez-Suñé, E. & X. Sanchez-Vila 1996b. Cálculo del balance y recarga en la Ciudad de Barcelona. La Recarga Natural de Aculferos en la Planificacion Hidrológica. AIH-GE/ITGE, Madrid.

Groundwater in the Urban Environment: Problems, Processes and Management, Chilton et al. (eds)
© 1997 Balkema, Rotterdam, ISBN 90 5410 837 1

Setting goals for the protection and remediation of groundwaters in industrial catchments

Bob C. Harris

National Groundwater and Contaminated Land Centre, Environment Agency, Olton, Solihull, UK

ABSTRACT: This paper reviews the current state of knowledge about groundwater contamination in the UK and the legislative means to enable remediation to take place. It discusses the approaches that could be used to determine groundwater clean-up values on a site specific basis within a risk-based framework and outlines the methodologies that are emerging. Learning from experiences in other countries is invaluable to avoid setting unrealistic and unnecessary goals for remediation in the deep consolidated aquifers which provide the majority of the groundwater which is abstracted in the UK. Concerns over the use of pump and treat as a remedial technique are highlighted in this context. The growing interest in intrinsic bioremediation is discussed and conclusions drawn that much research is urgently needed to underpin with sound science the decision making over the choice of available options.

1 INTRODUCTION

The lowland areas of the United Kingdom are amongst the most densely populated and highly industrialised regions of the world. The origins of the industrial revolution can be found in the English Midlands and 250 years of this historical legacy remain recorded within the subsurface environment. Groundwater is a vital component of the drinking water resources of England and Wales, providing around 35% of the total demand with the large majority of this (75%) being used for potable supplies. The proportion is variable and is much higher in some parts of the country, particularly in the south, east and the Midlands where there are also the greatest pressures on land use and demands on water resources. Industrial cities such as Birmingham and Liverpool overlie the Triassic sandstone which is the second most important aquifer in the UK.

There is very little information about the overall extent and nature of groundwater pollution and as groundwater is "out of sight" beneath the ground it is often "out of mind" in the consideration of potentially damaging land use activities on the surface. The balancing of interests between the different uses of land for industry, agriculture and living space and the need to protect valuable water resources is difficult. The Environment Agency of England and Wales and its predecessor, the National Rivers Authority, recognised these deficiencies in its Policy and Practice for the Protection of Groundwater (NRA 1992). This considers the degree of protection needed in the context of groundwater vulnerability. Thus the greatest efforts in preventative work and resources for regulation are put into those areas of the country where the preservation of groundwater resources is most important. The policy provides a framework for the assessment of new proposals and existing activity in terms of risk, providing appropriate tools in the form of groundwater vulnerability maps and source protection zones around each borehole from which groundwater is abstracted for public supply or other sensitive uses.

2 GROUNDWATER CONTAMINATION

In order to target regulatory effort where it is most needed, it is important to understand what activities present the greatest threats to groundwater quality. To this end a limited study was undertaken in 1995 to identify the main sources of groundwater contamination in England and Wales as they affect the major aquifers (De Hénaut et al. 1996).

There are significant concentrations of polluted sites around the major conurbations and industrial areas which overlie Major Aquifers[1]. This reflects a bias in the study related to the intensity and history of industry in these locations and the level of new development which provides recent site investigation data. Other areas of historic industrial activity do not show so clearly since the scope of the study was largely confined to the outcrops of Major and Minor Aquifers[2]. For example limited information was collected for the London area where groundwater resources are confined at depth and the area around Tyneside and Teeside was similarly not highlighted because of the inherent protection afforded to groundwater resources by the thick layers of glacial deposits in the north-east.

Landfill sites are numerically the most significant category of land use identified as giving rise to groundwater pollution. However, in terms of their actual impact on groundwater they are considered to be less serious than other sources and types of pollutants. Metallic compounds are the most frequently occurring contaminant group but pollution by organic compounds (hydrocarbons, solvents and pesticides) outweighs problems with inorganic pollution. In those urban areas which overlie major aquifers, such as the Chalk and the Triassic sandstones, pollution by organic compounds has had a significant impact on groundwater. For example, the widespread use of chlorinated solvents in the metal manufacturing and associated industries in Birmingham and Coventry has given rise to large numbers of discrete pollution sources coalescing to give a diffuse effect, resulting in around 80% of sampled boreholes being contaminated to a greater or lesser extent. (Lerner and Tellam 1992). Although chlorinated solvents are also a threat in rural areas, the majority of the estimated 14 public supply boreholes contaminated with solvents, and which need treatment in order to comply with drinking water regulations, are located in urban areas. (Harris 1993).

The number of groundwater pollution incidents relating to pesticide contamination is relatively low in comparison. However, the seriousness of pesticide contamination compares with solvents. In contrast the majority of inorganic and landfill leachate contamination occurrences are considered to be the least serious.

---

[1] Major Aquifer: highly permeable formations which support strategic drinking resources

[2] Minor Aquifer: either fractured rocks which do not have a high primary permeability, or formations of variable permeability which are important for local supplies or base flow support to rivers.

This study is the most comprehensive to have been undertaken in the UK and therefore provides us with a better indication of the present character and extent of groundwater pollution from point sources in England and Wales than has hitherto been available. However, the dynamic character and limited scope of the data will necessitate further information gathering for it to be even part-way comprehensive. One deficiency of the study is the irregular nature of its geographical spread, but the types and severity of pollution sources can be taken to be typical of that found within the UK in general.

3   APPROACHES TO REMEDIATION

3.1   *Current Legal Framework*

The Environment Agency has duties under the Water Resources Act 1991 to monitor and protect water resources. With respect to groundwaters that are already contaminated as a result of past industrial practices, the Agency's powers to require remediation are currently limited. Section 85 of the Water Resources Act provides for powers of prosecution should pollution be caused or knowingly permitted without appropriate authorization, but the burden of proof for groundwater pollution is high. This is mainly because of the long time delay between causation and detection, and the difficulties of detection in the first place. Section 161 of the Water Resources Act gives the Agency powers to remedy or forestall pollution of controlled waters and reclaim the costs of so doing from the person(s) causing or knowingly permitting the pollution to occur. Thus, in theory, the Agency can enter any land and carry out remedial works where this is deemed necessary and appropriate. In reality it has seldom happened on any large scale because the Agency or its predecessors have not been financed in a way that allows the ready mobilisation of large sums of money with little prospect of it being refunded.

3.2   *Changes in the Environment Act 1995*

The Environment Act 1995 introduced specific legislation into the UK for the first time to deal with the remediation of contaminated land and also proper provisions for the regulation of historical groundwater pollution. Section 57 of the Act (to be implemented in 1997) requires Local Authorities to identify contaminated land within their boundaries and to serve Remediation Notices on "appropriate persons" (ie those who caused the pollution and/or the owner of the site identified as contaminated land). Where pollution of controlled waters is an issue then the Environment Agency must be consulted and its views taken into account. Groundwater is included for certain specific situations where the pollution linkage from a source within the soil zone is continuing to cause contamination. For particular categories of sites, known as "special sites", the Agency takes over executive responsibilities. Special sites include situations where groundwaters are contaminated by compounds defined in List I of the EC Groundwater Directive and those where potable groundwater abstractions are threatened.

In other situations where no pollutant linkage exists, because of natural circumstances or human intervention to remove the source or cut the pathway, a modification to Section 161 of the Water Resources Act 1991 can be used which allows works notices to be served on the person or persons who caused or knowingly permitted the pollution to arise, in order that it can be remedied or forestalled. Therefore, rather than undertake the work itself and reclaim the costs, the Agency will in future be able to require those responsible for the pollution to undertake the requisite work. There are severe penalties for not carrying out the agreed works. If such a person is unable to be found or identified, and if remediation is required, the taxpayer may eventually pay through work carried out by the Environment Agency.

3.3   *Risk based approach to clean-up*

As the Agency's Policy and Practice for the Protection of Groundwater provides a framework for a risk-based approach to groundwater protection, the setting of remediation objectives for the clean-up of historical pollution can be approached in a similar way. This is consistent with overall UK government policy on contaminated land. The policy document "Framework for Contaminated Land" (DoE 1994) states that clean-up should only take place "where the contamination poses unacceptable actual or potential risks to health or the environment" and then only where "there are appropriate and cost effective means available to do so, taking into account the actual or intended use of the site". This approach has been reinforced by the draft guidance documentation supporting the new Environment Act 1995 legislation on contaminated land (DoE 1996).

In many areas which have a long industrial history, groundwater is not a resource in the sense that it is a strategic source of drinking water. London and Tyneside have been mentioned above in this respect and there are other areas of the UK's industrial heartlands such as the West Midlands industrial conurbation, part of which is known as the Black Country because of its long association with manufacturing industry, where the underlying strata are not hydrogeologically significant. In such areas shallow subsurface groundwater flow provides base flow support to streams and rivers. Much of this groundwater has percolated through many layers of industrial debris and made-ground and as a consequence is of a comparative poor quality. In areas which have been mined for coal, but have been long since abandoned, a further groundwater contribution to stream flow is made from diffuse discharges from flooded workings. Some of these workings have been used for waste disposal purposes and the legacy of what was then considered "good practice" shows today in the form of polluted surface water discharges. The consequence of the combination of these effects is that diffuse pollution of urban watercourses is often a major handicap to achieving a cleaner overall environment in the major industrial towns and cities.

The objectives which are set for clean-up in such urban situations must therefore relate more to the desired surface water quality than to clean groundwater for drinking water, since the latter is an artificial use that will never be realised. A structured approach must be used so that the environmental targets are clearly defined and the consequential risks assessed. Remedial action will then be tailored to the site specific needs. The approach can be broken down into the following elements:

- identification of the contaminant species and properties, and assessment of their quantities.

- identification of the potential environmental targets and the pathways by which they may become affected.

- quantification of the probability and consequent contaminant impact on the environmental target(s).

- setting of objectives for the limitation of impact on the perceived target(s).

- design of remedial actions to prevent or minimise the impact and achieve compliance with objectives.

- construction and/or operation of remedial scheme.

- environmental monitoring to check compliance with objectives.

- redesign of scheme and/or reconsideration of objectives should site works and subsequent monitoring indicate non-compliance or unknown complications.

By addressing historical contamination problems in such a staged and considered way it should be possible to undertake cost effective remediation which is appropriate for the contaminant type and the hydrogeological setting.

This approach cannot be adopted for the prevention of pollution since the current EC Directive requires the protection of all groundwaters. However, where there has been significant historical impact the appropriateness of clean-up or the extent to which it should be employed is a major factor. The Groundwater Protection Policy of the Environment Agency (NRA 1992) recognises this in respect of urban contamination, such as in Liverpool or Birmingham where the aquifer has effectively been abandoned as a potable water resource. Policy statement D6 states "In areas where historical industrial development is known to have caused widespread groundwater contamination, the Environment Agency will review the merits and feasibility of groundwater clean-up depending upon local circumstances and available funding." Such decisions cannot be taken lightly so there is a need to gather considerable amounts of information in advance. Apart from a relatively few examples the standard of contaminated-site investigation in the UK is currently poor.

4   SETTING REMEDIATION TARGETS

The setting of remediation targets or goals for groundwater remediation projects has not been aided by any methodology to promote consistency. Groundwater remediation is in its infancy in the UK. Of the point sources of pollution identified in the 1995 study only 44% have had some form of remedial action applied and of these only 25% (11% of the total) involved positive remedial schemes utilising techniques other than surface capping or excavation of overlying soils. Pump and treat operations were carried out in only 8% of the occurrences identified (De Hénaut et al 1996).

4.1   *Groundwater Remediation Targets*

The US experience cautions against the use of generic clean-up standards. Drinking water standards are clearly unachievable in many situations and other goals may have to be set depending on circumstance. In almost all situations involving organic compounds there will be a residue left within the pore spaces of the rock which is adsorbed onto the rock matrix or simply dissolved at low concentrations in the relatively immobile porewater.

Remedial targets should be site specific, relate to the particular "use" of the groundwater and the likelihood of technical and cost-effective success. One approach is to relate the desired clean-up objective to the type of aquifer as categorised in the Agency's Groundwater Protection Policy. It accepts that the higher standards required for aquifers where the main use is for potable purposes may not be achieved in practice. The following table shows the general approach:-

	Ideal Remediation Standard	Acceptable Remediation Standard
Major Aquifer	background quality	drinking water standard
Minor Aquifer	background quality	drinking water standard, or abstraction use, or surface water quality
Non-aquifer	surface water quality, or abstraction use, or, if no water based environmental target, minimal action	

There has been considerable work carried out within the Department of the Environment's and Environment Agency's R&D programmes to consider clean-up values for soils to protect human health and other receptors (Ferguson and Denner 1995). The Agency is also working on methodologies which will allow for the setting of clean-up targets on a site specific basis for both historically polluted groundwaters and contaminated land/soils which continue to leach contaminants to the water environment (Turrell et al 1996; Quint et al 1996). The approaches are both tiered in as much as more conservative targets are set where the data is limited. There is a trade-off between the costs of gathering more site specific information and the possible reduced costs in understanding and interpreting the attenuating capacity of the unsaturated and saturated zones in reducing the impact of pollution at the environmental target. Such tiered approaches are finding widespread acceptance with the ASTM Risk Based Corrective Action (RBCA) programme being widely taken up within the USA and other developments promoted by CONCAWE and others (ASTM 1994).

In line with the DoE's preferred approach the Agency is keen not to be over prescriptive regarding the setting of targets and the groundwater clean-up methodology therefore allows for a site specific approach to be adopted. This involves selecting a target/receptor of concern (borehole abstraction; spring; watercourse) and considering the desired water quality that is required to be maintained, for example, drinking water standards at a public water supply abstraction, Environmental Quality Standards or Water Quality Objectives for a watercourse. The groundwater quality to be achieved at the place where the groundwater is known to be polluted (ie within the plume of groundwater contamination) can then be back-calculated, given some basic information about the characteristics of the aquifer in that particular location.

Groundwater clean-up is very expensive and will be long-term in its application if highly exacting standards are to be achieved. In the case of smaller firms who are faced with problems, funding may not be available. The methodology is intended to make use of the physical effects of dilution and dispersion and take account of the natural biochemical attenuation processes which can occur as groundwater flows through underground strata. It therefore allows for the balancing of costs and benefits and the adoption of a pragmatic approach.

A potential problem arises since the approach is based on the protection of an ultimate receptor which has a known use (borehole for drinking; river for drinking/fishing/recreation). In order to gain the maximum benefit from the natural clean-up processes, and balance the costs and benefits, the plume of contamination may be allowed to continue to migrate down the groundwater gradient and pollute currently unpolluted groundwater. The situation is dealt with in the methodology by inserting a virtual target/surrogate receptor downgradient to allow for a degree of attenuation without affecting unreasonably large areas of aquifer.

4.2   Choice of Remedial Method

The extent of groundwater pollution within the UK is only now beginning to be quantified and because of the lack of any legislative backing most clean-up has taken place at the point of abstraction. Thus the water supply industry, by putting in place treatment systems at several public supply abstractions, is the largest exponent of pump and treat in the country. The historical precedent has therefore been to treat at the point of abstraction rather than at the source of pollution. Both approaches may have a role to play.

The UK must be careful not to repeat the mistakes of other countries who have a longer history of awareness and remedial action. The USA and the Netherlands, for example, have for many years required clean-up to drinking water quality in aquifers that can be used for this purpose. Conventional clean-up techniques, such as pump and treat, have been applied at numerous sites but in the majority of cases remedial goals have not been achieved. This has been due to the complexity of the hydrogeological environment or the type of contaminant, or a combination of both. In a study published by the National Research Council of the USA, information was reviewed from 77 US sites where pump and treat was the main remedial scheme employed (National Academy Press, 1994). In fissured or heterogeneous multiple layered aquifer systems contaminated with non-aqueous phase liquids it was concluded that clean-up to drinking water standards would be unlikely and the objectives should be refocused on the containment of plumes.

In the UK the fissured and heterogeneous multiple layered aquifer categories respectively relate to the main public supply aquifers, the Chalk and the Triassic sandstones and in many situations therefore pump and treat will not be a suitable technique to use in isolation. In overabstracted aquifer units it may also be unsustainable to abstract the volumes of water necessary without impacting on other boreholes and wells, river flows and wetland habitats. Difficulty in disposing of the cleaned-up effluent to watercourse, sewer or back into groundwater is an added potential problem. While the methodology has an important role in containing plumes close to environmental targets, in most cases it will need to be used in combination with other techniques. However, other techniques, such as in-situ bioremediation, have a low applicability, or have not been proven, in deep groundwater situations. They, and pump and treat, are also very expensive where deep major aquifers are concerned and cost benefit considerations will need to be closely considered.

4.3   A Place for Intrinsic Bioremediation?

If conventional treatment techniques will not achieve useful levels of clean-up what alternatives are available? A whole industry has grown up in the USA in particular around the area of active groundwater bioremediation and many techniques have achieved considerable success in situations involving biodegradable pollutants and shallow aquifer systems that are not too difficult to access. Interest has also turned towards natural attenuation processes (intrinsic bioremediation). Natural processes of biodegradation have an important role to play and may reduce residual organic pollutants to background concentrations given the right conditions and sufficient time. The new enthusiasm for such low-cost passive techniques has been driven by the cost-benefit arguments in the face of many billions of dollars having being spent abortively on other means of active clean-up to unrealistic targets.

The alternatives seem to rest on two options which represent the opposite ends of a spectrum. Firstly a continuation of the past practice adopted in the UK of cleaning-up at the point of abstraction. Thus contaminated plumes would be allowed to continue to migrate and the abstractor treats the water as it is pumped from the borehole. In urban areas, where groundwater resources have largely been neglected in modern times, the output from several boreholes could be treated together. The problems with this approach are that:-

- the polluter pays principle would not be seen to work, and;
- presently clean groundwaters would continue to be polluted as the plume spreads.

The first concern could be dealt with by some private arrangement between the polluter and the abstractor but it is an area fraught with problems. Perhaps the Agency could have some role as "honest broker" but it is more likely to turn into a lucrative business opportunity for lawyers.

The second option is to hope that natural attenuation processes are effective in ameliorating the effects of pollution, if there is sufficient time for them to work. This criterion will be fulfilled more often in the intergranular aquifers, such as the Triassic sandstones and the Greensand, than it will in the Chalk where groundwater travel times can be an order of magnitude faster. However, without the research evidence that intrinsic bioattenuation is working now in UK aquifers it will be difficult for regulators to accept it as an option in any clean-up strategy proposed.

4.4   Research Needs

In the UK the regulatory structure is very different to the USA. In the former remediation, and the development of techniques for clean-up, has been driven more by land availability, economics and perceived civil liabilities rather than by regulatory

systems. It is therefore uncertain which techniques may be applicable to the geological conditions present within the UK and in particular the remediation procedures to adopt in the thick consolidated rocks which form our major aquifers. Proving biosparging works effectively in a 5 m thick superficial gravel deposit, for example, is a very different, and much more costly, technical task than doing the same in Triassic sandstones at 200 m. There are very few case histories to judge the effectiveness of methodologies and little significant research been undertaken to date.

There is therefore a clear need for an extensive research programme. Research into groundwater pollution from point sources in the UK has tended to be preoccupied with the potential impact of landfills and particularly the fate of the heavy metal component within leachate. Landfills have been perceived in the UK as the greatest point source threat to groundwater resources over the past twenty years or so, without a significant amount of evidence in terms of major pollution incidents, while industrial sources and incidents have been largely ignored. Various initiatives are now being promoted so that the issues can be evaluated in greater depth and improved understanding be applied across different land uses. The Engineering and Physical Sciences Research Council has promoted a focused programme of research (Waste and Pollution Management) which will fund, in association with industrial and public sector partners, investigations into natural attenuation of DNAPL and other organic plumes. The other research councils are also focusing their programmes more on "real world" problems which will give further opportunities. The Environment Agency has a programme of research and, besides feeding into projects within the research councils' programmes, carries out its own commissioned work. For example a major study with the British Geological Survey (BGS) is currently underway to investigate the development and fate of a pollution plume from a domestic landfill within the saturated zone of the Chalk. The aim is to understand the role of natural attenuation on the organic component of leachate and apply the results to other contaminant plumes with similar characteristics.

4.5   Regulatory Decision Making

When the relevant legislative powers are introduced the regulator from the Local Authority, or more likely the Agency, will have difficult decisions to make on remedial options and clean-up targets. Regulators will need to work closely with the problem holders and their technical experts. Apart from the questions highlighted above, others that will need to be asked include:-

- what options are available to achieve the objectives and how much do they cost?

- do the costs involved match the environmental benefits to be gained from clean-up?

- is the timescale for the chosen option acceptable?

Answers to these questions will be difficult and expensive to find. All too often there has been too little investment made into defining the problem and assessing the options. The implementor of a remediation scheme must be in control of the situation. Entering quickly into a pump and treat scheme after having drilled only a couple of investigatory boreholes is guaranteed to give poor value for money and may even make the situation worse.

CONCLUSIONS

The UK is addressing the remediation of groundwater pollution at a relatively late stage in comparison to some countries. The pragmatic approach that has been used in the absence of a strong regulatory regime is now finding favour outside the UK, but it must be underpinned with sound science and codified so that regulators can apply it in a consistent and transparent way.

The creation of the Environment Agency in England and Wales, and the Scottish Environmental Protection Agency in Scotland, presents an unprecedented opportunity to grasp the issues and give a co-ordinated lead in a way that has previously been impossible. The Agencies will be in a position to give a technical lead on approaches, methodologies and standards. Some industries have already displayed a determination to address their responsibilities by the recent formation of the Soil and Groundwater Technology Association (SAGTA) and they have been successful in their early days in bringing together the problem holders and the problem solvers (researchers). However, there remains an urgent need for the injection of large scale funding to research innovative and cost-effective solutions for groundwater remediation. Research Council and Environment Agency money will not be sufficient and industry will also need to

contribute significantly. The alternatives are that regulators will require expensive techniques to be used which, because of custom and practice, may be perceived to be acceptable but in reality are not effective. Industry already undertakes some of their own research by way of investigating problems on their own sites. However, little of this work finds its way into the public domain.

The problem of historical groundwater pollution is a common one in which all sectors of society have a share. Regulators, industry, researchers and the consulting community all need to work together to find solutions that are sensible both technically and economically. Natural attenuation presents a highly promising solution but more must be learnt rapidly in the UK hydrogeological context if it is to be accepted within the forthcoming legislative regime.

DISCLAIMER

The opinions expressed in this paper are those of the author and not necessarily those of the Environment Agency.

REFERENCES

American Society for Testing and Materials (ASTM). 1994. Emergency Standard Guide for Risk-Based Corrective Action Applied at Petroleum Release Sites, ASTM ES 38-94.

De Hénaut, P; Harris, R.C.; Vernon, C. and Haines, T. 1996. Evaluation of the Extent and Character of Groundwater Pollution from Point Sources in England and Wales; in: Proceedings of the 32nd Annual Conference of the Engineering Group of the Geological Society; Conference on Contaminated Land and Groundwater - Future Directions.

Department of the Environment. 1994. Framework for Contaminated Land, DoE, London.

Department of the Environment. 1996. Consultation on Draft Statutory Guidance on Contaminated Land, DoE, London.

Ferguson, C. and Denner, J. 1995. UK Action (or Intervention) Values for Contaminants in Soil for Protection of Human Health; in: Van den Brink, W.J., Bosman, R. and Arendt, F. (eds.), Contaminated Soil '95, pps 1199-1200.

Harris, R.C. 1993. Groundwater Pollution Risks from Underground Storage Tanks, *Land Contamination and Reclamation*, **1**, 197-200.

Lerner, D.N. and Tellam, J.H. 1992. The Protection of Urban Groundwater from Pollution, *J IWEM*, **6**, 28-37.

National Research Council, 1994. Alternatives for Groundwater Cleanup, National Academy Press, Washington D.C.

NRA 1992. Policy and Practice for the Protection of Groundwater, HMSO, London.

Turrell, J., Clark, L., Blackmore, J., Oakes, D., Buckland, J., Sims, P. and Wilkinson, M. 1996. A Methodology to Derive Groundwater Clean-up Standards; R&D Technical Report P12, Environment Agency, Bristol.

Quint, M., Alexander, J., Curtis, S. and Irving, I. 1996. Methodology to Determine the Degree of Soils Clean-up Required to Protect Water Resources; R&D Technical Report P13, Environment Agency, Bristol.

Groundwater in the Urban Environment: Problems, Processes and Management, Chilton et al. (eds)
© *1997 Balkema, Rotterdam, ISBN 90 5410 837 1*

Incorporating policies for groundwater protection into the urban planning process

Ken W.F. Howard
Groundwater Research Group, University of Toronto, Scarborough, Ont., Canada

ABSTRACT : Urban planning can no longer be regarded as a two-dimensional exercise. To provide adequate groundwater protection, planners must incorporate an understanding of the sub-surface into the deliberation/decision-making process and acknowledge, for example, hydrogeological complexity, groundwater flow dynamics and the extended time frames over which impacts of land use on groundwater can occur. The difficulties of incorporating policies for groundwater protection into the urban planning process are illustrated here by examining urban development to the north of Metropolitan Toronto, Ontario, Canada. Federal, Provincial and Municipal laws exist that may limit degradation from future development. However, it is not clear that the legislation is sufficiently versatile to deal with the wide range of potential urban contaminants and the nature of groundwater flow within the glacial aquifer system. From a planner's perspective, groundwater protection is best achieved by defining "standards of practice" which, for example, would exclude certain types of development and land use activity in areas specified as "hydrogeologically sensitive". Studies suggest, however, that such an approach is entirely inappropriate in southern Ontario where aquifer heterogeneities and transient flow systems prevent well capture zones from being defined with confidence. Instead, a "standards of performance" "reasonable use" approach is promoted which would retain flexibility of design and encourage planning innovation, but would put the onus on the proponent to perform the necessary sub-surface investigations and provide designs (including monitoring programs and contingency plans) that would ensure environmental guidelines are met for all time.

1 INTRODUCTION

Metropolitan Toronto and Region of southern Ontario, Canada shares a problem that is common to many cities throughout the world. It is undergoing explosive urban growth with serious questions being raised regarding the environmental sustainability of this development and the potential detrimental impact on groundwater resources. In recent years, the effects of urban development on the quality and quantity of groundwater have been well documented (Lerner, 1990a, 1990b, 1990c; Howard, 1997). The task remains, however, to explicitly incorporate these findings into the urban planning process - this is crucial if we are to avoid repeating the errors of our not so distant past. In this paper, I describe the results of chemical audits and field and model studies of groundwater impacts in and around Metropolitan Toronto, Canada, and discuss them in

the context of anticipated urban growth along the Oak Ridges Moraine (ORM; Figure 1), an undulating ridge of kettled topography just north of the city. I review and question the value of existing environmental legislation, and discuss alternative methods by which the urban planning process can be improved.

2 OAK RIDGES MORAINE - HYDROGEOLOGY

In the eastern part of the Great Lakes Basin, in south-central Ontario, the Oak Ridges Moraine (ORM; 1400 km^2) (Figures 1 and 2) is a nationally-significant groundwater resource that has become increasingly threatened by urban growth, notably along the northern margins of the Greater Toronto Area (GTA) (Howard *et al.*, 1995). Located approximately 50 km to the north of Toronto's urban

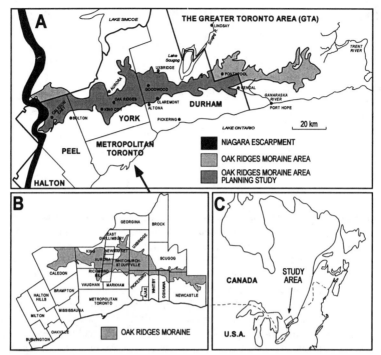

Figure 1. A) Location map showing the Oak Ridges Moraine (ORM) in relation to Metropolitan Toronto and the four Regions which together comprise the Greater Toronto Area (GTA); B) Local Townships; and C) Regional location (after Howard et al., 1995).

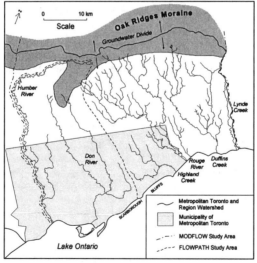

Figure 2. Metropolitan and Toronto Region Watershed (MTRW) showing location of study areas (after Howard et al., 1995).

core, the ORM forms a ridge between 5 and 20 km wide stretching for over 140 km eastward from the Niagara escarpment. It presently supports some 30,000 private wells, provides municipal water for several small towns and supplies the headwater for numerous streams, many of which drain southwards through the GTA to Lake Ontario.

The ORM is currently the focus of considerable debate concerning the potential impact of urbanisation and other anthropogenic activities on groundwater quality and supply. Current environmental pressures include thousands of septic systems, aggregate quarries, farms, and golf courses. Urbanization is expected to increase water demand and bring additional impacts such as leaking gasoline storage tanks, road deicing chemicals, fertilizers and pesticides. Sites are also required locally for the disposal of increasing quantities of municipal household waste. Fears have been voiced that the rate of urban development along and adjacent to the moraine will outpace our ability to make reliable estimates of potential impacts. Many communities, such as the town of Oak Ridges (Table 1), for example, anticipate significant population increases. Until recently, a moratorium on development along the ORM provided a window of opportunity for resource investigation and impact analysis. While some research issues have been addressed, others remain unanswered. A recent change in the leadership of the Provincial government now makes large-scale urban development of the ORM imminent.

3 PREVIOUS STUDIES

In 1991, the University of Toronto began a multi-disciplinary study of contaminant pathways in the Greater Toronto Area (GTA). The objectives of this work were to establish the potential for contamination of Lake Ontario via groundwater pathways, to quantify groundwater flow into the Lake, and to estimate long-term impacts on Lake water quality. Procedurally, this involved identifying and quantifying contaminant mass loadings for selected chemical parameters and estimating transport times for these parameters using a knowledge of groundwater flow paths and chemical retardation. To err on the side of conservatism, the potential for volatilisation and biodegradation of the contaminants during transport was ignored.

Table 1. Anticipated growth in "Oak Ridges", one of many small townships along the Oak Ridges Moraine.

Year	Population	Municipal Groundwater Abstraction m^3/day
1960	2,000	700
1970	2,900	1,000
1980	3,235	1,100
1990	6,400	2,200
1996	17,500[*]	6,000[*]
2000	30,000[*]	10,200[*]
2005	35,000[**]	12,000[**]
2010	44,000[**]	15,000[**]

[*] Predicted (Town of Richmond Hill, pers.comm.)
[**] Extrapolated

3.1 Contaminant source audit

A contaminant source audit was performed for a 700 km^2 sub-region of the GTA (FLOWPATH study area - Figure 2). Point sources of contamination (Figure 3) include 82 open and closed landfills (Howard et al., 1996), approximately 2125 underground storage tanks, 13 snow dumps, 10 coal tar sites and approximately 3000 septic systems. Non-point sources are represented by NaCl road de-icing salts applied to 4200 lane kilometres of roadway, and fertilizers applied to golf courses, parkland, domestic gardens and 180 km^2 of agricultural land. Details of the auditing approach are described by Howard & Livingstone (1997). Estimates considered contaminants known to have been stored or used in the study area up to the present time. For most chemicals, this means a time frame of about 30-50 years.

The audit showed that inorganic chemicals, and in particular, chloride derived from road de-icing salts represent the largest chemical loading to the sub-surface during the period. To establish chemical "threat", however, requires consideration of water quality standards and the potential degradation that will ensue. To make such an evaluation, the total mass of each chemical released was divided by the corresponding water quality standard. This procedure

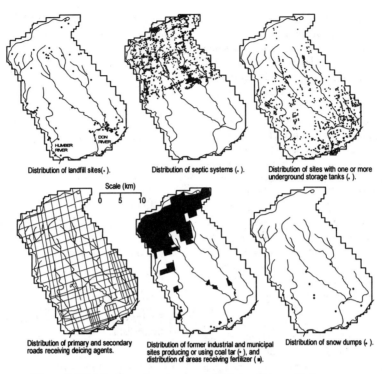

Figure 3. Distribution of contaminant sources within audited area

Table 2. Impact Potential (the volume of water in litres that would be contaminated by the available chemical mass to the local water quality standard)

PARAMETERS	LANDFILLS	SEPTIC SYSTEMS	UNDER-GROUND STORAGE TANKS	SNOW DUMPS	FORMER COAL TAR PLANTS	ROAD DEICING CHEMICALS	AGRICULTURE
INORGANICS:							
Chloride	3.7×10^{11}	1.4×10^{10}		8.7×10^{08}		3.7×10^{12}	1.3×10^{10}
Sodium	4.6×10^{12}			7.3×10^{08}		3.0×10^{12}	
Nitrate-N	7.9×10^{11}	3.1×10^{11}					2.4×10^{12}
Copper	4.0×10^{11}			6.3×10^{09}			
Lead	1.2×10^{13}			5.7×10^{11}			
Chromium	2.9×10^{12}						
Cyanide	3.5×10^{11}						
Mercury	1.0×10^{11}						
Arsenic	3.7×10^{11}			6.0×10^{09}			
ORGANICS:							
Benzene	1.7×10^{12}		3.0×10^{13}		4.0×10^{11}		
Ethylbenzene	9.7×10^{12}		4.2×10^{13}		7.1×10^{10}		
Tetrachloroethene	4.1×10^{10}						
Trichloroethene	1.1×10^{12}						
Dichloromethane	4.5×10^{11}	5.2×10^{09}					
Phenol	1.4×10^{16}						
1-4 Dichlorobenzene	1.4×10^{12}	2.0×10^{11}					
Toluene	2.3×10^{12}	3.3×10^{11}	2.1×10^{13}		2.3×10^{10}		
Xylene (total)	1.0×10^{12}		1.8×10^{12}		5.7×10^{08}		
Naphthalene	No Quality Standard						
Atrazine							6.0×10^{12}

34

essentially determines "impact potential" i.e. the volume of water that would be contaminated to the standard by the available mass (Table 2). To put the tabulated impact potentials in context, the volume of groundwater immediately underlying the study area is approximately 10^{13} litres and the volume of groundwater entering the study area each year as recharge and leaving as baseflow to urban streams is about 10^{11} litres (i.e. approximately 3×10^{12} litres over the past 30 years during which most of the contaminants have been released). Groundwater residence times average 100 years.

Reference to Table 2 reveals that impact potentials for the majority of contaminants listed exceed 3×10^{12} litres i.e. most give serious cause for concern. BTEX and phenols seem to represent the most serious problem, albeit that the risks are likely to be significantly alleviated by biodegradation and volatilisation. Other chemicals of concern include copper, lead and cyanide from landfills, sodium and chloride from road de-icing chemicals, and nitrate from a combination of sources. Field studies published by Pilon & Howard (1987) and Eyles & Howard (1988) confirm the extent of the inorganic contamination.

3.2 *Flow modelling*

The transport of contaminants in the audited area was initially modelled with FLOWPATH, a finite difference steady-state model which can simulate groundwater flow and perform particle tracking in heterogeneous, anisotropic confined/unconfined and leaky aquifers of two dimensions (Franz & Guiguer, 1990). This model was used to estimate transport times for the contaminants and predict the long-term impacts on receiving urban streams and Lake Ontario. To investigate, the potential impact of urban development along the Oak Ridges Moraine, the model was subsequently extended in regional extent and in three dimensions (Figure 4A) using Visual MODFLOW, an adaption of the United States Geological Survey (USGS) numerical finite difference model coded by McDonald and Harbaugh (1984). Modelling enabled groundwater flow paths (Figure 4B, for example) and transport times for the various contaminants to be estimated. In addition the transient capabilities of MODFLOW allowed the behaviour of the aquifer to be investigated under various long-term pumping and recharge scenarios. Preliminary results of the complete study have

been documented recently (University of Toronto, 1996; Howard *et al.*,1995). A combination of hydrochemistry and water balance studies reveals that recharge to the uppermost aquifer (the Oak Ridge Aquifer Complex (ORAC), modelled as Layer 1 (see Figure 4)) is not simply confined to areas of the moraine free of till cover, but is transmitted in significant amounts via a draping of Halton Till. Previously, this till, locally up to 10m thick, had been thought to inhibit recharge and provide a high degree of natural protection from percolating contaminants. Similarly, water balance studies (Gerber & Howard, 1997), isotope investigations (Gerber & Howard, 1996; Howard & Gerber, 1997) and modelling suggest that recharge to the ORAC (Model Layer 1) leaks, at least in part, through the underlying Northern Till aquitard and replenishes dozens of aquifers units to the north and south of the moraine (modelled to the south as Layers 2 and 3). Given that the Northern Till had previously been regarded as a low permeability unit and ideally suited for landfilling of municipal waste, this finding carries important implications. Ongoing work being undertaken in co-operation with researchers at Ontario's Waterloo Centre for Groundwater Research (WCGR) plans to investigate the effects of aquifer system heterogeneities on the 3-dimensional form and transient dynamics of well capture zones.

4 IMPLICATIONS FOR URBAN PLANNING AND GROUNDWATER PROTECTION

The results of the hydrochemical and hydrogeological studies confirm that urbanisation represents a serious threat to local groundwater quality. Federal, Provincial and Municipal laws exist that may limit future degradation. However, it is not clear that the legislation is sufficiently versatile to deal with the wide range of potential urban contaminants and the dynamics of groundwater flow within the complex glacial aquifer system. Three major problems are apparent:

i) the multi-jurisdictional structure of the land use planning process;

ii) the patchwork of statutes, policies, programs, regulations and guidelines that concern groundwater protection issues; and

iii) the inability of the planning process and its

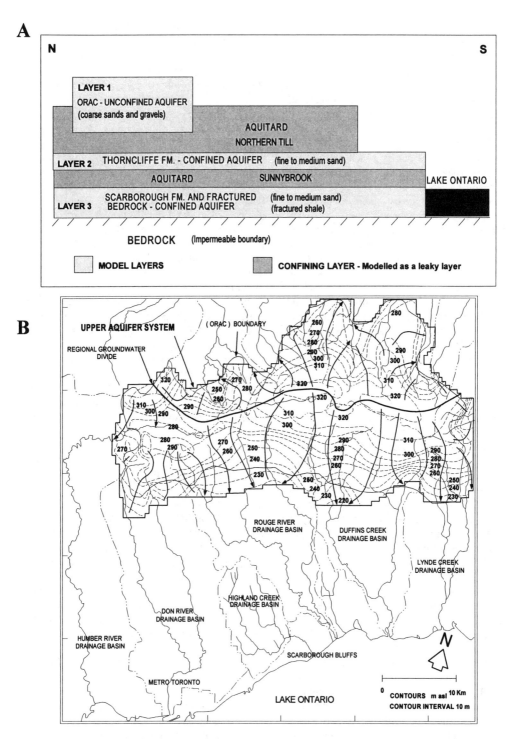

Figure 4. Aquifer modelling using Visual MODFLOW: A) Idealised three-layer model; B) Heads and flow directions in model layer 1 (upper aquifer immediately beneath the Oak Ridges Moraine).

associated regulations to recognise locally complex hydrogeological conditions, dynamic groundwater flow regimes, and the consequent difficulty of delineating well capture zones.

4.1 *Jurisdictional issues*

Prospective land developers are faced with a maze of legislation at virtually all levels of government. Under the 1995 Planning Act, the Ministry of Municipal Affairs (MMA) is responsible for the approval of official plans, official plan amendments (OPAs), subdivisions, consents and zoning order amendments. In practice, MMA regularly delegates approval authority for sub-divisions to regional municipalities (Counties and Townships). Municipalities are also, on occasion, delegated authority for the approval of OPAs. Legislative responsibility for the management and protection of ground and surface water, on the other hand, falls to the Ontario Ministry of Environment and Energy (MOEE). This authority is vested under the Ontario Water Resources Act, the Environmental Protection Act, and the Environmental Assessment Act, all passed into law by the Provincial government in 1990.

The planning policy issue begins to get complicated when other agencies enter the picture. Regional municipalities are responsible for providing services such as water, sewage treatment, waste disposal and roads. Conservation Authorities take an interest where the development is likely to affect valley lands and flood plains. The Ministry of Natural Resources (MNR) has no direct interest in water resources, but is responsible for protecting, aquatic habits, and areas designated as environmentally sensitive (ESAs) or determined to be of natural and scientific interest (ANSIs). MNR has also assumed primary responsibility for the protection of "special" areas of "local or Provincial interest". These areas include parts of the Oak Ridges Moraine and selected watersheds/sub-watersheds, even though such areas are designated largely on the basis of water resource issues, and should logically fall under the jurisdiction of MOEE.

To further complicate the process, certain groundwater issues also fall within the domain of District Health Units, the Ministry of Agriculture, Food and Rural Affairs (OMAFRA), the Waterfront Regeneration Trust, and the Federal Department of Fisheries and Oceans.

4.2 *Legislation*

Technical hydrogeological requirements pertaining to land use applications are summarised in a weighty document published by the Ontario Ministry of Environment and Energy (MOEE), 1995. This document was commissioned by the Office of the Provincial Facilitator of the Ministry of Municipal Affairs, and was prepared by external consultants to guide land development applicants (and, no doubt relevant government personnel) through those aspects of the planning process that are relevant to groundwater.

While the document is clearly useful for steering prospective developers through a minefield of statutes, policies, programs, regulations and guidelines, it also allows the many shortcomings of the process to be identified. For example, groundwater protection is not explicitly recognised in the urban planning process. In general, planning applications require hydrogeological investigations to be conducted where either:

a) groundwater is required for domestic supply (in which case the adequacy of resource and potential interference problems must be examined);

b) sewage systems are proposed that require subsurface disposal of waste via leaching beds or surface disposal using spray irrigation (in which case, impacts must fall within Provincial guidelines);

c) soil and/or ground water at the site is known or suspected to be contaminated; or

d) the site is located on areas which have been designated as hydrogeologically sensitive and therefore of "special" interest to the Province.

With the exception of case d) (see 4.3 below), where detailed studies are required to ensure both the quality and quantity of the groundwater resource will be maintained, the planning process fails to acknowledge modern hydrogeological thinking on the impacts of urban development on groundwater. It fails to understand the potential for groundwater replenishment via water distribution networks and sewage pipes. It fails to acknowledge the broad range, and large quantities of potential contaminants, that urban areas can eventually introduce to the sub-surface.

4.3 *The role of the sub-surface*

According to existing legislation, groundwater protection is only guaranteed in areas that have been designated as "hydrogeologically sensitive". In Ontario, the designation assumes that:

a) recharge to aquifers occurs almost exclusively in areas with little or no covering of glacial material; and

b) areas where recharge to underlying aquifers is highest are most in need of groundwater protection.

In the first place, numerous studies including Gerber & Howard (1996; 1997) and Howard & Gerber (1997) demonstrate that significant quantities of recharge can occur through glacial material, including tills previously regarded as essentially impermeable. As a result well capture zones are likely to be three-dimensionally complex, particularly in glacial sediments supporting multi-layered aquifer systems. Moreover, while it is true that higher recharge areas may require greatest protection from urban development, the reverse may be equally valid. This is because higher rates of infiltration will provide for greater attenuation of contaminants, and water levels in unconfined aquifers underlying recharge areas may, by virtue of a high specific yield, be less susceptible to gains or losses in recharge than water levels in semi-confined aquifers.

5 AN ALTERNATIVE APPROACH

In essence, the use of hydrogeological classification systems that attempt to define "recharge" zones or areas "most susceptible to pollution" tends to be effective only in geologically simple, steady state groundwater flow systems where hydrogeological conditions can be clearly and confidently defined. In most cases, classification schemes represent a gross simplification of the groundwater system at best, and provide a recipe for misinterpretation and abuse at their worst. They are particularly dangerous in the hands of individuals with limited hydrogeological knowledge and experience. Unfortunately, this "standards of practice" approach to groundwater protection is welcomed by planners because it is easy to administer and is readily incorporated into planning tools such as geographical information systems, thus enabling decisions to be made rapidly with a minimal degree of subjectivity.

Research in Ontario suggests that the standards of practice approach is particularly inappropriate where an irregular glacial stratigraphy and heterogeneous, multi-layer aquifers give rise to a complex groundwater flow system which can be highly sensitive to pumping. As an alternative, groundwater interests are best served by the incorporation of "performance standards" into the planning processes. Performance standards would designate limits for the degree of acceptable groundwater quality degradation, and may also, for example, require that recharge be maintained at pre-development levels. Such an approach would retain flexibility of design and encourage planning innovation.

As an appropriate model, it is suggested that "Reasonable Use Guidelines" (MOEE, 1994), presently applied with considerable success to the design and operation of municipal landfills in Ontario, be adapted and applied to all situations (e.g. urbanization, highway construction, golf course development, quarrying) where land use is significantly altered. Reasonable use guidelines recognise that some degree of impact is unavoidable and defines the degree of degradation permissible as a function of the historical background water quality, existing water quality, water quality standards and impacts from other sources that can be expected with a high degree of certainty. The standards of performance approach puts the onus on the proponent to perform the necessary sub-surface investigations and provide designs (including contingency plans) that would ensure environmental guidelines are met for all time. Proponents would also be required to install monitoring wells to enable environmental performance and compliance to be monitored by interested parties.

6 CONCLUDING SUMMARY

Common to many cities worldwide, Metropolitan Toronto is experiencing rapid urban growth with serious concerns being raised regarding the environmental sustainability of this development and the potential detrimental impacts on the quality and quantity of groundwater resources Recent hydrogeological and hydrochemical studies at the University of Toronto confirm that urbanisation represents a serious threat to local groundwater quality. While Federal, Provincial and Municipal laws exist that may limit future degradation, indications are that the legislation is complex, limited in extent and, with rare exceptions, fails to acknowledge either the wide range of potential urban contaminants or the dynamics of groundwater flow within glacial aquifer systems.

Urban planning should not continue to be treated as a two-dimensional exercise. In the interests of effective, long-term groundwater protection, planners and legislators must be asked to fully incorporate an understanding of the sub-surface into the deliberation/decision-making process. Where appropriate, they must acknowledge hydrogeological complexity, groundwater flow dynamics and the extended time frames over which impacts of land use on groundwater can occur. Clearly, the hydrogeologist has an important role to play if the urban planning process is to properly serve the interests of the groundwater industry. Traditionally, most contaminant hydrogeologists have worked in "reactive" mode, investigating and resolving problems as, and when, they arise. If groundwater protection policies are to be effectively incorporated into the urban planning process, hydrogeologists must be proactive and, if necessary, become directly involved in the development of planning policy.

In assuming this role, it is essential that we defend our hydrogeological understanding of the sub-surface and ensure that this knowledge is utilised in a sound, scientific manner. In particular, we should resist the standards of practice approach to groundwater protection that requires us to grossly simplify groundwater flow behaviour, simply to enable production of broad-based, two-dimensional hydrogeological classification schemes that can be readily incorporated into planning tools such as geographical information systems.

As an alternative, I would promote the universal incorporation of "standards of performance" into the urban planning process. This approach would maintain hydrogeological integrity, allow for flexibility of design and encourage planning innovation. The standards would designate limits for the degree to which degradation would be acceptable, and may also, for example, require that total, combined, direct and indirect recharge be maintained at pre-development levels. Standards of performance would encumber the proponent with the responsibility to perform the necessary sub-surface investigations and provide designs, together with monitoring programs and contingency plans that would enable environmental guidelines to be met for all time.

ACKNOWLEDGMENTS

The author gratefully acknowledge numerous University of Toronto students and colleagues who assisted in the collection and interpretation of the data. Particular thanks go to Nick Eyles, Rick Gerber, Sean Salvatori, Philip Smart, Joe Boyce, Mike Doughty, Tim Westgate and Steve Livingstone. Karina Gelo helped with the final preparation and formatting of the document. Irmi Pawlowski of the Ontario Ministry of Environment and Energy kindly provided key documentation. The work was supported by research grants to Howard and Eyles from the Great Lakes University Research Fund (GLURF) (sponsored by Environment Canada and the Natural Sciences and Engineering Research Council (NSERC)) and the Ontario Ministry of the Environment and Energy. The views presented here are those of the author and are not necessarily endorsed by colleagues or by the funding agencies.

REFERENCES

Eyles, N. & K.W.F. Howard, 1988. Urban landsliding caused by heavy rain; geochemical identification of recharge waters along Scarborough Bluffs, Toronto, Ontario. *Canadian Geotechnical Journal* 25, 455-466.

Franz, T. & N. Guiguer 1990. FLOWPATH, two dimensional horizontal aquifer simulation model: *Waterloo Hydrogeologic Software*, Waterloo, Ontario 74 pp.

Gerber, R.E. & K.W.F. Howard 1996. Evidence for recent groundwater flow through Late Wisconsinan till near Toronto, Canada. *Canadian Geotechnical Journal* 33, 538-555.

Gerber, R.E. & K.W.F. Howard, K.W.F. 1997, in press) Ground-water recharge to the Oak Ridges Moraine. In: Eyles, E. (ed.) *Environmental Geology of Urban Areas*. Special Publication of the Geological Association of Canada. Geotext #3, 173-192.

Howard, K.W.F., Eyles, N., Smart, P.J., Boyce, J.I., Gerber, R.E., Salvatori, S. & M. Doughty 1995. The Oak Ridges Moraine of southern Ontario: A groundwater resource at risk. *Geoscience Canada* 22, 101-120.

Howard, K.W.F., Eyles, N.& S. Livingstone 1996. Municipal Landfilling Practice and its impact on groundwater resources in and around urban Toronto. *Hydrogeology Journal* 4, no. 1, 64-79.

Howard, K.W.F. 1997. Impacts of Urban Development on Groundwater. In: Eyles, E. (ed.) *Environmental Geology of Urban Areas*. Special Publication of the Geological Association of Canada. Geotext #3, 93-104.

Howard, K.W.F. & S. Livingstone 1997. Contaminant source audits and ground-water quality assessment. In: Eyles, E. (ed.) *Environmental Geology of Urban Areas*. Special Publication of the Geological Association of Canada. Geotext #3, 105-118.

Howard, K.W.F. & R.E. Gerber 1997. Do tills beneath urban Toronto provide adequate groundwater protection? *Proceedings IAH XXVII Congress. Groundwater in the Urban Environment.* 21-27 September, 1997. Nottingham, U.K.

Gerber, R.E. & K.W.F. Howard. 1997. Ground-water recharge to the Oak Ridges Moraine. In: Eyles, E. (ed.) *Environmental Geology of Urban Areas*. Special Publication of the Geological Association of Canada. Geotext #3, 173-192

Lerner, D.N., 1990a. Recharge due to urbanization. Chapter 15 in Groundwater Recharge: A guide book for estimation natural recharge (eds. Lerner, D.N., Issar, A.S. and Simmers, I..). *International Association of Hydrogeologists, International Contributions of Hydrogeology* vol. 8; Hannover: Heise, 201-214.

Lerner, D.N., 1990b. Groundwater recharge in urban areas. *Atmospheric Environment* 24B, no.1, 29-33.

Lerner, D.N., 1990c. Groundwater recharge in urban areas. In: *Hydrologic Processes and Water Management in Urban Areas (Proceedings of the Duisberg Symposium, April, 1988). International Association of Hydrological Sciences (IAHS)* Publ. No. 198, 59-65.

McDonald, M.G. & A. Harbaugh 1984. A modular three-dimensional finite- difference groundwater flow model: *USGS Open File Report* 83-875. 528 pp.

Ontario Ministry of Environment and Energy 1994. Incorporation of the Reasonable Use Concept into MOEE groundwater management activities. Guideline B-7 (formerly 15-08). *OMOEE*, April, 1994.

Ontario Ministry of Environment and Energy 1995. MOEE Hydrogeological technical information requirements for land development applications. ISBN 0-778-4340-4. *OMOEE*, April, 1995.

Pilon P. and Howard, K.W.F. 1987. Contamination of sub-surface waters by road de-icing chemicals. *Water Pollution Research Journal of Canada* 22(1), 157-171.

University of Toronto 1996. The Hydrogeology of the Oak Ridges Moraine - Final report to the Ontario Ministry of Environment and Energy (MOEE). June, 1996. 60 pp.

Too much or too little: Recharge in urban areas

David N. Lerner
Groundwater Protection and Restoration Research Unit, University of Bradford, UK

ABSTRACT: Urban groundwater is under-used in the UK, mainly because of worries about the risks of pollution. Geotechnical problems have arisen as a consequence of rising water tables. In order to make full and wise use of the asset value, a clear understanding of the quantities of groundwater recharge is needed. Recharge sources are varied and complex in cities, with major changes to the hydrological pathways for precipitation, some of which can increase recharge compared to rural areas. In addition, much of the sizeable imports of water for public supplies finds its way to groundwater, through leaking mains and sewers, or by deliberate recharge in septic tanks and soakaways.

URBAN GROUNDWATER – AN ASSET OR A PROBLEM?

Urban groundwater is both an asset and a problem. It is an asset because of its value for water supply for drinking and industrial use. The distributed nature and low capital needed to pump groundwater make it equally valuable as a water supply for both high densities of small, domestic wells which are common in developing cities around the world, and for fewer, high volume wells such as are common in the UK. As an example of the latter, Nottingham has only some 20 wells in use, one for public supply and the others for industry. Another aspect of groundwater's use is as a route for disposal of liquid effluents, both excess runoff through soakaways and sewage through latrines and septic tanks. The asset value of this aspect is less clear cut, being of more value to the producers of effluent than the users of groundwater, who may suffer pollution as a consequence.

The problem side of urban groundwater is partly the health risk from pollution, but is principally the difficulties that arise through too much or too little groundwater. Over-abstraction causes falling water tables, which then require continual refurbishment of the water supply infrastructure as wells must be deepened or replaced. Falling levels can also cause subsidence, which has been a major problem in many cities around the world constructed on unconsolidated sediments. It becomes a more acute problem when deep boreholes replace shallow wells, increasing pumping, and lowering pore pressures in deep, fine-grained sediments.

Problems of too much groundwater are more common in the later stages of city development, for example in the UK and elsewhere in Europe. Too much groundwater is also found in some of the new, wealthy cities of the Middle East, as described later. Rising water tables can have nuisance value at the minimum, flooding basements, tunnels and underground carparks. There are also hazards, such as mobilising pollutants in the unsaturated zone, encouraging floating petroleum products to migrate into underground spaces, and affecting foundations. The latter are at risk as rising pore pressures decrease strengths and bearing capacities of strata.

A recent trend in the UK and other industrialised countries has been a move away from the use of urban groundwater for public potable supply. This has been due to pollution, sometimes with actual incidents of pollution occurring, while the perceived risk has been the cause in other cases. At the same time in the UK, there has been a downward trend in industrial pumping of groundwater. Although this is partly due to the changing nature of industry, there has been a move away from private supplies towards reliance on public supply from the mains. In contrast to these trends, there is growing pressure on rural groundwater. Water companies rightly see it as a valuable resource with good characteristics for exploitation. Irrigation of crops has not been widespread in the UK until recently, but demand for irrigation water is increasing because it can show extremely good financial returns by improving crops which have traditionally been grown without extra water. The ecological and environmental benefits of groundwater discharges to surface water have become better understood by the public and by environmental lobbyists, with widespread discontent about the drying up of springs and low flows in groundwater fed rivers. These are often streams which have recreational fishery and landscape value in affluent areas, and public pressure has led to a number of schemes to replenish flows.

Some of the problems associated with urban groundwater are related to pollution (or to potential pollution). Pumping is a primary control on many of the other issues, with both over- and under-abstraction causing difficulties. However recharge also has a part to play in the size of the problems. Urban recharge is complex, with many factors affecting whether it is higher or lower than in equivalent rural areas. The major part of this paper discusses recharge mechanisms in urban areas, with the final section looking at how the asset value of urban groundwater could be better managed, particularly in industrialised countries such as the UK.

RECHARGE PATHWAYS

The main sources of recharge water in urban areas are precipitation and the public water supply system.

Figure 1 shows a simplified model of the precipitation and recharge pathways for a natural or rural catchment. In the East Midlands, where Nottingham is, precipitation is about 650 mm/y, evapotranspiration is about 450 mm/y, with the remainder becoming recharge or runoff. More detail could be given in Figure 1 of some of the complications such as indirect and localised recharge as defined by Lerner et al. (1990). Localised recharge is an important feature in the UK, with patches of low permeability glacial cover causing runoff which infiltrates around the edges.

Urban effects on precipitation recharge

The classical view that cities reduce recharge because of the high proportion of impermeable surfaces is being recognised as incorrect. Although hydrologists have shown that urbanisation increases storm runoff, there is no direct evidence that the increase is at the expense of recharge, and it may well be at the expense of evapotranspiration, given the reduced plant cover in cities.

Hydrometeorologists have shown that cities have microclimates, with increased dust in the air and higher temperatures, which will affect rates of precipitation and evapotranspiration. More important for recharge are the ways that the hydrological pathways are altered, as illustrated in Figure 2. The main features are due to the interception of rainfall by relatively impermeable surfaces such as roofs, roads and other paving.

UK towns have a variety of types of sewer networks. Some have separate foul and storm

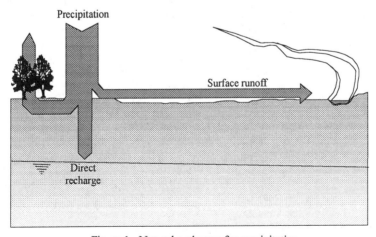

Figure 1. Natural pathways for precipitation

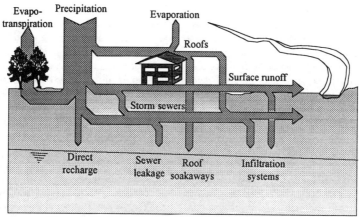

Figure 2. Urban pathways from precipitation to recharge

sewers, while others mix both types of water together. Some areas have partially separated systems, with storm runoff from roads and the fronts of houses carried by a storm sewer, while the rears are served by a foul sewer. The roof runoff from many houses, from at least the rear part of the house, is directed to soakaways to reduce the sewer loading. This latter system should increase recharge.

Roads and other paving might be expected to increase runoff, and they certainly do for higher intensity events. However some careful water balance studies on residential roads in Redbourn (UK) was carried out by Hollis and Ovenden (1988). They showed that only 11% of total rainfall became runoff, which increased to 28% if moderate and large storms (over 5 mm) were considered. They suggested that evaporation accounted for some of the missing water, and that the remainder was infiltrating through the road, particularly through gaps between kerbstones and cracks in the gutters. Deliberate recharge of road runoff is practised in some cities, through boreholes or in recharge basins. Detention basins are widely used to reduce peak runoff - these are likely to allow some infiltration to occur during the storage period, although silt may seal the bed unless it dries and cracks between events.

In many countries, there are no formal storm sewer systems, either because they are in (semi-)arid climates and runoff is rare, or because infrastructure installation is not complete due to rapid growth of the city. Runoff accumulates at the edge of paved areas, perhaps in ditches, and can infiltrate as well as take the intended route to surface water drainage.

There will certainly be some cities where recharge is increased because the paving reduces evapotranspiration and focuses the high runoff into these types of zones of localised recharge, the urban equivalent of the lower permeability geological cover mentioned above.

Even where storm sewers exist, they are unlikely to be watertight and leakage will occur. As with all sewers, leakage can be inwards and outwards, depending on the depth of the sewer relative to the water table, and the nature of the permeability around it. Sewers are often laid in permeable surrounds, such as sand or gravel placed as support material in the trench. This permeable path allows water trying to enter the sewer to flow laterally until it finds an opening. Conversely, water and pollutants leaking out of the sewer can flow laterally to find a convenient route to penetrate deeper into the aquifer. Even if a sewer is above the main water table, it will often run beneath a perched water table. On balance, most sewers collect extra water, that is more than enters through the drains and waste water pipes, and infiltration, as the waste water engineers call it, is a problem for design of sewer networks and waste water treatment plants. One example of an attempt to conduct a water balance on a sewer network is given by Lerner et al. (1993) for the city of Coventry, UK.

The vegetation cover of a city is very different from that of the countryside it replaced and will change evapotranspiration rates. An extreme and short term example where this change has altered recharge has been reported from Perth, Western Australia (Appleyard, 1995). The city is built on an extensive sand aquifer which is naturally covered by scrub vegetation, most of which is phreatophytic and draws moisture from the phreatic aquifer. The first step in the development of new housing areas is to clear the scrub, which immediately reduced evapotranspiration to nothing and permits much higher recharge to occur. Consequently the local water table can rise, and flooding of low-lying areas is a widespread feature of this city.

Water supply and sewerage networks

The water that is brought into cities for public water supplies is a major part of the water balance. Lerner (1990) quoted some examples from around the world. Imports ranged from 14 to 7500 mm/y, when the average flow was expressed in the same units as precipitation. The figures quoted are the extremes, with the very high value being for the central business district of Hong Kong. More typical values were in the range of 300-700 mm/y, which is more than average rainfall for most arid and semi-arid climates, and for many temperate zones. For example Birmingham, some 60 km from Nottingham, is typical of many UK cities and has almost equal average rainfall and water supply imports of some 700 mm/y for each.

Local groundwater may be added to the imported water to make up the total supply. For example, in Lima, Peru, 60% of the supply is local groundwater taken from several hundred municipal wells, while the remainder is river water. Local groundwater use may be restricted to certain areas where geology is favourable or where the supply infrastructure has not

been installed, or it may only be certain types of user. In Birmingham, UK, virtually all of the public supply is surface water, with groundwater restricted to industrial users.

Whatever the source, the water supply is distributed throughout the city to consumers, and then is collected for waste water disposal. It can find a variety of routes to recharge groundwater, as illustrated schematically in Figure 3. Elements of this network of paths are discussed in the following paragraphs.

A proportion of the water supplied to a city is consumed in the sense that it is evaporated to the atmosphere. Consumptive use by humans and in cooking is small, and the main consumption is in plant watering. This will be reasonably small in humid climates, but can rise rapidly in affluent cities where green gardens are desirable and affordable. In the UK, water consumption for gardening can be surprisingly high, with peak daily demands in a hot, dry period being three times the average, mainly due to garden watering.

A corollary of amenity irrigation is the high probability of excess irrigation giving rise to groundwater recharge, particularly with sandy and permeable soils. Over-irrigation of parks and gardens is common in urban areas. The water is not usually paid for, so there is little incentive to save. It will be applied by unskilled workers, for example by opening a valve on a large tanker and flooding the central reservation of a road. In affluent households, the value of a green garden will exceed the cost of almost any amount of water, even if metered, and again will often be applied by servants with little skill

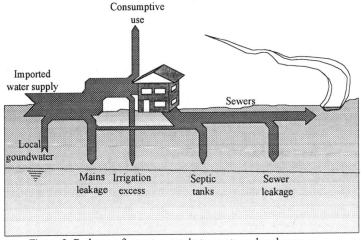

Figure 3. Pathways for water supply to waste and recharge

in judging the correct quantities. The result has been rising water tables and flooding of low lying areas and excavations in some Middle Eastern cities - an often cited example is Doha, Qatar, where the imported water supply is from desalination, an expensive source of water. In Riyadh, rising groundwater has also been a problem, and over-irrigation is partly the cause. Rushton and Al-Othman (1994) estimated that parks in Riyadh were receiving 22 mm/d of irrigation, while gardens were given 13 mm/d in an area with an average potential evapotranspiration of 8 mm/d. Another example is Perth in Western Australia (Sharma et al., 1996). Here the soils are hydrophobic and have low moisture retention capacity, so lawns are frequently and excessively watered to keep them green. Interestingly, the water table is not rising as a result because local groundwater, from shallow wells in each garden, is normally used for irrigation, leading to a net consumption of groundwater.

Leakage from water mains is a major source of urban recharge. The network of pressurised, unseen pipes can never be in perfect condition, and leaks are a recognised feature of water supply sizing and design. Loss rates of 20-25% are considered normal in the UK. The lowest rates occur in cities which have potential water resource shortages and aggressive leakage detection and repair programmes, of which Hong Kong is often cited as the best example with losses as low as 8%. At the other extreme are cities with old and under-maintained pipe networks, many illegal connections, and possibly in earthquake zones; loss rates up to 70% have been reported (Reed, 1980). Some caution must be exercised when converting loss rates to recharge because the reported rates are usually minimum night flows (MNFs) (Lerner, 1988). MNFs include legitimate uses at the time of measurement, such as night usage in factories and offices. MNFs also include leakage within premises which often flows to the sewer rather than into the ground and so does not become recharge. Literature reviews suggest that, internationally, 50% of MNFs may be leakage which can become recharge; for the UK, a rate of 20% of water supply has been suggested (Price and Read, 1989). A proportion of this recharge may be intercepted by sewers, which normally lie deeper than water mains. Nevertheless, recharge from water mains can exceed that from precipitation, even in temperate and humid climates.

Some of the issues of sewer leakage are discussed above in the context of storm systems, and apply equally to foul sewers. They can be expected to leak unless specially designed not to, leakage can be inward or outwards, and quantifying the recharge is difficult. In a study of a shallow aquifer system in Hong Kong, Lerner (1986) provided some chemical evidence (mainly BOD measurements) that groundwater was polluted by leaking sewers. In a later study in Coventry, his group again found evidence that some sewage leakage had occurred at the city scale, using ratios of boron and other chemical species (Nazari et al., 1993). In recent reviews of literature on sewer leakage and data from UK cities, both Lerner et al. (1994) and Misstear et al. (1995) showed that, although leakage occurs, there are almost no estimates of quantities, and no proven methods of identifying and quantifying it. Most of the straightforward chemical markers of sewage are present naturally in groundwater and occur in other sources of pollution. The only published regional estimate of sewer was that for Munich, which suggested that 5% losses occurred, equivalent to a recharge rate of 22 mm/y. A more detailed study of potential sewage marker species, which also attempts to quantify leakage is underway for Nottingham, and is reported by Barrett et al. (1997).

Not all cities have complete sewer systems to remove waste water for treatment, although they are almost universal in Northern Europe. In the UK for example, 97% of all households are sewered, not just in urban areas. The alternative disposal route for waterborne waste is through septic tanks and other soakaway systems. If used, these clearly return most waste water to the subsurface, as well as the chemicals it carries. Morris et al. (1994) give details of a shallow groundwater mound building up under Merida, Mexico, partly as a result of the recharge of most of the water supply through septic tanks. Another example was given by Thomson and Foster (1986) of Bermuda, where many urban areas are unsewered and rely on soakaway systems for waste water; roof catchments are used by many households for supply, thereby probably increasing recharge overall. Unfortunately the shallow fresh water lenses in the limestone aquifer are becoming more polluted by nitrate and other chemicals in the waste water. Well designed soakaway systems can reduce the microbiological and organic loads of sewage, particularly in intergranular aquifers with a substantial unsaturated zone and sufficient travel time. However they will not reduce the nitrogen loading, which will be ammonium or nitrate in anaerobic and aerobic aquifers respectively, unless there is volatilisation during oxidation of ammonium.

Table 1 Urbanisation effects on recharge in selected cities

City	Rainfall (mm/y)	Pre-urbanisation recharge (mm/y)	Current recharge (mm/y)	Increase in recharge due to urbanisation (%)
Merida, Mexico [A]	1000	100	600	600
Birmingham, UK [B]	730	137	132	-4

[A] Morris et al., 1994. [B] Knipe et al., 1993.

Hence dilution should be part of any strategy in which urban groundwater is to be used for both supply and disposal.

Net effects of urbanisation

Generalisation about the overall effects of urbanisation on precipitation recharge is not possible across all cities. We can say that the pathways are more numerous and more complex than in rural environments, and that many of them can enhance recharge to compensate for any loss of direct recharge due to impermeabilisation.

Similarly, the net effects of the water supply system cannot be generalised across all cities, although Foster et al. (1994) made a good attempt. Infrastructures, geologies and climates are too variable. We say that there will be substantial recharge from the water supply system, and that it will range from 90% of the supply in cool, unsewered cities to perhaps 10% in cities with extremely well maintained mains and sewers.

The complexity of urban infrastructure will always make it difficult to measure or estimate recharge rates. There remains much scope for research and studies of individual cities. A major need is for methods which can estimate areal average recharge rates, rather than point estimates, because the former will be of most value for modelling and water resource studies.

Two examples of the net effects of urbanisation are given in Table 1. Merida is rapidly developing and unsewered, while Birmingham is a mature, sewered city.

MANAGING THE ASSET AND THE PROBLEM

In the UK, the potential pollution problem associated with urban groundwater has led to a reduction in its use for public supply. This has inadvertently caused a second problem, that of rising groundwater and consequential geotechnical problems. This experience highlights the fact that cities are artificial environments and all facets must be actively managed. The asset value, as an under-used water resource in times of shortage and in the face of environmental pressures to reduce the use of rural groundwater, has been ignored. Recently some piecemeal re-development of public supply wells in cities has been started by individual water companies, but the UK not yet begun to manage the asset as a whole and consider its optimum use.

A risk-assessment framework can be used to view the groundwater management issue and assist decision making. The combination of source, pathway and target are schematically illustrated in Figure 4 to emphasise that all three must be considered to obtain a balanced view. Risk assessment presents its results in probabilistic terms, weighing up the likelihood of alternative outcomes. In a full assessment, it combines the probabilities of (a) possible source terms, that is types, quantities and frequencies of pollutant inputs, (b) attenuation (dilution and reaction) along the groundwater pathway, with (c) the effects on targets, whether health or financial. The analysis provides a rational way to chose between strategies for use or to consider methods of reducing risks. Even without a full probabilistic analysis, the risk assessment framework is still valuable to order consideration of the issue.

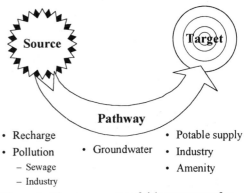

• Recharge
• Pollution
  – Sewage
  – Industry

• Groundwater

• Potable supply
• Industry
• Amenity

Figure 4. The components of risk assessment for groundwater

The main potential uses of urban groundwater (the targets of Figure 4) are:
- potable water supply,
- industrial use, and
- amenity water.

Amenity uses for urban groundwater range from refilling fountains and lakes to supporting canals or rivers at times of low flow. These uses may be less financially valuable than, say potable supply, but the hazards associated are much lower and lower quality water can be used. This in turn implies less concern about the source and pathway issues.

The pathway is of course from the surface through the aquifer, in both the saturated and vadose zones, to the outflow, which is normally a well. Classical vulnerability assessment provides a qualitative approach to understanding the likelihood of entry and attenuation of pollution. The sources for pollution are principally sewers and industry.

The source-pathway-target framework can be used to assess individual wells, or for urban groundwater as a whole. In either case use, aquifer protection and groundwater treatment can be balanced to take best advantage of the asset value while minimising the problems of urban recharge.

REFERENCES

Appleyard, S. J., 1993. Impact of stormwater infiltration basins on groundwater quality, Perth metropolitan region, Western Australia. Environmental Geology, 21, 227-236.

Barrett, M.H., K.M. Hiscock, S.J. Pedley, D.N. Lerner and J.H. Tellam, 1997. The use of marker species to establish the impact of the city of Nottingham (UK) on the quantity and quality of its underlying groundwater. Proc. IAH Congress, *Groundwater in the urban environment*, Nottingham 21-27 Sept 1997.

Foster, S.S.D., B.L. Morris and A.R. Laurence, 1994. Effects of urbanisation on groundwater recharge. In: W B Wilkinson (ed.), *Groundwater Problems in Urban Areas*, Thomas Telford, London, pp 43-63.

Greswell, R.B., J.W. Lloyd, D.N. Lerner & C.V. Knipe, 1994. Rising groundwater in the Birmingham area. W.B Wilkinson (ed.), *Groundwater Problems in Urban Areas*, Thomas Telford, London, 64-75, discussion 355-368.

Hollis, G.E. and J.C. Ovenden, 1988. The quantity of runoff from ten stretches of road, a car park and eight roofs in Hertfordshire, England during 1983. *Hydrological Processes*, 2, 227-243.

Knipe, C.V., J.W. Lloyd, D.N., Lerner, and R. Greswell, 1993. Rising groundwater levels in Birmingham and the engineering implications. CIRIA Special Publ. 92, 114 pages.

Lerner, D.N., 1986. Leaking pipes recharge groundwater. *Ground Water*, 24(5), 654-662.

Lerner, D.N., 1988. Unaccounted-for water a groundwater resource? *Aqua*, no. 1, 33-42.

Lerner, D.N., A. Issar & I. Simmers, 1990. *Groundwater recharge; a guide to understanding and estimating natural recharge.* Heise, Hannover, FRG. 345 pages.

Lerner, D.N., 1990. Groundwater recharge in urban areas. *Atmospheric Environment*, 24B(1), 29-33.

Lerner, D.N., M.W. Burston and P.K. Bishop, 1993. Hydrogeology of the Coventry region (UK): an urbanised, multi-layer dual-porosity aquifer system *Journal of Hydrology*, 149, 111-135.

Lerner, D.N., D. Halliday & J.M. Hoffman, 1994. The impact of sewers on groundwater quality. W.B Wilkinson (ed.), *Groundwater Problems in Urban Areas*, Thomas Telford, London, 330-341, discussion 197-211.

Misstear, B., M. White, P. Bishop and G. Anderson, 1995. Reliability of sewers in environmentally sensitive areas. CIRIA Funders report IP/14.

Morris, B.L., A.R. Lawrence and M.E. Stuart, 1994. The impact of urbanisation on groundwater quality (Project summary report), Tech. Rep. WC/94/56, British Geological Survey, Nottingham, UK.

Nazari, M.M., M.W. Burston, P.K. Bishop and D.N. Lerner, 1993. Urban groundwater pollution: a case study from Coventry, United Kingdom. *Ground Water*, 31(3), 417-424.

Price, M. And Reed, D.W., 1989. The influence of mains leakage and urban drainage on groundwate levels beneath conurbations in the UK. *Procs. Inst. Civ. Engrs. I*, 86, 31-39.

Reed, E.C., 1980. Report on water losses. *Aqua*, no. 8, 178-191.

Rushton and Al-Othman, 1994. Control of rising groundwater levels in Riyadh, Saudi Arabia. W.B Wilkinson (ed.), *Groundwater Problems in Urban Areas*, Thomas Telford, London, 299-309.

Sharma, M. L., D. E. Herner, J. D. Byrne and P. G. Kin, 1996. Nutrient discharge beneath urban lawns to a sandy coastal aquifer, Perth, Western Australia. *Hydrogeology Journal*, 4(1), 103-117.

Thomson, J.A.M. and S.S.D. Foster, 1986. Effect of urbanisation on the groundwater of limestone islands: an analysis of the Bermuda case. *Journal Institution of Water Engineers and Scientists*, 40(6), 527-540.

Rise of the groundwater table when flow is obstructed by shallow tunnels

Paul G. Marinos & Michael J. Kavvadas
Department of Civil Engineering, National Technical University of Athens, Greece

ABSTRACT: The paper investigates the steady-state rise of the groundwater table upstream of a shallow tunnel due to the obstruction of the groundwater flow in the direction normal to the tunnel axis, using a steady-state finite-element groundwater flow model. Based on the parametric results of the analyses, the paper proposes a simplified analytical method which gives reasonably accurate predictions of the magnitude of the water table rise via a closed-form analytical expression. It is shown that the predicted magnitude of the steady-state water table rise is proportional to the tunnel height and to the original hydraulic gradient in the direction normal to the tunnel axis. The predicted rise of the water table also depends on the depth of the tunnel below the original groundwater table. For uniform ground permeability, the predicted steady-state rise is independent of the hydraulic parameters of the aquifer. It is obvious, however, that the time required for the water table to rise and eventually reach the steady-state condition is dependent on the permeability and storativity characteristics of the aquifer. For typical values of the hydraulic gradient (2-5%), the predicted water table rise is in the order of   % of the tunnel height for tunnels located just below the water table.

1 INTRODUCTION

The enforcement of strict rules (mainly for environmental reasons) on the exploitation of groundwater in urban areas can result in significant water table rises and sometimes even in the reversal of the prevailing hydraulic gradients. Under such conditions, a rising shallow groundwater table can be a significant hazard for the structures in an urban environment. Even in rural areas, a rising water table can adversely affect the root system of the vegetation thus influencing the local ecosystem. In addition to the well-known factors causing fluctuations of the groundwater table (e.g. the seasonal discharge and recharge of shallow unconfined aquifers), the level of a water table may rise as a result of the construction of a long tunnel at a shallow depth below the piezometric surface if that tunnel obstructs the groundwater flow in a direction perpendicular to the tunnel axis. The purpose of this paper is to investigate these effects and estimate the magnitude of the water table rise due to the construction of shallow tunnels.

The types of structures considered to be at risk by a rising groundwater table include the basements and foundations of buildings and other tunnels or underground structures. In general, a rising water table can have the following adverse effects on adjacent structures:

1. Appreciable reduction of the bearing capacity of shallow foundations.

2. Development of uplift water pressures under foundations and floor slabs.

3. Possible ground heave due to the reduction of the effective stresses caused by the increasing pore water pressures.

4. Expansion of heavily compacted fills under the foundations of structures.

5. Appreciable settlements of poorly compacted fills upon wetting.

6. Possible ground collapse in the case of soils with high collapse potential in the zone which becomes saturated by the rising water table.

7. Potential leakage of groundwater (or simply the appearance of moisture) in basements of buildings and service ducts.

8. Increased loads on retaining systems and basement walls of buildings.

9. Increased need for drainage and the potential of instabilities in temporary excavations.

In addition to the above, the rising

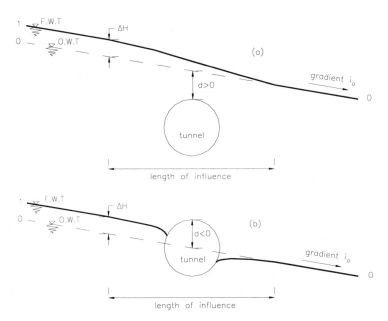

Figure 1. Sketch showing the rise (ΔH) of the Original Water Table (OWT) upstream of a tunnel located: (a) at a shallow depth below the water table and (b) at a depth intersecting the original water table. FWT=Final Water Table.

groundwater table can cause the propagation of contaminants contained in the previously partially saturated zone. Such previously harmless contaminants can be mobilised upon saturation, forced to migrate downstream and diffuse within the aquifer polluting the groundwater. Where the rising groundwater table can reach the surface, flooding and an increased risk of pollution of surface watercourses may become a problem. Finally, the rising of a near-surface groundwater table can affect the efficiency of highway drainage systems (Johnson, 1994).

The above adverse effects of the rising groundwater tables, in conjunction with the rapidly increasing number of underground transit systems in the urban environment, make necessary the investigation of the effects of such tunnels on the groundwater levels, since these systems are usually constructed at shallow depths close to the piezometric surface. The present paper studies these effects and proposes a method to estimate the magnitude of the groundwater table due to the presence of a tunnel.

2 THE EFFECT OF TUNNELS ON GROUNDWATER LEVELS

The construction of a tunnel at a shallow depth

below the groundwater table impedes the flow in the direction normal to the tunnel axis, thus causing a rise of the groundwater table in the upstream area. Figure 1 presents a sketch of the groundwater table levels before (Original Water Table - OWT) and after (Final Water Table - FWT) the construction of a tunnel in two cases: (a) a tunnel completely submerged below the original water table and (b) a tunnel located at a depth intersecting the original water table. The figure shows schematically the magnitude (ΔH) of the rise of the water table upstream of the tunnel. The existence of the tunnel forces the groundwater to circumvent it by locally increasing the length of the flow path and the corresponding flow velocity. The required extra energy loss is provided by the locally increased hydraulic gradient in the "length of influence"; the increased hydraulic gradient in turn causes a moderate rise of the water table in the upstream area. This effect extends to some distance in the upstream direction and fades in a large distance from the tunnel, since the disturbance in the flow regime caused by the construction of the tunnel can only be local. The water table fluctuation caused by the tunnel occurs progressively in a time-scale governed by the hydraulic conductivity of the aquifer and the magnitude of the long-term rise (ΔH).

50

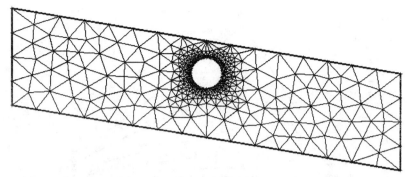

Figure 2. Typical finite element model used in the analysis of the steady-state flow around a cylindrical tunnel. The inclined top surface represents the originally uniform hydraulic gradient (i_o) in the direction perpendicular to the tunnel axis.

The magnitude of the rise of the groundwater table due to the construction of a shallow tunnel was investigated by analysing the two-dimensional steady-state flow around a cylindrical tunnel located at a depth (d) below the groundwater table. The groundwater table was assumed to have a uniform initial gradient (io) in the direction perpendicular to the tunnel axis. The analysis was performed using a two-dimensional finite element model of the steady-state groundwater flow around a cylindrical object simulating the tunnel. Figure 2 presents a typical finite element mesh layout used in the analyses. The inclined upper boundary presents the position of the original groundwater table. The depth (d) of the tunnel crest below the water table was varied to parametrically investigate its effect on the magnitude of the water table rise (ΔH). The quantities involved in the analyses are further described in Figure 1.

The finite element model used in the analyses is described by Kavvadas and Marinos (1994). The model is based on the Galerkin method of weighted residuals and solves the time-dependent, two-dimensional flow in a porous medium around a cylindrical object. While the model can study the time dependent evolution of the flow regime around the tunnel, only the final (steady-state) response was considered in the present study, by eliminating the time dependent terms. The reason for this simplification is that the steady-state response corresponds to the maximum water table rise and, since tunnels are permanent structures, the steady-state response will eventually occur during the life of the tunnel, regardless of the time required to reach that condition. The issue of the time required to reach the long-term steady-state condition is however briefly discussed at the end of the paper.

Figure 3 summarizes the results of the finite element analyses. The horizontal axis plots the depth (d) of the tunnel crest below the original position of the water table, normalized with the tunnel diameter. The vertical axis represents the magnitude of the steady-state water table rise (ΔH) upstream of the tunnel (also normalized with the tunnel diameter). The marks shown on the plot correspond to the computed data points for several values of the gradient (i_o) of the water table (equal to 1%, 2.5%, 5%, 10% and 15%). The figure also shows the best fit lines connecting the computed data points for the same value of the hydraulic gradient. For each value of the hydraulic gradient, the peak rise of the groundwater table is observed for d/D=0 i.e., when the tunnel is just fully submerged. The computed steady-state rise of the water table decreases gradually for negative values of (d), i.e., as part of the tunnel emerges above the groundwater table; the effect of the tunnel on the water table is obviously zero for d/D=-1, i.e., when the bottom of the tunnel is just above the water table. For a fully submerged tunnel, i.e., for positive values of the depth (d), the rise of the water table decreases gradually as the depth (d) increases; eventually the effect becomes practically negligible when the crest of the tunnel is at a depth of about two tunnel diameters below the original groundwater table.

3 THE PROPOSED SIMPLIFIED MODEL

The construction of a tunnel at a shallow depth below the groundwater table impedes the flow and as a result causes a moderate rise of the water table in the upstream area (Figure 1). The magnitude of the water table rise depends on the

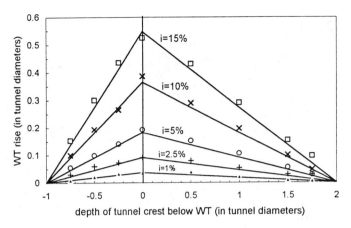

Figure 3. Finite-element predictions of the rise of the groundwater table as a function of the depth of the tunnel crest below the water table and the magnitude of the original hydraulic gradient (i) of the aquifer in the direction perpendicular to the tunnel axis.

size of the tunnel, its depth below the original water table and the hydraulic gradient in the direction perpendicular to the tunnel axis. The rise of the water table due to the construction of a tunnel is a time dependent process: the water table begins to rise when the tunnel is constructed and eventually the rise reaches a maximum value which corresponds to the steady-state condition. The time required to reach the steady-state condition depends on the geometrical characteristics of the project and the hydraulic parameters of the aquifer. However, since tunnels are permanent structures the steady-state condition will eventually be reached in practically all cases; it is thus usually justifiable to design for the steady-state rise of the water table. The previous section described the finite-element analyses performed and discussed the main results of a parametric investigation of this phenomenon. In the present section, a simple analytical model is proposed which results in a closed-form expression for the prediction of the steady-state rise of the water table due to the construction of a shallow tunnel. The model is based on the following assumptions:

1. The construction of the tunnel influences the groundwater table only in the direction perpendicular to its axis, i.e., the rise of the water table only depends on the component of the hydraulic gradient perpendicular to the tunnel axis. This is of course an obvious assumption.

2. The groundwater flow prior to the construction of the tunnel is spatially and temporally uniform.

3. When the steady-state condition is eventually re-established, the presence of the

tunnel does not alter the amount of the groundwater flow in the aquifer, i.e.,

$$Q_o = Q_f \qquad (1)$$

where (Q_o) is the original discharge and (Q_f) the final discharge in the domain influenced by the construction of the tunnel. Essentially, this assumption implies that the disturbance in the flow caused by the tunnel is only local and thus the hydraulic characteristics in the flow regime around the tunnel are gradually re-adjusted to maintain the same discharge as before the construction of the tunnel.

4. The tunnel influences the elevation of the surface of the groundwater table by an appreciable amount only if it is located within a shallow zone having a thickness equal to two-times its submerged thickness. This assumption is based on the results of the finite-element analyses (Figure 3) which show that the rise of the groundwater table for fully submerged tunnels is practically negligible for depths exceeding two tunnel diameters. Thus, for a fully submerged tunnel, the ratio of the cross sectional area of the flow domain before the construction of the tunnel (A_o) to that after the construction of the tunnel (A_f) is:

$$A_o / A_f = 3D/(3D-D) = 1.5 \qquad (2)$$

The same relationship also holds for partially submerged tunnels, since in such a case the near-surface zone influenced by the tunnel is also assumed to have a thickness equal to three-times the depth of the tunnel bottom below the water table.

5. The existence of the tunnel forces the groundwater to by-pass it by increasing the length

52

of the flow path. If (L_o) is the length of the initial straight line flow path and (L_f) the average length of the final flow path, then:

(a) It is assumed that the length of influence of the tunnel along the flow direction is equal to four tunnel diameters for a fully submerged tunnel (or more generally equal to four times the submerged depth of the tunnel), i.e., 1.5 diameters upstream of the tunnel and 1.5 diameters in the downstream. This assumption is based on the deformed shape of the flow lines computed from the finite-element analyses.

(b) The maximum length (L_m) of the final flow path corresponds to the stream-line which is tangent at the tunnel. Assuming that the shape of this stream-line is a circular arc tangent to the tunnel, then: $L_m/L_o = 1.16$ (for L_o equal to four tunnel diameters).

(c) The length (L) of any stream-line is in the range (L_m, L_o) as the distance of that stream-line from the tunnel increases. It is assumed that the length (L) of a stream-line decreases parabolically as the distance of that stream-line from the tunnel increases, i.e.,

$$L = L_o + \left(L_m - L_o\right)\left(1 - \frac{x}{3R}\right)^2 \qquad (3)$$

where (R) is the tunnel radius. For a fully submerged tunnel with its crest located at a depth equal to one tunnel diameter (i.e., for a symmetric split of the stream-lines above and below the tunnel), the average length (L_f) of the final flow path is:

$$L_f = \frac{1}{3R}\int_0^{3R} L\, dx = \left(1 + 0.333\left(\frac{L_m}{L_o} - 1\right)\right)L_o = 1.053\, L_o \,(4)$$

i.e., the average increase in the length of the flow path is about 5.3 % (for L_o equal to four tunnel diameters).

Using the above assumptions:

$$Q_f = Q_o \Rightarrow k \cdot i_f \cdot A_f = k \cdot i_o \cdot A_o \Rightarrow$$

$$\frac{\Delta h_f}{L_f} \cdot A_f = \frac{\Delta h_o}{L_o} \cdot A_o \Rightarrow$$

$$\Delta H \equiv \Delta h_f - \Delta h_o = i_o \cdot L_o \cdot \left\{\left(\frac{A_o}{A_f}\right)\left(\frac{L_f}{L_o}\right) - 1\right\} \Rightarrow$$

$$\frac{\Delta H}{D} = i_o \cdot \frac{L_o}{D} \cdot \left\{\left(\frac{A_o}{A_f}\right)\left(\frac{L_f}{L_o}\right) - 1\right\} = 2.32\, i_o \qquad (5)$$

i.e., the steady-state rise (ΔH) of the groundwater table upstream of a tunnel with its crest located at a depth $d=D$ below the water table is proportional to the hydraulic gradient (i_o) of the aquifer and to the tunnel diameter (D). This formula compares reasonably well with the predictions of the finite element analyses as shown in the following table:

Steady-state rise of the groundwater table (in meters) for a tunnel with its crest located at a depth equal to one tunnel diameter

Initial hydraulic gradient (%)	Tunnel diameter D=6m		Tunnel diameter D=10m	
	finite-element	Eq. (5)	finite-element	Eq. (5)
0.5	0.067	0.07	0.11	0.12
1.0	0.13	0.14	0.22	0.23
2.5	0.32	0.35	0.53	0.58
5.0	0.64	0.70	1.06	1.16
10.0	1.21	1.39	2.01	2.32

The above table gives the predicted rise of the groundwater table for a tunnel with its crest located at a depth equal to one tunnel diameter. For tunnels located at different depths, the finite-element results show that there exists a practically linear relationship between the predicted rise and the depth of the tunnel crest below the water table. Guided by these predictions and the simplified analytical model previously described, we can write the following approximate relationships for the magnitude of the steady-state water table rise (ΔH) in terms of the initial hydraulic gradient (i_o) of the aquifer, the tunnel diameter (D) and the depth (d) of the tunnel crest below the water table:

1. For fully submerged tunnels ($d > 0$):

$$\Delta H = 2.32 \cdot i_o \cdot D \cdot \left(2 - \frac{d}{D}\right) \qquad (6)$$

2. For partially submerged tunnels ($d < 0$):

$$\Delta H = 4.64 \cdot i_o \cdot D \cdot \left(1 + \frac{d}{D}\right) \qquad (7)$$

These relationships represent a linear variation of the water table rise with the depth (d) of the tunnel crest, as shown in Figure 3.

The above estimate of the water table rise represents the long-term value which can be reached in a time period governed by the hydraulic conductivity (k) of the aquifer and the magnitude (ΔH) of the long-term rise. The characteristic time (t_c) can be obtained by a dimensional analysis and is equal to $t_c = \Delta H / k$, where (k) is the engineering permeability (units: length / time). This time can vary between a few days in the case of a relatively pervious aquifer to several decades in the case of a ground with a very low permeability.

53

4 CONCLUSIONS

The paper investigates the steady-state rise of the groundwater table upstream of a shallow tunnel due to the obstruction of the groundwater flow in the direction normal to the tunnel axis. The effects are studied using a steady-state finite-element groundwater flow model. Based on the results of the finite-element analyses and reasonable arguments regarding the depth of influence of the tunnel (equal to three diameters) and the extent of the disturbance of the flow regime along the stream-lines (equal to four tunnel diameters), the paper proposes a simplified analytical method which gives reasonably accurate predictions of the magnitude of the water table rise via a closed-form analytical expression (equations 6 and 7). It is shown that the predicted magnitude of the steady-state water table rise is proportional to the tunnel height and proportional to the original hydraulic gradient of the aquifer in the direction normal to the tunnel axis. The predicted rise of the water table also depends on the depth of the tunnel below the original groundwater table. For uniform ground permeability, the predicted steady-state rise is independent of the hydraulic parameters of the aquifer, while the time required for the water table to gradually rise and eventually reach the steady-state condition is obviously dependent on the permeability and storativity characteristics of the aquifer. For typical values of the hydraulic gradient (0.5-5%), the predicted water table rise is in the order of 1-10% of the tunnel height for tunnels located just below the original level of the water table. For tunnels located at some depth below the water table or for partially submerged tunnels, the magnitude of the water table rise is lower.

REFERENCES

Johnson S.T. (1994) "Rising groundwater levels: engineering and environmental implications", *Proceedings of a Conference on Groundwater Problems in Urban Areas*, ICE, 285-297, Thomas Telford, London.

Kavvadas M. and Marinos P.G. (1994) "Prediction of groundwater table lowering for lignite open-cast mining in a karstic terrain in western Macedonia, Greece", *Quarterly Journal of Engineering Geology*, Vol 27, S41-S55.

Groundwater in the Urban Environment: Problems, Processes and Management, Chilton et al. (eds)
© 1997 Balkema, Rotterdam, ISBN 90 5410 837 1

Sustainable groundwater management for fast-growing cities: Mission achievable or mission impossible?

Brian L. Morris, Adrian R. Lawrence & Stephen S. D. Foster
Hydrogeology Group, British Geological Survey, Wallingford, UK

ABSTRACT: Urbanisation has a major impact on recharge to, and groundwater flow within, aquifers beneath cities. This results from factors which include the import of large quantities of water for supply, modifications to pluvial drainage, extensive use of the ground for effluent discharge and waste disposal and large-scale intra-urban groundwater abstraction. The consequences include problems of aquifer depletion, saline intrusion, land subsidence or, at the other extreme, locally troublesome rising groundwater levels. Furthermore, in most developing cities, population growth precedes the development of infrastructure to handle wastewater, leading to widespread contamination of shallow groundwater by domestic and industrial effluent. Given the large storage of most aquifers and their long residence times, there is often a major time lag before the problems of groundwater pollution become fully apparent. The net outcome is increasing water scarcity with escalating long-term marginal costs for water-supply. The traditional use of low-cost, minimally-treated groundwater for public water-supply in urban areas is being threatened and increasing health risks are involved in some hydrogeological environments. Against this background, urban groundwater management needs are assessed from the rather different perspectives of water-supply provision, wastewater/solid waste disposal and engineering infrastructure development and maintenance. The key to sustainable city development is the reconciliation of these three legitimate but different and potentially conflicting functions. A scheme of realistic policy strategies is proposed as a logical framework to help attain a balance between the three urban development needs. The paper does not include specific examples because of length constraints, but the policy paper from which it is drawn uses detailed studies of five developing world cities and selective study in five others.

1 URBAN GROUNDWATER MANAGEMENT ISSUES

1.1 *Analysis from different perspectives*

The principal urban services and facilities which relate to groundwater are (Figure 1):
- provision of water-supply
- wastewater elimination and solid waste disposal
- engineering infrastructure and buildings.

The first two of these impact directly upon the underlying groundwater system, and this can impose a number of serious constraints on or threats to urban development. There is a strong interaction between these functions because *benefits* from the use of the local subsurface (as aquifer, receptor or foundation medium) are apparent at the outset (Table 1) while many of the *costs* involved are longterm and not always appreciated at early, *ad hoc* stages of development. Yet professional and administrative

personnel in the municipal utilities concerned with the provision of each of these functions tend to have rather different perspectives on groundwater-related issues, perspectives which affect the development and maintenance of their respective services.

Water-supply: The provision of water-supply relates directly to groundwater, since it is frequently an important or major source both for the municipal water company, typically operating few high-yielding wells or wellfields, and for the private sector. In general terms the interests of the municipal water-supply companies and the private (residential and industrial) abstractors are similar. Both are concerned about issues of decreasing availability and deteriorating quality of groundwater, since they lead to rising water production costs, customer complaints about water quality nuisance factors, and/or to public health risks. They may also be concerned about the establishment or protection of legal rights to abstract groundwater. However, their priorities on these

Table 1. Balancing benefits and costs-urban use of the subsurface environment.

FUNCTION OF SUBSURFACE	INITIAL BENEFITS	LONG-TERM COSTS

Water-Supply Source	- low capital cost
	- staged development possible
	- initial water quality better
	- private and public supply can develop separately
		- excessive abstraction can lead to:
		  - abandonment/reduced efficiency of wells
		  - saline intrusion risk in coastal cities
		  - subsidence risk in susceptible environments

In-situ Sanitation Receptor	- low-cost community-built facilities possible - permits rapid expansion under sanitary conditions - uses natural attenuation capacity of subsoil	- sustainability of groundwater abstraction threatened if contaminant load exceeds aquifer assimilation capacity
Pluvial Drainage Receptor	- low capital costs - conserves water resources - less flood risk along downstream watercourses - roof runoff provides dilution of urban contaminants	- contamination from industrial/commercial area and most highways
Industrial Effluent/Solid Waste Disposal	- reduced manufacturing costs	- noxious effluent may prejudice groundwater quality - system favours irresponsible attitude to waste stream management

problems and on the options for tackling them are rather different.

The municipal water-supply utilities tend to take a broad view, and although affected by site specific problems are most concerned about overall resource scarcity and about water quality problems that are costly or impossible to treat. They can consider developing alternative water-supplies from beyond the city nucleus, into periurban areas and the rural hinterland. However, development of groundwater from beyond city limits may lead them into conflict with other major groundwater users, especially agricultural irrigators.

Private residential and industrial abstractors inevitably have to take a narrower view. They are primarily concerned about decreasing performance and deteriorating quality of the well(s) on the land they own or occupy. Furthermore, their options for dealing with any problems that arise are limited, since they are generally restricted to the specific site concerned. They may be able to treat the groundwater supply (at least for some quality problems) or deepen their wells (in efforts to overcome problems of yield reduction). Ultimately, the decision on continued use will depend upon the cost and reliability of the supply, compared to that available from the municipal water-supply utility.

Wastewater Elimination & Solid Waste Disposal: The subsurface is viewed from a very different perspective by those concerned with wastewater elimination, even where this function is also the responsibility of the municipal water-supply company and even more so where it is organised separately.

The first question that arises is whether it is feasible to dispose of liquid effluents to the ground, which may not be the case where soil infiltration capacity is low, due to shallow water-table or to relatively impermeable superficial strata. This may prevent the installation of conventional on-site sanitation units and exclude the possibility of disposing of larger quantities of wastewater through infiltration structures. A second set of issues is the impact of wastewater discharge and waste disposal on groundwater quality. In particular:

- whether the type and density of in-situ sanitation units is such as to seriously impact on groundwater quality
- whether the location and quality of downstream wastewater discharge from the mains sewerage system, together with its reuse for agricultural irrigation, is such as to prejudice the interests of groundwater users
- whether the siting, design and operation of landfills receiving solid wastes is acceptable from the point-of-view of leachate impacting on groundwater quality.

In the absence of a properly-resourced and adequately-empowered regulatory body, these issues rarely receive adequate consideration.

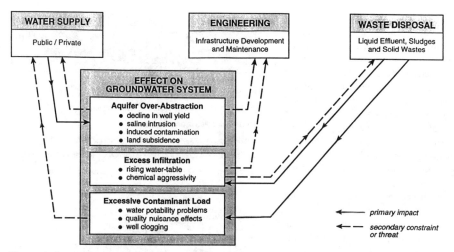

Figure 1. Interaction between urban services through the underlying groundwater system.

Engineering infrastructure: Groundwater-related issues which concern municipal engineers responsible for developing and maintaining urban buildings and infrastructure result from major lowering of groundwater levels (due to heavy abstraction for water-supply) in some ground conditions or from rising water-table (due to increased infiltration rates), where groundwater abstraction is absent/has decreased. Issues include:

- falling water-table: physical damage to buildings and to underground services, such as tunnels and sewers, as a result of land settlement and subsidence

- rising water-table: damage to subsurface engineering structures as a result of hydrostatic uplift or reduced bearing capacity, inundation of subsurface facilities, excessive ingress of groundwater to sewers, chemical attack on concrete foundations, subsurface facilities and underground structures.

Those responsible for maintaining the urban buildings and infrastructure are concerned about minimising such damage or trying to recover remedial costs, but it is rare that this can be achieved, since attribution to individual abstractors or polluters is difficult. At present it often has, unsatisfactorily, to be borne by the community at large, through urban taxes or rates, or even more unjustly by the owners of the damaged properties themselves.

1.2 *Interrelated and conflicting processes*

Hence effective management of urban aquifers has to reconcile the demands of water supply, waste disposal and urban subsurface engineering, even though in operation, these functions are not only strongly interrelated but also can be in conflict. Examining the effects each have on the subsurface can help develop the integrated approach so necessary to avoid serious long-term problems.

Groundwater resource effects: In most instances urbanisation affects underlying groundwater systems in two ways:

- by radically changing patterns and rates of aquifer recharge
- by adversely affecting the quality of groundwater.

The effect on recharge arises both from modifications to the natural infiltration system, such as surface impermeabilisation and changes in natural drainage, and from the introduction of the water service network, which is invariably associated with large volumes of water mains leakage and wastewater seepage (Foster et al, 1993).

The net effect on the quality of recharge is generally adverse, urbanisation processes being widely the cause of severe, but essentially diffuse, pollution of groundwater by nitrogen and sulphur compounds and rising levels of salinity (Morris et al, 1994). Quite widespread groundwater contamination by petroleum products, chlorinated hydrocarbons and other synthetic compounds, and on a more localised basis by pathogenic bacteria, protozoa and viruses, is also encountered (BGS et al, 1996). These adverse effects conflict with the use of groundwater for urban water-supply.

Consequences of groundwater abstraction: Groundwater abstraction necessarily results in a decline in aquifer water-levels. Where abstraction is limited, groundwater levels stabilise at a new equilibrium such that flow to the area of groundwater pumping balances abstraction. However, where groundwater withdrawal is heavy and concentrated, such that it greatl exceeds average rates of local recharge, water-levels may continue to decline over decades. Serious declines will lead to reducing well yields which can provoke an expensive and inefficient cycle of well deepening to regain productivity, or even premature loss of investment due to forced abandonment of wells.

Major changes in hydraulic head distribution within aquifers can lead to the reversal of groundwater flow directions, which can in turn induce serious water-quality deterioration as a result of ingress of sea water, up-coning/intrusion of other saline groundwater and induced downward leakage of polluted water from the surface. Thus severe depletion of groundwater resources is often compounded by major water-quality degradation.

In some unconsolidated aquifers groundwater quality also may suffer as a result of pumping-induced subsidence. Differential subsidence causes damage not only to individual buildings and roads, but also to piped services routed underground, by increasing water mains leakage and rupturing sewerage systems, oil pipelines and subsurface tanks. This can cause serious contamination of underlying aquifers.

Impacts of groundwater on urban infrastructure: The radical changes in frequency and rate of subsurface infiltration caused by urbanisation tend overall to increase the rate of groundwater recharge. If the underlying aquifer system is not utilised, or the shallow subsurface is not sufficiently permeable to transmit away the extra water, then groundwater levels will rise. As the water-table rises towards the land surface, initially tunnels and service ducts may suffer structural damage or be flooded. Both hydraulic and corrosion effects on building foundations and tunnel linings can follow. In extreme cases, where the water-table reaches the land surface, there may be a health hazard because septic tanks malfunction and water polluted with pathogens may accumulate in surface depressions.

On the other hand, where the city is underlain by a productive shallow aquifer and groundwater abstraction is significant, a declining water table will mask the presence of increased urban infiltration rates and indeed in some unconsolidated aquifers the geotechnical problems associated with pumping-induced subsidence can result. However, as cities evolve, intra-urban abstraction often declines, either as a direct result of groundwater quality deterioration or as a consequence of unrelated economic factors.

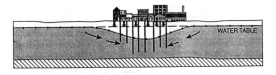

(a) town becomes city

- Water table lowered beneath city, wells deepened.

- Wastewater discharged to ground.

- Shallow groundwater in city centre becomes polluted.

- Subsidence can occur if aquifer is unconsolidated and interbedded.

- Expansion of pluvial drainage to ground and local watercourses.

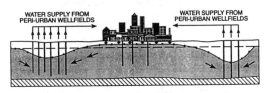

(b) city expands

- Aquifer beneath city largely abandoned because of contamination.

- Water table begins to rise beneath city due to cessation of pumping and high urban recharge.

- Significant water table decline in city periphery due to heavy abstraction from wellfields.

- Incipient contamination of urban wellfields by groundwater recharged beneath city centre.

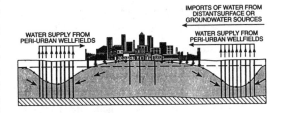

(c) city expands further

- Wellfields unable to cope with increased demand and threatened by outward growth of city.

- Expensive water imports from distant sources or conjunctive use schemes necessary.

- Water table rises beneath city nucleus - problems of flooding, wastewater disposal etc.

- Scope reduced for (low cost) pluvial drainage to ground.

Figure 2. Evolution of water supply and waste disposal in a typical city underlain by a shallow aquifer.

In these circumstances, the groundwater table begins to recover and may eventually (over decades) rise to levels higher than pre-urbanisation, as a result of the additional urban recharge (Figure 2).

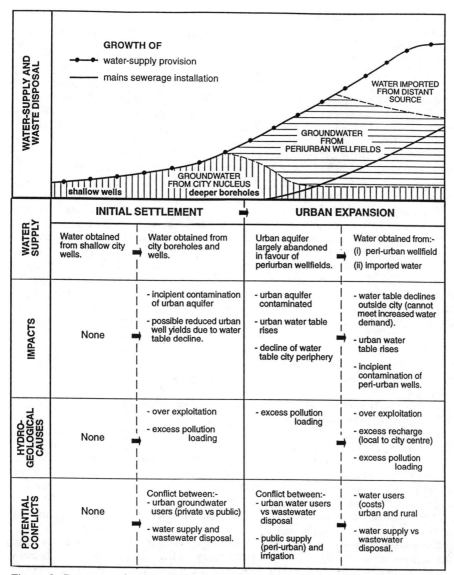

Figure 3. Processes of urban evolution from the groundwater resources perspective; pattern and stage.

This can provide a widespread threat to a well-established urban infrastructure constructed when foundation and cabled/piped services design did not need to take account of a near-surface water table. Thus the hydrogeological regime continues to exert a major control over an urban infrastructure, even when the city in question has ceased to depend significantly on local groundwater for water-supply.

1.3 *Pattern and stage of urban evolution*

Pattern: All cities evolve from small settlements, a process which in the more developed economies tended to take place over centuries (Figure 3). However, in the developing world, where most of the world's population growth is currently occurring, growth rates are unparalleled in human history. It took the population of Greater London from 1800 to 1910 to grow from 1.1 to 7.3 million, yet similar growth rates have been recorded in some Latin American and Asian cities in a few decades (Black, 1994).

One inevitable result in many fast-developing cities has been the appearance of informal settlements located on marginal land or in burgeoning periurban districts. The proportion of urban poor in such settlements is typically between 30-60% of the overall urban population and it is estimated by the year 2000 that over 1,000 million dwellers will be living in this type of settlement, many of which increasingly depend on the subsurface for water-supply and as a waste receptor (Earthscan,1990).

Stage: The effect of urban water-supply and wastewater disposal will not be limited to the geographic area occupied by the city itself. This is because cities, especially those undergoing major expansion, are intimately linked with their hinterlands. For instance, as cities grow, water supplies that were originally obtained from shallow underlying aquifers may no longer be sufficient, either because the available resource is too limited or because of quality deterioration from pollution. The extra water resources required will either be tapped from deeper aquifers, or more often will be drawn from aquifers or surface water bodies in the city hinterland area, invariably at ever-increasing distance and marginal cost, often competing with a prior use (notably agriculture) too.

The relative importance of the different roles the subsurface plays in city infrastructure is much more dependent on the development stage which a city has reached than on its size. For instance, as cities expand, they may envelop their own periurban wellfields, and progressive deterioration in groundwater quality may result either from direct urban encroachment or by infiltration from polluted surface watercourses in downstream riparian areas. There will be an inevitable hidden economic cost in such expansion, either from increased water treatment requirements or from the need to substitute new water sources from more distant areas.

Incipient versus mature condition: In fact, the time element is a crucial consideration when considering groundwater problems because:
- groundwater problems normally evolve over long periods
- mature problems are usually very much more difficult to address than incipient ones
- the benefits of management actions normally only accrue on a fairly long time-scale.

Mature problems usually develop where controls over groundwater abstraction and subsurface contaminant loading are weak, and there is no effective long-term groundwater management strategy in place. A further complication arises where groundwater is exploited by a large number of private boreholes. All too often, when fears of groundwater overexploitation arise, municipal abstraction is constrained without corresponding restrictions enforced on private well drilling. The common consequence is an epidemic of private well drilling and replacement of a moderate number of municipal supplies, which were at least capable of being systematically controlled, monitored, protected and treated, by a very large number of private sources. These are usually of shallower depth, inadequately sited and poorly constructed, making them much more vulnerable to pollution. Moreover, they are generally used unmonitored and untreated, resulting in greater health risks.

There is rarely adequate knowledge of the total quantities of groundwater eventually being pumped, but in many cases the overall exploitation of groundwater increases, rather than decreases, despite fears about saline intrusion and/or land subsidence. Since many boreholes have inadequate sanitary seal, they can provide pathways for rapid downward migration of contaminants to deeper high-quality aquifers. Thus where shallow boreholes are progressively deepened to tap confined as well as shallow aquifers, they can act as conduits for cross-contamination to occur, driven by differences in head between the various aquifers.

2 IMPROVING GROUNDWATER RESOURCE MANAGEMENT

2.1 *Underlying causes of management problems*

The numerous groundwater management issues that the concurrent exercise of the water supply, waste disposal and urban engineering functions pose need to be addressed, if urban development is to be sustainable. In essence problems arise from two underlying causes (Table 2):
- inadequately-controlled groundwater abstraction
- excessive subsurface contaminant load.

Additionally, in some situations where abstraction is not possible or has been abandoned, excess urban infiltration may cause different types of problem.

Inadequately-controlled groundwater abstraction: In most cases where groundwater is the primary or sole source of urban water-supply, and urban abstraction wells are mainly within city limits, the overall rate of groundwater abstraction will significantly exceed the long-term rate of groundwater recharge. A series of negative economic consequences and environmental impacts will sooner or later follow. Exceptions to this general rule may exist, but in the vast majority of cases there will be a clear need (and long-term benefits) in imposing, at the very least, selective constraints on groundwater abstraction. Where municipal water-supply is obtained from periurban

Table 2. Urban groundwater problems and management requirements.

UNDERLYING CAUSE	RESULTANT GROUNDWATER PROBLEMS	MANAGEMENT REQUIREMENTS
Inadequately-Controlled Groundwater Abstraction	over-abstraction of good quality resource within city limits	reserve good quality (deeper) groundwater for sensitive uses and encourage use of shallow (poor-quality) groundwater for non-sensitive uses
	Over-abstraction of good quality resource around city periphery (competition between urban supply and agricultural irrigation)	reserve good-quality groundwater for potable water supply and substitute treated wastewater or shallow poor-quality groundwater for irrigation
Excessive Urban Infiltration	rising water-table beneath city causing: - basement flooding - malfunction of in-situ sanitation units - reversal of aquifer flow directions (with contamination of periurban wellfields by polluted urban groundwater)	reduce urban infiltration by: - control of mains leakage - reducing seepage from on-site sanitation unit by mains sewerage installation increase abstraction of shallow (polluted) groundwater for non-sensitive uses
Excessive Subsurface Contaminant Load	contamination of municipal water-supply boreholes/wellfields	define source protection zones for priority control of surface contamination load
	general widespread contamination of groundwater	reduce contaminant load in selective areas, especially where aquifer is highly vulnerable, by appropriate planning provisions or mitigation measures plan wastewater treatment/disposal taking account of groundwater interest and impacts

wellfields, control over abstraction is required to avoid potential conflict with agricultural irrigation users.

The situation is, however, rarely as simple as this. In practice, where the abstraction of high-quality groundwater is excessive, substantial volumes of lower-quality groundwater will often be available and suitable for many uses. Thus incentives for the exploitation of lower-quality groundwater (such as that which has suffered saline intrusion or anthropogenic pollution) for non-potable private or industrial uses are required. Conversely, it may be necessary in some situations, for public health reasons, to prohibit the drilling or use of private wells for potable, or other sensitive, uses in seriously-polluted shallow aquifers.

Excessive subsurface contaminant load: It must be recognised that it is practically impossible to prevent the pollution of shallow aquifers in urban areas. However, it is vital in the interests of potable groundwater abstractors to constrain the imposition of subsurface contaminant loads to below critical levels, according to the vulnerability of underlying aquifers, the characteristics of the water pollutants involved and the pattern and purpose of groundwater abstraction.

All too often the urbanisation process proceeds without any recognition or consideration of groundwater pollution hazards. These are still rarely taken into account when considering maximum acceptable density for residential development served by on-site sanitation systems, priorities for the installation of mains sewerage systems (and the location and treatment arrangements for their discharge), the location of high-risk industries and landfill waste disposal sites, etc.

Excess urban infiltration: The overall rates of infiltration, especially in wholly unsewered areas, will be substantially greater than those existing naturally, prior to the urbanisation process. Groundwater abstraction may not however have developed as a result of unfavourable aquifer characteristics or adverse natural water quality, or it may have been abandoned as a result of anthropogenic pollution. The resultant rising water-table problems referred to earlier may also, less dramatically, accompany the reversal of natural groundwater flow directions and the transport of urban-derived contaminants towards periurban municipal wellfields.

The goal of urban groundwater management should be to strike a reasonable balance between maintaining water-supply availability and quality, preserving the urban infrastructure and ensuring the

Table 3. Urban groundwater-supply management: objectives, problems and mitigation measures.

OBJECTIVES	PROBLEMS EXPERIENCED	TARGETS	MITIGATION MEASURES
Maintain Groundwater Supplies	- decline in well yields due to falling water-table	constrain groundwater levels	- redistribute/reduce abstraction - increase urban recharge
Safeguard Groundwater Quality	- unacceptable water quality for potable use - excessive treatment costs - secondary quality nuisance effects	moderate subsurface contaminant load	- restrict contaminant loading by identified sources, especially on vulnerable aquifers - restrict density of residential development in vulnerable areas - selective control of industrial activities/effluents - zone land for different uses - control landfill location and design - separate waste disposal from groundwater supply spatially
	- increasing salinity from seawater intrusion - induced contamination	constrain groundwater levels	- redistribute and/or reduce abstraction - use scavenger boreholes - modify depths of water-supply boreholes
	- contaminants mobilised from contaminated land by rising water-table	constrain groundwater levels	- increase abstraction of shallow polluted groundwater for non-sensitive uses - reduce urban recharge

safe disposal of wastes. These requirements can be translated into the following groundwater resource objectives (Foster et al, 1996):

1- improving the sustainability of resource exploitation in and around cities by avoiding quasi-irreversible degradation of aquifer systems

2- more efficient use of available resources, avoiding anarchy in their exploitation and in land contaminant discharge.

We believe that these objectives would be acceptable to most national resource administrators and policy makers. In practical hydrogeological and environmental terms, the targets to achieve these strategic goals are (Table 3):

- constrain groundwater levels in aquifers underlying urban areas within a tolerable range, by controlling the magnitude of, and the end-use of, groundwater abstraction

- moderate subsurface contaminant load to acceptable levels, given local aquifer pollution vulnerability, by land-use planning to reduce potential pollution sources and selective controls over effluent discharges and other existing pollution sources.

To achieve the above targets a strong institutional framework is regarded by some as a prerequisite and by most as desirable. The ideal framework would include legislation to:

- render groundwater resources the property of the state, with the granting of licences for their legal exploitation in an approved manner

- prescribe the discharge of liquid effluents to the ground, the land disposal of solid wastes, and other potentially-polluting activities, by means of legal consents and/or planning approvals

- require that national or local government set-up a regulatory agency with the technical expertise, financial resources and legal backing to supervise the various licensing processes and to police their enforcement.

Other necessary activities for the regulatory agency would be to conduct appropriate levels of resource monitoring, surveillance of potable water-supply quality and effluent discharges and inspection of potentially-polluting activities.

However, the presence of an adequate legal framework does not, on its own, guarantee adequate management and protection of groundwater resources. In practice, where groundwater is concerned there are relatively few examples worldwide of regulatory agencies operating proactively to manage and protect resources. Complacency is widespread and regulatory measures and their enforcement vary considerably between nations, and also, in some cases between the capital and other cities in the same nation. Proactive regulation is also often handicapped by hydrogeological uncertainties about the size of the resource, inadequate information from unsuitable monitoring networks, insufficient personnel and logistic support and, frequently, interference with the regulatory process by powerful political groups, industrial and agricultural lobbyists.

In order to make real progress it will be necessary to set priorities systematically, based on the realistic economic value of the groundwater resource concerned. There will also be a need to balance the use of direct regulatory controls and of economic instruments (financial incentives and sanctions) to achieve the same ends. The options open to urban water resource managers need not be constrained to the one or the other; there could be much to gain by imaginative combinations of the financial carrot and the regulatory stick.

2.2 Achieving management targets

Constraining abstraction: The unrestricted exploitation of groundwater resources, free from all control, can only be considered tolerable in the case of (a) extensive aquifers with very large storage reserves in situations where, (b) the consequences of temporary over-development will not be reversible, (c) no account needs to be taken of reductions in spring discharge and river baseflow and (d) it will not cause increasing social inequity between water-users or (e) unacceptable deterioration in water quality. The most effective approach to the control of groundwater abstraction, of necessity, will be significantly different for aquifers in the early stages of development when there are no incipient signs of overexploitation, andaquifers where reductions in the total groundwater abstraction need to be achieved to mitigate the effects of overexploitation.

The regulation of groundwater exploitation is more directly and readily achieved through control of waterwell drilling than through subsequently licensing their pumping, although both elements need to be present in a balanced policy. Once the new water well is constructed the applicant would normally request an abstraction licence from the regulator, who should charge an annual fee for groundwater abstraction based upon a robust method of estimating actual abstraction by metering or indirect methods. All too often, the charging for groundwater abstraction has been nominal and does not even cover the administrative costs of the regulatory body. There is an urgent need, worldwide, to reform this situation and to levy charges which are realistic and based on one or more of the following criteria, depending on the local water resource situation:

-   recovering the full cost of the regulatory body in administering the exploitation of groundwater resources and investing in their evaluation and monitoring for management purposes
-   the cost of alternative raw water-supplies to the users concerned, if local groundwater resources

are lost through irreversible degradation
-   the full economic value, including an allowance for the cost of probable environmental externalities occasioned by groundwater abstraction.

The most rational approach to defining individual annual groundwater charges is that a weighting factor should be applied to the charge per unit volume dependent *inter alia* upon:
-   the proportion of (truly) consumptive use involved in water utilisation
-   the quality and location (in terms of potential for subsequent reuse) of the effluent generated
-   the overall environmental sensitivity of the abstraction, in terms of its location and timing, with a higher weighting factor where abstraction will only occur in the dry season or where it is located in coastal areas or near groundwater-fed environmentally-sensitive features
-   the quality of the groundwater supply obtained, with much lower weighting where poor quality water is abstracted, providing an element of additional protection for neighbouring high-quality groundwater sources.

It is only through adoption of a scheme of abstraction charging which encompasses such features that appropriate incentives will be present to optimise the use of scarce high-quality groundwater resources in the vicinity of some urban areas. The question of whether, within this scheme, discounts should be provided for large-scale public water-supply abstraction is a complex one (Postel, 1984). It should be noted that raising raw water abstraction charges provides an incentive for more effective demand management in urban areas. This will include the reduction of water-mains leakage losses to more tolerable levels and the payment of appropriate rates for luxury non-essential domestic uses, such as garden watering, car washing, etc.

For any abstraction control policy to be effective, enforceable sanctions are required against those who construct water wells without permit or exceed the licensed abstraction, eg well-use prohibitions.

Recuperation of overexploited aquifers: In the case of already overexploited aquifers, abstraction control will often need to include measures to prohibit the construction of new waterwells and to reduce abstraction in existing wells. As this can involve the complex legal area of redefining abstraction rights, the pragmatic approach is to declare special areas for the protection of groundwater resources in the greater public interest, by some form of local decree which prohibits or greatly restricts the circumstances under which new waterwells can be constructed, and imposes abstraction charges on all existing waterwell operators.

In all situations where a reduction of abstraction from overexploited aquifers is contemplated, it will be technically and economically more feasible if the policy can be implemented through some form of water-user group organised within the community or municipal framework (Briscoe, 1993). This will facilitate the introduction of more realistic abstraction charges and may make possible the use of more sophisticated economic instruments such as:

- encouraging non-sensitive groundwater users to switch from the exploitation of high-quality aquifers to shallow, poorer quality groundwater, with major reduction in their abstraction charges
- restricting or withdrawing groundwater abstraction rights from industrial companies that have not installed water efficient technologies
- trading treated wastewater for groundwater abstraction rights with agricultural irrigators in fringe urban areas
- providing subsidies for improving irrigation water-use efficiency in fringe urban areas in exchange for groundwater abstraction rights.

The problem of constraining abstraction is much simpler in those cities where the bulk of groundwater exploitation is by a few major water-supply utility and industrial boreholes, than where there are many individually-small, privately-operated domestic, commercial and industrial wells because:

- more information is normally available in the former case on quantities pumped, aquifer water levels and water quality, and thus on the state of overall resource development
- private individual abstractors are usually focused only on obtaining sufficient water for immediate needs and not on the collective long-term good of the city community.

Thus, city administrations allow an escalation of uncontrolled private water well construction at their peril. This approach uses groundwater levels to guide resource exploitation policy. Whichever package of measures is employed, the objective of abstraction control policy should on the one hand be to reduce the likelihood of suffering the more serious consequences associated with irrational and/or excessive exploitation, but on the other to avoid over-regulation, which will have high bureaucratic cost and will discourage economic development.

Controlling subsurface contaminant load: In developing strategies for groundwater pollution control it is important to distinguish between the threat to the resource or aquifer as a whole and that to a particular individual public water-supply source. A realistic balance between resource protection and source protection needs to be struck according to local circumstances. While in theory it is possible to manage land entirely in the interest of groundwater gathering, this is rarely acceptable on socio-economic grounds. In practice, it is generally necessary to define groundwater protection strategies which, while they constrain land-use activity, accept trade-offs between competing interests. To implement such strategies effectively we have to mesh hydrogeological understanding and requirements into land-use policies, which often have strong economic and sometimes emotive foundation. We also have to confront long-established practices and the problem of different professions not understanding each other's methodologies or priorities. Simple and robust matrices need to be established, which indicate what activities are possible where at an acceptable risk to groundwater. Instead of applying universal controls over land or soil use and effluent discharge to the ground, it is more effective, and less prejudicial to economic development, to utilise the natural contaminant attenuation capacity of the strata overlying the saturated aquifer and to recognise that the most rigorous controls are only required in the more vulnerable areas. This implies prioritisation and in effect, requires the zoning of the land surface on simple but consistent criteria. It can be approached by mapping aquifer pollution vulnerability. The vulnerability concept is not scientifically precise and has some serious limitations in a scientific sense, but it does provide a general framework within which to base groundwater protection policy.

Superimposed upon this division of the land surface will be special protection areas around individual public water-supply sources. For this purpose a hybrid system, based on estimates of groundwater catchment or capture zone and saturated zone flow times, is now becoming widely adopted. Once again the complexity of groundwater flow and pollutant transport means that only approximations to the true catchments are possible.

The two approaches to groundwater pollution prevention (resource protection and source protection) are complementary and the emphasis placed on one or other will depend on the source development situation and the prevailing hydrogeological conditions. Strategies which are predominantly source-oriented are best suited to more uniform, non-consolidated, aquifers, exploited only by a relatively small and fixed number of high-yielding municipal water-supply boreholes with stable pumping regimes. They cannot be so readily applied where there are very large and rapidly growing numbers of individual abstractors, as the joint problems of zone interference and the transient

64

nature of the flow regime render consideration of individual sources and the establishment of fixed zones impracticable. Moreover, data deficiencies and scientific uncertainties, especially in heterogenous aquifers, can render the estimation and reliability of protection zones difficult without costly fieldwork.

It has to be recognised that shallow groundwater in urban areas is often likely to be contaminated, especially in the absence of a comprehensive mains sewerage system. However, to avoid *excessive* loads of persistent pollutants, which may be transferred to deeper, less-vulnerable, aquifers in the longer term, the contaminant loading on vulnerable aquifers can be restricted by:

(a) selectively prioritising mains sewerage extension to areas of high groundwater vulnerability and/or source protection areas

(b) restricting the density of residential development served by in situ sanitation

(c) directing the location of landfill solid waste disposal facilities to areas of negligible or low groundwater pollution vulnerability

(d) restricting the disposal of industrial effluents to the ground in vulnerable areas, through introduction of effluent discharge permits and appropriate charging to favour recycling and waste reduction

(e) special measures for the handling of chemicals and effluents at any industrial sites located in vulnerable areas

(f) improving the location and quality of wastewater discharge from main sewerage systems after consideration of the potential impacts on periurban and downstream municipal wellfields.

Where appropriate it will be useful to define protection zones around municipal wells and wellfields, especially in periurban locations, delineating, as far as possible, the total capture area and a key isochron (such as the average horizontal 50-day travel time). In situations of extreme aquifer vulnerability it will be necessary to delineate these protection areas as total conservation zones and avoid most forms of economic development within them. This will only be possible in some periurban and hinterland situations.

3   CONCLUSIONS

(i) Urban groundwater in fast-growing cities will only be managed sustainably if the priorities and concerns of the three functions of water supply, waste disposal and urban subsurface engineering are acknowledged and their inter-relationships recognised.

(ii) Rapid urban development, especially if accompanied by the extension of on-site sanitation will inevitably lead to the widespread pollution of shallow groundwater. The simultaneous use of the subsurface for water supply and waste disposal can therefore only be accommodated if management objectives are set to reconcile the legitimate concerns of water supply and waste disposal interests.

(iii) The three functions come into conflict as a result of just three underlying causes:
- inadequately controlled groundwater abstraction
- excessive subsurface contaminant load relative to natural assimilation capacity
- excess urban infiltration (in those situations where abstraction is not possible or has been abandoned).

Urban groundwater management therefore needs to target these processes.

(iv) Each city is its own case, requiring specific diagnosis and the devising of locally appropriate and workable control policies. However it is clear that where a rapidly-growing city overlies a usable aquifer, these policies will always revolve around the twin goals of constraining/directing groundwater abstraction and controlling subsurface contaminant loading.

(v) The control of groundwater abstraction should seek to conserve high-quality water for urban drinking water-supply and other near-potable uses. In many cases, where the abstraction of such high-quality water is excessive, substantial volumes of lower-quality water will often be available and provide a suitable subsitute for many other uses.

(vi) Control does not have to be exclusively by means of regulation; carefully considered economic instruments can often play an important constraining role. In fact a combination of financial incentives and user-group endorsed regulation is likely to be the most effective means of achieving sustainable abstraction for public and private user alike.

(vii) In view of the time lag in the response of many aquifers to imposed contaminant loads, it is not appropriate to wait for proof of pollution before acting to control such loads. Just as it is axiomatic in public health programmes worldwide that preventive healthcare projects are much more effective than curative medicine, so in urban groundwater management the cost and technical challenge of many pollutant remediation programmes dictate that the emphasis must be on pollution prevention rather than remediation.

(viii) Land-use planning is inescapable for effective preventive control. A widely recommended approach which accepts that planning exists to achieve trade-offs between competing interests involves zoning the land surface to identify the areas most vulnerable to aquifer pollution. Aquifer vulnerability mapping, however, has to be matched to simple robust matrices which indicate what activities are acceptable, while strenuous community relations programmes will be needed to raise awareness of the role and susceptibility of the subsurface to contamination. The success of the latter will significantly influence the extent to which sanctions and policing will need to be applied.

(ix) Effective urban groundwater management has to be active, not passive, and to be effective requires a strong institutional framework to bring together groundwater stakeholders, inform water-user interest groups and enact regulatory and economic instruments.

(x) Finally, for management policy to be informed, it must stem from a coherent understanding of the local groundwater/aquifer system. Each city is unique in its particular groundwater setting and the urban environment where so many of us now choose to live merits more than standardised management prescriptions imposed without hydrogeological awareness.

ACKNOWLEDGEMENTS

This paper is published by permission of the Director, British Geological Survey (NERC) and is based on the World Bank Technical Paper Ref (Foster et al, in press) undertaken by the authors with the support of the British Department for International Development. The conclusions expressed here are those of the authors and do not necessarily represent the views of the DFID, the World Bank or any of their affiliated organisations.

REFERENCES

Black M (1994) *Mega-Slums: the coming sanitary crisis.* WaterAid, London

Briscoe J (1993) When the cup is half full. *Environment* 35(4) 7-37

BGS,ODA, UNEP and WHO (1996) *Characterisation and assessment of groundwater quality concerns in Asia-Pacific Region,* Eds Lawrence A R & Foster SSD UNEP/DEIA/AR.96-1, Nairobi Kenya

Earthscan (1990) *The Poor Die Young.* Eds Cairncross S, Hardoy JE & Satterthwaite D. Earthscan..

Foster SSD, Morris BL., & Lawrence AR. (1993) Effects of urbanisation on groundwater recharge. In proceedings of the ICE International Conference: *"Groundwater Problems in Urban Areas".* London, June 1993 pp 43-63.

Foster SSD, Lawrence AR & Morris BL (1996) Groundwater resources beneath rapidly urbanizing cities-implications and priorities for water supply management in: Report of the *Habitat II Conference* Beijing China 18-21 March 1996 pp 356-365

Foster SSD, Lawrence AR & Morris BL (in press, 1997) *Groundwater in Urban Development-Assessing management needs and formulating policy strategies.* World Bank Technical paper #.. World Bank Washington DC

Morris BL, Lawrence AR & Stuart ME (1994). *The impact of urbanisation on groundwater quality* (project summary report). BGS Technical Report WC/94/56. Keyworth UK

Postel S (1984) *Water: rethinking management in an age of scarcity.* Worldwatch Paper 62, Worldwatch Washington DC

Smith FB (1979) *The People's Health* 1830-1910. Croom Helm London

UNCHS (1987) *Global Report on Human settlements.* United Nations Centre for Human Settlements. Oxford University Press, New York.

Ground-water supply issues in urban and urbanizing areas

John M. Sharp, Jr
Department of Geological Sciences, The University of Texas, Austin, Tex., USA

ABSTRACT: Ground-water supply issues in urban and urbanizing areas include those of public perception, aquifer depletion, urban growth, and environmental degradation. Many urban areas are located along major rivers. The construction of major reservoirs and centralized water treatment systems with a few large intakes, as opposed to a larger number of wells, has led many urban areas to rely principally upon surface water. Smaller urban (and rural) areas, however, have traditionally relied upon ground water. As urban populations and urbanized areas grow and because sites for new reservoirs are limited, conjunctive use of ground water and surface water must become more common. Conjunctive use gives insurance against droughts, provides potentially vast sources of uncontaminated water, and allows the possibility of providing inexpensive, high-quality water resources to urban and urbanizing areas. Case histories, illustrated by examples from the American southwest and Texas in particular, demonstrate concerns involving aquifer overdraft or overexploitation and concomitant environmental issues. Long-term and cyclical overdrafts can create a perception that ground-water resources are unreliable, but actual declines are slow and predictable enough that alternative sources have been able to be brought on-line. Effects that accompany aquifer overdrafting include aquifer depletion, salt-water intrusion, subsidence, and deterioration of natural areas. Urbanization is commonly accompanied by ground-water deterioration, so urban expansion must be designed to protect ground waters and other resources. New technologies will offer challenges and opportunities. In order to address urban water-supply issues, sufficient hydrogeological data and valid interpretations must be available *a priori*.

1 INTRODUCTION

In 1900, only 10% of the Earth's population lived in cities. More than half will be living in urban areas by 2000 (United Nations 1991), and urban areas will accommodate most of the projected increases in population for both developed and developing countries. Many of the latter have population doubling times on the order of 25 years. However, even in the United States with a relatively low rate of overall population growth, urban populations in many areas (such as the Austin-San Antonio region in Texas) are expected to double in the next 25-50 years. Rates of areal expansion (urban sprawl) are also impressive indeed. In the New York City metropolitan region there was a 61% increase in urbanized area between 1964 and 1989, but the population growth was much less. Bangkok has expanded at a rate over 3,200 hectares per year for the past decade (Lowe 1992). Even smaller urban areas are sprawling. North of Austin, Texas, in 1997, ranch land is being subdivided for residential and commercial development at a rate of 3.3 hectares per day. In the United States, our urbanized areas are growing at rate equivalent to the area of two New York Cities per year. Table 1 lists

Table 1. The world's 10 largest metropolitan regions 2000 (United Nations, 1991).

City	Millions
Mexico City	25.6
Sao Paulo	22.1
Tokyo	19.0
Shanghai	17.0
New York	16.8
Calcutta	15.7
Bombay	15.4
Beijing	14.0
Los Angeles	13.9
Jakarta	13.7

the 10 largest metropolitan areas in the world. In the developing countries much of this growth occurs in illegal and unplanned squatter settlements. In Africa much of the urban growth is due to immigration from the rural areas, in other areas it is due equally to high birthrates in urban areas.

The people in urban and urbanizing areas require water, and ground-water supply issues stem from these demands. Specific solutions are complex because of competing political and economic interests, scientific uncertainties, and inadequate funds for resource development and scientific study. In principle, however, all solutions must follow one or more of three options -- increase water supplies, reduce water demands, or use available waters more efficiently.

Increased supplies can come from new surface- or ground-water sources, harvesting rain water, or utilization of presently unpotable waters. This last includes desalination and the use of unpotable water for bathing, washing, irrigation, sewage disposal, and industrial use. Dual distribution systems may be useful in this regard, but are very costly to install or to retrofit. Decreased demands for water can be achieved by limiting population growth (and concomitant water use), increased water prices, rationing, or public appeals to reduce water consumption. Limiting population growth is an ideal solution, but does not seem to be generally achievable. The developing countries have high rates of growth. Even in the developed countries, urbanization is proceeding rapidly. In the United States, there have been cases in which citizens voluntarily reduced water usage during drought, but the water prices were increased proportionately because operating costs for the water supply system are mostly for personnel and construction financing. Finally, we can find ways to operate more efficiently with existing water resources by conjunctive use, use of treated waste waters, artificial recharge, and water conservation measures.

In this discussion of ground-water supply issues for urban and urbanizing areas, I draw upon examples from the American southwest and, in particular, Texas, because Texas has undergone a metamorphosis similar to worldwide trends. In 1900 Texas was a rural society dominated by ranching, farming, and petroleum production. It has since become an urban society with an economy dominated by the manufacturing and service industries. In addition, Texas surface waters are already overallocated.

In the past many urban areas relied on ground water, but have switched to surface water because of economies of scale, resource adequacy, and public health concerns. Chlorination of water supplies in American cities became a requirement at the turn of the century (Havlick 1974). It was more economical to limit the number of water treatment plants, and the costs of surface-water development (in the United States) are commonly subsidized by the federal government.

There are also perception problems. When the public learns that water levels in supply wells have dropped, there is concern that the wells will "dry up." Water stored in a reservoir seems more reassuring than a well in the ground. Lubbock, Texas, directly overlies the prolific Ogallala aquifer, but obtains water from a reservoir nearly 200 kilometres away. Increasing salinity in the reservoir, however, is forcing the city to redevelop its ground-water resources. Lubbock is presently examining the development of several well fields as a supplementary source and for mixing with surface waters to minimize treatment costs. Interestingly, the disposal of urban storm runoff in playas as well as diminished pumpage of ground water has created rising water tables in places beneath the city to the point of causing foundation problems.

Other key issues for the use of ground water for urban populations include: aquifer location, aquifer overexploitation or overdraft, and water pollution. However, ground water offers unique advantages. It may be more widely available, less vulnerable to climatic variability, of superior quality, and cheaper to develop and to distribute.

2 LOCATION

Ground water exists everywhere beneath the land surface, but major surface-water bodies are rare in arid and semi-arid zones. Where local surface waters are not sufficient to meet urban demands, construction of reservoirs and long pipelines may be required. Urban areas in southern California obtain much of their water by transfer from the Colorado River to the east and from northern California. In other areas, surface waters are badly polluted. In much of the world the location of the major aquifers is known. For instance, in the U. S., these were inventoried and mapped by Meinzer (1923). In Heath's (1988) more recent map, major aquifers are essentially the same as those identified by Meinzer. Even where major aquifers do not exist (such as Precambrian shields), wells can be used to meet domestic needs.

In urbanizing areas, however, more detailed hydrogeological mapping is required to reduce uncertainty and to allow utilization of ground waters. This is especially critical when various water-supply options are estimated. Detailed hydrogeological maps are also important for urban planning issues. The Grundwasserschutzgebiete in Germany and the protected zones in Hong Kong demonstrate how hydrogeologic knowledge can be utilized propitiously in urban areas to protect ground-water resources. These areas can also serve as park lands and wildlife refuges. In many areas, however, there are insufficient data to delineate protection zones adequately.

In areas of limited recharge, urban areas may have to locate well fields, like surface-water reservoirs, many kilometres distant from the city. This is true for much of the American southwest.

3 OVERDRAFT/OVEREXPLOITATION

Although ground water exists under nearly all of the major urban areas, aquifer overdraft can cause aquifer depletion and the "secondary effects" of subsidence, salt-water intrusion, and degradation of special or sensitive natural environments.

3.1 *Aquifer depletion*

In general, aquifers run little chance of being exhausted. Exceptions may occur in arid or semi-arid regions. For instance, Tucson, Arizona, uses ground water from the Avra Valley which receives minimal recharge so that this aquifer is essentially being mined. Permanent depletion by ground-water mining can be a threat in such areas. Although these cases are limited, conjunctive use and long-range planning are required so that additional resources can be brought on-line as others are depleted by "mining."

Although permanent depletion is not generally a threat, it is easy for growing city's demands to exceed the safe or permissive yield of an aquifer. Of concern are situations in which water levels drop so far that pumping becomes very expensive or water yields are severely diminished. Artesian aquifers in Waco and Dallas, Texas, formerly provided free flowing wells, but water levels have fallen many tens of metres. These cities have largely switched to surface water resources for their potable supplies. Shallow wells in unconfined aquifers may no longer prove reliable where water levels drop very low, as has happened during droughts in the San Antonio and Austin, Texas, urban areas. In El Paso, the Hueco Bolson aquifer can no longer meet demands of the growing city; El Paso must look elsewhere for additional water supplies.

3. 2 *Subsidence*

Overdraft has caused severe subsidence in coastal cities, including Houston, Jakarta, Shanghai, Venice, and Calcutta, but even in interior cities, such as Mexico City and Las Vegas, differential subsidence disrupts road and utility systems and causes structural damage. Subsidence may create flooding problems where it changes the slope of drainage ditches and natural streams. In these situations, confined aquifers underlay or are intercalated with compressible clay layers. In Houston where over two metres of subsidence have occurred, one major subdivision (Figure 1) dropped below sea level and, after construction of expensive levees and pump-out systems, it was finally abandoned. Figure 2 depicts the historical subsidence trend for the Houston suburb of Pasadena. The decline in the rate of subsidence in the 1980s is the result of limiting the pumpage of ground water in the area as Houston, like some other coastal areas, switched to surface waters and relocated well fields farther inland.

Now, however, differential subsidence in these more inland areas has created problems with drainage systems and led to flooding by local streams. A procedure for controlling differential subsidence is to use careful hydrogeological analyses in order to plan the locations and rates of pumping in order to minimize the effects of subsidence. The negative effects of coastal subsidence and inundation can also be minimized or eliminated by land-use planning. The solution is very simple: control construction and development in low-lying areas. This also makes sense when we consider the potential effects of both coastal storms and eustatic sea-level rise caused of greenhouse warming. Nevertheless, in many countries the development of low-lying coastal areas will continue because of demands for land by a growing population, the desirability of being located on the

Figure 1. Brownwood subdivision house near Houston which was abandoned because of subsidence.

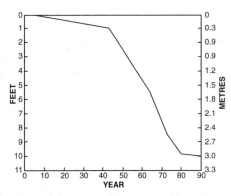

Figure 2. Subsidence in Pasadena, Texas, a suburb of Houston (Holzschuh, 1991). Subsidence accelerated with rapid urbanization near the beginning of the Second World War. The rate of subsidence has slowed because of controlled pumpage and the switching to nonlocal sources of water.

coast, or the fact that these areas may possess very fertile deltaic soils.

3.3 *Salt-water intrusion*

Overdraft can cause the intrusion of poor-quality water. This is especially important for cities on oceanic islands or in close proximity to the coastline where salt water underlies or is otherwise adjacent to the fresh waters. Once the intrusion has occurred, it takes a much longer period of time of reduced pumping for the aquifer to recover. However, salt-water intrusion can also occur inland. For instance, south of Kansas City, Missouri, overdraft of the Ordovician carbonate aquifers has induced downwards intrusion of saline water from overlying Pennsylvanian clastic rocks. In El Paso, Texas, overdrafts have reversed the hydraulic gradient with the Rio Grande, and poor-quality, brackish river water is infiltrating into the El Paso's major aquifer, the alluvium of the Hueco Bolson. Figure 3 shows the ground water declines from 1903 to 1988. The Rio Grande in the urban area has changed from an effluent to an influent (losing) stream. Because of upstream irrigation, the salinity of the Rio Grande, except in flood, exceeds drinking-water standards. In addition, the city is pumping water from the Hueco Bolson alluvial aquifer at rates in excess of recharge. New data since 1988 have evaluated the entire urban area that includes the larger adjoining

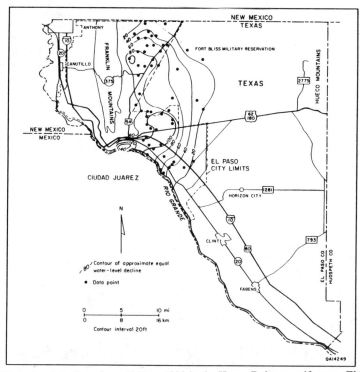

Figure 3. Water-level declines from 1903 to 1989 in the Hueco Bolson aquifer near El Paso, Texas (Ashworth, 1990). This overdraft has caused deteriorating water quality from recharge of brackish water from the Rio Grande. Water levels are continue to decline.

Mexico City of Juarez. Water levels under both cities have continued to drop in some areas by many metres.

Responses to salt-water intrusion vary and require either water importation, limiting ground-water extraction, or desalination of brackish or saline water. In some cases, surface waters can be utilized in lieu of ground water. In southern California, a pump tax on ground water was instituted to raise the costs of otherwise cheap ground water and to justify the high costs of long-distance imported water. In Hawaii, infiltration galleries have been installed in the islands' volcanic rocks. These limit the water-table decline and, consequently, the amount of salt-water intrusion. They also limit water yields in periods of low recharge. In The Netherlands, artificial recharge has been used to maintain a hydraulic barrier to salt-water intrusion. An ultimate response to salt-water intrusion is very expensive -- desalination -- but brackish ground water, depending upon the technology employed, may be easier to desalinate than sea water.

In El Paso, the city is experimenting with artificial recharge of reclaimed water from their sewage treatment plants and is examining the importation of ground water from sources up to 200 kilometres distant. Surface-water solutions appear unlikely; ground water will have be utilized. The long-term prospects for water supply in the El Paso-Juarez metroplex remain uncertain.

3.4 Protection of special environments

The protection of wetland environments that are fed by ground-water discharge (including those of threatened or endangered species) is becoming an important issue. A prime example is the Edwards aquifer of Texas. This aquifer supplies over two million people, including the city of San Antonio. Natural aquifer discharge is to a number of large springs but, with increasing pumpage, spring flows have decreased. U. S. courts have ruled that minimum discharges of >8.5 cubic metres/second (300 cubic feet per second) must be maintained at two of the spring systems in order to ensure the survival of several species of flora and fauna. These species exist only in waters emanating from the springs (McKinney & Sharp, 1995). Data from 1934 to the present show wide variations in recharge to the aquifer and increasing discharge by wells, largely for San Antonio (Figure 4). These data are plotted as 5-year, linearly-weighted running averages to minimize recharge variability and show the general trends.

The yearly water budgets in the aquifer (Figure 5) show that the fluctuations have become much more severe during recent years. This is because pumpage is increasing and there have been a number of large recharge events. It is manifest from Figures 4 and 5 that when conditions similar to those of the drought of record (1947-1956) occur again, the court-prescribed springflows and current

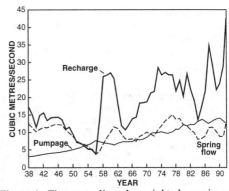

Figure 4. Five-year, linearly-weighted, running averages for recharge and discharge by wells and springs for the San Antonio segment of the Edwards aquifer, Texas. 1 cubic metre/second = 35.31 cubic feet/second.

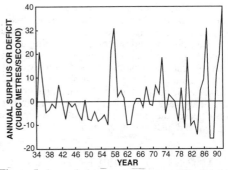

Figure 5. Annual changes in storage of the Edwards aquifer. Note the greater fluctuations in storage with time as heavy pumpage has been created by urban demands.

levels of pumping can not both be maintained. Because San Antonio is projected to double in population in the next 25 to 50 years, drought effects will be exacerbated.

There are few unused surface-water resources available, and there is a need to maintain fresh-water inflows to maintain the bay and estuarine environments of the Gulf of Mexico. Therefore, San Antonio's options are limited: long-distance surface-water importation, elimination of irrigated agriculture, growth controls, water conservation, reuse of treated sewage, or augmentation of springflow. The last option maintains court-prescribed minimal springflows by one or more of several options (Uliana & Sharp 1996): injection wells, enhanced natural recharge along losing streams that largely recharge the Edwards aquifer, exfiltration galleries near the springs, or direct addition of water to the spring lakes. Because all options for San Antonio are either expensive or leave a large volume of high quality water unused in the aquifer, no consensus course of action has yet been achieved.

4 QUALITY

Water-quality considerations are also an extremely important issue for urban ground-water supply . At the turn of the century, many cities were serviced by multiple shallow wells. Pollution of these shallow aquifers and the resulting health threats led to the establishment of centralized water-supply and -treatment systems. Shallow aquifers and surface waters in urban settings are subject to pollution by runoff from paved surfaces, hydrocarbons from leaky storage tanks and surface spills, illegal dumping of hazardous waste, leaky sewage lines, and lack of sanitation facilities. With urban growth it is expected that contamination of water resources will increase. Especially in developing countries, this may limit the use of shallow wells as a source of drinking water. Declining water levels can also cause water-quality deterioration from encroachment of poor-quality water or by changing hydrochemical conditions. Near Beijing, ground water is becoming more oxidized. Deep aquifers, however, may be relatively protected from urban pollution. Modern water-treatment plants are sophisticated and compact and, coupled with the fact that ground waters may require less sophisticated treatment, should ease the need for highly centralized treatment and distribution systems.

5 FACTORS TO CONSIDER FOR USE OF GROUND WATER

The increase in urban populations and the expansion of urban areas will place great demands on our water resources. Ground water will be required to meet these needs and is, in many cases, the best alternative. We shall need detailed hydro-geological investigations in order to use ground waters effectively and to estimate the costs of various water-supply and -management options. There is a need to use ground- and surface-water resources conjunctively. In this context, ground water offers drought insurance, redundancy to permit water distribution in the event of natural emergencies, and reliable supplies at a low cost. There is also need to protect existing and future ground-water resources and environmentally sensitive areas as urbanization proceeds. New technologies, such as aquifer storage and recovery (ASR) and dual-distribution systems, must be considered.

5.1 Drought insurance

Residence times are typically much longer in ground water than in surface waters; the former is commonly less sensitive to short-term climatic variations. Conjunctive-use systems pump ground water when surface waters are low during drought and allow ground water to recharge during times of surface water availability. The great advantage of wells over surface-water reservoirs is that wells can be drilled as needed, if distribution and treatment systems are designed to accept them.

Aquifer storage and recovery (ASR) can be adopted in this regard. In an ASR system, water is artificially recharged into aquifers during periods of excess water availability (floods, periods of high rainfall, etc.). Water is withdrawn from aquifer storage when needed. Lower capital costs can be a major advantage of ASR over the construction of supplemental surface-water reservoirs, detrimental environmental effects from reservoir construction and operation are also avoided. In addition, reclaimed industrial or sewage waters can be injected when their water quality is suitable.

5.2 Redundancy

Conjunctive use offers redundancy because highly centralized, single-source systems may lack the flexibility to meet unexpected events, such as natural disasters. The 1993 floods in the American Midwest disabled the water-treatment and -supply systems of cities that utilized surface waters. The public was without potable water for extended periods of time because there was no back-up system (no redundancy). Distributed wells offer multiple sources in the case of such emergencies. Surface waters can become contaminated with unexpected pollutants (caused perhaps by flooding, algal blooms, industrial accident, or sabotage). If such contamination occurs, if treatment plants malfunction, or if reservoir levels drop below intake levels, the urban water system depending solely upon a few large surface reservoirs or a few large intakes becomes essentially inoperable.

5.3 Costs

In the United States, the use of surface waters has been subsidized heavily by immense federal public-works programs. Dams, reservoirs, and their water distribution systems were constructed and maintained by agencies such as the Army Corps of Engineers and the Bureau of Reclamation. On the other hand, the costs of well-field development and the distribution systems from the well field were and generally continue to be the responsibility of local communities. Therefore, the financial incentives were and remain strong to use surface water if available. In several cases, major urban areas developed because of the promise by the federal government of a stable, abundant, and inexpensive source of water (Reisner 1986).

6 CONCLUSIONS

With the spread of urbanized areas, contamination of shallow aquifers is a major threat. Increase of impervious cover and storm sewers can reduce recharge and lower water tables. On the other hand, urban areas can suffer from rising water tables if they switch from ground-water to surface-water resources or if storm drainage disposal is not properly engineered. Urban development must be controlled or managed to protect future water resources and environmentally sensitive areas. This requires detailed hydrogeological maps, data, and analyses before decisions are made.

A key point is to understand how urbanization has affected or can affect hydrogeologic processes. For instance, utility lines, tunnels, and utility trenches backfilled with gravel or riprap create the equivalent of a karst conduit. Contaminated ground waters can flow rapidly towards areas that do not appear to be down gradient naturally. This makes prediction and control of contamination plumes exceedingly difficult. Sump pumps, leaky water and sewer mains, and storm-sewage disposal can create significant local hydraulic gradients. Paved surface surfaces limit and alter the natural distribution of areal recharge from precipitation. Consequently, the prediction of contaminant transport in urban areas is haphazard at best.

5.5 *New technologies*

New technologies offer new opportunities. Aquifer storage and recovery uses the aquifer as a temporary storage reservoir. Artificial recharge of suitable quality water by spreading basins or, typically, injection wells stores water from periods of excess precipitation and extracts it during periods of drought. In El Paso, tertiary-treated sewage is injected into the alluvial aquifer and pumped out down the flow path. In temperate areas, warm water from industrial plants can be injected in the summer and then pumped in the winter months and its heat extracted. Karstic aquifers can serve as natural canals or pipelines for transmission of water from areas of recharge to the cities. Where feasible, this could save on construction and associated costs.

Desalination or partial desalination of otherwise unusable waters, including ground waters, will become more feasible because of the relatively great financial resources of the urban areas. Such waters can be mixed with other waters to reach a suitable quality. Such expensive water should, however, be carefully conserved; this option might best be integrated with dual-distribution systems. These systems provide the possibility of conserving high quality expensive drinking water and of using brackish waters that are currently "lying fallow" for industrial and other nonconsumption uses.

Because many of the urban areas located on major rivers, of hygienic water treatment requirements, and of problems associated with aquifer overdraft, cities tend to rely excessively on surface waters. For instance, Havlik's (1974) figure of the urbanized hydrologic cycle completely omits ground water as an urban resource.

Ground water, however, offers unique advantages for supplying water to the urbanizing Earth. Careful aquifer development and conjunctive use can provide low-cost, redundant systems to address growing demands. Deep aquifers are relatively insulated from urban pollution and from climatic extremes. They can provide insurance against droughts and catastrophic contamination events. In addition, the costs of ground-water alternatives are often less than for new supplies from surface-water resources.

Hydrogeological data are required to prevent water-quality deterioration and the critical overdraft of the aquifers with potential deleterious secondary effects. These secondary effects include subsidence, salt-water intrusion, degradation of ground-water quality, and loss of critical natural habitats, as well as aquifer depletion. New and continually evolving technologies create opportunities for the use of ground water in urban areas. These now include aquifer storage and recovery, ground-water heat pumps, integration of ground-water supply into dual distribution systems, artificial recharge, and using aquifers to reclaim treated sewage waters. Detailed hydrogeological mapping and analyses must be accomplished before key decisions are made so that we can effectively use all of our water resources. Too often we are forced to make decisions in the absence of key data and the eventual consequences can be costly. We must begin to evaluate our hydrogeological resources on a scale more detailed than has been commonly done previously.

ACKNOWLEDGMENTS

Manuscript and presentation preparation costs were supported by the Chevron Centennial Professorship and by the Owen-Coates Fund of the Geology Foundation of The University of Texas at Austin. I gratefully acknowledge the comments of my graduate seminar students in discussing major urban water-supply issues. The technical editing of J. P. Chilton and Rosemary Barker are also deeply appreciated.

REFERENCES

Ashworth, J. B., 1990, Water resources of the El Paso area, Texas. In C. W. Kreitler & J. M. Sharp, Jr. (eds.), *Hydrogeology of Trans-Pecos Texas.* Austin, Texas: Bureau of Economic Geology.

Havlick, S. W. 1974 *The Urban Organism.*, New York: Macmillan.

Heath, R. C. 1988 Hydrogeologic setting of regions. In W. Back, J. S. Rosenshein & P. R. Seaber (eds.), *Hydrogeology*, v. O-2, Geology of North America, Boulder: Geological Society of America.

Holzschuh, J. C. 1991. *Land Subsidence in Houston, Texas, USA,* Fourth International Symposium on Land Subsidence: Houston.

Lowe, M. D. 1992. Shaping Cities. In *State of the World 1992*. New York: W. W. Norton.

McKinney, D. C., & J. M. Sharp, Jr. 1995. *Springflow Augmentation of Comal and San Marcos Springs, Texas: Phase I - Feasibility Study,* University of Texas Center for Research in Water Resources Report 247: Austin.

Meinzer, O. E. 1923. *Ground-water regions of the United States*, U. S. Geological Survey Water-Supply Paper 2242.

Reisner, M. 1986. *Cadillac Desert:*, New York: Viking Penguin.

Uliana, M., & Sharp, J. M., Jr., 1996, *Springflow augmentation possibilities at Comal and San Marcos springs, Edwards* aquifer, Transactions, Gulf Coast Assoc. Geol. Societies, v. 46.

United Nations, 1991. *World Urbanization Prospects, 1990.* New York.

1 Urban groundwater processes

Topic co-editors:

Kevin Hiscock
University of East Anglia

Paul Younger
University of Newcastle

Groundwater in the Urban Environment: Problems, Processes and Management, Chilton et al. (eds)
© *1997 Balkema, Rotterdam, ISBN 90 5410 837 1*

Geophysical logs and X-ray images of a DNAPL contaminated sand core

R. Ian Acworth
Groundwater Centre, Water Research Laboratory, University of New South Wales, Manly Vale, N.S.W., Australia

Jerzy Jankowski
Groundwater Centre, Department of Applied Geology, University of New South Wales, Sydney, N.S.W., Australia

ABSTRACT: Minimally disturbed cores of a 25 m unconsolidated sand and clay section were recovered using a modified triple-tube core barrel from an industrially contaminated site in the Botany Sands aquifer in Sydney. Physical and chemical analyses of the core sub-sections demonstrate that the formation is comprised predominantly of fine to medium sand from the surface to a depth of 21.4 m. A clay zone at 23.4 m overlies sandstone bedrock at 25.3 m. DNAPL occurs between 21.4 m and 23.4 m. Free phase DNAPL mixture was recovered from several of the core sub-sections, although the distribution was very erratic. A thin high TDS band associated with the top of the zone containing DNAPL forms a sharp bulk electrical conductivity anomaly and sodium to chloride ratios below 0.65 in this zone indicate that breakdown of the DNAPL mixture is occurring. Detailed measurements are presented for a 5 m section at the base of the aquifer and correlated with x-ray images of the cores and grain size determinations carried out on each 90 mm core sub-section.

1 INTRODUCTION

Contamination by DNAPLs in the Botany Sands aquifer at Banksmeadow in southern Sydney has recently been described by Acworth et al. (1995) and Woodward Clyde (1996). The Botany Sands is a heavily developed urban aquifer with extensive contamination in the industrial southern part of the aquifer adjacent to Botany Bay. The occurrence of a number of chlorinated hydrocarbons (DNAPL's) was identified from a comprehensive programme of drilling and testing at the site. A small site was examined in detail to determine the physical and chemical properties of the aquifer in the vicinity of the contamination. Four conductivity cone penetration test (CCPT) probes, a bundled piezometer, and four cored holes were established in an area of approximately 3000 m^2. The water table at the site is close to the ground surface.

The Botany Sands aquifer at the site comprises aeolian sands, with occasional peaty sand horizons, to a depth of approximately 21.5 m. Between this depth and the Triassic sandstone, which forms the basement at 25.3 m, a sequence of sandy silts and clays occurs with minor coarse sands. A DNAPL mixture was detected at the base of the aeolian sands, and has penetrated the lower hydraulic conductivity material. DNAPL was detected at 21 m depth in each of the four bores; however the distribution in individual bores was highly variable.

The cores were acquired in clear PET liners. Colour photography of the cores, combined with X-rays of the same core material has been particularly useful in linking together the various physical and chemical property measurements. The combined data set provides a useful example of the occurrence of DNAPL at depth in a sandy aquifer and is described for one of the sites in detail in this paper.

2 FIELD AND LABORATORY METHODS

Cone conductivity penetration tests were carried out at the site prior to any drilling activity. These revealed the presence of dense sands between 16 m and 20 m and a bulk electrical conductivity peak at approximately 21.5 m depth. The conductivity profile is shown in Figure 1.

A bundled piezometer was installed to a depth of 25 m with 13 intakes at various depths down the column. The individual mini-piezometers were formed from 5 mm internal diameter (ID) PVC tubes strapped to a central core and terminated in screen elements of 5 cm length. Bentonite packers were installed between the piezometer intakes to minimise the risk of cross contamination. A peristaltic pump was used to abstract water from the PVC tubes. Piezometers above 22 m produced water with no difficulty but the piezometers below this depth produced little if any water. The mini-piezometer at 21 m depth produced a small sample of DNAPL. The sample was lifted to the surface as discrete globules in the groundwater stream and settled to the base of the sampling container. The sample contained a mixture in which Carbon Tetrachloride (CTC), Tetrachloro Ethylene (PCE), 1:1:2:2 Tetrachloro Ethane (PCA), Chloroform (CFM), Trichloro Ethylene (TCE), 1:1:1 Trichloro Ethane (TCA), Hexachloro Ethane (HCA), Hexachloro Buta-1:3 Diene (HCBD), and Hexachloro Benzene (HCB) were identified. The sample density was 1.347g/ml at 20^0C.

A cored hole was constructed approximately 2 metres from the bundled piezometer. To obtain good quality minimally disturbed core samples in the sands, an HQ triple tube (HQ3) coring system was modified to recover core from the interior of 250 mm hollow flight augers using a wire-line system. The inner sample barrel from the HQ3 drilling system was adapted to engage a casing advance latch mechanism installed in the lead auger. The inner barrel fitted inside and protruded through the bottom cutting face of the lead auger. The latch mechanism located the sample barrel inside the lead auger and enabled the sample barrel to remain free from the rotation of the auger. This was achieved by use of a thrust bearing and ball race incorporated into the latch mechanism. The latch mechanism allowed for easy recovery of the 1.5 m long sample barrel via the use of standard wire line recovery techniques.

The sample barrel was lined with a clear PET liner and the core was acquired inside the liner. To prevent cross contamination, the use of water was limited to core barrel withdrawl. The sample barrel containing the liner and core were recovered to the surface using the wire line. The core and liner were then expelled from the sample barrel and the ends of the PET liner capped with PET caps. This method of core recovery achieved minimal disruption of the core and maintained the pore fluids in place. A new PET liner was inserted and the sample barrel lowered back into the bore until the latch mechanism engaged the barrel at the correct depth.

When the final core was withdrawn, the hole was backfilled with a bentonite mud and the augers withdrawn. A temporary casing was installed and

five metres of HQ3 core obtained from the Triassic sandstone basement using standard wire-line equipment. The hole was completed with 70 mm ABS casing, weighted with clean water and grouted in position.

Geophysical logging was carried out inside the ABS casing and included natural gamma, bulk electrical conductivity using induction, neutron, and gamma gamma (density) logs.

The cores were transfered from the field to an X-ray facility where they were imaged and photographed. They were then transfered to a cool room and stored in the vertical position prior to core cutting and logging.

The cores were cut into 90 mm sections. This was achieved by use of a liquid carbon dioxide jacket wrapped around the core to snap freeze the pore fluids. Individual core elements were then again sealed by new PET caps and placed back in storage. Complex conductivity measurements were carried out on each core section before a small (5 g) sub-sample from each core was taken axially for analysis using GC/MS techniques (Beck & Acworth 1996). Time constraints required this process to be limited to one sub-sample per 90 mm core sub-section. The complex conductivity data are not presented here.

The core was divided and placed in a centrifuge (3200 rpm) where the pore fluids were extracted using a specially constructed sealed nylon flask that contained a filter unit, comprising a filter paper between two perforated stainless steel discs supported on a perforated plastic base, separating the sample from the displaced liquid. The fluid EC, pH and major ion chemistry (Na^+, K^+, Ca^{2+}, Mg^{2+}, SO_4^{2-}, Cl^-) was then determined. In some cases, DNAPL mixture was also collected during the centrifuging. Grain size measurements were carried out on all the samples after extraction of pore fluids and an estimate of hydraulic conductivity established using Hazen's method.

3 RESULTS

The results of the geophysical measurements, the CCPT, the estimated hydraulic conductivity, the ratio of sodium to chloride in the pore fluids and the pore fluid EC are presented in Figure 1 for the section between 21.3 m and 26 m. The hydraulic conductivity data show a thin clay band at 21.6 m

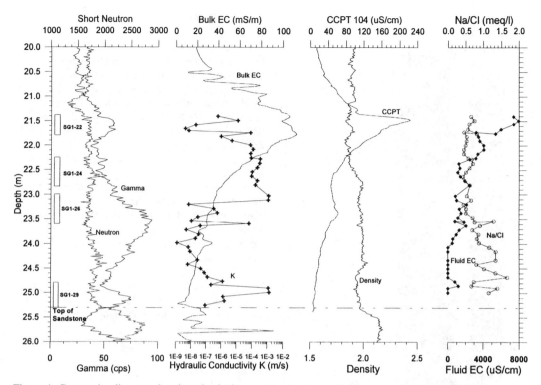

Figure 1. Composite diagram showing physical properties for the section between 21.3 m and 26.0 m.

and a thicker clay band between 23.15 m and 24.8 m. A thin sand unit is indicated just above the basement between 24.8 m and 25.1 m. Both clay bands can be clearly seen in the gamma ray activity log (Figure 1).

The upper (thin) layer has supported a thin pool of DNAPL, some of which was recovered from the bundled piezometer intake at 21 m. The neutron log shows a minimum at this depth, also indicating DNAPL (Schneider & Greenhouse 1992).

The bulk electrical conductivity log shows a broad peak centered on the clay zone, whereas the CCPT log shows a very sharp peak centered on the sand above the clay at 21.5 m depth. This is confirmed by the fluid electrical conductivity data measured on pore fluids centrifuged from the individual core sub-sections. The fluid EC peak is dominated by sodium chloride. Note also the rapidly varying ratio of sodium to chloride shown in Figure 1.

There is an excess of chloride over sodium in the zone between 21.5 m and 23.5 m, associated with DNAPL. Below this depth, sodium exceeds chloride.

The normal ratio of sodium to chloride in the southern zone of the aquifer is 0.98 (Acworth & Jankowski 1993) while the ratio of sodium to chloride in sea water is 0.87.

The DNAPL extract data indicate that DNAPL has penetrated the upper clay zone and extends downward to the base of the sand zone at 23.2 m depth. The photograph and X-ray of core SG1-26 (Figure 2) clearly show this boundary. The X-ray data also indicates fracturing and possible channeling of DNAPL through the clay for approximately 200 mm. No DNAPL was recovered from below this depth. Data are presented in Figure 2 for each of the core sub-sections. Values of hydraulic conductivity (K m/s), pH, EC (µS/cm) and the quantity of water obtained (spun) from each section (ml) are shown. The DNAPL data (mg/kg) are from the GC/MS analyses of the mini-cores taken axially from the core sub-sections. DNAPL levels in the top of core SG1-22 were approximately 800, 3,900 and 3,000 mg/kg for TCE, PCE and PCA respectively. The levels recorded at the base of the zone, as shown in Figure 2, were much lower.

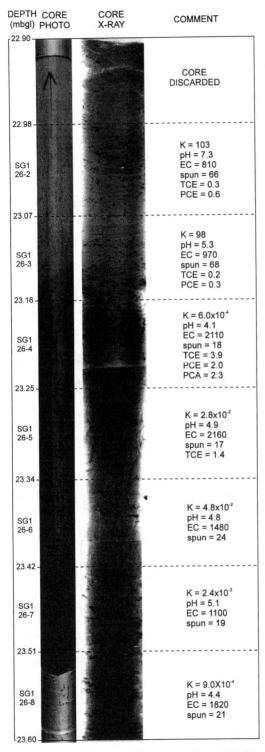

DEPTH (mbgl)	CORE PHOTO	CORE X-RAY	COMMENT
22.90			CORE DISCARDED
22.98	SG1 26-2		K = 103 pH = 7.3 EC = 810 spun = 66 TCE = 0.3 PCE = 0.6
23.07	SG1 26-3		K = 98 pH = 5.3 EC = 970 spun = 68 TCE = 0.2 PCE = 0.3
23.16	SG1 26-4		K = 6.0x10⁻⁴ pH = 4.1 EC = 2110 spun = 18 TCE = 3.9 PCE = 2.0 PCA = 2.3
23.25	SG1 26-5		K = 2.8x10⁻² pH = 4.9 EC = 2160 spun = 17 TCE = 1.4
23.34	SG1 26-6		K = 4.8x10⁻² pH = 4.8 EC = 1480 spun = 24
23.42	SG1 26-7		K = 2.4x10⁻³ pH = 5.1 EC = 1100 spun = 19
23.51	SG1 26-8		K = 9.0X10⁻⁴ pH = 4.4 EC = 1820 spun = 21
23.60			

Figure 2. Photograph and X-ray log of Core SG1-26.

4 CONCLUSIONS

The integrated data set shows that DNAPL at this site has moved downwards through sands to pool on clay layers. The DNAPL appears to have penetrated both the thin upper layer of clay and is also found within the top 200 mm of the thicker lower clay. At other bores, DNAPL was recovered from the underlying sandstone. The sodium/chloride ratio in the aquifer zone containing DNAPL is much reduced compared to background values. This is taken as an indication of DNAPL degradation and the release of chloride ions. In the lower clay layer, sodium exceeds chloride, indicating ion exchange with the clay matrix. The thin zone of high fluid conductivity shown in Figure 1 indicates that the top of the DNAPL zone is also associated with the dissolution of marine salts.

This paper demonstrates the usefulness of integrated geological, hydrogeological, geophysical and hydrochemical investigation techniques at DNAPL contaminated sites.

REFERENCES

Acworth, R.I. & J. Jankowski 1993. Hydrogeochemical zonation of groundwater in the Botany Sands aquifer, Sydney. *AGSO J. Aust. Geol. Geophys.* 14: 193-199.

Acworth, R.I., R.W. Beck, M.A. Groskops & N. Lavitt 1995. CRC WMPC Integrated Mapping Technologies Data Report. *Water Res.. Lab. Tech. Rep.* No. 95/04. University of New South Wales.

Beck, R.W. & R.I. Acworth 1996. A GC/MS method for the analysis of DNAPL contamination in the range 10 ppm to 2000 ppm. *Water Res. Lab. Res. Rep.* No. 192.

Schneider, G.S. & J.P. Greenhouse 1992. Geophysical detection of perchloroethylene in a sandy aquifer using resistivity and nuclear logging techniques. In R.S. Bell (ed.), *Proc. Symp. App. Geophys. Eng. Environ. Prob.*, SAGEEP, Denver, USA. Published by The Society of Engineering and Mineral Exploration Geophysicists.

Woodward Clyde 1996. ICI Botany Groundwater Stage 2 Survey, Published by Woodward Clyde, 486-494 Pacific Highway, St Leonards, NSW 2065.

Analysis of test pumping under conditions of variable viscosity recharge

Isam E. Amin
Department of Geological Sciences, California State University, Long Beach, Calif., USA

Michael E. Campana
Department of Earth and Planetary Sciences, University of New Mexico, Albuquerque, N.Mex., USA

ABSTRACT: A method for calculating the rate of groundwater recharge that occurs during pumping has been developed. The need for such a method is evident in the urban environment if the recharge water is contaminated or surface water-groundwater interactions are under investigation. The technique calculates recharge from a variety of sources: natural and artificial surface water bodies; other aquifers (via leaky layers); and infiltration from precipitation. The method accounts for dynamic viscosity differences between the recharge water and native groundwater; assuming density differences are negligible. The technique is based upon the well-known Cooper-Jacob method and uses semilogarithmic plots of time-drawdown data. It is thus appropriate for confined aquifers but is applicable to unconfined aquifers when drawdowns are small compared to the aquifer's saturated thickness. The method correctly predicts the special cases of no recharge; impervious boundary; a region of different transmissivity; and recharge rate greater than, equal to, or less than the pumping rate.

1 INTRODUCTION

A method is developed here for calculating the rate of groundwater recharge received by aquifers during pumping. The need for such a method is evident in the urban environment when the recharge water is contaminated or when surface-subsurface water interactions induced by pumpage are under investigation. The method calculates recharge from a variety of sources-natural and artificial surface water bodies (rivers, lakes, reservoirs); other aquifers (via leaky layers); and infiltration from precipitation. The method assumes negligible density differences between the recharge water and the native aquifer water, but takes into account differences in dynamic viscosity between the two waters. For example, the two waters can have different temperatures and hence different dynamic viscosities, which in turn influence the aquifer's hydraulic conductivity and transmissivity, and thus the rate of recharge.

Groundwater remediation and aquifer restoration are two areas for application of the proposed method. When the recharge water is contaminated, quantification of the recharge rate can assist in estimating the amount of contaminated fluid. This information is a prerequisite for designing an optimal system for groundwater remediation. Another application includes surface-subsurface water interactions. In this case, the volume of water lost from surface water bodies to groundwater systems (e.g., recharge induced by groundwater pumpage) can be calculated.

The proposed method utilizes the usual time-drawdown data obtained from aquifer tests, and employs the well-known Cooper-Jacob method (Cooper & Jacob 1946). Therefore, the limitations of the Cooper-Jacob method also apply to the proposed method. Primarily, u must be ≤ 0.05 (where $u = r^2 S/4Tt$, r is the radial distance from the pumped well, S is the aquifer's storativity, T is the aquifer's transmissivity, and t is the time since pumping started), so that straight lines can approximate the late time data on a chart of drawdown versus the log of time.

The proposed method is applicable to confined and unconfined aquifers. Application to unconfined aquifers is valid as long as their transmissivities can be determined by the Cooper-Jacob method, i.e., when drawdowns are small, compared to the original saturated thickness of the aquifer.

2 PROPOSED METHOD

The proposed method is discussed below.

2.1 Assumptions

The proposed method is based on the following assumptions, although these can he relaxed:

1. The aquifer is homogeneous and isotropic over the area influenced by pumping.

2. The aquifer has an infinite areal extent and uniform thickness over the area influenced by pumping.

3. The aquifer is pumped at a constant rate.

4. The pumped well penetrates and receives water from the entire thickness of the aquifer.

5. The pumped well is 100 percent efficient.

6. Prior to pumping, the potentiometric surface or the water table is horizontal over the area that will be influenced by pumping.

7. Flow is laminar.

8. $u \leq 0.05$.

9. The aquifer receives recharge during the pumping period.

10. Before the start of recharge, all water pumped from the well comes from the aquifer storage and water removed from storage is discharged instantaneously with decline of head.

11. Differences between the density of the recharge water and the host aquifer water are negligible, but the two waters can have different viscosities.

The Cooper-Jacob equation is an approximation of the Theis non-equilibriurn equation (Theis 1935); it is a reasonable approximation when $u \leq 0.05$. The proposed method is thus subject to the Theis assumptions, 1 through 7 above. Assumption 8 concerns the validity of the Cooper-Jacob method, and the last three assumptions are introduced to account for the effects of recharge.

2.2 Recharge effects on time-drawdown data

If an aquifer is receiving recharge during a pumping period, then the effects of recharge will be shown by semilogarithmic graphs of time-drawdown data (Figure 1) collected from observation wells or pumping wells with no well losses. As Figure 1 shows, the graph will consist of two parts. The first part is not affected by recharge and shows that the cone of depression is expanding up to time $t = t^*$. The second part is affected by recharge, which is encountered by the cone of depression immediately after time $t = t^*$. The slope of the second part is less than that of the first part, indicating that recharge has caused the cone of depression to enlarge at a slower rate than during the period of no recharge ($t \leq t^*$).

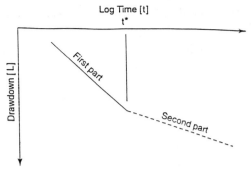

Figure 1. Effects of recharge on time-drawdown data.

Note that drawdowns of the first part are caused by pumping alone (recharge has not started yet), whereas those of the second part are caused by the net effect of pumping and recharge.

It should be emphasized that slope changes in time-drawdown data are not always a result of recharge, but could reflect aquifer heterogeneity as the cone of depression expands. In addition, changes in the pumping rate, casing storage, and interference drawdown also affect time-drawdown data. Therefore, the proposed method should only be used when changes in slope are believed to be caused by recharge.

2.3 Method development

Define:
Q_1 = pumping rate (L³/T),
ΔQ = recharge rate (L³/T),
Q_2 = net pumping rate, the algebraic sum of the pumping rate and the recharge rate (L³/T):

$$Q_2 = Q_1 - \Delta Q \qquad (1)$$

(Note that recharge is the negative of discharge.)
Δs_1 = slope of the first part of the time-drawdown graph (Figure 1) per one log cycle of time, and
Δs_2 = slope of the second part of the time-drawdown graph (Figure 1) per one log cycle of time.

Q_2, the net pumping rate, is an "adjusted" pumping rate (i.e., the pumping rate adjusted by the recharge rate).

The hydraulic conductivity (K) is defined as: $K = k\rho g/\mu$, where k is the intrinsic permeability, g is the acceleration of gravity, and ρ and μ are the density and dynamic viscosity of water, respectively. We assume that differences between the density of the recharge water and the aquifer water are negligible (assumption 11). However, the two waters may have different viscosities. In this case, the value of the hydraulic conductivity after recharge (K_2) will be different to that before recharge (K_1). For example, the hydraulic conductivity may double for a change in temperature of $0°$ to $20°$ (i.e., viscosity changes almost by half from $0°$ to $20°$ such as what may be observed seasonally from river recharge in northern US states. The approach defines $a = K_2/K_1 = \mu_1/\mu_2$, where μ_1 is the viscosity before recharge and μ_2 is the viscosity after recharge.

In confined aquifers, the saturated thickness of the aquifer *(b)* does not change by pumping or recharge. Therefore, in confined aquifers, the ratio of the transmissivity after recharge ($T_2 = bK$) to that before recharge ($T_1 = bK_1$) is also equal to *a*. The Cooper-Jacob method can be used to determine the transmissivity before recharge (T_1) as follows:

$$T_1 = 2.3 \, Q_2/4\pi\Delta S_1 \tag{2}$$

The transmissivity after recharge (T_2) can be determined as follows:

$$T_2 = 2.3 \, Q_2/4\pi\Delta s_2 \tag{3a}$$

T_1 can also be calculated using the data collected after recharge is encountered as follows:

$$T_1 = 2.3 \, Q_2/4\pi\Delta s_2' \tag{3b}$$

where $s_2' = as_2 =$ drawdown measured after recharge and corrected for viscosity variations, and $\Delta s_2'$ is the slope per one log cycle of the corrected drawdown.

In unconfined aquifers, the saturated thickness will change by pumping or recharge. The Cooper-Jacob method, however, is applicable to unconfined aquifers if the change in saturated thickness is relatively small in comparison with the original saturated thickness of the aquifer, in which case both equations 2 and 3 are applicable.

Equating equations 2 and 3b, and substituting equation 1 gives:

$$\Delta Q = Q_1 \, [1 - (\Delta s_2'/\Delta s_1)] \tag{4}$$

Equation 4 calculates the rate of groundwater recharge encountered during pumping periods. Equation 4 states that the recharge rate (ΔQ) can be determined from the pumping rate (Q_1), the slope of the time-drawdown graph not affected by recharge (Δs_1), and the slope of the time-drawdown graph affected by recharge, which is corrected for viscosity differences ($\Delta s_2'$).

Note that the value of Δs_1 always has a positive

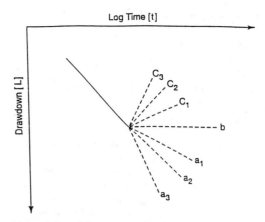

Figure 2. Possible responses for the second part of the time-drawdown data.

sign, if the graph is drawn in such a way that the drawdown increases downward as shown in Figure 1, whereas the value of $\Delta s_2'$ can be positive, zero, or negative. These values are shown in Figure 2. The three signs of $\Delta s_2'$ are discussed below.

1. $\Delta s_2' = 0$:

This case describes a constant water level (i.e., no increase or decrease in the drawdown, as shown on line b of Figure 2). Physically, this situation could only exist if the pumping rate is counterbalanced by an equal recharge rate. Therefore, equation 4 should predict the recharge rate to be equal to the pumping rate in this case. Substituting $\Delta s_2' = 0$ into equation 4 gives a $\Delta Q = Q_1$. Using a qualitative approach, Driscoll (1986) also concluded that the recharge rate is equal to the pumping rate when the second part of the graph is horizontal.

2. Positive $\Delta s_2'$:

As shown by the a lines of Figure 2, positive values of $\Delta s_2'$ can be: a) less than Δs_1 or b) equal to Δs_1 or c) greater than Δs_1,

a) $\Delta s_2' < \Delta s_1$ (Line a_1 of Figure 2):

In this case, both Δs_1 and $\Delta s_2'$ are positive. Therefore, ($\Delta s_2'/\Delta s_1$) is positive and < 1, and $[1 - (\Delta s_2'/\Delta s_1)]$ < 1. Accordingly, equation 4 predicts a $\Delta Q < Q_1$, and the recharge rate is less than the pumping rate in this case. Driscoll (1986) also reached this conclusion qualitatively.

b) $\Delta s_2' = \Delta s_1$ (Line a_2 of Figure 2):

In this case, both Δs_1 and $\Delta s_2'$ are positive and $(\Delta s_2'/\Delta s_1) = 1$. Therefore, $[1 - (\Delta s_2'/\Delta s_1)] = 0$, and equation 4 predicts $\Delta Q = 0$. In other words, equation 4 predicts no recharge in this case.

c) $\Delta s_2' > \Delta s_1$ (Line a_3 of Figure 2):

In this case both Δs_1 and $\Delta s_2'$ are positive and $(\Delta s_2'/\Delta s_1) > 1$. Hence, $[1 - (\Delta s_2'/\Delta s_1)] < 0$, and equation 4 predicts the recharge rate to have a negative value. Note that a negative recharge value physically means discharge. Therefore, equation 4 in this case predicts either an impervious boundary (transmissivity = 0) or a region of different transmissivity.

3. *Negative $\Delta s_2'$* (C lines on Figure 2):

Negative values of $\Delta s_2'$ can be a) less than Δs_1, or b) equal to Δs_1, or c) greater than Δs .

In these cases, the quantity $(\Delta s_2'/\Delta s_1)$ is negative, since Δs_1 is positive. Therefore, $[1 - (\Delta s_2'/\Delta s_1)] > 1$ regardless of whether $\Delta s_2' < \Delta s_1$ (line c_1), $\Delta s_2' = \Delta s_1$ (line c_2), or $\Delta s_2' > \Delta s$ (line c_3). Thus, in this case, equation 4 always predicts the recharge rate (ΔQ) to be greater than the pumping rate (Q_1). Note that Δs_2 in this case represents the slope of water levels that are physically increasing as pumping continues. It should be noted that, in the case of negative $\Delta s_2'$, equation 4 reads

$$\Delta Q = Q_1 [1 + (\Delta s_2'/\Delta s_1)] \qquad (5)$$

where the quantity $(\Delta s_2'/\Delta s_1)$ is the absolute value of the ratio of the two slopes.

3 PROCEDURE

Drawdowns measured after the start of recharge are multiplied by $a = \mu_1/\mu_2$ (values of μ_1 and μ_2 can be determined from the temperature of groundwater samples collected before and after recharge, respectively) to correct for viscosity variations. The corrected drawdowns are plotted on the semilogarithmic graph paper on which drawdowns measured before recharge were plotted. The rate of recharge can be calculated with equation 4 or 5 after $\Delta s_2'$ and Δs_1 are determined.

4 CONCLUSIONS

A method is presented here for calculating the rate of groundwater recharge that may occur during periods of pumping. Possible recharge sources include natural and artificial surface water bodies, leaky layers and infiltration of precipitation. The method is useful when the recharge water is contaminated or when surface-subsurface water interactions are being investigated. The method utilizes time-drawdown data obtained from aquifer tests, and employs the well-known Cooper-Jacob method. Therefore, the method is only valid when application of the Cooper-Jacob method is valid. The method is applicable to confined and, if their transmissivities can be determined by the Cooper-Jacob method, to unconfined aquifers.

REFERENCES

Cooper, H.H., Jr., & C.E. Jacob 1946. A generalized graphical method for evaluating formation constants and summarizing well-field history. *Transactions, American Geophysical Union* 27: 526-534.

Driscoll, F.G 1986. *Groundwater and Wells*, 2nd ed. St. Paul: Johnson Division.

Theis, C.V 1935. The relation between the lowering of the piezometric surface and the rate and duration of discharge of a well using ground-water storage. *Transactions, American Geophysical Union* 16. 519-524.

The use of marker species to establish the impact of the city of Nottingham, UK on the quantity and quality of its underlying groundwater

Mike H. Barrett & D. N. Lerner
Groundwater Protection and Restoration Research Unit, University of Bradford, UK

Kevin M. Hiscock
School of Environmental Sciences, University of East Anglia, Norwich, UK

Steve J. Pedley
Robens Institute, University of Surrey, UK

John H. Tellam
Department of Earth Sciences, University of Birmingham, UK

ABSTRACT: The aim of this study is to resolve much of the uncertainty surrounding the impact of cities on the quantity and quality of their underlying groundwater. Urban groundwater is a potentially valuable and underused resource in the UK. A better understanding of recharge sources such as leaking sewers should lead to improved management of urban aquifers. The study area is the city of Nottingham (UK) which overlies the Sherwood Sandstone aquifer. The underlying methodology for the study is to use chemical signatures to identify sources of recharge to the aquifer, relying upon differences in water qualities for the different recharge sources. It is important to establish species that may be used as indicators of particular recharge sources. The marker species which have proved most useful in establishing the presence of sewage contamination of groundwater for this study are nitrogen isotopes and microbiological indicators. These indicate multi-point source sewage contamination of shallow groundwater in Nottingham.

1 INTRODUCTION

Urban groundwater is a potentially valuable and underused resource in the UK. It is often at risk of contamination from the overlying city and a better understanding of the impact of recharge sources, such as sewers and mains leakage, should lead to improved management of urban aquifers. An overview of urban groundwater issues in the UK is given by Lerner and Barrett (1996). The overall aim of this study is to resolve much of the uncertainty surrounding the impact of cities on groundwater in the UK. The collation of better data will begin to answer questions such as what proportion of leakage from water mains recharges groundwater and what are the effects of sewers and other diffuse urban pollution sources on groundwater quality.

The study area is the city of Nottingham (UK), a major industrial city since the 18th century based largely on pharmaceutical and manufacturing industries. The city overlies the Triassic Sherwood Sandstone aquifer, which is unconfined beneath much of the city (confined to the east by Mercia Mudstone), relatively free of drift, and has a shallow groundwater table beneath the city centre (where rising water levels have resulted in flooded basements) and the industrial Basford area 4 km to the northwest. A hydrogeological map is shown in Figure 1. Groundwater abstraction began in 1850 and grew rapidly, supplying industrial and public needs. The aquifer extends north of Nottingham, underlying an agricultural area. Although the aquifer remains the principal water resource for the city, abstractions for public supply are restricted to the rural area due to concerns regarding the quality of the water underlying the city; abstractions from the city area continue for private industrial use.

The underlying methodology for the study is to use chemical signatures to identify the various sources of recharge to the aquifer, and so relies upon differences in water qualities for urban water supply, natural recharge and sewage. It is important to establish species that may be used as indicators of particular recharge sources, and much of the study has focused on establishing suitable marker species for detecting sewage recharge within groundwater.

2 SAMPLING IN THE NOTTINGHAM AREA

2.1 *Sampling networks*

A network of sampling points was established for this study. Deep groundwater samples were taken from all the currently abstracting industrial boreholes in Nottingham and additionally from the public water supply boreholes situated to the north and east of the city (Figure 1). Shallow groundwater samples were taken from purpose-installed monitoring boreholes in the Meadows housing estate near the city centre (Figure 1). Samples of shallow groundwater were also obtained from

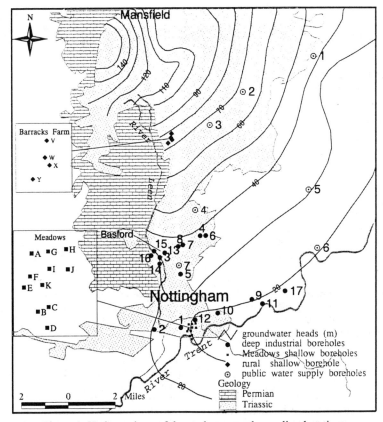

Figure 1. Hydrogeology of the study area and sampling locations.

flooded caves beneath the city centre, although these are not ideal as they are subject to atmospheric alteration. Sampling of raw sewage, rainfall, river water (from the Rivers Leen and Trent) was also carried out, and data on mains water quality within all of the Nottingham supply zones were made available by Severn Trent Water plc.

2.2 *General groundwater quality*

In general, the urban inorganic groundwater quality is less good beneath the city than beneath the surrounding rural land, although the degradation is not as serious as might be expected beneath a city with an industrial history as long as that of Nottingham. As would be expected, the shallow groundwater is more contaminated than the deep groundwaters, and the least good groundwater quality is found in the industrial Basford area.

3 MARKER SPECIES

Ideal marker species are those which, when present in groundwater, indicate recharge from a specific source. This requires that the species should be unique to one recharge source, and be easily detectable in both the recharge source water and in groundwater. In reality there are probably no completely ideal markers. Generally markers are present in more than one recharge source, requiring a multi-solute mass balancing exercise to quantify recharges. Alternatively, 'finger printing' can be used; although specific individual species may not be unique to a particular recharge source, specific combinations of species may be considered to be a 'fingerprint' for that source.

For the purpose of this project, several marker species for sewage were investigated following a literature survey, and then rejected for various reasons. Coprostanol (a faecal steroid) has been described in the literature as a useful species for determining the degree to which coastal waters have been contaminated by sewage by analysing sediment samples (Hatcher and McGillivary 1979, Kelly 1995). However, coprostanol is not suitable for use in groundwater studies as it is highly hydrophobic and tends to remain within sewage sludge, rather than the liquid portion. Optical brighteners were considered, but again rejected on the basis that they were unlikely to be present in groundwater in detectable quantities. Optical brighteners such as diaminostilbene disulphonic acid derivatives and disyryl biphenyl derivatives are used in detergent manufacture. However, they typically make up <0.1% of the total detergent (Soap and Detergent Industry Association 1995) and are designed to adsorb to clothes when in the wash solution. Considering further dilution of the optical brighteners remaining in the wash solution in the sewage system and still further dilution after leakage to the groundwater system, detection in groundwater samples is unlikely. EDTA, a complexing agent used in detergents, has been used as a marker species in previous studies (Grischek et al., 1994), but the cost of analysis at commercial laboratories proved prohibitive for this study.

Synthetic oestrogens (17α-ethynylestradiol and mestranol) would provide an interesting line of investigation, having been found to be present in river waters receiving treated sewage effluent (FWR 1992), but facilities for the analysis of this species were not made available during this study. Additionally oestrogen mimics such as alkyl phenol ethoxylates (APEs) may be present in industrial effluents, being used during production of intermediates for the detergents, adhesives and plastics industries (ENDS 1996), as well as domestic wastes. A survey of licences granted to industries to discharge wastes to the sewerage system revealed that cyanide (food industry) and silver (photographic processors) could be potential tracers, but neither of these were detected in groundwater samples (in fact CN was not detected in raw sewage samples and Ag was present at just 40μg/l). The marker species found to be of most use for detecting sewage effluent in groundwater during this study were stable nitrogen isotopes and microbiological indicators.

3.1 Nitrogen isotopes

Nitrogen occurs in both oxidised and reduced forms in groundwater, as well as in its elemental state. Of the nitrogen compounds, nitrate and ammonium are of most interest to this study. There is a wide variety of N-sources, including atmospheric loading and deposition of nitrate via rainfall, sewer leakage, nitrogen-based chemicals, fertilisers, urea used as a road de-icing agent, and ammonium as a by-product of many industrial

processes (Ford and Tellam, 1994). Variations in the stable isotopic composition of naturally occurring elements result from equilibrium and kinetic fractionation effects during physico-chemical processes (Rivers et al., 1996). Nitrogen has two stable isotopes, ^{15}N and ^{14}N, and their relative abundances are measured with respect to atmospheric nitrogen. If R is the ratio of the heavier isotope to the lighter isotope, then the relative fractionation is expressed thus:

$$\delta^{15}N = (R_{spl}/R_{std} - 1)1000 \qquad (1)$$

where $R_{spl} = {}^{15}N/{}^{14}N$ is the ratio of the sample and $R_{std} = {}^{15}N/{}^{14}N$ is the ratio of air.

Results are given in deviations of parts per thousand ($^o/_{oo}$); if $\delta^{15}N$ is positive, the sample is isotopically heavy, and vice-versa, relative to the air standard ($\delta^{15}N = 0$ $^o/_{oo}$). Nitrogen isotopes may be used to distinguish between different pollution sources by comparing the $\delta^{15}N$ value of the groundwater to that of the potential recharge sources. Interpretation must be cautious given the overlap between the variable isotopic compositions of potential sources and because of isotopic fractionation during nitrogen transformation processes. Processes that affect the nitrogen isotope composition of groundwater nitrate include denitrification (Heaton 1986) and groundwater mixing (Mariotti et al., 1988). Wilson et al. (1994) conclude that the distribution of isotope compositions is controlled by nitrogen inputs from a variety of sources. Figure 2 shows the nitrogen isotope signatures considered typical of particular recharge sources. Groundwater samples were obtained from the city centre caves, the deep industrial abstraction boreholes and shallow purpose-installed monitoring boreholes in the Meadows residential area near the city centre where the depth to groundwater is 2-5m. The depth of sewers in this area is 2-6m, all the sewers being either foul or combined (i.e. mixed foul and surface water). The $\delta^{15}N$ values in the deep boreholes ranged from +2.8 $^o/_{oo}$ to +12.2$^o/_{oo}$, with the cave samples having heavy signatures ranging from +13.4 $^o/_{oo}$ to +16.9 $^o/_{oo}$ (Rivers et al. 1996). The cave samples have $\delta^{15}N$ values in excess of the +10 $^o/_{oo}$ threshold considered to be indicative of localised pollution by sewage waste. The values in the Meadows area range from +7.9 $^o/_{oo}$ to +24.3 $^o/_{oo}$ with 70% of sites exceeding +10 $^o/_{oo}$ (Fairbairn 1996). Both the deep and shallow groundwaters in the study area are oxidising in nature and so denitrification is unlikely to explain the enriched isotope signatures obtained. The conclusion regarding the deep boreholes is that the majority have nitrate from a soil organic nitrogen source, presumably originating in the adjacent rural area (upstream), but that at least 3 have a component of

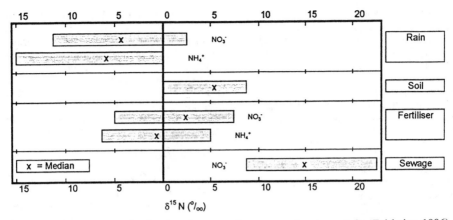

Figure 2. Typical nitrogen isotope signatures for sources of recharge (after Fairbairn, 1996).

sewage-derived nitrogen. Clearly, and as might be expected, many of the shallow groundwater samples are impacted by sewage effluent.

3.2 *Microbiological indicators*

A microbiological survey was carried out using groundwater samples taken from the Meadows boreholes and the results are displayed in Table 1 (Pedley, 1996). Analyses for bacteria, bacteriophage and enterovirus were carried out. Coliform bacteria (including *Escherichia coli*), faecal streptococci and sulphate reducing clostridia were the bacteria targeted as indicators of faecal (sewage) contamination. Bacterial indicators of faecal contamination were isolated from all borehole water samples. The density of indicator bacteria and the relative proportion of each indicator varied between sample points, but only 2 of the borehole water samples, borehole C and borehole I, were found to contain low densities of all types of faecal indicator bacteria. A high number of total coliform bacteria were isolated from boreholes B, D, E, G and H. Borehole E was most heavily contaminated with total coliform bacteria, whereas the adjacent borehole F (at 100m separation) contained a very low density of total coliform bacteria.

E. coli was isolated from all boreholes; six sites contained levels in excess of 10mpn (most probable number)/100ml, with boreholes G and H having levels in excess of 50mpn/100ml. Faecal streptococci were isolated from all boreholes with bacterial densities in excess of 100mpn/100ml at boreholes E, F, G, H and K.

In addition to bacteria, analysis was carried out for bacteriophage (viruses which use bacteria as a host organism). Whereas it is not easy to determine the presence of viruses (such as enterovirus) in

groundwater samples due to low efficiency of virus recovery, the presence of bacteriophage are readily determined. For example, 10 litres of sample are required to perform enterovirus analysis whereas just 20ml are required to perform coliphage analysis (Pedley, 1996). Coliphage virus (host organism *E.coli*) was isolated from boreholes B, C, D, F and J, although only 1pfu (plaque forming unit)/ml was detected at these sites. Analysis for enterovirus was carried out. There were no positive detections in the groundwaters sampled. During this study, only one set of samples was taken for microbiological analysis so the results represent a snapshot and take no account of quality variations with time. The density of faecal bacteria in water taken from some of the boreholes implies faecal contamination of the groundwater. The proximity of the source cannot be precisely determined, but some indication can be gained from the relative persistence of the different indicator organisms in the environment.

Faecal streptococci and *E.coli* are found in high numbers in the faeces of humans and animals (10^9-10^{10}/g). In fresh faeces, the number of *E.coli* is usually an order of magnitude greater than the number of faecal streptococci. As there is no known environmental reservoir of these organisms, their presence in water confirms faecal contamination. *E.coli* is very sensitive to environmental stress and is not considered to survive very long in water under ideal conditions. Thus, a high number of *E.coli* relative to the number of faecal streptococci indicates recent or local contamination. The relative level of the two indicators is reversed if the contamination is spatially or temporally remote.

Using these criteria, borehole H may be considered closest to a source of contamination and boreholes E and F as more remote.

The total coliform group of bacteria includes some species that may survive and proliferate in the

Table 1. Microbiology of shallow groundwater in the Meadows, Nottingham.

Site	Total coliforms (mpn/100ml)	E.coli (mpn/100ml)	faecal streptococci (mpn/100ml)	coliphage (pfu/ml)	Enterovirus (pfu/10l)
A	13	13	9	0	0
B	170	20	33	1	0
C	5	5	2	1	0
D	540	22	9	1	0
E	910	1	180	0	0
F	4	2	160	1	0
G	110	75	160	0	0
H	160	160	160	0	0
I	1	1	2	0	0
J	13	13	3	1	0
K	9	9	160	0	0

Table 2. Isotopic and microbiological indication of sewage contamination of shallow groundwater in the Meadows, Nottingham (numbers refer to rank order; 1=highest value).

Site	Land Use	Depth To Water Table (m)	$\delta^{15}N$	Total coliforms	E.coli	Faecal streptococci	Sewage	Notes
A	Parkland	2.59	11	6	5	7	N	
B	Parkland	3.98	2	3	4	6	F	Roadside, near public lavatories
C	Parkland	2.23	4	9	8	10		
D	Parkland	1.50	1	2	3	7	F	Roadside, near combined sewer
E	1970s housing	4.20	3	1	10	1	F, R	
F	1970s housing	3.48	5	10	9	2	R	
G	1970s housing	3.23	6	5	2	2		High Cl
H	1970s housing	3.68	8	4	1	2	C	High Cl
I	1970s housing	4.00	9	11	10	10	N	
J	1970s housing	4.90	10	6	5	9	N	
K	C19th housing	5.74	7	8	7	2		

N: No contamination ($\delta^{15}N<10°/_{oo}$; Total Coliforms<100mpn/100ml; E.coli<50mpn/100ml; F.strep<50mpn/100ml)
C: Close to source of microbiological contamination
F: Faecal contamination confirmed
R: Remote from source of microbiological contamination

environment in low numbers so the presence of this group of bacteria does not necessarily confirm faecal contamination but high numbers in a water sample may be considered indicative of contamination. Water from boreholes D and E contained particularly high numbers of total coliform bacteria, confirming the presence of faecal contamination. The conclusion of the microbiological survey is that 9 of the 11 shallow boreholes are faecally contaminated. The correlation between the microbiological survey and the nitrogen isotope survey is good. There is strong evidence of sewage contamination at all sites except boreholes A and I.

4 CONCLUSIONS

The marker species which have proved most useful in establishing the likely presence of sewage contamination of groundwater in this study are nitrogen isotopes and microbiological indicators. The fact that the two surveys (isotopic and microbiological) broadly corroborate each other suggests that such an approach provides a means of 'fingerprinting' sewage contamination.

Table 2 summarises the two sets of results for the shallow boreholes in the Meadows area, ranking the 11 sites numerically in order of most enriched nitrogen isotope value/greatest microbiological contamination (1 being the highest). The table shows that greatest sewage contamination is at boreholes D and E, with A, I, and J being least contaminated by sewage. Boreholes E and F are likely to be remote from the contaminant source and borehole H close to a source.

The spread of sewage contamination over the area is suggestive of a diffusive source, but is more likely a result of a multi-point source input. It is also considered that the most likely sources of sewage contamination are not the main sewers (which are largely below groundwater level and therefore, even if not water tight, are likely to be a sink for groundwater rather than a source of sewage leakage) but the connecting pipes to individual properties.

Further work is required if these marker species are to be used for more precise predictions of the locations of point source sewage contamination. Amongst the topics to be looked at in more detail are the fate of faecal indicator bacteria and viruses in groundwater and the transformations of nitrogen species (such as nitrification of ammonium) in sewage in the unsaturated zone and the effect of such processes on the groundwater isotopic signature.

REFERENCES

ENDS 1996. Chemical firms in the spotlight over oestrogen discharges. ENDS Report 263.

Fairbairn, J. 1996. Application of nitrogen isotope techniques to assess the impact of sewer leakage on shallow urban groundwater quality in the Sherwood Sandstone aquifer of Nottingham. Unpublished M.Sc. thesis, University of East Anglia, UK.

Ford, M. & J.H.Tellam 1994. Source, type and extent of inorganic contamination within the Birmingham urban aquifer system, UK. *J. Hydrol.* 156: 101-135.

FWR 1992. Effects of trace organics on fish. Foundation for Water Research final report on research commissioned by the Department of the Environment (UK) (FR/D 0008).

Grischek, T., W.Nestler, J.Dehnert & P.Neitzel 1994. Groundwater/river interaction in the Elbe river basin in Saxony. Second international conference on ground water ecology, U.S. Environmental Protection Agency, American Water Resources Association. 309-318.

Hatcher, P.G. & P.A.McGillivary 1979. Sewage contamination in the New York Bight. Coprostanol as an indicator. *Environ. Sci. Technol.* 13(10): 1225-1229.

Heaton, T.H.E 1986. Isotopic studies of nitrogen pollution in the hydrosphere and atmosphere: a review. *Chemical Geology.* 59: 87-102.

Kelly, A.G. 1995. Accumulation and persistence of chlorobiphenyls, organochlorine pesticides and faecal sterols at the Garroch Head sewage sludge disposal site, Firth of Clyde. *Environ. Pollut.* 88: 207-217.

Lerner, D.N. & M.H.Barrett 1996. Urban groundwater issues in the United Kingdom. *Hydrogeology Journal.* 4(1): 80-89.

Mariotti, A, A.Landreau & B.Simon 1988. ^{15}N isotope biogeochemistry and natural denitrification processes in groundwater: application to the Chalk aquifer of Northern France. *Geochimica Cosmochimica Acta.* 52: 1869-1878.

Pedley, S. 1996. Microbiological survey of shallow groundwater at the Meadows Estate, Nottingham. Robens Institute, University of Surrey, Report RI96/EHM/019.

Rivers, C.N., M.H.Barrett, K.M.Hiscock, P.F.Dennis, N.A.Feast & D.N.Lerner 1996. Use of nitrogen isotopes to identify nitrogen contamination of the Sherwood Sandstone aquifer beneath the city of Nottingham, United Kingdom. *Hydrogeology Journal.* 4(1): 90-102.

Soap and Detergent Industry Association 1995. *pers com.*

Wilson, G.B., J.N.Andrews & A.H.Bath 1994. The nitrogen isotope composition of groundwater nitrates from the East Midlands Triassic sandstone aquifer, England. *J. Hydrol.* 157: 35-46.

ACKNOWLEDGEMENTS

Funding provided by: EPSRC, MAFF, Environment Agency, Severn Trent Water plc, Stanton plc.

Groundwater in the Urban Environment: Problems, Processes and Management, Chilton et al. (eds)
© 1997 Balkema, Rotterdam, ISBN 90 5410 837 1

Application of a hydrogeological model to analyze and manage groundwater processes in the urban environment: A case study in the Milan area, Italy

T. Bonomi
Dipartimento di Scienze dell'Ambiente e del Territorio, Università degli Studi di Milano, Italy

A. Cavallin
Centro di Studio per la Geodinamica Alpina e Quaternaria, CNR, Milano, Italy

ABSTRACT: Within the framework of GIS, a distributed groundwater model is applied to evaluate the groundwater processes of the Milan hydrogeological system. The historical sequences of all the different mass balance factors for the period 1975-1994 have been analysed to evaluate their synergistic relationships. The model calibration was applied to 1990; then model applications were evaluated to test the effect of five years with high intensity rainfall (1975-1979) on groundwater and to simulate the piezometric fluctuations in the Milan area.

1 INTRODUCTION

A groundwater resource assessment is important for management and planning. The hydrogeological model applications are an important technique to analyse resource availability. To evaluate the groundwater balance and to simulate piezometric fluctuations, the structure and the factors of the hydrogeological system have to be determinated.

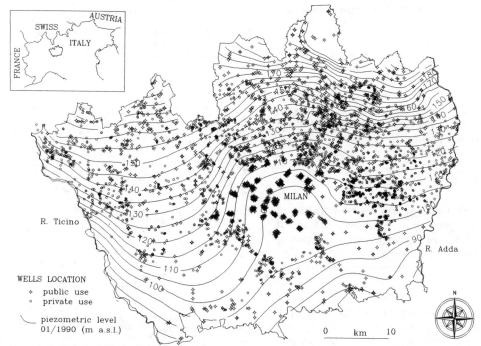

Figure 1. Studied area in the Po Plain, northen Italy.

2 STUDIED AREA HYDROGEOLOGY

The studied area is a province located in the Po Plain (Figure 1) and it is characterised by the highest density of urban, industrial and agricultural activities in Italy. The Milan province covers 1989 km², among which urban and industrial areas cover 29%, with the remainder used for agricultural purposes.

In 1990, the inhabitants were 3,794,925, with a groundwater pumping of more than 1 billion m³/y, among which nearly 700 million m³/y came from 1,499 public wells. In the area, 4,859 wells were identified and located, among which 2784 wells have stratigraphic logs.

The natural drainage network is constituted by the Adda and Ticino rivers, respectively in the eastern and western boundaries, where they drain groundwaters from the Plain (Figure 1). The hydrogeological system consists of fluvial and fluvio-glacial deposits, in which gravels and sands are predominant. The studied area can be considered an unconfined aquifer (Beretta et al. 1985; Cavallin et al. 1983).

The 4859 wells are filed in a database (Bonomi et al. 1995a), and they are referenced by geographic coordinates and well stratigraphic logs, translated into alphanumeric codes. A software, linked to the database, has permitted evaluation of the predominant textures within a layer defined between the topographic surface and the base of the aquifer. The application of geostatistical techniques (Bonomi et al. 1995b; EPA 1988) has permitted definition of the percent distribution of gravel, sand and clay. Gravel increases southward with a positive correlation (R=0.7), sand decreases south-westward with a negative correlation (R=0.65), and clay has a random distribution.

3 MASS BALANCE FACTORS

The hydrogeological system has been determined according to geometrical (depth and thickness of the aquifer) and hydrogeological parameters (permeability, transmissivity and storage coefficient). Inputs and outputs represent the mass balance factors.

The geometries of the hydrogeological system are identified by two static surfaces, the topography (DTM) and the base of the aquifer, and a dynamic one, the water table. Piezometric data are related to a monitoring network in 249 wells with a monthly frequency, active in Milan province since 1975 (Figure 2).

In 1915 the water table depth, quite close to Milan city, was about 1 m below ground surface; in 1930 2 m; in 1940 about 4 m; and in 1960 5-6 m. Since the 1950's, all piezometric wells indicate a decreasing aquifer level. This can be due mainly to two different causes: the irrigation decreasing and pumping increasing. The groundwater table decreased quickly, with an historical minimum in the 1970's, some 40 m below ground surface (Comune di Milano 1989) (Figure 3).

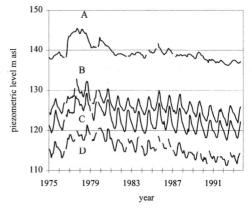

Figure 2. Monthly piezometric levels in the Milan area (northen part A, central part B, C and D) for the period 1975-1994.

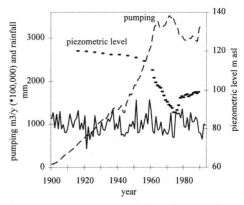

Figure 3. Yearly piezometric level (dotted line), pumping (dashed line) and rainfall (solid line) in Milan town, for the period 1900-1994.

At the end of the 1970's there was a general groundwater increase in the province (Casati 1988), with differing intensity. It reached maximum positive fluctuations in the 1980's (Figure 2). Many causes can justify this increase: precipitation, economic crisis, new industrial technologies. After the 1980's a new groundwater lowering developed (Figure 2), reaching the 1970's level.

In the last years (1993-1996) the situation in Milan is getting worse. Many areas of the town's subsurface (parking, underground, houses) are now flooded by groundwater.

The historical sequences of all the different factors of the mass transfer, for the period 1975-1994, have been analysed to evaluate their synergistic relationships: monthly piezometric levels; monthly rain and temperature data; irrigation water delivered by Canale Villoresi; the pumping wells; socio-economic data.

Around the town, where the irrigation practices are not common, a relationship between rainfall and groundwater table (Figure 4) is observed; where the irrigation is common the monthly correspondence between irrigation data and piezometric level (Figure 5) is observed.

In the metropolitan area, for the period 1960-1980, the more evident relationship is between pumping increase and water table lowering (Figure 3).

In general, the analysis of the relationships between the different factors established that there is no unique correspondence between only one of the input and output factors and the water table fluctuations, but all the factors contribute synergistically.

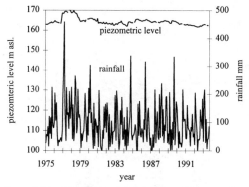

Figure 4. Monthly piezometric level, in the northen part of the Milan area, and monthly rainfall for the period 1975-1994.

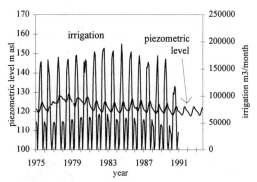

Figure 5. Monthly piezometric level and monthly irrigation, in the central part of the Milan area, for the period 1975-1994.

The maximum piezometric level in the latest 20 years has been analysed and simulated with regard to precipitation.

4   EXTREME METEOROLOGICAL EVENTS AND THEIR EFFECTS ON GROUNDWATER

From 1975 to 1979 two extreme, different meteorological events occurred:

1) rainfall more than 30% greater than the yearly average (997 mm/y) during the five years 1975-1979 when 6300 mm of rain occurred (Figure 3);

2) maximum monthly rainfall, 373 mm in October 1976; the maximum recorded for the period 1900-1993 (Figure 4).

These events produced different effects on the hydrogeological system. In particular the observed cases were:

1) direct effect between monthly rainfall and positive groundwater fluctuations both as an entity and as a sequence; these positive fluctuations were 35 m during October 1976;

2) cumulative and sometimes direct effect between monthly rainfall and positive groundwater fluctuations. In the northen part of the area, the maximum positive peak was 25 m above the previous period, and during all five years the average value was 10-15 m higher than the previous period;

3) cumulative effect, as in the last case, but the positive result was only 4-8 m with an irrigation influence recorded, in the central part of the area;

4) no effect in the spring zone, southward.

5 GROUNDWATER LEVEL SIMULATION LINKED TO EXTREME METEOROLOGICAL EVENTS

A distributed three-dimensional finite-difference groundwater flow model (MODFLOW, McDonald & Harbauch 1988) has been applied to evaluate the mass transfer of the hydrogeological system for 1990 (Bonomi 1995; Bonomi & Cavallin 1996) This calibration phase was used for the model applications described below.

Computer techniques were developed to link the model to software for data entry. The region was rasterized (using GIS ILWIS, Valenzuela 1988) on a 500 m grid consisting of 104 rows and 136 columns. Using this grid, all of the parameters (groundwater level, permeability, porosity, depth to the base of the aquifer, recharge) were rasterized.

The model boundaries were: constant heads, westward (Ticino river) and eastward (Adda river) and southward (spring line); and groundwater flux northward.

The model applications were able to reproduce periods with high intensity rainfall (1975-1979) and simulate groundwater fluctuations in the Milan area. The model was applied starting from the piezometric level of 1990 which is similar to the 1975 groundwater level (Figure 2).

The first simulation was for one month with a rainfall recharge of 373 mm (as in October 1976); the simulated positive groundwater fluctuations were 1-2 m with peaks of 3 m.

In the second simulation the total rainfall period for 1975-79 was covered. Mass balance factors were estimated; drawing about 1 billion m^3/y, with recharge (irrigation and precipitation about 4 billions m^3/y.

The simulated water table (Figure 6) has a flux direction and a gradient similar to the actual one (Figure 1). The simulated positive fluctuation is variable from 2 m to 14 m (Figure 7).

These results can be compared with the real fluctuations, in particular for cases 2, 3 and 4 of the preceding section. In case 1, where the aquifer has a high secondary porosity and the deposits are conglomerate, the model cannot simulate the higher value.

The good response of the model was due to the correct distribution and quantity of input and output factors (Peck et al. 1988).

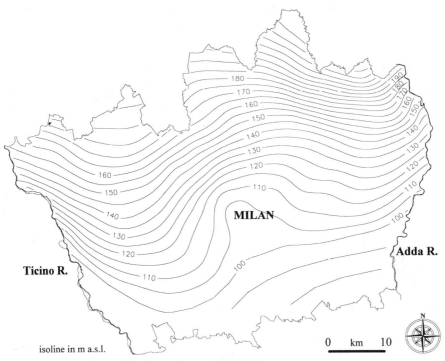

Figure 6. Simulated piezometric level after five years (1975-1979).

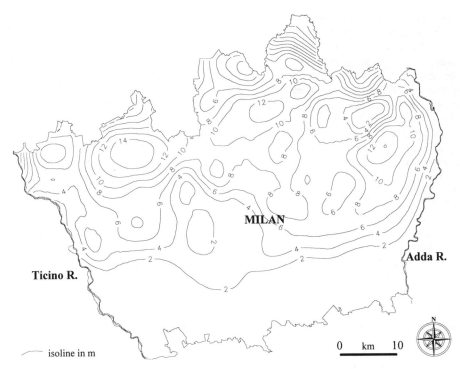

— isoline in m

0 km 10

Figure 7. Simulated positive fluctuations after five years (1975-1979).

6 CONCLUSIONS

Many factors can cause groundwater fluctuations. Meteorological extreme events can present hazards in the urban hydrogeological system (parking, underground, houses).

One single event, even if very intense, cannot produce as much damage as a long period of medium-high rainfall. In fact, the recorded data and the distributed model have verified that:
- during a period with rainfall 30% greater than the yearly average (997 mm/y), the positive groundwater fluctuations were, on average, 10-12 m;
- during one single maximum monthly event, the positive groundwater fluctuations were 2-4 m in the porous aquifer.

If a new meteorological extreme event were now to occur, the effects could be very hazardous. In fact the groundwater level during the period 1993-1996 increased by 4-6 m, such that extreme events could flood many infrastructures.

In the next few years many industries will close and new technologies will have better water use efficiency. Hence, groundwater levels are expexted to rise, regardless of meteorological events.

To forecast different hazard scenarios, it is necessary to define the hydrogeological system, to identify the mass balance factors and their relationships and to apply distributed models. All these approaches can be a great asset in evaluating groundwater development within urban planning.

Besides this, the application of distributed groundwater models within the framework of GIS permits us to update, to standardise and to integrate data continually; to minimise errors linked to single data points; to use the best software to solve problems with interchange of the results; and to assess groundwater availability according to the hydrogeological system studied.

REFERENCES

Beretta, G.P., A. Cavallin, S. Mazzarella. & A. Pagotto 1985. Primo bilancio idrogeologico della pianura milanese. Acque sotterranee, Milano, 2: 37-46, 3: 37-47, 4: 32-51.
Bonomi, T. 1995. Sistemi Informativi territoriali per la valutazione del bilancio del sistema

idrogeologico milanese. Fondazione Lombardia
Ambiente, Minima Naturalia n.11 , Milano.

Bonomi, T.& A. Cavallin 1996. GIS and
hydrological model: a case study in the Milan
area,. Italy. In *International Conference on
Application of GIS in Hydrology and Water
Resources Management, Vienna April 1996*, pp.
15-22.

Bonomi, T., A. Cavallin.& M. De Amicis 1995a.
Un database per pozzi: Tangram. In Atti 2°
Convegno Nazionale sulla protezione e gestione
delle acque sotterranee: metodologie, tecnologie e
obiettivi. Modena, Quad. Geol. Appl., suppl. n.3
1/95, pp. 3.461-3.465.

Bonomi, T., A. Cavallin., P. Cerutti & G.
Rotondaro 1995b. First results in identification of
aquifer parameters by statistical analysis of water
well data reports. *XXV IAH Congress prints,
Adelaide, Australia*, pp. 63-68.

Cavallin, A., V. Francani. & S. Mazzarella 1983.
Studio idrogeologico della pianura compresa tra
Adda e Ticino. Costruzioni, anno XXXII, Milano,
326: 1-25, 327: 26-39.

Casati, P. 1988. Acque sotterranee in Lombardia.
Coop. Edit. Nuova Brianza, Milano, 128 pp.

Comune di Milano 1989. L'acquedotto di Milano.
3v.

EPA 1988. Geostatistical Environmental
Assessment Software . GEO-EAS. User's Guide.
Las Vegas.

McDonald, M.G. & G. Harbauch 1988. A modular
three-dimensional finite-difference ground-water
flow model. Scientific Software Group, U.S.,
Washington, 528 pp.

Peck, A., S. Gorelick, G. De Marsily, S. Forster &
V. Kovalevsky 1988. Consequences of spatial
variability in aquifer properties and data
limitations for groundwater modelling practice.
IAHS Publication no. 175.

Valenzuela, C.R. 1988. ILWIS overview. "ITC
Journal", 12.

Natural retardation of industrial fluids in the Birmingham urban Triassic Sandstone aquifer

Stephen R. Buss, John H. Tellam & John W. Lloyd
Department of Earth Sciences, University of Birmingham, UK

Bob C. Harris
National Groundwater and Contaminated Land Centre, Environment Agency, Birmingham, UK

ABSTRACT: High concentrations of industries are often found in urban areas, and many industrial processes have the potential to cause considerable groundwater pollution. Foremost among these are the metal processing and finishing industries, which use hazardous fluids, often with extreme pHs and metal loading. Relatively little is known of the interactions of such fluids with aquifer materials. Laboratory work has begun to examine rock-fluid interaction in the Birmingham Triassic sandstone aquifer. Birmingham has a very long history of both ferrous and non-ferrous metal working. It is shown that acid attenuation reactions are dependent on the sandstone mineralogy; the near-surface weathered rock attenuates by ion exchange and silicate and iron oxyhydroxide dissolution, whilst deeper sandstones have additional buffering capacity involving calcite dissolution. Batch experiments have been conducted leading to a simple, but practical and quantitative, multi-substrate ion-exchange model for protons that allows pH-dependent acid buffering capacities to be estimated.

1 INTRODUCTION

The city of Birmingham is built upon an unconfined Triassic sandstone aquifer. The metal-working industry has always been predominant in the town. Strong acids have been used for centuries, often containing very high levels of heavy metals. The groundwater is now locally contaminated by pollution from metal-working sites (Ford & Tellam 1994). A project was therefore instigated to investigate the interactions of the pollutant fluids with the aquifer sandstone. The first part of the study is concerned with the acid buffering capacity of the sandstones, important since it is clearly being exceeded (Ford et al. 1992); this paper describes the progress to date.

1.1 *Geology*

The Sherwood Sandstone Group, the main unit of the Birmingham aquifer, comprises moderately well sorted fine- to coarse-grained sub-arkosic sandstones. Red iron oxide coatings are ubiquitous but of variable extent near the top of the sequence. Calcite cementation is variable throughout and has

been leached out entirely for approximately twenty metres near the surface. The sandstones contain a few percent clays, mostly kaolinite, and have very low organic carbon concentrations.

1.2 *The Birmingham metal industry*

The Birmingham metal industry is mainly based upon equipment manufacture and surface finishing. Both activities require oxide removal by acid (mostly sulphuric and hydrochloric) treatment and/or degreasing with alkalis or chlorinated solvents. The various surface finishing treatments involve elaborate preparation as well as the main treatment. For pre-treatment, sulphuric and hydrochloric acids are most commonly used for oxide removal. Electroplating solutions often have low or high pHs to retain high concentrations of metals in solution.

The potential pollutants may enter the aquifer by a variety of channels including leaking underground storage tanks or treatment ponds, or by accidental release outdoors. Before the environmental legislations of the 1970s, these fluids had been disposed of through drains, canals and rivers, down boreholes or by seepage into the ground.

Table 1. Proton-promoted dissolution reactions for Triassic sandstone minerals.

Mineral	Dissolution reaction	Weight % of rock	Buffering capacity (mol H^+/m^3 rock)
Calcite	$CaCO_3 + 2H^+ \rightarrow Ca^{2+} + H_2CO_3*$	10 (where present)	4 236
Goethite	$FeOOH + 3H^+ \rightarrow Fe^{3+} + 2H_2O$	1	238
Kaolinite	$Al_2Si_2O_5(OH)_4 + 6H^+ \rightarrow 2Al^{3+} + 2H_4SiO_4 + H_2O$	5	411
Orthoclase	$KAlSi_3O_8 + 4H^+ + 4H_2O \rightarrow K^+ + Al^{3+} + 3H_4SiO_4$	5	381

2 ACID POLLUTION

Acid inputs are buffered by two main mechanisms: protonation of oxide surface oxygens, and aquifer matrix dissolution. The following sections describe these in detail and estimate buffering capacity for each. In the calculations, a porosity of 20% and a bulk dry density of 2120kg/m^3 are assumed.

2.1 Proton sorption

Surface oxygens of oxide minerals take up protons from solution thus:

$$MO^- + 2H^+ \leftrightarrow MOH + H^+ \leftrightarrow MOH_2^+$$

This produces a variably charged mineral surface according to the ambient pH. This charge can be zero when the oxygens are protonated just enough to compensate for broken bonds and an internal charge. The pH at which the surface charge is zero is the 'point of zero charge' (pzc).

In a rock, there are a number of minerals with differing pzc's and sorption capacities. In the Triassic sandstone the two main ion exchangers are iron oxyhydroxides (pzc $\approx$ 6 - 8) and clays (pzc $\approx$ <3 - 5). The total exchange capacity and the ratio of surface areas, clay:FeOx, determine the total buffering capacity with respect to pH. A solution of pH4, for example, will be poorly buffered by a substrate with a pzc of 6 since at pH4, its exchange sites will be saturated with protons.

A simplistic view of the proton sorption capacity is that it will equal twice the maximum cation exchange capacity (CEC). This is only approximate since the CEC in these sandstones can vary with different exchanging cations (El-Ghomeny 1997) and protons may not be adsorbed hydrated, as are the cations in CEC tests. These factors will lead the measured CEC to underestimate the total proton sorption capacity. A typical CEC for the Triassic sandstone is 2.5meq/100g.

2.2 Mineral dissolution

Mineral dissolution occurs at different rates for the various minerals in the sandstone. Calcite, if present, will dissolve most rapidly; iron oxides and silicates will take longer. Table 1 shows the dissolution reactions and buffering capacities of the common Triassic sandstone minerals.

The calcite dissolution rate will depend on its dispersal throughout the rock and by transport of H_2CO_3* from the active surface. It would probably be valid, however, to assume equilibrium over short timescales of days.

Iron oxides are mostly goethite; the main silicate minerals present are kaolinite, potassium feldspar and quartz. The clays and iron oxides will dissolve most rapidly because they are the most unstable (Figure 1), with high specific surface areas. The half-lives given for the minerals in Figure 1 indicate that for the iron oxides and silicates, equilibrium is reached more slowly - over timescales of years.

In the real aquifer, these half-lives are likely to be further increased. Moss & Edmunds (1992) found that orthoclase dissolved 10-50 times faster in the laboratory than in the field. The probable reasons for this were: inadequate mixing in low-flow pores, the shielding of reactive minerals by neighbouring minerals, locally high dissolved aluminium concentrations in porewaters inhibiting the Al^{3+} producing dissolution reactions, and higher ambient temperatures in the laboratory.

2.3 Total buffering capacity

Figure 2 shows the estimated total acid buffering capacity of the Triassic sandstone. Where present, calcite clearly dominates the system. In calcite-free zones mineral dissolution still dominates, but proton sorption provides a significant capacity and, most importantly, the first available proton sink in a newly polluted system.

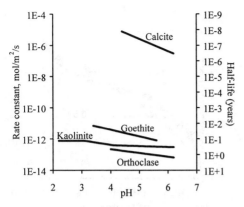

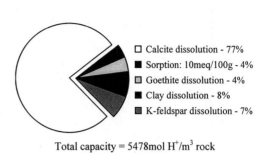

Total capacity = 5478mol H^+/m^3 rock

Figure 1. Dissolution rate constants and half-lives (25°C) for Triassic sandstone minerals. After Stumm & Morgan (1996) and Moss & Edmunds (1992)

Figure 2. Relative contributions to the acid buffering capacity of Triassic sandstone with mineralogy as in Table 1. The value for sorptive buffering is taken from experimental results in Section 3.2.

3 SORPTION BUFFERING MODEL

3.1 Model derivation

A model of proton sorption buffering in the sandstone has been developed based upon the assumption of limited exchange site availability (cf. the Langmuir sorption isotherm) and takes the form,

$$\left(H^+\right)_{sorbed} = \frac{k \cdot c \cdot \left(H^+\right)^2_{solution}}{1 + k \cdot \left(H^+\right)^2_{solution}} \qquad (1)$$

for one exchanging substrate, where (H^+) is the proton activity in solution or on exchange sites, c is an exchange capacity (meq/100g), and k is given by $k = 10^{2 \cdot pzc}$. This gives the relationship shown as curve 1 in Figure 3.

Rock systems, generally having more than one main sorption substrate, are inadequately represented by Equation (1), so are modelled using the relationship,

$$\left(H^+\right)_{Total} = \left(H^+\right)_{solution} + \sum_i \left(H^+\right)_{i \; sorbed} \qquad (2)$$

for i substrates. For example, a system with two substrates would yield curves like that in Figure 3, with points of inflection in the buffering response at around the values of the pzc's.

3.2 Experiments

A number of rock suspension/acid titrations have been conducted to validate the model in Section 3.1. In each, 3g of calcite-free Triassic sandstone was suspended in 20ml of distilled water and aliquots of hydrochloric acid were added. The suspensions were agitated continuously, and the pH monitored. Readings were taken five minutes after the addition of the acid to allow for sorption equilibration. The combined results are shown in Figure 4. Two curves also shown are the result of applying the following parameters to Equation (2):

$pzc_1 = 1.7$; $c_1 = 7$meq/100g
$pzc_2 = 6.5$; $c_2 = 0.14$meq/100g

The parameters were chosen to reproduce the two main points of inflection in the data, but it is clear that the Triassic sandstone cannot be realistically modelled with only two active surfaces. The data indicate the presence of a number of phases with intermediate pzc's. The third curve on Figure 3 shows that by the addition of two further surfaces, a reasonable agreement with the data can be obtained, however, the values chosen for their pzc's were chosen arbitrarily to provide a good match.

The total buffering capacity appears to exceed 10meq/100g - approximately four times the measured CEC; probably for the reasons suggested in section 2.1.

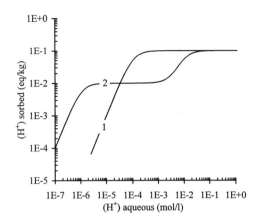

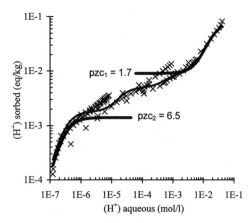

Figure 3. Modelled proton sorption isotherms.
Curve 1: pzc = 4, c = 10meq/100g (Equation 1)
Curve 2: pzc_1 = 2, c_1 = 9meq/100g
           pzc_2 = 6, c_2 = 1meq/100g

Figure 4. Rock suspension/acid titration results and modelled response curves.
- The two bold lines fit the obvious inflection points.
- The third line shows the effect of four surfaces.

4 CONCLUSIONS

Acid industrial fluids are entering the Birmingham aquifer. The upper carbonate-free parts of the aquifer have an instantaneous buffering capacity of around 200 mol H^+/m^3 rock, primarily by proton exchange on clays and oxyhydroxides. A slower-acting capacity of the order of 1 kmol H^+/m^3 rock derives from silicate and oxide dissolution, and may take decades or centuries to be fully realised. The rapid buffering capacity of the deep aquifer is around 4.4 kmol H^+/m^3 rock - mostly by calcite dissolution.

A simple model of the buffering capacity has been developed and tested against acid/rock titrations. It indicates that there are several active ion exchanging surfaces with pzc's between 1.7 and 6.5. The model allows the calculation of pH recovery following a pollution incident. For example, a 1m^3 spill of molar HCl directly into calcite-free rock will be buffered to pH6 by about 35m^3 rock. Precipitation equilibria control dissolved metal levels in the pollutant so significant concentrations of metal are not expected to migrate out of that volume below the spillage. A typical flow rate of 2m/year (Greswell 1992) would move the fluid through that volume of aquifer in approximately three and a half years. Comparison with the mineral half-lives in Figure 1 suggests that there will be some dissolution.

Further work is needed to validate the model and examine the effects of proton - cation competition. Long-term dissolution experiments will determine the relative importance of the buffering mechanisms.

ACKNOWLEDGEMENTS

The Environment Agency and the School of Earth Sciences, University of Birmingham are gratefully acknowledged for funding this project.

REFERENCES

El-Ghomeny, H.M.R 1997. *Laboratory experiments for quantifying and describing cation exchange capacity in UK Triassic Sandstones.* Unpublished PhD thesis, University of Birmingham.

Ford, M. & J.H. Tellam 1994. Source, type and extent of inorganic contamination within the Birmingham urban aquifer system, UK. *J. Hydrol.* 156:101-135.

Ford, M., J.H. Tellam & M. Hughes 1992. Pollution-related acidification in the urban aquifer, Birmingham, UK. *J. Hydrol.* 140:297-312.

Greswell, R 1992. *The modelling of groundwater rise in the Birmingham area.* Unpublished MSc thesis, University of Birmingham.

Moss, P.D. & W.M. Edmunds 1992. Processes controlling acid attenuation in the unsaturated zone of a Triassic sandstone aquifer (UK) in the absence of carbonate minerals. *Appl. Geochem.* 7:573-583.

Stumm, W. & J.J. Morgan 1996. *Aquatic chemistry (3rd ed).* New York: Wiley.

Environmental isotopic tracing of water in the urban environment of Pretoria, South Africa

Michael J. Butler & Balthazar Th. Verhagen

Schonland Research Centre, University of the Witwatersrand, Johannesburg, South Africa

ABSTRACT: Environmental isotopes contribute to an understanding of hydrological processes in urban environments in South Africa. Isotopic contrasts between mains water and ground water are found in Gauteng Province. Results for numerous private boreholes reflect considerable hydrological differences due to differing topographic relief and leakages, with concentrations of mains water in ground water ranging from 10% to 100%. An abrupt change in isotope values of mains water provides a useful time marker.

1 INTRODUCTION

The study of urban hydrology increases in importance as cities develop and expand, with impacts on the balance and quality of both surface and ground water. In South Africa, ground water is widely extracted by private householders. With increasing fresh water scarcity, management and protection of this resource requires the development of novel approaches for the study of ground water in the urban environment.

The chemistry of infiltrating water may change radically in the vadose zone, in particular in carbonate alkalinity, whilst the isotopes of hydrogen and oxygen are conservative tracers. Rand Water (RW) mains water is used by many municipalities in the highly industrialised and urbanised Gauteng province in which Pretoria is situated. This supply was found to have a distinctive δD - $\delta^{18}O$ composition (Figure 1), where δ values are a) much more positive than weighted average for Pretoria rain (IAEA 1992) and b) lie close to the world meteoric water line. This signal probably results from unique moisture conditions over the shallow, but extensive Vaal Dam, the principal storage reservoir for the RW mains supply. This isotopic composition readily distinguishes mains water from a) most naturally recharged ground water and b) water subject to surface evaporation. RW mains contains tritium at about 4 TU.

The $\delta^{18}O$ - δD values of mains water and most natural ground water differ by some 30x the standard deviation of measurement, allowing the detection of 5-10% of RW mains water in ground water.

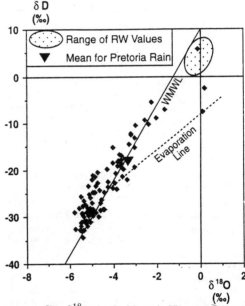

Figure 1. δD - $\delta^{18}O$ plot for Mountain View ground water, showing the WMWL, evaporation line and the range of values measured in RW mains water.

2 TRACING IMPORTED WATER IN THE SUB-SURFACE

Numerous private boreholes in the northern suburbs of Pretoria were used as sampling points. Mountain

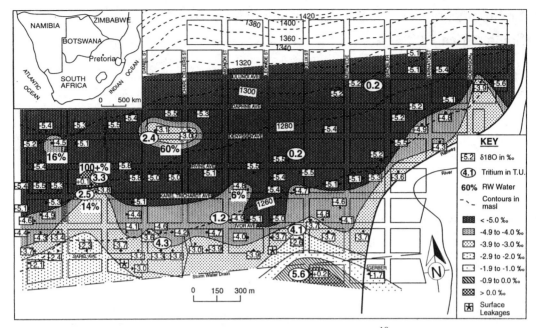

Figure 2. Map of the township of Mountain View showing topographic contours, individual $\delta^{18}O$ values, zones of equal $\delta^{18}O$, tritium values and calculated percent mains water.

View township (Figure 2) lies on a steep, south-facing hill slope. The areal distribution of $\delta^{18}O$ shows an increase of values downdip over the entire E-W extent of the township. Most δD - $\delta^{18}O$ values fall close to the WMWL (Figure 1), assumed to reflect both a gradient in recharge selectivity and admixed mains water.

Values of $\delta^{18}O$ considerably lighter (as low as -5.6‰) than the weighted mean in Pretoria precipitation ($\delta^{18}O$ = -3.7‰; IAEA 1992) occur where the slope is greatest, i.e. at the highest point in the township. The low $\delta^{18}O$ values are ascribed to rainfall selectivity, enhanced by higher runoff and interflow components.

Figure 3 shows a schematic section of the area, with the only three boreholes for which the depth could be ascertained. No rest levels could be determined; the ground water level had to be inferred. The borehole depths higher up the slope suggest that water was struck deep in fractured quartzite, well below the water table. This model is supported by tritium values of 0.2 TU, indicating mean residence times > 200 years. In the valley, higher $\delta^{18}O$ values, accompanied by higher tritium values around 4 TU, indicating mean residence times of about 30 years, are for shallower boreholes in weathered material.

The correlation of total dissolved solids (as E.C.) and $\delta^{18}O$ (Figure 4) shows a distribution of E.C. similar to $\delta^{18}O$. The dominant ion is HCO_3 as seen

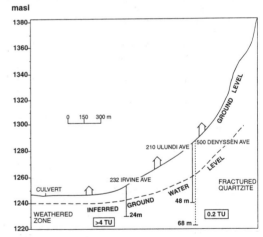

Figure 3. Schematic section of Mountain View, showing topographic slope and inferred rest water level contour and borehole depths.

in the correlation of alkalinity with E.C. (Figure 5). The chemistry of RW mains, initially at low alkalinity, therefore changes through accumulation mainly of bicarbonate on infiltration in a manner similar to rain water recharge whilst the isotopic signature is retained. In a few cases, δD - $\delta^{18}O$ values which are positive with respect to their

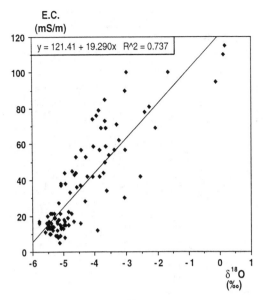

E.C.
(mS/m)

$y = 121.41 + 19.290x \quad R^2 = 0.737$

$\delta^{18}O$
(‰)

Figure 4. Plot of E.C. - $\delta^{18}O$ for Mountain View ground water.

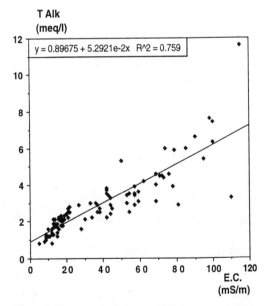

T Alk
(meq/l)

$y = 0.89675 + 5.2921e\text{-}2x \quad R^2 = 0.759$

E.C.
(mS/m)

Figure 5. Plot of total alkalinity - E.C. for Mountain View ground water.

immediate surroundings or stable isotope zone, are interpreted as admixture of mains water. Most values lie close to the WMWL/mixing line (Figure 1). Two values, with E.C > 110 mS/m, lie well to the right of the WMWL and show evaporation. A possible evaporation line is shown by way of illustration.

The percentage of point source mains water p_m can be calculated from:

$$p_m = \frac{\delta - \delta_g}{\delta_m - \delta_g} \quad \times 100\% \qquad (1)$$

where δ = measured value, δ_g = background for the area, δ_m = value in mains water, taken as $\delta^{18}O$ = -0.5‰. Assuming a mains water end member, the proportions calculated for the anomalous sampling points range from 6% to 100% (Figure 2).

The regular gradient of $\delta^{18}O$ values confirms reports that the reticulation system has recently been substantially rehabilitated. Only a few point sources could be identified. The high $\delta^{18}O$ values at the bottom of the slope are taken to be the result largely of downslope flushing of infiltrated mains water. The observed isotopic and E.C. patterns may therefore change with time.

3 EASTERN TOWNSHIPS

Townships to the east of Mountain View, at the foot of the hills (Figure 6), differ from Mountain View in a) the many suspected water mains leakages and b) ground water levels reflecting the much gentler surface slope.

The comparative frequency histograms in Figure 7 show only partial overlap in ground water δD values for Mountain View and the eastern townships. No clear geographic systematics are seen in the latter (Figure 6). Figure 8 shows practically no correlation of E.C. with isotopic composition in the eastern suburbs, showing a) the slower drainage due to the lower surface slope and b) the expected existence of numerous mains leaks.

With some scatter, δD - $\delta^{18}O$ fall effectively on the WMWL/mixing line (Figure 9). However, in the absence of zones of equal isotope values, a different approach is required for assessing the percentage mains water.

A substantial number of points have $\delta D > -7‰$, taken to show undoubted mains water influence. Removing these positive values gives a mean for the remaining points of $\delta D = -11‰$. This is taken as the natural ground water end member δ_g for the eastern suburbs. The percentage mains water values p_m were calculated using eqn. 1 and shown in Figure 6. The lowest value used ($\delta = -6‰$) gives a conservative value of $p_m = 31$ %. Lower percentages were regarded as too imprecise as δ_g is probably too positive. δ should reflect also diffuse infiltration mains water (garden irrigation, spillages).

The estimate of 100% mains for one borehole is supported by tritium at 4.6 TU; others show between 30% and 56% mains water, confirming the suspected numerous mains leaks which are seen to cluster, possibly resulting from the sampling coverage.

103

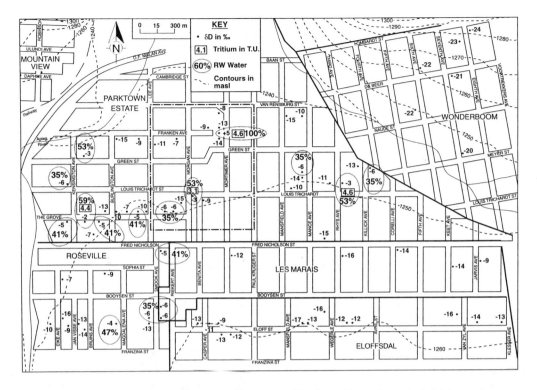

Figure 6. Map of eastern townships showing topographic contours, δD values, tritium values and calculated percent mains water. Detail: see Figure 11.

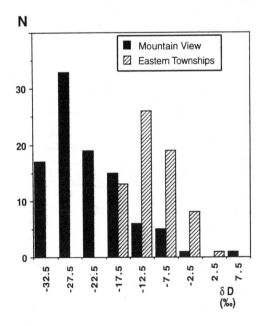

Figure 7. Comparative δD frequency histograms for Mountain View and eastern townships ground water.

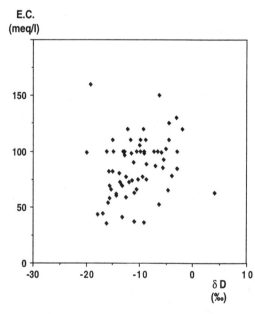

Figure 8. Plot of E.C. - δD for eastern townships ground water.

104

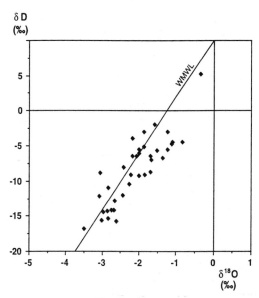

Figure 9. Plot δD - δ^{18}O for eastern townships ground water.

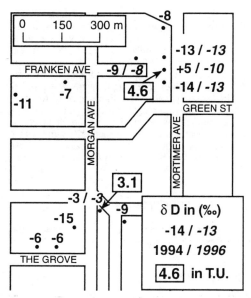

Figure 11. Detail from Figure 6, showing tritium values, and δD values for 1994 and 1996.

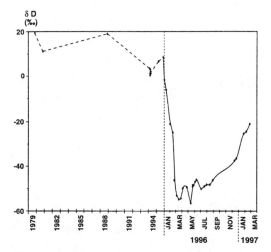

Figure 10. Past and recent δD trends for RW mains water.

4 CHANGE IN MAINS ISOTOPIC VALUES

The distinctive isotopic composition of RW mains water (plotted for δD in Figure 10) existed since the late 70's with some fluctuations. The exceptional 1995/1996 rainfall season, with individual rainstorm values reaching lows of δ^{18}O = -11.3‰ and δD = -71‰, produced a drop of 60‰ in δD in mains water, and therefore of the reservoir, implying complete isotopic resetting of Vaal Dam during this period.

This pronounced isotope signal was sought for in the study area. The borehole interpreted as showing the greatest influence of mains leakage (~100%) and others in the vicinity were resampled soon after the observed sharp drop in isotopic values. Figure 11 shows the original and new deuterium values for the resampled boreholes. The borehole which originally gave δD = +5‰ showed a drop of 15‰, whilst δD for the closely adjacent boreholes, which previously had produced "normal" ground water, remained unchanged. This confirmed the earlier interpretation of mains leakage, that it is localised in nature and probably not of long duration. The borehole further south which had previously been identified as producing 53% mains water as yet showed no change. The lower tritium value appears to confirm the slower response.

The lack of response of the "normal" boreholes to the heavy rainfall with exceptionally negative isotopic values shows the damping of some 10m of unsaturated zone on the infiltration of rain water.

5 CONCLUSIONS

This study has shown that environmental isotope techniques are indispensible in the study of urban hydrology, uniquely identifying recharge and geohydrological processes. Numerous mains leakages could be pinpointed. For a more quantitative interpretation, the importance of establishing a local terrain background has been clearly identified. The assessment of this background will depend on the particular circumstances in the area of study.

The isotopic transient in mains water is a convenient time marker for systems with constant mains input. Previous transients may have gone unnoticed, but are unlikely to have been of the magnitude of the 1995/96 event. At the time of writing, Vaal Dam is rapidly returning to its pre-1996 isotopic values. The unique mains water signal used in this study is therefore likely to be restored.

Although environmental tritium in southern African rainfall has returned to pre-bomb levels, it remains a useful tool for estimating ground water mean residence times. This is a basic parameter needed to assess urban ground water vulnerability to pollution.

6 ACKNOWLEDGEMENTS

This project was undertaken under contract to the Water Research Commission.

7 REFERENCE

International Atomic Energy Agency 1992. Statistical treatment of data on environmental isotopes in precipitation. Tech. Rep. Series # 331. IAEA, Vienna.

Groundwater in the Urban Environment: Problems, Processes and Management, Chilton et al. (eds)
© *1997 Balkema, Rotterdam, ISBN 90 5410 837 1*

Water-sensitive urban planning: Concept and preliminary analysis

N. Carmon
Faculty of Architecture and Town Planning, Technion, Israel Institute of Technology, Haifa, Israel

U. Shamir
Faculty of Civil Engineering, Technion, Israel Institute of Technology, Haifa, Israel

ABSTRACT: In the context of sustainable development, there is a need to promulgate guidelines for urban planning which will consider the effects of the built environment on water resources. Our current work is a first step on the way towards Water-Sensitive Urban Planning (WSUP). It focuses on groundwater protection, and includes: a review of the state of knowledge regarding the effect of urban development on runoff and infiltration, assessment of these effects for the coastal aquifer in Israel, identification of relevant components of WSUP, preliminary practical proposals, and recommendations for further research.

1 INTRODUCTION

Water-Sensitive Urban Planning (WSUP) is an important component of sustainable development, whose goals, approaches, methods and results are predicated upon consideration and care for the long-term effects of development projects on the natural resources and on their usefulness to mankind, both now and in the future.

WSUP considers the effects of urban development on water resources. It has two aspects: the effects on the quantity and quality of water resources, and the effects on water use and on generation of wastewater. Our work relates to the first of these, and focuses on groundwater. In this context, the goal of WSUP is to increase the quantity of good quality water which infiltrates into the ground and eventually reaches the groundwater.

Rapid urban development over aquifers is occurring and is expected to grow in many places, including Israel's coastal plain. In view of this, we have posed three objectives for our work:

1. To review the current state of knowledge about the influence of urban development on groundwater;

2. To create the knowledge basis for WSUP, which relates to planning guidelines (including housing patterns) and to installation of facilities for mitigating potential negative effects;

3. To explore the application of the above to Israel's coastal plain, where extensive urban development is expected over the next two decades.

The research project is ongoing. In this paper we review the literature survey conducted, report interim results of the analysis carried out, propose some guidelines, and outline a plan for further research.

2 LITERATURE SURVEY

2.1 *Urban land use and the quantity of groundwater*

Common wisdom, reflected in publications on hydrology, is that urban construction of buildings, roads and parking areas increases surface runoff by creating more impervious surfaces, which translates into a reduction in infiltration and, therefore, less groundwater recharge (Maidment 1993; Harbor 1994; Singh 1995). However, several studies have indicated that the effect of urban development on the hydrological balance is not quite so pronounced, and that, in effect, the percentage of rainfall which infiltrates is greater than often thought (Van de Ven 1985; WAWA 1987; Ferguson 1994). This is particularly true if measures are taken to increase infiltration (Ishizaki et al. undated; Fujita 1992; Herath et al. 1993).

Hence, the first question we posed for this research was: is it correct that urban development reduces groundwater recharge? There are several ways to approach an answer. One is direct measurement of the effect on groundwater (Water Sensitive Urban Design Research Group 1989) and computation of the groundwater balance equation. This requires measurements which are difficult and computations which are error-prone, and hence is seldom done. An indirect way would be to measure rainfall, runoff and evaporation, and compute infiltration as the remaining unknown in the balance equation at the surface. Again, few measurements exist of the runoff in urban areas (Herath et al. 1993; Gerti et al. 1993). A third way is to use models which accept rainfall data and compute infiltration, evaporation and runoff, using a description of the watershed and the properties of soil and land cover (Singh 1995). This is the approach we have taken in the meantime, as long as measurements are not available.

2.2 Urban land use and the quality of groundwater

Land uses affect the quality of surface runoff and the water which infiltrates into the ground. Urban development is accompanied by an increase in the quantities of several pollutants, the ones of most concern include chloride, nitrate and heavy metals (Berry & Horton 1974; Atwood & Barder 1989; Christensen & Rea 1993; Kappen 1993; Pitt et al. 1994).

Assessing the effect of urban development on groundwater quality faces even more severe difficulties than those mentioned above for quantity. The processes are complex and diffuse, soil properties which are not readily measurable in situ have a significant influence, and, most important, the process may take several decades before the effects of land uses reach the groundwater (Ronen et al. 1986; Barringer et al. 1990). From the perspective of our work, it is quite certain that the cleanest water for infiltration is rain which falls on houses and their yards and gardens, in particular the water which can be collected directly from roofs.

3 ESTIMATING LOSSES TO GROUNDWATER RECHARGE DUE TO URBAN DEVELOPMENT: A CASE STUDY IN ISRAEL'S COASTAL PLAIN

The population growth and the rapidly rising standards of living in Israel have resulted in extensive urban growth. About half of the total increase has taken place, and is expected to take place in the future, in the coastal plain. The core of the accelerated development is in the metropolitan area of Tel Aviv, which lies above Israel's largest and most important multi-year reservoir of water, the coastal aquifer. The phreatic sandstone aquifer lies beneath an area of some 1900 square kilometers, with a thickness ranging from a few meters to about 200 m. The water table, below which the aquifer is saturated, lies 5 to 20 m below the land surface.

We decided to concentrate on the main bulk of urban development: the residential area including the associated services (social services, commercial areas, local roads, parking spaces and small open spaces). We left out industrial areas and main transportation corridors.

The first objective of the case study was to provide initial estimation of the losses to groundwater recharge, resulting from the pattern of urban construction which is typical of Israel of the 1990s. Another objective was to identify the components of urban planning that seem to directly influence groundwater recharge.

3.1 The Test Location - Kiryat Ganim

The neighborhood of Kiryat Ganim, a newly constructed urban area on the coastal plain of Israel, was selected for our case study (Meiron-Pistiner 1995). Its construction began in 1991. By 1994 its population reached about 6,400 residents in 1,770 households. The neighborhood is part of Rishon Le-Zion, a city south of Tel Aviv that has grown from about 50,000 in the early 1970's to 100,000 ten years later, and to more than 150,000 inhabitants in the early 1990's. The population of the area and the physical plan of the neighborhood are typical of the urban sprawl at the heart of the State of Israel, the core that spreads above the coastal aquifer.

The climate in the area is Mediterranean, mild, with an average of 58 days of rainfall (over 0.1 mm) a year, from about October to April, dry the rest of the year. The annual rainfall averages 536 mm (maximum 912 mm, minimum 312 mm. The highest monthly rainfall is in December, with an average of 146 mm.

The soil on which Kiryat Ganim was constructed is primarily sandy, about 160-180 m thick to the impervious layer below. The groundwater in this area shows concentrations of chloride in the range of 110 to 230 mg/l, and nitrate (as NO_3) in the range of 40 to 75 mg/l (the acceptable concentrations are: Cl^-, 250 mg/l for potable and unrestricted agricultural use; NO_3, 45 mg/l for unrestricted potable use, with an upper limit of 90 mg/l). Hence, the groundwater in this area is suitable for most uses, but the concentrations are approaching critical limits.

Kiryat Ganim has an area of 560 dunams (560,000 m^2) with 57% covered by residential buildings and their yards; the remaining 43% include: 21% open space, 10% roads (those not within the residential area), 9% public and commercial services, and 3%

undeveloped open spaces.

The building patterns of Kiryat Ganim are typical of the recent (1990s) urban sprawl above the coastal aquifer of Israel. Out of the average area per person in the housing area (without public services, main roads, neighborhood open spaces, etc.), about one quarter is covered by roofs, 40% (!) are paved areas, and the remainder (about one third) is green (mostly private gardens). As can be expected, the lower the density of housing units per dunam, the higher the total area per person (2.5 times higher in low density than in high density). It might be expected that in lower densities, a larger percentage of the area per person will be open and green, but this is not the case in Kiryat Ganim; the percentage of green areas is the same in higher and lower densities, and hence, the impervious area per person in low density is 2.5 times larger than in high density.

3.2 *Computational Methods*

Because of the difficulties in field measurements, as discussed above, we used two methods to estimate the loss of infiltration due to the construction of Kiryat Ganim: the Soil Conservation Service (SCS) method (SCS 1975; Harbor 1994; Ferguson 1996) and the Storm Water Management Model (SWMM) (Huber & Dickinson 1988; Huber 1995).

According to the SCS method, the volume of runoff from each storm is a function of a Curve Number (CN), taken from tables. The CN value is assigned according to the land uses on the watershed. The more impervious the area, the higher its CN value, and the larger the runoff volume. The computation is carried out for each rainstorm, and the runoff from all storms is totalled over the year. It is then assumed that the increase in runoff translates into an equal reduction in infiltration.

SWMM performs a continuous simulation, using sub-models of the hydrologic processes in the watershed (evaporation, infiltration and runoff) with parameters assigned to each sub-model according to watershed shape and area, soil properties, and evaporation rates. The computed values of each variable are totalled over a year's simulation period, to yield the annual volumes of runoff and infiltration. SWMM uses variable time intervals in the computations: a short interval (typically five minutes) during rainfall, and longer intervals corresponding to the time between storms.

3.3 *Data and Results*

Rainfall records from the nearby Beit Dagan meteorological station were examined, and five years were selected, according to their total rainfall amount: one close to the long term average, two close to the upper and lower extremes, and two more in between.

For the SCS method, eight land uses were identified in Kiryat Ganim, and for each of them the total area and the division into pervious (CN=49), cultivated (CN=39) and impervious (CN=98) areas were measured on a detailed map. The impervious area is further separated into roofs and paved surfaces, as required for a later analysis.

SWMM was run for the same years. The area was divided into six sub-basins, the Green-Ampt model was used for infiltration, and parameter values were taken from the manual (Huber & Dickinson 1988).

Three development conditions were considered: before development; after development, where all roofs and paved areas are impervious; and after development but with the roof drains connected to the garden/yard, adding their area to that of the pervious area.

Detailed results for SCS have been reported in Carmon & Shamir (1997a), and those for SWMM in Carmon & Shamir (1997b). Table 1 presents a summary of the average results for the five years: the lost infiltration per square kilometer due to urban development according to current practice, and the percentage of that loss which can be saved by connecting roof drains to the ground.

Table 1. Loss of infiltration due to urban development, and percent saved by connecting roof drains to the ground.

	Computation by the SCS model	Computation by the SWMM model
Increased runoff per km² due to urban development	71,000 m³/year (14 % of the rain)	240,000 m³/year (47 % of the rain)
Percent saved by connecting roof drains to the ground	35 %	32 %

4 TOWARDS WATER-SENSITIVE URBAN PLANNING

A planning team has been preparing, since 1990, a master plan for Israel into the 21st century. It includes forecasts of population and the built areas, to the year 2020 (Mazor & Trop 1994). According to these forecasts, the urban area in Israel's coastal plain in 2020 will be double its value in 1990 (from about 650 km^2 to 1275 km^2). Taking the results computed for Kiryat Ganim and projecting them to the entire area of the coastal aquifer according to these forecasts indicates that the lost infiltration will be (by the two computational methods) between 90 and 300 million m^3/year, half from existing urban areas and the other half from new ones. This is a very significant amount of water, in particular in the Middle East, where water shortage may have to be alleviated through expensive desalination.

Reducing this amount by WSUP will yield other benefits, especially a decrease in surface runoff which will enable reduction in the size and cost of the drainage systems. Other potential benefits would be reduction in the magnitude and severity of flooding in the urban area itself, and in the waterways and coastal waters to which the drainage is directed. Needless to say, consideration must be given to the effect on groundwater quality of changing from the conventional to the proposed urban development scheme.

Our conclusion is that sustainable development and preservation of the water resources require a joint effort by researchers and planners to develop and implement guidelines for WSUP. In this concluding section of the paper, we propose to contribute in this effort, by: (a) identifying the relevant components of urban planning, (b) providing preliminary practical suggestions for planners, and (c) proposing a plan for further research.

4.1 *Relevant Components of Urban Planning*

Based on the work conducted so far, i.e. study of the literature and the investigation of Kiryat Ganim, we identify five components of urban planning which should be considered in connection with their effect on runoff and infiltration:

1. The proportion of built and paved areas versus open spaces (impervious versus pervious land cover), in common building patterns.

2. The distribution of open (pervious) spaces over the area. There are ways to "break" the impervious area by patches and strips of pervious area, where water accumulated over the impervious part has a chance to penetrate into the ground.

3. Pervious paving materials for sidewalks, parking areas, paths, squares, and interior roads. Water quality has to be considered when dealing with roads and parking lots, but paved areas in yards, gardens and sidewalks are probably safe from the point of view of quality.

4. Sub-division of the area into small "micro" catchments. Each building, with its small yard/garden and a low stone wall around it, can become an infiltration basin.

5. Incorporation into the urban fabric facilities designed to intercept, detain and infiltrate water from precipitation. Such facilities may be at several scales: the individual lot and building, the urban cluster (urban block), and the larger urban area and region.

Information about the effectiveness and cost of several facilities and means to reduce urban runoff and increase infiltration is available in the literature (Schueler et al. 1992; Kennedy Engineers 1992; Ishizaki et al. undated; Fujita 1993; Ferguson 1994; Konrad et al. 1995).

4.2 *Preliminary Practical Proposals*

Urban development is expected to continue, even over aquifers whose waters are important, because of the economic pressures which are usually much more powerful than the forces of preservation. Still, we hope that by identifying actions for preserving groundwater quantity and quality, which can be harmonized with urban development, the goal of sustainable development will be served.

Given the state of knowledge at this time, as revealed in our study, we cannot as yet provide well founded recommendations, even though such are urgently needed. We can, however, already make the following initial proposals:

1. The public, relevant authorities, urban planners and designers should be made aware of the opportunities for reducing the negative effects of urban development on groundwater quantity and quality;

2. Open spaces, especially green tracts, should be interspersed in the area to be developed, in a manner which will allow as much of the surface runoff to be intercepted by pervious areas as possible;

3. Wherever possible, rainwater should be captured on site, before it flows and becomes polluted; special attention should be paid to using yards as micro-catchments;

4. In the first stage of planning of an urban area, the sensitivity of the area in terms of potential damage to groundwater should be assessed. The

sensitivity assessment is intended:
- to identify small areas above phreatic aquifers which serve as important natural infiltration basins, due to specific topographical or geological structure, and to inhibit or limit construction above them;
- to identify larger vulnerable areas above phreatic aquifers, the soil of which is permeable and the quality of groundwater underneath them is high, and to direct planners to use the best knowledge available to them in order to increase infiltration and care for the quality of the infiltrated water.

4.3 *Recommendations for Further Research*

To establish planning guidelines for WSUP on a sound basis, much more research is required. Assembly of an adequate information and knowledge base requires years of field measurements and analytical studies. We should, however, not wait for these to be completed before issuing some recommendations which seem justified on the basis of what we can conclude in a shorter period of time. Urban development is progressing rapidly in many areas underlain by groundwater aquifers, and we must try to protect their waters while we continue to conduct further studies.

Hence, a two-phase strategy is proposed. The goal of the short-term phase is to issue recommendations for WSUP based on knowledge obtained from the studies already conducted and elicited from experts. The goal of the long-term phase is to issue affirmative planning guidelines, based on valid and reliable empirical research that explains cause and effect relationships between urban land uses and groundwater quantity and quality, in addition to investigation of the technical, economic, social and administrative feasibility and effectiveness of the proposed guidelines.

The short-term effort is based on existing knowledge; the assembly of information, summary, analysis and conclusions on:
1. The effect of different ratios of pervious areas in an urban zone, and their spatial distribution (few and large or small and many), on the quantity and quality of surface runoff infiltrating into the ground;
2. The effects of devices and facilities designed to increase infiltration of surface runoff, including: stone walls around gardens that create a micro-detention and recharge basin; roof drains connected to the surface of the yard or garden, or to an underground "recharge well"; pervious paving materials; pervious ("leaking") drainage pipes; small detention ponds (temporary or permanent); temporary

use of playgrounds as detention and recharge facilities.

For each one of these, the analysis should address two aspects:
1. The physical consequences - effects on the water resource, on the drainage system, on the environment, and on the urban landscape. These conclusions should be relevant to other regions and countries, with similar conditions;
2. Feasibility of implementation - technical, economic, administrative and social considerations of introducing planning guidelines, installing devices or facilities, and maintaining them. Some of the conclusions may be specific to the location, while others may be more universal.

Our current work focuses on these short-term tasks. In parallel with the above plan for the short-term, there is need for a concerted long-term effort to improve knowledge and generate the information upon which policies can be based, with confidence. Empirical investigations must be a central element of this effort. The objective is to collect and analyze field data on the relationships between tractable (independent) variables (land uses, building types, and facilities installed in the urban area) and the dependent variables (quantity and quality of runoff and groundwater), with appropriate attention to intervening variables such as meteorology and soil types. These tests must be conducted over periods of years.

Measurement facilities for surface runoff and its quality should be installed at the micro scale (house with yard/garden), at the meso scale (urban block) and at the macro scale (large sections of a city). Location of the measuring stations and the frequency of measurement need careful planning, to maximize the benefit of the data gathered. Some information of this type has been collected in several places in the world; it should be assembled and analyzed to provide the initial basis for the data collection effort. Groundwater quantity and especially quality should be measured directly by observation wells, in the unsaturated and saturated zones of aquifers to detect the influence of land uses and activities at the surface. Such monitoring systems require a dense network of wells, because of the local nature of the pollution, but do not need frequent measurements in time, since the processes are usually quite slow.

Models of urban hydrology should be modified to incorporate knowledge generated by field studies. Most existing models have concentrated on surface runoff, and even those which compute infiltration directly (for example SWMM) do not deal fully with the effect of the spatial distribution of pervious and impervious sub-areas and the effect of the temporal and spatial variability of rainfall on infiltration.

5 CONCLUDING REMARKS

In this paper, we have concentrated on one main aspect of WSUP, namely its effect on groundwater, in particular the quantity of infiltration. Other important aspects include: groundwater quality, effects on other water resources, water consumption in the area, effects on the drainage system and impacts on the downstream environment.

We believe it is feasible to reduce substantially the negative effects of urban development on the quantity and quality of groundwater in underlying aquifers, and maybe even bring about an improvement relative to conditions prior to urban construction. This leads to a new paradigm: urban runoff is a resource, not a nuisance.

Groundwater recharge is one aspect of WSUP. We believe that in its broadest sense WSUP has the potential to be viable technically, economically and socially, and contribute to sustainable development. We have examined some of the other aspects, are continuing the study, and seek to cooperate with researchers and practitioners who see the benefit in promoting Water-Sensitive Urban Planning.

ACKNOWLEDGEMENT

The work was carried out under contract to the Water Commission and the Ministry for Environmental Protection, and supported in part by the Fund for the Promotion of Research at the Technion. We are grateful to many who have worked on the project or helped in advice and data: Sigalit Meiron-Pistiner, Lea Kroneveter, Avner Kessler, Aryeh Ben-Zvi, Rami Gerti, Moshe Getker, Shmuel Arbel, Israel Gev.

REFERENCES

Atwood, D.F & C. Barder 1989. The effect of Perth's urbanization on groundwater quality - a comparison with case histories in the USA, in: G. Lowe (Ed.) *Proceedings of the Swan Costal Plain Groundwater Management Conference.*

Barringer, T., D. Dunn, W. Battaglin & E. Vowinkel 1990. Problems and methods involved in relating land use to groundwater quality, *Water Res. Bull.,* American Water Resources Association, 26(1):1-9.

Berry, B.J.L. & F.E. Horton 1974 *Urban Environmental Management: Planning for Pollution Control.* New Jersey: Prentice Hall.

Carmon, N. & T. Trop 1993. *Population, Education, and Labor Force in Israel - Trends and Forecasts, 1990-2020,* Report # 15 of the Second Stage of "Israel 2020 - A Master Plan for Israel in the 2000s". Haifa: Technion - Israel Institute of Technology.

Carmon, N. & U. Shamir 1997a Water-sensitive urban planning: protecting groundwater, *J. of Env. Planning and Management,* 40(4).

Carmon, N. & U. Shamir 1997b. *Water Sensitive Urban Planning,* Haifa: Technion - Israel Institute of Technology (in Hebrew).

Christensen, S. & A. Rea 1993. Ground water quality in the Oklahoma City urban area, in: W.M. Alley (Ed.) *Regional Ground-Water Quality.* New York: Van Norstrand Reinhold.

Ferguson, B.K. 1994. *Stormwater Infiltration.* Boca Raton: CRC Press, Lewis Publishers.

Ferguson, B.K. 1996. Estimation of direct runoff in the Thornthwaite water balance, *Professional Geographer* 48(3):263-271.

Fujita, S. 1992. Infiltration facilities in Tokyo: their purpose and practice. In *Urban Stormwater Infiltration.* Klintholm Havn, Denmark, 5th European Junior Scientist Workshop, 1-4 October 1992.

Gerti, R., S. Arbel & M. Getker 1993. Urbanization increases peak flows and runoff volumes: truth or myth? Special report #M-43. Israel Ministry of Agriculture, Erosion Research Station (in Hebrew).

Harbor, J.M. 1994. A practical method for estimating the impact of land-use change on surface runoff, groundwater recharge and wetland hydrology, *J. American Planning Association,* 60(1):95-107.

Herath, S., K. Musiake & S. Hironaka 1993. Evaluation of basin scale effects of infiltration systems. In H. Torno & J. Marsalek (Eds.) *Proc. 6th Conference on Urban Storm Drainage* American Society of Civil Engineers, September 12-17, 1993.

Huber, W.C. 1995. Storm water management model (SWMM). In V.P. Singh (Ed.) *Computer Models of Watershed Hydrology,* Colorado: Water Resources Publications.

Huber, W.C. & R.E. Dickinson 1988. *Storm Water Management Model: User's Manual.* Athens, Ga: Environmental Protection Agency.

Ishizaki, K., M. Seiji, A. Kagawa, T. Mochizuki & M. Imbe (undated) Rainwater infiltration technology for urban areas. Paper received from the authors.

Kappen, P.M. 1993. *Planning for Water Source Protection*. Chicago IL: American Planning Association, Council for Planning Libraries, CPL Bibliography 299.

Kennedy Engineers 1992. *Handbook of Best Management Practices for Stormwater Management and Erosion and Sedimentation Control*. Spokane, Washington.

Konrad, C.P., B.W. Jensen, S.J. Burges & L.E. Reinelt 1995. *On-site Residential Stormwater Management Alternatives*. Seattle, WA: University of Washington, Dept. of Civil Eng.

Maidment, D.R. (Ed.) 1993. *Handbook of Hydrology*. USA: McGraw-Hill.

Mazor, A. & T. Trop (Eds.) 1994. *Spatial Alternatives for Israel in the 2000's*, Report #21 of the Second Stage of "Israel 2020 - A Master Plan for Israel in the 2000's". Haifa: Technion - Israel Institute of Technology.

Meiron-Pistiner, S. 1995. *Water Sensitive Urban Planning: Towards Planning Guidelines*, Msc Thesis, Urban and Regional Planning, Technion - Israel Institute of Technology (Hebrew, with English Abstract).

Pitt, R., S. Clark & K. Parmer 1994. Potential groundwater contamination from intentional and nonintentional stormwater infiltration. Report EPA/600/R-94/051, U.S. Environmental Protection Agency.

Ronen, D., Y. Kanfy & M. Magaritz 1986. Nitrogen presence in ground water as affected by the unsaturated zone. In B. Yaron, G. Dagan & Y. Goldshmid (Eds.) *Pollutants in Porous Media*. New York: Springer Verlag.

Schueler, T.R., P.A. Kumble & M.A. Heraty 1992. *A Current Measurement of Urban Best Management Practices: Techniques for Reducing Non-Point Source Pollution in the Coastal Zone*. Metropolitan Washington Council of Governments.

Sheaffer, J.R., K.R. Wright, W.C. Taggart & R.M. Wright 1982. *Urban Storm Drainage Management*. New York: Marcel Dekker.

Singh, V. P. (Ed.) 1995. *Computer Models of Watershed Hydrology*. New York: Water Resources Publications.

Soil Conservation Service (SCS) 1975. *Urban Hydrology for Small Watersheds*. Technical Release No. 55, Engineering Division, Soil Conservation Service, U.S. Department of Agriculture)

Van de Ven, F. 1985. From rainfall to sewer flow: a process with consequences, in: *Water in Urban Areas*, The Hague: Proceedings of Technical Meeting No. 42, TNO Committee on Hydrological Research.

WAWA 1987. *Perth Urban Water Balance Study: Executive Summary*. Perth, Australia: Western Australia Water Authority.

Water Sensitive Urban Design Research Group 1989. *Water Sensitive Residential Design: An Investigation into its Purpose and Potential in the Perth Metropolitan Region*. Leederville, Western Australia: The Western Australia Water Resources Council.

© *1997 Balkema, Rotterdam, ISBN 90 5410 837 1*

The effects of urbanisation on groundwater recharge in the Ruhr region of Germany

Wilhelm Georg Coldewey & Johannes Messer
DMT-Gesellschaft für Forschung und Prüfung mbH, Essen, Germany

ABSTRACT: The influence of urban climate and soil sealing were investigated in order to make an initial assessment of the effects of urbanisation on groundwater recharge in the Ruhr region. The water budget parameters of evapotranspiration, direct runoff and groundwater recharge were calculated as a function of soil sealing in order to expand on this assessment. The calculations were carried out for catchment areas in the central Ruhr region and were followed by an evaluation of the effect of urbanisation. These kinds of calculations are of particular importance in the restoration of running waters. Water budget calculations permitted an estimate to be made of the low-water discharge in a running water after separation of the waste-water component.

1 INTRODUCTION

With a population of 5.4 million and an area of 4,400 km^2, the Ruhr region is one of the largest conurbations in Europe. Hydrological conditions, particularly the drainage capability, have been subjected to massive disturbances as the result of subsidences caused by coal mining which can amount to more than 20 m. The impaired drainage capability led to increasing marshiness and subsequently the outbreak of typhus and cholera epidemics. For this reason, a decision was made to regulate the central river of the Ruhr region - the Emscher - and to use it and its tributaries as open interceptors. All waste water is treated in a water treatment plant at the mouth of the Emscher and discharged into the Rhine. Today, now that the mining subsidences have abated, the ecological reshaping of these waterways is the most important component in the ecological and economic renewal of the region. The ecological reshaping of the Emscher encompasses:
- the separation of pure water and waste water,
- the decentralisation of waste water treatment,
- the removal of trapezoidal waste water receiving channels, and

- the creation of ecologically reshaped streams.

The groundwater recharge is of particular importance to the last item. Water budget totals must be drawn up for the catchment area of the body of water to be reshaped in order to calculate the low water runoff after separation of the waste water.

Water management intervention and above all soil sealing alter the components of the hydrologic cycle. Urbanisation leads to:
- the channeling in of additional water to satisfy the demand,
- a decrease in the evapotranspiration over the entire surface area, and
- an increase in the total runoff.

The direct runoff into the receiving channels increases due to the drainage of precipitation which accumulates on sealed surfaces, while at the same time the dry water flow decreases (Udluft et al. 1983; Wessolek 1988). The path of the water no longer runs from the recharged groundwater to the receiving channel, but rather is shortened by the direct conveyance of the precipitation to the bodies of water. The low retention capacity of sealed surfaces and the increased flow rates lead to higher flood peaks.

Table 1. Change in the potential (Et_{pot}) and actual (Et_{act}) evapotranspiration for different climate types as compared to the open land evapotranspiration according to Heger (1978) and Schendel (1968).

Climate type	Soil sealing	HEGER		SCHENDEL	
		Et_{pot}	Et_{act}	Et_{pot}	Et_{act}
Inner city climate	80 - 100%	36%	27%	16%	12%
Town climate	50 - 80%	8%	6%	6%	4%
Settlement climate	20 - 50%	-1%	-2%	1%	0%

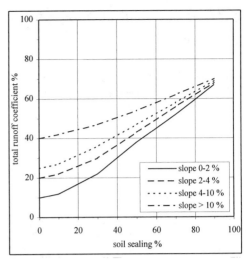

Figure 1. Total runoff coefficients as a function of soil sealing at various slope graduations for loamy soils (Messer 1996).

2 THE INFLUENCE OF URBANISATION ON THE WATER BUDGET

2.1 Urban climate

A "synthetic climate function map" with a gradual breakdown of the urban heat islands is available for the Ruhr region (Stock 1992). According to this map, a distinction is made not only between open land, forest and open water climates, but also between park, settlement, town and inner city climate types. Climate data from the City of Dortmund's climate analysis (Stock et al. 1986) were used to assess the influence of the urban climate on evapotranspiration. As compared to that of the open land climate, the average potential evapotranspiration is 26% higher in the inner city climate, and 7% higher in the town climate (Table 1). The potential evapotranspiration in the settlement climate corresponds to that of the open land climate. The increase in the actual evapotranspiration is somewhat less.

In order to study the effects of urbanisation on precipitation more closely, the 100-year precipitation development was evaluated at two weather stations in the central Ruhr region. No distinct trend towards an increase in precipitation - as is cited in the literature for other regions - could be determined based on the available data.

2.2 The influence of soil sealing on direct runoff

Soil sealing is the isolation of the pedosphere and the bedrock from the atmosphere, hydrosphere and biosphere due to packing (Berlekamp & Pranzas 1990). The degree of the isolating effect is influenced by various building materials. The transition from sealed to partially sealed to open soil is fluid and therefore a distinction must be made when considering the resulting consequences. For example, the percentage of seepage from precipitation on surfaces covered with concrete paving stones and lattice stones can be greater than on lawns (Siegert 1984).

A detailed mapping survey of the soil sealing was conducted in the central Ruhr region on 14 plots representing different types of building development (Messer 1996). The total area amounted to 571,000 m^2. A distinction was made between 16 types of soil sealing. Consideration was also given to whether the plots were connected to the sewerage system or drain off to open surfaces. The individual map units were assigned to 5 soil sealing classes, each representing an interval of 20%.

Using data from the literature, corresponding runoff and seepage ranges can be stated for the major soil sealing types under level conditions and the total runoff coefficient thus calculated. The dependence of the total runoff coefficient on the degree of soil sealing was calculated at various slopes (Figure 1).

3 THE EFFECTS OF URBANISATION ON THE WATER BUDGET PARAMETERS

The calculated increase in potential and actual

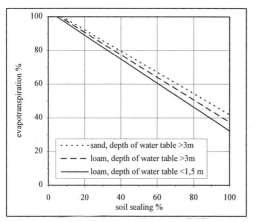

Figure 2. Evapotranspiration as a function of soil sealing for various soils and water table depths (Messer 1996).

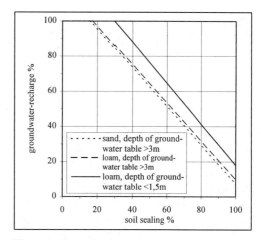

Figure 3. Groundwater recharge as a function of soil sealing for various soils and water table depths (Messer 1996).

evapotranspiration and the results of the soil sealing mapping enable the influence of urbanisation on the water budget to be quantified. The water budget parameters were determined for the 14 sample plots used in the soil sealing mapping.

The evapotranspiration calculations show a direct dependence between the degree of soil sealing and the decrease in evapotranspiration (Figure 2). An increase in soil sealing of 10% corresponds to a decrease in evapotranspiration of 6 to 7% and, at 100% sealing, the evapotranspiration is 32 to 42% that of the open land.

The increase in evapotranspiration on the remaining unsealed surfaces due to the effects of the urban climate first becomes evident at sealing degrees of over 50%. However, the significance of open surfaces to the total evapotranspiration decreases markedly above a sealing degree of 50%, so that the increase due to the urban climate is relatively small at 2 to 4%. The influence of the urban climate is more significant on open surfaces in inner city areas, such as wastelands and parks.

Soil sealing has no effect on direct runoff until it reaches portions upwards of 10%. A 10% increase in soil sealing causes a 7 to 9% increase in the direct runoff component of the overall precipitation. At 100% soil sealing, the direct runoff component amounts to a maximum of 75%, while the remaining 25% seeps through partially permeable coverings or evapotranspirates.

The evapotranspiration decreases continuously with increasing soil sealing, while the direct runoff increases. Due to the fact that the direct runoff increases more drastically than the evapotranspiration decreases, the groundwater recharge drops with increasing soil sealing.

The effects of soil sealing on the groundwater recharge first become evident on surfaces sealed by more than 15% (sandy soils, Figure 3). The decrease in groundwater recharge amounts to 11 to 12% at an increase in soil sealing of 10%. The groundwater recharge is still 7.7% of its initial value at 100% soil sealing and is exclusively attributable to the seepage through partially permeable surface coverings.

In addition to the influences described above, consideration must also be given to direct water management intervention measures, which cannot be quantified in general terms, but rather determined only in individual cases. These include the abstraction of drinking and industrial process water, groundwater withdrawal for building projects and decreases in the groundwater level due to the deepening and regulation of receiving channels. All of these measures result in an increase in the depth to the water table. For the vegetation this means a drop in the evapotranspiration capacity (Renger et al. 1986). The overall effect of these changes is an increase in the groundwater recharge.

Different types of pipes also influence the groundwater recharge. Leakage from water supply pipes and drainage pipes can have a positive effect on the groundwater recharge. It is also possible for pipes to carry out a drainage function. This also applies, for example, to the sand beds associated with different kinds of pipe laid in slightly permeable soils. This can increase the direct runoff and thus reduce the groundwater recharge.

4 CASTROP PLATEAU STUDY SITE

The findings on urban hydrology described here were integrated in a procedure for calculating the groundwater recharge differentiated according to area. This procedure was applied to the Castrop Plateau in the central Ruhr region and compared to runoff measurements (Messer 1996). The geological/hydrogeological conditions are virtually optimal for drawing up a water budget balance. The Emschermergel semi-aquiclude underlies the aquifer formed by the main terrace sediment, so that the groundwaters emerge in springs and feed streams in all directions (Coldewey 1991). The partial catchment areas surveyed make up a total area of 26.5 km^2 and are between 0.2 km^2 and 5.8 km^2 in size. The degree of building development varies widely up to 71% (an average of 38.4%). The degree of soil sealing reaches a maximum of 42%.

If the calculation results for the individual partial catchment areas are plotted as a function of the soil sealing, it becomes evident - as would be expected - that increasing soil sealing corresponds to a decrease in evapotranspiration and an increase in direct runoff (Figure 4). A 10% increase in soil sealing in the

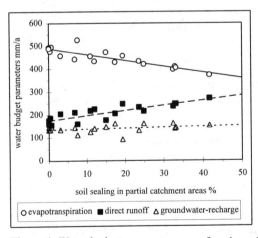

Figure 4. Water budget parameters as a function of soil sealing in the region of the Castrop Plateau (Messer 1996).

partial catchment areas of the Castrop Plateau leads to an average decrease in evapotranspiration of 27 mm/year or 5.3% and an increase in direct runoff of 22 mm/year or 12.6% (soil sealing up to 42%).

While the water budget parameters evapotranspiration and direct runoff show opposite reactions, the groundwater recharge shows no distinct dependence until the soil sealing reaches a maximum of 42%. This is due to the high amount of runoff which is over 50%, even on undeveloped surfaces. The high runoff, in turn, is caused by the high inclinations and the wide occurrence of loamy soils used for crop fields and grasslands. Accordingly, only those surfaces with a degree of sealing over 60% have a marked effect on the water budget. However, these surfaces generally make up only small fractions of the partial catchment areas.

5 EMSCHER RIVER SYSTEM CASE STUDY

The question now arises as to where these procedures for calculating water budget parameters can be applied in urban regions. As mentioned previously, receiving channels polluted with waste water are currently being ecologically reshaped. After the waste water is removed, only the groundwater outflow remains in the receiving channel. Due to the fact that the catchment areas of the streams have largely been sealed over the last 100 years, it was questionable whether the groundwater outflow could provide permanent runoff.

Using water budget calculations, the groundwater recharge was determined for 707 km^2 of the Emscher river system divided into 66 partial catchment areas and the results were used to estimate the low water discharge (Coldewey & Messer 1991).

Figure 5 shows a section of this study. The calculations resulted in an average groundwater recharge of 154 mm/year and an average low water specific discharge of 1.4 l/s·km^2. Due to the insufficient low water specific discharge, ecological reshaping is not advisable for 38% of the partial catchment areas and questionable for 36%. Ecological reshaping with sufficient natural low water specific discharge is possible for only 26% of the partial catchment areas. However, the influence of contaminated deposits which have an effect on the possibilities for ecological reshaping must also be examined.

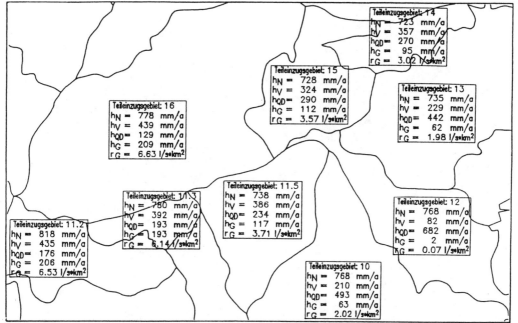

Figure 5. Water balance in partial catchment areas (Teileinzugsgebiet) of the Emscher river system (h_N = precipitation, h_V=evapotranspiration, h_{QD} direct runoff, h_G, r_G=groundwater outflow).

6 REFERENCES

Berlekamp, L.-R. & N. Pranzas 1990. Erhebung von Bodenversiegelungen in Ballungsräumen. - In: Rosenkranz, D.; Einsele, G. & Harres, H.-M.: Bodenschutz - Ergänzbares Handbuch der Maßnahmen und Empfehlungen für Schutz, Pflege und Sanierung von Böden, Landschaft und Grundwasser, Kennz. 3355, p. 1-24; Berlin.

Coldewey, W.G. & J. Meßer 1991. Gutachten über die geologischen und hydrologischen Verhältnisse im Emschergebiet im Hinblick auf die ökologische Umgestaltung; Bochum.

Coldewey, W.G. 1991. Hydrogeologie des Ruhrgebietes - Bedeutung für Wasserwirtschaft und Hydrographie. - In: Schumacher, H. & Thiesmeier, B.: Urbane Gewässer, p. 413-426; Essen.

Heger, K. 1978. Bestimmung der potentiellen Evapotranspiration über unterschiedlichen landwirtschaftlichen Kulturen. - Mitt. Dtsch. Bodenkundl. Ges., 26: p. 21-40; Göttingen.

Meßer, J. 1996. Auswirkungen der Urbanisierung auf die Grundwasser-Neubildung im Ruhrgebiet unter besoderer Berücksichtigung der Castroper Hochfläche und des Stadtgebietes Herne. - Dissertation TU Clausthal.

Renger, M.; O. Strebel; G. Wessolek & W.H.M. Duynisveld 1986. Evapotranspiration and Groundwater Recharge - A case study for different climate, crop patterns, soil properties and groundwater depth conditions. - Z. Pflanzenernaehr. Bodenk., 149: 371-381; Weinheim.

Schendel, U. 1968. Messungen mit Grundwasserlysimetern über den Wasserverbrauch aus oberflächennahem Grundwasser. - Z. f. Kulturtechn. u. Flurberein., 9: 314-326; Berlin.

Siegert, G. 1984. Entwicklung eines Verfahrens zur Messung und Berechnung der Versickerung von Regenwasser durch teildurchlässige Flächen bei Verwendung einer „Feuchte-Tiefensonde" (Neutronensonde). - Dissertation TU Berlin FB 21; Berlin.

Stock, P. 1992. Synthetische Klimafunktionskarte Ruhrgebiet. - Kommunalverband Ruhrgebiet, Essen.

Stock, P.; W. Bekröge; O. Kiese; W. Kuttler & H. Lüftner 1986. Klimaanalyse Stadt Dortmund - Planungshefte Ruhrgebiet, P 018, Kommunalverband Ruhrgebiet, Essen.

Udluft, P.; B. Merkel & G. Nemeth 1983. Einfluß urbaner Besiedlung auf Quantität und Qualität der Grundwasserneubildung im Bereich quartärer Karbonatschotter. - Z. dt. geol. Ges., 134: 621-639; Hannover.

Wessolek, G. 1988. Auswirkungen der Bodenversiegelung auf Boden und Wasser. - Informationen zur Raumentwicklung, Bundesforschungsanstalt für Landeskunde und Raumordnung, 8/9, p. 535-541; Bonn.

© *1997 Balkema, Rotterdam, ISBN 90 5410 837 1*

Transport of reactive solutes in a heterogeneous aquifer: Simulations with a stochastic approach

U. Döring
Martin Luther University, Halle, Germany

O. Neuendorf
Comma-Soft GmbH, Bonn, Germany

R. Seidemann
Rheinische Friedrich-Wilhelms University, Bonn, Germany

U. Jaekel & H. Vereecken
Research Center Jülich, Germany

ABSTRACT: In an integrated approach of field experiments, laboratory experiments and numerical simulations, the transport of uranin and lithium was investigated at a test site near Krauthausen (Germany). Physical and chemical aquifer heterogeneities were determined by insitu and laboratory measurements. The spatial variability of chemical parameters such as sorption capacity and specific surface was of the same order of magnitude as the spatial variability of the hydraulic conductivity. The influence of aquifer heterogeneities (sorption parameters and hydraulic conductivity) on solute transport was investigated with numerical simulations. Stochastic transport modelling showed that the variability of sorption parameters increased the uncertainty in predicting the plume arrival time while the shape of the plume was hardly affected. Laboratory and field observations suggest that chemical reaction processes like an incomplete sorption reversibility and sorption kinetics have a significant influence on the transport behaviour of the solutes.

1 INTRODUCTION

The transport of reactive contaminants in natural aquifers has been a field of intensive research during the last decade. The investigations focused on chemical reaction processes on one hand and on the influence of heterogeneity which is a characteristic of all natural soils and aquifers on the other hand. The effect of spatially variable hydraulic conductivity has been intensively studied theoretically (e.g. Dagan 1989) and by field experiments (Gelhar et al. 1992). Less research was done with respect to chemical heterogeneity of soils and aquifer sediments. Mainly, theoretical investigations were performed for different kinds of chemical reaction processes. For linearly sorbing solutes, analytical results were published e.g. by Destouni & Cvetkovic (1991) or Bellin et al. (1993). For nonlinear adsorption, Bosma et al. (1994) investigated the influence of spatially variable sorption capacity combined with spatial variability of the hydraulic conductivity. Since only few measurements are available to characterize chemical heterogeneity at the field or regional scale, most of these theoretical investigations are based on hypothetical parameter distributions.

In field tracer tests reactive solutes showed a transport behaviour which could hardly be predicted. Brusseau (1994) attributed these difficulties to physical and chemical sediment heterogeneities as well as to chemical reaction processes which are still not understood and quantified thoroughly enough. He

concluded that all of these different processes have to be considered to arrive at better predictions of solute (contaminant) transport.

In this work we present a research project which integrates field scale and laboratory experiments with numerical modelling to identify relevant transport mechanisms for reactive solutes. During the first project period which is described in this paper, the investigations focused on the effect of physical and chemical heterogeneities.

2 FIELD SITE

In order to follow the spatial and temporal distribution of tracer substances, as well as to obtain sediment material for the characterization of aquifer heterogeneities, 62 wells were installed at the test site each with one or more specific functions (Figure 1). The wells were set up in three clusters (25 m, 50 m and 100 m from injection) and along the main flow path to obtain a relatively detailed picture of the 3D solute plumes.

The unconfined aquifer is formed by about 11 m of Quaternary sands and gravels which were deposited in several fluvial terraces. The aquifer base is built by clay and silt belonging to the late Pliocene.

Sediment samples were taken in cores during the installation of the site. In situ measurements were performed to characterize the spatial distribution of

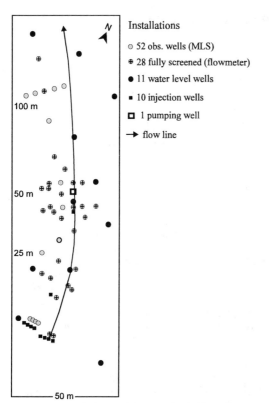

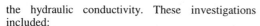

Figure 1. Installations of the test site in Krauthausen, W. Germany (50 km from Cologne).

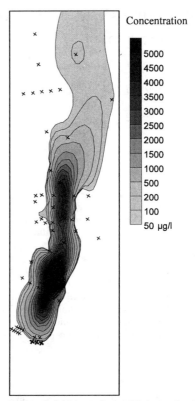

Figure 2. Lithium plume 85 days after injection. The concentration is averaged over the aquifer depth.

the hydraulic conductivity. These investigations included:

- a large scale pumping test,
- insitu borehole flowmeter measurements,
- insitu velocity measurements by ^{82}Br-dillution (Drost & Hoehn 1989).

The observation wells are equipped with multi-level samplers (MLS) which are 0.3 m apart so that a high resolution could be obtained in the vertical direction. In the horizontal direction observation wells are not closer than 5 m, except for the injection wells which are set up 2 m apart.

2.1 Natural gradient tracer experiments

For the main tracer test uranin ($C_{20}H_{10}O_5Na_2$) and lithium (Li^+) were used as a weakly sorbing anion and cation respectively. 2 kg of uranin and 120 kg of LiCl were dissolved in 4.5 m^3 groundwater and injected into 3 wells over a period of 5 hours. A tracer test with bromide as a conservative substance followed

one year later. The tracer solutions were injected over a depth between 7-8 m below surface. The main tracer test was observed for 450 days. During this period about 12,000 water samples were taken and analyzed. Sampling concentrated on snapshots of the spatial evolution of the plumes (Figure 2).

A spatial moment analysis was performed for all tracers to get more detailed information of the plume evolution (Vereecken 1996). Further break through curves were recorded at several wells with high time resolution and analyzed in order to identify chemical reaction processes and field scale sorption (Jaekel et al. 1996).

3 AQUIFER HETEROGENEITY

The characterization of aquifer heterogeneities included physical and chemical sediment parameters. Most parameters were determined on sediment samples, for the determination of hydraulic conductivity also insitu measurements were performed (see above). About 400 sediment samples of 0.1-0.2 m length were taken (liners, dry drilling) and statistically evaluated. 250 of these samples were taken from three boreholes in the vertical direction, 150 samples were taken from 50 drillings at a depth between 6-8 m in the horizontal direction.

3.1 Physical sediment parameters

For physical parameter characterization, the porosity and grain size distribution of the sediment samples were measured. From the latter, parameters like representative grain sizes and hydraulic conductivity were calculated. Here several empirical equations were used and compared to results of the insitu measurements (Döring 1997). Figure 3 shows a vertical profile of the hydraulic conductivity (K) calculated with the equation by Seiler (1973).

The profile shows a clear difference between the Rur and the Rhine terraces. For the statistical and geostatistical analysis both layers were evaluated separately. The heterogeneity was larger in the horizontal than in the vertical direction. The log-transformed variance of the Seiler K (Var ln K) was 0.57 in the horizontal and 0.81 in the vertical direction for the Rhine gravel. The Rur gravel had a significantly higher variance with values larger than 3 vertically.

A comparison of the different methods used to determine the hydraulic conductivity is listed in Table 1. The highest value was determined with the pumping test while the other methods resulted in comparable mean values of 2×10^{-3} m/s for the horizontal samples. Of the grain size methods the Seiler equation showed the best agreement with the in situ measurements.

Table 1. Hydraulic conductivity [m/s] determined at the test site (Rhine gravel).

Method	Mean	Var ln K	Factor 1σ	λv [m]
Pumptest	3.8 E-3	---	---	---
Velocity*	2.1 E-3	---	---	---
Flowmeter*	2.1 E-3	0.88	6	0.3
K (Seiler) *	2.0 E-3	0.81	5	0.6

*vertical direction

The number of samples/measurements was 70, 500 and 150 (velocity, flowmeter, K Seiler) respectively. The variance of the ln K values indicates a relatively low heterogeneity within the Rhine gravel. The lower and upper limits of one standard deviation differ by a factor of 5-6. The vertical correlation length (λv) was several decimeters (exponential model), the determination of the horizontal correlation length is still under way.

3.2 Chemical sediment parameters

For chemical parameter characterization, the organic carbon content (Corg), cation exchange capacity (CEC) and the specific surface area (sp. surf.) were measured on 400 sediment samples.

All parameters were determined at the sediment fraction <2 mm and then recalculated for the whole sediment by assuming that the larger fractions do not contribute any significant amount. Since up to 50 % of the sediment was larger than 2 mm, this method is probably a simplification which may underestimate the chemical capacity of the complete sediment. Together with these parameters the clay

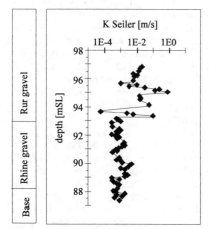

Figure 3. Vertical profile of the hydraulic conductivity.

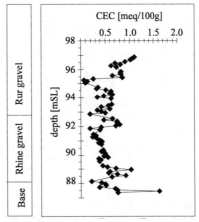

Figure 4. Vertical profile of the cation exchange capacity.

123

Table 2. Chemical sediment parameters (Rhine gravel) determined at the test site.

Parameter	Dimens.	Mean	Factor 1σ	λv [m]
CEC*	meq/100g	0.3	3	0.4
Sp. surf.*	m^2/g	0.7	2	---
Clay*	%	1.1	2	0.6
Fines*	%	3.6	2	---

* vertical direction

Table 3. Variation of uranin sorption capacity (Cs).

Parameter	Dimens.	Mean	Factor 1σ	λv [m]
Cs*	µg/kg sed.	30	2	---

* calculated for Cw=100 µg/l, vertical direction

content and the fraction of fines (<0.1 mm) were statistically analyzed.

The chemical parameters did not show the distinct difference between the terraces (Figure 4) as the physical parameters. This can be attributed to a low content of the fraction <2 mm, but at the same time a higher clay content of the Rur gravel which leads to a loss of layer differences. For the statistical analysis the differentiation between the terraces was kept for a better comparability of all data. The results for the chemical parameters are listed in Table 2. The Corg content could not be evaluated because the measured variance only resembled the analytical error.

3.3 Sorption parameters

The sorption behaviour of uranin and lithium was measured on 75 sediment samples (2 boreholes). Both substances showed a nonlinear sorption which was fitted by a Freundlich isotherm (equation 1). The sorption parameters (n and k) were determined with batch experiments, where again only the sediment

fraction <2 mm was measured. The determined sorption parameters were recalculated for the entire sediment as described in section 3.2.

$$Cs = k \cdot Cw^n \qquad (1)$$

where Cw and Cs are the concentration in solution and on the solid surface, n and k are sorption parameters.

Figure 5 shows a vertical profile of the uranin n- and k-values as well as of the resulting sorption capacity of the aquifer sediment. The sorption capacity exhibits a distinct depth variation which is larger than the analytical error of about 12 %. When the sorption capacity is compared to the CEC profile in Figure 4, both parameters show a similar trend. The correlation coefficient between the chemical parameters and the sorption capacity ranged between 0.6 and 0.8.

In the statistical analysis only 35 samples could be evaluated for the Rhine gravel. Therefore no attempt was made to determine correlation lengths. Table 3 lists the variation (Factor 1σ) of the uranin sorption capacity which corresponds perfectly to the variation of the chemical parameters in Table 2.

3.4 Comparison of sediment heterogeneities

A comparison of Tables 1, 2 and 3 shows that the variation of chemical and sorption parameters is smaller (about 1/3) than the variation of the hydraulic conductivity, but in the same order of magnitude. Further a weak negative correlation was observed between the hydraulic conductivity and the sorption capacity as well as the chemical parameters. For example the correlation coefficient between the uranin sorption capacity and the hydraulic conductivity calculated after Seiler was -0.5. The correlation coefficients between the hydraulic conductivity and the other chemical parameters ranged from -0.2 to -0.5 within the Rhine gravel. In general the more permcable sediments seem to have a lower chemical reaction capacity.

The negative correlation between sorption capacity and hydraulic conductivity should result in an enhanced spreading of the uranin plume in comparison to a conservative substance (e.g. Destouni & Cvetkovic 1991).

The (vertical) geological structure as measured

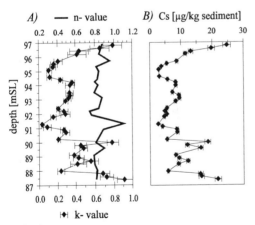

Figure 5. Vertical profile of uranin sorption. A: Freundlich n- and k- parameters. B: The resulting sorption capacity of the sediment (Cs) calculated for a solute concentration (Cw) of 100 µg/l.

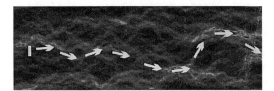

Figure 6. Stochastic flow field with flow direction. Black = low, white = high velocity components.

by the vertical correlation length seems to be identical for physical and chemical parameters.

4 NUMERICAL SIMULATIONS

After the determination of physical and chemical aquifer heterogeneities, numerical modelling was used as a tool to investigate the effect of these heterogeneities on solute transport. The consideration of heterogeneity requires stochastic flow- and transport models which have a high computational demand. Therefore during the research project a flow- and a transport model were developed which run on massively parallel computers such as the Intel Paragon or Cray T3D (Neuendorf et al. 1995).

4.1 Stochastic flow field

Based on the spatial structure of the hydraulic conductivity determined after Seiler (1973), a 2D stochastic flow field was computed (Figure 6). The (log transformed) K-field was created with a mean value of 2×10^{-3} m/s, a variance of ln K of 0.81 and a horizontal correlation length of 5 m. The resulting flow field had a mean flow velocity of 1.7 m/d with a velocity range between 0.2 and 9.1 m/d.

4.2 Effect of spatially variable sorption parameters

In one example the influence of spatially variable sorption parameters was investigated with by numerical simulations. On the basis of the heterogeneous flow field of Figure 6 two realizations (A, B) of heterogeneous n- and k-fields were created to calculate the uranin transport. The statistical data for both realizations were as followes:
  k: 0.55 mean and 0.027 variance
  n: 0.81 mean and 0.001 variance
Both parameters were log transformed, the horizontal correlation length was assumed to be 5 m without any correlation with the hydraulic conductivity.

The resulting solute transport was calculated with the transport model PARTRACE (Neuendorf 1997), which is a particle tracking code. The field was

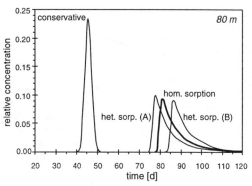

Figure 7. Break through curves of one element 80 m distant from injection for homogeneous (hom.) and heterogeneous (het. A, B) sorption parameters.

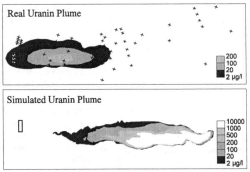

Figure 8. Real and simulated uranin plume 80 days after injection.

discretized in 0.5x0.5x0.2 m elements for a field of a 150x50x0.2 m extension. 2 million particles were used for the simulations. The starting concentration was 230 mg/l uranin in a volume of 2x6x0.2 m³.

The simulations clearly show the difference between the transport of a conservative and a nonlinear sorptive solute. The sorptive solute (here uranin) is retarded and exhibits the typical tailing (Figure 7). In the simulations with heterogeneous sorption parameters (n and k spatially variable) the shape of the plumes hardly differs but the arrival times vary. This first qualitative result agrees with the findings of Bosma et al. (1994) who concluded (with a hypothetical data set) that a combined variation of hydraulic conductivity and sorption parameters increases the uncertainty of the plume position, while the tail dominates the plume dimension. More realizations have to be performed to quantify the influence of the measured sorption heterogeneity on the tracer transport.

4.3 *Reality versus simulation*

The next step of the investigation was a comparison between simulated prediction and reality. First results are shown in Figure 8. The real uranin plume is slower and has significantly lower concentrations than the simulated one. These differences increased with increasing travel time. The discrepancies of the transport velocities may partly be attributed to a remaining uncertainty about the water flow velocity, because even the 'conservative' bromide had lower flow velocities than should expected from the value of the hydraulic conductivity.

The large discrepancy in solute concentration can neither be attributed to heterogeneity of the hydraulic conductivity nor of sorption parameters. The described simulations showed that the shape (concentration) of the plume is hardly affected by sorption heterogeneity. Even if a negative correlation between hydraulic conductivity and sorption capacity is considered, this will probably not explain the observed mass loss.

After the present results of the tracer tests and the numerical simulations it seems that aquifer heterogeneity cannot be the exclusive cause for the discrepancy between the simulated prediction and the real solute transport.

First results of the field break through curves and laboratory column experiments indicate that chemical reaction processes like a slow desorption rate and an incomplete sorption reversibility are important transport processes. Also the temporal variation of the flow field and local downward flow may have a significant influence on the tracer movement. These processes are the focus of further research activities.

5 CONCLUSIONS

The present results of the field, laboratory and numerical investigations indicate that aquifer heterogeneity cannot be the only cause of the difficulty in predicting solute transport. Chemical reaction processes need to be quantified accurately as well, in order to determine the relevant processes of solute transport. Investigations and numerical modelling should consider these different transport mechanisms.

REFERENCES

Bellin, A., A. Rinaldo, W.J.P. Bosma, S.E.A.T.M. Van der Zee & J. Rubin 1993. Linear equilibrium adsorbing solute transport in physically and chemically heterogeneous porous formations - 1. Analytical solution. *Water Resources Res.*, 29: 4019-4030.

Bosma, W.J.P., S.E.A.T.M. Van der Zee, A. Bellin & A. Rinaldo 1994. Instantaneous injection of a nonlinearly adsorbing solute in a heterogeneous aquifer. In Dracos, Th. & Stauffer, F. (eds.): *Transport and Reactive Processes in Aquifers, IAHR/AIRH Symposium.* Rotterdam: Balkema.

Brusseau, M.L. 1994. Transport of reactive contaminants in porous media: Review of field experiments. In Dracos, Th. & Stauffer, F. (eds.): *Transport and Reactive Processes in Aquifers, IAHR/AIRH Symposium.* Rotterdam: Balkema.

Dagan G. 1989. *Flow and Transport in Porous Formations.* Berlin: Springer.

Destouni, G. & V. Cvetkovic 1991. Field scale mass arrival of sorptive solute into the ground water. *Water Resources Res.*, 27: 1315-1325.

Döring, U. 1997. *Transport der reaktiven Stoffe Eosin, Uranin und Lithium in einem heterogenen Grundwasserleiter.* PhD Thesis, Berichte des Forschungszentrums Jülich.

Drost, W. & E. Hoehn 1989. Macrodispersivity in granular aquifers determined with single-well techniques using ^{82}Br as a tracer. *Radiochimica Acta*, 47: 13-20.

Gelhar, L.W., C. Welty & K.R. Rehfeld 1992. A critical review of data on field-scale dispersion in aquifers. *Water Resources Res.*, 28: 1955-1974.

Jaekel, U., A. Georgescu & H. Vereecken 1996. Asymptotic analysis of nonlinear equilibrium solute transport in porous media. *Water Resources Res.*, 32: 3093-309825.

Neuendorf, O., U. Döring, U. Jaekel, & H. Vereecken 1995. Numerical simulation of solute transport in heterogeneous porous media. *Zentralblatt für Geologie und Paläontologie*, Teil 1, Heft 11-12.

Neuendorf, O. 1997. *Numerische 3-D Simulation des Stofftransports in einem heterogenen Aquifer.* PhD Thesis, Berichte des Forschungszentrums Jülich. In Preparation.

Seiler, K.-P. 1973. Durchlässigkeit, Porosität und Kornverteilung quartärer Kies-Sand-Ablagerungen des bayerischen Alpenvorlands. *Gas- und Wasserfach*, 114: 353-358.

Vereeckcn, H. 1996. *Analysis of solute transport in a heterogeneous aquifer: the Krauthausen test site.* Habilitationsschrift, Universität Bonn.

Acknowledments. This research project was funded by the European Union under the contract EV5VCT920214 and by the Research Center Jülich.

Carbonate karst in the Moscow region and its development under urban conditions

R.G. Dzhamalov & V.L. Zlobina
Water Problems Institute, Moscow, Russia

ABSTRACT: High-rate exploitation of karst water leads to intensification of karst suffosion and erosion processes and renewed development of ancient covered karst. Prolonged and high-rate withdrawal of groundwater substantially changes, as a rule, the hydrogeological conditions. In urban areas, groundwater is subjected to many different stresses. One of these, high-rate groundwater withdrawal contributes to the formation of hydrodynamic, hydrogeochemical and thermal anomalies within the developed aquifer and to the intensification of karstification and suffosion. The lowering of piezometric heads in the Carboniferous aquifers of the central Moscow basin has resulted in substantial areal distribution of not only hydrodynamic anomalies but also hydrochemical, hydrobiological and thermal anomalies.

1 INTRODUCTION

It was usually considered that karst develops slowly. But today there is evidence which contradicts this opinion. New sinkholes may be formed within a few decades or at the beginning of high-rate development of carbonate aquifers, even in areas where sinkholes were not previously observed. Formation of sinkholes results from washout of ancient sediments. The presence of active karstification in urban areas leads not only to the deformation and destruction of structures and communication networks, but also to an increase in construction costs. The carrying out of regional investigations under urban conditions has its problems and requires appreciable funds. In this connection, it is important to establish the succession of the investigations. The increasing effect of urban and industrial centres on the environment involves pollution of environmental components: precipitation, soil and natural waters. The action of point and non-point pollution sources substantially deteriorates the state of aquifers and leads to their degradation. The chemical composition of groundwater changes as a result of pollution by infiltration of surface and soil waters. In urban areas groundwater is subjected to many different stresses. There are many particular environmental problems in the urban areas. Among them:

• influence of increasing human activities,
• groundwater pollution,
• sinkholes developing,
• surface collapses and subsidences.

2 THE PROBLEM AND METHODS OF INVESTIGATION

The region investigated is located in the Central Moscow Artesian Basin. At present, there are hundreds of pumping wells in the area. Water demands have increased with the development of industry. For this reason, the number of artesian wells has increased in the Upper, Middle and Lower Carboniferous aquifers.

The research area is situated in Moscow where about 25% of the entire territory of the city can be classified as karst. Carboniferous karstified aquifers have been used for public and industrial water supply for almost a century. The water supply wells have depths from 50 to 300 m and are irregularly distributed over the area of investigation. The investigated area comprises 900 km^2. In the area under investigation karstified limestones occur at depths ranging from 20 to 150 m under a cover of Jurassic sediments and moraine, fluvioglacial and alluvial Quaternary deposits. Clayey Jurassic deposits, 5-20 m thick, are generally eroded in the river valleys where the interaction between confined and unconfined groundwater and surface water is most pronounced. Solution cavities of various volumes and lengths are mainly located in the Upper and Middle Carboniferous rocks (Zlobina 1986). The depths and dimensions of cavities in the carbonate rocks were established during the course of drilling in only a few areas of detailed investigation.

Karst water is an integral part of the environment and, therefore, environmental changes affect groundwater actively and rapidly. Groundwater in karstic areas is closely associated with its recharge sources, such as stream flow and precipitation. The water-balance model showed that up to 80% of the karst water recharge results from percolation of precipitation and surface water within new manmade recharge areas. The groundwater development has resulted in changed leakage conditions, in the formation of large cones of depression, and in the leaching of clogging material from the chemical composition of groundwater due to mixing of surface water and groundwater with various chemical compositions. Water quality has rapidly deteriorated in aquifers composed of carbonate rocks. The use of multiple techniques of investigation is a principal method utilised for hydrogeological investigation in karst areas.

Further water withdrawal has resulted in a change in groundwater movement, an increase in flow velocities, and intensification of leakage from above. The transformation of the natural hydrogeological conditions has led to an increase in the dissolved solids content, concentrations of sulphate and chloride in the water of karstified aquifers.

Water abstraction is a man-induced factor that has the most pronounced effect on the quality of ground water under exploitation. Under aquifer overexploitation conditions, changes in redox and acid-base conditions are observed. More dynamic changes in confined water chemical composition are observed in intensive water withdrawal areas. Water samples for determining chemical, microbiological and isotopic concentrations were taken from all available water-supply wells during 1978-1995. In addition to standard hydrogeological studies, methods such as remote sensing, geophysical techniques, and isotopic and indicator methods are applied. Many different investigative methods or combinations of methods are used to delineate karst zones.

Table 1. Variations in some parameters within the Middle Carboniferous aquifer during the period of abstraction (within the manmade recharge areas).

Parameters	1935 year	1995 year
pH	7.72 - 8.4	6.0 - 6.8
Ca (mg/L)	43 - 64	96 - 152
Temp °C	7 - 8	9.5 - 15.7
Residence time (years)	100	2 - 5
S_{ca}	0.01 - 0.134	-3.17 to -2.54

Nota: S_{ca} = calcite saturation index

3 RESULTS

Water samples from water-supply wells were taken from 1978 to 1995. Rapid testing of a large number of water-supply wells, which are numerous in the urban area, make it possible to identify and delineate a karst area. A helium survey has been performed over an area of about 1000 km^2.

In the area under investigation, by 1987, three anomalies, mainly confined to fault zones and associated palaeovalleys, cutting Jurassic clays were found. Two of these anomalies had a large area (73 and 136 km^2). The area of the third anomaly was not greater than 40 km^2. In subsequent years the anomalies expanded with a tendency to merge. The analysis of the data showed that under the effect of groundwater withdrawal, marked changes occur in hydrochemical conditions. During recent decades a decrease in pH values from 7-8 to 4.9-5.2 was recorded in the Quaternary aquifers. Therefore, the dissolution and leaching of carbonate rocks had intensified 15-20 fold. Thermodynamic calculations make it possible to determine the indices of calcite and dolomite saturation. The spatial study of the karst water dissolving capacity for the area of investigation showed that within the area, nine zones are distinguished with a calcite saturation index of less than zero. These zones are large in size and, according to the integrated data of water, helium and tritium surveys, they are confined to areas of recharge of the aquifer under study. Some results are listed in Table 1 (and Figure 1).

Carbonate undersaturation of the karstic water considerably decreased from 1962 to 1996 (see Figures 2 and 3).

In addition, the thermodynamic simulation showed that the karstic water is considerably undersaturated relative to celestine.

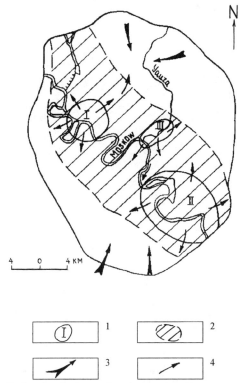

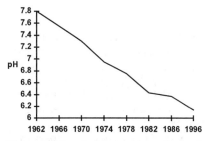

Figure 2. Trends in changing pH (in the Middle Carboniferous aquifer with overexploitation).

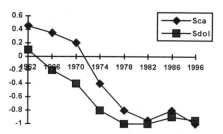

Figure 3. Trends in changing S_{ca} and S_{dol} (in the Middle Carboniferous aquifer with overexploitation).

Figure 1. Scheme of hydrogeological condition changes under groundwater overexploitation of the Middle Carboniferous aquifer within Moscow city area.

The thermodynamic modelling showed complex changes in the indices of water saturation in Carboniferous aquifers over time and area. As a result water becomes undersaturated by calcite, dolomite and other minerals (Dzhamalov & Zlobina 1991).

Heliometric investigations were conducted every year for studying the dynamics of the temporal change in the hydrogeological conditions. So, as a result of unconfined ground water and river water intrusion into the confined aquifer being developed, changes in karst water quality and dissolving capacity increase are observed. The largest karst water chemical composition changes are in zones of immediate contact between Quaternary and Carboniferous deposits. Species of microorganisms in groundwater were determined. Organic acids are products of their activity and affect limestone karstification. 43 species of micro-organisms, including filamentous bacteria, diatoms, green algae, blue-green algae etc. were found (Brekhovskikh et al. 1987).

After obtaining regional information for aquifers under investigation, other studies (hydrogeochemical, biological and limited investigation of the ground water flow mechanism using models) were carried out.

4 CONCLUSIONS

Changes in hydrodynamic conditions have activated processes of leaching and dissolution of carbonate rocks. Mixing of waters of various composition and origin has resulted in stable and regional change in the physicochemical equilibrium in the water-rock system of the aquifers.

The overexploitation of confined water from the Carboniferous aquifer has resulted in the formation of three extensive and prolonged recharge areas. These areas are also thermal, hydrochemical, and microbiological anomalies .

REFERENCES

Dzhamalov, R.G. & V.L. Zlobina 1991. The elfect of aquifer overexploitation on recharge area formation. *XXIII Congress I.A.H.: Aquifer overexploitalion Spain.* 133-137

Zlobina, V.L. 1986. Effect of groundwater exploitation on karstic and suffosion development. Nauka Publ. Moscow.

Brekhovskikh, V.F., V.L. Zlobina & N.S. Zolotareva 1987. Particularities of formation of hydrochemical regime and biocenosis composition of confined ground water being intensely exploited. *Vodnye Resursy* 1: 133-138.

Groundwater pollution from infiltration of urban stormwater runoff

J. Bryan Ellis
Natural Environment Research Council, Swindon, UK

ABSTRACT: There is increasing interest in the use of source control techniques for the disposal of urban stormwater runoff. Given the proven poor quality of such drainage waters, the operational performance and potential impacts of filtration devices on urban groundwater quality are reviewed and compared to available guidelines for various water uses. Erratic pollutant removal efficiencies and high failure rates are noted and pre-treatment of stormwater runoff is recommended prior to discharge to filtration systems. A tiered approach to the assessment of the groundwater polluting potential of urban runoff is proposed, although the use of runoff for direct recharge is not advocated.

1 INTRODUCTION

Strategies for the sustainable development of water resources and integrated catchment planning (ICP) are all now seeking to divert, attenuate and dispose of impermeable urban surface water at source and a number of UK water companies are investigating the potential of aquifer storage and recovery (ASR) although none yet involve direct stormwater recharge. The US, Netherlands and Australia have successfully harvested roof and street drainage through infiltration to groundwater as a basis for mains water replacement for secondary uses such as irrigation and recreation (Argue 1994). Whilst rising urban groundwater levels have been widely recognised as a problem, there are considerable uncertainties as to whether long term source disposal of urban stormwater runoff is likely to cause widespread contamination of urban groundwaters.

The impacts of episodic discharges from impermeable urban surfaces upon receiving surface water systems are now well documented (Ellis & Hvitved-Jacobsen 1996) but there are relatively few field assessments available to evaluate actual impacts of stormwater infiltration to urban groundwaters. The potential for highway discharges to contaminate local aquifers has certainly been recognised, especially where roadside filter or fin drains can directly infiltrate to underlying fissured strata (Price 1994; Luker &

Montague 1994). In the UK, it is now Environment Agency (EA) policy not to allow major highway and motorway discharges within designated Zone I (Inner Source Protection) regions and will only be acceptable under exceptional circumstances in Outer Source Protection Zones.

Within the context of ICP, regulatory authorities are increasingly identifyinging a range of source control techniques which are perceived as comprising a suite of Best Management Practices (BMPs) for the sustainable management of intermittent urban runoff (CIRIA 1992). As most source control systems divert surface runoff to groundwater, it can be argued that they comprise a valuable source of aquifer recharge. The theoretical risks they present to groundwater pollution must therefore be set against the potential benefits to be gained from, for example, the possible strategic recharge of some 208M m^3 per annum that could be generated from an average annual 500mm of rainfall falling on some 416 km^2 (52,000 km) of highway surfaces laid on the Chalk of S E England.

2 STORMWATER INFILTRATION AND QUALITY STANDARDS

The type and range of pollutants associated with

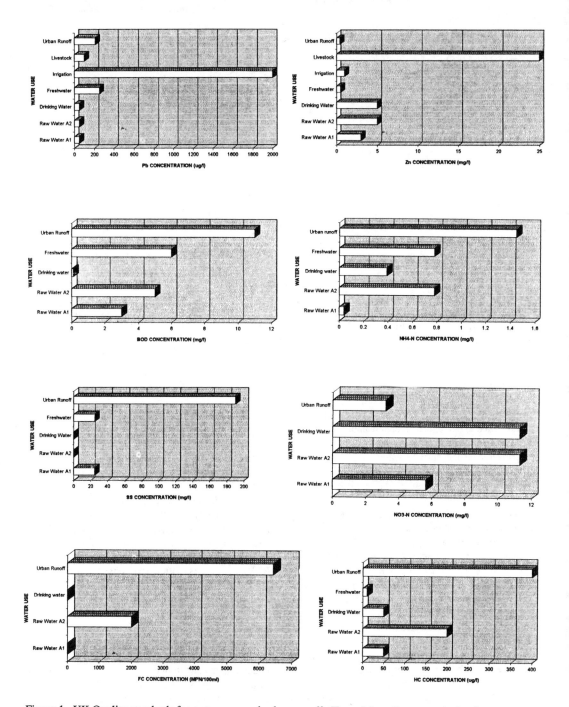

Figure 1. UK Quality standards for water uses and urban runoff (Event Mean Concentration) values.

urban stormwater is extremely variable (Ellis 1986) but five pollutant groups are of principal concern in terms of the potential use of urban runoff for ASR. Figure 1 compares overall pollutant event mean concentration (EMC) values recorded for urban runoff discharges within the UK with prevailing EU standards for various water uses. In terms of potential secondary re-use, of particular concern are raw waters (including groundwater) intended for potable use requiring either minimum A1 treatment (disinfection) or flocculation and sedimentation (A2).

2.1 *Solids and heavy metals*

A significant proportion of the total and toxic polluting load arising from urban surfaces is associated with the fine (<63 μm) particulate fraction of the discharge. Average lead levels in urban stormwaters considerably exceed most current UK quality standards with the exception of waters intended for irrigation (Figure 1). In general, levels of other metals such as zinc, cadmium, copper and chromium fall within the water use guidelines. The suspended solids (SS) concentration range is typically two orders of magnitude and the 190 mg/1 EMC value for stormwater runoff is of significance to ASR because fine solids are a primary cause of clogging of injection wells. In addition, this fraction may contain over 90% of inorganic lead as well as 70% of the copper, chromium and hydrocarbons. Whilst settleable and insoluble materials may not lead to any immediate failure of water quality standards, they could be leached out of infiltration systems through release of mobile, colloidal particulate in association with elevated DOC levels (10-12 mg/1) into the underlying saturated zone.

2.1.1 *Field Tests*

Most studies that have been undertaken of infiltration system performance have shown high but erratic

pollutant removal rates. This variability in performance is confirmed from a field study of a submerged aerobic biological filtration device to treat outflows from a stormwater detention basin receiving stormflows from a 440 hectare suburban catchment (Table 1). The filter medium used in the test was an inert expanded schist (nominal diameter 3-6mm) which is similar to that used for *biocarbone* treatment for water and industrial wastewaters and the test was conducted under a continuous flow regime without spiking.

Net losses of nutrients occur with extended retention times and backwashed concentrations of SS and Zn were as high as 265 mg/l and 43 μg/1 respectively suggesting that sloughed biomass and associated particulate clogging increase headloss and reduce efficiency quite rapidly. The erratic metal concentration depth profiles noted in the field tests are probably the result of variable precipitation with sulphide and adsorption onto Fe and Mn (hydr)oxides under changing redox conditions. Monthly backwashing would be required to maintain an optimum performance and based on a 50% removal target for SS, TOC, PO_4 and Pb for a 2-year, 1 hour duration design storm generating 7500m^3 of runoff, filter surface area would need to be about 1200 m^2. This would pose considerable space, cost and maintenance difficulties in urban areas and alongside highway verges.

2.1.2 *Failure rates and design.*

There are general high levels of failure reported for infiltration-based techniques with 5-year failure rates for trenches and porous pavements being 50 and 75% respectively for systems in the US Mid-Atlantic region (Schueler et al. 1992). There has likewise been a high failure rate of monolithic porous asphalt and concrete reported from the eastern US, and other countries such as Australia have abandoned this "best practice" altogether. Whilst many failures may be related to

Table 1. Field test filter performance.

Run Number	Hydraulic Retention Time (hr)	Surface Loading Rate (m/hr)	Flow Rate (l/min)	Removal Efficiency (%)					
				SS	TOC	PO_4	NH_4	Pb	Zn
1	1.0	0.45	6.4	94	10	21	59	nd	nd
2	1.5	0.30	4.3	92	13	-7	97	27	66
3	2.5	0.18	2.6	89	30	-100	-88	nd	nd

nd = not detectable

inappropriate sizing relative to catchment area or to lack of maintenance, the majority are the result of lack of solids pre-treatment and of groundwater mounding. Sand and other media (peat, compost, geotextiles) filter basins, which have gained substantial popularity in the US as stormwater BMPs, are also subject to high and early failure rates. Urbonas et al (1996) have reported cumulative total SS removal rates falling by 70% within one year of installation with flow-through (hydraulic conductivity) rates being throttled from an initial 1 m/hr to less than 0.02 m/hr causing frequent and severe flow by-passing. Infiltration and filter devices must be properly sized for the expected maintenance cycle that matches both the average annual runoff volume and the average annual total SS EMC in the runoff. If the control device cannot be made large enough to pass through the design event without backing-up water when it is partially clogged, sufficient stormwater detention volume or equivalent attenuation must be provided upstream to provide solids pre-treatment and to balance a clogged flow-through rate of about 10-12 mm/hr. Good engineering design practice can mitigate some of the problems associated with conventional infiltration and porous paving systems but they cannot provide a fail-safe guarantee of long term groundwater protection and neither are they able to predict a target pollutant removal rate.

2.2 Hydrocarbons and pesticides

Hydrocarbons and pesticides (including herbicides) are List I substances under the terms of the EC Groundwater Directive and thus direct discharge of stormwater runoff containing these substances to groundwater is not permitted, although the regulatory authorities have yet to establish Water Quality Objectives (WQOs) for groundwater. Until these are developed, the EA will advise on the standards which must be satisfied for individual aquifers. The Groundwater Protection Policies (GPPs) contained in the 1992 NRA framework document "Policy and Practice for Protection of Groundwater" also limit locations where indirect (via soakaways, infiltration trenches etc.) discharges are feasible, with oil interceptors required wherever either Source or Resource protection is necessary under Acceptibility Matrix 3c of the policy framework. Also relevant to the disposal of impermeable urban and highway runoff are the Groundwater Policy Statements concerning diffuse pollution of groundwater (Policies G1-G4) particularly with reference to the leaching of

herbicides from roadside verges and landscaped areas.

Total oil (hydrocarbon) levels in urban runoff average 10-20 mg/l (Figure 1) with motorway and trunk drainage averaging 25-30 mg/l and reaching as high as 100-400 mg/l during short intense storm events (Colwill et al. 1984). Suburban roads have a lower range varying between 2-28 mg/l. The significance of such oil contamination is difficult to quantify in terms of UK legislative requirements although EA discharge consents to surface waters of River Ecosystem Classes 1, 2 and 3 (General Quality Assessment Grades A, B and C) are in the region of 5-10 mg/l. For discharges to ground, oil interceptors and infiltration devices will have a negligble effect on the concentration of trace organics present in a dissolved or colloidal form. Whilst PAHs are generally insoluble and solid-associated, their cosolvent properties can enhance their solubility. Monocyclic aromatic hydrocarbons such as benzene and toluene are quite mobile as are the low molecular weight phenols, and in nutrient deficient aquifers their degradation is likely to be slow. Thus, unless there is specific local knowledge to indicate that degradation or attenuation will be assured, it should be assumed that none will occur.

Herbicides have become an integral part of urban management strategies for the control of vegetation by local county, highway and airport authorities as well as rail track operators (Ellis et al. 1997). The non-agricultural applications of herbicides represent 2-3% (550 tonnes) of the total amount of active ingredient applied each year in the UK. Figure 2 shows the exceedances of the 0.1 μg/l EU drinking water standard resulting from the use of non-agricultural herbicides in 1993 and 1994 expressed as a percentage of all pesticide exceedances by water utility regions. Herbicide losses from hard surfaces now account for more than 30% of pesticide exceedances in five regions and more than 15% in seven of the ten regions. The current UK regulatory approach to determining the impact on water resources of such applications in urban areas is to assume that 100% of the applied product will have the potential to be washed off and thus lead to contaminated drainage water being infiltrated down to groundwater. Whilst the use of the triazine group (atrazine and simazine) was revoked in 1993, there has been a switch to other compounds notably to diuron, chlorotoluron and isoproturon. In 1994, the latter was responsible for over 50% of all UK exceedances of the drinking water standard compared to only 7% and 2% for atrazine and simazine respectively. The transport mechanisms and underlying governing factors that determine the movement and fate of herbicides from hard surfaces to groundwater are still very poorly understood. Until this situation changes allowing the formulation of more robust impact risk assessments, the continued use of herbicides in urban areas will remain a significant issue for groundwater protection.

2.3 Bacteria

Concentrations of faecal coliform bacteria in urban stormwater are high (Figure 1) being significantly above the guidelines for all specified uses. Pathogenic organisms are also regularly found in impermeable stormwater runoff and biological treatment through grass swales and/or wetland systems would be needed

to provide a full groundwater protection. US EPA regulations set aside the natural degradation of pathogens in aquifers and require full tertiary treatment and disinfection prior to recharge where stormwater is to be reclaimed for use as a potential drinking water supply (National Research Council 1994). In Europe, it is common practice to allow a minimum 50-day residence time of recharge water in aquifers to enable die-off of pathogens but survival times and resuscitation mechanisms for enteric organisms in groundwater are still uncertain.

3 GROUNDWATER ASSESSMENT

A tiered approach is recommended for assessing the groundwater pollution potential of impermeable urban

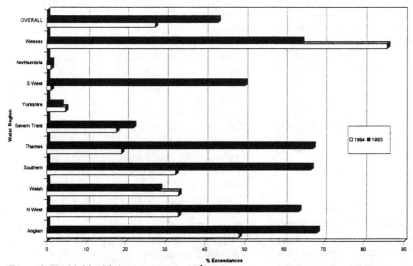

Figure 2. Herbicide drinking water exceedances.

Table 2. Urban stormwater drainage treatment systems.

Treatment System	Capital Cost (£k)	Maintenance Cost (£k/pa)	Removal Efficiency (%)					
			Zn_{tot}	Cu_{diss}	Fe	Pb	SS	HCs
Kerb/Gully/Pipe System	180-220	1000	<---------------------- 10 - 30 -------------------->					
Oil interceptors	10-30	300	30-50	<10	30-40	40-60	30-80	40-80
Combined Filter/French Drains	160-200	-	70-80	10-30	80-90	80-90	80-90	70-90
Infiltration Basin	20-50	2500	70-80	10-30	80-90	80-90	60-90	70-90
Sedimentation Lagoon	60-100	2000	60-80	20-30	90+	80-90	60-90	70-90
Detention Pond	15-30	350	30-40	<10	30-50	40-60	40-70	30-60
Grass Swales	15-40	350	70-90	50-70	90+	80-90	60-90	70-90
Wetland Systems	15-60	2500	<---------------------- 50 - 80 -------------------->					
Sedimentation Tank	30-60	300	30-50	<10	30-40	40-60	30-80	40-80

drainage. At the first stage, the methods published in CIRIA (Luker & Montague 1994) can be applied. In this method, an annual build-up rate for pollutants accumulating on the impermeable surface is assumed according to the appropriate land use and average traffic volume. All of the pollutant material is assumed to be washed off the surface, diluted by the total annual effective rainfall for the site to derive a calculated runoff concentration for specified pollutants. It is also further assumed that there is no removal or attenuation by the soakaway or infiltration device.

Given the greater vulnerability in terms of the potential and costs of remediation of groundwater to pollution, the conservative assessment is appropriate. Where the calculated concentration in the runoff is greater than the relevant EQS or specified guideline values, more detailed evaluation will be required to determine whether and what additional pollution control measures are needed. Table 2 provides a first order screening of the removal efficiencies afforded by various treatment systems that can be considered for urban drainage intended for groundwater recharge together with estimates of capital and maintenance costs. However, the design approach should adopt a "treatment train" combination of two or more source control systems to provide sufficient safeguard against diffuse groundwater pollution from impermeable urban runoff.

4 CONCLUSIONS

Considerable caution is needed in advocating the widespread introduction of dispersed source control techniques for impermeable urban stormwater management where there is likelihood of long term infiltration of such drainage waters to groundwater. Urban runoff is certainly not suitable for direct injection into aquifers to generate drinking water supplies and pre-treatment in detention or wetland basins is recommended for infiltration to be used for secondary irrigation or livestock supplies. Particular constraints on the sustainable reuse of stormwater from source disposal arises from trace organics (especially herbicides), pathogenic bacteria and possibly from dissolved metals and hydrocarbons. Much further evidence is required to characterise, quantify and predict their rates of degradation in both infiltration systems and within the saturated zone before these source control devices can be advocated for groundwater recharge. The recent EA inventory of aquifer pollution in England and Wales resulting from point sources such as landfill and the legal difficulties of implementing remedial measures, provides a clear warning of the dangers of similarly conceding to widespread source disposal of contaminated urban stormwater to groundwater.

REFERENCES

Argue, J.R. 1994. A new streetscape for stormwater management in mediterranean-climate cities. Proc. 17th *Biennal Conf., Int Assoc. Water Quality, Budapest,* Hungary. 23-32. IAWQ, London.

CIRIA. 1992. *Scope for control of urban runoff.* Report 124, Construction Ind. Research. Inf. Assoc., London.

Colwill, D.M., C.J. Peters, & R. Perry. 1984. *Water quality of highway runoff.* Report 823. Transport & Road Research Lab., Crowthorne, Berks. UK.

Ellis, J.B. 1993. Achieving standards for the recreational use of urban waters. In D Kay & R Hanbury (eds), *Recreational water quality management.* 155-174. Ellis Horwood, London.

Ellis, J.B & T. Hvitved-Jacobsen. 1996. Urban drainage impacts on receiving waters. *J.Hydr.Research,* 34(6): 771-783.

Ellis, J.B., D.M. Revitt & N. Llewelyn. 1997. Transport and the environment: Effects of organic pollutants on water quality. *J.Chart.Inst Water & Env Mgt.,* (In Press).

Luker, M & K. Montague. 1994. *Control of pollution from highway drainage discharges.* Report 142, Construction Ind. Research Inf. Assoc., London.

National Research Council. 1994. *Groundwater recharge using water of impaired quality.* Nat. Academic Press, Washington DC.

Price, M. 1994. Drainage from roads and airfields to soakaways. *J.Chart.Inst.Water & Env Mgt.,* 8: 468-479.

Raimbault, G & T.D. Balades, 1987. Realisations de structures reservoirs en voirie urbaine. *Voirie Urbaine,* 64:39-47.

Schueler, T.R., P.A. Kumble, & M.A. Heraty, 1992. *A current assessment of urban best management practices.* Metrop.Washington Council of Governments., Washington DC.

Urbonas, B., J.T. Doerfer & L.S. Tucker, 1996. *Stormwater sand filtration: A solution or a problem.* APWA Reporter, Amer.Public Works Assoc., Washington DC.

Modeling of contaminant transport and seawater encroachment in coastal aquifers

Abdulhamid M.Ghazali & Jamal O.El-Sheikh Ali
Department of Civil Engineering, Al Fateh University, Tripoli, Libya

ABSTRACT: In this paper groundwater flow, contaminant transport, and seawater movement in coastal aquifers are simulated using the USGS three dimensional heat and transport model (HST3D). The heat transport equation was converted via parameter transformation to simulate conservative species solute transport (i.e. salt). This use of the model has been verified by comparisons with existing results for documented cases. The model is being implemented for a coastal aquifer site with a contaminant source due to leakage from an underground fuel oil storage tank. Preliminary results for this case are presented showing the effects of seawater encroachment and water extraction systems on the propagation of the contaminant.

1 INTRODUCTION

Extensive groundwater extraction in urban coastal areas for agricultural, industrial, and domestic uses over prolonged periods of time with minimal surface recharge, as in the case of some areas of North Africa, has caused substantial seawater encroachment into aquifer systems. This problem combined with contaminant spreading from industrial spills, underground storage-tank leaks, sewer leaks, farm wastewater, and/or waste disposal sites can cause deteriorating quality of a very precious groundwater resource.

Groundwater flow and transport models are valuable tools in assessing present aquifer conditions and in predicting future aquifer situations and can be used to establish remedial action plans to attenuate the groundwater quality deterioration.

The HST3D model was developed by the U.S. Geological Survey to simulate groundwater flow in association with heat and solute transport, accounting for concentration and thermal effects on flow density (Kipp 1987). The model solves equations for flow, single solute species transport, and heat balance. However, it can not be applied to solve both contaminant transport and salt water movement in its basic formulation. Practical needs for simulating flow and the transport of organic solvent originating from sites in coastal aquifers necessitated the need to model flow, solute transport, and salt water movement simultaneously. In order to achieve this requirement, the heat balance equation of the HST3D model was converted using parameter transformation to second conservative solute species transport equation (Ghazali & Findikakis 1993).

This use of the model was verified by performing a series of verification tests and was confirmed by comparisons to existing published results (Ghazali & Findikakis 1993). The effects of salt water intrusion on the migration of contaminant plumes were demonstrated. Furthermore, this model is being implemented to simulate the movement of leaked fuel oil from an underground storage tank in a coastal aquifer. In this paper some preliminary results of this assessment are presented.

2 TRANSFORMATION OF THE HEAT EQUATION

The heat equation used in the HST3D model is:

$$\frac{\partial}{\partial t}(\varepsilon \rho c_f + (1-\varepsilon)\rho_s c_s)T = \nabla.(\varepsilon K_f +$$

$$(1-\varepsilon)K_s)I\nabla T + \nabla.\varepsilon D_H \nabla T - \nabla.\varepsilon \rho c_f vT +$$

$$q_H + q\rho^* c_f T^* \qquad (1)$$

where:

T is the fluid and porous medium temperature
T^* is the temperature of the fluid source
ε is the effective porosity
v is the seepage velocity
ρ is the fluid density
ρ^* is the density of the fluid source
ρ_s is the density of the solid phase
c_f is the heat capacity of the fluid phase at constant pressure
c_s is the heat capacity of the solid phase at constant pressure
K_f is the thermal conductivity of the fluid phase
K_s is the thermal conductivity of the solid phase
D_H is the thermo-mechanical dispersion tensor
q_H is the heat-source intensity
I is the identity matrix of rank 3

Setting the following physical parameters in the above heat transport equation as:

$c_f = 1$, $c_s = 0$, $K_f = c_f \rho D_m$, $K_s = 0$, $D_H = c_f \rho D_s$, and $q_H = 0$, the partial differential equation then becomes:

$$\frac{\partial}{\partial t}(\varepsilon \rho T) = \nabla . \varepsilon \rho D_m I \nabla T + \nabla . \varepsilon \rho D_s \nabla T - \nabla . \varepsilon \rho v T$$

$$+ q \rho^* T^* \qquad (2)$$

where:

D_m is the effective molecular diffusivity of the solute
D_s is the dispersion coefficient tensor

The converted equation represents the mechanism of transport of a solute species (T), namely advection, diffusion and dispersion, and a source term without including the two terms representing solute decay, and sorption. It therefore can be used to simulate a conservative solute such as chloride.

3 VALIDATION OF THE TRANSFORMED MODEL

The classical Henry's problem (Henry 1964) was used in the validation of this transformed model. A confined coastal aquifer represented by a two-dimensional vertical slice (200m long, 100m deep, and 1 m wide) with homogeneous material having a hydraulic conductivity of 1 m/day and a porosity of 0.35 was used for saltwater intrusion simulations. A seawater boundary condition is applied at one end of the model while a fresh water flux of 6.6×10^{-3} m/day is applied at the land side boundary. The model was discretized into 21 by 11 by 2 nodes for the finite

difference grid used by the HST3D model. Steady state solution of the seawater intrusion was performed using the original solute transport equation first, and using the transformed heat equation second. The results were identical. The results were further compared with the previously presented results by Huyakorn (1987), Frind (1982), and Henry (1964) for the case of constant diffusion/dispersion. This was achieved by setting the diffusion coefficient equal to 6.6×10^{-2} m^2/day and dispersivity equal to zero, with the results shown in Figure 1. The results show good agreement with the published results. A varying diffusion/dispersion case was simulated by setting the diffusion coefficient equal to zero and dispersivity equal to 3.5 m. Figure 2 shows the model results for this case which are in good agreement with results by Huyakorn (1987) and Frind (1964).

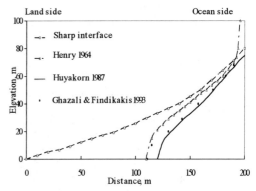

Figure 1. Concentration distributions (50% isochlor) for constant dispersion case.

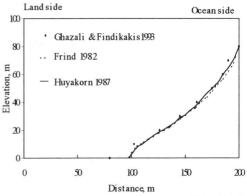

Figure 2. Concentration distributions (50% isochlor) for variable dispersion case.

138

4 EFFECTS OF SEAWATER PRESENCE ON CONTAMINANT TRANSPORT

Effects of seawater intrusion on contaminant plume migration were analyzed using this model. An initial condition of a contaminant plume was introduced to the previously described aquifer. The migration of the plume was first simulated in a uniform density flow regime without seawater present. The results of 10-year simulation are presented in Figures 3a and 3b. The same initial plume was then simulated in the presence of seawater intrusion. The results after 10 years of simulation are shown in Figures 4a and 4b. The effects of the seawater intrusion on the flow field and plume migration are evident near the coastline. The plume extends along an inclined plane represented approximately by the 50% isochlor line. It is evident that the dilution of concentrations are larger for this case than for the uniform flow condition case. This was attributed to higher advection and dispersion resulting from the non-uniform flow field in the case of seawater intrusion. It is worth noting that although larger dilutions are evident in the case of seawater intrusion, higher concentrations are present at shallower depths near the coastline for this case compared with the uniform flow condition case.

5 SIMULATION OF A CONTAMINATED COASTAL AQUIFER SITE

The model is being used to assess the present conditions of a coastal aquifer due to a possible leak from an underground fuel oil tank. Local well users have detected traces of fuel oil in the extracted water and possible contaminant sources are being considered. In this paper only preliminary results will be presented due to client confidentiality and limited availability of field data at present. In order to make preliminary assessments of contaminant migration, the transformed model was implemented for the upper confined aquifer using a two-dimensional vertical slice 2 km long extending from the coastline, 1 m wide, and 160 m deep that covers the area of concern. A varying head-boundary condition was set at the land side boundary of the aquifer based on some recorded well data for water levels. The suspected source of contamination was modeled as a surface contaminant source. Four wells were also included in the simulation to represent effects of water extraction on both the saltwater intrusion and contaminant plume migration as shown in Figure 5.

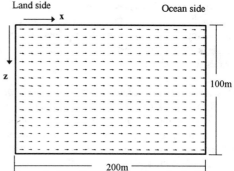

Figure 3a. Flow field for the uniform density flow

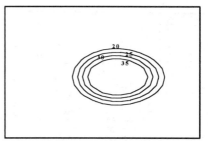

Figure 3b. Plume concentration distribution in ppm for the uniform density flow

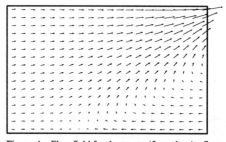

Figure 4a. Flow field for the non-uniform density flow

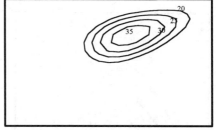

Figure 4b. Plume concentration distribution in ppm for the non-uniform density flow

Several oil-fuel leak-rates of the source were simulated for the last ten years in order to calibrate the model using collected field data. Figure 5a displays the flow field and the effects of both seawater intrusion and water extraction on the aquifer system.

Results of 10-year simulation of contaminant plume spreading for a leak rate of 200 *l*/day of oil fuel are shown on Figure 5b. It is clear that both wells at the a & b locations show traces of the contamination. Figure 5c shows the extent of the intrusion of saltwater into the aquifer.

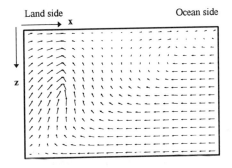

Figure 5a. Flow field for 10-year simulation.

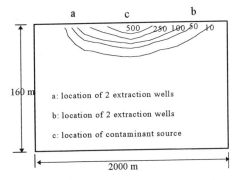

a: location of 2 extraction wells

b: location of 2 extraction wells

c: location of contaminant source

Figure 5b. Plume concentrations distribution in ppm for 10-year simulation

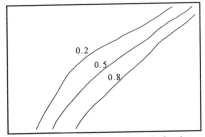

Figure 5c. Salinity concentration (in fraction, isochlor lines)for 10-year simulation.

6 CONCLUSIONS

The U.S. Geological Survey model HST3D was used to simulate multi-species solute transport. The heat balance equation of the model was converted using parameter transformation to a second species solute transport equation. The model therefore can be readily used to simulate the transport of contaminant plumes in coastal aquifers where normally the problem of seawater intrusion is persistent. The model was validated by conducting verification tests and comparisons to existing data and good agreement was achieved. The effects of the seawater intrusion on the migration of contaminant plumes were demonstrated. It was found that the contaminant plumes migrate along an inclined line representing the salt-fresh water interface. Higher plume dilution resulted in the case of seawater intrusion but higher concentrations were detected at shallower depths than that for the uniform density flow conditions. The model was applied to actual contaminated coastal aquifer condition and two-dimensional preliminary results were presented to determine the effects of the possible contamination sources. The effects of both water extraction and seawater encroachment on the spreading of the contaminant plume were shown. A three-dimensional model is under development for this site.

REFERENCES

Frind, E. O. 1982. Simulation of long- term transient density-dependent transport in groundwater. Adv. Water Resour. 5:73-88.

Ghazali,A. and Findikakis, A. 1993. Verification tests for transport modeling in coastal aquifers. ASCE Engineering Hydrology Conference. San Francisco, California.

Henry, H. R. 1964. Effects of dispersion on salt encroachment in coastal aquifers. U.S. Geol. Surv.Water Supply Pap. 1613C.

Huyakorn, P. S., P. Anderson, J. Mercer and H. White, JR 1987. Salt water intrusion in aquifer: Development and testing of a three-dimensional finite element model. Water Res. Research. 23:293-312.

Kipp, L. L. 1987. HST3D: A computer code for simulation of heat and solute transport in three-dimensional ground water flow system. U.S. Geol. Surv. Water-Resource Invest. Rep. 86-4095.

Artificial radionuclides as a tool for ground water contamination assessment: Experience following the Chernobyl disaster

V.Goudzenko
Research & Development Centre of Radiohydroecological Investigations, Kyiv, Ukraine

ABSTRACT: This paper presents the results of a groundwater contamination study in the regions influenced by radioactive fallout after the Chernobyl disaster on 26 April 1986. The presence of fission products such as ^{137}Cs (seldom ^{134}Cs) and ^{90}Sr in waters and water bearing rocks to comparatively great depth, taking into account the considerable difference between their chemical properties and controlling retardation characteristics, make this couple a unique tool for ground water vulnerability assay. A marked mobility of ^{90}Sr and relative immobility of ^{137}Cs allow an overlap of a wide range of contaminant retardation features.

1 INTRODUCTION

Numerous stable and radioactive isotopes (nuclides) have long served as tracers during various natural and artificial process investigations in the geological environment. Water molecule components such as ^{2}H, ^{3}H(T), ^{18}O and ^{17}O are the classical set for hydrology. As mentioned above, a wide range of water-soluble components including radionuclides is successfully used for the mass transfer study. Industrial development led to advancing contamination of the environment. Prolonged operation of nuclear fuel cycle facilities, and especially accidents and disasters in these, are the cause of the considerable accumulation of long living decay and activation products in the geosphere. Side by side with the obvious negative consequence of biosphere contamination, this occurrence may be partly used for a positive aim - radionuclides released may serve as tracers of contaminant penetration from the ground surface to groundwater and in this way may validate diverse models of contaminant transport. Exceptional sensitivity of radionuclide determination as compared with a majority of other contaminants allows a search for the trends of soil and groundwater pollution.

The disaster on 26 April 1986 in the 4th unit of the Chernobyl Nuclear Power Plant (ChNPP) led to the release of a large amount of fission and decay products, often including those situated in the fuel matrix (UO_2). Their radioactivity lead to significant contamination of soils and superficial waters reaching up to Mega-Bequerels per square meter (for ^{137}Cs and ^{90}Sr) in the vicinity of the ChNPP. Areal contamination along the tracks of atmospheric fallout reached levels of tens to hundreds of kBq/m^2 over distances of some hundred km from the damaged unit. The area under study here is located between ChNPP and the Kyivan Urban and Industrial Agglomeration (KUIA). The distribution of fission products in the soil profiles, water bearing rocks, aquitards and groundwaters has been studied here since 1986 to assay the protection of municipal water-supply sources and to forecast their possible contamination.

According to existing conceptions, vulnerability of groundwaters located within aquifers separated from the ground surface by thick aquicludes seems to be negligible. Nevertheless measurable concentrations of ^{90}Sr and ^{137}Cs (rarely ^{134}Cs) have been determined since 1989 in waters from municipal water supply wells in the city of Kyiv, which exploits Cretaceous and Jurassic aquifers, lying at depths of 150 to 250 m.

The Chernobyl origin of these radionuclides or at last some portion of them, had been confirmed in 1988-1989 by determination of short living ^{134}Cs in waters extracted from 26 wells, including artesian ones (Goudzenko 1993).The depth varies from 50 to 250 m, with aquifers from upper Jurassic and upper Cretaceous within the town of Kyiv to Palaeogene in suburban area. The presence of ^{134}Cs in artesian wells was of particular importance because it allowed the exclusion of the possibility of water contamination through the annular-weakened permeable zones in the aquitard around the well casings. The existence of such zones until then seemed to be the only reason for groundwater contamination observed by many hydrogeologists.

2 HYDROGEOLOGICAL FEATURES

The study area is located along the contact between the Ukrainian crystalline shield and the Dnieper-Don depression. The main aquifers and complexes are strata within Quaternary, Palaeogene, Cretaceous and Jurassic deposits. Aquicludes and aquitards (thickness from 10 to 100 m) which are widespread in the territory are: Palaeogene marls, marl-chalk formations of the upper Cretaceous and clay-siltstone fommations of lower Cretaceous-upper Jurassic layers. Interbeds of clays, clayey sandstones and siltstones throughout the sedimentary profile serve as local aquitards. A hydrogeological cross-section of the area is shown in Figure l. Groundwater is used for municipal and private water supplies: from the Quaternary deposits - in the rural settlements for individual consumers; from the Palaeogene deposits - for the municipal water supply systems in the small towns and collective fanns, and from the Cretaceous and Jurassic aquifers - for the municipal water intake within the KUIA (city of Kyiv and suburbs). The long operation of the latter has caused large depression cones to reach up to 100 and 140 km in diameter for the upper-middle Cretaceous and middle Jurassic aquifers respectively. Decline of water tables has exceeded some tens of meters. Redistribution of groundwater pressures led to a significant amplification of infiltration recharge (Shestopalov et al. 1991) and may be considered as one of the main reasons for relatively quick radionuclide penetration from the surface to groundwaters.

3 GROUNDWATER CONTAMINATION

Despite numerous critical views, the retardation concept remains the leading approach to the prediction of contaminant migration. Among the main factors controlling the retardation, the kinetics of the interaction between the pollutant and rocks on the filtration pathway, and the hydrodynamic dispersion of flow are of major importance. Kinetics in turn are controlled by pollutant and rock chemical properties. The most general mechanism of

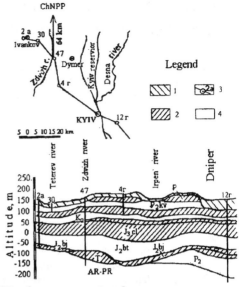

Numbers near rectangles mean:
1- undifferentiated Quaternary deposits; 2- main confined aquifers in Palaeogene, Cretaceous, Jurassic, and occasioned Triassic deposits; 3- cross-section line, well and its number; 4- main aquitards in middle Palaeogene, Upper Cretaceous and Middle Jurassic and partly Permiam deposits.

Figure 1. Hydrogeological cross-section along the SE trace of fallouts.

interaction seems to be cation exchange, but sometimes pollutants can make stronger chemical compounds with me matrix. Proceeding from these simple statements we can suppose, that if retardation is high, water bearing rocks on the filtration pathway will be polluted significantly, but groundwaters from the underlying aquifer will be clean and vice versa. The decade of observations of pore solutions, groundwaters soils and rocks contaminated with infiltrating ^{137}Cs and ^{90}Sr (undertaken in the alienated zone around ChNPP and in KUIA area) have shown that this natural phenomenon is not uniform. Some results of these observations are shown in Table 1.

Pore solutions have been collected from the upper parts of the soil profiles, so results may have been elevated due to an uncontrolled filtration of suspended particles. The presence of measurable amounts of ^{137}Cs at a rather great depth (more than several hundred of meters) confirms the existence of radionuclide transport to groundwater.

Table 1. Maximum concentrations of ^{137}Cs (Bq/l, Bq/kg) in the geological media one decade after the disaster.

Substance under study	Geological index	Alienated zone	KUIA
Pore solution	Q	up to 45	da
	P	da	da
Groundwater	Q	up to 200**	up to 0.7
	P	up tp 3	up to 0.01
Soils (Rocks)*	Q	30 (6 m), 280 (2.5 m)	20 (1 m), 1.5 (6 m)
	P	up to 5	up to 7

da - data absent
* - concentrations in the soils and rocks, collected from a depth greater than suspended particles can penetrate.
** - concentrations measured near the broken unit of ChNPP
Q - Quaternary; P - Palaeogene

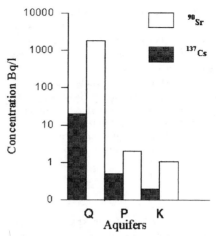

Figure 3. Radionuclides in the groundwater of the alienated zone.
Q - Quaternary; P - Palaeogene; K - Cretaceous

Concentrations of ^{90}Sr in the same parts of the geological media are less than ^{137}Cs, excluding the most contaminated areas around the 4th unit, where the density of both radionuclides' fallout are similar. Average concentrations of radionuclides of the groundwaters of the main aquifers used for potable water supply in KUIA in 1995 are shown in Figure 2.

The same data, drawn for the groundwaters of the exclusion zone, are shown in Figure 3. The comparison of Figures 2 and 3 shows a large difference between both nuclide concentrations in the water of the upper horizon which decreases with depth. Contamination of the main aquifers (K_2 and J_2) far enough from the power station is obvious, although essentially below dangerous levels.

The retardation of caesium and strontium compounds moving with an infiltration flow from the polluted surface downwards, has been studied by numerous investigators and techniques. The range of retardation factor (R_f) values, as controlled by distribution coefficients (K_d), is very broad for both ^{137}Cs and ^{90}Sr. Some recent results of their determinations are shown in Table 2.

The results obtained in the laboratory, as usual are higher than the in situ observations, especially for ^{137}Cs. Therefore the first should be used carefully in the forecast of groundwater vulnerability.

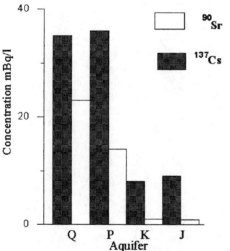

Figure 2. Radionuclides in the groundwater of KUIA in 1995.
Q - Quaternary; P - Palaeogene; K - Cretaceous; J - Jurassic

Table 2. Range of K_d values for soils and rocks of the area under study.

Techniques	^{137}Cs		^{90}Sr		Reference
	from	to	from	to	
"Batch"	626	7000	8.4	73	Shehtman et al 1996
In situ observation	5	293	1.1	32	Goudzenko Borodavko, 1996
In situ observation	-	-	0.5	2.0	Dzhepo et al. 1995

143

The wide range of retardation properties of ^{137}Cs and ^{90}Sr allow the use of R_f values, obtained by the observation of the behavior of these nuclides in the environment, for the most realistic groundwater contamination forecasts: strontium data for the conservative scenario and caesium data for the immobile pollutants. In reality the ^{90}Sr velocity in the unsaturated zone at times is about that for Tritium. "Break through" of the strontium spikes has been observed on some indicator sites around the ChNPP (Goudzenko & Borodavko 1996).

4 CONCLUSIONS

1. Ten years after the Chernobyl disaster, and about 40 years after the maximum of atmospheric nuclear weapon testing, ^{137}Cs and ^{90}Sr are determined in the groundwaters and rocks of the different aquifers at depths of more than 100 m in the areas with diverse surface contamination.

2. Side by side with the man-made pathways, such as the weak zones around the water wells, me geological medium has zones of increased permeability, where infiltration is signifilcantly higher man average.

3. A small portion of the radionuclides or other surface pollutants migrates in negative or neutral chemical forms, with practically no interaction with water bearing rocks.

4. The high sensitivity of radionuclide determination and their wide spread use due to the nuclear industry operation, make them outstanding tracers of mass transfer in the environment. Retardation charactenstics, obtained by direct field observabon of ^{137}Cs and ^{90}Sr migration for the specfic region, seem to be the most useful, taking into account artiflcial (depression cones, for example) as well as natural disturbances of the environment.

5. A wide range of retardation characteristics for both nuclides make them a suitable tool for predicting the behaviour of other pollutants whose characteristics lay between that of Cs and Sr.

REFERENCES

Dzhepo, S.P., A.S. Skal'skij, D.A. Bugaj, V.V. Goudzenko, S.A. Mogilny & N.l. Proskura 1995. Field characterization of radionuclide migration to groundwater at the "Red Forest" radioactive waste disposal site. In *Problems of the Chernobyl Exclusion Zone:* Naukova Dumka Publishing House, 2:77-83, (in Russian).

Goudzenko, V.V. 1993. Radiocaesium in the underground water of Kiev. *Journal of Ecological Chemistry* 4: 229-233.

Goudzenko, V.V.& I.V.Borodavko, 1996. Some results of tracers movement in the aeration zone. In *Proc. "Chernobyl-94" Int. Conf.*, 7:93-96. (in Russian).

Shehtman, L.M., V.T. Baranov, G.F.Nesterenko, E.A.Kishinskaja, V.M.Chernaja, & E.A.Yakovlev 1996. Geological media resisting possibility assay for the "Vector" facility site in the 30-km zone around the ChNPP. In *Problems of the Chernobyl: Exclusion Zone*: Naukova Dumka Publishing House, Kyiv,3: 134-145. (in Russian).

Shestopalov, V.M. (Chicf editor). 1991. *Water exchange in the hydrogeological strucfures of Ihe Ukraine. Water exchange under disturbed conditions.* Kyiv: Naukova dumka (in Russian).

Groundwater in the Urban Environment: Problems, Processes and Management, Chilton et al. (eds)
© *1997 Balkema, Rotterdam, ISBN 90 5410 837 1*

Study of the dynamic nature of the groundwater flow system in a basaltic aquifer, Mauritius

M.D.Nowbuth & A.Chan Chim Yuk
Civil Engineering Department, University of Mauritius, Reduit, Mauritius
A.Butler
Department of Civil Engineering, Imperial College of Science, Technology and Medicine, London, UK

ABSTRACT: Mauritius is a volcanic basaltic oceanic island having a highly heterogeneous hydrogeological structure. A conceptual groundwater flow model developed for the northern aquifer of the island, based on the concept of hydrostatigraphic units, indicated that localised regions of highly heterogeneous properties have major influence on the general groundwater flow pattern. A three dimensional picture of the aquifer on a regional basis does not highlight these localised heterogeneity. Detailed localised studies are needed to characterise the degree of influence of these features on the regional groundwater flow of this area.

1 INTRODUCTION

The island of Mauritius is situated in the Indian Ocean, between latitudes 19°59' S and 20°32'S, and between longitudes 57°18'E and 57°47'E, at a distance of 2000 km to the East of Africa (Figure 1). It was formed during two major volcanic activity periods, commencing some ten million years ago.

The first and hence older volcanic series emitted thick compact lava flows and these are acting as a hydraulic basement to the aquifers. The latest lava flows are thinner and much more permeable, forming the aquifers of the island. Groundwater resources are increasingly being exploited to supplement surface water, in order to meet the water demand. Over the last ten years, groundwater contribution to domestic water supply has increased from 20% to 50%. However, since the aquifers are coastal in nature such a practice can lead to salt water intrusion in the long run. Past studies (CWA 1990), reported that the groundwater basins can be further exploited but due to the heterogeneity of the aquifers, detailed studies of individual groundwater flow systems are required. Of the four main groundwater basins of the island, the Northern Plains Aquifer is the one most sensitive to salt water intrusion (FAO 1972). A conceptual model of this aquifer has been developed by integrating hydrogeological and meteorological data.

2 THE NORTHERN PLAINS AQUIFER

The Northern Plains Aquifer (Figure 2), covers a surface area of around 193 km². The boundaries of this basin were defined by Sentenac (1963) through electrical resistivity surveys. The aquifer was formed during the latest volcanic activities and is characterised by highly vesicular and fractured lava. However, the erratic emissions of lava, ashes and

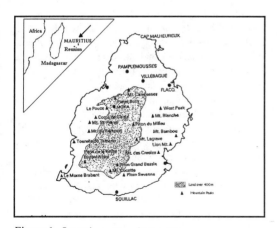

Figure 1. Location map of Mauritius.

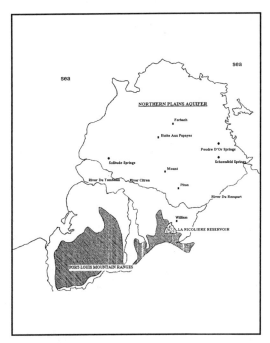

Figure 2. Boundaries of the Northern Plains Aquifer.

and the main groundwater flow controlling features highlighted.

3.1 Direction of Groundwater Flow

Depths to groundwater levels are measured once every month at thirty boreholes located randomly over the study area. At several boreholes the depths to groundwater during the wet season vary significantly from those during the dry season. So as to illustrate the general groundwater flow pattern over the study area, isopotential lines were drawn based upon mean hydraulic head values, using data over the past ten years (Figure 3).

The pattern of isopotential lines indicated clearly that groundwater flowed in the North East and North West directions mostly, and there was very little tendency for the flow to take place directly northwards (Figure 3). Core analysis and literature review on the geological studies over the island (Huntings 1973), revealed the presence of a volcanic vent, Butte Aux Papayes, which was extruded during the early stage of the late volcanic activity period. The lava emitted by this volcano was relatively much less permeable; these lava flows thus acted as a geological barrier, preventing groundwater flow directly northwards, and consequently isolating the northern tip of the basin. Negative hydraulic heads (these being calculated with respect to mean sea level), had been noted within this region, thus confirming the deduction.

Another interesting feature highlighted by the isopotential lines was the location of the recharge zone around la Nicoliere Reservoir, (Figure 3). This reservoir is located within the regions receiving highest rainfall annually, 2500mm on average, as compared to 1500mm annual average for the entire study area. However, apart from the rainfall pattern, it was also suspected that the reservoir itself might be in hydraulic contact with the groundwater basin, but this needed further investigation.

Hydraulic gradients in general fell under the range of 2 - 3%, though values around 5% were also obtained at a few locations. These steep hydraulic gradients were in most cases due to significant changes in base elevation over small distances. These values gave an indication of the rate of flow through the groundwater system and consequently towards the sea. This observation emphasised the volume of water that was being lost to the sea and that could be used more effectively.

pyroclastics, together with varying degree of weathering, rendered the subsurface media highly heterogeneous. Flow of groundwater through this subsurface is controlled by preferential pathways and exploitation of this resource is very complex. Because of its highly permeable geology, the study area has a poor hydrometric network and consequently surface water resources only cannot meet water demand. Thus, around 90% of the domestic water supply comes from groundwater resources (Gujjallu 1989). Further exploitation of groundwater can lead to salt water intrusion in some zones, owing to the highly permeable geology. The present study describes how a conceptual model was developed and emphasised the importance of such a model to providing sound basis for groundwater management options.

3 CONCEPTUALISATION OF THE NORTHERN PLAINS AQUIFER

Effective groundwater management plans are possible only through a clear understanding of the response of the groundwater basin to recharge and discharge mechanisms. Hydrogeological and meteorological data have been integrally analysed

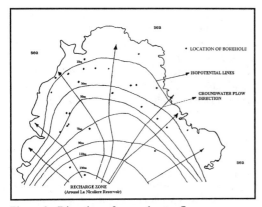

Figure 3. Direction of groundwater flow.

3.2 Dynamism of the Groundwater System

Here, the aim was to understand the rate at which the groundwater system responded to rainfall events. Plots of borehole hydrographs were analysed with respect to rainfall events. The response of the groundwater basin to rainfall events, reflected in the borehole hydrographs, varied with location. A distinct pattern was clearly observed; hydrographs of boreholes located inland exhibited highly fluctuating patterns whereas those located near the coast were rather dampened, in that they showed no response to rainfall events. Hydrographs of boreholes nearer to the coast could be under the influence of the sea level which would explain why no response was noted.

Comparison of the plots of borehole hydrographs also highlighted another interesting feature; several boreholes located near the coast had highly fluctuating hydrographs compared to the other nearby boreholes. This observation could be explained by the presence of preferred pathways in the form of connecting channels from recharge zones to drier regions. Nearby irrigation practices could also have influenced the hydrographs, but this would not have applied to specific boreholes.

3.3 Hydrostratigraphic Subunits

Around fifty core logs available over the study area were used to define hydrostratigraphic subunits in this section. Corelog details had been described with respect to physical properties and plots of these details revealed the degree of heterogeneity of the subsurface basin, such as: the successive lava layers, erratic emissions of pyroclastics, varying degree of weathering and varying types of weathering

products. Thus stratigraphic correlation of nearby corelogs was not an easy task.

The concept of hydrostratigraphic subunits were then introduced to picture the groundwater flow system in three dimensions. Anderson and Woessner (1992) reported that regional aquifer system analysis was rendered more practical by the implementation of hydrostratigraphic subunits. The principles behind the definition of such units are simple and logical (Mercer 1964); however, because of the extremely varying physical nature of hydrostratigraphic units it would not be realistic to comply with international standard guidelines for defining hydrostratigraphic subunits (Seaber 1988). Nevertheless, based upon the principles governing the water bearing and water transmitting properties of subsurface media, a set of hydrostratigraphic subunits were defined. For example, zones having the following properties: grey compact basalt, completely weathered rock to clay size particles, fractured basalt with tight joints, vesicular basalt with completely filled vesicles and tuff; were considered under the same hydrostratigraphic subunit, having a hydraulic conductivity of 10^{-9} m/s.

The core logs were then reinterpreted, this time based upon the concept of hydrostratigraphic subunits. Elevation of potential aquifer zones were noted and these were plotted on a location map at varying elevation intervals. For example, at elevation of 300 meters, if only 2 corelogs had potential aquifer zones, then these two coreholes were plotted on an x/y axis, where x and y are the eastings and northings respectively. A series of layers representing varying elevations were thus produced, starting at lowest elevation -110 meters going up to 310 meters. Superposition of these layers, then revealed the three dimensional nature of the potential aquifer (Figure 4). In the region around La Nicoliere Reservoir, the aquifer is smaller in areal extent and is of smaller depth. The depth increased significantly further from the Reservoir in the middle of the area and then decreased as it reached the coastal zone. A fairly steep change in base elevation was noted moving from the inland regions towards the coastal one.

The simplest representation of the aquifer (Figure 4) would be described as a highly potential aquifer zone sandwiched between a relatively less permeable layer above it and a highly impermeable layer below it. If the layers were produced based on a small elevation interval, 5m, then a different picture of the three dimensional nature of the aquifer system would have been obtained. However, before going into the

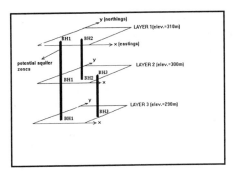

Figure 4. Location of Potential Aquifer Zones.

complexity of a subsurface system, a simpler geological model is always helpful.

4 DISCUSSIONS & CONCLUSIONS

The hydrogeological study has revealed several interesting features characterising the groundwater basin. Firstly, a small part found at the northern tip of the area was seen to be completely isolated from the entire groundwater basin. As average annual rainfall is relatively very low in this zone, locating a pumping station within this zone would induce salt water intrusion; specially that this being a zone already highly sensitive to salt water intrusion owing to its relatively permeable geology.

Another important feature noted was the influence of La Nicoliere Reservoir on the groundwater basin. The recharge zone around this reservoir would imply a strong hydraulic connection with the groundwater system. Thus, any major change to this reservoir, either by increasing the capacity or by reducing the inflow into it, would have a very significant impact on the groundwater flow.

The rate of groundwater being lost to the sea was noted to be high, an observation inviting further groundwater exploitation. The three dimensional nature of the aquifer indicated that residential areas were located within that potential aquifer zones. Any further groundwater exploitation would increase the rate at which polluting sources migrated towards the groundwater basin.

A two-month time lag to rainfall events, does indicate a very dynamic surface/subsurface interaction. Therefore, this observation puts emphasis on the location of polluting activities over the study area, these should be located away from recharge zones.

Though at this stage fairly important information has been obtained through this study, site specific studies would be required in order to devise groundwater management plans at a particular location. The heterogeneous nature of the study area might exhibit a different groundwater flow pattern on a small area, as compared to the regional study.

REFERENCES

Anderson, M. P. & W. W. Woessner 1992. *Applied groundwater modeling: simulation of flow and advective transport*. London: Academic Press.

Central Water Authority 1990. *Updating of Master Plan for Water Resources, Conclusions and Recommendations*. Government of Mauritius: Ministry of Energy, Water Resources and Postal Services.

FAO 1972. *Land and Water Resources Survey, Volume 4, Geology and Hydrogeology*. . The Government of Mauritius: United Nations Development.

Gujallu, S. 1989. *Water Supply in Mauritius*. Unpublished report submitted to the Central Water Authority.

Huntings Technical Services Ltd & Sir M. MacDonald & Partners 1973. *Northern Plains irrigation feasibility study - Supporting Report 1, Engineering and Hydrology*. The Government of Mauritius: The Overseas Development Administration.

Maxey, G. B. 1964. Hydrostratigraphic units. *Journal of Hydrology*, 2: 124-129.

Seaber, P. R. 1988. Hydrostratigraphic Units. *The Geology of North America*. Volume O-2.

Sentenac, R. 1963. *Recherches D'Eau Souterraine a l'Ile Maurice*. Mauritius Sugar Industry Research Institute. Occasional Paper No. 12 Volume 1.

Finite element simulation of isothermal multiphase flow and pollutant transport in deforming porous media

Norhan Abd. Rahman & Roland W. Lewis
Department of Civil Engineering, University of Wales, Swansea, UK

ABSTRACT: The simulation of groundwater contamination by nonaqueous phase liquids (NAPLs), such as organic solvents and petroleum hydrocarbons, requires a solution of the multiphase flow equations in a deforming porous medium. A numerical model is developed that describes the multiphase fluid flow through soil: namely gas, water and nonaqueous phase liquid. Also, the contaminant can exist within the gas and water phases. The governing partial differential equations, in terms of soil displacements, fluid pressures and concentrations are coupled and behave non-linearly and can be solved by the finite element method. In order to apply the finite element model to a specific problem a number of parameters must be evaluated. These include relative permeabilities, saturation-pressure relations, mass transfer coefficients and densities. As a demonstration of the model's applicability, the migration of a contaminant in a soil column is simulated.

1 INTRODUCTION

Spill and leaks of organic chemicals within the environment have resulted in widespread contamination of subsurface systems. Many of these pollutants are slightly water soluble and highly volatile fluids and thus may exist as nonaqueous phase liquids (NAPLs). In the unsaturated zone, residual NAPL, as well as NAPL dissolved in the water phase, may also volatilize into the soil gas phase. The remaining nonaqueous phase liquids may persist for long periods of time, slowly dissolving into the groundwater and moving in the water phase through advection and dispersion.

Within the last decade, several numerical models have been developed in order to study the movement of organic pollutants in subsurface systems. The multiphase flow and transport models of Abriola & Pinder (1985), Forsyth (1988), Kaluarachchi & Parker (1990), Sleep & Sykes (1993) and Zhan (1995) all assumed interphase equilibrium for NAPL-aqueous phase mass exchange. Other models have been developed especially to simulate volatile organics, but only at the cost of other limitations, such as Sleep & Sykes (1989), Falta et al. (1989) and Dorgaten & Tsang (1992). While these codes have found fairly wide application in simulating NAPL transport in shallow systems, these simulators were developed for use in isothermal problems and do not consider the

deformation problem. A fully coupled model for water flow and airflow incorporate pollutant transport in deformable porous media has been studied by Schrefler (1995) which does not consider interphase mass transfer in the simulation model.

The main objective of this study is to develop a model that describes the flow of multiphase fluids in a deforming porous medium in partially water-saturated soils. The flow of all multiphase fluids, as well as the water and gas phase transport, are included. Interphase mass transfer is taken into account by means of kinetic formulations for dissolution, volatilization and gas-water partitioning. The governing equations which describe the displacement of soil, multiphase fluid pressures and pollutant transport are coupled and the resulting non-linear partial differential equations are solved by the finite element method. Nonlinear saturation and relative permeability functions are incorporated into a Galerkin finite element model that is used to simulate the vertical infiltration of fluids in partially water-saturated porous media.

2 PHYSICAL MODEL

In order to describe mathematically the flow of immiscible fluids through a porous medium, it is necessary to determine functional expressions that best define the relationship between the hydraulic properties of the porous medium, i.e., saturation, relative permeability and capillary pressure. The distribution of zones as a function of capillary pressures are defined as follows;

I. water only$[P_{cgw} \leq P_{dgw}, \quad P_{cnw} \leq P_{dnw}]$

$$S_w = 1.0$$

II. water & gas$[P_{cgw} > P_{dgw}]$

$$S_w = S_{max}\left[\frac{P_{dgw}}{P_{cgw}}\right]^\lambda + S_{rw} \quad S_g = 1 - S_w$$

III. water & NAPL$[P_{cnw} > P_{dnw}, \quad P_{cgn} \leq P_{dgn}]$

$$S_w = S_{max}\left[\frac{P_{dnw}}{P_{cnw}}\right]^\lambda + S_{rw} \quad S_n = 1 - S_w$$

where,

$$S_{max} = 1 - S_{rw} - S_{rn} - S_{rg}$$

where, water(w), gas(g), NAPL(n), P_{cgw} is the capillary pressure between the gas and water phases, P_{cnw} is the capillary pressure between the NAPL and water phases, P_{cgn} is the capillary pressure between the gas and NAPL phases, P_{dgw} is the displacement pressure for a gas and water system, P_{dnw} is the displacement pressure for a NAPL and water system, P_{dgn} is the displacement pressure for a gas and NAPL system, S is the phase saturation, S_r is the residual saturation and λ is the pore size distribution index. The relative permeabilities for the water, k_{rw} and gas, k_{rg} phases are calculated from capillary pressure values using the Brooks & Corey (1964) equations and relative permeability for NAPL, k_{rn} based on Lujan (1985), i.e

$$k_{rw} = S_{we}^{\frac{(2+3\lambda)}{\lambda}} \tag{1}$$

$$k_{rg} = (1 - S_{te})^2(1 - S_{te}^{\frac{(2+\lambda)}{\lambda}}) \tag{2}$$

$$k_{rn} = (S_{te} - S_{we})^2(S_{te}^{\frac{(2+\lambda)}{\lambda}} - S_{we}^{\frac{(2+\lambda)}{\lambda}}) \tag{3}$$

which,

$$S_{we} = \left(\frac{S_w - S_{rw}}{S_{max}}\right), \quad S_{te} = \left(\frac{1 - S_g - S_{rw} - S_{rn}}{S_{max}}\right)$$

where S_{we} is the effective water saturation and S_{te} is the total effective liquid saturation. In addition to the above constitutive relations, the equations of state are needed to determine the fluid densities as functions of pressures. These equations are given as follows

$$\rho_w = \rho_{wo}[1 - \beta_w(T - T_o) + 1/K_w(P_w - P_{wo})] \tag{4}$$

$$\rho_n = \rho_{no}[1 - \beta_n(T - T_o) + 1/K_n(P_n - P_{no})] \tag{5}$$

$$\rho_g = \rho_{go}P_gT_o/(P_{go}T) \tag{6}$$

where the subscript zero indicates an initial steady state, β is the thermal expansion coefficient of fluid phase, ρ is the fluid density, P is the fluid pressure, K_w is the bulk modulus of the water phase, K_n is the bulk modulus of the NAPL phase and T is the absolute temperature.

For low-solubility organic contaminants, a proper description of water and gas phase transport requires the consideration of interphase mass transfer. Dissolution and volatilization of the NAPL phase are responsible for the input of the pollutants into the groundwater and soil gas, and gas-water partitioning can significantly affect transport within these phases (Dorgaten & Tsang 1992). In a kinetic formulation, the dissolution rate is controlled by C_{wm} which is the equilibrium concentration of the organic matter in the water phase, C_w is the concentration of organic matter in the water phase and is controlled by a rate coefficient κ_{nw}, where

$$\frac{\partial C_w}{\partial t} = \kappa_{nw}(C_{wm} - C_w) \tag{7}$$

Volatilization is of the same importance for the gas phase as dissolution is for the water phase. According to the physical similarity, its mathematical formulation is similar to equation (7), with gas phase instead of water phase parameters, i.e

$$\frac{\partial C_g}{\partial t} = \kappa_{ng}(C_{gm} - C_g) \tag{8}$$

where C_{gm} is the equilibrium concentration in the vapour phase, C_g is the concentration of organic constituent in the gas phase and κ_{ng} is the mass transfer coefficient for volatilization of organic compounds in the vapour phase.

Interphase mass transfer by dissolution and volatilization will generally be the dominating phase exchange in regions where a significant amount of the NAPL phase is present. In other regions, in contrast, the mass transfer between the water and gas phases is important. Gas-water partitioning is mainly controlled by Henry's Law a constant value of H that expresses the relation between C_g and C_w at equilibrium. Again, the transfer rate is represented by a kinetic formulation, which may be written as

$$\frac{\partial C_g}{\partial t} = \kappa_{wg}(HC_w - C_g) \tag{9}$$

where, $H = C_{gm}/C_{wm}$ and κ_{wg} is the mass transfer coefficient for gas-liquid partitioning between the water and gas phases.

3 MATHEMATICAL MODEL

A general equilibrium equation requires both the effective stress relationship and a constitutive law which relates the effective stress to the strains of the solid skeleton. The effective stress relationship is given by

$$\sigma = \sigma' - mP \tag{10}$$

where σ' is the effective stress and m $[1\ 1\ 0]^T$ is equal to unity for normal stress components. The equilibrium equation for the soil phase, relating the total stress to the body forces and boundary tractions is derived using the principle of virtual work.

$$\int_\Omega \delta\varepsilon^T d\sigma d\Omega - \int_\Omega \delta u^T db d\Omega - \int_\Gamma \delta u^T d\hat{t} d\Gamma = 0 \tag{11}$$

where ε represents the total strain of the soil skeleton and u means displacement. Incorporating the concept of effective stress and the constitutive relationship into the equilibrium equation, and dividing by dt, the final general equation is given as

$$\int_\Omega \delta\varepsilon^T D_T \frac{\partial\varepsilon}{\partial t} d\Omega - \int_\Omega \delta\varepsilon^T m \frac{\partial\overline{p}}{\partial t} d\Omega - \int_\Omega \delta\varepsilon^T c d\Omega$$

$$+ \int_\Omega \delta\varepsilon^T D_T m \frac{\partial\overline{p}}{\partial t} \frac{1}{3K_s} d\Omega - \int_\Omega \delta\varepsilon^T \frac{\partial\varepsilon_o}{\partial t} d\Omega$$

$$- \int_\Omega \delta u^T \frac{\partial b}{\partial t} d\Omega - \int_\Gamma \delta u^T \frac{\partial\hat{t}}{\partial t} d\Gamma = 0 \tag{12}$$

where K_s, $\hat{t}$, b, c and D_T are the bulk modulus of the solid skeleton, boundary traction factor, body force vector, creep function and tangent matrix respectively. In all examples, a linear elastic material behaviour is assumed for the soil deformation. In this paper, the effective average pore pressure, $\overline{p}$, is calculated from

$$\frac{\partial\overline{p}}{\partial t} = S_n \frac{\partial P_n}{\partial t} + P_n \frac{\partial S_n}{\partial t} + S_w \frac{\partial P_w}{\partial t} + P_w \frac{\partial S_w}{\partial t}$$

$$+ S_g \frac{\partial P_g}{\partial t} + P_g \frac{\partial S_g}{\partial t} \tag{13}$$

The system of three nonlinear partial differential equations is also time dependent because of the term $\frac{\partial S_\alpha}{\partial t}$. In order to solve the system we need to rewrite this term as a function of pressure. Using the chain rule,

$$\frac{\partial S_\alpha(P_{cnw}, P_{cgw})}{\partial t} = \frac{dS_\alpha}{dP_{cnw}} \frac{\partial P_{cnw}}{\partial t} + \frac{dS_\alpha}{dP_{cgw}} \frac{\partial P_{cgw}}{\partial t} \tag{14}$$

Finally, we have

$$\frac{\partial\overline{p}}{\partial t} = [S_n + P_n \frac{dS_n}{dP_{cnw}} + P_w \frac{dS_w}{dP_{cnw}} + P_g \frac{dS_g}{dP_{cnw}}] \frac{\partial P_n}{\partial t}$$

$$+ [S_g + P_n \frac{dS_n}{dP_{cgw}} + P_w \frac{dS_w}{dP_{cgw}} + P_g \frac{dS_g}{dP_{cgw}}] \frac{\partial P_g}{\partial t}$$

$$+ [S_w - P_n (\frac{dS_n}{dP_{cnw}} + \frac{dS_n}{dP_{cgw}}) - P_w (\frac{dS_w}{dP_{cnw}}$$

$$+ \frac{dS_w}{dP_{cgw}}) - P_g (\frac{dS_g}{dP_{cnw}} + \frac{dS_g}{dP_{cgw}})] \frac{\partial P_w}{\partial t} \tag{15}$$

The fluid phase behaviour has been described by Lewis and Schrefler (1987). The equation governing the behaviour of incompressible and multi-phase fluids flowing in a deforming porous medium can be obtained by combining Darcy's linear flow law with a mass conservation balance for each of the flowing phases. Incorporating the formation volume factor, B, and the relative permeability, into the continuity equations for each fluid phase α [i.e water, gas, NAPL], gives

$$\nabla\left[K \frac{k_{r\alpha}(S_\alpha)\rho_\alpha}{\mu_\alpha B_\alpha(P_\alpha)} \nabla(P_\alpha + \rho_\alpha gh)\right] = \Omega \tag{16}$$

In this formulation, K is the absolute permeability matrix of the medium, μ is the dynamic viscosity of the fluid, g is the gravitational constant, Ω is the rate of fluid accumulation and h is the head above a datum. On taking into account several factors which contribute to the rate of fluid accumulation, the general form of the continuity equation for each flowing phase may be expressed as follows:

$$-\nabla^T\left[\frac{Kk_{r\alpha}\rho_\alpha}{\mu_\alpha B_\alpha} \nabla(P_\alpha + \rho_\alpha gh)\right] + \phi\frac{\partial}{\partial t}\left(\frac{\rho_\alpha S_\alpha}{B_\alpha}\right)$$

$$+\rho_\alpha\frac{S_\alpha}{B_\alpha}\left[\left(m^T - \frac{m^T D_T}{3K_s}\right)\frac{\partial\varepsilon}{\partial t} + \frac{m^T D_T c}{3K_s}\right.$$

$$+ \left.\left(\frac{1-\phi}{K_s} - \frac{m^T D_T m}{3K_s^2}\right)\frac{\partial\overline{p}}{\partial t}\right] + \rho_\alpha Q_\alpha + \Gamma_\alpha = 0 \tag{17}$$

where ϕ is the porosity, Q represents external sinks and sources, while Γ represents internal sinks and sources due to interphase mass transfer. Equation (17) represents the general governing equations for multiphase incompressible fluid flow with interphase mass transfer and isotropic soil in a deforming porous medium. The mobility terms in this equation are strongly dependent on the unknowns, for example, the relative permeabilities depend on the fluid saturations. The governing equation for multiphase transport may be obtained

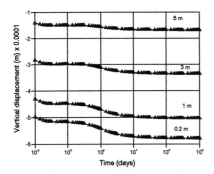

Figure 1: Profile of vertical displacement vs time (solid line-present code, triangle-Schrefler et al.).

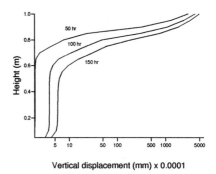

Figure 2: Profile of vertical displacement throughout soil column.

by incorporating the combined mass flux equation into the continuity equation for mass transport,

$$\frac{\partial}{\partial t}(\phi S_\theta C_\theta) + \nabla.(V_\theta C_\theta) - \nabla.(\phi S_\theta D_\theta \nabla C_\theta)$$
$$+ \overline{C}_\theta Q_\theta + \Gamma_\theta = 0 \qquad (18)$$

where θ denotes phase (water/gas), V is the Darcy velocity, D is the tensor of hydrodynamic dispersion, $\overline{C}$ is the concentration of sink/source flux Q and all other parameters have been defined previously. To solve the governing equations for the unknown u, P_w, P_g, P_n, C_w and C_g a knowledge of the constitutive parameters of the initial conditions and of the boundary conditions is required. The initial conditions within the porous medium are specified as,

$$u_i = u_i^o, \qquad P_\alpha = P_\alpha^o, \qquad C_\theta = C_\theta^o$$

The boundary conditions are specified as either prescribed values or fluxes,

$$u = u^b, \qquad P_\alpha = P_\alpha^b, \qquad C_\theta = C_\theta^b$$

$$q_\theta = -\frac{K k_{r\theta} \rho_\theta}{\mu_\theta} \nabla (P_\theta + \rho_\theta g h) n$$

where b_i is the body force, q is the flux, o represents the initial conditions and n is the vector normal to the boundary.

4 FINITE ELEMENT MODEL

The finite element discretization of the equilibrium, flow and pollutant transport equations may now be expressed in terms of the nodal displacements, u, nodal fluid pressures and concentrations, i.e. P_n, P_w, P_g, C_w and C_g by using the Galerkin method. Nine-noded quadrilateral elements and the respective associated shape function are used (Schrefler 1995). The unknowns are related to their nodal values by the following expressions:

$$p = N^T P, \qquad \varepsilon = BU, \qquad u = N^T U \qquad (19)$$

where N and B are the shape function and linear operators, respectively. The equations developed in Section 3 may be more concisely written as

$$A\overline{x} + Bx = F \qquad (20)$$

where $x = [u, P_w, P_g, P_n, C_w, C_g]$ and the matrices A, B and F are obtained by inspection. Equation (20) forms a coupled, nonsymmetric and nonlinear system of ordinary differential equations in time and is solved by an implicit scheme with the time weighting parameter set to one. The integration of the coupling terms A_{ij} and B_{ij} requires the use of a numerical technique. Here however, a two-dimensional Simpson rule integration method is employed, involving 9 integration points.

The coupling terms are evaluated for each element using this numerical technique, and then assembled into the global matrix. The format in the elemental matrices and the global matrix differs in the ordering of unknown variables. Thus it is necessary to transform the coupling terms from the elemental matrices to the global matrix, when assembling the global matrix. Once the global matrix has been fully assembled, the partial differential equations have been transformed into first order ordinary differential equations. A linear variation of the unknown variables in time is assumed to approximate the first order time derivatives. The generalised mid-point method is employed to discretize the time derivatives which yields the recurrence scheme,

$$(A + \theta \Delta t B)x_{n+1} = [A - (1 - \theta)\Delta t B]x_n + \Delta t F \quad (21)$$

where Δt is the time step length, x_{n+1} and x_n are state vectors at time instants t_{n+1} and t_n and θ is a time weighting parameter, usually $0 \leq \theta \leq 1$. The matrices are evaluated at the time level $n + \theta$. Because of the nonlinearities involved a solution

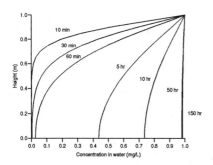

Figure 3: Profile of C_w with no interphase mass transfer.

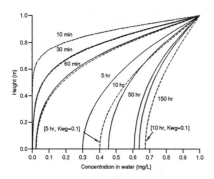

Figure 4: Profile of C_w with interphase mass transfer $\kappa_{nw} = \kappa_{ng} = \kappa_{wg} = 0.1\ hour^{-1}$ (solid line) and $\kappa_{wg} = 0.1\ hour^{-1}$ (dotted line).

scheme of the fixed point type is used within every time step. The convergence criteria implemented is based on the maximum change in the unknown variables between time steps.

5 NUMERICAL EXAMPLES

For the purpose of verification of the immiscible phase, the code was validated assuming partially saturated conditions based on a study by Schrefler et al. (1995). A column of 7 m height and 2 m width of a linear elastic material with Young Modulus, E=6 MPa and Poisson ratio, v=0.4 was subjected to an external surface load of 1.0 KPa. The top surface is the only drained boundary whilst the rest are assumed to be closed. The initial condition for pressures P_w and P_g depend on the initial saturation profiles. The other data for the porous medium were assumed to be the same as for Schrefler et al.(1995). The results obtained in Figure 1 using the developed code agree well when compared with those presented by Schrefler et al.(1995).

When the nonaqueous phase is immobilized, it is not necessary to write a flow equation for the NAPL phase. Changes in the nonaqueous phase saturation level occur only as a result of volatilization and dissolution. If it is assumed that water and gas phase pressures are independent of pressures in the immobilized NAPL phase then P_{cnw} is not required. The example of a soil column, 1 m in height, simulates the transport of a small amount of pollutant (constant concentration in the water, 1 mg/L) introduced at the top of the soil column, with pore water pressure changes and the initial water saturation is 0.445.

The initial pore water pressure was -280 KPa and the boundary pore water pressure was instantaneously changed to a value of -420 KPa at the surface. The soil column was assumed to be bounded at the lateral and bottom surfaces, preventing any fluid from crossing these boundaries, i.e. q_w and q_g are zero. The parameters for the soil are as follows: E=10 MPa, v=0.2, porosity 0.5, bulk modulus 6 x 10^{13} Pa and density 1800 kg/m^3. Absolute permeability of the medium is 0.55 x 10^{14} m^2, water dispersivity is 2.0 x 10^{-5} m^2/s, gas dispersivity is 1 x 10^{-5} m^2/s and H=0.3. Also, the soil was assumed to be unsaturated and the system assumed to be initially in a state of equilibrium. Thus for this example, the interphase mass transfer coefficients are expressed as;

$$\Gamma_w = -\phi S_w \kappa_{nw}(C_{wm} - C_w) + \phi S_g \kappa_{wg}(HC_w - C_g)$$

$$\Gamma_g = -\phi S_g \kappa_{ng}(C_{gm} - C_g) - \phi S_g \kappa_{wg}(HC_w - C_g)$$

Figure 2 shows the vertical displacement for no interphase mass transfer when infiltration occurs for a deformable soil. Figure 3 shows the pollutant concentration in the water phase throughout the soil column, when the mass transfer coefficient is equal to zero. Figure 4 shows the concentration in the water phase, when the mass transfer coefficient $(\kappa_{nw} = \kappa_{ng} = \kappa_{wg})$ is equal to 0.1 $hour^{-1}$ and $\kappa_{wg} = 0.1\ hour^{-1}$. On comparing the results in Figure 4, the degree of concentration in the water is visibly lower with a mass transfer coefficient after 5 hours because the concentration in the water phase reduces more rapidly as the mass transfer coefficient increases, due to the faster partitioning between the two fluid phases. Also, Figure 4 shows that an interphase mass transfer with $\kappa_{nw} = \kappa_{ng} = \kappa_{wg}$ improved the results compared with only κ_{wg} for decreasing the concentration in the water phase.

Figure 5 show the corresponding concentration profiles in the gas phase. The concentration in the gas increases rapidly and attains an almost equal concentration distribution throughout the soil column after 10 hr, due to the scale of the model. The results indicate that the mass transfer coefficients have significant importance for dissolution,

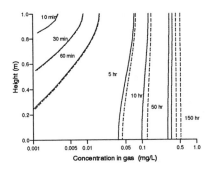

Figure 5: Profile of C_g with interphase mass transfer $\kappa_{nw} = \kappa_{ng} = \kappa_{wg} = 0.1\ hour^{-1}$ (solid line) and $\kappa_{wg} = 0.1\ hour^{-1}$ (dotted line).

volatilization and gas-water partitioning of the immobilized NAPL. Thus, the coupled consideration of interphase mass transfer, water and gas phase transport in conjuction with multiphase flow in deforming porous medium , is necessary for the prediction of subsurface contamination problems.

6 CONCLUSIONS

A general formulation and solution procedure for multiphase flow and pollutant transport in deforming porous material has been presented. Nonlinear saturation and relative permeability functions are incorporated into a Galerkin finite element model. The governing equations, in terms of soil displacements, fluid pressures and concentrations are given in the form of coupled non-linear partial differential equations. After a discussion of the physical processes and their mathematical formulation, the model was applied to study the migration of a contaminant in a soil column and the results show the usefulness of the present model in deforming porous media including the dissolution, volatilization and gas-water partitioning processes.

REFERENCES

Abriola, L.M. & G.F. Pinder 1985. A multiphase approach to the modeling of porous media contamination by organic compounds 1. equation development. *Water Resour. Res.* 21:11-18.

Brooks, R.H. & A.T. Corey 1964. *Hydraulics properties of porous media.* Hydrol. Pap.3, Colo. State Univ., Fort Collins.

Dorgaten, H.W. & C.F. Tsang 1992. Three-phase simulation of organic contaminations in aquifer systems. In K.U.Weyer (ed.), *Proc. Int. Conf. on Subsurface Contamination by Immiscible Fluids*:149-158, Calgary, Canada, Rotterdam: Balkema.

Falta, R.W., I. Javandel, K. Pruess & P.A. Witherspoon 1989. Density-driven flow of gas in the unsaturated zone due to the evaporation of volatile organic compounds. *Water Resour. Res.* 25:2159-2169.

Forsyth, P.A. 1988. Simulation of nonaqueous phase groundwater contamination. *Adv. Water Resour.* 11:74-83.

Kaluarachchi, J.J. & J.C. Parker 1990. Modeling multicomponent organic chemical transport in three-fluid-phase porous media. *J. Contaminant Hydrology* 5:349-374.

Lewis R.W. & B.A. Schrefler 1987. *The finite element method in the deformation and consolidation of porous media.* Chichester: John Wiley.

Lujan, C.A. 1985. Three-phase flow analysis of oil spills in partially water-saturated soils. *Ph.D. thesis,* Dep. of Civ. Eng., Colo. State Univ., Fort Collins.

Schrefler, B.A. 1995. F.E. in environmental engineering: coupled thermo-hydro-mechanical processes in porous media including pollutant transport, *Archive of Computational Methods in Engineering*, 2, 3:1-54.

Schrefler, B.A., X. Zhan & L. Simoni 1995. A coupled model for water flow, airflow and heat flow in deformable porous media. *Int. J. Numer. Methods Heat Fluid Flow* 5:531-547.

Sleep, B.E. & J.F. Sykes 1989. Modeling the transport of volatile organics in variably saturated media. *Water Resour. Res.* 25:81-92.

Sleep, B.E. & J.F. Sykes 1993. Compositional simulation of groundwater contamination by organic compounds. 1, Model development and verification, *Water Resour. Res.* 29:1697-1708.

Zhan, X. 1995. Numerical simulation of two-phase flow and solute transport with interphase exchange in porous media. *Comm. Numerical Methods Eng.* 12:433-444.

Occurrence of groundwater in metropolitan Detroit, Michigan, USA

D.T. Rogers
Clayton Environmental Consultants, Inc., Detroit, Mich., USA

K.S. Murray
The University of Michigan-Dearborn, Mich., USA

ABSTRACT: Metropolitan Detroit (USA) is underlain by unconsolidated sediments of glacial, glacial-lacustrine and fluvial origin. These sediments form a complex series of confined aquifers overlain by an extensive unconfined surficial aquifer. All surface water within metropolitan Detroit originates from this complex system of aquifers. Groundwater within the near-surface unconfined aquifer discharges directly into the Rouge River, the dominant river in the metropolitan area. The Rouge River is a major tributary to the Detroit River, which empties into Lake Erie. Thousands of sites of environmental contamination are located within metropolitan Detroit. The combination of contaminated sites and near-surface groundwater that flows and discharges into the Rouge River creates a significant potential for contamination to eventually migrate to the Great Lakes. The Rouge River is currently identified as an area of concern by the International Joint Commission (IJC) and represents a significant source of pollution to the Great Lakes.

1 INTRODUCTION

Development in metropolitan Detroit has transformed the area into an industrial region with several million residents. As a result, pollution and quality of life have become issues of high priority. In the past 10 years, several thousand sites of environmental contamination have been identified within the region (MDNR 1995). In addition, the dominant river in metropolitan Detroit, the Rouge River, has been identified as an area of concern by the International Joint Commission (IJC) (Hartig and Zarnell 1991) and as a significant source of pollution to the Great Lakes (Murray and Bona 1993).

The study of near-surface aquifers has become increasingly important in evaluating the impact of sites of environmental contamination, especially in urban areas such as metropolitan Detroit. Near-surface aquifers tend to act as pathways for contaminants in groundwater to migrate to sensitive habitats or areas where humans could be exposed to the contaminants.

Historically, near-surface aquifers in the region were not studied because (1) abundant water supplies were available from surface water sources (i.e., Detroit River), (2) near-surface groundwater was not considered potable, (3) reliable sources of groundwater were lacking (Mozola 1954; 1969), and (3) environmental contamination was not a concern. Only recently have near-surface aquifers become the focus of studies to evaluate their significance with respect to contaminant migration and overall environmental impact. This study used geologic and hydrogeologic information obtained from hundreds of sites of environmental contamination in metropolitan Detroit to evaluate urban groundwater in the region.

2 GEOLOGY AND HYDROGEOLOGY

Unconsolidated glacial deposits more than 10,000 years old cover nearly all of Michigan (Farrand 1988). In metropolitan Detroit, they range from 20 to 50 meters thick (Reick 1981). Bedrock consisting of limestones, shales and sandstones of Paleozoic age underlies the unconsolidated glacial deposits (Dorr and Eschman 1988).

These unconsolidated sediments in metropolitan Detroit were historically mapped for identifying potential natural and agricultural resources for future development and exploitation (Sherzer 1913). Historical geologic maps were based primarily on surface observation and did not

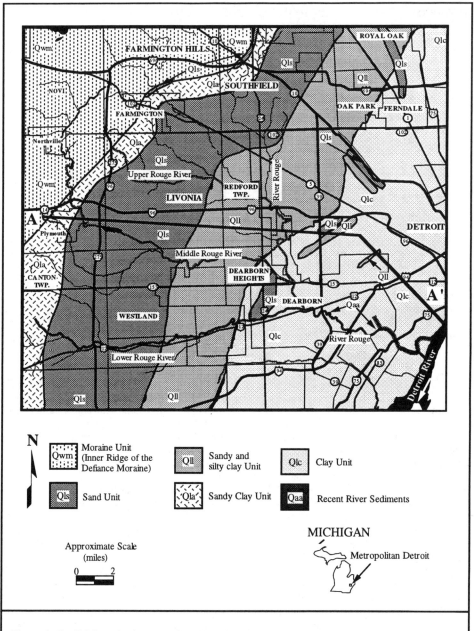

Figure 1. Surficial geologic map of metropolitan Detroit, USA.

address near-surface groundwater. Therefore, historical geologic maps are not adequate for environmental purposes. Therefore, an updated geologic map was compiled that not only used historical information, but also included geologic and hydrogeologic data gathered from over 2,500 investigations conducted at sites of environmental contamination (Rogers 1996a). The updated geologic map has revealed eight distinct geologic units:

1. Moraine Unit (glacial origin)
2. Sandy Clay Unit (glacial-lacustrine origin)
3. Sand Unit (glacial-lacustrine origin)
4. Sandy and Silty Clay Unit (glacial-lacustrine origin)
5. Upper Clay Unit (glacial-lacustrine origin)
6. Recent River Sediments (fluvial origin)
7. Lower Clay Unit (glacial origin)
8. Sand, Gravel and Cobble Unit (fluvial origin)

Figures 1 and 2 show the horizontal and vertical distribution of the geologic units.

2.1 *Moraine Unit*

The Moraine Unit consists of deposits associated with the Defiance Moraine (Inner Ridge). This unit is located along the western edge of metropolitan Detroit where rapid development is occurring. The Moraine Unit consists of sands, silts, gravels, and clays of varying thickness. Glacial erratics are also present within the unit. Subunits identified within the Moraine Unit include (1) kames, (2) eskers, and (3) historical glacial outwash zones. The Moraine Unit is stratigraphically the most complex and the least understood geologic unit within metropolitan Detroit because of the nature of the units' deposition.

Groundwater within the Moraine Unit is confined and unconfined. Multiple saturated zones are present within the unit; these zones range in thickness from less than 1 meter to more than 10 meters. Groundwater is present in layers of sediment that range from fine-grained sand to large cobbles. At some locations, near-surface groundwater (within 7 meters of the ground surface) is present and can be pumped in large volumes at a sustained rate (greater than 100 liters per minute). Groundwater within the Moraine Unit is a significant source of public and domestic potable water.

Recharge of groundwater to aquifers within the Moraine Unit is believed to be from lakes and surface infiltration through kames and historical glacial outwash zones.

2.2 *Sandy Clay Unit*

The Sandy Clay Unit is located east of the Moraine unit. The unit is generally described as a light-brown to gray sandy clay with occasional pebbles. The Sandy Clay Unit ranges from 1 to 5 kilometers wide and is generally less than 2 meters thick. Groundwater within the unit is unconfined, discontinuous, and not present in large volumes that could be pumped at a sustained rate. Groundwater within the Sandy Clay Unit may be hydraulically connected to groundwater within the Sand Unit, especially along the contact between these units. Generally, groundwater within the Sandy Clay Unit flows toward surface water. The Sandy Clay Unit has not been used as a source of potable water because of insufficient yield.

2.3 *Sand Unit*

The Sand Unit is located east of the Sandy Clay Unit and, like the Moraine Unit, it is located in an area of rapid development. The unit is characterized as a moderate yellowish-brown to light-olive-gray, fine- to coarse-grained quartz sand that becomes less coarse with depth. At many locations, the Sand Unit is stratified and has well developed cross-bedding, ripple marks, and scour and fill features. In addition, localized evidence of reworking and eolian deposition are present within the upper portion of the unit (Rogers 1996b). The Sand Unit ranges from 3 to 10 kilometers wide and from 1 to more than 10 meters thick.

Groundwater within the Sand Unit is unconfined. The direction of groundwater flow is generally toward the Rouge River. Groundwater has been observed seeping from the ground and discharging into the river at hundreds of locations (Rogers 1996; Murray 1997). Groundwater within the Sand Unit accounts for as much as 80% of the base flow in the Rouge River (Villar 1995). The saturated thickness of groundwater within the unit ranges from 1 to more than 7 meters.

The degree and nature of urbanization within metropolitan Detroit have affected the rate and direction of groundwater flow within the Sand Unit. Roads, storm sewers, retention basins and ditches constructed within the Sand Unit act as additional points for groundwater to discharge to surface water (e.g., Rouge River). Therefore, the residence time of groundwater within the aquifer has most likely decreased as a result of urbanization.

Groundwater within the Sand Unit is recharged by surface infiltration because the unit is encountered at or near the surface of the ground at most locations. Extraction wells in the unit pump groundwater at rates ranging from 2 to 200 liters per minute. The average yield from the unit ranges from 20 to 40 liters per minute. The Sand Unit has been used as a source of potable water.

2.4 Sandy and Silty Clay Unit and Upper Clay Unit

The Sandy and Silty Clay Unit and Upper Clay Unit are located adjacent to and east of the Sand Unit. They are characterized as a medium to light olive gray, mottled, pebble-bearing, sandy to silty clay or clay. Discontinuous fine-grained sand lenses may also be present within the units especially along their western margin. The width of each unit ranges from 5 to 10 kilometers. The thickness of each unit ranges from 3 to 10 meters.

The presence of groundwater in the clay units is relatively rare. When groundwater is present, it (1) is not present in large quantities, (2) flows toward surface water, and (3) is not used as a source of potable water. Groundwater within these two units most often occurs within sand and silt lenses and/or at the contact with the Lower Clay Unit.

Hairline fractures are present in these units. These fractures are caused by stress changes from wetting and drying cycles and/or freezing and thawing (Freeze and Cherry 1979). The occurrence of the fractures decreases with depth. These fractures and discontinuous sand lenses are the most likely causes of hydraulic conductivities in these units being slightly higher than what would normally be expected (refer to the table).

2.5 Recent River Sediments

Sediments composed of interbedded fine-grained sands, silts, and clays are located immediately along the Rouge River. These sediments may be as thick as 20 meters and may extend as far as 200 meters from the banks of the river. Groundwater has been encountered in these sediments at many locations along the river. Groundwater within these re-worked fluvial sediments is almost certainly hydraulically connected to the Rouge River.

As the population of Detroit grew during the 19th and early 20th century, open dumps and heavy manufacturing facilities were located along the Rouge River. Groundwater migrates through and beneath these sites to the Rouge River, making many of these sites significant sources of metal

and other types of pollution to the river (Murray 1996; 1997).

2.6 Subsurface Geology

Beneath the near-surface units, a thick clay unit of glacial origin (ground moraine) underlies the entire region. This clay unit, called the Lower Clay Unit, ranges in thickness from 16 to 60 meters and is characterized as a medium bluish-gray clay with pebbles and cobbles, and rarely a boulder. The Lower Clay Unit can be differentiated from the Upper Clay Unit by lithology and color.

Groundwater is not present in the Lower Clay Unit at sufficient quantities to be pumped. The hydraulic conductivity of the unit (refer to the table) is nearly uniform horizontally and vertically. The unit is an effective aquiclude because of its thickness, distribution, and low hydraulic conductivity. With the exception of the contact with the near-surface units, fractures have not been observed. This is likely due to the unit being at a sufficient depth beneath the surface to be unaffected by freezing and thawing or wetting and drying cycles.

The Lower Clay Unit has influenced near-surface groundwater discharge on a regional basis. The presence of this unit has essentially prevented groundwater from migrating to lower aquifers. Therefore, groundwater in near-surface aquifers discharges to surface water.

A discontinuous Sand, Gravel, and Cobble Unit is beneath the Lower Clay Unit and overlies bedrock. This unit ranges from 1.5 to 16 meters thick. Groundwater in this unit is confined. Wells installed in this unit have pumped as much as 2,000 liters of water per minute. Groundwater recharge from the Lower Clay Unit is most likely insignificant. Primary sources of recharge are more likely to occur from the Great Lakes or from bedrock aquifers.

3 DISCUSSION

The geologic units that are most sensitive to urbanization and contamination in metropolitan Detroit are the Moraine Unit and the Sand Unit. These units are sensitive because (1) they are composed of highly permeable sediments, (2) they contain large amounts of groundwater, which flows toward and discharges into the Rouge River, (3) they account for the majority of the base flow of the Rouge River, and (4) they are areas of groundwater recharge. The Moraine Unit is especially significant because it is a source of

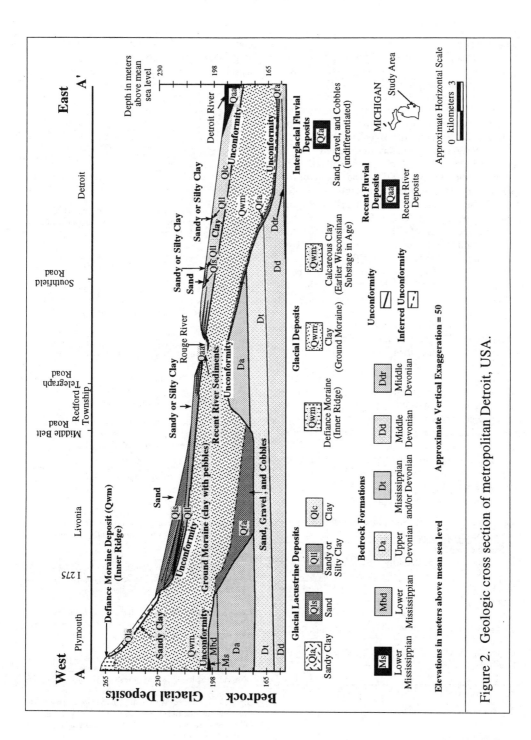

Figure 2. Geologic cross section of metropolitan Detroit, USA.

159

potable water.

This sensitivity has been documented from numerous sites of environmental contamination located within the Sand Unit where volatile organic compound (VOC) and heavy metal contamination has been detected in groundwater (1) near springs located immediately along the river which then enter the river (Rogers 1996a), (2) at locations immediately upgradient of the river, and (3) within the river or river sediment (Murray 1996; MDNR 1995). Data quantifying total contaminant loading from groundwater for VOCs, heavy metals and other types of contaminants to the Rouge River are lacking. However, the results of this study suggest that the Sand Unit most likely accounts for the majority of contaminant loading to the Rouge River.

The Moraine Unit and Sand Unit are both located in area of rapid urban development and occupy approximately 50% of the land surface of metropolitan Detroit.

Because of the Lower Clay Unit, near-surface groundwater in metropolitan Detroit has no migratory outlet other than surface water. This is environmentally significant because (1) contaminated groundwater will eventually discharge into the Rouge River and other surface water bodies if it is not controlled, captured, or biodegraded, and (2) groundwater is a source of pollution in the Rouge River and subsequently the Great Lakes.

The likelihood of encountering groundwater within 3 meters of the ground surface is summarized in the table below.

Table. Occurrence of groundwater within 3 meters of the ground surface.

Geologic Unit	Groundwater Probability	Hydraulic Conductivity (cm/s)*
Moraine Unit	35%	1.0×10^{-5} to $1.0 \times 10^{+1}$
Sandy Clay Unit	14%	1.0×10^{-4}
Sand Unit	97%	1.0×10^{-4} to 1.0×10^{-1}
Sandy and Silty Clay Unit	15%	1.0×10^{-5} to 1.0×10^{-2}
Upper Clay Unit	11%	1.0×10^{-6} to 1.0×10^{-3}
Lower Clay Unit	Nearly Zero	1.0×10^{-8} to 8.3×10^{-8}

*cm/s = centimeters per second

4 CONCLUSION

This study documents the environmental significance of near-surface groundwater in an urban environment. Furthermore, it demonstrates that a comprehensive and thorough understanding of geologic and hydrogeologic processes in urban regions profoundly influences the preservation of natural resources by identifying areas that are geologically sensitive to contamination and urbanization.

REFERENCES

Dorr, John A. & D. Eschman. 1988. *Geology of Michigan*. The University of Michigan Press. Ann Arbor: Michigan.

Farrand, W. R. 1988. *The Glacial Lakes Around Michigan*. Michigan Department of Natural Resources Bulletin No. 4. Lansing, Michigan. 15p.

Freeze, R. A. & J. A. Cherry. 1979. *Groundwater*. Prentice-Hall, Inc. Englewood Cliffs: New Jersey.

Hartig, J. H. & M.A. Zarull. 1991. Methods of Restoring Degraded Areas in the Great Lakes. *Reviews of Environmental Contamination and Toxicology* 117: 127-154.

Michigan Department of Natural Resources. 1995. *Michigan Sites of Environmental Contamination*. Environmental Response Division. Lansing, Michigan.

Mozola, A. J. 1954. *A Survey of the Groundwater Resources in Oakland County, Michigan*. Michigan Geological Survey. Publication 48, Part II. Lansing: Michigan.

Mozola, A. J. 1969. *Geology for Land and Groundwater Development in Wayne County, Michigan*. Michigan Geological Survey. Lansing: Michigan.

Murray, K. 1996. Statistical Comparison of Heavy-Metal Concentrations in River Sediment. *Environmental Geology* 27: 54-58.

Murray, K. A. Farkas, M. Brennan, M. Czach & M. Mayfield. 1997. Analysis of Surface Water Quality: Rouge River, Southeastern, Michigan. *Michigan Academician* 29: No. 2. 152-172.

Murray, J.E. & J.M. Bona. 1993. *Rouge River National Wei Weather Demonstration Project*. Wayne County, Michigan.

Rieck, R. L. 1981. Map. Glacial drift thickness, Southern Peninsula. Plate 15. *Hydrogeologic Atlas of Michigan*. Western Michigan University. Kalamazoo, Michigan.

Rogers, D.T. 1996a. *Environmental Geology of Metropolitan Detroit*. Clayton Environmental Consultants, Inc. Novi: Michigan.

Rogers, D.T. 1996b. The Geology and Depositional History of a Pleistocene Beach Sand in Southeastern, Michigan. *Proc. Michigan Geologic Survey Symposium*. 4-5. Lansing: Michigan.

Villar, L. 1995. *Groundwater, The Main Contributor of Water Recharge on the Lower Branch of the Rouge River*. Unpublished Thesis. The University of Michigan - Dearborn. Dearborn: Michigan.

Groundwater in the Urban Environment: Problems, Processes and Management, Chilton et al. (eds)
© *1997 Balkema, Rotterdam, ISBN 90 5410 837 1*

Ground collapse in an urban environment: A hydrogeological study of leakage from sewage systems

Dietmar Schenk & Ute Peth
Institute for Geoscience, University of Mainz, Germany

ABSTRACT: The study area "Oppenheim" is a town located in the northern part of the Oberrheingraben near Frankfurt a. M. In the oldest part of the town there exists a complex system of cellars, which are connected by a great number of tunnels. The construction of the cellar system originates from the 13th century and was built in a slope area, where the main soil material is loess. At present, leakage out of the urban sewage system, especially at the connection to private households, and uncontrolled access of surface water to the underground leads to water penetration into the cellar systems. Due to this process, suberosion phenomena lead to caverns and cavities and can cause damage to buildings at the surface. The hydrogeological system, a combination between natural and artificial flow systems, is monitored by water/wastewater balances. The origin of the water is to be clarified by its chemical composition. Furthermore, through the observation of the ground water and sewage water flow characteristics, climatic indicators must be found which account for the penetration of water into the cellar system.

1 INTRODUCTION

Oppenheim lies in the northern part of the Oberrheingraben, an active graben, near Frankfurt on the Main. The oldest part of the town originates from the 13th century and was built along a slope with an extension of 0,32 km[2]. The geology consists of Pleistocene loess with an average thickness of 8 m over Oligocene limestones. In the loess, which is a good foundation soil in dry conditions, there exists a widely ramified cellar system connected over three floors. The oldest parts of the cellars were probably built in the 13th century and are of European interest in terms of protection of historical monuments. After a break in a water pipe in 1986, settlement damages occurred in a street and under some buildings. The damage is a consequence of suberosion phenomena in the loess. The uncontrolled water outflow of the broken water pipe produced, in a very short time, caverns in the subsoil with an average diameter of 3 m. Sometimes these caves collapse in a dramatic manner under overlying weight (Fig. 1). The local authorities knew nothing about the problems concerning the subsoil and the cellar system, the latter being also affected by these leakages, and hence did not take any measures with regard to the

urban renewal. As a consequence of the damages an extensive survey programme and remediation process, which also includes a reha-bilitation of the sanitation system, was initiated to protect the citizens of Oppenheim from such harm.

Observations over the last few years have shown that the main reason for subsidence and subsequent settlement were the uncontrolled waterflow in the subsoil. Therefore, the survey programme was

Figure 1. Collapsed cavern after leakage of water pipeline.

expanded to include hydrogeological and hydrochemical studies.

1.1 Geology of the working area

Oppenheim is situated at the boundary between the 'Mainzer Becken', a Tertiary basin, and the western trench fault of the 'Oberrheingraben' (Fig. 2).

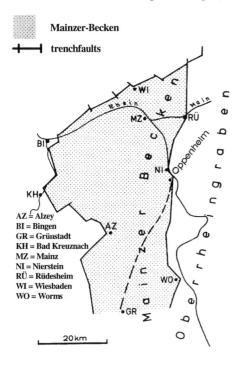

Figure 2. Geographic position of Oppenheim (After Rothausen & Sonne 1984).

The stratigraphic formations of the working area consist of Tertiary sediments of the 'Mainzer-Becken' and the 'Oberrheingraben'. The layers of interest in the oldest part of the town are (from the bottom to the top): green grey micaceous finesands followed by a layer with grey blue argillaceous marls and, lastly, silty fine sandy marls. These sediments, from the middle Oligocene, are summarized in the literature (Rothausen & Sonne 1984) as 'Mergeltertiär'. It is followed by Upper Oligocene to lower Miocene limestones called 'Kalktertiär'. Structural analysis of aerial photographs and satellite images shows that the working area is characterized by a strong tectonic stress. This indicates that the incompetent limestone may demonstrate a high density of fractures. This preliminary result has to be taken into account for the interpretation of the hydraulic conditions in the subsoil.

1.2. Problem definition of the subsoil exploration in Oppenheim

The main problem of the subsoil in Oppenheim is uncontrolled water flow, especially when encountering loess as the soil material. Water causes suberosion phenomena, which expand into unstable caverns. In the case of subsidence the buildings at the surface could suffer strongly. The source of the water can be of different origins: beside natural groundwater, leakages of the sewage system or the drinking water pipes as well as improper input of water from the gutters can be responsible. These are all triggers for the suberosion in association with subsidence. The observer may perceive the following picture. In the cellars inrush of water often happens in combination with initiation of breaks in the walls. Many times the source of water is unknown. Arising from this is the question of how the water source can be revealed. Another problem relates to detection of unnoticed fractures or leakages in the waste-water pipeline, which will lose water in situations such as after a heavy rainfall event.

2 URBAN INFLUENCE OF THE GROUND-WATER

Because of the problems explained above, the hydrogeological and hydrochemical situation in Oppenheim and the near surroundings were studied. The determination of the chemical composition of the groundwater should provide the key parameters, which are characteristic for the source of water.

2.1 Methods

A monitoring network, with 13 groundwater observation wells, is used to determine the chemical proportion of the geogenic input in the town. To record the different water types present, samples were taken at different locations. These include private cellar wells and four screened wells, situated in the oldest part of the town, and, moreover, all accessible spots where water inflow takes place in the cellar system. The results are compared with the geogenic input of the surrounding area to determine the urban influence. Furthermore, the whole sewage system including the private house connections are monitored for damages. Discharge measurements in the sewage system of the town are intended for

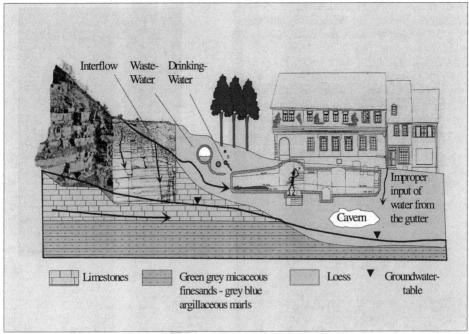

	Limestones		Green grey micaceous finesands - grey blue argillaceous marls		Loess	▼	Groundwater-table

Figure 3. Schematic hydrogeological cross-section.

quantitative aspects, which allow from consideration of the daily water consumption, a better relation between precipitation and discharge. In a GIS (ARC/INFO) the data will be stored and analysed with regard to the geographic features of the area.

2.2 Hydrogeological situation

The hydrogeological conditions in the subsoil of Oppenheim and the surrounding area can be divided into two principal parts: the upper aquifer, which consists of 'Kalktertiär' and the lower aquifer consisting of 'Mergeltertiär'. The upper aquifer is a joined aquifer with a free water table while the deeper aquifer with its sandy layers is a porous aquifer with a confined water table. Pumping tests in the 'Mergeltertär' have yielded low groundwater discharge. For the old town the following structural model can be made (Fig. 3).

With the natural input of seepage water, the water flow follows the hydraulic gradient via interflow, and lower groundwater flow through the oldest part of the town, in the direction of the River Rhine. At the interface of the two aquifers, groundwater flows into the adjacent loess. This is assumed by the observation of free spring discharge in a cellar where the stratigraphic boundary is intersected. Up to this point, where the lower aquifer formation comes in

contact with the loess, the two groundwater horizons do not correspond to each other. Nevertheless a correspondence between them along larger faults cannot be excluded.

2.3 Hydrochemical situation

In the first section of the project the chemical composition of all water types were determined. The following different types of water samples can be distinguished:

- bank-filtration water from the River Rhine
- water in the cellars
- surface water
- samples from the observation wells in the old town
- samples from the screened wells in the surroundings of Oppenheim

The analytical results give the first promising clues for a chemical classification of the different water-types. The distribution of the cations (Fig. 4) shows, for example, an apparent movement from the alkaline earth elements in the surroundings of Oppenheim to the alkali elements in the urban environment. Whether there are any mixing processes or adsorption- desorption mechanisms responsible for differences could not be determined at this point of the project. Nevertheless changes in the chemical composition of the groundwater are remarkable. A similar situation was found for the distribution of the anions (Fig. 5). The sulphate values of the ground-water in the town are lower in comparison with the sulphate values of the surrounding area. The high values of the latter may have a geogenic source (some gypsum and anhydrite layers) which dissolve

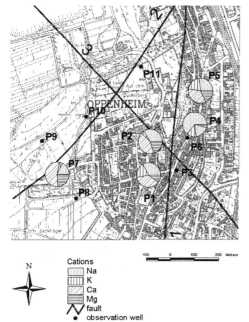

Figure 4. Distribution of cations in water wells in and around Oppenheim.

sulphate after contact with groundwater. This assumption is supported by the absence of any anthropogenic source in the field of study.

3 CONCLUSION

The results of the hydrogeological and hydrochemical studies in Oppenheim provide the first evidence of an urban influence on the chemical composition of the groundwater. With the water characteristics and the genesis of the waters a classification of water types is possible. This gives hints for the source of the water in the cellars. As a result of the initial project, it was determined that the water sources could be identified by chemical classification. When the sources are finally located the council can act to avoid uncontrolled water inflow. In the second phase of the project, a closed

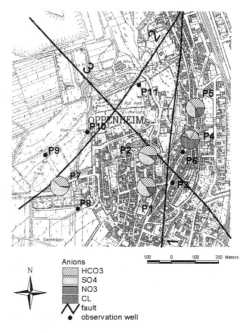

Figure 5. Distribuition of anions in water wells in and around Oppenheim.

water balance is to be achieved. This includes all masses of water flow going into and out of the urban region. A comparison between natural recharge and drinking water delivery on one hand and the amount of sewage water on the other hand will provide a quality control system for the rehabilitation of the sanitation system.

REFERENCES:

Rothausen, K. & V. Sonne 1984. Mainzer Becken. Sammlung geologischer Führer. 79: 203 S. Stuttgart: Gebr. Bornträger.

Modelling groundwater rebound after coalfield closure

Julia M. Sherwood & Paul L. Younger
Department of Civil Engineering, University of Newcastle-upon-Tyne, UK

ABSTRACT: The changes that have taken place in the British Coal Industry over the last five years have meant that in many coalfields the last deep mines have closed. When a coalfield is deep mined it is necessary to pump the groundwater to a low level to allow access to the coal measures. Pyrite in these rocks is thus exposed to air and oxidised. When a coalfield is abandoned and pumping ceases, groundwater is allowed to rise. The iron oxides, sulphates and proton acidity that are the products of the oxidised pyrite are dissolved into solution as the groundwater rises through the coal measures. If this water is allowed to discharge at the surface the iron oxides precipitate as an orange ochre. In addition to ground and surface water pollution other possible impacts are erosion of subsurface infrastructure, methane emissions and leaching from landfills.

Modelling abandoned coalfields is fraught with problems. Standard groundwater modelling software applies Darcian principles which assume simple porous media and laminar flow. An abandoned coalfield is riddled with roadways and collapsed strata. Flow through the roadways is likely to bear more resemblance to turbulent stream flow than laminar groundwater flow. There is also a scarcity of appropriate hydrogeological data. The strata in their present form have not been exposed to water and so accurate estimation of hydrogeological parameters is at least problematic. A lumped parameter model GRAM (Groundwater Rebound in Abandoned Mineworkings) has been developed. This model conceptualises a coalfield as a group of 'ponds'. Each pond is an area of coalfield that has been extensively worked and can be considered as a single hydraulic unit. The ponds are connected by roadways along which flow is assumed to be turbulent. The data requirements for GRAM are modest and its simplicity makes it ideal for Monte Carlo Simulation.

1 INTRODUCTION

Coal extraction was the driving force of the Industrial Revolution. Therefore rising groundwater levels in abandoned coalfields can be seen as a legacy of industrialisation and urbanisation in the UK as a whole.

The downsizing of the British coal industry announced in October 1992 has resulted in the closure of the last deep mines in many coalfields. This means that the dewatering of these coalfields to protect working mines is no longer necessary. As a result of the reduced water table associated with mining, pyrite in the coal measures is exposed to air and oxidises. If pumping is ceased, the rising groundwater will dissolve the iron oxides, sulphates and proton acidity that are the products of pyrite oxidation. This results in the generation of a form of pollution known as acid mine drainage (AMD).

The potential impacts of rising water levels and the production of AMD on a large scale are numerous. If the groundwater level is allowed to rise unchecked, pollution of surface waters can occur, with consequences for both the fauna of the water course and its economic use.

The high sulphate content of AMD is a particular problem if the rising water levels intersect urban infrastructure. Sulphates in solution react with tricalcium alluminate within Portland Cement causing expansion, which leads to the breakdown of concrete and brickwork constructions (National Coal Board 1975).

Inundation of abandoned mineworkings is generally regarded as having a beneficial effect on the long term stability of workings. It is thought that the water will add buoyancy and reduce the stress taken by the supporting walls and pillars (Henton 1974; National Coal Board 1975; Whittaker & Reddish

1989; Turner 1993). However Denby et al. (1982) argue that water can significantly reduce the shear strength of coal measure rocks.

The rising groundwater may also displace methane causing it to be emitted at the surface (G. Reeves University of Newcastle upon Tyne, Personal Communication 1993). However should it form pockets trapped in the voids left by mining there would be an increase in the probability of explosions (Turner 1993).

Where the rising minewater comes into contact with a landfill site an increase in leachate production, the mobilisation of heavy metals and the production of landfill gas can occur (Jackson 1993).

The numerous detrimental impacts of rising minewaters necessitate the prediction of its rate of rise and the identification of potential discharge points. Modelling is therefore an invaluable tool for the planning of remediation strategies.

2 PROBLEMS OF MODELLING THE COAL-FIELD ENVIRONMENT

A fundamental problem with modelling the hydrogeology of the coalfield environment is that the strata for which hydrogeological information is required have commonly not contained water since they were mined. This makes the estimation of appropriate data for modelling problematic and prone to inaccuracies.

Structural data are often available, however it is commonly too detailed or too sparse to be of much use. The most crucial information for the prediction of the location of discharges is the extent of extraction close to the surface; but these workings are the oldest and least well recorded. It was not until 1872 that it became a requirement to lodge mine plans with the mining records office, and 1947 (when the industry was nationalised) before comprehensive plans were kept (Richardson 1983).

The heterogeneous nature of mineworkings is a further problem associated with modelling. This is compounded by the changing methods of extraction with improvements in technology. Aljoe & Hawkins (1994) studied flow in mines that have experienced widespread roof collapse and concluded that both Darcian and pseudokarst type flow conditions exist. Aldous et al. (1986) describe stream flow along some of the main roadways of mined coal measures.

Traditional modelling techniques use Darcy's law which assumes simple porous media in which laminar flow occurs. Perry (1993) argues that models which are based on such idealised flow are inappropriate for the fractured and highly disturbed strata which result from mining. The heterogeneous coal mine environment is likely to have Darcian flow in the unworked coal measures, but turbulent flow similar to stream flow in the worked areas.

3 GROUNDWATER REBOUND IN ABAN-DONED MINEWORKINGS (GRAM)

The problems of lack of appropriate data and the varying type of flow that are likely to occur in mined strata mean that a modelling approach is needed that does not require large quantities of data and recognises the limitations of what data are available.

3.1 The Pond Concept

Minett (1987) describes the National Coal Board's conceptualisation of a coalfield as a series of 'ponds' (worked areas) separated by barriers of unworked coal or major faults which are relatively impermeable. GRAM takes this concept and incorporates it into a lumped parameter model. It is a simple transient model, with run times short enough to allow Monte Carlo simulation of the parameters whose estimation is most doubtful.

GRAM conceptualises a coalfield as a series of ponds connected by pipes. A coalfield can be divided up into these ponds and pipes using structural and water level data. The ponds can form any shape in plan, however they must be bounded by vertical walls of intact coal through which there is assumed to be no flow.

The hydraulic gradient within the ponds is assumed to be flat, hence the hydraulic conductivity is presumed to be large enough to allow the water to form this flat hydraulic gradient. This means that all flow to and from the pond is applied over its entirety.

Figure 1 shows the Dysart-Leven coalfield in eastern Fife, which has been divided into five ponds. The ponds represent the workings of the last five interconnected working collieries in the coalfield. The differences in the relative water levels are an indication of how difficult it would be to model this coalfield using traditional methods.

3.2 Hydrogeological Parameters

The data requirements of GRAM are small,

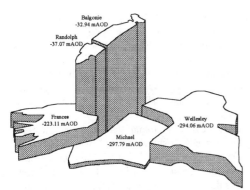

Figure 1. Depths to water within the ponds in the Dysart-Leven Coalfield in the autumn of 1994.

realistically aimed at the limited data sets that are available. The assumption of a flat hydraulic gradient means that flow is only directly modelled using pipeflow equations. Therefore values of hydraulic conductivity are not needed, as they would be for traditional groundwater modelling.

Parameter values for the pipeflow equations are however required. Much of these data can be obtained from structural records and mine plans, but the remainder, in particular, the pipe roughness coefficient k, must be calibrated against observed water level data.

Recharge to the model is a simple mechanism that can be easily adapted to the level of data which is available. Effective rainfall can be attenuated over a number of timesteps to allow a nominal representation of the time it takes recharge to pass through the unsaturated zone to the water table.

3.3 Calculation of Pipeflow

The transfer of water between ponds and discharge to the surface is represented using pipeflow equations. Flow along the pipes is modelled only for the case where the pipe is submerged, so that it flows full. Connections between mineworkings are commonly in the form of roadways, hence the use of pipeflow equations gives a realistic method of representing the nature of flow. A schematic diagram of how two ponds would interact is shown in Figure 2.

The Bernoulli equation is applied to the head loss between the ponds. The total head loss is the sum of the friction head loss and the minor head losses: entry loss and velocity head (Featherstone & Nalluri 1982).

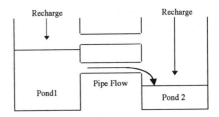

Figure 2. Schematic diagram of two ponds and their connections.

The Darcy-Weisbach equation is used to represent the friction head loss:

$$H = \frac{0.5V^2}{2g} + \frac{V^2}{2g} + \frac{\lambda L V^2}{2gD} \qquad (1)$$

| Gross Head Loss | Entry Loss | Velocity Head | Friction Head Loss |

Where V is the velocity of flow in the pipe (m/s), H is the head difference between the ponds (m), g is acceleration due to gravity (m/s²), D is the pipe diameter (m), L is the pipe length (m) and λ is a non-dimensional coefficient.

λ is a function of the roughness and diameter of the pipe. There are numerous methods of finding a value for λ, however the most frequently used method is the Colebrook-White equation for turbulent pipeflow:

$$\frac{1}{\sqrt{\lambda}} = -2\log\left[\frac{k}{3.7D} + \frac{2.51}{Re\sqrt{\lambda}}\right] \qquad (2)$$

Where k is the surface roughness (m), and Re is the Reynolds number. Which is given by:

$$Re = \frac{VD}{\nu} \qquad (3)$$

Where ν is the kinematic viscosity, which is generally assumed to be 1×10^{-6} m²/s.

These equations can be solved by initially neglecting the minor head losses in the Bernoulli equation, calculating a value for friction head loss and iterating to a solution. GRAM has the facility to use this method, however its use is associated with long run times.

An alternative method, offered by GRAM is the Prandtl and Nikuradse equation (Featherstone & Nalluri 1982). This method divides turbulent flow into three zones. In the rough turbulent zone λ is only a function of the relative roughness. Equation 4 represents the relationship for λ in the rough turbulent zone.

$$\frac{1}{\sqrt{\lambda}} = 2 \log \frac{3.7 D}{k} \qquad (4)$$

This equation has the major advantage that it does not need iteration to solve. As a consequence, the calculation time is kept to a minimum. This is important because the Bernoulli equation is a steady state equation, so the time step must be kept as small as is practical for minimisation of run-time.

GRAM was applied to the Dysart-Leven coalfield using both pipeflow equations. A comparison showed that the volume calculated by the Prandtl and Nikuradse equation is consistently larger than that calculated by the Colebrook-White by less than 1×10^{-3} % of the total pipeflow, where flow is in the rough-turbulent zone. This is a negligible variation when compared with the difference in run-time (the Colebrook-White option takes approximately thirty times as long as the Prandtl and Nikuradse to run).

3.4 Varying Storage Coefficient

GRAM has the facility to allow the storage coefficient in the ponds to vary vertically. Thus GRAM can represent the difference in storage coefficient between collapsed workings and the less porous intervening strata.

Lancaster (1995) studied the Ladysmith and Tindale shafts, south of the Butterknowle fault in the Durham Coalfield. Water level data which start three to four years after pumping was ceased, show a stepped rebound, indicative of a vertically varying storage coefficient.

3.5 The Iron Component

A simple iron model has been added to GRAM. The iron content of each pond is assumed to be homogeneous until discharge starts to occur, when the code differentiates between the vestigial and juvenile acidity (cf. Younger 1997).

There are three sources of iron represented by GRAM: recharge, seepage and the pyritic sulphur content of the coal seams. The flow between ponds carries dissolved iron with it. As the water levels rise in the ponds they pass through areas of variable

storage coefficient which represent the coal seams. The total iron content of each pond is increased as the water level rises through each seam. This is quantified using the sulphur content of each seam, the percentage of this sulphur which is in the pollution-generating pyritic form and the proportion of this sulphur which is oxidised and available to be dissolved.

Casagrande (1987) found that high and medium sulphur content coals associated with marine or brackish depositional environments have approximately equal proportions of pyritic and non-pyritic sulphur. On the other hand, in low sulphur content coals associated with freshwater depositional environments the pyritic sulphur amounts to only 20 - 30 % of the total sulphur content.

There is considerable uncertainty when estimating the proportion of the pyritic sulphur which is oxidised and available to be dissolved. Bullen Consultants (1994) used values in the range 0.1 - 10 % of the total pyritic sulphur, but stated that 10 % was probably an excessively high estimate.

3.6 Monte Carlo Simulation

The simplicity and relatively short run-times associated with GRAM make it ideal for Monte Carlo simulation. A range of parameters can be represented by probability distributions, however, two factors influence the choice of which parameters should be converted. Firstly the perceived reliability of the data and secondly how sensitive GRAM is to errors in their estimation.

GRAM in its general form has the capacity to allow values for the storage coefficient, the percentage run-off (and therefore indirectly the recharge rate) and the dimensions of any pipe to be taken from a probability distribution data set. However should it be deemed necessary, minor adjustments would make it possible to allow virtually any of the input data to be taken from a probability distribution.

3.7 Model Input

Data are input to the model in a series of ASCII files, however a Visual Basic 3.0 pre-processor has been developed for the uninitiated user. This displays the input files in a form which allows the user to easily identify and edit different pieces of data.

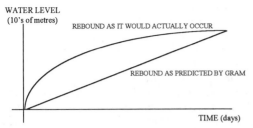

Figure 3. Notional comparison of the likely actual progress of groundwater rebound and groundwater rebound as predicted by GRAM

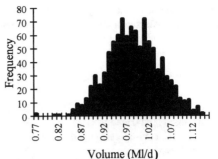

Figure 4. Volume of discharge from Wellesley shafts: probability distribution created by 1000 Monte Carlo simulations

3.8 Model Output

GRAM outputs a timeseries of water level data for each pond. During calibration, this can be compared to recorded datasets both graphically and statistically using a post processor in the form of a Visual Basic Macro in Excel 5.0.

Data sets are also produced for:
◊ the time of the first flow from each surface discharge point,
◊ the volume of each surface discharge over time,
◊ the iron content of each surface discharge over time
◊ and the average volume of flow from each surface discharge point.

When GRAM is run using Monte Carlo simulation these output data sets form probability distributions.

GRAM writes a water balance file. This contains a comparison of the change in storage volume and the difference between the volume of water entering and leaving the system in each timestep.

represented as discharge to the surface through a discrete point, like all other surface discharges. Therefore baseflow in its traditional form is unquantified. Recharge induced by a river is completely neglected. However this is likely to be a negligible proportion of the water balance of a modelled area.

The flat hydraulic gradient assumed over the ponds means that graphs of rebound at the pumping shafts have a uniform gradient; (see Figure 3). In actuality, these are more likely to be curved as the hydraulic gradient around the pumps flattens and voids fill. The curve will be at its steepest initially as the voids in the 'cone of depression' caused by pumping fill.

Thus the initial predictions of water level will be inaccurate. However the estimate of the total time taken for the pond to fill remains valid as the most significant factors controlling the system are recharge and storage volume.

3.9 Limitations of GRAM

The hydrogeological datasets used in this model are likely to be sparse due to the nature of the coal mining environment. In particular, the model is sensitive to the storage parameter. The estimation of this is particularly difficult and is perhaps the greatest source of error.

GRAM does not incorporate any modelling of the unsaturated zone or of soil moisture. This shortcoming can be mitigated by incorporating recharge as one of the values in the Monte Carlo simulation.

GRAM does not directly consider rivers that may flow across the model area. Baseflow can only be

4 CONCLUSIONS

GRAM has been applied most extensively to the Dysart-Leven coalfield (cf. Younger et al. 1995). The coalfield geometry and the large change in water level over a relatively short distance makes modelling with traditional methods virtually impossible (see Figure 1). However GRAM was fitted to the available water level data and was able to predict the rate of groundwater rise, and the timing and flow of discharges.

Monte Carlo simulation was used to represent the storage coefficient, the percentage run-off and the dimensions of one of the pipes which was not submerged during the calibration. A probability distribution for one of the discharge points is shown in Figure 4. The small standard deviation of the data set allows some confidence in the results.

ACKNOWLEDGEMENTS

We thank Bob Sargent of the Forth River Purification Board and Hendry Barbour of Bullen Consultants for their co-operation and the provision of data on the Dysart-Leven coalfield.

REFERENCES

Aldous, P.J., P.L.Smart & J.A.Black 1986. Groundwater management problems in abandoned coal-mined aquifers: a case study of the Forest of Dean, England. *Quarterly Journal of Engineering Geology.* London. 19:375-388.

Aljoe, W.W. & J.W.Hawkins 1994. Application of Aquifer Testing in Surface and Underground Coal Mines. *Proceedings of the 5th International Mine Water Congress,* Nottingham. 1:3-21.

Bullen Consultants 1994. *Report on the Effect of Ceasing Pumping from the Frances and Michael Collieries.* Final Report to Forth River Purification Board. Bullen Consultants, Glasgow. 70 pp.

Casagrande, D.J. 1987. Sulphur in Peat and Coal. *In* Scott, A.C. (Ed) *Coal and Coal-Bearing Strata: Recent Advances.* Geological Society Special Publication 32:87-105.

Chadwick, A. & J.Morfett 1994. *Hydraulics in Civil and Environmental Engineering.* E & F.N. Spon, London. 557 pp.

Denby B., F.P.Hassani & M.J.Scoble 1982. The influence of water on the shear strength of coal measures rocks and discontinuities in surface mining. *Proceedings of the 1st International Mine Water Congress of the International Mine Water Association.* Budapest, Hungary. 334-345.

Featherstone R.E. & C.Nalluri 1982. *Civil Engineering Hydraulics.* (2nd Edn.) BSP Professional Books, London. 373 pp.

Henton, M.P. 1974. Hydrogeological Problems Associated with Waste Disposal into Abandoned Coal Workings. *Water Services.* October. 349-352.

Jackson, K.B. 1993. *The Environmental Impact of the Cessation in Mine Dewatering upon the Waste Disposal Sites within County Durham.* Unpublished M.Sc. Thesis, University of Newcastle upon Tyne.

Lancaster, D. 1995. *Delineating the Catchment Area and Flow System of a Major Polluted Spring in County Durham.* Unpublished M.Sc. Thesis, University of Newcastle upon Tyne.

Minett, S.T. 1987. *The Hydrogeology of Parts of the Northumberland and Durham Coalfield Related to Opencast Mining Operation.* Unpublished Ph.D. Thesis, University of Newcastle upon Tyne.

National Coal Board 1975. *Subsidence Engineers Handbook.* 111 pp.

Perry, A.O. 1993. Hydrologic Models Used by the U.S. Bureau of Mines. *Proceedings of the Federal Interagency Workshop on Hydrologic Modelling Demands for the 90's.* U.S. Geological Society Water Resources Investigations Report 93-4018. 1.16-1.23.

Richardson, G. 1983. *Geological Notes and Local Details for 1:100000 Sheets NZ26NW, NE, SW, SE (Newcastle upon Tyne and Gateshead).* Geological Survey of England and Wales, Natural Environment Research Council.

Turner, I. 1993. *A Geotechnical Assessment of Groundwater Rise through Mineworkings in Gateshead.* Unpublished M.Sc. Thesis, University of Newcastle upon Tyne.

Whittaker, B.N. & D.J.Reddish 1989. Subsidence - Occurrence, Prediction and Control. *Developments in Geotechnical Engineering.* 56.

Younger, P.L. 1997. The Longevity of Minewater Pollution: A Basis for Decision-Making. *Science of the Total Environment.* 194/195:457-466.

Younger, P.L., M.H.Barbour & J.M.Sherwood 1995. Predicting the Consequences of Ceasing Pumping from the Frances and Michael Collieries, Fife Scotland. *British Hydrological Society 5th National Hydrology Symposium,* Edinburgh. 2.25-2.33.

Groundwater in the Urban Environment: Problems, Processes and Management, Chilton et al. (eds)
© 1997 Balkema, Rotterdam, ISBN 90 5410 837 1

Assessment and forecast of groundwater and rock contamination within the Kyiv industrial agglomeration influenced by Chernobyl fallout

V. M. Shestopalov, V. V. Goudzenko, Yu. F. Rudenko, V. N. Bublias & A. S. Boguslavsky
Scientific-Engineering Centre for Radioecological Studies, NAS of Ukraine, Kyiv, Ukraine

ABSTRACT: Results of recently obtained measurements and modelling balance assessments are presented for groundwater and water-bearing rocks contaminated by Chernobyl ^{137}Cs and ^{90}Sr within the Kyiv Industrial Agglomeration (KIA). Results show that existing and forecasted groundwater and rock contamination may be explained by the existence of fast migration pathways in conditions of high downward infiltration velocities in the KIA region induced by intensive prolonged exploitation of deep aquifers for water supply. Nevertheless the water-bearing rocks in the upper zone of intensive vertical water exchange, owing to their high sorption capacity, remain a powerful protection buffer within the biosphere.

1 INTRODUCTION

It was accepted by the majority of radioecologists, hydrologists and hydrogeologists that radionuclide pollution hazards are negligible for groundwater aquifers, which were considered a highly protected water source. The reality of Chernobyl, however, has dispelled such a delusion.

By summer 1987, the fission products, including the short-lived cerium-144, ruthenium-106, and caesium-134, resulting from the Chernobyl accident, had been detected in traceable amounts in water sampled from wells within the 30-km exclusion zone around the Chernobyl NPP. More recently, ^{137}Cs and ^{90}Sr of Chernobyl origin were found in confined aquifers both near the Chernobyl NPP and in other locations, including the Kyiv City water intake, which supplies potable water from Jurassic aquifers of 250-300 m depth.

Such unusual behaviour of radionuclides has led to a search for the mechanisms responsible for such fast migration of pollutants towards aquifers. Special emphasis was placed on the so-called active zones, those with enhanced mass- and heat exchange between shallow and deep layers of the earth's crust.

In this paper the latest data on groundwater and rock contamination with Chernobyl ^{137}Cs and ^{90}Sr are presented, obtained from boreholes located within the Kyiv Industrial Agglomeration. Based on these data,

model predictions are given for possible groundwater and rock contamination with ^{137}Cs for the next fifty year period.

2 DATA FROM NEW OBSERVATIONS

2.1 *Contamination of groundwater*

Starting in 1991, research has been conducted on the assessment and forecasting of groundwater contamination within the Kyiv Industrial Agglomeration (KIA) for radionuclides of Chernobyl origin (Shestopalov et al. 1992).

The KIA territory includes the city of Kyiv, satellite towns (Vyshgorod, Irpin, Brovary, Boryspil, and others) and adjacent areas within a radius of 60-70 km around Kyiv. In a vertical section the four aquifers being studied are: (1) Quaternary (depths to 20 m), (2) Eocene (depths to 130 m), (3) Cenomanian-Callovian (depths to 200 m), and (4) Bajocian (depths to 300 m). As a result of intensive exploitation of groundwater for town water supply during many years, depression cones of 20 to 60 km radius have formed in the deeper aquifers. In all aquifers, including the Bajocian (depths of 300 m), the contamination of groundwater with the most dangerous long-lived radionuclides ^{137}Cs and ^{90}Sr is observed with concentrations ranging within 5-200 and 1-50 mBq/l respectively.

Table 1. ^{137}Cs and ^{90}Sr concentrations in ground-water of the principal aquifers within the KIA.

Aquifer	^{137}Cs				^{90}Sr		
Range mBq/l	<10	10-50	50-150	>150	<10	10-50	>50
1	24%	56%	14%	6%	53%	40%	7%
2	45%	41%	9%	5%	71%	21%	8%
3	46%	31%	13%	10%	80%	20%	-
4	47%	28%	15%	10%	62%	35%	3%

Note: Aquifer numbers 1-4 are explained in the text.

In total, 500 groundwater samples were analysed for ^{137}Cs and 300 for ^{90}Sr concentrations. The results are presented in Table 1 for the four aquifers mentioned above, as percentages of the total number of measurements for given concentration ranges. These concentrations have the tendency to increase with time, and within the KIA borders they are higher in aquifers at depths of 200-300 m than out in the regions at depths of 2-20 and 45-130 m where the aquifers are not being exploited.

It should be noted that these findings are in contradiction with the generally accepted concept that the groundwater of deep aquifers are safely protected against external contaminants.

2.2 Contamination of rocks

Recently, in 1996-1997, some measurements have been performed to assess the ^{137}Cs content in rock samples taken from boreholes within KIA (see Figure 2) to depths of 100 m. These measurements have shown that the rocks are significantly contaminated, showing activities in the range of 1-10 Bq per kg of dry rock.

The reliability of sampling seems to be sufficiently high: the boreholes were drilled at undisturbed field sites, the core material extracted, packed to avoid external contamination, and analysed under laboratory conditions.

Figure 1 is a borehole profile for ^{137}Cs concentration taken at the south-western border of Kyiv (the Teremki site, see the location map on Figure 2), which reveals a decreasing trend with depth.

The data from a borehole on the Kyiv Plateau (right bank of the Dneeper, Yasnogorodka, Figure 2) show the values in the same range (1-7 Bq/kg) but of more scattered pattern with depth, while the two

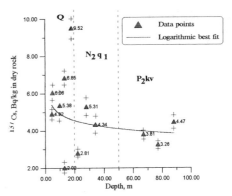

Figure 1. ^{137}Cs content in rock samples from the borehole of Teremki (the south-western margin of Kyiv). Crosses show possible error of measurements. Q; N_2q_1; P_{2kv} - Quaternary, Neogene, and Paleogene deposits respectively.

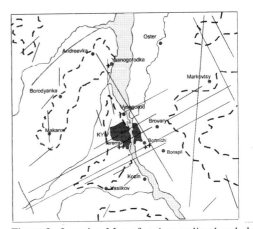

Figure 2. Location Map of rock-sampling boreholes (indicated by crosses) and fast migration zones within the KIA (straight lines show general direction of crustal weakness, associated with tectonic breaks, dashed contours enclose areas of relatively high occurrence of depression morphosculptures).

boreholes on the left bank (Bortnichi site) have shown smaller values in the range of 0-5 Bq/kg.

3 PATHWAYS OF FAST MIGRATION

The question arising from the data presented above is how can relatively high radionuclide concentrations appear at such depths? In the course of analysis of mechanisms of radioactive pollutant transport into groundwater, along with traditional infiltration pathways, the anomalously fast migration of contaminants was revealed which is associated with weak zones in sedimentary rocks. This revealed the heterogeneity in permeability of unconsolidated sediments, in contrast to usual zones of weakness in crystalline rocks and karstic limestones. It is most probable that such zones, which frequently appear in the surface relief as depression morphosculptures, are the objects primarily responsible for fast water and contaminant transport through the unsaturated zone (Shestopalov et al. 1996). Preliminary results for the location of such zones in the KIA are shown in Figure 2. Bold dashed contours enclose areas which are characterized, according to our preliminary analysis of field data, by high occurrence of fast migration zones - lineaments and circular depressions ("dishes"). Straight lines show the general direction of tectonic breaks.

The investigations concluded that the important characteristic of depression morphosculptures is an essential inhomogeneity of filtration and migration properties. The zones of anomalously rapid migration occur within linear and circular landscape depressions characterized by unconsolidated sediments with increased moisture and electrical conductivity. The soil profile cut in these zones differs from that of the background areas; the ground water levels dynamically react to rainfall, as is clear from anomalously high infiltration rates and formation of spreading mounds of groundwater level after intensive rainfall. Analysis of the radionuclide content in the solid phase of soil profiles indicates more intensive vertical migration in the active zones.

Characteristic of the KIA region are the mainly linear active zones (lineaments) which cover up to 10-15% of the area. In conditions of high vertical piezometric gradients induced by intensive exploitation of groundwater within the KIA (the average vertical infiltration rate ranges up to 300 mm per year, that is 3 times greater than outside of the region), these pathways may play an essential role in the observed fast penetration of radionuclides into aquifers.

4 MODELLING ASSESSMENT

Using the latest data, the preliminary balance assessment and forecast of water-bearing media contamination have been performed using the one-dimensional model for vertical concentration distribution $C(z,t)$ based on the convection-dispersion equation (Luckner & Shestakov 1986):

$$\frac{\partial}{\partial z}\left(D(z)\frac{\partial C}{\partial z} - wC\right) - \lambda C = (n + K_d) \tag{1}$$

taking into account the equilibrium sorption of contaminant by water-bearing rock characterized by distribution coefficient K_d. For our model assessment, which should be treated as approximate and preliminary, we have taken the depth-averaged value for downward velocity $w = 100$ mm/year, active porosity $n=0.1$, and $K_d= 5$ units. The generalized dispersion coefficient $D(z)$ was adjusted in the course of model calibration so as to fit the observed concentration in the liquid phase at control depths and at fixed time. Equation (1) was solved numerically for a typical 100 m depth vertical profile with the following upper boundary condition:

$$C(0,t) = C_o e^{-\lambda t} \tag{2}$$

where $\lambda = \ln 2/T$, (T -half-life for ^{137}Cs = 30 years) is the constant of radioactive decay. The surface initial concentration of ^{137}Cs in the liquid phase ($C_o = 40$ mBq/l was taken as corresponding to average assessments for surface water during Chernobyl fallouts in 1986.

According to the predictions obtained, the maximum groundwater contamination by ^{137}Cs for the most exploited Cenomanian aquifer will be observed in the Kyiv region in 2000-2005, ranging in concentration from 25 to 30 mBq/l.

Another task of the modelling was to obtain a balance assessment of the total amount of radionuclide accumulated in the 100 m-thick upper rock layer with changing time. This was done using profiles of $C(z,t)$ at given times and integrating over depth concentrations in the solid phase $N(z,t)$, using the equation of linear sorption kinetics:

$$N(z,t) = K_d\, C(z,t) \tag{3}$$

The balance was checked so as to fit to the total amount of contaminant calculated by equation (2) in which C_o is the total surface fallout contamination. The results are presented in undimensional form relative to the initial contamination taken as 1 at $t=0$ (Figure 3).

To improve this approximate assessment, the variability of the vertical iltration velocity field within KIA is presently being improved by use of a large-scale 3D model of groundwater flow in the region under study. It is very important also to clarify the

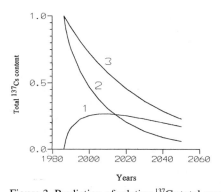

Figure 3. Prediction of relative ^{137}Cs total content in a 100 m thick geological medium of KIA:
1-accumulation by rocks in the 1-100 m depth range;
2- accumulation by upper 1 m layer;
3-total fallout initially taken as 1.

surface dynamics of radioactive contaminants as influenced by various processes of surface lateral transport (primarily, surface runoff during rainfall) and their distribution between the zones of fast migration and background areas.

5 CONCLUSIONS

1. The analysis of groundwater and rock sampling data and preliminary modelling assessment for vertical distributions of ^{137}Cs concentration in the region of KIA enables us to accept the possibility of accumulation in the host rock of up to 25% of the sum of initial surface fallout contamination (within the range of influence of the zones of radionuclide fast migration. This states in favour of the existence of pathways of anomalously fast radionuclide migration from the surface into groundwater, but on the other hand, indicates the important role of geological media as a powerful protection buffer within the biosphere.

2. The results obtained by direct measurements of ^{90}Sr provide evidence that observed maxima concentrations are sufflciently lower than the maximum permissible concentrations. Nevertheless, these data need to be periodically refined based on monitoring.

3. Results of a preliminary balance assessment for the average ^{137}Cs content in the upper 100 m layer of the geological rock medium in KIA show that in spite of the possible existence of fast migration pathways in the upper part of the active water exchange zone, the geological medium is a powerful buffer to radionuclide vertical migration, and that groundwater from deep aquifers is still a reliable source of potable water supply.

4. The model assessment given above for the total possible accumulation of radionuclides in the geological medium and groundwater was carried out for a typical site in the region under study with downward infiltration. For this reason, it may be somewhat overestimated. To obtain more precise forecasts, a more detailed regional study is necessary to evaluate the vertical filtration velocity component, and refine the boundaries of the regions of groundwater recharge and discharge.

ACKNOWLEDGEMENTS

This work has partly been undertaken with the support of the International Atomic Energy Agency (Research Contract No 9244).

Shestopalov, V.M., V.V. Goudzenko, Y.F. Rudenko, & A. S. Boguslavskij 1992. Combined Analysis, Modelling and Forecast of Long-Term Underground Water Contamination Inside the Chernobyl Fallout Influenced Zone. In *"Hydrological Impact of Nuclear Power Plant Systems":* 23-25.09.1992 *International Hydrological Programme. UNESCO Chernobyl programme.* Paris.

Shestopalov, V.M., V.N. Bublias, V.V. Goudzenko, I.P. Onishchenko, I.V. Borodavko 1996. Studying of the process of fast vertical migration of radionuclides in the geological environment. In *IV International Scientific Conference "Chernobyl-94. Summing up 8 years of work on eliminating the consequences of Chernobyl NPP accident",* Chernobyl: 11 0-1 1 9. (In Russian).

Luckner, L. & W.M. Schestakow. 1986. *Modelling of groundwater migration.* Moscow: "Nedra" Publisher. (In Russian).

Hydraulic conductivity across bedding planes: A critical control on conjunctive-use management in Albuquerque, New Mexico

John W. Shomaker
John Shomaker & Associates, Albuquerque, N. Mex., USA

ABSTRACT: Albuquerque, New Mexico, USA, lies above, and has produced its entire water supply from, a valley-fill aquifer more than 1,000 m thick and hydraulically connected with the Rio Grande. Water-management decisions have assumed the aquifer to be a continuous body of permeable material, recharged freely by the river; its ability to supply water was thought limited only by availability of water in the river. Water-level hydrographs now show the aquifer to be a sequence of semi-confined zones; pumping has led to head differences of more than 16 m between producing zones and the water table, in about 35 years. Model studies show recharge occurs at lower rates than expected, and is strongly dependent on irrigation. Supply from ground water alone is now known not to be sustainable, partly because of potential subsidence problems; this compels major change in urban planning, and water-rights administration in the Rio Grande Basin.

1 INTRODUCTION

Albuquerque, New Mexico, lies in the valley of the Rio Grande in the Albuquerque-Belen Basin (Fig. 1). Mean annual discharge of the Rio Grande at Albuquerque is 1.29 x 10^9 m^3/y. The range in annual discharge is large, from 0.32 x 10^9 m^3/y to 2.22 x 10^9 m^3/y for the 23-year period of record since completion of the most recent upstream reservoir.

The Albuquerque-Belen Basin is a deep, complex graben, one of a series of en echelon grabens that form the Rio Grande rift. Valley-fill sediments are braided-stream sands and gravels, intertonguing with alluvial fan deposits, playa lake clays, and aeolian sands, with basalt flows and pyroclastic units. The oldest valley fill is late Oligocene; most of the sediments are Miocene and Pliocene (Hawley & Haase 1992). All of the fill, except for middle Pleistocene and younger alluvium and piedmont deposits, is assigned to the Santa Fe Formation.

A very large volume of ground water is stored in the Santa Fe Formation aquifer, which ranges up to more than 4,500 m thick. Estimates of ground water in storage are very crude, but are in excess of 10^{11} m^3, at least 2,000 times the present annual abstraction.

The 1994 water budget of the Albuquerque-Belen Basin (Fig. 1) included abstraction of 0.21 x 10^9 m^3/y of ground water, almost all for municipal and industrial use; about 0.11 x 10^9 m^3/y was returned to the river as treated wastewater. Depletion of streamflow in the Rio Grande was estimated at 0.14 x 10^9 m^3/y, of which 0.08 x 10^9 m^3/y recharged the aquifer (Hansen 1995); the remainder was lost to evapotrans-piration of irrigation water.

The climate is semi-arid; precipitation in Albuquerque averages 200 mm/y, but is highly variable from year to year. Recharge occurs along the mountain front bordering the valley, but probably not on the valley floor itself except occasionally through the beds of large, normally dry, watercourses. Under natural conditions, ground water discharged to the Rio Grande but ground-water abstraction has reversed the gradient between river and aquifer in much of the valley near Albuquerque.

2 EARLY MODEL STUDIES

The U.S. Geological Survey and the New Mexico State Engineer Office (Reeder et al. 1967) predicted water-level declines for the period 1960-2000. The

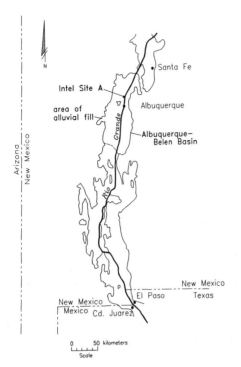

Figure 1. Map showing Albuquerque-Belen Basin and Intel Site A.

modeling was based on summation of the drawdown effects caused by pumping of each existing and predicted well. calculated by the Theis equation (Theis 1935).

The model was not tested by history-matching because there had been little pumping stress by 1960 and most wells had very short records of water-level measurements, and because, even if depletion of surface flows in the Rio Grande had been equivalent to a large fraction of the amount pumped, it would have been unmeasurably small compared with the average annual flow of the river. By 1960, total abstraction of ground water was equivalent to less than 6% of average Rio Grande flow, and change in stream discharge due to pumping could not have been measured precisely enough to guide model development.

The hydrogeological study upon which Reeder's work was based (Bjorklund & Maxwell 1961), gives the conception of the aquifer as it was at the time. The Santa Fe Formation was thought, at least as a first approximation, to be more-or-less consistent in character from place to place in the basin, and with depth. There had been few deep

water-supply wells tested outside Albuquerque, and in the absence of information, it was assumed that all of the valley fill had similar properties.

The Theis-equation method implied homogeneity of the aquifer, and full penetration by the river. Reeder and his colleagues understood that neither of these conditions was met, and explained carefully the potential for error in drawdown estimates, but the basic patterns of the system were thought to be correctly understood.

Depletion of streamflow, the replacement of water abstracted from the aquifer, was estimated by the State Engineer for administrative purposes through application of the Glover-Balmer (1954) equation; Glover-Balmer implies the same conditions as the Theis equation.

The concept of copious replenishment of ground water as it was withdrawn was tacitly accepted by professionals familiar with the basin, and was seized upon enthusiastically by those interested in the city's growth. The city already controlled some water rights in the river, and purchased additional water to be delivered to the Rio Grande from the Colorado River Basin. Urban planning went forward with confidence that Albuquerque had no fear of water shortage.

Transmissivity and distance from the Rio Grande were thought to be the dominant controls on long-term performance of wells. It was reasonable to assume that, with ample flows in the Rio Grande, depletion of streamflow would almost keep pace with ground-water depletion, and ground-water levels would not be far from equilibrium, as demand grew.

3 SYMPTOMS

In the mid-1980s, the writer's design-analysis studies for new supply wells revealed significantly greater water-level declines than had been predicted by the Reeder model, even though Reeder's work assumed much greater growth in demand than had actually occurred.

Storage coefficient, as calculated from long pumping tests of production wells that had been in service for years, was in the confined-aquifer range, not approaching the specific yield.

Several test wells to about 1,000 m, as compared with the 300 m to 450 m depths of then-existing production wells, showed that high-conductivity beds were not present below the part of the aquifer that had been developed.

4 RECENT MODEL STUDIES

The U.S. Geological Survey (Kernodle & Scott 1986; Kernodle et al. 1987) prepared the first multi-layer model of the Albuquerque-Belen Basin, in which flow across bedding planes could be taken into account. This model was based on the U.S. Geological Survey MODFLOW code (McDonald & Harbaugh 1983). The model was adjusted so that predictions matched the steady-state (1930s) distribution of ground-water head, and the heads as of 1960-61. A ratio of 1:500 between hydraulic conductivity parallel with and across bedding planes, was found consistent with the data.

The writer and colleagues prepared a three-layer model, of the northern part of the basin, in which full history-matching for hydrographs from pre-development conditions up to 1992 guided the

estimates of aquifer properties. The best history-match was found with a vertical-to-horizontal-conductivity ratio of 1:500. This was a MODFLOW-based superposition model, in which change from pre-development conditions, rather than actual ground-water head, was predicted. Figure 2 shows the comparison of predicted and observed trends in water-level change for four of the wells used in history-matching.

A more detailed and comprehensive MODFLOW model has been prepared by the U.S. Geological Survey (Kernodle et al. 1995), and is still being refined. New geological studies (Hawley & Haase 1992; Thorn et al. 1993; Hawley & Whitworth 1997) are guiding the modeling. The present understanding of the basin fill is much different from that of the 1960s, in that the highly conductive beds in which the earlier Albuquerque wells were

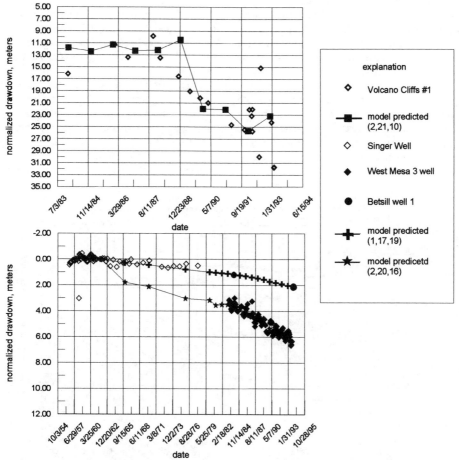

Figure 2. Comparison of predicted and observed trend in water-level change for selected wells, Shomaker & Associates' model of northern Albuquerque-Belen Basin.

completed have been found to be restricted to a relatively small area of the basin, and to occur only in the upper few hundred meters of the aquifer.The conductivity across bedding in the current versionof the model is 1/200th of the harmonic mean of the horizontal conductivity values of each pair of model layers.

Figure 3 shows hydrographs of six piezometers at a site about 2,500 m from the Rio Grande (Fig. 1); these hydrographs show clearly how the large abstractions in the basin are reflected by change in ground-water head. There are many nearby wells producing at relatively small rates from close to the water table, but the piezometer nest is close to irrigated lands. The screened intervals in nearby large-capacity abstraction wells are from about 200 to 600 m, corresponding with the three deeper piezometers. At this location, the difference in ground-water head between the water table and the principal producing interval had reached 9.8 m by March 1995, and increased by 6.4 m in the ensuing 17 months. Although water is recharged to the shallowest part of the aquifer from the river and the irrigation system, drawdown in beds deeper in the aquifer continues to increase rapidly in response to pumping.

In general, there is continuous saturation beneath the river, but a zone of incomplete saturation may develop if drawdowns increase further, and recharge from the river may reach a limit beyond which further increase in pumping will not lead to increase in recharge.

5 CONCLUSIONS

Hydraulic conductivity across the bedding planes is not a factor that can be neglected or treated lightly, but in fact governs the relation between aquifer and river, and thus the availability of a sustainable supply for Albuquerque.

1. Continued reliance on local ground-water supplies, assuming the projected rate of demand growth, will lead to total drawdown of 80 m beneath a large area of Albuquerque, and will approach 90 m in places, by 2060 (Brown et al. 1996). The threshold at which serious subsidence is likely to begin is estimated at 80 to 120 m (Haneberg 1996).

Albuquerque could continue to depend entirely on ground water for many years before physical constraints began to apply, but conversion to surface-water supply must be made very soon, for two reasons:

1. If the city were to wait until subsidence began to occur, and then attempted to convert, there would remain no ground-water reserve for drought, and there would probably be no Rio Grande water rights available.

2. The Rio Grande is already fully appropriated, and may be over-appropriated, in terms of water-rights administration. The surface-water supply that is presently controlled by the city, although no direct use has yet been made of it, is equivalent to about 86.3×10^6 m^3/y. Return-flow of treated wastewater is about 50% of total abstraction, so the

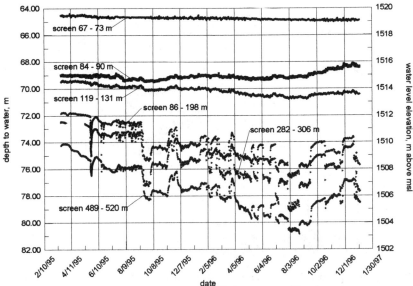

Figure 3. Hydrographs of Intel piezometers, Site A.

present surface-water rights would provide about 173 x 10^6 m^3/y to the system. Demand is now about 160 x 10^6 m^3/y, and is expected to reach 250 x 10^6 m^3/y by 2060.

Additional water, in the form of agricultural rights, is for sale, but restoration of the aquifer depends on continued recharge from irrigation canals and irrigated lands, and there are limits on the amount of water that should be converted to municipal use.

Downstream users may perceive efforts by Albuquerque to use more Rio Grande water as an attempt to, in effect, control two water supplies: the ground water that could continue to supply the city for many decades to come, and the river. Population growth is very rapid in the border region of New Mexico, western Texas, and northern Mexico, and water supplies are already under stress. Although Mexico's share of Rio Grande water is fixed by treaty, demand pressure is very great and may eventually lead to new arrangements.

Mexico's allocation of Rio Grande water is equivalent to only about 5.5% of the water that reaches Albuquerque. Ciudad Juarez is entirely dependent on ground water now, and water-level declines are much greater than in Albuquerque. The surface-water allocation is equivalent to only about one-half of the present demand. The population of the Ciudad Juarez area is probably already greater than that of the entire Rio Grande Basin above, and is growing at least as rapidly.

Albuquerque's situation shows that even a city blessed with a vast store of ground water beneath it, may quickly find that its only sustainable supply must come from surface water. The usefulness of the ground water in storage may be largely as a reserve for drought. It is ironic that the volume of ground water in storage was probably estimated reasonably well in early studies, but we now find that only a tiny fraction of the total can be used without incurring dire consequences.

REFERENCES

Bjorklund, L.J. & B.W. Maxwell 1961. *Availability of ground water in the Albuquerque area, Bernalillo and Sandoval Counties, New Mexico.* New Mexico State Engineer Tech. Rept. 21.

Brown, F.L., S.C. Nunn, J.W. Shomaker & G. Woodard 1996. *The Value of Water.* Consultants' report to City of Albuquerque.

Glover, R.E. & C.G. Balmer 1954. *River depletion resulting from pumping a well near a river.* Amer. Geophys. Union Trans., 35, pt 3: 468-470.

Haneberg, W.C. 1996. *Depth-porosity relationships and virgin specific storage estimates for the upper Santa Fe Group aquifer, central Albuquerque Basin.* New Mexico Bureau of Mines and Min. Res., New Mexico Geology 17, no. 4: 62-71.

Hansen, S. & C. Gorbach 1997. *Middle Rio Grande Water Assessment, Final Report.* U.S. Bureau of Reclamation.

Hawley, J.W. & C.S. Haase 1992. *Hydrogeologic framework of the northern Albuquerque Basin.* New Mexico Bureau of Mines and Min. Res., Open-File Rept. 387.

Hawley, J.W. & T.M. Whitworth 1997. *Hydrogeology of potential recharge areas and hydrogeochemical modeling of proposed artificial-recharge methods in basin- and valley-fill aquifer systems, Albuquerque Basin, New Mexico.* New Mexico Bureau of Mines and Min. Res., Open-File Rept. 402D.

Kernodle, J.M. & W.B. Scott 1986. *Three-dimensional model simulation of steady-state ground-water flow in the Albuquerque-Belen Basin, New Mexico.* U.S. Geological Survey Water-Resources Investigations Report 84-4353.

Kernodle, J.M., R.S. Miller & W.B. Scott 1987. *Three-dimensional model simulation of transient ground-water flow in the Albuquerque-Belen Basin, New Mexico.* U.S. Geological Survey Water-Resources Investigations Report 86-4194.

Kernodle, J.M., D.P. McAda & C.R. Thorn 1995. *Simulation of ground-water flow in the Albuquerque Basin, Central New Mexico, 1901-1994, with projects to 2020.* U.S. Geological Survey Water-Resources Investigations Report 94-4251.

McDonald, M.G. & A.W. Harbaugh 1983. *A modular three-dimensional finite-difference ground-water flow model.* U.S. Geological Survey Open-File Report 83-875.

Reeder, H.O., L.J. Bjorklund & G.A. Dinwiddie 1967. *Quantitative analysis of water resources in the Albuquerque area, New Mexico.* New Mexico State Engineer Tech. Rept. 33.

Theis, C.V. 1935. *The relation between the lowering of the piezometric surface and the rate and duration of a well using ground-water storage.* Trans. Amer. Geophys. Union, 2: 519-534.

Thorn, C.R., D.P. McAda & J.M. Kernodle 1993. *Geohydrologic framework and hydrologic conditions in the Albuquerque Basin, central New Mexico.* U.S. Geological Survey Water-Resources Investigations Report 86-4194.

Groundwater in the Urban Environment: Problems, Processes and Management, Chilton et al. (eds)
© 1997 Balkema, Rotterdam, ISBN 90 5410 837 1

Migration and attenuation of organic contaminants in the unsaturated zone: Field experiments in the Western Cape, South Africa

O.T.N.Sililo
Cape Water Programme, CSIR, Stellenbosch, South Africa

ABSTRACT: Field infiltration experiments were conducted on top of an unconfined sand aquifer to examine the migration and attenuation of organic contaminants from the surface, through the unsaturated zone to the water table. During the experiments, wastewater containing aliphatic hydrocarbons was irrigated on the site. Four other organic compounds: toluene, butyric acid, phenol and aniline were also introduced. Two days after the experiment, water samples were collected to examine concentration changes of the compounds with depth. Aniline and butyric acid were not detected in any of the samples. Phenol was only detected at 1 m and toluene had migrated up to 4 m. The aliphatic hydrocarbons were detected in all the soil water and groundwater samples indicating that rapid migration of contaminants can occur in the area. This finding implies that current waste disposal activities in the area could be polluting the groundwater resources.

1 INTRODUCTION

The Cape flats aquifer in the Western Cape, South Africa, is considered an important water supply source for the local urban communities and can supply ten percent of Cape Town's water supply needs. This unconfined aquifer is located in an urban environment where human settlement and industrialization are expanding rapidly. Early urban planners disregarded the potential impact of waste disposal activities on groundwater and a number of solid and liquid disposal sites were located in the area. Monitoring exercises at these sites have yielded contradictory results. In certain cases, no groundwater pollution has been detected giving an impression that current activities could continue unabated. Some studies have, however, shown that groundwater pollution is occurring (Tredoux 1981). The latter mainly occurred at sites where either the pollution loading was high or the water table was quite shallow. The question that is of interest here is: under what conditions can the unsaturated zone be depended upon to immobilize potential contaminants? To answer this question requires integrated laboratory, field and modelling studies. In this paper, we report on field infiltration experiments which were initiated to contribute to the understanding of the attenuation characteristics of the sands. This study was conducted as part of a Water Research Commission (WRC) project aimed at "assessing the contaminant attenuation characteristics of the soil aquifer system with special emphasis on the vadose zone". The ultimate aim of the WRC project is to provide planners with information regarding the extent to which natural attenuation can be depended upon to immobilize potential contaminants.

1.1 Assessment of attenuation

Attenuation can be defined as a process by which a decrease in concentration of a given species occurs for some fixed time or distance travelled. A number of physical, chemical and biological processes will occur in the subsurface which will work to reduce the concentration of contaminants. In order to assess whether natural attenuation is occurring at any given site, data on concentration changes must be collected. A decrease in concentration in time or in space may be indicative of natural attenuation. In this study the approach adopted is to assess concentration changes along the main flow path. The basis of this approach is that if natural attenuation is occurring, the contaminant concentration will decrease with distance from the source.

1.2. Study area

The study site is located on the Cape Flats aquifer. This consists of Quaternary-age deposits, mainly silica sand underlain by impervious pre-Cambrian Malmesbury Shales or Cape Granite. Sedimentation initially occurred in a shallow marine environment, subsequently progressing to intermediate beach and

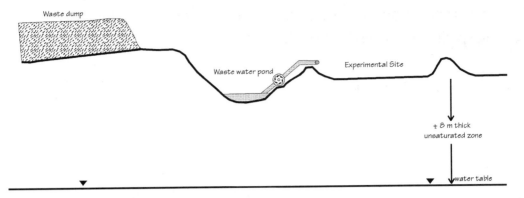

Figure 1. Cross section through the study site (not to scale).

wind blown deposits, and finally aeolian and marsh (peat) conditions. A characteristic feature of the sediments is the presence of shelly material over most of the area. The sand body is generally stratified horizontally. Portions of the area are covered by calcareous sands and surface limestone deposits, while silcrete, marine clays and bottom sediments of small inland water bodies occur sporadically. At the study site, the sands consist mainly of moderately sorted medium grained quartzitic sands with subordinate shelly and biogenic fragments. A number of calcretised horizons are present within the sand units. The measured fraction of organic carbon (f_{oc}) of the sands varies between 0.0029 and 0.0042. In situ permeability tests in the area yielded saturated hydraulic conductivity values ranging between 20 m and 40 m/day. The water table is about 8 metres deep.

The climate is typically Mediterranean with the winter rainy season from May to August. The average rainfall recorded at various stations in the Cape Flats ranges from 500-700 mm/annum.

The study plot, 3 m x 1.5m, is located approximately 30 metres away from a domestic waste site. Adjacent to the waste site is a pond (Figure 1) in which unauthorised dumping of various types of waste has occurred over the years. During the rainy season, the pond fills up with water.

2 METHOD OF STUDY

2.1 Objectives of field study

The main objective of the field study was to obtain data on the migration and attenuation of contaminants from the surface, through the unsaturated zone to the water table. A groundwater observation well installed at the site was used to obtain samples from the saturated zone while suction lysimeters were used in the unsaturated zone. A neutron probe access hole was

also installed to help monitor the migration of the wetting front during experimentation.

2.2 Lysimeters

Lysimeters (porous suction samplers) are the most frequently used type of in situ pore liquid samplers. A review of lysimeters has been given by Liator (1988), Everett and McMillion (1985) and Wilson et al. (1995). The principles of their operation are as follows: when placed in the unsaturated zone, the pores in the porous sampler of a lysimeter will form a continuum with pores in the surrounding medium. When a vacuum greater than soil water suction is applied within the sampler, a hydraulic gradient is created toward the sampler. If menisci of the liquid in the soil or porous cup are unable to withstand the applied suction, liquid water will be drawn across the porous wall into the cup. The ability of the menisci to withstand applied suction decreases with increasing pore radii of the porous segment. If the maximum pore radii are too large, the menisci are not able to withstand the applied suction and as a result, they break down and air enters the sampler. Once water enters the sampler, it can be drawn to the surface by applying pressure to the pressure vacuum line.

The design of the lysimeters used in this study is shown in Figure 2. The lysimeters were assembled by heat shrinking a 5 cm ceramic porous cup on to the bottom end of a 60 cm long and 5 cm diameter PVC cylindrical tube. The upper end was fitted with an airtight 5 cm PVC cap. The latter was then fitted with two 6 mm plastic tubing. One of the tubes, the sampling line, was fitted such that it extended from the bottom of the porous cup while the other tube, the pressure vacuum line, terminated just below the end cap. The pressure line was fitted with a 0.25 kPa non-return valve to maintain a vacuum within the lysimeter. After construction all lysimeters were

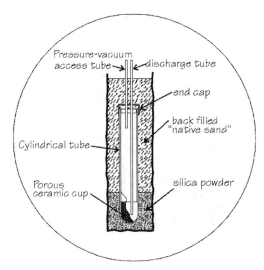

Figure 2. Lysimeter design and installation.

Table 1: General characteristics of selected organic compounds used in the study.

Parameter	Toluene[a]	Aniline[b]	Phenol[a]
Formula weight	92.14	93.13	94.11
Log octanol : water partition coefficient (Log K_{ow})	2.73	0.90	1.48
Log K_{oc}	2.06	1.41	1.43
Solubility in water (mg/L)	515	34 000	82 000
Henrys constant atm.m³/mol	0.007	0.136	2.7×10^7

Butyric acid is highly soluble in water

[a] Montgomery and Welkom (1991)
[b] Montgomery (1991)

checked to ensure that they were free of any leaks.

In order to install lysimeters on the site, a number of boreholes were drilled by rotary percussion, without adding any water. The general procedure of installation was as follows: silica powder was poured into the hole to cover the base. The lysimeter assembly was then lowered down until the porous cup rested on the silica powder. Additional silica was then added until the porous cup was completely covered by silica. The hole was then backfilled with native sand material, tamping thoroughly in the process. A total of 6 lysimeters were installed at the following depths from the surface: 1 m, 2 m, 3 m, 4 m, 5 m and 6 m.

2.3 Sprinkler system

The site was instrumented with two types of sprinkler system. The first type consisted of four spray sprinklers which were placed on the surface while the second type consisted of five drip lines, which were buried about 5 cm below the soil surface (Figure 3).

2.4 Infiltration experiments

Wastewater from pond A (Figure 3) was used to drive the infiltration process. During the course of the experiment, four organic compounds: toluene, butyric acid, phenol and aniline were also introduced. The organic compound solutions were prepared by mixing 16 g of a given compound with 400 litres of water giving 40 mg/L solutions. The general characteristics of selected organic compounds used in the study are shown in Table 1.

Just before infiltration experiments were initiated, soil moisture samples were collected from all the lysimeters and the observation borehole. The sampling procedure for the lysimeters involved applying a vacuum to the vacuum line using a vacuum pump while the sampling line remained shut. After 1 hour, the sampling (or discharge) line was opened and pressure applied to the pressure line. This caused the sample to move up to the surface through the discharge line. The samples were then collected in sample bottles and immediately stored in cooler bags. The samples were then transported to the laboratory where they were refrigerated at 4°C until they were analyzed. Lysimeters at 3m and 6m did not yield any samples.

Neutron probe readings were also taken to get an indication of initial moisture conditions.

The infiltration experiments were conducted in four phases, with each phase involving introduction of a different organic compound. During each phase, irrigation was initiated by pumping wastewater from pond A on to the field plot B at a rate of 1.0 l/s. A total of 7 m³ of wastewater was irrigated during the experiment. Twenty minutes after the onset of each irrigation cycle, 400 litres of the organic compound solution from tank C was introduced via the buried drip lines at a rate of 0.9 l/s.

At the end of each irrigation cycle, neutron probe measurements were taken. The objective of the latter was to observe progressive moisture changes during the experiment.

Two days after the experiment, sampling of the borehole and lysimeters commenced. The sampling procedure followed is as described above. Again, lysimeters at 3 m and 6 m did not yield any samples.

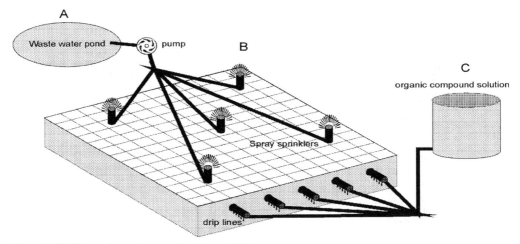

Figure 3. Field experimental setup showing sprinkler system.

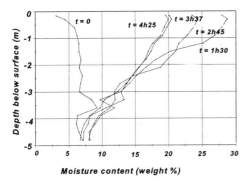

Moisture content (weight %)

Figure 4. Neutron probe moisture content vs. depth.
t = time after infiltration started.

2.5 Method of analysis

For organic analysis, the EPA method 3500 was used as a basis for the extraction of the water samples. The water samples were extracted three times with 10 ml methylene chloride. All extraction glassware had been heated to 400°C and prerinsed with methylene chloride. The use of a wrist-action shaker for 10 minutes was utilised. The extracts were combined and dried with anhydrous sodium sulphate, prior to injection.

The combined extracts were injected into a Varian Saturn 2000 Gas Chromatograph-Mass Spectrometer. EPA method 8260 was used as a basis for the GC-MS analysis. A 30m DB-5 column was used. The GC was temperature programmed from 30°C (6 min hold) to 70°C at 7°C/min and then to 280°C at 10°C/min. The mass spectrometer was set to scan from 40 to 450 mass units, at 0.810 seconds/scan. The injection port temperature was set at 260°C and the transfer line

Table 2: Organic contaminants (ppm) in wastewater

Decane	1.06
Tridecane	1.42
Tetradecane	0.95
Pentadecane	0.36

between GC and MS at 280°C. The ion trap of the MS was set at 120°C and the trap manifold was set at 45°C.

Peak identities were determined by comparison of mass spectra obtained for the extracts against mass spectra of external standards. Compound concentrations were determined by constructing calibration curves of external standards, using the peak areas under each reconstructed ion peak for the specific standard, as designated by EPA 8260.

Recovery efficiencies were calculated by spiking deionised water samples with known amounts of standards. These results were used to calculate the final compound concentrations.

3 RESULTS

Figure 4 shows the interpreted neutron probe readings, giving the change in moisture content with depth. It is evident from the graph that the wetting front had migrated beyond 3 metres in under 4 hours.

Table 2 shows the aliphatic hydrocarbons that were identified in the wastewater from pond A. It is noted that concentration of various organic compounds in the pond are likely to vary. As this variation in concentration was not determined, the data in Table 2 should be viewed as semi-quantitative.

Table 3: Aliphatic hydrocarbons (ppm) detected in soil water and groundwater samples

	1m	2m	4m	5m	Ground-water (~8m)
			Depth from the surface		
Decane	0.18	ND	0.16	ND	ND
Undecane	0.22	ND	0.25	ND	ND
Dodecane	0.41	1.36	1.08	1.41	0.63
Tridecane	0.49	1.70	1.73	1.68	0.83
Tetradecane	0.29	1.17	0.91	1.01	0.48
Pentadecane	0.14	0.44	0.38	0.35	0.16

ND = not detected
Detection limit = 0.005 mg/L.

Table 4: Toluene and its derivatives (ppm)

	Depth from the surface (m)	
	1 m	4 m
Toluene	ND	0.01
Benzoic acid	0.01	ND
Benzyl alcohol	0.77	ND

The organic compounds shown in Table 2 were not detected in the soilwater and groundwater samples which were collected before the infiltration experiments were initiated. They were, however, detected in all the soil water samples and the groundwater samples which were collected after the infiltration experiment. Shorter-chain alkanes (decane and undecane) were detected at 1 m and 4 m (Table 3). Of the organic compounds added at the surface, aniline and butyric acid were not detected in the water samples. Phenol was only detected at 1 m (0.2 ppm). Toluene was detected at 4 m and its derivatives at 1 m (Table 4).

4 DISCUSSION

The infiltration experiments were conducted to examine the vertical movement of organic compounds at this site. The main interest here was to examine whether the concentration of these compounds would decrease with depth during infiltration, and especially whether these compounds would penetrate through the 8 m thick unsaturated zone to reach the water table. The aliphatic hydrocarbons, although not the main focus of this study, have provided evidence that some organic contaminants will migrate rapidly through the unsaturated zone in this area. These compounds were detected in the groundwater two days after the infiltration experiment. This finding implies that

groundwater pollution may be occurring in this area as a result of water seepage from the wastewater pond.

Results of the organic contaminants added during the experiment indicate possible attenuation. Butyric acid and aniline were not detected in any of the water samples. Phenol was only detected at 1m and was not detected at depth.

It is interesting to note that toluene had penetrated up to a depth of 4 m. The organic compounds benzoic acid and benzyl alcohol identified at 1 m are known to be biodegradation products of toluene (Montgomery and Welkom, 1991). As noted by Muszkat (1993), although known to be biodegradable, toluene was added to the list of pollutants of major concern due to their persistence and transportability. The fraction of organic carbon (f_{oc}) of the sands (0.3 -0.4 %) is relatively low, as such sorption is not likely to be high.

A number of assumptions were made in assessing these results. Firstly, it was assumed that the flow was strictly vertical and lateral movement of water was minimal. Results of the neutron probe measurements provide a basis to justify this assumption because a rapid vertical movement of the wetting front was observed. It was also assumed that sorption of organic compounds on the silica powder and the porous cups was minimal and that the volatilization of the organic compounds during sampling was insignificant. These assumptions will have to be examined during the next phase of the study.

5 CONCLUSIONS

The experiments conducted here have demonstrated that organic contaminants can migrate rapidly through the unsaturated zone in this area. Aliphatic hydrocarbons penetrated through the 8 m thick unsaturated zone and reached the water table in less than two days. Phenol had penetrated to a depth of 1m while toluene had reached 4 m during the same period. These findings imply that current solid and liquid waste disposal activities in the area could be polluting the groundwater resources.

Extreme caution should be exercised when making assumptions on the ability of the unsaturated zone to attenuate and immobilise contaminants. While certain chemicals will be attenuated by the subsurface matrix, others will travel through rapidly to contaminate groundwater reserves. The field experiment conducted in this study serves to emphasize the danger of extrapolating attenuation capabilities from one study area to another in the urban environment.

ACKNOWLEDGEMENTS

A. Hön and B. Eigenhuis are thanked for assistance with the field experiment and P Engelbrecht and L. Cavé for preparation of the figures and final manuscript. M. Froneman and B. Visser did the organic analysis. Finally I would like to thank the WRC for permission to publish this paper.

REFERENCES

Everett, L.J. & L.G. McMillion 1985. Operational ranges for suction lysimeters. *Groundwater monitoring review* 51(5):51-60.

Liator, M.I. 1988. Review of solution samplers. *Water Resource Research* 24:727-733.

Montgomery, J.H. 1991. *Groundwater chemicals desk reference. Vol. 2.* Lewis publishers, Michigan.

Montgomery, J.H. and Welkom, L.H. 1991. *Groundwater chemicals desk reference.* Lewis publishers, Michigan.

Muszkat, L., D. Raucher, M. Magaritz, D. Ronen and A.J. Amiel 1993. *Unsaturated zone and ground-water contamination by organic pollutants in a sewage-effluent-irrigated site.* Ground Water 31(4), 556-565.

Tredoux, G. 1984. The groundwater pollution hazard in the Cape Flats. *Water Pollution Control* 83(4): 473-483.

Wilson, L.J., D.W. Dorrance, W.R. Bond, L.G. Everett & S.J. Cullen 1995. In situ pore-liquid sampling in the vadose zone. In L.J. Wilson, L.G. Everett & S.J. Cullen (eds), *Handbook of vadoze zone characterization & monitoring. Geraghty & Miller environmental science and engineering series*:477-521. Lewis Publishers.

Groundwater in the Urban Environment: Problems, Processes and Management, Chilton et al. (eds)
© 1997 Balkema, Rotterdam, ISBN 90 5410 837 1

Colloidal populations in urban and rural groundwaters, UK

Kim A. Stagg, U. Kleinert, John H. Tellam & John W. Lloyd
Department of Earth Sciences, University of Birmingham, UK

ABSTRACT: Colloids have been rarely studied in the UK major water resource aquifers, yet in addition to the possibility of affecting contaminant travel times and pollutant mass transport, they may also provide information concerning sources of pollution. Investigation of colloidal populations and the contaminants sorbed to them has thus been initiated, with samples being taken from urban and rural boreholes in one of the UK's main aquifers, the Triassic Sandstone, and the overlying Quaternary deposits. Preliminary results have been obtained from boreholes in Lancashire, Nottingham and Birmingham, and initial findings suggest higher colloidal populations (10^{12} particles/litre) within the shallow and urban sites compared with low populations (10^{10} p/l) in the rural deep boreholes. The deeper groundwaters contain higher proportions of inorganic material, and the shallow boreholes, higher organic proportions. In no case investigated did the heavy metal mass associated with the colloids form more than a small fraction of metals in solution. However, urban pollution sources were indicated by the metal content of individual colloidal particles.

1 INTRODUCTION

It is now widely recognised that colloids may affect both contaminant travel times and total mass transfer (McCarthy & Zachara 1989). Most investigations have concerned colloidal radionuclide transport, specifically within fractured formations (Grindrod 1993; Smith & Degueldre 1993; Kim et al. 1994). However, natural colloidal populations have been rarely studied specifically in major water resource aquifers, and especially in the UK.

Colloids are defined as suspended particles having a dimension between 1 and 1000 nm in at least one direction (Stumm 1993). Due to their dimensions, colloids possess an extensive surface area and numerous reactive surface sites per unit mass. This provides considerable sorption potential for contaminants such as heavy metals, radionuclides and organic compounds. Very low settling velocities will facilitate colloid transport over considerable distances, thereby increasing contaminant fluxes. Colloidal material can include: rock fragments detached from a geological matrix; re-suspended cement material eroded by groundwater flow or released following geochemical change; precipitates from supersaturated groundwaters; secondary minerals formed by equilibration of the suspended particles with changing geochemical conditions; and organic or bioorganic materials (humic acids, bacteria and viruses).

This research has been initiated to identify the colloidal populations and the contaminants sorbed to them within one of the UK's main aquifer systems, the Triassic Sandstone. Sampling regions were chosen to research different land-use environments. Preliminary results have been obtained from rural boreholes in Lancashire, urban shallow and deep boreholes in Nottingham, and urban deep industrial boreholes in Birmingham.

2 METHODS

In the present study, samples have been obtained from industrial, high abstraction, deep (>100m) boreholes, and from shallow (<10m) piezometers. Sampling from abstraction boreholes is convenient and avoids the need for special purging. However, the samples obtained, being mixtures of waters extracted from varying depths, can be inherently unstable, and thus colloidal sized artefacts can occur after sampling. In addition, the high abstraction rates may result in mobilisation of particulate matter in the aquifer, although in many cases most of the easily mobilised particulates may already have been flushed out of the system.

Sampling of industrial boreholes is performed using on-line, closed-system ultrafiltration. Groundwater, direct from the rising main, was passed through a 1 μm prefilter into a holding reservoir under an inert atmosphere of nitrogen and 1 % carbon dioxide. The groundwater was then circulated through a 10,000 molecular weight cut off (MWCO) tangential filter concentrating the colloidal fraction from 500l of groundwater to 5l, within the holding reservoir. On-line measurements of flow-rate, pH, conductivity, temperature and alkalinity of the permeate were performed.

Samples of raw and prefiltered water, permeate and concentrate were obtained to determine colloidal masses, each fraction being analysed by inductively coupled plasma - atomic emission spectrometry (ICP-AES) and colorimetry. The colloidal mass was mounted onto transmission electron microscope (TEM) grids in the field using an adaptation of the method proposed by Perret et al. (1991). Colloids were embedded in nanoplast resin and mounted on copper grids previously covered with a 10-50 nm thick film of collodion and a 5-10 nm thick carbon coating. This allows visual assessment by a scanning tunnelling electron microscope (STEM) and individual chemical analysis by energy dispersive x-ray analysis (EDX).

Sampling from piezometers is generally less convenient. However, although the systems sampled are less well flushed of particles than abstraction boreholes, and therefore purging has be performed, the samples obtained are less likely to represent mixtures of extreme chemistries. In this particular study, the piezometers were purged for over 10 borehole volumes using a positive pressure pump. 10.5l of groundwater was then collected in pre-sterilised high density polyethene (HDPE) bottles. Once in the laboratory the water was passed through a 1 μm prefilter before subjection to tangential filtration under an inert atmosphere. Further concentration by centrifugation allowed TEM grid mounting as above. In some cases, sub-samples were seeded with humic acid colloids, and mounted for STEM examination. Being powerful sorbers, the humic colloids scavenge species particles at very low dissolved concentrations; EDX analysis can then be used to identify the species present.

To date, samples have been collected from nine industrial boreholes within the Birmingham aquifer, fourteen industrial boreholes in the Nottingham aquifer and two public water supply boreholes from the Lancashire aquifer. In addition eight shallow monitoring piezometers have been sampled from Quaternary Gravels overlying the Triassic Sandstone aquifer in Nottingham.

3 HYDROGEOCHEMICAL ENVIRONMENTS

The Birmingham aquifer comprises a confined-unconfined Triassic Sandstone sequence overlain by Quaternary deposits of clays and gravels. The Birmingham conurbation covers the entire aquifer. The main industries that abstract groundwater are associated with various types of metal-working, most of which have been established for over a century. Other major industries include chemical and vehicle manufacture. Abstraction of groundwater is purely for industrial purpose and due to a decline in demand, groundwater levels are now rising.

Previous work on the hydrochemistry of the Birmingham aquifer groundwaters has been undertaken by Jackson & Lloyd (1983) and Ford & Tellam (1994). In general Eh values are oxidising with pH ranging from 6-8. Lower pH values are commonly associated with shallow waters. Typically groundwaters sampled are calcium (magnesium) - bicarbonate sulphate waters. Iron, copper, nickel and zinc are commonly found above detection limits, but only locally at mg/l levels. Saturation indices suggest over-saturation of iron species and quartz in the water samples. In general, Birmingham provides a set of localised, high concentration, metal-rich pollution sources enabling assessment of the impact of urban industrial environments on colloidal populations.

The conurbation of Nottingham covers a large proportion of an unconfined Triassic Sandstone aquifer. The major industry is textile manufacture and dying with some metal plating and food processing. The hydrochemistry of the aquifer and the impact of urban contamination have also been widely researched (Edmunds et al. 1982). Typically the Triassic Sandstone groundwater is of calcium (magnesium) -bicarbonate type. The pH values are neutral to slightly alkaline, with diverse ionic strengths. Saturation indices of sampled waters suggest over-saturation of calcite, dolomite, barite, quartz, and in some instances iron species.

Quaternary gravels associated with the River Trent overlie the Triassic Sandstone in the south of Nottingham. Eight piezometers were sampled within the city centre section of the flood plain. Typical groundwater analyses show a calcium (magnesium) - bicarbonate (sulphate) oxidising water of neutral pH and moderate ionic strength. Heavy metals are below detectable limits. Saturation indices suggest over-saturation in iron species, quartz, barite and in some instances calcite, dolomite, and rhodochrosite.

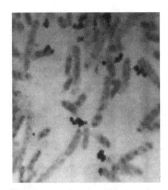

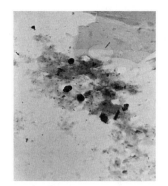

Figure 1. Bacteria and bioorganic matter.

Figure 2. Dense silicates with aluminosilicates and evaporites with associated iron and titanium.

Figure 3. Oval organic particles bound by an organic mass.

Scale Bar: 1 μm

The boreholes sampled in Lancashire are located within the unconfined section of the Lower Mersey Basin Region, also within the Triassic Sandstone. They are characteristic of a rural agricultural area, with little surrounding development. Groundwaters sampled typically are of calcium (magnesium) - bicarbonate (sulphate) type some with high levels of sodium. The waters are slightly acidic with low to moderate ionic strength. Nitrate levels are low and heavy metals are below detectable limits. Saturation indices of sampled water suggest over-saturation of iron species, barite and quartz.

4 RESULTS

4.1 Colloidal populations

Colloidal populations were estimated by two specific methods: calculations based on the colloidal mass determined from analysis of the various groundwater filter fractions; and visually by particle counting from STEM grids. Both these methods necessitate assumptions about, and including: homogeneous populations; particle sizes; and particle separation. However, comparison of the values obtained by the two methods, indicate agreement to within about an order of magnitude.

Particle estimates determined by STEM counting from the Birmingham groundwaters suggest populations of approximately 10^{10}-10^{11} particles per litre (p/l). Assuming particles to be quartz spheres of between 100-200 nm diameter, this would produce a colloid concentration population of 0.2-1 mgSi/l. Masses of colloidal materials calculated by ultrafiltration fractionation suggest values of approximately 300 μg/l. Particle estimates for the Lancashire aquifer show slightly higher colloidal populations of approximately 400 μg/l. Although one Lancashire groundwater shows three times more dissolved solids, colloidal populations remain equal at approximately 10^{10}-10^{11} p/l.

The Nottingham Triassic Sandstone aquifer colloid populations are more diverse with concentrations ranging from 200 μg/l to 15 mg/l. The majority of the boreholes contain concentrations between 200 μg/l to 800 μg/l, which correspond to a colloidal population of approximately 10^{11} p/l. However, the more contaminated boreholes show concentrations up to 15 mg/l equivalent to a colloidal population of 10^{12}-10^{13} p/l. The Nottingham Quaternary gravels show similar levels of colloids with fractions of between 10 to 50 mg/l, corresponding to a population of 10^{12}-10^{13} p/l.

4.2 Colloidal compositions

Colloids observed using the electron microscope have been classified according to morphology, density, aggregation and chemical composition.

The colloidal populations of the samples taken in the rural Lancashire aquifer are largely dominated by round and irregular, dense silicate particles with associated aluminium and iron. A very small amount of organic material is present, mostly within the stronger ionic strength groundwaters consisting primarily of irregular and elongate, transparent masses composed of carbon, nitrogen, oxygen and sulphur sometimes incorporating calcium, sodium and magnesium. Dense, spherical aggregates of

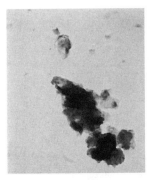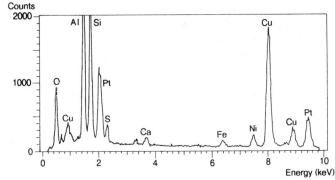

Figure 4. Aluminosilicate particle, approximately 750 nm in length, with EDX spectra showing platinum, nickel and iron. The copper and sulphur peaks are due to mountings.

silica and oxygen are sometimes present. Bacteria have been detected in one of the groundwaters.

Colloid particles in the urban Birmingham aquifer groundwaters comprise: anhedral particles, mostly of silica and oxygen, with aluminium, sulphur and iron; euhedral particles composed of silica, oxygen and aluminium; weak, acicular particles of calcium sulphate, possibly precipitation artefacts; and considerable quantities of bacteria and bio-fragments (Figure 1). Some sulphur and nitrogen rich colloids are present, likely to be associated with organics.

Perhaps the most intriguing particles are dense, siliceous spheres sometimes with associated aluminium, sulphur and heavy metals. They occur on STEM grids separately, or as cluster or chain aggregates. These particles mainly consist of silica with trace sulphur. They clearly represent silica precipitation, but at which stage is uncertain, and they are the subjects of ongoing investigation. Particle sources include precipitation following mixing in the wells, influx from atmospheric and/or made ground sources (e.g. PFA), or contamination following sampling.

Silicate and aluminosilicate particles consistently dominate the colloidal populations of the samples abstracted from the urban Nottingham industrial boreholes (Figure 2). The silicate particles mainly consist of irregular and rounded fragments. The aluminosilicate particles have more diverse morphologies, including irregular, rounded, spherical and globular. Some irregular and rounded, dense organic matter is present surrounding the silicate material. Iron oxides and calcium sulphates occur dominantly within the higher ionic strength groundwaters. Heavy metals are found mostly associated with the siliceous phase. Bacteria and bioorganic particles are also commonly present.

The majority of the colloids from the Nottingham shallow gravel groundwaters are composed of organic matter, with a small proportion of silicate and aluminosilicate particles. Small, oval, dense particles form the major proportion of the organic material, with irregular organic masses also present on the grids (Figure 3). Transparent fibres sometimes incorporating calcium and sodium, and aluminosilicate particles are also present. The inorganic material, composed mainly of dense, round and irregular particles is mostly bound by the organic matter to form large masses on the grids. Two of the groundwaters, however, contain mostly irregular and round, dense, silicate material with some aluminosilicate particles and considerably smaller amounts of organics. Some precipitates, particularly calcium sulphate, are present especially in the high ionic strength groundwaters, possibly as post-sampling artefacts. Abundant bacteria and bioorganic matter is present in all of the groundwaters and the heavy metals tend to be associated with the organic masses or on the siliceous material.

4.3 Metals associated with colloids

Data concerning the metals associated with the colloidal proportion were obtained from filtered groundwater fractions and EDX analysis. The former technique requires considerable quantities of contaminant to be present on the colloidal phase for detection. However, much lower contaminant levels can be detected using the EDX technique. Problems, however, are encountered in using the EDX technique to quantify chemistries of the colloidal populations due to the small number of samples

Table 1. Summary table of colloidal populations and associated contaminants.

Sites	Birmingham	Nottingham Deep	Nottingham Shallow	Lancashire
Colloidal Populations	10^{10}-10^{11} p/l	10^{11}-10^{13} p/l	10^{12}-10^{13} p/l	10^{10}-10^{11} p/l
Colloidal Composition:				
Inorganic	Al/Si, Si	Al/Si, Si	A few Al/Si, Si	Al/Si, Si
Organic	Very few	Very few	Humics, fibres	None
Possible Artefacts	$CaSO_4$	$CaSO_4$, FeO, NaCl, KCl	$CaSO_4$	None
Bacteria Frequency	Moderate	Moderate	High	Low
Metals:				
% total mass on colloids	< 1%	< 1%	< 1%	< 1%
Occurrence Frequency	High	Moderate	Low	Low
Metals present on	Inorganics	Inorganics	Inorganics & organics	-

which can be analysed, and the difficulty of randomly choosing particles.

Bulk ICP-AES analysis of groundwater samples abstracted from the Birmingham aquifer indicate the presence of chromium and zinc concentrations at levels close to the detection limit: occasionally concentrations in pumped waters reach mg/l levels, and one sample contained nickel at 800 mg/l. However, within all the groundwaters sampled, the mass associated with colloids never exceeds one percent. Within the Nottingham Triassic Sandstone aquifer, a few samples show zinc to be above detection limits and chromium is only rarely detected. The mass of these contaminants associated with colloids again never exceeds one percent. No metals are above ICP-AES detection limits within the samples from the Nottingham gravels, and as expected no metals are detectable in the samples collected from the Lancashire rural boreholes. It is, therefore, concluded that negligible mass is associated with the colloidal phase in the sampled groundwaters.

Using the EDX technique, nickel, chromium, titanium, zinc, cobalt and tin have been found on colloids from the Birmingham aquifer. However, the frequency of occurrence is only a few percent for each metal. The sample with the highest content of dissolved metals has the highest concentration of metals associated with colloids. However, some samples with moderate metal concentrations in solution, specifically chromium and zinc, frequently have metal-bearing colloids, whilst other samples of similar dissolved metal concentrations have few metal-bearing colloids. The addition of humic colloids to the groundwater recovered manganese and cerium, from solution.

EDX analyses from the Lancashire aquifer show only iron present, which is to be expected in the relatively iron-rich sandstone environment. Seeding of this groundwater with humic colloids does

however, show the presence of titanium and zinc, but at very low levels.

The majority of the Nottingham Triassic Sandstone aquifer industrial groundwaters have very low quantities of metals associated with colloids, with iron occurring in the majority of boreholes and traces of titanium in approximately 10 percent. However, one contaminated groundwater shows considerable frequency of occurrences of iron, nickel, platinum, titanium and zinc, and also infrequent traces of lead, manganese and chromium (Figure 4). Seeding with humic colloids increased the number of metals detected in most cases: elements most frequently found were zinc, titanium, barium and cerium. Seeding of the most contaminated borehole sample also produced tin.

The groundwaters sampled from the Nottingham gravels show different characteristics with fewer metals associated with colloids. No iron was present in any of the samples, titanium occurred in approximately 30 percent of the samples, and lead in one groundwater sample. Seeding, however, did result in the uptake of iron onto the humic colloids.

5 DISCUSSION AND CONCLUSIONS

Only a few sites were sampled in this survey and sampling conditions were not ideal. However, distinct colloidal populations have been identified within the selected areas. Table 1 summarises these populations and associated contaminants.

Generally, on a regional scale, the transport of colloidal mass within both the urban and rural Triassic Sandstone aquifers of the UK is not considerable, and thus colloids do not appear to be affecting the overall rates or velocities of transport of contaminants in these aquifers. However, it is possible that colloid-facilitated metal transport may occur to a significant extent at a much more local scale, and this possibility needs investigation. Near surface Quaternary deposits sampled in Nottingham have higher colloid concentrations than the underlying sandstones, though the colloidal mass still remains small compared to the dissolved mass.

The colloidal populations within the Triassic Sandstone are dominated by silica and aluminosilicate particles, as expected, with few organics. Some particles collected on grids are likely to be artefacts (e.g. $CaSO_4$, KCl, $NaCl$); others are possibly artefacts (e.g. SiO_2 spheres), though this has yet to be established.

Within the urban groundwater samples, metals are commonly found associated with colloids (e.g. iron, titanium, zinc, nickel, manganese, cobalt, tin, platinum). The rural sites are typically metal free, though even here metals are occasionally detected (e.g. iron, titanium). Seeding of the groundwater samples with humic colloids has enabled further recovery of metals from solution from samples from both the urban (e.g. lead, tin, chromium, cerium, antimony, lanthanum) and rural (e.g. zinc) sites.

The shallow urban groundwaters within the Nottingham gravels show different characteristics with larger proportions of organic colloids. Explanations for these differences include: proximity to the soil layer; immaturity of the borehole and thus inclusion of artefacts from drilling and made ground; lack of degradation of the organic material; and instability of aluminosilicate and silicate particles within the groundwater. The groundwaters contain larger colloidal populations, which again could be due to immaturity of the boreholes, but also could be a feature of the lack of straining of the aquifer media in comparison to the Triassic Sandstone. The shallow urban groundwater samples also show considerably less frequent occurrence of metals associated with the colloids (e.g. titanium, iron) in comparison with the deep sandstone boreholes.

It is concluded that although colloid-facilitated transport of contaminants may be of limited nature in UK urban Triassic Sandstone aquifers, colloids are potentially very useful in sourcing groundwaters in the complex urban environment. Metal-rich colloids were found not only where metals were detectable by bulk solution analysis, but also where metals were not detected. The industrial borehole groundwaters of Birmingham and Nottingham clearly show the effect of the urban environment, with greater frequency and diversity of heavy metals associated with the colloidal material present. This is in contrast with the rural sites where considerably fewer metals are present. Seeding of the groundwater with humic colloids is also potentially a very useful tool by further enhancing the detection of species present at very low concentrations.

Further investigation is necessary to substantiate these conclusions and produce a more detailed appraisal. Specific work is required to understand and ultimately diminish, if possible, the processes giving rise to the artefacts. More complete identification of the organic matter is necessary to allow better sourcing and understanding of provenance. There is considerable scope for using highly sorbant seeding colloids to further identify very low concentrations of heavy metals. Identification of colloidal populations at a smaller sample scale is necessary to enable assessment of more local colloidal transport. These investigations will allow more accurate indication of colloidal and heavy metal sources, within the groundwaters, thus enabling identification of specific pollutant sources and thus the tracing of groundwater itself.

ACKNOWLEDGEMENTS
This work is funded by NERC and the EC. Professor Miro Ivanovich is thanked for his help in establishing the methods.

REFERENCES

Edmunds, W.M., A.H. Bath & D.L. Miles 1982. Hydrochemical evolution of the East Midlands Triassic Sandstone aquifer. *Geochim. Cosmochim. Acta* 46: 2069-2081.

Ford, M. & J.H. Tellam 1994. Source, type and extent of inorganic contamination within the Birmingham urban aquifer system, *UK. Hydrol.* 156: 101-135.

Grindrod, P. 1993. The impact of colloids on the migration and dispersal of radionuclides within fractured rock. *J. Contam. Hydrol.* 13: 167-181.

Jackson, D. & J.W. Lloyd 1983. Groundwater chemistry of the Birmingham Triassic sandstone aquifer and its relation to structure. *Q.J.Eng.Geol.* 16: 135-142.

McCarthy, J.F. & J.M. Zachara 1989. Subsurface transport of Contaminants. *Envir. Sci. & Tech.* 23,5: 496-502.

Perret, D., G.G. Leppard, M. Muller, N. Belzile, R. De Vitre & J. Buffle 1991. Electron microscopy of aquatic colloids. *Water Research* 25: 1333-1343.

Smith, P.A. & C. Degueldre 1993. Colloid-facilitated transport of radionuclides through fractured media. *J. Contam. Hydrol.* 13: 143-166.

Stumm, W. 1993. Aquatic colloids as chemical reactants: surface structure and reactivity. *Colloids and Surfaces A-Physiochemical* 73: 1-18.

Groundwater in the Urban Environment: Problems, Processes and Management, Chilton et al. (eds)
© 1997 Balkema, Rotterdam, ISBN 90 5410 837 1

Groundwater quality implications of wastewater irrigation in León, Mexico

Marianne E. Stuart & Chris J. Milne
Hydrogeology Group, British Geological Survey, Wallingford, UK

ABSTRACT: Wastewater from the city of León, Mexico, has been used for irrigation of agricultural land close to the city for the last 40 years. The wastewater contains a significant percentage of industrial effluent from the extensive tanning industry, including high concentrations of salt and hexavalent chromium compounds, and is used untreated. The irrigated area overlies an aquifer which provides an important part of the municipal water supply. Infiltration of the irrigated water has led to the formation of a localised layer of shallow, poor-quality water above the regional aquifer. Investigation has shown changes in the quality of the infiltrating wastewater as it passes through the soil and shallow aquifer layers. These significantly reduce the concentrations of chromium, sodium, sulphate and nitrogen. However, high chloride concentrations remain to pose an immediate threat to groundwater quality in the lower part of the aquifer and chloride concentrations in groundwater from some deep municipal supply boreholes are now rising rapidly.

1 INTRODUCTION

The city of León in Guanajuato State, is situated in a wide upland valley at an altitude of 1800 m, about 500 km north of Mexico City. It has one of the fastest growing populations in Mexico, which is highly dependent on groundwater resources for public water supply. The climate is semi-arid, so there is also a heavy dependence on irrigation for agricultural crops. Groundwater is drawn from a complex aquifer system in the alluvial valley fill downstream of the city, including areas which have been subjected to wastewater reuse for agricultural irrigation for up to 40 years (Figure 1).

Wastewater generated in the city is highly polluted due to effluent derived from the prominent leather processing and shoe manufacturing industry. Several of the leather manufacturing processes give rise to highly polluting effluents. Sodium chloride, used to preserve hides before tanning, and hexavalent chromium are of particular concern here. The effluents are combined with domestic wastewater via sewers which feed into a series of open canals carrying the wastewater directly into the irrigation area. The subsequent distribution system is complex and subject to change depending on operational requirements. There are two large, dammed, settlement lagoons, but only a fraction of the water passes through the first of these holding lagoons before being applied directly to crops, mainly by flood irrigation. The second lagoon is further downstream and only intercepts water which has already passed through the study area. Infiltration of excess irrigated wastewater is sustaining a shallow groundwater body beneath the wastewater area, superimposed on rapidly declining regional groundwater levels.

This chemical study forms part of a wider project whose overall objective was to determine the effects of wastewater reuse on groundwater resources including quantity, quality and management issues (Chilton et al., 1997). As part of this aim, a regular programme of quality monitoring of both deep and shallow groundwater was established, surface geophysical techniques were employed to estimate the depth of penetration and lateral extent of poor quality water and both soil profiling and the drilling of cored observation wells were used to investigate the vertical dimension of groundwater quality variation. A more detailed description of the procedures used is provided in BGS et al. (1996). This paper is concerned with describing the observed chemical behaviour of the wastewater and the consequent effects on and implications for groundwater quality.

A separate detailed study of the area immediately surrounding the plant producing chromium chemicals for the tanning industry has delineated a plume of groundwater heavily contaminated with hexavalent chromium derived from the spoil heaps at the rear of the factory (Armienta and Quéré, 1995).

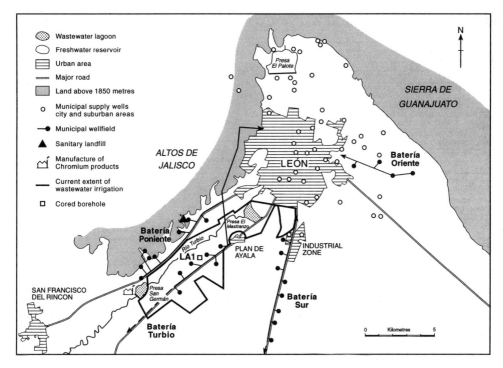

Figure 1. Location map showing wastewater irrigation area and municipal well fields.

2 PROCESSES IN THE DISTRIBUTION SYSTEM AND SHALLOW SOILS

Wastewater samples were collected as part of the regular monitoring programme at a series of points in the wastewater distribution system. A summary of the typical analyses is presented in Table 1. The dilution of the tannery effluents by other industrial and domestic waste during progression through the system can be clearly seen. It is also clear, from comparison of the quality of the collector canals and the lagoon outfall, that the lagoons act as highly efficient chromium removal sinks.

Soil core samples were taken from sites with a range of irrigation histories including: former settlement lagoon beds; fields irrigated with water from different wastewater sources; and fields irrigated with wastewater over different timescales. Control samples were obtained from fields which had never been irrigated with wastewater. Sampling of sediments from active storage lagoons was impractical for reasons of safety and hygiene. At each site, simple sub-sampling and field averaging procedures were used to try to improve the representativeness of samples. The final composited samples were analyzed for chromium and other heavy metals using a dilute nitric acid extraction and ICP-OES.

The analytical results provide clear evidence that chromium is accumulating in the soils affected by wastewater irrigation. All sites which have been exposed to varying durations of wastewater irrigation had extractable chromium contents at least one order of magnitude higher than unexposed samples. The degree of accumulation is related to the total period of irrigation although it must be remembered that the accelerating expansion of industry will not give rise to a constant accumulation rate. The variation in other heavy metals, such as Zn, Cu and Pb is not so pronounced, but elevated concentrations are still associated with the use of wastewater.

The soil analyses also confirm the picture of metal accumulation in lagoon sediments, evidenced by the very high concentrations in the sediment from the bed of the disused lagoon at Presa Blanca, to the north of the present Presa El Mastranzo.

There is unequivocal evidence of a decrease of metal concentrations with depth, particularly for chromium. At all sites the major fraction of chromium is contained within the top 0.3 m of the profile. Below 0.6 m concentrations are at, or close to, background concentrations, even at those sites which have the highest concentrations in the uppermost horizons (Figure 2). This pattern agrees well with other studies reported in the literature (McGrath, 1995).

Table 1. Typical values of key water quality parameters at the different stages of the wastewater distribution system.

Water type	Total Cr (mg/l)	Total N (mg/l)	Chemical oxygen demand (mg/l)	Conductivity (μS/cm)	pH
Tannery discharge	200	400	-	20000	8.0
Industrial collector	40	240	5000	9000	9.0
Domestic collector	20	100	1000	3500	8.4
River Turbio	4-29	50	250	1800	8.3
Lagoon exits	0.1-0.4	40-80	170-350	2000-2300	8.3
Irrigation canal	0.06	40	200	1200	7.9
Shallow polluted groundwater	0.002-0.005	2-14 (as NO_3)	10-60	2700	6.7
Regional background quality	0.002-0.005	0-2 (as NO_3)	0-4	480	7.2

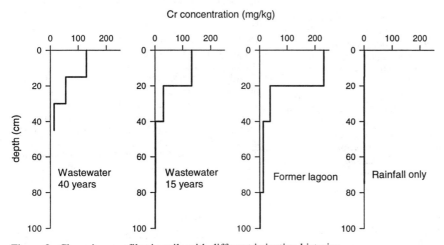

Figure 2. Chromium profiles in soils with different irrigation histories.

The mechanism of sorption of chromium by organic matter is not clear. Cr(VI) is not strongly sorbed to soils, but Cr(III) is readily precipitated as $Cr(OH)_3$ and can also be chelated by organic molecules attached to mineral surfaces (James and Bartlett, 1983). Cr(VI) can be reduced to Cr(III) in soils by aqueous inorganic species or by organic species such as carbohydrates or soil fulvic acids. Soil fulvic acids have been shown to reduce Cr(VI) effectively at pH 7 or below (Wittbrodt and Palmer, 1995).

The data in Table 1 also show considerable improvements in the concentrations of nitrogen and organic carbon (as indicated by chemical oxygen demand) within the lagoons. The nitrogen loading may be reduced by degradation of organic nitrogen directly to ammonia, which is then volatilized, or by denitrification of inorganic nitrate to nitrogen gas in the anaerobic bottom sediments of the lagoons and canals. Soil under continuous alfalfa cover and receiving large quantities of organic matter in wastewater is also likely to remain anaerobic for much of the irrigation cycle. Ammonia may be leached from the soil, but is not very mobile. Organic matter in the wastewater is more likely to be oxidised to carbon dioxide or bicarbonate in the shallow groundwater which tends to remain slightly aerobic.

3 CHEMICAL PROCESSES IN THE AQUIFER

Regional groundwater quality is generally very good, consistent with meteoric water originating from the volcanics which form the valley margins. The waters are of mixed calcium/sodium type (see Figure 3) with

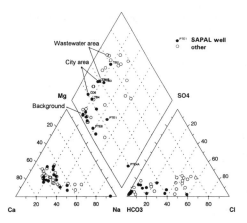

Figure 3. Piper trilinear diagram showing the impact of wastewater infiltration on groundwater

low concentrations of chloride and sulphate and the unpolluted waters have significant concentrations of dissolved oxygen, even at depth. This low level of background mineralization makes the impact of infiltrating wastewater readily distinguishable. Within the area of wastewater reuse all of the relatively shallow private irrigation wells which were sampled have a distinctive and characteristic major ion chemistry. Samples from within the wastewater area are found in the upper portion of the trilinear plot in Figure 3, reflecting their higher proportion of chloride. Samples from the deep municipal supply boreholes (SAPAL) located within the wastewater area are also found in this part of the diagram.

The infiltrating wastewater undergoes a sequence of chemical changes in the shallow layers of the aquifer. These are illustrated by a depth profile of porewater from borehole LA drilled in the wastewater area (Figure 4). There are heavy evaporation losses during the irrigation process so that porewaters in the unsaturated zone have about double the concentrations of major ions of the original wastewater. Oxidation of organic matter to carbon dioxide, which dissolves to form carbonic acid, leads to cation dissolution from the aquifer matrix to form bicarbonates. This process combined with cation exchange results in the replacement of the majority of the sodium in the original water by calcium. The sodium concentration falls rapidly from 600-800 mg/l at the surface to below 100 mg/l by 25 m, with a corresponding rise in calcium to 400 mg/l.

Cation exchange sites are thought to occur on clay particles of the aquifer matrix and to contain significant amounts of calcium and magnesium. The collapse of soil structures caused by similar exchange processes where irrigation water contains excess sodium are well known. This hazard is quantified for irrigation waters using the sodium adsorption ratio (Pescod, 1992).

Sulphate concentrations also decline over the interval 20-35m, although sulphate species do not appear to be saturated in the porewaters.

Assuming that chloride ions are conservative, the decline in concentration indicates dilution of the infiltration by better quality residual water, throughflow from beneath the city or recharge from the valley sides. Below 35 m no further changes in the relative ratios of the major ions are seen. Nitrate

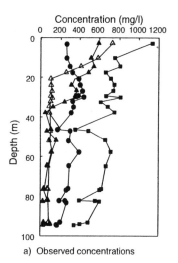

a) Observed concentrations

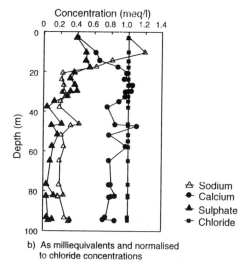

b) As milliequivalents and normalised to chloride concentrations

Figure 4. Profiles of porewater chemistry for borehole LA.

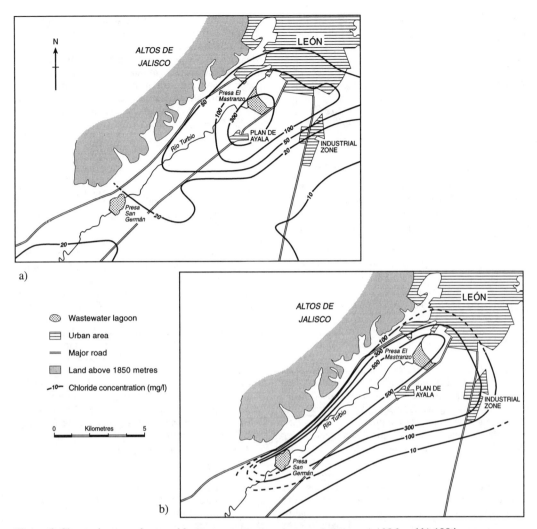

Figure 5. Change in groundwater chloride concentration contours between a) 1986 and b) 1994.

concentrations remain relatively modest, in the range 2-14 mg/l (as N).

The other two boreholes showed a similar pattern, although less clearly, but no simple relationship between history of irrigation and depth of penetration of poor quality water could be observed. This was due to the highly variable nature of the deposits forming the aquifer and the local impact on hydraulic conditions of high discharge pumping.

Shallow wells in the wastewater area retain higher concentrations of heavy metals other than chromium compared to background levels, although these are well below potable limits. Traces of uranium are also seen. These are thought to be derived from mobilisation of disseminated uranium in the aquifer matrix by infiltrating bicarbonate.

4 TIMESCALE OF WATER QUALITY CHANGES

Shallow wells close to one of the most recently developed areas of wastewater reuse have shown a dramatic increase in all major ions since 1986. The areal extent of shallow aquifer contamination is demonstrated by comparison of the regional chloride concentrations in 1986 and 1994. Elevated concentrations of chloride in groundwater have spread south-eastwards down the river valley away from the city (Figure 5).

More seriously, municipal boreholes situated within the wastewater area are now showing a rapid deterioration in quality. These draw water from the lower part of the aquifer sequence and are screened from 200 to 400 m. The rate of increase of chloride

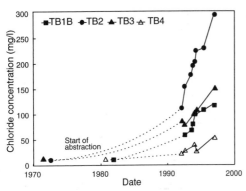

Figure 6. Progressively increasing chloride concentrations in groundwaters from municipal supply boreholes of the Bateria Turbio in the wastewater area.

concentration is currently approximately 40 mg/l/a and chloride is likely to exceed the national standard for drinking water (250 mg/l) in the worst affected borehole (TB2) very soon (Figure 6).

5 IMPLICATIONS

To date the results indicate that salt has been the most mobile of the pollutants originating in the applied wastewater. The pollutant loadings of metals, organic carbon and pathogens appear unlikely to penetrate through the thick aquifer system to deep abstraction boreholes. Therefore, for the municipal water undertaking, the most pressing issue in relation to the security of potable supplies is the future trend in salinity in the wellfields closest to the wastewater area. These currently supply some 16% of the city's water. A modelled projection of water quality over the next 30 years under the present regime shows that quality in the upper part of the aquifer will continue to deteriorate and the salinity will rise to values approaching those of the infiltrating water.

Consideration of a number of options available to tackle this problem suggests that the most important is to implement separate collection and disposal of industrial effluents, the major source of salinity. Other measures such as increased abstraction from the shallow aquifer and improved irrigation efficiency will also lead to long term amelioration of deep water quality.

ACKNOWLEDGEMENTS

This project was funded jointly by the UK Government Overseas Development Administration (ODA) and the Commission of the European Communities (CI1*-CT92-0043). We are very grateful for extensive collaboration and logistical support from the Comisión Nacional del Agua (CNA), and the Sistema de Agua Potable y Alcantarillado del Municipio de León (SAPAL) in Mexico, without both of whom the project would not have happened. This paper is published with the permission of the Director of the British Geological Survey, a component institute of the Natural Environment Research Council.

REFERENCES

Armienta, M.A. and A. Quéré 1995 Hydrochemical behaviour of chromium in the unsaturated zone and in the aquifer of Leon valley, Mexico. *Water, Air and Soil Poll.*, 84: 11-29

British Geological Survey, Comision Nacional del Agua, Sistema de Agua Potable y Alcantarillado del Municipio del León & Universidad Autónoma de Chihuahua 1996. Effects of wastewater reuse on urban groundwater resources of Leon, Mexico. *British Geological Survey Technical Report WD/95/64.*

Chilton, P.J., M.E Stuart, O. Escolero, R.J. Marks, A. Gonzalez and C.J. Milne 1997. Groundwater recharge and pollutant transport beneath wastewater irrigation: the case of León, Mexico. Geol. Soc. Spec. Pub: Groundwater pollution, aquifer recharge and vulnerability. In press

James, B.R. and R.J Bartlett 1983 Behaviour of chromium in soils. VI. Interactions between oxidation-reduction and organic complexation. *J. Environ. Qual.*, 12(2): 173-176.

McGrath, S. P. 1995. Chromium and nickel. In B. J. Alloway (ed), *Heavy metals in soils*. Blackie.

Pescod, M.B. 1992 Wastewater treatment and use in agriculture. *FAO Irrigation and Drainage Paper 47*, Rome.

Wittbrodt, P.R and C.D. Palmer 1995 Reduction of Cr(VI) in the presence of excess soil fulvic acid. *Environ. Sci.& Technol.*, 29: 255-263.

Groundwater in the Urban Environment: Problems, Processes and Management, Chilton et al. (eds)
© *1997 Balkema, Rotterdam, ISBN 90 5410 837 1*

An experimental study on migration of TCE in the unsaturated zone

Changyuan Tang & Shizuo Shindo
Center for Environmental Remote Sensing, Chiba University, Japan

Masahito Yoshimura
Department of Earth Science, Chiba University, Japan

Tatemasa Hirata
Faculty of System Engineering, Wagayama University, Eitani, Japan

ABSTRACT: Lysimeter experiments were conducted to study the behaviour of non-aqueous phase liquids (NAPLs), using trichloroethene (TCE) in simulated rains. By comparing the vertical profiles of tritium and TCE, it was found that TCE migration in the unsaturated zone could be divided into three stages during the rain event. At first, TCE dissolved into water that moved down during rain events. Next, when rainwater infiltrated into the ground, TCE gas moved down due to soil air compression, due to diffusion as well as density. Finally, after the rain events, TCE gas concentration remained constant, there was little movement of pure TCE and aqueous phase TCE moved because of water redistribution in the unsaturated zone. The results of our experiments also show that the infiltrating water not only dissolved TCE and made it mobile, but also enhanced TCE gas moving down by sealing pores and compressing gases in the unsaturated zone.

1 INTRODUCTION

A number of non-aqueous phase liquids (NAPLs) are common in groundwater through leakage, spillage, or disposal at manufacturing sites or at chemical waste disposal facilities. Unfortunately, even at concentrations in the part per billion ranges these contaminants can make the groundwater unusable. It is important to acquire a proper understanding of the relevant physics describing the transport and fate of NAPLs in both the unsaturated zone and groundwater.

Several experimental studies have been undertaken investigating the dissolution of NAPLs within the saturated zone (Fried et al. 1979; Anderson et al. 1992; Miller et al. 1990; Borden & Kao 1992; Powers et al. 1992; Geller & Hunt 1993). Based on those data, dissolution of NAPLs incorporates the specific interfacial area for dissolution between NAPL ganglia and flowing water. In fact, different pore structures yield different ganglia sizes and shapes and thus different specific interfacial areas for dissolution.

As NAPLs migrate through the subsurface, interfacial forces act to retain "globules" or "blobs" of the organic liquid in the unsaturated and saturated zones. These immobile blobs are difficult to remove by conventional remediation techniques and create a long-term source of pollution. The experimental work quantifying dissolution of NAPLs trapped at residual saturation below the water table has provided a better understanding of factors affecting NAPL concentrations in water leaving such zones. However,

fewer experiments have been undertaken to show the behaviour of residual NAPLs in the unsaturated zone. NAPL distribution in the unsaturated zone is affected greatly by the behaviour of water there, especially during periods of rain. In fact, many research projects in both in the laboratory and field have shown that DNAPL behaviour at field scale is too complicated to explain with the results obtained from the laboratory.

It is clearly necessary to fill the gaps between the two scales to understand DNAPL migration in the saturated and unsaturated zones. This paper describes an experimental study with a lysimeter, which tries to examine the dissolution of TCE in the unsaturated zone affected by infiltration.

2 MATERIALS AND METHODS

Infiltration experiments were conducted with the lysimeter (140 cm × 140 cm × 230 cm) shown in Figure 1. The thickness of the walls were 10 cm, therefore the sand volume in the lysimeter was 120 cm × 120 cm × 20 cm. Tensiometers, soil water samplers and gas sample pipes as well as thermometers were set at depths of 10 cm, 32 cm, 55 cm, 77 cm, 100 cm, 122 cm, 145 cm, 167 cm, 190 cm and 212 cm, respectively. In the middle of the lysimeter, a nuclear water meter access tube was set to measure the water vertical profile before and after experiments. Additionally, five TDR (time domain reflectometer) sensors were set at depths of 10 cm,

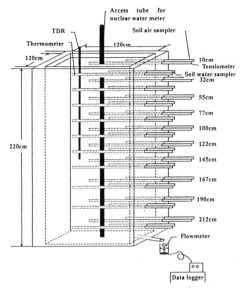

Figure 1. Lysimeter used in the experiments.

Ten experiments were conducted to study the behaviour of trichloroethene (TCE) during simulated rain events. Water was sprinkled by a rainfall simulator from the top of the lysimeter with an intensity of 25 mm/h. There were 33.3 mm in the first eight experiments, and 66.6 mm and 15.6 mm in the last two experiments, respectively. At the beginning of the first experiment, 2420 ml pure TCE and tritium-dated water were put at the depths of 10 cm from the top of the lysimeter.

The porous material used in experiments consisted of sand (88%), silt (4%) and clay (8%), with a hydraulic conductivity of 2.9×10^{-3} cm/s. The trichloroethene (TCE) used here was analytic special grade, produced by Wako Pure Chemical Industries.

Soil water and soil gas in the unsaturated zone were sampled during and after rain events. TCE extracted from the effluents or soil gas was analyzed by gas chromatography on a Shimadzu GC-14B equipped with a flame ionization detector (FID). Variations of tritium concentration in the effluents and soil waters were analyzed with a liquid scintillation counter (Packard Tri Cab 1050).

32 cm, 55 cm, 77 cm, 100 cm, 122 cm, respectively. Soil suctions, temperatures and effluent water from the bottom of the lysimeter were measured automatically and recorded in a data-logger. Hydraulic potentials were calculated by setting the lysimeter surface as zero. TDR values were measured once per 10 minutes during experiments. TCE and tritium were used to trace the behaviour of DNAPL and water, respectively.

3 RESULTS

Figure 2 shows the variations of hydraulic potentials during the experiments where the water table was set at 170 cm depth. At the beginning of experiments, hydraulic potentials were almost the same with depth, which means no vertical flow movement occurred.

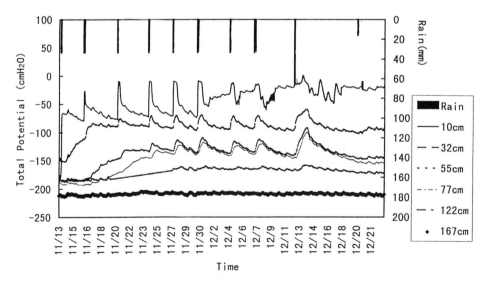

Figure 2. Variations of hydraulic potentials during the experiments.

However, during the first rain period, hydraulic potentials increased at depths of 10 cm and 32 cm. During the second rain period, hydraulic potentials in 10 cm, 32 cm, 55 cm and 77 cm increased to 65 cm , 55 cm, 95 cm and 100 cm water respectively. At the third rain period, hydraulic potentials increased at all depths. After the 4th rain period, patterns of hydraulic potentials responding to rain were the same at each depth, which means there a steady state existed in the lysimeter. During the rain period, hydraulic potentials responded to rain one by one at depths of 10 cm, 32 cm, 55 cm and 77 cm. However, hydraulic potentials at depths of 122 cm and 167 cm responded to rain less since the discharge would occur as soon as the infiltration front reached the top of capillary zone which was located at about 50 cm above the water table.

Initial soil water contents ranged from 20% at the surface to about 30% at the top of the capillary zone. During the rain event, water in the top layer increased first. With the infiltration, water contents increased with depth. At the end of the 10th experiment, water contents were more than 30% in the unsaturated zone.

Figure 3 shows the variations of vertical profile for ^3H with time. In general, the peaks of ^3H showed the movement of water during the experiments. As the infiltration water moved down, the peaks of ^3H became lower and lower with time. If a line is drawn to connect peaks of ^3H and consideration given to the lapsed days from the beginning of the first experiment, the velocity of the infiltration water in the lysimeter can be calculated. From Figure 3, it was found that the peak of ^3H reached a depth of 50 cm in the first 10 days. After that, movement of ^3H slowed down and reached a depth of 80 cm after 20 days. That means the velocity of infiltrating water was 5 cm/day and 3 cm/day in the first ten days and the second ten days, respectively.

Figure 4 shows the variations of vertical distribution for TCE gas concentrations. Before the experiments, TCE gas concentrations were zero ppm in the lysimeter. About half an hour after beginning the experiments, TCE gas was detected at 0.034 ppm and 0.006 ppm at depths of 32 cm and 55 cm, respectively. About five days later, TCE gas was detected at 0.04 ppm and 0.029 ppm at depths of 100 cm and 122 cm, respectively. That means that the TCE gas moved quickly into the soil. The high TCE gas concentration was detected on the 10th day. After that, this peak of TCE gas moved down by keeping the same gradient. The highest TCE concentration was found to be 176 ppm about 17 days and 20 hours after the beginning of experiments, and at the same time TCE gas concentration was 7.5 ppm at the depth of 122 cm. As the TCE moved down the lysimeter, the peak concentrations for TCE gas became lower and

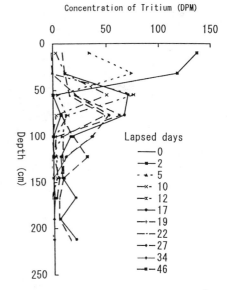

Figure 3. Variations of vertical profile for ^3H.

lower. The block of TCE gas at 100 ppm moved down quickly at about the 30th day and moved up in the 40th day. On the other hand, the block of TCE gas at 50 ppm moved down quickly at about 23 days and slowly before 45 days. This block of TCE gas moved down quickly again at 45 days. By considering the rain, it seems that movement of TCE gas corresponded well with infiltration water. Looking at the iso-concentration line for zero ppm, it was found that it shifted down quickly from five to ten days, and 25 days. At the depth of 167 cm, the soil was in the saturated zone where TCE gas could not be detected, although TCE was detected at 2.3 ppm in the effluent. Clearly, different from ^3H, TCE could either move down or keep still in high concentration at the topsoil layer where there existed pure TCE globules or blobs.

4 DISCUSSION

NAPLs that enter the subsurface through spills or leaks may create long-lived groundwater contamination problems. NAPL distribution in the unsaturated zone is affected greatly by the behaviour of water there, especially during the period of rain. By comparing the vertical profiles of tritium (Figure 3) and TCE (Figure 4), it was found that pure TCE liquid did not move straight downward in the unsaturated zone. The front of tritium matched well to the depths where the TCE concentration was about 20 ppm. This means that TCE could move more quickly than

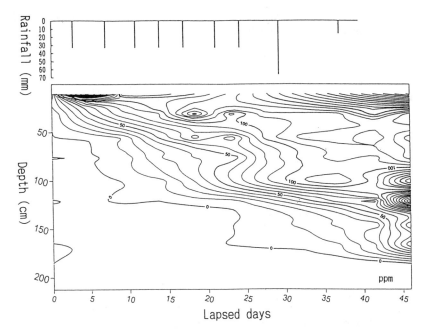

Figure 4. Vertical variations of TCE concentration during the experiments.

water in the unsaturated zone where TCE migration in the gas phase is very important. Generally, infiltrating water can push both TCE-dissolved-water and TCE gas downward during rain events. Considering the relationship between water content and TCE concentration, it is important to assess TCE migration processes in the unsaturated zone in infiltration conditions.

4.1 Pure TCE migration in soil

When the liquid (water or NAPLs) flowed down into the unsaturated porous zone, soil would be coated by it, and become the passage for the liquid. In this study, residual TCE could be found in the unsaturated zone. This is also true for water. Once the passage was available, both water and TCE moved down as preferential flows with mass transfer between them. According to Tang et al. (1995), the TCE body kept still without changing its shape, and water continued to infiltrate downward around the TCE body as it was trapped by water. The trapped TCE body did not move in the saturated zone in spite of water table changes. As soon as the water film has broken on the topside of the TCE body during the water table decline, the force balance which kept TCE maintained in the saturated zone was distorted. As a result, the TCE body changed its shape from a flat to long bar, which

increased the entry potential because of its thickness. If the entry potential of the TCE body was large enough, TCE would begin to move down. The TCE body could also increase its entry potential by joining other trapped TCE bodies when it moved down.

The lysimeter experiment results show that TCE acted as variable blocks against water movement. Rainwater could infiltrate to groundwater by making its way through the NAPL's zone where soil particles were wetted by water before. From the viewpoint of TCE dissolution, only the effective pores through which water could infiltrate were important. In field conditions, TCE gas concentrations in void pores might be much higher than that in infiltrating water. Because no forces would be available to drive the gas out except for diffusion, more pure TCE would stay in the unsaturated zone, and only TCE dissolved in solution would move down with infiltration. By comparison with groundwater, TCE will stay in the unsaturated zone much longer than that in groundwater.

In steady state conditions, the TCE dissolution rate can be defined as:

$$D = \frac{dm}{dt} = QCe \qquad (1)$$

where D is dissolution rate, m mass of TCE, Q the

202

flow rate and Ce the average concentration. Assuming M is the mass of residual TCE in the unsaturated zone, R is a effective dissolution rate, the volume of water for complete dissolution (Vw) can be calculated from:

$$Vw = \frac{QM}{R} \qquad (2)$$

According to the experimental results, the actual dissolution time would be longer, because the effective pores vary with rain infiltration conditions and dissolution rate would decrease with time.

As a result, water and TCE move in the subsurface in different ways. Water moves along wetting soils, and TCE made its way in the soil coated by itself. Since less water is available in the unsaturated zone than in groundwater, TCE would persist for a long time and be dissolved by infiltrating water in the unsaturated zone, causing long-term pollution.

4.2 TCE migration with infiltration water

Lysimeter experiments have been designed and conducted to investigate TCE behaviour as well as the factors affecting its dissolution in the unsaturated zone during the rain infiltration processes.

During steady state, TCE concentrations in effluents changed little. Considering the effective pore for TCE dissolution, the larger the particle size is, the higher the TCE concentration. Rain infiltration also enhanced TCE dissolution by pushing both TCE gas and the high TCE concentration water downwards.

By comparison with Figure 3 and Figure 4, we could identify the movements of water with TCE during the experiments. In fact, peaks of tritium coincided with the TCE iso-concentration line of 50 ppm. Therefore, the velocity of water was less than that of TCE. However, the depth where tritium could be detected coincided with TCE concentrations of zero ppm and 20 ppm. Furthermore, TCE gas was found at the place where no tritium could be detected. That means that water was one of the important carriers for TCE migration in the unsaturated zone. At the same time, gas movement was also important for TCE moving in the soil.

In general, the exchange coefficient for TCE dissolution was found to be dependent upon the velocity of the aqueous phase and time, but the solute concentration in the aqueous phase was only slightly dependent upon the aqueous phase velocity. These were interpreted as supporting the notion of a local equilibrium between TCE and the aqueous phase.

After pure TCE entered the lysimeter, the unsaturated zone became more heterogeneous.

Rainfall percolating through NAPL-contaminated zones was found to contain levels of dissolved TCE that were close to aqueous solubility. Following the weathering phase, infiltration water was applied, and subsequent analysis of infiltrated water samples revealed that dissolution was described by equilibrium conditions.

4.3 Effects of infiltration on TCE gas migration

According to Figure 4, it could be considered there existed residual pure TCE blocks at a depth of 10 cm where TCE gas concentration was 364.9 ppm five days after the beginning of the experiments. In ten days, TCE gas concentration decreased to 47.2 ppm at a depth of 32 cm, which means the pure TCE had not reached that depth. However, TCE gases were detected at 0.034 ppm and 0.006 ppm at depths of 32 cm and 55 cm, respectively. The results hinted that TCE gas moved down quickly, and the movement of TCE gas was very important at initial conditions.

Therefore, the one of important mechanisms for TCE migration was diffusion caused by air pressure gradient in the soil. During rain periods in the experiments, soil gas pressures increased quickly causing TCE gas to move down.

4.4 TCE migration processes during events

According to the results shown here, it was found that TCE migration in the lysimeter could be divided into three stages during the rain events. At first, TCE dissolved into water that moved down during rain events. TCE gas concentration increased with the increase of soil water content. Secondly, when rainwater infiltrated into the ground, TCE gas moved down due to soil air compression, diffusion as well as density. TCE gas concentration increased greatly with less change in soil water content. Thirdly, during soil water redistribution after the rain events, TCE gas concentration kept constant when soil water content decreased. TCE moved little since soil water was enough to prevent it escaping from the soil particles. Our experiments show that the infiltrating water not only dissolved TCE and made it movable, but also enhanced TCE gas moving down by sealing pores and compressing gases in the unsaturated zone.

5 CONCLUSIONS

Lysimeter experiments were conducted to study the behaviour of NAPLs with trichloroethene (TCE) in simulated rain. TCE and tritium were used in the experiments to trace the behaviour of DNAPL and water. At the same time, soil water potential was measured with tensiometers and a nuclear soil water meter.

By comparing the vertical profiles of tritium and those of TCE, it was found that pure TCE liquid did not move straight downward and TCE that could move more quickly than water in the unsaturated zone where TCE migration in the gas phase was very important.

Generally, infiltrating water can push both TCE aqueous phase and TCE gas downward during rain events. It means that TCE can move with infiltrating water by dissolution and TCE gas can move down through the soil due to sealing porous pores and compressing gases in the unsaturated zone during the events.

The effective pores through which rainwater infiltrated affected TCE dissolution. Since water and TCE move in the subsurface through different ways, TCE can continue to be dissolved by infiltrating water in the unsaturated zone for a long time.

ACKNOWLEDGMENTS

We gratefully acknowledge the assistance provided by Professor Sakura, Y. of Chiba University, and Dr. Komae, T. of National Research Institute of Agricultural Engineering. This research was supported partly by Showa Shell Sekiyu Foundation for Promotion of Environmental Research.

REFERENCES

Anderson, M.R., R.L. Johnson, & J.F. Pankow 1992. Dissolution of dense chlorinated solvents into ground water, 1, Dissolution from a well-defined residual source. *Ground Water*, 30: 250-256.

Borden, R.C. & C.M. Kao 1992. Evolution of groundwater extraction for remediation of petroleum contaminated groundwater. *Water Resour. Res.*, 64: 28-36.

Fried, J.J., P. Muntzer & I. Zilliox 1979. Groundwater pollution by transfer of soil hydrocarbons. *Ground Water*, 17: 1921-1925.

Geller, J.T.& J.R. Hunt 1993. Mass transfer from nonaqueous phase organic liquids in water-saturated porous media. *Water Resour. Res.*, 29: 833-845.

Miller, C.T., M.M. Poirier-McNeill & A.S. Mayer 1990. Dissolution of trapped non-aqueous phase liquids: Mass transfer characteristics. *Water Resour. Res.*, 26: 2783-2796.

Powers, S.E., L.M. Abriola & W.J. Weber, Jr. 1992. An experimental investigation of nonaqueous phase liquid dissolution in saturated subsurface system: Steady state mass transfer rates. *Water Resour. Res.*, 10: 2691-2705.

Tang, C., S. Shindo, S., M. Hirata & Y. Sakura 1995. Experiments on behaviour of NAPLs in unsaturated-saturated zone under the conditions of a changing water table. *IAHS Pub.*, 227: 157-164.

Groundwater in the Urban Environment: Problems, Processes and Management, Chilton et al. (eds)
© 1997 Balkema, Rotterdam, ISBN 90 5410 837 1

International practice for the disposal of urban runoff using infiltration drainage systems

David C. Watkins
Camborne School of Mines, University of Exeter, UK

ABSTRACT: The use of pluvial drainage soakaways is a well established infiltration drainage method in the UK. These are generally small devices in which urban runoff from roofs and paved areas may be stored and allowed to drain into the ground. Elsewhere in Europe larger scale devices are often favoured. These may be in the form of trenches or basins. In the US these schemes are often on an even larger scale and can form part of an integrated water management plan. The policy and practice in a number of different countries is reviewed. There is no consistent methodology or management practice between, or even within, different countries.

1 INTRODUCTION

Infiltration drainage systems can be used to dispose of stormwater runoff from roofs and paved areas. They are devices which store water and allow time for it to percolate into the ground (Figure 1). These differ from detention ponds because the receiving water is groundwater. They also differ from groundwater injection systems by the fact that water is discharged to the unsaturated zone some distance above the water table.

The advantages of infiltration drainage over piped sewerage systems include:

1. They can be used where access to piped drainage is impractical or where the sewerage system is already fully loaded.

2. They reduce the impact of urbanisation on river flooding by reducing the rapid passage of water into surface water bodies.

3. They promote groundwater recharge and increase river baseflow.

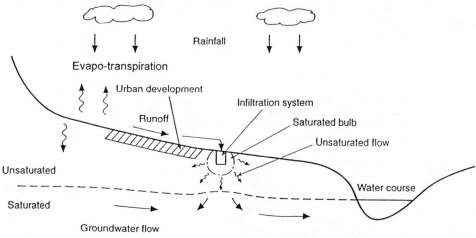

Figure 1. Diagrammatic representation of infiltration drainage.

There are also a number of disadvantages which include:

1. There is a potential for contaminants to enter the aquifer with the urban runoff.

2. The maintenance requirement is difficult to assess and often neglected. There is a potential for siltation and clogging of the infiltration surface which can lead to a decrease in performance with time.

3. Design methods in use vary considerably.

4. A rising water table in a shallow aquifer beneath an urban area can lead to a variety of problems.

5. They are not feasible in all situations.

The use of infiltration drainage methods is actively promoted in many parts of Europe, North America and Japan, but the types of system in use vary considerably.

2 TYPES OF SYSTEM

Infiltration systems can come in many forms. Innovative designs may be applied to suit the requirements of a particular site. Sometimes they are linked to other infiltration systems or to piped sewerage systems. The infiltration surface may be constructed either at or below ground level.

Ground level systems include:

1. Permeable roads and paved areas using porous asphalt or open lattice concrete blocks. These may be referred to as plane infiltration methods as infiltration is one dimensional.

2. Infiltration basins. These may be relatively large scale and may be designed to remain wet as small wetlands or to drain quickly allowing recreational use on a grassed surface.

3. Swales. These are essentially vegetated drainage ditches, often with check dams to promote seepage of the water into the ground.

According to CIRIA (1992) a distinct advantage of ground level systems is that they are visible; the operation and performance is readily observed and maintenance is easier to undertake and monitor.

Below ground systems include:

1. Soakaways, sometimes referred to as dry wells or percolation shafts. These may be square, rectangular or circular in plan and constructed with perforated concrete rings or dry brick lined walls. They may be empty chambers, to maximise storage, or stone filled to provide structural support.

2. Infiltration trenches. These are similar to soakaways but constructed as a long trench to maximise the infiltration surface area. They are usually stone filled and may include a horizontal perforated pipe to evenly distribute water. Harrington (1988) describes these as long narrow excavations, 1 to 4 m in depth, typically serving drainage areas up to 2.5 ha.

3 INTERNATIONAL PRACTICE

The benefits of infiltration drainage are recognised in suitable urban areas in many parts of the world. In the UK, small scale soakaways are commonly used. These serve and are located on individual properties. Elsewhere in Europe larger scale systems such as trenches and basins are often favoured. These may be referred to as "centralised" systems if more than one property is served. In the USA these schemes are often on an even larger scale and may form part of a city-wide water management plan.

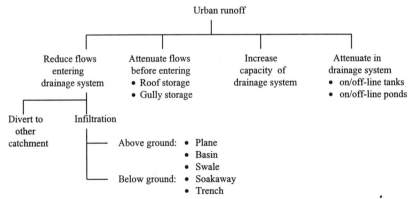

Figure 2. Options for the control of urban runoff (adapted from CIRIA 1992)

3.1 UK

Although a few innovative schemes involving infiltration basins and permeable pavements are occasionally used, traditional soakaways are the main infiltration method. Their use is firmly established with well in excess of 50,000 soakaways constructed each year in England and Wales (Watkins & Pratt 1995).

The first UK national guideline on soakaway design was published in the mid 1970's (BRE 1973). This method was found to be too restrictive, allowing only soakaways with equal depth and diameter to be designed. Guidelines were later developed to allow other geometries to be designed, including infiltration trenches (BRE 1991).

In the 1980's and 1990's, infiltration drainage was identified as an important method of source control, minimising the hydrological impact of urbanisation (CIRIA 1992).

Watkins (1991) developed an analytical frame-work for the hydraulic design of soakaways taking account of both infiltration and storage. This procedure was developed further to apply to all other types and shapes of infiltration system, without varying the basic assumptions, which allowed further guidelines and examples of good practice to be issued (Bettess 1996).

3.2 USA

A great deal of research was conducted in the 1970's and 1980's into the use of permeable pavements (e.g. Thelan et al. 1972; Diniz 1980; Field et al. 1982).

Ferguson (1991) refers to artificial infiltration being practised in Denver, Colorado, as early as 1889. Infiltration basins are firmly established in Southern California and have been extensively used in New York State. On Long Island, in the early 1930's legislation was enacted requiring developers to design and install recharge basins. More than 3000 such basins exist today within an area of glacial outwash deposits (Ferguson 1990). This has had the effect of protecting wells from saline intrusion problems. It has also led to an estimated increase in water table level of 1.5 m compared to a decrease of 0.9 m in areas where infiltration drainage is not used (Ku & Simmonds 1986).

In Maryland, state legislation enacted in 1982 required all developers to consider the use of infiltration drainage as an essential part of the stormwater management programme (MDNR 1984). Despite the implementation of maintenance procedures, a post project appraisal showed standing water in many of the basins (Pencyl & Clement 1987) and infiltration is no longer actively encouraged.

Basins in Florida frequently function as ephemeral ponds with their base below the natural water table, a feature common to Florida's natural environment according to Ferguson (1990).

In Arizona, due to low rainfall, standing water rarely occurs in basins and designers are able to integrate basin design with surrounding urban landscapes.

The state of Maine provides detailed guidance to developers and promotes infiltration drainage in terms of best management practices (MDEP 1995).

The US EPA estimated that there were some 90,000 soakaways in use in 38 states in 1987 (Wilson 1990).

3.3 Canada

Some twenty infiltration basins were constructed in the 1970's in Guelph, Ontario. These are now believed to have sealed and become wetlands, indicating the need for some form of pre-treatment to remove fine material from the water entering the infiltration system. Recent experience with other types of infiltration systems has proved more successful.

In Ontario, guidelines promote the use of infiltration drainage following a treatment train approach. If the ground is suitably permeable, roof drainage is disposed of to soakaways. The next options to be considered are conveyance controls such as swales, followed by end of pipe controls such as infiltration trenches, basins and wetlands (OMEE 1994).

3.4 Australia

Suitable conditions exist for infiltration around Perth, Western Australia (Davis et al. 1996). Infiltration of stormwater through basins, trenches and swales are the subject of best management practice guidelines (Whelans et al. 1993). Perth is considered to be unusual in this respect because extensive areas of the Perth metropolitan region are located on sandy soils where the water table is sufficiently deep for infiltration of stormwater to be a preferred option.

It is believed that some experimentation with infiltration drainage has also taken place in Adelaide, South Australia.

3.5 *Germany*

German guidelines are available for single property infiltration systems (ATV 1990). The term "area percolation" is used for systems where water is infiltrated in the open by surface flow to grassed verges or through constructed permeable surfaces.

"Trough percolation" is described as a variant of area percolation with which temporary storage of water is allowed. The inflow may therefore exceed the infiltration rate during a design storm. This method may be used with urban green areas, verges of foot and cycle paths and minor tracks.

With "trench" percolation, the water is either fed above ground to an open gravel filled trench or below ground to a perforated distribution pipe in a gravel filled trench. These are often laid at the base of grassed storage troughs in which further infiltration and storage can occur.

ATV (1990) use the term "shaft percolation" where water is stored in a permeable shaft (soakaway) from where it can slowly percolate into the soil. This method is recommended for detached house plots and other small drainage projects.

There are also many schemes and guidelines elsewhere in Western Europe including France, Switzerland and Holland.

3.6 *Scandinavia*

Hogland et al (1987) describe investigations into permeable road surfaces in Sweden termed "unit superstructures".

General design guidelines are available for infiltration systems (SWSWA 1983). This allows the design of vegetated infiltration surfaces and also below ground methods (Stahre & Urbonas 1988).

Stormwater infiltration is becoming increasingly accepted in Denmark. Systems used include direct discharge of roof runoff to grass lawns, road drainage through permeable asphalt surfaces, roadside swales, infiltration trenches and shafts or soakaways (Mikkelsen et al 1996).

3.7 *Japan*

Many different innovative systems are in use in Japan. Progress is made toward combination systems which feed firstly to soakaways or trenches but overflow to surface water or combined sewer systems (Fujita & Koyama 1990). In Tokyo, an area of more than 1400 ha has been drained to 33450 soakaways, 286 km of infiltration trenches and nearly 500000 m^2 of permeable pavement since 1980 (Mikkelsen et al 1996).

4 DESIGN METHODS

Due to the nature of extreme rainfall events it is impractical to design an infiltration system to cope with every conceivable event. It is necessary to accept the fact that the system will occasionally fail, by overflowing, when the design storm event is exceeded.

Design methods for calculating the required size of infiltration system vary considerably, both between countries and also within each country. Many successful schemes have been designed using local experience with no theoretical foundation, though the occasional bad experience can lead to a loss of confidence in the techniques. Design guidelines have been developed only relatively recently.

The simplest method is to allow storage of a set rainfall depth, such as 25 mm over the area drained. This approach, however, takes no account of soil permeability and can lead to infiltration systems being designed in unsuitable locations. A better approach is to base calculations on an estimated infiltration rate. Various attempts have been made to relate infiltration to permeability through Darcy's Law. ATV (1990) provide complex formulae to relate infiltration area to system geometry. Watkins (1991) compared various techniques in use with unsaturated flow modelling through numerical solution of the Richards equation. It was found that a simple assumption of a uniform and constant rate of infiltration through the wetted infiltration surface area provided a good approximation to soakaway performance; better than using many of the more sophisticated assumptions. If a unit hydraulic gradient is assumed then the infiltration rate is equivalent to the saturated hydraulic conductivity of the surrounding soil. The unit hydraulic gradient is valid for long term vertical infiltration from a ponded surface (Philip 1969) but less accurate for infiltration through the sides of an infiltration system (Watkins 1991).

In Australia, Davis et al (1996) feel that this type of approach leads to over-conservative designs and propose that numerical techniques based on unsaturated flow using the Green and Ampt solution provide a better design methodology.

The methodology developed in the UK by Watkins (Bettess et al. 1996) provides a simple approach to plane infiltration systems, more complex analytical equations for vertical sided systems such as soakaways and trenches and non-linear solutions for sloping sided systems such as basins and swales which require an approximate time-stepping solution procedure.

A number of guidelines quote a threshold value of infiltration rate, below which infiltration drainage should not be used. This restriction is economic rather than technical (Mikkelsen et al. 1996) as, technically, an infiltration system will work if large enough. In an urban environment, however, large systems are not always practical.

Table 1 lists set minimum infiltration rates adopted in various guidelines.

Table 1. Threshold infiltration rates.

country	infiltration rate		reference
	(mm/h)	(m/s)	
Sweden	72	2×10^{-5}	SWSWA (1983)
USA	12.5	3.5×10^{-6}	Harrington (1988)
USA	12.5	3.5×10^{-6}	MDEP (1995)
Germany	9.0	2.5×10^{-6}	ATV (1990)
USA	4.3	1.2×10^{-6}	Shaver (1986)
UK	1.0	2.8×10^{-7}	Bettess et al (1996)

5 OTHER ISSUES

There are many aspects of infiltration drainage to consider and this paper has only provided an overview of some.

Water quality issues are of paramount importance. Surface water quality is often the reason given for using infiltration drainage. Though care must be taken with salted roads, infiltration of storm water runoff to the ground above the water table, and especially through vegetated surfaces, provides a form of treatment. However, care must be taken to avoid polluting drinking water aquifers.

Geotechnical issues must also be considered. Steep slopes are not suitable for infiltration drainage as water can break out at the surface or destabilise the slope. Water should not be discharged too close to building foundations. This can be difficult to achieve in an urban environment.

Maintenance of the infiltration surface and pre-treatment of runoff using settlement or vegetated surfaces is important in ensuring a long working life for the system.

6 CONCLUSIONS

Under appropriate conditions infiltration drainage is a useful method of disposing of urban storm water runoff.

The main advantage is in mitigating the impact of urbanisation on surface water hydrology, which otherwise leads to increased flood peaks and low river baseflows.

Techniques are available to allow the design of a wide range of types of infiltration drainage system. Flexible but consistent methodologies such as those endorsed in the UK (Bettess, 1996) allow the designer a choice and can lead to effective and innovative designs to meet particular situations. It should be recognised that, although infiltration drainage can be used in many locations, not all locations are suitable on hydrogeological grounds.

There is work to be done on agreeing the best design and management practices at an international level.

ACKNOWLEDGEMENTS

The author is grateful for information provided by contacts overseas. In particular I wish to thank the following:

Doug Andrews of Ontario, Canada,
David Corwin of New York, USA,
Jack McCabe of California, USA,
John Hopeck of Maine, USA,
Sander van Hall of Perth, Australia,

REFERENCES

ATV 1990. *Construction and dimensioning of facilities for decentralised percolation of non-harmful polluted precipitation water*. Abwasser-techniche Vereinigunu e.V. standard A138. German Association for Water Pollution Control.

Bettess, R. 1996. *Infiltration drainage: manual of good practice*. Report 156. Construction Industry Research and Information Association, London, UK.

Bettess, R., A. Davies & D.C. Watkins 1996. *Infiltration drainage: hydraulic design*. Project record 23. Construction Industry Research and Information Association, London, UK.

BRE 1973. *Digest 151, soakaways*. Building Research Establishment, Watford, UK.

BRE 1991. *Digest 365, soakaway design*. Building Research Establishment, Watford, UK.

CIRIA 1992. *Scope for control of urban runoff*. Report 123. Construction Industry Research and Information Association, London, UK.

Davis, J., P. Davis, J. Robinson & D. Sim 1996. Design of infiltration basins, trenches and swales. *Local government engineering conference, March 1996*, Perth, Western Australia.

Diniz, E.V. 1980. *Porous pavement phase 1 - design and operational criteria*. United States Environmental Protection Agency report no. EPA-600/2-80-135.

Ferguson, B.K. 1990. Urban stormwater infiltration: purposes, implementation, results. *Journal of Soil and Water Conservation* 45(6): 605-609.

Ferguson, B.K. 1991. Taking advantage of stormwater control basins in urban landscapes. *Journal of Soil and Water Conservation* 46(2).

Field, R., H. Masters & M. Singer 1982. Porous pavement: research, development and demonstration. ASCE Proceedings, *Journal of Transportation Engineering* 108(TE3).

Fujita, S & T. Koyama 1990. Pollution abatement in the experimental sewer system. *Proc. 5th Int. Conf. on Urban Storm Drainage, Suita, Osaka, Japan, July 23-27*, (2):799-804.

Harrington, B.W. 1988. Design and construction of infiltration trenches. In: Urbonas, B., L.A. Roesner & M.B. Sonnen (eds.) *Design of urban runoff quality controls*, A.S.C.E.

Hogland W., J. Niemczynowicz & T. Wahlman 1987. The unit superstructure during the construction period. *The Science of the Total Environment* 59: 411-424.

Ku, H.F. & D.L. Simmonds 1986. *Effect of urban stormwater runoff on ground water beneath recharge basins on Long Island, New York*. Water Resources Investigations Report 85-4088, US Geological Survey, Washington DC, USA.

MDEP 1995. *Stormwater management for Maine: best management practices*. Maine Department of Environmental Protection, Augusta, Maine, USA.

MDNR 1984. *Standards and specifications for infiltration practices*. Maryland Dept. Natural Resources, Adminis. Stormwater Manage. Div., Annapolis, Maryland, USA.

Mikkelsen, P.S., P. Jacobsen & S Fujita 1996. Infiltration practice for control of urban stromwater. *Journal of Hydraulic Research* 36 (6): 827-840.

OMEE 1994. *Stormwater management practices, planning and design manual*. Ontario Ministry of Environment and Energy, June 1994, Ontario, Canada.

Pencyl, L.K. & P.F. Clement 1987. *Results of the State of Maryland infiltration practices survey*. Dept. Environ., Sediment and Stormwater Division, Annapolis, Maryland, USA.

Philip, J.R. 1969. The theory of infiltration. In: Chow, V.T. (ed.) *Advances in Hydroscience* (5): 215-296.

Shaver, H.E. 1986. Infiltration as a stormwater management component. In: Urbonas B. & L.A. Roesner (eds.) *Urban runoff quality - impact and quality enhancement technology*, American Society of Civil Engineers.

Stahre, P. & B.R.Urbonas 1988. Swedish approach to infiltration and percolation design. In: Urbonas, B., L.A. Roesner & M.B. Sonnen (eds.) *Design of urban runoff quality controls*, A.S.C.E.

SWSWA 1983. *Local infiltration of stormwater, instructions and comments* (in Swedish). Publication VAV P46, Swedish Water and Sewage Works Association.

Thelan E., W.C. Grover, A.J. Hoiberg & T.I. Haigh 1972. *Investigation of porous pavements for urban runoff control*. The Franklin Institute Research Laboratories, Philadephia, USA.

Watkins D.C. & C.J. Pratt 1995. *Infiltration drainage: survey of practice*. CIRIA Project record, Hydraulics Research, Wallingford, UK.

Watkins D.C. 1991. *The hydraulic design and performance of soakaways*. Report SR 271, Hydraulics Research, Wallingford, UK.

Whelan, Halpern Glick Maunsell in Association with Thompson Palmer and Murdoch University 1993. *Water sensitive urban (residential) design guidelines for the Perth metropolitan region. Schedule of best management practices*. Department of Planning and Urban Development, Water Authority of Western Australia and Environmental Protection Authority

Wilson, L.G. 1990. The ground water recharge and pollution potential of dry wells in Pima County, Arizona. *Ground Water Monitoring Review* 10 (3).

2 Geotechnical and construction problems

Topic co-editors:
Brian Morris
British Geological Survey

Shaminder Puri
Scott Wilson Kirkpatrick

Groundwater in the Urban Environment: Problems, Processes and Management, Chilton et al. (eds)
© 1997 Balkema, Rotterdam, ISBN 90 5410 837 1

Groundwater rise in Greater Cairo: Cause and effects on antiquities

A. M. Amer & M. M. Sherif
Irrigation and Hydraulics Department, Faculty of Engineering, Cairo University, Giza, Egypt

D. Masuch
Department for Engineering Geology and Hydrogeology, Aachen University of Technology, Germany

ABSTRACT: In the area of Greater Cairo a rising groundwater table has been observed east of the Nile over the last two decades. The groundwater rise can be linked to the specific hydrogeological setting of the Egyptian capital as well as to human activities. The Nile valley Pleistocene aquifer is constantly being recharged by vast quantities of irrigation water and leakage losses from both the sewer system and the public water supply network. Greater Cairo area contains many precious monuments of the pharaonic, Christian and Islamic periods. The rise of groundwater level is among the most serious menaces to the antique structures with a large number of them already being affected by foundation damage. Some selected cases of affected sites are presented. In any case, thorough investigations are recommended to select applicable rehabilitation techniques. The problem should be considered at the city-wide scale of the Greater Cairo area and not at the local scale for each antiquity site.

1 INTRODUCTION AND PROBLEM IDENTIFICATION

The population of Greater Cairo is expected to exceed 12.5 million inhabitants by the year 2000. The surrounding cities recently have experienced the most rapid growth rates in Egypt. Daily domestic water consumption of Cairo city amounts some 3.25 million m^3/day. The domestic water supply network was originally designed to serve a population of about 2 million only. Leakage losses through the exhausted water supply network exceed 60 %. The sewer system of Cairo was designed as an open channel flow with a maximum discharge of 1.5 million m^3/day in 1915 to serve a population of one million only. Nowadays, the network is receiving twice the design capacity under pressurized flow conditions. Leakage losses from this exhausted network are around 1/3 million m^3/day (i.e. 10 % of the effluent received). This has even resulted in frequent waste water flooding in several areas of the city with a considerable impact on groundwater quantity and quality as well as on public health.

Since the early seventies, problems related to water table rise have been observed east of the Nile in central parts of the city where a number of antiquity sites are located. High contents of chlorides and sulphates in groundwater contribute to endangering foundations in of some of Cairo's most densely populated areas such as Al-Sayida Zaynab, Al-Gamaliya and Al-Azhar. Harmful effects on subsoil

structures are encountered in places where groundwater rise is high enough to reach the structure itself. In some of the historic parts of Old Cairo groundwater has already submerged basements and structural elements and has caused severe damage. The problem is significant in the central part of the city, which is considered to be a depression zone. The area is subject to both lateral movement of subsoil water towards the depression and upward groundwater leakage.

2 GEOLOGY OF GREATER CAIRO RELATED TO GROUNDWATER HYDRAULICS

The principal results of previous geological investigations in Cairo area are summarized in Shata (1988), while Said (1975) outlined the subsurface geology of Cairo based on a number of boreholes. The following presentation of Greater Cairo geology focuses only on strata relevant to groundwater hydraulics.

Rubbish deposits, anthropogenic fill, aeolian sands, and alluvial Nile deposits cover a great part of central Cairo and are recorded also in the subsurface. The Recent and Pleistocene deposits are reported from top to bottom as follows:

2.1 Sub-Recent: Fill or Rubbish unit
Many parts of medieval Cairo have a bed of man-made fill consisting of decayed buildings and

rubbish. The sequence is of a thickness of up to 20 m and is reported from numerous shallow borings and excavations. Intercalated layers of silt and clay can be related to Nile floodplain origin.

2.2 Holocene: Silt-clay

The silt-clay unit represents the top of the Nile floodplain, but is also reported from its fringes and the channels of the major wadis as well as in the form of benches of 1 to 10 m thickness. Average thicknesses of the sediments are about 10 m. They consist of a successive accumulation of the suspended matter of the Nile during flood seasons and stand for the youngest of the Neonile deposits. Said (1975) estimated the rate of sedimentation before the construction of the Aswan High Dam as 10.3 cm/100 years. Montmorillonite is the major constituent clay mineral in this unit. The silt-clay layer marks the top of the Nile valley aquifer in the Cairo region.

2.3 Late Pleistocene: Coarse massive sand and gravel unit

Exposed in the northwest of Cairo this unit is being extensively quarried. The quarries reveal a section of uniform, crossbedded, loose floodplain sands, transported and deposited by the Prenile from source rocks south of Egypt. The subsurface thickness lies between 10-70 m and increases rapidly to about several hundred meters in the central delta. The coarse massive sand and gravel unit constitutes the main Nile valley aquifer in the Greater Cairo area. It includes clayey intercalations and sand lenses.

2.4 Lower Pliocene: Plastic clay

Separated from the Upper Pleistocene by a disconformity, the lower Pliocene plastic clay can be found in the subsurface between Abassia and Heliopolis. Sloping to the northwest the surface of the plastic clay is found at a depth of 25 m below ground surface of Nasr City, while in Heliopolis the top of the same layer is found at a depth of 80 m below ground surface. The clay is found to have a varying thickness from 16 m at Heliopolis to over 67

m at Abu Roash oil well No. 1 to 98 m in the western floodplain southeast of Cairo. The thick layer of plastic clay is found at the bottom of the Nile valley aquifer within the Cairo region and contains intercalated sand, gravel, and marl of lower Pliocene age. The bottom itself is underlain either by Eocene sediments or by Pliocene marine clay acting as an aquiclude.

3 GROUNDWATER SYSTEM OF GREATER CAIRO

The Greater Cairo aquifer represents the hydraulic connection between the Nile delta aquifer in the north and the Nile valley aquifer in the south. The aquifers are continuously being recharged by seepage from excessive use of irrigation water (Hefny 1982).

The Greater Cairo aquifer is a leaky aquifer system consisting of a semi-pervious silty clay layer acting as an aquitard on top of the graded sand and gravel unit constituting the aquifer itself. The aquifer is under semi-confined conditions where it is topped by the silty clay cap. At the eastern and western boundaries of the Nile valley the aquifer becomes phreatic due to the absence of the silty clay cap at the valley's fringes. The leaky aquifer is characterized by two inter-connected groundwater systems with the upper one being the subsoil water of the semi-pervious silty clay cap aquitard and the lower one forming the main aquifer itself. Groundwater pressure of the reservoir is referred to as piezometric head, whereas the subsoil phreatic water surface is referred to as shallow water table.

Vertical water movements through the clay cap unit are caused by the difference in levels between the piezometric head and the shallow water table. Vertical movement of groundwater is either upward or downward depending on their relative positions. Due to lack of information about the shallow water table levels of the aquitard in Central Cairo, recently

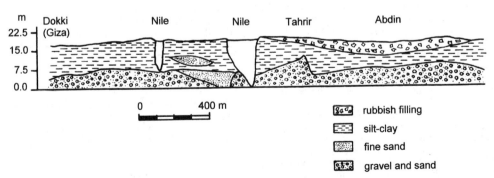

Fig. 1: Cross section through central Cairo
(after Hefny 1982).

214

nine shallow observation wells were drilled at selected sites. The wells are under the control of the Research Institute for Groundwater (RIGW) and the Irrigation and Hydraulics Department of Cairo University. Water table levels at these wells were recorded during 1991 and reveal a varying water table from less than 10 cm to a maximum of 2 m below ground surface. The shallow water is being recharged by a number of contributors:

- seepage from the irrigation channel network
- infiltration of surplus irrigation water
- leakage from the sewer network embedded in the strata
- losses from potable water supply network
- local upward flux from the aquifer

As indicated by several boreholes most districts of eastern Cairo are built on the alluvial Nile plain. The majority of medieval Cairo has a bed fill of sub-recent rubbish and waste deposits representing the remainders of successively decayed buildings covering the entire area from Al-Fustat in the south of the city to east Abassia. The clay cap thus can be regarded as a heterogeneous anisotropic formation constituting semi-permeable top boundary of the Greater Cairo aquifer.

The aquifer has a thickness of 20 m to 100 m in the central part of the urban area. Thicknesses increase to the northeast and decrease southeastward.

The bottom of the aquifer is marked by a thick layer of plastic clay having a maximum thickness of 80 m (Korany & Abdel-Aal 1988). The extent of the aquifer system is limited due to the existence of the eastern and western limestone escarpments. These lateral boundaries are limited by faults.

The Greater Cairo aquifer is partially penetrated by the Nile. Due to direct hydraulic contact between the river and the aquifer, flow conditions within the aquifer consequently changed after the construction of the High Aswan Dam. Before the completion of the dam, Nile water levels experienced an annual flood season from July through September and low levels during January and February. The groundwater regime in Greater Cairo reflected this cycle with some lag. Piezometric heads attained high levels during flood period and low levels during winter. Accordingly the Nile had a double function:

- recharging the aquifer during the flood season,
- draining the aquifer during the low stages period.

After the construction of the High Aswan Dam Nile water levels have been stabilized throughout the year at average levels presently some 35 cm higher. Fluctuations of water levels recently became limited. This indicates that the hydraulic interaction between the water budget of the Nile and the Cairo aquifer

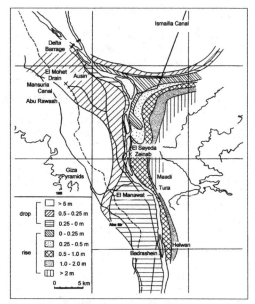

Fig. 2: Zones of rise and drop of groundwater levels in Greater Cairo from 1972 - 1981 (Hefny 1982)

now entirely depends on the changes in the aquifer piezometric heads.

In the eastern parts of Cairo a continuous rise in piezometric heads is being observed. This can be attributed to infiltration of irrigation water and leakage losses from both the water supply network and the sewer system due to new expansions of housing areas. Recent data from 9 shallow wells in Central Cairo are suggesting a significant upward flux of groundwater in the central and eastern parts of the capital (Sherif 1992). Whereas excessive withdrawals from wells in the areas east of the Nile led to local lowering of the water table level of 3 m, groundwater is continuously rising in the eastern parts of Greater Cairo (Shahin 1990).

A considerable amount of the input to the sewer system is being lost to the shallow layers of the Cairo aquifer causing serious contamination (Shahin 1990). Vertical recharge to the aquifer was estimated to be in the order of 800 million. m^3/ year. Net supply to the aquifer from the Nile amounts about 450 million m^3/year. The amount remaining in storage is about 10 million m^3/year, causing a general rise in the water level of 3 to 4 cm/year (Shahin 1990). Several quarters in Cairo frequently are inundated.

4 EXAMPLES OF AFFECTED SITES

Harmful effects of groundwater rise in Cairo to buildings and structures in the eastern parts of the city have already occurred to a number of outstanding architectural and historic antiquities.

4.1 Qalawun Complex (1284 - 1285, Bahri Mamluk period)

Situated on Sharia Muizz li-Dinn Allah, the former main street of Fatimid Cairo, the complex of Qalawun is a center of interest to both scientists and tourists. The mausoleum chamber is the best preserved part and is considered one of the most beautifully decorated medieval buildings in Cairo.

On its eastern side Qalawun Complex is surrounded by a trench covered with sand. The shallow groundwater table already rose to entirely inundate the trench. During summer 1991 groundwater levels began to decline due to pumping measures still in operation. The site would be flooded again immediately if pumping were to be stopped.

The most obvious example of damage related to groundwater rise is capillary ascent of water into the foundation and masonry. Severe damage is affecting not only the building stones but also is a threat to the stability of the structure itself. Columns and walls inside the mausoleum are extensively wet and are partly covered with waterlogged mud. Places of higher evaporation (especially those exposed to the sun) are covered with crusts of salt. These crusts can exceed thicknesses of some few centimeters. Capillary ascent of water has left its marks up to a height of three meters.

Qalawun Complex was subject to detailed geotechnical studies as part of project activities at the Irrigation and Hydraulics Department of Cairo University during 1991 and 1992. Previous works provided the logs of three boreholes drilled in April 1987. Another two boreholes were drilled at the site during 1991 using six inches diameter pipes and four inches diameter samplers. Subsoil conditions proved to be inhomogeneous with the areal extent of the soil layers changing within only a few meters. A correlation between the logs is highly insecure due

Table 1: chemical analyses of two groundwater samples from Qalawun Complex (September 1991) after Sabry 1992 in Amer 1992.

	Sample No. 1	sample No. 2
electric conductivity [μS/cm]	3400	3800
total dissolved solids [mg/l]	2620	2860
Cl⁻ [mg/l]	480	300
SO_4^{2-} [mg/l]	900	780

to heterogeneous proportions of gravel, sand, silt, and clay layers. Groundwater levels were encountered at very low depths in all borings with the shallow water table already having turned into surface water in one of the boreholes. Groundwater analyses confirmed bacteriological contamination originating from leakage of waste water from the rotten sewer network.

Due to its already endangered stability Qalawun Complex suffered severely from the earthquake that struck Cairo in 1992.

4.2 Al-Salah Talaah Mosque (1160, Fatimid Period)

The mosque of Al-Salah Talaah is the last and most beautiful mosque erected under the Fatimid dynasty. It is located at Ahmad Maher street opposite of Bab Zuweila.

Similar to the Qalawun Complex, the mosque is surrounded by a trench on its northern and western sides. The trench presently is inundated with water indicating the shallow water table. The trench also is being misused for waste and garbage disposal. Two pumps are installed on the northern side of the mosque, withdrawing phreatic shallow water from the silty clay cap for discharge into the sewer network.

The inner court of the mosque reveals surface unevenness that occurred during the last few years with the beginning of the pumping measures. The settlements are not caused by overburden pressure. They are the results of instabilities of the foundation soils that can be related to uncontrolled dewatering that caused differential settlement.

5 DISCUSSION AND ANALYSIS

In greater Cairo, alterations to the geotechnical properties of the soils are encountered in places where there is a chance for groundwater to rise to reach the structure itself or its foundation. Groundwater attacks subsoil structures located in areas of relatively low altitude. For this reason groundwater rise is much more severe in central areas of Cairo city, specially in old districts, where most of the precious antiques are located. In these areas groundwater has submerged the basements and substructural elements causing serious damage.

The problem of groundwater rise and its effects on Greater Cairo antiquities is a multi-disciplinary problem involving different elements including geohydrology, geochemistry, antiquity restoration, and geotechnics. Every structure must rest on earth foundations that are capable of supporting the weight of the structure without harmful settlement or other detrimental movements. For groundwater rise control, basic approaches may be used utilizing drainage processes for lowering water table and safely removing water which flows towards the site. The kind of dewatering system needed and its cost depend, among other factors, on the size and depth of the proposed work, subsurface soil and groundwater conditions, which must be thoroughly evaluated in advance.

The problem of groundwater rise in Greater Cairo should not be solved separately at the specific sites of the antiques. The aquifer under consideration should better be demonstrated to act as one unit, where the water table and/or piezometric head could be lowered in the entire region of the Greater Cairo and not be lowered at the sites of antiques only. Lowering the water table at one point would cause more lateral flux to this specific point due to the anticipated increase in the gradient of the piezometric head. Shallow water would restore its initial level rapidly under such activity. The solution of the problem is highly linked to the ongoing rehabilitation of the drinking water and sewerage networks in the Greater Cairo area. Considerable amounts of water are lost under current conditions to the underlying aquifer. This leakage problem should be tackled first, before undertaking any other measures to control the rise in water table.

Careful investigation is needed to identify sources of replenishment of the regional groundwater. Pumping at large rates usually produces drastic lowering of the water table. Consolidation of soil formations under adjacent buildings could take place with detrimental settlement of the structures.

6 CONCLUSION

Groundwater rise in greater Cairo is a major cause of antiquity defects and failures. Its destructive role might be in the form of corroding the building material and alteration of soil properties, mainly clay minerals. The effect of the groundwater rise problem on the antiqities becomes apparent after some time (months or even years) after the environmental changes imposed on the subsurface medium. Any change in water level and/or quality will affect the antiquity one way or the other. The problem should be solved at the city-wide scale of Greater Cairo, though it appears severely at the local scale of the antiquities sites. Special attention should be paid to soil-antiquity behaviour under dewatering conditions. Thorough investigations should be carried out to select the appropriate rehabilitation technique without causing more damage to the already deteriorated monuments.

7 REFERENCES

Hefny, K. [ed.] 1982. Groundwater studies project for Greater Cairo. Internal report, in Arabic and annexes in English. *Research Institute for Groundwater and Academy of Research and Technology.* 190 pp. Cairo.

Korany, E. A. & Abdel-Aal, M. E. 1988. Groundwater response in the urban sectors of Cairo environs, Egypt. *Hydrological processes and water management in urban areas. Urban water '88. Proceedings of the conference*: 429-436. Duisburg, Germany.

Sabry, M. A. 1992. Geotechnical investigations. In: Amer, A. [ed.]. 1992. *Groundwater effects on Greater Cairo antiques. Final report.* Faculty of Engineering. Cairo University.

Said, R. 1975. Subsurface geology of Cairo area. *Memoire de L'Institute d'Egypte, Tome Soixante.* 70 pp. Cairo.

Shahin, M. M. A. 1990. Impacts of urbanisation of the Greater Cairo area on the groundwater in the underlying aquifer. *Hydrological processes and water management in urban areas*: 198: 243-249. Wallingford.

Shata, A. A. 1988. Geology of Cairo, Egypt. *Bull. Assoc. Eng. Geologists*: XXV/2:149-183.

Sherif, M. M. 1992. Effect of groundwater on Greater Cairo antiques. In: Amer, A. [ed.]. 1992. *Groundwater effects on Greater Cairo antiques. Final report.* Faculty of Engineering. Cairo University.

Groundwater in the Urban Environment: Problems, Processes and Management, Chilton et al. (eds)
© 1997 Balkema, Rotterdam, ISBN 90 5410 837 1

Impact on groundwater level when tunnelling in urban areas

D.Cesano & B.Olofsson
Division of Land and Water Resources, Royal Institute of Technology (KTH), Stockholm, Sweden

ABSTRACT: Groundwater flows into underground constructions and the related drawdown of the groundwater level often cause detrimental effects on the environment as well as increasing construction costs. Data analysis from the 3 km long full bored section of the *Ormen* tunnel (the Snake) located right beneath the centre of Stockholm, Sweden, gave a unique possibility to study the parameters which influence water inflows and particularly the drawdown in hard crystalline rock terrain in urban areas. More than 80% of the measurement sites were affected by the tunnel over a short period. The drawdown as well as the leakages were controlled by a number of topographical, geological and technical parameters. An increased use of pregrouting in fracture zones is obviously effective in reducing immediate drawdown and inflows, whereas the effectiveness for long term impacts on the groundwater levels cannot be verified.

1 INTRODUCTION

Water leakage into tunnels and rock caverns generally causes problems for the rock construction as well as for the environment. Inflow of large quantities of water may endanger the labour force and lead to stability problems. Drainage of groundwater from the soil may lead to geotechnical problems such as ground subsidence and serious damage to foundations of buildings due to rotting and bacterial decomposition of wooden piles as a result of an increased access of oxygen. The geotechnical problems in the Stockholm area due to lowering of the groundwater levels have been frequently described in literature (Tyrén & Sund 1971, Morfeldt 1972, Lindskoug & Nilsson 1974). Drawdown of the groundwater levels due to construction of tunnels and rock caverns has sometimes been detrimental to the water supply (Ahlberg & Lundgren 1977, Nordberg 1980, Olofsson 1991).

Some studies of the drawdown in rock and soil around tunnels and rock caverns in crystalline rocks have previously been carried out in Scandinavia (Lindskoug & Nilsson 1974, Ahlberg & Lundgren 1977, Larsson et al 1977, Sund et al 1977, Olofsson 1991). Most of them are carried out in rural areas or in the suburbs of Stockholm and no systematic studies of the drawdown process have previously been carried out in the most densely built areas of Stockholm. The construction of a 3.7 km long bored tunnel in the centre of Stockholm gave therefore a unique possibility to study the hard crystalline rocks and the influence of underground excavations on the groundwater levels in a highly urbanised area.

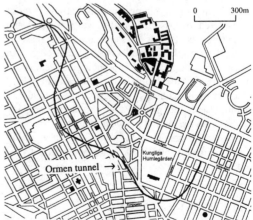

Figure 1. The centre of Stockholm and the bored section of the *Ormen* tunnel (540-3300m).

2 THE *ORMEN* TUNNEL

The Stockholm waste and rainwater network and the Henriksdal's waste water treatment plant does not have sufficient capacity to cope with the huge amount of water produced during periods of heavy precipitation. To avoid flooding, the surplus mixture of rain and waste water is allowed to overflow and to be temporarily stored in the nearest water course of the *Ormen* tunnel (the Snake), which occupies a sinuous route beneath the centre of Stockholm. When the pressure on pipelines has reduced, the surplus water is then pumped to Henriksdal's waste water treatment plant. The tunnel was constructed during 1990-1993 and has a storage capacity of 35000 m³. Most of the tunnel was excavated by the used of a tunnel boring machine for hard rock with a cutterhead diameter of 3.5 m. The completed tunnel has a cross sectional diameter of 9.6 m² and the tunnel slopes from both directions down towards a pumping station approximately 55 m below street level.

3 GEOLOGY AND HYDROLOGY

The bedrock in the Stockholm region belongs to the Svecocarelian orogeny 2000-1800 million years ago and mainly consists of crystalline rocks such as metasedimentary gneiss, gneiss-granite and undeformed granite which form a highly complex pattern in the city centre. The rock types are crossed by several major tectonic zones, which have been active during several periods. The bedrock topography is strongly undulating.

Unconsolidated drift deposits formed during and after the last glaciation period (70000 - 10000 y. b. p.) and consist of a thin or sometimes absent layer of till covered by assorted, partly wave washed and redeposited drift such as sand and in depressions overlaid by glacial as well as postglacial clays. An important geological and morphological feature in the centre of Stockholm is the "Stockholm esker" which wholly consists of glaciofluvial material (mainly sand and gravel) and stretches along the south-western side of the *Ormen* tunnel.

The annual precipitation in the Stockholm region is approximately 600 - 700 mm, predominantly as rain in late summer.

4 METHODS OF EVALUATION

The analyses of the impact on the groundwater comprised:

- A statistical evaluation of fracture data collected during the construction of the *Ormen* tunnel by the use of generalised tunnel maps showing the main geological features along the tunnel alignment. The tunnel map was compiled by the consultant company Mineconsult AB, Stockholm. Geological data have been statistically treated and graphically displayed using a computer programme developed by Olofsson, one of the authors.

- A calculation of the drawdown on 72 observation sites surrounding the *Ormen* tunnel. Three innovative methods were used for the calculation: two linear regression methods developed and described by Olofsson (1991), and a median method described by Cesano (1995)

- Statistical analyses using ANOVA (ANalysis Of VAriance) of the drawdown in relation to topographical, geological and technical parameters in the tunnel as well as on the surface.

5 EVALUATION OF FRACTURE DATA

Fracture density varies along the tunnel section 540m - 3300m as shown in Figure 2. The main fracture concentration is located at Stureplan (2700m- 2800m of the bored section), right beneath the centre of Stockholm. The predominant orientations of fractures along this section are N40-70W, N/S and E/W, Figure 3, and there is no distinct

Figure 2. Number of fractures (per 100m sections) in the bored part of the *Ormen* tunnel (540-3300m).

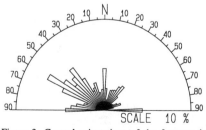

Figure 3. General orientations of the fractures in the bored section of the *Ormen* tunnel (540-3300m).

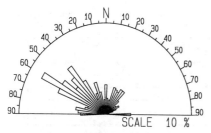

Figure 4. Orientation of the leaking fractures in the bored section of the *Ormen* tunnel (540-3300m).

Figure 5. Number of leaking fractures (per 100m sections) in the bored part of the *Ormen* tunnel (540-3300m).

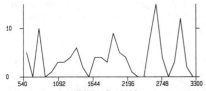

Figure 6. Number of mineral filled fractures (per 100m sections) in the bored part of the *Ormen* tunnel (540-3300m).

difference of the fracture pattern between the three main rock types granite, gneiss-granite and dark gneiss. The dip of the fractures is generally steep.

This can increase leakages in the tunnel since groundwater flows directly from the contact zone between drift and bedrock to deeper parts of the bedrock aquifer. The majority of the broad fractures with a width greater than 0.2m is mainly orientated N40-70W. Little correlation between these broad fractures and leaking fractures exists. The orientation of leaking fractures in the *Ormen* tunnel is similar to the predominant fracture family (N40-70W), Figure 3 and Figure 4. From a statistical point of view, granite has more leaking fractures than the other rock types. A distinct increase of leakages in the tunnel is correlated to the zones of increased fracturing, Figure 2 and Figure 5. The drop of leakages around section 3000m in spite of the increased fracture frequency might be due to the impervious properties of the mineral filling, Figure 2, Figure 5 and Figure 6.

6 CALCULATION OF THE DRAWDOWN

As a result of ground subsidence occurring in the 1970's after the construction of some tunnel projects, the municipality of Stockholm has set up a rigorous groundwater control system consisting of more than 900 wells in the city area. Among these, 72 wells were selected by the municipal authorities to be included in a special control programme for the construction of the *Ormen* tunnel. The normal measurement frequency is 0 - 6 times per year. During the construction period, measurements were taken at least twice per month.

The drawdown was calculated by two linear regression methods between the groundwater levels

Before tunnel construction   Average = -0.098 m
                                  Median = -0.1 m
After tunnel construction   Average = -0.263 m
                                  Average difference = -0.163 m
Lowest value = -0.55 m on 12/3/1991, Lowest annual value = -0.259 m in 1991

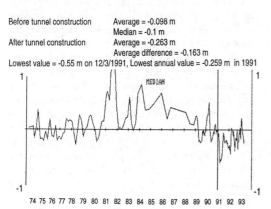

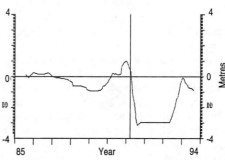

Figure 7. Calculation of drawdown using the Median (left) and Stepwise regression (right) methods at two different sites. The vertical line shows the time of the tunnel construction at the site. The positive drawdown during the years 1980-1989 in the left picture could be due to leaking pipes.

Table 1. ANOVA results: relation between a number of topographical/geological/technical parameters and leakages, average and maximum (peak values) drawdown on surrounding wells.

RECODED VARIABLE	INLEAKAGES	DRAWDOWN	MAXIMUM DRAWDOWN
Number of leakages per 100m of tunnel section		/	- - -
Distance of the well from the tunnel	/	- -	- - -
Altitude of wells - meters above sea level	- - -	/	+
Geology at the tunnel	***	/	*
Amount of pregrouting (tons/100m)	+++	/	- - -

Codes: +++/- - - strong direct/inverse correlation $F_{(0.00-0.05)}$; ++/- - moderate direct/inverse correlation $F_{(0.05-0.10)}$;
+/- weak direct/inverse correlation $F_{(0.10-0.20)}$; ***/**/* strong/moderate/weak correlation, non numerical variable;
/ no clear correlation $F_{(>0.2)}$

at investigation sites (dependent variables) and reference sites (independent variables) using the least squares method. The reference levels of groundwater were collected from observation wells belonging to the Swedish national groundwater network and located 20 - 40 km away from the *Ormen* tunnel. The best reference well for each measurement site was selected by correlation analyses comprising all sites.

The progress of the drawdown was analysed using a type of stepwise linear regression analysis based on repeated regression analyses versus a reference site.

Due to low correlation coefficients, a third method based on calculation of the differences from the median or average values of groundwater levels before the construction of the tunnel was applied. In order to evaluate the long time and instant effect on the groundwater system, the average and maximum value of the drawdown after tunnelling was also calculated over the study period (1990-1993).

The graphical outputs of data both for the median and the stepwise regression methods were similar, Figure 7. The curves show the calculated drawdown. In the ideal case this curve should fall along the horizontal line (no lowering of the groundwater level). The vertical line indicates the time the tunnel face passed the measurement site. The horizontal scale gives the time and the vertical scale shows the drawdown.

The calculation of the drawdown permitted the assessment of the hydrogeological impact of the *Ormen* tunnel on the local aquifer. 53% of the wells were affected if considering just the average drawdown (>0.1m), while 85% had a lowering of the groundwater level bigger than 0.3m if considering the maximum (peak) values of the drawdown over the study period. At some wells, the time of influence started from -60 days before the tunnel face passed the sites. This implies a good connectivity of the fracture systems, as well as heterogeneity and anisotropy in the fracture pattern.

7 RELATION BETWEEN DRAWDOWN AND TOPOGRAPHICAL, GEOLOGICAL AND TECHNICAL VARIABLES

In order to evaluate the influence of various variables on the drawdown, statistical analyses were applied with the ANOVA method (=ANalysis Of VAriance). Topographical features for each measurement site were taken from topographical maps, whereas geological and technical parameters were collected from tunnel maps, boring protocols and working reports.

ANOVA compares the variances and the means of different groups of values in order to clarify the variation among the data within each group and between the groups. It was then possible to study the variables in relation to average and maximum drawdown, as well as to the number of leakages. The main results are listed in Table 1.

8 DISCUSSION

From the analyses of fracture data within the *Ormen* tunnel, granite shows to be the main water bearing rock type due to its brittle behaviour that allows the creation of fractures in several orientations. The orientation of leaking fractures and heavy leaking fractures confirms that groundwater paths in hard rocks seem to be controlled by a finite number of major shear zones or family of discontinuities. The main drawdown of the groundwater level in the soil also followed the predominant orientation of the major tectonic zones in Stockholm, Figure 8. Fracture width seems to play a minor role for leakages, while natural impervious mineral filling showed to have a damping effect for groundwater inflows.

Previous investigations of the drawdown in dug wells, observation tubes and boreholes as a result of tunnelling in Swedish crystalline bedrock (Ahlberg & Lundgren 1977, Sund et al 1977) have shown a

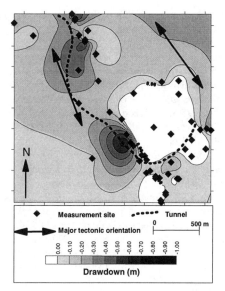

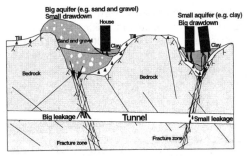

Figure 9. Relationship between drawdown and groundwater storage in the Stockholm area.

Figure 8. Map of the average drawdown (year 1993) around the Ormen tunnel. The two arrows indicate the orientation of the tectonic structures, showing a clear correlation with the preferential anisotropic direction of the drawdown .

few affected sites. The results are anyhow questionable since the method used for calculating the drawdown could only identify the sites where the drawdown was 1.0m or more. This study shows that the Ormen tunnel had a clear impact on the local groundwater levels.

The wide time interval of the beginning of the drawdown is explained by the hydraulic heterogeneity and anisotropy of the rock and overlying drift, where single fractures can drain distant located areas, and the usually highly varying hydraulic conductivity values. The recovery occurred no later than 1.5-2 years after the tunnel crossed the measurement site. Anyhow, a few wells were still affected after the last measurement day (3 years of influence) probably because of small recharge from precipitation due to the low permeability of the ground surface (asphalt cover of roads) and to the channelling of runoff rain water by artificial drainage systems.

The distance between the measurement sites and the tunnel is usually one of the most fundamental factors controlling the drawdown. Previous studies (Olofsson, 1991) have shown that declines of the groundwater levels are roughly logarithmic correlated to the distance. At the Ormen tunnel a weak inverse correlation between drawdown and distance was found, especially within a zone of 100 m from the tunnel. However this relation was

rather complex because of the heterogeneous and anisotropic properties of the groundwater flow in the rock.

Geological features such as rock type, number and orientation of fractures and mineral filling, played a major role for the drainage of areas around the Ormen tunnel and especially for the leakages. The most important hydrogeological features were the storage capacity of the drift and the number of leakages encountered in the tunnel. The rock type in the tunnel played a major role within the leaking process, but it was of secondary importance for the drawdown. Although red granite was strongly related to groundwater flows into the Ormen tunnel and hence problematic from a constructional point of view, single leaking fractures in gneiss and gneiss-granite are of more impact on the groundwater levels in the overburden.

Pregrouting was of primary importance to reduce the peak values of drawdown and probably for the biggest instant water inflows to the tunnel. However, the study has not been able to show that the average drawdown in the area has been reduced. An explanation for such a behaviour is that peak values of the drawdown are more closely related to the instant leakages, while the average drawdown is more related to the total amount of water flowing into the tunnel during the period of construction. Previous studies in Stockholm have shown that depending on the hydrogeological characteristics of the overburden, the rock and the aquifers, even small leakages can consistently lower the groundwater level, e.g. in aquifers where limited amount of groundwater is available (Knutsson & Morfeldt 1995), Figure 9. Therefore, depletion of small aquifers can have terrific consequences on the surrounding environments if the natural groundwater recharge is a slow process.

The clear correlation between altitude of the wells and the amount of leaking fractures points

223

out that topographic lows consist of more fractured rock and a bigger amount of leaking fractures. On the other hand, areas at a low altitude are discharge areas which have a larger storage of groundwater and therefore represent smaller impacts on the groundwater levels compared to areas at higher altitude.

9 CONCLUSIONS

Statistical analyses of geological data from the *Ormen* tunnel data, Stockholm, Sweden, show that the most likely combination for water leakage in the Stockholm area seems to be a fracture pattern with orientation N40-70W and N/S in red granite, while gneiss and gneiss-granite areas seem to be more sensitive to drawdowns. These fracture orientations are correlated to the main principal stress orientation calculated in eastern Sweden (Stephansson 1993). Granite is the most leaking rock due to its more brittle behaviour that increases the fracturing degree and therefore the storativity, while gneiss and gneiss-granite showed a stronger impact on the groundwater levels probably due to lower storage capacity and good hydraulic connections to the overburden through single leaking fractures.

The present study concludes that 53% of the wells had a visible lowering of the groundwater level over a long period, while 85% of the wells were instantly affected. Pregrouting seems to be effective for reduction of the instant effects on the groundwater level whereas no clear effect in the long term can be seen. Estimations on the drawdown of groundwater levels due to tunnelling is strongly dependent upon the method used to calculate the impact. The methodology and methods used in this study can easily be implemented in automatic groundwater control programmes in urban areas as well as used for construction purposes.

ACKNOWLEDGEMENTS

We wish to thank Mr. Daniel Morfeldt, Mineconsult AB, Stockholm, and Stockholm Vatten for their co-operation and for providing us with data.

REFERENCES

Ahlberg, P. & T. Lundgren 1977. *Groundwater lowering as a consequence of tunnel blasting.* Report no 1, SGI (Swedish Geotechnical Institute), Linköping. (In Swedish, English summary).

Cesano, D. 1995. *Hydrogeological impact when tunnelling in urban areas - evaluation of the drawdown in the Stockholm area due to the construction of the Ormen tunnel.* Thesis report, TR:1995:5, Division of Land and Water Resources, Royal Institute of Technology, Stockholm.

Knutsson, G. & C-O. Morfeldt 1995. *Groundwater - theory and applications.* Svensk Byggtjänst. (In Swedish)

Larsson, I., A. Flexter & B. Rosén 1977. Effects on groundwater caused by excavation of rock store caverns. *Engineering Geology*, 11: 279-294.

Lindskoug, N-E. & L-Y. Nilsson 1974. *Groundwater and urban planning.* Report R20:1974, Swedish Council for Building Research (BFR).

Morfeldt, C-O. 1972. Drainage problem in connection with tunnel construction in Precambrian granitic bedrock (in Sweden). *Proceedings of the Symposium Percolation Through Fissured Rock, Stuttgart,* T4-G: 1-9. Essen, Germany: Deutsche Gesellschaft fur Erd- und Grundbau.

Nordberg, L. 1980. Who took the water from our wells - the water power company or Nature herself?. *Proceedings of the 6th Nordic Hydrological Conference, 10-16 Aug. 1980,* in UNGI Report: 52 (321-332).

Olofsson, B. 1991. *Impact on groundwater conditions by tunnelling in hard crystalline rocks..* PhD Report Trita-Kut/91:1063, Division of Land and Water Resources, Royal Institute of Technology (KTH), Stockholm, Sweden.

Stephansson, O. 1993: Rock stress in the fennoscandian shield. In *Comprehensive Rock Engineering - principles, practice & projects,* John A. Hudson (ed.), Pergamon Press, 3: 445-459.

Sund, B., H. Roosaar & G. Bergman 1977. *Water leakage in rock tunnels - its impact and ray of influence.* Report R36:1977, Swedish Council for Building Research (BFR), Stockholm. (In Swedish, English summary).

Tyrén, S. & Sund, B. 1971. *Lowering of groundwater at Mariatorget in Stockholm.* Report R6:1971, Swedish Council for Building Research (BFR). (In Swedish).

Groundwater in the Urban Environment: Problems, Processes and Management, Chilton et al. (eds)
© *1997 Balkema, Rotterdam, ISBN 90 5410 837 1*

Groundwater modelling to predict the impact of a tunnel on the behavior of a water table aquifer in urban conditions

Alain Dassargues
Laboratoires de Géologie de l'Ingénieur, d'Hydrogéologie, et de Prospection Géophysique (L.G.I.H.), University of Liège, Belgium

ABSTRACT: In alluvial sediments, big civil engineering works often cause often significant changes in groundwater conditions, inducing possible damage in urban areas. Before construction of a tunnel, the impact of this new and artificial impervious barrier must be studied in detail. For example, an eventual strong rise of the water table must be computed and predicted in order to anticipate the risk of cellar flooding in houses and to take avoidance measures.

In this context, the construction of a tunnel longer than 500 m in the alluvial plain of the River Meuse and River Ourthe, in the city of Liège (Belgium), was considered as a possible factor which could induce water table changes. The alluvial aquifer is crossed transversally by the new tunnel whose the base lies on the less-pervious bed-rock. A finite difference model has been built including all the complex features interacting with groundwater in an urban environment: river-aquifer interactions through embankments, leakage from other surface water bodies, irregular boundary conditions. After calibration of the model on historical data measured in extreme piezometric conditions (floods and lowest water levels), the heterogeneous hydraulic conductivity distribution has been checked against the well-known geological description of the zone. Then, many simulations have been performed for different transient groundwater and surface water conditions (extreme water levels). Drainage 'windows' through the tunnel base have been proposed in order to decrease the 'barrier effect' in the alluvial aquifer. The results of the simulations with and without such a window has provided the information needed about the impact on the water table aquifer behaviour.

1 INTRODUCTION

The geological and hydrogeological data of the studied zone were collected previously so that more emphasis is given here to the modelling approach (Dassargues & Monjoie 1994). In the city of Liège (Figure 1), a new tunnel is planned for the alluvial plain of the River Meuse, near the junction between the Rivers Meuse and Ourthe. This tunnel, whose base is lying on the less-pervious bed-rock, will cross transversally the alluvial aquifer along a distance of 550 m.

Measured piezometric levels of the water table aquifer are given on figures 2 and 3 respectively for situations corresponding to the lowest water levels and to the highest water levels. Due to the geographic layout and the high permeability of the river embankments, these extreme piezometric levels are largely influenced by the water levels in the River Ourthe (north-east zone) and in the River Meuse (south-west zone).

2 MODEL AND DISCRETIZATION

To compute the eventual rise of the water table due to the presence in the alluvial aquifer of this new

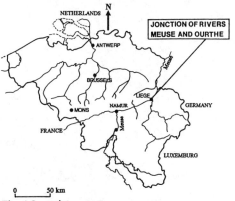

Fig. 1 Location map.

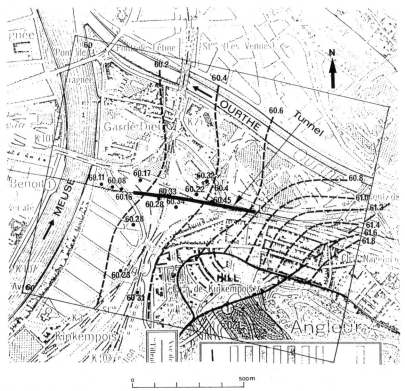

Fig.2 Measured piezometric map in conditions of the lowest water levels (October 1994).

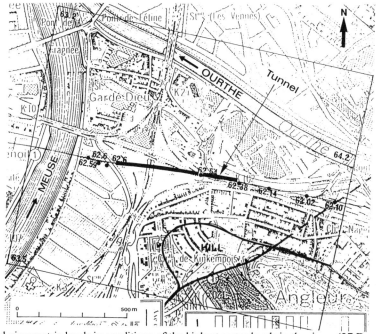

Fig.3 Measured piezometric levels in conditions of the highest water levels in the rivers (27 December 1993).

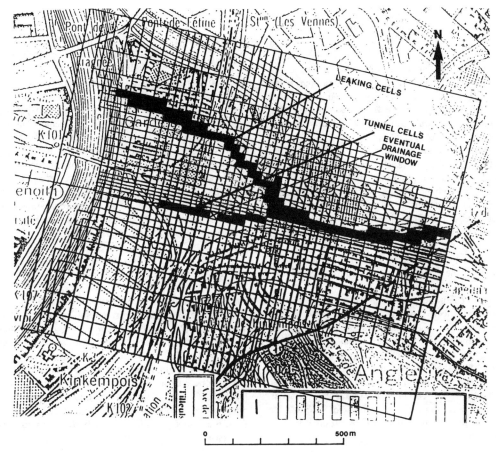

Fig.4 Finite difference grid, 'leaking cells' for infiltration from surface water bodies, and tunnel cells with or without a 'drainage window'.

impervious barrier, quasi steady state conditions are considered for each of these extreme piezometric situations. The finite-difference method was adopted, using a two-layer local network of rectangular cells. MODFLOW (McDonald & Harbaugh 1988), together with the PM3 pre- and postprocessor (Chiang & Kinzelbach 1992) were used.

The spatial discretization of the domain was realized with two layers of 1070 rectangular cells covering an area of 1.7 km², the total thickness of the alluvial sediments is about 7 m. The smallest cells have dimensions of 25 m x 25 m.

The chosen boundary conditions can be described as following:

1. on the western boundary, prescribed piezometric heads were taken in equilibrium with the water levels in the River Meuse (60.0 m in the lowest conditions and 63.2 to 63.5 m in the highest conditions),

2. on the northern to north-eastern boundary, prescribed piezometric heads were taken in equilibrium with the water levels in the River Ourthe (60.0 to 60.8 m in the lowest conditions and 63.2 to 64.2 m in the highest conditions),

3. on the southern boundary, prescribed piezometric conditions were deduced from extrapolated measured piezometric heads in the alluvial plain and in the foothill (in both type of conditions),

4. on the eastern boundary, prescribed piezometric heads were deduced from measurements in the alluvial plain of the River Ourthe (in both type of conditions).

At the bottom of the model, an impervious boundary was used to represent the low-pervious bed-rock.

On basis of pumping tests results, the permeability values characterizing the alluvial aquifer range from $1\ 10^{-3}$ to $2\ 10^{-2}$ m/s. However, it is known that these sediments can be affected locally by lower permeability values in more silty to loamy zones and by higher values in coarse and clean gravels (Dassargues & Lox 1991). A uniform value of storage coefficient of 0.05 was chosen (for computing eventual transient conditions of the highest water levels conditions).

Infiltration due to rainfall can be neglected as the infiltration surface is drastically reduced in urban conditions, but an important infiltration flow (or leakage) is coming from a surface water channel linking the River Ourthe to the River Meuse. The water level of this channel is maintained constant by two locks. Leakage conditions were introduced in the corresponding cells of the upper layer (figure 4). The permeability coefficient and the thickness of the bottom of the channel were taken respectively to 1.10^{-7} m/s and 0.5 m.

After calibration of the model, predictive simulations were performed with the tunnel represented by a line of impervious cells in the two layers of the model. Since the beginning, it was also foreseen to simulate the effect of an eventual (3 m x 30 m) 'drainage window' through the tunnel base (Figure 4). Although the construction of this 'window' would certainly not be easy for civil engineering reasons, it was proposed in order to decrease the barrier effect of the tunnel in the alluvial aquifer.

3 CALIBRATION

The first step of the calibration procedure was made using permeability coefficients that were calculated from pumping-test results. As a second step of the calibration, using a trial-and-error approach, more localized zones of different hydraulic conductivity values were introduced. This optimization process continued until no significant improvement in the calibration on the two extreme measured situations (lowest and highest conditions) was obtained. Figure 5 shows the spatial distribution of the hydraulic conductivity values obtained at the end of this double-calibration procedure of the model on both situations. The corresponding computed piezometric maps are shown for the lowest water levels (Figure 6) and for the highest water levels (Figure 7).

4 PREDICTIVE SIMULATIONS

Predictive simulations were performed, in a first step, with impervious cells representing the tunnel and without any 'drainage window' through it. Then, simulations with the tunnel and the 'drainage window' (as described previously) were also done. These two scenarios were computed in both extreme piezometric conditions (the lowest and highest water levels). Consequently four computed piezometric maps were calculated and differentiation was made from the respective reference calibrated situations of figures 6 and 7.

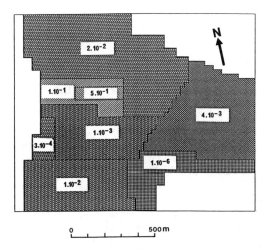

Fig.5 Horizontal hydraulic conductivity in both layers.

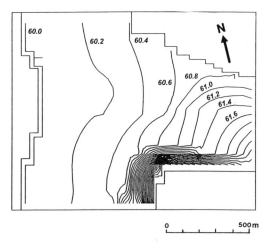

Fig.6 Calibrated simulated piezometric map in conditions of the lowest levels.

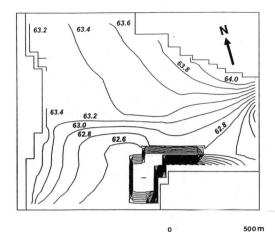

Fig.7 Calibrated simulated piezometric map in conditions of the highest water levels (after 2 days).

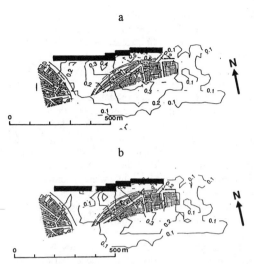

Fig.8 Conditions of the lowest water levels: rise of the piezometric heads due to the tunnel (a) without, and (b) with the 'drainage window'.

In conditions of the lowest water levels, a differential piezometric rise, due to the presence of the tunnel in the alluvial sediments, was computed in the area to the south of the proposed tunnel lineation with a maximum of 0.6 m (Figure 8a). When including the presence of the 'drainage window', nearly no change was found (Figure 8b), the maximum difference reached not more than 0.15.

In conditions of the highest water levels, a piezometric difference of 1.6 m was computed in this area to the south of the proposed tunnel. In fact, in these conditions, the tunnel acts as a protection wall against important and rapid piezometric rises induced mainly by the overwhelming influence of the River Ourthe in such extreme conditions. In such conditions, this area to the south of the proposed tunnel should be better protected against cellar flooding and sewer exfiltration than before. After two days with the highest water levels in both rivers (flood conditions), the comparison between the piezometric situations computed with and without the tunnel, shows clearly that the tunnel is responsible for a slower rising of the piezometric levels in the zone of the alluvial aquifer located just in the south of the tunnel (Figure 9a). Of course, when including the presence of the 'drainage window', this 'protective influence' is partially annihilated (Figure 9b).

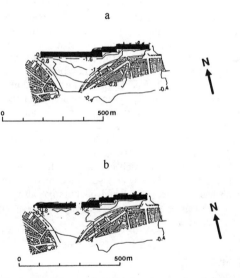

Fig.9 Conditions of the highest water levels (after 2 days): rise of the piezometric heads due to the tunnel (a) without and (b) with the 'drainage window'.

5 CONCLUSIONS

On basis of the computed results, quantitative results were provided to answer the following practical question: what is the expected impact of a tunnel construction on the piezometric levels of an alluvial aquifer in urban conditions. Before that modelling exercise, the impact of this artificial impervious barrier was difficult to assess even if large values of hydraulic conductivity were found by analytical interpretation of pumping tests.

An eventual strong rise of the water table was still to be considered in order to anticipate the risk of cellar flooding in the houses and eventually to take the needed steps to avoid it.

All the important features interacting with groundwater in an urban environment were taken into account : river-aquifer interactions through embankments, leakage from other surface water bodies, irregular geometry of the boundaries, etc. After calibration of the model on historical data measured in two extreme piezometric conditions (the highest and the lowest water levels), the obtained heterogeneous hydraulic conductivity distribution has been checked in relation with the geological description of the zone. Then, using the calibrated model the simulations have provided results showing that:

1. in conditions of the lowest water levels, and in steady conditions, a rise of the piezometric levels can be expected in the zone located in the south of the tunnel with a maximum of about 0.6 m.

2. in flood conditions corresponding to the highest water levels, and after two days of such extreme conditions in the rivers, the strong rise of the piezometric levels in the aquifer is restrained in this same zone in the south of the tunnel. In this case, creating an impervious barrier in the sediments, the tunnel has a protective (but transient) effect on the piezometric levels in this zone.

3. the influence of an eventual 'drainage window' through the tunnel is negligible in conditions of the lowest water levels, and is certainly not favourable when the piezometric levels are rising, due to the overwhelming influence of the River Ourthe water levels on the piezometric levels in the studied zone.

The modelling approach has allowed to integrate all the data, parameters, and scenarios in one tool which has provided useful and quantitative answers and which can be easily modified to simulate eventual other scenarios.

REFERENCES

Chiang, W.H. & W.Kinzelbach. 1992 *Processing MODFLOW: pre- and postprocessors for simulation of flow and contaminants transport in groundwater systems with MODFLOW, MODPATH and MT3D Version 3.0*, Dpt of Civil Engineering, Kassel University, Germany, 62 p.

Dassargues, A. & A.Lox. 1991 *Modélisation mathématique de la nappe alluviale de la Meuse en aval de Liège (Belgique)*. In "Le système hydrologique de la région frontalière Liège-Maasbracht, résultats des recherches 1985-1990". *Rapport et notes n° 26, CHO-TNO*, Delft, pp. 27-54.

Dassargues, A. & A.Monjoie. 1994 *Modélisation de l'impact du tunnel de Kinkempois sur la nappe alluviale de la Meuse à Liège (Belgique)*. Report LGIH-University of Liège (unpublished), 89p.

Mc Donald, M.G. & A.W.Harbaugh. 1988 *A modular three-dimensional finite-difference groundwater flow model*. Techniques of the Water-Resources Investigations of the United States Geological Survey: book 6, Modeling techniques, Scientific Software Group, P.O. Box 23041, Washington, D.C. 20026- 3041.

Groundwater in the Urban Environment: Problems, Processes and Management, Chilton et al. (eds)
© *1997 Balkema, Rotterdam, ISBN 90 5410 837 1*

Construction dewatering in Hong Kong

R.A.Forth
Department of Civil Engineering, University of Newcastle-upon-Tyne, UK

C.B.B.Thorley
Gutteridge Haskins and Davey Pty Ltd, Brisbane, Qld, Australia

ABSTRACT: The construction of the Island Line (ISL) of the Mass Transit Railway (MTR) in Hong Kong involved dewatering for deep excavations, extensive grouting and compressed air tunnelling. These activities had a significant effect on ground and building movements adjacent to the ISL and contributed to settlements of up to 200 mm of multi-storey buildings founded on piles. Careful and lengthy monitoring of buildings adjacent to the ISL enabled the excavation - and dewatering - induced settlement to be established. It was also noticeable that after the compressed air was switched off the buildings "rebounded". This paper provides case histories of buildings subject to substantial adjacent dewatering processes.

1 INTRODUCTION

Hong Kong is one of the most densely populated cities in the world and therefore a logical place for an underground mass transit railway system. The Island Line (ISL) of the Mass Transit Railway (MTR) was the second part of the system following the success of the first lines built on the Kowloon side of the harbour connecting Hong Kong Island via a submerged tube. A large part of the initial system was constructed using cut and cover techniques, but it was decided that this would be too disruptive to traffic on Hong Kong Island and the line would be built by tunnelling methods.

Twelve new stations were constructed during the period 1982 to 1986 along with modifications and extensions to the existing stations in Central and Admiralty. Twin bored tunnels, 6 m in diameter, were driven from Central to Shaukiwan with the station tunnels being 8 m in diameter. The station concourses were large box-like structures generally constructed by top-down methods and connected to the tunnels by adits. Beyond Shaukiwan in the east the line was at ground level either in rock tunnels or at grade. This paper therefore provides case studies from excavations and tunnelling in soft ground in the Western to Shaukiwan section of the ISL.

2 GEOLOGY

The geological profile along the ISL is variable, as indicated by Fig. 1. In general there is a variable thickness of fill, overlying soft alluvial and marine deposits (with occasionally colluvium), which in turn overlies weathered rock, usually granite. Since the invert level of the tunnels was approximately 26 m below ground, the excavations for the concourses were generally around 30 m below ground level.

3 DEEP EXCAVATIONS

In almost all cases the concourse excavation commenced with the installation of diaphragm walls which were extended down to bedrock, or, if too deep, grouting was carried out at the base of the walls to create an impermeable barrier. The excavation within the diaphragm wall "box" proceeded usually in a top-down fashion (Fig. 2) with dewatering within the box advancing ahead of the excavation in order to keep it dry. As groundwater level was just a few metres below ground surface the groundwater level within the box was ultimately drawn down some 25 to 30 metres.

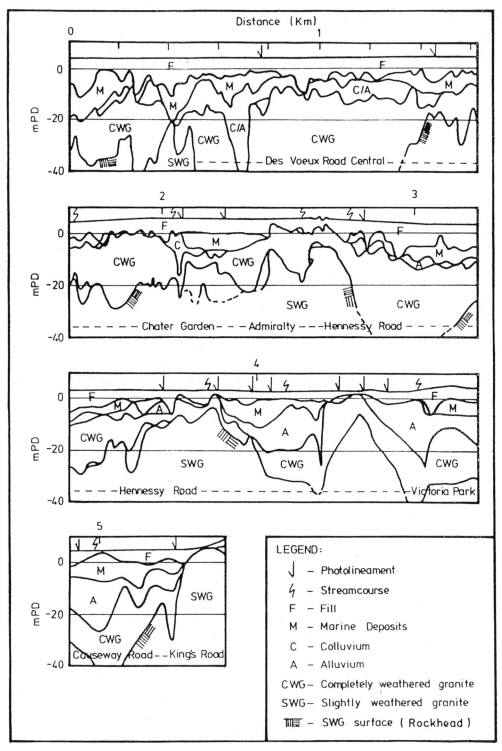

Figure 1. Geological Section - Central to Victoria Park

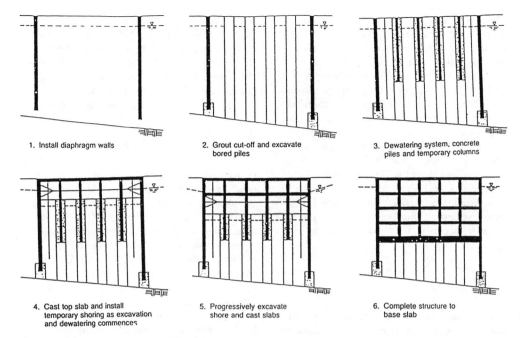

1. Install diaphragm walls

2. Grout cut-off and excavate bored piles

3. Dewatering system, concrete piles and temporary columns

4. Cast top slab and install temporary shoring as excavation and dewatering commences

5. Progressively excavate shore and cast slabs

6. Complete structure to base slab

Figure 2. Top down excavation procedure

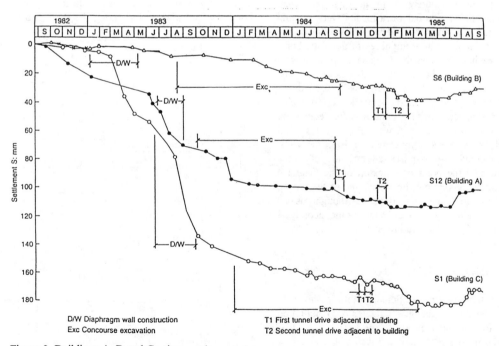

D/W Diaphragm wall construction
Exc Concourse excavation

T1 First tunnel drive adjacent to building
T2 Second tunnel drive adjacent to building

Figure 3. Buildings A, B and C: time-settlement plots

233

These activities obviously could have had a potential impact on adjacent buildings, all of which were monitored during construction. By carefully correlating activity with time it was possible to correlate the settlement of adjacent buildings with a particular activity. However it was not possible to separate the settlement due to excavation and dewatering as these proceeded more or less simultaneously.

Prior to the works commencing an estimate of settlement and hence potential damage to all adjacent buildings along the ISL was made. As has been reported elsewhere (Forth & Thorley 1996) the predictions generally substantially under-estimated settlement for diaphragm walling but were fairly accurate for bulk excavation and dewatering.

4 TUNNELLING

Tunnelling between station concourses was generally carried out using open-faced shields in compressed air. Air pressure of about 3 bars was used to maintain a dry tunnel. Extensive grouting was also carried out along the ISL. The running tunnels, approximately 6 m in diameter, were usually side by side but occasionally were situated one on top of the other. They often followed the route of the main thoroughfares through the built-up area but occasionally deviated to pass directly under existing buildings. Estimates of the settlement of adjacent buildings were carried out based on the Peck method (Peck 1969) which requires an estimate of ground loss (or "equivalent face loss", EFL) to be made. Back analysis and previous experience suggested an EFL of 1-3%. The method also requires an estimate of i, the distance of the point of inflexion of the Gaussian settlement curve from the centre line of the tunnel, in relation to Z, the tunnel depth. Although this can vary considerably with changes in the geological profile i = 0.5 Z was used reasonably successfully.

5 CASE HISTORIES

An example of time settlement plots is shown in Fig. 3 for three buildings (Buildings A, B and C) on piled foundations adjacent to the Island Line. It is clear from the plots that a substantial amount of settlement was caused by diaphragm walling, particularly in the case of Buildings B and C. Bulk

excavation and dewatering caused a significant amount of settlement, but tunnelling activities generally produced little surface settlement. Of particular interest is the "rebound" of the buildings after the compressed air was turned off and groundwater levels re-established. This was between 10 and 15 mm for Buildings B and C.

6 GROUNDWATER CONTROL

Groundwater control was achieved by a combination of methods. For the deep excavations the diaphragm walls were very effective when founded in bedrock. However where bedrock was deeper than the base of the excavation grout was injected beneath the walls. In the context of the ISL project the grout was only required to be fully effective for about a year or two as there were no significant delays in the programme of construction. However research is needed into the performance of the grout in the longer term, where, for example, building programmes are delayed for technical or, more likely, financial reasons.

For tunnelling, groundwater control was achieved by grouting and compressed air. The use of compressed air meant that all site investigation boreholes and piezometers along the route had to

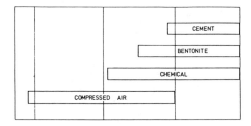

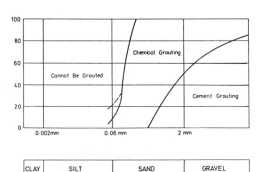

Figure 4. Grout Penetration Ranges

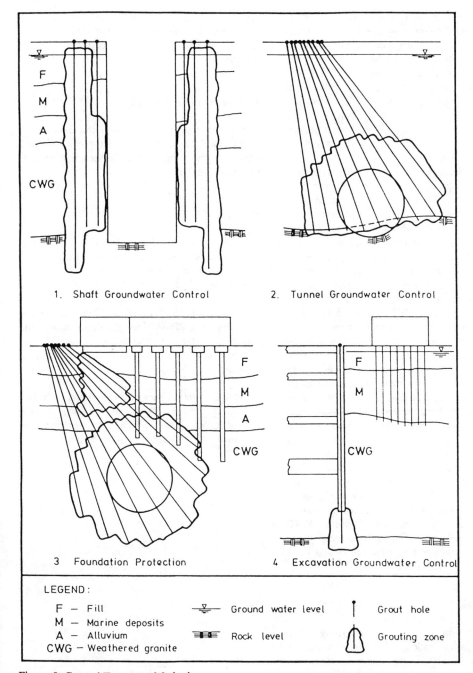

1. Shaft Groundwater Control

2. Tunnel Groundwater Control

3 Foundation Protection

4 Excavation Groundwater Control

LEGEND:

F — Fill
M — Marine deposits
A — Alluvium
CWG — Weathered granite

▽ — Ground water level

≡▆≡ Rock level

Grout hole

Grouting zone

Figure 5. Ground Treatment Methods

be backfilled and thoroughly sealed which, of course, prevented the collection of groundwater level data during the tunnelling phase.

Ground treatment designs were based on the soil conditions for each particular site and were generally specified as a grout percentage of the soil volume, and an injection pressure. In most cases grouting for groundwater control was two stage; cement-bentonite followed by chemical, with grout volumes specified for each type. Typical volumes for cement-bentonite grout were 5% to 30%, depending on soil type (fill through to CWG) and for chemical grouts 20% to 40%. Jet Grout piling or Jet Special Grouting was also employed and may use greater than 50% grout by volume. The chemical grouts most commonly used were Sodium Silicates with hardener volumes depending on setting times required.

Grouting pressures were dependent on depth of grouting and desired permeation rates, and were usually in excess of overburden or water pressure. Injection methods used varied from site to site and include, in soil, Tube-a-Manchette, Lag and Jet Special grouting (a replacement method). Rock grouting was generally done using a staged method.

Generally the soil grouting was effective both as groundwater control and ground consolidation. The chemical grouts appear to be able to permeate soils with up to 10% to 20% passing the 75 micron size, although this was by no means a general rule, as the cement-bentonite grouts can penetrate the coarser sands and gravel sizes. In most cases the soils encountered were able to be effectively grouted using these two stage mixes. The major problems which were encountered tended to be in the loose alluvial sands (Cater et al. 1984). These coarser sands provided resistance to grouting. It is not known whether this was due to groundwater flows or excessive grout travel or a chemical effect. Consequently they often provided an opening in the grout curtain allowing water ingress during excavation or tunnelling. Figure 4 shows the grout-penetration ranges in the Hong Kong soils as determined from experience gained by the MTRC on the ISL. Included as Figure 5 are some typical grout hole arrangements adopted for various types of problem on the ISL.

7 SUMMARY

The construction of the ISL in Hong Kong presented a major challenge due to the intensity of urbanisation and the geotechnical conditions. Comprehensive structural surveys of all buildings along the ISL were carried out prior to commencement of the project. Estimates of settlement and damage were made and precautions taken during construction included frequent monitoring to ensure public safety. Only one significant failure occurred when an advancing shield encountered an unexpected inclined bed of running sand, causing collapse of roadway at the surface.

ACKNOWLEDGEMENTS

The authors wish to acknowledge the assistance of their former colleagues in the Geotechnical Control Office of the Hong Kong Government in data monitoring and drafting of figures.

REFERENCES

Cater, R W, Shirlaw, J N, Sullivan, C A and Chan, W T 1984. Tunnels constructed for the Hong Kong mass transit railway. *Hong Kong Engineer*, Vol. 12, No. 10, p. 37-49.

Forth, R A and Thorley, C B B 1996. Hong Kong Island Line - Predictions and Performance. *Int. Symp. on Geotechnical Aspects of Underground Construction in Soft Ground, London*, p. 677-682.

Peck, R B 1969. Deep excavations and tunnelling in soft ground. *Proc. 7th Int. Conf. on Soil Mechanics and Foundation Engineering, Mexico City*, State-of-the-Art Volume, p. 266-290.

Groundwater in the Urban Environment: Problems, Processes and Management, Chilton et al. (eds)
© 1997 Balkema, Rotterdam, ISBN 90 5410 837 1

Impact of rising piezometric levels on Greater Buenos Aires due to partial changing of water services infrastructure

Mario A. Hernández & Nilda González
Cátedra de Hidrogeología, Facultad de Ciencias Naturales, Universidad Nacional de La Plata, Argentine

ABSTRACT: The intensive exploitation, since the beginning of the century, of a semiconfined aquifer in Buenos Aires City (Argentina) and its surrounding areas has caused large drawdown cones by the coalescence of smaller ones. The population of the area is about 11 million inhabitants. The climate is subhumid-humid with a mean annual rainfall of 1050 mm/year and a surplus of 270 mm/year. Some of the effects caused by the intensive exploitation have been saline intrusion and leakage from the phreatic aquifer through the aquitard, which caused a fall of the water table. As a consequence of the demand increase and closing of production wells due to salinization and nitrate content, treated water from the La Plata River began to be imported. The recovery of piezometric levels has caused the phreatic levels to rise, with a serious impact on the urban infrastructure, established some decades ago. Based on successive flow-nets, on the system parameters T,S,K,K',T' and on the value of imported yields, a monitoring system with forecast capacity is proposed, as well as an operative model for phenomena control, using alternative pumping on both aquifers.

1 INTRODUCTION

The city of Buenos Aires and its urban surroundings (Fig. 1) are the areas with the highest demographic and industrial density in Argentina, with 10,835,000 inhabitants and approximately 44,880 industries in an area of 3,380 km². The

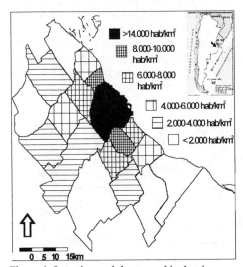

Figure 1. Location and demographic density.

average rainfall is 1050 mm/y and the excess rainfall - mainly from May to November - is 270 mm/y. The landscape is extremely flat (with a slope of 1.10^{-3}), and developed on Quaternary sediments following the right margin of the Río de La Plata River.

The original supply of water obtained directly from the river and shallow wells since 1851 has been replaced by treated water from the river in Buenos Aires (future Planta Palermo Plant); and since the end of the 19th century in the city, and in particular the urban area surrounding it, it has been replaced by water obtained from wells in a semiconfined aquifer located 35 m deep. Groundwater is mainly used for public and industrial supply, the industrial growth of the area dating from the 1920s. There is also a strong horticultural use in the periphery of the urban areas (De Felippi et al 1991).

The intensive exploitation of the resource caused the appearance of wide drawdown cones (Fig. 2) and the intrusion of saline groundwaters, which resulted in a considerable number of abandoned holes. In order to satisfy the requirements, the public service is being expanded by the use of surface waters from the Planta Palermo Plant and the construction of a new Plant (Planta Bernal),

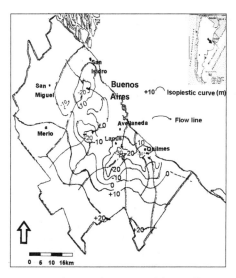

Figure 2. Piezometric map, Puelche aquifer.

from which vast volumes of inland water are imported.

The negative effects of this import - mainly the recovery of the piezometric and phreatic levels - on an urban and industrial structure established during a period of deep groundwater levels are here analysed.

2 GEOHYDROLOGICAL SYSTEM CHARACTERISTICS

The active geohydrologic sub-system is contained in continental Pleistocene sediments, except for the coastal area where there are outcrops of marine deposits.

The base of the active sub-system are marine clays (*Formación* Paraná, Pliocene) with aquiclude characteristics, under which aquifers are confined

and saline. Above the sub-system there are pluvial sands (*Formación Arenas* Puelches, Lower Pleistocene) containing the semiconfined aquifer "Puelche", which is the main supply source in the region. The rest of the sequence up to the surface is formed by loessic silts (*Formación Pampeano*, Middle-Upper Pleistocene) containing two aquifers hydraulically very connected, the lower one, semi-unconfined, and the phreatic one, used only by the population without public service. The base of this formation is clayey to silty-clayey and acts as an aquitard of the Puelche aquifer.

Table I and Figure 3a show the characteristics and geometry of the system, indicating depths and thicknesses.

The average geohydrologic parameters for the area, obtained from numerous pumping tests, are shown in Table II.

The recharge of the system is local and regional, from the excess of the water balance. The recharge of the Puelche aquifer comes from the phreatic aquifer and through the Pampeano, by means of leakage through the aquitard. The normal transit time, about 500 years according to ^{14}C dated studies in the area, has been reduced due to the difference of the hydraulic head, consequence of the intensive exploitation.

The original discharge went to the Río de La Plata river and its tributaries, but, as illustrated in Figure 2, the existence of the great drawdown cones has inverted in many places the direction of the flow, and has turned surface flow into downward leakage (Hernández, 1975). The main discharge of the system is currently due to pumping. The annual volume obtained from the Puelche aquifer alone is greater than 900 Hm^3/year. Unfortunately, this evolution cannot be quantitatively demonstrated, since statistics of the extracted volumes are faulty in the case of the public service and non-existent in the case of the industrial sector - which is more than 30 % of the total.

Table I Geohydrological system.

UNIT	FORMATION	AGE	BEHAVIOUR	THICKNESS	WATER QUALITY
Phreatic	Upper Pampeano	Pleist-Holocene	Aquifer	variable (10m)	Fresh/Brackish
Pampeano	Pampeano	Pleistocene	Aquifer	15 m	Fresh
Aquitard	Lower Pampeano	Pleistocene	Aquitard	8 m	
Puelche	Arenas Puelches	Lower Pleist.	Aquifer	15 m	Fresh>Brackish
Marine Clays	Paraná	Pliocene	Aquiclude	20 m	
Paraná	Paraná	Pliocene	Aquifer	> 30 m	Saline

Table II: Characteristic geohydrological parameters.

UNIT	K (m/day)	T (m²/day)	S (--)	K' (m/day)	T' (day⁻¹)
Phreatic aquifer	5	50	1.10^{-1}		
Pampeano aquifer	10	150	2.10^{-2}		
Aquitard (lower Pampeano)				$4.5 .10^{-2}$	$3 .10^{-3}$
Puelche aquifer	30-50	700-1000	$5.10^{-3} - 3.10^{-4}$		

Flow direction inside the system has evolved as shown in Figure 3. The phreatic levels were initially positive with reference to the piezometric ones of the Puelche. The value of the head difference grew with the exploitation, as well as leakage, with a descending vertical movement predominance.

The water of the phreatic and Pampeano aquifers contains sodium-calcium bicarbonate except for the areas near the river and its tributaries, where it contains sodium chloride. The water of the Puelche aquifer contains natural sodium bicarbonate, with the same exception as in the previous case.

3   EFFECTS   OF   THE   INTENSIVE EXPLOITATION

The exploitation of the Puelche aquifer started growing during the 1920's, mainly due to World War I industrial growth and the resulting demographic explosion. This expansion of the use of the aquifer developed in a haphazard way due to the lack of norms for the optimisation of the location of industrial and service wells, which resulted in interference between the wells' drawdown cones. This provoked a progressive coalescence, which in time resulted in large, composite cones covering almost all the urban area surrounding the city of Buenos Aires (Fig. 2), especially the southern sector (Hernández 1978).

The apexes of the main cones reached   -35m to - 40m a.s.l., their original position being + 5m to + 15m. The drawdown lower limit was given by the top of the aquifer, where it behaved as a free aquifer. When the extraction rate was accordingly adjusted, the extension of the area was increasing due to the need of new wells and the incorporation, in the periphery, of horticultural irrigation with waters from the Puelche. Figure 3 a-b shows the evolution from an original situation corresponding to the end of the 19th century (Artaza 1943) to the 1980's, when it reached its maximum drawdown.

This in turn caused another, very important, effect: the intrusion of the saline waters (with sodium chloride) from the aquifer itself, lying on

the alluvial plain of the Río de La Plata river and its main tributaries (discharge zones), saline due to a long run with a minimal final speed. Studies based on ²H and ¹⁸O isotopes showed the origin of saline waters, showing that salinization occurred due to a long residence time and not due to marine or paleo-marine waters (Hernández, 1978). This intrusion was one of the causes for the abandonment of the wells, along with the increment of the concentration of nitrates caused by the lack of a piped sewage system in 70% of the urban area and also due to the ingress of industrial polluting agents.

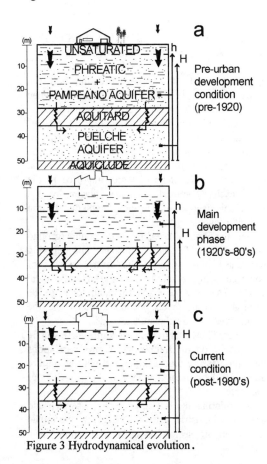

Figure 3 Hydrodynamical evolution.

The increase of the hydraulic head difference between the semiconfined aquifer and the phreatic-Pampeano complex caused an acceleration of the leakage through the aquitard, with an important fall of the phreatic surface. Constructions realised during that period, as a consequence of the speedy urban and industrial development, found a non-saturated zone, where sub-surface structures were emplaced (foundations, subsoils, underground parking lots, boiler rooms, machine rooms, etc.). Excavations more than 10 m deep did not reach the phreatic level, which had declined to a greater depth due to descending leakage (Fig. 3b).

As a way of meeting the need for water, the service was expanded with surface water treated at the Planta Palermo and the more modern Planta Bernal (1979). This import of water introduced new contributions to the system from leaks and on-site sanitation returns, apart from the volumes no longer extracted due to this replacement, with the resulting consequences detailed in the following section.

4 IMPACT OF THE GROUNDWATER LEVELS RISING AND CONTROL PROPOSAL.

The first effect of the new situation was the recovery of the piezometric levels (Figure 4) when more than 150 wells were abandoned. The difference of hydraulic head grew gradually smaller, as well as leakage rate, and the phreatic surface slowly rose with the maintenance of the contributions to the system. In addition to this, there was a percentage of water imported to the local cycle, favoured in many places by the individual disposal of sewage waters due to the lack of a sewage system.

Thus, the phreatic levels reached the underground constructions, flooding subsoils and forcing permanent dewatering in the central sectors of some cities in the southern area (Hernández et al 1991). This is a new situation and tends to be general as rising levels become regional and the area served by pluvial waters spreads.

It is very likely that in the near future there will be also effects on the framework of the foundations and sub-pressure on the support structures. Figure 3c shows the current tendency of the behaviour of the system.

Since during the last few years the service and control of industrial waters passed from the public to the private sector, no corrective actions have

been made in this regard in spite of the existence of a Regulatory Body. This Regulatory Body - which is supposed to control the operation of the service and which represents the State and the Provinces but not the users - has been so far concerned mainly with water charges, technical claims from the users, service improvement and fiscal issues rather than with the maintenance of the exploitation. Unfortunately, this situation is possible due to the weakness of the regulatory legal frame. On this basis, a proposal including follow-up and control actions, as well as norms to stop the advance of a situation which may cause a severe impact, are proposed.

4.1 Monitoring of the present situation.

A first, quite easily implementable step, would be to select existing, strategically located wells, and, when abandoning them, seal them only after placing a plastic observation pipe, so as to form a monitoring network to keep a piezometric and hydrochemical control of the Puelche aquifer. Small piezometers should be built near some of the active wells in order to perform pumping tests for a densification of the values of T, S, and K, and

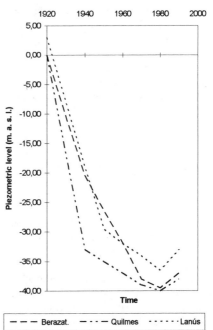

Figure 4 Piezometric level changes (Puelche Aquifer)

240

specially the aquitard coefficients T' and K'.

To complete the hydrodynamic scheme it would be necessary to drill some small-diameter, observation wells in the phreatic aquifer. The information obtained and the hydrometric series would be useful for the development of a 3D flow model which, once calibrated, would be used to simulate and forecast the evolution of the phreatic levels. The need for a 3D model comes from the fact that the main problems in the area are caused by vertical transference mechanisms (infiltration, leakage, level recovery), which cannot be directly reproduced in a bidimensional spatial model. Hydrochemical data are very valuable for the corroboration of the dynamic phenomenon in the initial analytical model and its refinement.

Model operation would be used to issue an early alert and to select the areas where control activities should be practised, since it is almost impossible to cover the whole area.

4.2 Control proposal

In some sectors, selected according to the model, a series of actions to stop the phenomenon could be put into practice, the most important being the installation of a piped sewage system in order to reduce the local recharge from water importation.

A recommended practice is to continue with the pumping in some of the wells to be abandoned in order to maintain the leakage rate. The volumes thus extracted would be sent to surface water courses (highly polluted in the area) in order to produce an ecologically useful dilution, or, alternatively, to pluvial drains. Obviously this operation should be suspended during the rainy season in order to avoid flooding in the area.

If these activities are combined with the simulation and forecasting model, pumping may even be automated with reference to a critical safety value, and in case of a dangerous rise, the phreatic aquifer could be also pumped (alternative pumping) by means of a close network of dewatering wells.

Since the adjustment of the model and pumping control activities will demand a certain amount of time, it is advisable to begin as soon as possible, with pilot tests run in the most critical sectors.

Naturally, these activities can only be carried out within a regulatory framework for a sustained use of the hydric resource. This framework does not exist yet, since the concession of the service of both surface and underground water supply has not considered the effects arising from a combined but not harmonic use of the resource.

Of course, financial support to solve the problem and to prevent its extension can only be granted if there are regulations to control water exploitation.

However, it is not likely that the correction of the situation will be achieved in the near future, since it was not included in the conditions of the concession. A negotiation process will be necessary in order to create this regulatory body.

Another factor of importance is the lack of participation of the users and scientists, as proclaimed at the Dublin'91 Conference. Technical knowledge is available, therefore the only step to be taken in order to correct the situation is the creation of a regulatory body.

5 CONCLUSIONS

The abandonment of the service wells in the urban area surrounding the city of Buenos Aires and their replacement by treated pluvial waters has caused a rise in the phreatic levels due to the recovery of the piezometric levels of the semiconfined aquifer, leakage having been reduced.

This rise of the level is causing important problems due to the flooding of underground constructions (basements, underground parking lots, machine rooms, etc.) in the central sectors, making dewatering pumping inside the facilities necessary. It is possible that in time there will be also effects on the foundations of the buildings and even sub-pressure on the structures.

The operation of a monitoring network using the existing wells, even those to be abandoned, would be useful to build and operate a three-dimensional simulation and forecasting model to select the sectors where control activities are necessary.

Pumping maintenance in selected positions and the use of the extracted volumes for an ecologically attractive dilution of the highly polluted water courses in the area is one of the recommended steps to be taken, this activity being controlled by the model itself.

It would be advisable to create a regulatory body that considers the participation of the scientific sector and the users in order to put these activities into practice.

REFERENCES

Artaza, E. 1943. *Saneamiento urbano en la República Argentina. Provisión de agua y desagües urbanos.* Cuaderno 6. Facultad de Ciencias Fisico-matemáticas. La Plata.

De Felippi, R., N. González, M.A. Hernández, V. Paredes y G. Pepe 1991. *Abastecimiento de agua en el Area Metropolitana de Buenos Aires y Gran La Plata.* Senado de la Nación-UN CEPAL-CELADE. Buenos Aires.

Hernández, M.A. 1975 *Efectos de la sobreexplotación de aguas subterráneas en el Gran Buenos Aires y alrededores. República Argentina.* II Congreso Iberoamericano de Geología Económica, I:435-450. Buenos Aires.

Hernández, M.A. 1978. *Reconocimiento hidrodinámico e hidroquímico de la interfase agua dulce-agua salada en las aguas subterráneas del estuario del Plata, Partidos de Quilmes y Berazategui.* VII Congreso Geológico Argentino, Actas, II:273-285. Buenos Aires.

Hernández, M.A., J. Fasano y E. Bocanegra 1991. *Prevención de riesgos en la recuperación de niveles piezométricos en áreas urbanas de Argentina.* Segunda Conferencia Latinoamericana de Hidrología Urbana, Actas, 130-138. ALFHSUD-UBA-IDRC. Buenos Aires.

Groundwater in the Urban Environment: Problems, Processes and Management, Chilton et al. (eds)
© *1997 Balkema, Rotterdam, ISBN 90 5410 837 1*

Modelling falling and rising groundwater levels in cities

M. Mavroulidou & R. I. Woods
Department of Civil Engineering, University of Surrey, UK

M. J. Gunn
Division of Civil Engineering, South Bank University, London, UK

ABSTRACT: Engineers need better modelling tools if they are to design successful dewatering schemes to counteract the effects of rising groundwater levels in cities. The paper describes the numerical modelling of pumping incorporating possible desaturation of materials. The model is applied to a simplified geology representing 50m of clay overlying a sand aquifer. The techniques used show promise and are sufficiently flexible to be applied to other lithologies.

1 INTRODUCTION

In many large cities, such as London, groundwater (piezometric) levels are rising. If no remedial measures are taken, many buildings and structures will be subject to flooding and differential movements associated with changes in effective stresses in the ground. The authors have been engaged on research (sponsored by the Engineering and Physical Sciences Research Council) which has as its aim the use of numerical modelling to determine the likely consequence of these rising groundwater levels on surface and subsurface structures and also to evaluate alternative schemes for pumping to protect the structures against damage.

CIRIA Special Publication 69 (Simpson et al. 1989) considered in some detail the situation in London where the water level in the aquifer below the city centre is rising at a rate of between 0.5m and 1.5m per year. Here generally a few metres of recent and Quaternary deposits overly approximately 50m of London Clay. Beneath these deposits are the Lower London Tertiaries consisting of layers of clays and sands above the Chalk, a consolidated fine grained limestone. There are several scour hollows in the London Clay and a few of these extend right through the clays into the underlying permeable materials. Simpson et al (1989) considered possible strategies for dealing with the rising groundwater levels and concluded that the most cost effective

solution would be regional pumping. This would involve abstracting up to 30 Ml/day (in total) from between 5 to 30 wells located in central London.

The main concern for geotechnical engineers in this situation is to obtain estimates of how the pore pressures in the clay will vary with time during pumping. In this paper we describe an approach to numerical modelling which allows us to consider the development of groundwater flow in both a layer of clay and the underlying aquifer in a single integrated calculation which includes the possibility of progressive desaturation of either the clay or the aquifer.

2 MODELLING TECHNIQUES

In the civil engineering field both analytical and numerical solutions are used to estimate pumping rates and drawdowns associated with dewatering systems. Calculation of steady state flow rates and drawdowns for both confined and unconfined aquifers is often based on the assumption of predominantly horizontal flow. Soil consolidation theories (e.g. Biot 1941) are used to estimate the times needed to achieve particular drawdowns where the flow is confined. Powrie and Preene (1994) present various analytical solutions based on soil consolidation theory and compare theoretical predictions with data obtained from case studies of dewatering fine grained soils.

Solutions of the type described above are based on assumptions of homogeneous permeability and compressibility of the soil. The equations obtained are similar to those found in other application areas, for example the conduction of heat through solids. Use can therefore be made of standard solutions for heat conduction (e.g. Carslaw and Jaeger, 1948). Also, as these solutions are all linear, the principle of superposition can be employed. For example, the effect of pumping from several wells can be found by superposing several instances of a single well solution.

There are usually significant discrepancies between observed field data and analytical solutions (Preene and Powrie, 1993; Powrie and Preene, 1994). Well known difficulties in using analytical solutions include deciding appropriate boundary conditions and the permeability of the soil. When soil desaturates we can expect higher volumes of water extracted from the ground. This is because flows in the saturated case are linked to the volumetric strain of the soil skeleton (i.e. the classical assumption in soil consolidation theory). On the other hand during desaturation an elemental volume of soil releases water as part of a completely different physical process.

Numerical techniques such as finite differences or finite elements have been increasingly applied to groundwater modelling over the past thirty years, in particular to unconfined flow through dams or aquifers. Two distinct approaches to modelling unconfined flow have been used with finite elements. The first approach is the variable mesh technique (Taylor and Brown 1967) which employs a finite element mesh for the zone of saturated soil below the phreatic surface. As the position of the phreatic surface is usually not known *a priori*, the geometry of the mesh is adjusted as part of the solution procedure. The second approach is the fixed mesh technique (Desai 1976) which adjusts the permeability of the soil above the phreatic surface, usually reducing it by a factor of 1000. This approach seems to be intended mainly as a numerical artifice (to eliminate flow above the phreatic surface) rather than an attempt to model the behaviour above the phreatic surface in a realistic fashion.

When time dependent movement of the phreatic surface is modelled the usual approach is to apply a flow term along the phreatic surface, corresponding to the water released by the soil as the phreatic surface moves (e.g. Bathe et al; 1982). The specific yield of the soil is used to quantify this term.

The authors have developed a formulation which considers flow above (as well as below) the phreatic surface. The permeability and storage coefficient which are used in the calculations are continuous functions of pressure head based on real soils data. The position of the phreatic surface emerges as a by-product of the calculation (the boundary between positive and negative pore water pressures) rather than being calculated explicitly as part of the solution process.

3 PROPOSED NUMERICAL MODEL

The basic equation governing flow of water through the soil is:

$$\frac{\partial}{\partial x}(K_x(\psi)\frac{\partial h}{\partial x}) + \frac{\partial}{\partial y}(K_y(\psi)\frac{\partial h}{\partial y}) + \frac{\partial}{\partial z}(K_z(\psi)\frac{\partial h}{\partial z}) + Q = S\frac{\partial h}{\partial t}$$

(1.a)

or for axisymmetric conditions

$$\frac{1}{r}\frac{\partial}{\partial r}(r\,K_r(\psi)\frac{\partial h}{\partial r}) + \frac{\partial}{\partial z}(K_z(\psi)\frac{\partial h}{\partial z}) + Q = S\frac{\partial h}{\partial t}$$

(1.b)

where h is the total head, ψ is the pressure head. K_x, K_y and K_z are the permeabilities in the x, y and z directions respectively, given as functions of pressure head. Q represents point sources or sinks. S is the storage coefficient relating changes in the volumetric water content to changes in pressure head. When $\psi > 0$ we make the normal assumptions of soil consolidation theory (Biot 1941): soil particles and water are both volumetrically incompressible. Changes in soil volume are due to changes in the volume of the pore space which can be found from the effective stress principle and the elastic compressibility of the soil skeleton. Thus when $\psi > 0$ S is the elastic storage coefficient. When $\psi < 0$ the soil may become desaturated and we obtain S from the slope of an experimentally determined curve relating volumetric water content to pressure head.

We have adopted the following basic expressions for the relationship of volumetric moisture content and permeability to pressure head (when $\psi < 0$):

$$\theta(\psi) = \theta_s \frac{1}{1 + a_1|\psi|^{n_1}}$$

$$\qquad (2)$$

$$K(\psi) = K_s \frac{1}{1 + a_2|\psi|^{n_2}}$$

$$\qquad (3)$$

In the present work, typical data given for a silty sand by Vauclin et al. (1976) and Jurong clay provided by Leong and Rahardjo have been used (1995) (see Fig.1a and 1b). The values of the parameters a_1,n_1 and a_2,n_2 as back-fitted by the above mentioned authors have been adopted.

For the derivation of Eqn (1) validity of Darcy's law in both the saturated and the unsaturated zones has been assumed throughout the analysis. The dependence of both the permeability and storage

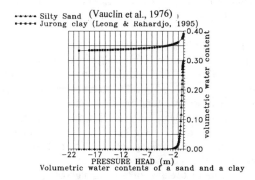

Figure 1a. Volumetric water contents of the soils used in the present model.

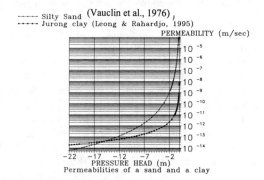

Figure 1b. Hydraulic conductivities of the soils used in the present model.

terms on the pressure head variations causes (1) to be strongly non-linear. For the linearization of the equation a Picard iterative scheme was adopted and a backward Euler finite-difference scheme was used for time integration.

4 PUMPING ANALYSIS

As mentioned in the introduction, one possible strategy for counteracting the effect of rising groundwater levels in cities regional dewatering using a number of wells. A number of saturated-unsaturated analyses have therefore been performed, in order to study the effectiveness of pumping from such a grid of wells, 100m deep and spaced 1km apart. The simplified geology assumed considers an upper 50m layer of clay and a lower 150m layer of sand which is being dewatered. The initial impetus for our research was the situation in London, as described in the introduction. As we do not have the permeability and storage properties for London Clay, the Lower London Tertiaries and the Chalk in the form required for our analyses, we have adopted the material properties for Jurong clay and the silty sand described in the previous section. Our intention is to demonstrate the viability of technique in a situation which resembles the London situation in broad terms (i.e. a clay layer overlying an aquifer).

In our analyses we have taken as the starting condition an initial hydrostatic state of pore pressure in both the clay and the underlying aquifer. Thus in the analyses presented here we are addressing the issue of whether we can model the original pumping from the aquifer to produce a depressed water table (i.e. the condition before the recovery of the water table that is currently taking place).

If a single well of the grid (remote from the edge) is being analyzed, the remote boundary conditions can be assumed to be completely impermeable, because of symmetry (Figure 2). It is assumed that the water is produced from a constant head, corresponding to an initial sudden drawdown of 90m in the well (Figure 3). Although the type of fixed head boundary conditions in the well is less usual in water resources and geotechnical compared with petroleum engineering practice, it has been chosen as more appropriate in the modelling of pumping from fine-grained soils. In fact, according to Powrie and Preene (1993), constant rate boundary conditions are not well-suited to modelling pumping from fine grained soils (saturated hydraulic conductivity<10^{-5} m/s) because, as the authors say 'in practice, in fine soils, the capacity of the pumping equipment will normally be much greater than ... [the yield] of the well, so that after the first few minutes of pumping, the drawdown in the wells will remain constant, while the flow rate decreases'. We have assumed that the pressure head at the top of the clay is zero. Field measurements of pore pressures in central London (in the London Clay) have indicated near hydrostatic distributions at the top of the clay layer (Simpson et al; 1989) consistent with a perched water table.

In order to determine the effect of the pressure head dependent permeabilities and water volumetric content term we have performed two analyses (case A and case B). In case A the permeabilities are held constant at the saturated values (7.8×10^{-9} m/s for the clay and 9.7×10^{-5} m/s for the sand) and the volumetric responses are governed solely by the elastic storage coefficients. Figure 4 (a), (b) and (c)

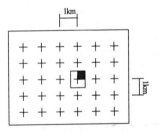

Figure 2. Plan view.

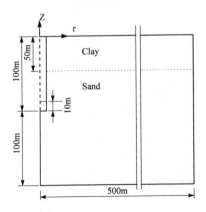

Figure 3. Section.

show the calculated variations of pore pressure with depth at times of 7.3 days, 109.5 days and 1460 days for case A. In case B the permeabilities and the volumetric responses vary with negative pressure head according to the relationships defined in Section 3 above. Figure 4 (d), (e) and (f) show the calculated variations of pore pressure with depth at times of 7.3 days, 109.5 days and 1460 days for case B.

The analysis with constant permeabilities quickly develops a pore pressure profile typical of those measured in the London Clay and consistent with its under-drainage. The development of horizontal drainage in the sand (towards the well) can also be clearly seen (Figure 4 (a)). The final state is one of steady downwards seepage above the new water table and the pore pressure profile (Figure 4(c)) is consistent with this (nearly all the head drop is across the clay and this leads to the suction profile in the clay and top of the sand).

From an examination of Figures 4(d) to 4(f) it is clear that the development of this flow regime is retarded in the analysis with varying permeabilities and storage terms. Examination of similar pore pressure profiles at much larger times (not shown here) indicate that the system is heading towards the same final state as the analysis with constant permeabilities. This slowing down of the flow process seems physically reasonable and is consistent with desaturation of the sand.

It is not so clear, however, that the final state is physically realistic. We have attempted to model desaturation by varying permability and storage coefficient. The analysis assumes that we have a continuous distribution of head throughout the mesh. It is not clear that assigning heads to sand from which the water has drained has physical meaning. Air will be introduced into the unsaturated zone, and it might make more sense to take air pressures as defining the boundary condition on the bottom of the clay. These type of considerations would lead to significant extra complexities in the modelling process (e.g. multi-phase flow), and there would be significant advantages if we could retain with the present single phase model.

Figure 5 shows how the calculated flow rates of water extraction from the well develop with time for the two analyses. The calculated flow rate is of the same order of magnitude as that calculated by Simpson et al (1989). This agreement is clearly fortuitous bearing in mind that the analysis results are for 50m of Jurong clay overlying a silty sand

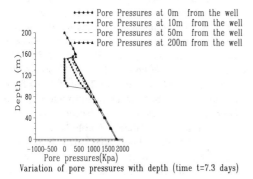

Variation of pore pressures with depth (time t=7.3 days)

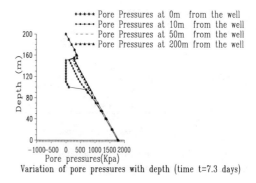

Variation of pore pressures with depth (time t=7.3 days)

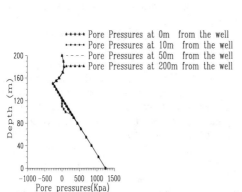

Variation of pore pressures with depth (time t=109.5 days)

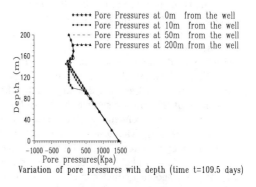

Variation of pore pressures with depth (time t=109.5 days)

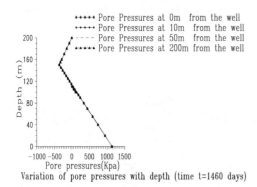

Variation of pore pressures with depth (time t=1460 days)

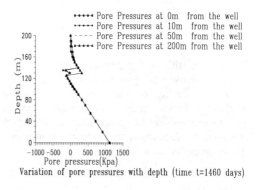

Variation of pore pressures with depth (time t=1460 days)

Figure 4a, 4b and 4c (above) Variation of pore pressures with depth at various time levels for case A. In this analysis the permeability and storage cofficient terms were held constant at the saturated values.

Figure 4d, 4e and 4f (above) Variation of pore pressures with depth at various time levels for case B. In this analysis the permeability and storage coefficient terms varied with pressure head according to the relationships defined in section 3.

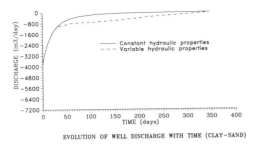

EVOLUTION OF WELL DISCHARGE WITH TIME (CLAY–SAND)

Figure 5. Comparative well discharge plots for constant and varying hydraulic properties.

aquifer. It is interesting to note that the flow rates for the analysis with a variable storage coefficient are larger than those where just elastic storage effects are present. This is to be expected and is consistent with draining water from the sand during desaturation. However, the total volume of water pumped seems to be less than that implied by the new position of the phreatic surface in the sand and the volumetric water content -pressure relation for the sand (Figure 1(a)). The desaturation of the sand takes place over a narrow range of pressure head change (2m) and it is likely that some points in our mesh are overshooting this range. This point requires detailed further investigation.

5 CONCLUSIONS

Our analysis with varying permeabilities and storage properties shows some promise of providing a more realistic modelling of the process of pumping involving some desaturation. The techniques used are quite general and can be applied to other lithologies, assuming the data characterising permeabilities and storage properties are available.

REFERENCES

Bathe, K.J., Sonnad, V., Domigan, P., "Some Experiences Using Finite Element Methods for Fluid Flow Problems", *Proceedings of the 4th conference on finite element methods in water resources*, Hannover, West Germany, June 1982, pp.9.3-9.16.

Biot, M.A., "General theory of three dimensional consolidation", *Journal of Applied Physics,* 12, 1941, pp155-164.

Carslaw, H.S. and Jaeger, J.C. *Conduction of Heat in Solids,* (2ed), Clarendon Press, Oxford, 1959.

Desai, C.S., "Finite residual schemes for unconfined flow", *International Journal for numerical methods in engineering* , 10, 1976, pp. 1415-1418.

Leong & Rahardjo, "Typical Soil-Water Characteristic Curves for two Residual Soils from Granitic and Sedimentary Formations", *1st International Conference on Unsaturated Soils,* Vol. 2, Balkema, Rotterdam/Ecole Nationale des Ponts et Chaussées, Paris, pp519-524, 1995.

Powrie W. & Preene, M., Time-drawdown behaviour of construction dewatering systems in fine soils, *Géotechnique*, 44, (1), 1994, pp. 83-100.

Preene M. & Powrie, W., "Steady-state performance of construction dewatering systems in fine soils", *Géotechnique*, 43, (2), 1993, pp. 191-205.

Simpson B., Blower T., Craig R.N. and Wilkinson W.B., "The Engineering Applications of Rising Groundwater Levels in the Deep Aquifer below London", *C.I.R.I.A. Special Publication 69,* C.I.R.I.A., London, 1989

Taylor R., Brown C.B., "Darcy flow solutions with a free surface", *A.S.C.E. Journal of the Hydraulics Division*, March 1967, pp. 25-33.

Vauclin M., Khanji D., Vachaud G., "Etude expérimentale et numérique du drainage et de la recharge des nappes à surface libre, avec prise en compte de la zone non saturée", *Journal de Mécanique*, Vol 15 (2), 1976, pp. 307-348.

Groundwater in the Urban Environment: Problems, Processes and Management, Chilton et al. (eds)
© 1997 Balkema, Rotterdam, ISBN 90 5410 837 1

Modelling of the groundwater impacts of a new underground railway through an urban area

N. P. Merrick
National Centre for Groundwater Management, University of Technology, Sydney, N.S.W., Australia

ABSTRACT: A key infrastructure project in Sydney (Australia) prior to the 2000 Olympics is the construction of an underground railway to link the city with the international and domestic airports. As the railway route passes through the only significant aquifer close to Sydney, the contractor has to comply with a uniform Condition of Approval which limits groundwater inflow to the tunnel. A regional model of the aquifer has been used to assess the dynamic impacts on groundwater levels and velocities of tunnelling, excavation, construction and shaft dismantling over a period of 44 months. Separate best case and worst case estimates of groundwater inflows have been used to justify a variation to the Condition. The time for the system to reach 95% of equilibrium levels varies from 2 to 10 years, due to spatial differences in stress and hydraulic conductivity. It is clear from sensitivity analysis that drawdown predictions are robust and are not affected significantly by uncertainty in hydraulic conductivity.

1 INTRODUCTION

Near Sydney, Australia, the only significant source of groundwater is the Botany Sands aquifer, which underlies Sydney's south-eastern suburbs - an area of dense urban and industrial development. The northern rim of the Botany Basin (Figure 1) is about 3 km south of the city of Sydney.

Following European settlement in 1788, the Botany area consisted of occasional sandhills on generally flat sandy land with low shrubs. Further south there were extensive swamps up to at least the 1830s, but by the 1860s most had dried up due to the activities of man, cattle and horses, and the introduction of a water supply scheme for Sydney in 1852. The land supported agriculture and the more noxious industries which could not be located in the inner city. Stream contamination in the Botany area was reported more than a century ago.

The aquifer has the distinction of being the oldest producing groundwater system in Australia which is still in active use. Prior to 1930, water was withdrawn from open dams, timbered shafts and brick wells but intensive exploitation of the sand aquifer did not occur until the introduction of the borehole pump. In 1942, when the aquifer was investigated as an emergency water supply during wartime, groundwater was being used for a wide range of industries and irrigation of recreation space. Due to a long history of urban occupation and industrial development, the aquifer has been degraded in many places and is constantly under threat from anthropogenic activities. The major users of groundwater today are petrochemical and paper manufacturing plants, as well as numerous golf courses which flank environmentally significant wetlands. Groundwater accounts for about 40% of industrial water demand, 15% of commercial use, and 20% of all water used in the Northern Zone of the Botany Basin. Residential use of groundwater is negligible. The groundwater extracted from the Botany area, currently about 11,000 ML/a, accounts for only 1-2% of Sydney's total water usage.

The area also supports major transport and freight infrastructure in the form of Sydney Airport and Port Botany. During 1996, construction commenced on another major infrastructure project - the New Southern Railway - which will link the city of Sydney with Sydney Airport by an underground railway, in time for the 2000 Olympics. As a substantial length of the 10 km tunnel will intersect the sandbeds of the Botany Basin, there is concern that seepage of groundwater into the tunnel could disturb equilibrium conditions in the sand aquifer and could mobilise contaminated groundwater into "pristine" areas.

Following the environmental impact study, the Department of Planning placed on the constructors of the rail link, Transfield Bouygues Joint Venture, the following Condition of Approval:- *"Groundwater inflow into the tunnel shall be controlled during the construction and operational stage so as not to exceed 50 m^3/day/km unless otherwise approved by*

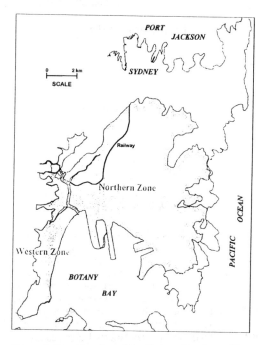

Figure 1. Locality plan of the Botany Sands aquifer.

the Department of Water Resources." This condition was based on a modelling study which considered four alternative uniform inflow rates from 5 to 1500 m3/day/km. However, because the tunnel had to pass through rock at the northern end and sandy sediments at the southern end, it became apparent that, instead of a uniform inflow rate along the railway route, the hard rock portion of the tunnel would have a higher rate than that specified in the Condition of Approval, and the soft ground tunnel would have a rate much lower than specified. Four underground railway stations to be constructed along the route are also expected to have much higher inflows than the specified uniform rate. More detailed modelling has been undertaken to allow Transfield Bouygues Joint Venture to build a case for a reasonable variation in the Condition of Approval.

1.1 *Hydrogeology*

The basin consists of Quaternary unconsolidated sediments which overlie a Triassic bedrock of sandstone and shale, which are of much lower permeability. The Botany Sands vary in thickness from about 1 m to 75 m, generally thickening towards the south and south-east. They form an intermittent depositional sequence that ranges upwards from fluvial through estuarine, to terrestrial swamp and aeolian deposits. The upper section consists mainly of sandy deposits but can contain discontinuous peat beds and layers of indurated

sandrock. The lower section is comprised of layers of interbedded clays, peats and sands.

Good recharge occurs in the more elevated north, where rainfall averages 1300 mm/year. Rainfall infiltration into the unconsolidated sediments is high in open space areas, particularly at five golf courses, Randwick Racecourse, Centennial Park, Moore Park and grassed borders of the Lachlan Lakes. Additional recharge occurs from street runoff in urban and industrial areas after heavy rain. Average rainfall reduces to about 1100 mm/year near the airport. Modelling suggests that the amount of infiltration varies from about 6 percent (on estuarine sediments) to about 37 percent (on sandy sediments). Recharge from rainfall is in the order of 22 ML/day in a dry year and 44 ML/day in a wet year.

Shallow regional and local groundwater discharges into the Lachlan Lakes and Alexandra Canal, which drains into Cooks River at the junction of the Northern and Western Zones. Deep groundwater discharges into Botany Bay. Modelling studies show that the discharge to the Bay and Cooks River is in the order of 8 ML/day in a dry year and double in a wet year. To the canal the groundwater loss is about 9-12 ML/day. As the Lachlan Lakes form a series of stepped dams, they vary from influent to effluent along their length. The net discharge to the lakes is about 8 ML/day in a wet period; in a dry period a similar rate passes from the lakes to the aquifer.

Groundwater levels in the basin range from 0 m to 40 m AHD (Australian Height Datum) and are generally less than 9 m below ground surface. The saturated thickness of the aquifer is typically 15-20 m. The water table is in a state of dynamic equilibrium, constrained by surface water bodies and subjected to variations in rainfall and abstraction. Groundwater flows in a south to southwest direction along a fairly uniform hydraulic gradient (about 1:120). To the immediate north of Botany Bay, where clay and peat beds form barriers to vertical flow, piezometric head decreases with depth.

Laboratory measurements of hydraulic conductivity range from 12 to 29 m/day while various pump tests exhibit a range of 20 to 85 m/day. Storage coefficient ranges from 0.0004 to 0.24.

1.2 *Construction Technology*

The railway will pass beneath some of Sydney's most populated areas, industrial sites, the main airport runway, heritage buildings, ancient fig trees, six lanes of the Princes Highway and Cooks River. The project, to be finished in the year 2000 at a cost of $650 million, has seven separate construction sites.

Four underground railway stations are being constructed using diaphragm wall techniques in which the station box walls are constructed in the ground before excavation begins. The use of a bentonite slurry to maintain pressure at each wall panel minimises groundwater drawdown. The soil and rock within the station box is removed with a trench cutter rig. Different technologies are being used for the northern and southern tunnels. From Prince Alfred Park to Green Square Station (Figure 2), tunnelling through Hawkesbury Sandstone is being done by two road headers, one working south and the other working north from a 26 m deep shaft at Green Square. A tunnel boring machine (TBM) manufactured in Germany, 11 m diameter and 80 m long, is being used to drive the tunnel through soft sediments from Tempe Reserve to Green Square, using expertise gained from the English Channel Tunnel, Paris Metro and Cairo Metro. The tunnel is supported by precast concrete lining segments which are erected at the rear of the TBM as it advances. Joints are filled with continuous rubber seals to minimise groundwater ingress. The void outside the tunnel shell is grouted as the TBM moves forward.

2 NUMERICAL MODEL

The groundwater model has been used for a range of practical applications, including the potential impact of a new runway at Sydney Airport on groundwater levels in the Botany Sands aquifer. Predictions were made, not only for changes to the shoreline by construction of the runway, but also for substantial changes in sea level and rainfall (the "greenhouse effect"). The third runway came into use in late 1994.

The aquifer is essentially unconfined to the north but in the south is partially confined by clay and peat

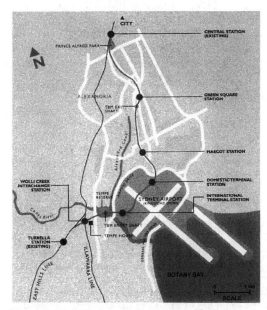

Figure 2. New Southern Railway route alignment

lenses. On a regional scale, it is reasonable to conceptualise the aquifer as a single layer varying from unconfined to semi-confined, because the lateral continuity of peat and clay beds is in the order of 100 m. The basin rim is assumed to contribute negligible inflow. The various water bodies (lakes, canal, river, bay), which define boundary conditions, are taken to be static for long-term modelling. The imposed dynamic stresses on the system are rainfall, abstraction and irrigation of recreation space.

The groundwater model (Merrick 1994) has been developed using Aquifem-1 finite element software. The grid has 578 elements and 326 nodes. Element dimensions vary from about 100 m to 1300 m.

Hydraulic conductivity, storage coefficient, bottom elevation and thickness are specified at each node. A leakage coefficient is specified at lake nodes, along with observed lake levels. Nodes which track the shoreline, Cooks River and Alexandra Canal are given fixed heads.

Most of the external boundary is presumed to allow no lateral flow into the aquifer, except where it cuts an alluvial valley on the southeast edge.

Groundwater abstraction by pumping is simulated by negative fluxes at 53 nodes which incorporate the extraction histories of 91 production bores. Forty-three bores are used to irrigate parks and golf courses, thereby returning a fraction to the groundwater system. A recharge flux is added at 59 elements to account for the irrigation return. Water used for industrial purposes is assumed to be lost from the system by piped sewerage disposal.

The study area has been divided into six land use regions to each of which has been assigned an infiltration factor determined during model calibration. The study area is divided into two rainfall regions associated with monitored climate stations.

There is considerable spatial variability in hydraulic conductivity. In the model there are eight discrete values ranging from 2 to 36 m/d.

2.1 Construction Algorithm

To isolate the effects of railway construction, the usual dynamic stresses on the system have been held at constant rates. Rainfall has been set at long term mean rates and abstraction from bores has been set at current rates. The only stresses which vary with time are the groundwater inflows to the tunnel, stations and temporary shaft.

The total length of the underground railway (excluding cut and cover sections) is 8224 m. Of this, the length within the model boundary is 7748 m because the model represents only the unconsolidated sediments within the Botany Basin. A realistic construction schedule has been followed (Figure 3) with tunnelling and excavation activities in parallel with separate rates of progress for the

251

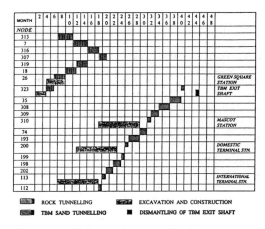

Figure 3. New Southern Railway excavation, construction and tunnelling schedule

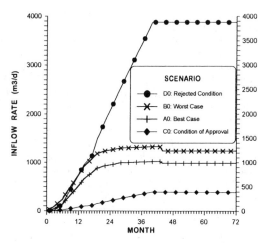

Figure 4. Cumulative inflow rates for four scenarios.

northern rock tunnel, the southern rock tunnel, the sand tunnel, and station and shaft excavations. The route is defined by 22 nodes (two of which lie on the boundary). The internal 20 nodes are considered as effective groundwater "pumps" which become active progressively at different months as construction proceeds. Four of the nodes along the route represent stations at which a higher inflow is anticipated during construction and one node represents the TBM exit shaft which remains open until month 44. An example of the cumulative inflow rates for four scenarios is shown in Figure 4.

Special purpose software was written to track the progress of parallel construction activities, to identify when a route node becomes active from any one of nine possible construction activities, and to allocate projected groundwater inflows to appropriate model nodes. The variables in the program are the separate lengths, durations and inflow rates for two tunnels, four stations and one shaft. The algorithm allows for a reduction in inflow to the TBM exit shaft when it is dismantled. Some simulations allowed for reduced inflow to station boxes after grouting had taken place. Best estimates of anticipated inflow rates were derived by independent multi-layer cross-sectional modelling.

3 STEADY STATE SCENARIOS

Because of the uncertainty in chosen hydraulic conductivity values, steady state simulations for pre-construction conditions were run for the base model and for two perturbed models, in which hydraulic conductivities were varied by ±25% for elements close to the railway route.

In the vicinity of the railway route, velocities vary from 0.01 m/d to 1.9 m/d but are generally below 1

m/d. The natural lateral flows are expected to vary from about 240 to 4400 $m^3/d/km$, but the sensitivity analysis extends this range from 210 to 4800 $m^3/d/km$. The volume of groundwater crossing the tunnel route (under pre-construction conditions) is about 13.7 ML/d, at an average of 1760 $m^3/d/km$.

4 TRANSIENT SCENARIOS

Many scenarios have been run for a range of possible inflows to the various excavation components, for both calibrated and perturbed hydraulic conductivity distributions. The results are compared with a scenario which simulates the Condition of Approval.

4.1 Best Case Scenario

Scenario A investigates the effect of seepage to the tunnel for the *best case* set of prescribed inflow rates. The three uncertain components of inflow are: rock tunnel 300 $m^3/d/km$, Green Square station 700 $m^3/d/km$, TBM exit shaft 3000 $m^3/d/km$. The equilibrium inflow is 7.2% of the natural groundwater flow which crosses the railway route. For comparison, the Condition of Approval scenario intercepts 2.8% of the natural groundwater flow.

Comparison with the base steady state scenario shows an increase in velocity in the northern half of the model area from a maximum 1.9 to 2.0 m/d. The maximum increase in hydraulic gradient is about 50% at the northern end of the rock tunnel, but the flow magnitudes there are quite low (about 250 $m^3/d/km$). The increase in gradient at Green Square is about 5%. The average increase in gradient from Green Square to the northern boundary is about 19%. To the south of Green Square the gradients are reduced by 7% on average. The maximum reduction in gradient is 26% at the southern end of the route at Alexandra Canal; this is a beneficial impact because contaminated groundwater from the airport will discharge to the canal and Cooks River at a lower rate. The flow directions change by about 5 degrees at the railway nodes to the north, but vary by an average of only 1 degree to the south.

After 48 months, the maximum drawdown is about 2.2 m at the northern edge of the model where low permeability is used to represent residual clay. Water level is predicted to fall by about 0.1 m near Mascot Station and Domestic Terminal Station, by about 0.05 m at the International Terminal Station, and by about 0.7 m near Green Square Station. After 50 years, the maximum drawdown is about 3.1 m.

The time required to reach equilibrium varies along the rail route. It is a minimum near the International Terminal Station and a maximum at the northern end of the route where stresses are more severe and permeabilities are lower. The predicted time varies from 2.0 to 9.5 years at the 95% level, and from 4.9 to 14.9 years at the 99% level.

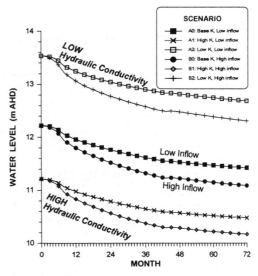

Figure 5. Simulated hydrographs at Green Square Station for each scenario.

4.2 Worst Case Scenario

Scenario B investigates the effect of seepage to the tunnel for the *worst case* set of prescribed inflow rates. The three uncertain components of inflow are: rock tunnel 400 m³/d/km, Green Square station 1500 m³/d/km, TBM exit shaft 7000 m³/d/km. The equilibrium inflow is 9.1% of the natural groundwater flow which crosses the railway route.

There is very little discernible difference in velocities between the best case and worst case scenarios. The maximum increase in hydraulic gradient is about 90% at the northern end of the rock tunnel. The increase in gradient at Green Square is about 7%. The average increase in gradient from Green Square to the northern boundary is about 31%. To the south of Green Square the gradients are reduced except for a minor increase at one node. The maximum reduction in gradient is 26% at the southern end of the route at Alexandra Canal, but this is a beneficial impact. The average decrease in gradient from Green Square to the southern boundary is about 7%. The flow directions change by about 6 degrees at the railway nodes to the north, but vary by an average of only 1 degree to the south.

After 48 months, the maximum drawdown is about 3.0 m at the northern edge of the model. Water level is predicted to fall by about 0.1 m near Mascot Station and Domestic Terminal Station, by about 0.05 m at the International Terminal Station, and by almost 1 m near Green Square Station. After 50 years, the maximum drawdown is about 4.5 m.

The equilibrium time varies along the rail route from a minimum near the International Terminal Station to a maximum at the northern end of the

route. The predicted time to reach equilibrium varies from 2.0 to 9.6 years at the 95% level, and from 3.6 to 15.1 years at the 99% level.

4.3 Sensitivity Analysis

The drawdown in water table level as excavation and tunnelling proceed at the planned rates can be tracked dynamically by the model in the form of simulated hydrographs. Figure 5 shows that uncertainty in hydraulic conductivity results in a change in water elevation of about 10% at Green Square, and that uncertainty in inflow rates accounts for an uncertainty of about 0.4 m in drawdown.

The maximum increase in hydraulic gradient for the best case scenario is in the range 44% to 72% at the northern end of the rail route. Gradients are increased at only Green Square Station, where the expected increase is in the range 2.9% to 6.1%. The maximum reduction in gradient ranges from 23% to 31% at the southern end of the route at the Canal.

The maximum increase in hydraulic gradient for the worst case scenario is in the range 66% to 163% at the northern end of the rail route. Gradients are increased at only Green Square Station, where the expected increase ranges from 4.9% to 9.7%. At the southern end of the route, the maximum reduction in gradient ranges from 23% to 31%.

For comparison, the Condition of Approval scenario has a maximum increase in hydraulic gradient of 5.9% to the north of Green Square and a maximum reduction in gradient of about 14% at the southern end of the route at Alexandra Canal.

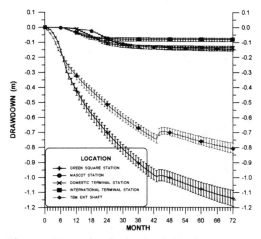

Figure 6. Uncertainty in simulated drawdown at each station for the worst case scenario.

Gradients are increased at only Green Square Station, where the expected increase is 1.0%.

The uncertainty in hydraulic conductivity affects the magnitude of predicted drawdown. The sensitivity runs for each scenario have been used to estimate the standard error for drawdown. The drawdown responses with error bars are shown in Figure 6 for the worst case scenario. Although uncertainty in hydraulic conductivity can cause substantial changes in predicted water elevation, the variation in drawdown is insignificant. The maximum deviation from the mean is no more than 5 cm in the worst case. It is clear from this sensitivity analysis that the drawdown predictions are robust and are not affected significantly by uncertainty in the assigned hydraulic conductivity distribution.

5 CONCLUSION

The original Condition of Approval made no distinction between soft sand and hard rock tunnelling, which use different drilling technologies and incur different seepage rates. The current design rates vary from a minimum of 10 m^3/d/km for the sand tunnel to a maximum of 400 m^3/d/km for the rock tunnel. Higher rates over short distances are anticipated for the station excavations (500 m^3/d/km in sand, 1500 m^3/d/km maximum in rock) and for the exit shaft for the sand boring equipment (7000 m^3/d/km maximum). This study has assessed the impact of likely variable inflow rates which take into account different lithologies and construction technologies for tunnels in sand and rock. The timing of the inflows follows a realistic construction schedule over a period of 44 months, and the effects have been simulated for a total time period of 50 years. Two limiting scenarios have been considered:

a *low inflow* case which intercepts 7.2% (1.0 ML/d) of steady state groundwater flow, and a *higher inflow* case which intercepts 9.1% (1.2 ML/d) of steady state groundwater flow.

The maximum drawdown in groundwater level will be at the northern edge of the model. The expected maximum values are 3.1 m (low inflow case) and 4.5 m (higher inflow case) at equilibrium. There are no known nearby users of the groundwater resource who are likely to be affected adversely by the lowering of the water table. It is clear from the sensitivity analysis that the drawdown predictions made in this study are robust and are not affected significantly by uncertainty in the assigned hydraulic conductivity distribution.

The time required to reach equilibrium varies along the rail route. It is a minimum near the International Terminal Station and a maximum at the northern end of the route where stresses are more severe and permeabilities are lower. The predicted time varies from 2.0 to 9.6 years to reach 95% of the final equilibrium level.

It is only in areas of increased hydraulic gradient where the tunnel could have a negative impact by accelerating groundwater flow beyond its natural rate, and possibly mobilising contaminated groundwater into areas of better quality. The groundwater hydraulic gradient is expected to increase substantially at the northern end of the rail route where the tunnel is driven through sandstone and shale. The maximum increase should be 50-90%. Minor changes in hydraulic gradient are expected at Green Square Station, with expected values of 5-7%. From Green Square southwards, the consistent reduction in hydraulic gradient has a positive effect because any occurrences of contaminated water will not be mobilised beyond what would occur under natural conditions. In the southern part of the route, hydraulic gradient will be reduced by about 26% near Alexandra Canal without any change in direction. This is a beneficial impact because contaminated groundwater beneath the airport will discharge to Alexandra Canal and Cooks River more slowly. There is no risk of saltwater intrusion for the variable inflow scenarios investigated in this study.

ACKNOWLEDGEMENT

Transfield Bouygues Joint Venture is acknowledged for permission to publish this paper.

REFERENCES

Merrick, N. P., 1994, A groundwater flow model of the Botany Basin. IEA and IAH Water Down Under 94 Conference, Preprints of Papers, Vol.2, Part A, 113-118.

Groundwater in the Urban Environment: Problems, Processes and Management, Chilton et al. (eds)
© *1997 Balkema, Rotterdam, ISBN 90 5410 837 1*

Engineering investigation and technological solutions for the groundwater lowering in the city of Dessau, Germany

U. Riemann
HGN Hydrogeologie GmbH, Nordhausen, Germany

ABSTRACT: In the town of Dessau, Germany rebounding groundwater levels have caused flooding of existing buildings and structures over large areas. The rise has been due to strongly declining groundwater withdrawal. Since 1990, abstraction for drinking water supply, industry and agriculture declined from about 50,000 m^3/d to as little as about 5,000 m^3/d. As a result of this, in some parts of the town groundwater levels are now as high as 0.5-1.0 m below surface. Heavy rains in 1994 led to an extreme situation with large-scale flooding particularly in the municipal district of Alten. To minimise or prevent consequential damage, extensive engineering studies were conducted and the following installations were set up for controlling groundwater levels:
· A pumping system of ten wells for dewatering one district.
· A radio controlled measuring network for groundwater level monitoring and pumping system control.

1 INITIAL SITUATION

The German town of Dessau in the Land of Saxony-Anhalt (Figure 1) has a population of about 100,000, and is a major industrial centre for engineering. The groundwater flow regime is strongly influenced by the confluence of the Rivers Mulde and Elbe. As the town developed, surrounding villages were integrated into the municipal area. Due to the presence of the two rivers, the town expanded mainly towards the west and south. The development of new residential and industrial areas has changed the natural landscape and influenced the surface water, soil water and groundwater regimes.

The aquifer in the Dessau region is about 15 m thick and consists of Quaternary and Tertiary deposits (Figure 2). The dominating Quaternary consists mainly of Pleistocene deposits of the Elsterian and Saale glacial periods. These are overlain by Young Pleistocene to Holocene formations including native and forest soils and meadow loam.

The aquifer has calculated transmissivities of 1 x 10^{-2} to 1 x 10^{-4} m^2/s, hence permeability is quite suitable for groundwater movement. The Mesooligocene Rupelian clay of the Tertiary forms the base of the aquifer over large areas.

Until 1989/90, public water supply, industry and agriculture each day pumped about 50,000 m^3 of groundwater. As a result, groundwater levels fell by 2-3 m over large areas. With the construction of the residential area of the Zoberberg district in the western part of the town, systems for controlling groundwater levels were first established up in the

Figure 1. Location map.

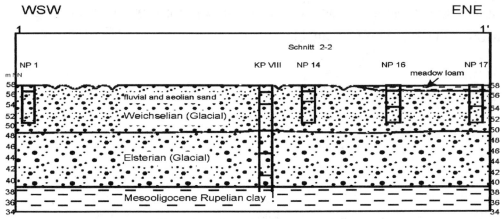

Figure 2. Hydrogeological cross-section.

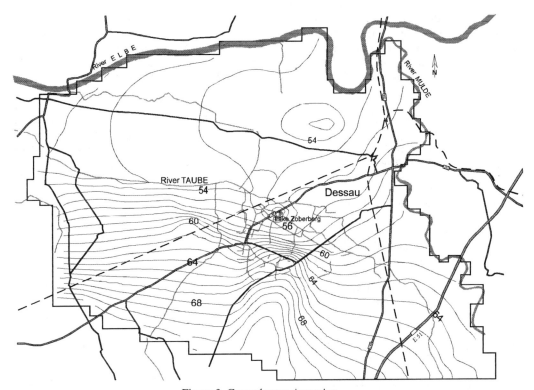

Figure 3. Groundwater dynamics.

1970s. Lake Zoberberg (which originated from the excavation of materials for building) and single wells were used for that purpose. Figure 3 shows the groundwater flow pattern as influenced by such conditions.

The storm water system of the new residential areas was connected to the lake. The storm water drain entering at a level of 52.5 m above sea level imposes a maximum permissible lake level which requires the periodic withdrawal of water from the

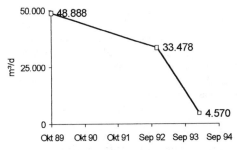

Figure 4. Abstraction trends in Dessau.

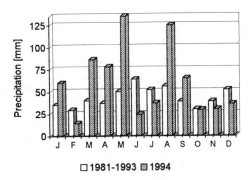

Figure 5. Precipitation at the Quellendorf meteorological station.

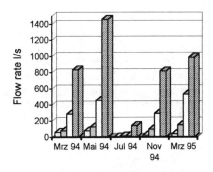

☐ MP 1 ☐ MP 3 ☐ MP 6 ▨ MP 7

Figure 6. Flow measurements in the ditch system.

lake. Without such withdrawal, the lake level would rise by about 3 m, a process that back up drainage through the rain water system.

In Figure 3 one can also see the groundwater flow from south to north. In the area where River Mulde flows into River Elbe it turn east towards an east-west direction. These receiving waters drain the areas under review.

2 CHANGES IN THE GROUNDWATER FLOW PATTERN IN THE DESSAU REGION

After the closure of the drinking water works in the Dessau region in 1990 and the end of groundwater withdrawal for industrial process water in 1990-1992, the delivery rates declined to about 5,000 m^3/d (Figure 4), and the groundwater level started to rise again. Temporary and localised groundwater withdrawal in connection with construction work in 1994 only temporarily influenced the overall situation in the urban district of Dessau. Heavy rainfall caused the situation to get even worse in 1994.

According to measurements by the German Weather Service, total precipitation recorded at Quellendorf (the meteorological station relevant for the Dessau region) was 690 mm in 1994, i.e. about 30% more than the long-term average of 527 mm (Figure 5).

In some locations in Dessau the groundwater level is less than metre below surface. Following heavy rains, groundwater levels in the area under review were 0.2 to 0.3 m higher after about five days. In Dessau-Alten and Zoberberg in particular, groundwater had penetrated into the cellars of existing buildings.

In such situations an efficient drainage system is an urgent necessity for receiving and discharging both surface water and groundwater. The drainage system in the Dessau region is formed by the River Taube and its tributary drainage ditches. The drainage ditches are shallow and narrow (decimate range). Only the ditches south-west of Dessau cut deeper into the aquifer - a result of land improvement. That system, however had little effect due to weeds, litter and refuse in the ditches and interference from construction work. It had also to be considered in the subsequent studies as it is used for discharge the pumped groundwater.

3 ENGINEERING STUDIES AND WORK TO PREVENT FOUNDATION FLOODING

The current groundwater dynamics in the urban district of Dessau were recorded in the first stage of the study. Periodical measurement of groundwater levels provided information on water level trends. At the same time the hydraulic effect of the ditch system was determined by measuring flow rates. Taking into account reported temporary groundwater withdrawal in connection with construction work and the associated discharge into the ditch system,

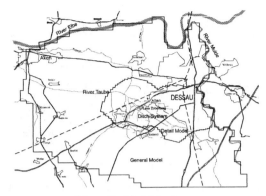

Figure 7. Model limits.

The data thus collected were used as the basis for setting up a general geohydraulic model which was used for simulating both the flow situation and the changes that had occurred in the groundwater dynamics over an area of above 100 km², and to show the first effects of keeping groundwater levels as low as necessary.

4 TECHNICAL INSTALLATIONS FOR GROUNDWATER DEWATERING

Further investigations were concentrated on the district of Dessau-Alten and the new residential area of Zoberberg. There already existed the above-mentioned water lowering facilitie.s in the Zoberberg residential area (individual wells, Lake Zoberberg) which, however, due to partial ferric incrustation had lost much of their effect on the surrounding area. Following the general model, a regional detailed model was then developed for an area of about 30 km² (Figure 7). Finer resolution resulted in a more precise model translation of local conditions, making allowance also for the discharge of the pumped groundwater into the ditch system.

With the more detailed model the effectiveness of

preliminary information was obtained regarding the interactions between surface water and groundwater.

Depending on the amount of rain, flow in the lower reaches of the River Taube at the southern edge of Dessau was between 10 and 80 l/s (MP 1). It increased to 25 to 450 l/s at the western edge of the urban district of Dessau (MP 6) north of Mosigkau (Figure 6). Those measurements furnished proof of the partial connection between the ditch system and groundwater.

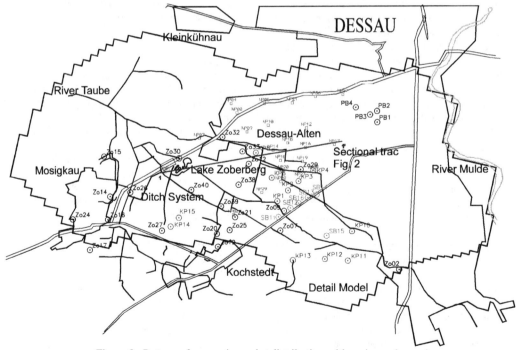

Figure 8. Pattern of measuring point distribution with main roads.

the new dewatering systems on the surrounding area was demonstrated. This helps to optimise the siting and operation of the systems. Technically, groundwater lowering is accomplished by a new pumping field of ten wells. The groundwater obtained is discharged into the ditch system of the River Taube in its upper reaches. Relevant groundwater level measurements are an essential prerequisite for the efficient and hence low-cost operation of the groundwater lowering systems. In conformance with the foundation depth of the buildings, groundwater levels in the new residential area should not exceed 56 m a.s.l.

Thirty newly sunk groundwater measuring points (100 mm diameter) have been equipped with in well data loggers (sensors) for automatic measurement of groundwater level and temperature. Measurements are taken twice a day and passed on by telemetry link. The latter is connected, via modem, to a computer for data processing, storage and output.

The measuring network automatically records the contours of the groundwater surface in an area of about 10 km^2. Allowing for set threshold water level, this provides for efficient control of the new pumping field.

The measurements are managed in a database that can be complemented and updated with data from other measuring points as well as with water levels in the ditch system and in the main receiving waters, and relevant groundwater withdrawal and/or flow rates. With this information the groundwater dynamics in the urban area of Dessau can be compiled and documented area-wide for a given period. The database can also be used to update and re-calibrate the existing geohydraulic model. Interference with the system can thus be checked and assessed quickly.

5 CONCLUSIONS

Starting from the Dessau experience, the following stages are proposed for setting up groundwater lowering systems in built-up areas:

1. Recording site-specific groundwater flow regimes. Regional surface waters have to be included in the investigations.

2. Constructing a geohydraulic model to show the effects of groundwater lowering systems on their surroundings. The model helps to optimise the scope and structure of the technical systems.

3. Setting up new groundwater measuring points for populating the database. Later, those measuring points can be used for efficient system control.

4. Construction work for erecting the groundwater lowering system, including requisite preliminary planning.

5. Testing the new systems in a field experiment. Measurement of the changed contour of the groundwater dynamics for comparison with the model results.

REFERENCES

Busch, K.-F., & L. Luckner 1972. *Geohydraulik.* Leipzig: VEB Dt. Verl. f. Grundstoffindustries.
Matthelß, G. 1990. *Die Beschaffenheit des Grundwassers.* Berlin-Stuttgart: Verh Gebruder Borntraeger.

Evaluation of potential geotechnical problems associated with rising groundwater level in Riyadh city, Saudi Arabia

A.S.Stipho
Al Asker Consulting Engineers, Riyadh, Saudi Arabia

ABSTRACT: The harsh environment and hot climate in Saudi Arabia coupled with the impact of substantial modernization have caused significant changes to the long established soil water regime. Shallow groundwater levels rising at alarming rate have shown an impact on many engineering structures in several major cities. This is due to changes in the historically stable water sensitive soil layers that prevail in the area. This study is directed towards investigating the influence of moisture change on the water sensitive collapsible desert soil in both natural and compacted forms. It was concluded that such soil undergoes sizable volume change or loses its trength upon inundation with water, resulting in severe structural problems.

1 INTRODUCTION

The geological and environmental features in the desert countries of the Middle East, in general, have produced a unique balance between soil behaviour and the status of groundwater.

The pre-dominant harsh and hot environment of Saudi Arabia coupled with geological processes have developed a repeated typical pattern of soil profile at many sites. These geological and environmental features are in turn reflected in the soil contents and behaviour in the Riyadh area and elsewhere.

The recent substantial modern developments in the area have introduced major challenges to practising engineers. They touched the long established environmental balance in the area, and disturbed it. The disturbance is clearly reflected in the soil-water regime. Modern Saudi Arabia is well known for its massive exploitation of underground water resources. The excessive use and exploitation of groundwater have brought about significant urban changes. Consequently, they have led to rapid rises in shallow urban groundwater levels to an alarming rate (Al Towegeri and Tabbaa 1992).

Rising groundwater levels are reported as a potential problem for engineering structures in a number of cities throughout the world (Hurst & Wilkinson 1985, Brassington & Rushton 1987). Groundwater has become noticeable at many shallow excavations and some recent wet soils at street level were found at many sites in Riyadh city.

This phenomenon has resulted in widespread structural distress related to soil volume change, foundation movements, concrete deterioration, steel corrosion, flooding of cellars, basements, lift shafts and more recently the flooding of transport underpasses.

Though many government agencies in Riyadh are monitoring groundwater movements closely and providing solutions, the lack of national historical observation data and records on groundwater makes it difficult to address and explain the nature of each factor involved. The widespread structural damage has given the incentive to conduct this study. This paper is not intended to discuss the hydrogeological regime or analyse its models, it is mainly an attempt to correlate the consequences of groundwater movement with the behaviour of water sensitive soil, which is widely encountered in this area.

2 GEOLOGICAL CONSIDERATIONS

The natural and geological conditions in Saudi Arabia are defined by well divided topographic units (Oweis & Bowmann 1981, Stipho 1984). Most of the plain unit is found along the coastlines and inland at the foothills. Lithologically, this unit is characterized by wind blown sand and fine deposits from the weathering of the nearby hills, above a relatively impermeable rock bed.

Soil particles in this unit are loosely bonded with intercalated layers of halite and gypsum. Thus the soil is quite varied in texture, density, consistency and strength. The degree of cementation depends on the type of cementing agent and percent of fines content.

The silt and clay deposits encountered, are often found to contain specific active minerals, such as montmorillonite. Active minerals are unstable and usually found in an extremely desiccated condition, which makes them very sensitive to water. Groundwater movement is governed by Darcy's Law, which makes permeability an important factor in this context. Fissures, cavities, cracks, and layers of coarse grained beds, that are known to exist widely in Saudi Arabia, influence the overall permeability of the soil and subsurface in all directions.

3 GROUNDWATER CONDITION

Due to the rapid increase in population, modernization and industrialization, the demand for water in Saudi Arabia has increased drastically (Table 1). Rainfall amount and frequency in Saudi Arabia is very limited, while the evaporation rate is excessive and leads by a ratio of 30: 1 (Dahkail & Al Gahtani 1982, Stipho 1984). The lack of rain or surface sources of freshwater, makes underground water the most economic source of supply.

Deep wells with pumping facilities are installed all over the country for municipal and irrigation use. Some of these wells have to be deepened every six months to stay functional, while the shallow groundwater level in Riyadh city is continuously rising. An average rise of 1 m/year is reported, while in some districts during 1983-1988 the rise reached an average of 3 m/year (Al Shaikh et al. 1992).

The rise in the shallow groundwater level in Riyadh is attributed to: I) the drastic increase in water consumption, II) the massive demographic changes and modernization, III) the expansion of green areas and over-irrigation, IV) the excessive leakage from the water distribution systems and V) the nature of the geological formations of the area.

Groundwater movements alter the capillary fringe zone and moisture content of the soil down the profile. These changes are taking place at or above the foundation level of most structures. Moisture in soil activates chemical reactions, changes the soil conductivity and alters soil structure, (Fookes et al. 1985, James & Little 1986). Clay minerals in the desert may retain relatively stable structures for many years as a result of past increased overburden pressure, provided they stay away from water or some salts (Milton 1970).

The rise in groundwater level may not only change soil moisture and salt contents, but destabilize soil structure, and erode fine particles. Under loads, such soil undergoes hydro-compaction, a sudden settlement (collapse), different to the classical consolidation process. It takes place with no water

Table 1. Water consumption and losses in the Riyadh area (1000 m^3/day).

Year	1983	1984	1985	1986	1987
Daily rates of drinking water provision	371	460	584	683	765
Waste water received at the sewerage treatment plants	97	121	175	232	293
Total rate of loss	274	339	409	451	472

(After Riyadh Development Authority technical report 1988).

being forced out of the soil, but while the soil is losing its strength, it absorbs additional water. Shale formations however, show different failure patterns upon saturation, and tend to swell and increase in volume upon absorbing water (expansive soil).

4 SALT ATTACK

The hyper-depositional environment typical of deserts supplies a considerable amount of salts. Once the groundwater reaches the surface it becomes enriched with the encrusted salts and extremely aggressive to concrete. The principal salts which are widely encountered in the groundwater of Riyadh include; calcium, magnesium, sulfate and chloride (Table 2). The moisture fluctuations in soil with a high content of salts are liable to produce the worst condition that encourages salt attack and inflicts severe deterioration on concrete and steel.

Unprotected ordinary concrete elements are the most affected and warrant strict precautionary measures. Salt attack will significantly shorten the functional life of unprotected steel and exposed reinforced concrete. Sulfate and chloride attack the concrete and corrode the reinforcing steel. The calcium aluminum hydrate in the hardened concrete reacts with the sulfates to produce calcium sulfate aluminate crystal, which has a volume 227% greater than that of the original crystals. Crystallization of these salts in the concrete pores often leads to slow persistent disintegration of the element.

On the other hand soil resistivity is highly influenced by the presence of salts. Moisture in soil enhances the flow of electrical current while soluble salt triggers the process of corrosion of metals.

Table 2. Typical range of chemical properties of shallow groundwater in the Riyadh area (Al Towegeri & Tabbaa 1992).

Parameter	Range (mg/l)
Cl	221-1841
SO_4	284-173
HCO_3	57-459
NO_3	4-424
Ca	440-1800
Mg	16-420
pH	7.2-9.8
TDS	11040-6326

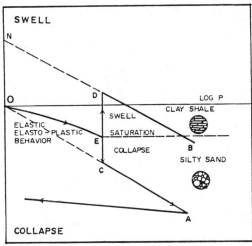

Figure 1. Schematic model diagram for water sensitive soil.

Corrosion of steel is a major cause of deterioration of concrete structures in the world. This problem costs the United States alone about 300 billion dollars each year, (Chaker 1996).

Due to the nature of shallow groundwater in Riyadh and the leaks from drainage systems, it becomes a good media for bacteria, which could cause health hazards. Some bacteria influence the chemical and physical properties of soil. They convert sulfides to sulfates while others are capable of fixing atmospheric nitrogen to a form useful to plant life. The high permeability encountered in Riyadh soil makes air circulation within the top layer of soil very easy, thus corrosion of embedded steel becomes as easy as that which occurs in the atmosphere.

5 MODEL BEHAVIOUR OF SENSITIVE SOIL

Water sensitive soil is special and largely prevails in the arid environment. Such soil is characterized by its severe desiccation and high sensitivity to water ingress. With the exception of solid rock, most of the soil in Saudi Arabia may be considered as sensitive to water. The highly dissociated clay, silt, clayey sands and those salt bonded eolian deposits are particularly vulnerable to water ingress. Dhowian & Touma (1991), gave a detailed account of the different water sensitive soils which are encountered in the area. The behaviour of water sensitive soil is idealized and modelled under loading in both dry and soaked condition. Figure 1 is a schematic diagram to represent the typical (p-e) relationship for water sensitive soil. The generalized model behaviour is idealized to fall within two well defined parallel lines, OA and NB. In the first stage, the behaviour of dry soil under increased loading follows a defined elastic to elasto-plastic pattern which analytical methods in the literature are capable of predicting to a high degree of accuracy.

At a particular loading level, e.g. point E, and after inundation with water it may either follow path EC or ED depending upon the nature of soil, and its fines content. Path EC represent the collapse of soil upon saturation under loading, which is typical behaviour for the silty, clayey sands and salt rich eolian deposits.

The extend of the collapse is gauged by the parameter CP, (collapse potential), which represents a guide to the severity of the collapse. It is defined as:

$$CP = \frac{\Delta e_c}{1 + e_o}$$

where: Δe_c = change in void ratio upon wetting, e_o = initial void ratio.

Soil with dominant clay shale may, on the other hand, expand upon saturation following path ED. Dhowian et al. (1985) reported 14% swell in the top few meters of some clay shale found in Saudi Arabia. Upon increased load intensity (P), the normal consolidation process was proceeded along lines DB and CA.

6 TEST PROGRAM

A test program was established to study soil behaviour in natural conditions upon inundation with water. Typical soil samples from Al Rabowa, a domestic residential area in Riyadh, were studied. One borehole was sunk to a depth of 11 m, while a test pit of 3 m depth was dug to obtain undisturbed soil samples. The subsurface soil profile for the site is shown in Figure 2. Groundwater was found at 6.5 m from the surface,

DEPTH (M)	BORE HOLE LOG	SPT (N)	SOIL DESCRIPTION
0.00 – 1.0 – 2.0		18 23 27	MEDIUM DENSE DRY, YELLOW BROWN MEDIUM TO FINE SAND WITH TRACES OF SILT.
3.0 – 4.0		19 26 30	RUST BROWN POORLY SORTED CEMENTED SAND WITH GYPSUM INTRUSION. (SHLBY 2.50 –2.85M)
5.0 – 6.0 – 7.0		32 29 40	DITTO, VERY DENSE WITH TRACE OF CLAY SHALE.
8.0 – 9.0 – 10.0		37 54 42	WEATHERED MODERATELY STRONG, YELLOWISH WHITE LIMESTONE WITH WEAK ZONE OF BROWN SANDY SILT.
11.0			END OF DRILLING

Figure 2. Borehole log of the site.

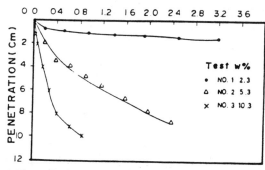

CONE RESISTANCE (Kg/cm²)

Test w%
- NO. 1 2.3
△ NO. 2 5.3
× NO. 3 10.3

Figure 3. Cone penetration resistance.

(in November). The top few meters of the profile were found to be hard and very dry, dominated by alluvial deposits, silty sand with traces of crystallized gypsum. The moisture content down the profile increased from 0.7% to 6.8% at the bottom of the pit. The average dry field density was found to vary between 1.4 and 1.48 kg/cm³, and the maximum dry density from a standard compaction test was averaged to 1.77 kg/cm³ at optimum moisture content of 11.0%.

At typical foundation depths of 1.5 m, a standard hand operated cone penetrometer was used to evaluate the bearing resistance at natural moisture content and then immediately after inundation with water and after 24 hr. from the time of flooding.

In a series of tests, undisturbed bulk samples were carefully carved from the exposed faces and trimmed by hand to fit consolidometer rings. All samples were taken from above the water table and tested in their natural moisture condition. Soil samples were tested under an applied consolidometer ring seating load of 0.5 kg (0.143 kg/cm²), for 24 hr. At the end of which, the load was doubled each time until it reached 16 kg (4.57 kg/cm²). The samples were saturated at different load levels then the consolidation and unloading processes were continued in the same increase/ decrease manner. Other samples were kept for 24 hr. after inundation with water and then unloaded in the same manner. Further tests were carried out on compacted soil samples at optimum moisture content. Soil specimens were compacted in a standard ASTM mold under standard compaction effort to maximum dry density. Test specimens were then carved to fit into the consolidometer ring and placed under the same consolidation, inundation process as before. Tests results are depicted in Figures 3-6.

7 TEST RESULTS

A marked decrease in the bearing resistance was found after inundation with water. Cone penetration resistance was found to be highest when the soil was in its natural moisture condition (w = 2.3%) and dropped by 70% percent only 24 hr. after flooding with water, as shown in Figure 3. The sharp reduction in bearing resistance both immediately and after 24 hr. of flooding is attributed partly to the release of the confining stresses, the loss of capillary effect and loss of bonding forces. The nature of bonding of soil particles is complex, but the fast and immediate loss of strength after flooding (test no.2) could be mainly due to the loss of confining stresses and the capillary effect, but the further loss observed after 24 hr., (test no.3), could be attributed to the loss of chemical bonding and some electrochemical effects. This fast and sharp reduction in bearing resistance is mainly due to the high porosity of the soil under study.

Figures 4 and 5 show the consolidation/collapse behaviour of the undisturbed soil samples. During the first stage of consolidation, all samples followed a typical linear deformation pattern as postulated in the analytical model herein.

Large collapse potentials were observed while testing the soil under high loads as reported by Stipho (1993), Clemence and Fibarr (1981). In the second stage of consolidation sharp linear consolidation curves were again observed. The linearity in behaviour during this stage suggests that some mechanism other than consolidation is taking place; a slow chemical reaction is the most likely suspect.

After achieving the desired loading levels, all samples were allowed to rebound in decrements while the soil was still in a wet condition. Once again clear linear elastic behaviour with very little rebound was observed. Lower collapse levels were observed with compacted soil specimens at optimum moisture

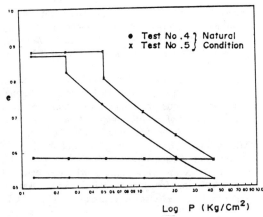

Figure 4. Consolidation/collapse of cemented alluvial desert soil.

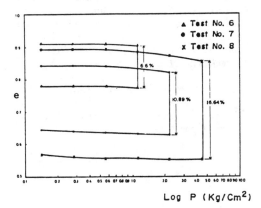

Figure 5. Variation of collapse potential with level of loading of flooding.

Table 3. Collapse potential values.

CP%	Severity of the problem
0-1	No problem
1-5	Moderate problem
5-10	Trouble
10-20	Severe trouble
>20	Very severe trouble

content upon inundation at load intensities similar to those of tests 6 and 7, as shown in Figure 6.

The collapse potential CP under 200 kpa loading (calculated from test 7) was equal to 10.89%. In comparison with Jenning & Knight's (1975) criteria for severity of the problem shown in Table 3, the

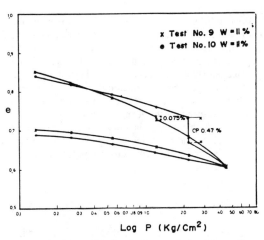

Figure 6. Consolidation/collapse behaviour of compacted alluvial desert soil.

observed values represent severe trouble. This information may not be quantitatively justifiable for all sites, but it gives a good guide for estimating the magnitude of the problem.

8 CONCLUSIONS

The loss of bearing resistance in water sensitive soil is predominantly divided between the loss in chemical binding forces and the loss of intergranular confining stresses. The collapse is immediate upon inundation when the bonding is provided physically while it is slower in the case of chemical cementing. Both chemical and physical bonding are typically available in hot-climate, loose-consistency alluvial deposits that are altered by wind, blown sand and hillwash.

Soil collapse and its consequential effects on foundations and engineering structures are raising serious concern. Test results on soil samples from the area under study showed larger than average collapse potential, indicating that severe damage may take place once the groundwater reaches foundation level.

The collapse potential seems to increase with increasing stress intensity at which flooding takes place (Figure 5). On the other hand, the collapse potential was found to be very small in compacted soil at optimum moisture content, indicating that groundwater poses relatively smaller risk to buildings founded on selected compacted engineering fill rather than natural soil. Thus the consideration to control groundwater level at its existing position is a very important task for maintaining foundations and engineering structures in a stabilized condition.

Further, the widely accepted local criterion of using bearing capacity results obtained in the natural

265

dry condition, needs to be revised and investigation of the soil water sensitivity should always be on the requirements of any geotechnical report. Though the present and future fragmentation of ground water management and expectations has been the concern of many government agencies in Saudi Arabia, efforts have led to a number of national decisions to lower the groundwater level at many sites.

The results presented herein are related to the area investigated and the opinions expressed are those of the author and do not necessarily apply to other sites or conditions.

REFERENCES

AL Towegeri A., & M. Tabbaa 1992. Rise of the groundwater table in Riyadh and its effect on the structures. *Proceedings of the Pan Arab Conf. on Building Deterioration in the Arab World and Methods of repairs, Riyadh*, 367-388.

AL Shaikh, A., T. AL Rifeai, & Zaolouk 1992. Building Deterioration in Riyadh City, Case Study. *Proceedings of Pan Arab Conf. on the Building Deterioration in the Arab World and Methods of Repair, Riyadh*, 400-412.

Brassington, F. K. Rushton 1987. Rising water table in central Liverpool, *Quarterly Journal of Engineering Geology*, London, Vol.20, 151 - 158.

Chaker, V. 1996. Measuring Soil Resistivity, Choosing the right Method, *ASTM Journal of Standardization*, ASTM, June 16-22.

Clemence, S. & A. Fibarr 1981. Design considerations for collapsible soils, *Journal Geotechnical Eng. Div. ASCE, GT3*, 305-316.

Dahkail F. & A.S. AlGahtani 1982. The deterioration of concrete structures in the environment of eastern of Saudi Arabia, *The Arabian J. for Sciences and engineering Vol.7, No.3*, 191.

Dhowian A., A. Ruwaih, O. Erol, & A. Youssef 1985. The distribution and evaluation of expansive soil in Saudi Arabia, *Proceedings of the 2nd Saudi Engineers Conf.* Vol. 1, 308-326.

Dhowian A., & F. Touma 1991. Water sensitive soils in Saudi Arabia *Proc. 3rd Saudi engineers conf.* Nov., Riyadh, 110-115.

Fookes, P., W. French & S.M. Rise 1985. The influence of Ground and groundwater geochemistry on construction in the Middle East. *Quarterly Journal of Engineering Geology*, London, Vol.18, 101-127.

Hurst, C. & W. Wilkinson 1985. Rising groundwater levels in Cities. *Proceedings of conf. on Groundwater in Engineering Geology*, Geological Society of London, UK.

James A.N., & A.L. Little 1986. Discussion on the influence of ground and groundwater geochemistry on construction in the Middle East. *Quarterly Journal of Engineering Geology*, London, Vol.19, 209-214.

Jennings, J. & F. Knight 1975. A guide to construction on or with materials exhibiting additional settlements due to collapse of grain structure, *Proceedings of the 6th regional Conf. for African soil Mechanics and Foundation Eng.* 99-105.

Milton, G. 1970. *Geology of clays*, Published by Springger-Verlag, 176.

Owies, I. & J. Bowmann 1981. Geotechnical consideration for construction in Saudi Arabia, *Journal Geotechnical Engineering*, GT. 3 ASCE, Vol. 107, 319-338.

Stipho A. 1993. The impact of rising groundwater level on the Geotechnical behaviour of soil in hot climate Regions, *Proceedings of 3rd Int. Conf. on Case Histories*, St. Louis, 1-6 June.

Stipho, A. 1984. Soil conditions and foundation problems in the desert regions of the Middle East. *Proceedings 1st Int. Conf. on Case Histories in Geotechnical Engineering*, Roulla Missouri, Vol. 21.

The higher Commission for the Development of Riyadh, Environmental Management program, 1988. The rising of groundwater table in Riyadh city Progress report No. 15.

Rising groundwater levels in Barcelona: Evolution and effects on urban structures

E. Vázquez-Suñé, X. Sánchez-Vila, J. Carrera & M. Marizza
Escola de Camins, Universitat Politècnica de Catalunya, Barcelona, Spain

R. Arandes
Ajuntament de Barcelona, Spain

L. A. Gutiérrez
Clavegueram de Barcelona S.A. (CLABSA), Spain

ABSTRACT: During the last few years, the continuous rising of groundwater levels beneath the city of Barcelona has become a serious problem to urban structures, such as the metropolitan subway and underground parking areas. This rise is mainly due to a decline in groundwater exploitation, following a reduction in high water-consuming industrial activity in the city. We relate historical data regarding groundwater levels and water chemical composition with information about changes in land use with time. We also present an evaluation of the main terms affecting recharge in the city. The outcome is a global groundwater balance for the period 1965-1995. We have quantified that a total rate of 40 million m³ per year should be pumped from the aquifers underneath the city in order to keep to the present groundwater levels. A lesser amount would lead to a rise in levels, and to continuing problems. Finally, we suggest possible uses for this additional water.

1 INTRODUCTION AND PRESENT GROUNDWATER SITUATION

Barcelona is located in north-eastern Spain, between a mountain range named Serra de Collcerola and the Mediterranean Sea (see Figure 1), both boundaries running approximately in the NNE-SSW direction. The other boundaries are two rivers, Llobregat and Besós, which form a simple rectangular shape with a slight slope going from the mountain range to the sea. Some hills break this slope, the main one being Montjuic, near the sea. Other hills are located near the mountain range, forming local steep slopes that give rise to some streams, although most of them are presently urbanised.

In the subsurface of Barcelona we can separate different aquifers which can be characterised by their geological age. A schematic representation of the aquifers can be seen in Figure 1.

The Palaeozoic aquifer is composed of shales and granites. Catchments in this aquifer are located in the topographic highs of the city and production is from both wells and mines. Quaternary aquifers can be found in the rest of the city; in topographic low areas, they correspond to the alluvial and deltaic sediments of the Llobregat and Besós rivers; in intermediate areas, they correspond to piedmont cones and to coarse alluvial sediments.

Since the middle of the XIXth Century, the aquifers underneath Barcelona have been supporting heavy water extraction, particularly the two deltaic aquifers, where production is highest due to the large transmissivity values

associated with the alluvial material. Historically this extraction produced very large drawdowns, leading to groundwater levels below the sea at certain points, with the associated impacts on the chemical quality of the water due to seawater intrusion. Since the 1970's, urban pressures have caused many industries to migrate from the city to other areas. This resulted in a decrease in total extraction and a progressive recovery in the groundwater levels.

During the last few years, the continuous rise in the groundwater levels has become a serious threat to some underground urban structures. In the last 30 years, rises

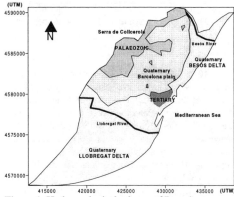

Figure 1. Hydrogeological scheme of Barcelona area.

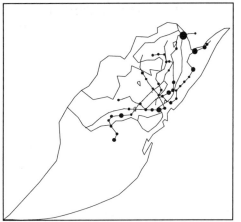

Figure 2. Location of seepage problems in the subway system. Size points are proportional to seepage.

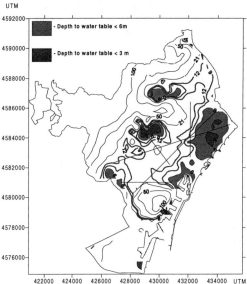

Figure 3. Depth to groundwater table in December 1996 (in meters).

from 1 to 10 m in the water table have been observed in certain areas. Many urban structures were designed and constructed at times of minimum water levels, and the possibility of water reaching the structure level was never considered. The rise in groundwater levels has produced increasing seepage into public and private structures, such as the metropolitan subway, sewage network, and underground parking areas. The total amount of water that is currently being pumped from the metropolitan subway is about 12 million m³/year. The problem is not restricted to a few points, but is quite general (see Figure 2).

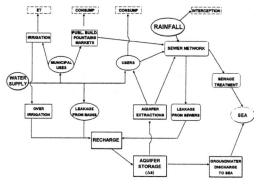

Figure 4. Conceptualisation of urban hydrogeological cycle in Barcelona.

The effect upon urban underground structures is also spread throughout the city. Figure 3 is a map of the depth from the surface to the water level. This map has been obtained by subtracting the piezometric map corresponding to December 1996 from the topography. The piezometric map was obtained by interpolation from more than 30 piezometer data values. We see that in a large area of the city, the depth to the water level is less than 6 m, which corresponds to two underground car park floors. This figure demonstrates the extent of the impact on underground structures throughout the city.

The economic impact of maintaining these structures under the new groundwater conditions is very high. To the need for drainage works, such as impermeabilisation, installation of pumps, and pipes for the seepage water, must be added the energy cost of continuously pumping rather high flows. It is important to further note that the use of the city sewage system for evacuating all the seepage water is not a very good solution, as it can affect the proper functioning of the system during periods of critical need, such as summer storms.

2 URBAN HYDROLOGICAL BALANCE

A good knowledge of urban hydrology requires a detailed analysis of the water flows: their magnitude, relative importance, and dependence upon hydrological parameters (Lerner 1990). The analysis must consider both the quantity and the quality of the water, from the moment the water enters the system (by precipitation or by direct import from other zones), to when it leaves (by runoff, evaporation, extraction). To complete the full hydrological cycle a lot of data are needed, which includes climatology, flows in the supply and sewage system, and outflow to the sea. The conceptual scheme of the groundwater balance in Barcelona is shown in Figure 4.

The overall balance is divided into two sub-balances. The first one corresponds to water in the supply plus sewage networks; the second is a proper groundwater balance. To evaluate the different terms in the balance we needed some

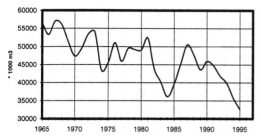

Figure 5. Evolution of water losses pertaining to the supply system.

historical data, provided by the local supply and sewage companies and the local authorities.

We have established an annual balance for the period 1965-95. Some of the missing data have been obtained by interpolations or extrapolations. This causes some uncertainty in the closure of the balance.

The different terms taking part in the balance are briefly described and quantified next:

Water supply system:

There are two basic numbers that are known with a very small error: The total volume of water supplied to the distribution system, and the amount of water actually used by the consumers. The difference are losses in the network, which are an input to the water balance system. During the period 1965-95, both the total supply volume and the computed factor of losses (ratio between losses and total supply) have been diminishing with time, mainly due to the progressive modernisation of the network. Figure 5 shows the evolution of the total water losses during the study period. This value is the most significant in quantitative terms of the full groundwater balance.

Rainfall:

We used data, from a representative point in the city, corresponding to instantaneous rainfall and outflow rates in the sewage system, measured ¨on line¨. It was found that 85-90% of the rainfall is directly diverted to the sewage system. The remaining 10-15% can be divided into surface runoff (which is considered negligible for rains with a return period smaller than ten years), surface retention, and infiltration. Surface retention is evaluated from the response to single episodes of rainfall. It is found that rainfall below a threshold of 1 mm produces no changes in the sewage flow rates. This value is adopted as representative of surface retention, accounting for 10% of the total rainfall in an average year. Infiltration is then estimated between 0-5%, with a mean value of 2% (Vázquez-Suñé and Sánchez-Vila, 1997). We do not distinguish infiltration in non-urbanised zones, as urbanisation in the city is very intensive.

Sewage water

Water flowing into the sewage network comes from different sources: Rainfall, return from users, return from irrigation, and water coming from the subway or underground constructions. Parés et al. (1985) evaluate

the return from users as 90% of the total water supplied to users. This value agrees with the data from Lerner (1990), who estimates a consumption of 20 l/hab/day, which turns out to be around 8% of the water supply in Barcelona. Losses from the sewage system, which is an input in the balance, are estimated about 5% of the total flowing water. The remaining water discharges to the sea.

Return of irrigation

This quantity is equal to the difference between the water supplied for irrigation and the actual evapotranspiration (ETR). Data about irrigation rates is supplied by the local authorities. The ETR is assumed equal to the ETP (1000 mm according to Hernández and Vázquez-Suñé, 1995).

Water mines and subway

There are a number of ancient water mines draining the Palaeozoic aquifer. The annual volume extracted from these mines is about 1.2 million m^3.

The subway system drained 13.1 million m^3 during 1995. This value is difficult to extrapolate to the past, as it is known that seepage to the subway system has increased during the last years, but it is not known in what amount. The water coming from both mines and the subway system goes directly to the sewage system.

Pumping wells for industrial and private supply purposes

In the Lower Valley of the Besós River, the amount of groundwater pumped for industrial and private supply purposes during the 60's was as high as 60 million m^3/year. Since the late 70's there has been an increase in urbanisation, and many heavy industries have moved out of the city. The total amount of the water extracted at present from the aquifers is about 5 million m^3/year.

Groundwater discharge to sea

This term can be computed from Darcy's law. During the study period this value ranged from 2 - 7 million m^3/year.

When all the previous values are input into the conceptual balance in Figure 4, the storage variation can be estimated. We consider the initial situation to correspond to 1965, although it was already a period where the groundwater levels were below the ones applicable to a steady state case.

In Figure 6 we see the evolution of Δs (change of aquifer storage) with time; this gives us an indication of the evolution of global groundwater levels with time. From 1965 to 1975 we see that the levels went down, as the aquifers were still being exploited above their recharge rates. At that time, and due to a world economic crisis, several industries shut down, extraction diminished, and levels started recovering. Around 1987, the late 80s, levels were again at the same situation as in 1965. Finally, during the last 10 years levels have progressively increased from 1 to 10 m depending on the zone.

From the balance we conclude that a total of around 40 million m^3/year should pumped to keep the present groundwater levels. This figure includes present day rates of industrial pumping and seepage to the subway, in an amount of 20 million m^3. The remaining 20 million m^3 are causing groundwater levels to rise. Unless additional

Figure 6. Evolution of water storage during the period 1965-95.

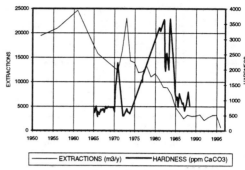

Figure 7. Extraction and quality groundwater evolution.

pumping takes place the situation would get worse in the future. The local authorities should either undertake pumping themselves or allow industries to increase their groundwater consumption by fiscal incentives.

3 GROUNDWATER QUALITY AND HYDROCHEMISTRY

The first quantitative information about the hydrochemical characteristics of the groundwater flow in Barcelona goes back to 1960. In addition, we have performed two new sampling rounds in 1996, with at least 50 control points from a few private wells and from water seepage into the subway tunnels.

Wells located in the northwest part of the city yield water with low quantities of Cl and Mg, as they are close to the highest recharge zone, where the aquifer comprises metamorphic rocks and granites.

Groundwater from the Barcelona plain shows a zonation, according to Piper classification, from sodium sulphate chloride, near the mountains, to magnesium calcium chloride, close to the sea. The increasing quantity of Ca and Mg is probably due to the interaction with the aquifer materials. Also, over this entire area, high concentrations of NO_3 are detected, with values around 100 ppm. We found low NO_3 concentrations in the old town area, probably due to two reasons: 1) In the middle of the 80's, a significant part of the sewage system was replaced, thus reducing seepage; 2) The aquifer in that area is less permeable, giving large renewal times, so that denitrification processes can take place.

Groundwater from the Llobregat delta area contains high Cl concentrations, and the relations rMg/rCa and $rCl/rHCO_3$ increase towards the sea, thus indicating seawater intrusion caused by both the high extraction rates, and the recent works that have enlarged the Barcelona Harbour.

In the Besós delta, east of the city, data available suggests that since the 60s there has been a significant seawater intrusion, as a consequence of intensive water extraction due to industrial activities (MOP, 1966; Custodio et al. 1976). In the Poble Nou area, the seawater front intruded as much as 1.5 km from the shore.

Water in that area contained 15000 ppm Cl and 36400 μS/cm of Electrical Conductivity. The rMg/rCa ratio had risen up to 5, while the $rCl/rHCO_3$ ratio had surpassed 10.

During the 70's the progressive degradation of groundwater caused by seawater intrusion led to a significant reduction in industrial extraction, and in particular to the closure of some urban water supply wells located 3-4 km from sea. The migration of several industries to other areas outside the city, and the subsequent reduction in water extraction led to a slow recovery of the water quality and the retreat of this intrusion front.

At present, Cl concentrations in the city vary from 500 to 4000 ppm, the ratio rMg/rCl is around 1 - 2, $rCl/rHCO_3$ goes from 2 - 10, and rSO_4/rCl is between 0.2 - 1. All these values confirm the progressive recuperation of groundwater levels and the increase in the amount of water flowing from the aquifers to the sea.

Figure 7 shows the evolution in quality, at one well located 3 km inland, related to the total extraction in that area. The well was originally used for supply to the city. We see that between 1970 and 1983 there was a great degradation in the quality, which led to the closure of the well for supply purposes. Since then, extraction in the area has fallen rapidly, and the quality in this and nearby wells has slowly recovered.

Table 1 shows the evolution of Cl and some ionic ratios in another well in the same area and its significant decrease since 1966.

4 POSSIBLE USES OF GROUNDWATER IN THE CITY

From the previous paragraphs it is clear that the actual rate of extraction is not enough to hold the water levels in their present position. Some additional water should be pumped from the aquifers. It has also been found that this water is, for many uses, of acceptable quality, although it cannot be used for drinking purposes.

The additional water should not be diverted into the

270

Table 1.- Quality evolution in Besós delta aquifer.

"Frigo" well	rMg/rCa	rCl/rHCO3	Cl (ppm)
1966	1.5	20	9000
1980	0.75	3.8	1079
1996	0.61	0.58	149

sewage system, but could otherwise be put to a number of possible uses in what can be considered as an integrated and rational management of the total hydraulic resources. In this spirit, we consider two possible applications:

Substitute potable water by groundwater, whenever this is possible use within technical and economical constrains. The idea is to use groundwater in all the applications where we do not need to meet the standards of potable water; that is, garden watering, street cleaning, sewage network cleaning, among others. An idea that is currently under consideration is to suply the new areas under construction with a secondary water supply line, with lower quality water (and so, less expensive) to be used in toilets, refrigeration systems, and so on.

Regenerate the Besós river-bed, by supplying an ecologically beneficial, good-quality water, without having to further treat the water.

REFERENCES

Custodio, E., Suárez, M. and Galofré, A. (1976). Ensayos para el análisis de la recarga de aguas residuales tratadas en el delta del Río Besós. II Asamblea Nacional de Geodesia y Geofísica. Barcelona

Hernández, E. and Vázquez-Suñé, E. (1995). *Estudio sobre el funcionamiento hidráulico de la laguna de la Ricarda*. Fundación C.I.H.S. Informe interno.

Lerner, D.N. (1990). Recharge due to urbanisation. *Groundwater Recharge*. E. Issar & J. Simmer (ed.), IAH International Contributions to Hydrogeology, Heise, 8: 210-214.

MOP (1966). *Estudio de los recursos hidráulicos totales de las cuencas de los ríos Besós y Bajo Llobregat*. Comisaría de Aguas del Pirineo Oriental and Servicio Geológico de Obras Públicas. Barcelona. 4 volumes.

Parés, Pou and Terrades, (1985). *Ecologia d'una ciutat: Barcelona*. Col·lecció descobrir el medi urbà. V. 2. Ajuntament de Barcelona.

Vázquez-Suñé, E. and Sánchez-Vila, X. (1997). Cálculo del balance y recarga en la Ciudad de Barcelona. *La Recarga Natural de Acuíferos en la Planificación Hidrológica* AIH-GE/ITGE. Madrid (in press).

Groundwater in the Urban Environment: Problems, Processes and Management, Chilton et al. (eds)
© *1997 Balkema, Rotterdam, ISBN 90 5410 837 1*

Rising groundwater breaks surface: A case study from the Arabian Gulf

Nick R.G. Walton
Department of Geology, University of Portsmouth, UK

ABSTRACT: This paper presents an extreme example of a rising water table situation typical of that currently occurring in a number of Arabian Gulf cities where a fast expanding, affluent population has demanded the production of large quantities of desalinated seawater. This has resulted in estimated infiltration volumes from a combination of leaking pipes and sewers, septic tanks and garden watering of more than two hundred times the natural rainfall recharge to the pre-urbanised area. The consequence of such a massive overloading of the natural groundwater system is a predictable rise in the water table. This has already resulted in breakthrough of poor quality groundwater to the surface in the lower lying areas of the city, leaving them either permanently flooded or permanently damp and salty from the high evaporation rates, with consequent deleterious effects on roads and built structures .

1 INTRODUCTION

Problems caused by rising water tables due to irrigation of dry lands have beset every civilisation since Mesopotamian times and continue to this day in many arid and semi-arid areas of the world where crop irrigation is practised (Kazmann 1965). However, in very recent times, rising water tables have begun to cause a variety of problems in cities and urban/industrial areas under one of two quite different scenarios:

1. In some of the older, industrial cities of the western world. These were originally developed around heavy water-using industries, many of which derived their supplies from their own on-site or local boreholes. Much subsequent urban development has therefore occurred during an era of artificially lowered water tables. The closure or relocation of these old, heavy industries over the past few decades has led to groundwater rebound which is now threatening the integrity of underground services, structures and foundations, (Brassington 1990).

2. In some of the very modern cities of the Arabian Gulf. Oil wealth has fuelled a rapid expansion of the population, the majority of whom now live in just a few major cities in the region and demand large quantities of fresh water which can only be met in this arid zone by desalination of seawater. A combination of low relief and low shallow subsurface permeability has caused this artificial influx of fresh water to overwhelm the natural drainage and groundwater dispersion systems, (George 1992).

This paper takes one example of an Arabian Gulf city which is typical of a number of others in the region in respect of geology, topography and climate, as well as size, growth rate and consumer water demand patterns. It evaluates the various contributing inputs to groundwater recharge, shows the inexorable rise and, by extrapolating the groundwater hydrographs (Figure 1), predicts the eventual breakthrough at the surface which has already occurred in the lower lying areas of the city, (Figure 2).

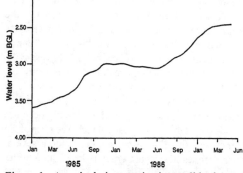

Figure 1. A typical city monitoring well hydrograph.

Figure 2. Groundwater level appearing just below surface in a typical downtown housing complex.

2 CAUSES OF RISING WATER TABLES IN SOME MIDDLE EASTERN CITIES

The population of a number of key capital cities of the region has risen from a few thousand to several hundred thousand over the last three decades, and water consumption per capita has risen from less than 100 1/p/d to more than 500 l/p/d. This has demanded massive increases in fresh water supplies which, from the 1970s, could only be met by desalinating seawater in ever larger and more sophisticated desalination plants.

Unfortunately, the construction of a sewerage system generally lagged about a decade behind the provision of household freshwater supplies, which were initially delivered by tanker prior to installing a full mains distribution system. A combination of rapid population growth being supplied with increasing volumes of initially free or very low cost desalinated seawater at rates of a few hundred l/p/d, most of which then entered the ground either directly as garden watering or indirectly via septic tank discharges, resulted in a rise in the groundwater level at rates typically between 0.3 and 0.8 m/a, (Figure 1).

Many of the Arabian Gulf cities are coastal cities with flat hinterlands comprising alternating sequences of marine sedimentary limestone, evaporite and shale formations. Such lithologies can typically be classified as medium to poor aquifers or aquitards.

Annual rainfall in the region is less than 80 mm/a with recharge rates typically of around 10%, due to the very high evaporation in the region. Consequently, the water table would naturally be found close to sea level which typically would be only a few metres below ground level. Since a typical Gulf city occupies around 10-15 km^2 of area, natural recharge rates of the order of 100,000 m^3/a are calculable, which is several hundred times less than typical desalinated water production rates.

With only a limited sewerage system initially installed, this large input of fresh water caused a significant rise in the water table. Continued expansion of the sewerage systems, which took place mainly in the early 1980s, substantially reduced the input of desalinated water to the ground, leaving garden watering as the major source of ground water recharge by the end of the decade although water mains leakage is also significant, (Table 1). Interestingly, as the rising water table encountered the newly dug sewerage system, the sand filled sewer trenches began to act as significant drainage pathways, leading excess water away towards the coastal pumping stations and seepage to the sea.

Table 1 presents the groundwater budget for an unnamed but typical Gulf coastal city of some 250,000 inhabitants within an area of approx. 16 km^2 and shows that the net annual addition to groundwater storage is 0.9 Mm^3 or 3.0% of the total of all identified inputs to the annual recharge. This is sufficient to cause the observed mean annual rise in groundwater level of some 0.3-0.4 m averaged across the city, with proportionately higher increases under the main city centre recharge mound. This water budget result equates to an average effective porosity of some 14-18% which is a little higher than typical measured values of 2-12% in the underlying chalky limestone

Table 1. Groundwater budget for one typical Gulf coastal city.

Groundwater recharge/outflow	Mm^3/a	% of total
Recharge source		
1. Garden irrigation returns	13.7	45.1
2. Effective rainfall recharge	0.2	2.6
3. Potable water system leaks	9.2	30.2
4. Septic tanks/soakways	6.7	22.1
Total	29.8	
Outflow source		
1. Seepage and channelling to coast	13.3	46.3
2. Groundwater abstraction	6.0	20.9
3. Drainage into sewerage system	5.3	18.5
4. Storm-water drainage	2.0	6.9
5. Groundwater flow inland	1.8	5.6
6. Groundwater evaporation	0.5	1.8
Total	28.9	

lithology but is of the correct order, indicating a reasonably good agreement between the calculated water budget and the observed groundwater level rise.

Most of the Gulf cities undertook comprehensive surveys of their rising water tables during the mid-late 1980s, producing water balance models to identify the inputs, stores and outputs to the system. George, (1992) lists and comments upon a number of these studies and gives details of the Riyadh situation, studied by Salih and Swann (1989) whose groundwater budget is presented in Table 2 below.

A comparison between the two city groundwater budgets depicted in Tables 1 and 2 shows that although the total amount of water involved is some four times greater in the Riyadh situation, the percentage breakdown amongst the components is remarkably similar. This is indicative of the similarities in climate, geology and economic development which extend throughout much of the Arabian Gulf region.

Table 2 Estimated groundwater budget for the main drainage area of Ar Riyadh, based upon data from Salih and Swann, (1989).

Groundwater recharge/outflows	Mm³/a	% of total
Main inputs to groundwater		
Man-made		
Potable system leaks	40.5	32.7
Septic tanks/soakaways	20.8	16.8
Irrigation returns	48.9	39.5
Sub-total	*110.2*	*89.0*
Natural		
Rainfall infiltration	5.1	4.1
Subsurface inflow	8.4	6.8
Sub-total	*13.5*	*10.9*
Total inputs to groundwater	*123.7*	
Main outputs from groundwater		
Man-made		
Net flow to stormwater system	40.9	37.1
Well abstractions	25.5	23.2
Net flow to foul drainage	25.5	23.2
Sub-total	*91.9*	*83.5*
Natural		
Subsurface out-flow	18.3	16.6
Total outputs from groundwater	*110.2*	

The author's involvement with one particular study of a Gulf coastal city produced the groundwater budget shown in Table 1, where garden irrigation can be seen to be the major recharge source (40%) and seepage to the coast (45%) the main discharge component.

The construction of a network of groundwater monitoring wells throughout the city during the early 1980s allowed a database of well hydrographs to be set up which enabled predictions of surface breakthrough to be estimated for the early 1990's, e.g. Figure 1. Figure 1 also clearly shows that the form of the annual hydrograph is the opposite of what might naturally be expected, with the steepest rise in groundwater level occurring during the very hot, dry summer months (May-September) and a stable plateau appearing during the winter months when the main winter rainfall recharge occurs. This is not a time lag effect, due to the proximity of the groundwater table to the surface, but simply reflects the dominance of recharge from garden watering (Table 1) which reaches its peak in the summer months, and reduces to very low levels during the winter season.

Interestingly, as the densely populated downtown areas became connected into the sewerage system and the wastewater recharge started reducing, construction of large villas in the expanding city perimeter areas contributed proportionately much more recharge from their extensive garden watering, thereby increasing direct recharge substantially. This has had the recent effect of shifting the focus of the recharge mound away from the city centre and out into the suburbs offering some relief to the lower lying central areas but creating an annular recharge mound instead.

3 EFFECTS OF THE RISING WATER TABLE

There are a number of quite diverse effects which can be summarised as follows:

- Flooding of underground services, basements, car parks, underpasses etc.
- Damage to services, structures and roads from water, salt, heave and subsidence.
- Overloading of sewerage systems and sewage treatment plants due to sewer exfiltration.
- Salinisation and waterlogging of soils with subsequent adverse effects on vegetation.
- Health hazards due to standing pools of poor quality water.

Whilst the geotechnical effects caused by heave and flooding will be similar to those found in other rising water table situations throughout the industrial world, (Simpson et al 1989) a special Middle Eastern dimension is added with the presence of both underlying evaporite deposits and evaporative salinisation of the near-surface. Furthermore, the recharge of aggressive, low TDS desalinated waters has a significant dissolution effect on underlying gypsum/anhydrite layers as well as carbonate rocks, causing relatively rapid enlargement of underground cavities which ultimately collapse causing substantial damage, (Al Rifaiy 1990). The dissolution of evaporative salts causes the already aggressive, desalinated water to become more harmful to concrete and reinforcing materials leading to progressive structural weakening of typical modern city buildings and infrastructure.

4 REMEDIATION AND CONTROL MEASURES

Initially, many of the affected areas responded by implementing site specific drainage solutions. However, once the regional nature of the problem became known, a range of water table control strategies were planned and implemented. These included networks of herringbone pattern sub-surface collector drains, vertical drainage/ recharge to lower aquifers, water demand control strategies based upon metering and pricing, and leak detection and network maintenance for the potable water distribution system.

Additionally, recent advances in membrane water treatment technology are now being pursued with a view to recovering and rehabilitating some of this abundant but poor quality ground water as a recyclable resource for further industrial and municipal usage.

REFERENCES

Al Rifaiy, I.A. 1990. Land subsidence in the Al-Dahr residential area in Kuwait: a case history study. *Quarterly Journal of Engineering Geology*, 23: 337-346

Brassington, F.C. 1990. Rising groundwater levels in the United Kingdom. *Proceedings of the Institution of Civil Engineers*, Part 1, 88: 1037-1057

George, D.J. 1992. Rising groundwater: a problem of development in some urban areas of the Middle East. In McCall, Laming and Scott (eds) *Geohazards - natural and manmade*. Chapman and Hall.

Kazmann, R.G. 1965. Modern Hydrology, New York, Harper and Row.

Salih, A & Swann, L. 1989. Geotechnical problems associated with the rising groundwater in Ar Riyadh. *Second Symposium on geotechnical problems in Saudi Arabia*, Riyadh: 235-238.

Simpson, B., Blower, T., Craig, R.N. & Wilkinson, W.B. 1989. The engineering implications of rising groundwater levels in the deep aquifer beneath London. *Construction Industry Research & Information Association - Special Publication No. 69*, CIRIA, London.

3 Water supply experiences

Topic co-editors:
Harriet Nash
Wardell Armstrong

Phil Aldous
Thames Water

Groundwater in the Urban Environment: Problems, Processes and Management, Chilton et al. (eds)
© 1997 Balkema, Rotterdam, ISBN 90 5410 837 1

Groundwater quality classification and mapping: The Palermo Plain, NW Sicily, Italy

G. M. Adorni, M. Battaglia & P. Bonfanti
Istituto di Geologia e Geofisica, University of Catania, Italy

A. Cimino
Istituto di Geofisica Mineraria, University of Palermo, Italy

ABSTRACT: In most of Italy, groundwaters provide the main contribution to meeting the water demand for potable use. Consequently, these resources are much exposed to overexploitation and risk of derogation of quality, especially due to the demographic and industrial growth of the last fifty years. The effectiveness of groundwater management in urban planning is closely linked to a good knowledge of aquifer systems; but it is difficult to give an adequate description of groundwater quality without falling back on a subjective assessment. Recently, a classification and mapping methodology for groundwater resources has been developed: this method represents a good attempt to standardise the definition of groundwater quality.

The Palermo Plain area, studied by numerous authors from geological, hydrogeological and geochemical viewpoints, seems particularly suitable for the experimental application of this methodology. The aquifer in the arenaceous deposits is fed by surrounding limestone mountains and has great strategic interest. However, it becomes poor in quantity and quality due to overexploitation by over 2000 wells and the impact of the conurbation of the Palermo area. It is highly vulnerable to inorganic and organic pollution that may worse groundwater quality. Using GIS, a groundwater quality map of this area has been prepared. The map clearly shows an extremely serious environmental picture and large variability of chemical parameters.

The results of this research show that the Palermo Plain area is characterised by groundwater unsuitable for potable use, with some reservations for irrigation and industrial uses. This situation is probably the combined consequence of hydrogeological factors and high urbanisation.

1 INTRODUCTION

In Italy, groundwater supplies most of the required amount to satisfy human water needs. This important resource is considerably exposed to risks connected with excessive exploitation and deterioration of quality, mainly due to the demographic and economic growth of the last fifty years. Therefore, the state of knowledge with respect to development and preservation strategies is elementary. In particular, the description of groundwater quality has been in the past bound to subjective evaluations related to the experience of individual authors.

To define the so-called "*base quality*", Civita et al. (1993) have recently developed a methodology designed to prepare plans to protect groundwater resources. This constitutes an attempt to standardise the description of this important parameter.

The Palermo area has been thoroughly examined by many authors with various methodologies (geology, hydrogeology, geophysics, geochemistry). Because of the high quality and large quantity of data collected, the area is suitable for applying this methodology to classify and map groundwater quality. In the Palermo Plain, groundwaters are stored in an alluvial sandy-arenaceous aquifer which is recharged by surrounding carbonate mountains. Despite the fact that this resource has been overexploited and becomes poor in quality, it still constitutes an important reserve. This aquifer is intensely exploited by a large number of wells (over 2000), for potable, irrigation and industrial uses. Moreover, since it includes almost all the urbanised territory of Palermo, it is particularly vulnerable and subject to organic and inorganic pollution.

The environmental features of this area have stimulated the authors of this paper to prepare a groundwater quality map utilising the mentioned procedure. The purpose is to outline the "state of health" of water resources and readily identify the suitable use of groundwaters. This map has been constructed using computerised systems, taking into account the necessity to easily update the information shown; since the quality characteristics of groundwaters can be subject to deterioration or improvement in a relatively short time. Furthermore, computerised mapping will be a valuable aid to the authorities responsible for developing and protecting groundwater resources.

2 HYDROGEOLOGY AND VULNERABILITY OF THE PALERMO PLAIN AQUIFERS

The hydrogeological setting of the Palermo Plain is summarised in this paper, because it has already been exhaustively described by many authors (Cimino et al. 1971; Cusimano & Liguori 1980). The aquifers of the Palermo Plain are indirectly supplied by hydrogeological units of limestones and dolomite-limestones outcropping in the Palermo Mountains, which are characterised by karst permeability. Within the plain, terrains belong to the complex of Quaternary white/yellow organogenic calcarenites. They present sandy and/or clayey-sandy interbeddings, and are more or less cemented. Below this complex, a clayey-arenaceous unit occurs, at depths of a few meters to over 80 m. This formation represents the permeability threshold for the carbonate mountains which surround the plain, and it constitutes the lower confining layer for the groundwaters stored in the overlying calcarenites.

The environmental setting of the plain (Cusimano & Di Cara 1995) is characterised by the presence of highly concentrated pollution sources, largely due to the direct introduction of unpurified urban and industrial waste waters in streams and channels of the hydraulic defence of Palermo town (i.e. the *Passo di Rigano Channel*). These courses are not water-proofed, and carry polluting substances directly to the underlying aquifers. Indeed, the peripheral zones of the town, along the foothills of the carbonate mountains, still lack a sewerage network: the drainage of waste waters takes place through disposal wells. Lastly, further pollution sources are related to fertilisers used in agriculture as well as to dumping of various wastes, often inside old open caves or galleries. The presence of the Bellolampo municipal tip in the western sector of the town should also be mentioned. This tip is situated in very permeable karst terrain. The greatest deterioration of groundwater quality occurs in zones with a significant density of real or potential pollution sources (*Brancaccio, Partanna, Mondello*), in which numerous cavities are present (*Resuttana*, talus of Pellegrino Mt., *Acquasanta*), and close to water courses turned into sewer channels (Oreto River and *Passo di Rigano* channel).

Some areas are also vulnerable to sea water intrusion due to overpumping of groundwaters. Indeed, significant phenomena of salt water pollution occur through the intensely fractured carbonate units as well as along the sandy-arenaceous coastal belt (*Partanna-Mondello, Favorita, Sferracavallo, Cardillo*).

3 THE CLASSIFICATION METHODOLOGY AND MAPPING CRITERIA

A quick classification methodology and mapping of quality of groundwater resources (*Risorse Idriche Sotterranee, RIS*) has been proposed by Civita et al. (1993). It is in accordance with Enclosure no. 1 of the Italian presidential decree no. 236/88, wich identifies the quality requisites for waters assigned to human needs.

The quoted authors selected a small number of chemical-physical analytic parameters: total hardness (Th), conductivity, SO_4, Cl, NO_3, related to undesirable substances: Fe, Mn and NH_4. Those parameters are particularly significant for an initial quality characterisation of waters for potable use and to define any pollution phenomena. Values of the selected parameters are subdivided into three intervals, defined on the basis of the VG (guide value) and the CMA (maximum admissible concentration) (Table 1). VG and CMA are imposed by decree no. 236/88. For unspecified limits, the authors based them on notes and observations according to the law or *good technique criteria*.

Table 1. Groundwaters classification scheme according to Civita et al., 1993

		Parameters group							
		1 (chemical-physical)					*2 (undesirable substances)*		
Description	*Class*	*Th* (°F)	*El.Cond.* μS/cm	*SO4* (mg/l)	*Cl* (mg/l)	*NO3* (mg/l)	*Fe* (mg/l)	*Mn* (mg/l)	*NH4* (mg/l)
Very good	A	15 - 30	< 1000	< 50	< 50	< 10	< 0,05	< 0,02	< 0,05
Acceptable	B	30 - 50	1000 - 2000	50 - 250	50 - 200	10 - 50	0,05 - 0,2	0,02 - 0,2	0,05 - 0,5
Poor	C	> 50	> 2000	> 250	> 200	> 50	> 0,2	> 0,05	> 0,5

Class	Description
A	Drinking water without treatment; suitable for almost all industrial and irrigation use.
B	Water drinking without treatment; some restriction for industrial and irrigation use.
C	Water unsuitable for drinking without treatment and with restrictions for other uses.
C1	Must be subjected to specific treatment.
C2	Must be subjected to simple or extensive treatment.

The described intervals correspond to progressively worse quality classes, to which a use assessment is given: thus, class "A" corresponds to waters with optimal quality characteristics, class "B" to waters with average quality. Lastly, class "C" includes definitely poor waters. In order to obtain a classification of water quality, first indicates the class of parameters of group 1, then the one of the group 2. For example, if all values of groups 1 and 2 belong to class "B", it is a B_1B_2 type water: on the other hand, even if only one of parameters of the first group belongs in the "C" class interval, the water is classified as C_1B_2.

This methodology has already been applied in several areas of Italy, including the Modena and Vercelli plains (Civita et al. 1993), Apennine alluvial plains such as the Conca Ternana and the Valle Umbra (Giuliano et al. 1993) and the Campania valleys (middle course of Volturno river, Corniello et al. 1995). The aim was to verify - in various hydrogeological and hydrochemical settings - the capability and the sensitivity of the methodology to represent disparate situations of groundwater quality.

4 CHEMICAL FEATURES OF GROUND WATERS OF PALERMO PLAIN

Detailed studies on waters of the Palermo Plain (Alaimo et al. 1984) have shown a bicarbonate-alkaline earth chemical type. It evolves towards chloride-sulphate-alkaline earth and to chloride-sulphate-alkaline types.

The lowest salinity values represent bicarbonate-alkaline earth waters, originating from the carbonate mountains surrounding the plain. High salinity waters are probably caused by sea-water encroachment (or up-coning), while waters with an intermediate salinity denote the mixing processes between the low and high salinity waters. Sea intrusion paths (see arrows in figure 1) should be at least two, both influenced by tectonics. The first one starts from the *Sferracavallo-Tommaso Natale* zone (#1 in Fig.1), reaching and bordering Castellaccio Mt.; the second one, perpendicular to the first direction, cuts the Pellegrino Mt. relief (#2 in Fig.1).

Figure 1 shows the water conductivity contours for the studied area, confirming the existence of the quoted pollution trend. Likewise, this map displays a third path in the *Acqua dei Corsari* zone(#3 in figure 1).

Subsequently, Cimino et al. (1987) have applied geochemical and geophysical methodologies to investigate pollution phenomena of the Palermo Plain aquifers. They took a particular interest in the ion exchange properties of the Numidian Flysch clays

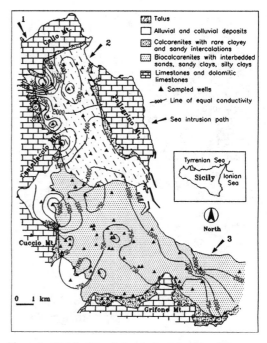

Figure 1 - Distribution of electrical conductivity (EC).

that constitute the impervious substratum of the studied aquifers. The authors believed that ion exchange phenomena significantly affect the composition of groundwaters, owing to their Na deficit with respect to the Na/Cl ratio of sea water. However, Alaimo et al. (1984) have attributed the Na deficit to anthropogenic processes connected with the heavy urbanisation.

With regard to the nitrogen cycle compounds, it has to be emphasised that the available data indicate extremely diffuse organic pollution, confirmed by the high correlation with certain bacteriological indices. In particular, as already mentioned above and confirmed by the interpretation of the ammonium contour map (Figure 2), the highest pollution values are found in areas with no sewerage network.

The chemical composition of Plain waters is the result of the overlapping of a complicated series of elements, among which a noticeable role is played by: 1) the direct contribution of rainfall as well as water from the carbonate mountains surrounding theplain; 2) the interaction with the lithological elements of the aquifer (rock dissolution and ion exchange); 3) mixing with sea water that penetrates principally through tectonic structures; 4) pollution due to the heavy anthropogenic load in the area (infiltration of waste waters into aquifers, industrial pollution, fertilisers in agriculture).

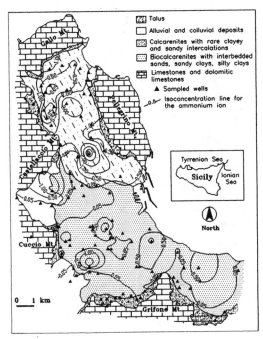

Figure 2 - Distribution of ammonium.

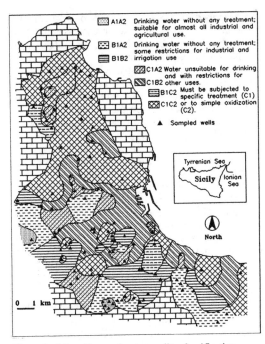

Figure 3 - Map of groundwater quality classification.

5 CLASSIFICATION AND QUALITY MAPPING OF GROUNDWATER RESOURCES (RIS) OF THE PALERMO PLAIN

The classification and mapping described by Civita (1993) and performed here, used chemical data from a hundred sampled wells (Alaimo et al. 1984), combined with further data furnished by the Municipal Water Supply Company of Palermo town.

5.1 *Mapping procedure*

The network of sampling points, represented in Figure 3 shows a fairly even distribution. Indeed, the density of the wells is not particularly affected by the rather uniform permeability of the plain terrains, so permitting a homogeneous exploitation of the RIS. Consequently, the proposed example is considered to be statistically representative of the whole population of waters of the Palermo Plain.

The mapping procedure, using GIS, is as follows:
- construction, by means of spot data interpolation, of the contours for the geochemical parameters of groups 1 and 2;
- codification of value intervals into the "A", "B" and "C" classes;
- preparation of the two codified maps of groups 1 and 2;

- overlaying the two maps and determination of codified sub-areas with both classes.

5.2 *Groundwater quality and conclusions*

A first reading of the map of groundwaters so constructed (Figure 3) shows an extremely compromised situation, characterised by a notable variability in quality. It is immediately manifest that most of the plain territory is distinguished by groundwaters unsuited for potable supply, but suitable for limited industrial and irrigation uses ("C1" class).

For the western sector of the plain, the characterisation is mainly determined by high total hardness, chloride and - partially - by nitrate. For the southern sector of the plain, the assignment to class "C1" is definitely caused by high nitrate values.

The described situation has to be attributed to the superimposition of hydrogeological factors (high hardness due to the carbonate water contribution from the nearby mountains and chloride from sea water mixing in coastal zones) and to high anthropogenic loads (nitrate from sewer networks).

Moreover, from the distribution of parameters of group 2, further sub-areas have been defined for which the distinguishing factor is essentially the ammonium ratio. This is connected to the direct introduction into the aquifer of untreated urban sewage. Fe and Mn have instead low concentrations, even included in the interval of the "A" class (Fe < 0.05 ppm; Mn < 0.02 ppm).

The western sector of the plain seems to be have suffered the most deterioration: waters exploited in this zone are mostly included in the C_1C_2 class. This area is characterised by a high intrinsic vulnerability (Cusimano & Di Cara 1995), having a good primary permeability; it is also subject to the greatest contaminant load. Better quality waters are pumped in the peripheral southern sectors of the plain, close to the Cuccio and Grifone Mts., which are the most productive hydrogeological structures supplying the plain.

It is also evident that, moving away these last structures, water quality undergoes a rapid deterioration as regards parameters of the second group (essentially ammonium), changing from an excellent to a poor classification.

ACKNOWLEDGEMENTS

The authors wish to thank the Municipal Water Supply Company of Palermo, who very kindly furnished part of the hydrochemical data, utilised in this paper.

The research was executed with a grant from the Italian National Research Council (CNR), Strategic Project "Environment and Territory", sub-Project "Criticism of water availabilities to be utilized for potable purposes".

REFERENCES

Alaimo, R., P. Ferla & S. Hauser 1984. *Idrogeochimica delle acque della Piana di Palermo*. Palermo: Ila Palma.

Cimino, A., P. Cosentino & G. Cusimano 1971. Studio idrogeologico della Piana di Palermo. *Proc. Symp. Int. sulle Acq. Sott. in Rocce Crist.*, Cagliari, 25-26 October 1971: 63-81. Cagliari:

Cimino, A., G. Dongarrà, R. Abbate & B. Marchese 1987. L'uso integrato di metodi geofisici e geochimici nello studio e controllo di acquiferi in aree costiere. *Mem. Soc. Geol. It.* 37:427-436.

Civita, M., A. Dal Prà, V. Francani, G: Giuliano, G. Olivero, M. Pellegrini & A. Zavatti 1993. Proposta di classificazione e mappatura della qualità delle acque sotterranee. *Inquinamento* 35: 8-17.

Corniello, A., D. Ducci & P. Napolitano 1995. Piana del medio corso del F. Volturno (Campania): carta della qualità delle acque sotterranee. *Quaderni di Geologia Applicata* 1/95:3499-3505.

Cusimano, G. & A. Di Cara 1995. Carta della vulnerabilità all'inquinamento degli acquiferi del territorio del Comune di Palermo. *Quaderni di Geologia Applicata* 1/95: 3203-3214.

Cusimano, G. & V. Liguori 1980. Idrogeologia della Piana di Palermo. *III Conf. Int. su Pianificazione Acque, Acireale, 17-21 February 1980*. Unpubl.

Giuliano, G., G. Marchetti & L. Peruzzi 1993. Classificazione e mappatura della qualità delle acque sotterranee in pianure alluvionali intra-appenniniche. *Quaderni di Tecn. di Protez. Amb.* 49: 205-226.

Environmental impact of new settlements in Egypt

Nahed E. El Arabi
Research Institute for Groundwater (RIGW), National Water Research Center, Kanater, Egypt

ABSTRACT: Egypt is faced with a continuous increase in population in limited urban areas confined to the banks of the Nile; the developed area of the country represents about 11% of its total physical area. As a result of the increase in population, a considerable part of the agricultural land has been urbanized. Government policy in the last two decades has concentrated on the extension of agricultural land into reclaimed desert areas and the redistribution of population, starting at the peripheries of existing cities.

A number of new settlements have been established, accompanied by the initiation of industrial and agricultural activities. Two of the problems facing the new settlements are sustainable water supply and wastewater disposal. In these new areas, groundwater is the main source of water supply. Sewage water is disposed of into unlined oxidation ponds or used directly for irrigation.

This paper discusses the hydrogeological conditions in one of the first new settlements, the Tenth of Ramadan city, and the problems facing the sustainability of the water supply. The Tenth of Ramadan area is ranked as a high pollution risk area, due to the high infiltration rate of the existing oxidation ponds and the wastewater based-irrigation in the reclaimed desert. The infiltration of polluted wastewater to the aquifer and consequently the migration of pollutants are simulated with the help of a numerical model. Calculations indicate that the well field might be affected by pollutants in forthcoming years. Mitigation actions are proposed.

1 INTRODUCTION

Egypt covers an area of about one million square kilometers. The population is estimated at 60 million (1996). About 99% of the population is concentrated on only 11% of Egypt's area, confined to the Nile banks. The increase in population and subsequent urbanization along the Nile has resulted in considerable loss of agricultural lands. Government policy therefore concentrates on the extension of agricultural lands into reclaimed desert areas and the redistribution of the population, starting at the peripheries of the existing cities.

The contribution of industrial activities to the national income is steadily increasing. The development of new cities with industrial facilities has contributed significantly to this process. The new cities depend to a large extent on groundwater for their water supply, although the exploited aquifers are also normally highly vulnerable to pollution. Therefore the cities are directly confronted with the need for proper disposal of wastewater in order to protect the groundwater resources.

The pressure on groundwater resources should be considered within the wider context of the increasing role of groundwater in Egyptian water resources management. Groundwater is the second source of water in Egypt, the first being Egypt's annual share of Nile water of 55.5 billion m^3. Annual groundwater extraction from the Nile aquifer system is about 4.4 billion m^3. Groundwater extraction from the Nile system and fringes is expected to increase to 7.5 billion m^3 in the forthcoming twenty years.

One of the first new settlements accompanied by a large industrial area is the Tenth of Ramadan city, located on the fringes of the Eastern Nile Delta region (Figure 1). Industrial and domestic wastewater is partly disposed of into oxidation ponds east of city. Another part is used for restricted irrigation. As the groundwater is used for water supply of the city, the risk of pollution from the wastewater requires studies and monitoring.

This study discusses the prevailing hydrogeological conditions in the Tenth of Ramadan area. The sustainability of groundwater as the main source of water supply is also discussed. A numerical flow and

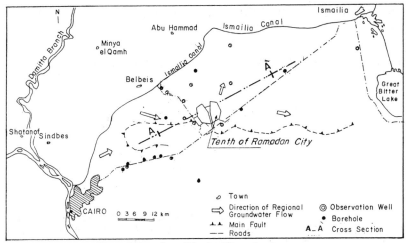

Figure 1. Location of Tenth of Ramadan Area.

solute transport model is used to simulate the flow system and to assess the extension of the groundwater pollution originating from the oxidation ponds where the industrial wastewater is collected. Protection measures for the water supply well field are indicated.

2 PHYSICAL AND HYDROGEOLOGICAL SETTING OF TENTH OF RAMADAN CITY

Tenth of Ramadan city consists of two main parts (Figure 2):

1. an urban zone and two small industrial zones for small scale industries (north of the Cairo - Ismailia road); and
2. a large industrial zone for all types of industries south of the road. More than 700 industries have been established since the city was founded in the early 1980s.

The daytime population of the total area is estimated as about 150,000.

The study area is bounded in the north and west by the Ismailia canal (Figure 1). The area of Tenth of Ramadan is dissected by several dry wadis. The topsoils consist of rounded gravels. The main aquifer in the area consists of Plio-Pleistocene sands. The aquifer thickness ranges from 75 - 200 m, decreasing towards the south. The aquifer is underlain by a low permeability limestone (Figure 3). The regional groundwater flow was mainly directed to the east and north-east before the urbanization. Now some anomalies exist due to local groundwater extraction schemes and infiltration from oxidation ponds. The average groundwater heads vary from 6 to 16 m (+MSL). The groundwater salinity (TDS) in the study

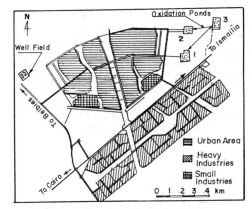

Figure 2. Layout of Tenth of Ramadan Area.

area varies between 750 and 950 mg/l.

Sources of groundwater recharge are seepage from the Ismailia canal, excess irrigation from the agricultural lands and infiltration from the oxidation ponds. Groundwater abstraction takes place at a well field northwest of the city where 24 wells, with a maximum total discharge of about 40,000 m³/day, are operated as a source of drinking water supply.

Since 1980 the domestic and industrial wastewater of the city has been collected and disposed of in three oxidation ponds (Figure 2). Overflow from the ponds is discharged into Wadi el Watan about 15 km northeast of the city. Oxidation pond No. 1 collects the effluent of domestic wastewater from the urban areas, about 14,000 m³/day. Oxidation pond No.2 collects domestic and part of the industrial wastewater with an average inflow of about 13,000 m³/day. Oxidation pond No. 3 collects the effluent from heavy industries at an average of about 25,000 m³/day.

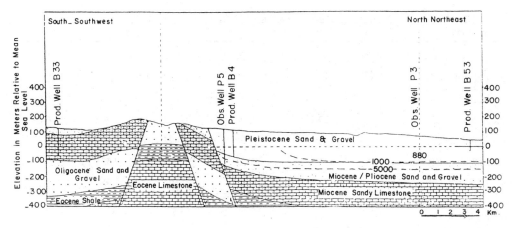

Figure 3. Hydrogeological cross section through the study area.

3 THE NEED FOR ENVIRONMENTAL ASSESSMENT

In the past, the promotion of economic growth as the motor for increased well-being was the main development thrust, with little sensitivity to adverse social or environmental impacts. The need to avoid adverse impacts and to ensure long term benefits led to the concept of sustainability. The environmental impacts assessment (EIA) procedure was developed in the 1970s (Dougherty and Hall 1995).

Tenth of Ramadan city being the first new industrial settlement, an EIA was not considered in the original planning. After 17 years, the need for an EIA was found to be important to provide an opportunity to mitigate against negative impacts and enhance positive impacts. Scoping of the environmental issues of this settlement, infiltration of polluted wastewater to the aquifer and consequent pollutant migration are considered to be the main environmental issues to be addressed.

4 GROUNDWATER VULNERABILITY AND POLLUTION RISK ASSESSMENT

Based on the field investigation and existing hydrogeological information of the study area and the Nile delta region (RIGW 1991), a groundwater vulnerability map has been produced. Groundwater in the study area is classified as of medium vulnerability due to the high infiltration capacity of the upper layer.

Most of the southern part of Tenth of Ramadan City is occupied by heavy industries in particular. Oxidation pond no. 3 contains heavily polluted water, as shown by some metal analyses. Table 1 shows that the industrial effluent and the groundwater in the vicinity of pond no. 3 are also heavily polluted with

iron, manganese and lead. Groundwater pollution risk is the combination of groundwater vulnerability and pollution load. This concept is used in the study to identify aquifer zones needing protection measures and pollution control. Figure 4 shows that the area of oxidation ponds and its surroundings are classified as zones of high pollution risk. Groundwater in these zones is already polluted. Migration of the polluted groundwater may affect the city's well field located downstream of the recharge area, after the formation of a groundwater mound as a result of the infiltration from the oxidation ponds.

5 MODELLING OF GROUNDWATER FLOW AND QUALITY

5.1 Groundwater flow model application

At the early development stage, a well field consisting of 24 wells was constructed to supply a maximum discharge of 40,000 m³/day. A numerical groundwater flow model was used to simulate the different abstraction scenarios and to predict their effect on groundwater heads for the next 10 years, regardless of the quality and pollution transport aspects. This resulted in a recommended long-term operation rate of 20,000 m³/day with an expected drawdown of 6 m (RIGW 1980). At that stage the effect of infiltration from the oxidation ponds was not included in the analysis.

5.2 Solute transport model application

Field data (Table 1) have shown that groundwater in the study area is at risk. Therefore a two dimensional numerical groundwater flow and solute transport model, GWTRAN (Warner 1981) was used to simulate

287

Table 1. Concentrations of selected heavy metals in pond no. 3 and observation wells (mg/l)

Sampling point[1]	Fe	Mn	Pb	Zn	Cu
1. gw 500 m from OP3[2]	63.68	2.46	1.274	4.38	0.13
2. gw 150 m from OP3	16.42	0.49	0.412	0.77	UDL
3. inlet OP3 [3]	4.54	0.19	0.160	0.56	0.04
4. gw 25 m from OP3	29.4	1.647	0.199	0.402	0.070
6. gw 25 m from OP3	216.4	10.530	0.493	0.801	0.358
8. gw 25 m from OP3	485.4	3.744	0.395	0.533	0.152
9. gw 25 m from OP3	657.9	5.396	0.108	1.354	0.614
Standard for discharging treated industrial liquid effluent into groundwater (law 48/82)	1	0.05	0.05	1	1
Standard for drinking water (Ministry of Health, 1995)	0.3	0.05	0.05	5	1

[1] Samples taken in September 1996 (nos. 1-3) and December 1996 (4-9).
[2] gw = groundwater, OP3 = Oxidation pond no.3.
[3] Note that large variations occur in the inlet water. Differences in groundwater concentrations also need further attention.

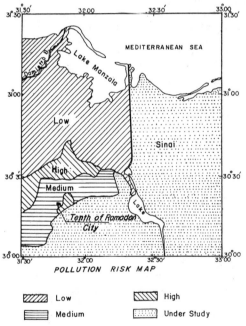

POLLUTION RISK MAP

Low   High
Medium   Under Study

Figure 4. Pollution risk map.

groundwater flow and predict the migration of pollution originating from the high pollution-risk zone. The area of the simulated region is about 220 km² with the following boundary conditions: (1) the western boundary is represented by a groundwater contour line; (2) the north-west boundary is represented by the Ismailia canal; (3) the southern boundary is represented by a main fault which is considered to be a no-flow boundary. The calibration of the model was executed with average groundwater levels.

The calculated groundwater levels are in agreement with the observed trends (Figure 5), allowing the use of the model for preliminary conservative calculations of solute transport, taking into consideration only advection and dispersion. Due to its non-reactive characteristics, chloride was chosen as an indicator for the spreading of the pollution plume originating from the oxidation ponds. The average chloride concentration of the recharged water is 390 mg/l and the initial concentration in the aquifer is 210 mg/l, giving a concentration ratio of 0.54. Based on field data resulting from pumping tests, the effective porosity is set at 0.15. For the prevailing hydrogeological situation a dispersivity of 1,500 m is regarded as representative. A sensitivity analysis has been performed for these two parameters.

Figure 6 presents the regional extension of the calculated concentration ratio of 0.6 after 20 and 50 years, while Figure 7 presents the calculated concentration ratio at the well field itself. The breakthrough curve for the concentration ratio at the well field shows a gradual increase of the concentration ratio starting after 10 years of operation. A rapid increase of concentrations at the well field is expected after about 15-20 years, which coincides with the period since the start of the operation of the well

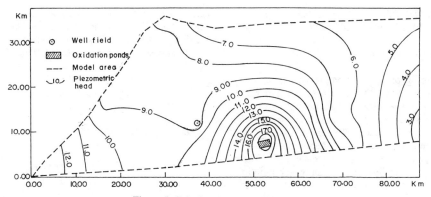

Figure 5. Calculated groundwater levels.

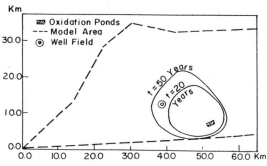

Figure 6. Extension of concentration ratio 0.6.

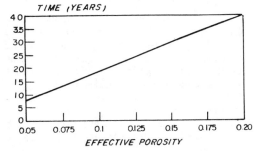

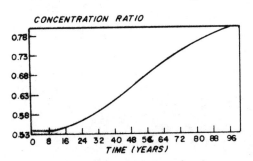

Figure 7. Breakthrough curve at the well field.

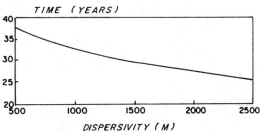

Figure 8. Sensitivity analysis for effective porosity (a) and dispersivity (b).

field and the oxidation ponds. After 30 years the concentration ratio has reached 0.58, which corresponds to an increase in concentration of 10% in relation to the original concentration.

A sensitivity analysis has been performed for the influence of the effective porosity and the dispersivity on the breakthrough time at the well field. In the analysis the breakthrough time is the operation time after which the concentration ratio increased to 10% (to 0.58). Effective porosity is assumed to vary from a minimum of 0.075 to a maximum of 0.2, influencing

to a large extent the breakthrough time for the concentration ratio of 0.58 (varying from 13 to 40 years, see Figure 8a). Field values for dispersivity are assumed to fall in the range of 500 - 2,500 m, resulting in a variation of breakthrough time between 26 and 37 years (Figure 8b).

From the figures of groundwater flow and concentration distribution, it can be concluded that the pollutants such as the heavy metals detected in the groundwater samples in the vicinity of the industrial effluent pond will reach the well field or might have reached it already. Monitoring the water quality with respect to these parameters at the well field is therefore urgently required.

289

6 ENVIRONMENTAL MANAGEMENT OF GROUNDWATER RESOURCES

6.1 *Preventative measures*

Nowadays in Egypt the pollution prevention hierarchy (source reduction, recycling, treatment and disposal) is beginning to receive substantial attention. Industries in the Tenth of Ramadan City are involved in a pollution prevention project funded by USAID. The last method in the prevention hierarchy is effluent disposal which should be at the permitted environmental limits. These measures will gradually reduce groundwater pollution, but will not prevent the migration of the existing groundwater pollution.

6.2 *Mitigation measures*

In the case of the well field of Tenth of Ramadan City, risks to public health are expected within the forthcoming years. As a first step the installation a local early warning groundwater quality monitoring network is urgently required. As mitigative actions the following scenarios can be considered:

* treatment of polluted water;
* closing of polluted wells and drilling of new wells at a greater distance, or increasing the discharge of other wells;
* construction of interceptor pumping wells, treatment of the water and eventually reinjecting the treated water;
* isolation of the polluted groundwater using injection wells to create a hydraulic barrier. Injected water might originate from the well field itself or from surface water.

All these options need technical and economic evaluation.

REFERENCES

Dougherty, T.C. and A.W. Hall 1995. A Guide to the Environmental Impact Assessment of Irrigation and Drainage Project in Developing Countries. *Report OD 131*. March 1995, Sponsored by FAO and ODA.

RIGW 1980. *Groundwater Studies For Tenth of Ramadan City.* Ministry of Irrigation, Water Research Center, Cairo, Egypt.

RIGW 1991. *Hydrogeological map of Egypt, Belbeis Map Sheet, Scale 1:100000.* Research Institute for Groundwater, National Water Research Center, Cairo, Egypt.

Warner, J.W. 1981. *Finite Element 2-D Transport Model of Groundwater restoration for in Situ Solution Mining of Uranium.* Ph.D Dissertation, Colorado State University Fort Collins, Colorado, Fall 1981, USA.

Groundwater in the Urban Environment: Problems, Processes and Management, Chilton et al. (eds)
© 1997 Balkema, Rotterdam, ISBN 90 5410 837 1

The rise, fall and potential renaissance of the English spa town

David Banks
Norges Geologiske Undersøkelse, Trondheim, Norway

Harriet Nash
Wardell Armstrong, Newcastle-under-Lyme, UK

ABSTRACT: The occurrence of mineral waters in England is controlled by the interplay of three factors (i) structural; (ii) hydrochemical evolutionary and stratigraphical factors; and (iii) specific mineralogies. The paper examines the interaction between the development of mineral water resources for spas and urbanization, focusing on the spas of the Derbyshire Peak District and of London. In some cases, mineral waters have been the catalyst for urban development (e.g. Buxton or Bath); in some cases, industrial activity (mining) has largely been responsible for the public availability of mineral waters (e.g. Matlock or Droitwich); in many cases, however, rapid industrialization and urbanization has been dependent on external factors and much of England's spa heritage has been lost (e.g. London), the only reminders being found in place names and chemical nomenclature (Epsom salts).

1 INTRODUCTION

The theme "Urban Groundwater" usually addresses the threats posed to groundwater resources by urban development. It should not be forgotten, however, that the availability of groundwater and, in particular, mineral water resources, has sometimes been instrumental in determining the direction of urban development. This paper briefly reviews the hydrogeological and hydrochemical features of English mineral waters and the impact that these have had on the development of spa towns.

England lies outside major tectonically active zones and hence its mineral and thermal water resources are less spectacular than those found in other locations in Europe (e.g. Bohemia, the Rhine Graben). Britain's warmest spa waters are found at Bath (up to 45.3 °C - Kellaway 1991) and Buxton (up to 27.7 °C).

England has nevertheless a rich heritage of spas (Edmunds et al. 1969, Albu et al. 1997), most of them reaching the peak of their popularity in the 19th Century. Currently, however, very few of the historic spa waters are anything other than a tourist curiosity. Bottled water is in fashion in the U.K., although the British palate is as yet uneducated in the appreciation of true mineral waters to the same degree as central and eastern European connoisseurs. British consumers tend to prefer bland, unmineralised bottled waters, for which the traditional English spas are largely unsuited (with the exception of Buxton water - see below). Many British bottled waters are simply normal groundwaters, abstracted from wells or boreholes.

2 ENGLISH SPAS AND GEOLOGY

The occurrence of the spas of England is controlled by one or more of three factors (Figure 1):

1. Structural features. Several spas occur where faults or anticlinal structures permit the emergence of deep, warm or mineralised waters at the surface (e.g. faults at Buxton, Harrogate, Matlock; anticlinal structures at Bath, Harrogate);

2. Hydrochemical evolutionary and stratigraphical factors. Spas occur at localities where groundwaters emerge after long evolutionary pathways and high residence times, such as at the edges of aquifer outcrops (e.g. Buxton, Matlock) or where deep brines emerge via erosional incisions or man-made wells (e.g. Woodhall Spa);

3. Specific mineralogies, such as pyritic mudstones at Harrogate (Hudson 1938, Edmunds 1993, Bottrell et al. 1996), Matlock Bank, Epsom and several London spas; evaporites at Droitwich (Mitchell et al. 1961) and Leamington; iron-sands at Tunbridge Wells and Hampstead Heath.

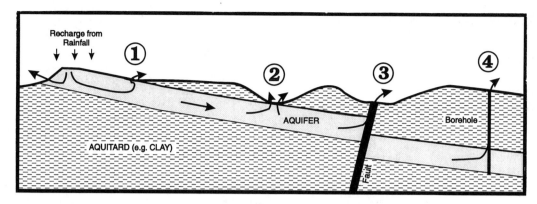

Figure 1. Modes of spa occurrence. 1 = long deep flow path emerging at feather edge of confining strata (e.g. Buxton, Matlock); 2 = erosional incision; 3 = fault; 4 = borehole tapping deep mineral water (e.g. Woodhall). Modified after Albu et al. (1997).

3 THE RISE AND FALL OF THE ENGLISH SPA

Several English spas were known to the Romans, including Bath (Aquae Sulis Minerva) and Buxton (Aquae Arnemetiae), but these fell to a large degree into obscurity after the Romans departed. With the exception of Bath, which continued to be used by the Saxons and thereafter the Church, little is heard of England's spas until the latter 16th and 17th Centuries, when increased mobility and the emergence of a leisured class led to royals, aristocrats and adventurous travellers visiting some of the spas. Returning travellers, having discovered the rich spa culture of Continental Europe sought the existence of suitable waters in England. In the 18th Century royal patronage and the establishment of hydrotherapeutic hospitals at, for example, Bath and Buxton, dramatically increased the spas' popularity. This continued into the 19th Century, when rail travel became widely available to the middle classes, with many spas reaching their zenith. Attractive towns expanded rapidly around the most popular spas. They were popular meeting places for the country's governing elite.

The 20th Century saw the end of this run of prosperity. Some spas, such as Harrogate, found a role in treating war-wounded in the 2nd World War, but the death knell was sounded by the advent of the National Health Service after 1948. Spa treatment continued to be offered by the National Health Service for a while, but gradually doctors came to favour the application of medical drugs and hydrotherapy in more controlled forms and no longer sent their patients to spas for treatment. A handful of spas continued to offer limited hydrotherapy, including Woodhall, Bath, Leamington and Buxton. Of these, only the Devonshire Royal Hospital at Buxton is still operational in the public sector.

4 SPAS AND URBANISATION

The processes of spa development and urbanisation often occurred in parallel, but the interaction was complex:

1. Industrial activity or urbanisation may have resulted in a spa source being discovered or developed. Examples include thermal and mineral springs discovered during lead mining at Matlock and the use of brine mines at Droitwich as spas.

2. The prosperity stimulated by the spa may have promoted urban, leisure and commercial development; often the spa may have been the single most important stimulus for growth. This has occurred at, for example, Bath, Buxton and Harrogate.

3. Urbanisation may have threatened spa sources, either by derogation of the source, pollution or simply by the spa-related economy becoming subordinate to other commercial, residential and industrial interests and being "smothered". This appears to have been the case at many of the London spas.

5 SPAS AS A STIMULUS FOR URBAN DEVELOPMENT - BUXTON

The warm springs of Buxton (Edmunds 1971) emerge near the edge of the outcrop of the Carboniferous limestone aquifer of the Derbyshire Peak District, near the junction with the overlying lower permeability Millstone Grit shales. The springs thus represent the end-point of a deep, long flowpath resulting in an evolved, warm water. The town was known to the Romans. The first document from the mediaeval period recording the spa is from 1460 and at about the same time another writer described

Buxton as (Langham & Wells 1986): "Halywell (or Holy Well), the source of the water of (the River) Wye, in the County of Derby, about 100 miles from London, makes many miracles making the infirm healthy, and in winter it is warm, even as honeyed milk".

Buxton's most famous visitor was Mary Queen of Scots, who sought relief from her chronic arthritis in the period 1573 to 1583. At around this time, a medical practitioner described the properties of water in perhaps a little too much detail (Langham & Wells 1986): "The Waters Helpe Women that by reason of overmuch moisture, or contrary temperature be unapt to conceave.....(and)...al such as have their whisker too abundant and be overwatry....weak men that be unfruitful...Likewise for all that have Priapismus and that be perboyled in Venus Gulf......Beneficial for such as vomit blood. Good for the continued desire to make water and unordinary desire to going to the stoole, doing nothing or very little with great payne. The haemmorroydes and pyles it soon mendeth....... The greene sickness perfectly it cureth and the Morphawe soon it expelleth"

By 1572, a 30-person bath-house existed (Naylor 1983), to be replaced in 1670 by a larger "Great Hall". In the 18th century, George III established a Charity hospital to aid the poor in seeking a water cure. There was a catch, though (Devonshire Royal Hospital 1990): the poor had to come from more than 7 miles away, arrive only between April and November, not stay longer than 5 weeks and not receive more than 6 shillings per week (in 1785). The blockade of raw cotton from America during the Civil War led to an acute need for places of convalescence for victims of the cotton industry recession in NW England. In, and shortly after, 1878, the Duke of Devonshire and the Cotton Districts Relief Fund financed the construction of a huge dome over the entire hospital site. This, the Devonshire Royal Hospital, is Britain's only surviving large-scale hydropathic establishment based on natural spa water and operated under the auspices of the National Health Service.

Both cold and thermal waters can be found in Buxton. The Natural Baths were originally fed by several warm springs at a rate of some 9.8 l/s (Stephens 1929). Manganese used to precipitate out in the baths as a purple-brown mud, also containing barium, lead, cobalt, molybdenum and several other elements (Langham & Wells 1986). The temperature of the waters is constant at around 27.7°C. The waters are somewhat radioactive, containing radium and dissolved radon at 0.034 Bq/l and 77 Bq/l respectively, with 2.78 µg/l uranium, for good measure (Andrews 1991).

The spa has influenced the town's development strongly, encouraging rich architecture and tourism. A well-known opera house still flourishes in what would almost certainly otherwise be a modest Pennine market town ! Most of the famous thermal springs were located in the grand Crescent of 1794, built by John Carr. The spring area, which fed the so-called gentleman's Natural Baths, can still be observed in the basement of the right wing of the Crescent, in the town's tourist office. Water is piped from here, across town to Perrier's bottling plant where "Buxton Mineral Water", one of the U.K.'s most popular bottled waters, is produced. This spring also feeds the hydrotherapy unit of the Devonshire Royal Hospital and the town's public swimming pool. Although Buxton water can be regarded as a true spa water due to its temperature, it differs little in its major ion composition (calcium bicarbonate) from normal limestone groundwaters (this "blandness" makes it an attractive bottled water for the U.K market). The thermal waters of the Peak District (Figure 2), including Buxton, tend however to be slightly enriched in a number of parameters, notably Sr, Br, I, and Mg, and depleted in NO_3^- (Edmunds 1971).

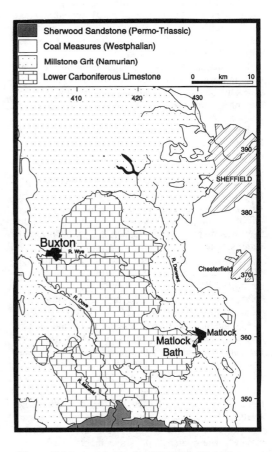

Figure 2. Map of the Derbyshire Peak District.

6 INDUSTRY AS A STIMULUS OF SPA DEVELOPMENT - MATLOCK BATH

Matlock Bath is the next most important thermal spa of the Carboniferous Limestone of the Peak District (Edmunds 1971), situated in the gorge of the River Derwent. Again, it is situated at the junction of the limestone outcrop with overlying Millstone Grit shales. Faulting expedites the ascent, from depths of up to 600 m (Smith et al. 1967), of evolved, warm groundwaters to the surface. While some of the springs emerge naturally at the surface, others were intercepted during the intensive mining of the rich subvertical lead-ore veins ('rakes') in the area, an activity which predated the area's importance as a civilised and polite spa resort. Indeed, a visitor of 1732 reported (Flindall & Hayes 1976): "Here are no inhabitants, except for a few Groovers (miners) who dig lead oar, and whose Hutts are not higher than a good Hogstye...I cannot omit observing to you the natural Innocence of these People....I was up early in the Morning...when came out of one of these Hutts a Woman, I may say, Naked, for I am sure she had no Shift on, at least but a Piece of one. I was surpriz'd at the Impudence of the Woman, and she as much surpriz'd to see me !". At this time there was no road passable by coach to Matlock.

The thermal waters encountered during mining emerged from drainage adits (or soughs). The Wragg (or Bath) Sough, for example, was about 440 m long, tapping several thermal springs, ranging in temperature from 17 to 22°C, issuing from fissures associated with the Bacon Rake Fault (Flindall & Hayes 1976, Rieuwerts 1987). The waters flowed down the sough, were diluted with cold water inflows, and then drained out of the sough into the River Derwent. By 1791, wooden pipes were built within the adit from the thermal springs, preventing mixing with cold waters. The Fountain Baths, erected at the tail of the sough, have now been demolished, and the flow was diverted to supplement the town's drinking water supply.

The earliest documented use of the springs at Matlock Bath was in 1698. The "Old Bath" thermal spring, initially utilised by the clergy, fell into the hands of George Wragg, who built a bath-house and made provision for visitors (Naylor 1983). From the 1730s, the road to Matlock was improved and the spa began to take on a life of its own, growing more independent of the former mining economy. Urban development took on a character similar to that of other popular spa resorts such as Buxton.

By 1800, hotel accommodation had increased further. Flindall & Hayes (1976) note that the "Natural Innocence" of the people had now changed to a more familiar "single-minded desire for visitors' money". The opening up of a number of mines as "show caves" after 1800 attracted further visitors to the resort, and hydrotherapy establishments flourished. At the height of its popularity, three main springs were utilized at Matlock Bath; at the New Bath Hotel (for swimming pool, ornamental ponds and pump room), the Royal Hotel (for the hotel and official pump room) and the Thermal Swimming Baths (Stephens 1929). At present, Matlock is a popular tourist destination, but its popularity is based on its show caves, leisure parks, architecture and natural setting, rather than its thermal waters. Currently, the waters are only used to supply a public drinking fountain in the tourist centre, some ponds and to feed a private swimming pool at the New Bath Hotel.

7 CONFLICT BETWEEN SPAS AND CITIES - LONDON

The area occupied by the London conurbation today consisted, not so very long ago, of the City of London, surrounded by smaller villages such as Islington, Hampstead and Bayswater. It was an area rich in a variety of mineral waters.

The early development of London was controlled by the availability of groundwater and settlements grew up based on springs and wells in the flood plain of the Thames and its sand and gravel terraces (Buchan 1938), e.g. Holywell, Clerkenwell, Sadler's Well and Clement's Well. Intervening areas underlain by Eocene London Clay developed significantly later, with the advent of piped supply. In 1725, the first deep well was sunk through the London Clay at Kilburn, below which high quality water from the Lower London Tertiaries and Cretaceous Chalk aquifers could be obtained (Woodward & Bromehead 1922).

Following the development of the deep aquifers, shallow springs and wells from the Eocene London Clay and overlying Bagshot Beds and Quaternary deposits continued to be used for medicinal and spa purposes, owing to their often unusual chemistries (Woodward 1909). Among these, one can mention (Whitaker 1912, Albu et al. 1997):

1. Dulwich, whose waters may have been in use by c.1640. The water "purges quickly - not sinking, but raising the spirits...It is found to be diuretic". Another account tells of a well sunk in 1739 to 18 m depth in pyritic (presumably London) clay. Its use declined after around 1780.

2. At Wellfield House near Streatham, agricultural weeders accidentally discovered the purgative and emetic properies of springs from the London Clay in 1660. Three wells were eventually developed here and were famous for purging intestinal worms. One customer reported that he "got rid of four worms, the least 5 ft long and one 8¼ ft. There were giants in those days".

3. The popular Beulah Spa in the London Clay at Norwood (Woodward & Bromehead 1922) had fallen into a "languid and deserted condition" in 1851 according to The Times (Trench & Hillman 1993), but was still in use as a hydrotherapeutic establishment in 1909 (Woodward 1909).

4. Jessop's Well at Stoke D'Abernon. Once, during cleaning of the well, a man stood "bare legg'd" in the water for three hours and was "purged so severely for a week that he said that he would not venture, on any account, thus to clean the well again".

5. The Epsom source achieved world renown due to its derived mineral, Epsom Salts (or Epsomite, $Mg^{2+}SO_4^{2-}.7H_2O$). The Epsom Water began as a small muddy hole, discovered in 1618. That cattle would not drink from it was taken as an indicator of its special properties, and the water was initially used as an external medicinal treatment. In 1630, yet another bunch of hapless labourers discovered the water's purgative properties upon ingestion. The original spring was replaced by two new wells in around 1708. Whitaker (1912) suggests that these were not the "Real McCoy" and the spa gradually lost its reputation.

6. Acton Wells, again with purging properties. These were closed in 1776 due to lack of demand (Trench & Hillman 1993).

7. Well Walk in Hampstead boasted a popular ferruginous spring, derived from the basal spring line of an outcrop of sandy, ironstone-rich Bagshot Beds, which cap the London Clay on high ground.

Those readers who are especially interested in gastrointestinal disorders will note that several of the above-mentioned sources tended to result in long sessions in the latrine. These sources, whose active ingredient is magnesium sulphate, are mostly springs in the pyritic London Clay. On weathering, pyrite releases iron, acid and sulphate:

$$2FeS_2 + 7O_2 + 2H_2O = 2Fe^{2+} + 4SO_4^{2-} + 4H^+_{(aq)}$$

The magnesium is likely to be derived from ion exchange reactions in the clay, possibly for iron.

None of the above springs is in use today and most of them are difficult to trace at all. What caused the demise of these spas? Whitaker (1912) blames two aspects of urbanisation for the decline of many of London's springs:

1. Some springs, particularly those in Chalk or Lower London Tertiaries may have been derogated by over-abstraction of deep artesian wells in the Chalk. Derogation of other, shallower springs may also have been caused by tunnelling activities.

2. Contamination from urban activity; cesspits, sewage farms, cemeteries, industry.

In addition to these factors, the demise of the spas can be explained as a simple smothering by urban expansion as London burst out of the constraints of its old city walls in the 16th Century (Trench & Hillman 1993). The urbanisation of the spa areas was not stimulated by the spas themselves, but rather by the rapid geographical and economic expansion of London as a commercial, industrial and residential centre. Its wealth not being based on its spa resources, the city had no interest in maintaining their infrastructure or quality.

8 RENAISSANCE

England's spa heritage is still in a sorry state, but there are signs of a potential renaissance. Some spa towns, such as Matlock, Buxton and Bath (Figure 3), have continued to succeed as tourist destinations, although this has largely been due to their rich history, architecture and pleasant surroundings than to actual use of their waters. At other spas, too there are signs of awareness of future potential.

Bath's Roman baths are a major tourist attraction and, additionally, boreholes supply the Pump Room and Cross Bath with microbiologically pure water. Plans have been put forward by a leading hotelier to bottle "Bath Spa Water" and a private sector company is considering the option of redeveloping the Stall Street Baths as a full modern health and leisure spa.

At Harrogate, the only bathing facilities left today are the beautiful Turkish Baths, which sadly use standard tap water, not genuine spa water. The only mineral water which is still drunk at Harrogate is that of the Sulphur Wells, at the town museum. Plans have been proposed to restore Harrogate's Royal Baths, by privatizing the Turkish Baths and opening a casino. An attempt to sell Harrogate waters as medicinal waters failed, due to the excessive costs associated with testing to comply with UK and European medical legislation. Drilling has recently taken place, with the intention of finding a low mineralisation, non-sulphide water for bottling.

At Buxton itself, the Crescent has been restored, but the baths themselves are partly converted to a shopping complex and the pump room is currently closed. The future of hydrotherapy at the Devonshire Royal Hospital is also in doubt. The bottled water business appears to flourish, however.

At Leamington Spa, the Baths, where hydrotherapy had been practised on the National Health Service since the 1950s, were closed in 1990. Currently, the only public access to the spa waters is via a drinking water tap. Plans are underway to redevelop the hydrotherapy baths within the private sector, but using mains water.

The brines of Droitwich Spa are used in their undiluted form at the Brine Baths (the old public baths of 1836, re-opened in 1985), operated by a private company offering hydrotherapeutic treatment.

The brine also supplies the Droitwich Lido (public bath) after dilution by a factor of around ten, to seawater concentration.

In London, most of the spas are difficult to trace now, although local authorities at Epsom have recently refurbished one of the wells and are building a visitor centre nearby.

9 SPA PROTECTION AND PROMOTION

In the case of many spas, such as Buxton and Harrogate, it has been established that the spa waters are a mixture of old, deeply circulating waters and young waters with relatively shallow flow paths. This poses some problems for the definition of recharge areas and hence protection zones. Currently, the Environment Agency is establishing protection zones for public supply wells and there are plans to extend this work to private supplies for spas and bottling plants in the next few years. Clearly, the immediate concern should be to define recharge areas for waters that are bottled for consumption. Often, these are relatively young waters, at greater risk from industrial and agricultural contamination. In the long term, however, the recharge areas for older, traditional spa sources must also be defined and protected to ensure the quality of the resource in perpetuity.

The British Spas Federation exists to promote the economic interests of the spa towns of England, Scotland and Wales. It is to be hoped that their planned renaissance will not just focus on casinos, architecture and fashionable arcades, but will also stimulate interest in the sine qua non of every spa town - the waters themselves.

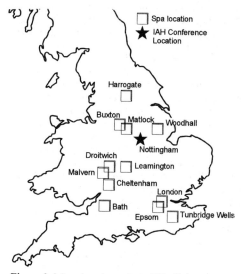

Figure 3. Map showing selected English spas.

REFERENCES

Albu, M., D. Banks & H. Nash 1997. *Mineral and thermal groundwater resources.* London: Chapman and Hall (in press).

Andrews, J.N. 1991. Radioactivity and dissolved gases in the thermal waters of Bath. In Kellaway (1991), pp. 157-170.

Bottrell, S.H., R. Raiswell, R. & M.A. Leosson 1996. The influence of sulphur redox reactions and mixing on the chemistry of shallow groundwaters: the Harrogate mineral waters. *J. Geol. Soc.* 153, 231-242.

Buchan, S. 1938. *The Water Supply of the County of London from Underground Sources.* Memoirs of the Geological Survey of Great Britain, HMSO.

Devonshire Royal Hospital 1990. *Devonshire Royal Hospital, Buxton - Handbook.* Devonshire Royal Hospital, Buxton.

Edmunds, W.M., B.J. Taylor & R.A. Downing 1969. Mineral and thermal waters of the United Kingdom. In M. Malkovský & G. Kacura (eds) *Report of the 23rd Session of the International Geological Congress, Czechoslovakia, 1968, Proceedings of Symposium II:* "Mineral and thermal waters of the world. A - Europe", 139-158.

Edmunds, W.M. 1971. Hydrogeochemistry of groundwaters in the Derbyshire Dome with special reference to trace constituents. *Institute of Geological Sciences Report* No. 71/7, London: HMSO.

Edmunds, W.M. 1993. In A.H. Cooper & I.C. Burgess (eds.), *Geology of the Country around Harrogate,* British Geological Survey Memoir for 1:50000 geological sheet 62. London: HMSO.

Flindall, R. & A. Hayes 1976. *The Caverns and Mines of Matlock Bath. 1: The Nestus Mines: Rutland and Masson Caverns.* Moorland Publishing Co., U.K.

Hudson, R.G.S. 1938. The Harrogate mineral waters. *Proc. Geol. Assoc.* 49, 349-352.

Kellaway, G.A. (ed.) 1991. *Hot Springs of Bath.* Bath City Council.

Langham, M. & C. Wells. 1986. *Buxton Waters - a History of Buxton the Spa.* Derby: J.H.Hall & Sons.

Mitchell, G.H., R.W. Pocock & J.H. Taylor 1961. *Geology of the Country around Droitwich, Abberley and Kidderminster (Explanation of sheet 182).* Memoirs of the Geological Survey of Great Britain. London: HMSO.

Naylor, P.J. 1983. *Ancient wells and springs of Derbyshire.* Cromford: Scarthin Books.

Rieuwerts, J.H. 1987. *History and Gazetteer of the Lead Mine Soughs of Derbyshire.* Publ. J.H.Rieuwerts.

Smith, E.G., G.H. Rhys & R.A. Eden 1967. *The Geology of the Country around Chesterfield, Matlock and Mansfield.* Memoirs of the Geological Survey of Great Britain. London: HMSO.

Stephens, J.V. 1929. *Wells and springs of Derbyshire.* Memoirs of the Geological Survey. London: HMSO.

Trench, R. & E. Hillman 1993. London under London - a subterranean guide (2nd edn.). London: John Murray Ltd.

Whitaker, W. 1912. *The Water Supply of Surrey from Underground Sources.* Mem. Geol. Survey of England & Wales, HMSO.

Woodward, H.B. 1909. *The Geology of the London District.* Memoirs of the Geological Survey, England and Wales.

Woodward, H.B. & C.E.N. Bromehead 1922. *The Geology of the London District.* Memoirs of the Geological Survey, England and Wales, 2nd edition. HMSO.

Groundwater in the Urban Environment: Problems, Processes and Management, Chilton et al. (eds)
© 1997 Balkema, Rotterdam, ISBN 90 5410 837 1

Groundwater pollution threat to public water supplies from urbanisation

D.S.Chadha
Environment Agency, North East Region (Dales Area), York, UK

S.Kirk
Geraghty & Miller, Cambridge, UK

J.Watkins
Yorkshire Water Services (Environmental), Bradford, UK

ABSTRACT: More than one hundred years ago, deep shafts and approximately 1.5 km long adit systems around three boreholes were built in the semi-confined East Yorkshire Chalk aquifer to supply drinking water to the City of Hull, England. Over the years the land around these groundwater sources which supply on average 65 Ml/d has been developed and at present three out of four sources are semi-urbanised. In the absence of a public sewer there is a tendency to build septic tanks thereby increasing the threat of groundwater pollution.

A study was undertaken to identify pollution risk to public groundwater supply from septic tanks. The study has showed that human enteroviruses have been found at two different sites and rotavirus at one site within the study area. Nitrate and bacterial contaminants have also been found in the Chalk groundwater. These pollutants are thought to be derived from septic tank systems which operate in this area.

Bacteriophage tracing exercises in the saturated zone indicate that the rate of movement of Chalk groundwater towards Dunswell and Cottingham Public Supply boreholes can be as great as 160 metres per day.

Surface derived contaminants in the area infiltrate to the Chalk aquifer below. Given the groundwater velocities in the Chalk aquifer, it is anticipated that some viral pollution will reach both the public supply and private abstractions within the study area.

High Chalk groundwater velocities will control the shape and size of the groundwater protection zones around public supplies in the urban area. Enforcement of groundwater protection policy in the inner 50 day travel time zone will put constraints on future urban development.

1 INTRODUCTION

A desk study report (Kool 1987) highlighted the potential risk of pollution of groundwater sources including public supplies from septic tanks in the Chalk aquifer. The area under study was not sewered. Therefore, a field investigation was undertaken to identify and quantify the risk to public supplies, and to find justification for capital spending to lay a new sewerage system (Kirk & Chadha 1989).

The study included the following:
- An extensive literature review of similar investigations.
- Hydrogeological exploration and mapping following drilling, multi-aquifer groundwater level monitoring and a surface geophysical survey.
- A water quality survey of drift and Chalk groundwaters.
- Pollution sampling.
- The use of microbiological tracers to determine groundwater flow paths and travel times.
- The interpretation of the results, as presented in this paper.

2 GEOLOGY AND HYDROGEOLOGY

Within the study area (Figure 1) the chalk aquifer is overlain by a variety of drift and alluvial deposits. The Chalk is a fine grained, fissured limestone of Cretaceous age. The drift deposits consist of Pleistocene Boulder Clay and Glacial sands and gravels. These are in places overlain by fluvial sands, gravels and alluvium. The drift deposits generally reach a thickness of 10 m.

Regionally the Boulder Clay forms an almost continuous blanket within the drift deposits overlying the Chalk from the coast to the Chalk outcrop in the west. Locally, however, the Boulder Clay is known

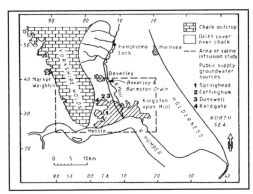

Figure 1 Study Area, East Yorkshire Chalk

to be thin or absent. Lithological cross sections have been drawn which show that the Boulder Clay thins out where there are thick sand and gravel deposits. This was subsequently proven in a borehole drilled in the north-west corner of the study area.

A geophysical survey (Hawkins 1988) was undertaken to identify any discontinuities of the Boulder Clay. The survey was unsuccessful due to insufficient resistivity contrast between the Boulder Clay and adjacent deposits.

3   GROUNDWATER FLOW

Groundwater flow and storage in the Chalk aquifer is dominantly within the bedding planes and joints, which have been widened by solution during the long-term circulation of groundwater. This secondary permeability has developed preferentially in the zone of water table fluctuation. There is layered permeability within the Chalk as was proven when a second lower adit system, sunk at Cottingham pumping station, failed to yield water.

The Cottingham area experiences extreme water levels of low in summer and high in winter. A general depression develops with water levels below Ordnance Datum during low water levels. This is usually wiped out by the winter recharge and positive hydraulic gradients are restored in the Chalk aquifer.

In four purpose built observation boreholes, data loggers were installed in various aquifers to gain knowledge about the degree of hydraulic connection between the drift aquifers and the Chalk aquifer below. The observations of the groundwater level recessions show that there is a relatively high degree of connection between the drift aquifer beneath the Boulder Clay and the Chalk aquifer it overlies. It therefore follows that any pollutant infiltrating below

the Boulder Clay layer would eventually move towards the pumping stations. The relationship between the drift aquifer above the Boulder Clay and the aquifers below presents a more complicated picture.

In some parts the drift and the Chalk water levels behave independently whereas at other places there is hydraulic connection between them. This occurs at places where the Boulder Clay is absent within the drift and the drift water moves laterally above the Boulder Clay and drains through the 'windows' into the Chalk aquifer when it becomes unconfined.

During high water levels the Chalk and the drift aquifer immediately above it become fully saturated and sub-artesian heads may be observed. The drift aquifer above the Boulder Clay may also become saturated; only partial drainage of this uppermost aquifer being achieved by the network of drainage ditches.

It is therefore concluded that during late autumn and low groundwater levels, the Drift aquifers contribute water to the Chalk aquifer. Furthermore the upper drift aquifer may become fully drained in the areas where the clay layer fails to act as a barrier to the infiltration process. Hence there is a large contribution to the public and private supply boreholes from the storage in the drift.

On the average 65 Ml/d are abstracted from the Hull area Chalk aquifer for public water supply. This abstraction is controlled using control curves developed by Yorkshire Water in 1979 and later refined by the Chalk groundwater resources model (Salmon et al 1996).

4   SOURCES OF POLLUTION

The study area is not covered by a public sewer. Therefore disposal of sewage is via septic tanks from isolated rural properties north of Cottingham.

Household size septic tanks are placed in approximately 3 m deep excavations with overflow being discharged via a surface irrigation system. They represent both a source of contaminants and a possible means of puncturing the clay layer which would otherwise protect the Chalk groundwater below from surface derived pollution. Due to similar considerations the drainage ditches in the area, including Creyke Beck, also required investigation. The depth to which they cut into the drift material represented potential weak points in the clay layer. It is possible that at certain locations the Boulder Clay within the drift area over the Chalk aquifer is absent, and contaminated drift water can be recharged to the Chalk aquifer during low summer and drought water levels. Soakaways by comparison are usually constructed at shallow depths and would only convey roof and surface runoff into the drift material, which would not normally be considered a serious pollution threat. Therefore, in the absence of a public sewer the most obvious groundwater pollution hazard is that associated with septic tank effluent discharged to the underground strata and entering the Chalk aquifer.

5 LITERATURE REVIEW OF SEPTIC TANK POLLUTION INCIDENTS

The vast majority of the relevant literature originates from the United States. This is not surprising given that some 70 million people in the United States are dependant upon septic tanks for sewage disposal (Hershaft 1976). In the United States, septic tank systems are frequently reported sources of localised groundwater pollution and in some cases regional groundwater problems have also been recognised in areas of high septic tank density. Historical concerns have focused on bacterial and nitrate pollution; more recently synthetic organic chemicals and viruses have been detected in groundwater having originated from septic tank discharges. One common reason for degradation of above is that the capacity of the soil to absorb effluent from the tank has been exceeded, and the waste added to the system moves upwards. Another occurrence of greater significance to groundwater contamination is the rapid movement of pollutants through the soil or substrata. Many soils with high permeability can be rapidly overloaded with organic and inorganic chemicals and microorganisms, thus permitting rapid movement of contaminants from the unsaturated zone to the groundwater zone (Canter & Know 1985).

A review of the literature suggests that microbiological and especially viral contamination is the major hazard associated with septic tanks which serve domestic premises; most other contaminants being rendered innocuous by the attenuation process described earlier. Contamination of drinking supplies by malfunctioning septic tank systems has caused many outbreaks of waterborne communicable diseases. In the USA, between 1971 and 1978, Craun reports:

".... overflow or seepage of sewage primarily from septic tanks or cesspools was responsible for 41% of the outbreaks and 66% of the illness caused by contaminated underground water. These percentages include outbreaks where contaminants travelled through limestone or fissured rock." (Craun 1981)

Documented cases of infectious hepatitis (so far rare in the UK) have been traced to contaminated groundwater. Many other pathogens, such as typhoid, cholera, streptococci, salmonella, poliomyelitis, and protozoans are transmitted by septic tank systems. Many of these pathogenic organisms have a slow die-off rate in the subsurface environment and may persist for several months (Bitton & Gerba 1984). In fractured rocks, where groundwater velocities can be high, this is sufficient time to produce transport distances of many kilometres (Freeze & Cherry 1979).

Although much of the research in this field has been carried out in the United States, investigations in the United Kingdom have produced similar conclusions. For example, a study carried out by Southern Water, in the Chalk aquifer at Snowdown, Kent, singled out viruses as "the most important potential pollutants arising from the introduction of discharges from septic tanks into the Chalk." (Montgomery 1988).

Moreover, human enteroviruses have been found in water from a Chalk well with a history of excellent bacteriological quality (Bexley Well in the South London Division of the Thames Water Authority). The viruses were detected in the complete absence of bacterial indicators and a proportion of these viruses survived disinfection treatment which consisted of a nominal 1 mg/l of free chlorine maintained for a minimum contact period of 15 minutes (Slade 1985). The paper concluded that "viruses may occur in underground sources which have consistently proven to be satisfactory in routine monitoring tests for bacterial indicators of faecal pollution." The pollution is thought to have been derived from a leaking sewer, and to have travelled through several metres of drift deposits (alluvium, sand and gravel) and then into the groundwater of the Chalk aquifer.

The presence of human enteric viruses in drinking water is considered undesirable by many authorities, as they believe them to have a very low minimum infective dose (possibly as little as one virus particle) and also that the present of even relatively harmless types may indicate the possible presence of much more dangerous viruses (WHO 1979).

A recent national (UK) groundwater quality survey cites the increasing numbers of septic tanks as an area of growing concern in terms of the potential degradation of groundwater quality (Halcrow & Partners 1988). Clearly in the UK there is growing awareness of the pollution potential of these systems and the results of this investigation contributes to the picture.

6   GROUNDWATER TRACER TEST

Three bacteriophage tracers, Serratia marcescens, coliphage MS2, and Enterobacter cloacae bacteriaphage were injected at three different sites in boreholes in boreholes in the saturated part of the Chalk aquifer.

Samples were collected at the Cottingham public supply borehole using auto-samplers and analysed for total coliforms, Escherichia coli, enterococci, chlostridia, enterovirus, and rotavirus. The sampling and monitoring continued for 77 days.

7   RESULTS

The bacteriophage tracing exercise indicated that the rate of movement of Chalk groundwater towards the pumping stations ranges between 54 and 160 metres/day.

Another recent tracer exercise in the Chalk aquifer around Kilham (East Yorkshire) has shown groundwater velocities of 130-475 m/day thus showing karstic behaviour of the Chalk (Ward et al).

Enteroviruses were found in two privately owned borehole supplies which penetrate the Chalk aquifer. Rotavirus, enterococci and clostridia were detected in Chalk groundwater abstracted from an observation borehole. All three sites are served by septic tanks. No viruses were detected in the groundwater recovered at Cottingham pumping station.

8   HIGH   GROUNDWATER   VELOCITY IMPLICATION   TO   GROUNDWATER PROTECTION ZONES

The National Rivers Authority (NRA) Policy of Practice for the Protection of Groundwater (1992) has now been adopted by the Environment Agency (the Agency).

The Policy covers all types of threat to groundwater. It helps the Agency and other organisations to implement the laws which can be used to protect groundwater.

Around each groundwater source, the Agency has defined three Source Protection Zones. These vary in their size, shape, and relationships according to the particular situation at any one place. The type of soil, the geology, the rainfall and the amount of water pumped out of the ground all have to be considered.

Zone I is a 50 day travel time for pathogens. Zone II is a 400 day travel time and Zone III is the total catchment zone for the groundwater source. If a 50 day travel zone has to be established using groundwater velocity of 160 metres/day then at least 8 km long zone would be required in the up gradient direction of groundwater flow. This would put constraints on future developments in the urban area where disposal of sewage is required via septic tanks. The alternative would be to build a public sewer with high specifications so that there are no leaks to the Chalk aquifer. This may not be cost effective in some parts of the Cottingham area. However, if the urbanisation and in-filling of domestic, agricultural and industrial properties continues then they will pose serious threat to the quality of public water supply.

CONCLUSIONS

- Groundwater tracing work has shown that contaminants including enteroviruses, rotavirus, nitrate and bacterial pollution from septic tanks can infiltrate to the Chalk aquifer.
- Given the short travel time from infiltration point to abstraction point, it is anticipated that some viral pollution may reach public supply and private abstraction boreholes.
- High groundwater velocities in the chalk aquifer indicate it to be karstic, which will influence the shape and size of the groundwater protection zones.
- Constraints should be put on future development in the urban area requiring disposal of sewage from septic tanks.

REFERENCES

Bitton, G & C P Gerba. 1984. *Groundwater Pollution Microbiology (ed).* John Wiley & Sons: p377.

Canter, W & R Know. 1985. *Septic Tank* System Effects on Groundwater Quality. Lewis Publishers inc: p336

Freeze, R A & J A Cherry. 1979. *Groundwater.* Prentice Hall, New Jersey.

Craun, G F. 1981. Outbreaks of Waterborne Disease in the United States, 1971-78. *J Amer Wes Wks Assoc 73.*

Halcrow, W & Partners. 1988. An Overview of Groundwater Quality in England & Wales. *Hydrogeological Group Meeting, Geol. Soc. of Lond.*

Hawkins, T R W. 1988. *Geophysical Survey at Cottingham.* Humberside.

Hershaft, A. 1976. The Plight & Promise of On-site Wastewater Treatment. *Compost Science, Vol 17, No 5: 6-13.*

Kirk, S. Chadha, D S. 1989. Investigation of pollution risk to groundwater sources from developments around Dunswell Road and North Moor Lane, Cottingham. *Internal report, Yorkshire Wate*r, *36 p.*

Kool, E. 1987. Criteria for Siting Septic Tanks Within Protection Zones of the Chalk Aquifer of East Yorkshire. *Academic Report, Agricultural University.* Wageningen, the Netherlands.

Montgomery, H A C. 1982. *Water Quality Changes in a Septic Tank Effluent Discharged to the Chalk.* Jour. IWEM.

National Rivers Authority. 1992. *Policy & Practice for the Protection of Groundwater.* Bristol, UK.

Salmon, S. Chadha, D S & Smith D B, 1996. Development of Groundwater Resource Model for the Yorkshire Chalk. *Jour. CIWEM Vol. 10 No 6 415-422.*

Slade, J S. 1985. Viruses & Bacteria in a Chalk Well. *Wat Sci Tech Vol 17 111-125.* Bilthoven.

Ward, R S. Williams, A T & Chadha, D S. 1997. The Use of Groundwater Tracers for Assessment of Protection Zones Around Public Supply Boreholes. *7th Internationalsymposium on Water Tracing.* Portoroz, Slovenia.

ACKNOWLEDGEMENTS

The authors wish to express their gratitude to Emma Freeman and Neil Suffield in putting together this paper with diagram. The views expressed in the paper are those of the authors and do not necessarily reflect the views of their respective organisations.

The impact of falling levels in the sedimentary aquifer supplying São Paulo International Airport, Brazil

H. N. Diniz, S. Y. Pereira & P. R. B. Pereira
Geological Institute of São Paulo State, São Paulo, Brazil

U. Duarte
Geosciences Institute of São Paulo University, Brazil

ABSTRACT: The São Paulo Metropolitan Region, in southeastern Brazil, is largely located within a Tertiary and Quaternary tectonic sedimentary basin. The sedimentary aquifer has been exploited intensively for four decades and has shown unmistakable signs of exhaustion. In spite of the water surplus from rain and runoff, the soil, which is very clayey and the urban conurbations make the terrain impervious and the recharge deficient. Due to these factors the aquifer is being depleted. This paper shows the process of water depletion in the sedimentary aquifer in the São Paulo International Airport area and proposes solutions for the recovery of the aquifer with the employment of artificial recharge.

1 LOCALIZATION AND PHYSIOGRAPHIC ASPECTS

São Paulo International Airport (SPIA) is situated in Guarulhos Municipality in the Metropolitan Region of São Paulo, 23° 30' S latitude 46 30' W longitude. The SPIA is located in the hydrographic basin of the Baquirivu-Guaçu River, a tributary to the Tietê River, the most important river of São Paulo State.

In the central part of the basin, in the Paulistan Plateau Zone, north of the area, Tertiary and Quaternary continental sedimentary deposits occur. The crystalline rocks north of that area belong to the São Roque Mountain Zone, separated from the sedimentary deposits by a large fault transcurrent zone known as Taxaquara-Jaguari.

The relief is relatively low within the São Paulo sedimentary basin and very hilly in the north portion of the airport area, in the Itaberaba and Bananal ridges, where the crystalline basement is composed of metamorphosed sedimentary, volcanic and igneous rocks (granitic and dioritic), which belong to the São Roque Group. The mountains and hills formed by the metamorphic rocks are 750 to 1,200 m high, while the sedimentary deposits of the river Baquirivu-Guaçu basin have altitudes varying between 720 and 820 m.

The average rainfall in the Baquirivu-Guaçu hydrographic basin is around 1,400 mm/year, the average annual temperature around 18° C and the annual potential evaporation around 850 mm/year. The parameters described allow the climate to be classified, according to Koeppen (in Setzer, 1943), as Cwb of the Continental Savannah Plateau with moderate summers.

2 THE LOCAL GEOLOGY - THE BAQUIRIVU-GUAÇU GRABEN

The São Paulo sedimentary basin is structured as a hemispherical graben tilted NNW and has a maximum continuous thickness of sediments of the order of 256 m. Melo et al. (1986) recognized four sedimentary facies in the Baquirivu-Guaçu region: alluvial fan deposits, fluvial plain deposits, transitional deposits between alluvial fans and fluvial plains and lacustrine deposits. The alluvial fan and transitional facies and portions of the fluvial plain deposits characterize a braided fluvial system. Some deposits on the fluvial plain mark a transition to a fluvial braided system and to an upper fluvial meander system.

Two major tectonic structures cross the Baquirivu-Guaçu Basin (Figure 1). One is the Jaguari River Fault (Emplasa 1980), normal and trending ENE-WSW, which intercepts the Basin in the northern area of the Airport. The other, perhaps more important from the hydrogeological viewpoint, is younger and crosses the whole Baquirivu-Guaçu basin in a NE-SW direction. This structure was formed by tectonic compression and is composed of successive square-shaped grabens and horsts with variable lengths of a few meters to 4 km. This structure is filled with sediments, with generally coarse, angular and mineralogically immature grains.

These characteristics indicate the proximity of the source area and the depositional events. This tectonic feature is more recent than the Jaguari River Fault and was probably active at the end of the Oligocene and

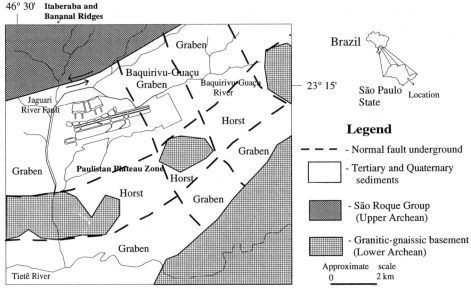

Figure 1. Geological map of the São Paulo International Airport area .

during the Miocene and constitutes the Baquirivu-Guaçu Graben.

The definition of the Baquirivu-Guaçu Graben was only possible in the course of hydrogeological surveys carried out in the region.

3 HYDROGEOLOGICAL ASPECTS OF SPIA AREA

A hydrogeological study requested by INFRAERO (Brazilian Enterprise for Airport Infrastructure) from the DAEE (State of São Paulo Water and Electric Energy Departament) in 1982 showed that the water supply of the SPIA by wells corresponded to 1.3% of the cost of surface water supply. Because this, in 1984 four wells (W-1, W-2, W-3 and W-4) were constructed. Nowadays the SPIA is totally supplied by groundwater tapped by 7 wells, all penetrating the São Paulo sedimentary basin aquifer. The depth of the wells varies between 115.5 and 195.5 m, and they furnish 2,700 m³/d of water. These wells are labelled W-1', W-2', W-3', W-4', W-5, W-6 and W-8 in Figure 2.

The aquifer is composed of sandstones, argillites and consolidated and unconsolidated conglomerates, of the Resende Formation of the São Paulo sedimentary basin. The SPIA was built on a swamp formed on the plain of the Baquirivu-Guaçu hydrographic basin, which contains a sequence of organic clay beds near the surface. These beds cause pronounced impermeability and hence the recharge of the aquifer is very slow. The aquifer is composed of sand and sandstone beds positioned topographically and stratigraphically below the clay and mudstone beds.

Many abstraction wells have been installed to meet the increasing demands of the Air Companies and travellers. Due to this fact the renewable groundwater resource is being quickly depleted because, as soon as the slow infiltration reaches the aquifer, it is quickly tapped by well pumps. Nowadays the wells yield an average of 35 m³/hour but at the beginning the wells could supply 120 m³/hour.

Despite of all these facts, the Airport Maintenance Sector has always taken care of the conservation of the sedimentary aquifer, allowing less than 12 hours/day of pumping and equivalent periods of recovery.

Once the renewable groundwater resources were exhausted, the wells started to exploit the permanent reserve and this provoked the widespread fall of the water level in the aquifer. The aquifer is predominantly unconfined and the fall of water levels cause changes in the storage coefficient values of the sediments situated in the area of influence of the wells, because this parameter depends on the ratio between the saturated and unsaturated thickness of the aquifer, as shown by Kováks (1981).

The decrease of storage coefficient values in the neighborhood of the pumping wells caused an increase of the influence area that provoked general interference among the wells. This interference, allied to the high rate of abstraction cause a rate of decline of the water level of 0.4 m/month. The water tables attained a depth of 66 m in November 1996, a total of more than 55 m decline. Hence the loss of well productivity was very high.

Table 1 lists the hydraulic parameters of the sedimentary aquifer at the well sites and their

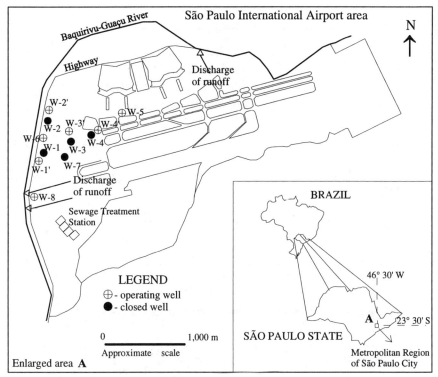

Figure 2. Well location in the São Paulo International Airport.

pumping test rates of discharge. The values of storage coefficient obtained show that the aquifer is very depleted at the sites of wells W-01', W-02', W-06 and W-08 and has best conditions of storage at sites of wells W-3', W-4' and W-5.

The transmissivity values indicate that the most permeable aquifer zones are in the areas of wells W-2', W-4', W-5 and W-8. The discharge rates of the wells confirm the transmissivity values obtained.

4 MONITORING OF SPIA WELLS

The water levels in the SPIA wells have been constantly monitored by INFRAERO. Daily measurements are taken one hour before pumping in the morning and the dynamic level is measured immediately before the pumping equipment is switched off. The wells were constructed after March 1989, in substitution for wells which were plugged and deactivated, due to the deterioration of the galvanic iron screens. The water volumes extracted are likewise measured with discharge meters. In most of the wells, the correlation between water table and dynamic levels is very high, about 95% and 99%. The correlation rates found show that the drawdown caused by groundwater exploitation (about 2,700 m³/d), although measured through a plastic tube

Table 1. Hydraulic characteristics of the sedimentary aquifer at the well sites.

Well number	S (dimensionless)	T (m²/d)	Discharge (m³/h)
W-01'	0.0033	76	39.8
W-02'	0.0006	133	50.3
W-03'	0.04	67	30.0
W-04'	0.012	131	47.5
W-05	0.0025	147	44.2
W-06	0.0004	71	36.5
W-08	0.0001	138	56.8

installed in the wells, reflects the drawdown in the aquifer.

One hypothesis developed to explain the high drawdown in the pumping wells was that the groundwater in the wells loses hydraulic pressure as a function of the blockage of the filter screens by iron oxides produced by iron bacteria. This explanation is not adequate because such a situation would yield a discrepancy between the water table level and dynamic levels. The correlation rate of 95% indicates

305

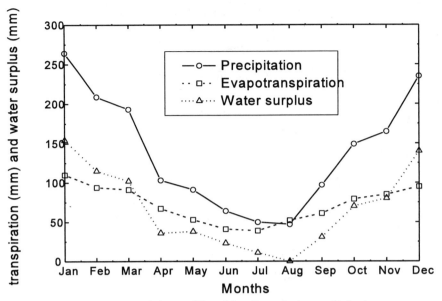

Figure 3. Water balance of Baquirivu-Guaçu hydrographic basin.

clearly that the continued drawdown represents the depletion of the aquifer sedimentary beds.

5 THE WATER BALANCE OF THE BAQUIRIVU-GUAÇU BASIN

In the neighborhood of the SPIA, near Bonsucesso Village, there is a rainfall station, monitored by DAEE, labeled E3-002. This station is located in the middle part of the hydrographic basin of the river Baquirivu-Guaçu, at 23° 25' S latitude and 46 24' longitude, and has provided daily rainfall data since 1965.

The hydrometereological data of the Bonsucesso Station was used to prepare the water balance for the Baquirivu-Guaçu river hydrographic basin, based on Thornthwaite's (1955) model adapted to southwest Brazilian climatic conditions. The average temperatures used in the model were obtained from monthly average rates for the southwest region of Brazil (Camargo & Ghizzi 1991). The field capacity, which indicates the minimum storage value of a specific soil to enable deep recharge, was estimated as 125 mm, and considered uniform throughout the basin.

The values found for the water balance, calculated for 1965-1994 were:
-annual average precipitation:1667 mm
-annual average actual evapotranspiration: 865 mm
-annual average water surplus: 802 mm.

Figure 3 shows that there are two main climatic periods during the year: a rainfall period occurring from October to March, with precipitation higher than 100 mm/month, and a dry period from April to September, with precipitation lower than 100 mm/month. The climate is classified as Mesothermic humid.

The monthly potential evapotranspiration does not exceed the monthly precipitation and it is equal to the actual evapotranspira-tion, about 865 mm/year. Soil moisture deficits do not occur and water is not taken from the soil to compensate for the evapotranspiration processes. The volume available to supply the aquifer by infiltration or runoff ís high, between 650 and 850 mm/year (average of 802 mm/year). Only during the If the total area of the runways in SPIA are considered, which are 1 km wide and 4 km long, the water surplus corresponds to: 802 mm/year multiplied by 1 km and 4 km, giving 3,208,000 m³/year.

The SPIA water consumption is around 2,700 m³/day or 985,000 m³/year. In other words, the water surplus of the precipitation on the runways alone would be enough to supply the aquifer three times more than the current requirement.

6 THE PROPOSAL FOR THE AQUIFER RECOVERY

In view of the hydrodynamic parameters of the sedimentary aquifer and due to the present conditions of well explotation, the best way to recover the local sedimentary aquifer is by artificial recharge using surplus rain via injection wells.

As previously verified, the sedimentary aquifer is set in a closed basin originating from the strong Tertiary tectonism, which limited its lateral size. This

306

aquifer has high permeability and storage capacity but with limited recharge areas due to the clayey layer near the surface, which limits infiltration of the superficial flow to the sand beds below.

7 AQUIFER RECHARGE

In view of the considerable annual volume of water surplus in the SPIA area, the most adequate alternative for rainwater storage (in terms of quality and quantity) is its infiltration by injection wells.

The high surface water surplus (of about 0.8 m^3/m^2/year) permits the use of pluvial water as recharge. The pluvial water is to be stored in surface reservoirs connected to injection wells. This proposal would bring two advantages: recovery well yields and the reduction of flood peaks in urban areas situated downstream.

To make the artificial recharge effective, the pluvial waters must be pumped to underground reservoirs which can accept the equivalent of 100 mm/day of precipitation, since in the region these value are rarely exceeded. These reservoirs must be connected to a well or several wells which would drive the water directly in the aquifer, by pumping or gravity. The water must be cleaned from the dirt which comes from drainage pipes with the aid of sand filters. Health control would be made effective by chlorination or other treatments at the surface.

For injection of the surface water and the monitoring of the levels and quality of the groundwater, the infiltration wells and piezometres would be constructed at depths of between 100 and 150 m.

Estimates of potential infiltration are about 100 m^3/hour, based on the typical abstraction rates of the wells before the high drawdowns occurred.

The best areas to construct the injection wells are in the Baquirivu-Guaçu Graben, in the vicinity of the pumping wells. The plugged wells (W-01, W-02, W-03 and W-04) could be used for this objective after some recovery procedures.

REFERENCES

Camargo, A.P.& S.M. Ghizzi 1991. Estimativa da temperatura média mensal com base em cartas de temperatura potencial normal ao nível do mar para a região sudeste do Brasil. *Boletim Técnico* 141, 17p. and 12 maps. Campinas, Agronomic Institute of São Paulo State.

Emplasa - São Paulo Metropolitan Enterprise of Planning. 1980. *Geologic map in scale 1:100,000 of São Paulo Metropolitan Region*. São Paulo Secretary of Metropolitan Trade, 2 maps. São Paulo Government.

Kováks, G. 1981. Seepage hydraulics. *Developments in water science, 10* (Translation of A szivárgás hidraulikáya),. Budapeste: Elsevier Scientific Publishing Company.

Melo, M.S., S.L.V.Caetano & A.M.Coimbra 1986. Tectônica e sedimentação na área das Bacias de São Paulo e Taubaté. *Brazilian Congress of Geology*, 34, v.1:321-336. Goiania: Brazilian Society of Geology.

Ponçano, W.L., C.D.R.Carneiro, C.A.Bistrichi, F.F.M.Almeida& F.L.Prandini 1981. *Mapa geomorfológico do Estado de São Paulo*. Publication 1183, Monografia 5. São Paulo: Institute of Technological Research.

Setzer, J. 1943. Clima do Estado de São Paulo. *Boletim do DER*, 9(33):52-61, oct.1943. São Paulo.

Thornthwaite, C.W. 1955. The water balance. *Publications in climatology*, 8(1), 104p. New Jersey.

Groundwater in the Urban Environment: Problems, Processes and Management, Chilton et al. (eds)
© *1997 Balkema, Rotterdam, ISBN 90 5410 837 1*

Groundwater flow evolution in the circum-Vesuvian plain, Italy

L. Esposito & V. Piscopo
Dipartimento di Geofisica e Vulcanologia, Università di Napoli 'Federico II', Italy

ABSTRACT: The variations in groundwater flow rates and direction of the plain around Vesuvius over the last twenty years were examined. The following aspects were found: an overall decline in the water table which is more pronounced to the east of Naples rather than the Sarno plain; several changes in the direction of groundwater flow; a decrease in the size of the Sarno groundwater basin with a corresponding increase in the size of the basin east of Naples; a reduction in aquifer storage (approximately 56×10^6 m^3, between 1978 and 1993), amounting to 38% of average annual recharge. The main cause would seem to be increased pumping of the aquifer, which currently accounts for some 54% of groundwater outflow. Pumping particularly affects the groundwater resources of the plain lying east of Naples where it accounts for 98% of groundwater outflow.

1 INTRODUCTION

The research area covers the plain around the Somma-Vesuvius volcano situated between the city of Naples, the limestone mountains of Lattari, Sarno and Avella and the Gulf of Naples (Fig.1). It is essentially a flat area which has undergone a major transformation especially over the last twenty years, with a substantial rise in population (currently about 2600 inhabitants per km^2). As a result, urbanization has increased along with a correlated reduction in agriculture and an expansion in industrial development. This has led to an inevitable repercussion on groundwater flow rates and direction. In order to study the phenomenon, the current state of the water table has been compared with the situation reported in studies from the 1970s, taking into account the complex geological and hydrogeological features.

2 GEOLOGICAL AND HYDROGEOLOGICAL FEATURES

The study area (approximately 500 km^2) is the southern sector of the wider Campanian Plain, a structural depression on the Tyrrhenian Coast. The graben began to form during the Pliocene, between Mesozoic carbonate sequences outcropping to the

east and south of the plain (Fig. 1). During the Pleistocene this structural depression was filled with products of Neapolitan volcanoes (Phlegrean Fields and Somma-Vesuvius) and alluvial and marine sediments to a thickness of some thousands of metres.

The first few hundred metres beneath the soil of the circum-Vesuvian plain, the zone of the most active groundwater circulation, are made up of pyroclastic deposits (ashes, pumice, scoriae and tuffs) and alluvial deposits, interposed with marine sediments (mainly sandy and partly clayey), marshy layers (mainly silt) and palaeosols. Travertines, debris and conglomerates lie at the base of the limestone mountains, while approaching the Somma-Vesuvius volcano lava flows prevail, interbedded with pyroclastic deposits.

The limestone mountains are the most important aquifers (average yield from 20 to 25 l/s/km^2). They feed a few high discharge springs (approximately 11 m^3/s in 1978), located at the boundaries of the plain (Fig.1).

The carbonate aquifers also feed the aquifer of the plain, especially where a thick layer of debris and conglomerates flanks the mountains (Celico, 1983).

The Somma-Vesuvius volcano has a radial water table and groundwater flows towards the sea and also feeds the aquifer of the surrounding plain (Celico, 1983).

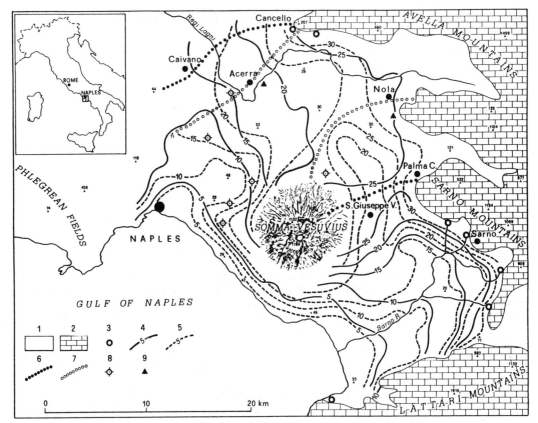

Fig. 1 - Hydrogeological scheme: 1. Pyroclastic and alluvial deposits; 2. Limestone; 3. Main springs; 4. Piezometric contour lines in 1993; 5. Piezometric contour lines in 1978 (after Celico, 1983); 6. Groundwater divide in 1993; 7. Groundwater divide in 1978; 8. ARIN and Acquedotto Vesuviano wells; 9. SIMN piezometric station.

The aquifer of the circum-Vesuvian plain is characteristically extremely heterogeneous due to granulometric variations in the unconsolidated sediments, the degree of fissuring of rock and complex stratification of both deposits and rock. This gives rise to communicating overlapping aquifers, due to the non-continuous nature of aquitards (silt, ashes and palaeosols) or the discontinuities of tuffs (Celico, 1983).

3 DATA, INTERPRETATION AND RESULTS

The study was conducted considering the data referring to the period 1978-1993, though less complete data referring to the period 1924-1970 were also utilized. In particular, the morphology of the water table as it stood in 1993 was reconstructed

and compared with 1978 and a partial reconstruction of 1924; seasonal and annual changes in groundwater levels were examined; the extent of aquifer recharge was assessed; groundwater outflow from the aquifer was estimated.

3.1 *Water table morphology in 1993*

The water table morphology in 1993 was reconstructed on the basis of measurements in around 400 wells of varying depth (from 5 to 200 m), from April to May. By interpolating the water levels it was found that they correspond to a single water table surface, which confirmed that the various aquifers locally identified are communicating.

The map in Figure 1 shows that groundwater flows from NE to SW and highlights the presence of two axes of groundwater drainage, one to the east of Naples and one parallel to the River Sarno. Between the two runs a groundwater divide (between S. Giuseppe V. and Palma C.); a second groundwater divide bounds the area under examination to the north (between Cancello and Caivano).

The hydraulic gradient varies from a few units per thousand to a few units per hundred. In particular, the highest values of the piezometric gradient found at the foot of the Lattari mountains (Fig. 1) may be related to high inflow from carbonate aquifers where transmissivity is high (10^{-1}-10^{-2} m²/s) compared with values in other areas of the plain (10^{-2}-10^{-6} m²/s).

The relationship between the volcanic aquifer and the aquifer of the plain is such that the former feeds the latter. This is particularly evident in the southern and eastern areas of the volcano (Fig. 1).

3.2 Comparison between water table morphology in 1993 and the past

The water table morphology in 1993 was compared with the one of 1978 (Fig. 1). The latter was reconstructed utilising fewer wells (approximately 200) and measurements do not relate to a completely homogeneous period. Nevertheless, the water table morphology of 1978 allowed the study of large scale variations in groundwater flow from the 1970s to the 1990s.

From 1978 to 1993 there was an overall decline of the water table of an average 4 metres. Around the limestone mountains, variations in level exceed 5 metres and reach the maximum (approximately 7 m) near Sarno mountains, where the aquifer is poorly transmissive (10^{-4} -10^{-6} m²/s). A lesser decline (approximately 2 m) was recorded in the River Sarno plain due to considerable inflow from the Lattari aquifer. Major falls (between 5 and 10 m), on the other hand, were recorded in the plain east of Naples, where considerable and continuous pumping from major well fields takes place (Fig. 1).

By comparing the two reconstructions the presence of a deep drawdown to the east of Naples corresponding to the local well fields was found. On the northern slopes of Somma-Vesuvius the piezometric contour lines, which indicated that the aquifer of the volcano fed the aquifer of the plain in 1978, no longer show this phenomenon (Fig. 1). The groundwater divide between the northern and southern sectors of the plain (S. Giuseppe V.- Palma C.) has shifted southwards; the northern groundwater divide has shifted northwards (Fig. 1). This effectively means that from 1978 to 1993 the aquifer

of the plain underwent a reduction in storage and the groundwater basin of the plain lying east of Naples was enlarged, mainly at the expense of the Sarno plain, which was highlighted in 1989 (Celico & De Paola, 1992).

The water table reconstructions of 1978 and 1993 were also compared with a partial reconstruction of 1924 (Fiorelli, 1926). This refers to a limited sector east of Naples (Fig. 2). The main point which emerges from this comparison, besides a fall in water table levels, is an increase of groundwater inflow from the Somma-Vesuvius to the aquifer of the plain lying east of Naples.

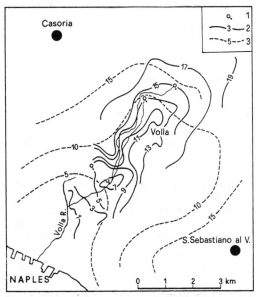

Fig. 2 - Water table morphology east of Naples in 1924 (Fiorelli, 1926, modified): 1. Springs present in 1924; 2. piezometric contour lines in 1924; 3. piezometric contour lines in 1978.

3.3 Seasonal and annual fluctuations of groundwater level

In order to confirm the results of the water table analysis (cf. par. 3.2), the piezometric levels measured in the observation stations of the Servizio Idrografico Mareografico Nazionale (SIMN, 1926-1990) were considered. Available data concern piezometric levels taken generally every three days in 11 stations from 1930 to 1990. Few stations however have complete data for the period.

An examination of seasonal fluctuations of the piezometric level (Fig. 3) reveals that, on average, they do not exceed 2 metres. Furthermore, the

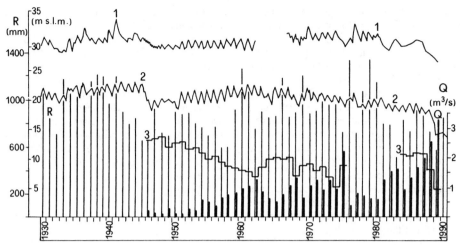

Fig. 3 - Correlation between piezometric levels, rainfall (R) and pumping discharge (Q): 1. Nola SIMN station; 2. Acerra SIMN station; 3. Groundwater level of ARIN well field.

smallest seasonal variations (< 2 m) were recorded in the Sarno plain, where groundwater inflow from the volcano and especially from the Lattari mountains is considerable (cf. par. 3.4).

The seasonal changes relating to the period 1930-1990 were compared with those determined during 1992-1993 from 350 wells (Fig. 4). In this case it appears that variations in the transmissivity of the aquifer are not sufficient to account for changes exceeding 3 metres (up to a maximum of 5 m), recorded in the area of the main well fields or near industrial sites.

Among the piezometric stations of the SIMN the most complete sequence and reliable data come from Acerra and Nola (Figs. 1 and 3). Over the period 1930-1990 piezometric levels show a falling trend, heightened in the period 1980-1990, with a fall of up to 5 metres. Furthermore, according to other sources in the literature it appears that the Cimitile and Nola wells were dry in the summers of 1989 and 1990 (Ducci & Onorati, 1993).

Level fluctuations over the period 1930-1990 were also examined taking into account precipitation over the same period. The period 1980-1990 was relatively dry, although the piezometric decrease recorded in these years cannot be due to precipitation alone, since similar dry periods did not produce the same effects (Fig. 3).

3.4 *Aquifer recharge*

In order to assess the impact of pumping on

groundwater resources of the plain, the aquifer recharge of the study area (507.7 km^2) was evaluated.

Taking into account the hydrogeological scheme (cf. par. 3.1) the main contributions to aquifer recharge are provided by direct precipitation and groundwater inflow from the nearby volcanic and carbonate aquifers (sewage and pipe leakage only marginally affect the total recharge).

In order to assess direct infiltration, rainfall and temperature data over the period 1960 - 1990 were considered (SIMN, 1926-1990); to calculate evapotranspiration the Thornthwaite method was used. To calculate effective infiltration the plain was divided into two, according to whether the area was given over to irrigation (284.1 km^2) or vine and orchard cultivation (127.7 km^2).

For the area given over to irrigation, since in the dry season potential monthly evapotranspiration was higher than rainfall contribution, the difference was made equal to groundwater outflow lost from the aquifer under irrigation. Subtracting the difference from the effective precipitation of the wet season the mean annual effective infiltration was calculated, taking away irrigation consumption. This turned out to be equal to 57 mm, equivalent to a volume of 16.2 x 10^6 m^3/year.

For the areas given over to vine and orchard cultivation actual evapotranspiration was calculated, since irrigation consumption had a negligible effect on the total. The mean annual effective infiltration was calculated at 467 mm, equivalent to a volume of 59.6 x 10^6 m^3/year. Thus, taking into account irrigation consumption, the overall mean effective infiltration of the whole plain was 75.8×10^6 m³/year.

On the basis of flow nets constructed for 1993 and aquifer transmissivity, inflow from nearby volcanic and carbonate aquifers was calculated. The main sources were the Lattari mountains (1.00 m³/s), Somma-Vesuvius (0.87 m³/s) and the Sarno and Avella mountains (0.40 m³/s), amounting overall to 71.6×10^6 m³/year. Thus, groundwater inflow from bordering aquifers plays a fundamental role in aquifer recharge of the plain.

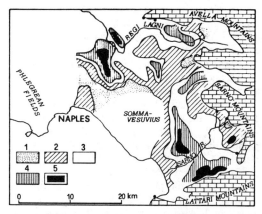

Fig.4 - Map of seasonal piezometric fluctuations in 1992-1993: 1. <0.5 m; 2. 0.5-1.0 m; 3. 1.0-1.5 m; 4. 1.5-2.0 m; 5. 2.0-5.0 m.

3.5 Groundwater outflow and pumping

The main outflows of groundwater from the plain are to the sea and rivers.

In order to calculate groundwater outflow to the sea, flow nets of the coastal area referring to 1993 and relative values of transmissivity were employed.

The outflow from the plain lying east of Naples amounted to 2.2×10^6 m³/year, while that from the Sarno plain amounted to 13.2×10^6 m³/year.

In order to calculate groundwater outflow to rivers, the Regi Lagni Canals and the Sarno River were considered (Fig. 1). In the Regi Lagni Canals water exchange with the aquifer is negligible due to the overall decline of the water table and the cemented river-bed. Groundwater still discharges into the Sarno River: measurements for 1992-1993 show an increase in river flow of 57.1×10^6 m³/year.

After calculating irrigation use (cf. par. 3.4), the volume of industrial and waterworks pumping was evaluated.

An assessment of industrial consumption was made taking into account the nature of industry, number of personnel (ISTAT, 1985), the productive cycle and the period in function; in addition, appropriate sampling took place. From available data regarding the 1980s the volume of water drawn from the aquifer amounted to approximately 34×10^6 m³/year.

The main waterworks which fall within the area under observation are the well fields of the local companies (Acquedotto Vesuviano and ARIN). The Acquedotto Vesuviano drew an average of approximately 13×10^6 m³/year over the last ten-year period. From 1960 to 1990 ARIN consumed an average of approximately 40×10^6 m³/year (Fig. 3). A minimum percentage of pumped groundwater returns to the aquifer.

4 DISCUSSION

From an analysis of all the data available, though not completely homogeneous, it would seem that the water balance of the plain has changed considerably over the last twenty years.

Drawdown exceeding 3 metres, highlighted in the comparison of the two water table reconstructions (1978 and 1993) cannot be due to the different period of measurement of the wells or to a variation in precipitation.

Piezometric data recorded by SIMN from 1969 to 1990 do, in fact, show average seasonal variations of 1-2 metres, a reduced reaction of water levels to variations in precipitation and an accelerated fall in levels, at least in some stations, from 1980 onwards (cf. par. 3.3).

Storage reduction of the aquifer is further confirmed by a coincidence of the highest changes in the period 1978-1993 and the areas in which consumption is highest (cf. par. 3.2).

This aspect may also be deduced by seasonal piezometric changes in the hydrologic year 1992-1993. In this case the greatest decline (from 2 to 5 m), recorded in areas of industrial development and the main well fields, cannot be traced to variations in aquifer transmissivity (cf. par. 3.3).

Storage reduction of the aquifer over the last twenty years has been more considerable in the plain lying east of Naples than in the Sarno plain.

The groundwater basin of the latter has in fact decreased by 50 km², giving rise not only to a reduction of the areas of direct recharge but also to a reduction in groundwater inflow from the Sarno mountains and Somma-Vesuvius volcano.

Hydrogeological relationships between the plain and the volcanic aquifer, moreover, have clearly changed over the last twenty years; a comparison of the piezometric contour lines of 1978 and 1993 shows a reduction of the section of inflow towards the aquifer of the plain (cf. par. 3.2). The area in which this variation in the direction of flow has taken place is affected by pumping from the wells of the Acquedotto Vesuviano.

Pumping from the aquifer of the plain influences storage reduction. It appears from an evaluation of total groundwater outflow from the plain that 54% is due to pumping. In particular, for the sector of the plain east of Naples pumping (approximately 68 x 10^6 m^3/year) represents 98% of outflow.

The incidence of urban growth on effective infiltration would seem, on the other hand, to be minimal. Even with an urban growth of 254%, recorded between 1954 and 1988, a 6% reduction in volume of infiltration water has been recorded, as urbanization has tended to take away the land from irrigation areas (cf. par. 3.3).

Though it has not been possible to assess all the various factors in the water balance in reference to an homogeneous period, the results do show that the storage reduction taking place is not sufficient to allow seawater intrusion. Indeed groundwater outflow into the sea is still present, though reduced, from the plain lying east of Naples (approximately 70 l/s). In this sector seawater intrusion is contained thanks to a reduced transmissivity of the aquifer close to the coast.

Nevertheless, there is a distinct imbalance between the plain east of Naples and that of the Sarno, with drawing of groundwater from the latter to the former. This is apparent also from an estimation of storage reduction in the period 1978-1993, amounting to 56 x 10^6 m^3, taking into account an average effective porosity of 6%. A total of 77% relates to the plain east of Naples. For this sector it should be considered that the springs slightly to the east of Naples (Fig. 2), with a discharge of 1.4 m^3/s up to the 1930s, falling by some 100 l/s in 1977 (Viparelli, 1978), disappeared completely in 1978. Thus, reduction in storage has speeded up over the last twenty years (from less than 1 x 10^6 m^3/year between 1930 and 1970 to approximately 3 x 10^6 m^3/year over the period 1978-1993). Should this phenomenon continue it is easy to predict a further decrease of the groundwater basin of the Sarno plain, besides a variation in the hydrogeological equilibrium between the bordering carbonate aquifers and the plain itself. There are already some signs of this variation. The water table fall of the plain has provoked a corresponding drop in the base level of the carbonate aquifers, which is partly responsible for the discharge reduction of the springs located at the edges of the plain (Fig. 1). An example of this is the disappearance of the S.Maria La Foce spring located at the highest point among the Sarno springs (from a discharge of 2.3 m^3/s in 1969-1971 it had fallen to 0 l/s in 1991).

5 CONCLUSIONS

The study of variations in groundwater flow of the plain around Vesuvius over the last twenty years has highlighted the following aspects: an overall decline in the water table which is more pronounced to the east of Naples rather than the Sarno plain; several changes in the direction of groundwater flow; a decrease of the Sarno groundwater basin with a corresponding increase in the basin east of Naples; a reduction in aquifer storage (approximately 56 x 10^6 m^3, between 1978 and 1993), amounting to 38% of average annual recharge.

The main cause would seem to be increased pumping of the aquifer, which currently accounts for some 54% of groundwater outflow. Pumping particularly affects the groundwater resources of the plain lying east of Naples where it accounts for 98% of groundwater outflow. Although the fall in the water table of the plain has not allowed seawater intrusion, at least not yet, it has made a considerable impact on bordering carbonate aquifers. Indeed, the fall in the level of the water-table at the base of limestone mountains is partly responsible for the reduced discharge of some springs fed by the fractured aquifers.

REFERENCES

Celico P. 1983. Idrogeologia dei massicci carbonatici, delle piane quaternarie e delle aree vulcaniche dell'Italia centro-meridionale. *Quad. Cassa Mezzogiorno* 4/2: 117-190. Roma.

Celico P. & De Paola P. 1992. La falda dell'area napoletana: ipotesi sui meccanismi naturali di protezione e sulle modalità di inquinamento. *Gr. Scient. It., Studi e Ricerche*: 387C-412 C.

Ducci D. & Onorati G. 1993. Analisi di una lunga serie di dati piezometrici in Piana Campana. *Atti 2° Conv. Intern. Geoidr.*, Firenze, 1993: 339-357.

Fiorelli T. 1926. Cenni sull'andamento della falda acquifera nel sottosuolo della zona tra Napoli e Pomigliano d'Arco. *Annali Genio Civile*, 1926, VII: 93-102. Roma.

ISTAT 1985. 6° Censimento generale dell'industria, del commercio, dei servizi e dell'artigianato. II, 1. Roma.

SIMN 1926-1990, *Annali idrologici*, I-II. Napoli.

Viparelli M. 1978. Le acque sotterranee ad oriente di Napoli. *Fond. Pol. Mezz. d'Italia*, 111: 1-48. Napoli.

Groundwater in the Urban Environment: Problems, Processes and Management, Chilton et al. (eds)
© 1997 Balkema, Rotterdam, ISBN 90 5410 837 1

Impact of additional exploitation on the littoral aquifers in the north of Senegal

S. Faye, C.B.Gaye, A.Faye & R.Malou
Department of Geology, University of Cheikh A. Diop, Dakar, Senegal

ABSTRACT: Simulation of additional exploitation of 35,000 m^3/d using the finite difference method (MODFLOW) has shown a decline of the piezometric head, which is accompanied by saltwater intrusion in the north west of the aquifer system. The inflow across boundaries increases by about 20,000 m^3/d and sea water intrusion advance in the north west is suspected to contribute to this input. In addition to sea water intrusion, agricultural practices are also a threat to the resource quality.

1 INTRODUCTION

Dakar, the capital city of Senegal, with a population of 1,500,000, is experiencing a serious water supply shortage, which is estimated at 100,000 m^3/d. The groundwater resources which feed the distribution network are aquifer systems situation in the north and mid-western part of Senegal.

The littoral north aquifer system provides up to 20,000 m^3/d to the network distribution for Daka, 7,000 m^3/d to local industries and 104,500 m^3/d for villages and agricultural consumption in the region. Decline of the piezometric head and sea water intrusion in the north west of the aquifer have been observed.

In order to satisfy the demand in Dakar and surrounding areas, the Water Authorities (Ministère de l'Hydraulique/PNUD 1994) plan to abstract an additional 35,000 m^3/d from the north littoral system. The objective of this paper is to simulate this planned exploitation using MODFLOW (McDonald & Harbaugh 1988) and to assess the system sensitivities with regard to sea water advance. Assessing the impact of agricultural practices on the resource quality is another objective.

2 HYDROGEOLOGICAI, SETTING AND CONCEPTUAL MODEL

The aquifer system extends over about 8,600 km^2 (Figure 1). It belongs geologically to the Senegalese sedimentary basin and is composed of two main aquifers:
• the Quaternary sandstone aquifer situated in the west, with a thickness varying between 20 and 160 m, is composed of unconsolidated sands and clays, and lies directly over an impervious marly substratum;
• the Lutetian limestone aquifer situated in the east is karstic in parts and has a mean thickness of 30 m.

These two aquifers are hydraulically linked by a fault which has brought them into contact.

The piezometric head distribution of the Quaternary sandstone aquifer shows flow directions from a dome 35 m high (located in the south west) towards the north, the ocean and the limestone aquifer.

Water from the aquifer system was chemically analysed from 115 wells for major cations and anions during a three year (1992, 1993 and 1994) period.

For most of the water samples, values of the total dissolved solids are relatively low (less than 1 g/l), except those found in the saline intrusion zone in the north west of Louga (up to 8 g/l) and in the brackish water zone in the north and north east of Louga (10 g/l). Water in the Quaternary sandstone aquifer is of sodium chloride and calcium chloride facies, whereas water from the limestone aquifer is of calcium bicarbonate facies (Kane 1995).

Saltwater intrusion has been proved in the north west of the studied area by geophysical electric methods (Diouf 1995), and the saline front, which is at 5 m depth, evolves from a sharp slope near the coast to a subhorizontal position inland.

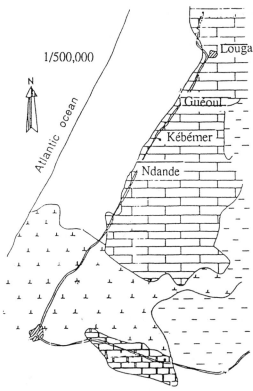

1/500,000

N

Atlantic ocean

Louga

Guéoul

Kébémer

Ndande

☐ ₁ Quaternary sandstone

☐ ₂ Lutetian limestone

☐ ₃ Lower Eocene limestones

☐ ₄ Eocene marly limestone

☐ ₅ Eocene marl

Figure 1. Aquifer distribution.

The conceptual model is represented by an unconfined one-layer aquifer system, in transient state, with 2D linear flow where saltwater intrusion occurs.

Boundary conditions are characterised by (Faye 1995):

• a specified head (zero) boundary along the coastal zone;

• specified head boundaries in the north, north east and eastern limits of the system (the measured heads are stable during the transient state period);

• an hydraulic no flow boundary at the line of groundwater divide of the piezometric mound. The aquifer system is recharged mainly in this zone.

The modelled area was divided into a mesh with cells of 2 x 2 km. The distribution of the

hydrodynamic and geometric parameters were performed using geostatistical methods (variograms and kriging techniques) in order to reduce estimation errors.

3 CALIBRATION AND SIMULATION

Calibration of the model was carried out in two steps:

• a steady state calibration using initial conditions of 1975. In fact, piezometric head changes of the aquifer system began at this time due to industrial development (mining and chemical industries) and exploitation of groundwater to supply Daka. Calibration (Figure 2) was achieved by changing values of the permeability, with regard to the nature of the reservoir and also to its variation trend, then values of infiltration which range from 0 to 5 mm/y (Faye, 1995).

• transient state calibration was referred to the piezometry of 1994 and adjustments were made only to the values of infiltration and the storage coefficient. Results of this later step, shown in the water budget (Table 1), indicated clearly that the aquifer system is fed mainly by rainwater infiltration and the main output from the system is discharge towards the ocean and through evaporation.

Table 1 Water budget in m^3/d calculated after calibration.

	Input	Output
Recharge	86,669	
Discharge		156,560
Boundaries	29,543	30,701
Storage	175,330	2.18
Wells		104,480
Total	291,540	291,740

The simulation scenario took into account three factors:

• the pumping rate of 35,000 m^3/d which is planned by the Water Authorities;

• the location of the abstraction wells at Guéoul and Ndande, which are near to the distribution network;

• the duration of 25 years.

4 RESULTS AND INTERPRETATION

Results (Figure 3) showed a drawdown zone along the line between the two planned exploitation zones, with a maximum drawdown of 10 m.

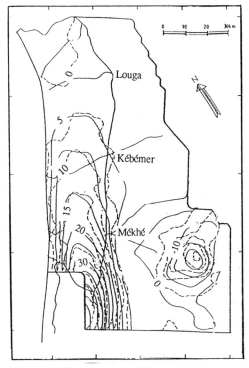

Figure 2. Calibration results (in metres) of the steady state model (measured 1975 head in dashed line, simulated head in continuous line).

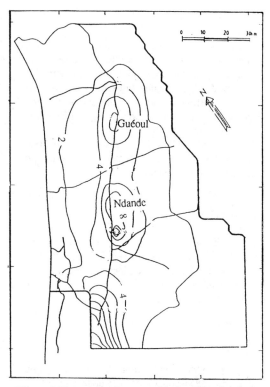

Figure 3. Drawdown (in metres) induced by simulation of 35,000 m³/d additional abstraction (curve of equal drawdown value).

The water budget (Table 2) showed a decreased output and increased input along the system limits compared to Table 1.

On the other hand, the system storage is slightly increased (58 m³/d) compared to the boundaries input which would increase from 29,543 to 48,870 m³/d. This increase is suspected to be mainly due to saline intrusion advance.

5 RESOURCE QUALITY

High nitrate content (up to 230 mg/l) waters are found mainly in the coastal "niayes" (local term used to designate coastal depression zones where the aquifer outcrops and where agricultural practices are developed). These concentrations indicate pollution from either degradation of organic matter or direct input of nitrate in the aquifer through use of fertiliser. Table 3 shows ranges of values of nitrate found in the different samples per year.

However, urban development in some places (Tivaouane, Mékhé, Kébémer and Louga) has not

Table 2. Water budget in m³/d calculated after simulation.

	Input	Output
Recharge	86,659	
Discharge		156,560
Boundaries	48,870	26,343
Storage	185,530	58.78
Wells		137,410
Total	321,060	320,360

Table 3. Number of samples per class and per year.

	1992	1993	1994
$NO_3^- < 30$ mg/l	83	59	68
$30 < NO_3^- < 50$ mg/l	11	4	10
$NO_3^- > 50$ mg/l	21	15	15

affected water quality; this could be explained by the thickness of the unsaturated zone which ranges between 20 and 35 m.

317

6 CONCLUSIONS

Because of its unconfined nature and its location, the aquifer system is particularly vulnerable to sea water intrusion. Simulation of an additional abstraction of 35,000 m³/d indicated a threat of saline front advance and it is therefore important in the real abstraction phase to control water specific conductivities in the north west of the system.

The second problem is the high nitrate content found in the "niayes" zone which could be due to organic matter degradation of fertiliser.

ACKNOWLEDGEMENTS

This work was financially supported by the International Development Research Centre (IDRC). The authors wish to thank Pierre Gélinas and his research associates from Laval University of Quebec (Canada) for their collaboration.

REFERENCES

Diouf, S. 1995. Application de la géophysique (électrique et sismique) à l'étude de la géométrie du réservoir de l'aquifère du littoral nord du Sénégal (de Taïba à Rao). *Mém. DEA, Univ. de Dakar,* 105p + annexes.

Faye, S. 1995. Modélisation hydrodynamique des nappes du littoral nord entre Cayar et St Louis. Impact des futurs prélèvements envisagés dans le cadre de l'approvisionnement en eau de Dakar et de ses environs. *Thèse Doct. Ing., Université C.A. Diop de Dakar,* 166p.

Kane C.H. 1995. Contribution à l'étude hydrochimique de la nappe des sables quaternaires du littoral nord du Sénégal entre Cayar et Saint Louis. *Thèse 3 éme cycle, Univ. C.A. Diop de Dakar,* 131p + annexes.

MacDonald, M.G. & A.W. Harbaugh 1988. A modular Three Dimensional finite difference groundwater flow model. *Techniques of water resources investigations of the U.S. Geological Survey, Book 6, Modelling techniques.*

Ministère de l'Hydraulique/PNUD. 1994. Bilan-Diagnostic de resources en eau du Sénégal. *Rapport MH/PNUD/DASG-SEN/87/006.*

Groundwater in the Urban Environment: Problems, Processes and Management, Chilton et al. (eds)
© *1997 Balkema, Rotterdam, ISBN 90 5410 837 1*

Recharge and discharge of aquifer systems in Curitiba, Brazil

João Nogueira Filho
Programa de Pos-Graduação em Geologia, Universidade Federal do Paraná, Brazil

Paulo Cesar Soares
Departamento de Geologia, Universidade Federal do Paraná, Brazil

ABSTRACT: Curitiba city, in 1996, had 1.5 million inhabitants with an estimated population growth of 4%/year. Privately drilled wells, in fractured rocks, provide as much as 20% of the 6.0 m³/s potable water demand. Groundwater exploitation has been made without aquifer conservation plans, because little is known about the local groundwater dynamics. Recharge and discharge areas have not been mapped yet, which makes understanding the aquifer systems difficult. Appropriate parameters delimited by geostatistics, show relevant groundwater variation patterns. Geochemical, isobath and piezometric contour maps reveal that the Curitiba sedimentary basin and related structure is the most important geological entity controlling all groundwater flow. This discovery allowed delimitation of recharge and discharge areas, followed by indication of areas favourable for protection and exploitation.

1 INTRODUCTION

Curitiba city, with about 1.5 million inhabitants is located in South Brazil and is the capital of the Paraná State (Figure 1). It is situated on the Atlantic plateau, with a mean altitude of 900 m, where the main river basins begin (Figure 2).

The main geological characteristics of the area are presented in Figure 3. Paleoproterozoic gneiss and migmatites, Neoproterozoic metasedimentary rocks, Jurassic and Cretaceous basic dykes and Tertiary-Quaternary sediments crop out in the city area. The

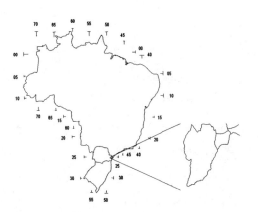

Figure 1. Geographic location of the studied area in South America, with the boundaries of Brazil, Paraná State and the Curitiba city municipality.

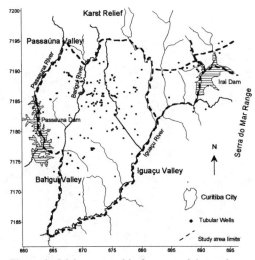

Figure 2. Main geographic features of the study area and the location of analysed wells. Coordinates are UTM (km).

semiconsolidated sediments correspond to the Guabirotuba Formation of the Curitiba sedimentary basin, and the metamorphics to its basement (Figure 4). The regional basement was highly structured in the late Proterozoic, and fractured in the Phanerozoic, including the more recent tectonic events that affected the basin.

Fracture systems in the gneissic-migmatitic rocks of the basement host small aquifers whose average discharge reaches up to 3.5 m^3/h/well. To the north of Curitiba, metasedimentary rocks include phyllites, metacarbonates and quartzites, deformed by regional tectonic events that took place during the Late Proterozoic and resulted in a NE-SW structural trend. Weathering of the metacarbonates led to the

formation of a karstic aquifer system with total discharge potential of about 10 m^3/s.

The basic dykes cut the metamorphics in a N40-60W trend. The walls of these dykes are discontinuities which provide preferential ways through which groundwater accumulates and percolates the crystalline basement (Figure 3).

The development of the Curitiba Basin resulted from Cenozoic tectonism in a semi-arid climate. The sediments that filled the basin include mainly sandy mudstones, with montmorilonitic clays. This cover reaches a maximum preserved thickness of less than 100 m and in the basal section, occasional arkose sand lenses occur. In these lenses, water production reaches 100 m^3/h/well.

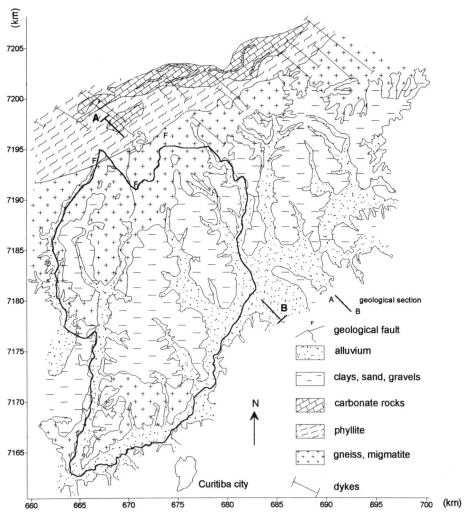

Figure 3. Geological map of the area and the boundaries of Curitiba municipality (CPRM, 1988). Coordinates are UTM (km).

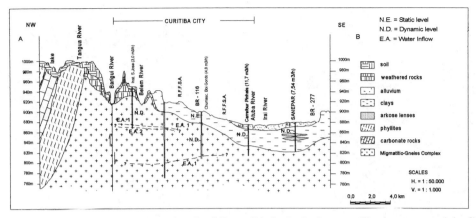

Figure 4. Geologic section portraying the different lithologies in the crystalline basement and the Curitiba sedimentary basin.

The aquifers in the crystalline basement are the most exploited ones, but because of their random distribution and spatial irregularity, little is known about their hydraulic parameters.

All these strongly structured lithologies demand studies on the geologic control that they exert on the aquifers they host. However, in densely populated areas, there are some extra difficulties in studying geologic entities, because geologic structures are obliterated by buildings and roads, wells are irregularly distributed and electricity lines interfere with geophysical works. Estimation of aquifer-related data over undrilled areas can help to overcome such difficulties.

The recharge of all the aquifers could be mainly either through the base of Cenozoic cover, large fractures or soil/sediment percolation. The role that these geologic entities play in the recharge of aquifers is very important to the sustainable use of groundwater.

2 METHODS

The well data used correspond to an irregular set of aquifer sampling, as shown in Figure 2. The geometry of the basement dipping toward the trough of the Curitiba Sedimentary Basin induces a strong trend to the investigated variables. This trend was studied by using trend surface analysis with a third-order polynomial surface because of the best gain in correlation coefficients. The surface generated provides values for unsampled points and the

residuals for sampled ones. Variographic analysis and kriging was applied to some variable residuals, but due to the highly irregular sampling, the results were not satisfactory. At the margin of the worked area the trend may result in large errors.

The estimations were carried out for several variables. The altimetry and depth of piezometric level, contours of the sedimentary basement, fracture patterns, water production and main chemical components were investigated in order to evaluate the proposed discharge and recharge entities and their positioning with respect to the urban area. Only the main results in order to of the conclusions are presented here, in view of space restrictions.

The use of trend surfaces resulted in contour maps of some of the variables involved, which reflect the groundwater percolation and other aspects of the aquifers.

The integration of layers of information resulted in a thematic map in which recharge and discharge areas are delimited. Together with the different patterns of occupation, the map can be used to locate areas requiring environmental protection.

3 TREND SURFACE MAPS

The results of the interpolation of piezometric data from 242 wells, by a third-order polynomial surface, were superposed on the geological map of Curitiba (Figure 5). The higher piezometric levels are located towards the north and south-east; flow lines are inferred towards the low level in the NE-SW axial zone of the basin.

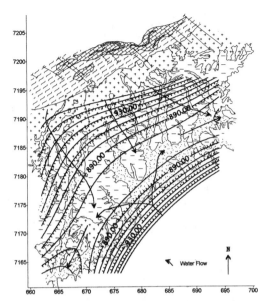

Figure 5. Superposition of the piezometric contour map obtained from a third-order polynomial (242 wells) and the geological map. Coordinates are UTM (km). Contours in meters.

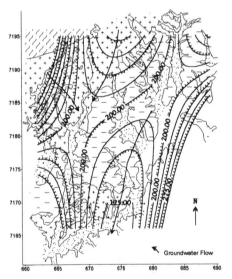

Figure 6 - Superposition of the TDS map obtained from a third-order surface (158 wells) and the geological map. TDS values in ppm. Coordinates are UTM (km).

Geochemical analysis of major ions reveals similar distribution trends, which are summarised in the total

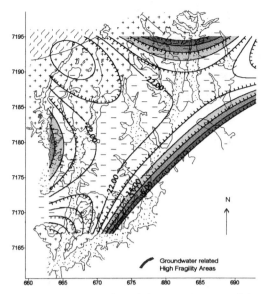

Figure 7. Superposition of the isobath map and the geological map (1:20.000, 4.0 m equidistant curves). Coordinates are UTM (km).

dissolved solids (TDS) trend surface map (Figure 6). The higher TDS values are towards the basement, especially the karst zone in the north, and less (higher dilution) in the central part of the sedimentary cover.

The isobathic map of piezometric level was obtained from the grid that resulted from the differences between the digital terrain model (DTM) and piezometric values (Figure 7). This map shows the zones where the inflow to the aquifer is potentially higher because the piezometric level is closer to the surface.

The superposition of layers made it possible to infer the main areas of recharge, discharge and the more susceptible zones for contamination, which are plotted together with the zoning of human occupation (Figure 8).

4 DISCUSSION

The contour maps reveal the coherence between the trend surfaces of the variables involved. The groundwater flow patterns converge towards the trough of the basin. From this trough, the groundwater flows in two directions: one to the north-east toward the Ribeira do Iguape hydrographic basin, and the other to the south-west, toward the Iguacu hydrographic basin. This trend was also detected in

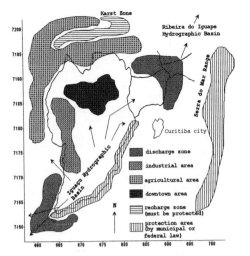

Figure 8. Districts of Curitiba and the localisation of recharge and discharge areas. The different types of occupation are also plotted. Coordinates are UTM (km).

TDS and piezometric trend surfaces indicate a secondary groundwater flow directed toward the northwest, where it reaches an important NE fault system along which the Passauna River flows.

Surface lineaments interpreted from Landsat images and a digital terrain model, and subsurface anomalies interpreted from processed gravimetric data, reveal the presence of important geological discontinuities related to fault zones (Nogueira F° & Soares 1996), either in the basement or in the cover, such as the fault systems underlying Passauna, Iguacu (NE) and Barigui (N) rivers.

Anomalous values of the studied variables in such zones show the role these discontinuities play in the recharge, discharge, flow and production of water.

studies of the spatial behaviour of the recharge areas, in the behaviour of the interface between the sediments of the Curitiba Basin and its basement and also in a local study of the groundwater flow through the arkose lenses (Nogueira F° et al, 1996).

In the northern part of the area, because of the higher relief, the contours are directly influenced by groundwater flow from the karstic aquifers. The carbonate-rich water migrates to the depressed trough of the basin through interconnected fractures in the basement and the margins of the diabase dykes. This trend had already been detected by local geochemical analysis (Nogueira F.° & Bittencourt, 1995). Both

5 CONCLUSIONS

The behaviour of the variables studied indicates that groundwater flow in the interconnected aquifers follows highly structure-influenced flow patterns. Despite the strong irregularity of the groundwater flow within fractured aquifers in crystalline rocks, the aquifer properties are well described by trend surfaces, implying that these aquifers are inter-connected by fractures. The piezometric, TDS and isobath maps related to basement configuration and fracture zones were good indicators of the discharge and recharge zones.

The interconnection between the aquifers allows groundwater to flow from recharge zones to the central depression of the sedimentary basin. The thin sedimentary cover behaves as an aquiclude, because of its clayey composition, protecting the basement fracture aquifers.

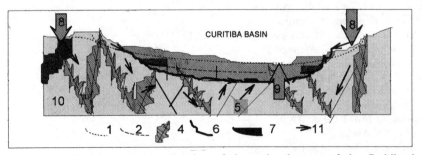

Figure 9. Diagrammatic representation of the main elements of the Curitiba basin aquifer system. (1) piezometric trend level; (2) water entry trend level; (3) sedimentary cover aquiclude; (4) fracture zone aquifer; (S) fracture connection; (6) unconformity connection; (7) arkose lens aquifer; (8) recharge zone; (9) discharge zone; (10) crystalline basement; (11) water flow; (12) karst aquifer system connection.

Thus the Curitiba basin aquifer system is made up of the interconnection of small basement fracture aquifers by horizontal flow throughout the undercover unconformity, the main fault zones and the dyke walls, and vertical flow through cover fractures, all protected by the sedimentary aquiclude of the Guabirotuba Formation (Figure 9).

The map results made it possible to locate the recharge and discharge zones of the Curitiba basin aquifer system and to associate with the city zoning based on their environmental peculiarities. The recharge areas are situated mostly over the northern parts of the city, over areas where karstic aquifers are present and in the south-east, from the Serra do Mar range. The discharge areas are concentrated along the trough of the Curitiba Basin and show two main discharge zones: one to the Rio Ribeira do Iguape hydrographic basin, to the Northeast of the study area, and the other, to the Rio Iguaçu hydrographic basin.

ACKNOWLEDGEMENTS

The authors are grateful to CAPES and CNPq for personal financial support. To UFPR and FINEPIPADCT for the research facilities. Special thanks to Acquasul Po,cos Artesianos Ltda. e Hidropel Hidrogeologia e Perfuracoes Ltda., for the opening of their data files. This research is part of the Master in Geology thesis of the first author.

6   REFERENCES

CPRM. 1988. *Projeto Integracao Geologica da Regiao Metropolitana de Curitiba.* Sao Paulo. SP.

Nogueira F°.J. e Bittencourt, A.V.L. 1995. Caracterizacao hidroquimica e implicacoes ambientais dos aquiferos da regiao de Curitiba. *Simposio Sul-Brasileiro de Geologia VI/Encontro de Geologia do Cone Sul, I, Boletim de Resumos Expandidos*, Porto Alegre-RS, 371-374.

Nogueira F°., J.; Lisboa, A.A.; Rosa F°, E.F. 1996. Estudos preliminares sobe tend8ncias de fluxo subterraneo da bacia hidrografica do Alto Iguacu - *Curitiba/Pr. IX Congresso Brasileiro de Aguas Subterraneas*, Salvador-BA, ABAS.

Nogueira F°, J. e Soares, P.C. 1996. Analise da distribuicao da agua subterranea em Curitiba atraves de geoprocessamento. *II Congresso e Feira para Usuarios de Geoprocessamento. Anais...* SAGRES, Curitiba-Pr, 261-272.

Causes and consequences of extreme water shortage in Ta'iz, Yemen

C. Handley
Department of Geography, School of Oriental and African Studies, London, UK

J. Dottridge
Department of Geological Sciences, University College London, UK

ABSTRACT: The people of Ta'iz in the southern highlands of Yemen experience severe water shortages, receiving water from public supply only once in every 15 to 40 days. Deterioration in the frequency and quality of the water supplied has resulted in private water treatment and distribution schemes. The problems of water supply are aggravated by rapid population growth. Ta'iz is supplied from boreholes located down-gradient of the city, which have become contaminated, and by a wellfield which suffers from declining water levels and falling yields, due to depletion of the limited alluvial aquifer. Recent emergency drilling of 18 boreholes in volcanic rocks produced a combined yield of only 35 l/s, but exploratory boreholes in the Cretaceous sandstone aquifer had greater potential, despite limited outcrop and unknown recharge. Attempts to supply the city from the more distant sandstone aquifer were met with hostility by the local people.

1 INTRODUCTION

1.1 *Current situation*

During the past two years, mains water supply to the city of Ta'iz has been connected between once every 15 and once every 40 days. The water delivery crisis reached a peak during summer 1995. Mains water is of poor quality, with electrical conductivity averaging 2000 µS/cm. The poor delivery results in many people purchasing tankered water for washing and sanitation, and the poor quality necessitates purchase of drinking water from water purification companies. Water sales, storage tank manufacture and water processing and distribution activities have proliferated as the private sector has responded to the demand. Water collection from standpipes has become a facet of everyday life for most families. On the day mains water arrives, the household water-related activity is intense. The sociological and economic repercussions resulting from a sudden reduction in supply are extreme. Opinions indicate that the irregularity of supply is the most difficult aspect to handle. The causes of the severe water shortage can be traced primarily to the failure of the main wellfield on which the city was dependent.

1.2 *Geographical setting*

Ta'iz is located within the upper catchment of Wadi Rasyan, in an area forming a low plateau within the Southern Highlands of Yemen (Figure 1). The plateau lies in a faulted graben 25 km wide, aligned east-west and descending from 1500 m above sea level in the east to 900 m in the west, in a series of step-faulted blocks of stratified volcanics, which dip to the east or north east. The eastern edge of the area is occupied by a flat loess covered plateau, forming the surface water divide between the Red Sea and the Indian Ocean. To the north and south, the graben is bounded by highlands rising to 3000 m composed respectively of volcanic rocks and granite. These highlands receive some of the largest quantities of rainfall in the Arabian Peninsula. Spate runoff from the highlands enters the alluvial valleys (Figure 1), and infiltrates rapidly into the coarse wadi alluvium. The alluvium can reach 60 m in thickness, but may be unsaturated as at Al Hayma.

Socio-economically, the area serves as the hinterland of the city of Ta'iz with a population of 350,000. The exploitation of water resources is dominated by agriculture, and to a lesser extent by the domestic and industrial needs of the city for both

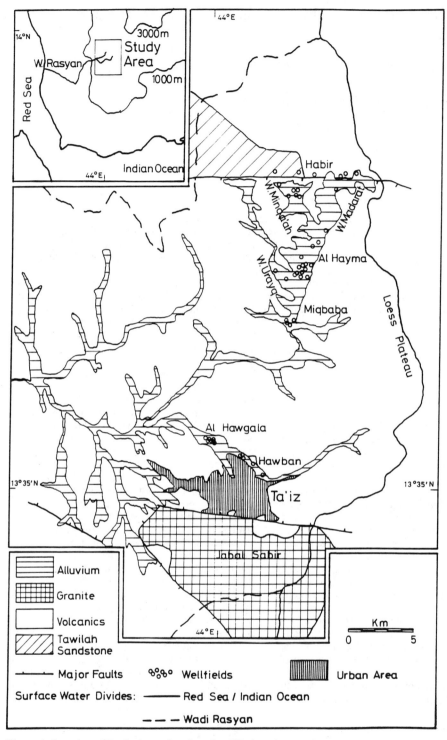

Figure 1 Location of Study Area, showing simplified geology and main wellfields

water and food. From an estimated total water use of 200 Mm³/year in the upper catchment of Wadi Rasyan, 95% is for agriculture, 4.5% for domestic and 0.5% for industrial use. Approximately 50% of the water abstracted returns to groundwater.

2 HYDROGEOLOGY

The volcanic rocks of the Ta'iz graben comprise a thick sequence of fractured basic and acidic lavas, tuff and ash, which form an unconfined aquifer. Storage is low, mostly limited to fractures, and hydraulic conductivity is also low, typically 0.04 m/d. This unit is not considered adequate as an aquifer to supply the city of Ta'iz, due to the large separation necessary between boreholes in a wellfield, low storage and low probability of intersecting significant fracture conduits. These factors preclude the successful development of a wellfield in the volcanics.

Since the 1960s, the water supply of Ta'iz has been derived from nearby alluvial deposits. Pumping tests in the alluvium indicate that the hydraulic conductivity for 70% of wells ranges between 4.5 and 61 m/d, averaging 16.5 m/d. No storage coefficients are available. Some parts of the alluvial aquifer, which were originally in a confined condition, are now unconfined due to excessive drawdowns. The first wellfields to be developed, Hawban and Al Hawgala, were located immediately downstream of the city (Montgomery 1974). With increasing population, water supply and sewage disposal, the water quality deteriorated, with an EC in 1996 of 5000 μS/cm. Recirculation of waste water from the city to the wellfield through the alluvium has maintained groundwater levels in the wellfields, despite continuing abstraction (as an emergency supply) until 1997.

Declining water quality and population growth led to the development of another alluvial aquifer, at Al Hayma, 15 km north of Ta'iz. Exploratory drilling took place in the late 1970s (Leggette et al 1977) and the wellfield was developed during the 1980s. The trends in abstraction and water level declines are shown in Figures 2 and 3. The increase in abstraction with population growth during the 1980s and the sharp decline in supply during summer 1995 are particularly apparent.

The Cretaceous Tawilah Sandstone outcrops to the north of the graben and is thought to occur throughout the graben beneath the volcanic sequence. The sandstone is approximately 200 m thick. Pumping tests in 6 exploratory boreholes in the Habir area indicate a hydraulic conductivity of between 1 and 8 m/d and an unconfined storage coefficient of around 7%. The sandstone is unexploited and represents the most promising future resource, although its recharge pattern has not

been determined and groundwater mining may take place. Where affected by volcanic extrusions and dykes, the sandstone may be altered to quartzite with a reduction in porosity.

In response to the water crisis of 1995, an emergency drilling programme within the city of Ta'iz constructed 18 wells in the volcanics, providing a total of 35 l/s. Three of the exploratory wells in the sandstone at Habir were also utilized, yielding 32 l/s. The poor yield of the wells in the volcanics is thought to be at least partly due to the low hydraulic conductivity, whilst the sandstone well yields were also disappointing. The latter may be affected by low well efficiencies due to inadequate well development, but this has not been confirmed by step tests. These average yields were derived from the total monthly discharge and are

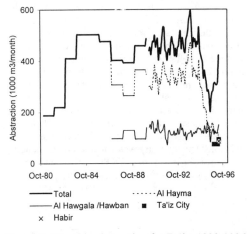

Figure 2. Monthly abstraction for Ta'iz, 1980-1996

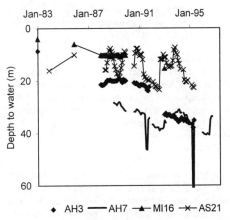

Figure 3. Hydrographs of observation wells, Al Hayma

thus reduced by operating inefficiencies and stoppages. As a result of the emergency drilling and use of the Habir wells, mains water delivery improved from 40 days between connections to 15 days.

3 CAUSES OF THE WATER CRISIS

3.1 *Depletion of the Al Hayma Aquifer*

The Al Hayma valley occupies 26 km^2, within a catchment of 205 km^2. The 1995 water crisis in Ta'iz was essentially caused by the steady depletion of the Al Hayma aquifer over the preceding 10 years, and consequent declining yields in the wellfield. This worsening situation reached crisis point in early 1995, precipitating a rapid deterioration in water delivery.

The original wellfield design was based on the assumption that the Ta'iz water supply scheme would intercept all groundwater recharge to the aquifer and the entire surface inflow to the valley (Leggette et al 1977). As there would be no water remaining for irrigation, a compensation package for farmers was planned. An annual abstraction of 10 Mm^3 was envisaged, but actual abstraction has never exceeded 6 Mm^3/year. Design calculations indicated a possible abstraction of 9 Mm^3/year $\pm$ 20%, but then stated that a yield of 10 Mm^3/year was obtainable. This quantity was considered adequate to supply a population of 178,000, the anticipated population of Ta'iz in 1990. However, population growth during the period from 1975 to 1994 has been much faster, as shown by the census data in Figure 4.

3.2 *Incorrect assumptions in the wellfield design*

The failure of the Al Hayma wellfield is due to a number of unrealistic assumptions made by the designers (Leggette et al 1977).

Agricultural abstraction

It was assumed that all agricultural abstraction would cease, but instead, the farmers deepened their wells to keep pace with declining water levels. Irrigation provides a valuable second, cash crop, whereas rainfed agriculture only provides a subsistence crop.

Rainfall

Annual rainfall was assumed to be between 600 and 650 mm. Annual rainfall distribution is bimodal with peaks in April/May and August/September and lower rainfall in June and July. The dry season lasts from mid-October to mid-March. Summer rains are associated with convective storms. Cloud cover builds up from midday with rains usually in the afternoon. Rainfall intensity measurements during 1995 (Handley in preparation) indicated that 85% of the annual rainfall (708 mm total) in the Ta'iz area fell during short duration events totalling twelve hours. Storms are very localised with considerable differences in rainfall from a single event over distances of less than 500 m. The annual totals measured at a single station can vary considerably, depending on how many storms are centred on the station during the year.

Although no monitoring stations have been established in the Al Hayma area since the project design, field observations of storm movement and satellite image interpretation of vegetation density indicate that the total annual rainfall in the Al Hayma valley is less than at the nearest monitoring station, and is also less than the design value. Rainfall in the catchment above Al Hayma, however, is thought to be similar, or even higher, than the design value. Estimates of the amount of water reaching the Al Hayma valley depend on the rainfall-runoff ratio assumed.

Runoff

During the wellfield exploration period, the wadi was perennial over its whole course, with a flow of 3 to 3.5 Mm^3/yr. Today flows are restricted to major rainfall events, when short duration flows occur only in the upper reach of the alluvial valley and transmission losses over this section account for all the spate water. It is thus not possible to compare modern runoff with that of 20 years ago. In the wellfield design, a rainfall-runoff ratio of 7% was assumed for the whole catchment. Rudimentary measurements of storm flow in wadis on the northern slopes of Jabal Sabir indicate rainfall-runoff ratios as high as 26%, but typically between 0 and 5.5% depending on duration and intensity

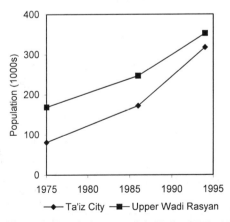

Figure 4. Population growth in Ta'iz, 1975 - 1995

328

(Handley in preparation). A threshold of about 6 mm rainfall, below which no runoff occurs, and an average annual runoff of approximately 3.6 % are indicated. The catchment monitored has very similar climatic, land use and slope characteristics to the area providing runoff to the upper part of Wadi Al Hayma.

Recharge

Recharge and runoff calculations in the design report included a mass balance of chloride for rainfall and runoff, assuming that all the chloride entering the catchment is from rainfall. However, it is likely that seepage of more saline groundwater into the Al Hayma valley from the east and human activity increases the chloride content of the groundwater, thus the assumption of a closed system cannot be maintained.

3.3 *Agricultural Water Use*

The application of irrigation water was determined from assessment of current cropping patterns and crop water requirements (Handley in preparation). This application is in addition to water received by direct rainfall and by run-on from adjacent areas. The latter was calculated using a rainfall/runoff ratio of 35%, derived from field measurements by Eger (1986) of rainwater harvesting in similar terrain in Amran, Yemen. This ratio was only applied to rainfall events which exceeded the threshold of 6 mm rainfall, as observed in the Ta'iz area (Handley in preparation), and may be an overestimate for Ta'iz. Alderwish (1995) measured an irrigation return of 25% for similar soils in the Sana'a basin. Estimates of agricultural water requirements and aquifer recharge are summarised in Table 1.

In 1975, there were 25 agricultural wells, which were estimated to irrigate 552 ha. Satellite imagery indicates that by 1985/6, 578 ha were under irrigation. Interviews with farmers suggest that this period coincided approximately with the peak abstraction for irrigation. In 1996, the total number of dug wells in the Al Hayma valley was 142, of which 110 were dry, and 23 were in use. There are 118 drilled wells in the valley, 33 of which are dry and 40 are operational, and a further 56 boreholes are used for water supply to Ta'iz. Satellite imagery from 1994/5 indicates a total irrigated area of 488 ha, and the irrigation intensity also appears to have declined since the mid 1980s. There has been a very noticeable shift in irrigation from the downstream end (Miqbaba) to the upstream (Wadi Madarat and Upper Al Hayma), as the wells in the lower valley have dried up and upstream users have drilled wells to irrigate potatoes and qat (a mild amphetamine, which is a high value crop). Actual irrigation of qat appears to be much less than the theoretical crop water requirement.

Table 1 Water supply for agriculture in the Al Hayma valley

Area	Rainfall Mm^3/yr	Irrigation use (except qat) Mm^3/yr	Return to aquifer Mm^3/yr
Madarat	0.27	0.37	0.25
Upper Al Hayma	0.84	2.17	1.15
Lower Al Hayma and Wadi Urayq	0.51	1.18	0.51
Miqbaba	0.22	0.41	0.20
Minqa'ah	0.85	1.74	0.78
Total	3.49	7.54	3.59

4 CURRENT RESEARCH

Current research (Handley in preparation) aims to provide more reliable figures for the water balance components. Before a water balance can be determined with any degree of confidence, it is hoped to calibrate a groundwater model of the Al Hayma alluvial aquifer against historical records of water levels, and using estimates of past abstractions derived from satellite imagery. Although the accuracy of this research is limited by lack of long-term monitoring of many parameters, two particular aspects of the work are considered to be worth further investigation. It is hoped that stream gauging during the flash floods will give a more accurate and verified rainfall-runoff coefficient, and that it will be possible to measure infiltration of rainfall through the soil profile during and immediately after rainfall events. These measurements will be related to the rates of evapotranspiration calculated from meteorological parameters measured over the same period.

5 CONCLUSIONS

The city of Ta'iz has now embarked on a new phase of water supply, through the exploitation of the Tawilah Sandstone. Although good yields are expected, the extent of recharge to the sandstone, which has a very limited area of outcrop, remains to be proven. Groundwater mining may occur in future, and, if there is very little recharge, may have already taken place with the present low levels of abstraction.

However, local politics are likely to exert a greater influence than any hydrogeological criteria on the development of future resources. The lessons from Al Hayma have been learned by many farmers in the area. Not only has the alluvial aquifer been exhausted, but so has the farmers' patience with the government. Consequently, there was violent hostility from local people to exploratory drilling in the sandstone.

Although many reports assessing the water resources of the area have been produced, they are all flawed by the lack of hydrological data, in particular, on which to base their analyses and recommendations. Establishment of a monitoring network is therefore an urgent priority for the Ta'iz area, to collect data on rainfall, wadi flows, abstraction and groundwater levels, which are essential to improve the evaluation of available resources and provide long-term solutions to the water supply crisis in Ta'iz.

REFERENCES

Alderwish, A.M 1995. *Estimation of groundwater recharge to aquifers of Sana'a basin, Yemen,.* unpublished PhD thesis, University of London.

Eger, H., 1986. *Runoff Agriculture. A Case Study About the Yemeni Highlands.* Unpublished PhD thesis, Tubingen University.

Handley, C.D., in preparation. *Water Stress. A case study of Ta'iz, Yemen.* M.Phil. thesis, University of London

Leggette, Brashears and Graham, 1977. *Hydrogeologic investigation for well field development in Al Haima basin. YAR.,* report for NWSA, Yemen.

Montgomery, J.M. Consulting Engineers, 1974. *Feasibility study of water and sewerage for Ta'iz, YAR., Vol II, Water Resources Evaluation,* report for USAID, contract no. AID/ASIA-C-1081.

ACKNOWLEDGMENTS

We would like to thank the UNDDSMS in Sana'a for providing access to the well inventory for the Ta'iz area and for purchasing the satellite images, Prof J A Allan (SOAS, University of London) for advice and direction in conducting the research, and Hiro Yoshida (SOAS) for processing the satellite images.

Groundwater for urban water supply in northern China

Han Zaisheng
Administration of Mineral Resources, Ministry of Geology and Mineral Resources, Beijing, People's Republic of China

ABSTRACT: Groundwater plays an important role in urban and industrial water supply in northern China. More than 1000 groundwater wellfields have been explored and installed. Groundwater provides about half of the urban water supply. A complete set of regulations for the use and methods of exploration of groundwater have been established in China. Serious over-exploitation of groundwater has created environmental problems in some cities. Some safeguarding measures for groundwater resource protection have been taken.

1 GROUNDWATER EXPLORATION FOR URBAN WATER SUPPLY

A complete set of regulations and methods for the exploration of groundwater have been established in P.R.China, and form the basis of national and industry standards, which are regularly revised. These include: GB 15218-94 Standards of Classification for Groundwater Resources; GBJ 27-88 Hydrogeologic Exploration Specification of Water Supply; GB/T14497-93 Requirements for the Operation of Groundwater Resources Management Models; GB/T14848-93 Standards of Groundwater Quality; GB/T 14157-93 Hydrogeologic Terminology; DZ44-86 Hydrogeologic Exploration Specification of Urban and Industrial Water Supply; DL/T 5034-94 Technical Code for The Hydrogeological Investigation of Water Supply for Thermal Plants; CJJ16-88 Hydrogeologic Exploration Specification for Urban Water Supply.

Conventional groundwater exploration utilizes hydrogeological mapping, hydrogeophysical prospecting, investigative drilling, pumping tests and groundwater observation, amongst other methods. Some relatively new techniques such as remote sensing, isotopic studies, shallow seismic prospecting and velocity logging are also applied in exploration (Yin Changping et al. 1993).

In China, the exploration of groundwater is divided into three stages; reconnaissance, detailed survey and prospecting. Table 1 shows these three stages and their respective requirements (Han Zaisheng 1994).

2 GROUNDWATER RESOURCE EVALUATION

Groundwater resource evaluations are in progress for urban water supply in most cities in China. To determine the allowable abstraction of a wellfield, the groundwater budget is estimated from information about such things as precipitation, surface water hydrology and other components of the groundwater system. The balance and its alteration by groundwater replenishment, storage and discharge should be appraised rationally. In some complex situations, the exploitable yield of a wellfield is determined by trial-exploitation pumping tests.

On the basis of a conceptual hydrogeological model, a mathematical model is established for groundwater evaluation. Numerical simulations with finite element or finite difference methods have been used widely during the last twenty years.

Environmental problems that may emerge after the groundwater has been exploited are predicted during the exploration. The analysis of the influence of groundwater abstraction on the environment has become an essential requirement for establishing a new wellfield.

3 EXPLOITATION OF GROUNDWATER FOR URBAN WATER SUPPLY

Groundwater plays an important role in urban and industrial water supply in northern China. More than 1000 wellfields have been explored and established. Categorized by aquifer type, 73 percent are in

Table l. The requirements of three stages of groundwater exploration in China

Stage	Reconnaissance	Detailed Survey	Prospecting
Scale of mapping	1:200000-1:50000	1:50000-1:25000	1:25000-1:0000
Scope of exploration	Natural system	Section rich in groundwater	Wellfield and surroundings
Geophysical exploration	Data collection	Surface geophysical prospecting	Well logging and additional surface exploration
Investigation Drilling	A little	Some exploration wells	Exploration - production wells
Pumping Test	Simple pumping test	Multiple wells pumping test	Trial-exploitation pumping test
Groundwater Observation	Existing data collection	Establish observation wells	Improve observation net

unconsolidated deposits, 21 percent in karst and 6 percent in fractured aquifers. The unconsolidated aquifers are mainly Quaternary deposits. In the alluvial plain of northern and north-eastern China, groundwater has been exploited for more than 3000 years. The karst aquifers in northern China mainly consist of Ordovician and Cambrian limestones and dolomites. Some large springs in karst areas are used for industrial water supply directly. The fractured aquifers in hard rock have little significance for urban water supply in northern China (Ji Chuanmao et al. 1996).

Most cities in northern China are situated by rivers, so riverside groundwater is important for urban and industrial water supply. There are about 300 riverside wellfields in northern China. Eight provincial capitals are situated along the Yellow River and its tributaries. All of these cities use groundwater for their urban water supply. There are more than 50 riverside wellfields situated along this valley. There are 16 large and medium cities in the Haihe river valley, including Beijing and Tianjin. Most cities in this area make use of groundwater for their water supply. Among them, riverside aquifers are the most sure source of groundwater, which is widely investigated and exploited in suitable areas.

Groundwater provides about half of the total quantity of urban water supply in northern China. Table 2 shows groundwater abstraction for some cities. There are also many industrial sites including power plants, chemical plants and petrochemical works using groundwater for their water supply.

4 ENVIRONMENTAL DETERIORATION

Groundwater over-exploitation has caused large and continuous drawdown of groundwater levels in some cities of northern China. Table 3 summarises the groundwater level status during the last 50 years (Shi Zhenhua & Li Chuanyao 1993). Several environmental deterioration effects have appeared, caused by groundwater overexploitation in some cities.

Land subsidence has occurred in the cities of Tianjin, Cangxhou, Xuchang, Langfang, Jining and Dezhou. This results in poor drainage and an increased risk of flooding. For example in the Tanggu region of Tianjin city, the ground surface had subsided to below sea level, and the area has had to be protected by an embankment. Land subsidence in Cangzhou city, Hebei province has reached more than 1.5 m in the last thirty years (Fei Jin 1988).

Surface collapses have appeared in some cities with karst aquifers, such as Tangshan, Baoding, Laiwu, Qinhuangdao and Taian. Tangshan is one of the most important cities in northern China, and was rebuilt on the ruins of the great earthquake of 1976 which measured 7.8 on the Richter scale. However a number of karst collapses took place from 1976 to 1991. The collapses occurred in 20 places and their area of influence has reached 20 km^2 in downtown Tangshan.

The mechanisms of karst collapse in Tangshan and other cities of northern China are as follows: over-pumping groundwater; drawdown both in the karst and the Quaternary sediments, erosion by infiltrating water; gravity collapse. All of the collapses have similar hydrogeological conditions. The shallow karst

Table 2. Groundwater abstraction for the main cities in northern China

Scale	Amount (10⁶ m³/d)	City
Very large	>1.0	Beijing, Xian, Shenyang, Tangshan, Taiyuan, Liaoyang, Shijiazhuang, Urumqi
Large	0.5 - 1.0	Jinzhou, Harbin
Middle	0.2 - 0.5	Lanzhou, Huhehot, Jinan, Qiqihar, Kaifeng, Zhengzhou, Datong, Xining, Baotou, Yingkou, Xinxian, Anyang
Small	<0.2	Changchun, Tinchuan, Siping, Anshan, Jiamusi

Table 3. Groundwater level status in selected cities

City	Beijing	Zhengzhou	Shenyang	Taiyuan	Datong	Shijiazhuang	Liaoyang
Balance	1949-1968	1950-1971	1949-1962	1956-1967	1958-1978	1957-1965	1944-1970
Slow Decline	1968-1975	1971-1978	1962-1980	1967-1980	1978-1983	1965-1979	1970-1978
Fast Decline	1975-now	1978-now	1980-now	1980-now	1983-now	1979-now	1978-now

is well developed. The thickness of Quaternary sediments, overlying the carbonate rock is generally less than 50 m. The severe change in groundwater flow is derived from over-pumping of karst water. The deformation of the soil layer is the main cause of karst collapse.

A decrease or ceasing of karst spring discharge has occurred at Baotu spring in Jinin, Jinci spring in Taiyuan and Bai spring in Xingtai. Some of these large karst springs were important urban water supplies. For example, Jinan city in Shandong province is famous as a spring city for its 72 springs, including Baotu spring. Because of the over-exploitation of karst water, Baotu spring and others ceased frequently from 1974. All the springs in Jinan were dry in 1989 due to the short period of precipitation in that year. The tourist trade, for which spring sightseeing is the main attraction, was damaged.

Sea water intrusion is found in the coastal cities around the Bohai sea such as Dalian, Qingdao, Laizhou, Longkou, Yantai and Qinghuangdao. In downtown Dalian, the area of sea water intrusion increased from 84 km² to 220 km² from 1997 to 1986.

Sea water intrusion took place in 7 regions near utilized groundwater sources. The concentration of chloride of groundwater has increased to more than 130 mg/l in some wells. Fresh water of high quality is more valued in the coastal cities than in others.

Groundwater in the urban areas has been contaminated to varying degrees. Deterioration of groundwater quality has become a striking environmental problem in half of the cities of northern China. Table 4 shows selected analytical results for pollutants in groundwater of selected cities.

5 GROUNDWATER MANAGEMENT

The rational exploitation and utilization of groundwater are very important for sustainable development of cities. Some measures for groundwater protection have been taken in many cities. The trends in deterioration of water quality and over use of urban groundwater are being reversed by water allocation projects and protection measures. For urban water pollution control, urban sewage and industrial wastewater will increasingly be treated and reused. Protection areas have been delimited for both surface water and groundwater resources in important water supply regions. The over-exploitation of groundwater is controlled by increased infiltration, making full use of artificial recharge. The application and dissemination of water-saving techniques economizes on water. The legal system will be improved for strengthening management and for effective protection of groundwater resources. For

Table 4. Pollutants in groundwater of selected cities   Units: mg/L

City	Beijing	Tianjin	Lanzhou	Dalian	Xian	Shenyang
NO_2	0.01-3.5	0.00-0.89	0.00-6.0	0.00-0.38	0.00-0.02	0.01-0.02
NO_3	0.18-4.0	0.00-6.0	2.0-41.6	0.00-5.37	0.20-4.60	0.00-3.20
Phenol	0.00-0.09	0.00-0.076	<0.002	0.10-0.134	0.00-0.005	0.001-0.022
Cyanide	0.00-0.08	0.00-0.014	0.00-0.026	<0.004	0.002-0.011	0.01-0.065
Arsenic	0.00-0.16	0.00-0.02	<0.01	0.00-0.012	0.00-0.026	0.001-0.015
Mercury	0.00024-0.01	>0.00002	<0.001	0.00-0.0012	0.00-0.0016	0.001-0.003
Cadmium	0.001-0.38	0.002-0.29	<0.004	0.00-0.344	0.00-0.10	0.001-0.45
Fluoride	0.25-1.45	0.42-6.33	0.10-0.20	0.00-9.0	0.30-0.90	0.10-0.45
Number of wells	769	306	59	383	Wei river side	Hun river side

water shortages, long-distance water allocation and transfer schemes have been put into effect for some cities.

In Beijing, the capital city of China, the economic structure has ben adjusted to encourage water saving. The industrial enterprises which use large amounts of water and those causing pollution have been controlled and transformed water-saving techniques such as spray irrigation, drip irrigation and conveyance of water in pipes have been encouraged in the suburban areas. These water-saving techniques for irrigation have been applied over about 2000 km² and groundwater withdrawal for agriculture has decreased considerably in the last 10 years. The Yonding river and Chaobai river are the two major water systems in Beijing and conjunctive management of groundwater and surface water has been implemented. Artificial recharge of groundwater has taken place in the western and northern suburban areas. By these measures, the continuous drawdown of groundwater levels has been controlled, and groundwater levels rose by 0.2-5.6 m from 1994 to 1995 in most of the area. Along-distance water transference scheme from the Yangtze river to the north China plain is in progress. This could be the solution for sustainable water supply of Beijing.

Overall targets are to accelerate the use of water-saving techniques to help alleviate the crisis of urban water shortage, to protect groundwater resources in the over-exploited areas, to improve the coordination between socioeconomic development and environmental improvement and to seek sustainable utilization of groundwater resources.

6 CONCLUSIONS

Groundwater plays an important role in urban water supply in northern China. Serious over-exploitation of groundwater has created environmental problems in some cities. Some measures for groundwater protection have been taken. These include economizing on water usage, regulation of groundwater levels, making full use of artificial recharge, pollution control and strengthening management of groundwater resources. The cities in northern China cannot develop further unless groundwater is used in a sustainable way.

REFERENCES

Fei Jin 1988. Resources in the North China Plain. *Environmental Geology and Water Sciences*, New York, Springer International, 12(1), 63-67.
Han Zaisheng 1994. Classification of Groundwater Resources and Categorization of Exploration Level. *Hydrogeology and Engineering Geology*, Beijing, China. Vol. 21, No. 2, 31-33.
Ji Chuanmao, Hou Jingyan & Wang Zhaoxin 1996. *Groundwater Development in the World and Guidelines for International Cooperation*. Seismological Press, Beijing.
Shi Zhenhua and Li Chuanyao 1993. *The Manual of Urban Groundwater Engineering and Management*. Construction Press of China.
Yin Changping, Sun Tingfang, Jin Liangyu, Wen Tingzuo and Long Shaodu 1993. *Exploration and Evaluation of Groundwater Well Fields*. Geological Publishing House, Beijing, China.

Hydrogeology of the Kearney, Nebraska, wellfield

William E. Kelly
School of Engineering, Catholic University of America, Washington, D.C., USA

Mohammad F. Dahab
Department of Civil Engineering, University of Nebraska, Lincoln, Nebr., USA

ABSTRACT: Ground water contamination caused the city of Kearney, Nebraska to move its primary ground water supply to an island in the Platte River. Recently, the island wellfield was expanded and a study was undertaken to determine the maximum yield of the wellfield and what alternatives the city has to further increase its supply. The yield of the wellfield is controlled by flow in the Platte River. Detailed water level, temperature, pumpage, and stage data were collected for the years 1990 -1992 and used to estimate the maximum sustained yield of the wellfield. At the same time, alternative sites away from the river were studied to see if they could be used to augment the city supply during periods of low or no river recharge. Extensive numerical flow and transport modeling was done to study the yield of the wellfield under various river flow scenarios.

1 INTRODUCTION

The City of Kearney, Nebraska depends entirely on ground water for its public water supply. Originally, the city's wells were located in the city proper but yield and quality problems led to establishment of its main wellfield on an island in the Platte River.

In assessing the capability of the wellfield to meet the city's long-term needs, both the quantity and quality of the supply must be evaluated. The yield of the wellfield is heavily dependent on flow conditions in the Platte River. In the event that the river becomes dry for a period of time, or the flow in the river is confined to channels remote from the wellfield, excessive drawdowns can be expected.

During periods of little or no flow in the Platte, there is also the possibility that poor quality ground water - primarily high nitrate ground water from north of the river - could invade the wellfield. The purpose of this study was to evaluate the hydrogeology of the wellfield as a basis for determining the long-term yield with respect to both quantity and quality of the water supply.

2 BACKGROUND

The wellfield is located on the western end of what is known as Killgore Island in the Platte River about

1.2 km southeast of Kearney, Nebraska. The island is bounded by two branches of the Middle Channel of the Platte River; the two branches are referred to herein as the north and south branches. There are currently 12 supply wells with 6 having been installed in 1983 and 6 in 1992. The island is underlain by coarse alluvial materials filling the Platte River Valley. The alluvium is approximately 15 m thick and is underlain by the Ogallala Formation (Sheurs 1956). The Ogallala is relatively fine grained and all of the supply wells are screened from the base of the alluvium through about one-half the aquifer thickness (Miller and Associates 1992).

3 AQUIFER PROPERTIES

3.1 *Pump test results*

In 1983, Well 83-1 was pump tested (Layne Western 1983). This well is located on the north side of the island adjacent to the north branch. For pump testing, four observation wells were installed and 83-1 was pumped at a constant rate of 0.095 m^3/s for two days. Two of the observation wells were located on a line parallel to the river and two perpendicular to the river. Water levels in the river and the aquifer were approximately the same at the

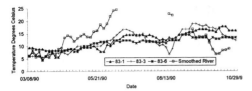

Figure 1. Temperature data 1990.

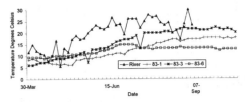

Figure 2. Temperature data 1991.

start of the test. Drawdowns in the pumping well and the observation wells leveled off after one day of pumping, indicating recharge from the north branch of the river.

Analysis of the equilibrium drawdown results using the method of Schaefer and Kaser (1965) yielded a transmissivity of 2,700 m^2/day and an "a" distance of 76 m. Well 83-1 is about 72 m from the edge of the north branch and these results indicate a highly permeable aquifer in essentially full hydraulic connection with the Platte River.

3.2 Temperature data analysis

Temperature data are commonly used to characterize the connection between surface and ground water. During this study, temperature data were collected for the north branch through most of 1990 and 1991. Surface elevations and river temperatures were measured from a bridge to the island across the north branch about 1 km northeast of 83-1.

Temperature in the aquifer lags behind the temperature changes in the river, following the expected sinusoidal pattern observed with induced infiltration (Todd 1980). However, important departures from this pattern occur during periods of low flow when one or both of the branches go dry. When the branch adjacent to a production well goes dry in the summer months, the temperature of the well drops reflecting the loss of recharge of warm river water.

In the wellfield, the temperature behavior of wells along the south and north branches is clearly different. In the summer of 1990, all pumpage on the island was from Wells 83-1 through 83-6.

During this period, the flow on the Platte was low. Conditions on the south branch were not observed although it was probably dry. Measurements of surface water elevation and temperature were made from the bridge across the north branch. The north branch was observed to be dry on most of the measurement days and flow at the Kearney gage

during July was less than 8.5 m^3/s much of this time. When the north branch went dry, the temperature in 83-1, which had been rising following the seasonal trend in the surface water temperature, stabilized and then dropped to a new equilibrium reflecting the loss of recharge (Figure 1). The drop in 83-3 which is only about 38 m from the north branch was even sharper. When flow returned to the branch for a few days in August, this was immediately reflected by increasing temperatures in well 83-1.

Well 83-6 is adjacent to the south branch and about 1 km east of 83-1. Conditions on the south branch were not observed in 1990 but were probably dry from May onwards. The temperature first increased in May and then leveled off until it increased in August, apparently reflecting recharge from high flows on the Platte.

In August of 1991, flow conditions were again low, although the north branch was only observed to be dry on August 26 and 30. Low flows persisted through September but there still was flow in the north branch. During this period, no-flow conditions on the south branch were observed for much of the period starting in late June. In late June, the temperature in 83-6 peaked and then leveled off (Figure 2). However, the temperature in Wells 83-1 and 83-3 continued to increase until the north branch went dry in September.

3.3 Flow data

The river flow data are from a U.S. Geological Survey gaging station located 1.2 km west of the island. Flow in the vicinity of the island can be quite variable and appears to control the yield of the wellfield. During extreme low flow periods, flow is restricted to the Middle Channel of the Platte which is about 600 m south of the wellfield. As the flow drops during periods of low flow, the south branch goes dry and eventually, if the flow is low enough, the north branch goes dry. For wellfield yield, the critical condition occurs when the south branch is

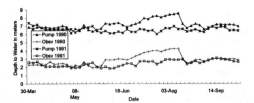

Figure 3. Water level data.

dry and the north branch is going dry. Measurements of surface elevations at the bridge and observations of the north branch flows were correlated with flows at the Kearney gage. No-flow conditions were not observed above about 8.5 m³/s at the Kearney gage. At higher flows, there was a good correlation between the elevation at the bridge and the Kearney gage flow.

3.4 *Water levels*

Figure 3 shows the depth to water data for Well 83- and observation well #1 which is located about 46 m north of 83-1, for the summers of 1990 and 1991. The north branch went dry in late June 1990. During this period, Well 83-1 was pumping continuously at about 0.095 m³/s and water levels declined continuously indicating that water was coming primarily from ground water storage. During the period water levels declined until flow returned to the branch in August. In 1991, the north branch had flow and the water levels did not decline for any extended period (Figure 3).

4 ANALYSIS

Conditions at Well 83-1 were used to develop and test a preliminary model for estimating the yield of the existing wellfield. Well 83-1, as constructed, is highly efficient. The radius of the well is approximately 53 cm and the drawdown due to the aquifer alone after one day of pumping would be approximately 3.11 m versus the 3.93 m actually observed.

The well was not tested at different rates so a well loss coefficient could not be calculated. However, theoretical corrections for dewatering and partial penetration suggest the contribution to total drawdown from well loss is very small.

With water in both branches, the saturated thickness at the island wellfield is controlled by the

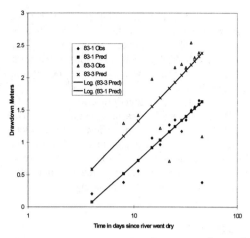

Figure 4. Drawdowns after flow ceases in north branch.

stage in the river. At the time of the pump test, the stage on the north branch was 644.6 m which corresponded to a saturated thickness of 14.3 m. After one day of pumping at 0.095 m³/s the drawdown was 3.9 m, leaving about 4.6 m of saturated aquifer above the well screen.

As the flow drops, the south branch goes dry leaving a single line of recharge - the north branch. During continuous pumping, the wells furthest from the north branch would be expected to experience excessive drawdowns first. This situation was analyzed using an image well model with a single recharge boundary. With recharge only from the north branch, pumping from the wellfield can continue but at a reduced rate. Wells 83-2, 83-4 and 83-6 would be most affected since they are furthest from the recharge line. When there is no flow in either branch, the yield of the wellfield is dependent on storage. Data from the summer of 1990 indicated that withdrawals cannot be sustained for longer than about 30 days.

The data for the extended period of no-flow in 1990 were analyzed to estimate the yield for Well 83-1. The depth to ground water with the north branch flowing just before it goes dry is approximately 6.86 m. When the branch goes dry, drawdowns increase. The drawdown on June 28, 1990 was 6.88 m and was taken as representative of the drawdown just before the north branch went dry. The additional drawdown occurring due to loss of recharge is plotted versus log time in Figure 4. The top of the screen is approximately 9.45 m below the measuring point. If a limit of 1.0 m above the screen is taken as controlling the yield, then the maximum drawdown is 6.45 m or approximately 1.68 m of additional drawdown. Thus approximately 45 days after flow stops in the north branch, the elevation would have dropped to the limiting elevation.

For Well 83-3 the starting drawdown is about 7.32 m. The depth from the measuring point to the top of the screen is about 9.45 m. Allowing for a safety factor of one meter, the maximum drawdown would be 8.45 m or an additional 1.13 m. From Figure 4, the critical drawdown would be reached after only about ten days of continuous pumping.

5 DISCUSSSION

Analysis of data gathered during this study indicates that the yield of the Kearney wellfield is almost entirely dependent on the flow conditions in the Platte River as reflected in the flow in the branches on the north and south sides of the island.

Analysis of pump test data shows that a "recharge line" and the location of the north branch are coincident, indicating good hydraulic connection. Temperature data further demonstrate a close hydraulic connection between the river and the wellfield. Wells on the north and south sides of the island demonstrate distinctly different temperature behavior, reflecting different flow conditions on the north and south sides of the island during periods of declining flow.

While flow continues in the north branch, the drawdowns in Well 83-1 can be modeled with a single image well representing recharge from the river. With flow in the north branch, pumping from the well can be sustained at a rate of 0.095 m³/s. The limit for some flow in the north branch corresponds to a flow at the Kearney gage of about 8.5 m³/s under river conditions in 1990.

For analyzing yield after the north branch goes dry, the water level is taken to represent the equilibrium groundwater level at the branch's low flow stage. The additional drawdown is plotted versus time since the branch went dry to estimate the time to reach a critical drawdown defining the minimum pumping level.

Records for two wells were used to estimate the maximum period that the wellfield can support these withdrawals without recharge. For the two wells, the periods were approximately 45 and 10 days for Wells 83-1 and 83-3, respectively. This means that the yield of the wellfield would decline after ten days.

An investigation of alternate sites indicated that there were no sites with acceptable yields in areas where water quality could be assured. Ground water which is not influenced by river recharge generally has high nitrate levels. The wells in the city proper appear to have the best yield characteristics and one strategy would be to maintain and protect these wells and use them to augment the island wells during periods of prolonged low or no river recharge. Blending of the water would allow quality to be maintained for some period of time. Other alternatives are being evaluated.

REFERENCES

Layne Western 1983, *Hydrologic engineering investigation city of Kearney*, Kearney, *Nebraska*, August.

Miller and Associates 1992, *Phase I wellfield research program*, Kearney, Nebraska, May.

Shaefer, E.J. and Kaser, P. 1965, Graphical aids for the solution of formulas used in analyzing induced infiltration tests, *Ohio Department Natural Resources, Division Water Technology Report 6*

Scheurs, R.I. 1956, Geology and ground-water resources of Buffalo County and adjacent areas Nebraska, *U.S. Geological Survey Water-Supply Paper 1358.*

Todd, D.K. 1980 *Groundwater Hydrology*, 2nd Edition: New York, John Wiley & Sons.

Sustainable management of a coastal urban aquifer

Hugo A. Loáiciga
Department of Geography, University of California, Santa Barbara, Calif., USA

ABSTRACT: Sustainable aquifer management occurs when (1) the rate of aquifer exploitation maintains aquifer storage within pre-specified and adequate levels, (2) ground water quality meets acceptable criteria, and (3) negative long-term environmental impacts associated with ground water pumping are avoided. It is demonstrated in this article that sustainable aquifer management is compatible with criteria of economic efficiency, as long as the natural process of ground water recharge is properly accounted for and aquifer pumping and storage are constrained to meet conditions (1)-(3) cited above. A model for sustainable aquifer management is developed in this work, and key economic and hydrogeologic variables defining feasible ground water pumping strategies are identified and quantified. Ground water pumping in a layered aquifer of central California illustrates the principles of sustainable ground water management laid out in this work.

1 INTRODUCTION

The roots of sustainability as a global paradigm in water resources utilization can be traced back to the Mar del Plata (Argentina) 1977 United Nations Water Conference (United Nations 1978). There, a consensus arose as to the importance of assuring long-term water supplies of suitable quality to all peoples. Expressed in terms of assured and suitable water supplies for human consumption and the global economy, water management took a crude, anthropocentric view. Ever since, water management has evolved to encompass environmental and aesthetic concerns. Beyond the understandable priority lent to humans and the economy, water management today seeks to preserve, and restore, the natural landscape and its flora and fauna. It is in the context of this harmonious human-environment coexistence that the concept of sustainability has become the paradigm of water management in the latter part of this century. Ground water exploitation, in particular, plays an important role in sustainable water management, as it constitutes about one half of the estimated 3,500 km^3 of water used by humans currently on a global basis every year (Zektser & Loáiciga 1993, Cohen 1995, Loáiciga et al. 1996).

Many of the qualities associated with "sustainable" water management, such as adequate water on a long-term basis and environmental protection, are, however, too broad to serve as guidelines upon which to devise specific aquifer management strategies. As an alternative, we seek to reconcile criteria of economic efficiency with the renewable nature of most ground water in the quest to develop sustainable aquifer management principles. It is our view that sustainable water management will not take hold in practice unless economic criteria are allowed their vital role. This requires recognition of the fact that water has a market price and a production and opportunity cost whatever its intended use. Vague criteria, such as potential tradeoffs caused by water consumption today at the expense of future consumption are of little utility in framing sustainable aquifer management strategies. Thus, sustainable ground water management is posed in this work as a problem involving the exploitation of a renewable resource, i.e., ground water, subject to constraints on pumping rates and aquifer storage. Such constraints must be specified externally, by administrative, legal, environmental, or institutional sources and agents, and it is they that ensure sustainability of aquifer management.

2 HYDRAULICS OF RENEWABLE GROUND WATER

Consider the situation illustrated in Figure 1, where a confined aquifer with a hydraulic head h_2 is overlain by an unconfined aquifer whose water table is at an elevation h_3. The storage coefficients of the unconfined and confined aquifers are S_3 and S_2, respectively. A horizontal aquitard, of thickness b_2 and hydraulic conductivity K_2, separates the confined and unconfined aquifers. The unconfined and confined aquifers are recharged by a bedrock aquifer that has a hydraulic head h_1 and storage coefficient S_1. A vertical aquitard, of thickness b_1 and hydraulic conductivity K_1, separates the bedrock aquifer from the unconfined and confined aquifers. The situation depicted in Figure 1 is a simplified representation of the hydraulic interaction and ground water recharge observed in coastal aquifers of central California (and other parts of the world): a coastal range formed by fractured rocks serves as a conduit for deep ground water recharge to confined and unconfined aquifers, where the latter, in addition, receives recharge from channel seepage (represented by r_3 in Figure 1). The bedrock aquifer is recharged by percolating precipitation in the highlands (r_1 in Figure 1). Typically, the confined aquifer, due to its better water quality, is the source of water supply to coastal communities. The pumping rate of the confined aquifer is represented by Q in Figure 1. The relative magnitudes of the hydraulic heads in the unconfined and confined aquifers determine the direction of water exchange among them. Discharge is typically from the coastal aquifers to the ocean (of water density $\rho_S = 1.025$ g/cm^3) , that has a mean seal level elevation, h_S, although this can be reversed by low hydraulic heads in the aquifers. The Darcian flows between the coastal aquifers and the ocean are regulated by the intervening hydraulic heads and the thickness (b_S) and hydraulic conductivity (K_S) of the ocean bottom sediments. The rates of recharge r_1 and r_3 are a function of the amount of yearly precipitation, but they also depend on the hydraulic status of the aquifers receiving percolating water and channel seepage. The dimensions of the aquifers are denoted according to the notation of Figure 1, where it is assumed that the width of aquifers perpendicular to the plane of the Figure is W. The following system of differential equations describes the time evolution of hydraulic heads (h) in the various aquifers of Figure 1:

$$\begin{bmatrix} \dot{h}_1 \\ \dot{h}_2 \\ \dot{h}_3 \end{bmatrix} = \begin{bmatrix} a & b & c \\ d & e & f \\ g & k & m \end{bmatrix} \begin{bmatrix} h_1 \\ h_2 \\ h_3 \end{bmatrix} + \begin{bmatrix} n \\ p \\ q \end{bmatrix} \qquad (1)$$

in which $\dot{h}$ denotes the rate of time change of a hydraulic head, and the parameters a, b, c, d, e, f, g, k, m, n, p, q are given by the following:
$a = -K_1L_{V2}/(S_1L_1b_1)-K_1L_{V3}/(S_1L_1b_1)$; $b = K_1L_{V2}/(S_1L_1b_1)$; $c = K_1L_{V3}/(S_1L_1b_1)$; $d = K_1L_{V2}/(S_2L_2b_1)$; $e = -K_2/(S_2b_2)-K_1L_{V2}/(S_2L_2b_1)-K_SL_{V2}/(S_2L_2b_S)$; $f = K_2/(S_2b_2)$; $g = K_1L_{V3}/(S_3L_2b_1)$; $k = K_2/(S_3b_2)$; $m = -K_2/(S_3b_2)-K_SL_S/(S_3L_2b_S)-K_1L_{V3}/(S_3L_2b_1)$; $n = r_1/S_1$; $p = K_SL_{V2}\,\rho_Sh_S/(S_2L_2b_S)-Q/(S_2L_2W)$; $q = K_SL_S\rho_Sh_S/(S_3L_2b_S) + r_3/S_3$.

Notice that in equation (1) the vector components n, p, and q contain the external stresses and variables that drive aquifer dynamics, i.e., the recharge and pumping rate.

The system of differential equations in (1) can be written in compact form as follows:

$$\dot{h} = Ah + B(t) \qquad (2)$$

with initial condition $h(t=0) = h_0$. The (3 x 3) coefficient matrix A is (approximately) constant (see further elaboration in Section 4) while the (3 x 1) "forcing" vector B can vary with time. Letting E(t) be the 3 x 3 matrix whose i-th (i = 1, 2, or 3) column equals $e^{\lambda_i t}v_i$, where λ_i and v_i denote an eigenvalue and eigenvector of the matrix A, respectively, it can be shown that the solution of equation (2) is given by the following expression:

$$h(t) = E(t)E(0)^{-1}h_0 + E(t)\int_0^t E(\tau)^{-1}B(\tau)d\tau \quad (3)$$

Equation (3) gives a close-form solution for aquifer hydraulic heads as a function of time, aquifer recharge, and pumping rate. The pumping rate is a decision variable. Aquifer recharge is largely driven by climate, and thus, it is subject to the stochastic variations in precipitation. The next section explains the coupling of aquifer hydraulics and management objectives to complete the sustainable optimization model of this work.

3 SUSTAINABLE AQUIFER MANAGEMENT

3.1 Aquifer Hydraulics

Sustainable aquifer exploitation occurs when a

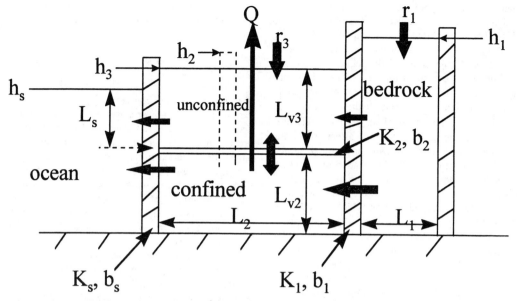

Figure 1. Diagram of the coastal aquifer system.

pumping rate (constant or variable) is applied over a predetermined time period without negative environmental or water resource impacts. Furthermore, our definition of sustainability incorporates criteria of economic efficiency. Barring political initiative tailored to exempt specific aquifers from ground water withdrawal, environmental and water resource protection schemes that disregard the economic benefits derived from ground water use ultimately cause more harm than good. Thus the emphasis in this study is to reconcile environmental and economic concerns. An obvious question is whether or not such dual objective of pairing seemingly conflicting goals is possible. The answer, in our opinion, is positive, provided that there is a full understanding of what economic benefits are being traded off for the environmental benefits that accrue from constraints imposed on ground water withdrawal. Ultimately, the balance between economic and environmental objectives must be judged from a broader perspective than mathematical modeling can allow, such as considerations of social welfare and the changing social, economic, and political landscape of a region or nation. A key to developing truly optimal sustainable aquifer exploitation policies, it appears, is to have adequate quantification of economic, water resource, and environmental impacts , and making those impacts known to the public. Final choices among possible

policies must be resolved through established democratic channels.

The model for sustainable aquifer exploitation presented below, thus, must be seen as a potentially useful tool in the larger process of ground water management. To this end, the model is designed to provide feasible solutions. More specifically, the economic benefits stemming from aquifer exploitation will be shown to depend on the initial aquifer storage, pumping rate, the time horizon over which the aquifer is pumped, the market price of ground water, the cost of producing ground water, the natural ground water recharge, and all constraints that ensure environmental viability. Thus, this study strives to identify critical parameters that influence the economic and water resources performance of an aquifer pumping scheme. This information is then available to the public and decision maker who make the final choices.

3.2 The objective function and constraints

The objective function of the sustainable aquifer management problem maximizes the present value of net revenue that accrues from extracting and selling ground water over a time period. The search for a constant pumping rate that achieves such optimal revenue, however, is constrained by bounds imposed on the pumping rate and on aquifer hydraulic head to meet sustainability criteria. It was

341

stated above that only the confined aquifer, with hydraulic head h_2, is subject to pumping. The head h_2 can be obtained directly from equation (3), and is equal to the second row of the vectorial expression on the right-hand side of that equation. The key environmental constraint on the confined hydraulic head is that it be equal to or larger than the fresh-water equivalent of the ocean hydraulic head (= ρ_S h_S, where ρ_S is the density of sea water). In addition, pumping in the confined aquifer affects the water table elevation in the overlaying unconfined aquifer, h_3: as the confined hydraulic head drops, leakage through the horizontal aquitard may be induced vertically downward. This lowers the water table level in the unconfined aquifer, which must also be at all times equal to or larger than the fresh-water equivalent of the ocean hydraulic head. Notice that the water table elevation, h_3, is given directly by the third row of the right-hand-side of equation (3).

Let P = market price of water per unit of water; C = d^* - $b^*\cdot$ h_2 , the cost of pumping one unit of ground water when the hydraulic head in the confined aquifer is h_2, where d^* and b^* are constants; s = the real discount rate; $f_S(s)$ = the probability density function of the discount rate; $f_R(r)$ the probability density function of the recharge rate r_1 (this is the most important recharge component, while r_3 is negligible in relative terms); NR = present value of the net revenue stream accruing from aquifer exploitation; $\Pi(h_2)$ = P - C(h_2) = the net revenue per unit of ground water sold. The net revenue $\Pi(h_2)$ is a function of the hydraulic head in the confined aquifer, which, in turn, depends on the pumping rate Q and recharge rate in a nonlinear fashion. The objective function, F, of the sustainable management problem represents the maximization of the present value of expected net revenue. Maximization is with respect to pumping rate Q. F is given by (t >> 0):

$$F = \int_0^\infty \int_0^\infty \int_0^t \Pi[Q,r']Qe^{-s't'}f_S(s')f_R(r')d^3x \quad (4)$$

(where d^3x = dt' ds' dr'). F is subject to the following constraints on the expected values of aquifer hydraulic heads (denoted by the overbar on h_1 and h_2) :

$$\bar{h}_2(t) \geq \rho_S\, h_S \quad (5)$$

$$\bar{h}_3(t) \geq \rho_S\, h_S \quad (6)$$

The gamma distribution is a suitable choice for the probability density function of the real interest rate:

$$f_S(s) = \frac{\varphi^{\gamma+1}s^\gamma e^{-\varphi s}}{\Gamma(\gamma+1)} \quad (7)$$

in which φ and γ are constants, and $\Gamma(\ )$ denotes the gamma function. The seepage recharge r_3 is treated deterministically and set equal to 1% of mean annual precipitation. The recharge r_1 is a fraction of the annual precipitation in any given year. Specifically, r_1 = f_1 P, where f_1 = 0.15. Therefore, the probability distribution of the recharge r_1 is obtained by scaling the distribution of precipitation. Precipitation follows a gamma distribution with mean of 0.46 m/yr and a standard deviation of 0.25 m/yr. The status of aquifer hydraulic heads affects mainly the recharge to the unconfined aquifer. Given, however, that seepage through channel beds to the underlying aquifer is relatively small, treating the recharge r_3 as a fixed percentage of mean annual precipitation is adequate while introducing significant computational simplifications.

3.3 Model parameters

The model developed above is applied to the storage unit II aquifer of Santa Barbara, California (Santa Barbara County Water Agency, 1996). Table 1 shows a list of model parameters that appear in equation (4) and their dimensions. These parameter characterize: (1) hydrogeologic processes of aquifer flow; (2) economics of ground water extraction and marketing; (3) stochastic variability of discount recharge; and (4) aquifer geometry. Table 2 shows initial hydraulic heads. Four alternative sets of initial hydraulic heads were used in solving the optimization problem embodied by equation (4). The purpose was to ascertain the role of antecedent hydrologic conditions in long-term aquifer management .

4 SELECTED RESULTS

Solutions to problem (4) were obtained for four levels of initial hydraulic heads, as follows:

Notice that the sea level h_S = 75 m above the datum, which in this case coincides with the bottom of the confined aquifer. Note also that the thickness of the unconfined aquifer L_{V3} = h_3 - (L_{V2} + b_2), and it

Table 1. Parameters of the management problem.

Parameter	Value (or range)	Dimension
$b*$	9.0×10^3	$/m
$d*$	10^6	$
P	8.0×10^5	$/10^3$ AF
h_0	$\geq h_S \rho_S = 76.875$	m
γ	0.69315	none
φ	15.625	none
$S_1 = S_3$	0.1	none
S_2	0.005	none
K_1	0.5	m day^{-1}
K_2	0.1	m day^{-1}
K_S	0.01	m day^{-1}
r_3	0.02	m yr^{-1}
f_1	0.15	none
L_1	0.75×10^3	m
L_2	2.5×10^3	m
L_{V2}	50	m
L_{V3}	variable	m
L_S	20	m
W	5.0×10^3	m
b_1	10	m
b_2	5	m
b_S	5	m

Table 2. Initial conditions in aquifer system.

Code	Initial head (in m)		
	h_1^0	h_2^0	h_3^0
$h_0 = 5$	150	135	130
$h_0 = 3$	150	125	130
$h_0 = 2$	125	100	110
$h_0 = 1$	125	90	110

varies with the elevation of the water table h_3. In each simulation L_{V3} is set equal to the initial water table elevation (h_3^0) minus 55 (= L_{V2} + b_2). Initial condition 5 represents aquifer conditions at high storage.

Initial conditions 3, 2, and 1, on the other hand, initialize the aquifer system at progressively lower storage relative to initial condition 5. The planning horizon duration t in equation (4) was set arbitrarily large (i.e., $t \rightarrow \infty$)

Figure 2 displays the results for each set of initial conditions. The following conclusions are drawn:

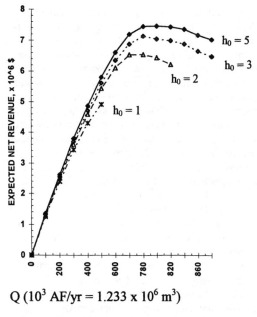

$$Q (10^3 \text{ AF/yr} = 1.233 \times 10^6 \text{ m}^3)$$

Figure 2. Present value of expected net revenue as a function of pumping rate (Q) and initial conditions.

1. The present value of expected net revenue(in 10^6 US $) increases with increasing pumping rate (pumping rate is expressed here in 10^3 AF/yr, where 1 AF = 1 acre foot = 1,233 m^3) over a wide range of pumping rates;

2. For initial conditions 2, 3, and 5, the expected next revenue shows a well-defined maximizing pumping rate; the expected revenue declines once that pumping rate is exceeded;

3. For initial condition 1, synonymous to low storage in the aquifer system, the expected revenue increases monotonically with increasing pumping rate; beyond a pumping rate of 550 AF/yr, at which the expected net revenue is highest, hydraulic heads become infeasible;

4. The feasible range of pumping rates in Figure 2 is determined by constraints on hydraulic heads h_2 and h_3; in all cases, these constraints occur at the points where the expected net revenue graphs are cutoff, i.e., at pumping rates of about 550, 800, 900 and 900 AF/yr for initial conditions 1, 2, 3, and 5, respectively.

5 CONCLUSIONS

A model for sustainable ground water management has been developed and implemented in this study.

A definition of sustainable aquifer management implied by the principles of this article can be summarized as follows: " Sustainable aquifer management is a strategy for ground water pumping (and recharge) that can be maintained over a specified period of time, and which meets economic, environmental, and institutional criteria with a high probability". This definition stresses key factors in sustainable management: (1) the time element over which implementation of sustainable aquifer management occurs; (2) criteria to be met, which involve economic efficiency as well as environmental constraints; (3) the stochastic nature of ground water recharge, which is driven by climate; (4) the statistical fluctuations of the real interest rate. Factors (3) and (4) imply that due to the inherent statistical nature of sustainable management, it must be posed as a probabilistic problem. A mathematical model for sustainable aquifer management has been developed in this article. It includes stochastic elements, economic criteria, and the hydraulic dynamics of a coastal aquifer system. Environmental criteria have been imposed via constraints on hydraulic heads. Preliminary results were obtained for a set of initial aquifer conditions. Our results show well defined optima of expected net revenue for given aquifer dynamics and other factors considered in the mathematical model of sustainable management. Further calculations and optimizations will be pursued in the future, aimed at assessing the sensitivity of results to model parameters.

REFERENCES

Cohen, J.E. 1995. *How many people can the earth support?*. New York: Norton & Co.
Loáiciga, H.A., J.B. Valdes, R. Vogel, J. Garvey & H. Schwarz. 1996. Global warming and the hydrologic cycle. *Journal of Hydrology*, 174:83-128.
Santa Barbara County. 1996. *Ground Water Resources Report, Santa Barbara, California*: Santa Barbara County Water Agency, Santa Barbara, California.
United Nations. 1978. Water development and management: *Procs. of the United Nations Water Conference*, Mar del Plata, Argentina. Oxford, United Kingdom: Pergamon Press.
Zektser, I.S. & H.A. Loáiciga. 1993. Ground water fluxes in the hydrologic cycle: past, present, and future. *Journal of Hydrology*, 144:405-427.

Falling groundwater levels of Ljubljana aquifer

Z. Mikulič
Hydrometeorological Institute of Slovenia, Ljubljana, Slovenia

ABSTRACT: Ljubljana, the capital of Slovenia, is situated at the southern part of the Ljubljana Plain, the most important aquifer on national scale. The pumping of groundwater for organised water supply started in 1890 and ever since the groundwater level has been decreasing for various reasons, as described in the paper. The fact that the city is sitting on an aquifer influenced the urbanisation greatly, leaving large area open for the protection zone of the Kleče pumping station. This policy secured for to the city drinking water of superb quality, fed to the water supply system for most of the time in its natural form without additional treatment.

1 HISTORY OF LJUBLJANA WATER SUPPLY

In the mid 19th century the main Vienna-Trieste railway line reached Ljubljana, being at that time small provincial capital of the Province of Carinthia. It boosted the industry growth and influenced the way of life of the population like no other event in the history of the town. At the beginning, the other public services could not cope with the pace of development. The citizens still had to fetch water from open wells. During dry seasons the public wells dried out, while the owners of private wells cut the supply to the other users.

The frequent shortages of water caused outcry of the general public, forcing the authorities to decree in 1883 that Ljubljana should have modern water supply (Sonc 1934). The matter was obviously pressing, since after some deliberations the Water Supply Committee ordered geological investigation by the Imperial Geological Survey in Vienna. That institution paid due attention to the problem, and the director conducted the investigation and prepared the geological report (Stur 1887). Several options were studied, including use of water from the springs in the Ljubljana vicinity and the pumping of the groundwater from the Ljubljana aquifer. In 1888 the Committee came to the decision to construct a pumping station at Kleče, some three kilometres north of the town. Following the completion of design (Smreker 1888), construction started the same year.

On 17th May 1890 Ljubljana Water Supply Company begun to deliver water to 606 out of 900 households (Karpe 1990), and ever since the Kleče pumping station has been in operation. In the first year of operation the groundwater was abstracted from the aquifer at a rate of 0.016 m^3/sec. It had increased to 1.39 m^3/sec by upgrading the Kleče pumping station and introduction of other pumping stations. Nevertheless, all the time the original pumping site has been the major supplier of the water, still accounting for one half of the city's consumption.

2 HYDROGEOLOGIC SETTING

The Ljubljana Plain is a roughly 15 km long and 4 km wide flat area, gently sloping to the east. It is a young tectonic depression filled with gravel and cemented sediments to a thickness of up to 100 m, as shown in the cross section of Figure 1. Subsidence started at the beginning of the Quaternary and, a varying rate has continued to the present time. During the glacial periods of Pleistocene, the glacial streams deposited gravel material from the frontal moraines of the Julian Alps foothills (Žlebnik 1971). During interglacial stages the degradation was the prevailing process. The streams cut their beds into the last already cemented fill, while the ground surface weathered to clay and clayey gravel. Apparently, by analogy with neighbouring plains, there are four fills corresponding to four glaciations. The top fills are

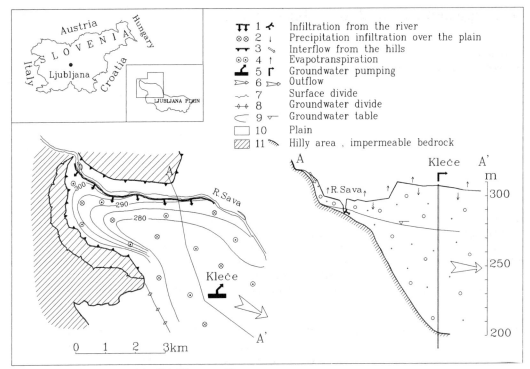

Figure 1. Conceptual model of Ljubljana aquifer.

quite well investigated, while the data on older ones are rather scarce, due to the insufficient number of deep boreholes.

At the surface of the major part of the plain is the Pleistocene Gravel terrace. Only close to the Sava river is low Holocene terrace, 0.5 to 2 km wide. Both terraces consist of sandy gravel, the thickness of fills varying between 4 and 13 m. The gravel is covered by only a thin layer of humus, so the infiltration of rainfall into the aquifer is high. The older Pleistocene fills beneath the gravel are cemented to a variable degree. Cemented zones are not very extensive. Also, the layers of clay separating the fills are missing or interrupted in most parts of the aquifer, due to erosion prior to the accumulation of the next fill. The shallow clay layer is continuous only in the western part of the plain in a one kilometre wide belt along the hilly area. The discontinuity of clay and cemented zones enables free circulation of water through the entire aquifer.

The bedrock to the gravel is impermeable Permian-Carboniferous clayey shale, quartz sandstone and conglomerate. Along the Sava river the bedrock is shallow, at depth only 5 to 15 m. For short reaches, the river bed is even cut into clayey shale. Towards the middle of the plain the bedrock steeply drops, and the thickness of gravel increases, reaching maximum of 101 m at Kleče pumping station. To the east, the depth to the bedrock decreases again, being about 50 m over the major part of the plain.

Most of the aquifer comprises sandy gravel, an excellent water collector. The water table is continuous over the entire area. Along the western hilly area, perched shallow groundwater overflows the edge of the clay layer into the deeper main water body. The groundwater regime is controlled by boundary conditions similar to those in other Slovenian intergranular porosity aquifers (Mikulič 1992). As shown in Figure 1, the inflow is by drainage from the Sava river, infiltration of precipitation from the ground surface, and interflow from the hilly area bordering the plain. The total flow through the aquifer is estimated to be roughly 5 m^3/sec. The drainage from the river contributes about 50%, precipitation infiltration about 40%, while the interflow from the hills amounts to less than 10 % (Brilly 1989). The losses and outflows are by evapotranspiration, pumping of groundwater and outflow from the system by draining into the river at the downstream end of the aquifer.

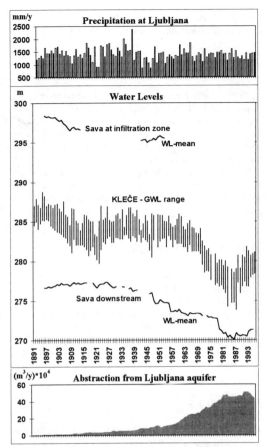

Figure 2. Falling groundwater levels of Ljublana aquifer at Kleče pumping station.

3 FALLING GROUNDWATER LEVELS

The groundwater level has been measured daily at Kleče pumping station up to present, since the start of pumping in 1890. The data are kept in the archives of Ljubljana Water Supply Company. Apart from mere tabulation (Sketelj 1974), so far they have not been systematically processed. In Figure 2, groundwater levels are represented by the annual range.

The major factor contributing to falling groundwater table was changes in the river bed of the Sava(Žibrik & Meden 1969, Breznik 1985). In early 1890s the Save, in the reach along the plain, was a typical braided stream, with numerous meanders in a zone wide up to 1.5 km wide, as seen in Figure 3. The altitude of the river bed was quite stable. In the period 1895 to 1908, water flow was channelled by river trainig structures into an artificial narrow bed about 50 m wide. By cutting across the meanders the slope of the stream increased, it became faster and

erosion took place instead of the previous balanced sedimentation - erosion process. By 1922 erosion along the river in the upper part of the plain was coupled with aggradation on the downstream reach. The measured erosion between 1896 and 1922 at the infiltration reach was 4.5 m , causing a fall of water table about 5 m. During the 1923 floods, the high water destroyed the river control structures, and the Sava assumed more natural stable flow. By the early 1950s, the river elevation increased gradually by 2 m, stabilising the groundwater table. In 1952 and 1953 two power schemes were completed on the Sava upstream of Ljubljana, interrupting sediment transport. The erosion started again, this time along the entire reach of the river bordering the aquifer. At first, it caused the groundwater level to fall, as at the turn of the century. In the 1970s and 1980s the influence of the hydropower schemes was enhanced, by dredging of gravel in the stream for construction material, and increased water pumping. All these factors increased the rate of groundwater level fall. The all time minimum was reached in 1987, with the groundwater table about 10 m lower than in the first year of operation of Kleče pumping station.

It is apparent that in a period of one hundred years there was no climatic change regarding the amount of precipitation. The annual rainfall changes modified the groundwater regime in years of excessive draught or anomalous wet seasons The droughts of 1920, 1921 and 1947 caught the management of pumping station by surprise, leaving pumps at Kleče occasionally dry.

The lessons of one hundred years of operation have been taken into account in the most recent period. The river erosion is under control by several low weirs, made of nature-friendly rip-rap. The groundwater level has been rising again, also due to a lower pumping rate. The restructuring of the economy in the nineties, by abandoning resource-wasteful industries, led to decreased water consumption. Nowadays the groundwater level still about 5 m lower than that in 1890.

4 URBAN ASPECTS

The depth to the groundwater table in the urbanised area of Ljubljana is typically between 15 and 25 m. It is deeper than the usual foundation depth of the structures, so the oscillations so far did not cause the type of problems known in some other cities.

The location of the major pumping station at Kleče, close to the city, however, influenced urbanisation greatly in last 100 years. In 19th century Ljubljana was a small town at the foothills of the Castle Hill. The steep wooded hills in the vicinity did not allow the urban area to spread to the east and west. It would be

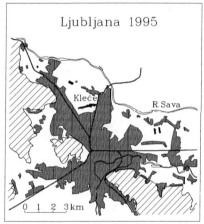

Figure 3. Urbanisation of Ljubljana, as influenced by location of pumping stations.

natural to urbanise the area to the north, in the Ljubljana Plain. This has been blocked by the waterworks of Ljubljana Water Supply Company. As seen in Figure 3, the area of groundwater flow from the Sava river to Kleče has been left uninhabited, to protect the water quality. The total area of the protection zones of all the Ljubljana pumping stations is about 20 km^2, quite a lot compared to 77 km^2 area of entire Ljubljana Plain.

In the 1970s, there was a lot of discussion to find a new source of drinking water for the city. The cost of a new water supply system proved to be prohibitive, so the existing pumping stations remained intact. Sometimes, their location imposes additional costs on the construction projects. For the new motorway, passing just south of Kleče pumping station, costly additional structures were built to prevent infiltration from the road surface into the aquifer.

Certainly, groundwater protection is an obstacle to free city growth, but sometime in the near future it could be regarded as a blessing to have a vast potential recreational zone amidst the very urban area.

5 CONCLUSIONS

For proper aquifer management a good knowledge is required of both the hydrogeological conditions and the sensitivity of the groundwater system to change. The groundwater level in the Ljubljana aquifer has been decreasing mostly due to human intervention into the flow of the Sava river.

The Ljubljana case shows that drinking water is so vital to the city that water protection policy has influenced radically the spatial spread of the urban area.

ACKNOWLEDGEMENTS

The author is grateful to Franc Karpe for interesting discussions and for providing unpublished records of Ljubljana Water Supply Company. The help in data processing by Niko Trišič and Primož Gajsar is appreciated. Vlado Savić is thanked for help in drafting the figures, while Jože Miklavčič helped to produce printouts meeting the requirements set by the publisher.

REFERENCES

Breznik, M. 1985. Outlooks and problems of groundwater use. *Proc. 4th Goljevšeek memorial day*: 301-340. Ljubljana: FAGG&VGI.

Brilly, M. 1989. Groundwater model of Ljubljana aquifer. *Proc. 8th Goljevšeek memorial day*: 404-414. Ljubljana: FAGG&VGI.

Karpe, F. 1990. *Ljubljana water supply company, one hundred years 1890-1990*. Ljubljana: Centenary publication of Ljubljana water supply company.

Mikuliè, Z. 1992. Hydrological aspects of groundwater protection in Slovenia. *Ujma* 6: 133-139.

Sketelj, J. 1974. *Development of Ljubljana waterworks and statistical data 1890-1971*. Ljubljana: FAGG.

Smreker, O. 1888. *Design project of Ljubljana waterworks* (unpublished internal report in archives of Ljubljana water supply company). Ljubljana.

Sonc, S. 1934. Development of Ljubljana water supply company. *Kronika slovenskih mest* 1: 310-312.

Stur, D. 1887. *To the question of water supply of the provincial capital Ljubljana*. Vienna: Imperial Geology Survey.

Žibrik, K. & Meden, S. 1969. *Hydrological state of existing groundwater regime at Ljubljana plain* (internal report). Ljubljana: Hydrometeorological Institute of Slovenia.

Žlebnik, L. 1971. Pleistocene of Kranj, Sora and Ljubljana plain. *Geologija* 14: 5-50.

Groundwater in the Urban Environment: Problems, Processes and Management, Chilton et al. (eds)
© *1997 Balkema, Rotterdam, ISBN 90 5410 837 1*

Groundwater contamination control at an urban well field in Vilnius, Lithuania

B. Paukstys & N. Seirys
Hydrogeological Company GROTA, Vilnius, Lithuania

ABSTRACT: The results of a hydrogeological study carried out in the vicinity of a well field located in a heavily urbanised area of Vilnius city, Lithuania are described in the paper. Oil storage and a mound of salt/sand mixture are located upstream of the well field at a distance of less than 1 km, and they are the main sources of soil and groundwater contamination. As a result of human activity shallow groundwater is contaminated by chloride and hydrocarbons over an area of more than 200,000 m². A polluted groundwater plume has been detected 250 m east of the well field and is migrating towards a discharge zone. The contaminated shallow aquifer is hydraulically connected with the productive aquifer, and traces of pollution are also observed in the productive aquifer. A hydraulic barrier consisting of 6 wells has been installed upstream, between the pollution sources and the well field. Pumping tests on the barrier wells have been performed. The data collected prove that it is possible to prevent polluted groundwater from seeping into the productive aquifer containing the well field by artificially changing the hydraulic relationship between the aquifers.

1 DESCRIPTION OF THE PROBLEM

A small well field, abstracting about 1000 m³ per day of groundwater, used for drinking and industrial purposes, is located in the valley of the second largest Lithuanian river (the Neris) in a groundwater discharge zone, within the industrial area of Vilnius city. Upgradient of the well field are located a large municipal oil storage, a sand-salt pile used for the deicing of winter roads, and a powerful heating plant. The distance to these pollutant sources from the well field varies from 300 to 900 m (Figure 1).

The oil storage site has been used since 1949 and spills of oil products often occurred on the site. The salt/s and mixture mound is located in a former sand pit. After the sand was excavated the salt mixture was deposited on the permeable sandy soil without any lining at the base. These are favourable conditions for subsurface contamination.

As a consequence of these human activities, shallow groundwater has been contaminated by hydrocarbons and chloride. The area of soil and shallow groundwater contamination by hydrocarbons is more than 200,000 m² and almost twice as big an area is contaminated by chloride. The boundary of contaminated shallow groundwater lies 200-250 m from the edge of the well field. The concentration of chloride in shallow groundwater ranges from 620 to 810 mg/l (maximum allowable concentration (MAC) for drinking water is 250 mg/l), and the BTEX concentration reaches 17.2 mg/l. Elevated chloride concentrations (up to 360 mg/l) are also observed in some production wells. The possibility of protecting the groundwater resources at the well field has been examined.

2 GEOLOGY AND HYDROGEOLOGY

The Quaternary sand and gravel aquifer lying at a depth of 19-23 m (55-75 m abs. level) is being exploited with a yield of 1000 m³/d from 4-6 abstraction wells. The aquifer is covered by a 3-9 m thick low-permeability moraine till and 7-20 m thick alluvial sand (Figure 1). The till layer is discontinuous and has so-called "permeable windows". This increases the vulnerability of the productive aquifer. The aquifer contains fresh, good quality groundwater of bicarbonate-calcium composition. The TDS of water samples ranges from 0.5 g/l to 0.65 g/l, total

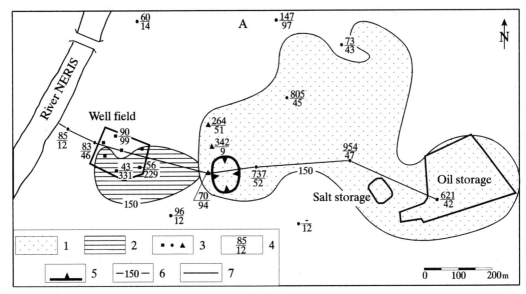

1-2 areas of groundwater contamination by chloride : 1- unconfined (shallow) aquifer, 2 - productive aqui-fer; 3 - groundwater observation station: production, monitoring and hydraulic barrier well; 4-concentration of chloride, mg/l : in numerator - unconfined aquifer, in denominator - productive aquifer; 5 - seepage zone of unconfined aquifer into productive aquifer; 6- isoline of chloride concentration, mg/l; 7- geological cross-section line.

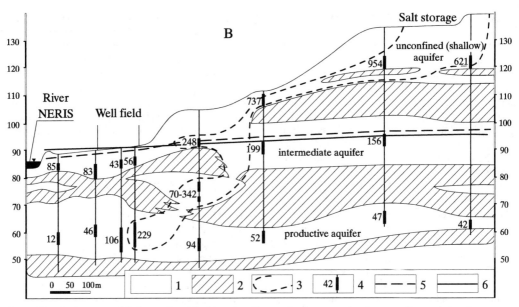

1- aquifer; 2 - impermeable layer; 3 - chloride migration route; 4 - groundwater sampling point and concen-tration of chloride, mg/l; 5 - 6 groundwater level: 5 - intermediate aquifer, 6 - productive aquifer.

Figure 1.   Distribution of chloride contamination in the vicinity of the well field (A) and geological cross-
-section (B).

hardness (as Ca+Mg) reaches 7-9 meq/l. Very high iron concentrations in abstracted groundwater (up to 7-11 mg/l, MAC=0.3 mg/l) necessitated construction of a plant at the waterworks to remove the iron.

The aquifer is underlain by the Cretaceous clay and silt that serves as an aquiclude between the Quaternary sands and Middle Devonian dolomites. The depth to the Devonian dolomites at the well field is 68 m. The possibility to abstract groundwater from the Devonian aquifer has been examined, but it has been found that groundwater contains 2.8 g/l TDS and exceeds by 2.8 the limits allowed by the drinking water standard (1 g/l). The total hardness of the water reaches 34.5 meq/l, almost 5 times the drinking water standard (7 meq/l). It was thus shown that groundwater of such quality cannot be used for drinking purposes.

The productive aquifer is overlain by intermoraine water-bearing sands and gravels, which cover all the investigated area, except for a narrow (100-150 m wide) strip on the left bank of the Neris river. The depth to this intermediate aquifer varies from 16 m to 41 m, and its thickness reaches 17.4-25 m. In the vicinity of the well field the aquifer contains unconfined groundwater with elevated sodium and chloride concentrations. This shows hydraulic connection between the intermediate and the overlying shallow polluted aquifer.

The uppermost aquifer is alluvial sand and gravel. Groundwater from this aquifer, as well as from the other aquifers, discharges to the Neris river valley. Outside the boundaries of the well field the aquifer is heavily polluted with chloride and oil products (mainly BTEX). The maximum concentration of chloride near the sand/salt pile reaches 4.3 g/l and exceeds by a factor of 17 the MAC for drinking water. The concentration of dissolved BTEX in the groundwater near the oil storage facility fluctuates from 0.17 to 17.2 mg/l.

The hydrodynamic relations between the aquifers are rather complicated. Near the pollution sources (oil storage and salt/sand mixture pile) the level of contaminated unconfined groundwater is 7 m higher than the productive aquifer but in the area of the well field, close to the groundwater discharge zone, the water level in the productive aquifer is 1.25 m higher than that of the unconfined water table. Due to groundwater extraction the water level in the productive aquifer is declining and a possibility of seepage of contaminated unconfined groundwater is created.

3 RESULTS OF INVESTIGATIONS

A detailed hydrogeological study was conducted in 1995/1996 in the vicinity of the well field, with the purpose of evaluating the possibilities for protection of drinking water resources. It was found that the hazardous zone where productive groundwater can be polluted occupies a 300 m long and 250 m wide zone. In this zone shallow groundwater seepage into the productive aquifer is observed. The chloride concentration in the uppermost (unconfined) aquifer ranges from 621 to 954 mg/l, in the intermediate aquifer this concentration decreases to 248-740 mg/l and in the productive aquifer it reaches values of 163 to 331 mg/l. The background chloride concentrations in the productive aquifer are at a level of only 10 to 15 mg/l.

A hydraulic barrier consisting of 3 well pairs (total 6 wells) was installed between the well field and the pollution sources. The well pairs were drilled at a distance of 55 to 80 m from each other, at depths from 31 to 62 m. Three wells were installed into the intermediate aquifer and three other wells reached the productive aquifer. In addition, 9 monitoring boreholes for observation of fluctuations of groundwater chemical composition and levels were installed around the well field.

The main purpose of the hydraulic barrier is to develop artificial drawdown of contaminated groundwater in order to prevent seepage into the productive aquifer. The drawdown has to occupy all the area of the polluted groundwater plume, and the water level of the intermediate aquifer has to be lower than in the productive aquifer.

Pumping tests performed in the hydraulic barrier wells revealed that changes of hydraulic relations between the aquifers are followed not only by groundwater level fluctuations, but also by changes of the chemical composition of water. Developing the drawdown of the intermediate aquifer below the level of the productive one, the leakage of fresh groundwater from the productive into the contaminated aquifer is increased. When pumping groundwater from the hydraulic barrier wells abstracting from the intermediate aquifer, the concentration of chloride after 1 pumping day was reduced by 40 per cent: from 69.6 mg/l to 39.05 mg/l. The TDS decreased from 716 mg/l to 646 mg/l during the same pumping period. When pumping groundwater from the productive aquifer, the opposite picture was observed. The chloride concentration increased from 94 mg/l to 135 mg/l and the TDS from 470 to 546 mg/l. The conclusion was made that a water level decline in the contaminated aquifer increases the upward leakage of fresh groundwater, which dilutes the contaminated aquifer and vice versa: lowering the water table of the productive aquifer increases its salinity and chloride concentration. These data confirm the good hydraulic continuity between the productive and overlying aquifers.

The optimum groundwater extraction rate of the barrier wells was calculated and abstraction quantities in the well field estimated after the pumping tests. Two conditions have to be fulfilled for the hydraulic barrier to work effectively: 1) groundwater drawdown has to reach such an extent that it prevents migration of all of the contaminated plume, and 2) inversion of the groundwater levels has to be created, i.e. the level of productive aquifer has to be higher than the contaminated groundwater level.

Pumping tests revealed that when pumping three hydraulic barrier wells installed into the intermediate aquifer with yields of 10 m^3/h, 4 m^3/h and 4 m^3/h it is possible to create the desired drawdown of more than 1.7 m in 12-15 days of continuous abstraction. Creation of this amount of drawdown in the contaminated aquifer will prevent the migration and downwards filtration of contaminants. Extracted groundwater will be transferred to a water treatment plant.

It has been also calculated that the total abstraction from the well field should not be higher than 1700 m^3/day. If the proposed pollution prevention measures are implemented they can serve as a long term solution for the protection of potable groundwater resources.

A groundwater monitoring programme was prepared and is considered to be a very important pollution prevention measure.

4 CONCLUSIONS

Detailed hydrogeological investigations were carried out in 1995/1996 in the vicinity of a well field, located in the urbanised area of Vilnius city, Lithuania. Oil and sand/salt storage are the main groundwater pollution sources that have caused soil and groundwater contamination over an area of more than 200,000 m^2. Concentrations of chloride in the uppermost aquifer reaches 4300 mg/l and dissolved BTEX concentration values are up to 17.2 mg/l. The polluted unconfined aquifer is hydraulically connected with the intermediate and productive aquifers. This was proved by elevated chloride concentrations in both aquifers. The productive aquifer is being abstracted by

4-6 wells with a total yield of 1000 m^3/day. The boundary of the contaminated groundwater plume at present is 200-250 m east of the boundary of the well field.

Six wells have been drilled between the pollution sources and the well field. Pumping tests were performed at the barrier wells. Data collected show that if a drawdown is created in the intermediate aquifer pumping three wells with appropriate yields it can prevent downward filtration of contaminated groundwater.

REFERENCES

Marcinonis, A. 1991. Remediation of shallow groundwater contaminated by hydrocarbons. *Groundwater regime, resources and protection in Lithuania. Informational bulletin.* Vilnius: 42-45. [in Lithuanian].

Marcinonis, A. 1993. Subsurface contamination by hydrocarbons and its investigations in Lithuania. *Groundwater monitoring in Lithuania. Informational bulletin.* Vilnius: 69-74. [in Lithuanian].

Overexploitation effects of the aquifer system of México City

L. F. Sánchez-Díaz & C. Gutiérrez-Ojeda
Instituto Mexicano de Tecnología del Agua, Morelos, Mexico

ABSTRACT: Mexico City is located in the South-Central part of the Mexican Republic, within a closed basin which has experienced intensive tectonic activity from Late Cretaceous to Quaternary times. The required water supply (58 m^3/s) for more than twenty million people who inhabit the urban area, comes from subsurface sources (internal 41.1 m^3/s; external 4.9 m^3/s) and external surface sources (12 m^3/s). Several geological-geophysical studies, transmissivity and specific capacity were used to identify four different hydrogeologic units within the aquifer system below Mexico City: i) Andesitic; ii) Tarango; iii) Alluvial and iv) Basaltic. The main production aquifer currently in use is composed of intermixed clastic and alluvial materials which are overlaid (confined) by a lacustrine clay deposit. The exploitation of the Mexico City´s aquifer system started in the late 1920s. Nowadays, it is estimated that groundwater abstraction within the internal basin is twice the recharge. The alluvial aquifer overexploitation has caused i) drawdowns of more than three m/year; ii) lower discharge rates; iii) groundwater quality decline; iv) land subsidence of 0.10-0.40 m/year; and v) depletion of springs. Saline pore water and high compressibility of the clay layer are respectively associated with groundwater quality decline and land subsidence due to groundwater abstraction.

1 INTRODUCTION

Mexico City is situated in the south-central part of the Mexican Republic (Figure 1), between 100°00' and 100°00' W-longitude and between 25°00' and 26°00' N-latitude. It covers a total area of about 4,700 km^2 and includes the states of Distrito Federal and Mexico. Land surface elevations of the city range between 2,230 to 3,000 meters above sea level (masl) with an average of 2,400 masl. The city has a population of more than twenty million people with a required water supply of 58 m^3/s.

The climate in the area is temperate most of the time with a well defined winter season and an average temperature of 15°C. Most of the precipitation occurs in the summer (the rainy season is from May to October): the mean annual precipitation is 700 mm with a distribution that is influenced by the topographic conditions.

2 GEOLOGY

The City is located in a closed basin which belongs to a very active tectonic zone referred to as the Transmexican Volcanic Belt (Mooser 1975). Several geological and geophysical studies have described the

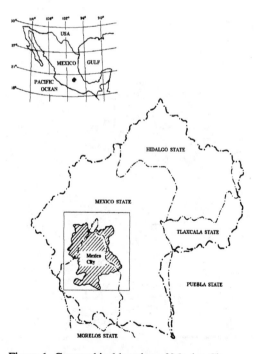

Figure 1. Geographical location of Mexico City.

stratigraphic sequence within the basin as quite erratic.

The area experienced intense volcanic activity that produced huge volumes of sediments which were transported and reworked by the extensive drainage system developed on the valley floor. The sediments filling the valley are mainly composed of intermixed clastic and alluvial materials. They constitute the main aquifer below Mexico City.

The volcanic events of the late Quaternary blocked the natural valley drainage system to the south and resulted in the formation of a series of interconnected large lakes which covered a considerable portion of the valley floor (Mooser, 1978). A thick lacustrine clay layer was then deposited over the alluvial-fluvial sediments.

The high clay compressibility has given this layer unique characteristics within the area (Rudolph et al., 1989):

i) it acts as a semiconfining aquitard with a considerable leakage flux that can supply important volumes of water to the main aquifer during pumping, and

ii) it accounts for the high degree of land subsidence related to groundwater abstraction.

The clay deposits range from a few cm thick in the valley perimeter to 200 m in the Texcoco lake area (Figure 2).

3 HYDROGEOLOGY

The geologic evolution of the Valley of Mexico produced the formation of several types of rocks which have different physical and hydrogeologic characteristics. According with the geologic analysis previously stated and with several hydrogeologic studies there are four different types of aquifers (Sánchez, 1989) within the valley. Figure 3 shows the surficial contact between the four aquifers.

i) Andesitic. Contained in porphyro-andesitic rocks (in some cases densely fractured) with a high infiltration capacity:

$$1 < Q_s < 1.3 \text{ l/s/m}$$
$$T = 0.3 \text{ m}^2/\text{s}$$
$$K = 0.003 \text{ m/s} \qquad (1)$$

where Q_s = specific capacity, T = transmissivity and K = hydraulic conductivity.

These characteristics are found only in some areas; in most places the andesitic rocks are completely unproductive.

ii) Tarango. Contained in fluvial sands, conglomerate and pyroclastic materials. Their hydrogeologic characteristics are also influenced by the particle size distribution, compaction, fracture density and lithostratigraphic lateral changes:

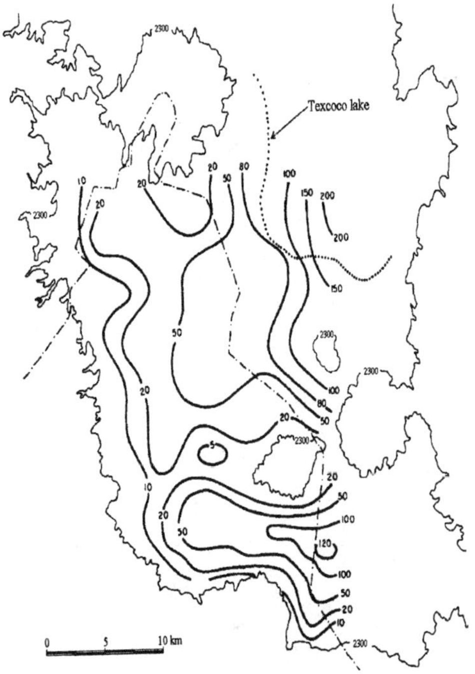

Figure 2. Thickness of the lacustrine layer (m).

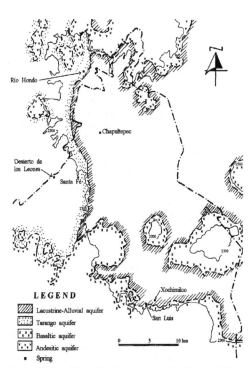

Figure 3. Aquifers distribution within Mexico City.

$0.3 < Q_s < 1.3$ l/s/m
$0.005 < T < 0.002$ m²/s
$0.0005 < S < 0.0015$ (2)

•

where S = storage coefficient.

iii) Alluvial. This aquifer is formed by gravels, sands and lenses of silt and clay deposited in the bottom of the lakes and it is overlaid (confined) by a lacustrine clay deposit (Figure 2).

The deposits' shape, particle size distribution and the lithostratigraphic changes (lateral and vertical) control the hydrogeologic characteristics of these alluvial lacustrine deposits:

$1.4 < Q_s < 5.5$ l/s/m
$T = 0.01$ m²/s
$S = 0.2$ (3)

iv) Basaltic. Contained in lava spills and pyroclastic materials, this aquifer is mainly found in the central part of the Distrito Federal.

$Q_s > 200$ l/s/m
$0.1 < T < 0.4$ m²/s
$0.10 < S < 0.15$ (4)

The aquifers are mainly confined in the central part of the basin and unconfined towards the surrounding mountains which are composed of basalts, andesitic rocks and deposits of the Tarango Formation.

4 WATER RESOURCES DEVELOPMENT

Since the foundation of Mexico City in 1325, up until 1867, the water supply came from the Chapultepec and Santa Fe springs (0.22 m³/s) located to the west of the City (Figure 3). During the Republican period (1867-1900) the increasing water demand was covered with the Desierto de los Leones and Rio Hondo springs (0.50 m³/s) as well as with 1,100 domestic boreholes (Sánchez 1994). From 1900 to 1928 the City incorporated the Xochimilco and San Luis springs, located to the south, into its water supply network, while the Chapultepec spring was abandoned due to contamination.

More than 1,000 wells were drilled from 1929 to 1978 to cover the increasing water demands of more than 9.0 million people: 450 were municipal and 870 were private wells. From 1979 to 1993, 200 more wells were drilled for the same purposes. Nowadays the City requires 58 m³/s of which 41.1 m³/s come from the Valley of Mexico aquifer system (internal basin), 12 m³/s from Cutzamala system (surface external source) and 4.9 m³/s from the Lerma aquifer (external source).

5 EXPLOTATION INDICES

It is estimated that groundwater abstraction within the internal basin is twice the recharge. This aquifer overexploitation has caused :
i) drawdowns of more than 3 m/year;
ii) a reduction in well yields;
iii) groundwater quality decline;
iv) land subsidence of 0.10 - 0.40 m/year; and
v) spring depletion.

5.1 *Drawdowns*

The aquifer system has experienced a dramatic decrease of the piezometric surface in the last 40 years. At the end of 1950s the depth to the piezometric surface was 5 to 8 m. By 1991 this range increased to 30-60 m (Figure 4). Water level fluctuations are attributed to several causes: change in water storage, soil consolidation and inefficient well design.

The mean drawdowns observed in the period 1986-1991 were of 0.60 to 1.60 m/year (Figure 5). Their areal distribution is consistent with the well density: highest values in the center of the basin and lower values towards the surrounding mountains. It is considered that if the water demand continues its

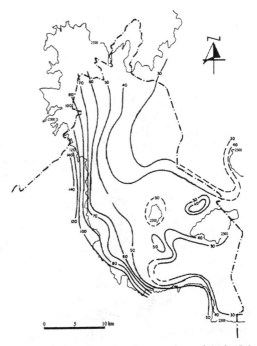

Figure 4. Depth to the piezometric surface in July-1991 (m).

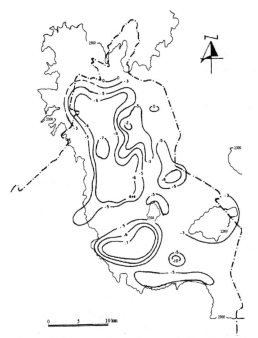

Figure 5. Piezometric surface evolution from Aug-1986 to Jul-1991 (m).

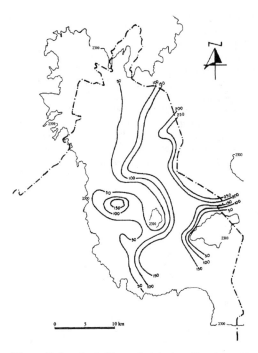

Figure 7. Land subsidence in Mexico City from 1976 to 1985 (cm).

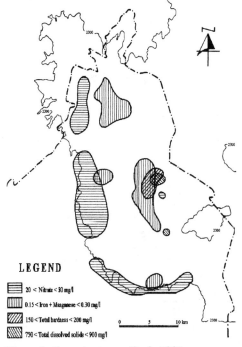

LEGEND

▤	20 < Nitrate < 30 mg/l
▥	0.15 < Iron + Manganese < 0.30 mg/l
▧	150 < Total hardness < 200 mg/l
▨	750 < Total dissolved solids < 900 mg/l

Figure 6. Groundwater quality in 1985.

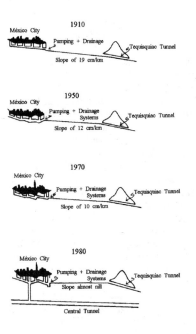

Figure 8. Surface slope changes during 1910-1980 (and their effects on the Mexico City drainage system).

356

growth tendency, the mean drawdowns could reach the value of 2 m/year.

5.2 *Well discharge reduction*

Several wells drilled during the period 1929-1978 experienced a reduction in yield due to the water level decrease. Fifteen years ago the Federal Government implemented a restoration program to extend the life span of the wells.

5.3 *Groundwater quality decline*

Recent investigations have shown that vertical gradients acting on the lacustrine clay deposit can induce the infiltration of surface contamination. Pumpage is also inducing recharge from municipal and industrial sewerage systems, as well as the movement of pore water contained in the clay deposits, which have a high organic matter content. Figure 6 shows the areas with high concentration of nitrate, iron + manganese, total hardness and total dissolved solids.

5.4 *Land subsidence*

Nabor Carrillo (1942) established that the piezometric head reduction in the semiconfined aquifer of Mexico City had caused consolidation of the clays. Several reference (height) levels installed in the last century revealed a land subsidence of 3.0 to 8.5 m during the period 1891-1970, with a subsidence rate of 4 to 11 cm/year. Due to pumpage increase, the subsidence rate also increased, to 6-28 cm/year during the period 1976-1985 (Figure 7). This has caused the failure of surface structures, rupturing of pipelines and surface slope changes (Figure 8).

6 CONCLUSIONS

Overexploitation of the aquifer will continue to cause undesirable effects on the area, unless abstraction be considerable reduced to levels close to the natural recharge. Artificial recharge of wastewater by injection wells should be considered as an alternative to attenuate the overexploitation effects.

REFERENCES

Carrillo N., 1942, Simple two and threedimensional cases in the theory of consolidation of soils, Journal of Math. and Phy., Vol. XXI, No. 1.

Mooser F., 1975, Historia geológica de la cuenca de Mexico, in Memorias-Obras del Sistema de Drenaje Profundo, Dept. Dist. Fed., 9-38.

Mooser F., 1978, Geología del relleno Cuaternario de la cuenca de Mexico, in El subsuelo y la Ingeniería de Cimentaciones en el Area Urbana del Valle de Mexico, Symposium proceedings, 9-13.

Rudolph D.L., Herrera I. and Yates R., 1989, Groundwater flow and solute transport in the industrial well fields of the Texcoco saline aquifer system near Mexico City, Geof. Int., Vol. 28-2. pp. 363-408.

Sánchez D.L.F., 1989, Los acuíferos de la Ciudad de Mexico, su estado actual y alternativas de solución para su control y conservación, Tesis de Maestría, Escuela Superior de Ingeniería y Arquitectura, IPN.

Sánchez D.L.F., 1994, Los acuíferos de la Ciudad de Mexico, origen, aprovechamiento y efectos colaterales a su explotación, II Congreso Latinoamericano de Hidrología Subterránea, Santiago de Chile.

Groundwater for coastal holiday towns to satisfy peak summer demand

John M.C. Weaver
Division of Water, Environment and Forestry Technology, CSIR, Stellenbosch, South Africa

ABSTRACT: In 1994 the African National Congress, under the leadership of Nelson Mandela, won the majority of votes and thus formed the new government of South Africa. Consequently, there has been an increase in efforts to ensure that all of the population has access to basic water supply - 25 litres per person per day within 200 metres of their dwelling. The realignment of available funding has caused coastal holiday towns to look carefully at available water supply options. Surface water schemes cost at least twice that of groundwater schemes, both for capital costs and for running costs. The population of coastal holiday towns is highly seasonal, with the population increasing five to eight times over the four weeks of Christmas/New Year. This causes a similar peak in demand for water. Increasingly these towns are looking towards groundwater to supply this demand.

1 POLITICS OF WATER-SUPPLY FUNDING IN SOUTH AFRICA

The first elections in which the total population (above the age of 18) of South Africa was allowed to vote were held in 1994. Previously the country was governed by the white minority (about 5 out of 40 million). This government was under the control of the National Party from 1948 until 1994, and instituted the racial separation policy which was known as apartheid or separate development.

In 1994 the general election resulted in the African National Congress (ANC), under the leadership of Nelson Mandela, winning the majority of votes and becoming the new South African government. The ANC voter support base is South Africa's black population, both rural and urban. With this change of voter support base has come a shift in emphasis of government activities and priorities from supporting the white population towards supporting the total population and making good the historical lack of attention towards the black population.

The post of Minister of Department of Water Affairs and Forestry (DWAF) has in the past been a reward for politicians who have served the party well, and who brought varying degrees of activity to the post. The appointment of Professor (of law) Kader Asmal to the post has introduced a new dynamism and flurry of activity to DWAF.

The guiding principle of the revitalised DWAF is "Ensuring some for all ... forever" (DWAF Homepage). The details of their policies are described in the DWAF White Paper (1994) in which the basic water supply policy is stated as to ensure the supply of 25 litres of good quality water per person per day within 200 metres of their dwelling, increasing to 50 litres per person per day by the year 2002.

It is estimated that 12 million of South Africa's population lack access to even this low level of supply. Consequently, energy and funding has been directed towards satisfying these basic needs. The task has been given a high priority and a new section has been formed within DWAF called Water Supply and Sanitation. This section has been delegated the job of reducing the lack of water supply and has been given a large budget for this task.

Consumers of water that have been negatively affected by these changes include the coastal holiday resorts. These are characterized by the following features:

• predominantly white owned
• occupancy mainly over summer (Dec/Jan)
• low permanent occupancy, typically 10 - 20%.

Having these characteristics, funding for the development of water-supplies for coastal holiday towns has dropped to the low priority end of the scale.

2 COASTAL PHYSIOGRAPHY AND TYPE OF WATER SUPPLY

South Africa's coastline is mostly rugged and rather

straight with a lack of protected bays and inlets. There are no fjords. The majority of rivers have silted estuaries, open only to small boats. The geology of about one third of the coastline comprises quartzites of the Table Mountain Group. These Ordovician age quartzites form spectacular scenery with mountains and valleys close to the coast.

The consequence of this is that reservoir (dam) sites are often available within 50 km of most coastal towns. Historically South Africa's water-supply has been dominated by surface water supply mostly from dams which fill during the rainy season.

Thus coastal towns have often relied on dams. However, these are relatively expensive and the reduced availability of funding has meant that these towns are now increasingly looking towards groundwater as a less expensive source.

3 ECONOMICS OF SURFACE WATER VERSUS GROUNDWATER SUPPLIES IN SOUTH AFRICA

Surface water schemes have always been more expensive than groundwater schemes. Johnstone and Snell (1985) assessed the relative cost of South African surface and groundwater schemes. The average capital cost of 5 groundwater schemes was US$ 0.48 million per scheme versus an average of US$ 0.9 for 8 surface water schemes. For these same schemes the average cost of water (operating cost plus interest and capital redemption) was 8.9 US cents/m^3 for groundwater and 18.7 US cents/m^3 for surface water.

The combination of reduced Government support and cost implications has resulted in many of the coastal towns looking towards groundwater for water-supply.

4 CASE EXAMPLE: STILBAAI

Stilbaai is 280 km east of Cape Town. Stilbaai means the still or quiet bay, which is a reflection of this being the only safe anchorage for small boats for 50 kilometres on either side. Groundwater for this town is obtained from the contact between calcretised fossil sand dunes of Cenozoic age (50 my) overlying quartzites of the Table Mountain Group (Ordovician 450 my). The groundwater is collected from a number of springs and also from boreholes.

Typically for a coastal holiday resort, the summer population of 20,000 for the four weeks over Christmas/New Year far exceeds the permanent population of 2,500 persons. Figure 1 below shows the water-demand over a year, December 1994 was a particularly dry month, whereas rain during December 1995 reduced demand. Note the slight increase in

demand for April 1995 which is due to the Easter school holiday. Taking into account vacant plots and future developments, the expected demand for the year 2002 is some 200,000 m^3 for the month of December.

To develop this additional water supply, the choice is either to develop a wellfield 8 km outside town or to build a weir on the river above the tidal influence, which is 16 km inland. The capital cost (1997 estimate) of the wellfield is US$ 600,000 and for the weir option is US$ 1,640,000. Running costs for the wellfield would be about 20 US cents per m^3 versus 53 US cents per m^3 for the surface water option.

Stilbaai will probably choose the wellfield option. This information is from Weaver (1996) and Scott de Waal (1989).

5 CASE EXAMPLE: STRUISBAAI

Struisbaai is 170 km east of Cape Town. Struisbaai is derived from the Dutch name Vogelstruijsbaai recorded in 1672, meaning bay of ostriches. The bay provides the only protected harbour for 60 km to the west and 25 km to the east. In addition to the holiday resort population there is also a small commercial handline fishery. The permanent population is 1,700 of whom about half are fisher-folk. The summer population is estimated at about 9,000.

Until the mid-1980s Struisbaai was supplied by 5 boreholes. These boreholes are drilled through relatively thin (5 to 40 m) calcretised fossil sand dunes (Cenozoic 50 my) into quartzites of the Table Mountain Group (Ordovician 450 my). The boreholes are 90 to 150 m deep and are between 600 and 1000 m from the coast.

Lack of a management system and increased demand led to over-pumping and consequent saline water intrusion. The aquifer is a fractured rock aquifer with no primary porosity. The high hydraulic conductivities of the fractures compounded the mismanagement. Thus in the mid 1980s it was decided to develop an alternate source of water. A surface-water option was an inland dam with a 40 km pipeline and treatment works. Alternatively the choice was to move inland and re-establish the wellfield. In current costs the surface water choice is US$ 2,000,000, while the groundwater scheme is US$ 270,000. The groundwater option was chosen and established in 1990. The advantage of groundwater is that additional boreholes can be drilled as additional supplies are needed, as there are no other groundwater users of significance for 20 km inland.

This information from Struisbaai Municipality (1997), VKE (1991) and Meyer (1986).

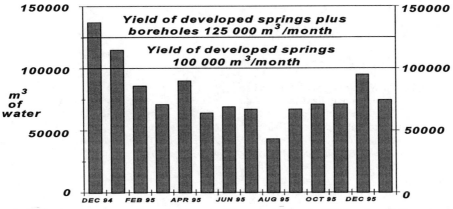

Figure 1. Stilbaai water consumption, showing monthly consumption for 1995 and available water supply.

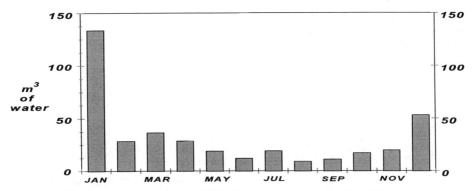

Figure 2.   Struisbaai water consumption for 1996. The metering period is 15 to 15 of next month, thus the 133,560 m³ consumption for January is for the total peak holiday season of December/January.

6 COMMENT

The combination of changing political demands and economics is inducing local councils to increasingly look to groundwater as a source of water. Mistrust by local officials of the reliability of groundwater is a real problem facing South African hydrogeologists when trying to persuade municipalities to investigate the groundwater option. The fact that more than 90% of the aquifers are fractured rock aquifers does not make the task easier.

The factors that are taken into consideration when deciding on whether to choose a surface or groundwater scheme are the cost of the scheme, quantity of water and quality of water. Although all three factors are important, invariably the deciding factor is financial. If funding is freely available, then a surface water scheme will probably be chosen, reflecting the mistrust of the reliability of groundwater, the "invisible" resource. However, when money becomes a limiting factor, then the lower cost of a groundwater scheme encourages its implementation.

Quantity of water could be an issue limiting the use of groundwater in areas where suitable zones of fractured rock are not developed.   However, approximately one third of the coastline is quartzites of the Table Mountain Group, which usually have zones of well developed fracturing, suitable for developing wellfields.

Quality can be an issue, as coastal aquifers often have elevated salinity from wind-blown sea-spray. In contrast surface water will have low salinities. This could tip the scale in favour of surface water schemes. However this will be a minor consideration in comparison to the financial aspects.

REFERENCES

DWAF, 1994. *Water Supply and Sanitation White Paper*, Department of Water Affairs and Forestry, South Africa.
DWAF Homepage: http://www.gov.za/dwaf/

Johnstone A.C. and E F A Snell, 1985. An assessment of the relative costs of surface and groundwater as a water resource. Conference proceedings *"Africa needs groundwater"* Groundwater Division, Geological Society of South Africa.

Meyer, P.S., 1986. 'n Waardering van Struisbaai se grondwater-voorsiening in die lig van verwagte groei na inskakeling by die nasionale netwerk. *Report G3485*, Department of Water Affairs and Forestry, South Africa.

Scott de Waal, 1989. *An additional water-supply for Stilbaai*. Consulting report for Stilbaai Municipality.

Struisbaai Municipality, 1997. Municipal records of water consumption.

VKE, 1991. *The exploration for additional water on erf 920*. Consulting report for Essential Sterolin Products.

Weaver, 1996. *Stilbaai: Assessment of the groundwater resource*. Consulting report for Stilbaai Municipality.

4 Groundwater pollution hazards

Topic co-editors
John Tellam
University of Birmingham

Richard Kimblin
CES

Identification of the main source of chromium pollution from various potential sources

M.A.Armienta, R.Rodríguez, N.Ceniceros, O.Cruz & A.Aguayo
Instituto de Geofísica, Universidad Nacional Autónoma de México, Mexico

ABSTRACT: In Buenavista, south of León, Guanajuato, México, hexavalent chromium concentrations up to 50 mg L^{-1} were detected in groundwater. A chromate factory with five different deposits of solid wastes, wastewater from two tanneries and fumes from the factory were identified as potential pollution sources. Chemical analyses of soils, aquifer material, groundwater and wastes were performed. The water table depth was measured in the wells exploited in the area and in five boreholes. One of the solid waste deposits was identified as the main source of chromium in the underlying groundwater. Secondary sources of chromium are irrigation with polluted water containing hexavalent chromium, and the fumes from the chromate factory. Tannery wastewater was not an important source of pollution of the groundwater in this area.

1 INTRODUCTION

In urban areas, groundwater is vulnerable to different potential contaminants coming from various industrial activities. In some cases different sources of the same substance may be present in a limited area, making it difficult to establish adequate remediation strategies. The first step in the cleaning up of a polluted aquifer is to identify the origin of the pollutant. To accomplish this objective, geochemical, hydrological and chemical information must be collected and interpreted. When the pollutant is a polivalent element, its chemical form may be an important approach for distinguishing among its sources.

León city, with more than one million inhabitants, is one of the most important industrial centres of México. More than 550 tanneries are located in this city. Most of them use chromium as a tanning agent and discharge their wastewaters without treatment to the León river.

In the León valley, in the centre of México, groundwater pollution by chromium has been reported. The presence of chromium is due to both anthropogenic and natural sources. The weathering of ultramafic rocks in the northeast of the valley has produced hexavalent chromium,

Cr(VI), concentrations in the groundwater between 0.004 and 0.015 mg L^{-1}. The use of rubble ashes from brick factories as fertilizer has resulted in Cr(VI) concentrations up to 0.04 mg L^{-1} in most of the valley groundwaters. The highest concentrations up to 50 mg L^{-1} were found at Buenavista, 13 km southwest of León, near to a chromate factory "Química Central" (QC, Figure 1). Wastewaters from the leather industry were not found to be a source of chromium pollution in the groundwater of the valley (Armienta et al. 1993).

The factory (QC), produced Na_2CrO_4 and $CrOHSO_4$, mostly from chromite. In this area of around 5 km^2 there are also various potential pollution sources. In the QC yards, three different kinds of solid wastes were piled without protective cover (1, 2, 3, Figure 1). There are also two landfills containing residues from the factory process, one located in the factory yard (4, Figure 1), and the other about 1500 m southwest of QC (5, Figure 1). Besides, in this zone two tanneries (A,B, Figure 1) which use chromium in their manufacturing processes are located. The tannery wastewaters are discharged through canals to a reservoir located behind QC. The water from this impoundment (San Germán Dam) is used for

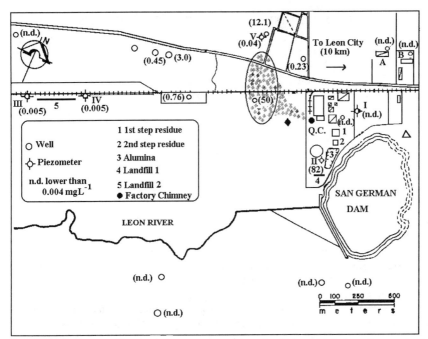

Figure 1. Study area. The shaded area corresponds to the highest total chromium contents in soils. Groundwater Cr(VI) concentrations (mg L^{-1}) in parenthesis.

irrigation.

The objective of the study presented here was to determine the main source of chromium in groundwater in the most polluted part of the León valley.

2 CHEMISTRY OF CHROMIUM IN THE ENVIRONMENT

Chromium in the environment may be present as Cr(VI) or Cr(III), each having specific chemical and toxicological properties. Hexavalent chromium is the toxic form of the element, whereas trivalent chromium is an essential element for man (Doisy et al. 1976; Fishbein 1984). Their behaviour in groundwater is also different, since Cr(VI) is present mainly as an anion and Cr(III) as a cation. Cr(VI) is highly soluble, and Cr(III) precipitates at normal groundwater pH (Hem 1977; Sass & Rai 1987). The adsorption processes are also different for each of the oxidation states. Although both Cr(III) and Cr(VI) may adsorb on clays, and on iron and manganese oxides and hydroxides, the extent of the adsorption, and its

dependence on the pH is different (James & Bartlett 1983).

If disposed of on the soil, chromium may react chemically with the different soil fractions and be retained on a temporary or permanent basis. The chromium content of the different soil constituents is relevant for its transport to aquifers.

3 METHODOLOGY

Water samples were obtained from the wells located in the area. The samples were analysed for physico-chemical parameters, and Cr(VI) following standard procedures. Cr(VI) was analysed by colorimetry through its reaction with diphenyl-carbazide, and total chromium by atomic absorption spectrophotometry (APHA 1989).

Five boreholes, each 30m deep, were drilled without drilling mud near the potential pollution site (Figure 1). The cores were analyzed for Cr(VI), total chromium, iron and manganese. Water obtained at three depths was analyzed for Cr(VI). Concentrations of Cr(VI) and total

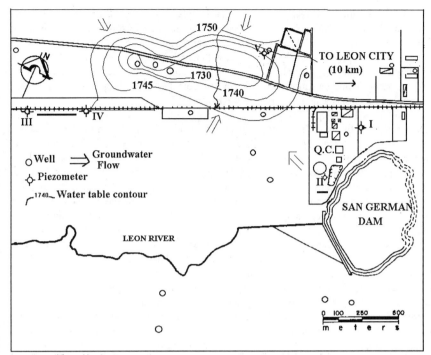

Figure 2. Piezometric depression at the Buenavista area. (contour values in m above sea level)

chromium in the solid wastes were also determined. Granulometric analyses of the cores were performed by standard procedures.

For the chemical analyses of the cores, samples were taken every 0.6 m. The samples were ground and quartered. For the determination of total chromium, 1 g of the quartered sample was dissolved with HNO_3 and HCl. The obtained solution was analyzed by atomic absorption spectrophotometry. Cr(VI) was determined by leaching 1g of the quartered sample with water and analyzing by colorimetry.

Soil sampling was performed at 70 sites, located on a 200 m or 100 m grid. The location of the sampling area was chosen based on the prevailing southeast-northwest wind direction. Some reference points were placed upwind from QC. At each sampling point, two soil samples were obtained, one at the surface and the other at a depth of 0.3 m. Chemical analyses included exchangeable chromium, mainly Cr(VI) considered as the fraction leached with distilled water, and total chromium, (Cr(III) plus Cr(VI)), obtained from acid digestion.

A more detailed sequential extraction procedure (Tessier et al. 1979) was applied to four selected soil samples. Chromium bound to the carbonate phase, iron and manganese oxides, organic matter and residual was determined.

4 RESULTS AND DISCUSSION

Two of the wells had very high concentrations of chromium, 50 mg L^{-1} and 12.1 mg L^{-1} of Cr(VI), both far above the Mexican drinking water standard of 0.05 mg L^{-1}. Values of 0.05 mg L^{-1} to 2.3 mg L^{-1} were measured for five other wells. All of these polluted wells are located west of QC (Figure 1).

From the granulometric analyses, the following units of Quaternary fluvial deposits were identified: a) Light orange to brown clay, b) Fine grained light brown silty clay, c) Fine to coarse grained light brown sandy clay, d) Grey silt, e) Light brown to grey gravel and sand, f) Coarse to fine grained silty sand g) Fine grained light grey to dark brown sand. These units are found in different orders in each of the boreholes.

The local aquifer comprises the following formations down to 100 m depth: an aquitard, a semi-confined aquifer, a confining bed, and a confined aquifer. Interbedding of units with different permeability within the aquitard, allows vertical and horizontal hydraulic communication. The boreholes drilled in this formation located the piezometric level of the aquitard at 10 m depth.

Most of the soil samples with high total chromium concentrations (up to 1000 mg kg^{-1}), resulted from the transportation of powder from the factory chimney by the prevailing SE to NW winds (Figure 1). Only low concentrations of chromium were found upwind from the chimney. This dust was produced in the grinding and calcination of chromite. The release of dust was eliminated in 1989 when electrostatic precipitators were installed.

Eighteen soil samples had detectable amounts of Cr(VI). The highest concentration (65 mg kg^{-1}) was found in a former small water reservoir (♦, Figure 1) that stored Cr(VI) contaminated groundwater (260 mg L^{-1} in 1976, decreasing to 50 mg L^{-1} in 1985) pumped from a nearby well. Irrigation with groundwater containing 12.1 mg L^{-1} Cr(VI) (in December, 1995), pumped from a well located about 500 m to the northwest of QC, accounts for the presence of Cr(VI) in the soils next to it.

Total chromium concentrations of up to 3000 mg kg^{-1} were detected northeast of San Germán Dam (Δ, Figure 1). Hexavalent chromium was not detected at this point. Chromium in this area, located near the canals transporting tannery wastewaters, may originate from the overflows of the San German Dam and of the canal's waters, and from irrigation with León River water. Chromium in these samples is mainly Cr(III), coming from the tannery wastes.

Total chromium contents for the samples obtained at 0.3 m depth were generally lower (up to 500 mg kg^{-1}) than those of the superficial layer. Neverthless, the areas with higher contents appear identical to those of the surficial samples.

Cr(VI) was detected in two of the samples treated by the sequential extraction procedure. These samples also had the highest concentrations of total chromium (more than 12,000 mg kg^{-1}). At one of the points, located in the small abandoned water reservoir, Cr(VI) was detected both in the surface (10 mg kg^{-1}) and in the 0.3 m sample (32 mg kg^{-1}). By contrast, at the other point, located next to the landfill, Cr(VI) was found only in the surficial sample (2.5 mg kg^{-1}). This difference may be caused by the specific source of chromium. At the first site, Cr(VI) came from the infiltration of water with a high Cr(VI) content, easily transported through the soil. At the second point, Cr(VI) originated from the solid chromium wastes stored in the landfill.

Chromium in the sample located near the León river, was found to be mostly in the sulphides and organic phase fraction of the soil. This sample, in spite of having a high concentration of total chromium (2469 mg kg^{-1} for the surficial sample) did not present any Cr(VI). This lack of Cr(VI) is expected in such a reducing environment.

Cr(VI) concentrations in the water obtained from the piezometers has been analyzed every 15 days since January 1991. The results for the first sampling obtained about 2 m below the water level are presented in Figure 1. Cr(VI) concentrations in the water from the piezometers show a decreasing gradient to the northwest of QC, having the maximum value in the piezometer located within the factory yard (Piezometer II). Although the absolute values have changed over time (Table 1), the relative concentrations in the five piezometers have remained constant except for Piezometer V. The particular behaviour of this piezometer may be explained by its location about 5 m from a highly contaminated well (12.1 mg L^{-1} of Cr(VI)) with an intensive abstraction regime. On the other hand, in spite of its location next to the canals transporting tannery wastewaters, Piezometer I only occasionally showed concentrations of Cr(VI) above the detection limit.

The water level measurements showed a piezometric depression northwest of QC (Figure 2). This depression, generated by local pumping explains the Cr(VI) distribution in the groundwater.

Concentrations of Cr(VI) in the solid cores also showed maximum values for Piezometer II and non detectable amounts for Piezometer I. The highest Cr(VI) content (within the saturated zone) was obtained for borehole II with 65 mg kg^{-1} at 12 m depth, followed by Borehole V with 0.7 mg kg^{-1} at 14 m depth, Borehole III with 0.06 mg kg^{-1} at 18 m depth, and Borehole IV with 0.05 mg kg^{-1} at 15 m depth, Cr(VI) was not detected in borehole I at any depth (Armienta & Queré 1995).

The chemical composition of the solid residues is given in Table 2. The highest concentrations of soluble hexavalent chromium were obtained for the alumina residue, which is located about 5 m from Piezometer number II (Figure 1). The other

368

Table 1. Cr(VI) concentrations (mg L^{-1}) in the water from the piezometers at 2 m below the water level for selected dates.

Date	I	II	III	IV	V
Jan 15/91	n.d.	81.700	0.005	0.005	0.040
Feb 1/91	n.d.	18.670	n.d.	n.d.	0.058
Feb 15/91	n.d.	10.910	0.009	n.d.	7.220
Mar 1/91	0.018	6.420	n.d.	0.072	9.680
Mar 15/91	n.d.	1.627	n.d.	0.176	1.672
Apr 1/91	0.006	1.537	n.d.	0.398	7.570
Apr 15/91	n.d.	-	n.d.	0.161	-
May 1/91	n.d.	1.270	n.d.	0.583	4.840
Dec 15/94	n.d.	16.450	0.334	n.d.	5.724
Jul 15/96	n.d.	3.608	0.266	0.005	0.501

n.d.= lower than 0.004 mg L^{-1}

residues have a lower content of Cr(VI). The chromate landfills were built by piling the deposits of the 1st and 2nd step residues onto a plastic sheet. The alumina was put in plastic bags and piled in a hole 6 m deep. This pile reached a height of 14 m above the ground. After the bags became torn, the alumina spilled and a pool rich in chromium was formed by the action of rain. The pool base was located over a sand and gravel layer, facilitating hydraulic communication with the aquifer, which at this site has a piezometric level of 9.8 m below ground level.

Based on the distribution of groundwater pollution found in the boreholes (Figure 1), on the higher content of Cr(VI) in the alumina residue, and on the characteristics of its disposal, the alumina was considered to be the main pollution source in the area. No evidence of leakage from the landfills

Table 2. Total and hexavalent chromium concentrations for various residues.

Residue	Total Cr *	Cr(VI)*
1st·step	2.10%	0.17%
2nd step	2.26%	0.14%
Alumina	15.55%	6.12%
Tannery wastewater	73.2 mg L^{-1}	n.d.
Landfill 1	2.2%	3.7%
Landfill 2	2.2%	3.5%

* Dry basis; n.d.= lower than 0.004 mg L^{-1}

was found. Chromium from the tannery wastewaters was not found to be percolating through the soil to the groundwater, and no evidence of Cr(III) oxidation was observed.

The QC managers were advised to remove the alumina pile. This is currently being done. The relevance of this pollution source was confirmed as the bottom of the pile, formed by high permeability material (gravel and sand), was exposed.

5 CONCLUSIONS

The Cr(VI) distribution in the groundwater, along with its content in the solid residues, and the characteristics of the disposition of the waste deposits, indicated that the most probable source of chromium in groundwater was the alumina pile. The high permeability of the material found in the layer with the greatest Cr(VI) concentrations in the piezometer located near the alumina, allowed chromium movement after its leaching. The extraction regime of the wells in this area produced a drawdown cone which pulled the contaminant from the QC yard toward the northwest. The kind of material forming the bottom of the alumina pile, exposed during its removal, confirmed the easiness of Cr(VI) infiltration into the aquifer.

Secondary sources of groundwater chromium in the Buenavista area are irrigation with Cr(VI) polluted water, and the fumes from the chromate factory. Tannery wastewaters were not found to be a source for groundwater pollution in this area.

The identification of the main pollution source allowed the proposal of an aquifer remediation strategy in the Buenavista area. The clean-up programme, which is currently underway, is based on the removal of the main pollution source, the reprocessing of the wastes and the pumping and treatment of the most polluted wells.

REFERENCES

APHA 1989. *Standard methods for the examination of water and wastewater.* Washington AWWA, WPCF.

Armienta M.A., R.Rodríguez, A.Queré, F. Juárez, N.Ceniceros, A.Aguayo 1993. Groundwater pollution with chromium in Leon valley, Mexico. *Intern. J. Environ. Anal. Chem.* 54:1-13.

Armienta M.A. & A.Queré 1995. Hydrogeochemical behavior of chromium in the unsaturated zone and in the aquifer of Leon valley, Mexico. *Water, Air and Soil Pollut.* 84:11-29.

Doisy, R. J., H. P. Streeten, J. M. Freiberg, & A. J. Schneider 1976. Chromium metabolism in man and biochemical effects in: A. S. Prasad (ed.), *Trace elements in human health and disease.* New York: Academic Press.

Fishbein, L. 1984. Metals in biological and environmental samples. *Intern. J. Environ. Anal. Chem.* 17:113-170.

Hem, J.D. 1977. Reactions of metal ions at surfaces of hydrous iron oxide. *Geochim.Cosmochim. Acta* 41: 527-538.

James B.R. & R.J. Bartlett 1983. Behavior of chromium in soils. VII. Adsorption and reduction of hexavalent forms. *J. Environ. Qual.* 12: 177-181

Sass, B.M. & D.Rai 1987. Solubility of amorphous chromium(III)-iron(III) hydroxide solutions. *Inorg. Chem.* 26:2228-2232.

Tessier, A. , P. G. Campbell & M.Bisson 1979. Sequential extraction procedure for the speciation of particulate metals. *Anal. Chem.* 51:884-851.

Groundwater in the Urban Environment: Problems, Processes and Management, Chilton et al. (eds)
© 1997 Balkema, Rotterdam, ISBN 90 5410 837 1

An expert system for managing hydrocarbon risks

Bridget E. Butler & Judith I. Petts
Centre for Hazard and Risk Management, Loughborough University, UK

ABSTRACT: Risk assessment and risk management now underpin environmental protection in the UK. Risk assessment provides for a structured and systematic analysis of a problem. It is now accepted as providing an objective tool to inform risk management decisions. In particular, risk assessment can assist in the prioritisation of management activities more effectively to direct resources to significant risks. However, the application of risk assessment remains ad hoc and often focused on quantified approaches. The problem of how to integrate the results of a risk assessment into decision-making processes remains. Intelligent expert/knowledge-based systems offer considerable potential to support regulatory decision-making relating to environmental risks. Such systems utilise expert knowledge to solve specific problems as an expert would but without requiring specialist or skilled users. This paper describes the development of a prototype decision-support tool to assist non-specialist regulatory personnel in the Environment Agency in the prioritisation of risks and management activities relating to groundwater threats from hydrocarbon point-sources such as petrol filling stations.

1 INTRODUCTION

Within the UK, the protection of water resources, particularly groundwater resources, is an important issue for regulatory authorities such as the Environment Agency, industry and the public in general. There is a diverse range of potential sources of groundwater pollution: both point and diffuse (Harris & Skinner 1992). Of the many substances with the potential to pollute groundwater, hydrocarbons present a particular risk due to their ubiquitous nature and potential mobility once released.

Hydrocarbon pollution sources, such as petrol filling stations, present both a large-scale and significant point-source pollution risk problem. A 1992 survey (Thompson 1993) in the London area identified that 52% of underground tanks used to store petroleum were over 20 years old, with 30% of leaks arising from tanks and 70% from associated pipework. In previous years 100-130 leaks had been recorded per year. The Institute of Petroleum's UK Marketing Survey for 1996 shows that the number of petrol filling stations in the UK has decreased since 1986, but that site throughput has increased (Table 1).

1.1 Risk assessment and risk management

Risk assessment is now accepted as a structured, objective and robust tool to assist risk management decisions (Herbert et al. 1995). This applies both in

Table 1. UK petrol filling stations 1986-1995 (Institute of Petroleum, 1996).

Year ending	Number of sites	Site throughput (million litres)
1995	16 244	1.76
1994	16 971	1.76
1993	17 969	1.72
1992	18 549	1.67
1991	19 247	1.62
1990	19 465	1.62
1989	19 756	1.56
1988	20 016	1.50
1987	20 197	1.41
1986	20 641	1.34

the regulatory context and within industry. Risk assessment can be used to prioritise management activities to ensure the most effective use of resources (time, personnel etc.). Regulatory developments both in the UK and Europe are encouraging, and in some cases specifically requiring, the adoption of a risk assessment approach, for example, in the design and siting of new landfills; the identification and assessment of contaminated sites, and in the protection of groundwater (e.g., Environment Act 1995).

Different stages and/or objectives of decision-making warrant different approaches to risk assessment. For example, the derivation of clean-up levels or the understanding of site-specific risks to human health, may require quantitative risk assessment (e.g., Goldsborough & Smit 1995). However, the rapid prioritisation of potential risk problems at different sites so as to identify where regulatory or other actions should be focused, may be performed effectively using semi-quantified or qualitative ranking tools (e.g., CCME Subcommittee on Classification of Contaminated Sites 1992; McFarland 1992).

The common feature of any application of risk assessment is a need for extensive user knowledge and understanding. The problem of integrating the results into the decision-making process remains. Part of this problem lies in designing systems which can be applied to allow effective and consistent decision-making.

The regulatory environment provides several barriers to the use of risk assessment and risk management approaches:
  (i) decisions are often complex, across a wide range of disciplines and need to be made quickly;
  (ii) there are relatively few experts;
  (iii) consistent decision-making is often difficult;
  (iv) decisions have to be made by relatively inexperienced staff; and
  (v) the concept of risk is not well understood.

1.2 A knowledge-based approach

The effect of high power, cheap computing has resulted in the development of a particular branch of artificial intelligence called expert or knowledge-based systems. Expert/knowledge-based systems offer considerable potential to support regulatory decision-making relating to environmental risks. Such systems are special-purpose computer programs designed to operate in a specific problem area; the program utilises human expertise and solves problems as a human expert would (Hayes-Roth et al. 1986). Knowledge-based systems can assist non-expert or less experienced personnel in solving complex problems that may exceed their current abilities. They do not replace human expertise but enhance it as the knowledge such a system holds is explicit and accessible, unlike more conventional programs (Waterman 1986).

The knowledge-based system approach to problem solving has been used in a wide variety of domains such as medicine, agriculture, engineering, geology and chemistry. The use of this approach in the environmental field is more recent but developing rapidly (Hushon 1989; Geraghty 1993; Warwick et al. 1993). Systems have been developed for use in regulatory support, site assessment and remediation, contaminant modelling and water resources management (Crowe & McClymont 1992; Hushon 1987).

The characteristics of groundwater pollution problems make them amenable to a knowledge-based approach, as highlighted by Crowe (1994): i.e.,
  (i) interdisciplinary knowledge is required to solve problems e.g., geology, toxicology etc.;
  (ii) natural systems exhibit complex behaviour, resulting in difficult decision-making;
  (iii) type, quantity and quality of information available to make these decisions is variable; and
  (iv) human experts with the requisite breadth of knowledge are rare.

2 SYSTEM STRUCTURE AND DEVELOPMENT

The remainder of this paper discusses the design of a system as a general risk-management support-tool that enables prioritisation of actions. It focuses on petrol-filling stations and their potential risk to groundwater due to petroleum leaks, spills etc. The system is not aimed at the groundwater specialist or expert risk assessor but at less experienced regulatory personnel.

Although the field of knowledge-based systems is expanding rapidly, effective design and development methodologies have only recently been laid down (Guida & Tasso 1994). Crucial to successful system development is adequate focus on system design, e.g., ensuring that there is a real need for the system, identification of suitable domain experts, identification of user needs etc. (Kidd 1987). If insufficient attention is paid to these areas, and a logical approach is not taken, then development of a successful system is less likely.

2.1 Stages of development

As a process, system development has been divided in this work into three stages:
  (i) Stage One - Framing the problem;
  (ii) Stage Two - Collecting and structuring the knowledge, and forming a conceptual model of the system; and
  (iii) Stage Three - Model and prototype computer system development.

2.1.1 Stage One - framing the problem

Stage One has involved identification of experts in the field and system users. Identification of a suitable expert who is able to contribute to development of a tool such as a knowledge-based system is a critical step. Development would be significantly hampered by an expert who is inaccessible, unenthusiastic or unable to communicate his knowledge (Welbank 1983). As this system was to be designed for a regulatory environment, a regulatory groundwater specialist with at least ten years of experience was identified. In order not to introduce undue regulatory bias, a second expert, an academic groundwater specialist, has also taken part in this study.

Equally important to the identification of human experts who provide their knowledge and experience

372

to form the basis of any system, are the potential system users. Users should be involved in system development and their needs clearly identified (Kidd 1987). Potential users for this study were identified as having less than ten years of experience, inexperienced risk assessors and non-specialist groundwater officers. They would, however, have some hydrogeological knowledge, such as water quality officers and waste regulation officers. Potential users were also identified from within industry, who may have responsibility for groundwater protection, such as environmental managers. A total of twenty potential users were interviewed.

Users were asked about their background, how many years experience they had, what their responsibilities were, what sort of information sources they use when fulfilling those responsibilities, and about their level of familiarity with computers.

Backgrounds varied widely: geology, hydrogeology, environmental science, microbiology, biology, and geography. Most had studied to first degree level. Years of experience also varied, from 2-12 years. Although responsibilities ranged from those of a water quality officer with the Environment Agency, to those of a local authority hydrogeologist, groundwater protection was not their sole responsibility. Information sources used included other more experienced members of staff, internal guidance documents, legislation and books. Most of those who took part in this study were familiar with the use of computers, although some were more frequent users than others.

From initial interviews carried out with the regulatory expert and potential users, it became clear that several apparently simple questions needed to be answered as fully as possible when an officer is presented with a polluting or potentially polluting situation:

(i)   What is the pollutant, where is it coming from?
(ii) Where can the pollutant go?
(iii) How will it get there and how long will it take?
(iv) What will be the impact on any identified target?

These equate with the understanding of the source (i) - pathway ((i) and (iii)) - target (iv) framework, which underpins environmental risk assessment. Clearly, for a system to be successful, what the users will require from it must be identified. Of those potential users interviewed, several requirements could be identified. The system must be easily understood and not use 'black box' programming. The need for data input must be kept to a minimum and a wide range of information must be provided to assist the user: e.g., types of pollutant; legislation; guidance documents; potential targets; and relevant human experts who could be contacted.

2.1.2 Stage Two - Knowledge acquisition and conceptual model formation

Stage Two of system formation, the collection and structuring of knowledge to form a conceptual model is often thought of as a 'bottleneck' (Feigenbaum 1983). The actual process of knowledge acquisition is time-consuming and difficult. There are a wide variety of acquisition techniques that have been used for knowledge-based system development. The most common however, is the interview. The technique is useful for eliciting background information and understanding the reasons why something is done in a certain way (Shadbolt & Burton 1995). Interviews can be structured, semi-structured or unstructured. A series of semi-structured interviews have been carried out with the regulatory groundwater specialist. During one of these interviews he was asked to describe a real-life problem scenario. From this a range of concepts were elicited that described the area of groundwater pollution and point-source hydrocarbon pollution in particular, taking into account variations in hydrology etc.

These elicited concepts were then utilised in another knowledge acquisition technique called concept or card sorting. This technique is useful for identifying relationships between concepts and building a conceptual model of the area (Neale 1988). Each concept was written onto a card and the cards sorted into various categories devised by the expert. For example the first sort divided the 90 concepts into source, pathway and target terms, with a fourth category of 'irrelevant' (Table 2).

During this study there were two main aims of using this particular technique: (i) to enable rules to be

Table 2. Categories devised by the expert.

Sort No.	Categories for sorting concepts	Example concepts
1	Source; pathway; target; irrelevant	Diesel spill; groundwater flow; surface water
2	High; medium; low risk; irrelevant	Depth to water table < 5m; minor aquifer; high dilution
3*	Critical, very important, important in risk terms; irrelevant	Volume of spill > 10,000l; high permeability;
4	Sufficient information to do something yourself; ask for more information; pass it onto a specialist; irrelevant	Containment - pea gravel; surface water nearby; remediation strategy
5	Do something immediately; longer-term action; little/no action; irrelevant	No unsaturated zone; no targets within 500m; non-aquifer

* Sort 3 is a sub-sort of 2 and is not discussed here

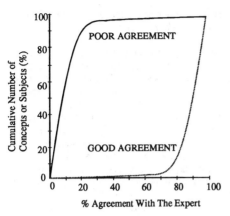

Figure 1. Illustration of agreement with the expert across all concepts.

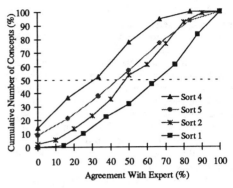

Figure 2. Measure of agreement with the expert across all concepts.

generated for a prototype system, and (ii) to identify whether there was a real need for the system. These aims were achieved by identifying the concepts that the expert used when problem-solving, identifying how he used these and investigating how others used them.

Sorts were also carried out with waste regulators, environmental managers and academics. Each sort was performed by between six and ten people. Comparing their results back to the expert allows for identification of areas of agreement and disagreement. Figure 1 illustrates a representation of the level of agreement with the expert across all concepts, so for example, a level of 90% of the concepts, might give 20% or less agreement with the expert in the case of poor agreement.

Figure 2 shows the level of agreement or disagreement that was actually obtained across all sorts when comparing back to the expert. Sort 1, when people were asked to sort the concepts into source, pathway and target terms, gave the highest agreement with the expert. For sort 1, 50% of concepts gave an agreement of 65% or less with the expert.

Overall agreement with the expert was generally low. Sort 1 gave the highest agreement, then sort 2 and sort 5 (Table 2). Those carrying out the concept sorting were able to agree with the expert at a higher rate for sorting concepts into source, pathway and target terms (sort 1) compared with both high, medium and low risks (sort 2) and reaction time when dealing with a problem (sort 5). Sort 4 showed the least agreement, which may be expected as those sorting the concepts were asked to decide whether they had enough information to deal with the problem. Those people who do not spend 100% of their time dealing with groundwater issues may feel they need more information to deal with a problem, than

say the groundwater specialist who is familiar with dealing with such problems on a regular basis. Variations in the hydrogeological environment for example are important, and are perhaps more apparent at a national level. The groundwater specialist who took part in this work is considered a national expert. Such divergence of understanding between expert and non-expert decision-makers confirms that this is a decision problem which could benefit from the use of a knowledge-based system.

The outcome of Stage Two of system development is the generation of a 'paper model' of the decision problem based on expert knowledge (Figure 3). The model is formed from blocks of information that the expert utilises when problem solving. The concepts of risk management (stages 1-8) have been applied to each section of information, which in turn forms a section of the prototype computer model.

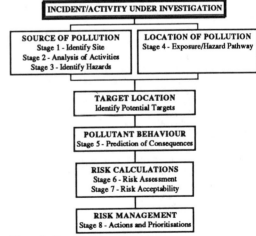

Figure 3. Prototype model structure.

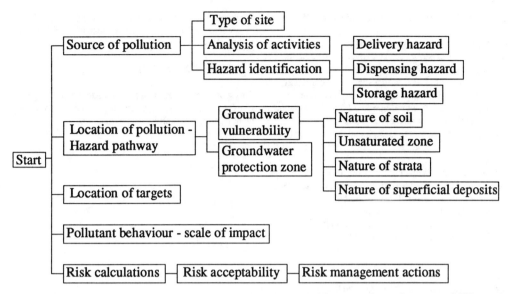

Figure 4. Arrangement of knowledge 'sections' using ESTA to assess risk to groundwater from a petrol filling station.

2.1.3 *Stage Three - Building the prototype computer system*

Stage Three of system development leads to the production of a prototype computer system. In this study, the prototype has been developed using a shell rather than using a programming language directly. A shell in this context is a knowledge-based system with all the problem-specific information removed. A shell environment allows a non-programmer to develop a knowledge-based system The shell chosen was ESTA (Expert System shell for Text Animation) produced by Prolog Development Center (1993). ESTA uses a Windows environment and can be interfaced with other applications such as Microsoft Excel. The knowledge-base developed with ESTA is based on rules and is shown as a 'tree-representation', the branches showing how the knowledge is arranged (Figure 4). The system is then built-up section by section until a working prototype is developed, which can then be tested and validated by the expert and potential users. A working prototype has been developed and has undergone preliminary testing.

3 CONCLUSIONS

Development of a knowledge-based system as a support tool for risk management decisions associated with point-source hydrocarbon groundwater pollution is a valid and valuable approach to the problem.

Although the system being developed focuses on petrol filling stations, once the knowledge has been acquired, the system can be expanded to incorporate other types of site. A computer-based knowledge system is more valuable than the many paper-based ranking tools which are being developed, for three primary reasons:

(i) it is explicitly and transparently based on expert knowledge;

(ii) it has been formulated on the basis of an understanding of how the non-expert responds to risk issues; and

(iii) it provides explicit and interactive help to the user.

REFERENCES

CCME Subcommittee on Classification of Contaminated Sites 1992. *National classification system for contaminated sites.* CCME EPC-CS39E. Canadian Council of Ministers of the Environment, Winnipeg, Manitoba.

Crowe, A.S. 1994. The application of expert systems to groundwater contamination protection, assessment, and remediation. *Groundwater contamination and control.* U. Zoller. New York, Marcel Dekker Inc 567-584.

Crowe, A.S. & G.L. McClymont 1992. An overview of expert systems developed for hydrogeological applications. *Proc. of the 1992 conference of the Canadian chapter of the International Association of Hydrogeologists.* Hamilton: Ontario.

Feigenbaum, E.A. 1983. Artificial intelligence. *IEEE Spectrum* 20: 77-79.

Geraghty, P.J. 1993. Environmental assessment and the application of expert systems: an overview. *Journal of Environmental Management* 39: 27-38.

Goldsborough, D.G. & P.J. Smit 1995. Risc: computer models for soil investigation, risk analysis and urgency estimation. *Proc. Contaminated Soil '95*. The Hague, Netherlands: Kluwer Academic Publishers.

Guida, G. & C. Tasso 1994. Design and development of knowledge-based systems. Chichester: John Wiley and Sons.

Harris, R.C. & A.C. Skinner 1992. Controlling diffuse pollution of groundwater from agriculture and industry. *Journal of the Institution of Water and Environmental Management* 6: 569-575.

Hayes-Roth, F., D.B. Lenat & D.A. Waterman 1986. *Building expert systems*, Reading, Massachusetts: Addison-Wesley Publishing Company Inc.

Herbert, S.M., M.R. Harris & J.M. Denner 1995. UK Standard Procedures for Contaminated Land. *Proc. Contaminated Soil '95*. The Hague, Netherlands: Kluwer Academic Publishers.

Hushon, J. 1989. Overview of Environmental Expert Systems. In *Expert systems for environmental applications*. Washington, DC: American Chemical Society.

Hushon, J.M. 1987. Expert systems for environmental problems. *Environmental Science and Technology* 21:838-841.

Institute of Petroleum 1996. UK retail marketing survey. *Petroleum Review* 50: supplement.

Kidd, A.L. 1987. Knowledge acquisition - an introductory framework. In *Knowledge acquisition for expert systems - a practical handbook*. (ed.) A.L. Kidd. New York, Plenum Press.

McFarland, R. 1992. Simple qualitative risk assessment technique for the prioritisation of chemically contaminated sites in New South Wales, Australia. *Proc. HSE conference on Risk Assessment*: 456-463. London: Health and Safety Executive, Bootle, Merseyside.

Neale, I.M. 1988. First generation expert systems: a review of knowledge acquisition methodologies. *The Knowledge Engineering Review* 3: 105-145.

Prolog Development Center 1993. ESTA expert system shell with interface to PDC Prolog, version 4.1.

Shadbolt, N. & M. Burton 1995. Knowledge elicitation: a systematic approach. In *Evaluation of human work - a practical ergonomics methodology*. (eds.) J. R. Wilson & E. N. Corlett. London: Taylor & Francis Ltd.

Thompson, J.A.J. 1993. Petrol filling stations: past problems and future solutions. *Industry and Environment* 16: 27-29.

Warwick, C.J., J.D. Mumford & G.A. Norton 1993. Environmental management expert systems. *Journal of Environmental Management* 39: 251-270.

Waterman, D.A. 1986. *A guide to expert systems*. Reading, Massachusetts: Addison-Wesley Publishing Company Inc.

Welbank, M. 1983. *A review of knowledge acquisition techniques for expert systems*. Ipswich: British Telecom Research Laboratories.

ACKNOWLEDGEMENTS

This work was funded as a postgraduate studentship by Loughborough University. The support of the Environment Agency is gratefully acknowledged.

Groundwater in the Urban Environment: Problems, Processes and Management, Chilton et al. (eds)
© *1997 Balkema, Rotterdam, ISBN 90 5410 837 1*

A risk based corrective action approach using computer modelling at an urban leaking underground storage tank site

W.A.Canavan
Lincoln Applied Geology, Inc., Somers, N.Y., USA

R.S.Vandenberg & S.Revell
Lincoln Applied Geology, Inc., Bristol, Vt., USA

ABSTRACT: Leaking underground storage tanks (LUSTs) at gasoline service stations are a major source of groundwater contamination in urban areas. Application of a Risk-Based Corrective Action (RBCA) approach at a gasoline-contaminated underground storage tank site indicated that implementation of extensive soil and groundwater remediation was not warranted, nor was it always the most effective method of addressing soil and groundwater contamination problems. Data collected at an urban site in Queens, New York were used to model contaminant transport to predict the impact of known gasoline contamination of soil on the underlying groundwater. Computer models were calibrated with known site characteristics and estimates of contaminant mass loading to groundwater. Downgradient receptor concentrations were also obtained. The results of the RBCA approach utilizing computer modelling indicated that minimal risk of future groundwater contamination exists at the site, and that additional investigation and/or remediation is unnecessary.

1 INTRODUCTION

Given the staggering number of documented petroleum release sites in the United States of America, and the fact that the majority of State regulatory agencies are under-staffed, the United States Environmental Protection Agency (USEPA) has endorsed the American Society of Testing and Materials (ASTM) Risk-Based Corrective Action (RBCA) as an alternative tool to address sites based on potential risks. RBCA was conceived so that sites can be expeditiously mitigated, especially in areas of low risk, while assuring that human health and the environment are adequately protected. The USEPA's current position on RBCA was outlined in a recent directive issued by the Office of Solid Waste and Emergency Response (USEPA OSWER Directive 9610.17). The impetus for the directive was the need to help individual States build corrective action programs that are based on both sound science and common sense, and are flexible and cost-effective.

RBCA is a consistent decision-making process for the assessment and response to a petroleum release, based on the protection of human health and the environment (ASTM 1995). RBCA is a process for determining the amount and urgency of corrective action(s) necessary at a petroleum release site. It has evolved out of an explicit need to master a work load that has grown too large and appears to be out of control (LUSTLINE 1994).

As of October 31, 1994, more than 270,000 petroleum releases had been reported nationwide. In 1994 alone, there were 34,000 confirmed releases reported nationwide. The upcoming 1998 USEPA deadline for upgrading, replacing, or closing UST systems is expected to increase the number of petroleum contaminated sites as contamination is discovered during the upgrade or removal process at existing UST facilities (USEPA 1995).

The New York State Department of Environmental Conservation (NYSDEC) which oversees corrective action at petroleum contaminated sites located in New York State, recently issued an interim document entitled "Interim Procedures for Inactivation of Petroleum-Impacted Sites" in January 1997. The document was developed to improve the corrective action decision making processes and to minimize delays related to closure of petroleum spill sites as well as to maximize the use of limited resources (NYSDEC 1997). The interim document was adapted from the tiered ASTM RBCA approach. It clarifies and expands current State guidelines for site closure to include the RBCA process for petroleum impacted sites.

The following study applies the RBCA approach using computer modelling at an urban LUST site. The purpose of the study was to predict if known vadose zone contamination could adversely impact groundwater beneath the site at levels exceeding state and federal drinking water standards.

Two different modules of the same soil and groundwater contaminant transport modelling package were used. The American Petroleum Institute (API) Decision Support System (DSS) was selected to model the study area because it incorporates widely accepted industry developed models for the RBCA approach.

2 STUDY AREA

The study site is located in Queens, New York, U.S.A. The site was chosen because it is located in an area where groundwater has been adversely impacted due to extreme urbanization.

The subject site consists of an active gasoline service station located in a commercial and residential area in the northern portion of Queens County, New York. Queens County is located at the western end of Long Island, New York (Figure 1). According to the 1990 census, the borough of Queens encompasses an area of approximately 285 km^2 and has a population of 1.95 million.

3 HYDROGEOLOGIC SETTING

Pleistocene (Wisconsin Stage) glacial drift deposits cover approximately eighty percent of Queens County, New York, including the subsurface beneath the site. The remainder of the county is covered by shore and salt marsh deposits and manmade fill of Holocene age. The subject site is located at the top of a long regional ridge underlain by what is known as the Harbor Hill Terminal Moraine, which marks the farthest advance of the Wisconsin age glaciation in Queens County (Figure 1) (Swarzenski 1963) (Soren 1971).

The unconsolidated sediments underlying the area consist of Late Cretaceous to Pleistocene deposits were deposited unconformably on crystalline bedrock of Precambrian (?) age (Soren 1971). The bedrock beneath the county dips about 24 m per 1.61 km to the southeast which allowed the deposition of unconsolidated deposits ranging in thickness from 0 m in northwestern Queens to 335 m in the southeastern part of the county (Figure 2).

Four distinct aquifers have been identified beneath the area and include in descending order: the upper glacial aquifer, the Jameco Aquifer, the Magothy Aquifer, and the Lloyd Aquifer (Soren 1971) (Figure 2). The upper glacial aquifer directly underlies the subject site, and thus will be discussed in detail.

The upper glacial aquifer consists mainly of glacial outwash deposits of sand and gravel. Groundwater occurs under unconfined conditions in most of the aquifer especially south of the Harbor Hill Moraine. The thickness of the aquifer ranges from approximately 1 m in northwestern Queens to about 46 m in the southern part of the county (Figure 2). The upper glacial aquifer is designated as a potable source of water by the NYSDEC and is extensively pumped as a commercial and residential water source in the central part of the county between the Harbor Hill Moraine and Jamaica Bay (Soren 1971). The groundwater immediately beneath the site is not utilized for supply purposes; however, the Jamaica Water Supply Company operates two municipal supply wells within a two kilometre radius of the site (Figure 1).

4 INVESTIGATION METHODOLOGY

Test borings were drilled around the existing UST area at an active gasoline service station using the hollow stem auger drilling method. Soil samples were collected during drilling and sent to a laboratory where they were analyzed for gasoline components using EPA certified methodologies. The borings were drilled to varying completion depths with the maximum depth being 28 m, due to the limitations of the drilling method and the nature of the sediments.

The geology beneath the study site consists of compact fine to medium sand with some silt and fine gravel which extends below a fill unit from 1.8 m to 28 m be-

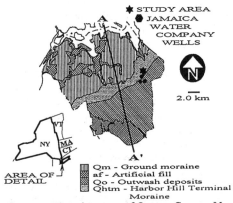

Figure 1. Plan view map of Queens County, New York; showing the surficial geology (adapted from Soren 1971).

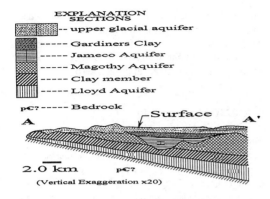

-- upper glacial aquifer
----- Gardiners Clay
----- Jameco Aquifer
----- Magothy Aquifer
----- Clay member
----- Lloyd Aquifer
pC? ----- Bedrock

Surface

A   A'

2.0 km   pC?
(Vertical Exaggeration x20)

Figure 2. North-south cross section of Queens County, New York; showing hydrogeologic units (adapted from Soren 1971).

low grade. The groundwater table was not encountered suggesting that it is present below 28 m in the area of the facility. The location of test boring and soil sampling locations, are shown on Figure 3.

Results of the drilling indicate that the sediments encountered during the study were consistent with descriptions of the upper glacial aquifer reported by Soren (1971) and Swarzenski (1963). The results of soil sampling and laboratory analysis indicate that soils beneath the site were impacted by petroleum hydrocarbon compounds (gasoline) in the vicinity of the UST area. The hydrocarbon impacted soils were the result of documented LUSTs located in the central portion of the site (Figure 3).

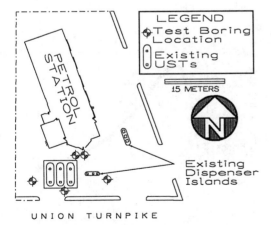

LEGEND
Test Boring Location
Existing USTs

15 METERS

N

Existing Dispenser Islands

PETROL STATION

UNION TURNPIKE

Figure 3. Site plan showing the study area.

5 CONCEPTUAL MODEL

To initiate the study, a conceptual model of the physical structure of the subsurface was developed using data collected from the subsurface investigation. The conceptual model included estimating the source area size, soil porosity, soil volumetric water content, depth to groundwater, and mass of adsorbed benzene contamination. The parameters obtained included the following: source area size = 8.53 m wide x 7.62 m long x 13.41 m thick; porosity = 0.35; volumetric water content = 0.15; depth to groundwater = 30.5 m; benzene concentration = 150 µg/kg.

For the purpose of the study, benzene (C_6H_6) was chosen as the indicator compound because it has the lowest NYSDEC Groundwater Quality Standard (0.7 µg/l), and it is also the most mobile of the aromatic hydrocarbons found in gasoline.

6 MODEL PREPARATION

A fate and transport model was prepared to evaluate the potential for adsorbed hydrocarbon contamination to migrate downward and impact the groundwater table beneath the site. The model was prepared because two Jamaica Water Company municipal supply wells are located within 1.6 km of the site.

The conceptual model parameters were used as input for two separate modules of the API DSS modelling package. The Jury unsaturated flow model was chosen to predict vadose zone contaminant transport and mass loading rates to groundwater, and the AT123D groundwater fate and transport model was subsequently utilized to predict contaminant travel times.

7 JURY UNSATURATED MODEL

The Jury model is an industry accepted unsaturated screening level model that estimates the chemical flux volatilizing from soil and time varying concentrations throughout the unsaturated zone (API 1994). The time varying concentration profiles are used to estimate the contaminant loading to the water table. According to Jury et. al. (1983) (1990), the model is based on the analytical solution of a differential mass balance equation that accounts for the following considerations: total soil concentration, time, first order decay of contaminants, chemical diffusion in the unsaturated zone, depth of the contamination, and contaminant velocity.

To address the modeling at the Queens site the Jury

model calculated the annual mass loading to groundwater from user specified site and chemical data. The Jury model required input of the following soil column data: volumetric water content (0.15), effective porosity (0.35), soil bulk density (1.65 g/cm³), fractional organic carbon (0.002 mg/mg), thickness of incorporation (13.41 m), thickness of soil cover (13.41 m), depth of unsaturated zone (30.50 m), x-dimension of contaminant source (8.53 m), y-dimension of source (7.62 m), thickness of boundary layer (0.5 cm), and infiltration rate (0.0173 cm/day). Chemical input data required in the Jury model include: total soil concentration (0.15 mg/kg), chemical air diffusion coefficient (7,517 cm²/day), chemical water diffusion coefficient(0.84 cm²/day), Henry's Law constant (0.25 mg/l/mg/l), K_{oc} (83 µg/g oc/µg/ml), chemical decay rate (0.00 1/day), and solubility (1,750 mg/l).

The Jury model was run using the API DSS software package as an interface. The model was run to predict mass loading rates to ground water 60 years into the future. The mass loading rates obtained were ultimately used in the AT123D ground water fate and transport model to predict resultant groundwater concentrations at a receptor point 17 m below and 10 m downgradient of the source.

8 JURY MODEL RESULTS

Results of the Jury model show that some benzene will migrate (leach) downward and enter the groundwater beneath the site (Figure 4). The highest mass loading calculated by the Jury model occurs between 8 and 18 years in the simulation. The peak mass loading occurs at 11 years at a rate of 1.75 g/yr. After 11 years, the mass loading rate declines steadily with some trace mass still entering the groundwater aquifer even at year 60 in the simulation.

As part of the computer modelling process, a sensitivity analysis was completed to evaluate Jury model input parameters. Volumetric water content, source size, and source concentration were determined to be the most sensitive variables.

Volumetric water content was determined to have the greatest impact on the resultant mass loading rates and arrival times. Changing the volumetric water content in the Jury model dramatically affects the mass loading rate to groundwater.

It is also important to note that the Jury model does allow for the input of a biodegradation factor, which was not used (set to 0.00 1/day) in the model so that the potential risk to groundwater and the environment was determined very conservatively. It is obvious that

biodegradation will occur as the mass of contamination migrates downward toward the groundwater table. If the Jury model was run to include a biodegradation factor the resultant benzene mass loading to the groundwater would likely approach zero.

9 AT123D MODEL

The AT123D groundwater contaminant fate and transport model was run to calculate hypothetical benzene concentrations in groundwater beneath and downgradient of the site. The AT123D model uses a Cartesian coordinate system to describe the source and the location of a hypothetical receptor point (Yeh, 1981). The receptor point is an important element in the RBCA approach, because it is the nearest downgradient point where risk to human health and the environment must be determined.

The AT123D model idealizes the saturated zone and assumes that flow is one dimensional, steady, and uniform in the downgradient direction (American Petroleum Institute 1994). The differential mass balance (advective-dispersion) equation:

$$D_l \frac{\partial^2 C}{\partial l^2} - \overline{v}_l \frac{\partial C}{\partial l} = \frac{\partial C}{\partial t} \tag{1}$$

(where, l = a curvilinear coordinate direction; $\overline{v}$ = average linear groundwater velocity; D_l = coefficient of hydrodynamic dispersion in the longitudinal direction; C = solute concentration) is internally solved to describe contaminant fate and transport in the saturated zone (Freeze & Cherry, 1979). Groundwater concentrations are then calculated across a number of equally-spaced vertical intervals using the following equation (American Petroleum Institute 1994):

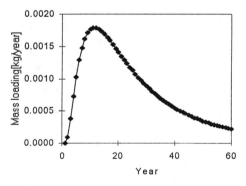

Figure 4. Predicted mass loading to ground water.

380

$$C_{well} = \sum_z \frac{C(z)}{N_z} \qquad (3)$$

where, C_{well} = vertically-averaged well concentration; $C(z)$ = concentration at depth z (mg/l); N_z = number of user specified intervals between top and bottom of the well screen. The concentrations are then internally vertically averaged. The method assigns equal weight to all vertical intervals between the top and bottom of the interval assigned.

To show maximum concentrations that could be present, a 1 m interval was chosen extending from the top of the water table into the saturated zone. The input data were again conservatively estimated where actual data were not available. The depth to groundwater was estimated to be approximately 30.5 m below the surface and approximately 17 m below the source of contamination. The hydraulic conductivity (k) of the aquifer material was estimated from the literature to be 1,112 m/yr (Freeze & Cherry 1979).

10 AT123D MODEL RESULTS

The results of running the AT123D model, using the Jury models' calculated mass loading values as input, conservatively show that very low concentrations of benzene are predicted in the ground water downgradient (10 m) of the source. Figure 5 graphically depicts the results obtained by the AT123D model.

Peak concentrations of benzene predicted for between 12 and 14 years at a maximum of 2.7 µg/l. After 12 to 14 years, concentrations decline to less than 0.5 µg/l, which is below NYSDEC Groundwater Quality Standards for benzene. The model was rerun to calculate concentrations of benzene at a greater dis-

tance from the source (100 m), and as expected, the results show that concentrations of benzene will be extremely low at this distance (<0.05 µg/l) and well below NYSDEC Groundwater Quality Standards.

The data presented on Figure 5 show some concentration-time oscillations that are the result of hydraulic conductivity and hydraulic gradient input values. These oscillations occur because of the relatively large time step internally used by the model (1 year time step) (Yeh 1981). Tests on the model have demonstrated that if small time steps are used (<0.1 years), the amplitude of the oscillations are not significant (Yeh 1981).

11 CONCLUSIONS

The results of a RBCA approach using computer modelling indicate that the source of adsorbed benzene contamination present in the subsurface at the study site will not significantly threaten groundwater. This type of RBCA approach was both cost effective, beneficial, and demonstrated these findings to the regulatory agency, without using more invasive and costly investigative techniques. In this instance the RBCA approach was used in lieu of the more traditional practice of basing clean-up requirements on generic environmental standards that may or may not be appropriate to site-specific situations.

REFERENCES

American Petroleum Institute. 1994. Decision Support System for Exposure and Risk Assessment Version 1.0. Manual Pages B-1 - B-12 and C-1 - C-21.

American Society of Testing and Materials, 1995. Risk-Based Corrective Action at Petroleum Release Sites. ASTM Paper No. ES 1739-95.

Freeze, R.A. & J. A. Cherry. 1979. *Groundwater*. Englewood Cliffs, NJ: Prentice Hall, Inc.

Jury, W.A., W.F. Spencer, and W.J. Farmer. 1983. Behavior Model for Trace Organics in oil. Model Description. Journal of Environmental Quality, 12. Pages 558 - 564.

Jury, W.A., D. Russo, G. Streile, and H.E. Elabd. 1990. Evaluation of Organic Chemicals Residing by the Soil Surface. Water Resources Research. Volume No.1, Pages 13- 20.

LUSTINE, 1994. New England Interstate Water Pollution Control Commission, Bulletin 21,

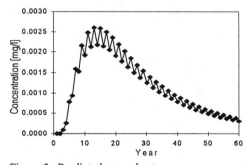

Figure 5. Predicted groundwater concentrations at the theoretical receptor point.

December, 1994. NYSDEC, 1991. NYCRR Parts 316 to 317, Ground Water And Surface Water Quality Regulations.

NYSDEC, 1997. Interim Procedures for Inactivation of Petroleum Impacted Sites.

Soren, J., 1971. Ground-Water and Geohydrologic Conditions in Queens County, Long Island, New York. Geological Survey Water Supply Paper No. 2001-A, 39 pgs.

Swarzenski, W.V., 1963. Hydrogeology of Northwestern Nassau and Queens Counties Long Island, New York. Geological Survey Water-Supply Paper No. 1657, 90 pgs.

United States Environmental Protection Agency. 1995. Directive #9610.17. Use of Risk Based OSWER Decision making in UST Corrective Action Programs.

Yeh, G. T. 1981. AT123D: Analytical Transient One, Two, and Three dimensional Simulation of Waste Transport in the Aquifer System. Oak Ridge National Laboratory, Oak Ridge, TN.

Predicting water quality impacts from future minewater outflows in an urbanized Scottish catchment

M.Chen & C.Soulsby
Department of Geography, University of Aberdeen, UK

P.L.Younger
Department of Civil Engineering, University of Newcastle-upon-Tyne, UK

ABSTRACT: One of the most important hydrogeological problems in urban Scotland is groundwater rebound in abandoned mining areas in the Central belt. The evolution of acid mine drainage causes groundwater contamination which, in turn, pollutes surface waters which are often important amenity and conservation resources within the urban environment. The Central Coalfield in West Lothian was extensively mined from Polkemmet and neighbouring collieries. Groundwater recovery is near its completion, following mine closure in 1985. Geochemical modelling indicates that pyrite oxidation, calcite dissolution and goethite precipitation are primarily responsible for the evolution of groundwater chemistry currently observed in both the Polkemmet and Riddochhill shafts. Predictive modelling suggests that minewater discharge would have marked effects on the River Almond, with goethite being precipitated at a rate of up to 36 kg/day, dissolved sulphate concentrations ranging between 170 and 800 mg/l, and pH being depressed to 6.5. This contamination will affect both the visual amenity and conservation value of the River which drains a highly urbanized catchment.

1 INTRODUCTION

Contamination of groundwater during water table rebound in abandoned coal mining areas constitutes a major hydrogeological problem in many parts of the world. These areas are often highly urbanized as a result of mining communities which have developed during the exploitation of mineral resources. Contamination of minewater is primarily attributed to the oxidation of pyrite in worked coal seams and subsequent dissolution due to water table recovery. The resulting acidic groundwater is rich in Fe and sulphate. When recovery is complete and groundwater discharges into surface waters extensive pollution can ensue. Receiving streams in urban areas are usually important amenity and conservation resources and the degradation in water quality resulting from minewater discharge can be serious. In many former mining areas this pollution usually adds to the often poor levels of environmental quality associated with economic decline.

The Central Coalfield in West Lothian, located in the urbanized upper catchment of the River Almond (Figure 1), has been extensively mined for over a century. Polkemmet Colliery was the last of several inter-connected collieries to close when it was flooded during the 1984/85 Miner's Strike (Younger 1995). Recent monitoring of the rebound at Polkemmet indicates that the rate of groundwater recovery is currently at 0.15 to 0.2 m per week (SRK 1995). If this trend continues, rebound will be complete, and the nearby River Almond will begin to receive minewater discharges before the year 2000.

Consequently there is an urgent need to assess the potential water quality impacts on the River Almond resulting from the closure of the Polkemmet Colliery. The objectives of this study are to (1) evaluate the chemical evolution of minewater quality using the computer code NETPATH (Plummer et al. 1994) and (2) assess environmental impacts of minewater discharges on the River Almond during summer low-flow conditions using a second computer code, PHREEQE (Parkhurst et al. 1980).

2 GEOLOGY, MINING OPERATION AND HYDROGEOLOGY OF THE STUDY AREA

The stratigraphy of the Central Coalfield comprises four Dinantian to Westphalian groups of strata: Limestone Coal Group, Upper Limestone Group, Passage Group, and Lower Coal Measures.

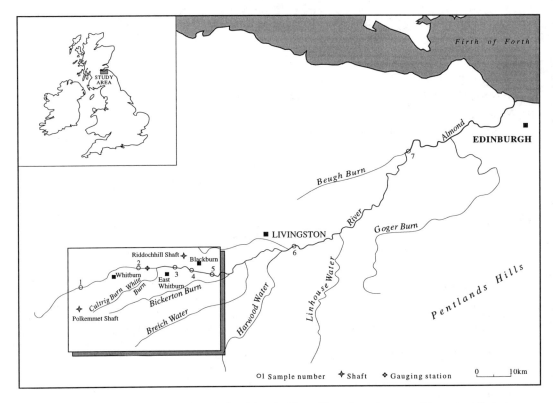

Figure 1. The study area showing coal mining regions, the River Almond catchment and its major tributaries.

The sediments consist of coals, limestones, mudstones, siltstones, sandstones and seatearths. These coal-bearing strata dip to the north-west in the study area (Figure 2). Coals occur in all Carboniferous groups, and those in the Limestone Coal Group and the Lower Coal Measures (Productive Measures) are economically the most important.

Shallow coal seams in the Lower Coal Measures and Limestone Coal Group were exploited first via both drifts and shafts. Deeper reserves in the Limestone Coal Group to the west were subsequently mined from Polkemmet, Riddochhill, Whitrigg and Foulshiels collieries.

Coal mining and associated dewatering has fundamentally changed the hydrogeology and hydrochemistry of the Coal Measures. The hydrogeology of the abandoned coalfield is dominated by flow through mined voids and associated collapsed strata. Consequently engineers have tended to conceptualise flooded workings in terms of "ponds", defined as discrete systems of inter-connected workings generally hydraulically separated from each other except for discrete overflow pathways (Younger et al. 1995). The composite mine plan in the Polkemmet system (Figure 2), shows the extent of connected and inter-connected ponds of workings on the Wilsontown Main and Jewel coal seams. The Polkemmet and Whitrigg Pond is the largest subsurface water body in the system, covering an east-west distance of 8 km from the deepest workings (at an elevation of approximately -350 m above sea level) to the outcrops in Whitrigg.

A potential future discharge location for minewater has been predicted at the entrance of a former drift mine in a topographically low area adjacent to the River Almond (SRK 1995). If this prediction is correct, minewater discharge would have a direct impact on the quality of the river. Conceptually, groundwater in the Polkemmet pond will rise and flow northeastward into the Whitrigg pond via the overflowing pathways A and B, while groundwater in the Loganlea, Foulshiels and

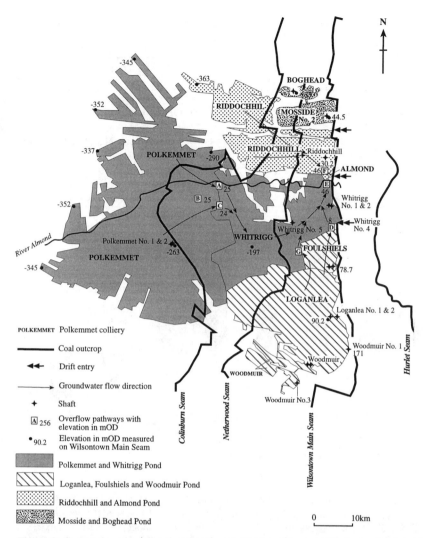

Figure 2. Composite mine plan showing the extent of working and likely groundwater flow directions and possible minewater discharge location (from SRK, 1995).

Woodmuir pond will flow northward into the Whitrigg via the pathways D and G. Groundwater from both the Riddochhill and Almond pond, and the Polkemmet and Whitrigg ponds is likely to mix and break out via the Almond Mine, before discharging into the river. Judging from historic pumping rates during dewatering, future discharge rates are estimated to be 2000 m³/d in the dry summer and 7500 m³/d in the winter (SRK 1995).

3 EVOLUTION OF MINEWATER GENERATION

Samples were collected from the River Almond during the low flow period in September 1996 and analysed using standard methods. Groundwater samples from the Polkemmet and Riddochhill shafts were collected and analysed by the Scottish Environment Protection Agency (SRK 1995). Hydrochemical data are shown in Table 1. NETPATH was used to identify the main hydrogeochemical processes which control the evolution of the groundwater chemistry at the

Table 1. Hydrochemistry for shaft groundwater, the River Almond and rain water (all units are in mg/l except where stated).

	pH	EC µS/cm	Alkalinity as CaCO₃	NO₃⁻	SO₄²⁻	Cl⁻	Na⁺	K⁺	Ca²⁺	Mg²⁺	Fe	Mn
a) Polkemmet *Average (n=5)*	7.16	1080.00	466.60	-	252.20	15.80	97.00	19.90	102.02	55.26	1.74	1.23
b) Riddochhill *Average (n=10)*	6.66	3380.00	368.16	-	1565.00	11.42	49.80	20.95	345.00	242.20	20.82	8.25
c) River Almond *Average (n=7)*	7.17	907.71	100.57	24.40	137.86	72.74	48.06	6.64	66.90	20.04	0.03	0.28
d) Rain Water	4.47	-	0	1.55	2.59	2.41	1.21	-	0.22	0.17	-	-

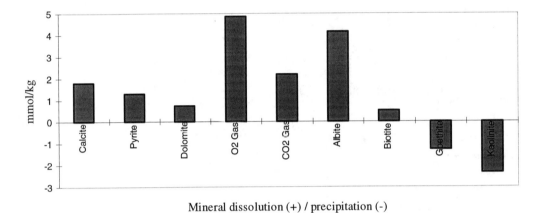

Mineral dissolution (+) / precipitation (-)

Figure 3. NETPATH model 1: from rain to groundwater at Polkemmet.

Polkemmet and Riddochhill shafts. NETPATH geochemical modelling requires the initial and final water to be in a hydrological path and/or both waters are evolutionary. This requirement can be easily satisfied by choosing the rain water as a starting water and current shaft groundwater as final waters. The rain water at Loch Leven (DOE 1990) was selected as the initial water, while the average chemical composition of unstratified shaft groundwater at Polkemmet, and the median Riddochhill groundwater chemistry at a depth of 98.5 m below the ground surface, have been used to represent the final waters.

Two models for the Polkemmet groundwater system were found that satisfied the chosen constraints (Figure 3). As anticipated, both models show that calcite and dolomite dissolution, pyrite oxidation and goethite precipitation, are the main processes governing the groundwater chemistry

evolution at the Polkemmet shaft. In model 1, carbon dioxide is used to contribute in the generation of alkalinity, whereas in model 2 carbon dioxide is replaced by dissolution of siderite ($FeCO_3$). Considering that both carbon dioxide and siderite may well be present in the deep workings, it is reasonable to conclude that they both may have participated in the geochemical reactions.

Only one model satisfied the constraints for groundwater at Riddochhill. This is generally similar to the models for Polkemmet in that controlling processes are calcite dissolution, pyrite oxidation and goethite precipitation. However a major difference is that 6.6 times more calcite (11.97 mmol/kg) has been dissolved, 10 times more pyrite (13.62 mmol/kg) has been oxidised, and 4 times more goethite (12.89 mmol/kg) has been precipitated, together with considerable CO_2 outgassing (Figure 3). This is perhaps due to the relatively samll amount of oxygen

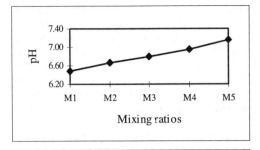

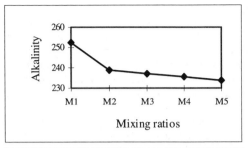

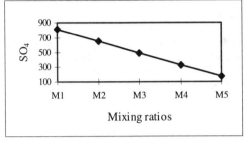

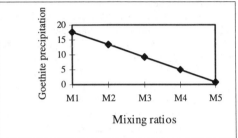

Figure 4. Results of PHREEQE simulation.

available for pyrite oxidation in the deep Polkemmet workings compared with the shallow Riddochhill site. Thus the acidity generated in the Polkemmet shaft was only able to dissolve a limited amount of calcite and other minerals.

4 IMPACTS ON SURFACE WATER QUALITY

PHREEQE geochemical modelling involves mixing the river water with minewater discharges (estimated chemical composition from shaft groundwater) and allowing goethite precipitation in oxidised riverine environments.

Assuming a total future minewater outflow of 2000 m^3/d, five scenarios were simulated by varying the discharge rate of these two groundwater components. Q_{95} of the River Almond is 5500 m^3/d (Figure 1). M1 is the worst possible scenario with the minewater discharge represented by 100% Riddochhill-type groundwater; the simulation is then progressed to M2, M3, M4, corresponding to 75%, 50%, 25% respectively of the Riddochhill-type groundwater in each simulation; in M5, minewater discharge is set at 100% Polkemmet-type groundwater. This range of scenarios is reasonable, since the Riddochhill shaft is nearest the predicted discharge location (at the drift entry of Almond mine) whereas the Polkemmet and Whitrigg pond is the largest subsurface water body.

The results of the PHREEQE simulation are shown in Figure 4. In the worst-case scenario (M1), it is predicted that minewater discharge would have dramatic effects on the River Almond with goethite being precipitated at a rate of 36 kg/day, sulphate reaching 800 mg/l, and pH being reduced to 6.5. For the other scenarios (M2-M5), predictions are that the River Almond would experience goethite precipitation rates ranging from 1.5 to 27 kg/day, sulphate between 170-650 mg/l, and alkalinity around 235 mg/l as $CaCO_3$.

Following the initial breakout, water quality would probably improve over a decade or two, with major cations and anions approaching their predicted lower ranges as Riddochhill-type water is gradually replaced by the Polkemmet-type groundwater (Figure 4). Subsequently, long-term minewater discharge with Fe loading ranging from 1.5 to 2 mg/l can be expected to persist for many decades. The longevity of the minewater pollution steps is caused by the pyrite oxidation and dissolution of its products in the unsaturated zone as the water table fluctuates.

Iron oxide precipitation as amorphous hydroxides or goethite, commonly known as ochre, is a primary environmental and ecological hazard. Ochre deposition in the stream bed not only inhibits photosynthesis, and but also generates additional acidity and contributes a highly reactive sediment to the stream.

SUMMARY

NETPATH and PHREEQE geochemical models were based on a number of plausible assumptions, but they do provide a good first approximation of minewater pollution and the water quality impacts of the River Almond as a result of the 1985 closure of Polkemmet Colliery.

Geochemical modelling predicts that the minewater discharge under the worst-case scenario would have dramatic effects on the River Almond. Although water quality would improve as minewater discharges are gradually dominated by the Polkemmet-type groundwater, residual pollution may last for many decades to come, if not centuries.

The River Almond is an important conservation and amenity resource in West Lothian. Despite a heavily urbanized catchment the river is extensively utilized by local residents and is an important component of the local landscape. Pollution from acid mine drainage would have a deleterious effect on this important resource and would contribute to a significant lowering of environmental quality in an area that has already suffered economic decline as result of the contraction of the mining industry. It is therefore important that hydrogeology is applied in the prediction of minewater impacts on surface waters so that appropriate remediation techniques (eg passive wetland treatment, restoration of pumping regimes *etc*.) can be developed to minimize the impacts of groundwater rebound in urban areas.

Active treatment of Riddochhill-type minewater by lime dosing and flocculation, followed by passive wetland treatment of the long-term Polkemmet-type minewater is recommended (Chen et al., 1997). The initial active treatment will reduce considerably the land area required for the subsequent passive treatment.

REFERENCES

Chen, M., C. Soulsby & P. L. Younger 1997. Predicting the generation of minewater pollution and its impacts on the quality of the River Almond following abandonment of Polkemmet colliery, Central Scotland. *Quarterly Journal of Engineering Geology*, in press.

DOE (Department of Environment) 1990. Acid deposition in the United Kingdom 1986-1988.

Parkhurst, D., D. Thorstenson, & L. Plummer 1980. PHREEQE - A computer program for geochemical calculations. US Geological Survey, *Water Resource Investigations Report* 80-96.

Plummer, L. N., E. C. Prestemon & D. L. Parkhurst 1994. An interactive code (NETPATH) for modeling net geological reactions along a flow path Version 2.0. *U.S. Geological Survey Water-Resources Investigations Report* 94-4196, 130pp.

SRK 1995. *Polkemmet Colliery - mine water recovery (Phase 1)*. Report prepared by Steffen Robertson and Kirsten for *the Forth River Purification Board*.

Younger, P. L. 1995. Minewater pollution in Britain: past, present and future. *Mineral Planning*, 65, 38-42.

Younger, P. L., M. H. Barbour & J. M. Sherwood 1995. Predicting the consequences of ceasing pumping from the Frances and Michael Collieries, Fife. *The fifth National Hydrology Symposium*, British Hydrological Society, 2.25-2.33.

Groundwater supply of Slatina city endangered by contaminants from the River Olt, Romania

Irina Dinu & Marius Albu
University of Bucharest, Romania

Victor Moldoveanu
PROED SA, Bucharest, Romania

Harriet Nash
Wardell Armstrong, Newcastle-under-Lyme, UK

ABSTRACT: The water supply of Slatina city is entirely from groundwater, both from shallow and deep aquifers. The water supply is now greatly endangered, not only by nitrates and nitrites from agricultural activity, but also by sodium and chloride discharged from chemical plants to the River Olt and thence to the alluvial aquifer in the Slatina area. Construction of storage lakes along the River Olt has changed the natural surface water and groundwater regime. The contaminants in the Olt River have polluted firstly the shallow aquifer by lateral migration and secondly the deep aquifer by leakage through an aquitard. The paper presents the hydrogeological conditions, an assessment of aquifer dispersivity, the groundwater chemistry and the preliminary conceptual model of the shallow and deep aquifers interconnected by the aquitard. The study represents the first step in the development of a groundwater management plan for the city.

1 GEOLOGICAL AND HYDROGEOLOGICAL CONDITIONS

1.1 *Geological background*

The city of Slatina is situated in the south-west of Romania, in the valley of the River Olt. The water supply of the city and villages in this area is entirely from groundwater.

The exploited aquifers are in Pliocene - Pleistocene formations and two main aquifers can be distinguished (Figure 1):
• a phreatic aquifer, 4 to 20 m thick, consisting of sands and gravels of the flood plain and terraces of River Olt;
• a confined aquifer complex, which reaches a depth of 140 m, comprising at least four sandy horizons separated by discontinuous clay intercalations.

Between the phreatic aquifer and the confined aquifer complex there is a continuous aquitard, from 1 to 32 m thick, consisting of clays and sandy clays (Moldoveanu 1995).

1.2 *Hydrogeological parameters and water use*

The following parameters were established during the course of the study and utilised in the groundwater flow model and water balance.

Phreatic aquifer
• surface area $A = 109$ km^2
• thickness $M = 4 - 20$ m
• transmissivity $T = 150 - 4000$ m^2/day
• hydraulic gradient $i = 0.0012 - 0.01$
• recharge from precipitation $q = 0.33$ l/(s·km^2)
• number of existing wells $N = 91$
• number of exploited wells $n = 47$
• total pumping rate at present $Q_{ex}{}^P = 135$ l/s
• total number of exploited wells after reconditioning of the wellfield $n1 = 70$
• total pumping rate after reconditioning of the wellfield $Q_{ex} = 300$ l/s.
Confined aquifer complex
• surface area $A = 335$ km^2
• thickness $M = 70 - 100$ m
• transmissivity $T = 360 - 7000$ m^2/day
• hydraulic gradient $i = 0.001 - 0.004$
• number of existing wells $N = 117$
• number of exploited wells $n = 98$
• total pumping rate at present $Q_{ex}{}^P = 385$ l/s
• total pumping rate after reconditioning of the wellfield $Q_{ex} = 593$ l/s.

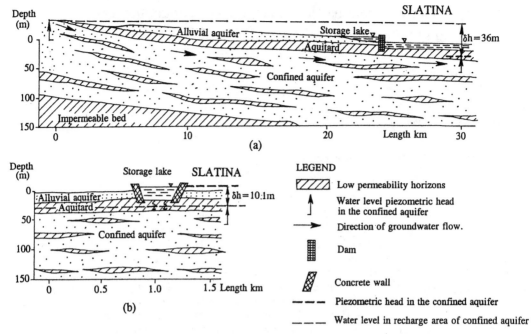

Figure 1. Schematic hydrogeological sections - (a) along and (b) across the Olt Valley.

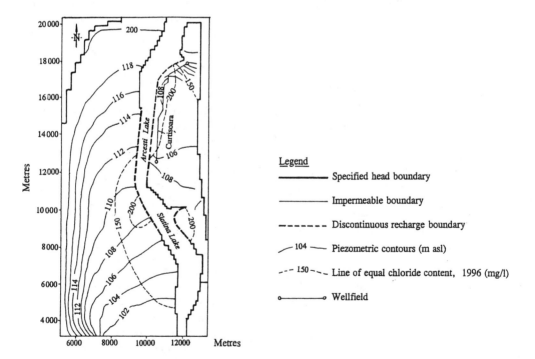

Figure 2. Model of the shallow aquifer.

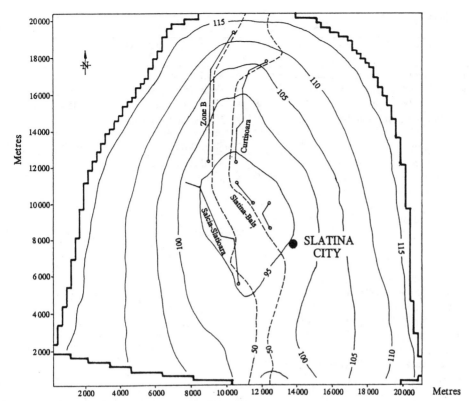

Figure 3. Model of the deep aquifer (legend as for Figure 2).

Aquitard
- leakage surface area $A = 17.9$ km^2
- average vertical hydraulic conductivity
  $K' = 2 \cdot 10^{-6} - 2 \cdot 10^{-4}$ m/day
- thickness $M' = 1 - 32$ m
- leakage parameter $K'/M' = 6 \cdot 10^{-8} - 2 \cdot 10^{-4}$ day^{-1}.

2 MODEL OF THE AQUIFERS

A simplified conceptual model of part of the aquifer system has been developed, and MODFLOW was used to simulate groundwater flow and refine the water balance. The model consists of three layers, the first corresponding to the shallow (phreatic) aquifer, the second to the aquitard and the third to the confined aquifer complex.

The phreatic aquifer is recharged by lateral flow through alluvial deposits along the northern and the western boundaries, from precipitation, and locally by discontinuous recharge from the storage lakes on the River Olt. Rainfall recharge was estimated as the average amount of precipitation less surface runoff and evapotranspiration, taking into account the altitude, the slope, the soil characteristics and the type of vegetation cover.

The deep aquifer extends further to the east and west than the shallow aquifer. It receives recharge by lateral flow along the western, northern and eastern boundaries, and by downwards leakage from the storage lakes.

Groundwater flow out of the study area is to the south in both aquifers.

Specified head (Dirichlet) conditions on the boundaries were prescribed by interpolation of measured piezometric heads. For the shallow aquifer the eastern limit is a no-flow boundary, represented by the limit of the flood plain. The storage lakes locally represent no-flow boundaries for the phreatic aquifer, the bottom of the aquifer being higher than the bottom of the lake (Figure 1). However, there are zones where the lake is in contact with the aquifer, giving discontinuous

Table 1. Water balance.

Aquifer	Inflow (m³/day)		Outflow (m³/day)	
phreatic aquifer	• northern and western boundaries	27577	• southern boundary	14310
	• lateral inflow from storage lakes on the River Olt	25258	• wellfields	22464
			• domestic wells	3456
	• effective infiltration from the surface	3172	• leakage to the confined aquifer complex	15777
	Total inflow	56007	Total outflow	56007
confined aquifer complex	• western, northern and eastern boundaries	43429	• southern boundary	7971
			• wellfields	51235
	• percolation by leakage from the phreatic aquifer and the storage lakes on the River Olt	15777		
	Total inflow	59206	Total outflow	59206

recharge boundaries; Dirichlet conditions were therefore also prescribed for these locations (Figure 2). For the confined aquifer complex Dirichlet conditions were prescribed for all the boundaries (Figure 3). The aquitard is modelled as a layer which allows groundwater transfer by leakage.

The calculated water balance for the two aquifers is shown in Table 1.

3 GEOCHEMISTRY OF GROUNDWATER

Chemical analyses of water samples both from the shallow aquifer and the confined aquifer complex were carried out in 1988 and 1996. The Piper diagram of the 1996 analyses (Figure 4) shows two types of water: calcium-chloride-bicarbonate water for the phreatic aquifer and sodium-chloride-bicarbonate water for the confined aquifer complex.

About 30 years ago, two chemical plants began to discharge sodium-chloride wastes to the Olt river. Consequently, downstream, the shallow aquifer became progressively more contaminated by sodium and chloride. The 1996 chemical analyses show a chloride content of over 200 mg/l locally in the shallow aquifer, in the area of the Curtisoara wellfield and close to the lakes (Figure 2). These values are close to those obtained in 1988. However, in recent years the contamination has extended to the deep aquifer, especially beneath the lakes, due to leakage (Figure 3). The 1988 analyses show a chloride content of almost 30 mg/l in the deep aquifer, in the Curtisoara wellfield, while 1996 analyses show more than 60 mg/l in the Curtisoara

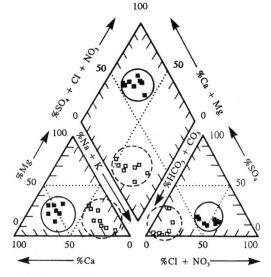

■ shallow aquifer
□ deep aquifer

Figure 4. Piper diagram.

wellfield and 185 mg/l in the Salcia-Slatioara wellfield.

Nitrate levels were found to be locally significant, in the northern part of the Curtisoara wellfield in the phreatic aquifer and in the Zone B wellfield in the deep aquifer. In 1996, the highest concentration of nitrate was 20 mg/l, in the shallow aquifer.

Some of the Romanian standards for drinking water are exceeded. The most polluted areas are in the Curtisoara and Salcia-Slatioara wellfields. Natural organic matter (consumption of O_2) reaches 18 mg/l, phosphates 6 mg/l and iron 1 mg/l in the Curtisoara wellfield. In the Salcia-Slatioara wellfield organic matter reaches 14 mg/l, phosphates 5 mg/l, nitrites 10 mg/l and ammonium 5 mg/l. The highest ammonium concentration (over 50 mg/l) was determined in the Zone B wellfield. Pesticides may also be present, but thay have not yet been analysed for.

A third of the wells in the shallow aquifer are not in use because of the high content of chloride, nitrate and nitrite. There is a high risk of further contamination of both aquifers.

4 ESTIMATION OF DISPERSION

The main pollution problem of Slatina is due to contaminants from the storage lakes on the River Olt, which have already reached the shallow aquifer. This is shown by the high chloride concentrations, which are over 200 mg/l locally. Chloride concentrations in the deep aquifer, which exceed 60 mg/l, show that this is also endangered.

Therefore both horizontal and vertical migration are assumed. The first is due to losses from the storage lakes to the phreatic aquifer, along the discontinuous recharge lines (Figure 2). The second is due to leakage from the bottom of the lakes to the deep aquifer and even by losses along the well casings.

Using chloride concentrations measured in wells close to the storage lakes, the coefficients of hydrodynamic dispersion were estimated from the analytical solution of Ogata & Banks (1961):

$$C\rho(t,l) = \frac{(C\rho)_0}{2}\left(erfc\frac{l-u_c t}{2\sqrt{Dt}} + e^{\frac{u_c l}{D}} \cdot erfc\frac{l+u_c t}{2\sqrt{Dt}} \right)$$

(4.1)

with the initial condition
$C\rho\ (0,\ l)= 0$ for $0 \le l < +\infty$

and the boundary conditions
$C\rho\ (t,\ 0)= (C\rho)_0 = const.$ and
$C\rho\ (t,\ +\infty)= 0$ for $t \ge 0$,
where: $(C\rho)_0$ is the contaminant concentration (kg/m^3) along the boundary of contamination, $C\rho(t,l)$ is the contaminant concentration (kg/m^3) in the aquifer at the moment t and the distance l, u_c is the migration velocity (m/day) of the contaminant in the l direction, D is the coefficient of hydrodynamic dispersion (m^2/day), t is the time passed since pollution started (days) and l is the distance (m).

In the case of the shallow aquifer, the following parameters are known:

- the chloride concentration $(C\rho)_0$ in the lake has the average value of 0.8 kg/m^3,
- the distances l from 50 m to 2250 m, between the lake and the wells were measured along the streamlines (Albu 1982),
- the time since pollution started is almost 30 years (10000 days),
- chloride concentrations determined on samples from the wells are from 114 to 241 mg/l.

For lateral migration, calculated values of the coefficient of hydrodynamic dispersion are from 0.05 to 1 m^2/day and those of migration velocities are from 0.001 to 0.21 m/day.

For vertical migration, the term l in formula (4.1) is equal to the thickness M' of the aquitard between the storage lakes and the confined aquifer complex. The chloride concentration $(C\rho)_0$ has the same value as for horizontal migration, the time t is the same and the vertical migration velocity is determined with the following formula:

$$u_c = \frac{K'}{M'} \cdot \frac{\delta h}{m}$$

(4.2)

where K' is the vertical hydraulic conductivity of the aquitard (m/day), δh is the average head difference between the lakes and the confined aquifer complex (m), m is the kinematic porosity of

Table 2. Calculated values of parameters for vertical migration

Storage lake	K'/M' (day^{-1})	Δh (m)	u_c (m/day)	D (m^2/day)	$C\rho$ (kg/m^3)
Arcesti	$4 \bullet 10^{-7}$	25.00	$1 \bullet 10^{-3}$	$1.5 \bullet 10^{-4}$	0.060
Slatina	$1 \bullet 10^{-6}$	12.43	$1.24 \bullet 10^{-3}$	$1.5 \bullet 10^{-4}$	0.055

for t = 10,000 days

the aquitard (dimensionless). The kinematic porosity of the aquitard under the lakes was estimated at 0.01, taking into account the available data from pumping tests.

Based on formulae (4.1) and (4.2), the vertical migration velocities of chloride through the aquitard, the vertical dispersion coefficients and chloride concentrations at the bottom of the aquitard were estimated. Table 2 shows these results.

These values represent a first attempt to assess the dispersion coefficients for lateral and vertical migration. Tracer tests, which are planned for the next stage of this study, will provide further information on transport parameters.

5 POLICY FOR WATER MANAGEMENT

The wellfields of Slatina city have been designed to provide a total abstraction rate of 1100 l/s of fresh water for domestic use and industry. From this total, 250 l/s should be provided by the shallow aquifer and 850 l/s by the deep aquifer. The abstraction rate decreased during the last 20 - 25 years and it reached 500 l/s in 1995 (150 l/s from the shallow aquifer and 350 l/s from the deep aquifer) and there are frequent water cuts in the city. The reasons for the decrease of capacity include construction of impermeable structures such as dams on the River Olt (which have resulted in less recharge to the shallow aquifer) and damage to the wells.

The required abstraction rate is estimated at 740 l/s for the year 2000 and 800 l/s for 2010, taking into account the decreasing requirements for industry and the movement of people away from the area.

A short-term project for rehabilitation of the wellfields involves works to improve the well efficiency and the abstraction system. When this has been completed, 260 l/s could be abstracted from the shallow aquifer and 590 l/s from the deep aquifer.

Hydrochemical and isotope studies are planned to provide information about the different pollutants and their transport paths. These will be helpful in testing remediation solutions and, if possible, in stopping the sources of pollution.

6 CONCLUSIONS

The alluvial aquifer system of Slatina is seriously polluted by chloride, nitrates and nitrites. Because of this, many wells in the shallow aquifer are no longer in use. Pollution, mainly by chloride, has already begun to extend to the deep aquifer. As a consequence, there are serious problems concerning the water supply in this area.

A more detailed study is necessary to provide more information about the contaminants and to find solutions to prevent further pollution and remedy the current situation.

In this first step, simple conceptual and numerical models of the aquifer system were developed, establishing boundary conditions, hydraulic parameters and the water balance for each aquifer. Hydrodynamic dispersion coefficients, both for lateral and vertical transfer, were estimated for later use in a transport model.

The next step in this study will be to obtain more detailed data concerning the natural limits of the aquifer system, evolution of piezometric heads, pumping rates and contaminant concentrations, in order to improve the numerical hydrodynamic model and develop a transport model. Results from numerical modelling will be useful in finding solutions for rational exploitation of the groundwater resources and remediation of groundwater quality.

REFERENCES

Albu, M. 1982. Propagation of pollution in an aquifer laterally bounded by a stream (in Romanian). *Hidrotehnica* 27 (5): 134-135.

Moldoveanu, V. 1995. *Hydrogeological study for the reconditioning of the drinking water source of Slatina city* (in Romanian). PROED SA

Ogata, Akio, & R.B. Banks 1961. A solution of the differential equation of longitudinal dispersion in porous media. *USGS Professional Paper 411.A.*

Groundwater in the Urban Environment: Problems, Processes and Management, Chilton et al. (eds)
© *1997 Balkema, Rotterdam, ISBN 90 5410 837 1*

Pollution of groundwaters on Donji Milanovac

V. Dragisic, B. Miladinovic & D. Milenic
Faculty of Mining and Geology, University of Belgrade, Yugoslavia

ABSTRACT: This paper describes a case example of excessive ground water pollution in a catchment area for domestic supply, from copper flotation effluent at Majdanpek. The copper ore deposit at Majdanpek is located in the Bor field, one of the largest copper-bearing basins of Europe. Flotation of low-copper ores produces waste water which is discharged to a tailing dump. This waste water contains increased contents of sulphate, iron, manganese, and other metallic constituents. Occasional failures at dumps result in uncontrolled seepage into surface streams and consequent contamination of both surface and ground water. The latest excessive pollution of ground water in May 1996 was caused by failure in the flotation-tailing dam at Majdanpek. The effluent seepage from the dump polluted the source of domestic water supply to the town of Donji Milanovac and a few more intake areas in rural communities of the Porecka Reka basin.

1 INTRODUCTION

In East Serbia there are several mines and plants for the processing of copper ore (Bor, Veliki Krivelj and Majdanpek). The process of copper ore treatment has produced large amounts of ore waste and flotation tailing heaps, located in the vicinity of the towns of Bor and Majdanpek. The waste and tailing heaps pollute the environment in a number of ways, sometimes to the extent of ecological catastrophes. The area of the town of Majdanpek has, thus, in the past twenty years witnessed two ecological disasters caused by uncontrolled discharge of large amounts of flotation tailings and waste waters into the surface streams and the surrounding karst and alluvial aquifers.

The Majdanpek copper deposit is situated in the vicinity of the town of Majdanpek, near the Yugoslav-Romanian border. Long exploitation and flotation processing of low-grade copper ore has taken place in the vicinity of the town, two flotation tailing heaps have been formed: the "Valja Fundata" and the "Saski potok".

In 1974, from the "Valja Fundata" tailing heap formed on a karstified foundation, an uncontrolled discharge of several million cubic metres of tailings and waste waters occurred, through activated underground streams. This resulted in pollution of karst aquifers, destruction of some speleological structures, contamination of surface waters of the Veliki Pek river and of the neighbouring aquifers. The most recent ecological disaster occurred in May 1996, when, due to the dam failure of the "Saski potok" flotation tailing heap, the tailings and the waste waters were discharged into the Porecka river. The accident resulted in the contamination of surface and underground waters in this river system and the elimination of the water source for the supply of the town of Donji Milanovac and a number of neighbouring settlements.

2 CHARACTERISTICS OF FLOTATION TAILINGS

Flotation tailings represent a mixture of comminuted ore-bearing andesites and water which is, in the form of a fluid mass, deposited into the tailings area after the concentration of copper and magnetite minerals. The solid phase of the tailings has a fine grain size distribution, with a 0.6 to 0.002 mm grain size. The chemical composition of the solid phase is shown in Table 1.

Table 1. Chemical composition of flotation tailings solid phase in % (Pavlovic & Trifunovic 1996).

Cu	Zn	Pb	As	Fe	S	Cd
0.05-	0.02-	0.001	0.00-	3.85-	1.64-	0.0003
0.10	0.04		0.02	5.30	2.90	

$CaCO_3$	Na_2O_3	K_2O_3	MgO	Al_2O_3	SiO_2
3.02-	1.26	3.29	0.91	10.20-	63.05-
3.78				14.43	69.10

Table 2. Chemical composition of waste waters in the tailings heap, surface and ground waters, after the accident.

Name		"Saski Potok" tailing	The Porecka river	Ground waters	MPC*
Date of sampling	Unit	22.05.1996.	22.05.1996.	04.06.1996	
pH		8.32	8.63	8.65	6.5-8.5
Elec.conductivity	µS/cm	3955	553	727	600
Nitrate	mg/l	0.003	0.004	0.001	0.005
Nitrite	mg/l	<0.46	0.90	1.13	10.00
Chloride	mg/l	33.63	12.39	25.0	200
Sulphate	mg/l	3927.00	129.28	275.00	200
$KMnO_4$	mg/l	28.44	18.96	12.55	8.0
Alkalinity	mg/l	74.16	33.18	50	-
Hardness	mg/l	210	18.34	20.20	20
Dry residue	mg/l	7337	750	804	800/1000
Calcium CaO	mg/l	701.40	109.30	-	200
Magnesium MgO	mg/l	1005.60	53.27	110.81	50
Iron Fe	mg/l	0.780	0.95	0.58	0.30
Manganese Mn	mg/l	1.450	0.25	0.14	0.05
Sodium Na	mg/l	36.30	18.24	-	150
Potassium K	mg/l	18.44	8.12	-	12
Arsenic As	mg/l	0.0018	0.0012	0	0.05
Copper Cu	mg/l	0.034	0.040	0.021	0.10
Zinc Zn	mg/l	0.280	0.052	0.064	5.0
Cadmium Cd	mg/l	<0.0005	<0.0005	0.0005	0.005
Lead Pb	mg/l	<0.005	<0.005	0.005	0.05
Chromium Cr	mg/l	0.014	0.008	0.006	0.05
Mercury Hg	mg/l	<0.0002	0.0002	0.0002	0.001
Nickel Ni	mg/l	0.018	0.006	0.001	0.05
Oxygen O_2	mg/l	7.44	9.76	-	6-8
BOD-5**	mg/l	6.08	7.86	-	2-4

*Maximum permissible concentration
**Biochemical oxygen demand (5 days)

The liquid phase of the flotation tailings (about 50%) consists of highly mineralized waste water with increased contents of sulphate, heavy metals, phenol and other toxic matters (Calic & Tomanec 1966). The chemical composition of waste waters of the Saski potok tailing heap, several days after the failure, is shown in Table 2.

3 DESCRIPTION AND CONSEQUENCES OF THE ACCIDENT

The most recent accident in the area of the town of Majdanpek occurred in the night between May 8 and 9, 1996. After a long rainy period the flotation dam broke and about 100,000 m^3 of tailings and a great amount of waste water was discharged. Part of the tailings was carried away by the river Danube, and

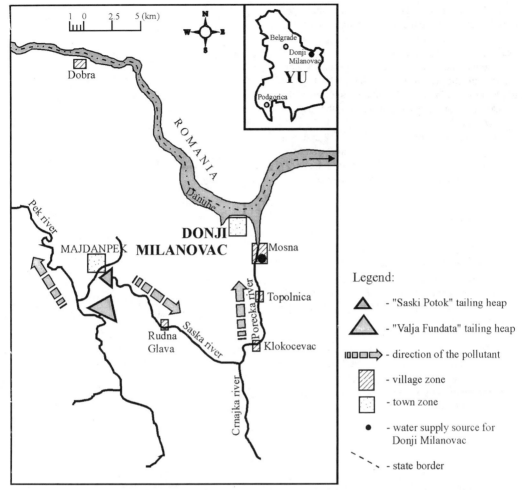

Figure 1. Geographical position of the place of accident and the zone of pollution near Donji Milanovac.

part was deposited in the alluvial plain of the Porecka river (Figure 1).

The consequences of the accident are still being investigated, but they are undoubtedly enormous. Besides the contamination of surface waters, ground waters in the Porecka river alluvial aquifer (Table 2) were also contaminated. The habitats, flora and fauna of the river banks were also damaged.

A water supplying structure was built in the alluvial aquifer of this river, to provide the town of Donji Milanovac with ground water. Due to direct hydraulic connection between the surface and the ground waters, the water in the structure was directly infiltrated into the underground through gravel and sand alluvium deposits.

As a consequence, the water structure was excluded from the system of water supply of Donji Milanovac, as well as a number of smaller water supplying structures in the villages of Mosna, Klokocevac, Topolnica and Rudna glava.

This accident particularly struck the town of Donji Milanovac, an important tourist resort in Serbia. After the accident, the population of the town has been supplied with water brought by cisterns from springs 30 km away from the town.

4 CONCLUSION

1. The latest failure of the "Saski potok" flotation

tailings heap in the vicinity of the town of Majdanpek in 1996 led to the contamination of surface and ground waters and the disturbance of the natural system of the Porecka river.

2. Contamination of surface and ground waters resulted in the exclusion of the ground water supplying structure from the alluvial aquifer of the Porecka river, particularly jeopardizing the town of Donji Milanovac.

3. Contamination of ground waters in the closer and the wider area of the town of Donji Milanovac produced huge problems for this tourist resort currently supplied with water from distant places.

REFERENCES

Calic, N. & R. Tomanec 1996. Mineral Processing in Environment Protection. Mining and Environmental Engineering. *Proceedings of the Yugoslav Conference with international participants:* 359-363. Belgrade: Faculty of Mining and Geology, Belgrade University.

Pavlovic, S. & S. Trifunovic 1996. Protection by Vegetative Cover of the Majdanpek Mine Tailing Heap. Mining and Environmental Engineering. *Proceedings of the Yugoslav Conference with international participants:* 381-385. Belgrade: Faculty of Mining and Geology, Belgrade University.

The impact of leaking sewers on urban groundwater

M. Eiswirth & H. Hötzl
Department of Applied Geology, University of Karlsruhe, Germany

ABSTRACT: Contamination of urban groundwater by sewage leakage from damaged sewers is an increasing matter of public and regulatory concern. It is estimated that in Germany several 100 million m^3 waste water leaks every year from partly damaged sewerage systems into soil and groundwater. In many cities damaged sewerage systems are the main sources for groundwater contamination with sulphate, chloride and nitrogen compounds. Besides the ecological point of view, damaged sewerage systems exhibit essential economic problems because groundwater can also infiltrate into the sewers. This paper presents the results of comprehensive groundwater-quality studies carried out during the last 3 years in the City of Rastatt situated in the Upper Rhine Valley, Southern Germany.

1 INTRODUCTION

Urban groundwater (or groundwater that underlies urban areas) is a distinct subdomain of hydrogeology (Lerner 1996). In contrast to rural areas, urban groundwater shows some specific features. For example, the recharge of urban groundwater is heavily affected by extensive sealing of surfaces, leaking water mains, sewers, and stormwater recharge. Additional large spatial variations in recharge rates are typical. Beside this, urban groundwater is also effected by geotechnical interactions (e.g. deep basements, tunnels). The quality of urban groundwater is mainly affected by the input of the muniplicity of urban features. Table 1 shows the main possible sources for urban groundwater contamination.

Table 1. Possible sources for urban groundwater contamination.

- waste sites and solid waste disposals
- septic tanks and cesspools
- polluted precipitation of surface runoff
- road deicing
- gasoline stations
- water treatment effluents
- mine tailings and brines
- runoff from tank pipeline and storage leakage
- industrial impacts (cooling water, process water)
- chemical dry cleaners
- agricultural impacts, e.g. parks and gardens (fertilisers, soil amendments, pesticides, animal wastes, stockpiles)
- traffic accidents (dangerous goods)
- deep buildings (grout injections within the groundwater)
- leaky sewerage systems (industrial and urban waste water)

In order to understand the impacts of leaky sewerage systems within the framework of a research and development project "leakage detection for old sewers and sewerage systems in areas with fluctuating groundwater tables", the correlation between damaged sewerage systems, soil and groundwater and contamination have been investigated by co - operation between science and municipal practice. The research has been carried out by the Department of Applied Geology, University of Karlsruhe and the Municipal Department of Civil Engineering, City of Rastatt and partly the Federal Institution of Hydraulic Engineering, Karlsruhe.

One scientific aim of the research and development project was to estimate the possible risk of sewage exfiltration into soil and groundwater and to develop and test nondestructive leakage detection methods for damaged sewers. This paper deals with the assessment of potential risks due to damaged sewers; the results of other parts of the project are presented elsewhere (e.g. Eiswirth et al. 1995a, 1995b).

The feasibility for detecting and ascertaining the extent of sewerage leakages has been tested on an old very damaged sewer pipe section in the City of Rastatt at "Rheinauer Murgdamm". This old sewer has been assembled in an earth dam, used as a flood dam for the River Murg (Eiswirth et al. 1994). Further research has been carried out in a specially constructed sewerage test site in a suburb of Rastatt, and hydrochemical investigations have been carried out in order to assess the influence of sewage effluents on groundwater and soil quality.

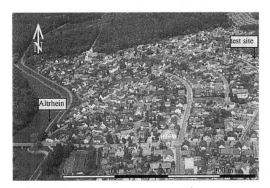

Figure 1. Aerial view of Plittersdorf (suburb of the City of Rastatt).

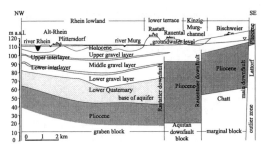

Figure 2. Geological cross section (NW-SE) through the Upper Rhine Valley in the area of Rastatt.

2 GEOLOGY AND HYDROGEOLOGY

In Plittersdorf, a suburb of the City of Rastatt, groundwater levels are mainly effected by natural fluctuations of the nearby River Rhine and its tributary river, the Altrhein (Figure 1).

The geology of the Upper Rhinegraben in the area of Rastatt/Plittersdorf can be divided into four main tectonic units: a graben block, a downfault block, a marginal block (fore hills), and an outlier zone (basement) (Figure 2). The graben is bordered by the Black Forest and the Vosges. During Holocene times, the river Rhine excavated the Lower Terrace Formations within the present Rhine depression and filled it up with recent material in various thickness. With a generally clearly rising slope, the Rhine depression borders the valley terrace that in this region corresponds to the uniform flat Lower Terrace plain. Along the mountain border, a Holocene channel was created by the rivers Kinzig, Murg and others coming down from the mountains. As shown in Figure 2 in the region of Rastatt the thickness of the Pleistocene sediments is some 60 m and increases continuously in northward direction (Bartz 1967).

On the graben block the thickness of the Upper and Middle Pleistocene gravel layer is about 33 m. Below, the Lower Pleistocene Rhine sediments follow: the base of the Quaternary sediments is build by impermeable Pliocene sediments at an elevation of about 55 m a.s.l. (Figure 2). The Quaternary can be divided into three gravel layers (main aquifers) separated by two less permeable intervals, and a lower less permeable sandy-silty layer (Lower Quaternary). The main aquifer (Upper gravel layer) in the area of Plittersdorf has a thickness of about 20 m.

The local geology of Plittersdorf is dominated by a 5 to 11 m thick gravel layer and by 1.5 to 4 m thick Holocene sands/silts in channels. Beside these sediments anthropogenic infill can be found everywhere in Plittersdorf (Figures 3 and 4).

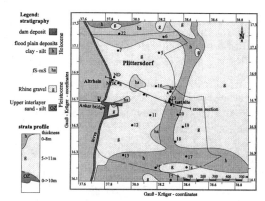

Figure 3. Schematic local geological map of Plittersdorf and location of groundwater observation wells.

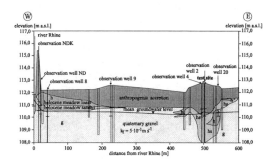

Figure 4. Schematic geological cross section (location is indicated in Figure 3).

The suburb of Plittersdorf is bordered by a levee against high floods from the Altrhein river in the west.

Groundwater flow in Plittersdorf during periods of low water level of the Altrhein river is in a northwest direction with a low hydraulic gradient of 0.26 % (Figure 5).

Groundwater velocities in this area have been calculated with the 3D numerical groundwater flow model FEFLOW®. For example the numerical model

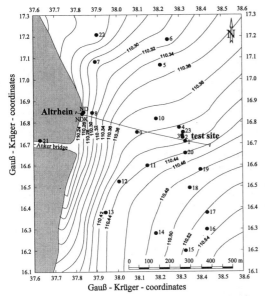

Figure 5. Map of groundwater level in Plittersdorf during low river water level on 10.11.1993 [m a.s.l.].

indicates a mean groundwater flow velocity during low water level at groundwater observation well 9 of about $v_x = 0.8$ m/d (to the west) and $v_y = 1.4$ m/d (to the north).

3 TEST SITE DESCRIPTION

In April 1993, an artificially constructed sewer test site was built in the area of the sewage pumping station in Plittersdorf. This sewer section, with separated storm and sanitary sewers, was connected directly to the separate sewerage system of the city (Figure 6).

This sewer test system allows flushing with municipal sewage as well as flushing of the storm sewer with rain water under nearly "natural" conditions. This kind of a mesoscale model was constructed to study physical, chemical and microbiotic processes in the soil and groundwater, including transport and degradation of leaking sewage. Details are presented in Eiswirth et al. (1995a,b).

4 HYDROCHEMICAL INVESTIGATIONS

Hydrochemical groundwater investigations can define the risk assessment for soil and groundwater caused by sewage exfiltration from damaged sewers. The subsurface migration behaviour of the contaminants is mainly influenced by the soil composition, e.g. content of clay, organic matter and pH-value. For detailed description of the hydrochemical changes in groundwater chemistry during subsurface transportation, water samples have been taken from bore holes along the line shown in Figure 5. Beside the seasonal and regional variation in groundwater chemistry, areas with anomalous chemistry diverge chemical contents have been detected (Figures 7-11).

The hydrochemical anomalies in groundwater below the test site (groundwater observation well 2) could only be caused by the influence and mixture with sewage leaking from the sewer. For example, consider the specific electric conductivity (SEC). The groundwater in observation well 2 is significantly influenced by waste water with a mean SEC of 1000 µS/cm (Figure 7). This is clear evidence for active leakage of sewage from the test site. This result is confirmed by the variations in sulphate and potassium concentration (Figure 8).

The mean sulphate concentrations in the groundwater of observation well 2 are low compared to the other observation wells (Figure 7). This is due to desulphurisation processes (mean sulphate concentration in waste water 80 mg/l) in the anaerobic groundwater zone below the damaged sewer test site.

Potassium concentrations in the groundwater of Plittersdorf are relatively constant at 8 mg/l. At observation well 2 the mean potassium contents are higher (11 mg/l) due to the influence of waste water

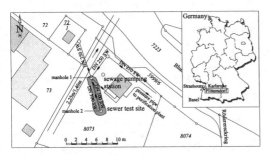

Figure 6. Location of waste water test site in Plittersdorf (Southern Germany).

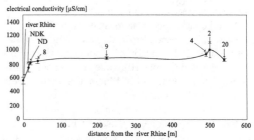

Fig. 7: Variations of the specific electric conductivity in groundwater along the hydrochemical profile (confidence of means with 95% level of significance).

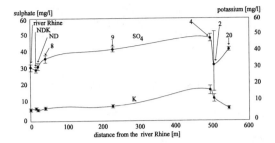

Figure 8. Variations of sulphate and potassium concentrations in groundwater along the hydrochemical profile.

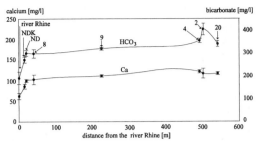

Figure 10. Variations of bicarbonate and calcium concentrations in groundwater along the hydrochemical profile.

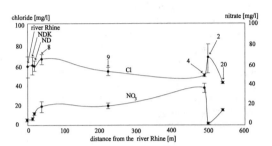

Figure 9. Variations of chloride and nitrate concentrations in groundwater along the hydrochemical profile.

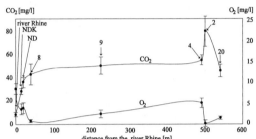

Figure 11. Variations of carbon dioxide and oxygen concentrations in groundwater along the hydrochemical profile.

(mean potassium concentration in waste water 38 mg/l).

The mean chloride concentrations in the groundwater of Plittersdorf are relatively constant. Only at observation well 2 the mean chloride contents are higher (69 mg/l) due to the influence of waste water (mean chloride concentration in waste water 110 mg/l).

The mean nitrate concentrations in the river water are very low (4 mg/l) compared to the high nitrate concentrations in the groundwater of Plittersdorf (Figure 9). At observation well 2 the nitrate concentrations are nearly zero (0.7 mg/l) due to (incomplete) denitrification / nitrification processes in the anaerobic zone below the test site. During these microbiological processes nitrate is mainly reduced to nitrogen gas (see equation 1 in section 5).

Bicarbonate concentrations in groundwater of Plittersdorf correspond to SEC variations. At observation well 2 the bicarbonate contents are significantly elevated (Figure 10) while calcium concentrations in the groundwater of Plittersdorf are relatively constant at 110 mg/l.

The CO_2-concentrations in the groundwater of Plittersdorf are relatively constant while at observation well 2 the mean CO_2 contents are higher (80 mg/l) due to microbial degradation of the waste water effluents in the sub-surface (Figure 11).

While CO_2 is produced by aerobic biodegradation in the unsaturated zone below the sewer leakages, oxygen is consumed. Therefore the mean O_2-concentrations in groundwater are nearly zero and anaerobic conditions have been established (Eiswirth & Hötzl 1996b).

The various transformation reactions occurring in the unsaturated subsurface below the damaged sewers as well as in groundwater are summarized in the following section.

5 TRANSFORMATION REACTIONS

Various transformation reactions occur in the subsurface environment of damaged sewers. For example, mineralisation of organic nitrogen produces nitrate, which may then be reduced to nitrogen gas (= denitrification, equation 1) or ammonium (= dissimilatory nitrate reduction, equation 2) as follows:

$$4 NO_3^- + 5 CH_2O = 2 N_2(g) + 5 HCO_3^- + H^+ + 2 H_2O \quad (1)$$

$$NO_3^- + H_2O + 2 CH_2O = NH_4^+ + 2 HCO_3^- \quad (2)$$

Microbial degradation of waste water in the subsurface is mainly influenced by the concentration and availability of free O_2 and other electron acceptors (e.g. sulphate and nitrate). Therefore organic matter is partly oxidized to ammonium (= ammonification, equation 3). If there is enough oxygen avail-

402

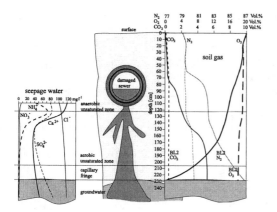

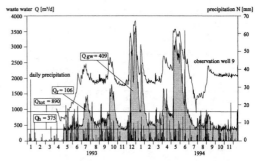

Figure 13. Waste water discharge and daily precipitation at the sewage pumping station in Plittersdorf for 1993 and 1994 (Q_{tot} = total discharge; Q_r = storm water runoff, Q_h = runoff from households; Q_{gw} = groundwater infiltration).

Figure 12. Variations in waste water chemistry and soil gas composition during the effluent seepage through the subsurface below a damaged sewer

able ammonium is mainly oxidized to nitrate (= nitrification, equation 4).

$$CH_2O(NH_3) + O_2 = NH_4^+ + HCO_3^- \qquad (3)$$

$$NH_4^+ + 2\,O_2 = NO_3^- + 2\,H^+ + H_2O \qquad (4)$$

The described aerobic biodegradation processes decrease the dissolved O_2 content and increases the dissolved CO_2 concentration in pore water and groundwater. The biodegradation can also be described using glucose $C_6H_{12}O_6$ representing organic matter (Brun and Engesgaard 1994, equation 5).

$$C_6H_{12}O_6 + 12\,H_2O \Rightarrow 6\,CO_3^{2-} + 36\,H^+ + 24\,e$$

$$CO_3^{2-} + 2\,H^+ \Rightarrow CO_2(aq) + H_2O \qquad (5)$$

Following a release, oxygen is depleted and carbon dioxide in the soil air is increased as a result of aerobic respiration (Figure 12). As soon oxygen levels diminish, anaerobic processes become dominant. Under highly anaerobic conditions the biodegradation can produce high levels of carbon dioxide and methane (equation 6):

$$C_6H_{12}O_6 \Rightarrow 3\,C_2H_4O_2 \Rightarrow 3\,CO_2 + 3\,CH_4 \qquad (6)$$

During the investigation in Plittersdorf the following major transformation processes have been identified during the seepage of waste water effluents through the subsurface below damaged sewers:

– precipitation of iron sulphides, anaerobic oxidation, fermentation and ammonification within a thin anaerobic zone immediately below the sewer leakages (Figure 12).
– biodegradation (oxidation) of organic matter, dissimilatory nitrate reduction and bicarbonate buffering within an aerobic unsaturated zone above the capillary fringe (Figure 12)

6 BALANCING THE IMPACT OF WASTE WATER EFFLUENTS

The sewerage system of Plittersdorf/Rastatt was built mainly in the years 1965 to 1970. The complete sewerage system can be subdivided into a total length of 9882 m storm water sewers (mean diameter 300 mm) and 9955 m waste water sewers (mean diameter 250 mm). In Plittersdorf about 87 % of the sewerage system is situated within the zone of fluctuation of the groundwater table. Therefore the groundwater level is influencing the ex- or infiltration behaviour of damaged sewers. As indicated in Figure 13 the waste water discharge at the sewage pumping station in Plittersdorf for 1993 and 1994 is strongly influenced by the groundwater level. The mean daily waste water discharge for Plittersdorf is 890 m³/d. Using the mean daily water demand for Plittersdorf (320 m³/d), a total of 570 m³/d of additional water was pumped through the pumping station. Subtracting the rain runoff from households (106 m³/d), the groundwater infiltration rate is calculated to be 409 m³/d for Plittersdorf (Figure 13). This means that nearly 52 % of the total waste water discharge is infiltrated by groundwater.

For Plittersdorf we calculated a groundwater infiltration rate of 46.6 l/d·km and a waste water exfiltration rate of 1.2 l/d·km. In other German cities, e.g. Hannover, infiltration of groundwater (198720 l/d·km) into the sewerage system is also higher than exfiltration of waste water (17300 l/d·km).

As listed in Table 2, in Plittersdorf the impact of leaking sewers on groundwater quality is indicated mainly from sodium (mean annual input 153 kg/ha·a), ammonium-N (80 kg/ha·a), potassium (55 kg/ha·a), sulphate (55 kg/ha·a), organic nitrogen (33 kg/ha·a) and phosphate (16 kg/ha·a). In Hannover it is mainly sulphate (160 kg/ha·a), chloride (120 kg/ha·a), ammonium-N (30 kg/ha·a), potassium (20 kg/ha·a) and phosphate (13 kg/ha·a) which are leaking into the subsurface from damaged sewers.

Table 2. Mean sewage composition and mean annual input from damaged sewers into soil and groundwater in two German cities (Rastatt and Hannover).

	Rastatt			Hannover[*]		
	mean concentration in sewage [mg·l⁻¹]	mean annual load 4400 m³·a⁻¹ [kg·a⁻¹]	mean annual input 0,030 km² [kg·ha⁻¹·a⁻¹]	mean concentration in sewage [mg·l⁻¹]	mean annual load 6,5·10⁶ km³·a⁻¹ [kg·a⁻¹]	mean annual input 84 km² [kg·ha⁻¹·a⁻¹]
potassium	38	167	55	25	160000	20
sodium	111	488	153			
ammonium-N	55	242	80	35	230000	30
organic nitrogen-N	23	101	33			
chloride	101	444	150	150	980000	120
nitrate	7	31	10			
sulphate	38	167	55	200	1300000	160
boron	1.96	9	3	1,7	10000	
phosphate	11	48	16	17	110000	13
lead	0.034	1.5	0.48	0.035	230	0.03
cadmium	0.005	0.022	0.007	0.003	15	0.002
chromium	0.0010	0.004	0.001	0.035	230	0.03
copper	0.062	0.27	0. 09	0.115	730	0.09
nickel	0.027	0.12	0.05	0.035	230	0.03
zinc	0.85	3.7	1.2	0.29	1900	0.22

[*] 395 km combined sewerage systems; separated systems: 1060 km waste water sewers. 845 km storm sewers; 84 km² area in which all waste water sewers are always above the groundwater level

7 CONCLUSIONS

The results of hydrochemical groundwater analysis and detailed investigations concerning the movement of sewage show that damaged sewerage systems are the main sources for groundwater contamination in Plittersdorf with sodium, chloride, nitrogen compounds and sulphate. The following migration and fate of the contaminants in soil and groundwater essentially depends on the geology und mineralogy of the sewer´s surrounding. Because most of the waste water compounds leaking to the underground are attenuated and biodegraded within the unsaturated zone the groundwater quality is influenced only within a narrow zone next to the sewer leakages. Therefore the the impact of leaking sewers on urban groundwater is strongly variable and the chemical content of industrial and urban effluents mainly produce the potential risk for soil and groundwater.

ACKNOWLEDGEMENTS

The work reported in this paper forms part of a general program of research into the restoration of sewerage systeme. The financial support of the former BMFT (Bumdesminister für Forschung und Technologie) is gratefully acknowledged.

REFERENCES

Bartz. J. 1967. Recent movements in the Upper Rhinegraben. between Rastatt and Mannheim. *Abh. Geol. L.* 6: 1-2.

Brun. A. & Engesgaard. P. 1994. A coupled microbiology-geochemistry transport model for saturated groundwater flow. - In: Dracos & Stauffer (eds). *Transport and Reactive Processes in Aquifers*: 457-462.

Eiswirth. M. & Hötzl. H. 1994. Groundwater contamination by leaky sewerage systems. *Proceedings of the 25th Congress of the International Association of Hydrogeologists „Water Down Under 94"*. Adelaide (Australia). 21 - 25 November 1994. Vol. A. p. 111-114.

Eiswirth. M. & Hötzl. H. & Merkler. G.-P. 1995a. Detection of contaminant transport from damaged sewerage systems and leaky landfills. In: Kovar. K. & Krásný. J. (Eds.) 1995. *Groundwater Quality: Remediation and Protection GQ´95*. - IAHS-Publ. No. 225: 337-346.

Eiswirth. M. & Hötzl. H. Kramp. J.. Lazar. C. & Merkler. G.-P. 1995b. Qualifying methods for leakage detection. *Proceedings of the 12. Int. No-Dig Conference*. Dresden. 19 - 22 Th. Sept. 1995: 195-208.

Eiswirth. M. & Hötzl. H. 1996b. Unsaturated zone investigations by soil gas surveys. *Proceedings of the 1 st. International Congress on „The impact of Industrial Activity on Groundwater Resources"*. Cernobbio. 22 - 24 th. May. 1996: 621-632.

Lerner. D.N. 1996. Guest Editor´s Preface to theme Issue: Urban groundwater. *Hydrogeological Journal* v. 4(1): 4-5.

Groundwater in the Urban Environment: Problems, Processes and Management, Chilton et al. (eds)
© 1997 Balkema, Rotterdam, ISBN 90 5410 837 1

Chemical transformations of groundwater beneath unsewered cities

Daren C. Gooddy, Adrian R. Lawrence, Brian L. Morris & P. John Chilton
Hydrogeology Group, British Geological Survey, Wallingford, UK

ABSTRACT: Geochemical processes that can occur in groundwater beneath unsewered cities are described. Examples are taken from Santa Cruz (Bolivia) and Hat Yai (Thailand), cities with moderately shallow and very shallow water tables respectively. A conceptual model previously developed for an analogous problem, leakage from a slurry lagoon into a carbonate aquifer, is applied to the two cities. Geochemical processes are dominated by reactions involving organic carbon and nitrogen, during progressive consumption of electron acceptors. Reduction of manganese, iron and sulphate occurs as the redox potential of the groundwater falls. If the buffering capacity of the aquifer is exceeded by the acidity produced during these reactions, pH falls. The depth to the water table is probably the most important factor determining availability of oxygen which in turn strongly influences the changes in redox potential and pH. This can significantly impact the mobility of trace elements.

1 INTRODUCTION

Many cities in developing countries use groundwater for urban water supply. However, shallow groundwater beneath these cities is frequently contaminated, largely as a result of the disposal of urban wastes which are rich in organic carbon and nitrogen. As a consequence, shallow aquifers are often abandoned in favour of deeper ones. Yet, pumping from these same deeper aquifers can impose vertical hydraulic gradients and induce significant leakage from shallow horizons. Groundwaters derived from shallow layers high in nitrate and chloride and relatively low in dissolved oxygen have been observed to percolate into deeper alluvial aquifers beneath the cities of Hat Yai (Thailand) and Santa Cruz (Bolivia).

A detailed study carried out by the BGS in a carbonate aquifer, at a site where an unlined lagoon had been receiving cattle slurry, revealed that complex geochemical processes were taking place. Most significant was the development of distinct redox zones. This paper shows that the type of reactions taking place beneath a slurry lagoon in the carbonate aquifer of southern England are analogous to the processes occurring beneath unsewered cities, and extends this theme to examine potential quality threats to urban groundwaters.

The work described here is based on chemical data from i) cored boreholes and porewaters obtained from beneath the slurry pit in the UK, ii) groundwater data collected over a period of 5 years in Santa Cruz, and iii) groundwater and porewater data from shallow piezometers specially constructed in Hat Yai.

2 SITE DESCRIPTIONS

Santa Cruz is located on the eastern plains of Bolivia about 25 km from the easternmost edge of the Andean cordillera. It is the second city of Bolivia with a population of about 700,000 within an area of roughly 145 km^2. Population density averages 70 ha^{-1} with a range of less than 40 ha^{-1} to more than 150 ha^{-1}. A considerable proportion of the area has been made impermeable by roofs and pavements. The city is situated entirely on the eastern bank of the Rio Pirai and lies at an elevation of about 415 m amsl. Local relief is subdued and a gentle 12 m high north-south ridge which bisects the city forms a surface water divide between the Rio Pirai and the Rio Grande river system. The climate is sub-tropical with an average annual temperature of 23.8°C and rainfall of 1540 mm a^{-1}. Rainfall distribution is seasonal with nearly half the annual rains falling between November and February. Open-pan evaporation is 1615 mm a^{-1} and this probably precludes recharge from rainfall during the March to October dry season. Annual effective rainfall over the remaining period averages 170 mm.

Hat Yai is the third largest city of Thailand with a municipal population of around 160,000 in an area of around 16 km^2. The population density averages 100 ha^{-1} ranging between 60 ha^{-1} and 150 ha^{-1} and like Santa Cruz, a considerable proportion of the area is impermeable. In common with many other cities in the region it is expanding rapidly. The area is situated in a low-lying valley, at an elevation of 5-10 m amsl, and bounded by low hills. Two rivers, the Khlong U-Tao Phao and Khlong Toei, flow down the valley in a generally northerly direction. The area has consistently high temperatures throughout the year; the annual average exceeds 27°C. Average rainfall is 1816 mm a^{-1}, with a distinct rainy season during October to December. Potential evaporation rates are high at more than 1850 mm a^{-1}. Infiltration to groundwater is believed to be of the order of 170 mm a^{-1}.

ADAS Bridgets is about 5 km east of Winchester in Hampshire, UK. In 1975 an unlined pit approximately 10 m deep and 40 m in diameter was created for the disposal of cattle slurry. During an 18 year lifetime roughly 10 million litres of dilute slurry were disposed of to the pit although some of this was subsequently removed for land application.

2.1 Santa Cruz geology and hydrogeology

Santa Cruz is situated on a plain comprising a deep tectonic mountain front trough which formed on the continental side of the Andean cordillera. The outwash plain deposits in this sedimentary basin exceed 1500 m thickness in the general area of the city and range from mid-Tertiary to Quaternary in age. The upper half of the sequence is of most significance hydrogeologically, comprising a complex alternating sequence of gravels, sands, silts and clays and their admixtures. These deposits form a highly productive but complex aquifer system, with groundwater able to move vertically as well as horizontally. The lenticularity of the upper 25 m of the aquifer implies that while vertical leakage may be impeded locally, the system as a whole can be regarded as in broad hydraulic continuity. The shallow groundwater level varies considerably across the city but typically exceeds a depth of 10 m in the city centre. Recharge from rainfall is augmented by river infiltration, water

mains and sewer leakage along with pluvial runoff to soakaways and wastewater from septic tanks. There is evidence that contaminants have penetrated to a depth in excess of 50 m (Morris et al., 1994). Regional groundwater flow is believed to be broadly southwest to northeast across the city although this could be locally modified by the intensive urban groundwater abstraction. Santa Cruz is totally dependent on groundwater for its water supply, which is derived entirely from wells located within the city limits.

2.2 Hat Yai geology and hydrogeology

The Hat Yai valley is underlain by a thick sequence of Quaternary and Recent alluvial sediments, resting unconformably on Permian metasediments. The valley is fault bounded with marginal Permian metasediments forming low but steep-sided hills. The alluvial sediments within the valley have a thickness which locally exceeds 250 m, and contain three major aquifer units of sand and gravel, separated by aquitards of poorly permeable fine sands, silts and clays.

Groundwater is drawn from a large number of privately-owned boreholes within the city for domestic purposes, for industry and for hotel supply. Hat Yai obtains about 50% of its urban water supply from groundwater, much of which is drawn from the semi-confined Hat Yai aquifer. This aquifer is overlain by some 30 m of sands, silts and clays. These upper, less permeable deposits possess a relatively shallow water table (<5 m bgl) which is maintained by high urban recharge originating from excess rainfall, leaking water mains, infiltration from canals and seepage from on-site sanitation systems. Monitoring of groundwater quality in the semi-confined Hat Yai aquifer has revealed elevated ammonia and chloride concentrations beneath the city centre, indicating incipient contamination. The main source of this contamination is believed to be seepage from canals, induced by the large volumes of groundwater which are abstracted in the centre of the city and whose influence dominates groundwater movement (Lawrence et al., 1994).

2.3 Bridgets Farm geology and hydrogeology

The lagoon at ADAS Bridgets is situated on the Cretaceous Upper Chalk, a calcium carbonate aquifer, at c. 110 m amsl. The Chalk here is estimated to be 170 m thick. The groundwater level has been measured at 58 m bgl and is believed to fluctuate by 1-

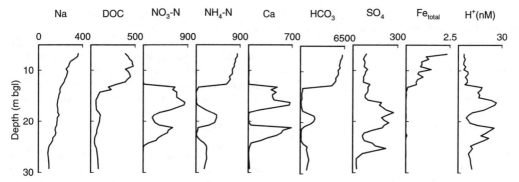

Figure 1. Porewater profiles from beneath a slurry lagoon at ADAS Bridgets, UK. Results are expressed as mg L^{-1} except hydrogen ion concentration (H$^+$) which is expressed in nM.

2 m annually. Although the unsaturated zone extends to 50 m, the moisture content of cores taken below the lagoon indicate the aquifer matrix is near saturation.

3 RESULTS

3.1 Geochemical processes at Bridgets Farm

Porewater profiles obtained from beneath the slurry lagoon are shown in Figure 1. It is clear that the slurry constituents have percolated through the Chalk, leading to high concentrations of sodium (Na), dissolved organic carbon (DOC) and nitrogen (N). Significant quantities of microorganisms (total viable counts commonly > 10^6 g^{-1}) were also found in the matrix throughout the profile although the original study concentrated on faecal indicators. The distribution of the nitrogen species, bicarbonate (HCO$_3$) and calcium (Ca) suggests more complex processes are occurring than relatively non-reactive piston drainage of the slurry. These distributions can be best explained by considering the effect of an organic load on microbially catalysed redox reactions and carbonate equilibrium.

In natural environments it is often observed that redox processes proceed sequentially from the highest energy yield downward and there are both chemical equilibrium and kinetic/microbial reasons why redox reactions follow such sequences. Table 1 shows the sequence of terminal electron transfer processes (TEAPs) commonly encountered in sub-surface environments. In some cases (where oxygen, nitrate or sulphate are present), the disappearance of a reactant is observed, while in other cases (when manganese, and iron are present in the reduced form) it is the appearance of a reactant product that is registered.

Table 1. Terminal electron acceptor processes common in sub-surface environments (after Lovley and Chapelle, 1995).

Process	Relative Energy Yield
Aerobic Respiration	100
Denitrification	93
Mn^{4+} Reduction	87
Fe^{3+} Reduction	84
Sulphate Reduction	6
Methane Production	3

In the top 12 m of the lagoon profile all the oxygen has been consumed and another TEAP is required for degradation of organic matter. Nitrate is no longer available having been consumed by denitrification (equation 1).

$$4NO_3^- + 5CH_2O \rightarrow 2N_2 + 4HCO_3^- + CO_2 + 3H_2O \quad (1)$$

No manganese is present in the Chalk matrix and iron from the slurry is already in its reduced (Fe^{2+}) form. Therefore sulphate reduction is the next TEAP and the reaction can proceed as in equation (2). When sulphate is reduced most of the iron will be precipitated as an insoluble sulphide.

$$SO_4^{2-} + 2CH_2O \rightarrow H_2S + 2HCO_3^- \quad (2)$$

Further investigation of the site revealed the presence of fractures at 12.5 and 21 m which were believed to be introducing oxygen into the system (Gooddy et al., 1994). When oxygen is used for the

TEAP, carbon dioxide is produced (equation 3) resulting in the formation of carbonic acid (equation 4) that reacts with carbonate minerals (equations 5-7).

$$CH_2O + O_2 \rightarrow CO_2 + H_2O \qquad (3)$$

$$H_2O + CO_2 \rightleftharpoons H_2CO_3 \qquad (4)$$

$$H_2CO_3 \rightleftharpoons H^+ + HCO_3^- \qquad (5)$$

$$HCO_3^- \rightleftharpoons H^+ + CO_3^{2-} \qquad (6)$$

$$CaCO_3 + 2H^+ \rightleftharpoons 2HCO_3^- + Ca^{2+} \qquad (7)$$

Geochemical calculations reveal the porewaters are saturated if not supersaturated with respect to calcite. The generation of bicarbonate during oxidation pushes the equilibrium over to the left hand side of the equation (7) and hence little calcite is dissolved. There is also an inhibiting effect on nucleation with high concentrations of organic matter (Amrhein and Suarez, 1987).

The introduction of oxygen leads to the precipitation of iron as Fe^{2+} is rapidly oxidised to Fe^{3+}. No iron is found below 12.5 m, confirming that it is derived from the slurry and hence not available as a TEAP in the sediment.

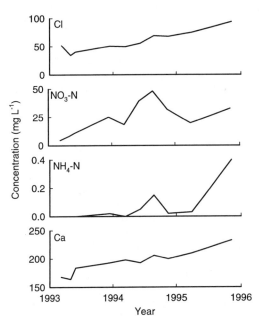

Figure 2. Groundwater monitoring data for a 36 m deep well, Santa Cruz city centre.

Nitrification is the process whereby ammonia or ammonium is oxidised by an organism as a means of producing energy (equation 8). The process is usually carried out by autotrophs who utilise carbon dioxide as a carbon source, but can also be achieved by heterotrophs. The sharp decline in DOC at around 12.5 m seems to infer heterotrophic activity.

$$NH_4^+ + 2O_2 \rightarrow NO_3^- + 2H^+ + H_2O \qquad (8)$$

The generation of protons predicted by this equation and the rise in hydrogen ion concentration occurs at the same time in the profile. This is despite the fact that Chalk matrix has almost infinite buffering capacity. When sulphate, nitrate, iron or manganese are the electron acceptors, bicarbonate is produced without generating acidity, and without significant carbonate dissolution .

In the absence of oxygen deeper in the profile, reducing conditions prevail. However, around 20 m some nitrate is available for reduction and this appears to delay the on-set of further sulphate reduction.

3.2 Geochemical processes in Santa Cruz

An example of data from the Santa Cruz sampling programme is shown in Figure 2. A gradual increase of chloride, nitrate and ammonia with time can be observed as wastewater from the city percolates downwards. In common with the slurry lagoon, nitrate is produced as large quantities of ammonia are oxidised. The protons released react with calcite in the matrix leading to increasing concentrations of calcium.

In several shallow wells which contain little nitrate, manganese is detected (Figure 3), while high concentrations of iron (>25 mg L^{-1}) are found in a few shallow wells where all the nitrate has been reduced. Manganese is also present in the latter but at lower concentrations. There has therefore been a shift in TEAP to iron reduction (equation 9) at the most reducing sites.

$$CH_2O + 3Fe(OH)_3 \rightarrow HCO_3^- + 3Fe^{2+} + 4OH^- + 3H_2O \quad (9)$$

3.3 Geochemical processes in Hat Yai

A porewater profile from the centre of Hat Yai is displayed in Figure 4.High concentrations of calcium quickly diminish with depth, whereas ammonia concentrations increase over the same depth range. The declining DOC concentrations imply a high

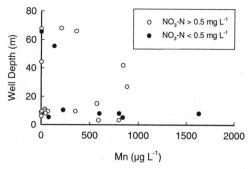

Figure 3. Concentration of manganese in Santa Cruz wells influenced by waste water.

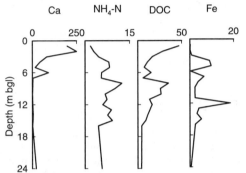

Figure 4. Porewater profiles from a city centre site in Hat Yai. Results in mg L^{-1}.

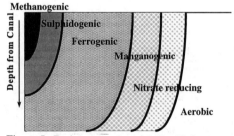

Figure 5. Redox zones beneath Hat Yai.

degree of microbial activity in the top 5 m. Nitrate is found only in the top few metres and probably generated through the oxidation of ammonia hence releasing protons and dissolving calcium and bicarbonate from calcite in the matrix.

The top 2-3 m represent the unsaturated zone and, beyond this, concentrations of iron begin to increase as

conditions become more reducing. The relatively low concentrations of iron and nitrate in the top few metres and the presence of ammonia could indicate pyrite oxidation (to reduce the oxidation state of iron) followed by nitrate reduction (equation 10). This reaction generates a large number of protons which would require buffering. The profile also contains high concentrations of manganese although iron reduction is the dominant TEAP in the top 12 m. Below this depth sulphate concentrations decline rapidly as sulphate reduction commences. Iron concentrations also fall as iron sulphides are formed and precipitated.

$$10Fe^{2+} + 2NO_3^- + 14H_2O \Rightarrow 10FeOOH + N_2 + 18H^+ \ (10)$$

Analysis of groundwaters from across the city has revealed the formation of a sequence of redox zones (Figure 5). The sequence is similar to those found at landfill sites (Lyngkilde and Christensen, 1992). The zone boundaries are often indistinct as reducing water moves into contact with relatively oxidising water and vice versa. The most reducing zone has yielded groundwater with arsenic concentrations up to 1 mg L^{-1} (twenty times the WHO guide value). Arsenic is likely to be present in the rock matrix as arsenopyrite or adsorbed to ferric hydroxides.

4 DISCUSSION

As observed at the slurry lagoon a mixture of organic carbon and nitrogen in the presence of an adaptive microbial community can react quite readily with the aquifer matrix. A highly reducing zone just beneath the lagoon has developed, causing sulphate reduction. No reduction of manganese or iron is observed as neither element is present in the matrix.

The introduction of atmospheric oxygen results in the oxidation of ammonia to nitrate. During this process a large number of protons are produced which causes a small fall in pH despite the large buffering capacity of the calcite matrix.

The sub-surface of Santa Cruz is generally unsaturated to at least 10 m. Oxygen in the unsaturated zone allows ammonia to be oxidised to nitrate. The calcite present in the rock matrix can buffer the protons generated and no fall in pH has been observed. In some shallow wells concentrated around the city centre it appears that reducing conditions are starting to occur. Reduction zones occur in isolated pockets elsewhere, but are more predominant in the city centre. This is mainly due to greater contamination but could reflect the highly seasonal recharge and localised impedance to groundwater movement caused by clay lenses.

Hat Yai has an unsaturated zone less than 5 m thick. Dissolved oxygen concentrations are negligible and most of the nitrate has been reduced. Ammonia concentrations greater than 15 mg L^{-1} are found at the water table. Porewater profiles reveal considerable depletion in base cations reflecting the geochemical evolution of the unsaturated zone as conditions became more reducing. Any future addition of protons could have a dramatic impact on the pH of the environment. Toxic metals such as cadmium and aluminium, which may be present in the aquifer matrix or in waste water, are more soluble at a lower pH and may therefore compound contamination.

Trace element mobility can also be increased through binding to organic matter (Christensen et al, 1996). Concentrations of nickel, copper and zinc were found to correlate closely ($r^2 > 0.75$) with DOC in the slurry lagoon porewater profile. However at both cities, groundwater concentrations of DOC are commonly less than 3 mg L^{-1} so the flux of trace metals reaching the water table by this mechanism is likely to be small. Nevertheless the indirect effect of a high organic load in the sub-surface is very important. Oxidation of organic matter can lead to the development of reducing conditions and so mobilise redox-sensitive elements some of which are highly toxic.

5 CONCLUSIONS

In groundwaters contaminated by wastewater, microbially mediated and abiotic chemical changes of organic compounds are closely linked to the geochemical environment. The development of reducing conditions depends upon the depth of the unsaturated zone, the availability of TEAPs and the presence of viable microorganisms. In turn, the transformation of significant quantities of organic matter affects groundwater chemistry in terms of aqueous speciation and pH, leading to mobilisation of potentially harmful contaminants.

REFERENCES

Amrhein C. & D.L. Suarez 1987. Calcite supersaturation in soils as a result of organic matter mineralization. *Soil Sci. Soc. Am. J.*, 51: 932-937.

Christensen J.B., D.L. Jensen & T.H.Christensen 1996. Effect of dissolved organic carbon on the mobility of cadmium, nickel and zinc in leachate polluted groundwater. *Wat. Res.* 30:3037-3039.

Gooddy D.C., P. J. Chilton, K.L. Smith, D.G. Kinniburgh & L.R. Bridge . 1994. Unsaturated zone drilling beneath a slurry pit on the Chalk at Bridgets Farm Winchester. *Brit. Geol. Surv. Tech. Rep.* WD/94/16.

Lawrence A.R. et al. 1994. Impact of urbanisation on groundwater: Hat Yai, Thailand. *Brit. Geol. Surv. Tech. Rep.* WD/94/16.

Lovley D.R. & F.H. Chapelle 1995. Deep subsurface microbial processes. *Rev. Geophys.* 33: 365-381.

Lyngkilde J. & T.H. Christensen 1992. Redox zones of a landfill leachate pollution plume. *J. Contam. Hydrol.*, 10: 273-289.

Morris B.L. et al. 1994. Impact of urbanisation on groundwater: Santa Cruz, Bolivia. *Brit. Geol. Surv. Tech. Rep.* WD/94/37.

ACKNOWLEDGMENTS

This study was funded by the Overseas Development Administration under project R5975. The authors would like to thank SAGUAPAC (Bolivia), DMR (Thailand) and the Prince of Songkla University (Thailand) for considerable assistance with groundwater sampling. This paper is published with the permission of the Director of the British Geological Survey (NERC).

In-situ remediation technologies on polluted groundwater

Li Guanghe, Zhang Xu & Liu Zhaochang
Department of Environmental Engineering, Tsinghua University, Beijing, People's Republic of China

Zhu Kun
Department of Environmental Engineering, Lanzhou Railway College, Gansu, People's Republic of China

Ja Daochang
Dawu Water Resources Management Office, Zibo, Shandong, People's Republic of China

ABSTRACT: In the east part, around 20 km^2, of the Dawu catchment, including the Xixia and Dongfeng abstraction areas, the groundwater has been polluted by discharge of petrochemical contaminants from an ethylene plant. Petrochemicals have spread over a significant area, up to 10 km^2, at concentrations of 20-48 mg/l. More than 60 organic species were detected in the groundwater. It is very important to control the spread of the polluted groundwater plumes and remove the contaminants remaining in the aquifers. In-situ integrated remediation technologies for groundwater polluted with petrochemicals have been researched in both laboratory and field. The results showed that a hydrodynamic capture technique can remove 80% of the petrochemicals and effectively control the spread of the pollution plume. Air sparging was used mainly to clean up the volatilizable contaminants and increase the dissolved oxygen in groundwater. Biodegradation and oxidation technologies can remove more than 50% of contaminants in groundwater. Through the operation of the integrated remediation zone, the concentration of the dissolved oxygen content increased from 2 mgL^{-1} to 5 mgL^{-1} and the petrochemical concentration was reduced from 2.1 mgL^{-1} to 0.7 mgL^{-1}, the removal rate reached 67%.

1 INTRODUCTION

Groundwater pollution by petrochemicals has become a serious environmental problem in recent years in China with the development of the petrochemical industry. This paper describes the research and development of remediation technologies for groundwater polluted with petrochemicals. The case study area is located in Zibo city, in the middle of Shandong province, in the east part of China (see Figure 1).

Since 1970, with the construction and development of production capacity of 0.3 million tonnes by the Qilu Petroleum Chemistry Corporation, Zibo city has become one of the most important petrochemical bases in China. Groundwater is the main water supply source for local industries and residents. In the Dawu catchment 0.45 million cubic metres are abstracted daily. Unfortunately, an area of serious groundwater pollution in the Dawu catchment, such as Liuhang- Hougao-Jinling area, has been identified caused by discharge of petrochemicals which have infiltrated through the soil into the groundwater. Petrochemicals have moved into a significant area of up to 10 km^2 at concentrations as high as 20-48 mgL^{-1}. More than 60 species of organic contaminants have been detected in groundwater.

The key problem is how to control the spread of the plumes of polluted groundwater and remove the contaminants remaining in the aquifer.

2 NATURAL CONDITIONS

The remediation area of approximately 21 km^2 is situated in an intermediate zone between a hilly region and a wide plain. The land surface dips from South to North at a gradient of 0.8%. The elevation of the study area ranges from 60 to 260 metres above sea level. The Zibo region is classified as a warm inland climate with a hot rainy summer and cold dry winter. The monthly average temperature ranges from -3.6 °C in January to 26.3 °C in August with an average annual temperature of 12.2 °C. Annual average precipitation is about 630 mm, and the annual average evaporation is 1790 mm.

The study area is located on the Zibo syncline. The land surface is composed of Quaternary pluvial and alluvial sedimentary layers which mainly consist of gray -yellow loam and silt, ranging in thickness from 5 m in the south to 40 m in the north. The area is underlain by Carboniferous (C) and middle Ordovician (O$_2$) rocks. Carboniferous marl strata, about 40 m in thickness, present in the northern part of the study area, have low permeability and form a natural barrier for groundwater flow. The middle Ordovician (O_2) limestone strata dip north-east across the whole 20 km^2 study area with a thickness of more than 400 m. These well karst-fractured strata ranging from 90 to 180 m below the land surface is an important karst aquifer storing a great quantity of groundwater. This forms the main aquifer for the water supply to Zibo city.

Groundwater is recharged from the rainfall infiltration and the groundwater inflow from the southern hilly area where there is little soil cover. The depth of the groundwater level below the land surface varies from 20 m in the rainy season to 60 m in the dry season. Generally, the regional groundwater flow is from the southern hills to the north-east plain, but flow, controlled by a local cone of depression, is from west to east, that is from Hougao where groundwater has been seriously polluted by petrochemicals towards Dongfang which is a very important potable water abstraction area in the Dawu catchment.

3 GROUNDWATER QUALITY

The field investigation indicated that the unsaturated zone in the ethylene plant was seriously polluted by petroleum. Results from 120 soil samples showed the petroleum concentration in the soil layers to range from 12 to 94050 mg/kg soil. It is obvious that the soil has become the direct pollution source for the groundwater in the study area. Groundwater quality data from 35 monitoring wells indicated that the groundwater has been seriously polluted by petroleum in some areas of Dawu. The contaminants were mainly of oil and benzene and have now penetrated a significant area (up to 10 km^2) of the karstic limestone aquifer. The distribution of the petroleum pollutants in the groundwater is illustrated in Figure 2. In some local areas such as Hougao and Liuhang the petroleum concentration was as high as 18 mgL^{-1} and more than 60 species of organic pollutants were detected in groundwater by means of gas chromatography/mass spectrometry. The

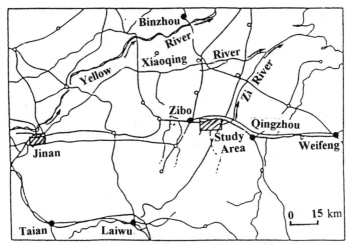

Figure1. Geographical position of the study area.

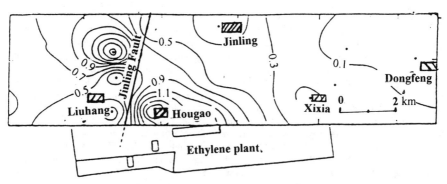

Figure 2. Distribution of total oil concentrations (mgL^{-1}) in the groundwater.

412

Table 1. Total oil concentrations (mgL^{-1}) at different depths below the groundwater level in Jinling.

Depth (m)	Mar. 1993	Apr. 1993	May 1993	Apr. 1994	Dec. 1994
0	0.253	0.143	0.075	0.23	0.29
10	0.02	0.054	0.05	0.175	0.15
30	0.05	0.058	0.05	0.05	0.05

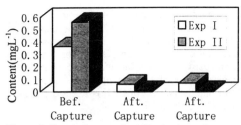

Figure 3. Simulation results of hydrodynamic capture.

monitoring results indicated that the pollution plume is starting to impact on the existing extraction wells, and threatening the operation of the Dongfeng potable water abstraction area.

Since 1992, groundwater quality at different depths of the aquifer in Jinling and Hougao has been investigated to determine the vertical distribution of the pollution plume in the aquifers. The results are shown in Table 1. It can be seen that the position of the pollution plume is from 0 to 30 m below the groundwater level in Jinling. The results lay the foundation for selecting reasonable remedial technologies and relevant parameters, such as the location of the capture zone, depth and position of the remedial wells, as well as the injection depth of gas and bacteria in biodegradation and air sparging zones.

4 REMEDIAL TECHNOLOGIES

The investigation of soil and groundwater quality indicates that in the study area the potential and direct pollution sources are widely distributed within the ethylene plant area. Waste water containing petrochemicals from the plant continuously leaks into the soil and the groundwater. Obviously, cutting off the pollution sources, blocking the spread of the polluted groundwater plume to the main water supply area and removing the contaminants from polluted groundwater has become the key problem in the recovery and remediation of the groundwater. Since 1990 a series of laboratory and in-situ simulation experiments have been carried out. Four remedial techniques: hydrodynamic capture, air sparging, biodegradation and chlorine dioxide oxidation were used in the in-situ underground remediation of the polluted groundwater. This paper focuses on a discussion of the remedial technologies and the relevant technical parameters for in-situ remediation of the groundwater.

4.1 Air sparging

For water treatment, air stripping is a promising method for removing volatile organic contamination from water at low cost(Lamarche & Droste 1989). From the laboratory experiments, it was evident that air venting could remove about 30%-45% of the petroleum from groundwater. Therefore air sparging by means of injection wells would be effective for removing the organic contaminants from the aquifer.

In addition, the experimental results indicated that the air sparging not only removed some petrochemicals, but also effectively increased the dissolved oxygen (DO) in groundwater. DO contents increased from 1 mgL^{-1} to 5-6 mgL^{-1} through the air sparging under the conditions of the simulation experiments.

4.2 Hydrodynamic capture

The principle of the hydrodynamic capture technique is to use grounwater abstraction to remove contaminants from the aquifer and to use the depression of the water table to halt the spread of pollution. This requires information on geology, hydrogeology, the distribution of sources and the properties of the pollution (Ahlfeld & Chartes 1990; Grubb 1993). The results of the simulation experiments, shown in Figure 3, and proved that the hydrodynamic capture technique can effectively clean up 80% of the petrochemicals in the groundwater and block the spread of the pollution plume.

In addition, the efficiency of the capture zone is mainly affected by the position of the abstraction well in the pollution plume. Based on the experimental results in the laboratory, the best position is at the centre of the pollution plume, and intersecting whole vertical section of the pollution plume thickness.

4.3 Chlorine dioxide oxidation technique

Chlorine dioxide has a very strong oxidation capacity, so it can break down the benzene ring, and can oxidize toxic organic components to nontoxic byproducts. Therefore chlorine dioxide is widely used in water pre-treatment. In order to determine the effects of the chlorine dioxide in removing the petrochemical contaminants and to obtain the relevant technical parameters for in-situ remediation, experiments have been done in the laboratory. The

413

results are showed in Figure 3 and Figure 4.

The results showed that, with the increase of the chlorine dioxide content, improvement of the removal rates of petroleum is not obvious. The reaction between the chlorine dioxide and the contaminants is quick process, optimum reaction time is 5 min, and the content of ClO_2 is 7.5mgL^{-1}, and the removal rate is about 55%.

4.4 Oxidation-hydrodynamic capture technique

The purpose of setting up the oxidation-hydrodynamic capture technique was to clean up the contaminants in the aquifer polluted with petroleum more effectively by joint action of chemical oxidation and hydrodynamic capture. In order to determine the feasibility and the relevant parameters for in-situ remediation of the polluted aquifer, laboratory experiments were carried out. The results showed that the petroleum concentration in water before chemical oxidation-capture remediation was 1 mg/l, however, after treatment this was redued to 0.15 mg/l, a removal rate of 85%. In addition, the analytical results from water samples from the monitoring wells indicated that the contents of the chlorine reached 9 mg/L from 0 to30 cm below the water level, which strongly enhanced the efficiency of the oxidation-capture technique. It is quite evident that the oxidation-capture remediation zone can efficiently reduce the contents of the petroleum and remove the contaminants in the groundwater. The technique has been selected to be used for the in-situ remediation of the groundwater pollution.

4.5 Bioremediation

Biodegradation experiments were carried out in the laboratory. The bacteria cleaning up the contaminants were from the local polluted grounwater in Hougao and Liuhang, and the optimal mixed bacteria which used oil as their unique carbon source were obtained by the selection, separation and culture of the bacteria in the laboratory. Biodegadation results, shown in Figure 6, indicated that the bacteria could effectively degrade the petrochemicals, and removal rates were about 90%.

5 IN-SITU IMPLEMENTATION OF REMEDIAL TECHNOLOGIES

All the five techniques described in section 4 were taken forward for on-site experimentation. Their implementation is illustrated in Figures 7 and 8.

The length of the remedial zone was a total of 280 m from the air sparging zone to the

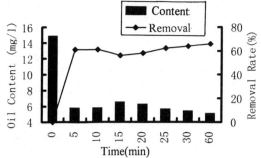

Figure 4. Relationship between the reaction time and the removal rates.

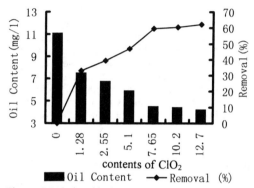

Figure 5. Relationship between the removal retes and the injection contents of ClO_2.

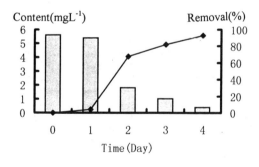

Figure 6. Biodegradation of the petroleum.

hydrodynamic capture zone. In the remedial area, a capture zone consisting of 10 pumping wells was established within the pollution plume of the aquifer. The depth and diameter of the pumping wells were 200 m and 0.4 m respectively. The daily total abstraction rates of 20000 cubic metres created an artificial groundwater valley of 3 m depth which

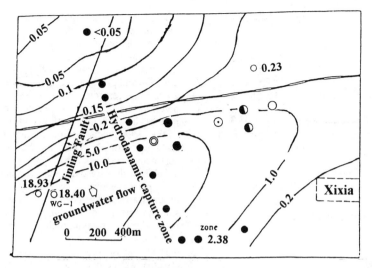

Figure 7. In-situ underground integrated remediation scheme of the polluted groundwater
◐ air sparging well;   ⊙ bacteria injection well;   ◎ oxidant injection well;   ● pumping well;
○ observation well;   --0.2-- contour of petrochemical concentration, mgL⁻¹(before remediation).

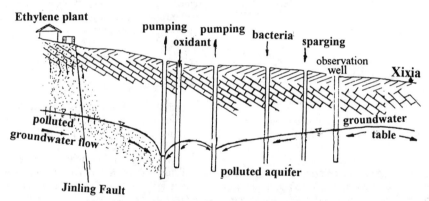

Figure 8. Section of integrated remediation scheme.

changed the groundwater flow direction and strongly blocked the expansion of the pollution plume.

In addition, a stable barrier formed by abstraction grounwater to prevent the further movement of the pollution plume in the Hougao and Liuhang. A part of the abstraction will be treated to be used in farmland irrigation and industry in future, a part mixed with chlorine dioxide on the land surface was injected back into the polluted aquifer into oxidation zone.

Many case studies have shown that chemical treatment methods are practical and successful for the recovery of contaminated soil using redox reactions. However it is rarely reported that chemical methods have been used directly for in-situ remediation in a polluted aquifer. In this study, the in-situ remediation results showed that when compared with other oxidants such as potassium permanganate, chlorine dioxide is a suitable oxidant to be used in in-situ remediation both in terms of the oxidation capacity and economy.

The removal rates of total petrochemical contaminants reached 70-80% by the chlorine dioxide technique. Other techniques, air sparging and biodegradation, have been shown to be efficient in the remediation of the polluted groundwater (Figure 9). Particularly air sparging could effectively increase the dissolved oxygen content in the polluted groundwater in the remedial zone, which obviously was helpful in increasing the activity of the bacteria removing the

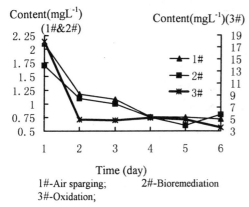

Content(mgL⁻¹)(1#&2#)

Content(mgL⁻¹)(3#)

Time (day)

1#-Air sparging;   2#-Bioremediation
3#-Oxidation;

Figure 9. In-situ remediation results.

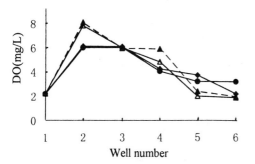

Well number

1-observation well   2&3-sparging wells
4-bio-remediation well   5&6-pumping wells

Figure 10. Dissolved oxygen contents in different remediation wells during in-situ remediation.

petrochemical contaminants and thus the efficiency of biodegradation 30 m down gradient. The monitoring results showed that the removal rate reached 53%, and 80% of the toxic organic components could be removed by biodegradation.

Through the operation of an integrated remediation zone, the concentration of dissolved oxygen increased from 2 mgL⁻¹ to 5 mgL⁻¹ (Figure 10), and the petrochemical concentration was reduced from 2.1 mgL⁻¹ to 0.7 mgL⁻¹, equivalent to a removal rate of 67%.

6 CONCLUSIONS

1. Groundwater in Zibo region is a critical resource that is known to have been both over exploited and polluted, and is likely to be threatened further by the expansion of the pollution plume. The field investigations showed that the groundwater pollution was caused by leakage of waste water containing petrochemicals. Petroleum and other organic compounds were found at high concentrations in groundwater.

2. Hydrodynamic capture of the pollution plume is an effective and practical technique. Setting up a capture zone in the remedial area is an effective way to halt deterioration of the groundwater quality. It was able to alter the groundwater flow and reduced the threat of the groundwater pollution plume moving towards the production wells in the Dongfeng main abstraction area.

3. Chlorine dioxide oxidation is effective in cleaning up petrochemical contaminants in polluted groundwater. It has been selected to be used for in-situ remediation of the groundwater pollution. The removal rate of total petrochemical contaminants was about 35-40%.

4. The oxidation-capture combined technique can effectively remove pollutants from groundwater.

5. By the operation of an integrated remediation zone the removal rate of total petrochemical pollutants reached 67%. The in-situ remediation results indicated that the integrated underground remediation technologies were effective in removing the petrochemicals in groundwater and aquifers and restoring groundwater quality in the Dawu water catchment.

REFERENCES

Ahlfeld, P.D. & S.S. Chartes 1990. Well location in capture zone design using simulation and optimization techniques. *Ground Water 28(4):* 507-512.
Grubb, S. 1993. Analytical model for estimation of steady-state capture zone of pumping wells in confined and unconfined aquifers. *Ground Water 31(1):*27-32
Lamarche P. & R.L. Droste 1989. Air- stripping mass transfer correlation for volatile organics. *J.of AWWA, 24(5):*46-54.

Groundwater in the Urban Environment: Problems, Processes and Management, Chilton et al. (eds)
© *1997 Balkema, Rotterdam, ISBN 90 5410 837 1*

Modelling subsurface phosphorus transport

A. Gupta & G. Destouni
Department of Civil and Environmental Engineering, Royal Institute of Technology (KTH), Stockholm, Sweden

M. B. Jensen
Department of Agricultural Sciences, Soil, Water and Plant Nutrition, Royal Veterinary and Agricultural University, Denmark

ABSTRACT: Subsurface transport of phosphorus (^{32}P) was studied by modelling the experimental breakthrough curves (BTCs) from tracer tests in two intact soil monoliths. The main advantage of the presented probablistic Lagrangian modelling approach is that it decouples hydrological transport (evaluated by non-reactive tracer tests) and chemical processes. The model interpretation of experimental results is as far as possible based on independently determined parameter values. The model results indicate that in the experimental soil monoliths water flows preferentially through about 25% of the total water content. In both monoliths, the modelling yields consistent first-order kinetic parameter values for the ^{32}P sorption-desorption.

1 INTRODUCTION

Urbanization generates increasing quantities of waste products which can be highly toxic and persistent, and with time leach from the subsurface to the groundwater. Hence, groundwater contamination by inorganic and organic chemicals in the subsurface has created a great impetus for the development of models of the transport processes in the unsaturated zone. In urban areas phosphorus may come from fertilizers, detergents, medicines, industries, automobile exhausts etc. The unsaturated zone usually contains large continuous macropores, the presence of which may cause surface applied chemicals to move rapidly through the soil profile. Leaching of phosphorus through such preferential flow paths may contribute to eutrophication of fresh waters.

In this paper, transport of phosphorus is studied by modelling the experimental BTCs from tracer tests in two intact soil monoliths. The modelling is based on the probabilistic Lagrangian approach to reactive subsurface transport (e.g., Cvetkovic & Dagan 1994) and a similar concept has been previously applied in chemical engineering by Villermaux (1974). The model involves non-reactive solute travel time probability density function (pdf) through the soil monoliths, coupled with a reaction model for linear, non-equilibrium sorption-desorption.

2 EXPERIMENTAL SETUP AND RESULTS

Two intact soil monoliths were excavated in agri-

Table 1. Characteristics of the field soil as determined from standard soil samples.

Horizon	Bulk density	Porosity	Clay	Silt	Fine sand
cm	g/cm^3		%	%	%
Ap 0-25	1.33	0.49	15	15	44
Eg 25-45	1.40	0.47	19	14	43
Bt1g 45-73	1.56	0.41	19	11	44
Bt2g 73-108	1.78	0.32	20	13	42

cultural loamy-sand field near Farre, Jutland in Denmark. The monoliths were sized 0.5m in diameter by 0.73m long and 0.5m in diameter by 1.0m long and are in the following referred to as L1 and L2, respectively.

The identified horizons of the monoliths are Ap, Eg, Bt1g and Bt2g (Table 1) with an average mineral density of 2.65g/cm^3. The texture was determined by sieving and sedimentation. The average porosity was based on 0.5m diameter samples. The subsoil contained two distinct types of macropores: biopores (earthworm burrows and some decayed root channels) and fractures.

For L1 the Ap-horizon was removed in the laboratory in order to focus the study on the subsoil. Monolith L2 contained all the soil horizons. In the laboratory, the monoliths were insulated and cooled to 1-2°C, controlled by a thermocouple. The experimental setup is shown in Figure 1.

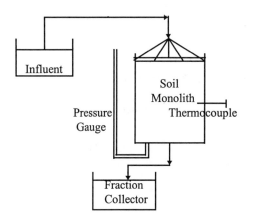

Fig. 1 Schematic representation of laboratory setup.

A full cone nozzle fed from a pressurized carboy applied influent to the surface of the soil monoliths, at a rate regulated with a timer-controlled magnetic valve. For tracer application, a secondary tracer carboy replaced the ordinary influent carboy by turning of a three way stop-cock. Effluent was collected from the bottom of the monoliths in a fraction collector. The flow rate was controlled by means of a peristaltic pump. The pressure head was measured by connecting an open-ended vertical tube to the bottom cover.

Tracer experiments were carried out under saturated, steady-state flow conditions. Pulses of both tritium (^3H_2O) and ^{32}P as $H_2{}^{32}PO_4^-$ were applied to the soil monoliths (Table 2). Effluent was sampled and analyzed for ^{32}P and ^3H_2O by scintillation counting. Aliquots of the applied pulse solutions were analyzed by the same procedure. The effluent concentration was multiplied with the volumetric flow rate, Q, yielding the solute mass flow rate.

The experimental cumulative BTCs were obtained by integrating the solute mass flow rate over time. Table 2 shows the mass recovery in the individual tracer tests for the two soil monoliths. The results indicate that tritium is a non-reactive tracer while ^{32}P is strongly adsorbed to the soil.

Table 2. Experimental parameters.

Mono-lith	Q ml/min	Tracer	Pulse vol. ml	Pulse conc. cpm/ml	Mass recov-ery %
L1	8.42	^3H_2O	670	1431500	81
		^{32}P	670	163650	0.78
L2	8.92	^3H_2O	500	277200	97
		^{32}P	500	907200	1.0

3 MODELLING OF TRITIUM BTCs

A probabilistic Lagrangian transport formulation has been used for model interpretation of the tritium BTCs. The approach is based on the assumption that the solute spreading is primarily an effect of variability in solute advection between different stream lines coupled with possible solute mass transfer between mobile and immobile water zones (Destouni & Cvetkovic 1991).

The modelled BTCs are based on available independently measured parameters, namely total water content, θ, and water flux q=Q/A, with A being the monolith cross-sectional area. They are compared with the experimental BTCs in order to identify and quantify possible effects of preferential flow and transport pathways. The transport model used for L1 is the advection dispersion equation (ADE) coupled with the effects of immobile water zones in terms of a mass transfer coefficient, α, between mobile and immobile water, quantified by the water content θ_m and θ_{im}, respectively. For a pulse injection at the soil surface the resulting solute travel time pdf, $f(t,z)$ at time t through the monolith effluent at depth z from the monolith surface (z=0), can be expressed as (Destouni & Cvetkovic 1991)

$$f(t,z) = \exp\left[-\frac{\alpha}{\theta_m}t\right]s_m(t;z) + \int_0^t \psi\left(t,\varsigma\right)s_m\left(\varsigma;z\right)d\varsigma \quad (1)$$

$$\psi\left(t,\varsigma\right) = \left(\alpha^2/\theta_m\theta_{im}\right)\varsigma \exp\left(-\frac{\alpha}{\theta_m}\varsigma - \frac{\alpha}{\theta_{im}}t + \frac{\alpha}{\theta_{im}}\varsigma\right) \cdot$$
$$\hat{I}\left[\left(\alpha^2/\theta_m\theta_{im}\right)\varsigma\left(t - \varsigma\right)\right]H\left(t - \varsigma\right) \quad (2)$$

where ς is a dummy variable, H(t) is the Heaviside step function, $\hat{I}(W) = I_1\left(2W^{1/2}\right)/W^{1/2}$, with I_1 being the modified Bessel function of the first kind of order one, and s_m is the normalized solution to the ADE for an instantaneous flux injection and flux detection of non-sorptive solute (Kreft & Zuber 1978) expressed as:

$$s_m(t;z) = \frac{1}{T\left[4\pi\left(\lambda/z\right)\left(t/T\right)^3\right]^{1/2}}\exp\left[-\frac{\left(1 - t/T\right)^2}{4\left(\lambda/z\right)\left(t/T\right)}\right] \quad (3)$$

In (3), $T = z\theta_m/q$, is the mean advective solute travel time to z, and λ is the local dispersivity. The agreement between the experimental and modelled cumulative BTCs (least squares method) is shown in Figure 2, where the modelled cumulative BTC is obtained by integrating the pdf, $f(t,z)$ over time. The fitted parameters for L1 are λ=0.10m, θ_m=0.10 and α=0.00008 min^{-1}, indicating 26% of the total water content, θ, to be mobile.

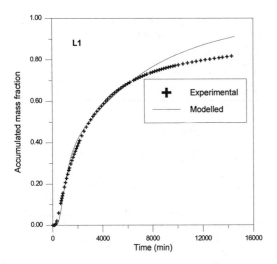

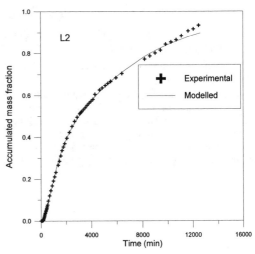

Fig. 2 Experimental and modelled tritium BTCs for soil monolith L1.

Fig. 3 Experimental and modelled tritium BTCs for soil monolith L2.

The independently known/measured parameters, z, θ, q for L1 are 0.73m, 0.38 and 4.3×10^{-5} m/min, respectively.

For monolith L2 a bimodal pdf of solute travel time, $f(t,z)$, is used to quantitatively handle solute advection variability through both preferential and slow flow paths. In this methodology all the water is assumed to be mobile and is distributed as θ_1 (water content in slow flow paths) and θ_2 (water content in preferential flow paths). The bimodal pdf is expressed as

$$f(t,z) = v f_1(t,z) + (1-v) f_2(t,z) \qquad (4)$$

$$f_i(t,z) = \frac{1}{t\sqrt{2\pi\sigma_i^2}} \exp\left[-\frac{1}{2} \frac{\left(\ln(t) - \ln(T_i^G)\right)^2}{\sigma_i^2} \right] \qquad (5)$$

where $f_i(t,z)$ is a log-normal distribution with T_i^G being the geometric mean and σ_i^2 the variance of ln t within the population of slow flow paths for i=1 and the population of preferential flow paths for i=2. Furthermore, v is a weighting coefficient, expressing the area fraction influenced by the slow flow paths, and is quantified as:

$$v = \theta_1(V/Q)\exp(-\sigma_1^2/2)/T_1^G \qquad (6)$$

where V is the total volume of soil in the monolith. The agreement between the experimental and modelled cumulative BTCs for L2 is shown in

Figure 3. The fitted parameters for L2 are $v=0.4$, $\sigma_1^2=0.4$, $\sigma_2^2=0.7$, $T_1^G=9460$min and $T_2^G=1644$min, indicating that 24% of the total water flows through preferential flow paths. The independently known/ measured parameters, z, θ, q for L2 are 1.0m, 0.42 and 4.5×10^{-5} m/min, respectively. The obtained θ_1, θ_2 are 0.32 and 0.10 respectively.

4 MODELLING OF ^{32}P BTCs

For modelling the phosphorus transport we extend the Lagrangian transport formulation, by quantifying sorption-desorption as it takes place along advection flow paths (e.g., Cvetkovic & Dagan 1994). The reactive transport along a streamline can be parameterized by a function, $\gamma(t,\tau)$, with τ being the non-reactive solute travel time in an individual streamline.

For the present experimental results it is assumed that the solute, ^{32}P is undergoing sorption-desorption controlled by linear, first-order kinetics. Thus, the actual mass flow rate, s, through the monolith can be expressed as (Destouni & Cvetkovic 1991)

$$s/M_0 = \int_0^\infty \gamma(t,\tau) f(\tau,z) d\tau \qquad (7)$$

$$\gamma(t,\tau) = \exp(-k_1 t)\delta(t - \tau) + \\ k_1 k_2 \tau \exp(-k_1\tau - k_2 t + k_2\tau) \hat{I}\left[k_1 k_2 \tau(t-\tau)\right] H(t-\tau) \qquad (8)$$

419

In (7), M_0 is the total input of tracer mass and $f(\tau,z)$ is given by the modelling of the tritium tracer BTCs. In (8) k_1 and k_2 are the sorption and desorption rate coefficients, respectively, and δ is the Dirac delta function.

Figures 4a and 4b show the experimental and modelled cumulative ^{32}P BTCs for L1 and L2, respectively, where the modelled cumulative BTCs are obtained by integrating the mass flow rate in (7) over time. The only fitting parameters for the modelled ^{32}P BTCs were k_1 and k_2, which are listed in Table 3.

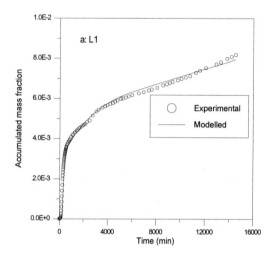

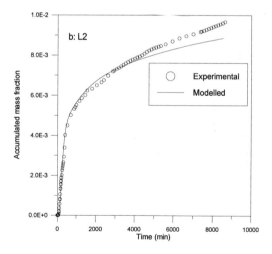

Fig. 4 Experimental and modelled cumulative ^{32}P BTCs for a) soil monolith L1 and b) soil monolith L2.

Table 3. Model parameter values for the first-order sorption-desorption kinetics.

Monolith	k_1 (min^{-1})	k_2 (min^{-1})
L1	0.007	0.002
L2	0.010	0.004

5 CONCLUSIONS

In this paper the probabilistic Lagrangian approach has been used for modelling phosphorus transport in controlled laboratory experiments. The main advantage of this approach is the decoupling of hydrological transport (evaluated by non-reactive tracer tests) and chemical processes. The model analysis indicates that preferential flow occurs in both experimental soil monoliths. For L1, the model results indicate that water flows preferentially through 26% of the total water content (obtained as θ_m/θ), while the corresponding result for L2 is 24% of the total water content (obtained as θ_2/θ).

The model results for ^{32}P yield kinetic parameters k_1 and k_2 of the same order of magnitude for the two different soil monoliths, even though different models were used for the non-reactive tracer BTCs. Furthermore, the resulting fit for the ^{32}P tracer tests was good in spite of the poorer model fit for the non-reactive tracer experiments.

The kinetic parameters calculated at the laboratory scale can be used to evaluate field-scale leaching of phosphorus by incorporating spatial variability in transport parameters due to scale transition. Further, the approach presented here can also be used for quantifying uncertainty and impact evaluation of increasing contaminants in urbanized environment.

REFERENCES

Cvetkovic, V. & G. Dagan 1994. Transport of kinetically sorbing solute by steady random velocity in heterogeneous porous formations. *J. Fluid Mech.* 265:189-215.

Destouni, G. & V. Cvetkovic 1991. Field scale mass arrival of sorptive solute into the groundwater. *Water Resour. Res.* 27:1315-1325.

Kreft, A. & A. Zuber 1978. On the physical meaning of the dispersion equation and its solutions for different initial and boundary conditions. *Chem. Engng. Sci.* 33:1471-1480.

Villermaux, J. 1974. Deformation of chromatographic peaks under the influence of mass transfer phenomena. *J. Chromatographic Sci.* 12:822-831.

Groundwater in the Urban Environment: Problems, Processes and Management, Chilton et al. (eds)
© 1997 Balkema, Rotterdam, ISBN 90 5410 837 1

Risk assessment of subsurface disposal of industrial residues in coal mines

Th. Himmelsbach
Lehrstuhl für Angewandte Geologie, Ruhr-Universität-Bochum, Germany

Ch. König
*Theorie der Tragwerke und Simulationstechnik, Fakultät für Bauingenieurwesen, Ruhr-Universität-Bochum,
Germany*

ABSTRACT: The subsurface storage of industrial residues in coal mines underneath densely populated urban areas is important for waste disposal in North-Rhine-Westfalia, Germany. The residues from electric
energy plants exist as filter ashes and desulphurization residues which are injected behind the long wall faces.
The use of coal mines as underground repositories requires proof that contaminants, like heavy metals, will
not return via slow groundwater flow to the biosphere. The quantitative risk assessment of such underground
storage facilities can only be done with the help of numerical models. The succesful modelling of the nearfield of the fractured host rock requires a stochastic fractured aquifer model which includes the physical
processes of fracture flow, matrix diffusion, sorption and desorption effects. This paper summarizes the evaluation methods used to obtain the model parameters, such as permeability and statistical fracture data,
effective diffusion and sorption coefficients. The parameters are used to perform numerical calculations to
predict the water table rise in the near field of the repository and the flow and transport velocities after the
coal mines are depleted.

1 INTRODUCTION

With regard to the increasing amount of industrial
residues from electric power plants, subsurface
storage in coal mines underneath densely populated urban areas is important in North-Rhine-
Westfalia, Germany (Jäger et al. 1990). The residues exist as filter ashes and desulphurization residues. The residues are collected and stored at a
few, still active coal mines where they are mixed
together with mining debris and water to obtain a
hydraulic suspension. A system of pipelines and
pumping stations transports this hydraulic suspension towards the subsurface repository.

The bulk volume assimilating the residues originates directly from the mining process itself. At
German coal mines the production is restricted to
areas of more or less subhorizontal bedding to render the coal production more effective by using a
system of large long wall faces. Only the long wall
face is protected by a strong safety shield covering
a width of approximately 5 m. As the coal production proceeds, the safety shields are moved
stepwise forward. Just behind the safety shield the
overlying bed rock collapses yielding a loose heap
of rock debris which provides enough bulk volume
to inject the hydraulic suspension. As the coal
mining proceeds, the rock debris and the industrial

residues filling the void space become increasingly
affected by the subsiding overburden. The increasing pressure and additional mineralogical reactions of some components of the injected suspension
lead to a new brecciform rock mass. Aside from
the subsurface waste disposal aspect, the injection
of industrial residues therefore also diminishes
subsurface subsidence and renders the ventilation
of the coal pits more effective (Striegel 1995). The
injection method is schematically depicted in
Figure 1.

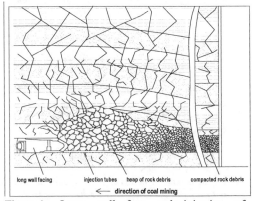

long wall facing   injection tubes   heap of rock debris   compacted rock debris
← direction of coal mining

Figure 1. Long wall face and injection of
residues.

The hydrogeological and geochemical investigations which have been carried out by Jäger et al. (1990) have shown that the most likely path by which dissolved contaminants could return to the biosphere is via groundwater flow after the mines are depleted and the pumping of groundwater has been stopped. The use of coal mines as longterm repositories requires a clear demonstration that contaminants, like heavy metals, which may reach the surface after thousands of years will not, due to dilution and sorption along the migration path, represent any harm to the biosphere.

2 PHYSICAL PROCESSES

In our study we consider the Carboniferous host rock as a fractured aquifer whose hydraulic behaviour is controlled by faults, fractures and fissures. Within the fractured system, advection may occur at much higher flow velocities than within the undisturbed porous matrix. The physical process of matrix diffusion is of particular relevance to those aqueous species which show only weak sorption and which would otherwise migrate at or near groundwater velocity from a repository towards the ground surface (Bradbury & Green 1985). Recent theoretical and experimental investigations, which were performed in connection with the burial of radioactive waste, indicated the importance of matrix diffusion as a retardation mechanism affecting solute transport processes in fractured host rock (Neretnieks 1980). The quantitative risk assessment of an underground storage facility can only be done with the help of a numerical model. Such models must consider the following physical processes:

- diffusion of contaminants into the rock matrix
- adsorption of contaminants in the matrix
- fast fracture flow within the fracture network
- and slow flow in the matrix.

For the numerical modelling the following problems have to be solved (Wendland & Schmid 1995):

- the generated, stochastical fracture network should reflect natural fracture patterns and must consider natural fracture length and spacing distributions
- the fracture network must be generated in a 3D-domain considering a random 3D-distribution of fractures
- any arbitrary cross section of the 3D-fracture network will lead to 2D-fracture traces which will be used for the further 2D-modelling of the problem

- the diffusion or adsorption of contaminants from the fracture into the porous matrix has to be approximated mathematically
- and the numerical coupling of the fast advective transport in the fractures and slow diffusive processes in the matrix has to be solved.

In the present study we consider the system as a coupled fracture-matrix model. The advection in the fractures and in the porous matrix is described by coupling the continuity and the Darcy equations. The formulation allows treatment of satured ($p>0$, $S_w=1$, $k_{rel}=1$) and unsatured ($p<0$, $0<S_w<1$, $k_{rel}<1$) conditions as well as the consideration of variable fluid density ρ:

$$\rho\left(s_w s_{op} + n\frac{dS_w}{dp}\right)\frac{\partial p}{\partial t} - \nabla\left[\rho K k_{rel}\frac{\rho g}{\mu}\nabla\left(\frac{p}{\rho g}+z\right)\right] = Q\rho \quad (1)$$

with:
- s_w saturation factor
- p hydraulic head
- k_{rel} permeabilty factor due to saturation
- K permeabilty

The permeability of the porous matrix has to be determined in the laboratory and the permeability of the fractures is assumed to follow the Cubic Law (Louis 1967):

$$K = \frac{2b^2}{12} \quad (2)$$

with b describing the half width of the fracture. The numerical application of this equation requires the definition of boundary conditions from the hydrogeological model (Figure 2).

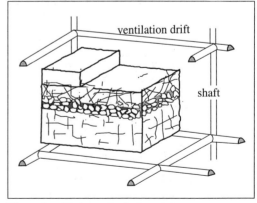

Figure 2. Hydrogeological model of the repository.

When the pumping at the shafts is stopped, the groundwater table will rise again. The groundwater rise will slow down when the deepest ventilation drift is reached and it will increase again until the next mining horizon is flooded. Since the coal pit has been drained for a long time period the host rock is only partially saturated. From the the surrounding shafts and ventilation drifts steep hydraulic gradients will therefore be orientated towards the disposal site. The transient propagation of the saturation front through the host rock will therefore be the most important load case which has to be described by the model.

3   DERIVATION OF PARAMETERS

The modelling of the nearfield of the fractured host rock requires the derivation of effective aquifer parameters such as the permeability of fractures and matrix, statistical fracture data, effective diffusion and sorption coefficients.

3.1   Fracture network generation

The generation of a fracture network depends on the scale of the model. Fractures can either be incorporated deterministically as discrete fracture sets or stochastically if the scale of observation becomes larger (Kulatilake et al. 1993). The present study requires a stochastic approach, because the number of fractures becomes too large for deterministic generation. This approach requires the evaluation of statistical fracture parameters from field measurements. The parameters are:

- direction and dip of main fracture patterns and their spherical variance
- statistical fracture length distribution
- statistical fracture spacing distribution
- mean fracture aperture and its distribution.

The evaluation of statistical parameters is performed by fitting statistical distribution models to observed field data. This can be done considering Gaussian, log-normal or exponetial distributions. Figure 3 shows an example depicting the fracture-length distribution for a sandstone outcrop where the considered log-normal distribution yields the best results. The obtained statistical information, which is consitent with real fracture patterns, can now be used to generate a three-dimensional random fracture network (Huewel 1995).

Figure 4 shows the 3D fracture domain which is cut by a vertical 2D cross section. The two-dimensional fracture traces on this cross section are used to perform simulations with the two-dimensional fracture model.

3.2   Determination of diffusion coefficients.

The determination of diffusion coefficients was performed using diffusion cells. Diffusion was measured through different rock samples of 52 mm diameter and 5 mm thickness. The rock disks were ealed into perspex holders which were mounted vertically between the two perspex halfs of the diffusion cell. One half of the diffusion cell contained the reservoir of the diffusing species, and the other was initially kept at zero concentration (Figure 5). The chosen experimental array considers the diffusion process through the rock sample to be a one-dimensional process and the data were evaluated considering Fick´s second law (LEVER et al. 1985). The experiments generally lasted a few weeks, with steady-state diffusion being reached after 1 - 3 weeks (Figure 6). All experimental data could be fitted reasonably well to the model and yielded consistent effective diffusivities ranging from $7 \cdot 10^{-9}$ cm²/s to $2 \cdot 10^{-8}$ cm²/s (Himmelsbach et al. 1995).

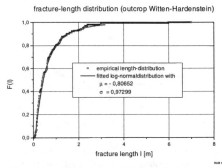

Figure 3.   Fitting a log-normal probability function to empirical outcrop data.

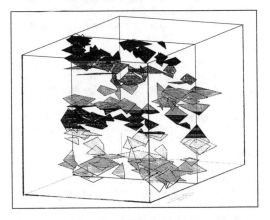

Figure 4.   Randomly generated fracture network.

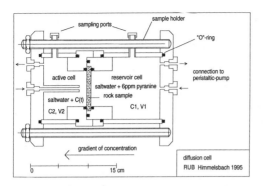

Figure 5. Schematic sketch of the diffusion cell.

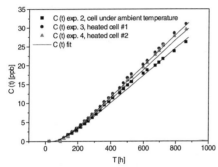

Figure 6. Diffusion experiments performed under different temperatures.

4 RESULTS OF FIRST SIMULATIONS

First simulations have been carried out to model the effect of the groundwater rise after the pumping at a coal mine has stopped. One aim was to test the model and to derive information about the likely spatial head distribution within the host rock. Another interest was how the fracture network would affect the general hydraulic behaviour which was compared with modelling results considering a conventional porous aquifer model (Wendland & Schmid 1995). The model incorporates an area of 500 m in length and 100 m in height. The fracture network was generated by using statistical fracture data, like dip direction and angle of dip, sperical variance of fracture clusters and length distribution, which were collected from subsurface and from surface outcrops of Carboniferous sandstones close to the Ruhr-valley, North-Rhine-Westfalia, Germany (Witthüser 1995).

The statistical data aquisition was restricted to sandstone outcrops, because siltstone layers, which also occur, will be treated later as anisotropic porous aquifers. Their fracture density is much higher than the fracture density of sandstones and can not be handled by the model. The model in its present form containes about 18000 fractures and the mesh generation leads to about 88000 elements (König & Himmelsbach 1995; Himmelsbach et al. 1995).

An example for the mesh generation is shown in Figure 7. It shows how the mesh generator refines the net in the neighbourhood of fractures. Such a net refinement in the neighbourhood of fractures is an important prerequisite for the coupling of fast fracture and slow matrix advection. At areas containing only few or isolated fractures having no or reduced interconnection with others, the mesh shows a smaller nodal density.

Figure 8 shows a section of the entire two-dimensional fracture model depicting the trace lengths of fractures resulting from an arbitrary cross section through the three-dimensional fracture network. The cross section depicted in Figure 8 demonstrates clearly the influence of heterogeneous fracture sets which consist in this study of three different fracture sets having different directions and angles of dip. The center points of all fractures are distributed randomly in space leading to a uniform spatial fracture density.

Like natural conditions, the fracture domain contains isolated as well as connected fractures having a limited extension. The interconnection between different single fractures demonstrates again the influence of anisotropic rock fragmentation. The latter becomes much more obvious if the spatial head distribution is calculated.

Figure 9 shows the influence of groundwater rise on the repository site. The ventilation drift at the lowest mining level is already flooded and the hydraulic head at this level corresponds to the groundwater level at the adjacent shafts. The highest hydraulic heads are therefore observed at the direct vicinity of the ventilation drift which is depicted as a circle in Figure 9. The spatial head distribution within a certain distance from the ventilation shaft becomes extremely heterogeneous and reflects the ansiotropic effect of the different fracture sets.

Only fractures which are connected to each other have a direct influence on the spatial head distribution. Isolated fractures, having no connections to others, do not influence the hydraulic head directly. At regions where fractures are located very close to each other, but do not intercept each other, the contour lines of hydraulic head are condensed. At other regions, where a good interconnection between different sets of fractures occurs, the contour lines of hydraulic head are more spreaded. In comparison to these results a normal porous aquifer model will never, even if a certain effect of anisotropy is considered, lead to such a heterogenous distribution of hydraulic head, which is characteristic for fractured aquifers.

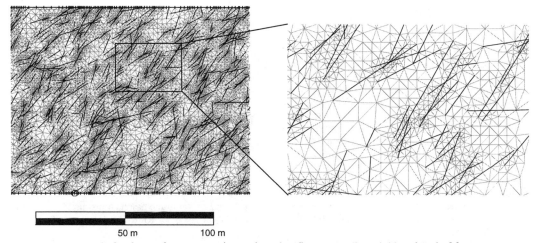

Figure 7:   Example for the mesh net generation and mesh refinement at the neighbourhood of fractures.

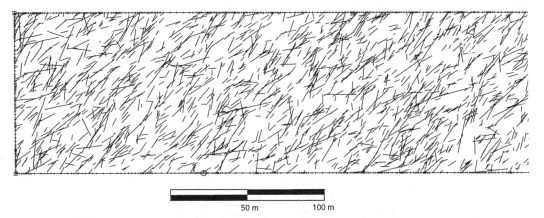

Figure 8:   2D fracture traces on an arbitrary, vertical cross section through the 3D fracture network.

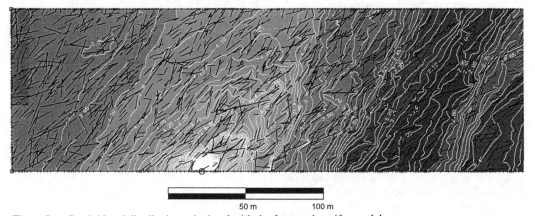

Figure 9:   Spatial head distribution calculated with the fractured aquifer model.

5   DISCUSSION

The German coal mines of the Ruhrgebiet are located in the most densely populated urban area of Germany. The productive Carboniferous sequences are overlain by Cretacious porous and fractured aquifers which are widely used for water supply of the northern part of the Ruhrgebiet. With regard to the sustainibility of these drinking water resources the use of coal mines for subsurface disposal of industrial residues needs proof that these aquifers will not be affected by aqueous solutions which may occur at the deep burial level during the phase when the depletion of the coal mines is stopped. In other words it must be shown that these aqueous solutions will not reach the biosphere or, if they do, they will be diluted and sorbed to such an extend, that their effect can be neglected.

The results presented in this paper still reflect a simplified hydrogeological model of the disposal site. Future work must therefore focus on the definition of a more realistic hydrogeological model describing the nearfield of the disposal site. The future model should therefore include both sedimentary units of the Carboniferous host rock, the sandstone and the siltstone laycrs. However, only the sandstone layers will be simulated as fractured aquifers, while the siltstone layers will be treated as conventional anisotropic porous aquifers. Only the combination of both types of sedimentary units will reflect realistic aquifer conditions and will help to estimate, for example, travel times in the nearfield of the repository when the repository will be flooded.

With regard to the general uncertainty of model input parameters, multiple simulations of different scenarios, reflecting different boundary conditions and aquifer properties, have to be performed. The resulting different scenarios will help us to understand the sensitivity of the model to the input of different aquifer parameters and properties.

6   LITERATURE

Berkowitz, B., J. Bear & C. Braester 1988. Contiuum models for contaminant transport in fractured porous formation. *Water Resour. Res.* 24(8): 1225 - 1236.

Bradbury, M.H. & A. Green 1985. Measurement of important parameters determining aqueous phase diffusion rates through crystalline rock matricies. *Journal of Hydrology* 82: 39-55.

König, Ch. & Th. Himmelsbach 1995. Modelltechnisches Konzept zur numerischen Berechnung der Transportprozesse im geklüfteten Steinkohlengebirge. In: „Prozeßsimulation im Kluftgestein" Aquifere und Geologische Barriere - Lehrgangsmaterialien: 31 S., Universität Hannover, Institut für Strömungsmechanik und elektronische Rechnen im Bauwesen.

Himmelsbach, Th., S. Harnischmacher & P. Obermann 1995. Determination of effective diffusivities by measuring aqueous phase diffusion. *GeoCongress* 1: 263 - 270, Sven von Loga, Cologne, Germany.

Himmelsbach, Th., Ch. König & E. Wendland 1995. Modelltechnisches Konzept zur Flutung von Grubenbauen im geklüfteten Steinkohlengebirge. *GeoCongress* 2: 193 - 198, Sven von Loga, Cologne, Germany.

Huewel, A. 1995. Erstellung eines Kluftgenerators in der Programmiersprache Fortran 90. Unpubl. diploma-thesis, Ruhr-University Bochum, Germany.

Jäger, B., P. Obermann & F-L. Wilke 1990. Studie zur Eignung von Steinkohlebergwerken im rechtsrheinischen Ruhrkohlenbezirk zur Untertageverbringung von Abfall- und Reststoffen, LUA, Düsseldorf, Germany.

Kulatilake, P.H.S.W., D.N. Wathugala & O. Stephansson 1993. Joint Network Modelling with a Validation Exercise in Stripa Mine Sweden, *Int. J. Rock Mech. Min & geochem Abstr.*, 30(5): 503-526.

Lever, D.A, M.H. Bradbury & S.J. Hemingway 1985. The effect of dead-end porosity on rock-matrix diffusion. *Journal of Hydrology* 80: 45-76.

Neretnieks, I. 1980 : Diffusion in the rock matrix: An important factor in radionuclide retardation? *Jour. of Geophys. Research* 85/B8: 4379-4397.

Striegel, K-H. 1995. Die Bedeutung der untertägigen Verwertung von Reststoffen für die Entsorgungswirtschaft. Vortrag anläßlich der ESSENER TAGUNG, 29.-31.3.95 in Aachen, unpubl. monograph, Essen, Germany.

Wendland E. & G. Schmid 1995. Flow phenomena in carboniferous fractured rock, Proc. of the 6th Int. Conf. on Computing in Civil Building Eng., Berlin, July 1995.

Witthüser, K. 1996. Geostatistische Methoden der Trennflächenanalyse geklüfteter Sandsteine - Mit Beispielen aus dem Ruhrkarbon. Unpubl. diploma-thesis, Ruhr-University Bochum, Germany.

Groundwater in the Urban Environment: Problems, Processes and Management, Chilton et al. (eds)
© *1997 Balkema, Rotterdam, ISBN 90 5410 837 1*

Experience in the use of stable nitrogen isotopes to distinguish groundwater contamination from leaking sewers in urban areas

K.M.Hiscock, P.F.Dennis, N.A.Feast & J.D.Fairbairn
School of Environmental Sciences, University of East Anglia, Norwich, UK

ABSTRACT: Leakage of sewage in urban areas can potentially contaminate groundwater with nitrogenous compounds. Raw sewage contains organic nitrogen and ammonium and undergoes biodegradation during recharge. To provide evidence of the impact of leaking sewers on groundwater and the nitrogen transformations that occur in the soil zone during sewage recharge, a survey of unconfined Chalk groundwaters in the London Basin and a controlled laboratory experiment were undertaken. It is concluded in this study and previous work that stable nitrogen isotopes are useful in identifying sewage leakage but should be corroborated with additional chemical and microbiological data. Soil type, rate of sewage loading and unsaturated zone thickness are key parameters that are likely to influence sewage transformations and should be considered in the assessment of the impact of leaking sewers on groundwater quality.

1 INTRODUCTION

Urban environments produce highly modified and artificial groundwater systems vulnerable to the risk of pollution. The leakage of mains water supplies and sewage wastes can potentially contaminate groundwater with nitrogenous compounds (Lerner & Barrett 1996). There is the widespread assumption that sewer leakage is extensive (Rauch & Stegner 1994) although evidence for this is not conclusive. A better understanding of the relative impact of pollution sources, such as mains and sewer leakage, should improve management of the urban environment. The application of existing and novel survey techniques, for example the application of stable nitrogen isotopes, is needed to assess groundwater quality and 'fingerprint' sources of recharge and pollution. Many examples exist of the application of the nitrogen isotope technique to contamination problems (for example Wassenaar 1996) and this paper aims to establish, using the nitrogen isotope technique, whether sewer leakage is a contributor to groundwater nitrate.

Two districts were chosen on the northern and southern limbs of the London Basin to assess the impact of urbanisation on the unconfined Chalk aquifer: the Colne Valley in the north and the area of Croydon in the south. It was thought that this choice of contrasting urban areas might reveal differences in the Chalk groundwater nitrogen isotopic compositions, when compared to adjacent rural areas. The Chalk aquifer is affected by nitrate contamination as a result of arable farming in the more rural areas but this is unlikely to be the case under urban areas.

The North London district contains several urban areas such as Harpenden in the north and Watford in the centre. The South London district is more urbanised with an amalgamation of urban centres. Figures 1 and 2 show the general geology and the distribution of sampling sites used in this study.

To investigate the influence of contrasting soil media on the transformation of nitrogen compounds contained in raw sewage, individual lysimeters were constructed and filled with three differing soil media. One contained a monolith of undisturbed soil collected from a grassed area in the Midland city of Nottingham (see Fairbairn (1996) for location and details of excavation). The other two were packed with soil media chosen to provide relative extremes of texture and chemical properties: an inert (combusted) course-grade sand and a richly organic (Irish Moss) peat.

2 NITROGEN ISOTOPE CHEMISTRY

Sources of nitrate in natural waters may be identified by comparison of the nitrogen isotope ratio of dissolved nitrate with that of potential sources (Heaton 1986). When comparing stable nitrogen isotopes, $\delta^{15}N$ is defined as $(R_{spl}/R_{std} - 1)$, where R_{spl} = $^{15}N/^{14}N$ ratio of the sample and $R_{std} = {}^{15}N/^{14}N$ ratio of the standard (purified air). Generally, stable isotope data are given in deviations of parts per thousand (‰). Sources of nitrate, and their typical ranges of $\delta^{15}N$ composition, include: nitrified soil organic nitrogen (+4‰ to +9‰); nitrogenous fertilisers (-4‰ to +4‰); and animal and sewage wastes (>+10‰). These ranges incorporate the majority of values associated with each source, although site specific conditions may cause the ranges to overlap. For example, fertiliser nitrate that has exchanged with soil nitrogen will have an isotopic value similar to that of nitrified soil organic nitrogen. Thus, a general 'agronomic' source of nitrate can be defined with an isotope composition in the range +4‰ to +9‰. Also, isotopic fractionation arising from hydrochemical processes such as denitrification can alter the original isotope ratios, typically resulting in a depletion of the heavier isotope (^{15}N) in the reaction products, and an enrichment in the residual nitrate (Mariotti et al. 1988). Dilution with water with a low nitrate concentration may decrease the nitrate concentration of a mixed water but will only affect, in a non-linear way, the isotopic composition if the isotopic compositions of the two end-members are different.

3 METHODOLOGY

3.1 Field sampling

In both sampling districts, Chalk groundwater samples were obtained from deep abstraction boreholes. Samples were collected for isotopic analysis of dissolved nitrate in 2 L or 5 L polyethylene bottles, depending on the presumed nitrate concentrations.

3.2 Lysimeter experiments

A range of laboratory tests were employed to analyse the soil materials (Fairbairn 1996). The results of the analyses of texture, bulk density, pH, cation exchange capacity (CEC), organic matter content

Table 1. Soil characterisation data for the three soil media used in the lysimeter experiments. T and B refer to the top and bottom sections of the Nottingham soil sample.

Soil type	Texture	Dry density (kg/m³)	Organic matter (%)	pH	CEC (*)	N (**)
Sand	Medium sand (†)	2190	0.1	8.54	3.8	0.35
Peat	Peat	830	98.5	3.96	30.8	1.40
Notts T	Silty loam	2180	11.7	6.42	39.0	0.58
Notts B	Fine silty loam	2180	10.5	8.05	26.9	0.84

* Cation exchange capacity in milli-equivalents per 100 grammes of soil.
** Nitrogen leaching potential in mg of nitrate per gramme of sample.
† Grade 0.60-1.18 mm.

and soil nitrogen content are given in Table 1. The in situ Nottingham soil, which could be described as a sandy loam, was observed to have a more organic-rich upper section and a sandier lower section. The inert sand control had an expected low CEC in contrast to the peat which had a high CEC (30.8 milli-equivalents per 100 grammes of soil) and available organic matter content (98.5%). The peat was found to leach 1.40 mg of nitrate per gramme of sample. On inspection, the Nottingham soil exhibited a relatively high organic matter content and CEC for normal mineral soils (Page 1980). It was found that the high organic content upper section leached less nitrogen (0.58 mg NO_3^- per gramme) than the sandier lower section (0.84 mg NO_3^- per gramme).

The lysimeters were constructed from 18 cm OD PVC sewage pipe cut into 75 cm sections. As shown in Figure 3, one end of the pipe was sharpened and fitted with a collection reservoir at the base. A woven wire mesh (0.9-1.1 mm) with a pack of glass beads (1.5 mm diameter) at the base of each lysimeter avoided any blockage of the outlet. The lysimeters were sealed with silicone grout and PVC sheeting. For the duration of the 6-day experiment, the lysimeters were installed in a greenhouse, to ensure constant environmental conditions, and continuously irrigated with raw sewage. Sampling of the outflow was undertaken every 12 hours. The addition of 0.05M mercuric chloride to each sample acted as a bio-poison prior to cold storage at 4°C.

3.3 Laboratory isotope methods

Preparation of samples for analysis of $\delta^{15}N$ followed the method of Feast & Dennis (1996). A distillation

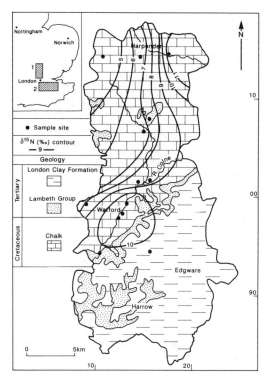

Figure 1. Sampling sites and results of $\delta^{15}N$ analysis of Chalk groundwaters in North London. The inset map shows (1) the North and (2) the South London study areas.

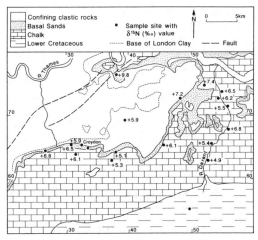

Figure 2. Sampling sites and results of $\delta^{15}N$ analysis of Chalk groundwaters in South London.

procedure was used to convert dissolved nitrate into ammonium sulphate, followed by combustion to produce nitrogen gas. Once purified, the $\delta^{15}N$ of the nitrogen gas produced was measured on a VG Isogas Sira II isotope-ratio mass spectrometer. The method yields a precision better than ± 0.2‰.

Samples from the lysimeters containing high ammonium concentrations were similarly prepared but in two stages. The first distillation to collect ammonium was carried out without Devardas alloy, followed by a second distillation using Devardas alloy to collect the nitrate.

4 RESULTS

4.1 *Chalk groundwater data*

A total of 43 samples were analysed for $\delta^{15}N$ values, of which 18 came from North London and 25 from South London. Nitrogen isotope values ranged from

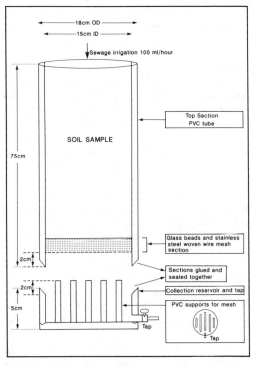

Figure 3. Design of lysimeter experiments.

+4.4‰ to +11.0‰. Nitrate concentrations for the same samples (analysed by ion chromatography) ranged between 19.9 mg/L and 54.4 mg/L (mean =

30.0 mg/L). The range of North London groundwater isotopic compositions spanned the total range for waters from the London area. Samples from South London were less variable, ranging from +4.9‰ to +9.8‰ (Figure 2). Figure 1 shows nitrogen isotope contours drawn for the North London district. There appears to be a spatial control on the $\delta^{15}N$ values, with heavier values (+9‰ to +11‰) around the central urban area of Watford and lighter values (+4‰ to +7‰) around the agricultural area west of Harpenden. A heavy isotope value (>+11‰) is recorded to the east of Harpenden. Figure 4 shows a histogram of nitrogen isotope compositions for both sampling areas. The North London district yielded a greater proportion of samples with a heavy $\delta^{15}N$ composition (>+10‰).

4.2 Lysimeter experimental data

The results of the lysimeter sewage irrigation experiments are shown in Table 2, which also lists nitrate and ammonium concentrations (NO_3^- analysed by ion selective electrode and NH_4^+ by colorimetry). Only the results for the first and last samples from the collection reservoirs are reported. The initial raw sewage contained 48.2 mg/L of nitrate and 48.3 mg/L of ammonium suggesting that some nitrification of ammonium to nitrate had occurred prior to the start of the experiments. The lysimeter containing inert sand initially leached a high nitrate concentration while, in the absence of a significant CEC, the ammonium concentration remained similar to the input concentration throughout the experiment. The peat lysimeter demonstrated a slight reduction in nitrate and a significant reduction in ammonium concentrations during the 6-day period. The Nottingham soil initially showed elevated nitrate (125.1 mg/L) and reduced ammonium (1.1 mg/L) in the outflow suggesting initial flushing of the soil nitrate and strong attenuation of ammonium.

During the experiment the ammonium concentration remained low, while the nitrate concentration gradually approached the concentration of the sewage input.

The first and last samples of lysimeter filtrate were analysed for stable nitrogen isotopes as reported in Table 2. Interpretation of the isotopic data should be treated with caution since it was found that the nitrogen species concentrations altered between collection of the filtrate and isotopic analysis, even with the addition of bio-poison and cold storage. The raw sewage input was measured to have a $\delta^{15}N_{NO3}$

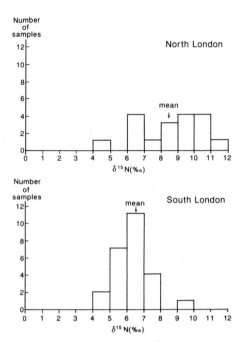

Figure 4. Comparison of $\delta^{15}N$ values in Chalk groundwaters in the London Basin.

value of +6.4‰ and a $\delta^{15}N_{NH4}$ value of +10.2‰. For the sand lysimeter, the $\delta^{15}N_{NO3}$ and $\delta^{15}N_{NH4}$ values showed no significant change in isotopic ratios during the experiment, and were similar in composition to the raw sewage solution. The peat lysimeter showed a trend of possibly increasing $\delta^{15}N_{NO3}$ composition during the experimental period while the $\delta^{15}N_{NH4}$ value decreased. The first sample of filtrate from the base of the Nottingham soil was isotopically depleted compared to the raw sewage ($\delta^{15}N_{NO3} = +2.6‰$) and only showed a slight isotopic enrichment ($\delta^{15}N_{NO3} = +3.2‰$) by the end of the 6-day period.

5 DISCUSSION

The $\delta^{15}N$ values recorded for Chalk groundwaters in the London Basin are similar to those recorded for limestone aquifers in the predominantly agricultural areas of Lincolnshire and Norfolk where similar hydrochemical conditions are encountered (Feast 1995). However, the high $\delta^{15}N$ values measured in the oxidising Chalk groundwaters near Watford, and which therefore cannot be the result of denitrification, probably reflect an urban source of

Table 2. Hydrochemical and stable nitrogen isotope results from the three soil lysimeter experiments.

Sample	pH	Cl⁻ (mg/L)	K⁺ (mg/L)	NO₃⁻ (mg/L)	NH₄⁺ (mg/L)	$\delta^{15}N_{NO3}$ (‰)	$\delta^{15}N_{NH4}$ (‰)
Raw sewage: (1 day)	7.06	221	27.2	48.2	48.3	+6.44	+10.24
Sand lysimeter:							
Start (1 day)	7.18	426	138.6	130.0	48.0	+5.85	+7.35
Finish (6 days)	7.96	232	32.1	70.0	35.7	+5.69	+7.00
Peat lysimeter:							
Start (1 day)	4.72	310	15.5	35.5	10.4	+5.75	+9.15
Finish (6 days)	3.89	150	8.0	30.0	9.5	+6.66	+5.83
Nottingham soil:							
Start (1 day)	7.16	120	18.6	125.1	1.1	+2.57	*
Finish (6 days)	7.15	276	8.1	80.0	0.8	+3.21	*

* Nitrogen gas yield too low for accurate isotopic measurement

isotopically-enriched nitrogen. The only likely sources in the urban environment would appear to be storm drain or foul sewer discharges or a sewage influence within the River Colne.

This investigation and previous studies have revealed enriched nitrogen isotopic signatures in urban groundwater. Kreitler et al. (1978) demonstrated an isotopic shift from $\delta^{15}N$ values between +2‰ to +9‰ in an agricultural area of Long Island, New York, to heavier values (two samples with $\delta^{15}N$ equal to +12.1‰ and +21.3‰) in an urban area with no agricultural activity. Kreitler et al. (1978) attributed the heavy values to leakage from the dense network of sewers. Kimmel (1972) had previously suggested that leakage from sewers had been a major source of recharge to the aquifer. Mariotti (1988) discovered that nitrogen isotope values from the unconfined Chalk aquifer of northern France varied between +3‰ and +7‰ in an agricultural area but were significantly higher (+8‰ to +10‰) in an urban area. Komor & Anderson (1993) reported $\delta^{15}N$ values for nitrate in residential areas with septic systems of only +6‰, while Rolston et al. (1994) demonstrated that septic sites in California produced nitrate with an isotopic composition of around +7.5‰. These values are within the range normally attributed to soil organic nitrogen such that in some cases animal wastes are indistinguishable from soil nitrogen sources. Rivers et al. (1996) found that groundwater abstracted from deep boreholes in the Sherwood Sandstone aquifer in Nottingham gave $\delta^{15}N$ values mostly in the range +4‰ to +8‰, but with some values in excess of +8‰, suggestive of point-source inputs from sewer leakage.

This study, and that of Rivers et al. (1996) who sampled raw sewage from the same treatment works in Nottingham, have shown that the nitrogen isotopic composition of sewage is relatively isotopically depleted (see Table 2) and within the range expected for an agronomic source of nitrate. These data confirm that it is not the animal waste itself which is isotopically heavy but partial volatilisation of ammonia depleted in ^{15}N during decomposition of urea in sewage that causes the residual ammonium and subsequent nitrate to become isotopically enriched (Kreitler 1979). The potential for such isotopic fractionation of the ammonium derived from human wastes in urban areas will depend on whether sewage leaks directly into groundwater or is in contact with a sufficiently large vapour phase above the water table to enable volatile loss of ammonia. Thus, it is possible that not all inputs of sewage to groundwater will have an isotopically heavy signature. This presents a problem when using the nitrogen isotope technique to demonstrate the presence or absence of nitrogen from a septic source or leaking sewers.

With no standard method for determining the impact of sewage systems on contamination of groundwater, lysimeters were used in this study to represent the field situation. Although the results from the lysimeter experiments proved inconclusive in verifying the suggested sub-surface isotopic enrichment of sewage by ammonia volatilisation, the in situ Nottingham soil demonstrated the potential contribution of soil-derived nitrogen in causing an isotopic shift of dissolved nitrogen species when raw sewage leaches from the soil zone.

6 CONCLUSIONS

It is concluded that stable nitrogen isotopes are useful in identifying sewage leakage but must be used with caution and corroborated with additional information such as major and minor ion analyses and microbiological parameters.

Following from the initial experience with lysimeters to assess sub-surface transformation of sewage products, it is concluded that further work is required, over longer time periods and with improved sample preservation, to model the inferred isotopic fractionation effects resulting from ammonia volatilisation. Soil type, rate of sewage loading and thickness of the unsaturated zone are key parameters that are likely to influence sewage transformations and should be considered in the assessment of the impact of leaking sewers on groundwater quality.

REFERENCES

Fairbairn, J.D. 1996. *Application of nitrogen isotope techniques to assess the impact of sewer leakage on shallow urban groundwater quality in the Sherwood Sandstone aquifer of Nottingham*. MSc Thesis, University of East Anglia, Norwich.

Feast, N.A. 1995. *Application of nitrogen and sulphur isotope hydrochemistry in groundwater studies*. PhD Thesis, University of East Anglia, Norwich.

Feast, N.A. & P.F. Dennis 1996. A comparison of methods for nitrogen isotope analysis of groundwater. *Chemical Geology (Isotope Geoscience Section)* 129: 167-171.

Heaton, T.H.E. 1986. Isotopic studies of nitrogen pollution in the hydrosphere and atmosphere: a review. *Chemical Geology (Isotope Geoscience Section)* 59: 87-102.

Kimmel, G.E. 1972. Nitrogen content of groundwater in King's County, Long Island, New York. *U.S. Geol. Surv. Prof. Paper 800-D*: D199-D203.

Komor, S.C. & H.W. Anderson 1993. Nitrogen isotopes as indicators of nitrate sources in Minnesota sand-plain aquifers. *Ground Water* 31: 260-270.

Kreitler, C.W. 1979. Nitrogen-isotope ratio studies of soils and groundwater nitrate from alluvial fan aquifers in Texas. *Journal of Hydrology* 42: 147-170.

Kreitler, C.W., S.E. Rayone & B.G. Katz 1978. $^{15}N/^{14}N$ ratios of ground-water nitrate, Long Island, New York. *Ground Water* 16: 404-409.

Lerner, D.N. & M.H. Barrett 1996. Urban groundwater issues in the United Kingdom. *Hydrogeology Journal* 4: 80-89.

Mariotti, A., A. Landreau & B. Simon 1988. ^{15}N isotope biogeochemistry and natural denitrification process in groundwater: application to the Chalk aquifer of northern France. *Geochem. et Cosmochim. Acta* 52: 1869-1878.

Page, A.L. (ed) 1982. *Methods of soil analysis Part 2: Chemical and microbiological properties (2nd edition)*. Agronomy Series No.9 Part II. American Society of Agronomy: Soil Science Society of America.

Rauch, W. & T. Stegner 1994. The collation of leaks in sewer systems during dry weather flow. *Water Science Technology* 30: 205-210.

Rivers, C.N., M.H. Barrett, K.M. Hiscock, P.F. Dennis, N.A. Feast & D.N. Lerner 1996. Use of nitrogen isotopes to identify nitrogen contamination of the Sherwood Sandstone aquifer beneath the city of Nottingham, UK. *Hydrogeology Journal* 4: 90-102.

Rolston, D.E., G.E. Fogg, D.L. Decker & D.T. Louie, 1994. Nitrogen isotope ratios of natural and anthropogenic nitrate in the subsurface. *Water Down Under, Adelaide, Australia, 21-25 November 1994*.

Wassenaar, L.I. 1996. Evaluation of the origin and fate of nitrate in the Abbotsford Aquifer using the isotopes of ^{15}N and ^{18}O in NO_3^-. *Applied Geochemistry* 10: 391-405.

ACKNOWLEDGEMENTS

We are grateful to Severn-Trent Water, the Three Valleys Water Company and Thames Water Utilities for their helpful assistance. Financial support was provided by the Natural Environment Research Council (NERC) and the University of East Anglia. Geological information contained in Figures 1 and 2 is reproduced by permission of the Director, British Geological Survey. ©NERC. All rights reserved. The views expressed in this paper are entirely those of the authors.

Groundwater in the Urban Environment: Problems, Processes and Management, Chilton et al. (eds)
© 1997 Balkema, Rotterdam, ISBN 90 5410 837 1

Do tills beneath urban Toronto provide adequate groundwater protection?

Ken W.F. Howard & Richard E. Gerber
University of Toronto, Scarborough, Ont., Canada

ABSTRACT : Urban activities have released numerous sources of contamination to the shallow subsurface beneath the Greater Toronto Area, Canada. However, the extent to which these sources contaminate deeper groundwater is largely determined by the degree to which aquitards restrict the vertical movement of shallow groundwater in which the contaminants are entrained. The general consensus has been that thick till sheets of late Wisconsinan age provide a considerable degree of natural protection to groundwaters in deep underlying aquifers. This is largely based on measurements of hydraulic conductivity which are typically in the range 10^{-11} to 10^{-9} m/s. Since the mid-1980's research at the University of Toronto has challenged traditional views, using water balance studies, major ion chemistry and environmental isotopes to demonstrate that the tills are more permeable to recharge than once believed. Recent tritium studies, for example, now confirm the existence of post-1952 water at depths within the till approaching 50 m. Ongoing work plans to characterize the till units fully and identify the groundwater transport paths. This is being achieved through additional isotope work, pumping tests and piezometer tests, tracer studies and numerical modelling.

1 INTRODUCTION

The Greater Toronto Area of south central Ontario (Figure 1) is one of the most densely populated regions in Canada. Throughout this area, industrial and urban development associated with human activity has introduced numerous sources of contamination to the shallow subsurface (Howard et al. 1996, Eyles & Livingstone 1996; Howard & Livingstone 1997). However, the extent to which these potential sources translate into observable degradation of groundwater quality is largely determined by the local hydrostratigraphy and, in particular, the degree to which aquitards restrict and retard the vertical movement of groundwater and entrained contaminants.

The Greater Toronto Area is underlain by a thick sequence of glacial sediments of Late Pleistocene age. These, in turn, overlie Paleozoic bedrock. The package of glacial sediments supports a large number of aquifers as, for example, in the Duffins Creek - Rouge River drainage basins where 14 aquifer units have been defined (Sibul et al. 1977; Howard & Beck 1986). The largest and most

important of the defined aquifer units is the Oak Ridges Moraine Aquifer Complex (ORAC) (Figures 1 and 2) (Howard et al. 1995) which provides the headwaters for most of the region's major rivers. The hydrogeological relationship between the ORAC and other aquifer units in the drainage basins is complex and has been the focus of considerable debate in recent years. The relationship is largely determined by the disposition, geometry and hydrogeological characteristics of the intervening till aquitards.

Studies by the Ontario Ministry of the Environment (Sibul et al. 1977), grouped aquifers into upper and lower systems separated by a low permeability aquitard designated the Northern till (Boyce et al. 1995) (Figure 2). This aquitard is now believed to be the most important control on regional groundwater flow. It determines the degree to which groundwater, most notably in the Oak Ridges Moraine Aquifer Complex, but also in shallow "upper" aquifers, is able to replenish deeper "lower" aquifers, several of which are heavily exploited for domestic supply. Moreover the hydrogeological nature of the Northern till determines the extent to which urban and industrial contaminants released to

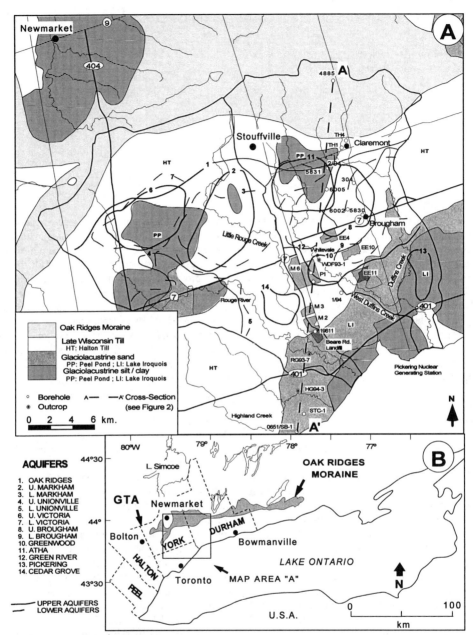

Figure 1   Study area (after Gerber & Howard 1996) showing location of the Greater Toronto Area and the Oak Ridges Moraine. Surficial geology is based on maps by Barnett et al. (1991) and Westgate (unpublished data on file with the Ontario Geological Survey).

the shallow subsurface threaten the quality of deep groundwaters.

In the Toronto area, the general consensus has been that thick till sheets of late Wisconsinan age,

including the Northern till, provide a considerable degree of natural protection to groundwaters in deep underlying aquifers.   Standard field and laboratory methods of determining hydraulic conductivity

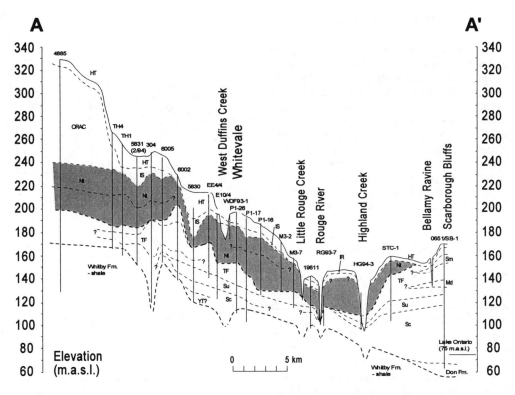

Stage	Unit	Age (Yrs.)	Lithology	Thickness (m)
Late Wisconsinan	Lake Iroquois (IR) Deposits	<12,500	Beach sands, gravels and lacustrine silt and clay deposited in high-level lake.	< 5m
	Halton Till (HT)	13,000	Silty/sandy till interbedded with sand and gravel.	< 25m
	Oak Ridges Aquifer Complex (ORAC)	13,000	Sand and gravel outwash	<100m
	Mackinaw Interstadial (IS)	13,300	Sandy fluvial gravel with lacustrine silt and clay	< 15m
	Northern till (Nt)	13.5-25,000	Silt till	< 60m
Middle Wisconsinan	Thorncliffe Formation (TF)	30-45,000	Deltaic sands, lacustrine silt and clay Sm Seminary diamict; Md Meadowvale diamict	< 40m
Early Wisconsinan	Sunnybrook Till (Su)	50,000	Clay till with laminated silty clay	< 20m
	Scarborough Formation (Sc)	70,000	Deltaic sands and glaciolacustrine silts and clays	< 40m
Sangamonian	Don Formation	125,000	Fluvial, interglacial clay and sand	
Illinoian	York Till (YT)	125,000	Sandy, shale-rich till	< 5m
	Whitby Formation	Late Ordovician Black shale		

Figure 2   North to south section across the region (from Gerber & Howard 1996). Location of section is shown on Figure 1.

characteristically yield values in the range 10^{-11} to 10^{-9} m/s and suggest vertical travel times of the order of hundreds to thousands of years. As a consequence, till is often the geologic medium of choice when selecting sites for landfills or other activities that threaten the quality of underground resources.

435

2 REGIONAL HYDROCHEMICAL STUDIES

During the mid-1980's, regional hydrochemical studies conducted by the Toronto research group challenged the traditionally held views by using inorganic groundwater chemistry to demonstrate that the inorganic chemical character of water in the upper aquifers is often mirrored in vertically adjacent lower aquifers (Howard & Beck 1986) (Figure 3). This implies that the upper and lower aquifers do not behave independently and that despite the supposed presence of the Northern till, sufficient hydraulic interaction is present to unify the sediments into a single aquifer system.

3 WATER BALANCE STUDIES

The ability of the Northern till to transmit water is further illustrated by water balance and regional model studies. Water balance studies (Gerber & Howard 1997) demonstrated that a component of water must be transmitted via the till to deeper, underlying aquifers if downstream baseflows are to be maintained. MODFLOW studies (Howard et al. 1995) subsequently showed that model calibration is best achieved when a small but significant leakage factor is assigned to the Northern till on a regional scale.

4 ISOTOPE STUDIES

Recently, attempts have been made to confirm the movement of groundwater through the Northern till by examining the isotope chemistry of porewaters. The work was carried out at two sites and involved tritium (Figure 4), deuterium and oxygen-18.

To obtain representative pore waters, a series of borehole cores was collected using both air- and mud-rotary techniques (Gerber & Howard 1996). Air-drilled wells provided an uncontaminated data set. The mud-cored boreholes allowed the integrity of the mud data set to be evaluated. Results from both sites reveal that tritiated (post-1952) water has penetrated the Northern till to considerable depths. As shown by Figure 4, for example, tritiated water is encountered at three locations, the deepest approaching 50 m. Oxygen-18 and deuterium data from the mud-drilled wells confirm that measures used to prevent sample contamination were effective. At present it is not clear whether the pathways for this movement are attributable to the local presence

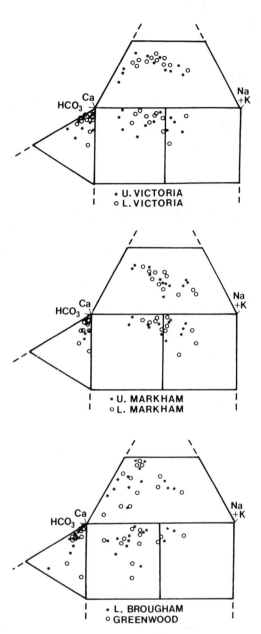

Figure 3. Chemical characteristics of groundwaters from adjacent upper and lower aquifer systems displayed on the upper fields of Durov diagrams (after Howard & Beck 1986). The location of aquifers is shown on Figure 1.

of more permeable till facies, facies variations, secondary structures, or simply very thin but interconnected sand lenses. However, the findings

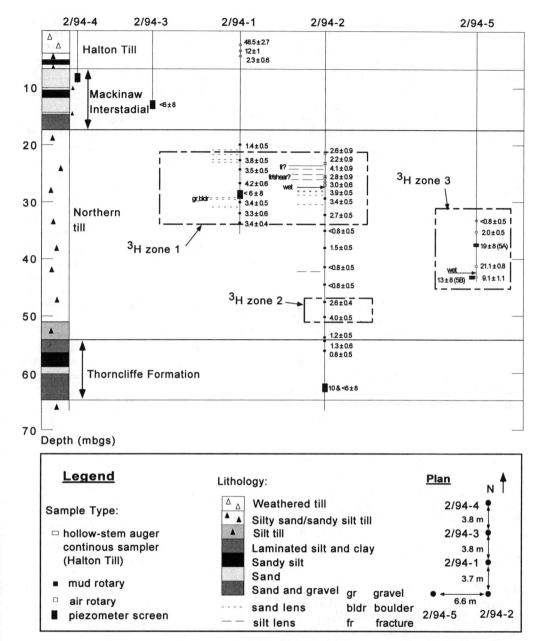

Figure 4   Stratigraphy and tritium section for Site 2/94 near Claremont (from Gerber& Howard 1996). Values in the figure are tritium concentrations shown in tritium units (T.U.). (The location of site is given in Figure 1).

have considerable implications for deep recharge and the transport of near surface contamination to deep aquifers.

5 CONCLUSIONS

Despite field and laboratory determinations of permeability that suggest the hydraulic conductivity

437

of the Northern till lies in the range 10^{-11} to 10^{-9} m/s, there is now a considerable volume of hydrochemical, water balance and modelling evidence that suggests these tills may be significantly more permeable. It would appear that the tills do not provide the degree of natural protection from urban and industrial contaminants that was once believed and this has important implications for the management and protection of the region's groundwater. Ongoing work plans to characterize the till units fully and identify the groundwater transport paths. This is being achieved through additional isotope work, pumping tests and piezometer tests, tracer studies and modelling (FRACTRAN (locally)) and Visual MODFLOW (regionally)).

6 ACKNOWLEDGMENTS

The authors gratefully acknowledge numerous University of Toronto students and colleagues who assisted in the collection and interpretation of the data. Particular thanks go to Sean Salvatori, Philip Smart, Joe Boyce, Mike Doughty, Tim Westgate and Steve Livingstone. Thanks are also extended to Vicki Remenda, Bob Drimmie and Nick Eyles who contributed to the discussion of the results. The work was supported by research grants to Howard and Eyles from the Great Lakes University Research Fund (GLURF) (sponsored by Environment Canada and the Natural Sciences and Engineering Research Council (NSERC)) and the Ontario Ministry of the Environment and Energy. The views presented here are those of the authors and are not necessarily endorsed by the funding agencies.

7 REFERENCES

Barnett, P. J., W.R. Cowan & A.P. Henry 1991. *Quaternary geology of Ontario, southern sheet.* Ontario Geological Survey, Map 2556.

Boyce, J. I., N. Eyles & A. Pugin 1995. Seismic reflection, borehole and outcrop geometry of Late Wisconsin tills at a proposed landfill near Toronto, Ontario. *Can. J. Earth Sci.* 32:423-428.

Gerber, R. E. & K.W.F. Howard 1996. Evidence for recent groundwater flow through Late Wisconsinan till near Toronto, Canada. *Canadian Geotechnical Journal* 33:538-555.

Gerber, R.E. & K.W.F. Howard 1997. Ground-water recharge to the Oak Ridges Moraine. In: Eyles, N. (ed.) *Environmental Geology of Urban Areas.* Special Publication of the Geological Association of Canada. Geotext #4:173-192.

Howard, K.W.F. & P. Beck 1986. Hydrochemical interpretation of groundwater flow systems in Quaternary sediments of Southern Ontario. *Canadian J. Earth Sci.* 23:938-947.

Howard, K.W.F., N. Eyles, P.J. Smart, J.I. Boyce, R.E. Gerber, S. Salvatori & M. Doughty 1995. The Oak Ridges Moraine of southern Ontario: A groundwater resource at risk. *Geoscience Canada* 22:101-120.

Howard, K.W.F., N. Eyles & S. Livingstone 1996. Municipal landfilling practice and its impact on groundwater resources in and around urban Toronto. *Hydrogeology Journal* 4(1):64-79.

Howard, K.W.F. & S. Livingstone 1997. Contaminant source audits and ground-water quality assessment. In: Eyles, N. (ed.) *Environmental Geology of Urban Areas.* Special Publication of the Geological Association of. Canada. Geotext #4:105-118.

Sibul, U., K.T. Wang & D. Vallery 1977. *Groundwater resources of the Duffins Creek - Rouge River drainage basins,.* MOE, Water Resources Branch, Toronto, Ont., Water Resources Report 8.

Development of a contaminant plume from a municipal landfill:
Redox reactions and plume variability

Jerzy Jankowski
Groundwater Centre, Department of Applied Geology, University of New South Wales, Sydney, N.S.W., Australia

R. Ian Acworth
Groundwater Centre, Water Research Laboratory, University of New South Wales, Manly Vale, N.S.W., Australia

ABSTRACT: A bundled-piezometer was installed down gradient of a municipal landfill in a sandy aquifer in the Botany Basin, Sydney, Australia. The geophysical and hydrogeochemical studies have shown that the leachate plume generated from the unsealed landfill varies both in time and space. These changes are believed to be associated with different mobilisation rates of contaminants as the result of a varying infiltration flux through the unlined landfill. The centre of the leachate plume is characterised by high TDS and low Eh values; an elevated concentration of the major ions Na^+, K^+, Ca^{2+}, Mg^{2+}, NH_4^+, Fe^{2+}, HCO_3^-, Cl^- and TIC; by the trace elements Mn^{2+}, Sr^{2+}, B, and F^-; and by the presence of S^{2-} and the absence of NO_3^-, SO_4^{2-} and DO. The low values and narrow ranges of oxidation-reduction potential are attributed to redox buffering associated with the high S^{2-} concentration. The pH range in the plume only varies between 6.0 and 6.6 indicating strong buffering with respect to H_2CO_3/HCO_3^-. During dry periods, the plume maximum concentration occurs between 8 m and 10 m depth. After major rainfall events the plume maximum concentration occurs between 5 m and 7 m depth. Redox processes in the leachate plume have been evaluated from an examination of field data for DO and Eh, and from computed redox potentials for the redox couples NO_3^-/NH_4^+, Fe^{3+}/Fe^{2+}, $Fe(OH)_3/Fe^{2+}$, SO_4^{2-}/S^{2-} and HCO_3^-/CH_4. Five redox zones have been established within the plume.

1 INTRODUCTION

Leachate plumes downgradient from municipal landfills are characterised by anaerobic conditions associated with an absence of DO, high concentrations of both major and minor ions, the presence of S^{2-} and CH_4 and the absence of NO_3^- and SO_4^{2-} (Baedecker & Back 1979a). The transport of reduced species and the different stages of their oxidation downgradient from a landfill lead to a characteristic redox zonation (Baedecker & Back 1979b; Lyngkilde & Christensen 1992).

The delineation of chemical reactions in a plume can be evaluated at different distances down flow (Baedecker & Back 1979a, b) by the installation of piezometers. Screen sections greater than one metre have typically been installed in these piezometers. Vertical variation in the contaminant plume can be evaluated from closely spaced multilevel sampling devices (Nicholson et al. 1983; Lyngkilde & Christensen 1992) where the screened section is only a few centimetres in length.

Measurements of the redox potential in natural and contaminated environments represent a mixed potential, which it is not possible in general to relate to a single dominant redox couple (Stumm & Morgan 1981; Lindberg & Runnells 1984). The Eh values for NO_3^-/NH_4^+, Fe^{3+}/Fe^{2+}, $Fe(OH)_3/Fe^{2+}$, SO_4^{2-}/S^{2-} and HCO_3^-/CH_4 redox couples can be computed using the Nernst equation and compared with field Eh measurements.

In this paper we describe the variation in redox zonation and the response to seasonal rainfall variation of a plume from an unlined landfill in Astrolabe Park at Daceyville, Sydney, Australia. The site is underlain by aeolian and alluvial deposits comprising the upper part of the Quaternary Botany Sands aquifer. Drilling and geophysical investigations around Astrolabe Park have determined the thickness of the unconsolidated sediments to be approximately 30 m.

The total volume of waste deposited was approximately 2×10^5 m^3. As the lateral extent of the landfill was estimated to be 4.7 ha, based upon examination of a series of aerial photographs, the average thickness of landfill was approximately 4.35

m. Hydrogeological, hydrochemical and geophysical investigations have described in detail this site (Jankowski et al. 1991; Acworth et al. 1994).

2 BULK EC AND FLUID EC VARIATION

The total depth of the drilled piezometer was 30 m, comprising 21 sampling points. Sampling points were every metre from the surface to 15 m and then every two metres to the base of the borehole. Three bulk EC profiles were measured in the central 50 mm diameter core of the bundle, and two fluid EC profiles established for the bundled piezometer points. These data are shown in Figure 1. This figure is limited to the top 16 m of the aquifer which contain the contamination plume. Uniform conditions exist between 16 m and the bedrock. The depth to the water table was 2.80 m in October 1995 and 2.38 m in December 1996. The gamma ray activity plot (not shown on Figure 1) indicates clean sand in the saturated section of the aquifer. Three bulk EC peaks are apparent in the data with significant variation in peak development in the three data sets. Low hydraulic conductivity is indicated in a thin zone at 7.25 m and again between 8.5 m and 9 m. These thin zones separate the bulk EC anomalies.

The fluid electrical conductivities for the two rounds of sampling are shown in Figure 1 and the anomalies are broadly similar to the bulk EC anomalies as would be expected. The fluid EC shows little variation between the two sampling rounds below 8 m, but a significant deviation above 8 m depth. In the October 1995 round of sampling the fluid EC decreases above 8 m, while a significant increase in fluid EC occurs in December, 1996. This is interpreted as an increase in flushing and increased mobilisation of contaminants through the landfill as a result of increased rainfall at that time. The relationship between plume development and rainfall is currently under investigation.

Fluid EC values peak at 740 µS/cm in 1995 and 930 µS/cm in 1996. These values are 3.4 and 4.3 times the background fluid EC values of local (uncontaminated) groundwater upgradient from Astrolabe Park.

3 CHEMICAL COMPOSITION OF THE LEACHATE PLUME

The vertical variation in chemical composition of the leachate plume is shown by a series of profiles from the bundled piezometer in Figure 2. The dominant ions in the leachate plume are HCO_3^-, Cl^-, Na^+, Mg^{2+}, Ca^{2+} and NH_4^+. Bicarbonate, magnesium, calcium and ammonia are all present at levels significantly above the background for groundwater in the aquifer as described by Acworth & Jankowski (1993). Bicarbonate is present at a concentration of 11 times (520 mg/l) the background values. Sodium and chloride concentrations are 40 mg/l and 48 mg/l respectively showing only slightly elevated concentrations above the background values of 15 mg/l and 28 mg/l (Figure 2a).

The high concentration of HCO_3^- and CO_2 in the leachate plume is the result of several processes. Carbon dioxide is produced in the soil zone and is transported to the aquifer by rainfall recharge. Carbon dioxide is also a significant by-product of redox reactions; the oxidation and decomposition of organic matter and fermentation reactions. Some of the CO_2 is used for the dissolution of carbonate minerals present in the landfill and the aquifer matrix. The vertical profile of HCO_3^- and TIC is shown in Figure 2b. At the top of the aquifer and in the upper part of the plume, elevated bicarbonate concentrations are considered to be the result of dissolution of shell material present in the aquifer. Mass balance calculations demonstrate that HCO_3^- concentrations from the dissolution of shell material can produce values as high as 100 mg/l. The

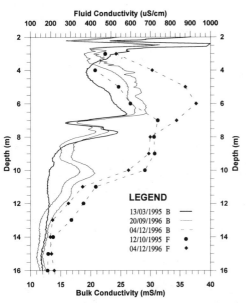

Figure 1. Variation of bulk and fluid EC with depth.

October 1995 and December 1996 are attributed to the higher rates of redox reactions, occurring as a result of increased fluxes of oxygen rich rain water, producing high concentrations of bicarbonate.

Concentrations of Ca^{2+} (Figure 2c) and Sr^{2+} (Figure 2d) between depths of 3 m and 5 m (above the plume) show the effect of dissolution of $CaCO_3$ shell debris present in silty and clayey sand layers in the Botany Sands aquifer (Jankowski et al. 1994). This process has an effect on pH values and TIC values at these depths which also effect dissolution-precipitation reactions in the top part of the leachate plume between 5 m and 6 m. The combination of dissolution processes producing enhanced bicarbonate above the plume and redox reactions within the plume, also producing bicarbonate, complicates the delineation of the plume top, based upon measurements of simple TDS or fluid and bulk EC.

Trace elements showed elevated concentrations of F (x 2), B (x 10), Sr^{2+} (x 20) (Figure 2d) and Mn^{2+} (x 20) (Figure 2e) over background concentrations. Maximum concentrations of F, B, Sr^{2+} and Mn^{2+} were 0.8 mg/l, 0.6 mg/l, 0.45 mg/l and 0.4 mg/l respectively. The leachate plume is also characterised by an absence of oxygen; the presence of S^{2-} and the absence of SO_4^{2-} (Figure 2f); a high concentration of NH_4^+ and very low concentration of NO_3^- (Figure 2g). The concentration of Fe^{2+} (Figure 2e) is high and is controlled by precipitation reactions within the plume.

A number of authors (Baedecker & Back 1979a; Nicholson et al. 1983) have reported a very narrow pH range (between 6.0 and 7.0 pH) in leachate plumes from contaminated sites. This occurs when similar concentration of acid and bases are present and is associated with the production of CO_2 from redox reactions; from the generation of ammonium and fermentation reactions; the presence of organic acids and the precipitation of carbonate minerals (Baedecker & Back 1979a; Kehew & Passero 1990). The Astrolabe Park landfill leachate has a pH range between 6.59 and 7.11.

The leachate plume from Astrolabe Park is characterised by high HCO_3^- and $CO_{2(aq)}$ and H_2CO_3 concentrations. In the presence of these high concentrations, very small changes of pH occur. The values in the major part of the plume vary between 6.04 and 6.65 in October 1995, and between 6.25 to 6.61 in December 1996 (Figure 2h). As the leachate

plume is undersaturated with respect to $CaCO_3$ (log IAP/K_{cal} = -0.40 - -2.10) and $CaMg(CO_3)_2$ (log IAP/k_{dol} = -1.04 - -4.43), pH buffering will play a major role in $CO_{2(aq)}$ and HCO_3^- equilibria. The pH decreases in the transition zone at the base of the plume and returns to a background value of 5.6 which is characteristic for uncontaminated local groundwaters (Acworth & Jankowski 1993).

4 REDOX REACTIONS

The Eh measurements were made using a platinum electrode calibrated in the field against Zobell's solution (Zobell 1946; Nordstrom 1977). The Eh values in the leachate plume are shown in Figure 2i. A strongly reducing environment is present with Eh values varying between -100 mV and -143 mV in 1995 and -116 mV and -152 mV in 1996. Dissolved oxygen was found to be negligible throughout the plume.

The vertical variation of NH_4^+ is shown in Figure 2g. A strong peak occurs in the leachate plume with maximum values of 49 mg/l (1995) and 31 mg/l (1996). The concentration of NH_4^+ is higher than NO_3^- which clearly indicates reduction of the NO_3^- present in the aquifer (concentrations up to 10 mg/l) as well as microbiological degradation of organic nitrogen present in putrescible waste in refuse. Above and below the leachate plume the NO_3^- concentration increases and becomes the dominant nitrogen species in the aqueous system.

The SO_4^{2-} and S^{2-} changes in the vertical profile show an absence of SO_4^{2-} in the leachate plume between 7 m depth and 12 m depth in 1995 and between 5 m depth and 10 m depth in 1996 (Figure 2f). This can be used to delineate the centre of the plume and indicates that full reduction of SO_4^{2-} is occurring. The highest concentration of S^{2-} in a leachate reaches 4.8 mg/l. Both above and below this zone, a transition zone is formed in which both sulphur species are present. Outside this transition zone, the concentration of SO_4^{2-} rapidly increases to background values.

Ferrous iron and manganese also have their highest concentrations in the leachate plume, where the strongest reducing environment is present. The strong reducing environment alters the equilibrium solubility for both metals. Colloidal iron is present in the most contaminated waters. Measurement of total Fe by digestion in 10% HNO_3 showed a

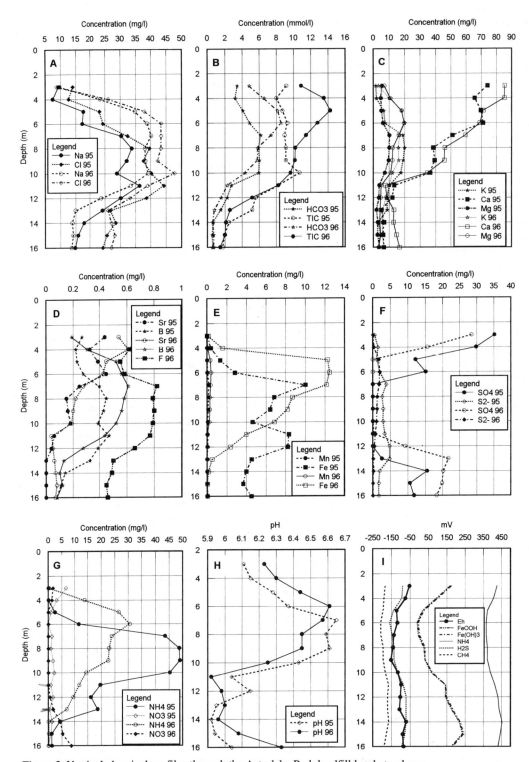

Figure 2. Vertical chemical profiles through the Astrolabe Park landfill leachate plume.

Fe by digestion in 10% HNO_3 showed a concentration of 18.5 mg/l compared to a measurement of 12.5 mg/l of Fe^{2+} measured by both ICP-AES and colorimetric methods.

The Eh measurement using a platinum electrode represents a mixed potential (Stumm & Morgan 1981; Lindberg & Runnells 1984) created by the redox couples present in solution. It is difficult to indicate which of the possible redox couples has the largest impact on the measured Eh values and for this reason the discussion which follows is based upon a theoretical calculation of redox couples. The measured Eh values shown above lie between those associated with the reduction of NO_3^- to NH_4^+ and the reduction of $Fe(OH)_3$ to Fe^{2+} (Champ et al. 1979; Stumm & Morgan 1981). In this leachate plume however SO_4^{2-} is completely reduced to S^{2-} and methane formation has occurred, so the theoretical value of Eh for pH 7 should be approximately -214 mV. This indicates that the measured redox potential by a platinum electrode does not represent a real single dominant redox couple in the leachate plume.

For the NO_3^-/NH_4^+, Fe^{3+}/Fe^{2+}, $Fe(OH)_3/Fe^{2+}$, SO_4^{2-}/S^{2-} and HCO_3^-/CH_4 redox couples, the Eh was calculated using the Nernst equation and the chemical equilibrium model WATEQ4F (Ball et al. 1987). The results are shown as a vertical profile in Figure 2i. The computed redox values, when compared with field Eh measurements, demonstrate that no single redox couple is dominant. The field values are the closest to calculated Eh values of the SO_4^{2-}/S^{2-} redox couple. The calculated data for the NO_3^-/NH_4^+, Fe^{3+}/Fe^{2+} and $Fe(OH)_3/Fe^{2+}$ redox couples show no relation to the field data. This is in agreement with the results presented by Baedecker & Cozzarelli (1992), who find that the SO_4^{2-}/S^{2-} and HCO_3^-/CH_4 couples gave the most reasonable Eh results for a contaminant environment. This environment is showing strong redox buffering which is demonstrated by the low variation in both measured and calculated Eh values. This buffering is considered to result from the high concentration of sulphide in the leachate plume.

5 VERTICAL REDOX ZONATION

Clear vertical redox zonation occurs in the leachate plume and is similar to the lateral biogeochemical zonation identified by Baedecker & Back (1979a, b); Nicholson et al. (1983); and Lyngkilde & Christensen (1992). Hounslow (1980) identified vertical zonation in a contaminant plume and demonstrated the existence of two anaerobic zones associated with the presence or absence of hydrogen sulphide. The following vertical redox zones have been established for the Astrolabe Park leachate plume:

Central Zone (A). An anaerobic zone which has the highest concentration of S^{2-}, NH_4^+, Fe^{2+}, Mn^{2+}, HCO_3^- and TIC. The pH occurs in a very narrow range, indicating pH buffering and the Eh values are the lowest in the section. Sulphate is absent in this zone and NO_3^- is absent or at very low concentrations. Sulphide and ammonia are significantly in excess of sulphate and nitrate. Dissolved oxygen is not detectable. Carbon dioxide is present between 7% and 11% by volume, and these values are slightly lower than those outside the main plume. This indicates CH_4 production via a fermentation reaction. The Eh values show little variability, indicating that this plume is buffered with respect to the redox couple SO_4^{2-}/S^{2-}. The zone is supersaturated with respect to goethite, siderite, pyrite and amorphous FeS.

Transition Zone 1 (B). This transition zone only occurs immediately below the central part of the plume at a depth of 13 m during dry periods and 11 m during wet periods. The zone is also characterised by strongly anaerobic conditions but there are traces of sulphate present, and the concentrations of S^{2-} and NH_4^+ are decreasing. The Fe^{2+} and Mn^{2+} concentration are lower but still present well above the background levels. Bicarbonate and TIC are high, but lower than in the main plume, with the CO_2 percentage volume a little higher, showing that CH_4 is oxidised to CO_2. This zone is supersaturated with respect to pyrite and FeS and becomes undersaturated with respect to siderite and goethite.

Transition Zone 2 (C). This transition zone occurs on both sides of the plume. The zone is still anaerobic. The concentration of SO_4^{2-} is higher than S^{2-} in this zone. Nitrate is present and the concentration of NH_4^+ is lower than the previous zones but remains significant. The manganese concentration is low with intermediate Fe^{2+} values. Bicarbonate is much lower than in the main plume while haematite and pyrite are supersaturated and FeS is close to equilibrium.

Transition Zone 3 (D). This zone is slightly anaerobic and occurs outside transition zone 2. Both sulphate and sulphide are present as well as nitrate and ammonium. Mn^{2+} and Fe^{2+} values are low, only

443

slightly above background levels. HCO_3^- is close to the concentration of local groundwaters. Pyrite is supersaturated, and haematite, goethite and FeS have variable saturation indices depending on the intensity of mixing between leachate and local groundwaters.

Background Zone (E). This zone only occurs below the leachate plume. Nearly all elements return to background values, however because the aquifer at this location is slightly anaerobic some redox species are variable and S^{2-}, NH_4^+ or Fe^{2+} can appear in higher concentration, but this is not associated with contamination from the Astrolabe Park landfill.

6 CONCLUSIONS

Detailed monitoring at closely spaced sampling points and the repetition of sampling in wet and dry periods are shown to be important in developing an understanding of the groundwater dynamics associated with plume development at contaminated sites. Where the expense of detailed and repeated sampling and analysis becomes prohibitive, then the use of bulk electrical logging is shown to be a valuable tool for determination of changes in the plume development. Five vertical redox zones were found in the aquifer downgradient from the landfill. The redox classification is based on the presence or absence of redox sensitive elements; their concentrations; and the saturation indices for iron minerals. The leachate plume represents a system which is under strong pH buffering with respect to H_2CO_3/HCO_3^-, and strong Eh buffering associated with the high S^{2-} concentration.

REFERENCES

Acworth, R.I. & J. Jankowski 1993. Hydrogeochemical zonation of groundwater in the Botany Sands aquifer, Sydney. *AGSO J. Aust. Geol. Geophys.* 14: 193-199.

Acworth, R.I., B. Kelly & J. Jankowski 1994. Improved contamination assessment of a domestic landfill using integrated geophysical, geochemical and hydrogeological methods. *Proc. 25th Cong. Int. Assoc. Hydrogeol., Adelaide, 21-25 November 1994*: 235-240.

Baedecker, M.J. & W. Back 1979a. Hydrogeological processes and chemical reactions at a landfill. *Ground Water* 17: 429-437.

Baedecker, M.J. & W. Back 1979b. Modern marine sediments as a natural analog to the chemically

stressed environment of a landfill. *J. Hydrol.* 43: 393-414.

Baedecker M.J. & I.M. Cozzarelli 1992. The determination and fate of unstable constituents of contaminated groundwater. In S. Lesage and R. E. Jackson (eds.), *Groundwater contamination and analysis at hazardous waste sites*: 425-461. New York: Marcel Dekker, Inc.

Ball, J.W., D.K. Nordstrom & D.W. Zachman 1987. *WATEQ4F a personal computer FORTRAN translation of the geochemical model WATEQ2 with revised data base*. USGS Open-File Rep. 87-50.

Champ, D.R., J. Gulens & R.E. Jackson 1979. Oxidation-reduction sequences in ground water flow systems. *Can. J. Earth Sci.* 16: 12-23.

Hounslow, A.W. 1980. Ground-water geochemistry: arsenic in landfills. *Ground Water* 18: 331-333.

Jankowski, J., P.W. Hitchcock, R.W. Beck & M.J. Knight 1991. Hydrogeology and hydrochemical processes near a landfill, Astrolabe Park, Sydney, Australia. *Proc. Int. Hydrol. Water Resources Symp. Perth, 2-4 October 1991*: 317-323.

Jankowski, J., R.I. Acworth & D.J. Evans 1994. Detailed hydrogeochemical sampling of an unconsolidated sand aquifer in the Botany Basin, Sydney, Australia: II. Hydrogeology and groundwater chemistry. *Proc. 3rd Int. Symp. Environ. Geochem., Cracow, 12-15 September 1994*: 170-172.

Kehew, A.E. & R.N. Passero 1990. pH and redox buffering mechanisms in a glacial drift aquifer contaminated by landfill leachate. *Ground Water* 28: 728-737.

Lindberg, R.D. & D.D. Runnells 1984. Ground water redox reactions: An analysis of equilibrium state applied to Eh measurements and geochemical modeling. *Science* 225: 925-927.

Lyngkilde, J. & T.H. Christensen 1992. Redox zones of a landfill leachate pollution plume. *J. Cont. Hydrol.* 10: 273-289.

Nicholson, R.V., J.A. Cherry & E.J. Reardon 1983. Migration of contaminants in groundwater at a landfill: A case study. 6. Hydrogeochemistry. *J. Hydrol.* 63: 131-176.

Nordstrom, D.K. 1977. Thermochemical redox equilibria of Zobell's solution. *Geochim. Cosmochim. Acta* 41: 1835-1841.

Stumm, W. & J.J. Morgan 1981. *Aquatic chemistry*. 2nd ed. New York: John Wiley & Sons.

Zobell, C.E. 1946. Studies on redox potential of marine sediments. *Bull. Amer. Assoc. Petrol. Geol.* 30: 477-513.

Groundwater in the Urban Environment: Problems, Processes and Management, Chilton et al. (eds)
© 1997 Balkema, Rotterdam, ISBN 90 5410 837 1

Vertical heterogeneity in the Botany Sands aquifer, Sydney, Australia: Implications for chemical variations and contaminant plume delineation

Jerzy Jankowski & Peter Beck
Groundwater Centre, Department of Applied Geology, University of New South Wales, Sydney, N.S.W., Australia

R. Ian Acworth
Groundwater Centre, Water Research Laboratory, University of New South Wales, Manly Vale, N.S.W., Australia

ABSTRACT: Recent studies in the Botany Sands aquifer, Sydney, have demonstrated that the aquifer, while homogenous and isotropic on a regional scale, is highly heterogeneous and anisotropic on the micro scale. Detailed hydrogeological and hydrochemical studies, supported by geological and geophysical data, have been carried out at an experimental site (7 m wide by 11 m long by 4 m saturated depth) and show that significant variation in both hydraulic conductivity and water chemistry is the result of changes in the depositional environment of the sediments. The hydraulic conductivity ranges between 2.1×10^{-5} m/s and 5.8×10^{-4} m/s. Groundwater chemical analyses at a depth of approximately 3.5 m below ground surface show high concentrations of HCO_3^-, Ca^{2+} and Sr^{2+} which are considered to be due to dissolution of shell material. The same zone contains a significant proportion of clay material and both components are considered to be aeolian. Evaporative concentration is considered to occur in the unsaturated zone of the aquifer, increasing the concentration of Na^+ and Cl^- above that in rainwater. Downward percolating rainwater in a recharge event mobilises the concentrated pore fluid water and acts as an enhanced source of Na^+ in cation exchange reactions with the clay, thus releasing Ca^{2+}. Mass balance modelling is used to demonstrate that dissolution of $CaCO_3$, ion exchange and reverse ion exchange between Na^+ and Ca^{2+}, the flux of CO_2 from the soil zone, and oxidation of pyrite are all important chemical reactions in this 4 m deep shallow section of aquifer.

1 INTRODUCTION

With the increased number of detailed hydrogeological studies at contaminated sites, where detailed hydraulic conductivity and contaminant distribution information are necessary to delineate solute movement, more attention must be given to detailed studies of the micro-scale environment. An aquifer which on a regional or even local scale was considered to be homogenous, when investigated on a micro-scale (site) is often highly heterogeneous. Detailed characterisation of aquifer material at a grain scale with grain fraction characterisation and distribution, mineralogy, and organic and inorganic material present (Ball et al. 1990) will provide detailed information about physical aquifer properties. Heterogeneity becomes increasingly important as the scale of the system decreases, with sometimes sharp concentration boundaries of chemical elements (Ronen et al. 1987).

The chemical composition of groundwater is principally a function of recharge water chemistry and mineralogy but these factors have little effect on the aquifer physical characterisation (Back & Baedecker 1989; Back et al. 1993). Small changes in mineralogy, not accounted on a regional scale, can produce large changes in chemical composition of groundwater on the micro scale. In a micro-scale system, either human activities or natural processes related to mineralogy may have significant effects on geochemical reactions (Smith et al. 1991; Postma et al. 1991; Bjerg & Christensen 1992; Ronen et al. 1987). In a vertical section, chemical heterogeneity may cause chemical zonation in the aquifer to develop on a scale from a few centimetres to tens of centimetres. In this paper are presented the results of detailed hydrogeochemical studies on a micro scale from 5 bundled shallow piezometers installed in the upper part of a coastal aeolian sand aquifer.

2 SITE DESCRIPTION

The study has been carried out at the Eastlakes Experimental Site (ELA) located in the middle of the northern zone of the Botany Sands aquifer, in

Sydney, Australia. The geological framework of the Botany Sands has been described by Albani (1981). Vertical heterogeneity is represented on a macro scale by 4 major units linked to changing depositional environments in Botany Bay. Unit 2 represents a Quaternary aeolian environment and is comprised entirely of quartz sand with a small proportion of $CaCO_3$ shell material evenly distributed throughout. This unit is present at the study site to a depth of 21 m where a peat layer occurs which has a radio-carbon age of 35,000 years. Average groundwater chemistry at the ELA site represents fresh dune recharge water in the Botany Sands aquifer (Acworth & Jankowski 1993).

The ELA site was established in 1992 for the detailed study of sorption, dispersion and advection of non-reactive and reactive solutes. A three dimensional network of 49 bundled piezometers has been installed within the upper shallow part of the aquifer on a grid of 7 m by 11 m. A total of 815 sampling points with a horizontal spacing of 1 m and vertical spacing of between 150 mm and 200 mm allows ready evaluation of hydrogeological and chemical heterogeneity at a micro-scale and for a 3-D delineation of chemical transport. The drilling methodology and piezometer installation are presented by Evans (1993) and Acworth et al. (1994). The site is located on the side of a dune above a weir controlled pond in the Botany wetlands. The aquifer is in hydraulic continuity with the pond which provides a stable fixed head boundary for the experiments.

The site lithology comprises quartz sand with 77 % - 95 % of medium sand, 3 % - 10 % fine sand and 2 % - 14 % silty-clay material. Grain size analyses show

that a high clay content exists between 7.5 m and 8.5 m a.s.l. This clay is generally yellow to brown in colour and correlates well with yellowish to brownish groundwaters which were recovered from these depths during the development and sampling process. The clay has also been identified using gamma logging (EM-39). The zone between 7.5 m and 8.5 m a.s.l. has a higher fine sand content (5 % to 8 %) than the aquifer above and below this layer (3 % to 4 %). The presence of the fine sand and the silt/clay contribute to a hydraulic conductivity value below 6×10^{-5} m/s.

The upper part of the aquifer is characterised by a medium sand layer of up to 1 m thickness containing silt and organic material weakly bound by a ferruginous cement. The layer is known locally as "Waterloo Rock".

The water level at the site is between 9.74 m and 9.35 m a.s.l. (between 0.70 m and 1.87 m below ground surface) with a variation of approximately 400 mm during rainfall events. The hydraulic gradient varies between 0.003 to 0.009 with an average value of 0.007 and is directed normal to the lake shore.

3 SPATIAL DISTRIBUTION OF HYDRAULIC CONDUCTIVITY

The spatial distribution of the hydraulic conductivity was determined for the three lines C, D and E and for row 7 at the site from 516 falling head measurements carried out by Evans (1993). This method was selected as the best for field determination in this type of mini-piezometers and

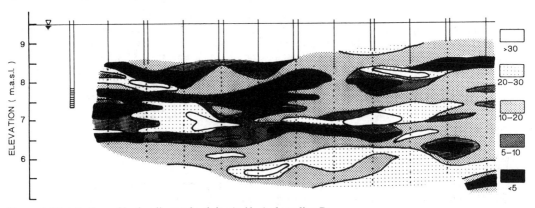

Figure 1. Distribution of hydraulic conductivity (m/day) along line D.

representative of permeameter falling head tests for undistorted core samples (Sudicky 1986). The summary of the hydraulic conductivity tests are presented in Table 1 and in Figure 1 which shows the spatial distribution of the hydraulic conductivity data along the central line D. The mean hydraulic conductivity value for the entire population at the ELA site is 1.69×10^{-4} m/s, with a maximum of 5.8×10^{-4} m/s (50 m/day) and a minimum of 2.1×10^{-5} m/s (1.8 m/day).

The presence of clay in the central part of the aquifer section results in a hydraulic conductivity which is an order of magnitude lower than the surrounding zones. This layer has a profound effect upon solute movement in the aquifer (Evans 1993). Several low hydraulic conductivity lenses exist as shown in Figure 1. These low conductivity zones can be classified as mini aquitards within the aquifer system causing the lower part of the section to be semi-confined to confined.

4 CHEMICAL HETEROGENEITY

The chemical composition of groundwater in this part of the aquifer demonstrates a large vertical variation with respect to both the chemical types of waters and the concentration of major elements. A summary of 88 groundwater samples collected along the central line D is presented in Table 1. The 4 m vertical section of aquifer is characterised by fairly oxidised waters in the upper and middle part and slightly reducing waters in the lower part. The reduced environment is associated with the peat layer at the base of the unconfined section of the aquifer (Evans 1993).

Both above and below the lower hydraulic conductivity middle zone, Na-Cl waters dominate. However, in the middle section at a depth of 3.5 m b.g.s. (7 m - 8 m a.s.l.) Ca-HCO$_3$ rich waters are present. The variation of fluid electrical conductivity in vertical section has the shape of a boomerang (Figure 2a). The pH is close to neutral where Ca-HCO$_3$ waters occur and decreases to a pH value below 5.5 in the upper and lower parts of the section. The presence of oxidised waters with a lack of contaminants in the vertical unconfined section above the peat layer produces a relatively simple composition consisting only of the major elements.

Boron is present throughout the section at low concentrations (Table 1) and Sr^{2+} is associated with

Table 1. Summary of chemical composition and hydraulic conductivity of groundwaters based on 88 chemical analyses and 516 hydraulic conductivity measurements.

Element	Mean	Min.	Max.	St. dev.
pH	6.64	4.80	7.30	0.54
EC (μS/cm)	371.41	184	492	60.33
TDS (mg/l)	251.78	85	367	57.87
Na (mmol/l)	0. 86	0.39	1.78	0.39
K (μmol/l)	95.7	2.6	154.5	37.3
Ca (mmol/l)	1.19	0.003	1.89	0.50
Mg (mmol/l)	0.07	0.00	0.67	0.57
Sr (μmol/l)	0.34	0.00	2.51	0.57
Fe (μmol/l)	0.18	0.00	7.34	1.25
HCO$_3$ (mmol/l)	1.82	0.08	3.04	0.72
SO$_4$ (mmol/l)	0.33	0.12	0.57	0.11
Cl (mmol/l)	1.05	0.74	1.50	0.20
B (μmol/l)	6.48	0.00	13.88	3.70
SI$_{Calcite}$	-1.30	-6.67	-0.35	1.21
SI$_{Dolomite}$	-4.84	-12.22	-2.05	2.37
SI$_{Strontianite}$	-4.51	-8.27	-2.61	1.48
Log$_{PCO2}$	-1.70	-2.32	-0.92	0.27
K^1 (all)	1.69×10^{-4}	2.1×10^{-5}	5.80×10^{-4}	1.08×10^{-4}
K^1 (line C)	1.72×10^{-4}	2.1×10^{-5}	5.57×10^{-4}	1.14×10^{-4}
K^1 (line D)	1.70×10^{-4}	2.1×10^{-5}	5.80×10^{-4}	9.67×10^{-5}
K^1 (line E)	1.65×10^{-4}	2.1×10^{-5}	4.62×10^{-4}	1.15×10^{-4}
K^1 (row 7)	1.64×10^{-4}	2.1×10^{-5}	5.80×10^{-4}	1.19×10^{-4}

Line C - N=126; Line D - N=200; Line E - N=126
Row 7 - N=112; ^{1} - m/s

Ca^{2+} and is a product of dissolution of shell material. With the exception of the peat layer, no Zn^{2+}, Li^+, Mn^{2+}, Fe^{2+}, heavy metals, NO_3^-, NH_4^+ and PO_4^{3-} have been detected in the aquifer.

Figures 2b and 2c show the cumulative vertical sections for all samples from the 5 bundled piezometers. Very sharp vertical changes occur in only 150 mm intervals for some of the major ions. The highest variation are between HCO_3^-, Ca^{2+} and Mg^{2+} in the interface between quartz sand and organic material zones where changes are 0.57 mg/mm, 0.27 mg/mm and 0.05 mg/mm respectively. No such sharp variation is noted for other ions which show much more stable concentrations in the vertical profile.

There is a strong negative correlation between Ca^{2+} and HCO_3^- versus Na^+ and Cl^- as seen in Figure 2b. The upper and lower less clayey parts of the aquifer are characterised by low concentrations of Ca^{2+} and HCO_3^- and high concentrations of Na^+ and Cl^-. The reverse holds true in the more clayey central section.

447

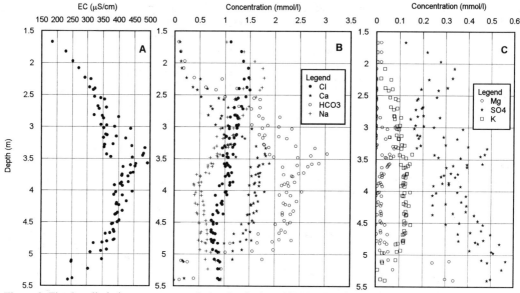

Figure 2. Five bundled piezometers cumulative depth plot of fluid EC and major ion chemistry.

The chloride concentration shows a decreasing trend with depth. The potassium and magnesium (Figure 2c) concentrations follow those of Ca^{2+} and HCO_3^- with the higher values in the middle part of the aquifer. Sulphate shows an increasing trend in concentration with depth (Figure 2c).

5 CHEMICAL REACTIONS AND MODELLING

Chemical reactions can be depicted by the relationship between different ions as shown by bivariate plots in Figure 3. The Na^+ versus Cl^- plot (Figure 3a) shows that groundwater with lower concentrations of both these ions is located below the 1:1 line. This indicates exchange of Na^+ for Ca^{2+} in water associated with quartz sand. The scatter of points is attributed to the mixing within the interface. With increasing Na^+ and Cl^- concentrations the data points in this plot move above the 1:1 line where the exchange of Ca^{2+} for Na^+ prevails.

The Ca^{2+} versus HCO_3^- plot (Figure 3b) shows good correlation as the concentrations of both these ions increase. This is associated with the dissolution of calcium carbonate shell material. Deviation from the 1:1 line is caused by HCO_3^- production from the CO_{2aq} which is supplied from CO_{2gas} present in the unsaturated zone and also from the oxidation of pyrite in organic material. Some bicarbonate is also derived from the dissolution of $SrCO_3$ and $CaMg(CO_3)_2$ present in shell material. The dissolution of $CaCO_3$ represents a typical open system keeping P_{CO2} constant during the dissolution processes. The ion exchange between Na^+ and Ca^{2+} throughout the aquifer is shown on the Ca^{2+} versus Na^+ plot (Figure 3c) where a negative correlation is associated with this process and is also shown in Figure 4 as a variation of Na/Cl ratios with depth.

The increase of SO_4^{2-} with depth is suggested here to be due to the process of oxidation of FeS_2 in the peat and organic material layers present in the aquifer. This process produces H^+ which lowers the pH and results in the dissolution of $CaCO_3$ in the clayey-sand layer. Sulphate is evenly distributed along the flow path due to dispersion across the aquifer, with the highest concentration near the source. The Fe^{2+} supplied from the oxidation of pyrite is present in the aquifer in reducing groundwaters. Very close to the water table, where strongly oxidised conditions are present, iron is precipitated as oxides (Fe_2O_3), hydroxides ($Fe(OH)_3$) and in the presence of high HCO_3^- and pH as carbonates ($FeCO_3$). In shallow water tables this process forms dense cemented ferruginous layers with iron concretions known as the "Waterloo Rock", which has been related by some authors to ancient water table fluctuations. However, this process can not be associated with the origin of similar cemented ferruginous layers in sand dunes approximately 8 or more meters above the

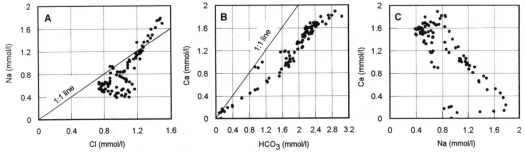

Figure 3. Bivariate plots of Na versus Cl, Ca versus HCO₃ and Ca versus Na.

present water table. The sand dune layers are most likely related to the leaching of iron rich soil horizons.

The dissolution of gypsum as a source of SO_4^{2-} is not possible, simply because all the investigated sediments are of terrestrial origin and no traces of gypsum are present. The process of concentration by evaporation of shallow groundwater after prolonged dry periods also will not produce gypsum because all the Ca^{2+} will be first taken out for the precipitation of $CaCO_3$. An origin from ocean generated rainfall and sea sprays will be possible if the concentration shows a decrease with depth, however, the reverse trend is present.

The high concentration of Sr^{2+} is associated with the Ca^{2+} and HCO_3^- peak and is due to the presence of Sr^{2+} in shell material. The low concentration of Mg^{2+} throughout the sandy and clayey-sand part of the aquifer is the result of low Mg^{2+} concentrations in shell material. Higher concentration of Mg^{2+} in the peat layer is the result of Mg^{2+} release under these more acidic conditions.

To test the chemical processes outlined above, a mass balance calculation has been undertaken using

the computer program NETPATH (Plummer et al. 1991). The plausible phases of CO_{2gas}, calcite, dolomite, NaCl, sylvite, pyrite, goethite and Ca/Na exchange have been modelled. The vertical profile of the mass balance variation from one of the bundled piezometers is presented in Figure 5. One end member is fresh water and the second end member is provided by the chemical data from the piezometer. Modelling has also been performed for rain water as an end member. The difference between these two end members is very small.

The chemical modelling shows that the chemical composition of groundwater in the vertical section is the result of a number of processes, including: dissolution of $CaCO_3$ and $CaMg(CO_3)_2$; the flux of CO_{2gas}; dissolution of NaCl and KCl; oxidation of pyrite; and the precipitation of $Fe(OH)_3$ and ion exchange processes. The Ca/Na exchange mass balance supports very well the field data presented in Figure 4. The selection of goethite for the mass balance calculations and not haematite does not change the sulphate flux to the groundwater system. The highest dissolution rate of $CaCO_3$ of 1.5 mmol/kg occurs in the clayey-sand and this is associated with the high Na/Ca ion exchange of 0.3

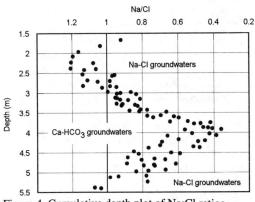

Figure 4. Cumulative depth plot of Na:Cl ratios.

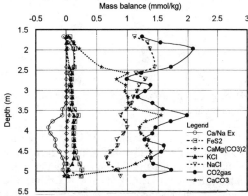

Figure 5. Mass balance for a bundled piezometer.

mmol/kg. The ion exchange is forced by the precipitation of calcite which would occur during a prolonged dry period (Evans 1993). The exchange reaction supplies Ca^{2+} to keep the carbonate system in equilibrium. During a wet period, groundwaters are undersaturated with respect to all carbonate minerals, and equilibrium is maintained only for waters with the highest Ca^{2+} and HCO_3^- concentrations causing further slow dissolution of shell material.

6 CONCLUSIONS

The installation of 49 bundled piezometers at the East Lakes Experimental site in an area of approximately 80 square metres has allowed a detailed investigation of the natural hydro-geochemical processes occurring in a sandy aquifer. Hydrochemical analyses and hydraulic conductivity data are presented along one line of selected bundled piezometers, comprising a total of 88 sampling points and 200 falling head measurements. This data set has shown that significant variation in hydraulic conductivity occurs in what was considered to be an isotropic and homogeneous aquifer. The lower hydraulic conductivity material contains fine sand, finely divided shell material and silty clay. The presence of this zone has a profound impact upon the hydrogeochemical evolution of ground water passing through the zone. The shell material acts as a major source of Ca^{2+} and HCO_3^- ions, while the clay provides cation exchange sites for sodium.

This study of the natural hydrogeochemical variation present in an aquifer indicates that significant vertical variation occurs in natural systems as well as the result of contamination, and that it is necessary to establish the true background processes present at a contaminated site before any conclusions can be drawn regarding the impact of contamination.

REFERENCES

Acworth, R.I. & J. Jankowski 1993. Hydrogeochemical zonation of groundwater in the Botany Sands aquifer, Sydney. *AGSO J. Aust. Geol. Geophys.* 14: 193-199.

Acworth, R.I., J. Jankowski, D.J. Evans & M. Groskops 1994. Detailed hydrogeochemical sampling of an unconsolidated sand aquifer in the Botany Basin, Sydney, Australia. I. Drilling and sampling methodology. *Proc. 3rd Int. Symp.*

Environ. Geochem., Cracow, 12-15 September 1994: 5-6.

Albani, A.D. 1981. Sedimentary environments and Pleistocene chronology of the Botany Basin, N.S.W., Australia. *Geo-Marine Lett.* 1: 163-167.

Back, W. & M.J. Baedecker 1989. Chemical hydrogeology in natural and contaminated environments. *J. Hydrol.* 106: 1-28.

Back, W., M.J. Baedecker & W.W. Wood 1993. Scales in chemical hydrogeology: A historical perspective. In W. M. Alley (ed.), *Regional ground-water quality*: 111-129. New York: Van Nostrand Reinhold.

Ball, W.P., Ch. Buehler, T.C. Harmon, D.M. Mackay & P.V. Roberts 1990. Characterisation of a sandy aquifer material at the grain scale. *J. Cont. Hydrol.* 5: 253-295.

Bjerg, P.L. & T.H. Christensen 1992. Spatial and temporal small-scale variation in groundwater quality of a shallow sandy aquifer. *J. Hydrol.* 131: 133-149.

Evans, D.J. 1993. A physical and hydrochemical characterisation of a sand aquifer in Sydney, Australia. *MAppSc Project Report*, UNSW.

Jankowski, J., R.I. Acworth & D.J. Evans 1994. Detailed hydrogeochemical sampling of an unconsolidated sand aquifer in the Botany Basin, Sydney, Australia: II. Hydrogeology and groundwater chemistry. *Proc. 3rd Int. Symp. Environ. Geochem., Cracow, 12-15 September 1994*: 170-172.

Plummer, L.N., E.C. Prestemon & D.L. Parkhurst 1991. *An interactive code (NETPATH) for modelling NET geochemical reactions along a flow PATH*. USGS Water Res. Invest. Rep. 91-4078.

Postma, D., C. Boesen, H. Kristiansen & F. Larsen 1991. Nitrate reduction in an unconfined sandy aquifer: Water chemistry, reduction processes, and geochemical modelling. *Water Resour, Res.* 27: 2027-2045.

Ronen, D., M. Magaritz, H. Gvirtzman & W. Garner 1987. Microscale chemical heterogeneity in groundwater. *J. Hydrol.* 92: 173-178.

Smith R.L., R.W. Harvey & D.R. LeBlanc 1991. Importance of closely spaced vertical sampling in delineating chemical and microbiological gradients in groundwater studies. *J. Cont. Hydrol.* 7: 285-300.

Sudicky, E.A. 1986. A natural gradient experiment on solute transport in a sand aquifer: Spatial variability of hydraulic conductivity and its role in the dispersion process. *Water Resour. Res.* 22: 2069-2082.

Groundwater in the Urban Environment: Problems, Processes and Management, Chilton et al. (eds)
© *1997 Balkema, Rotterdam, ISBN 90 5410 837 1*

Contamination in two urban industrial areas in South Korea

Michael A. Jones & Shaminder Puri
Scott Wilson Kirkpatrick, Basingstoke, UK

Sun-ki Kang
Samsung Engineering Research and Development Center, Youngin-Shi, Korea

Sang Hoon Lee
*Samsung Global Environment Research Center, Seoul, Korea (Presently: Korea Environmental Technology
Research Institute, Seoul, Korea)*

ABSTRACT: As part of its corporate environmental policy the Samsung Group is commencing a programme
of soil and groundwater contamination investigations and monitoring, progressing far beyond the scope of
current legislative requirements. Initial studies have targeted 10 manufacturing and industrial facilities
throughout South Korea to establish a contamination baseline, determine potential hazards, associated risks
and potential liabilities, and to prepare for the evolving regulatory requirements to control soil and
groundwater contamination. Part of these investigations has targeted the industrialised urban centres of
Suwon and Changwon, revealing inorganic and organic contaminants potentially derived from a range of
unconfirmed on-site and off-site sources. Numerous contaminant sources are to be expected in an urban
industrial area which has developed rapidly with limited regulatory controls, but the current assessment
indicates that the risk of environmental impact from these sites is generally low. The investigation
methodology adopted is to be developed for application at other Samsung facilities.

1 INTRODUCTION

There are many heavily industrialised areas in South
Korea which have undergone rapid development in
the last 10 years. Industrial complexes have
evolved and factories producing diverse products
are required by Korean legislation to adopt clean
technology to protect the environment. In this
context, environmental assessments have been
completed but legislation concerning soil and
groundwater contamination has only been enacted
recently, and mechanisms of enforcement by the
Ministry of Environment are developing slowly.
Nevertheless, corporate environmental policies are
driving investigations and monitoring far beyond
regulatory requirements.

As part of the Samsung Group environmental
policy, preliminary soil and groundwater
investigations have been carried out at 10 facilities
throughout South Korea. A large part of this study
concentrated on two industrialised urban areas
where Samsung has a number of diverse operations:

1. Suwon, 20 km south of Seoul, where Samsung
manufactures electronic and electrical goods.

2. Changwon, on the south coast, where
Samsung has manufacturing and heavy industrial
facilities.

2 AIMS OF THE STUDY

1. Establish a soil and groundwater
contamination baseline, and investigate on-site and
off-site contaminant sources in the areas of
concentrated industry.

2. Determine potential hazards and associated
risks, as well as investigating potential liabilities
arising from off-site contaminant migration.

3. Pre-empt requirements of regulations for the
control of soil and groundwater contamination.

4. Develop a methodology of soil and
groundwater contamination investigation for
application at other Samsung facilities.

3 SCOPE OF INVESTIGATIONS

The phased soil and groundwater investigation
comprised desk study, field reconnaissance, site
investigation (SI), contamination evaluation and

Table 1. Chemicals used at the Suwon and Changwon facilities.

Suwon	Changwon
Chlorinated solvents	Chlorinated solvents
Petroleum hydrocarbons	Petroleum hydrocarbons
Sodium hydroxide	Sodium hydroxide
Heavy metals	Heavy metals
	Polychlorinated
	biphenyls (PCBs)

Table 2. Soil and groundwater contaminants covered by current Korean standards.

Soil	Groundwater
Arsenic	Ammonia
Cadmium	Arsenic
Chromium (hexavalent)	Cadmium
Copper	Chloride
Cyanide (total)	Chromium (hexavalent)
Lead	Copper
Mercury	Cyanide (total)
Phenols	E.coli
Mineral oil	Fluoride
	Lead
	Manganese
	Mercury
	Nitrate
	Phenols
	Trichloroethene (TCE)
	Tetrachloroethene (PCE)

preliminary risk assessment. The desk study revealed a range of chemicals used on site in Suwon and Changwon (Table 1), plus a number of adjacent industrial and manufacturing sites, e.g. metal plating plant, ceramics, plastics and tuna processing factories, all potential contaminant sources.

The desk study revealed that Korean standards for soil contamination are limited to a few contaminants (Table 2), but a more comprehensive suite exists for groundwater in recognition of its importance as a source of drinking water.

Due to the wide range of potential contaminants identified, a broad screening survey for potential contaminants was carried out based on the UK ICRCL suite (* = soil only; + = groundwater only):

1. metals (As, Cd, Cr (total* & hexavalent), Cu, Ni*, Hg, Pb, Se, Zn);
2. boron;
3. cyanide and thiocyanate*;
4. sulphide*;
5. phosphate*;
6. total non-volatile aromatics (i.e. polyaromatic hydrocarbons; PAHs) and mineral oils;
7. phenols*;
8. total petroleum hydrocarbons (TPH)*, benzene, toluene, ethyl benzene, xylene (BTEX)+;
9. chlorinated solvents, e.g. TCE, PCE, dichloromethane (DCM).

Based on the desk study and field reconnaissance, the SI was designed to assess key areas of potential contamination from sources on site and off site, as well as the potential for contaminant migration off site. The SI comprised: (i) shallow monitoring wells; (ii) soil sampling and analysis; (iii) soil gas measurements; (iv) water sampling and analysis.

4 INVESTIGATIONS IN SUWON

4.1 *Site setting*

Samsung has four separate but adjacent facilities on the eastern edge of Suwon, and owing to their proximity they were considered as a single unit in this study. Electrical and electronic goods are manufactured here.

The complex lies on the eastern bank of the Won chun-chun River, while the western bank opposite the complex comprises paddy fields and greenhouse cultivation (Figure 1).

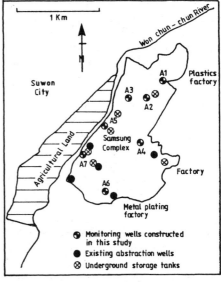

Figure 1. Location map of the Suwon complex.

There are several wells used to supply the manufacturing processes:
1. a 150 m deep well, used infrequently, 500 m upstream of monitoring well A4;
2. nine wells from 16 to 60 m deep in the south-west corner of the complex.

4.2 Hydrogeological model

The stratigraphic sequence on the published geological map comprises Quaternary alluvium overlying a basement of Jurassic biotite granites intruded into Precambrian biotite gneisses. Boreholes drilled in this investigation revealed:
1. made ground (0.6-1.7 m thick) of very poorly sorted clayey sands and gravels, with silts and clays;
2. alluvium (3-6.7 m thick) of sands, gravels and some clays;
3. igneous and metamorphic basement of weathered and some fresh granite and gneisses.

The hills east and north-east of the site are likely to be areas of recharge, with groundwater flowing towards the river, into which it probably discharges. Groundwater levels measured in this study have confirmed the hydraulic gradient is directed towards the river. Based on available data, the hydrogeological stratigraphy is interpreted as:
1. low/moderate permeability unsaturated zone of made ground, alluvial silts and clays;
2. minor unconfined alluvial aquifer;
3. fractured basement aquifer.

4.3 Site investigations

Seven boreholes were drilled at the Suwon complex, to depths of 8 to 10 mbgl (Figure 1). The locations were selected during field reconnaissance to investigate the concerns summarised in Table 3, including underground storage tanks (UST). Soil samples were collected for chemical analysis and a monitoring well completed in each borehole.

4.4 Contamination assessment

4.4.1 Soils

Many of the potential inorganic soil contaminants analysed are close to analytical reporting limits, while others meet Korean and international standards. The only inorganic contaminant at elevated levels is arsenic. Its concentrations exceed Korean standards at which management is required to limit contamination (20 mg/kg) at various depths

Table 3. Borehole locations at the Suwon complex (* = monitoring well dry).

Well No.	Location Rationale	No. of Samples	
		Soil	Ground water
A1	Downstream of plastics factory	12	1
A2	Downstream of plastics factory	12	1
A3	Hydrocarbon UST adjacent	10	1
A4	Downstream of off-site industry & on-site hydrocarbon UST	12	1
A5	Downstream boundary of site	10	1
A6	Downstream of metal plating factory	14	0*
A7	Downstream boundary of site	12	1

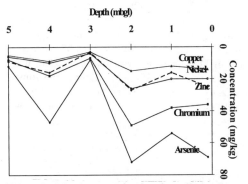

Figure 2. Metal contamination in soils at Suwon (borehole A1).

in A1 (Figure 2), A2, A5 and A6, and exceeds the standards at which treatment (50 mg/kg) is required at 3.4 mbgl in A5. However, only in A1 are there high arsenic levels at the ground surface. From its association with orange-brown and grey-green clays and clayey silts, it is inferred that arsenic is adsorbed onto hydrous iron oxides and combined with sulphides, respectively. Further, the similar variations shown by arsenic and other trace metals (Figure 2) suggest their distribution may be natural.

Depth variations of the organic contaminants investigated are similar to one another. TPH is at significant levels throughout each borehole, often with very high levels at about 1 mbgl, and almost always exceeds the Dutch 'B' (500 mg/kg) levels. These observations suggest that the alluvial aquifer is contaminated with petroleum hydrocarbons, although groundwater analyses for BTEX did not reveal any such contamination (Section 4.4.2) and significant soil gas concentrations were observed in only one sample. However, the TPH contamination pattern suggests there may be multiple off-site sources in the vicinity of A1 and A2, and on-site sources in the vicinity of A4 (e.g. UST upstream), A5, A6 (see below) and A7 (Table 3).

PAH levels are low except at depth in A5 and close to the surface in A6. At A6 there are several potential contaminant sources: (i) an oil interceptor treating surface runoff; (ii) a depression in the tarmac where oils have accumulated for some time; (iii) lube oil drums in a storage building; (iv) a metal plating factory upstream.

Several chlorinated solvents were detected: (i) TCE in A1, A2, A3, A7; (ii) DCM in all boreholes; (iii) DCE (cis-1,2-dichloroethene) in A1, A2, A3, A7; (iv) PCE at 5 mbgl in A2 but at only 15 μg/kg. TCE and DCE sometimes only occur in the unsaturated zone, with their distribution potentially controlled by lower permeability units restricting downward migration. However, in A3 there is a trace of TCE below a low permeability unit, while in A2 higher levels (85 μg/kg) occur in the alluvial aquifer, corresponding with the PCE occurrence, which suggests migration through the lower permeability unit. Solvent levels in A1 and A6 may relate to their proximity to upstream, off-site plastics and metal plating factories respectively.

4.4.2 Groundwater

Several inorganic species are close to reporting limits, while others meet the Korean standards. A few groundwater components exceed the Korean drinking water standards, including manganese and ammonia, the latter possibly related to leakage from waste water and sewerage systems. Even though high arsenic concentrations are found in the soil sequence, groundwater arsenic levels only exceed the Korean groundwater standards in two cases (A5, A7) and even here the levels are within Korean groundwater standards for industrial uses (0.1 mg/l). This is partly explained by the high soil arsenic levels occurring in the unsaturated zone.

Of the organic species, only TCE in A1 and A2 exceed Korean groundwater standards.

5 INVESTIGATIONS IN CHANGWON

5.1 Site setting

Changwon lies within an alluvial basin drained by the Chong wonchon and Namchon rivers, close to the head of Masan Bay. Samsung has a strong presence in Changwon, with three facilities in the industrial area on the southern edge of the town (Figure 3): (i) Heavy Industries, on the south bank of the Namchon River; (ii) Aerospace (1), to the south-east on the south river bank; (iii) Aerospace (2) upstream on the north bank of the Namchon. At Heavy Industries, steel goods and heavy vehicles are manufactured, with cameras, car springs and semi-conductor frames at the Aerospace sites.

There are six abstraction wells, 58 m to 100 m deep, at the Aerospace (1) site. It is our understanding that chlorinated solvents have caused extensive groundwater contamination beneath Changwon and its residential areas. This includes deep groundwater beneath Aerospace (1), but data are limited and the contaminant sources unclear.

5.2 Hydrogeological model

The stratigraphic sequence on the published geological map shows Quaternary alluvium in the Changwon basin underlain by Cretaceous andesites and granitoids intruded into a sedimentary basement. Boreholes in this investigation revealed:

1. made ground (1.5-3.4 m thick) of clayey sands and sandy clays with beds of granitoid cobbles;

2. alluvium (<4 m thick) of sands and gravels overlain by a thin black clay away from the river; at the Heavy Industries site the gravels and sands are also underlain by a black clay;

3. heavily weathered igneous basement.

The hills south of the site are thought to be areas of limited recharge, with groundwater flows in the basement towards the river, into which it may discharge. Away from the river, groundwater in the alluvium is confined by silty clays, but closer to the river where the silty clays are absent, the alluvium and made ground form a composite unconfined aquifer. Water level observations in previous engineering site investigations suggest that groundwater flows away from the river, implying a hydraulic connection between aquifer and river; as the tidal range is at least 1 m, the aquifer may discharge as river levels fall and recharge as river levels rise. Using available data, the

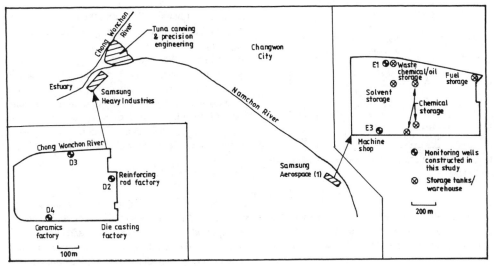

Figure 3. Location map of Changwon sites

hydrogeological stratigraphy is interpreted as:

    1. moderate/low permeability unsaturated zone of made ground and upper alluvium;

    2. alluvial clay aquitard, absent near the river;

    3. minor alluvial aquifer;

    4. aquitard of alluvial clays and weathered igneous rock;

    5. minor basement aquifer.

5.3 Site investigations

Seven boreholes were drilled in Changwon; two to 6.7 and 7.4 mbgl at the Aerospace (1) site, and three at the Heavy Industries site to depths of 4.3 to 5 mbgl (Figure 3). Their locations were selected to investigate particular concerns. Soil samples were collected for chemical analysis and a monitoring well completed in each borehole (see Table 4).

5.4 Contamination assessment

5.4.1 Soils

As in Suwon, many potential inorganic soil contaminants are close to analytical reporting limits, while others generally meet Korean and international standards. Only isolated soil samples exceed guidance levels, e.g. high levels of zinc and acid soluble sulphide in black clays at the Heavy Industries site which could relate to zinc sulphides recorded in the mineralised basement rocks.

    Potential organic contaminants at the Aerospace

Table 4. Borehole locations in Changwon (* = monitoring well dry).

Well No.	Location Rationale	No. of Samples	
		Soil	Ground water
D2	Downstream of reinforcing rod factory	4	1
D3	Downstream boundary of site	6	1
D4	Upstream boundary of site, downstream of ceramics factory	6	1
E1	Downstream boundary of site	4	0*
E3	Upstream boundary of site, downstream of machine shop	8	1

(1) site are at low levels, although TPH slightly exceeds Dutch 'B' levels. However, at the Heavy Industries site there is evidence for organic contamination, i.e. high levels of mineral oils occur in the black clays furthest from the river (Figure 4). The source of these mineral oils is uncertain and not easily reconciled with its low permeability, but these relatively young sediments may have been contaminated during deposition, perhaps related to spillages at the adjacent oil jetty. High TPH levels are found in much of the sequence, and it is possible the high concentrations in the made ground relate to local sources, e.g. reinforcing bar factory near D2.

455

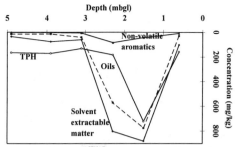

Figure 4. Metal contamination in soils at Changwon (borehole D4).

As chlorinated solvents had been detected previously in the Aerospace (1) abstraction wells, TCE and PCE were expected in the soil samples. However, most volatile organic compounds analysed were below analytical reporting limits, and no consistently elevated soil gas levels were detected. The only exceptions were 1,2-dichloroethane (48 μg/kg) and toluene (88 μg/kg) at 6.4 mbgl in E3, corresponding to high TPH levels.

5.4.2 Groundwater

Of the potential groundwater contaminants at the Aerospace (1) site, only coliforms exceed Korean drinking water standards. There are sewage storage tanks downstream of the monitoring well, which suggests an upstream, off site source.

At the Heavy Industries site, hydraulic connection of the aquifer with the tidal river influences its hydrochemistry. Saline intrusion may explain major ions (Na, K, Ca, Mg, Cl) exceeding drinking water standards in the groundwater. However, several other minor parameters are at elevated levels: (i) Cd and Mn in all three wells; (ii) Pb, Hg and NH_4-N in some cases; (iii) coliforms in the well furthest from the river. The NH_4-N levels may be natural, related to organic matter degradation in the alluvium, while Mn may relate to the sediment reducing conditions, but the Cd, Hg, Pb and coliforms may be from artificial sources.

None of the hydrocarbons and organic solvents analysed are above detection limits except for anionic surfactants, at both sites, and 1,1,1-trichloroethane at the Heavy Industries site (D3 and D4); their sources are uncertain.

Owing to previous occurrences of chlorinated solvents in groundwater at the Aerospace (1) site, they were expected in the shallow groundwater sampled in this study, but neither PCE or TCE were detected at either site. This, and the lack of TCE and PCE in soil samples, suggests solvents are not migrating downward from on-site sources to contaminate the basement aquifer. Possible explanations for the solvent contamination include: (i) on-site abstraction wells capturing contaminated groundwater from off site; (ii) migration of a dense non-aqueous phase liquid from sources north of the river; (iii) contaminant leakage into on-site abstraction wells via the wellhead chamber.

6 CONTAMINATION RISKS

The potential contamination hazards at all three sites are: (i) direct contact with contaminated soil and groundwater by gardening and engineering staff; (ii) direct contact with groundwater used in manufacturing; (iii) discharge of contaminated groundwater into adjacent rivers, affecting ecology and water users.

Although some soil contaminants exceed Korean regulatory standards, the risk of significant impact is low because of limited direct contact between site personnel and contaminated soils well below ground level. In addition, most groundwater meets Korean standards for industrial use, the only use to which groundwater is put at these sites. Further, the ground is partially protected from contamination by tarmac and concrete surfaces, a 2-4 m thick unsaturated zone, the lack of aquifer outcrops on site, and partial confinement of the alluvial aquifers. Thus in general, contamination may not present a high risk although any impact off site is uncertain.

7 CONCLUSIONS

This preliminary evaluation suggests that on-site and off-site activities have contaminated soil and groundwater at the Suwon and Changwon sites. At this stage of the site assessment, the overall risk of contamination causing a hazard to site personnel or other targets is judged to be low, except for staff who repeatedly come into contact with contaminated surface soils, and staff dealing with underground services and construction contractors in contact with deeper soils and groundwater, for whom the risk is moderate.

Development of a prototype contaminated land assessment system

C. Kelly, R. J. Lunn & R. Mackay
Centre for Land Use and Water Resources Research, University of Newcastle-upon-Tyne, UK

ABSTRACT: The future of industrially contaminated land is now a major concern for local authorities across the UK. The enforcement of the Environment Act 1995 early this year will require local authorities to undertake an audit of contaminated land within their boundaries, and establish an action plan for implementation of measures to mitigate health and environmental risks which are unacceptable with respect to statutory and non-statutory guidance. In preparation for meeting these obligations, Newcastle City Council (NCC) have initiated a programme of research at Newcastle University to develop a prototype Contaminated Land ASsessment System (CLASS) to map contaminated land within the city boundaries. This system has been developed within the framework of the Geographic Information System ARC/INFO. It comprises two main components. First, a comprehensive database for identification and characterisation of contaminant sources, pathways and targets within Newcastle city boundaries. Second, a hazard modelling system to classify each site in terms of its future pollution potential. The CLASS system will provide a valuable tool for NCC in prioritising future actions such as monitoring, site investigation and/or remediation of contaminated sites.

1 INTRODUCTION

The introduction in 1997 of "Statutory Guidance and Regulations on Contaminated Land" that will underpin Section 57 of the 1995 UK Environment Act will enable its enforcement early this year. The Act will require each local authority to inspect its area and determine whether land is contaminated land. For each site found to be contaminated, the persons who "caused" or "knowingly permitted" the pollution must be identified and will bear the costs of remediation. However, if those persons cannot be found, then the present owners or occupiers, in many cases the authorities themselves, may be liable. In preparation to meet such obligations this year, Newcastle City Council (NCC) initiated in 1996 a programme of research at Newcastle University to develop a prototype Contaminated Land ASsessment System (CLASS). The CLASS system would map potentially contaminated land and within the city boundaries and assesses its hazard potential .

The best established tool on which to base the CLASS system was that of the hazard assessment model DRASTIC (Aller et al. 1987). DRASTIC was created for the purpose of groundwater protection in the United States. It was designed to provide for

systematic evaluation of groundwater pollution potential in any hydrogeological setting. DRASTIC classes site areas using a combination of seven physical and chemical characteristics (Aller et al. 1987). The seven variables (from which the name of the model is derived) are Depth to water, Recharge, Aquifer media, Soil media, Topography, Impact of the vadose zone, and Conductivity (hydraulic). The classification system contains three parts: 1) weights; 2) ranges; and 3) ratings (Aller et al. 1987). Each DRASTIC parameter has been assigned a relative weight between 1 and 5, with 5 being considered most significant in regard to contamination potential and 1 being the least significant. In turn, each variable is subdivided into ranges and each range is given a rating. The final result for each hydrogeological setting is a numerical value, called the DRASTIC index. The higher the value is, the more susceptible the area in question is to groundwater pollution.

CLASS has been developed using a similar approach to that of the DRASTIC system of considering several physical and chemical properties on a site and classifying them into ranges. It uses a source-pathway-target approach to rank industrial and ex-industrial land in terms of its pollution risk potential. The locations of potentially polluting industries (both past and present) are identified from Ordnance Survey data. This information is then combined with physical and chemical attribute data to characterise pollution sources, pathways and targets for each site.

There are two factors within DRASTIC which required a different approach for development of the CLASS system for site hazard assessment in Newcastle. First, DRASTIC is designed to evaluate risk over large areas; its recommended usage is for areas greater than 100 acres. A typical example of its use is the assessment of groundwater vulnerability for the state of Nebraska (Rundquist et al. 1991). Application to such large areas implies that the hydrogeological assessment within DRASTIC can be made from classifying the different soils and lithologies present at each location. Within an area as small as Newcastle city, the soils and geology are basically the same everywhere and it is the thickness of each lithological layer that varies. Therefore, an approach has been developed within CLASS of modelling the travel times for pollutants via lateral subsurface flow from sites to their nearest targets. These travel times are then used to assess the hydrogeological implications of each site location.

Second, DRASTIC assesses the vulnerability of groundwater regions, rather than classifying existing sites. For this reason it assumes a generic pollutant with the mobility of water; an assumption that is not valid for sites in the Newcastle city area. The CLASS system identifies the chemicals that could be present given the industrial heritage of a site, and then assesses for each chemical independently, its potential risk to nearby targets.

The final hazard assessment index within CLASS is derived from combining ratings from five variables: time of travel to the nearest target; site area; toxicity; persistence; and sorption characteristics. CLASS has been applied to the Newcastle city area, and the sites identified have been assigned one of 10 hazard assessment indices. Results are presented in the form of hazard assessment maps, showing the locations of sites and their index. The database can also be easily interrogated to provide any chemical or physical property data on potential pollutants for an individual site. This system will form a valuable tool to aid NCC in prioritising future actions such as monitoring, site investigation and/or remediation of contaminated sites.

2 DATASETS

All CLASS datasets are held within the Geographical Information System ARC/INFO, which readily enables the storage of spatial data and other associated information. The spatial data are stored as raster maps and comprise source, pathway and target datasets; for example, site locations, geological data and river network data. The attribute data (associated information) comprise tables of industries, chemicals and physical properties that are linked to the spatial data.

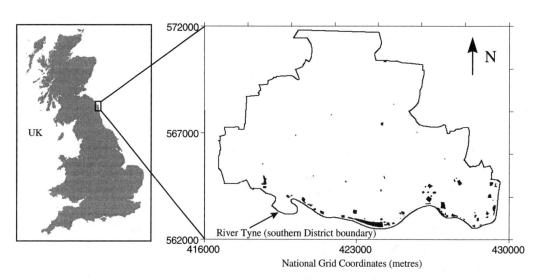

Figure 1. The industrial sites at the turn of the nineteenth century in the Newcastle District.

2.1 Source data

The source data comprise industrial site data and chemical data, the former being stored as spatial data and the latter stored as attribute data. The selection of chemicals was based on the following factors: causing pollution to the subsurface environment; being hazardous to human life; and commonly found on industrial sites. It was decided to extract chemical property data from the database provided by the U.S. EPA, since it is comprehensive and aptly fitted the needs of the project. The EPA database of 324 chemicals includes metals, organic and non-organic solvents and pesticides. The following physicochemical properties were selected as being important for site assessment: solubility; volatility; sorption; mobility; and persistence. Other chemical attributes recorded were carcinogenicity, acute toxicity, chronic toxicity and bioconcentration factor.

A list of industries liable to produce pollution and a list of potential contaminants associated with each industry were compiled using the Department of Environment Industry Profiles (Department of Environment 1995). Using information provided by Newcastle City Council's Standard Business Directory a list of present day industries found in Newcastle was drawn up and matched to industrial sites on the current Ordnance Survey (O.S.) topographic maps. Early edition O.S. maps (turn of the century) were used to provide information on the locations of older industrial developments, as shown in Figure 1. The number of old sites established is ninety-six and there are thirty-one on the current maps, some of which are coincident with the old sites. Each site is linked via the industrial database to the chemical by the process shown in Figure 2. This allows interrogation of a site to find a list of chemicals and their associated properties.

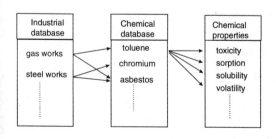

Figure 2. Schematic diagram illustrating how the attribute data are linked in Arc/Info.

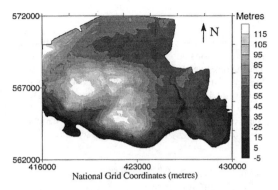

Figure 3. The digital terrain model for the Newcastle District.

2.2 Pathway data

These datasets comprise geological maps, associated hydraulic properties, and a digital terrain model. The digital terrain model (DTM) for the Newcastle District was derived from O.S. contours at a ten metre resolution, and is shown in Figure 3.

The local geology comprises a thick sequence of unconsolidated material overlying a predominantly sandstone sequence. The unconsolidated material comprises four main layers; from groundlevel these are made ground, sand, sandy-clay and boulder clay. Borehole data provided by the British Geological Survey allowed spatial elevation of each lithological layer to be estimated up to a depth of 30 metres below ground. Local hydraulic parameter data are not available so general values were taken from the literature (de Marsily 1986).

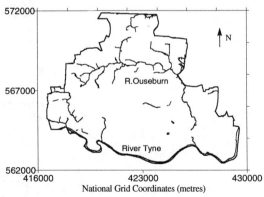

Figure 4. The surface water bodies in the Newcastle District.

459

2.3 *Target data*

For the prototype system, only surface water bodies have been considered as possible pollution targets. The surface water data were derived from Ordnance Survey Landline data. The river network for the Newcastle District is shown in Figure 4. Note that where the streams disappear, it is because they have been channelled underground. The main tributary north of the river Tyne is the river Ouseburn.

3 METHODOLOGY FOR SITE CLASSIFICATION

The hydrogeology of a site, site area, travel times to the nearest target, toxicity, persistence and sorptive properties of chemicals present on the site have all been used to classify its final hazard potential of each site. The classification system for sites currently in use was based upon calculations of shortest chemical travel times to provide information for establishing monitoring networks. A different approach has been taken for old sites, which were classed in terms of their remediation requirements. The modelling system described here (Figure 5) is that for the assessment of old sites.

The first step in the modelling system is to calculate the subsurface flow directions. These are assumed to follow the direction of the steepest descent of the ground surface, and have been calculated from the DTM. The next stage is to evaluate the distance to the nearest downstream target for each site. This distance is converted to an 'effective' distance to account for the angle of the target to the estimated on-site flow direction. Using the hydrogeological data, the travel times are then calculated for water from a site to reach its nearest target. To estimate these times, a conceptual model of the lateral flow pathways must be developed. First, the presence or absence of boulder clay beneath the site is established: if present, travel times are calculated assuming lateral flow via a perched water table above the boulder clay (assuming a mean transmissivity within the made ground, sand and sandy-clay); if absent, travel times are calculated for lateral transport within the underlying sandstone aquifer.

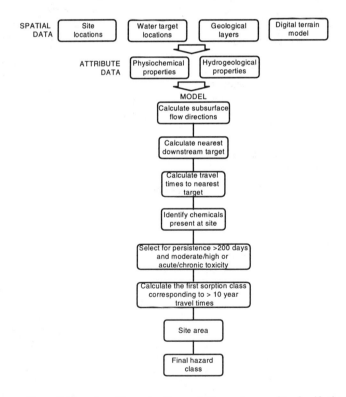

Figure 5. Flow chart illustrating the modelling system used to classify the sites.

At this stage in the modelling system, the industry on each site and hence its associated chemicals are identified. Only chemicals with a persistence greater than 200 days and with at least moderate toxicity are considered. The travel times of these remaining chemicals to the nearest target are then assessed.

The effective speed of travel of a chemical in water is equal to the water velocity multiplied by the chemical's retardation factor. Within this modelling system the retardation factor has been calculated assuming a linear sorption isotherm. Each chemical is placed into one of five sorption classes: no adsorption (< 50 L/kg); virtually no adsorption (50-150L/kg); moderate adsorption (150-2000L/kg); high adsorption (2000-20000L/kg); and very high adsorption (>20000L/kg) (Sawyer et al. 1994). From this classification their effective speed of migration from a site to its nearest target can be calculated. If chemicals are present on a site from each sorption class, this results in five different travel times for each site. In each case the travel time for the highest sorbing chemical on a site was considerably longer than the lapsed time since the site went out of use. Therefore, to distinguish between sites, the number of chemicals thought still to be present on the site was calculated. It was assumed that travel times of less than 10 years would imply that the chemical was no longer persistent (since the old sites were mapped at the turn of the century).

This method produced 3 chemical travel time classes (plus one no-threat class for all site travel times > 1000years). Calculation of the final hazard index for each was assessed by combining the information on chemical travel time with the size of the potentially contaminated site area (Figure 6). Site areas were divided into three classes: >10000 m^2; >1000 m^2; and <1000 m^2. Each chemical travel time class (1-3) was divided into 3 subclasses based on site area. An extra hazard index (10) was added to the system to represent sites that have no threat, either because no chemicals are sufficiently persistent and toxic, or because the shortest travel times are greater than 1000 years. The result is that each site has been given a hazard index of between one and ten; one representing the highest hazard potential, and ten representing the lowest hazard potential.

4 RESULTS

The distribution of old sites within each hazard index for the Newcastle District is given in Table 1. The industries that fall into index one tend to be close to the river Tyne; 8 of the 15 that come into class 1 are ceramic-cement-asphalt works; the others are metal works or dockyard/land areas.

Table 2 gives distribution of indices for each industrial type. This shows that any one industry is not tied down to a single index. For example, the first industry in the table, ceramic-cement-asphalt works, falls into six indices and it is interesting to note that these are at either end of the hazard index range. This indicates that the site area, the hydrogeology of the site and the distance to the river all play an important role in determining the hazard index.

5 CONCLUSIONS

A contaminated land assessment system, CLASS, has been developed and applied to the Newcastle District. CLASS has been designed around a source-pathway-target approach to predicting pollution migration. A category system of ranks and ranges, similar to that within the groundwater vulnerability estimator DRASTIC, has been applied to estimate a hazard index for all industrial and ex-industrial sites. Determination of a hazard index for ex-industrial

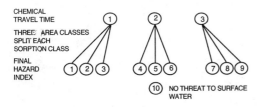

Figure 6. Three chemical travel time classes subdivided by three area classes giving nine hazard indices, onto which a tenth is added indicating no threat by the industry.

Table 1. Number of sites in each class for the old city.

CLASS	No of sites
1	15
2	18
3	9
4	1
5	4
6	3
7	3
8	20
9	10
10	13

461

Table 2. Distribution of the hazard index for each industrial type.

Industry Type	Hazard Index									
	1	2	3	4	5	6	7	8	9	10
Ceramics-cement-asphalt	X	X	X					X	X	X
Inorganic chemical works	X	X		X	X			X		X
Ordnance works			X							
Railway Engineering works	X									
Gas/Coke works		X						X		
Iron & Steel works								X	X	X
Oil refineries	X									
Pulp & Paper works		X								
Textile & Dye works			X		X					X
Timber products works							X	X		
Dry cleaners								X		
Glass manufacturing works										X
Animal processing works						X				X

sites is based upon an estimation of the distribution of chemical travel times to near-by surface water targets. The index is derived using five physical and chemical attributes: water travel time; contaminated site area; sorption; persistence; and toxicity.

Application of CLASS to the Newcastle District has identified 96 ex-industrial and 31 current industrial sites (some of which are coincident). The ex-industrial sites have been categorised into 10 indices for assessment of future hazard potential. The distribution of industrial sites within each of these indices shows that not only the type of industry, but also the location, area and hydrogeology of the site, all play a vital role in the assignment of the hazard index.

CLASS is a potentially powerful and valuable tool for identifying contaminated sites and assessing their hazard potential. It is hoped that it will form an integral part of Newcastle City Council's approach to planning site assessment, monitoring and remediation. The design of the system enables easy incorporation of new data as they become available from site investigation programmes, thus facilitating continuous updating of the database and increasing the reliability of the hazard indices for each site.

REFERENCES

Aller, L., T. Bennet, J.H. Lehr & R. J. Petty 1987. DRASTIC: A standardised system for evaluating groundwater pollution potential using hydrogeologic settings. *USEPA Document #EPA/600/2-85-018*.

Department of the Environment (DoE) *Industry Profiles*. 1995.Environment Act 1995: Statutory Guidance and Regulations on Contaminated Land.

ESRI 1995. *Understanding Geographical Information Systems GIS : The ARC/INFO method* Redlands, California: Environmental Systems Research Institute.

ESRI 1991. *ARC/INFO User's Guide, Version 6.0.* Redlands, California: Environmental Systems Research Institute.

Marsily, G. de 1986. *Quantitative Hydrogeology*. Academic Press.

Rundquist, D.C., A.J. Peters, L. Di, D.A. Rodekohr, R.L. Ehrman & G. Murray 1991. Statewide groundwater vulnerability assessment in Nebraska using the DRASTIC/GIS Model. *Geocarto International*. 6 (2): 51-57.

Sawyer, C.N., P.L. McCarthy, & G.F. Parkin 1994. *Chemisty for Environmental Engineering*. Fourth Edition. McGraw-Hill.

Impact of urbanization on shallow groundwater in Lithuania

A. Klimas
Vilnius Hydrogeology Ltd, Lithuania

ABSTRACT: The population of some Lithuanian cities and towns still use shallow groundwater from dug wells for drinking. In many places, this water recharges deeper aquifers. Therefore it is important to know, monitor and control the state of such groundwater in urbanized areas. Results of three-years of investigation in six cities served as a basis for working out an original methodology of hydrogeological studies in the cities, similar to that of GIS technologies. These studies do not require large financial means, since data of former investigations are usually used for assessment of the state of shallow groundwater in the cities.

1 INTRODUCTION

The influence of urbanization on the quality of shallow groundwater is important in two aspects: (1) well owners drink this water in city areas, where there are no centralized water supply systems; (2) this water recharges deeper aquifers, especially those which are intensively exploited.

During the last three to four years, we have carried out detailed studies of shallow groundwater quality in four Lithuanian cities (Klimas 1995; 1996). The location of the cities is shown in Figure 1. The results have shown that cities exert a negative influence on shallow groundwater (Figure 2). First of all, cities pollute water. Due to spills from underground pipe-lines and changes in groundwater recharge conditions in the built up areas, the groundwater table rises and causes flooding. Moreover, cities warm up the subsurface causing changes in microbiochemistry and shallow groundwater chemistry. Similar problems are known to occur in cities and towns in many countries (Lerner &Barrett 1996; Shwecov 1991). In order to investigate and map all these and other hydrogeological changes in the upper part of the geological section of Lithuania, we have proposed an original methodology (Klimas 1996). The present paper is to deal with the generalized results of such studies. Some data about the cities studied are given in Table 1 below.

Table 1. Some data about the cities studied.

City	Area, km^2	Population in 1996	Number of water intakes	Centralized water supply, m^3/d
Siauliai	69.33	146000	4	24500
Panevezys	29.78	132000	1	28000
Jonava	10.64	26000	1	6930
Varena	11.94	7000	1	3760

2 METHODS

The basic steps for the assessment of the effect of urbanization on urban hydrogeological conditions are as follows: (i) formation of computerized data bases (CDB); (ii) control investigations; (iii) mapping of the area; (iv) modelling of pollution processes, (v) monitoring optimization.

In special case a GIS (Geological Information Systems) approach has been effectively applied for identification of natural and anthropogenic factors limiting city growth and complicating groundwater protection (Klimas 1995).

2.1 *CDB Formation and control investigations*

Three basic information sources are used in

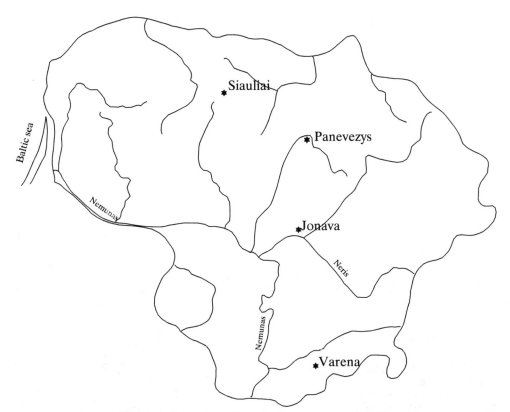

Figure 1. Location of studied urban areas in Lithuania.

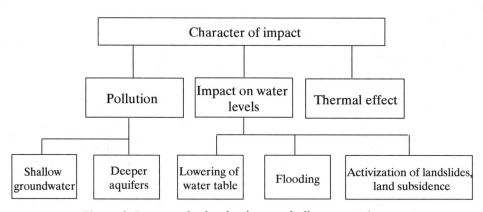

Figure 2. Impact of urbanization on shallow groundwater.

characterising the shallow groundwater: 1 - data from Public Health Care Centres concerning dug well investigations; 2 - data from geotechnical borings; 3 - data from monitoring boreholes. The size of the CDB is given in Table 2.

There are two basic CDB formation problems: (1) there are no dug wells in the industrial areas, and few geotechnical boreholes in the residential areas; (2) dug well data usually characterize the latest 5-10 year period, whereas those of geotechnical boreholes cover longer period.

Table 2. CDB structure and volume in the cities investigated.

City	Period covered by CDB	Dug wells* (1)	Dug wells* (2)	Geotechnical boreholes* (1)	Geotechnical boreholes* (2)
Siauliai	1957 - 1996	110	132	405	417
Panevezys	1958 - 1995	87	1190	500	503
Jonava	1962 - 1994	430	741	74	74
Varėna	1973 - 1996	59	331	47	49

*(1) number of boreholes and wells, (2) number of water chemical analyses

Statistical analyses of the data have shown that there arc no substantial differences between the dug well and geotechnical borehole data, whereas control investigations revealed the fact that anomalies in shallow groundwater pollution in the cities are stable in time and space. Therefore, in order to detect them, water analyses from different times could be used.

2.2 Mapping and modelling

The principle of the hydrogeological mapping of urban areas is similar to that of GIS. Usually three maps are compiled: urbanization, groundwater dynamics and hydrochemistry. Groundwater dynamics map shows lithology of water-bearing rocks, and groundwater flow structure, i.e., head contours and water flow lines.

Industrial, residential and green areas are distinguished in the urbanization map. Industrial and residential areas are further zoned with more details according to potential effect on shallow groundwater.

Hydrochemical maps contain isocones of various groundwater quality criteria drawn from CDB data by the kriging method. After all three maps are superimposed one on the another, the position of isocones is adjusted, and all the CDB data about groundwater quality are grouped according to their position in the above-mentioned urbanization and groundwater dynamics maps. After statistical treatment, the groundwater quality characteristics are obtained for certain urban areas reflecting different urban and hydrogeological conditions in a city. In order to get an integrated picture of the urban effect on shallow groundwater, the summarized anomaly coefficients are determined from groundwater quality indices, then after treatment by factorial analysis, the zones of greatest groundwater pollution and those of pollutant migration are defined. If necessary,

pollutant migration can be modelled, with compilation of conceptual, filtration and migration models for the urban areas. Such models enable evaluation of urban effects on deeper aquifers. Flooding phenomena in shallow aquifers are identified according to water level anomalies shown in the groundwater dynamics maps. The type of built-over areas, amount of underground communications, their density and state are taken into account.

Thermal impact of the urban areas on shallow groundwater is determined directly by measuring its temperature in the dug wells and monitoring wells, and distinguishing anomalies: anomalies in water chemistry also provide indirect evidence.

2.3 Groundwater monitoring

Mapping of shallow groundwater quality and its modelling enable us to propose a new system of groundwater monitoring or to optimize the existing ones. Such systems in the shallow aquifers should, first of all, control the groundwater state in the zones of pollution and pollutant migration.

3 URBAN IMPACT ON SHALLOW GROUNDWATER QUALITY

The effect of urbanization on shallow groundwater quality is expressed in three ways:
1. Groundwater is polluted by substances which do not occur naturally in the aquifer;
2. Pollution increases the concentration of already existing components;
3. Pollutants are transformed in the aquifer by means of interaction with water-bearing rocks, thus supplementing the groundwater chemistry with new compounds.

Typical representatives of the first category are hydrocarbons and detergents, the second - chlorides and sulphates, and the third - organic usually nitrogen-containing compounds.

Long-term data show that the composition of shallow groundwater under the impact of pollution is developing in a well ordered manner. The neutral oxygen-rich environment that prevailed in a clean hydrogeological medium is gradually being replaced by a slightly alkaline or alkaline anoxic environment under the conditions of intensive pollution (Klimas 1994).

The upper part of the geological section, being in good communication with the atmosphere, even under conditions of intensive pollution, has shallow groundwater that contains oxygen. The dominant reaction - the nitrification of organics containing nitrogen in the form of ammonium - occurs in two stages:

$$2NH_4^+ + 3O_2 \rightarrow 2NO_2^- + 2H_2^+ + 2H_2O \qquad (1)$$

$$2NO_2^- + O_2 \rightarrow 2NO_3^- \qquad (2)$$

Organic matter is also oxidized:

$$CH_2O + O_2 \rightarrow CO_2 + H_2O \qquad (3)$$

Carbonic acid produced in this reaction reacts with carbonaceous rocks - limestone and dolomite:

$$CO_2 + CaCO_3 + H_2O \Leftrightarrow Ca^{2+} + 2HCO_3^- \qquad (4)$$

$$2CO_2 + CaMg(CO_3)_2 + 2H_2O \Leftrightarrow Ca^{2+} + Mg^{2+} + +4HCO_3^- \qquad (5)$$

Because of this reason, the alkalinity and hardness of shallow groundwater increases. When the rate of pollution input into the groundwater exceeds the available supply of dissolved oxygen, e.g. in the areas built-over and under asphalt, nitrate reduction occurs, i.e. denitrification:

$$4NO_3^- + 5CH_2O \rightarrow 2N_2 + 4HCO_3^- + CO_2 + 3H_2O \qquad (6)$$

or ammonification:

$$NO_3^- + 2CH_2O + H_2O \rightarrow NH_4^+ + 2HCO_3^- \qquad (7)$$

Due to the above reactions, water alkalinity increases further, and ammonium accumulates. Analysis of the shallow groundwater chemistry in the above cities confirms that this is how shallow groundwater quality is developing in the urbanized areas. Only in rare cases the shallow aquifers achieve more reduced conditions, when manganese, iron and sulphates are reduced. These phenomena are more typical of deeper polluted aquifers (Klimas 1994). Dependence of chemistry in the cities on various factors is shown by the data presented in Table 3.

The data of Table 3 show that virtually all the cities studied have shallow groundwater more or less polluted with nitrate and non-oxidized organic. Moreover, water is more polluted in the larger cities. The quality of shallow groundwater depends less on rock composition and more on economic activities in some part of a city.

There are large differences in shallow groundwater chemistry as observed in industrial when compared with residential districts. There is a general tendency for shallow groundwater

of industrial areas to contain more sulphate and chloride, to be harder, and to be more mineralized. In residential areas it is more rich in nitrate and non-oxidized organic matter.

In order better to relate the groundwater chemistry and its transformations with certain types of economic activity and compositions of rocks, factor analysis of the entire hydrochemical information stored in CDB has been carried out. This analysis enabled the groundwater quality parameters to be grouped as follows:
1. Total mineralization, total hardness, chloride, sulphate, calcium and magnesium;
2. Permanganate oxidation, bicarbonate, ammonium, nitrate, nitrite.

The first group of parameters show anomalies in the industrial areas and second group - in residential areas. After these anomalies are drawn on the map, areas of industrial and municipal pollution of shallow groundwater are marked. When these areas are "shifted" according to the groundwater flow, pollutant migration zones also are distinguished.

4 IMPACT ON DEEPER AQUIFERS

The influence of urbanization on deeper semi-confined aquifers is revealed at the time when these aquifers are insufficiently isolated from polluted shallow groundwater or when they are being heavily pumped.

Our investigation in the cities mentioned shows that from the ground surface to a depth of about 30 m the confined water chemistry is similar to that of the shallow groundwater, except for the fact that the confined groundwater always contains less nitrate, but more ammonia and bicarbonate. Such changes in the confined groundwater chemistry are observed to depths of 70 to 100 m. Below these depths, the groundwater practically never contains nitrate and is enriched with iron and manganese, and sometimes with hydrogen sulphide. This indicates a change in redox environment in the polluted deeper aquifers compared with the unpolluted ones. Especially typical is the increase in alkalinity that is the result of redox reactions describes in section 3. Such phenomena are observed in Siauliai and Panevezys water intakes to depths of 180 to 250 m.

5 OTHER PROCESSES

Other geological-hydrogeological processes of

Table 3. Arithmetic average of some figures reflecting chemistry of shallow groundwater

Parameter	Dimension	Cities				Water containing rocks		Urbanization type	
		Siau-liai	Pane-vezys	Jona-va	Vare-na	sandy loam	sand	Indus-trial	Resi-dential
BM*	mg/l	910	959	676	401	915	760	911	830
BK*	mg-ekv/l	12.5	11.0	8.6	5.5	11.7	8.8	11.8	10.7
pH	-	7.3	7.4	7.4	7.4	7.3	7.4	7.4	7.4
PO*	mgO$_2$/l	4.7	5.0	3.8	2.5	5.1	3.9	4.2	4.8
Cl$^-$	mg/l	150	101	245	45	95	192	182	134
SO$_4^{2-}$	mg/l	187	137	105	50	141	110	185	119
HCO$_3^-$	mg/l	544	493	417	274	498	436	517	482
NO$_2^-$	mg/l	0.2	0.04	0.20	-	0.29	0.33	0.13	0.30
NO$_3^-$	mg/l	46	73	58	23	72	47	13	67
NH$_4^+$	mg/l	1.4	1.85	0.63	0.25	1.4	0.9	1.7	1.16
n *	mg/l	441	1880	857	380	1784	1453	678	2536

* BM - total mineralization, BK - total hardness, PO - permanganate oxidation, n - number of analyses

anthropogenic origin are less common than the shallow groundwater pollution described above.

A lowering of the water table is, first of all, observed at sites of intense water extraction. The water table can be lowered to a decrease in recharge in the areas under buildings and asphalt. All this can cause a negative impact on vegetation. However the most important thing is that in these cases the quality of shallow groundwater is always deteriorated. After the water level has been lowered, the slightly alkaline reducing environment usually prevailing in the shallow groundwater becomes slightly acid and oxidising. Atmospheric oxygen oxidizes organic matter stored in the polluted and dewatered soils; thus infiltrating water becomes more carbonic-acid-aggressive and hard. The dried up peatbogs show process of oxidation of pyrite and, hence, increase in iron and sulphate contents in shallow groundwater.

Rising groundwater tables or flooding are more common phenomena in the cities. To occur, certain geological- hydrogeological conditions are necessary as well as an additional groundwater recharge source. The most typical and important geological- hydrogeological precondition for flooding is a weak drainage capability in the area. The common additional infiltration source is leakage from underground pipelines. Such areas are notable for positive shallow groundwater table anomalies in the cities studied. Their height reaches 2-3 m, on average, but in Siauliai it is even higher - 6 m, in Panevezys - 5 m and Jonava - 4 m.

The thermal effect of urbanization on shallow groundwater is not very pronounced. For instance, the temperature anomaly in Varena differs from the background by 4°C. Most probably, thermal anomalies could also be distinguished according to anomalies in water chemistry, i.e. microbial activity is increased and so water aggressivity is increased, as well as alkalinity.

6 MONITORING

Usually some monitoring of groundwater is already carried out in the cities. For instance, the state of shallow groundwater in Lithuania is being regularly controlled by the Public Health Care Centres. Quantity, quality and levels of groundwater are measured in the samples taken from the centralized water intakes by the corresponding enterprises exploiting water. The influence of pollution sources on groundwater is also controlled by some other institutions. Therefore groundwater monitoring systems in the cities should not be created, just optimized. We have proposed the principles for such optimization. Their essence embraces distinguishing of monitoring priorities with determination of the first- and second-order monitoring.

The first-order monitoring should be organized in those sites where shallow groundwater is not only used but also polluted (1a). Pollution should be controlled in those sites where there is no groundwater users, but the polluted shallow groundwater contaminates or can contaminate deeper aquifers used as drinking water sources (1b). The second-order monitoring is organized in those sites where polluted but unusable shallow groundwater penetrates deeper and pollutes or can pollute still unused confined aquifers - potential sources of drinking water (2a). Such monitoring of shallow groundwater is also organized in those sites where this water (although not polluted) is still used by residents (2b), as well as in those sites where it is not used and exerts no influence on deeper layers but is being polluted (2c).

Practically, monitoring priority areas in the cities are determined according to GIS technology, by superimposition of maps compiled for drinking water sources, urbanization, groundwater quality anomalies and separate quality parameters.

7 CONCLUSIONS

Impacts of urbanization on shallow groundwater can be revealed by mapping chemical characteristics, physical characteristics, and directions of groundwater flow. The patterns in the maps compiled indicate a generalized form of spatial structures - anomalies. Analysis of the evolution of such patterns enable determination of not only changes in shallow groundwater quality and quantity, but also their causes. This, in turn, provides a basis for optimising monitoring systems for shallow groundwater. This enables control and management of the shallow groundwater.

REFERENCES

Klimas, A.A. 1994. Fresh groundwater quality formation regularities under technogenic impacts. *Scientific Papers 5 of the Geological Society of Lithuania:* 1 - 56.

Klimas, A. A. 1995. Impacts of urbanisation and protection of water resources in the Vilnius District, Lithuania. *Hydrogeology Journal 3/(1):* 24 - 35.

Klimas, A. A. 1996. Methology for mapping shallow groundwater quality in urbanized areas: A case study from Lithuania. *Environmental Geology* 27/(4): 320 - 328.

Lerner, D.N. & M.H. Barrett 1996. Urban groundwater issues in the United Kingdom. *Hydrogeology Journal* 4/(1): 80 - 102.

Shwecov P.F. (ed.) 1991. *Stationary models of hydrolithosphere in urban agglomerations (Moscow agglomeration).* Moscow: Nauka.

Pesticides and volatile organic compounds in shallow urban groundwater of the United States

D.W.Kolpin
US Geological Survey, Iowa City, Iowa, USA

P.J.Squillace & J.S.Zogorski
US Geological Survey, Rapid City, S.Dak., USA

J.E.Barbash
US Geological Survey, Menlo Park, Calif., USA

ABSTRACT: The widespread use of pesticides and volatile organic compounds (VOCs) over the past half century has led to their detection in many hydrologic systems in the United States. However, few systematic investigations of occurrence have been carried out over multistate regions using a consistent study design. Nine urban studies of shallow groundwater have been conducted to date as part of the U.S. Geological Survey's National Water-Quality Assessment Program. Pesticide compounds were detected in 48.6% of the 208 urban wells sampled. Sixteen different pesticide compounds were detected in samples from these wells. Prometon was by far the most frequently detected pesticide compound, being found in 8 of the 9 urban studies. VOCs were detected in 53.4% of the 208 urban wells sampled, with 36 different VOC compounds being found. Measured VOC concentrations exceeded current U.S. Environmental Protection Agency drinking water regulations in 19 wells. Methyl *tert*-butyl ether (MTBE), a common fuel oxygenate, was the most frequently detected VOC for this study.

1 INTRODUCTION

The widespread use of pesticides and volatile organic compounds (VOCs) over the past half century has led to their detection in many hydrologic systems in the United States. Contamination of groundwater by pesticides and VOCs is an important issue in the United States because groundwater is used for drinking water by about 50 percent of the population. A large number of studies have examined the occurrence of pesticides and VOCs in groundwater beneath selected areas of the United States over the past three decades. However, few systematic investigations have been carried out over multistate regions using a consistent study design (Barbash & Resek 1996). Few data are currently available in the United States on the effect of urban land use on groundwater quality -- particularly with respect to urban pesticide use.

In 1991, the U.S. Geological Survey (USGS) began full-scale implementation of the National Water-Quality Assessment (NAWQA) Program to examine the quality of ground and surface water resources in 60 major hydrologic basins (study units), covering about 50% of the contiguous United States (Leahy & Thompson 1994; Gilliom et al. 1995). The NAWQA study units are divided into three groups, to be intensively studied in 9-year cycles on a rotational schedule.

Land-use studies (Gilliom et al. 1995) are one component of the groundwater quality assessments conducted by each NAWQA study unit. These studies examine shallow groundwater quality within well-defined environmental settings characterized by specific types of land use and hydrogeology. A complete data set for land-use studies from the first 20 NAWQA study units is not yet available. However, a national assessment of groundwater quality—and the processes that control it—will be obtained by combining the results from NAWQA study-unit investigations from across the country, building over time as study-unit cycles are completed.

This paper describes the occurrence of pesticides and VOCs in shallow groundwater from the initial set of nine land-use studies completed in urban areas by the first group of 20 NAWQA study units. The objective of this discussion is to provide an initial summary of the concentrations and frequencies of detection of selected pesticides and VOCs in shallow groundwater within a variety of urban settings across the United States.

2 METHODS

The primary objective of each land-use study is to determine the quality of recently recharged groundwater (generally within the past 10 years) within a specific land-use and hydrogeologic setting (Gilliom et al. 1995). By focusing on recently recharged groundwater, the land-use studies provide a direct assessment of the effects of specific human activities on groundwater quality, and an early warning of the potential for contamination of major aquifers farther downgradient (vertically or horizontally) or nearby surface waters receiving groundwater discharge. Nine urban land-use studies, representing 208 wells, had sufficient data to be included in this initial summary of the pesticide and VOC results (Figure 1). Of these nine urban land-use studies, six were of unconsolidated and three were of bedrock aquifers. Most of these urbanized areas represent large (>1,000,000) population centers.

The types and locations of wells sampled and the manner in which they are selected can have a strong influence on which pesticides and VOCs are detected in a groundwater study, as well as the frequency and spatial distribution of the detections (Barbash & Resek 1996). In an attempt to make study results comparable among different areas, the groundwater sampling design of NAWQA employs specific rules regarding the procedures for selecting existing wells or locations for wells to be installed (Gilliom et al. 1995; Lapham et al. 1995; Squillace et al. 1996). The geographic domain of each land-use study is defined by a specific combination of hydrogeologic conditions and targeted land use.

To the extent possible, the sampling locations selected for each urban land-use study were randomly distributed throughout the hydrogeologic/ land-use setting of interest using a grid-based selection method (Scott 1990). Wells previously installed to investigate known or suspected contamination were avoided. Except for some "up-gradient" monitoring wells, sampled wells were either existing or newly installed low-capacity wells screened near the water table and located in what were presumed to be recharge areas, either within or directly downgradient from the land-use setting of interest.

All samples were collected by USGS personnel using established protocols and procedures designed to obtain water samples representative of the targeted aquifer (Koterba et al. 1995). Before water samples were collected, each site was pumped until field-measured values of pH, water temperature, specific conductance, and dissolved-oxygen concentration stabilized. Samples for pesticide analyses were passed through a 0.7 μm, baked, glass-fiber filter to remove suspended particles. One litre of sample was either (a) stored in an amber, baked glass bottle and immediately chilled prior to and during shipment to the laboratory, or (b) pumped through a solid-phase extraction cartridge, chilled, and shipped to the laboratory. Samples for VOC analyses were collected in an environmental chamber to protect the samples from airborne contamination, preserved with hydrochloric acid to a pH of 2 or less,

Figure 1. Location of 208 wells for the initial set of nine urban land–use studies conducted by the U.S. Geological Survey, National Water–Quality Assessment Program.

chilled, and shipped to the laboratory.

A capillary column gas chromatography/mass spectrometry method (Zaugg et al. 1995) was used to analyze for 25 herbicides, 17 insecticides, 2 herbicide degradates, and 2 insecticide degradates. The method detection limits for these pesticide compounds ranged from 0.001 to 0.018 µg/L. A purge-and-trap capillary column gas chromatography/mass spectrometry method (Rose & Schroeder 1995) was used to analyze for 60 VOCs. The analytical reporting limit for all VOCs in this method was 0.20 µg/L.

3 INITIAL PESTICIDE RESULTS

Pesticide compounds (i.e. parent compounds or degradates) were commonly detected in shallow urban groundwater, with one or more compounds detected in 48.6% of the 208 wells sampled for this study. Sixteen different pesticide compounds were detected in samples from these wells (Table 1). Herbicides were detected much more frequently than insecticides (44.7% versus 8.2%), reflecting, in part, the fact that herbicides are used far more extensively than insecticides in the United States (Aspelin 1994). Other factors such as variations in physical and chemical properties, and method or timing of application may also have contributed to the greater frequency of detection for the herbicides relative to the insecticides. The method detection limits for the pesticide compounds detected in the urban land-use studies were not consistent; thus, the relative rankings of the frequencies of detections listed in Table 1 may be somewhat misleading. Research has documented an inverse relation between method detection limits and the frequency of pesticide detection (Kolpin et al. 1995; Barbash & Resek 1996). To compensate for this inconsistency, Figure 2 presents the frequencies of pesticide detection after adjusting to a common reporting limit of 0.01 µg/L. Prometon was by far the most frequently detected compound (Figure 2), having been found in 8 of the 9 urban land-use studies. Prometon is unique among the pesticides examined in that it appears to be used only for non-agricultural purposes such as domestic and commercial applications to driveways and fence lines, on lawns and gardens, as an asphalt additive, or as a soil sterilant before asphalt is put in place (Pasquarell & Boyer 1996). There was a significant, positive relation (P=0.008; Spearman rank correlation) between population density (a surrogate for the intensity of urban land use) and the frequency of prometon detection in shallow groundwater (Figure 3). Thus, in general, the greater amount of urbanization near sampled wells, the greater the frequency of prometon detection in shallow groundwater. Earlier research also documented a direct relation between urban land use and prometon detection in groundwa-

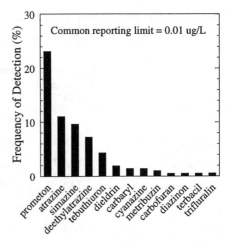

Figure 2. Frequency of detection of selected pesticide compounds in urban wells, following adjustment to a common reporting limit of 0.01 ug/L.

EXPLANATION

○   Agricultural Land-Use Studies

•   Urban Land-Use Studies

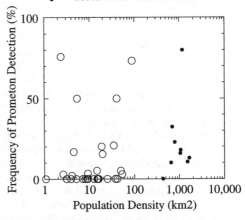

Figure 3. Relation between the frequency of prometon detection in shallow groundwater and the degree of urbanization within NAWQA land-use studies (based on median population density of sampled wells in each of the 40 initial land-use studies).

ter (Burkart & Kolpin 1993). The non-agricultural use of prometon (for example, use on rights-of-way or associated with hard-surface roads) may explain the frequent prometon detections in some agricul-

471

Table 1. Pesticide compounds in groundwater samples collected for the 9 urban land-use studies.
[MCL, maximum contaminant level; HA, health advisory level; ---, not established]

Compound	Frequency of detection (%)	Reporting limit (µg/L)	Maximum concentration (µg/L)	MCL, HA[1] (µg/L)	Number of wells exceeding an MCL or HA
Pesticides[2]					
Prometon	26.4	0.005	4.0	<u>100</u>	0
Atrazine	18.8	0.002	2.3	3	0
Deethylatrazine[3]	14.4	0.002	0.56	---	--
Simazine	10.6	0.005	1.1	4	0
Tebuthiuron	4.8	0.015	0.08	<u>500</u>	0
DDE, p,p'-[4]	2.9	0.002	0.002	---	--
Dieldrin[5]	2.4	0.005	0.045	---	--
Volatile Organic Compounds[6]					
Methyl *tert*-butyl ether	26.0	0.2	23,000	<u>20</u>[7]	6
Chloroform	24.5	0.2	12	100	0
Tetrachloroethene	21.1	0.2	4,800	5	9
Trichloroethene	10.1	0.2	230	5	3
cis-1,2 dichlorethene	6.7	0.2	82	70	1
1,1-Dichloroethane	5.3	0.2	2.2	--	--

[1]U.S. Environmental Protection Agency (1996)
[2]The following pesticide compounds were also detected in fewer than 2% of the wells: carbaryl, metolachlor, metribuzin, cyanazine, diazinon, carbofuran, propanil, terbacil, and trifluralin
[3]Formed from the degradation of atrazine or propazine
[4]Formed from the degradation of DDT
[5]Also could have been formed from the degradation of the insecticide, aldrin
[6]The following VOCs were also detected in fewer than 5% of the wells: dichlorobromomethane, carbon tetrachloride, chlorodibromomethane, toluene, benzene, chlorobenzene, chloroethane, ethylbenzene, methylene chloride, trichlorofluoromethane, 1,1-dichloroethene, 1,1,1-trichloroethane, 1,2-dichlorobenzene, 1,2-dichloropropane, *trans*-1,2-dichloroethene, 1,4-dichlorobenzene, dichlorodifluoromethane, naphthalene, vinyl chloride, 1,2,4-trimethylbenzene, isopropylbenzene, propylbenzene, 1,3,5-trimethylbenzene, butylbenzene, *sec*-butylbenzene, *tert*-butylbenzene, isopropyltoluene, trichlorotrifluoroethane, xylenes
[7]Lower value in estimated range for Draft Lifetime Health Advisory

tural land-use studies (Figure 3). Factors such as hydrogeology and soils also are likely important processes contributing to the transport of prometon to groundwater.

Although there are few data currently available on pesticide use in urban areas, the pesticides detected more frequently during the urban studies (Figure 2) are generally those used more commonly in urban settings (Barbash & Resek 1996; Gianessi & Puffer 1991). Indeed, with the exception of carbofuran and cyanazine, all of the pesticide compounds detected in the urban land-use studies (Figure 2) are known to be applied in non-agricultural settings (Barbash & Resek 1996; Gianessi & Puffer 1991; Meister 1995).

Although dacthal is known to have significant non-agricultural use, no dacthal was detected in this study. The absence of dacthal was not unexpected, however, because of the strong affinity of this compound for clay particles and organic matter in the soil and its low water solubility (U.S. Environmental Protection Agency 1992). Previous research, however, has noted frequent detections in groundwater of the principal dacthal degradation products in groundwater; these degradates having been more frequently detected in wells surrounded by higher amounts of urban land and golf courses (Kolpin et al. 1996; U.S. Environmental Protection Agency 1992)

No pesticide concentrations measured in these urban areas exceeded current U.S. Environmental Protection Agency drinking water regulations or health advisory levels (Table 1). This lack of exceedences, however, may provide an inaccurate picture of pesticides in shallow urban groundwater for several reasons. First, these drinking water criteria only consider the effects of individual compounds and do not account for the presence of multiple pesticide compounds. Research has indicated that some combinations of pesticide compounds can have additive or synergistic toxicity (Marinovich et al. 1996; Thompson 1996). For this study, 45.5% of the urban sampling sites where pesticides were detected had two or more compounds present. Second, other pesticide compounds not examined for this study, particularly pesticide degradates, have been detected in groundwater (Kolpin et al. 1997; Potter & Carpenter 1995) that also could have potential health effects (Bain & LeBlanc 1996; Tessier & Clark 1995). Finally, recent research suggests that some pesticide compounds may potentially cause deleterious health effects at levels considered safe by current standards (e.g. Biradar and Rayburn 1995).

4 INITIAL VOLATILE ORGANIC COMPOUND RESULTS

VOCs were commonly detected in shallow urban groundwater, with one or more VOCs detected in 53.4% of the 208 wells. A total of 36 different VOCs were detected in samples from these wells (Table 1). Measured VOC concentrations exceeded current U.S. Environmental Protection Agency drinking water regulations or health advisory levels in 19 wells (Table 1). Methyl *tert*-butyl ether (MTBE) was the most frequently detected VOC in this study. MTBE is the most commonly used gasoline oxygenate in the United States (Squillace et al. 1996). The use of oxygenates in gasoline is mandated by the 1990 Clean Air Act Amendments in some metropolitan areas in an effort to reduce atmospheric concen-

trations of carbon monoxide or ozone. MTBE is also used in many parts of the United States to increase the octane rating of gasoline.

Chloroform was the second most frequently detected VOC for this study. These detections may have been related to the presence of chloroform in chlorinated drinking water as a disinfection by-product. Chlorine is commonly added to public-water supplies and has been used in the United States since the early 1900's for preventing waterborne diseases (Cooper et al. 1993). In many urban areas, chlorinated water is used for the irrigation of lawns. Thus, chloroform may reach shallow groundwater in urban areas via transport in chlorinated irrigation water. The detections of two other disinfection by-products, dichlorobromomethane and chlorodibromomethane, support this hypothesis. However, there are many other sources of chloroform, including the degradation of other VOCS, that also may have contributed to its detection in shallow urban groundwater.

The remaining four VOCs detected in at least 5% of the sampled wells (Table 1) are chlorinated solvents. They are used as degreasers, chemical intermediates, and in the manufacture of carbon-based products such as plastics, rubber, perfumes, and lacquers. Some of the detections of these four VOCs may also have arisen from the degradation of other VOCs.

5 CONCLUSIONS

The NAWQA urban land-use studies represent the first systematic attempt to document the effects of urban land use on shallow groundwater quality in the United States on a national scale. Pesticides and VOCs were commonly detected in shallow groundwater beneath nine urban areas across the United States during the first set of these studies, with pesticide compounds being detected in 48.6% and VOCs in 53.4% of the 208 wells sampled. Sixteen different pesticides and 36 different VOCs were detected for this study. The detections of these compounds in shallow urban groundwater appeared to be related to their urban use.

REFERENCES

Aspelin, A.L. 1994. *Pesticides industry sales and usage, 1992 and 1993 market estimates.* U.S.Environmental Protection Agency, Office of Pesticide Programs, 733-K-94-001.
Bain, L.J. & G.A. LeBlanc 1996. Interaction of structurally diverse pesticides with the human *MDR1* gene product p-glycoprotein. *Toxic. Applied Pharm.* 141:288-298.

Biradar, D.P. & A.L. Rayburn 1995. Chromosomal damage induced by herbicide contamination at concentrations observed in public water supplies. *J. Environ. Qual.* 24:1222-1225.

Burkart, M.R. & D.W. Kolpin 1993. Hydrologic and land-use factors associated with herbicides and nitrate in near-surface aquifers. *J. Environ. Qual.* 22:646-656.

Barbash, J.E. & E.A. Resek 1996. *Pesticides in Ground Water: Distribution, Trends, and Governing Factors*. Chelsea, Michigan: Ann Arbor Press.

Cooper, W.J., E. Cadavid, M.G. Nickelsen, K. Lin, C.N. Kurucz, & T.D. Waite. 1993. Removing THMs from drinking water using high-energy electron-beam irradiation. *Journal AWWA* 85: 106-112.

Gianessi, L.P. & C. Puffer 1991. *Herbicide use in the United States*. Washington, D.C.: Resources for the Future, Inc.

Gilliom, R.J., W.M. Alley & M.E. Gurtz 1995. *Design of the national water-quality assessment program: Occurrence and distribution of water-quality conditions*. U.S. Geological Survey Circular No. 1112.

Kolpin, D.W., D.A. Goolsby & E.M. Thurman 1995. Pesticides in near-surface aquifers: An assessment using highly sensitive analytical methods and tritium. *J. Environ. Qual.* 24:1125-1132.

Kolpin, D.W., S.J. Kalkhoff, D.A. Goolsby, D.A. Sneck-Fahrer & E.M. Thurman 1997. Occurrence of selected herbicides and herbicide degradation products in Iowa's ground water, 1995. *Ground Water* (in press).

Kolpin, D.W., E.M. Thurman & D.A. Goolsby 1996. Occurrence of selected pesticides and their metabolites in near-surface aquifers of the midwestern United States. *Environ. Sci. Technol.* 30:335-340.

Koterba, M.T., F.D. Wilde & W.W. Lapham 1995. *Ground-water data-collection protocols and procedures for the National Water-Quality Assessment Program--collection and documentation of water-quality samples and data*. U.S. Geological Survey Open-File Report 95-399.

Lapham, W.W., F.D. Wilde & M.T. Koterba 1995. *Ground-water data-collection protocols and procedures for the National Water-Quality Assessment Program -- Selection, installation, and documentation of wells, and collection of related data*. U.S. Geological Survey Open-File Report 95-398.

Leahy, P.P. & T.H. Thompson 1994. *U.S. Geological Survey National Water-Quality Assessment Program*. U.S. Geological Survey Open-File Report 94-70.

Marinovich, M.R., F. Ghilardi & C.L. Galli 1996. Effect of pesticide mixtures on in vitro nervous cells. *Toxic.* 108:201-206.

Meister, R.T. (ed.) 1995. *Farm Chemicals Handbook '95*. Willoughby, OH: Meister Publishing Co.

Pasquarell, G.C. & D.G. Boyer 1996. Herbicides in karst groundwater in southeast West Virginia. *J. Environ. Qual.* 25:755-765.

Potter, T.L. & T.L. Carpenter 1995. Occurrence of alachlor environmental degradation products in groundwater. *Environ. Sci. Technol.* 29:1557-1563.

Rose, D.L. & M.P. Schroeder 1995. *Method of analysis by the U.S. Geological Survey National Water Quality Laboratory - determination of volatile organic compounds in water by purge and trap capillary gas chromatography/mass spectrometry*. U.S. Geological Survey Open-File Report 94-708.

Scott, J.C. 1990. *Computerized stratified random site-selection approaches for design of groundwater-quality sampling network*. U.S. Geological Survey Water Resources Investigations Report 90-4101.

Squillace, P.J., J.S. Zogorski, W.G. Wilber & C.V. Price 1996. Preliminary assessment of the occurrence and possible sources of MTBE in groundwater in the United States, 1993-1994. *Env. Sci. Technol.* 30:1721-1730.

Tessier, D.M. & J.M. Clark 1995. Quantitative assessment of the mutagenic potential of environmental degradative products of alachlor. *J. Agric. Food Chem.* 43:2504-2512.

Thompson, H.M. 1996. Interactions between pesticides; a review of reported effects and their implications for wildlife risk assessment. *Ecotoxic.* 5:59-81.

U.S. Environmental Protection Agency 1992. *Another look -- National survey of pesticides in drinking water wells, phase 2 report*. U.S. Environmental Protection Agency Report EPA/579/09-91/020.

U.S. Environmental Protection Agency 1996. *Drinking water regulations and health advisories*. U.S. Environmental Protection Agency Report EPA 822-R-96-001.

Zaugg, S.D., M.W. Sandstrom, S.G. Smith & K.M. Fehlberg 1995. *Methods of analysis by the U.S. Geological Survey National Water Quality Laboratory -- determination of pesticides in water by C-18 solid-phase extraction and capillary-column gas chromatography/mass spectrometry with selected ion monitoring*. U.S. Geological Survey Open-File Report 95-181.

Groundwater in the Urban Environment: Problems, Processes and Management, Chilton et al. (eds)
© *1997 Balkema, Rotterdam, ISBN 90 5410 837 1*

A risk assessment framework for contaminated groundwater

Kenneth A. MacDougall & George Fleming
Department of Civil Engineering, University of Strathclyde, Glasgow, UK

ABSTRACT: This paper describes the formulation of a risk assessment framework, aimed at identifying areas at risk from contaminated groundwater. Risk is dependent upon the nature of the end target population, for example, humans, fish, etc., the nature of the contact, the quantity and concentrations of the contaminant. The foundation for such a risk assessment must lie with an understanding of the local and regional groundwater flow regimes. The framework involves looking at the contaminant concentrations at specific locations, then determining the areas which may be at risk. Other factors which affect the determination of risk and how they may be incorporated into an overall risk value are discussed. Risk may then be determined by the exposure route and type, and concentrations of a particular contaminant which may pose a threat to the population in question.

1 INTRODUCTION

This paper presents a framework for assessing the potential risks posed by contaminated groundwater, and forms part of an ongoing research project. This framework is based upon the following definition of risk;
"the potential for inflicting damage upon a receptor".

Risk assessments are becoming ever increasingly utilised as a means of categorising amounts of contamination and determining remediation strategies. Techniques such as Risk Based Corrective Action - RBCA (ASTM 1995) in the USA have gained a wide and rapid acceptance since their release, partly because they introduce a more uniform, standardised approach to the risk assessment problem. In the UK the Contaminated Land Exposure Assessment (CLEA) model (Ferguson & Denner 1993) currently being developed, uses a risk based approach to assess contamination levels. To date many of the risk assessments which have been undertaken in this area have focused primarily on the public health aspects, and the potential harm to human beings, for example in the RBCA, risk assessment is defined as,
"an analysis of the potential for adverse health effects."

It must be borne in mind that humans are not the only population at risk from this type of contamination. There are a wide variety of receptors, or end targets, such as surface water quality of springs and rivers, plants, animals, fish, buried structures and utilities. In the developed world, the majority of groundwater abstractions for potable use undergo some form of preliminary treatment, so if contaminants are present then they can be removed before they reach the end user. Thus this system of risk assessment may be of greater benefit to human health in developing countries, where less treatment is available.

2 POTENTIAL FOR CONTAMINATION

In developed countries there are areas of historic lowering of groundwater tables, either due to abstractions for drinking water or to allow mining, as in many of the industrial areas. In such areas, these practices have been greatly reduced, or ceased completely, resulting in a rebound of the groundwater table in many such locations. As the water table rises there is the potential for contaminants previously locked within the soil matrix, to be released and contaminate the rising groundwater. This contaminated water may subsequently contaminate river systems, springs and pose a threat to the ecosystem they sustain. Should groundwater contain contaminants which are aggressive towards buried structures, such as sulphates towards concrete, then damage may occur which will have to be suitably repaired. This damage may be a slow process, but could cause many problems to structures and utilities which were designed when groundwater was not believed to be part of the design criteria. This is the type of situation where risk assessments have scope for further use, in examining effects of possible changes and their effects in the future.

3 RISK UNCERTAINTIES

There are numerous sources of uncertainty when dealing with movement of contaminated groundwater. This is taken a stage further, when the risk has to be estimated, yet more uncertainties are introduced into the problem.

The basic conceptual model underlying risk assessments is Source-Pathway-Receptor (Pollard et al. 1995). The component of this model with the greatest uncertainty is the pathway. Andricevic & Cvetkovic (1996) have shown that with groundwater transport, the main uncertainties occur within the pathway due to predominantly the geologic heterogeneities and estimates of sorption and general attenuation parameters. Time and financial constraints often rule out extensive investigations to gain more understanding of these parameters, and simpler models are adopted instead.

If effort is made to focus on the two remaining components, more useful information may be acquired. A detailed characterisation of the (potential) source will allow the type and concentrations of contaminants to be assessed. The same can be undertaken for the receptor. If they can both be subsequently monitored, this will provide both calibration and validation data for the assembled model.

4 CLASSIFICATION OF RISK

By assessing the source of contamination and determining the mode of release, the nature of the risk may be simply classified as illustrated in Figure 1. The quantity and mode of release of the contaminants will inevitably determine the potential risk. The actual amount of this potential which is realised will depend upon the pathway characteristics, attenuation factors, and the nature of the receptor. In a simplified model represented by Figure 1 and the relationship below, it is assumed that the pathway is through a homogeneous aquifer. The attenuation capacity is assumed to be capable of only dealing with a set percentage of the total (source) concentration at any one time. This will enable the contamination at the receptor to be determined.

The actual risk posed is a function of the source (S_F) and receptor (R_F) factors, the source factors being the nature of the source (N_S) and the attenuation capacity (A). The receptor factors include, the concentration reaching the receptor (C_R), the nature of the receptor (RC_N), sensitivity of the receptor (RC_S), exposure route (E) and social considerations (S_C).

$$\text{RISK } \alpha \ S_F \, R_F \qquad (3.1)$$

S_F = Source factor $= fn\,(\,N_S,\,A\,)$
R_F = Receptor Factor $= fn\,(C_R,\,RC_N,\,RC_S,\,E,\,S_C\,)$

Table 1 provides some examples of the factors which should be taken into account when determining R_F.

One of the single main factors in determining risk is the concentration at the receptor. This will ultimately determine quantity of contaminant potentially available.

The simple risk model developed here assigns only one value to summarise all attenuation processes, this represents a very simplistic approach, however, as the model develops further, various attenuation processes will be examined and represented in greater detail.

In Figure 1, the potential risk can be approximately related to behaving in a similar manner to that of the receptor concentration through time.

The nature of the receptor will determine what substances may be likely to cause harm, and the sensitivity will assign a further value of harm, depending on the resistance of sub-sets of a receptor to the substance in question. The exposure is the route by which the receptor comes into contact with the substance.

Table 1. Factors affecting risk

RISK FACTORS		EXAMPLES				
Nature of Receptor	(RC_N)	Human,	Animal,	Plant,	River,	Concrete
Sensitivity of Receptor	(RC_S)	Man,	Woman,	Child,	Baby,	Elderly
Exposure Route	(E)	Ingestion,	Inhalation,	Dermal		
Social Considerations	(S_C)	Public Perception,		Location of Contamination		

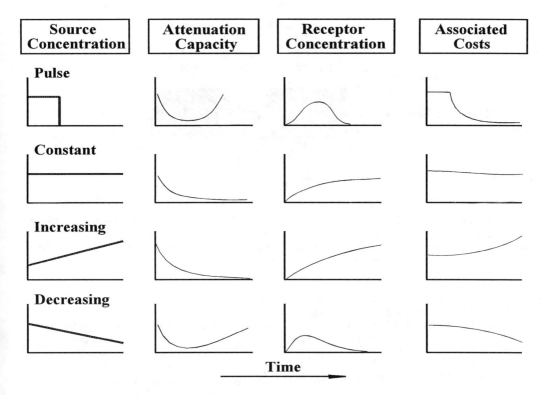

Source Concentration	Attenuation Capacity	Receptor Concentration	Associated Costs
Pulse			
Constant			
Increasing			
Decreasing			

Time

Figure 1. Schematic representation of source type, attenuation capacity, receptor concentration, and associated remediation costs

The inclusion of social considerations in the relationship introduces a term, which cannot be easily quantified. However, if risk assessments are to be developed as decision making tools, then it is necessary to include such parameters in the modelling process. With the increasing awareness of the general public of their environment, the power of public opinion and risk acceptance (Vrijling et al. 1995) have the potential to have major implications on decision making in the future.

Cost implications are illustrated in Figure 1, however, it is only displayed to provide a comparison between relative remediation costs for the different modes of contaminant release. Assessing the cost of prevention, protection or remediation must also account for several sensitive factors, each of which may be subjective. They include assigning costs to a responsibility for the preservation of the resource for future generations, maintaining and sustaining the present environment. Then there are ethical questions as to how important is the protection of human health, and the ecosystems that depend on what may be or become contaminated groundwater.

The approach taken when risk assessments are undertaken, can have a significant bearing on the outcome of the task. A worst case scenario may be adopted, where receptor concentrations are assumed to be equal to those at the source. The reality of this actually happening may be very unlikely, thus realism should be incorporated in to the assessment, this will allow solutions to be developed which tailor more accurately for the conditions expected. Attenuation of contaminants must be taken into account, as natural attenuation is adopted by some agencies as an acceptable method of remediation, especially with regard to hydrocarbon contamination (Buscheck & O'Reilly 1995).

5 MATRIX ANALYSIS

As part of the framework, an initial screening method of the contaminants present at a particular site should be undertaken, this will allow the main contaminants of concern to be identified. The matrix analysis provides a quick and easy method for recognising these parameters.

The observed contaminant levels are compared to, say drinking water standards, by means of a Contamination Index, where drinking water

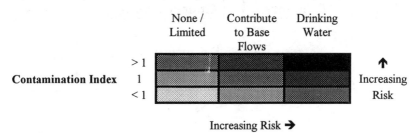

Use of Groundwater

	None / Limited	Contribute to Base Flows	Drinking Water	
> 1				↑
Contamination Index 1				Increasing
< 1				Risk

Increasing Risk ➔

Figure 2. Risk matrix analysis

standards are unity; good quality water is less than unity; and poor quality is greater than zero. This is then compared to the end use of the resource by the receptor(s) in question, or to identify the receptor(s). Figure 2 illustrates a typical matrix analysis form.

The matrix cells can be colour coded such that in the bottom left hand corner they are green, representing natural, relatively uncontaminated resource, blending through a yellow to a red in the top right hand corner, representing contamination which should be examined further. This allows an easily identifiable graphical image which can instantly provide an indication of the problem contaminants on a site.

Such a matrix analysis has further applications to different parameters, such as type of pollutant release and the approximate duration.

6 CONCLUSIONS

This paper outlines a risk assessment framework which recognises key factors which should be incorporated into risk assessment, as well as other factors which should be examined and considered in parallel with the risk assessment, such as cost. It is for regulators to assign cost to the increases in the risk to life, health or damage to receptors, a consideration which may be influenced by public opinion, especially if humans are the receptor at risk.

A simple model with a schematic outline of what it represents has been briefly explained. This framework will be expanded and developed to provide a quantitative analysis. Certain parameters will be subjective, and should be individually assigned for each particular application.

Matrix analysis has been briefly discussed, and could provide a valuable tool for initial assessment, and communication of results, both to professionals and lay persons due to its simplistic nature.

Risk assessment can and does provide a key tool for assessing current situations and dealing with future planning issues. The two parts of the framework described here, the initial screening matrix analysis, followed by the simple model are both tools which can aid in the development, and understanding of risk assessments.

REFERENCES

Andricevic, R. & V. Cvetkovic 1996. Evaluation of risk from contaminants migrating by groundwater. *Water Resources Research* 32(5): 611-622.

ASTM 1995. *Standard guide for risk-based corrective action applied at petroleum release sites*. American Society for Testing and Materials, West Conshohocken, PA.

Buscheck, T. & K. O'Reilly 1995. *Protocol for monitoring intrinsic bioremediation in groundwater*. Chevron Research and Technology Company.

Ferguson, C.C. & J Denner 1993. Soil guideline values in the uk: new risk-based approach. *Proc. 5th Int. Contaminated Soil Conf.* 365-371. Kluwer Academic Publishers.

Pollard, S.J., D.O. Harrop, P. Crowcroft, S.H. Mallett, S.R. Jeffries, & P.J. Young 1995. Risk assessment for environmental management: approaches and applications. *Journal of the Chartered Institute of Water and Environmental Management* 9: 621-628.

Vrijling, J.K., W. van Hengel & R.J. Houben 1995. A framework for risk evaluation. *Journal of Hazardous Materials* 43: 245-261.

© *1997 Balkema, Rotterdam, ISBN 90 5410 837 1*

An assessment of the risks associated with the disposal of nitrate effluent by spray irrigation at a major chemical factory in Johannesburg, South Africa

L. Magda
Steffen, Robertson and Kirsten (Africa), Johannesburg, South Africa

ABSTRACT: The disposal of nitrate rich effluents by spray irrigation has been practised for a number of years at a major chemical plant to the north of the Johannesburg city centre. The factory area, although large, is surrounded by urban developments many of which utilise groundwater for garden irrigation. The factory is also situated upstream of a major low cost and informal settlement, the residents of which use stream and borehole water indiscriminately. Various studies have been carried out in an effort to quantify the impacts of the effluent spray on the groundwater system and to assess the risks to adjacent property owners and possible downstream users. These have included an assessment of plant and soil nitrate uptake, flow and transport modelling of the groundwater system, and the evaluation of the risk to users following the source, pathway, target approach. The results of these studies are described and the conclusions relating to the future management options presented.

1 INTRODUCTION

A large chemical and explosives factory has disposed of its nitrogen-rich effluent by means of effluent spray activities since 1962. The spray area comprises about 1000 ha of undulating grass-covered land, and is situated along the north and west factory boundary. Although the factory, built at the turn of the century, was originally located far from urban areas, it is now surrounded by urban residential development.

The spray areas are situated on the tops and side slopes of gentle hills, with the residential areas as close as 30 m from the edge of some spray areas, and two streams located downgrade of the spray areas, within and outside the factory boundary. The existing residential areas are potentially at risk from the migration of contaminated groundwater. The future residents of the low cost informal settlement are potentially at risk both from groundwater contamination as well as stream contamination. Only the risks via groundwater contamination will be considered in this paper. The streamwater quality currently falls within the SA Drinking Water Guidelines.

The study area is underlain by granites, which are typically weathered to very shallow depths in the low-lying gulley areas and greater depths in higher areas. Three aquifer types have been identified on site, namely localised perched aquifers above local clay lenses, a regional weathered aquifer above the granite bedrock and deeper fractured aquifers, within discrete fractures in the granite. The regional weathered aquifer stores and transports the bulk of contaminated groundwater. Groundwater in the weathered aquifer often emerges as baseflow into the streams (SRK 1994a).

An investigation was undertaken to assess the potential health risks to groundwater users as a result of the effluent spray activities. The investigation comprised an assessment of the source-pathway-target scenarios for groundwater contamination.

2 RISK ASSESSMENT FOR GROUNDWATER

The source and pathway were simulated by using AQUA, a groundwater flow and transport model developed by Vatnaskil (1989). For the purposes of the model, the source is defined as that area of recharge to the weathered aquifer, at a specified volume and concentration. The pathway is defined as the transport of contaminants within the weathered aquifer system towards a potential target area.

The targets include groundwater users in the residential areas. The existing targets for groundwater contamination were identified during a borehole census carried out in the surrounding residential areas. A conceptual illustration of the source area and potential targets is indicated in Figure 1.

The groundwater model was established from available information including formation permeabilities, porosity and storage, records of

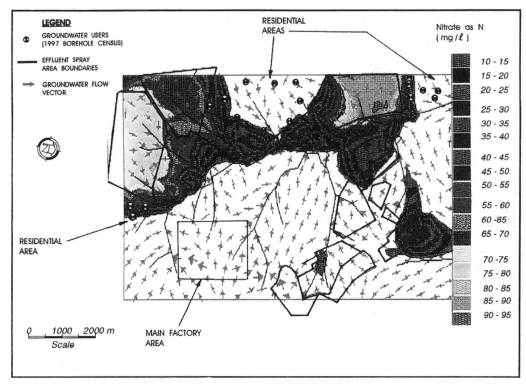

Figure 1. Conceptual model of the potential fate of the effluent spray water.

rainfall, effluent spray volumes and concentrations, estimates of evaporation and runoff, infiltration into the soils, evapotranspiration and natural attenuation, and the final volumes and concentrations recharged to groundwater. (SRK 1994b; 1996).

The model was calibrated using rest water levels and chemical analyses from available monitoring boreholes on site as well as from the boreholes sampled offsite. The evapotranspiration and natural attenuation capacity was assessed using the results of a soil and vegetation uptake study, and was also used to calibrate the model. The results of the model and the the locations of the groundwater users are presented in Figure 2.

The pathway constitutes groundwater flow within the weathered aquifer from higher lying areas to lower lying areas. The results of the model indicate that the spread of contamination is not only determined by natural piezometric gradients, but also occurs radially as a result of a localised mounding effect, which results in the development of artificial piezometric gradients around the perimeter of the spray area.

The existing targets comprise the groundwater users within the residential areas already affected by the groundwater contamination. Future targets include

potential groundwater users in future residential developments. The results of the borehole census and the transport modelling indicate that ten out of about 30 groundwater users approached are presently targets. The levels of nitrate contamination (NO$_3$ as N) at the targets vary from about 10 mg/l to 60 mg/l.

3 DATA INTERPRETATION

In terms of the source-pathway-target approach, the source has been defined as that component of contaminated effluent water, which after being sprayed, infiltrates through to groundwater. The source area includes the are of direct artificial recharge to groundwater.

These values are compared with the drinking water guideline of 10mg/l, from the South African Department of Water Affairs and Forestry (DWAF) guideline limits for Insignificant Risks to human health. In terms of risk characterisation, the concentration levels at the targets were assessed in the light of groundwater use, which includes garden irrigation, swimming pool fillings and drinking.

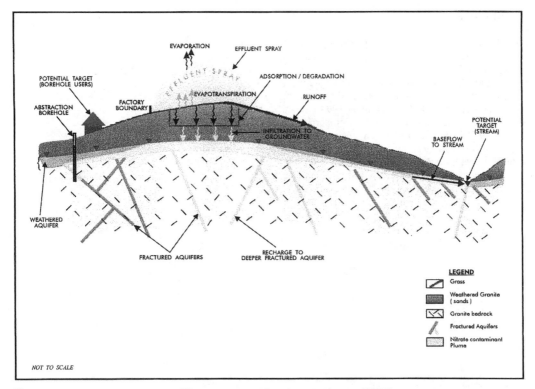

Figure 2. Transport model output - Nitrate concentrations in groundwater (1997)

4 CONCLUSIONS

The groundwater risk assessment has indicated that at present, at least 10 groundwater users are targets for the contaminated water. Due to present use of groundwater for garden irrigation, swimming pools and drinking water, risks to human health by ingestion or inhalation are present, and are highest within 40 - 50 m of spray area boundaries. The risks apply mainly to infants under three months of age due to the possible development of methaemoglobinaemia, a condition in which blood is unable to carry oxygen in the human body. Under certain conditions, nirtate may react in the human body with secondary and tertiary amines and amides, commonly derived from food, to form nitrosamines, which are known carcinogens.

In view of the low probability of ingestion of large volumes of groundwater, the risk to human health is nevertheless considered to be low to medium. This is due to the low recorded volumes ingested over long periods of time. The evaluation of the risk also includes the additional risk due to the possibility of future groundwater users. The factory has agreed to reduce these risks in the short term by informing the groundwater users of the potential hazards and will implement long-term management measures to reduce the impacts of their spray activities.

The long term measures will depend on the desired level of cleanup, as agreed with the authorities . These management methods are likely to include the following options:

1. A reduction of the source area by means of limiting the spray area to a specified distance from the factory boundary.

2. The installation of an interception trench to provide an interception point in the pathway. The trench could be situated along the factory boundary in areas where the contaminant plume is sufficiently concentrated, and would be used to prevent on-going migration of the contaminant plume towards the targets.

3. The construction of a denitrification plant to remove nitrogen from the effluent prior to spraying.

The implementation of these management methods will be used to eliminate the risk to groundwater users in the long term. In the interim, the groundwater users will be kept informed and alternative water supplies will be provided by the factory, as required.

REFERENCES

SRK 1994a. Ground water quality investigation of spray areas, Phase 1. Steffen, Robertson & Kirsten Report 197104, June 1994.

SRK 1994b. Ground water quality investigation of spray areas, Phase 2 - 4. Steffen, Robertson & Kirsten Report 197104/2 September 1994.

SRK 1996. Annual monitoring report October 1994 - October 1995. Steffen, Robertson & Kirsten Report 212681/4 March 1996.

Vatnaskil 1989. *AQUA3D Groundwater flow and transport model.* Vatnaskil Consulting Engineers Sudurlandsbraut 50, Reyjavik, Iceland.

The problem of groundwater contamination at waste disposal sites in Ukraine

V.G. Magmedov
Ministry for Environmental Protection and Nuclear Safety of Ukraine, Kyiv, Ukraine

L.I. Yakovleva
Ukrainian Scientific Centre for Protection of Waters, Kharkiv, Ukraine

ABSTRACT: This paper presents the results of an investigation of the use of biotesting and bioindication as methods for groundwater quality monitoring at waste disposal sites. The data obtained during three years of field and laboratory research have been used for the evaluation of biotests prior to establishing groundwater quality monitoring in areas adjoining landfills. The results support the concept that, in cases of uncertainty with identification of pollution sources and the level of groundwater contamination, toxicity can be used as an integral characteristic of groundwater quality.

1 INTRODUCTION

The problem of groundwater contamination at waste disposal sites is one of the most important ecological problems for the urban environment in Ukraine. The volume of domestic solid waste has been increasing constantly and now amounts to 38-40 million tonnes annually (Magmedov & Matorin 1997). The area occupied by landfills is more than 2600 hectares, according to official information, and may be twice that if uncontrolled dumping is accounted for. As all landfills are sources of contamination for groundwater, and may result in disease-related problems, the associated risk to the environment is considerable.

Many of the landfills have no groundwater monitoring system, or they are poorly operated. In most cases no special groundwater protection measures have been implemented. As a result, groundwater quality is affected, and in many places is equal to wastewater and has high toxicity. The extent of the problem has increased considerably in recent years as a result of the period of transition to a market economy. This restructuring has led to a decrease in both infrastructure and finances available for effective solid waste management and groundwater monitoring.

For these reasons, in 1994 a new project dealing with the problem of landfill influence on groundwater quality was initiated by the Ukrainian Scientific Center for Protection of Waters (USCPW). At one stage of the work a list of the solid waste landfills and their range according to the degree of negative influence they have on groundwater quality was prepared. However, taking into consideration the fact that in only 30% of cases the groundwater quality was being monitored, and the rest of the landfills had no information as to the degree of negative influence on the environment, there appeared to be a need to choose methods which would allow the characterisation of this influence (Magmedov & Yakovleva 1996).

Bioindication and biotesting were chosen as the methods of research. The Kharkiv city domestic landfill and the industrial solid waste disposal site of the "Electrotyazhmash" plant were selected as the experimental sites for testing the chosen methods for integral evaluation of groundwater quality, .

2 MONITORING NETWORK

The research was carried out between 1993 and 1996. Groundwater samples were taken during different seasons six times a year from seven wells at the industrial solid waste disposal site and from four control points near the city domestic waste landfill. In total, during the investigation, 132 samples have been taken and each sample was analysed three times. A plan of monitoring wells near the disposal site of "Electrotyazhmash" plant is shown in Figure 1.

The following monitoring wells were installed around the industrial solid waste disposal site:
- well 1- the control, situated up hydraulic gradient from the landfill at a distance of 300 m from the landfill;
- wells 2-5 - situated around the perimeter of the landfill, up and down the hydraulic gradient;
- well 6 - situated down hydraulic gradient at a distance of 100 m from the landfill;
- well 7 - situated down hydraulic gradient at a distance of 400 m from the landfill.

Table 1. Evaluation of the degree of water toxicity for the test-object *Daphnia magna*.

Length of life of 50% of test-objects (hours)	Qualitative evaluation of the toxicity	Quantitative evaluation of the toxicity
more than 20	zero	0
up to 20	low	1
up to 10	medium	2
up to 5	high	3
less than 2	very high	4

Table 2.   The influence of groundwater from around the industrial solid waste landfill on the different test objects (a summary of the data for spring and autumn sampling, years 1993 - 1996).

Test-objects	Level of toxicity						
Well No	1	2	3	4	5	6	7
Paramecium caudatum	0/0*	0/0	0/0	0/0	4/4	3/4	0/0
Daphnia magna	2/2	2/3	2/2	3/2	4/4	3/4	2/0
Lemna minor	2/2	2/4	4/3	2/2	4/4	0/4	4/2
Vallisneria spiralis	0/0	3/1	0/0	0/0	4/4	4/4	0/0
Scenedesmus quadricauda	0/0	0/0	0/0	0/0	2/4	4/4	0/0

* numerator - data for spring sampling/ denominator - data for autumn sampling

Table 3.   The influence of groundwater from around the domestic solid waste landfill on the different test objects (a summary of the data for spring and autumn sampling, years 1993 - 1996).

Test objects	Level of toxicity			
Point No	1	2	3	4
Paramecium caudatum	0/0	1/0	0/0	0/0
Daphnia magna	2/2	1/3	1/1	1/1
Lemna minor	0/2	1/2	0/2	0/0
Vallisneria spiralis	1/2	1/1	1/2	0/1
Scenedesmus quadricauda	0/3	2/3	4/3	0/2

* numerator - data for spring sampling/ denominator - data for autumn sampling

The Kharkiv city domestic solid waste landfill is situated at a distance of 300 m from Dergachie village. As the monitoring well network is absent in the landfill area, a selection of samples was taken from potable supply wells situated at the following distances from the landfill:
- point 1 - 300 m;
- point 2 - 330 m;
- point 3 - 350 m;
- point 4 - 1000 m.

3 METHODS AND MATERIALS

The research included qualitative and quantitative evaluation of the groundwater conditions. Chemical analyses of the water samples were carried out according to standard methods. For biological control, two methods were used (APHA 1985; USSR 1991; Oksiyuk et al. 1993):
- The first method was bioindication of the analysed samples by taxonomic groups of micro-organisms

484

and physiological groups of bacteria.
- The second method was biotesting of the samples, noting the following parameters for the test species ('test objects'):frequency of occurrence, species growth rate, frequency of protoplasm moving in cell.

Most attention was given to the search for test objects having the highest degree of sensitivity, informativity and ability to clearly register and reproduce the effect. Hence, in the process of research the following criteria for choosing the test objects were taken:
- a high level of sensitivity to a wide spectrum of pollutants, especially the toxic ones;
- the certainty in response to the influence (mortality rate);
- ecological diversity;
- the possibility of estimating the test object status;
- the level of reproducibility and certainty;

- the technical possibility of cultivating and using the test objects as part of the State Control System.

On the basis of the above mentioned criteria the following test-objects were chosen:
- at the level of population - green microscopic alga *Scenedesmus quadricauda* and the unicellular organism *Paramecium caudatum*;
- at the level of organism - *Daphnia magna(Crustacea)* and the high aquatic plant *Lemna minor*;
- at the level of cell - the high aquatic plant *Vallisneria spiralis*.

The toxicity of the monitored groundwater was evaluated in grades. In Table 1 the initial classification for the determination of water toxicity using *Daphnia magna* as the test object is given. Analogous classifications have been used for the determination of water toxicity using other test objects.

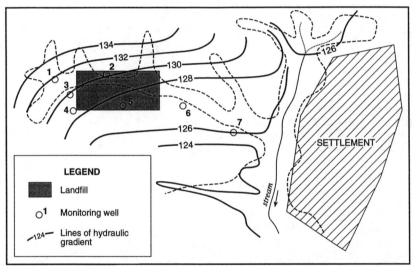

Figure 1. The industrial solid waste disposal site of the "Electrotyazhmash" plant and the groundwater monitoring network.

Table 4. Comparative data on biotesting of groundwater toxicity at the area adjacent to the landfills.

| Test-objects | % Toxic samples of total | | | | | | | | | | |
| | Well No | | | | | | | Point No | | | |
	1	2	3	4	5	6	7	1	2	3	4
Paramecium caudatum	100	100	50	100	100	100	50	100	50	100	100
Daphnia magna	60	80	75	100	100	80	60	30	75	100	100
Lemna minor	0	20	0	0	100	100	0	50	50	50	25
Vallisneria spiralis	0	33	0	0	40	83	33	75	25	50	25
Scenedesmus quadricauda	0	0	0	0	100	100	0	0	0	0	0

4 RESULTS AND DISCUSSION

The chemical and biological research on groundwater quality around landfills which was carried out in 1993-1996 demonstrated that it is not only contamination that happens. Even where there is no exceedence of Maximum Acceptable Concentrations (MAC) of individual pollutants, the groundwater becomes toxic for animals and human beings. So, in the area adjoining to the Kharkiv city solid waste landfill, the groundwater is not only contaminated by organic and mineral compounds, but is toxic in a radius of 1000 m from the boundary of the landfill. In Tables 2 and 3 the comparative results of groundwater biotesting in the area adjoining the domestic and industrial solid waste landfills are given for spring and autumn sampling. Table 4 shows a summary of the data on biotesting of the groundwater samples taken in 1993 - 1996.

The analysis of the data obtained demonstrates that the following test objects can be used as indicators of integral groundwater quality:

- *Daphnia magna*
- *Lemna minor*
- *Scenedesmus quadricauda*

The existence of acute toxicity of groundwater should be determined by brief biotesting with *Daphnia magna* and *Lemna minor*.

The existence of chronic toxicity of the groundwater should be determined by long term biotesting on *Daphnia magna* and *Lemna minor*. If additional toxicity research is necessary, the alga *Scenedesmus quadricauda* can be used as the test object.

For the express evaluation of the groundwater quality around landfills the use of the high aquatic plant *Vallisneria spiralis* with the duration of determination of 1.5 hours can be recommended.

5 CONCLUSIONS

As a first step to minimizing the negative influence of landfills on the environment an inventory of all landfills existing in Ukraine should be drawn up, ranking them according to the risk of groundwater pollution.

The analysis of groundwater chemical and biological data from the regions adjoining landfills demonstrates the reliability of biotesting and bioindication as integrating methods of groundwater quality assessment.

From the point of view of sensitivity to the contaminating substances the recommended test object should be ranked in the following way starting from the highest priority: *Daphnia magna, Lemna minor, Scenedesmus quadricauda.*

REFERENCES

American Public Health Association, American Water Works Association and Water Pollution Control Federation. 1985. Standard method for the examination of water and waste water, 16th edition. Washington DC.

Magmedov, V.G. & E.M. Matorin 1997. Solid waste management in Ukraine: what has to be done? *R '97-Recovery, Recycling, Re-Integration. Collected Papers of the R '97 International Congress*, Geneva, Switzerland, February 4 - 7, 1997, Vol.1, 210 - 215.

Magmedov, V.G. & L.I.Yakovleva 1996. Landfills: factors effecting groundwater contamination. *Proceedings of the International Conference on "Water Resources and Economical Development of Republic Belorus,"* 24 - 25 May 1996, Minsk, Vol.2, 25-26.

Oksiyuk, O.P. 1993. Complex ecological classification of the water quality. *Hydrobiological Journal*, 29, 4, 62 - 76.

USSR Ministry for Environmental Protection 1991. *Manual on water quality biotesting*, RD 118-02-90., Moscow.

An experiment in geophysical monitoring of a contaminated site

N. P. Merrick
National Centre for Groundwater Management, University of Technology, Sydney, N.S.W., Australia

ABSTRACT: Dynamic variations in aquifer resistivity, as might occur during the passage of a contaminant front or during the remediation of a contaminated site, can be monitored remotely by geophysical means. An experiment at a contaminated site near urban Sydney (Australia), which involved injection of fresh water into an aquifer contaminated with chlorinated hydrocarbons, afforded an opportunity for assessing the performance of several geophysical methods: electrical resistivity sounding, downhole electromagnetic logging, and transient electromagnetic sounding. Measurements were repeated over a period of four months at times which coincided with the onset, duration and cessation of the injection stress. This study has shown that, of the methods tested, the best resolution and best potential for monitoring is given by downhole induction logging. However, this is an invasive method, and is limited to a small region of influence. Of the non-invasive methods tested, transient electromagnetic soundings gave excellent lateral resolution and good vertical resolution.

1 INTRODUCTION

The Botany Sands aquifer is a shallow groundwater system within the Botany Basin which starts 3 km south of the site of the first colonial settlement in Sydney, Australia. Still in active use today, it is the oldest producing groundwater system in Australia. The first well was sunk by Lieutenant James Cook on 29th April 1770 at Kurnell on the southern shore of Botany Bay. In 1788, settlement commenced just beyond the northern rim of the Botany Basin at Port Jackson. Reports of water quality degradation date back to 1795 for the stream which provided the fledgling colony's water supply. Due to a long history of urban occupation and industrial development, the aquifer has been degraded in many places and is constantly under threat from anthropogenic activities. Its continued utility is all the more important because there is no other significant unconsolidated-sediment aquifer in the Sydney metropolitan area.

One particular contaminated site within the Botany Basin, at a distance of about 8 km due south of Sydney, has been the subject of considerable investigation and research. The site, contaminated with chlorinated hydrocarbons and inorganic compounds is soon to undergo remediation. As part of the research effort, a brief study was made of the potential for geophysical techniques for playing a role in monitoring the remediation process. If dynamic geophysical characteristics measured in the field can be shown to correlate with remediation activity, then long-term cost savings should accrue during the monitoring phase.

As remediation has not yet commenced, an independent injection experiment was used as a surrogate indicator of remediation activity. This experiment involved the continuous injection of fresh water into the aquifer for a period of 19 days (March 22 to April 9, 1995) at a rate of about 6 m^3d^{-1}, in order to evaluate the desorptive properties of the aquifer. The injection took place through slotted PVC casing at 14 m to 17 m depth in Bore WG74I, which is one of three neighbouring bores (WG74S, WG74I, WG74D) adjacent to two multilevel piezometers (Figure 1). Geophysical measurements were scheduled to coincide with significant stresses on the system. The first measurements followed completion (on December 20, 1994) of the installation of the multilevel piezometers, which drilling recharged the aquifer with a considerable volume of fresh water. Subsequent measurements were scheduled before, during and after the injection experiment.

The geophysical programme focussed on the geoelectrical properties of the sedimentary section. The methods used were:

1. Electrical resistivity soundings (DC);
2. Downhole electromagnetic induction logging (DHEM);
3. Transient electromagnetic soundings (TEM).

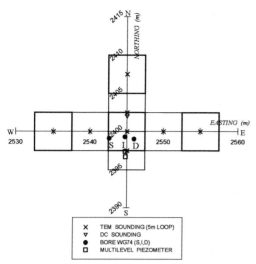

Figure 1. Relative locations of bores, soundings and TEM transmitter loops.

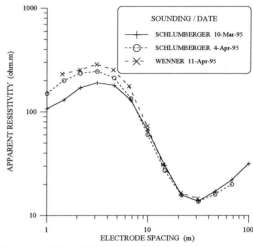

Figure 2. DC resistivity sounding curves repeated on three occasions.

2 ELECTRICAL RESISTIVITY

The electrical resistivity method uses a four-electrode array to inject electrical current into the ground and measure the resulting voltage set up at the earth's surface. By expanding the spacing between the current electrodes, information can be gleaned on the variation of ground resistivity with depth. Resistivity soundings using the ABEM Terrameter were performed on three occasions (March 10, April 4 and April 11, 1995) at the one site (Figure 2). On the first two dates, the Schlumberger electrode array was used. On the third occasion, a tripotential array was used to give Wenner α, β and γ soundings.

2.1 Interpretation

Each sounding has been interpreted quantitatively in terms of a horizontally layered earth by means of RINVERT for Windows inversion software (Merrick 1996). The reliability of the interpretations has been assessed by equivalence analyses.

The interpreted resistivity of the layer above bedrock is the parameter which is the diagnostic property under investigation in this monitoring programme. The resistivity soundings have poor stratigraphic resolution, and can resolve only four gross layers at this site:
1. Fill
2. Dry sand
3. Saturated Sand
4. Bedrock (sandstone)
The fill has severe equivalence because it

is only 0.4 m to 0.6 m thick. Its resistivity increased from about 70 Ωm to about 100 Ωm during the injection test. The dry sand has extreme equivalence. It can have a wide range in resistivity but is generally about 600 Ωm. The water table estimate, which varies from 1.7 m to 1.9 m on the three days, agrees closely with measured depths. Being thick, the saturated sand has mild/minor equivalence. It is well resolved but does require a constraint on thickness to force depth to that encountered in drilling. The resistivity of this layer increased by 13% during the injection experiment (11.2 to 12.7 Ωm). The bedrock layer has a poorly resolved resistivity.

3 DOWNHOLE ELECTROMAGNETICS

The electromagnetic method induces electrical currents and magnetic fields in the ground by passing a high frequency alternating current through a transmitter coil, and simultaneously measuring the resultant magnetic field at a receiver coil. The Century 9510 Slim Hole Induction Tool was used to provide downhole induction logs at bores WG74I and WG74D on four occasions. This tool measures natural gamma radiation, mandril temperature, temperature-compensated apparent conductivity, and apparent conductivity corrected for skin effect.

3.1 Time variation

Figure 3 shows the downhole induction logs acquired at bore WG74D on four occasions. The logs segregate clearly into four distinct curves (in order of

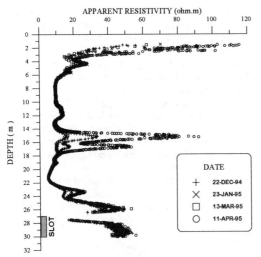

Figure 3. Downhole induction resistivity logs at bore WG74D repeated on four occasions.

decreasing resistivity) according to their associated events:

(a) 11-Apr-95 (after injection);
(b) 22-Dec-94 (after drilling);
(c) 23-Jan-95 (approaching equilibrium after drilling);
(d) 13-Mar-95 (at equilibrium before injection).

The difference between curves (a) and (b) shows that the injection experiment put more fresh water into the aquifer than did drilling. There is a pronounced increase in resistivity at the injection site (14-17 m depth at 1.3 m west). The effect of the injection is essentially confined to two thin sand zones from 14.5 m to 17 m depth; the layers are separated by a thin clayey (or peaty) seam. The lower sand layer near 17 m is not apparent at the two equilibrium dates because its natural conductivity matches that of neighbouring clayey/peaty zones.

There is a zone of increased resistivity near 3 m depth caused by the injection experiment, probably due to unintentional leakage or infiltration of fresh water into less resistive soil. At depths below the injection level, injection of water has had no effect on formation resistivity. However, at these depths, drilling waters have entered the aquifer, particularly near 23 m and 26 m depth.

4 TRANSIENT ELECTROMAGNETICS

The transient electromagnetic method (TEM) pulses a localised patch of ground with an electromagnetic field which is allowed to diffuse into the earth. A short direct current is passed through a transmitter

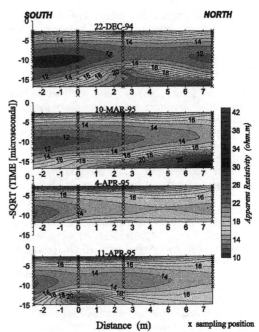

Figure 4. TEM resistivity pseudosections repeated on four occasions.

loop, to set up the field, then a receiver coil monitors the collapsing magnetic field after the current is switched off.

The Geonics Protem receiver and TEM47 transmitter were used to provide TEM soundings at eight contiguous positions in the vicinity of bore WG74I, as indicated in Figure 1. Soundings were conducted on four occasions: 22-Dec-1994, 10-Mar-1995, 4-Apr-1995, 11-Apr-1995.

The receiver coil was positioned 12.5 m from the centre of each 5 m square transmitter loop. For soundings in the North-South direction, the receiver loop was to the north of the transmitter loop. For soundings in an East-West direction, the receiver loop was to the west for soundings west of the origin and to the east for soundings east of the origin. This arrangement gave effective investigation over a length of 45 m east-west and 25 m north-south.

4.1 Pseudosections

The north-south dataset is displayed as a pseudosection in Figure 4. The vertical axis, the square root of the time of measurement, is a surrogate depth indicator. In very approximate terms, the maximum time shown (15 $\mu s^{1/2}$) is of the order of 30 m, and the scale can be taken to be roughly linear in depth. Injection took place at 0.7 m

489

south of the distance axis origin. The four images correspond to four events: 22-Dec-94 (after drilling), 10-Mar-95 (before injection), 4-Apr-95 (during injection), 11-Apr-95 (after injection). The overall impression is of a layered earth with three distinct zones: (a) a resistive surface, (b) a conductive section, (c) a resistive base. This sequence is consistent with information gathered from resistivity soundings and induction logs. The central section shows a variability in magnitude over time, indicating a change in formation resistivity in response to stresses on the system.

The section recorded during injection (4-Apr-95) shows a clear increase in resistivity in the central zone along the whole line. Prior to injection (10-Mar-95), the central zone showed conductivity increasing to the south from an apparent resistivity of 15 Ωm (north) to 12 Ωm (south). At 4-Apr-95, the apparent resistivities decline from 16 Ωm (north) to 13 Ωm (south). Two days after injection ceased (11-Apr-95), the central zone was slightly more conductive than during injection, but was still fresher than before injection. The northern half of the line had almost recovered pre-injection levels, but the region in the vicinity of the injection source (at 0.7 m South) was still much fresher. This behaviour is consistent with the downhole induction log response.

The earliest TEM section (22-Dec-94) is consistent in form but not in magnitude with the other sections. The conductive zone marked by the 12 Ωm contour is anomalously large in size and more conductive than expected, given that drilling recharged the aquifer with fresh water at the southern end of the line. It is probable that this section has a systematic offset due to less rigorous survey procedures. The survey on this date was done under very difficult conditions in heavy rain and loop positioning was not as precise as on other days. A systematic offset would explain the downhole log observation of increased resistivity at the intermediate slot (14-17 m), when compared with measurements taken immediately before the injection experiment.

For transient electromagnetics to be reliable as a remote monitor, it is vital that the transmitter loops be re-occupied precisely (within a few cm), and that the same orientations are used for the transmitter loop/receiver coil pair. If that is done, then it appears that TEM can detect changes in resistivity of better than 1 Ωm. This corresponds to a resolution of 4-10 mS/m in conductivity at typical formation resistivities (10-15 Ωm), which translates to a change in salinity of about 100-200 mg/L.

5 DISCUSSION

Resistivity soundings are appropriate for spot information, but their region of influence is not localised. They are inappropriate for investigating variations over small distances (about 10 m). For smaller scale spatial variations, resistivity imaging is preferred. Nevertheless, the method was successful in detecting a diagnostic variation in the resistivity of the saturated sand layer, when stressed by the injection experiment.

Downhole induction logs give excellent vertical resolution and are able to track small variations in conductivity with time. They are an excellent means of monitoring the dynamic behaviour of an aquifer system, provided that stresses on the system (such as remediation) cause changes in conductivity. Induction logs provide more detailed and more reliable stratigraphic information than can be expected of a driller's log. The geophysical log is a better indicator of bed boundaries but cannot assign lithologies unambiguously.

Transient electromagnetic soundings provide excellent lateral resolution and good vertical resolution of the geoelectrical signature of the subsurface. Presentation of data in pseudosection format allows recognition of dynamic variations in an aquifer, provided that stresses on the system (such as remediation) cause changes in conductivity. For transient electromagnetics to be reliable as a remote monitor, it is vital that the transmitter loops be re-occupied precisely, and that the same orientations are used for the transmitter loop/receiver coil pair. If that is done, then it appears that TEM can detect changes in resistivity of better than 1 Ωm (< 10 %).

The appropriateness of the methods investigated here, as a means of remote monitoring during remediation, depends upon there being a diagnostic change in conductivity during the remediation process. The petrophysical characteristics of the study site were beyond the scope of the present study but there are some indications in the literature that a change in hydrocarbon content in a medium will give rise to a measurable change in conductivity. Huang et al. (1995), for example, found that progressive diesel oil contamination of laboratory samples caused changes in resistivity of 20-50%.

REFERENCES

Huang, M., C. Liu, L. Shen, & D. Shattuck 1995. Monitoring soil contaminations using a contactless conductivity probe. *Geophysical Prospecting* 43: 759-778.

Merrick, N. P. 1996. The electrical resistivity method. In P. Zannetti (ed.), *Environmental Modeling Vol.3: Computer Methods and Software for Simulating Environmental Pollution and its Adverse Effects*: 329-370. Southampton: Computational Mechanics Publications.

Groundwater in the Urban Environment: Problems, Processes and Management, Chilton et al. (eds)
© *1997 Balkema, Rotterdam, ISBN 90 5410 837 1*

Groundwater contamination from sewers: Experience from Britain and Ireland

Bruce D. Misstear
Trinity College Dublin, Ireland

Philip K. Bishop
Mott MacDonald, Cambridge, UK

ABSTRACT: Following a discussion of the contaminating properties of sewage and an international overview of groundwater contamination from leaking sewers, the paper focuses on the situation in Britain and Ireland. Evidence of sewer-related groundwater contamination in Britain is considered on the basis of reported incidents and indirect evidence from groundwater quality data. Experience of groundwater contamination from sewers in Ireland is then reviewed, including a description of two major incidents affecting public water supply sources. Finally, the paper considers the implications of sewer-related contamination for groundwater protection.

1 INTRODUCTION

This paper details experience of groundwater contamination from sewers in Britain and Ireland. The authors were recently involved in a Construction Industry Research and Information Association (CIRIA) research contract (Misstear *et al.* 1996) examining the impact of leaking sewers on groundwater quality in England and Wales. Subsequent experience on the same issue has been gained in Ireland.

Britain (especially England) is a comparatively urbanised and industrialised country and many of its largest cities are underlain by major aquifers such as the Chalk and Sherwood Sandstone. The Irish Republic is less urbanised and the most important aquifers (which include Carboniferous limestones and glacial sands and gravels) are exploited in mainly rural areas. Notwithstanding these contrasts, evidence of sewer-related contamination is found in both countries.

2 PROPERTIES OF SEWAGE

Sewage originates from both domestic and industrial sources and comprises a complex mixture of natural inorganic and organic matter with a small proportion of man-made substances. The main source of contamination in domestic sewage is human excreta, with lesser contributions from food preparation, personal washing and laundry.

The broad components of sewage may be divided into organic matter, organisms and inorganic constituents. Most of the organic carbon can be attributed to the major organic groups: carbohydrates, fats, proteins, amino acids and volatile acids. The remainder comprises other organic molecules such as hormones, vitamins, chlorinated hydrocarbons and pesticides. Organisms found in sewage include bacteria, viruses, fungi and protozoans.

There are substantial inorganic constituents in sewage, especially compounds containing sodium, potassium, calcium, magnesium, boron, chloride, sulphate, phosphate, bicarbonate and ammonia. A major source of phosphate, chloride, sulphate and boron is synthetic detergents, the use of which has more than doubled in the last thirty years.

The chemical and physical nature of sewage can be further complicated by the inclusion of industrial wastes composed of strong spent liquors from industrial processes, and comparatively weak wastewaters from rinsing, washing, condensing and contaminated surface runoff.

3 INTERNATIONAL OVERVIEW

There does not appear to be a large amount of international material published regarding sewers as a source of groundwater contamination. The literature search for the CIRIA study uncovered fewer than 50 papers on this topic from outside Britain and Ireland, the majority originating from the USA and Germany. These can be categorised as:

1. Sewer-related groundwater contamination incidents.

2. Groundwater quality data as evidence of sewer-related contamination.

3. Studies of different sewer types and their potential for groundwater contamination.

Evidence of sewer-related groundwater contamination incidents was obtained from the USA, Sweden and Israel. The earliest reference found was that of Deutsch (1963) describing two cases of leaking sewers polluting groundwater in Michigan in 1945 and 1952. The most dramatic incident of sewer leakage traced internationally was that from Haifa in Israel in 1985, where leakage from a broken sewer into an adjacent village well resulted in epidemics of typhoid and dysentery (Anon 1985). In this case 6,000 people were affected and there was one fatality.

Many studies cite groundwater quality data as evidence of sewer-related contamination. Common indicators cited include bacteria, nitrate, ammonia and various organic compounds. In the USA nitrogen isotopes were used by Kreitler et al. (1978) to define the sources of nitrates in groundwater, with the conclusion that leaking sewers played a major role. In Germany chemical determinands have been used to estimate the degree of sewer leakage. Mull et al. (1992) estimated that between 5 and 8 million m^3 of sewage was contaminating groundwater in the Hanover area. Schleyer et al. (1992) state that the full extent of the potential hazard confronting groundwater in Germany from leaking sewers has only recently been recognised. They estimate that 10 to 15% of the 285,000 km of public sewers and 600,000 km of private sewers in the former West Germany have exceeded their life expectancy with approximately 300 million m^3 of wastewater seeping into groundwater each year.

Some of the most technical studies of sewer leakage are from Germany. In one example Eiswirth & Hötzl (1994) investigated the feasibility of detecting sewer leakages in an old sewerage scheme and in a specially constructed research system in Rastatt in southern Germany. Amongst their conclusions they suggest that closed-circuit television surveys cannot distinguish between those cracks and fractures which represent active or inactive leakage from sewer pipes.

4 ENGLAND AND WALES

Evidence of groundwater contamination from sewers in England and Wales can be divided into two categories, similar to those above for international studies:

1. Reported contamination incidents linked to leaking sewers.

2. Circumstantial evidence of leaking sewers from groundwater quality data.

4.1 Groundwater contamination incidents

The CIRIA study used a combined literature search and questionnaire survey to identify sewer-related contamination incidents. Eighteen incidents were uncovered by the literature search and 39 incidents were reported in the questionnaire responses (although there was some limited duplication). The study showed that older sewers were more prone to leakage than modern ones owing to the materials and practices employed and deterioration with age.

The earliest incident cited in the literature is that of Castle Springs, Bath in 1928, when a leaking sewer led to contamination of a well in a Jurassic limestone aquifer. This resulted in a typhoid outbreak and seven deaths. The most recent major incident was that at Bramham, Yorkshire in 1980, where leakage from a surcharged sewer contaminated a borehole exploiting the Magnesian Limestone aquifer. This resulted in 3,000 cases of gastro-enteritis (Short 1988). In this incident a contributory factor to the outbreak of illness was a breakdown in chlorination of the supply. The failure or lack of disinfection of potable supplies is common to all of the incidents where adverse health effects were reported.

The CIRIA study showed that most of the major aquifers in England and Wales have been impacted locally by sewer-related groundwater contamination (see Figure 1). However, the Chalk has been the focus of many more incidents than any other aquifer. While this is likely partly to reflect its status as the most extensively used aquifer, hydrogeological controls may also play an important role with regard to its vulnerability. The most productive horizons of the Chalk aquifer are generally located within the uppermost 10 to 20 m of strata which have well developed fissures. Thus, in the case of unconfined Chalk, shallow contaminated groundwater may move rapidly to abstraction boreholes with inadequate time for bacteria mortality.

The Triassic Sandstone is the second most important aquifer in England and shows far fewer sewer-related contamination incidents than the Chalk. This may reflect different flow mechanisms in the sandstone, with a stronger component of inter-granular flow and a more regular distribution of fissures with depth leading to slower overall groundwater velocities and therefore longer times for bacteria to die-off.

4.2 Evidence from groundwater quality data

Circumstantial evidence for leaking sewers is provided by the often poor quality of urban groundwaters in England. For example, Price and Reed (1989) state that evidence for sewer leakage is provided by the high nitrate concentrations present in

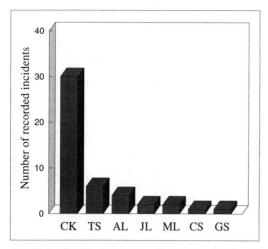

CK= Chalk, TS= Triassic Sandstone, AL= Alluvium, JL= Jurassic limestones, ML= Magnesian Limestone, CS= Carboniferous sandstones, GS= Greensand

Figure 1. Breakdown of sewer-related contamination incidents in England and Wales by aquifer.

groundwater beneath urban areas such as Liverpool and Birmingham. Halliday and Lerner (1992) report that shallow groundwater sampling in Birmingham shows sewer leakage to be a highly probable source of sulphate, chloride, phosphate and nitrate contamination.

Burston *et al.* (1993) suggest leaking sewers are an important source of boron in Coventry's groundwater, and may locally be responsible for some chlorinated solvent contamination of groundwater. In London, leaking sewers may be responsible for some localised high nitrate concentrations in the Thames gravels aquifer (CIRIA 1993).

5 INCIDENTS IN IRELAND

The problem of sewage pollution from septic tank effluent has received significant attention in Ireland in recent years, with studies showing that more than 50% of private wells are affected in some rural areas (e.g. Daly *et al.* 1993). Rather less is known about sewage contamination from sewers. As with the CIRIA study in Britain, the information available is often indicative rather than conclusive. A 1993 investigation of groundwater quality in Ireland (which focused on trace organic contaminants but also included sampling for other chemical and microbiological parameters) found 13 cases of groundwater contamination in which leaking sewers were either known or suspected to contribute to the

problem (K.T.Cullen and Co. 1994).

A subsequent desk study and questionnaire survey by MacMahon (1995) reported on a further seven groundwater contamination incidents which are thought to be sewer-related. The most serious of the incidents occurred in the town of Naas in 1991. Since MacMahon's survey, there has also been a major pollution incident at a well source in Nenagh which is believed to be sewer-related. The Naas and Nenagh incidents are described in turn below.

5.1 *The Naas incident*

The town of Naas is located about 40 km southwest of Dublin. In October 1991 a public water supply serving approximately 1,500 households in the town became grossly contaminated by sewage. About 4,000 people became ill, suffering varying degrees of gastro-intestinal disorders. The incident has been described by Garrett (1992) and by Moore (1992).

The source of the incident at Naas was a borehole known as Sunday's Well, located in what is now a housing estate. The borehole exploits a Quaternary sand and gravel aquifer. Problems with the Sunday's Well source commenced on 7 October 1991 with a consumer's complaint of a foul smell from the water after it was boiled. These complaints escalated and when the borehole was examined it was apparent that it had become contaminated by sewage. Initial water analyses showed presumptive coliforms of about 10^9 per ml and *E. coli* of about 10^7 per ml.

The contamination was traced to a blockage that had occurred in a sewer a few metres away from the borehole, resulting in the seepage of sewage into the borehole. Although the supply was chlorinated this apparently failed to cope with such high levels of pollution. Moreover, super-chlorination of the sourceworks and flushing of the mains took about two weeks to remedy the situation.

5.2 *The Nenagh incident*

The County Tipperary town of Nenagh, 150 km southwest of Dublin, until recently obtained part of its water supply from a well at Gortlandroe on the outskirts of the town. The well is reported to be 4.5 m deep and 5.5 m in diameter (Keohane 1996). The geology at the well site comprises approximately 4m of Boulder Clay overlying a shallow fissured Carboniferous Limestone aquifer.

Details of the site layout and the contamination incident are available from the Environmental Protection Agency (EPA 1996). The following is a brief synopsis only. The water supply well is located on the northern edge of an industrial estate, adjacent to a cosmetics plant and about 250 m from a small

493

plastics factory (Figure 2). There are a number of sewers and drains which run close to the well: one foul sewer passes 12.5 m to the west, another 15 m to the north, and there is a storm water drain 4 m to the east of the well.

On 3 August 1996 the water supply undertaker began to receive complaints from customers about the quality of the drinking water. Investigations initiated by the EPA, the local authorities and the health board showed that the well was contaminated. On visual inspection the well water was observed to have a "distinctive perfumed odour and milky colour", and subsequent water analyses indicated a high level of *E. coli* bacteria and low concentrations of organic chemicals including 1,1,1-trichloroethane (TCA, at 15 µg/l) and a siloxane compound known as OMCT siloxane (28 µg/l).

The presence of high levels of *E. coli* bacteria is a common indicator of sewage pollution. The contaminant TCA was also detected in the effluent from the plastics factory, and OMCT siloxane in samples of effluent which had leaked from a drain flange at the cosmetics plant site, about 75 m from the well (Figure 2).

Based on these and other findings, the EPA report concluded that the well was contaminated by both sewage and industrial effluent (although it should be added that some of the findings are disputed by other parties involved, and that investigations are continuing). Fortunately, this incident did not lead to the sort of health problems reported for Naas. Nevertheless, owing to the location of the well, its shallow depth and high vulnerability to pollution, the EPA concluded that the well is unsuitable as a source of public water supply.

6 GROUNDWATER PROTECTION

The protection of groundwater from pollution is a fundamental principle of European Union (EU) policy on water resources. Moreover, the current EU Groundwater Action Programme includes the statement "Remedial action should be taken towards leaking sewers in order to avoid pollution of groundwater" (European Commission 1996).

A groundwater protection policy has been in operation in England and Wales since 1992 (National Rivers Authority 1992). The main elements of this policy are a classification of groundwater vulnerability (based largely on soil and aquifer characteristics and depth to the watertable), definition of source protection zones or SPZs (based on travel times of pollutants and source catchment areas), and statements on groundwater protection policy in relation to potentially polluting activities. With regard to sewers, the policy indicates that the relevant regulatory authority (currently the

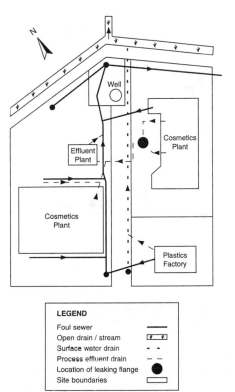

Figure 2. Sketch of the Nenagh site (after EPA 1996).

Environment Agency) would normally oppose the laying of new main sewerage systems within the innermost protection zone around a borehole (although the use of pipework which is less vulnerable to leakage would be considered on a case by case basis).

In Ireland a draft groundwater protection policy has been developed by the Geological Survey of Ireland (Daly 1995). This policy is similar in many respects to that covering England and Wales, although greater emphasis is given to the role of the subsoils rather than soils in groundwater vulnerability assessment. Policy statements with respect to potentially polluting activities are incorporated in a groundwater protection scheme matrix which also includes the vulnerability rating, SPZs and aquifer classification. To date a policy statement has not been prepared for sewers.

6.1 *Sewers in vulnerable areas*

The construction of new main sewers in a vulnerable area such as the inner protection zone around a water supply borehole should be avoided if at all possible. If sewers are to be permitted then measures need to

494

be taken to minimise the risks of leakage. Appropriate measures could include the adoption of double skin sewers of the kind used in Germany (ATV 1991). When assessing the need for rehabilitation of existing sewers, the groundwater vulnerability should be considered along with structural condition and hydraulic performance criteria.

Where sewers are present near to water supply boreholes then groundwater quality needs to be monitored carefully for indicators of sewage contamination. In addition to monitoring the raw water quality at the borehole, it may be appropriate to install shallow monitoring boreholes between the sewer(s) and the water supply borehole.

6.2 Borehole construction

Just as it is undesirable to construct a new main sewer near a water supply borehole so the opposite is also true. A risk assessment into the potential for sewage-related pollution should be carried out when locating a new borehole site, especially if this is within or close to an urban area.

Some of the sewage contamination incidents reported on in this paper involved old boreholes where the integrity of the upper lining materials was suspect or the annulus was poorly grouted. There is therefore a need to inspect the condition of existing boreholes regularly, and to carry out remedial works as necessary. For new boreholes good construction practices are essential to avoid these kind of problems in the future.

7 CONCLUSIONS

1. Despite a relatively sparse international database, there have been a sufficient number of incidents reported to indicate that sewers can be a significant source of contamination.

2. Where sewer-related contamination has coincided with breakdown or lack of chlorination, the effects on public health can be dramatic, as in the Haifa (Israel), Bramham (England) and Naas (Ireland) incidents.

3. There is a need to consider sewers in any groundwater protection policy. The construction of new main sewers close to water supply boreholes should be avoided, and groundwater protection should be considered in any maintenance strategy for existing sewers.

4. Good borehole construction practices can reduce the risk of sewer-related contamination of water supplies.

5. Monitoring of groundwater for indicators of sewage pollution is essential where sewers lie close to public water supply sources.

ACKNOWLEDGEMENTS

The authors would like to thank CIRIA and Mott MacDonald for their support in producing this paper. The funders of the CIRIA project are also gratefully acknowledged: the National Rivers Authority, North West Water, Northumbrian Water, Severn Trent Water, South West Water, Thames Water Utilities, Wessex Water and Stanton Plc. The authors would also like to acknowledge the data on the Nenagh investigation provided by the EPA report and Mr J. Keohane. The views in this paper are the authors' alone.

REFERENCES

ATV (Abwassertechnischen Vereinigung) 1991. *Sewers and drains in water extraction areas.* ATV.

Anon 1985. Leaking sewer causes typhoid in Israel. *World Water* 8.

Burston, M.W., M.M. Nazari, P.K. Bishop & D.N. Lerner 1993. Pollution of groundwater in the Coventry region (UK) by chlorinated hydrocarbon solvents. *J. Hydrol.* 149: 137-161.

CIRIA 1993. *A study of the impact of urbanisation on the Thames Gravels Aquifer.* London: CIRIA.

Daly, D. 1995. *Groundwater protection schemes in Ireland: a proposed approach - draft for consultation.* Dublin: Geological Survey of Ireland.

Daly, D., R.Thorn, & H.Henry 1993. *Septic tank systems and groundwater in Ireland.* Dublin: Geological Survey of Ireland.

Deutsch, M. 1963. Ground water contamination and legal controls in Michigan. *U.S. Geol. Surv. Wat. Supply Paper 1691.* Washington: U.S. Govt. Printing Office.

Eiswirth, M. & H. Hötzl 1994. Groundwater contamination by leaking sewage systems. *IAH Down Under '94*: 111-114.

EPA 1996. *Report on the contamination of the Gortlandroe well, Nenagh, Co. Tipperary.* Wexford: EPA.

European Commission 1996. Proposal for a European Parliament and Council Decision on an action programme for integrated groundwater protection and management. *Off. J. Eur. Comm.* 39: 1-18.

Garrett, P.G. 1992. Calling for the doctor at Kildare. *Water Bulletin* 4: 6-7.

Halliday, D. & D.N. Lerner 1992. *Sewers as a source of groundwater pollution in urban areas.* Unpublished report, Univ. of Birmingham.

Keohane, J. 1996. *Hydrogeological investigations of the Gortlandroe water supply well, Nenagh, County Tipperary.* Wexford: EPA.

Kreitler, C.W., S.E. Ragone & B.G. Katz 1978.
Nitrogen-15 / nitrogen-14 ratios of groundwater
nitrate, Long Island, New York. *Ground Water*
16: 404-409.

K.T.Cullen & Co. Ltd. 1994. *STRIDE:
Environmental Subprogramme Measure 3 - Trace
organic contaminants in Irish groundwaters.*
Report prepared on behalf of the Department of
the Environment in Dublin.

McMahon, S. 1995. *Groundwater contamination
due to leaking sewers in Ireland.* Unpublished
M.Sc dissertation, Trinity College Dublin.

Misstear, B.D., M. White, P.K. Bishop & G.
Anderson 1996. *Reliability of sewers in
environmentally vulnerable areas.* London: CIRIA

Moore, S. 1992. Naas water pollution incident 1991.
*Proc. of the 13th Env. Health Conf., Lahinch, 6-9
May 1992*: 43-53. Env. Health Officers Assoc.

Mull, R., F. Harig & M. Pielke 1992. Groundwater
management in the urban area of Hanover,
Germany. *J. Inst. Wat. & Env. Manag.* 6: 199-206.

National Rivers Authority 1992. *Policy and practice
for the protection of groundwater.* Bristol: NRA.

Price, M. & D.W. Reed 1989. The influence of mains
leakage and urban drainage on groundwater levels
beneath conurbations in the UK. *Proc. Instn. Civil.
Engrs. Part 1*, 86: 31-39.

Schleyer, R., G. Milde & K. Milde 1992. Wellhead
protection zones in Germany: delineation, research
and management. *J. Inst. Wat. & Env. Manag.* 6:
303-322.

Short, C.S. 1988. The Bramham incident, 1980 - an
outbreak of waterborne infection. *J. Inst. Wat. &
Env. Manag.* 2: 383-390.

Predicting and defining diesel contaminant flow in a fractured limestone aquifer

B. Miyazaki
ADVANCE, Whittier, Calif., USA

J. Bridenbaugh
Parsons Engineering Science, Honolulu, Hawaii, USA

ABSTRACT: Groundwater flow in fractured limestone aquifers is not linear (perpendicular to gradient), but follows a tortuous, "zigzag" path. As a result, migration of contaminants also follows a tortuous path. This paper summarizes pre-survey activities, subsurface field activities, and laboratory analytical results, for site investigations conducted at Kadena Air Base, Okinawa, Japan. Investigations were conducted, from 28 June to 25 October 1993, to identify possible sources of diesel fuel contamination found in a municipal water supply well, owned and operated by the Okinawa Enterprise Bureau, within the Air Base.

1 INTRODUCTION

Kadena Air Base (Kadena AB) is located on the island of Okinawa, Japan (Figure 1). It serves as a support base for U.S. Pacific Air Command and other Air Force missions in the Pacific rim region. Groundwater is a significant source of domestic water supply on Okinawa. A diesel spill of unknown origin contaminated this primary drinking water supply. This type of groundwater pollution is a common hazard in urban environments.

The Okinawa Enterprise Bureau (OEB) owns and operates 24 water wells located on Kadena AB. Well # 2, in the Washington Heights housing area, is located in the southwestern portion of Kadena AB. It was contaminated with diesel product in April, 1993. Since this municipal well created a major cone of depression, several potential release sources (locations) were possible.

Primary project tasks were: (1) identify the most probable diesel release source, and (2) delineate the areal extent of contamination. Defining aquifer geometry was critical to accomplishing these tasks.

A background search reduced the list of release sources to two possible locations. A soil gas survey identified one area with VOCs (volatile organic compounds) present, confirming that no more than two release sources were possible. Drilling and coring was conducted to confirm the presence of diesel in groundwater and identify the probable release source.

2 SETTING

2.1 Geologic and hydrologic setting

Okinawa is the exposed crest of a large curved submarine ridge, stretching 1,250 kilometers (km) from the southern tip of Hyushu, Japan to the northeast coast of Taiwan. The convex east and south side of this ridge is separated from the Philippine Sea basin by the Ryukkyu Trench (U.S. Army 1959).

Surface geology on Okinawa is divided into two zones. The southern zone is characterized by a thick succession of upper Tertiary clay, silt, sand, gravel, and limestone. The central and northern zone is comprised of Paleozoic and possible Mesozoic meta-sediments, along with intrusive rocks of unknown age. Near the coast, these intrusive rocks are overlain by upper Tertiary and Quaternary gravels and limestone (U.S. Army 1959).

Kadena AB is underlain by the Naha Formation (Fm), an organic limestone. It is buff to tan, indistinctly bedded, and rich in algal nodules. The Naha Fm grades laterally to impure and pure limestone beds, interfingered with unconsolidated non-calcareous gravel, sand, and silt (U.S. Army 1959). Based on aerial photographic interpretation, bedding in the vicinity of Well # 2 strikes east-northeast, and dips south at between 5 and 15 degrees.

Since Okinawa is part of a major north-northeast

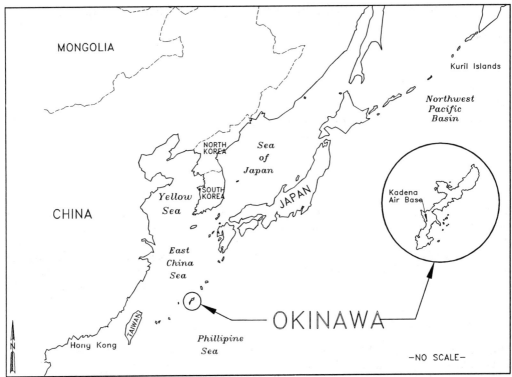

Figure 1. Location map, Okinawa, Japan.

trending island arc system, primary stress on the island is generally east-west compression. As a result, a set of dominant fracture trends is prevalent on the island. Development of major secondary solution porosity within the Kadena Aquifer of the Naha Fm is directly associated with preferential limestone dissolution along these dominant fractures. Consequently, groundwater flow and contaminant migration in this fractured limestone aquifer are not linear (perpendicular to gradient), but follow a tortuous, "zigzag" path. Since fractured limestone aquifers with secondary solution porosity are common in many parts of the world, this case study is relevant to global urban pollution hazards.

The Kadena Aquifer, underlying Well # 2, has an approximate areal extent of 20 square kilometers. (U.S. Army 1959). Water is present in primary porosity, as well as fractures and solution cavities. No published information on transmissivity or other aquifer characteristics was identified. Based on data collected during the pre-survey, general transmissivity was calculated to range between 370 and 500 square meters per day.

Regional gradient in the vicinity of Well # 2 is toward the west at 22 meters (m) per km. Depth to the top of the Kadena Aquifer at Well # 2 is 38 m below ground surface (10 m above mean sea level).

2.2 *Facilities*

A heat plant (Building 8111) with a 5,000 gallon diesel above-ground storage tank (AST) is located 20 m north of Well # 2 (see Figure 2). During May 1993, a concrete pad was constructed beneath the diesel tank. Subsurface fuel lines were abandoned, and left in-place. New subsurface fuel lines were installed to reduce the potential for undetected diesel fuel releases from the heat plant system. During the heat plant system upgrade, no evidence of subsurface diesel releases was detected.

3   INVESTIGATION PROCEDURES

In order to investigate other possible sources of diesel contamination in Well # 2, a pre-survey was

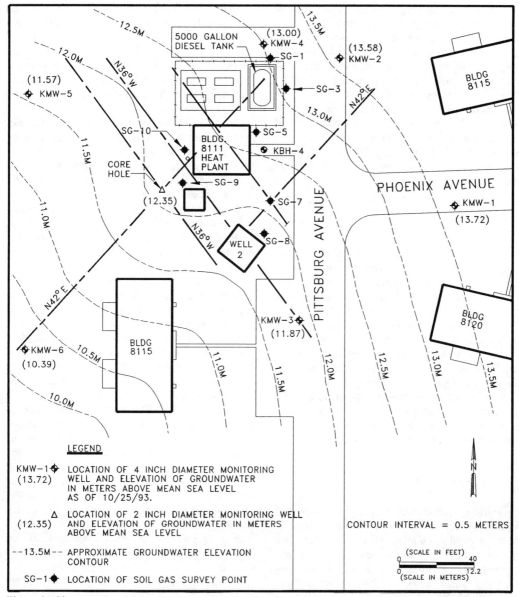

Figure 2. Site map showing monitoring well and soil gas sample locations, and 1993 groundwater contours.

conducted from 28 June to 05 July 1993. Based on the information gathered, ten potential diesel contamination sources were identified.

A subsurface investigation was conducted from 26 August to 03 November 1993. This included a soil gas survey, cutting a continuous core in proximity to Well # 2, constructing six groundwater monitoring wells, along with collecting and

analyzing groundwater samples.

Soil organic vapor (SOV) survey methods were used as a field reconnaissance tool to collect subsurface vapor samples for immediate on-site chemical analysis of volatile organic compounds (VOCs). Seven SOV points were installed around the Building 8111 heat plant. Samples were collected at depths between 1.0 and 1.2 m below ground surface. No signs of soil contamination were observed during probe installation.

Knowledge of dominant fracture orientation and its influence on secondary porosity development was used to position the six monitoring well locations. A field geologist measured 21 fracture orientations at excellently exposed Naha Fm outcrops on and around Kadena AB. Measurements were plotted on a geologic stereographic net, and two dominant vertical fracture trends become evident: (1) N36°W, and (2) N42°E (see Figure 2). Monitoring well and soil gas sample locations are shown on Figure 2.

4   RESULTS

Diesel vapors were detected at one (SG7) soil gas sample location. Diesel fuel was encountered in the core hole at a depth of 34.3 m below ground surface. No petroleum hydrocarbon contamination was detected in any of the groundwater samples.

Six of seven soil gas samples were reported free of hydrocarbon diesel vapors. Soil gas probe SG7, located 4.9 m north of Well # 2, had a diesel vapor concentration of 1.07 mg/m^3. Samples were analyzed using gas chromatography.

A continuous core was cut to provide direct information on lithology and aquifer characteristics. In the core hole, clear diesel fuel was detected in the vadose zone just above the groundwater table.

5   CONCLUSIONS

Diminishing contaminant recovery in Well # 2 support the conclusion that a one time release of diesel from the Building 8111 heat plant AST system was the most likely source of groundwater contamination. However, the source was not positively identified by the investigations conducted.

It is likely that secondary porosity development, and therefore the primary flow paths, follows the dominant fracture orientations identified. When these two fracture orientations are compared with the local groundwater contours shown on Figure 2, movement of diesel contamination through the aquifer can be inferred. Based on data obtained during the field investigation, dominant fracture trends, and the groundwater contours, the following conclusions were reached. These conclusions

assume the 5,000 gallon above ground diesel storage tank located adjacent to (north) Building 8111 is the contamination source.

1. Diesel contamination flowed southwest along fracture trend N42°E. It moved down gradient toward the core hole N42°E, past the west side of abandoned borehole KBH-4 (no visible signs of diesel contamination).

2. Due to localized variations of the groundwater gradient created by Well #2 (cone of depression), some diesel contamination flowed along intersecting fractures trending N36°W. Contamination moved downgradient (southeast) toward OEB Well # 2 and soil gas sample location SG7.

3. It appears that diesel contamination moved southeast along fracture trend N36°W is being captured by Well #2. Diesel vapors were not detected in gas probe SG8 (about 5 m south of SG7 and adjacent to the east side of Well # 2).

Based on the history of contamination and results obtained from the subsurface investigation, it appears that contamination is limited to specific flow pathways between the above ground diesel fuel storage tank and piping facilities north of heat plant Building 8111, and OEB Well # 2. It appears that the AST containment and subsurface piping replacement at heat plant Building 8111 eliminated further occurrences of contamination.

This case study illustrates the importance of understanding the factors controlling groundwater and contaminant flow through fractured limestone aquifers. In many cases, incorrect conclusions are drawn regarding potential pollution hazard levels based on lack of identified contamination in samples collected from this type of aquifer. Correct aquifer characterisation, along with a knowledge of the factors controlling fluid flow, are critical when addressing pollution in urban areas underlain by these aquifers.

6   REFERENCES

Engineering-Science, Inc. 1993. *Kadena Air Base, well contamination pre-survey report.*

Engineering-Science, Inc. 1994. *Kadena Air Base, well contamination field survey report.*

United States Army 1959. *Military geology of Okinawa-Jima, Ryukyu-Retto, Volume II: Water Resources, and Volume V: Geology.*

Groundwater in the Urban Environment: Problems, Processes and Management, Chilton et al. (eds)
© *1997 Balkema, Rotterdam, ISBN 90 5410 837 1*

Risk assessment of groundwater contamination from the southeastern Bucharest landfill

V.D.Mocanu & V.D.Mirca
PROED S.A., Bucharest, Romania

M.Albu
Faculty of Geology and Geophysics, University of Bucharest, Romania

ABSTRACT: 1,333 tonnes of industrial and domestic wastes from Bucharest are deposited daily in a former quarry on the southeastern edge of the city in the Dambovita valley. These wastes include dangerous substances from several hospitals and from the chemical industry. The contaminated water on the floor of the quarry is in hydraulic connection with shallow aquifers discharging to the Dambovita river and possibly to the deep aquifers of the Fratesti Strata. Some pollutants have already been identified in the deep aquifers, endangering the drinking water supply of the city. The paper presents the results of an investigation of the hydrogeologic conditions and the risk of uncontrolled groundwater contamination. Mitigation measures and remediation for protection of groundwater resources are suggested.

1 INTRODUCTION

Bucharest is a city of 2.1 million people producing 1,622 tonnes of domestic and industrial wastes daily. Of this only six tonnes are incinerated, 79 tonnes are recycled and 1,333 tonnes are deposited in the main landfill of Bucharest which is sited in a former quarry extending over 104 ha on the southeastern edge of the city. The remaining 204 tonnes are not collected and are disposed of by fly tipping around the city.

The void utilised for the landfill is about 2 million m^3, folmed by quarrying for clay. The clays are underlain by two shallow sand and gravel aquifers separated from deep sandy aquifers of the Fratesti Strata, by relatively impermeable clays and silts. The Fratesti Strata are formed by the three different permeable layers of sand and gravel, known as the A, B, and C layers, separated by clay levels (Figure 1). However, some local interconnection may exist between the different layers, whose total thickness can be estimated at about 70 to 100 m. This aquifer has good quality water and good protection against pollution, and provides 15% of the city's water supply.

The shallow aquifers are highly vulnerable to pollution because they extend from the surface down to depths of a few tens of meters. Nevertheless, these aquifers are exploited from domestic wells of the Leordeni and Glina suburban areas (Figure 2). The landfill has used about half of the void; it is unlined and its base is in the upper shallow aquifer. The wastes deposited include toxic substances and other contaminants from the chemical industry (Albu et al. 1994) and from several hospitals, including waste that may contain disease - carrying micro organisms. Pollution of groundwater around the landfill was identified during assessment of a nearby site for a new waste water treatment plant, where several domestic wells in the shallow aquifers had been closed due to contamination of the water. Following this, a preliminary hydrogeological investigation was required by Bucharest Municipality to establish the extent of pollution of the shallow aquifers and the risk of contaminantion of deep aquifers providing the water supply for the city.

2 HYDROGEOLOGICAL INVESTIGATION

The main investigation consisted of: surveying and mapping the area of the landfill; measuring the water level in six old and four new observation wells (piezometers) in the shallow aquifers; sampling and chemical analysis of the surface water and groundwater from the landfill and overflow drain wells in the shallow aquifers.

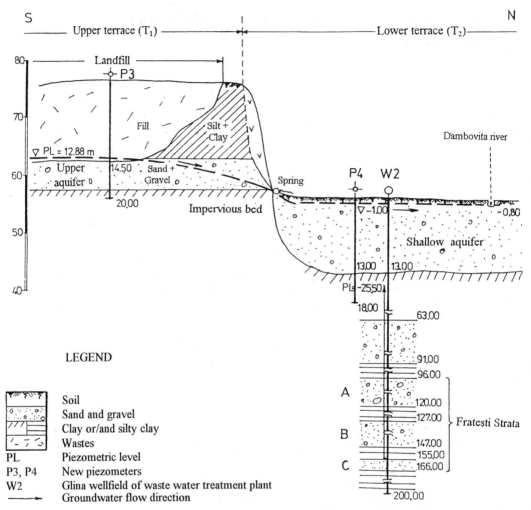

Figure 1. Cross section on Dambovita river in the area of the Glina landfill.

The investigation gave the following results:

• the landfill is not contained by continuous physical barriers and the pollution of groundwater is obvious both on the floor and on the northern edge of the landfill;

• in the landfill, the contaminants are dissolved and transported in leachate from the surface to the floor (Mather 1994) and afterwards by groundwater flow from the upper aquifer to the lower alluvial aquifer in the Dambovita flood plain (Figure 1);

• in the shallow aquifers, the groundwater flows from southwest to northeast, discharging to the Dambovita river;

• the water types are sodium bicarbonate in the landfill (Pl), sodium chloride in the overflow drain (P2), calcium bicarbonate in the upper aquifer (P3) and

sodium bicarbonate in the lower aquifer (P4), as shown in Figure 3;

• the first determinations of toxic components in the shallow aquifers indicate concentrations of chromium, nickel and cyanide above the limits for drinking water standards;

• at the site of the new waste water treatment plant (Figure 2), the water from the three deep wells is already undrinkable because of the increased content of ammonium and organic matter. Landfill leachate is considered the most likely source of pollution, as water levels in the wells are some 10 to 20 m below those in the shallow aquifers, due to pumping for the water supply of Bucharest (Mocanu 1994). The wells themselves may provide preferential flowpaths, behind the casings (Bretotean et al. 1994).

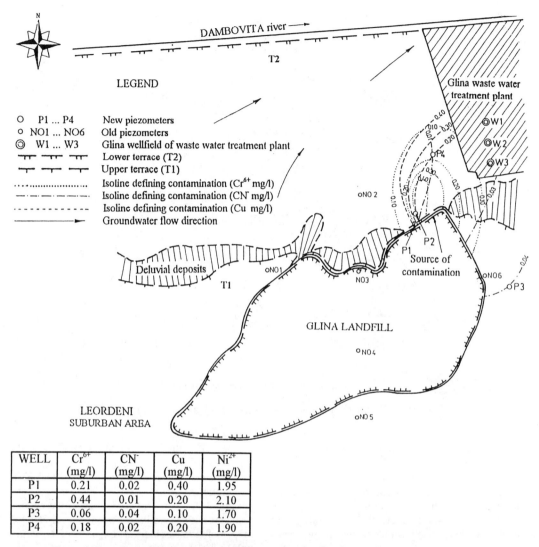

WELL	Cr^{6+} (mg/l)	CN^- (mg/l)	Cu (mg/l)	Ni^{2+} (mg/l)
P1	0.21	0.02	0.40	1.95
P2	0.44	0.01	0.20	2.10
P3	0.06	0.04	0.10	1.70
P4	0.18	0.02	0.20	1.90

Figure 2. Location of the Bucharest landfill area showing local groundwater contamination.

3 CONCLUSIONS AND PROPOSALS

The landfill on the southeastern edge of Bucharest is a major source of groundwater contamination, with toxic components such as chromium, nickel and cyanide. The contamination plume extends in the shallow aquifers from the northeastern corner of the landfill to the site of the new waste water treatment plant and farther to the Dambovita river (Figure 2). Moreover, there is a risk of contaminant penetration from the shallow aquifers to the deep aquifers of the Fratesti Strata not only by leakage through aquitards but also by preferential pathways around the casing of water supply wells.

The proposed mitigation measures include:

1. controlling the disposal of dangerous wastes from the chemical industry and from hospitals;

2. monitoring of surface water and groundwater quality for the whole area, and modelling to determine the most effective of the measures listed below to control the migration of leachate from the landfill:

• lining the floor of the remaining void before deposition of waste;

• covering the deposited wastes with an impervious layer;

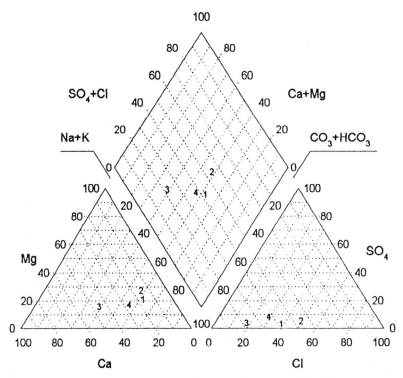

1,2,3,4: Water analyses from new piezometers P1 to P4

Figure 3. Classification of the groundwaters by means of a Piper diagram.

• collecting the water from precipitation by a drain around the landfill;

• surrounding the landfill by a physical barrier such as a bentonite cement wall, beginning with the northeastern corner of the landfill;

• hydraulic control of the shallow aquifers and controlling the contaminant plume by a pump - and - treat system;

3. improving waste collection and recycling, and environmental education (Mocanu 1994).

REFERENCES

Albu, M., G. Tomescu, M. Bretotean, & R. Pane 1994. Types of industrial impact on grouudwater resources in Romania, *Proceedings of the International Hydrogeological Symposium,* Constantza, Romania: 1-7 Bucharest: University Press.

Bretotean, M., S. Wagstaff, F. Zamfirescu, W.G. Burgess, & M. Albu 1994. Risque de la deterioration de la qualite des ressources en eau du s,vsteme aquifer descouclles de Fratesti dans la zone de Bucharest. *Proceedings of the International Hydrogeological Symposium,* Constantza, Romania: 26 - 36 Bucharest: University Press.

Mather, J.D. 1994. The attenuation of the organic component of landfill leachate in the unsaturated zone: a review. *Quart. J. Engineering Geol.* 22: 241 - 246.

Mocanu, V.D. 1994. *Technical studies and design for the upgrading and the expansion of the Bucharest water supply and sewerage systems.* Hydrogeological Report, PROED S.A. C370H/94.

Industrial legacy of contaminated land and urban groundwater pollution

I.K.Nevecherya
Laboratory of Geological Environment Protection, Moscow State University, Russia

V.L.Voronin & V.M.Shestakov
Department of Hydrogeology, Moscow State University, Russia

ABSTRACT: A new district of Moscow - Maryinsky Park - is built on land which 100 years ago was occupied by filtration fields for sewage wastes from the city. As a result of the long-term operation of this waste disposal system, serious pollution of groundwaters has occurred. The construction of the new district can potentially influence hydrogeological conditions greatly and may change the character of the spreading of accumulated pollution. Building of the new district may cause increasing flow of polluted groundwaters into deep aquifers which are used for water supply.

1 INTRODUCTION

The study area is located in the south-east of Moscow, in the river Moscow valley. It was the location, over a period of 100 years, of "filtration fields" for waste waters for the city. The area of the former filtration fields covers about 20 km². The western one quarter of the waste disposal area has in the 1970s been built over, becoming the Maryino district of Moscow. The other three quarters of the former filtration fields are also presently being built over. This is the new Moscow district of Maryinsky Park.

The operation of the filtration fields was as follows. The waters, after initial purifying, were deposited in spreading basins from which some water evaporated and the rest infiltrated into the ground. During the operation the basins gradually filled with fine-grained deposits. As a result of the waste water disposal, the unsaturated zone and the upper shallow aquifer below the site are grossly polluted.

The purpose of the paper is to draw together the previously published data on the area (Efremov & Bogdanov 1993; Shestakov et al. 1995) in order to assess the effect that the construction of the new Maryino district has had and is having on the spreading of the groundwater contamination.

2 GEOLOGICAL STRUCTURE

The geological sequence of the area consists of Carboniferous limestones overlain by Jurassic and Quaternary sediments (Shvetsov 1991). The younger sediments infill topography formed by three ancient drainage systems. The oldest system is cut into the Carboniferous sequence, and its valley was subsequently filled by Bathonian and Callovian (Jurassic) sediments. In preglacial times, a river system cut into the Jurassic rocks, and its valley was then filled in the early Quaternary by alluvial sands. The most recent drainage system has cut into the Quaternary sediments and its valley is now partly filled with recent alluvial sediments (Efremov & Klukvin 1989). In broad outline the three valley systems coincide, but examined closely it is clear that there exist complex cross-cutting inter-relationships, with the depth of downcutting being very variable. The modern river valley has a flood plain and three terraces.

The Maryinsky Park district is located on the flood plain and the first terrace: the second and third terraces surround it to the north and east. The Maryino district is located to the west, and it is bordered to the south by the Moscow River which here sharply changes direction from east-west to north-south.

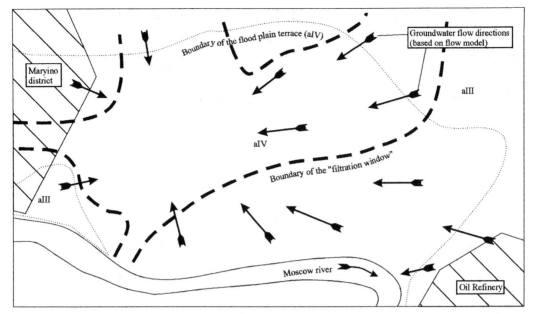

Figure 1. Ground water flow patterns in the Maryinsky Park area.

The oldest Mesozoic sediments of the area are Bathonian-Callovian sandy clays with beds of fine-grained sand, sandy loam, and loam. They lie on the eroded surface of middle Carboniferous rocks, filling in pre-Jurassic valleys, but they are absent in the central part of the study area where the preglacial valley has incised most deeply. The maximum thickness of these sediments is 32 m. The middle and upper Callovian sediments transgressively overlie the Bathonian-Callovian sediments. They are represented by a monotonous sequence of dense, darkly-coloured clays 2-6 m in thickness. In the central part of the area these clays are missing.

In the centre of the study area, Oxfordian Jurassic sediments are barely represented, but they occur in the east where they are present even in the modern river channel. They comprise dense grey and brown clays and black partly sandy clays, and are of 2-8 m in thickness. In the east, sand with clayey beds of Tithonian age occur.

The Quaternary sediments in the area are of glacial, fluvioglacial, and alluvial origin, and comprise sand, sandy loam, loam, clay, and peat. They reach over 20 m in thickness. They mainly overlie Callovian and Oxfordian clays, and where these are absent, Bathonian-Callovian sand and clay: where the Jurassic sequence has been removed by erosion, the Quaternary sediments directly overlie the Carboniferous limestones. Building rubble,

household waste, and the filtration bed deposits cover the Quaternary sediments to a depth of 0.2 to more than 3 m: in the following descriptions these deposits will be referred to as technogeneous sediments.

3 HYDROGEOLOGICAL CONDITIONS

The aquifer units present in the area are: the unconfined technogeneous sediments, the unconfined Quaternary sandy alluvial sediments, and the confined and unconfined Bathonian-Callovian sediments present in the ancient valleys. The Jurassic sediments have relatively low permeability. Confined, sometimes artesian, aquifers exist in the lower and middle Carboniferous sequence: these aquifers are used for public and industrial supplies for the region and for Moscow city.

The general regional groundwater flow direction is downwards. Recharge of the Quaternary aquifers occurs by infiltration of precipitation, waste water, and River Moscow water, the latter over half the year. Discharge of these aquifers occurs partially via flow to the Moscow River, but mainly via downwards flow to the deeper Jurassic aquifers in the ancient valleys where the regional Jurassic aquitard is eroded.

Although in general the Jurassic sequence acts as a regional aquitard, where these sediments are eroded, "filtration windows" allow direct connection between the Quaternary and middle Carboniferous aquifers. In the past, groundwater discharge would have occurred from the Carboniferous aquifers upwards through the filtration windows into the Quaternary aquifers, and thence into the Moscow River. However, abstraction has lowered groundwater levels in the Carboniferous aquifers and now water flows downwards from the Quaternary aquifers.

A mathematical model was developed to investigate the groundwater flow system in the Quaternary sediments. The interactions with the river and the deeper aquifers were taken into account by setting appropriate internal and external boundary conditions. Recharge was determined using an inverse approach based on measured groundwater heads: more than three hundred monitoring wells are available in the area, though after careful quality screening data from only 100 were used.

The modelling indicated that the groundwater flow direction in the Quaternary sediments is generally towards the filtration windows, and thence to the deeper aquifers (Figure 1).

4 GROUNDWATER POLLUTION

Both anthropogenic and natural factors have been important in causing pollution of surface and groundwaters. A major source of the pollution of the groundwaters in the Quaternary sediments is the waste water from the filtration fields. A secondary source is the fine-grained "mud" deposits in the filtration beds. The Jurassic and Carboniferous aquifers then receive the polluted recharge from the Quaternary sediments.

The migration of the waste waters is confirmed by distinctive concentrations of ammonium, manganese, cadmium, iron, and dissolved oil. Table 1 shows average concentrations of these determinands in the ground waters of the filtration basin muds, the Quaternary deposits, and the middle Carboniferous aquifers.

Another important source of pollution in the area is a large oil refinery contiguous with the filtration basins to the southwest. The refinery is more than 60 years old. The Quaternary aquifer is badly polluted by free and dissolved oil, with the total concentration of the dissolved oil reaching 70 mg/L. In the area of the refinery, the groundwater chemistry has changed greatly in composition. Hence, the groundwaters no longer contain appreciable concentrations of sulphate and nitrate. At the same time, bicarbonate and ammonium concentrations are increased, the latter up to 30 mg/L. As shown by Nevecherya & Voronin

Table 1. Average concentration of pollution indicator species in the filtration basin muds, the Quaternary deposits, and the middle Carboniferous aquifers (mg/L).

Unit	NH_4	Fe	Mn	Cd	Oil
Filtration basin mud	na	27208	381	70	731
Quaternary sediments	270	5.6	31	0.04	9.2
Middle Carboniferous aquifers	1.2	1.1	0.05	0.0012	0.26

(1997), the characteristics are typical of waters affected by long term petroleum pollution. The groundwater below the refinery is recharged, at least in part, to the Quaternary sediments elsewhere in the study area (Shestakov & Voronin 1997).

5 CHANGE IN HYDROGEOLOGICAL CONDITIONS FOLLOWING CONSTRUCTION OF MARYINSKY PARK

The construction of the Maryinsky Park district was accompanied by the removal of the filtration basin muds and the infilling of the basins with sand. The modelling work using the inverse method outlined above indicates that the recharge in the area developed in the 1970s is around 200 mm/y, much higher than the rate of infiltration through the original filtration basins (40 mm/y). This increase results from the removal of the low permeability muds and from leakage from water supply pipes and from sewers. To counteract the increase of infiltration, drainage systems have been installed. However, the inverse method modelling indicates that these measures have not been successful.

It would be expected that the cessation of the waste water dumping together with excavation of the filtration muds would result in improvement of the groundwater quality. However, given the extent of the pollution present in the unsaturated zone, little improvement is likely in the foreseeable future. The increase in recharge rates to the Quaternary sediments will be translated into an increase in the recharge to the deeper aquifers, thus threatening the water supplies to the city. Modelling indicates that the increase of flow to the middle Carboniferous aquifers is about fourfold relative to that prior to the urbanisation.

6 CONCLUSION

The existence of waste water filtration basins has resulted in the pollution of shallow groundwater systems in the Maryinsky Park district of Moscow. The shallow groundwater systems are connected to the deep Carboniferous aquifers used for water supply for the city. Hence these important aquifers are under threat.

ACKNOWLEDGEMENT

This study comprises part of the research undertaken on contract to Moscow City Committee of Nature Protection.

REFERENCES

Efremov D.I. & I.V. Bogdanov 1993. *Geoecological state of Lublinsky Filtration Fields* (in Russian). Moscow: CRGC - Geocentre-Moscow.

Efremov D.I. & A.N. Klukvin, 1989. Present state and prognosis of hydrogeological and technical condition, changes as a result of rising of groundwater levels in Moscow. *Geotechnique and hydrogeology of Moscow:* 46-69 (in Russian). Moscow.

Nevecherya I.K. & V.L. Voronin, 1997. *Changes of macrocomponent composition of groundwater affected by free oil plume* (in Russian). In preparation.

Shvetsov P.F. (ed.) 1991. *Constantly operating models of city agglomeration territories hydrolithosphere (an example of Moscow agglomeration),* in Russian). Moscow: Nauka.

Shestakov V.M., I.K. Nevecherya & E.A. Skovortsova, 1995. *Development of hydrogeoecological monitoring scheme on Lublinsky Filtration Fields* (in Russian). Moscow: Moscow State University.

Shestakov V.M. & V.L. Voronint 1997. *Oil contamination of groundwater at Moscow Refinery* (in Russian). In preparation.

Groundwater in the Urban Environment: Problems, Processes and Management, Chilton et al. (eds)
© *1997 Balkema, Rotterdam, ISBN 90 5410 837 1*

Geophysics for monitoring of groundwater contamination

B.Olofsson, J.Aaltonen & Å.Fleetwood
Division of Land and Water Resources, Royal Institute of Technology (KTH), Stockholm, Sweden

G.Blomqvist
Swedish National Road and Transport Research Institute (VTI), Linköping, Sweden

ABSTRACT: Geophysical methods have be used for groundwater contamination investigation programmes in urbanized areas at waste deposits and for studies of salt water intrusion. Such methods are valuable as basis for the setting up of chemical monitoring programmes, especially in heterogeneous and anisotropic media. The measurements are usually repeatable and can also be a part of a monitoring programme for direct identification of the spread of pollutants. The paper gives some examples of the use of environmental geophysics at urban areas in Sweden.

1 INTRODUCTION

Traditionally, investigation of groundwater quality around potential pollution sources, comprise drilling and inserting of measurement tubes, followed by water collecting and chemical analysis. The placing of the monitoring sites is often more or less randomly carried out since access to reliable hydrogeological site investigation material is often limited. Within hydraulically homogeneous conditions leachates might be sufficiently monitored by such sites, whereas under strongly heterogeneous and anisotropic conditions monitoring of the leakage pattern might fail. Drilling of control wells can also be a risk itself because it can puncture impermable layers and, hence, construct new pathways for the leakage. Therefore, in hydraulically heterogeneous areas, there is a great need for non-destructive measurement methods, which monitor properties in volumes instead of spot-wise randomly located sites.

Geophysical measurements have been used for a long time for groundwater exploration due to the fact that groundwater has different geophysical properties, such as electrical characteristics, than the soil or rock matrix. Analyses made on leakage from landfills often show a considerable increase in salinity compared to unaffected water (Chian & DeWalle 1976). Therefore, geoelectric methods have been used to detect groundwater with low resistivity such as contaminated groundwater at landfills (Seeman. 1986). In addition, electromagnetic methods such as the Slingram method and IP

(Induced Polarization) are useful for conductivity measurements.

Combined geophysical methods have be used in several different ways during the planning and construction phases and continously during the operation of landfills or other hazardous constructions. In summary the use can be for:

1. Determination of sites for landfills, roads and other hazardous land uses. Measurements can be carried out on a regional scale (using e.g. airborne geophysics) or on a detailed scale (using ground geophysics) in order to identify the most favourable location. The interpreted measurements can give information on geology and stratigraphy of rock and soil and on tectonic structures, and therefore give a base for design, detailed localization for drilling, and other more expensive investigation techniques as well as for the setting up of monitoring programmes.

2. Direct identification of polluted areas. Geophysical methods can to some extent be used for identifying the spread of pollutants and to clarify pathways. However, the pollutants must change the physical properties of the ground (e.g. the conductivity) and it might be difficult to distinguish small anomalies from the natural seasonal and geological variations. The methods have been used in order to detect salt water intrusion in coastal areas.

3. Regurlarly monitoring programmes carried out at landfills etc. Repeated measurements using geophysical methods along fixed control lines or at fixed positions can reveal changes of the physical

509

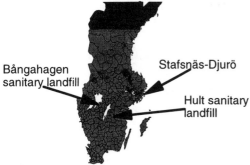

Figure 1. Locations of described examples in southern Sweden

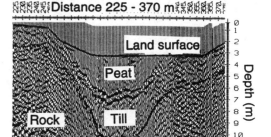

Figure 2. Interpreted results of a GPR profile intersecting a fracture zone at Bångahagen landfill.

properties, which in turn can be a result of spread of pollutants. For hazardous waste deposits etc, a fixed monitoring system can be set up with continous measurements.

4. *Identifying of hazardous objects* such as dumped barrels of chemicals covered by soil, dumped ammunition in lakes, industrial remnants etc.

Three examples from geophysical investigations for the study of stratigraphy and tracing of leachates at urban areas in Sweden are presented below.

2 EXPANSION OF A LANDFILL

2.1 Problems and aims

The aim of the project was to gain basic geological information, such as soil stratigraphy and soil depth in a planned expansion area adjacent to Bångahagen landfill (Figure 1). The present landfill is located on clay covered by peat whereas the planned new disposal area is located on glacial till with a few outcrops of crystalline hard rock.

2.2 Investigation methods and results

The geophysical methods VLF (Very Low Frequency) and GPR (Ground Penetrating Radar) were selected in combination with geological and tectonic field studies and conductivity measurements of water in ditches, observation tubes and dug pits.

The measurements revealed a rather small soil depth (1-3m) on top of a slightly undulating hard rock surface (Fleetwood & Olofsson 1993). However, two distinct depressions of the bedrock surface were encountered (Figure 2), formed by steep electrically conductive fracture zones. One of these zones extended into the present disposal area. Conductivity measurements along the zone also indicated a discharge area with increased salinity probably due to flow of leachate along the fracture zone, beneath the existing double system of water collecting ditches (Figure 3).

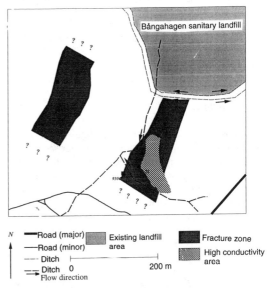

Figure 3. Interpretation from geophysical measurements south of Bångahagen landfill.

Complementary geophysical investigations south and north of the existing landfill showed that the tectonic zone diminished southwards forcing the leakage upwards to the land surface, whereas the extension of the zone north of the present landfill was highly electrically conductive beneath layers of peat and clay (Olofsson & Fleetwood 1994). A new observation tube placed in the north part of the zone indicated an escape of leachate northwards.

2.3 Conclusions

The existing monitoring programme based on water collecting from observation tubes and chemical analyses, which had been running for decades, had so far shown no signs of impact outside the collecting system of ditches. The combination between various geophysical measurements, geological field studies and quick conductivity measurements, which in total were carried out within four days revealed a clear indication of impact on groundwater along a previous unknown fracture zone. The measurements provide a basis for modifying and optimizing the existing monitoring programme.

3. SALT WATER INTRUSION

3.1 Problems and aims
A growth of population (especially during summers) in the area of Stafsnäs-Djurö in the Stockholm archipelago, has raised the need of fresh water. The islands mainly consist of bare outcrops with minor depressions usually filled with till and clay. At Stafsnäs-Djurö, several spots of sand and gravel have given the possibility to extract groundwater from dug wells in the sandy formations. However, the withdrawal has led to a raised content of salt in the groundwater, probably due to salt water intrusion. The aims were to test if a combination of various geophysical methods could identify the intrusion process in order to provide a basis for suggestions for remedial measures.

3.2 Methods and results
A comprehensive geophysical measurement programme was carried out using geoelectrical resistivity methods (vertical electrical sounding as well as electrical profiling), electromagnetic methods (using two types of ground conductivity meters), GPR and refraction seismic as well as drilling and water sampling.

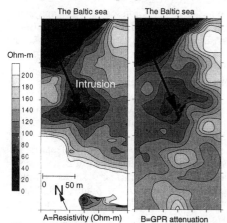

A=Resistivity (Ohm-m) B=GPR attenuation

Figure 4. A comparison between some geophysical methods at Stafsnäs-Djurö area. **A**=Ground conductivity measurements (using Slingram) recalculated as resistivity (ohm-m), coil separation 4m. B=GPR, radar wave attenuation (inverse relative scale).

The electrical measurements and the electromagnetic methods worked well in harmony in identifying areas of increased conductivity (Huber & Lundqvist 1995). GPR data were used for interpretation of soil stratigraphy and groundwater levels. However, using the radar wave attenuation as a variable, it was also possible to get a rough picture of the variation of conductivity which was highly correlated to the geoelectrical and electromagnetical methods (Figure 4).

The geophysical measurements revealed an advancing seawater intrusion. However, the intrusion showed a complex pattern indicating "tongued" flow.

3.3 Conclusions
A combination of ground penetrating radar, which can give information on stratigraphy of the soil and a rough picture of the conductivity pattern, and one of the geoelectrical or electromagnetical methods, which can identify zones of higher conductivity, seemed to be the most favourable combination for detection of the salt water intrusion. The investigation gave a much better understanding of the complex intrusion process, which could not have been obtained by random drilling and water sampling, due to the heterogeneity and anisotropy of the groundwater flow. However, the tongue flow of the intrusion, which took place in the central part of the investigation area, favours the possibilities of prevention measures such as hydraulic or artificial barriers.

4 MONITORING PROGRAMMES

4.1 Problems and aims
The sanitary landfill at Hult (Figure 1) is located in an area consisting of thich layers of peat (4-6m) above silt and clay. The regular monitoring programme consisted of groundwater sampling and chemical analyses in observation tubes. No traces of leakage through the existing double system of ditches have been recognized. The aims were to investigate the possibility of using geophysical methods regurlarly within the monitoring programme at the landfill as well as to investigate the soil stratigraphy of an area planned for expansion of the landfill.

4.2 Methods and results
The geophysical methods selected were GPR in order to clarify the soil stratigraphy and geoelectrical methods (using VES - vertical electrical sounding - and electrical profiling) in order to clarify the

resistivity distribution vertically as well as horizontally for the detection of leakages.

The VES-measurements which were carried out at sites previously measured six years earlier, revealed similar results and a clear repeatability of the geoelectrical measurements (Fleetwood & Olofsson 1996). Therefore, a control line for geoelectrical profiling along the whole southern and western sides of the landfill has been set up and background measurements have been carried out. Repeated measurements on an annual basis have been recommended. A special computer programme for data handling, calculations and presentations including an automatic alarm system for repeated geoelectrical measurements at landfills have been developed. The alarm starts if the resistivity decreases to a value lower than a fixed limit.

Analyses of GPR measurements in the planned expansion area were carried out using an interactive interpretation computer programme, which gives the possibility of pseudo3D interpretations. From profiles of radar data, an areal model using *kriging* was compiled (Figure 5). The analysis revealed that the thickness of the peat layer is much smaller than at the existing disposal area and the basement crops out at the eastern part of the area. The model gives the basis for the optimization of the placing of observation wells and also for the setting up of further geophysical investigations. A geophysical monitoring programme has been suggested.

4.3 Conclusions

The geophysical investigations have not indicated any leakage from the landfill. The local geology gives a high degree of repeatability of the geoelectrical measurements, which in turn favours the setting up of a complete geophysical control programme. Such a programme can reduce the need for chemical analyses, and hence reduce the costs for the monitoring programme. At the same time it increases the certainty of the control programme since it measures the whole volume along the measurement profile line.

FINAL CONCLUSIONS

The examples point out the advantages and possibilities of using geophysical methods for various kinds of monitoring programmes in urban areas. The geophysical methods can be applied interactively during the planning, construction and operation stages of a landfill and other hazardous land uses. Although the interpretation of geophysical data needs long experience, repeated measurements

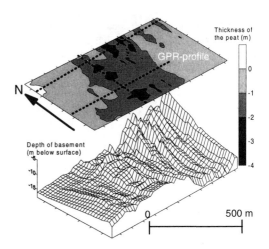

Figure 5 Calculated thickness of the peat in a planned new disposal area at Hult as well as the estimated depth to the basement. The models were compiled using kriging.

along control lines can be carried out routinely. Deviations from the previous measurements indicate that the physical properties (and hence the chemical properties) have changed.

REFERENCES

Chian, E.S.K. & F.B. DeWalle 1976. Sanitary landfill leachates and their treatment. *J.Environ.Eng.-ASCE* 102(2):411-431.

Fleetwood, Å. & B. Olofsson 1993. Geophysical investigations at the sanitary landfill Bångahagen, Mariestad. *Unpublished report*. Div.of Land and Water Resources, Royal Inst. of Technology, Stockholm.(In Swedish).

Fleetwood, Å. & B. Olofsson 1996.Geophysical control programme at Hult landfill. *Unpublished report*. Div.of Land and Water Resources, Royal Inst. of Technology, Stockholm.(In Swedish).

Huber, A. & A. Lundqvist 1995. Application of geophysical methods in salt water intrusion detection in a coastal aquifer system. *M.Sc Thesis report series* 1995:7. Div.of Land and Water Resources, Royal Inst. of Technology, Stockholm.

Olofsson, B. & Å. Fleetwood 1994. Geophysical investigations at the sanitary landfill Bångahagen, Mariestad - complementary measurements. *Unpublished report*. Div.of Land and Water Resources, Royal Inst. of Technology, Stockholm.(In Swedish).

Seeman, P-O. 1986. *Landfill leachate attenuation in soil and ground water, II*. Report Trita-Kut 1046. Royal Institute of Technology, Stockholm.

Feasibility of a dual pump recovery (DPR) system to recover a dense plume of contaminated groundwater

Claus J.Otto & Lloyd R.Townley
Centre for Groundwater Studies, CSIRO Land and Water, Perth, W.A., Australia

ABSTRACT: A leaking point source located in an urban area has resulted in a dense plume composed mainly of ammonium sulfate. The contaminant has accumulated in the bottom of a regional unconfined sandy limestone aquifer system. With a current conventional single-pump system of four recovery bores it would take 17 years to remediate the aquifer. The main limitation of the current remedial strategy is that the efficiency of recovery is decreasing due to downconing of the dense/freshwater interface and increasing dilution by freshwater. A dual pump recovery (DPR) system has been developed to enhance the efficiency of recovery operations and to reduced the duration of remediation. Results are presented for DPR trials in two adjacent bores and a single bore. It is estimated that a DPR system can halve the recovery time.

1 INTRODUCTION

The encroachment of new residential and commercial areas into areas of past industrial land use activities is of particular concern in the Perth metropolitan area, Western Australia. A leaking point source, now located within the metropolitan area, has resulted in a dense ammonium sulfate plume (up to 22 g L^{-1}), which has spread radially over an area of several square kilometres. The contaminant has accumulated in the lower 30-50% of a regional unconfined sandy limestone aquifer with a saturated thickness of about 20 m. It is estimated that the total volume of contaminated groundwater (EC >2000 μScm^{-1}) is 12.3 x 10^6 m^3 (based on 1994 data).

At the present time, four single-pump recovery bores extract on average 1166 m^3d^{-1}, well below the capacity of the bores. It is estimated that it would take about 17 years to remediate the aquifer (3/4 of contaminated groundwater recovered). The main limitation of the current remedial strategy is that the recovery efficiency of the existing bores is decreasing, due to downconing of the saline/freshwater interface and increasing dilution by freshwater. Recovery efficiency is defined here to be the recovered concentration relative to the concentration in the contaminated layer. Single-pump recovery in the density-stratified aquifer mixes the groundwater recovered from each layer and requires all recovered water to be treated. A dual pump recovery (DPR) system has been developed to counter-balance the downconing hydraulically and prevent the invasion of fresh water.

2 DUAL PUMP RECOVERY SYSTEM

The concept of a DPR system is simple and not new. Similar techniques have been used or have been proposed to prevent upconing of the seawater wedge in coastal aquifers (e.g. Underwood & Atherton 1964; Zack 1988), to recover dense coal tar wastes (Villaume et al. 1983) and to recover light oils which float on the water table (e.g. Wisniewski et al. 1985).

A DPR system consists of a pair of lower and upper pumps that can be used to recover dense contaminated groundwater in an aquifer that contains distinct layers of fresh and dense groundwater. The lower pump is the recovery pump, and the upper pump the control pump, so-called because it balances the rate of extraction from the recovery pump so as to ensure that contaminated water enters the recovery pump and relatively uncontaminated water enters the control pump. This relatively fresh water can be used for artificial recharge, irrigation or other water management purposes.

2.1 *Theory*

The principle of a DPR system is that, apart from local drawdown near a pump, groundwater flows horizontally towards a pumping bore, such that dense contaminated groundwater is captured by the lower recovery pump and freshwater is captured by the upper control pump. The elevation of the almost horizontal saline/freshwater interval remains stable at one or two aquifer thicknesses from the bore.

In the case of a fully-penetrating fully-screened bore, flow in both the near and far fields towards the bore is essentially horizontal (given large horizontal K values), i.e. the interface remains horizontal. Drawdown and vertical flow near the bore only become important when the degree of anisotropy increases, pumping rates are very high or the diameter of the bore is very small. The flow pattern in the near field is very different if partially penetrating or partially screened bores are used (e.g. one in the contaminated layer and one in the freshwater layer). However, flow directions are still horizontal in the far field, and the concentrations of recovered water will still depend on the location of the interface in the far field, regardless of the details of flow directions in the near field (as long as vertical dispersion is insignificant).

2.2 Pumping rates

Recovery of the contaminant is controlled adaptively by varying the ratio of pumping from the two pumps. Therefore a key issue is the appropriate selection of pumping rates. If at any stage the pumping rate of the control pump is too small, the concentration of contaminant in the recovered groundwater from the recovery pump will start to decrease. Conversely, if the pumping rate in the control pump is too large, the concentration of contaminant in the groundwater in the control pump will start to increase, thus limiting re-use and perhaps requiring treatment of the control water. During the operation of a DPR system, concentrations at the pump outlets need to be monitored frequently and pumping rates must be adjusted to changes in concentrations (or elevations of the interface in the far field), so as to maximise the efficiency and the rate of mass recovery of contaminated groundwater at all times.

3 RESULTS OF DPR FIELD TRIALS

The DPR system has been tested extensively in the field. For the first trials, a pair of pumps was installed in two adjacent bores screened below and above the interface within the aquifer. An inflatable packer separated the two screens. In a second field trial, the pumps were installed in a single fully-penetrating, fully-screened large-diameter bore. In either case, the intake of the recovery pump was

placed at the bottom of the contaminated zone, and the intake of the control pump was placed within the freshwater zone.

The hydraulic conductivity of the sandy limestone aquifer ($\sim$700 m d^{-1}) is more or less homogeneous and the interface is relatively sharp. It was reasoned that to pump at a combined or total rate of Q_T, the recovery pump should pumped at a rate of Q_r, where $Q_r = bQ_T$ and b is the ratio of the thickness of the dense layer relative to the total saturated thickness, and the control pump at $Q_c = (1-b)Q_T$. If the aquifer is not homogeneous, the pumping rates should theoretically be based on the ratio of transmissivities in the fresh and dense layers.

3.1 DPR in two adjacent bores

Two bores were drilled 1.5 m apart to the base of the unconfined aquifer. Bore 1 was screened from 29 m to the bottom at 32 m depth, and bore 2 was screened between 18 and 23 m depth. Initially, a fully slotted PVC monitoring bore was drilled 1.5 m from bores 1 and 2, to monitor the depth to the interface before and during pumping by measuring the electrical conductivity in the standing water column. Before pumping, the relatively sharp transition zone (EC: 3300 to 8800 μS cm^{-1}) was located between 24 and 25 m depth. The water table was at 14 m depth.

Figure 1 shows EC profiles measured in the fully slotted monitoring bore prior to pumping, with only the recovery pump operating and for various pumping ratios of the control and recovery pumps. The loss of recovery efficiency with only the recovery pump operating can clearly be seen. The EC at the recovery pump outlet decreased significantly and the interface was lowered because freshwater was invading from the upper layer. When both pumps were turned on, the interface shifted very close to the water table. Even when the pumping ratio Q_c:Q_r was 1 or even less, the increase in EC from the control pump and upward movement of the interface could not be avoided.

It was found that the fully slotted monitoring bore acted as a conduit to the control pump. This problem was solved by converting the monitoring bore to an unslotted bore and using an EM39 electromagnetic logging device to monitor the depth to the interface. Long-term DPR tests showed that a pumping ratio of 0.66 maintained a constant interface elevation and that the EC at the recovery bore levelled off at 10 000 μS cm^{-1}. The EC at the control pump outlet stabilised after several hours but remained higher than pre-pumping levels (Figure 2).

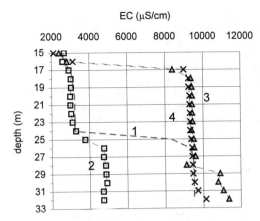

Figure 1. EC profiles after 3 hours of pumping. 1: pre-pumping; 2: $Q_r = 833$ L min^{-1}; 3: $Q_r = 400$ L min^{-1} and $Q_c = 628$ L min^{-1}; and 4: $Q_r = 833$ and $Q_c = 628$ L min^{-1}.

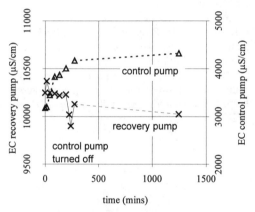

Figure 2. Concentrations at the pump outlets stabilised after several hours of pumping when a pumping ratio of 0.66 was applied.

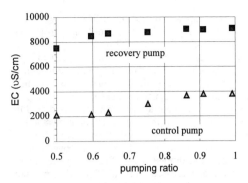

Figure 4. With increasing pumping ratio the concentration of groundwater from both the recovery pump and control pump increases. EC measurements were taken after several hours of DPR.

3.2 DPR in a single bore

A 30 cm diameter borehole was drilled to the base of the unconfined aquifer at a depth of about 31 m. The borehole was fully screened from the water table at about 14 m to the base. The upper section of the screen (14 to 22 m) was 25 cm wide to accommodate the control pump, and the cable and pipe from the lower recovery pump. The lower section of the screen was 20 cm in diameter. The interface was between 22 and 23 m depth. An unslotted monitoring bore was drilled 1.5 m from the DPR bore. The thickness of the dense layer at this location is nearly 52% of the saturated thickness of the unconfined aquifer, implying an initial pumping ratio (control pump to recovery pump) of about 0.88.

The results of the DPR tests in a single bore are summarised in Figure 3. A 14-day test was conducted for various pumping ratios which show very well the effect of the control pump on the efficiency of the recovery pump in terms of concentrations at the pump outlet. Initially, only the

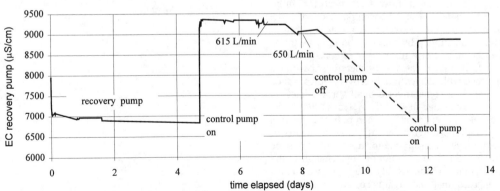

Figure 3. A 14 day DPR test demonstrated clearly the effect of the control pump on the recovery efficiency of the lower pump, see text for details.

515

recovery pump was turned on at 568 L min^{-1} for 5 days and as expected, the EC declined from pre-pumping levels of about 8500 μS cm^{-1}. The control pump was then turned on with a pumping ratio of 1:1. The EC at the recovery pump outlet rose immediately to values higher than 9000 μS cm^{-1}, which exceeded EC values measured prior to DPR operation. The pumping ratio was modified slightly to 0.9 and 0.86 during the test which resulted in minor changes in EC. On day 9 the control pump was turned off and the EC at the recovery pump outlet declined immediately. The EC at the control pump outlet increased from a 2800 μS cm^{-1} pre-pumping level to about 3600 μS cm^{-1} (for a pumping ratio of 0.86). In an additional 3-day test, the pumping rate of the control pump was reduced to 410 L min^{-1} and the recovery remained at a maximum rate of 635 L min^{-1} (ratio 0.65). In this test, EC values of less than 3000 μS cm^{-1} were achieved from the control pump outlet and a near-stable EC level of 9000 μ Scm^{-1} from the recovery pump.

Figure 4 is a summary of several long-term (days) and short-term (hours) DPR tests which were conducted for different pumping ratios. It shows that with an increasing pumping ratio the EC of water at both the recovery pump and control pump outlets increase. A pumping ratio between 0.6 and 0.7 is considered optimal for this case because the EC from the control pump is low enough for re-use, while maintaining a contaminant load from the recovery which is nearly double the load from a conventional single-pump recovery system. EC measurements with the EM39 in the adjacent monitoring bore showed that the interface remained stable during the DPR tests.

4 CONCLUSIONS

The DPR trials in one bore were more successful than in two adjacent bores, possibly due to a more pronounced horizontal flow field near the fully-screened bore. The concentrations of the contaminant in the recovered groundwater can be controlled adaptively by varying the ratio Q_c to Q_r. Since the drawdown in a fully-screened bore is minimal, pumping rates can therefore be much higher than with conventional recovery bores, which are generally screened over a small vertical interval. The only advantage of a DPR system is that if the dense water is kept separate, then only that fraction of Q_T would need treatment. If the water quality of the dense layer is unsuitable for treatment, it may be better to allow some dilution by changing the pumping ratio. The feasibility of a DPR system also pre-supposes that the quality of water from the control pump is suitable for disposal or re-use

without any treatment. It is implicit in any consideration of a DPR system that the "optimal" pumping ratio will vary with time, as recovery proceeds. If the quality from the control pump deteriorates with time, then the pumping ratio can be changed in such a way that some of the upper layer is drawn downwards towards the recovery pump. Characteristic diagrams for individual DPR bores such as shown in Figure 4 can be used to control the water quality.

5 REFERENCES

Underhill, H.W. & M.J. Atherton 1964. A coastal ground water study in Libya and a discussion of a double pumping technique. *J.Hydrology* 2: 52-64.

Villaume, J.F., P.C. Lowe and G.P. Lennon 1983. Coal tar recocery from a gravel aquifer, Stroudsburg, PA. *Proc. ASCE Conf on the Disposal of Solid, Liquid and Hazardous Wastes.* Bethlehem, Pennsylvania, April.

Wisniewski, G.M., G.P. Lennon, Villaume, J.F. & C.L. Young 1985. Response of a dense fluid under pumping stresses. *Toxic and Hazardous Wastes, Proc. 7th Mid-Atlantic Waste Conf.*

Zack, A.L. 1988. A well system to recover usable water from a freshwater-saltwater aquifer in Puerto Rico. *U.S. Geological Survey Water-Supply Paper*: 2328.

Groundwater in the Urban Environment: Problems, Processes and Management, Chilton et al. (eds)
© 1997 Balkema, Rotterdam, ISBN 90 5410 837 1

Remediation of contaminated land located on the Yorkshire Coal Measures aquifer, UK

Michael O. Rivett & R. John Aldrick
Environment Agency, Ridings Area, Leeds, UK

ABSTRACT: A review of contaminated land remediations undertaken at 87 sites on the Yorkshire Carboniferous "Coal Measures" aquifer is presented. The area contains a widespread legacy of contaminated land that is underlain by an aquifer of limited intrinsic resource value. The review leads on to discuss what degree of remediation is justified in environments such as the Yorkshire Coal Measures and provides a summary of issues that influence this question. Due to the widely different local sensitivities of sites, the authors advocate the need for site specific "source-pathway-receptor" assessments to reliably determine the necessary degree of remediation.

1 INTRODUCTION

In much of the industrialised world, "Contaminated Land" (CL) exists in conurbations that contain a multitude of industrial sources. Such conurbations may often overlie aquifers that have limited intrinsic groundwater resource value. The urbanised areas situated on the UK Yorkshire Carboniferous "Coal Measures" aquifer are a case in point. The frequency and severity of CL is high, whereas the intrinsic groundwater resource value is low, the Coal Measures being classified as a "Minor Aquifer" (NRA 1994).

There is debate as to what extent remediation of CL in localities such as the Yorkshire Coal Measures is justified. Remediation costs can be exceedingly high, whereas realised benefits may be low. This paper discusses this issue in relation to the Yorkshire Coal Measures. The issue is approached by reviewing CL consultations made to the UK regulator (Environment Agency) in recent years. The review leads on to a discussion of issues that influence the degree of remediation undertaken to protect the Coal Measures water environment and justification is provided for the remediation approach adopted to date.

2 BACKGROUND

The study area is described as the "Yorkshire Coal Measures aquifer" (Figure 1). It includes the Coal Measures aquifer within the Aire, Calder, Dearne, Don and Rother river catchments under the regulatory responsibility of the Environment Agency - Ridings Area. The area is mainly within West and South Yorkshire with a small portion in North Derbyshire.

The Coal Measures in the study area has geological boundaries to the west and north with the Carboniferous "Millstone Grits" and to the east with the Permian "Magnesian Limestones". The Coal Measures extend further south beyond the surface water divide boundary used in this study.

Industrialisation of the Yorkshire Coal Measures has been due to the historical exploitation of its coal resource. "Heavy industry" including coal, metal and textiles works were prominent; however, industrial decline in recent years has left substantial CL legacies. Major conurbations such as Leeds, Sheffield and Bradford, numerous smaller urban areas and out-of-town coal mining complexes contain significant CL.

The Carboniferous Coal Measures comprise a thick sequence of rocks that have extensive faulting and repeated sequences of mudstone, siltstone, coal and sandstone; the latter is the primary aquifer unit. The Coal Measures are a complex discontinuous multi-aquifer environment covered by variable glacial and recent drift deposits, alluvial gravels being the most permeable. Groundwater flow in the sandstone rock is primarily via fissure flow, with much less intergranular flow. Geological dip and groundwater flow are both generally eastward, following topography and surface water drainage. Groundwater often has elevated iron, manganese and chloride and groundwaters within former mine workings are acidic with elevated iron.

The Coal Measures are classified as a "Minor Aquifer" due to their limited resource value, a good borehole yield being 1000 m^3/day. There are currently 150 licensed groundwater abstractions from the Coal Measures (Figure 1) used for: general industrial or cooling 39%; domestic and agriculture; 24% spray irrigation 17%; water undertaking 5%;

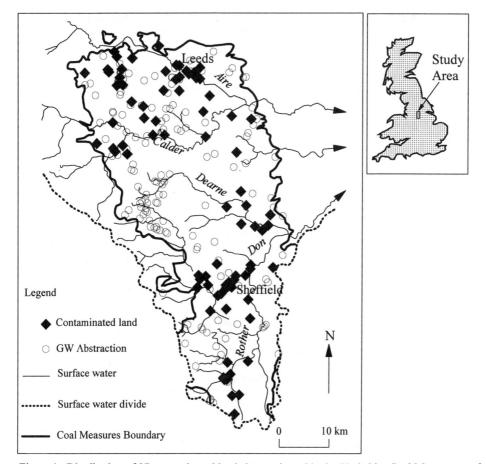

Figure 1. Distribution of 87 contaminated land sites reviewed in the Yorkshire Coal Measures study area.

miscellaneous 15%. Licence exempt abstractions (not shown) also exist relating to low volume abstractions which are mainly used for rural domestic supplies.

Most surface waters have their sources in the Pennine Hills to the west on the Carboniferous Millstone Grits, or Carboniferous Limestones. Toward the western margins of the Coal Measures, a number of ochrous discharges from long abandoned shallow coal workings impact the surface water quality. Further impacts from sewage and industrial discharges and CL arise within the urban areas. Many river sections have been classified within "poor" water quality classes. Although poor quality watercourses still remain, there have been recent improvements due to industry closure and increased environmental controls over discharges and contaminated land impacts.

3 CONCEPTUAL MODELS

"Source-Pathway-Receptor" (SPR) conceptual

models are required to assess risks associated with CL sites and to evaluate the principal contamination impacts to the water environment (DoE 1994a). Figure 2 provides a conceptual model of a generic Coal Measures environment with two example CL sites; "Site 1" impacts a shallow groundwater regime and "Site 2" a deep regime. For each site, the three main contaminant source types that cause groundwater contamination are illustrated and discussed below.

3.1 *Classical leaching scenario*

In the classical leaching scenario, the source of chemical contamination is the sorbed, or residual chemical held in the land, usually above the water table. Infiltrating water becomes contaminated as chemicals dissolve or desorb ("leach") and a plume of dissolved inorganic or organic solutes develops down gradient. Site 1 contaminates a shallow aquifer regime, groundwater in made ground, alluvium, drift,

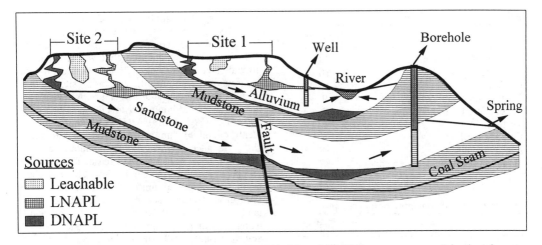

Figure 2. Conceptual model illustrating leachable, LNAPL and DNAPL source zones originating from two contaminated land (CL) sites in a generic Coal Measures environment. For clarity, dissolved-phase groundwater plumes arising from these source zones are not shown.

or weathered mudstones, which may subsequently impact a shallow groundwater abstraction, or surface water regime. Site 2 on a vulnerable sandstone outcrop causes contamination of a deep aquifer regime, dissolved contamination migrating within the sandstone and potentially impacting deep groundwater abstraction points, or spring discharges.

3.2 *LNAPL Scenario*

In the LNAPL (Light non-aqueous phase liquid) scenario, LNAPL held as immobile residual above the water table may dissolve in a similar way to the leaching scenario. LNAPL that reaches the water table will "float" and may act as a source of dissolved contamination generating a dissolved plume down gradient. Alternatively, LNAPL itself may laterally migrate on the water table and impact surface waters, or shallow groundwater abstractions. LNAPL examples include most hydrocarbon fuels and oils.

3.3 *DNAPL Scenario*

In the DNAPL (Dense non-aqueous phase liquid) scenario, DNAPL held as immobile residual above the water table may dissolve in a similar way to the leaching scenario. DNAPL that reaches the water table, may penetrate deep within the aquifer system leaving trails of residual DNAPL suspended below the water table, or form DNAPL "pools" on lower permeability horizons. Such DNAPL may act as a source of dissolved contamination and generate a plume in the aquifer down-gradient, alternatively the DNAPL itself may continue to migrate laterally and

occasionally accumulate in the bed of a surface water, or at the base of a groundwater well. DNAPL's include chlorinated solvents, PCB's and coal tars.

4 REVIEW OF CONSULTATIONS

A review of Coal Measures CL consultations made to the Groundwater Section of the Environment Agency - Ridings Area (formerly National Rivers Authority) during 1994-96 is presented. For sites selected, the applicant was of the opinion that the necessary site investigation works were largely complete. Figure 1 indicates the distribution of sites and shows a clustering around the conurbations. Data from the consultations are summarised in Tables 1 to 3.

4.1 *Site Investigations and Contamination Impacts*

Of the 87 sites reviewed, 75 had site investigation and remedial works completed as an integral part of a land re-development, usually under Planning Control. At 9 sites, surface water pollution incidents were the instigating force. Legal actions were threatened, or attempted at some sites; however, all 9 sites were ultimately remediated as part of a re-development, or voluntarily. Site owner's corporate environmental policy was the primary driving force for only 3 of the 87 sites. However, environmental policies of owners, or supporting financial institutions were often a significant driving force behind many of the remedial works conducted during site re-developments.

Table 1. Previous site uses.

Site Use	Number
Engineering / Metals	22
Landfill / Tips	10
Gasworks	10
Coking works and colliery	9
Petrol stations / Fuel depots	7
Textiles	6
Colliery spoil tips	5
Miscellaneous	18
Total number of sites reviewed:	87

Table 2. Observed contamination to receptors.

Receptor	Number
Off-site Surface water (SW) Impact	
Dissolved discharge to SW	5
LNAPL discharge to SW	2
DNAPL discharge to SW	2
Off-site Groundwater (GW) Impact	
Shallow GW aquifer	9
Deep GW aquifer	0
Licensed GW abstraction	0
Groundwater (GW) Below Site	
Dissolved plume	61
LNAPL accumulation	44
DNAPL accumulation (inferred)	8

Table 3. Principal site remediations undertaken.

Remediation	Number
Encapsulation - development / cap	59
Excavation to off-site landfill	47
Excavation to on-site landfill	9
Pump-and-treat LNAPL recovery	13
Bio-remediation in-situ	2
Bio-remediation ex-situ	2
Soil treatment ex-situ	1
Barrier wall containment	1
No remedial action	4

Previous site uses are summarised in Table 1. About 25% were occupied by metals or engineering works, a further 25% by gasworks, coking works or colliery spoil tips. Site area analysis shows 34 sites were less than 2 ha, 41 sites between 2-10 ha and 12 sites above 10 a, with 3 sites over 100 ha. The largest sites were occupied by colliery - coking works complexes.

Review of soil and groundwater monitoring indicated spatial sampling point densities generally decreased at larger sites and were always reduced for groundwater compared to soil. Sampling densities were often disturbingly low, particularly of groundwater. For example, 26 (30%) sites provided no groundwater monitoring and for 60 sites below 5 ha area, the mean spatial soil sampling density was just 15 points/ha compared to UK guidance of 25 points/ha (BSI 1988). Hence, the confident identification of "hot-spots" as outlined in recent UK guidance (DoE 1994b) could be low. Sometimes low densities were reasonable given the proposed scope of remedial works and associated testing, or expected uniformity of some sources. Poor groundwater assessment was attributed to the land re-development focus at many sites, works being primarily directed at land surface environmental health and building condition risks. The above resulted in further site investigation works being requested at many sites.

A low level of site investigation resulted in poor conceptual understanding of many sites and it was often difficult to infer which of the Figure 2 conceptual models were applicable. The majority (77 sites) were close to surface waters, a shallow groundwater flow regime to the surface water being the primary SPR route of concern. Reliable assessment of contaminant migration to deep groundwater regimes was rare as reasonable monitoring was only provided at 19 sites. The authors expect many individual sites may impact both shallow and deep groundwaters and contain a mixture of leaching, LNAPL and DNAPL sources.

Table 2 summarises the observed impact on water receptors. Of the 87 sites, only 9 (6 major coking works) had caused observable quality impacts to surface waters. Ochrous discharges were evident at 5 sites, LNAPL oil seepages at 2 sites and DNAPL coal tars seeped from river beds at 2 sites. Many sites probably caused some dissolved contamination in surface water base-flows; however, contaminant fluxes were often believed low, or river dilution so high, that surface water impacts were not measurable.

In relation to off-site groundwater receptors (Table 2), site boundary monitoring indicated shallow groundwater contamination was migrating off-site at 9 sites (additional to those sites causing surface water impacts). This figure was considered artificially low due to the frequent absence of relevant boundary monitoring. Off-site contamination of deep aquifer regimes was not directly confirmed at any sites, mainly due to a lack of suitable boundary monitoring. Deep groundwater regime assessments at the 19 sites identified earlier indicated 12 sites had deep dissolved plumes internal to sites, 8 had LNAPL on sandstone outcrops and 1 site had circumstantial evidence that DNAPL coal tars had migrated in deep sandstones.

None of the 87 sites were proven, or even strongly suspected, to have caused contamination of groundwater abstraction supplies.

In relation to the on-site groundwater "receptor" directly beneath CL sites, Table 2 indicates that of the 61 sites having groundwater monitoring available, some dissolved contamination was observed beneath all sites, LNAPL contamination beneath 44 (72%) sites and DNAPL contamination inferred beneath 8 (13%) sites. One can reasonably assume that similar percent occurrences apply to the total number of sites reviewed for dissolved and LNAPL contamination. Due to difficulties in locating DNAPL contamination, its percent occurrence in groundwater below sites is probably best estimated from suspected historical use data: 45 (52%) sites probably used DNAPL coal tars or solvents and hence DNAPL contamination at these sites is suspected. Although groundwater is classified as a receptor above, NAPL in the groundwater beneath CL acts as a principal source of dissolved plume contamination, as conceptualised in Figure 2.

4.2 Remediation

Table 3 summarises the principal remedial approaches applied to the 87 sites. The regulator's strategy was to agree approaches that removed, or contained source zones of contamination to the water environment. Most remediations aimed to reduce risks to surface water receptors contaminated via shallow groundwater regime pathways, or prevent continued contamination input to deep groundwater regimes. Remediations included the removal, or isolation of the following:
- "Hot spot" soil zones of high contaminant mass potentially leachable or mobile;
- Sub-surface tanks, pipelines and lagoons possibly mobilised if facilities rupture, or leak;
- Significant LNAPL accumulations on water tables potentially mobile or a source of dissolved plume;
- Shallow DNAPL contamination.

To evaluate remediation proposals, the authors derived SPR conceptual models for each specific site similar to Figure 2 using data provided, in-house data and further site investigation requested. Perceived risks of on-site sources to receptors determined the scope of remedial works on a site specific basis. Key issues evaluated were migration potential to surface waters, vulnerability of underlying aquifer units, and migration potential to water supplies. Modelling, or detailed risk assessments were not undertaken.

At the majority of sites, a combination of contaminant encapsulation (hard surface development or capping layers) and contaminant excavation to off-site landfill disposal was implemented. Excavation to landfills created on-site occurred at 9 large sites, 4 of these using open-cast coal extraction to offset remediation costs. Pump-and-treat LNAPL removal (ie local oil skimming) was used at 13 sites. Floating LNAPL was also removed at other sites during excavation works identified above. Table 3 lists a few other remediations; however, major pump-and-treat removal of dissolved plumes, in-situ soil treatments, and innovative NAPL remediations were not used.

All remediations were restricted to on-site areas. Recognising limitations of remediation technologies, complexity of the geologic environment, limited groundwater resource value, low risk and known impact to existing groundwater abstractions and very high cost-benefit ratios associated with off-site deep groundwater zone remediations, no such remediations were thought warranted for the sites reviewed.

5 WHAT REMEDIATION IS JUSTIFIED?

The question as to what degree of remediation is justified for the Yorkshire Coal Measures and similar environments worldwide is contentious. Degree of remediation is influenced by several general factors:
- Statutory environmental legislation;
- Political will and policy;
- Regulatory approach - eg. pragmatic or legalistic;
- Environmental policy and liability perceptions of site owners, purchasers and financial institutions;
- Public, pressure group and third party opinion;
- Funding available from public and private sectors;
- Technical investigation or remediation constraints.

These factors influence both the number and individual scale of remediations. In addition, a number of local Coal Measures issues, some of wider applicability, influence the degree of remediation undertaken:
- Recognising receptor vulnerability often decreases : Shallow groundwater > Surface watercourses > Deep groundwater > Groundwater abstractions;
- Shallow source-zone remediation is usually feasible and should normally be attempted to minimise long term significant impact to surface waters and groundwaters of (potential) value;
- Contamination at depth is difficult to remediate in this environment with current technology;
- A proportion of groundwaters may be impacted by currently rising poor quality deep minewaters;
- Many surface waters are "robust" receptors and major derogation is quite rare as CL contaminant fluxes are often low and river dilutions high;
- CL impacts to surface waters are often minor compared to high flow, low quality sewage effluent and minewaters discharges;

- Many CL sites cause surface water contamination via low base-flow seepages that is not easily discernible against industrial background quality;
- Increasing control of sewage and minewater discharges may cause CL impacts to surface waters to become more significant.

Differing views on the relative importance of the above issues will cause a divergence of opinion on the extent to which remediation of the Coal Measures is justified and should be undertaken. It is unrealistic, from cost-benefit, technical, risk, environmental and resource arguments to expect all CL sites to be remediated to the highest possible standard. Equally, it is unrealistic to argue that because the Coal Measures is generally of such limited water resource value and industrial contamination is so widespread, that no remediation is required.

The authors aimed to take a pragmatic, technically feasible approach to remediation that is within the current statutory framework. Specific aspects of this approach and types of remedial works arising have been detailed in Section 4.2. The authors advocate a balanced approach between the above general extremes and have developed a remediation strategy for the Coal Measures that examines the specific local sensitivity of individual sites. The heterogeneity of the Coal Measures and varying site proximities to surface waters and aquifer units (capable of, or in use) causes site risks to greatly vary. Hence, each site should be appraised on a site specific SPR basis using conceptual models similar to those of Figure 2.

With the approach taken, although remediations are perhaps not as extensive as those performed in similar environments worldwide, those implemented are believed adequate to minimise the principal risks. There are some drawbacks with the approach (see below); however, a balance has been struck between managing risks to the water environment and sustaining urban regeneration of "Brown Field" sites in accordance with government policy (DoE 1994c).

6 CONCLUSIONS AND CONCERNS

It is concluded that CL remediation on the Yorkshire Coal Measures should be approached using a site specific strategy. The local sensitivity of sites to the water environment varies enormously, dictating a need to approach sites on an individual basis and undertake site specific SPR analysis to identify an appropriate degree of site remedial action. The review is thought relevant to other conurbations worldwide that also contain widespread CL legacies overlying aquifers generally of low resource value.

Issues and concerns relevant to future CL remediation on the Yorkshire Coal Measures, some having wider significance, include the following.

1. The pending UK CL statutory regime to be implemented by S.57 of the Environment Act 1995 is based on SPR risk assessment. This review indicated the poor quality of many site assessments. Improvement would be required to enable confident risk assessment and decision making under the new regime. If "natural attenuation" remediation is proposed this, in particular, would need to be based on a robust SPR risk assessment and future confirmatory monitoring.

2. Remediation to date has largely been during site re-development works which can impose significant time and technical constraints on the remediation works. The S.57 regime should facilitate the remediation of "problem" CL sites not subject to re-development.

3. Remediation measures to date in the Coal Measures have been directed at remediation of shallow on-site sources. Remediation of DNAPL, or dissolved plumes in deep sandstones of potential resource value has not been undertaken. It remains to be seen how important and technically feasible it is to control, or remediate such contamination in this environment.

4. The vulnerability of Coal Measures sandstone units of potential resource value is variable. Availability of reliable vulnerability maps, particularly in urban areas, would facilitate determination of CL sensitivities.

REFERENCES

British Standards Institute, UK 1988. Code of practice for the identification of potentially contaminated land and its investigation. Draft for development DD 175. London: BSI.

Department of the Environment, UK 1994a. A framework for the assessment of contaminated land on groundwater and surface water. *Contaminated Land Research Report No.1.* London: HMSO.

Department of the Environment, UK 1994b. Sampling strategies for contaminated land. *Contaminated Land Research Report No.4.* London: HMSO.

Department of the Environment, UK 1994c. Framework for contaminated land. Outcome of the Government's policy review and consultation paper "Paying for our past". London: HMSO.

National Rivers Authority, UK 1994. Contaminated land and the water environment. *NRA Water Quality Series Report No. 15.* London: HMSO.

DISCLAIMER

Groundwater in the Urban Environment: Problems, Processes and Management, Chilton et al. (eds)
© *1997 Balkema, Rotterdam, ISBN 90 5410 837 1*

Delineating gasoline entrapped below the water table

G.A. Robbins, M.A. Butler, E.J. Gilbert, G.K. Binkhorst & C. Troskosky
Department of Geology and Geophysics, University of Connecticut, Storrs, Conn., USA

ABSTRACT: Gasoline contamination of groundwater in the urban environment is a ubiquitous problem in the United States. Although gasoline is a light non-aqueous phase liquid, it can become entrapped by capillary action below the water table when the water table fluctuates. Entrapped gasoline significantly contributes to difficulties in remediating groundwater contamination. Through the use of direct push tools, appropriate sampling schemes and on-site, real-time field contaminant analysis, the spatial distribution of gasoline entrapped below the water table can be assessed. Our research at sites that exhibit a variety of geological conditions would suggest that entrapped gasoline tends to be spread over a relatively small vertical extent (fractions of a metre to about a metre). This implies that excavating or focusing other remediation strategies on a relatively small vertical zone beneath the water table in the source area can greatly increase remediation effectiveness.

1 INTRODUCTION

The typical approach to site assessments in the U.S. at underground storage tank (UST) sites having gasoline releases entails conducting multiple phases of an investigation. The approach relies heavily on hollow stem auger drilling for soil sampling, on shallow monitoring wells for water quality sampling, free product detection and hydraulic testing, and on laboratory analysis for quantifying contamination. Robbins (1989), Robbins & Martin-Hayden (1991), and Martin-Hayden et al. (1991) have shown that this approach is problematic in that it does not take into account the three-dimensional distribution of contamination. Martin-Hayden & Robbins (1997) have shown that the current approach to site assessments can result in misleading contaminant delineation and ineffective remediation. Importantly, the current site assessment approach fails to consider the entrapment of gasoline by capillary action beneath the water table. Gasoline may become entrapped below the water table, especially in fine grained soil, if it is released from partially submerged tanks or if the water table fluctuates while gasoline is floating on the groundwater. Gasoline entrapment below the water table appears to be responsible for long term continuous sources of groundwater contamination at UST sites.

Over the last several years, direct push technologies have been commercialized. Direct push technologies involve using small diameter tools that are hydraulically rammed into the subsurface to perform sampling of soil and groundwater with depth (multilevel sampling). The use of direct push sampling has the potential to improve the three-dimensional delineation of contamination, especially below the water table.

The objective of this study was to evaluate methods to delineate gasoline entrapped below the water table using direct push tools. Results from two sites that have very different hydrogeologic characteristics are presented.

2 FIELD SITES AND METHODS

Table 1 summarizes the site characteristics of two field sites. The sites are located in Connecticut and have had gasoline releases. A GeoProbe® direct push device was used in conducting multilevel sampling of soil. Soil cores were obtained above the water table with an open ended sampler (Macro-Core Sampler®) and below the water table with a retractable drive point sampler (Large Bore Soil Sampler®). Groundwater samples were obtained using a variety of methods.

Table 1. Summary of site characteristics.

Site Information.	Colchester	Bethany
When contamination started or was discovered	Discovered: February 1991	Discovered: 1991 Probably leaking since early 1970s
Suspected source	Broken pipe fitting	Abandoned gasoline tanks
Approximate source location	CMW-4 to CML-19	BMW-1 to BMW-5
Stratigraphic conditions	Approximately 3.65 m of fine to coarse sands underlain by silt	Very fine grained soils - till (found thin perched layers)
Hydraulic conductivity (cm/sec)	Sands: 1×10^{-2}	1.8×10^{-5}
Typical depth to ground water	1.2 to 1.5 m below grade	1.5 to 3 m below grade (shallower near the source and deepening further away)
Direction of ground water flow	North - Northeast	South
Flow conditions	Primarily horizontal flow	Upward gradients observed at a several locations at the site

Samples were collected from clusters of piezometers, a mill slotted well screen, a GeoProbe® Screen Point 15 retractable sampler and a GeoInsight PowerPunch™.

Following soil collection, samples were preserved in methanol for laboratory analyses by EPA Method 8240B (GC/MSD). Soil concentrations are reported as total soil contamination. Groundwater samples were preserved in HCL and analyzed by EPA Method 624 (GC/MSD) for dissolved contaminants.

3 FIELD TEST RESULTS

The Bethany site is characterized by low hydraulic conductivity. This made multilevel sampling of groundwater impractical. Instead, soil sampling was used to delineate contamination. Figure 1 is a contour map of the maximum benzene concentration observed in each soil coring location. The contamination

follows a relatively narrow path to the south. Figure 2 is a cross section of the benzene contamination. The soil contamination is confined to a zone below the water table and has about a 1 metre vertical extent. Contamination levels are well below residual saturation. Hence, the gasoline is trapped below the table in an immobile state.

In contrast to the Bethany site, the Colchester site is characterized by relatively high hydraulic conductivity. This situation was conducive for both groundwater and soil sampling. Figure 3 is a groundwater contamination map for benzene in the area of the source. The map is based on contouring the maximum observed benzene concentration in any of the multilevel groundwater samplers. Figure 4 is a cross section of the benzene groundwater

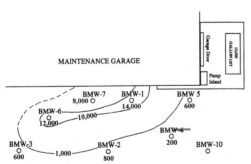

Figure 1. Maximum benzene soil contamination at Bethany (July 1996).

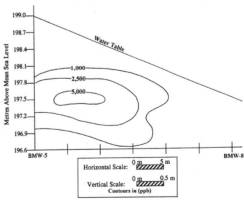

Figure 2. Cross section of benzene soil contamination at Bethany (July 1996).

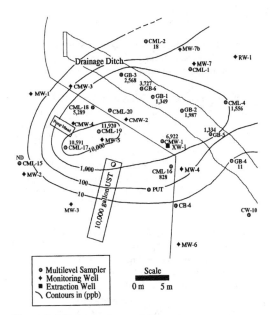

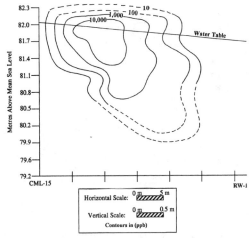

Figure 5. Cross section of benzene soil contamination at Colchester. (December 1995)

Figure 3. Maximum benzene groundwater contamination at Colchester (March 1996).

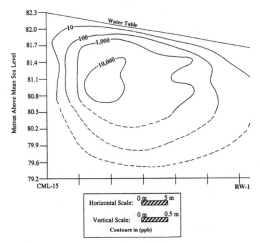

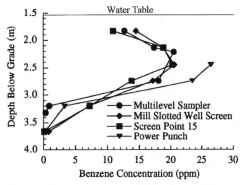

Figure 6. Comparison of groundwater sampling methods (August 1996).

Figure 4. Cross section of benzene groundwater contamination at Colchester (March 1996).

groundwater table. The zone of maximum entrapped product shown in Figure 5 is less than a metre in thickness and is at a higher elevation than the maximum groundwater contamination as indicated in Figure 4. This may be explained by increased aerobic biodegradation in the groundwater at shallower depths. At the location of maximum contamination, the oxygen level of the groundwater was found to diminish rapidly from about 4 mg/l near the water table to the ppb range within a depth of 0.75 m of the water table.

contamination along a vertical plane that goes through the source area. Most of the groundwater contamination stems from a narrow (about 1 metre) vertical zone below the water table.

Figure 5 shows the benzene soil contamination along the same cross section (although at a different time). The soil contamination straddles the

Tests were performed at several locations to evaluate different methods of groundwater sampling. Figure 6 shows the results for four different methods at CML-19. At this location and the others, the different sampling methods yielded about the same

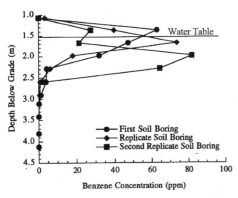

Figure 7. Replicate soil profiles (August 1996).

results. This implies that the different methods would provide about the same quality of information on the vertical distribution of groundwater contamination.

Soil borings were drilled adjacent to one another to test the reproducibility of profiling the soil contamination below the water table at both sites. Multiple soil borings were conducted at several locations at each site. Figure 7 exemplifies the results. The soil contamination exhibited high vertical concentration gradients. Soil contaminant distributions were similar in profile amongst adjacent borings at both sites. However, very significant concentration differences were observed at the same depths between adjacent borings. The concentration differences may be attributed to heterogeneity and problems in depth control in sampling, especially given the high vertical concentration gradients observed.

4 CONCLUSIONS

The study would suggest that entrapped gasoline tends to be spread over a relatively short vertical interval (fractions of a metre to about a metre) within the zone of water table fluctuation, irrespective of hydrogeologic conditions. This implies that excavating or focusing other remediation strategies on a relatively small vertical zone beneath the water table in the source area can greatly increase remediation effectiveness. We have found that equivalent levels of quantification of groundwater contamination with depth can be readily achieved with different methods of sampling in a highly permeable environment. However, profiling soil contamination with depth below the water table appears to be more prone to variation. Further information on this study may be found in Robbins & Butler (1997).

REFERENCES

Robbins, G.A. 1989. Influence of using purged and partially penetrating monitoring wells on contaminant detection, mapping, and modelling. *Ground Water*, 27,155-162.

Robbins, G.A. & J.M. Martin-Hayden 1991. Mass balance evaluation of monitoring well purging, part I. Theoretical models and implications for representative sampling. *J. Contaminant Hydrol.* 8, 203-224.

Martin-Hayden, J.M., G.A. Robbins, & R.D. Bristol 1991. Mass balance evaluation of monitoring well purging, part II. Field tests at a gasoline contamination site. *J. Contaminant Hydrol.* 8, 225-241.

Martin-Hayden, J.M. & G.A. Robbins 1997. Plume distortion and apparent attenuation due to concentration averaging in monitoring wells. *Ground Water*. 35, 339-346

Robbins G.A. & M.A. Butler 1997. *Recommended guidelines for multilevel sampling of soil and ground water in conducting expedited site investigations at underground storage tank sites in Connecticut.* A report submitted to the Connecticut Department of EnvironmentalProtection. Hartford, Connecticut.

Groundwater in the Urban Environment: Problems, Processes and Management, Chilton et al. (eds)
© *1997 Balkema, Rotterdam, ISBN 90 5410 837 1*

The role of mine waste disposal in the arsenic pollution of groundwater in Zimapán, México

R.Rodríguez C. & A.Armienta H.
Department of Natural Resources, Geophysics Institute, National Autonomous University of Mexico, Mexico

L.Longley
Department of Geology, Bates College, Lewiston Maine, Maine, USA

ABSTRACT: In 1992, the National Water Commission, CNA, found arsenic concentrations exceeding the drinking water standard (0.050 mg/L) in many of Zimapán's water sources. The maximum observed arsenic concentration in the municipal supply wells was 1.2 mg L^{-1}. More typical arsenic concentrations in local springs and dug wells range from 0.02 to 0.06 mg L^{-1}. Some water sources have undetectable arsenic concentrations. Two potentially significant arsenic sources include ore processing wastes and arsenic bearing minerals in the rocks. The Pb - Ag - Zn ore has many arsenic bearing contaminating minerals. Some of the most significantly polluted wells are located in the vicinity of ore processing waste piles which have been deposited at the periphery of the urban area of Zimapán. Groundwater may be contaminated as the water flows through fractured rocks and as precipitation percolates through the waste piles. Dry deposition of smelter particulates may also contribute to the problem.

1 PROBLEM DESCRIPTION

The Valley of Zimapán, State of Hidalgo, central Mexico is located in a semi-arid region where groundwater is the sole source of drinking water. There are no available surface water bodies. Until 1980, when the municipal wells were drilled, the 8700 residents used springs and shallow (< 30m) dug wells as a drinking water source (Figure 1).

The Zimapán region has been an important mining district since the seventeenth century. Ag, Zn and Pb have been refined by selective flotation, in facilities near the mines and in the town itself. Mining and processing wastes have routinely been disposed along the Tolimán River, which marks the southern edge of the urban area. Heaps of discarded smelter slag are common throughout the town. Currently, the ore processing plants are located several kilometres from the urban area.

In 1992, the National Water Commission, CNA, detected the presence of arsenic in the water supply as a result of a massive federal effort to detect cholera bacteria. Arsenic is not routinely included in chemical analyses of water supply systems. After that, in 1993, the Geophysics Institute of the National Autonomous University of Mexico, UNAM, began a study of the groundwater, rock and soil As concentrations. These efforts are all designed to evaluate the source and distribution of arsenic in the groundwater of the Valley of Zimapán (Armienta et al. 1993, 1995). In 1995, the National Science Foundation of the USA began funding for a Research Experiences for Undergraduates programme to supplement UNAM's effort.

Environmental, Water and Health authorities are concerned because long periods of ingestion of As polluted water could produce severe health effects. The maximum permissible arsenic concentration in drinking water is 0.05 mg L^{-1}. Induction of cancer is the most striking long term effect of chronic exposure to inorganic arsenic (Nriagu 1994). The municipal potable water system provided As concentrations in drinking water of about 0.2 to 0.3 mg L^{-1} until 1996.

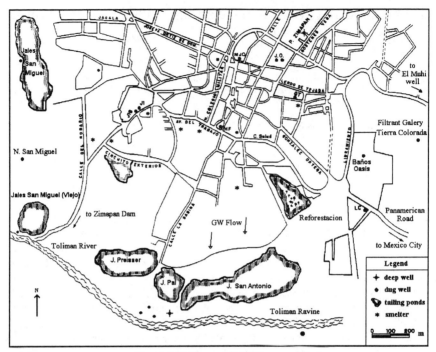

Figure 1. Tailing ponds in Zimapan, Mexico

Two small communities took water directly from the most polluted wells, El Muhi and Detzani. The first one had an arsenic concentration of 1.0 - 1.2 mg L^{-1} whereas the second one had 0.4 - 0.5 mg L^{-1}. Both of them had been drilled into the limestone section below the Tertiary volcanic cover. These wells were closed definitely in 1996. In these areas some people with skin problems like hyperpigmentation and keratosis of the hands and feet were detected.

2 THE AQUIFER SYSTEM

The regional geological framework is defined by the presence of fractured Cretaceous rocks: the Tamaulipas, Doctor and Soyatal Formations constituted by limestones. Tertiary rocks are represented by the El Morro Formation a limestone conglomerate. Volcanic deposits of basaltic and andesitic composition, Las Espinas formation, are located in the east of the valley.

The Zimapán fanglomerate is present in the north - west and south of the urban area.

The local geology defines a complex heterogeneous aquifer system with sharp lateral contrasts. The fanglomerate acts as an unconfined aquifer with partial hydraulic communication with the fractured limestones.

The limestone aquifer is exploited by deep wells. Perched aquifers are also present in some areas within the limestones, the fanglomerate and the volcanic rocks. In these are located shallow dug wells used for agriculture and services and occasionally for drinking water.

The volcanic rocks and the El Morro conglomerate have low permeability, but locally they may have some secondary permeability, defining perched aquifers.

The regional groundwater flow is in a south-easterly direction. Most of the aquifer recharge comes from the precipitation in the surrounding mountains. Precipitation in the valley proper is less than 400 mm/yr (Dueñas et al, 1992). Limited information on the formation intrinsic permeability and hydraulic conductivity is available (Ramos 1996; Turner 1997).

3 THE As SOURCES IN ZIMAPAN

The detected groundwater As is associated with three potential arsenic sources (Armienta et al,

1993): 1) the naturally occurring arsenic bearing minerals in the vicinity of the ore bodies; 2) the ore processing wastes; and 3) the particulate smelter fumes that were subsequently deposited on soils and sediments some distance from the former smelters.

3.1 Naturally occurring As bearing minerals

Many arsenic bearing minerals are known to occur in association with the Pb-Ag-Zn deposits including adamite (Zn_2AsO_4OH), arsenopyrite (FeAsS), hidalgoite ($PbAl_3$ (SO_4) (AsO_4) $(OH)_6$), mimetite (($PbClPb_4$)(AsO_4)$_3$, where (AsO_4) can be replaced by (PO_4) (Frye, 1981)), olivinite ($Cu_2(AsO_4)(OH)$) and tenantite ($3Cu_2SAs_2S_3$) (Simon & Mapes 1956). These minerals are related to intrusive bodies. Interactions with the groundwater may result in dissolution of arsenic from the mineral phase. The arsenic concentration in a pool of water standing in contact with a minor ore deposit was found to be 0.6 mg L^{-1} (Tichenor 1995). Two deep (about 150m) municipal wells (El Muhi and Detzani) which small communities were using directly had arsenic concentrations of 1.1 and 0.7 mg/l respectively. The As content in the deep wells could be explained by the oxidation of the arsenic-bearing rocks due to the oxygen dissolved in groundwater flowing through fractures. In these neighbourhoods, some people exhibited signs of chronic arsenic poisoning.

3.2 Smelter Stack Particulates

Until 1940, when the last smelter was closed, more than forty smelters had operated in the area. The smelters were located within the town limits. The smelter fume particulates probably contain arsenic (Rose et al. 1990). The dry deposition of particulates on the soil surface provides a potential arsenic source for infiltrating rain water. During a two and one half hour sediment (1 mg)/ water (25mL) experiment, soils from Zimapán were shown to contain 2 to 19 ppm of soluble arsenic (Armienta et al. 1995). Arsenic deposition and infiltration in the soil acted as a diffuse source. Shallow aquifer formations located around smelters were affected. There is not evidence of their influence on the deepest aquifers.

3.3 Ore Processing Wastes

Ore process waste piles (jales) are present in mining regions all over the world. In Zimapán these masses cover 2 km^2, 5 % of the urban area (Figure 1). The process waste overlies the Zimapán Fanglomerate and the El Morro and Las Espinas Formations along the Tolimán River. The river course is the contact between the Zimapán Fanglomerate and the volcanic rocks. The age of the oldest jales is not known. The older jales appear to be compacted and lithified. Their composition is quite heterogeneous. They are orange red in colour, presumably from iron oxidation. The San Miguel Nuevo Jales is still in use. The waste deposited there is a fine grey coloured powder.
The arsenic content of the jales material ranges from 0.68 to 4.07 wt % as As_2O_3 (Armienta et al. 1995). Water from dug wells in the near vicinity of a jales (within 100m) have arsenic concentrations of up to 0.43 mg/L. Water from shallow dug wells into the Fanglomerate upstream from the jales - out of the influence of smelters - have lower arsenic concentrations. The adverse health effects seen in the population around the El Muhi and Detzani wells are not detected in the persons living in close proximity to the jales. The risk level of the different routes of exposure, water ingestion and dust inhalation, acting in the jales areas is unknown. There are no studies related to the environmental effects of dusts coming from them. Trees planted on the jales Reforestación do not show any apparent systemic damage.
Geochemical similarities were observed between water from the dug wells located near jales and waste water from one of the mineral processing plants. Although the fanglomerate contains detritic material coming from arsenic-bearing rocks, the As concentration of ground water detected in those dug wells is lower than the dug wells polluted by jales.
Mechanical and wind erosion is also contributing to the pollution of the Tolimán River. The jales can contaminate soils and agriculture lands located around them.

4 CONCLUSIONS

The arsenic pollution of the ground waters in the Zimapán Basin is not due to a single process. Instead, at least three mechanisms must be carefully evaluated. First, dissolution of rocks and minerals by water may contribute As, particularly in the deeper wells. Second, water infiltrating the jales undoubtedly increases its arsenic concentration and contaminates shallow water sources near and/or downstream of the jales. The Tolimán River appears to act as a hydraulic barrier, preventing contamination of shallow aquifers to the south (Ramos 1996). The river is located at the contact between the fanglomerate and the volcanic rocks. The heterogeneity of the geological framework and the complex groundwater hydrodynamics have produced an irregular distribution of As in springs, dug and deep wells. Leaching of jales is affecting only dug wells located downstream and the surface water of the Tolimán River (García 1997).

Present - day mining activities can not be considered as pollutant sources for the Zimapán Valley, as on-going exploitation is located outside the Zimapán Basin. Most of the contemporary tailings are near the mines.

Lastly, the total impact of the potential leaching of smelter particulates is presumed to be less significant than that of the other arsenic sources mentioned above. It is necessary to carry out a more detailed study to assess the potential mobility of As coming from the jales leakages. We are continuing our efforts to evaluate these hypotheses.

REFERENCES

Armienta, A., R. Rodríguez, G. Villaseñor, A. Aguayo, N. Ceniceros, F. Juárez & Méndez, T. 1993. *Survey study of the arsenic pollution in the Zimapán zone*, Hgo. Tech. Report il. IGF-UNAM., México. 100 pp.

Armienta, A., R. Rodríguez, N. Ceniceros, A. Aguayo, & O. Cruz 1995. *Environmental risk assessment of the presence of arsenic in Zimapán Hgo*. Final Memoire MAPFRE Foundation, Spain. Mexico City. 50 pp.

Dueñas García, J. C., M. A. F. González, J. B. López, R. M. Palencia, & J. J. Rodríguez S.

1992. *Geological Mining Monograph of the State of Hidalgo*. Consejo de Recursos Minerales, México.

Frye, K. (ed.), 1981. The Encyclopaedia of mineralogy., PA, USA: Hutchison Ross Publishing Co., Stroudsburg .

García. A. 1997. *Distribution and speciation of arsenic in fluvial sediments of the Tolimán River in Zimapán Hgo*. Master Degree Thesis Earth Sciences Postgraduate Program. UNAM, Mexico. 76 pp.

Nriagu, J. O. (ed.) 1994. *Arsenic in the Environment, Part II: Human Health and Ecosystem Effects*. Advances in Environmental Sciences and Technology. New York, USA: John Wiley & Sons Inc.,.

Ramos, A. 1996. *Structural parameters that control groundwater hydrodynamics in the Zimapán Area, Hgo*. Master Degree Thesis. Earth Sciences Postgraduate Program. UNAM, Mexico.

Rose, A. W., H. E. Hawkes, & J. S. Webb, 1990. *Geochemistry in Mineral Exploration*. New York: Academic Press.

Simon, S. F. & V. E. Mapes, 1956. *Geology and Ore Deposits of the Zimapán Mining District, State of Hidalgo, Mexico*, Prof. Paper 284 USGS, Washington, USA.

Tichenor, S. E., 1996. *Hydrogeology of Zimapán, Mexico: A study of Arsenic in Local Bedrock and Groundwater*. Unpublished B. A. Thesis, Dept of Geology, Bates College, Lewiston, ME. USA. 68 pp.

Turner, B. H. 1997. *Intrinsic permeability of the Zoyatal Formation, Zimapán, Mexico*. Unpublished B.S. Thesis, Dept of Geology, Bates College, Lewiston, ME. USA. 105 pp.

Groundwater in the Urban Environment: Problems, Processes and Management, Chilton et al. (eds)
© *1997 Balkema, Rotterdam, ISBN 90 5410 837 1*

Reclamation of the Island Street Site Nottingham: A case study

Michael Rogers & Fiona Bryson
Wardell Armstrong, Birmingham, UK

ABSTRACT: The site of a former chemical factory has been reclaimed by AMEC Civil Engineering on behalf of Nottingham City Council. Contamination from previous site uses included heavy metals, ammonia, VOCs and PAHs within madeground over the Sherwood Sandstone aquifer. This paper comments on the legacy of contamination, focusing on the design and implementation of the reclamation strategy. Additionally, details are presented of the groundwater treatment system utilised during reclamation.

1 THE SITE

The Island Street Site, approximately 5.5 hectares in area is located some 700 m from Nottingham city centre. At the time of commencement of the works the site was occupied principally by buildings associated with a former pharmaceutical research facility. Other derelict industrial buildings were also distributed around the site. Following reclamation it is planned to redevelop the site for commercial usage.

The site has a long history of industrial usage including: former canals; railway viaducts; warehouses; board works; leather works; blacksmiths; lace works; gas works; a scrapyard; lead works; hide works and a pharmaceutical facility.

The historical development of the site is not restricted to the more recent industrial development outlined above. The site also has significant archaeological interest. Prior to the culverting and canalising of the river channels, the area was meadow land around the River Leen. A detailed archaeological watching brief was conducted during the reclamation works to examine all excavations.

1.1 *Site geology and ground conditions*

A full site investigation was undertaken in the early stages of the project to establish the existing ground conditions with respect to material types, ground contamination and the presence and status of any shallow groundwater. This investigation was undertaken in general accordance with DD175 (British Standards Institution 1998) and Department of the Environment guidance (Department of Environment 1994). The ground conditions at the site prior to remediation are illustrated in Figure 1. Madeground deposits comprised some 2.5 m to 3.5 m (though up to 5 m in the former canals) of variable soft to firm clays, brick rubble and sand. Minor constituents also include ash, wood and coal tar along with numerous foundations, cellars, service ducts and pipes. The former canals were generally infilled with brick rubble and frequently contained a layer of black odorous silt at the base.

Beneath the madeground an alluvial layer varying between 1.9 m and 6.5 m thick was encountered, comprising predominantly clayey material with some sands and sandy clays. This alluvial material was underlain by sand and gravel deposits overlying the Sherwood Sandstone.

1.2 *Hydrogeology*

A study of the regional hydrogeology indicated that groundwater flow beneath the site is from north-west to south-east. Water levels in boreholes in the Sherwood Sandstone aquifer underlying the site indicate that sub-artesian groundwater conditions prevailed in the Sherwood Sandstone aquifer. This sub-artesian water is confined or semi-confined by the overlying alluvial material.

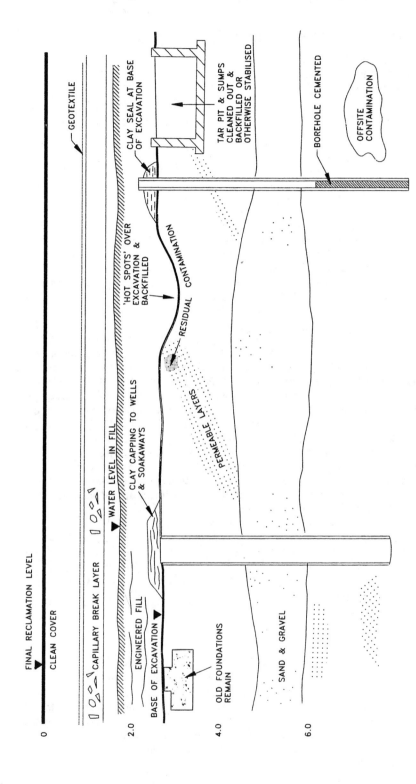

Figure 1. Ground conditions prior to remediation.

Simply stated, the ground conditions and the regional hydrogeological regime can be divided into the following hydrogeological units:

UNIT 1 Madeground. This comprises a mixture of brick, rubble and other waste material. Isolated groundwaters within this material are discrete or localised and typically rest on top of the alluvial clays etc. Generally, water levels range from about 1 m to 4 m below ground level.

UNIT 2 Alluvium. This comprises predominantly clay with silty and sandy layers, confining to an extent, groundwaters in the underlying Sherwood Sandstone Group, which is a significant regional aquifer

UNIT 3 Sherwood Sandstone Group. This comprises generally buff to pale red-brown sandstone with subordinate conglomerate, siltstone and mudstone. The unit forms a major aquifer contributing an important part of the regional water supply. Beneath the site piezometric levels from the aquifer range from 1 m to 3 m below ground level.

Historically local over abstraction of groundwater from the Sherwood Sandstone aquifer has resulted in depressed groundwater levels. This over abstraction is reported to have ceased and in recent years groundwater levels have been recorded as rising again. The sub-artesian groundwater levels recorded in recent boreholes may therefore not have always been present. Such over abstraction of groundwater may have enhanced the downward migration of contaminants from the madeground.

Protection of the Sherwood Sandstone aquifer from further contamination was an important driving force behind the reclamation. The National Rivers Authority (NRA) (subsequently incorporated into the UK Environment Agency in April 1996) were involved at all stages of the reclamation works.

1.3 Contamination status

As a consequence of the industrial history of the site, a number of problems presented themselves, of which a legacy of chemical contamination of both near-surface ground materials and associated groundwater was the most severe. Chemical contamination included heavy metals, ammoniacal nitrogen, volatile organic compounds (VOCs) and polyaromatic hydrocarbons (PAHs).

The distribution of contaminants throughout the site was largely found to be linked with the known site history. The site was classified into zones for remediation purposes. A summary of principal areas of contamination is given below:

Table 1. Maximum levels of determinands identified during site works.

Determinand and site specific	General site levels and comments
Organics	
VOC (1 mg kg^{-1})	Generally 2 to 30 mg kg^{-1} up to 310 mg kg^{-1}
PAH (100 mg kg^{-1})	Up to 1819 mg kg^{-1}
Inorganics	
NH$_3$ (4 mg l^{-1})	Widespread up to 14.1 mg l^{-1}
Cl (4 mg l^{-1})	Generally below limits
FCN (0.5 µg l^{-1})	Isolated above limits up to 9.2 mg l^{-1}
SO$_4$ (500 mg l^{-1})	Sporadically above limits up to 1600 mg l^{-1}
As (50 µg l^{-1})	Generally below limits
Cd (5 µg l^{-1})	Generally below limits
Cr (250 µg l^{-1})	Generally below limits
Cu (100 µg l^{-1})	Generally below limits
Pb (250 µg l^{-1})	Generally below limits
Hg (1 µg l^{-1})	Isolated above limits up to 2.5 µg l^{-1}
Ni (200 µg l^{-1})	Generally below limits
2n (500 µg l^{-1})	Generally below limits

- former scrapyard   PAH and inorganics;
- former chemical works   VOC;
- former canals   PAH and VOC;
- former gas works   PAH;
- bioremediation area   VOC.

Table 1 outlines in general terms, the levels of contamination identified at the site during the initial site investigation phase.

2 RECLAMATION

The initial proposals for the reclamation put forward by the client, Nottingham City Council, comprised the off site removal of all the madeground materials to a licensed landfill. Subsequently 'clean inert' material would have been imported to replace that removed. An alternative scheme was proposed whereby only the madeground that was severely contaminated would be removed. The remainder would be recompacted to bring the site up to a suitable level.

This reclamation strategy had the benefits of removing the reservoir of severe contamination, retaining the beneficial attenuating medium of the alluvial layers and through the selective re-use of the madeground, a greatly reduced project cost. Relevant clean up criteria were agreed with the Environment

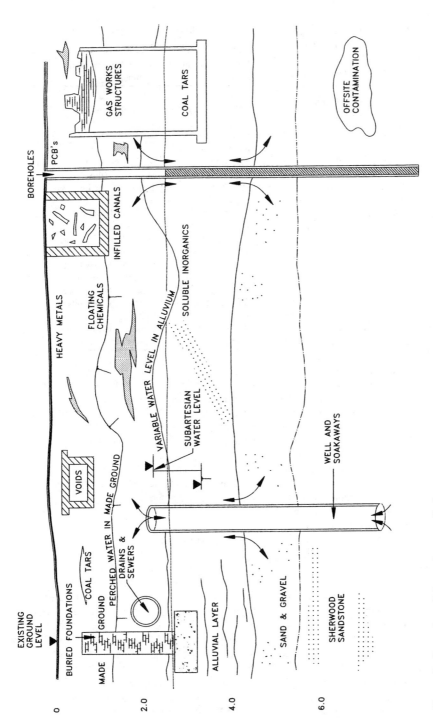

Figure 2. Ground conditions after remediation.

Table 2. Agreed clean up levels.

Determinand	NRA specified levels
Organics	
VOC (mg kg^{-1})	1
PAH (mg kg^{-1})	100
Inorganics	
NH$_3$ (mg l^{-1})	4
Cl (mg l^{-1})	400
FCN (μg l^{-1})	0.5
SO$_4$ (mg l^{-1})	Fill: 500 Capping: 500
	Average, 1,000 Maximum
As (μg l^{-1})	50
Cd (μg l^{-1})	5
Cr (μg l^{-1})	250
Cu (μg l^{-1})	100
Pb (μg l^{-1})	250
Hg (μg l^{-1})	1
Ni (μg l^{-1})	200
2n (μg l^{-1})	500

Note: The levels for inorganic compounds are based upon analysis of a leachate prepared using the NRA protocol (Lewin K et al 1994).

Agency for each of the contaminants believed likely to occur from a knowledge of the site history and previous site investigation. Table 2 summarises the relevant clean up criteria for the site.

The reclamation was tested on completion by confirmatory testing at eighty locations on an approximate 25 m grid. These locations were taken at varying depths an analysed for a full suite of determinands. Following minor retreatment works all of the test locations were within the agreed limits. Figure 2 illustrates the ground conditions at the site following completion of the reclamation works.

2.1 Groundwater treatment

In the initial reclamation strategy it was envisaged that significant volumes of water would be encountered, principally from:

- perched water in the madeground;
- water contained within the infilled canals;
- former culverts;
- rainwater.

The majority of this water was anticipated to be slightly contaminated (principally with heavy metals and organics) though localised pockets of severe contamination were likely.

A full review of the options for groundwater treatment, prior to discharge to sewer, was undertaken in order to determine the BPEO (Best Practicable Environmental Option). This was required by the regulator, the Environment Agency, due to the presence, in the groundwater, of 1,2-dichloroethane which is a "prescribed substance" (Anon 1991). This review included reference to recent CIRIA guidance (CIRIA Vol. VIII 1995). The slightly contaminated water was treated by an on-site treatment plant prior to ultimate discharge into the foul sewer system.

A site specific discharge limit of 30 μg l^{-1} 1,2-dichloroethane was authorised by HMIP with a maximum discharge rate of 10 l s^{-1}. The treatment plant comprised a settling tank (to remove suspended solids), an aeration section (using compressed air to drive off VOC's; a straw filter (to remove organics) and a settling tank with a floating oil boom (to screen off any floating product). The flow rate was monitored by a continuous, flow-proportional sampling system. Samples were analysed for VOC's on a weekly composite basis.

In one section of the site the perched groundwater was more severely contaminated with VOCs. In places the VOCs were recorded up to 2,500 times the agreed site limits consisting mainly of toluene, benzene, ethyl benzene, 1,2-dichloroethane and vinyl chloride.

This more severely contaminated water was pumped into holding tanks prior to off site tankering and disposal. Some 400 m^3 of this water was tankered off site for treatment at licensed facilities.

2.2 In-situ ground remediation

In one area of the site VOC compounds were detected at levels between 2 mg kg^{-1} and 36 mg kg^{-1} compared to a site limit of 1 mg kg^{-1}. An assessment of the options for ground remediation for VOC compounds was undertaken by approaches to a number of specialist remediation companies and reference to a series of reference publications (CIRIA Vol IV 1995; Smith 1995; Armshaw et al. 1992) As this area was not required for immediate excavation, in-situ bioremediation by air sparging was undertaken.

Steel tubes were drilled into the madeground across the area to be treated. Through the selective application of vacuum extraction on some of the tubes oxygen was drawn through the madeground. The oxygen had the twin effect of stripping the VOCs from the soil and encouraging biological breakdown of the organic components by the indigenous microbial population.

This process took 7 months and was undertaken by a specialist sub contractor, who monitored the work by measuring VOC vapours in the extraction boreholes. Post remediation testing of the soil to confirmed the success of the works. Some 3,500 m^3 of material were treated at a cost of £18 m^{-3} compared to a cost of around £30 m^{-3} for the more traditional "excavate and dump" approach.

2.3 Overall project statistics

The following statistics give an indication of the scale of the reclamation works:
- total material excavated   200,000 m^3
- contaminated material taken off site   55,000 m^3
- contaminated material remediated in-situ 3,500 m^3
- imported general fill   20,000 m^3
- contaminated water
  (treated and disposed of to sewer)   5,000 m^3
- highly contaminated water
  (tankered for off site disposal   400 m^3

These works were completed by AMEC during an 18 month contract period. The works were undertaken as a Design and Build contract jointly funded by Nottingham City Council and the EEC.

3 CONCLUSION

The long industrial history of the Island Street Site meant that the following factors were present:
- significant ground contamination
- extensive sub-surface structures and voids
- geotechnically unsuitable ground materials

The ultimate design of the reclamation strategy for the Island Street Site permitted a number of known (and some unknown) problems to be overcome, and allowed the site to be redeveloped in a cost effective manner.

The project is a good example of a successful contractor/consultant/client/regulator relationship in which flexibility and open discussions from an early stage of the project allowed ultimate goals to be successfully achieved.

ACKNOWLEDGEMENTS

The authors would like to thank AMEC Civil Engineering Limited for their permission to use the information from the reclamation scheme for this paper.

REFERENCES

Anon. 1991. *Environmental Protection (Prescribed Processes and Substances) Regulations.* Statutory Instrument No.472.

Armshaw, R. et al 1992. *Review of Innovative Contaminated Soil Clean-up Processes.* Report LR 819 (MR) Warren Spring Laboratory Publications, Stevenage, UK.

British Standards Institution 1988. *Code of practice for the identification of potentially contaminated land and its* investigation. Draft for Development DD175.

CIRIA 1995. Ex-situ remedial methods for contaminated groundwater and other liquids *Remedial Treatment for Contaminated Land.* Volume VIII,. Construction Industry Research and Information Association, Special Publication 108.

CIRIA 1995.Classification and selection of remedial methods, Volume IV In-situ methods of remediation Volume IX. *Remedial Treatment for Contaminated Land* Construction Industry Research and Information Association Special Publications 104 and 109.

Department of the Environment 1994. *Sampling Strategies for Contaminated Land.* Contaminated Land Research Report No.4.

Lewin K. et al 1994. Leaching Tests for Assessment of Contaminated Land: Interim National Rivers Authority (NRA) Guidance. Research and Development Note 301. Foundation for Water Research, Marlow, UK.

Smith M.A. (ed) 1985. *Contaminated Land Reclamation and Treatment.* Plenum Press, New York.

Groundwater in the Urban Environment: Problems, Processes and Management, Chilton et al. (eds)
© 1997 Balkema, Rotterdam, ISBN 90 5410 837 1

Preliminary assessment of the occurrence and possible sources of MTBE in groundwater in the United States, 1993-1994

P.J.Squillace, J.S.Zogorski & C.V.Price
US Geological Survey, Rapid City, S.Dak., USA

W.G.Wilber
US Geological Survey, Reston, Va., USA

ABSTRACT: Out of 60 volatile organic chemicals analyzed, MTBE was the second most frequently detected chemical in samples of shallow groundwater from urban areas that were collected during 1993-94 as part of the U.S. Geological Survey's National Water-Quality Assessment Program. Samples were collected from 5 drinking-water wells, 12 springs, and 193 monitoring wells in urban areas. At a reporting level of 0.2 µg/L, MTBE was detected most frequently in shallow groundwater from urban areas (27% of 210 wells and springs sampled in 8 areas) as compared to shallow groundwater from agricultural areas (1.3% of 549 wells sampled in 21 areas) or deeper groundwater from major aquifers (1.0% of 412 wells sampled in 9 areas). Only 3% of the shallow wells sampled in urban areas had concentrations of MTBE that exceed 20 µg/L, which is the estimated lower limit of the United States Environmental Protection Agency draft lifetime drinking-water health advisory. Because MTBE is persistent and mobile in groundwater, it can move from shallow to deeper aquifers with time. Possible sources of MTBE in groundwater include point sources, such as leaking storage tanks, and nonpoint sources, such as recharge of precipitation and storm-water runoff.

1. INTRODUCTION

The 1990 U.S. Clean Air Act Amendments require fuel oxygenates, such as methyl *tert*-butyl ether (MTBE) or ethanol, to be added to gasoline used in some metropolitan areas to reduce atmospheric concentrations of carbon monoxide or ozone (Figure 1). The Clean Air Act Amendments require the use of oxygenated fuels during the winter when the concentrations of carbon monoxide are largest. Nine metropolitan areas that have the most severe ozone pollution are required to use a special blend of gasoline called reformulated gasoline year round, a requirement that became effective in January, 1995.

MTBE is a potentially important groundwater contaminant because of its mobility and persistence (Garrett et al. 1986), and because it is tentatively classified by the U.S. Environmental Protection Agency (USEPA) as a possible human carcinogen. In nonoxygenated gasoline, the monocyclic aromatic hydrocarbons, which include benzene, toluene, ethylbenzene, and the three xylenes, m-, o-, and p- (BTEX compounds), are the most soluble and most mobile components in gasoline. In oxygenated gasoline, MTBE is even more soluble and mobile than any of the BTEX compounds (Garrett et al. 1986; Barker et al. 1990; Luhrs & Pyott 1992; Odermatt 1994). In fact, evidence indicates that MTBE

moves as rapidly as a conservative tracer (Barker et al. 1990; Hubbard et al. 1994). MTBE persists in groundwater under both aerobic and anaerobic conditions (Barker et al. 1990; Hubbard et al. 1994; Suflita & Mormile 1993; Mormile et al. 1994; Yeh & Novak 1994) because it resists physical, chemical, and microbial degradation. That is not to say that MTBE will never degrade or that microbes can not be engineered to degrade MTBE.

2 STUDY METHODS

The U.S. Geological Survey's National Water-Quality Assessment (NAWQA) Program is designed to describe current water-quality conditions for 59 of the largest and most important river basins and aquifer systems nationwide by the year 2000 (Leahy & Thompson 1994). Investigations in these 60 areas, referred to as "Study Units," are the principal areas where water quality data are collected for the NAWQA Program (Figure 1). Additional information on the NAWQA Program is available at "http://wwwrvares.er.usgs.gov/nawqa/nawqa_home.html." Some groundwater quality data for volatile organic chemicals (VOCs) from the first 20 Study Units are summarized in this paper.

The NAWQA Program for groundwater focuses

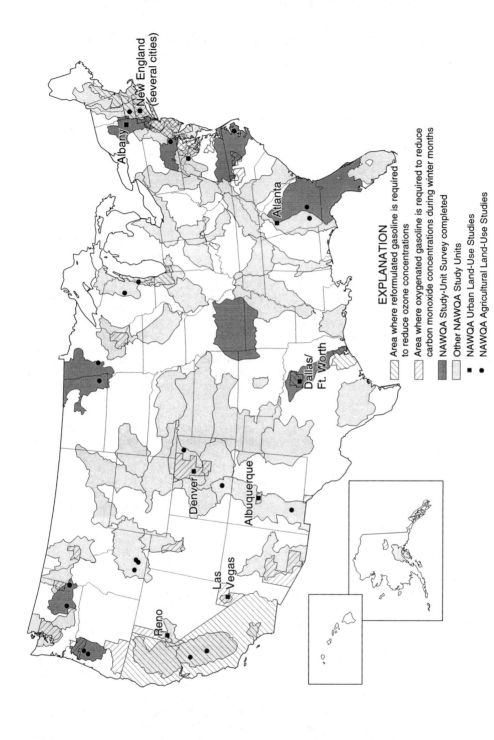

Figure 1. Location of areas using oxygenated or reformulated gasoline, U.S. Geological Survey National Water-Quality Assessment (NAWQA) Study Units, and Urban and Agricultural Land-Use Studies, 1993-1994.

EXPLANATION

Area where reformulated gasoline is required to reduce ozone concentrations

Area where oxygenated gasoline is required to reduce carbon monoxide concentrations during winter months

NAWQA Study-Unit Survey completed

Other NAWQA Study Units

■ NAWQA Urban Land-Use Studies

● NAWQA Agricultural Land-Use Studies

New England (several cities)

Albany

Atlanta

Dallas/ Ft. Worth

Denver

Albuquerque

Las Vegas

Reno

on assessing (1) the water-quality conditions of major aquifers, and (2) the quality of recently recharged groundwater associated with recent land-use activities (Gilliom et al. 1995). The sampling design is based on the need to examine ground-water quality at a range of spatial scales. Focused at the largest scale, "Study-Unit Surveys" are used in conjunction with an analysis of historical water-quality data to characterize groundwater quality across large portions of individual study units. The spatial density of wells sampled for a Study Unit Survey is generally one well per 100 km^2. However, a higher priority is placed on sampling aqui-fers from which groundwater is currently being withdrawn (typically for industry, irrigation, public or domestic water supply) relative to aquifers where the groundwater is not currently being used. "Land-Use Studies" are carried out on an intermediate scale to build an understanding of the potential effects of land use on shallow groundwater quality. The Land-Use Studies are directed toward under-standing the effects of human activities on shallow groundwater quality. Wells selected for a Land-Use Study are randomly distributed throughout the land-use setting of interest using a grid-based random sampling approach (Scott 1990).

VOC analyses were performed using purge and trap capillary gas chromatography/mass spectrome-try. The method of analysis is discussed in detail by Raese et al. (1995) and Rose & Schroeder (1995) and is similar to USEPA Method 524.2, revision 3.0.

3 STUDY RESULTS

3.1 Occurrence of MTBE in shallow groundwater

Of the 210 urban wells and springs sampled, 28% contained chloroform; 27% contained MTBE; 18% contained tetrachloroethene; 10% contained trichlo-roethene; 7% contained cis-1,2 dichloroethene; 5% contained 1,1-dichloroethane; and 5% contained benzene. MTBE generally was not found with BTEX compounds, which commonly are associated with point-source spills of gasoline. Of 210 urban wells and springs sampled, 61 wells and 1 spring had concentrations of MTBE or BTEX. Among these 61 wells and 1 spring, 79% had MTBE only, 13% had MTBE and BTEX, and 8% had BTEX compounds only.

MTBE was detected more frequently, and in larger concentrations, in shallow ambient groundwater in urban areas compared to shal-low groundwater in agricultural areas. At a reporting level of 0.2 μg/L, MTBE was detected in 27% of 210 shallow urban wells

and springs, and in only 1.3% of 549 shallow agricultural wells sampled. MTBE was detected in samples of shallow groundwater in all eight urban Land-Use Studies areas but in only 3 of 21 Agricultural Land-Use Studies. In urban areas, MTBE was detected in shallow groundwater in Denver, Colorado; New England (specifically urban areas within Con-necticut, Massachusetts, and Vermont); Reno, Nevada; Albany, New York; Dallas/Fort Worth, Texas; Las Vegas, Nevada; Atlanta, Georgia; and Albuquerque, New Mexico (Fig-ure 2). In agricultural areas, MTBE was detected in southern Colorado, New England, and eastern Pennsylvania.

MTBE was detected most frequently in samples of shallow urban groundwater in Denver, Colorado, and New England (Figure 2), but the reason for its frequent detection is not known. In Denver, samples from 79% of the shallow urban wells (23 of 29 wells) had detectable concentrations of MTBE, and in New England, samples from 37% of the wells (13 of 35 wells) had detectable concentrations of MTBE. The frequent detection of MTBE in these two areas may be related to the fact that the aquifer, and the overlying unsaturated zone, consists of very conductive sand and gravel and that the median depth to water was very shallow-- 4.3 m in Denver and 2.8 m in New England. However, the mean annual precipitation is about three times greater in New England than in Denver (39), and therefore the groundwater recharge in these two areas may be substantially different.

Of the 210 shallow Urban Land-Use wells and springs sampled, 73% had concentrations less than the reporting level of 0.2 μg/L, 24% had concentra-tions of MTBE ranging from 0.2 to 20.0 μg/L, and 3% had concentrations exceeding 20.0 μg/L, which is the estimated lower limit of the USEPA draft life-time drinking-water health advisory level (U.S. Environmental Protection Agency 1996). None of the samples from the 549 Agricultural Land-Use wells or 412 Study-Unit Survey wells had concen-trations of MTBE that exceeded 20.0 μg/L. The maximum concentration of MTBE detected in shallow groundwater in urban areas were over 100 μg/L whereas the maximum concentration in shallow groundwater in agricultural areas was 1.3 μg/L.

3.2 Possible sources of MTBE in groundwater

MTBE in groundwater can originate from point and nonpoint sources. Possible point sources of MTBE include industry, leaking gas tanks, pipelines, land-fill sites, dumps, spills, underground injection, and refueling facilities. The infrequent concurrent

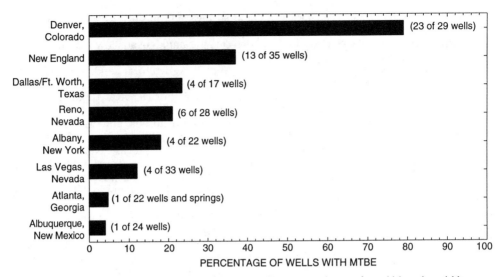

Figure 2. Frequency of detection of MTBE in shallow groundwater from Urban Land-Use Study areas, 1993-94.

detection of MTBE with BTEX compounds suggest that point-source leaks are not the principal source of the MTBE detected in urban groundwater, although the lack of association does not completely rule out point-source spills as a potential source.

Possible nonpoint sources of MTBE include atmospheric deposition and stormwater runoff. Once in the atmosphere, MTBE can partition into precipitation and be transported in stormwater runoff into streams or into shallow groundwater with recharge from stormwater runoff or infiltration of precipitation. The transfer of MTBE from atmospheric gases to rainwater is dependent on the temperature and concentrations of MTBE in the air. The U.S. Geological Survey sampled stormwater in 16 cities and metropolitan areas from 1991 through 1995 (Delzer et al. 1996) to help municipalities meet the National Pollutant Discharge Elimination System (NPDES) monitoring requirements set by the USEPA. MTBE was detected in 6.9% of the 592 samples collected. Eighty-three percent of all detected concentrations of MTBE occurred between October and March, which corresponds with the expected winter use of oxygenated gasoline. Concentrations of MTBE ranged from the lowest reporting level of 0.2 to 8.7 µg/L.

4 CONCLUSIONS AND ADDITIONAL STUDY NEEDS

Based on the USEPA's current understanding of MTBE's carcinogenicity, the concentrations in groundwater reported in this study in most cases do not represent a risk to human health; samples from only 3% of the shallow wells and springs in urban areas had concentrations of MTBE that exceeded 20 µg/L, which is the estimated lower limit of the USEPA's draft drinking-water health advisory. Currently, MTBE is not a required analyte of monitoring programme of public water supplies and drinking water; however, MTBE can be analyzed by purge and trap, capillary column gas chromatography/mass spectrometry (Rose & Schroeder 1995), which is extensively used for VOC analysis by public-water utilities. Given the preliminary information discussed in this paper, it is advisable for urban water utilities to consider adding MTBE to their existing VOC analytical schedule on a voluntary basis.

How MTBE enters shallow urban groundwater is not clear, and existing environmental monitoring programme may not be adequately designed to answer this question. Federal, state and local government agencies have made substantial investments to protect the quality of the environment, and the effectiveness of these efforts has been evaluated by assessing the resource that was focused for protection (e.g. air, surface water, or groundwater). The integration of monitoring programme would help to insure that efforts to protect or improve one component of the environment do not adversely affect another. Integrated environmental monitoring in a few major cities would provide an improved understanding of the source, transport, and fate of MTBE in groundwater in urban areas.

Defining the source of MTBE in shallow groundwater is essential to prevent further contamination, and to protect other vulnerable aquifers in the United States from contamination by MTBE or similar compounds. Questions related to the source of MTBE include: (1) Is the frequency of detection of MTBE in shallow groundwater more related to its use or to aquifer vulnerability? (2) Is the source of MTBE in shallow ambient urban groundwater primarily from nonpoint sources of contamination, such as precipitation and urban runoff? There may be areas of the United States where the use of MTBE will not result in its infiltration to shallow or deeper groundwater. However, before this can be determined, seasonal information is needed on how much MTBE is being used in major metropolitan areas. This information can be related to the frequency of detection of MTBE and to aquifer vulnerability. To define nonpoint sources of MTBE contamination, information is needed on the release of MTBE to the atmosphere from various activities. MTBE can be released to the atmosphere from a variety of sources including industrial stack and fugitive emissions, refueling at service stations, and mobile sources, such as automobiles. With the possible exception of industrial emissions, the amount of MTBE released to the urban atmosphere from these other sources is not well documented. Once MTBE is in the atmosphere, some can be returned with precipitation, but more research is needed to determine the concentrations of MTBE in precipitation and in surface runoff on a seasonal basis.

A better understanding of the transport of MTBE from land surface to shallow groundwater, and from shallow to deeper aquifers would be used to protect public water supplies and in developing well head protection plans for public water supplies. Questions related to the transport of MTBE include: (1) Can MTBE in precipitation or stormwater runoff recharge the shallow groundwater; if so, under what conditions, timeframes, and in what concentrations? (2) How quickly, and at what concentrations, can MTBE be transported from shallow to deeper groundwater? (3) What is the maximum extent of a MTBE plume originating from a point source relative to the BTEX compounds? Depth to water, recharge rates, permeability of the unsaturated zone, evapotranspiration, and other characteristics are likely to affect the transport of MTBE through the unsaturated zone. Because MTBE is mobile and persistent in groundwater, it is reasonable to expect that it will move from shallow to deep groundwater with time, but it is not known how quickly and at what concentrations. Knowledge on the maximum extent of a MTBE plume relative to BTEX compounds originating from a single gasoline contamination source will help determine if point source contamination is responsible for the widespread detection of small concentrations of MTBE in the absence of BTEX compounds.

Additional study and data on the fate of MTBE are needed to determine if MTBE, or its degradation products, will accumulate in groundwater over time. The accumulation of MTBE in groundwater may not necessarily result in an increase in concentrations with time, but its detection would become more frequent. The degradation of some organic chemicals in aquifers can be very slow, with a half life of years, decades or longer, to breakdown to carbon dioxide and water. The degradation products of some organic chemicals can be toxic. Questions related to the fate of MTBE include: (1) What is the long-term fate of MTBE, and its degradation products, in groundwater? (2) What is the half-life of MTBE in groundwater under aerobic and anaerobic conditions in various aquifers? (3) Are the degradation products of MTBE a human health concern. There also may be degradation products of MTBE in the air, such as *tert*-butyl formate (Japar et al. 1991), which enter shallow groundwater with recharge water. Investigation of these degradation products is necessary to a full understanding of the fate of MTBE.

In order to determine if MTBE concentrations are likely to rise above current levels and potentially rise to levels that pose a health threat it is necessary to understand three things about the compound: (1) the pathways by which it enters the groundwater, (2) the processes by which it is transported in groundwater, and (3) the rates at which it degrades. Only when all three of these issues are reasonably well understood can meaningful projections be made of the potential for MTBE reaching dangerous levels over long periods of use. The U.S. Geological Survey is beginning to conduct research on aspects of all of these processes and is in close communication with other scientists studying these questions. In addition, the NAWQA Program will continue to monitor some wells in all Study Units, providing a continuing empirical check on the changes in levels of MTBE in groundwater. The U. S. Geological Survey will continue to report to the public, regulatory agencies, industry, and the scientific community on the results of its research and monitoring on this emerging water-quality issue.

REFERENCES

Barker, J.F., C.E. Hubbard & L.A. Lemon 1990. The influence of methanol and MTBE on the fate and persistence of monoaromatic hydrocarbons in ground water: *Ground Water Management-- Proceedings of Petroleum Hydrocarbons and Organic Chemicals in Ground Water--Prevention, Detection, and Restoration*, Oct 31-Nov. 2,

1990: 113-127. American Petroleum Institute and Association of Ground Water Scientists and Engineers. Houston, Tex.

Delzer, G.C., J.S. Zogorski, T.J. Lopes & R.L. Bosshart 1996. *Occurrence of the gasoline oxygenate MTBE and BTEX compounds in urban stormwater in the United States, 1991-95.* U.S. Geological Survey Water-Resources Investigation Report 96-4145.

Garrett, P., M. Moreau & J. Lowry 1986. MTBE as a ground water contaminant. In *Proceedings of Petroleum Hydrocarbons and Organic Chemicals in Ground Water--Prevention, Detection and Restoration*, National Water Well Association and American Petroleum Institute: 227-238. Houston Tex.

Gilliom, R.J., W.M. Alley & M.E. Gurtz 1995. *Design of the National Water-Quality Assessment Program--Occurrence and distribution of water-quality conditions.* U. S. Geological Survey Circular 1112.

Hubbard, C.E., J.F. Barker, S.F. O'Hannes, M. Vandegriendt & R.W. Gillham 1994. *Transport and fate of dissolved methanol, methyl-tertiary-butyl-ether, and monoaromatic hydrocarbons in a shallow sand aquifer.* American Petroleum Institute Publication Number 4601. Washington, DC.

Japar, S.M., T.J. Wallington, S.J. Rudy, & T.Y. Chang, 1991, Ozone-forming potential of a series of oxygenated organic compounds. *Environ. Sci. Technol.* 25: 415-420.

Leahy, P.P. & T.H. Thompson 1994. *U.S. Geological Survey National Water-Quality Assessment Program.* U.S. Geological Survey Open-File Report 94-70.

Luhrs, R.C. & C.J. Pyott 1992. Trilinear plots a powerful new application for mapping gasoline contamination. In *Proceedings of Petroleum Hydrocarbons and Organic Chemicals in Ground Water--Prevention, Detection and Restoration Eastern Regional Ground Water Issues*; Nov. 4-6, 1992: 85-100. American Petroleum Institute and Association of Ground Water Scientists and Engineers: Houston, Tex.

Mormile, M.R., S. Liu & J.M. Suflita 1994. Anaerobic biodegradation of gasoline oxygenates: Extrapolation of information to multiple sites and redox conditions. *Environ. Sci. Technol.* 28:1727-1732.

Odermatt, J.R. 1994. Natural chromatographic separation of benzene, toluene, ethylbenzene and xylenes (BTEX compounds) in a gasoline contaminated ground water aquifer. *Org. Geochem.* 21:1141-1150.

Raese, J.W., D.L. Rose & M.W. Sandstrom 1995. *U.S. Geological Survey Laboratory method for methyl tert-butyl ether and other fuel oxygenates.* U.S. Geological Survey Fact Sheet FS-219-95.

Rose, D.L. & M.P. Schroeder 1995. *Method of analysis by the U.S. Geological Survey National Water-Quality Laboratory--Determination of volatile organic compounds in water by purge and trap capillary gas chromatography/mass spectrometry.* U.S. Geological Survey Open-File Report 94-708.

Scott, J.C. 1990. *Computerized stratified random site-selection approaches for design of ground-water- quality sampling network.* U.S. Geological Survey Water-Resources Investigations Report 90-4101.

Suflita, J.M. & M.R. Mormile 1993. Anaerobic biodegradation of known and potential gasoline oxygenates in the terrestrial subsurface. *Environ. Sci. Technol.* 27:976-978.

U.S. Environmental Protection Agency 1996. *Drinking water regulations and health advisories.* Washington, D.C.: Office of Water.

Yeh, C.K. & J.T. Novak 1994. Anaerobic biodegradation of gasoline oxygenates in soils. *Water Environ. Research* 66:744-752.

Urban impacts on a mineral water source, Serbia

Zoran Stevanovic, Bojan Hajdin, Petar Dokmanovic & Igor Jemcov
Faculty of Mining and Geology, Institute of Hydrogeology, Belgrade, Yugoslavia

ABSTRACT: This paper is a contribution to the methodology of research on the protection of groundwater in a geologically complex and sensitive area. The problems of an urban area where there is little or no regulated protection of groundwater are described. A number of potential and identified polluters have been registered around the mineral water source in the urban zone of Smederevska Palanka, Serbia. The absence of preventive actions, the occurrence of industrial and agricultural activities, and roads in the area, as well as the lack of elementary physical protection of the intake structures, have all resulted in deterioration of mineral water quality. The investigations form the basis for proposed sanitary protection zones and remedial actions designed to permit the continued exploitation of the local natural resource.

1 INTRODUCTION

General aspects of the protection of the mineral water resource at Smederevska Palanka have been presented by the researchers of the Faculty of Mining & Geology (Stevanovic et al.1993, 1995; Bozovic et al. 1995). In the meantime, as predicted, the resource of this mineral water has become polluted by chemical and microbiological contaminants in the production well area. The incident prompted (unfortunately delayed) urgent detailed hydrogeological, hydro-chemical and microbiological investigations, and remedial steps (in October 1994).

2 HYDROGEOLOGICAL CHARACTERISTICS, WATER QUALITY AND POLLUTION

The mineral water source area of Kiseljak is located between the rivers Jasenica and Kubrsnica. The oldest lithostratigraphic unit consists of Paleozoic crystalline schists under Neogene deposits. The latter exceed 900 m in thickness, and consist of sand, clay and sand-clay deposits. Quaternary deposits in the Jasenica and the Kubrsnica alluvial plains are up to 15 m thick. Tectonically, the area is characterized by recent and older faulting. Carbon dioxide gas is rising from deep horizons. The explored aquifer of carbon dioxide-rich water, Palanacki Kiseljak, is present in the alluvial sand-gravel deposits.

The shallowest aquifer of carbon dioxide-rich water (TDS range 1.6-2.3 g/l) is susceptible to pollution from the ground surface as a result of the unfavourable local hydrogeology and geology (shallow depth, permeability of overlying beds, hydraulic communication with surface waters, etc.) and many anthropogenic factors.

Problems associated with the maintenance of the Palanacki Kiseljak water quality are much older than the last contamination incident of 1994, but they were not given adequate consideration. Actually, there is not a single provision in the Regulations on the location of protection zones for drinking water supply sources.

Bacteriologically, sporadic impurity was registered in the period 1992-1994, with *Escherichia coli* and *Streptococcus faecalis* being detected. The situation has deteriorated, especially in low-water periods, and since 3rd August 1994 new faecal contamination of mineral water was registered, with a progressive increase in bacterial levels in the following days. The contamination affected shallow wells on the left bank of the river, which are pumped for water bottling. The water quality deterioration coincided with the construction of a manhole in the regional water distribution system located by the Kiseljak intakes. The manhole cut through the partly protective surficial alluvium, and thus provided for vertical infiltration of polluted surface waters.

This incident confirmed the risk of serious contamination during low water periods when the hydraulic balance becomes disturbed. The drawdown in groundwater levels allows infiltration of polluted water from distant localities, from the ground surface, or directly from the Kubrsnica river.

More than twenty potential polluters, whose localities are shown in Figure 1, were registered in October-November 1994 during the field mapping. The foci of pollution are the residential area, the site of GOSA metal industry, and the bottling plant, which have the majority of the waste disposal sites.

The general microbiological analysis of mineral waters in the source areas was followed by a detailed microbiological analysis of selected samples by the APPI-STRIP method (Jankovic 1980). The analytical results obtained showed significant quantitative and qualitative bacterial similarities in a number of localities, including the river and the manhole.

On the basis of the microbiological water analysis of Oct. 1994, the mineral water source area (Figure 2) is divided into three characteristic subareas:

Table 1.   Microbiological analysis of water from representative sampling locations.

No	Location	Coli index x 10^3	Total count of aerobic mesoph. bact. x 10^3	Identifications
1	Mineral well B-1	24	8.2	*Cytrobacter Klebsiella sp., Enterobact. sp.*
2	Waterworks manhole	24	19	*Klebsiella sp.*
3	Kubrsnica river	380	300	*E. Coli*
4	GOSA well	240	260	*Enterobacter, Klebsiella sp.*
5	Borehole P-4	3.8	160	*Klebsiella sp.*

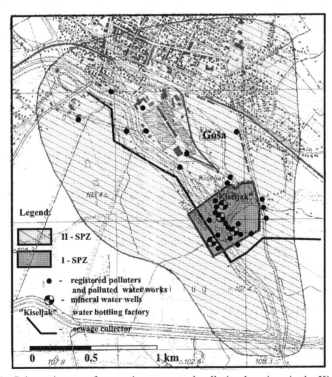

Figure 1. Schematic map of protection zones and pollution locations in the Kiseljak area.

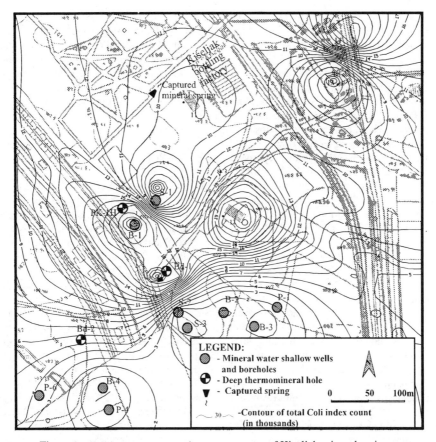

Figure 2. Coli index concentration contour map of Kiseljak mineral spring zone.

Area I, the area of mineral water abstraction sites, where the microbiological pollution was recorded after the faecal contamination incident.

Area II, an area of abandoned wells, where the Coli index (total Coli bacteria count per litre by MPN method) was low but measurable. Water from these wells is also characterized by an autochthonous microflora.

Area III, on the left bank of the Kubrsnica is characterized by microbiologically much better water.

3 PROBLEMS OF URBAN AREA MULTIPLE USE AND PROTECTIVE MEASURES

Water from this source with inadequate sanitary protection has been commercially used for years as a table mineral water. The inadequacies of the protection and preparation are many:

- The source is unprotected and unfenced;
- The area of the source is used for more than one purpose: park, promenade, rural homesteads (gardens, stables, septic tanks, pastures), improvised disposal of various litter, swimming pool;
- In ignorance, sewerage construction occurred at the border of the source zone (Figure 1), and the water supply works (including a relief manhole near one of the production wells). These works cut through one of the abandoned and unprotected wells which penetrates the water-bearing strata.

Each of the stated factors is not necessarily a direct source of mineral water pollution, but is certainly contributing to the present poor water quality.

The present multipurpose use of the bottled-water production zone, where groundwater is not naturally protected from contamination, ideally should not be continued; alternatively the activities should be significantly reduced and subjected to a strict sanitary control.

The first imperative step is the definition of sanitary protection zones (SPZ), a preliminary action for all subsequent steps. The areas of SPZ I and II are shown in Figure 1. Zones are determinated in compliance with the legal regulations in Yugoslavia. Zone I is the physical protection area of water wells and zone II corresponds to a well's cone of depression (neutral flow line). The zoning, particularly SPZ I, had to consider the given situation (the multi-purpose use of the land); thus the SPZ areas are compromises. SPZ III should include the entire urbanized area of Smederevska Palanka and large parts of the Jasenica and Kubrsnica river areas.

On the basis of hydrogeological investigations, a design was proposed for localized, remedial and protective measures (some of these activities have been completed and resulted in improved water quality). The major measures in protection zone I proper are: fencing the zone of strict protection and control of access allowing entrance only to persons employed on the works; riverbed sealing or concreting of the Kubrsnica through the protection zone; soil stripping in several localities where there are old refuse heaps, and recapping with fresh soil; relocation of several farm homesteads from the zone; discontinuation of any activity unrelated to mineral water production; relocation of the sewage collector line; relocation of water supply lines and the manhole; sanitation, cleaning and decontamination of all Kiseljak water wells, all conduit pipes, reservoirs, filters, and other water system elements; definition and observation of working rules in surrounding works which are potential polluters in protection zone II (GOSA industry, barracks, petrol-filling station, etc.); assign the zone a special protection regime status like a natural reservation, to raise awareness of the presence of a natural mineral water of high quality and its almost hundred years of exploitation; continuous monitoring of the mineral water exploitation (including maintenance of shallow drawdowns by operation of several wells), and water quality monitoring for early detection of any contamination.

4 CONCLUSION

The considered case example shows the complexity of a multi-purpose area in an urban environment. The attempt of town planners to convert the area where mineral water is abstracted and bottled for table use into a park for sports and social amenities has failed as a result of uncontrolled activities (housing, water supply and sewerage pipings, roads, local refuse heaps, etc.). Priorities in the land use have to be established and a strict control introduced for prevention of undesirable effects on the natural mineral water resource.

REFERENCES

Bozovic, M. and Z. Stevanovic, P. Papic 1995. Bioloski i hemijski indikatori ekscesnog zagadjenja mineralnih voda "Kiseljaka" u Smederevskoj Palanci. (Biological and chemical indicators of excessive pollution of mineral water Kiseljak in S. Palanka). *Proceedings of Symp. "Zastita voda '95" ("Water protection '95").*p..283-287. Tara.

Jankovic, M. 1980. Mikrobilogija. p.1-235. Beograd: Naucna knjiga.

Stevanovic, Z. and B. Filipovic, B. Hajdin 1993: Generalni aspekti zastite mineralnih voda Smederevske Palanke (General aspects of protection of mineral water of S. Palanka). *Proceedings of Symp. "Zastita voda '93" "Water Protection '93").* p.16-21. Arandjelovac.

Stevanovic, Z. and B. Filipovic, B. Hajdin, P. Dokmanovic, I. Jemcov 1995. Mere zastite mineralnih ugljokiselih voda u sklopu višenamenskog koriscenja prostora u Smederevskoj Palanci, (Protective measures of mineral carbondioxide water of S.Palanka). *Proceedings of Symp. "Zastita voda '95" ("Water protection '95").*p.273-277. Tara.

Groundwater contamination from waste-engine oil recycling in Western Australia

Peter Thorpe & John Waterhouse
Golder Associates, Perth, W.A., Australia

ABSTRACT The successful remediation of a contaminated site, in terms of technical and financial goals, cannot be achieved unless the hydrogeology and the nature and extent of contamination is understood in advance of the selection of a remedial strategy. The metropolitan area of Perth, Western Australia contains at least 700 contaminated sites excluding petrol stations, each of which has the potential to pollute shallow unconfined sand aquifers which supply 40% of Perth's public water supply and private irrigators. The site considered in this paper consists of an abandoned brick-clay pit, 7 m deep, filled with the by-products of a waste oil refinery and builders' rubble. The wastes below the water table contain concentrated sulphuric acid, heavy metals, PAH, BTEX, phenols and oil. Leachate from the pit has a TDS of 87 000 mg/L.

1 INTRODUCTION

Perth, Western Australia overlies major aquifers that provide about 70% of the total water usage and 30% of the public drinking water supply. Urban and industrial development in Perth has created at least 700 potentially contaminated sites excluding petrol stations with underground fuel tanks. The investigation of these sites is at a formative stage and only a small number have been remediated.

The site described in this paper is considered to be one of the worst cases as it consists of a 7 m former brick-clay pit with several smaller pits nearby, within a residential area and used for the disposal of oil re-refining wastes which include sulphuric acid, waste oil and grease, engine deposits containing metals, Fullers Earth, PAH and phenols. The problem for remediation is compounded by back-filling of the pit with builders' rubble, plaster and steel scrap, giving a total waste volume of about 13 000 m³. The waste is largely submerged beneath the water table and groundwater contamination has previously been observed both below the pit within a deeper aquifer and laterally at least 13 m from the pit perimeter (Thorpe 1995).

Golder Associates was commissioned in 1996 by the Department of Environmental Protection to undertake a detailed review of existing data and a site investigation to provide practical options for remediation.

2 HYDROGEOLOGICAL SETTING

The site is located in an eastern residential suburb of Perth 17 km east of the city centre (Figure 1). The area is part of a major Mesozoic sedimentary basin which extends for 1 000 km along the south-west coast of Western Australia.

The site has a surface elevation of 19 m AHD (Australian Height Datum) and is underlain by sediments of the Quaternary superficial formations (Guildford Clay) in turn underlain by the Cretaceous Leederville Formation.

The Guildford Clay consists of about a 16 m thickness of sandy clay and clayey sand with minor sand beds with a saturated thickness of about 13 m. Individual sand beds form confined aquifers which are likely to be laterally discontinuous. Regional groundwater flow is to the south-west.

The underlying Leederville Formation consists of interbedded sands and clays and forms a major confined aquifer with a potentiometric head of about 15 m AHD. The regional direction of groundwater flow is to the west at a rate estimated to be about 1 to 4 m/day in the Perth area. Downgradient from the site the nearest public drinking water supply bore is at Leederville, about 20 km from the site.

Groundwater supplies suitable for domestic irrigation bores are limited within the Guildford Clay due to its high clay content. Most domestic bores in the area are located at greater depth in the upper part of the Leederville aquifer and are used

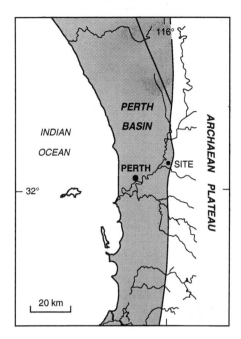

FIGURE 1: LOCALITY PLAN

for garden reticulation only. Locally the salinity of groundwater in the Guildford Clay is variable from fresh to marginal quality (890 to 4 000 mg/L Total Dissolved Solids) and is of marginal quality in the Leederville aquifer (1 000 - 1 200 mg/L TDS).

3   INVESTIGATION PROGRAMME

The scope of work at the site involved the following:

- Hazard characterisation of the pit wastes
- Shallow and deeper evaluation of soil and groundwater contamination
- Preliminary design of groundwater inflow control system
- Assessing options for remediation.

Figure 2 is a plan showing the layout of the site and Figure 3 presents a section through it.

3.1   Hazard characterisation

The liquid wastes within the major pit were characterised chemically as an initial step to determine the suite of compounds to be tested for outside the pit. Liquid (oil and water) samples were collected from bore OM2 within the centre of the major pit. Sample OM2B/1 comprised mainly oil and OM2B/2 comprised mainly water.

In the following sections the test results in Table 1 are compared to accepted guidelines for the assessment of contaminated sites in Western Australia. These include the ANZECC (1992) guidelines which specify environmental investigation levels of some compounds. If soils at a site exceed this investigation level further studies of the site are required. The ANZECC guidelines cover only a limited number of chemicals within soil only and they defer to the equivalent Dutch guidelines for soil and water (Assink & van den Brink 1985). Exceedance of the Dutch B guidelines indicates that further site investigation is required, and exceedance of Dutch C indicates that site clean-up is required.

The filtered water sample with TDS=87 000 mg/L has an equivalent density to hypersaline water. It has a greater density than the surrounding groundwater (TDS ~ 2 000 mg/L) and has the potential to sink and displace lower density groundwater below the base of the pit and at the sides.

3.2   Shallow and deeper evaluation

Twelve shallow (< 12 m) and three deeper (< 40 m) bores were drilled at strategic locations to assess the extent of contamination in the Guildford Clay and the underlying Leederville aquifer and to characterise the contamination status of other infilled clay pits and drains nearby.

The results, summarised in Table 1, showed:

- The highest level of groundwater contamination at the site occurs beneath and downgradient from the major pit within about the upper 10 m of the Leederville aquifer. This upper section of the aquifer is underlain by low permeability black clay and silt which is interpreted as being laterally continuous across the area at about -5 to -10 m AHD. Offsite groundwater contamination of the upper Leederville aquifer is apparent from bores drilled to the west. Groundwater flow may have transported contaminants about 100 m down hydraulic-gradient from the major pit.
- Groundwater in the Guildford Clay aquifer adjacent to the major pit is virtually uncontaminated in terms of the guidelines. Sulphur concentrations are high and in a small number of bores concentrations of total phenols exceed the Dutch guidelines.
- Soils adjacent to the major pit are variably contaminated with hydrocarbons up to and above the Dutch C guideline in some cases to a depth of 4 to 5 m, about 10 m from the pit perimeter.
- The origin of the high levels of sulphur in groundwater and soil in the area is not clear, as there are at least two other potential major sources

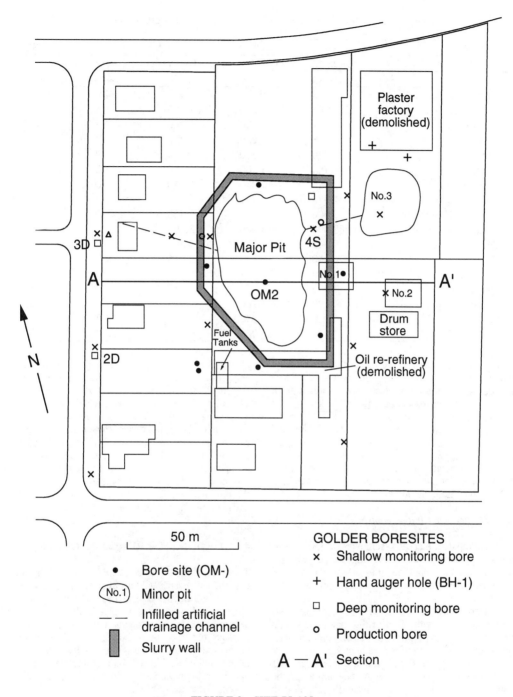

Plaster factory (demolished)

No.3

3D

Major Pit 4S

A OM2 No.1 A'

×No.2

Drum store

Fuel Tanks

2D

Oil re-refinery (demolished)

N

50 m

GOLDER BORESITES

- Bore site (OM-)

No.1 Minor pit

- - Infilled artificial drainage channel

Slurry wall

× Shallow monitoring bore

+ Hand auger hole (BH-1)

□ Deep monitoring bore

○ Production bore

A−A' Section

FIGURE 2: SITE PLAN

Table 1: Summary of chemistry of oil/water wastes and contaminated groundwater.

Bore	OM2	OM2	4S	2D	3D
Sample Type	oil in pit	water in pit	groundwater	groundwater	groundwater
Unit	mg/kg	µg/L	µg/L	µg/L	µg/L
Sample interval (m)	6.0-6.9	6.0-6.9	5.0-8.0	18.0-24.0	16.0-22.0
Cadmium	0.2	200	<2.5	<2.5	<2.5
Chromium	8.7	20,000	5.6	<2.5	8.0
Copper	6.8	2,000	5.2	13	13
Lead	730	8,300	<2.5	7	7
Nickel	0.4	5,000	10	160	120
Zinc	14	440,000	10	520	460
PAH, total	1,370	281	<10	<10	<10
Aliphatic hydrocarbons	23,600	5,560	155	<20	<20
Complex hydrocarbons	680,000	14,000	25,000	2,200	330
Benzene	62	11	<1	<1	<1
Toluene	440	32	<5	<5	<5
Ethylbenzene	350	<1	<10	<10	<10
xylene	2,000	71	<10	<10	<10
Phenols, total	100	5,200	17	25	28
pH	4.0	1.0	6.3	3.2	3.2
TDS, mg/L	n/a	87,000	2,600	470	4,900

of sulphur in the area as well as the sulphuric acid residues from the oil re-refining wastes. These include the dissolution of plaster wastes and natural sources such as oxidation of sulphides in the sediments.

Two of the deeper test bores off-site and downgradient were contaminated with complex hydrocarbons, zinc, nickel, phenols, sulphur and acidity. Groundwater sampled up gradient from the major pit at similar depth above the black clay beds showed no contamination.

3.3 Groundwater inflow control

It is anticipated that any removal of the wastes would require control of the adjacent unconfined groundwater to stabilize the pit walls and to minimize the volume of grossly contaminated water.

Two constant-rate 24 hour pumping tests were undertaken with 10 m of the major pit within the Guildford Clay aquifer to assess potential well yields and estimate aquifer parameters.

Following testing, groundwater level data were assessed to develop an understanding of the behaviour of the groundwater system's response to pumping. An initial prediction was made of the likely pit dewatering requirements during excavation of the wastes within the major pit. Using an analytical approximation of drawdown and superposition of a number of pumping bores, it is estimated that eight production bores located

around the perimeter of the major pit would be required. Hydraulic parameters adopted were transmissivity of 5 m^2/day and storage coefficient of 0.002. Bores would need to be pumped at an average rate of 9.5 kL/day for a period of 30 days, by which time groundwater heads adjacent to the pit are predicted to be lowered to below the base of the pit floor. After this, the bores would be pumped at a reduced rate to maintain the lowered groundwater levels to allow separate pumping of the liquid wastes from the major pit and subsequent excavation of the solid waste.

4 OPTIONS FOR REMEDIATION

The remediation works should take into account that the oil wastes will produce a strong odour of sulphur and oil when disturbed. If large quantities are exposed or aerated then a health hazard may develop. Air monitoring will be required to manage the risk of a health hazard developing during excavation of the wastes. Close community liaison and education will be required as a nuisance odour problem is very likely to develop well in advance of a health hazard.

The options identified for the remediation of the site are:

Option 1: Isolate and leave in situ
This involves the installation around the major pit of a low permeability, chemical resistant

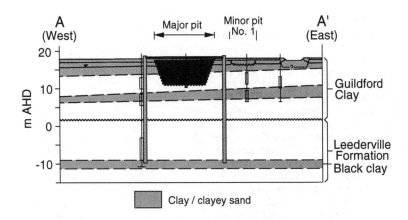

FIGURE 3: SECTION THROUGH SITE

grout curtain or slurry wall, anchored into the clay at about 30 m depth. This option would prevent the spread of contamination farther off-site, a pre-requisite for any of the following remediation methods. It would also assist any other remediation work by reducing the groundwater inflow during excavation of the wastes and would allow the pit to be deepened if necessary.

Option 2: On-site treatment and containment

The waste consists of two phases (solid/semi-solid and liquid). The liquid phase would not be accepted in an on-site containment cell, and would first have to be treated at a liquid waste plant. The containment cell would need to be constructed above the existing ground surface to protect the shallow aquifer.

Option 3: Incineration

High temperature destruction of similar wastes has successfully been employed in various countries. The liquid phase of the waste could be treated by low-rate injection into cement kilns, or destruction in a purpose-built burner. The remaining ash and solid phase of the waste would require removal to an approved site.

Option 4: Removal to local landfill

This envisages removal of the waste to an approved Perth landfill. The liquid phase would have to be disposed of separately as described above. The solid phase of the waste would also need pre-treatment to be acceptable at a local landfill.

Option 5: Removal to Mount Walton

This envisages removal of all the wastes to the intractable waste disposal facility at Mount Walton, 500 km east of Perth.

These options were ranked according to a number of criteria and Options 5, 1 and 4 (in order of acceptability) were selected. The preferred Option 5, Removal to Mount Walton IWDF, has been broadly outlined and costed at five to six million dollars.

Remediation techniques such as in situ soil washing and in situ biodegradation of the wastes have been discounted as impractical due to the chemical and physical composition of the wastes. Major restrictions to the success of these techniques are that the wastes are low permeability, heterogeneous bituminous sludges, submerged below the water table, waste liquids and solids are highly acidic, and waste disturbance is likely to produce unpleasant odours with possible health risks.

5   DISCUSSION AND CONCLUSIONS

The past disposal of oil re-refining wastes into an abandoned, groundwater-connected, clay pit has created an environmental hazard in a residential area in Perth, Western Australia. The wastes contain sulphuric acid, heavy metals, PAH, BTEX, phenols and waste oil.

The separated water fraction within the liquid wastes at the base of the pit is highly contaminated with a TDS of 87 000 mg/L which has the potential to migrate downwards by displacement of the adjacent, less dense groundwater (TDS 1 000 to 2 000 mg/L). This mechanism probably explains why most of the contaminated groundwater was found both near to the major pit and at greater depth within sandier layers from 15 to 25 m depth above a thick black clay layer and down gradient from the major pit. This clay layer appears to act as a barrier to further vertical movement of the contamination from the major pit.

Dewatering trials around the perimeter of the major pit showed that the shallow aquifer is confined and has a low groundwater yield. Based on average hydraulic properties it is estimated that eight dewatering bores, each pumped at 9.5 kL/day for 30 days, would lower groundwater heads below the base of the major pit, allowing pumping and excavation of the oil re-refining wastes.

Five practical options for remediation of the site include: isolate in situ, on-site treatment and containment, incineration, removal to local landfill, and removal to a remote intractable waste site. The last is the preferred option and has been costed at five to six million dollars, about 20 times the value of the land affected by the contamination.

REFERENCES

ANZECC 1992, *Australian and New Zealand Guidelines for the assessment and management of contaminated sites*. Australian and New Zealand Environment and Conservation Council, National Health and Medical Research Council.

Assink, J.W. & van den Brink, W.J. 1985, *Contaminated soil*. First International TNO Conference on Contaminated Soil 11-15 November 1985: 399-405 Martinus Nijhoff Publishers, The Netherlands 1986.

Thorpe, P.M. 1995, *Investigation of groundwater and soil contamination at the OMEX site, Clayton Street, Bellevue*. Western Australian Geological Survey Hydrogeology Report No. 1995/41 (unpub).

Detection of polar organic contaminants in raw water in Berlin

U. Tröger
Institute of Applied Geosciences II, Technical University Berlin, Germany

ABSTRACT: The region of Berlin is dominated by Pleistoceniec sediments. Coarse to fine grained sands form a multiaquifer system with tills as aquiclude in intercallation. Clofibric acid, a medicament was detected first in groundwater samples of different depths from the sewage farms south of Berlin. The acid had passed even through the aquicludes. Later it was detected together with other medicine in the drinking water produced from Berlin water works. Some sewage farms of Berlin are situated in the catchment area of the production wells. Drained water from the sewage farms reaches the river Spree upstream of Berlin. The river water is used for artificial recharge in large areas surrounded by water wells. Some wells of the public water works produce bank filtered groundwater. The research target is the identification of more medicaments and the determination of the pathway.

1 A SHORT GEOLOGY OF BERLIN

Berlin is situated on Pleistocene sediments which cover all of northern Germany. Miocene clay deposits overlain by lignite sands form the base upon which a variable Pleistocene sequence of porous sandy sediments and tills were laid down. The sands display a wide range of grain sizes, although hydrogeological conditions within each strata are relatively homogeneous.

Different types of rivers, which formed in front of and underneath the melting ice, characterize the sedimentation of fine to coarse sands. The melting ice beneath the ice tunneled out channels in the Pleistocene sediments, eroding older sediments down to the Miocene (fig.1). In several cases the glacial tills were completely removed and the sequenece of sand-till-sand interrupted.

The intercallation of tills and sandy layers forms a multiaquifer system. Channels of coarse sand form windows in the impermeable till. During the latter stages of the ice age the Berlin-Warsaw marginal valley was formed where today the river Spree is located. The movement of the glaciers left many small to large scale depressions in the flat topography in which lakes were formed (LGRB & Sen. Stadt. Um. Berlin 1995).

In the central part of Berlin the Weichsel sediments were completely eroded allowing the sands of the Weichsel aquifer to crop out. In the marginal valley approximatly 70 m of permeable sediments build up an exellent aquifer. North and south of the marginal valley (fig.2) the upland area is formed of Weichsel sediments with a permeable layer on the top followed by a till.

2 HYDROGEOLOGY

Hydrogeologically the glacial sediments found in Berlin and the surrounding represent excellent aquifers. Because of the glacier erosion in some cases the vulnerability of the groundwater obviously is high. This is the case especially in the marginal valley where many water works are situated (fig.3).

2.1 *Aquifers and aquicludes*

The Pleistocene sediments can be divided into two types based on their permeability (Tröger & Asbrand 1995). In general a top layer of highly permeable sands (k_f-values ranging from 2 E-3 m/s to 1 E-4 m/s) is underlain by relatively impermeable Weichsel tills (typically less than 2 m thick, $k_f = 1$ E-7 m/s to 1 E-8 m/s).

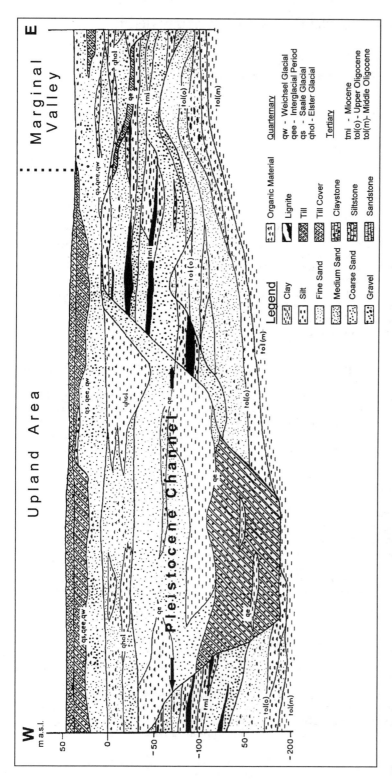

Figure 1. Cross Section of Central South Berlin, horizontal distance approximately 10 km (after Brühl 1985).

The older sediments of Saale age represent the main aquifer. The permeability of the medium grained sands is approximately 1 E-3 m/s. The aquiclude of the same age is 10-20 m thick and slug tests indicate k_f-values of 1 E-7 m/s to 1 E-8 m/s.

2.2 *Groundwater flow*

Groundwater flow follows the morphology both northwards and southwards from the large areas of moraines towards the river Spree. The rivers influence the cones of the water works wells, although the amount of surface water extracted is small. However, because of the direction of flow, any groundwater contamination will eventually reach the water works wells.

To the north and south of the marginal ice valley the gradient of groundwater flow in the unconfined aquifer is ca. 1 E-3. In the east-west striking valley itself the gradient is approximately 1 E-4. The horizontal flow of groundwater varies from 3 E-7 m/s to 1 E-7 m/s.

2.3 *Water supply*

Berlin has an independant water supply system. The potable groundwater is of excellent quality. All water works are located within the city of Berlin. The groundwater comes from water wells situated along the rivers and lakes and from wells located in the large forest areas inside the city boundaries. On average 250 Mio. m^3 groundwater was extracted annually, or ca. 1,5 m^3 groundwater per day from 1200 wells. The wells are 26 to 170 m deep with extraction rates from 40 to 400 m^3/h. Two wells with horizontal filters can pump up to 1600 m^3/h (Berliner Wasserbetriebe 1995).

The potable water supply of Berlin is based on three different types of extraction: natural groundwater recharge, bank filtration and artificial groundwater recharge:

2.3.1 Natural groundwater recharge & bank filtration

Most wells pump groundwater which is naturally recharged in the unsealed areas of Berlin. Water wells around the shore of the lake Mueggelsee and along the banks of the Havel pump a small but unquantified amount of surface water, which is filtered through loamy sand. The pathway between the lake Mueggelsee and the water wells is particularly short, which caused in former times of high water levels during winter periods caused problems in quality.

2.3.2 Artificial groundwater recharge

Artificial groundwater recharge was started by the water works as a self-sufficient necessity whilst the city was still divided. The water for the recharge process is taken from the river Havel and river Spree. After natural aeration the water passes through a micro-sieve to a large sand filter. These sand filters are excavated in the top of the main aquifer, enabling the recharge water to directly feed the aquifer without any underground pipes. Groundwater extraction wells are placed adjacent to these filters, with the water needing about 50 days or more to reach the well filter screens.

In the early 1980's treatment of surface water was upgraded to increase the recharge capacity from 15 to 55 million cubicmeter per year.

3 MEDICINES IN THE GROUNDWATER

Medicines must be both highly soluble and at a specific dosis to reach their target and be adsorbed in the human body. Hormones were suspected to be in over dosis, with equal amounts being retained as leaving the body. However it was difficult to imagine that minute amounts of specific medicaments could be recognized in sewage water.

The sewage farms in the south of Berlin have been partly transformed into farm land. Fertilizer and pesticides were used in both cases. In a research project started in 1992 the state of soil and groundwater contamination was analysed. The search for contaminants included pesticides and for the first time clofibric acid was identified in groundwater in sewage farm recharge areas (Stan et al. 1994; Stey et al. 1994; Heberer & Stan 1996).

The pathway taken by clofibric acid has been traced to the deepest aquifer in the region. To do so, it passed through apparently good till aquitards, although no accumulations of the acid were found in the water samples analysed from these layers. In addition, there appeared to be no specific distribution pattern for the acid, from which one inferred that contaminated sewage contained different concentrations at different times.

During the period of operation some areas of the sewage farms were flooded with up to 10 m of sewage annually. The farms were connected to large drainage channels and to natural gullies, through

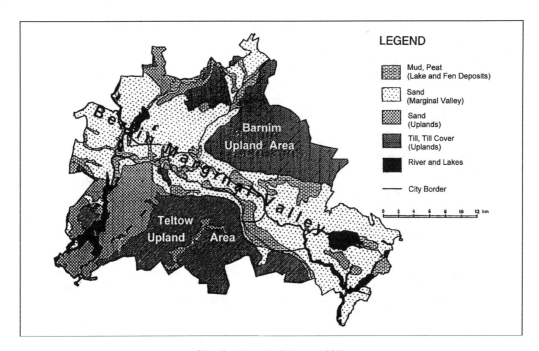

Figure 2. Simplified geological map of Berlin (Sen. Stadt. Um. 1992).

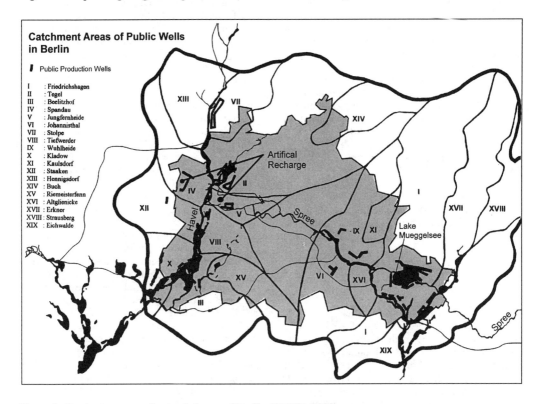

Figure 3. Catchment areas of extended area of Berlin (BUND 1993).

which most of the sewage passed via a short soil path (ca. 2m). The non polar organic acid was not adsorbed in the clay or in the organic load of the sewage. The run-off from the sewage farms flowed to the rivers as well as drainage effluent, an unquantified part of which reaching the river Spree upstream of Berlin.

3.1 Clofibric acid

Clofibric acid is used for lipid control in the blood. In particular triglycerid is lowered, whilst cholesterine is not so strongly affected. The retention time in the blood varies between 2-12 hours depending on the medicine. 29 million day-doses are used annually in Germany and between 15-21 t of clofibric acid are released with the sewage. In cities with large populations the amount of acid is especially concentrated.

Clofibric acid can be analysed in very low quantities (Heberer et al. 1995). The detection limit is 1 ng/l, the determination limit 10 ng/l. No changes in chemical composition are known and the acid can even be identified after 30 years retention in the groundwater. Clofibric acid behaves like a tracer. The concentration found in groundwater below sewage farms reaches values of more than 2000 ng/l. In drinking water concentrations of 270 ng/l were detected.

4 POSSIBLE PATHS FOR CLOFIBRIC ACID FROM SEWAGE TO DRINKING WATER

The detection of clofibric acid in the deepest aquifer beneath sewage farms is a clear demonstration of the unbounded dispersion of the medicine. It has been detected in different Eh and pH environments. Neither clay nor organic matter abundant in sewage retained the acid on its path through the groundwater, as shown by observation wells around sewage farms.

Clofibric acid has also been found in the drinking water of Berlin's water works. The distance between the sewage farms and the water works

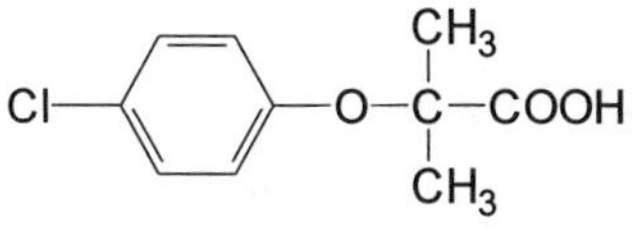

Figure 4. Formula of Clofibric acid.

wells is too great for a direct link in the aquifer. Modelling a high dispersion coefficient and a homogenous aquifer several hundred years would still be necessary for the acid to reach the well.

When the sewage farms were drained groundwater recharge did not occur on a large scale. Only a minor portion of the drained water reached the Spree upstream of Berlin. Given, that only a small amount of sewage water reaches the groundwater beneath the sewage farms and in the groundwater concentrations of over 2000 ng/l were recorded, the load of clofibric acid in the drainage water should be much higher. It is assumed that dilution of medicine takes place and that the concentration varies with run off.

In general the river is effluent changing to influent in the cones of the water works wells. Clofibric acid is stable throughout the whole cycle in surface water and groundwater prior to artificial recharge. Hence, the two sources of clofibric acid in drinking water can be identified: bank filtration from the Spree and artificial groundwater recharge, both comimg from the same source.

A third but very minor source of clofibric acid in drinking water could be minor cracks in damaged sewer systems. Big sewage losses are unlikely as most large scale war damage was repaired. In the event of minor leaks clofibric acid could be used as tracer.

5 CONCLUSIONS

Stable compounds of medicines taken in higher doses than the body can absorb may reach the sewage. Clofibric acid and N-(phenylsulfonyl)-sarcosine were the first such compounds detected in groundwater. They remain in groundwater after passing all kinds of treatments and have been detected in drinking water. The accummulation cycle sewage water - surface water - groundwater - drinking water identified in Berlin may appear under the same conditions in other cities.

Medicament compounds can be used as tracers because they remain unchanged even after long periods in groundwater. Many other compounds, other than the two substances identified may presently contaminate the groundwater. This is clearly a very important area for more research as it is clearly unacceptable to have drinking water containing drugs. In addition, medicines could form metabolites with toxic effects which will need to be identified and eliminated from the water cycle.

REFERENCES

Brühl, H.K. & Otto, R. 1985. Hydrochemie, Thermometrie und Hydraulik des Grundwassers in den südlichen Stadtbezirken von Berlin (West). Institut für Angewandte Geologie. Freie Universität Berlin.

Bund für Umwelt und Naturschutz Deutschland 1993. Konzeption einer ressourcenschonenden Wasserbewirtschaftung für die Region Berlin. *BUND* Landesverband Berlin e.V. Arbeitskreis Wasser. Berlin

Heberer, T., Butz, S. & Stan, H.-J. 1995. Analysis of phenoxycarboxylic acids and otheracidic compounds in tap, ground, surface and sewage water at the low ppt level. *Int. J. Environ. Anal. Chem.*,**58**, 53-54.

LGBR Landesamt für Geowissenschaften und Rohstoffe Brandenburg & Senator für Stadtentwicklung und Umweltschutz Berlin 1995. Geologische Übersichtskarte von Berlin und Umgebung: Kleinmachnow und Berlin.

Senatsverwaltung für Stadtentwicklung und Umweltschutz 1992. Digitale Basiskarte k 100, Berlin.

Stan, H.-J., Heberer, T. & Linkerhägner, M. 1994. Vorkommen von Clofibrinsäure im aquatischen System - Führt die therapeutische Anwendung zu einer Belastung von Oberflächen-, Trink und Grundwasser? *Vom Wasser*,**83**, 57-68.

Stey, W., Rejman-Rasinska, E. & Tröger, U. 1994. 2 - (4) - Chlorphenoxy -2- methlpropionsäure ein neuer Indikator für abwasserbelastetes Grundwasser, *14. Jahrestagung der Fachsektion Hydro-geologie* der Deutschen Geologischen Gesell-schaft, Flächenhafte Schadstoffeinträge in das Grundwasser, Mainz, 93.

Tröger, U. & Asbrand, M. 1995. Belastung des Grundwassers durch Schadstoffverlagerung im Verbreitungsgebiet der Rieselfelder südlich Berlins. *Studien und Tagungsberichte, Landesumweltamt Brandenburg*, **9**, 43-55.

Groundwater in the Urban Environment: Problems, Processes and Management, Chilton et al. (eds)
© 1997 Balkema, Rotterdam, ISBN 90 5410 837 1

Groundwater quality in Taubaté landfill, Brazil

I. Vendrame & M. F. Pinho
Aeronautics Technology Institute, São Paulo, Brazil

ABSTRACT: A two-dimensional, numerical mass transport and flow model, UNMOC (Charbeneau 1990) combined with chemical data and the computed hydraulic heads was simultaneously applied to both the new and the inactive landfill of Taubaté, a 265 700 m^2 facility. The UNMOC model was applied to study the quality of the local groundwater. It was noticed that ammonium, chloride, sodium, magnesium and calcium contribute to the increase in conductivity in the groundwater in the area. Ammonium, and chloride turned out to be particular indicators of the municipal waste pollution. The development of a contamination plume from the landfill was modelled for chloride, for the current year and for the next five years showing that no contamination from groundwater would be detected in the nearby stream. The results and validity of the application of such a model are discussed.

1 INTRODUCTION

The majority of developing countries require economic and industrial progress to remove their population from poverty. Pollution and deterioration of natural resources seem to be an unavoidable phase in the fight for a better life. Thus, the land is transformed into a storage ground for solid and liquid wastes, from domestic to industrial waste in addition to storage of toxic and nuclear waste.

In Brazil, despite the efforts that have been made since 1977 when the Interministerial Commission (ABAS 1984) was created to study the exploitation of groundwater, there have been no legislation or even preventative programmes to protect groundwater. However, in 1993 the law, number 8275, was established to fill this gap.

Waste disposal is a major cause of groundwater pollution. In some circumstances waste disposal facilities are designed to promote the leakage of large quantities of liquid waste into the ground. In other cases, landfills are designed to be leakproof when constructed but do, in fact, allow leakage of liquid waste. Even though a landfill is covered, leachate will certainly form by the infiltration and percolation of the rain through the garbage. Many substances are removed from the leachate as it moves through the ground, but others may pollute groundwater and even streams if the leachate discharges at land surface as springs or seeps.

This sort of pollution is particularly important between the big towns of Rio de Janeiro and São Paulo, where the mean annual rainfall is 1600 mm, generating nearly 1.6 million l of leachate per year,

per hectare of a landfill situated in this region.

This paper presents the results of a ground water quality simulation at the 265 700 m^2 Taubaté municipal landfill in the state of São Paulo. The landfill was enlarged in 1991, and is now composed of two areas: the inactive landfill and the new landfill.

A two-dimensional analytical and numerical mass transport and flow code, UNMOC (Charbeneau 1990), was used to model the site. Chemical data for inactive and new landfills were obtained from, respectively, USC (1996) and Guiguer (1987). Hydraulic heads data were obtained from Guiguer (1987).

2 TAUBATE LANDFILL CHARACTERISTICS

The municipal landfill is operating under a CETESB (Sanitation Company at São Paulo) license. In the first operating year 700 m^3 of chemical and metallurgical wastes were dumped in the landfill. But, this kind of waste was suspended by CETESB in 1979.

A summary of general data is presented in Table1.

2.1 Chemical parameters

USC (1996) presents the maximum and minimum values found for chemical parameters of leachate from inactive and working landfills in the south of Brazil, as shown in Table 2. The samples were collected from the leachate drainage system.

The total measured iron concentrations were high (reaching 72.0 mg/l) at 25 m downhill the old Taubaté landfill but, they were low correlated to the electric conductivity. These high concentrations can be ascribed to ferric oxide dissolution from sediments.

In Table 2 all figures in mg/l except pH (in standard units) and:
TVS- total volatile solids
TSS- total suspended solids
TDS- total dissolved solids
COD- chemical oxygen demand

2.2 Topography and climate

The landfill area is situated in a region presenting a mean altitude of 600 m and the topography is hilly. The Taubaté Basin is part of the sedimentary Hill subzone of middle Paraiba River Valley, zone of the Atlantic Plateau, in the east part of the state of São Paulo (Ponçano et al. 1981).

The climate is Cwd (mesothermal with dry winter and wet summer), mean annual temperature 20 °C, mean annual rainfall 1600 mm and potential evapotranspiration 1000 mm. The original vegetation is fields and bushes. In the alluvial plain there are rice plantations and pastures.

2.3 Geology

The site is located in the Taubaté Tertiary Sedimentary Basin, where Cenozoic layers overlie pre-Cambrian crystalline basement. The sediments are mainly layers of clayish rock, shale and sandstone.

The sediments are 200 m thick in the study area according to the isopach maps of geologic formations of the region (IPT 1978).

Observations of sediment outcrop show clearly alternating clay and sand beds typically of decimetric thickness.

Soil samples extracted from the study-area show that the sediments range from a silty-sandy clay to a silty-clayey sand.

3. UNMOC MODEL APPLICATION

The program UNMOC (Charbeneau 1990) simulates the fate and transport of a miscible pollutant in an unconfined aquifer. UNMOC is a modified version of the United States Geological Survey's MOC computer code originally released with the document "Computer Model of Two-Dimensional Solute Transport and Dispersion in Groundwater" (Konikow & Bredehoeft 1978).

The basic structure of the original code has been retained. The modified model is designed for

Table1. Physical landfill characteristics

Parameter	Value
Population	240 000
Daily waste production	150 t
Total designed area	265 700 m^2
Il working period	1979 - 1992
Nl working period	1992 - 1997
Total stored waste	985 500 t

Il - inactive landfill and Nl - new landfill

Table 2. Chemical parameter ranges for inactive and working landfills in Southern Brazil.

Parameter	Inactive landfills		New landfills	
	min	max	min	max
Alkalinity	225	6137	4412	7309
TVS	257	1322	1238	2410
pH	6.05	7.51	7.30	7.84
TSS	58	140	226	633
TDS	402	6794	5296	8893
COD	90	2000	1672	2500
Total N	16.8	1414	599	1279
Ammoniacal N	14	1080	308	1192
Total P	0.057	2.312	0.960	4.107
Chloride	275	1949	1474	2324
Aluminium	0.081	3.9	0.218	4.14
Cadmium	-	0.033	0.070	0.055
Chromium	0.005	0.056	-	0.048
Copper	0.008	0.190	0.025	0.128
Iron	4.504	9.90	5.860	10.56
Nickel	-	0.333	0.063	0.404
Lead	0.021	0.700	0.106	0.809
Zinc	0.040	0.350	0.081	0.725

application to unconfined aquifers since these are most susceptible to contamination from surface or near-surface sources of pollutants. The model is applicable to one or two-dimensional problems involving steady-state or transient flow. The model computes changes in concentration over time caused by the processes of advective transport, hydrodynamic dispersion and mixing (or dilution) from fluid sources. The model assumes that the solute is non-reactive and that gradients of fluid density, velocity, and temperature do not affect the velocity distribution. However, the aquifer may be heterogenous and/or anisotropic.

The model couples the groundwater flow equation with the solute-transport equation. The advection terms are handled by looking upstream along characteristics rather than releasing particles and letting them migrate downstream along the flow lines. Because of this, there is no need to keep track of the location of the particles as there was in the original code.

3.1 Model calibration

The first step in the model calibration was to apply the PLASM model (Prickett & Lonquist 1971) to solve for the head distribution, which was then used as the initial condition in a later UNMOC model simulation. All boundaries were assumed to be coincident with the catchment boundaries where flux was considered to be zero. In the nodal points coinciding with the stream it was assumed that the hydraulic heads were limited by a maximum value, equal to the topographic height of the nodal point.

In order to verify the accuracy of the solution it was necessary to match the computed heads with the heads measured at a number of points in the field (Guiguer 1987). The measured topographic profile and water table levels downhill from the landfill are shown in Figure 1. The PLASM model was run many times assuming steady-state to undertake the calibration.

The infiltration rate was considered as a percentage of a constant and uniform total year rainfall. It was observed that when the infiltration rate varied from 125 mm/year to 50 mm/year the head levels presented little decrease. When the infiltration rate varied from 125 mm/year to 200 mm/year the head levels presented some increase. The infiltration rate was set 100 mm/year to match the measured field heads.

When the hydraulic conductivity varied from 10 m/day to 0.1 m/day the hydraulic heads significantly changed. Keeping the same infiltration rate, for higher hydraulic conductivities the groundwater moved more rapidly and the heads were lower than those for lower hydraulic conductivity values. The hydraulic conductivity was set 0.3 m/day.

For higher values of the coefficient of storage the heads were higher and in contrast, the heads decreased for lower coefficient of storage values. This can be explained by the hydraulic diffusivity concept, which states that groundwater flow is in direct proportion to transmissivity and in inverse proportion to the coefficient of storage. Thus, for a high coefficient of storage value, the hydraulic diffusivity of an aquifer is lower, making groundwater flow difficult and consequently increasing the heads. As the aquifer is unconfined the coefficient of storage can be taken as the effective porosity of the aquifer. The heads computed by the PLASM model matched the field measured values for a coefficient of storage of 0.2.

The best set of parameters found to match the field measured head values was: coefficient of storage, 0.2; hydraulic conductivity, 0.3 m /day; infiltration rate, 100 mm/year, and aquifer thickness 4.0 m.

The PLASM model (1971) was applied to obtain the heads, which were kept constant during the UNMOC model simulations.

The UNMOC model was run twenty times to be calibrated to match the chemical concentrations measured at a number of points in the field (Guiguer 1987). The area boundaries were considered impermeable.

Firstly the effect of varying the ratio between the longitudinal and the transverse dispersivity was investigated. When this ratio varied from 1 to 10 appreciable concentration differences occurred in time. When the ratio varied from 10 to 100 little difference in concentration with time was noticed. This fact is ascribed to the transverse dispersivity effects as they become negligible when compared to the longitudinal dispersivity and advection effects.

The retardation factor represents the interaction between the subsurface environment and the pollutant. Geochemical interactions can retard the pollutant movement. Higher retardation factor values lead to significant effects on the contamination plume movement and also affect the simulation time. To model chloride, a conservative pollutant, the retardation coefficient was set at 1.0.

The best set of parameters, for the UNMOC model, to match the field measured chloride concentrations (Guiguer 1987) was: effective porosity, 0.25 %; longitudinal dispersivity, 5.0 m; transverse dispersivity, 0.5 m; retardation coefficient, 1.0 and hydraulic conductivity, 3.0 m/day. The parameters requested by UNMOC model to assure a stability criterion were adjusted by sucessive simulations till the error in the mass balance was less than 10 %. The parameters were: NITP, number of iteration parameters (usually 4-7); ITMAX, maximum number of iterations for hydraulics; TOL, convergence criteria for hydraulics (usually<0.01) and, CELDIS, maximum advection step per particle move.

3.2 Data used and results

Used data were the chemical data obtained from the inactive landfill (USC 1996) and from the new landfill (Guiguer 1987), and the computed hydraulic heads from PLASM. Chloride, sodium and ammonium were highly correlated with groundwater conductivity, which is a good indicator of water mineralization. As chloride is the most conservative solute and turned out to be a particular indicator of the municipal waste pollution, the development of contamination plumes was modelled for this element for the current year and for the next 5 years. In the first case, in 1996, measured chloride concentrations 50 m downhill of the new facilitiy were 500 mg/l. On the first row of the inactive landfill the chloride concentrations were set at 100 mg/l, as recommended (USC 1996), for a landfill which has been inactive for 5 years. These 1996 chloride concentration values were set on the first row of cells to simulate the development of a plume for the end of 1997 and 2001. For the other cells the concentrations were set zero. The modelled plumes for the first case for 1997 and 2001 are shown in Figures 2 and 3, respectively.

561

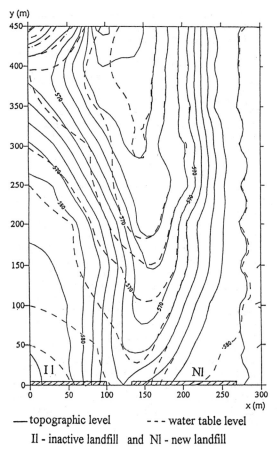

y (m)

— topographic level   - - - water table level

Il - inactive landfill   and   Nl - new landfill

Figure 1. Observed topographic profile and water table levels.

In the second case, as a first step, the UNMOC model was run setting 500mg/l of chloride concentration at the   first   row of cells for the inactive landfill site from 1979 to 1992 to model the chloride concentration matrix. For the following run, for 1993, chloride concentrations were set 500 mg/l and   400 mg/l in the first row of cells for the new and   the   inactive   landfills,   respectively.   The concentrations were set to zero for the other rows in front of the new landfill. On the other hand, in front of the inactive landfill the previously modelled concentration matrix for the end of 1992 was taken into account. For 1994, the concentration matrix for the whole site was replaced by the modelled concentration matrix for 1993. For the following runs, the concentration matrix was replaced for the modelled concentration matrix for the previous year, while chloride concentrations were set 500 mg/l on the first row of cells for the new landfill and the concentration decrease was assumed linear (USC

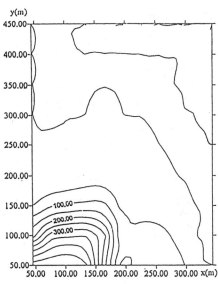

Figure 2. Chloride concentrations (mg/l) considering an homogeneous and isotropic aquifer, for 1997. Flows before 1997 implicitly accounted for using boundary concentrations.

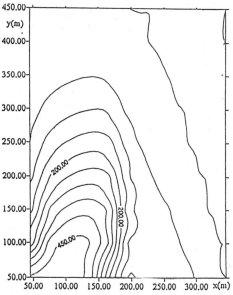

Figure 3. Chloride concentrations (mg/l) considering an homogeneous and isotropic aquifer, for 2001. Flows before 1997 implicitly accounted for using boundary concentrations.

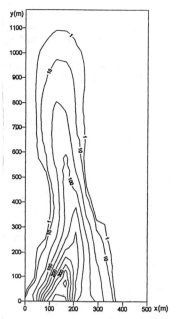

Figure 4. Chloride concentrations (mg/l) considering an homogenous and isotropic aquifer, for 1997, explicitly taking into account the flows before 1997.

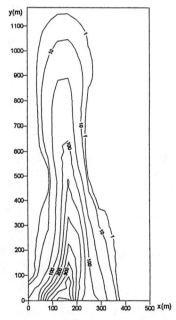

Figure 5. Chloride concentrations (mg/l) considering an homogenous and isotropic aquifer, for 2001, explicitly taking into account the flows before 97.

1996) on the first row of cells for the inactive landfill. The modelled plumes for the second case for 1997 and 2001 are shown in Figures 4 and 5, respectively. To run the model it was set a 330 m wide and 1200 m long area. The finite-difference cell size chosen was 30 m in the x-direction and 50m in the y-direction. The aquifer was assumed to be homogeneous and isotropic in respect of the solute transport parameters.

4 DISCUSSION OF RESULTS

According to Figure 2, chloride concentrations are nearly 500 times the background concentration (1 mg/l) at 50 m from the landfill, for the current year (1997). Chloride concentrations decrease to the background value at nearly 350 m downhill from the landfill. According to Figure 3 chloride concentrations are nearly 500 times the background concentration at 50 m from the landfill in 2001. Chloride concentrations decrease to the background value nearly 500 m downhill the landfill in the next five years.

According to these calculations the potability limit (250mg /l) which is in 1997 at nearly 150 m from the landfill would be at 250 m in 2001. At this distance there is a cattle farm which would therefore have some food contamination problems.

According to Figure 4, chloride concentrations decrease to background value at nearly 1075 m downhill from the landfill in 1997. According to Figure 5, chloride concentrations decrease to the background value 1175 m downhill from the landfill in the next five years. The potability limit (250 mg/l) which is predicted to be in 1997 at nearly 190 m would be at 240 m in 2001.

The modelled plumes for the second case, which takes into account the flows before 97, are more realistic than those modelled for the first case, which does not explicitly take into account the flows before 1997. Comparing the results for the two cases it is shown that for the higher concentrations the results are quite similar but, for the lower concentrations the plume length is larger for the second case as was expected.

It was shown that the numerical model can be applied to the studied-site with some reservations, when compared to the observed results presented by Guiguer (1987). The numerical model considers that the velocity vectors are parallel and present constant values along the analysed reach. This fact is aggravated by the local soil stratification presenting different vertical section velocities, which are considered as a mean velocity by the numerical model.

It was observed in the field data, that when the water table rises the electric conductivity increases. This can be ascribed to the higher infiltration in the summer, through the landfill producing more leachate.

At some points more distant from the landfill, but situated in the same lithologic environment, the superficial water and the groundwater were a little mineralized, in 1996. The water collected from a stream at 600 m downhill from the landfill was 8μ Ω/cm, while a sample collected from a shallow well in a farm 800 m from the landfill was 15μ Ω/cm. According to these measured data, for points situated far from the landfill, the modelled values are close to the observed values.

Also, it was noticed that deeper observation wells were needed for a better model calibration. In fact, the maximum solute concentrations occur just underneath the landfill bottom and they decrease with depth, due to dispersion associated with high soil moisture contents.

5. CONCLUSIONS

1. Chloride, sodium and ammonium turned out to be good indicators of the municipal waste pollution.

2. The simulation results showed that the groundwater and the streams are likely to be polluted up to 1175 m from the landfill over the next 5 years.

3. The hydraulic conductivity proved to be the most sensitive parameter in the calibration model process.

4. Deeper observation wells are necessary to colect water samples at different depths to permit a better model calibration.

REFERENCES

ABAS (Associação Brasileira Águas Subterrâneas) 1984. Proposta de lei federal sobre o uso das águas subterrâneas. *Anais Forum Brasileiro de Legisllação do uso de águas subterrâneas.* Belo Horizonte, Minas Gerais:ABAS.
Charbeneau, R. 1990. *Program UNMOC users guide.* University of Texas at Austin.
Guiguer Jr., N. 1987. *Poluição das águas subterrâneas causadas por aterros sanitários: uma abordagem matemático experimental.* Tese de mestrado. Universidade São Paulo, 250 p.
IPT 1978. *Geologia da região administrativa 3(vale do Paraiba) e parte da região administrativa 2* Publicação IPT no.1106, São Paulo 78 pp.
Konikow, L. F. & J.D. Bredehoeft. 1978. *Computer models of two-dimensional solute transport and dispersion in groundwater.* Technical Water Resources Investigations, Book 7, Chap C2, 90 pp. Reston, Virginia: US Geol Survey.
Ponçano, W. L., C.D.R. Carneiro, C.A. Bistrichi, F.F.M. Almeida & F.L. Prandini. 1981. Mapa geomorfológico do estado de São Paulo, IPT. *Ser. Mon.* 5(1): 94 pp.

Prickett, T. A & C.G. Lonquist. 1971. PLASM - *ComputerTechniques for Groundwater Resource Evaluation.*(Illinois State Water Survey Bulletin 55) 62 pp.
USC (Caxias do Sul University) 1996. *São Giácomo Remediation System Report.*

5 Groundwater management and urban planning

Topic co-editors
Sue Hennings
Environment Agency

John Chilton
British Geological Survey

Current legislation to manage the impacts of mining on ground water in South Africa

Ian Cameron-Clarke
Steffen Robertson and Kirsten (Africa), Johannesburg, South Africa

ABSTRACT: Johannesburg has been the centre of the gold mining industry in South Africa for many decades and has a history of environmental problems associated with the effects of mining on the ground water system. To the west of the city, along the so called West Wits Line, dewatering of dolomite aquifers has resulted in the formation of sinkholes, sometimes with disastrous consequences. To the east continuous pumping to maintain the ground water below current mining levels has resulted in the disposal of acidic water to surface water bodies with possible adverse impacts. Shallow mining has caused the destruction of shallow aquifer systems with loss of a resource, and the construction of large tailings disposal facilities and waste rock dumps with potentially acid generating materials has led to the seepage of acid water into the ground water and surface water systems. Many of these impacts can be reduced or prevented with appropriate management. Current legislation requires all owners of mines to prepare an Environmental Management Programme before mining can commence. Management actions identified in the Environmental Management Programme Report (the EMPR) are legally enforceable. The impacts themselves are described and current procedures and legislation to provide effective management are given.

1 INTRODUCTION

The Gauteng Province of South Africa is the largest urban area in the country. It developed initially as a result of the gold mining industry and is characterised by significant urban and business development intermingled with mine shafts, mine waste dumps and undermining at various depths. Small, largely defunct coal mining operations, also occur within the eastern parts of the province.

Environmental impacts of past and present mining activities have been severe in some cases. Those associated with impacts on the ground water system include aquifer dewatering, with the consequential formation of sinkholes in dolomitic areas, aquifer contamination as a result of seepage of acid water from mine workings and mine waste dumps, destruction of resources in areas of shallow mining, and contamination of surface water bodies by the discharge of contaminated mine water.

The mining industry in South Africa has for many years operated without a framework of legislation relating to broad environmental protection. The growing awareness both nationally and internationally of the need to protect the environment led the Government to promulgate the Minerals Act of 1991 (Pretorius J.J. 1991) which requires the owner of any mine to submit and obtain approval for an Environmental Management Programme before mining can commence.

This paper describes in general terms the impacts of mining on the ground water systems in the urban areas of Gauteng, and indicates the procedures now required by law prior to the commencement of mining to protect the environment.

2 MINING IMPACTS ON URBAN GROUND WATER

Mining impacts on the ground water environment in the Gauteng area can be divided generally into impacts associated with aquifer dewatering and impacts associated with the acidic rock drainage into the ground water. Ground water occurs mainly in secondary weathered and fractured aquifer systems at depths varying from 20 m to 70 m, although local shallow perched aquifers occur at many locations on horizons of hardpan laterite. Parts of the area are underlain by dolomitic rocks with typical karstic aquifer conditions.

2.1 *Aquifer Dewatering*

Aquifer dewatering as a result of mining manifests itself in the following two ways:
- A resource of significance to the local community is lost or depleted.
- Sinkholes and dolines develop as a result of the lowering of the water table.

In the Gauteng Province domestic water is supplied to most urban residents by the local water board (Rand Water). Many properties however have boreholes which are used for garden irrigation, and in periurban areas small holding owners frequently use ground water for domestic purposes. The main areas which have been affected in this way are those where the depth of mining is shallow (<100 m - 200 m) resulting in the destruction of the rock mass integrity such that drainage into the workings occurs. These are limited to a relatively narrow zone along the gold reef outcrop workings which extend for a distance of about 100 km from the East Rand Goldfield to the east of Johannesburg to the West Rand Goldfield to the west, and to localized areas where shallow coal mining has occurred. The coal workings are now frequently flooded with ground water of dubious quality. In areas underlain by dolomite, particularly where there is no cover of younger formations, dewatering has in some instances resulted in reductions of sustainable yields.

Sinkhole formation due to the lowering of the water table in areas underlain by dolomite has in the past had some catastrophic consequences, particularly in the western parts of the Province. The mechanism of sinkhole formation is now largely understood, however, and with appropriate urban planning and development the impact on the environment is usually minimised.

2.2 *Acid Rock Drainage*

Waste materials from both gold and coal mining activities generate acidic leachate which will cause contamination of the ground water if allowed to enter the ground water system. In the Gauteng Province the scale of gold mining has required the disposal of very large volumes of tailings in surface tailings dams. Seepage from these dams has had a significant impact on ground water, to the extent that in many instances there is very little that can now be done to remedy the situation. Shallow perched aquifers, which usually discharge as seepage into surface drainage features, are however often more severely contaminated, with the result that surface water is the most severely affected receiving water.

3 ENVIRONMENTAL MANAGEMENT PROGRAMMES

In November 1992 the Department of Mineral and Energy Affairs (DMEA) published a document entitled the Aide-Memoire for the Preparation of Environmental Management Programme Reports (EMPR) for Prospecting and Mining (Department of Mineral and Energy Affairs 1992) to " assist applicants for, and holders of, prospecting permits or mining authorisations to draw up environmental management programmes in accordance with an established approach which is acceptable to all the regulating authorities and to secure the approval thereof ".

3.1 *Environmental Management Programme Reports*

The objectives of an EMPR are seen as follows:
- To meet the environmental requirements and directives under the Minerals Act, No 50 of 1991 and its regulations.
- To provide a single document that would satisfy the various authorities concerned with the regulation of the environmental impacts of mining.
- To give reasons for the need for, and the overall benefits of, the proposed project.
- To describe the relevant baseline conditions at and around the proposed site.
- To describe briefly the prospecting or mining method and associated activities so that an assessment can be made of the significant impacts that the project is likely to have on the environment during and after mining.
- To describe how the environmental impacts will be managed and how the positive impacts will be maximised.
- Ground water use
- The hydrogeological conditions, including a conceptual model of the aquifer likely to be affected by mining.
- Estimates of interflow between ground water and surface water in areas where stream diversions are planned.

The compilation of this section of the EMPR

requires information about the site itself. All too often however site specific details are not available and the costs required to obtain the information may be regarded by the mining company as excessive. Consequently authors of reports are forced into making generalisations which are inadequate for a proper assessment of possible impacts and to meet the needs of the regulatory authority.

Section 5.2.9 of the EMPR should include "an assessment of the impacts of mining activities on ground water in the affected zone, the impact on boreholes, and the impact on ground water users" . This broad statement is intended to cover all likely impacts on the ground water system from construction to post-closure. Unfortunately the Aide Memoire does not provide adequate guidelines to more specific requirements of the authorities, and has resulted in several costly misunderstandings when EMPRs have been prepared by mine personnel not experienced in hydrogeology. The actual requirements of Section 5.2.9 are detailed descriptions of each potential source of impact on the ground water system and at least a semi-quantified estimate of the impact in terms of changes of quality and reduction of yields with time, right through from construction to decommissioning and post-closure.

The requirements of Section 6.2.9 are that the EMPR should indicate strategies for:

- Optimising surface rehabilitation to minimise adverse ground water impacts.
- Meeting the requirements of legitimate ground water users in the affected zone.
- controlling seepage into and out of diverted river sections.

In reality this section of the document often contains a programme of activities which are intended to assess and quantify the hydrogeological conditions specific to the site (which should be included in Section 2.10), and thereafter to monitor the effects of mining on the ground water system. It is a requirement of the authorities, however, that specific operational plans are in place in the event of adverse impacts being identified during monitoring.

- To set out the environmental management criteria that will be used during the life of the project so that a closure certificate can be issued.
- To indicate that financial resources will be made available to implement the environmental management programme set out in the document.

It is required that the EMPR be divided into the following sections:

Part 1   Brief Project Description
Part 2   Description of the Pre-mining Environment
Part 3   Motivation for the Proposed Project
Part 4   Detailed Description of the Proposed Project
Part 5   Environmental Impact Assessment
Part 6   Environmental Management Programme
Part 7   Conclusions
Part 8   Statutory Requirements
Part 9   Amendments (with time)
Part 10 Supporting Documentation
Part 11 Confidential Material

The regulatory authority, which in the case of ground water, is the Department of Water Affairs and Forestry, recognises that many of the mines in South Africa and particularly those in the Gauteng Province have been operational for many years, and that baseline information relating to the pre-mining environment is often impossible to obtain and generally of little real consequence in managing the impacts from current and future activities.

The greatest emphasis is placed on Parts 5 and 6 wherein the impacts themselves are described and quantified, and a programme of actions is provided to manage and minimise the impacts. Part 5 is required to take account of the various types of impacts which will occur during the different phases of the project from construction through operation to decommissioning.   Part 6, the Environmental Management Programme is legally binding although open to review and variation with the approval of the authorities.

3.2 Ground Water in the EMPR

Sections 2.10, 5.2.9 and 6.2.9 of the EMPR deal specifically with ground water.   Section 2.10 is required to describe the ground water regime in terms of:

- The depth of the water table
- The presence of boreholes and springs and their estimated yields
- Ground water quality

4 PROBLEM AREAS

Several problem areas have emerged with the preparation and approval of EMPRs. These are frequently related to water issues which, in most cases, are paramount in terms of environmental impacts. The problems encountered revolve around the amount of detail required for broader environmental aspects, the resultant cost of the overall document, and, as a consequence, the amount of money "available" for investigating the ground water issues in sufficient detail to provide definitive assessments of the likely impacts and management options to minimise the impacts. In many instances, environmental issues relating to original land use, wildlife and undisturbed vegetation types for example, are of limited concern in areas where baseline conditions are far from pristine. They nevertheless need to be addressed in some detail to meet the requirements of the Aide-Memoire which does not highlight the importance of the ground and surface water aspects.

Many mining companies carry out EMPR projects by tender, with the lowest cost often being the ruling criterion. The scope of work in terms of data availability and data collection requirements is often not clear. Consequently bidders who provide realistic amounts to cover data collection may not be awarded the project and with this knowledge costs are cut down to win the work .

There has been a steep learning curve for both the authorities and consultants in the preparation of EMPRs. Reports produced now are significantly better than those produced a few years ago and despite the difficulties that have been encountered, the effect on "cleaning up" the mining industry, and reducing the impacts on the ground water in urban areas has been significant.

REFERENCES

Department of Mineral and Energy Affairs. November 1992. Aide-Memoire for the preparation of Environmental Management Programme Reports for Prospecting and Mining.

Pretorius J.J. (Advocate of the Supreme Court Of SA). 1991. Minerals Act (Act 50 of 1991)

High-school summer action on protecting groundwater quality

Peter Dillon & Paul Pavelic
Centre for Groundwater Studies & CSIRO Land and Water, Adelaide, S.A., Australia

ABSTRACT: Student volunteers from 32 South Australian high schools participated in a summer vacation groundwater education and sampling program, which provided valuable quality-assured data. This resulted in an increased awareness of urban groundwater by students, bore owners, and the community at large via the considerable media attention the program received. It also yielded valuable information on the impact of more than 100 years of urbanisation on groundwater quality in the watertable aquifer of metropolitan Adelaide in three areas, which were selected for their different land use histories and physiographic features. In each area there is evidence of widespread nitrate and bacterial (coliform and aeromonas) contamination of groundwater. There were also isolated incidences of TCE and benzene contamination. In 3 of 99 wells the potential beneficial uses of the water (using Australian water quality guidelines) were impeded by the anthropogenic contamination. Most of the sampled water was too saline to be considered a drinking water supply, but was adequate for irrigation. The data showed that there is no room for complacency in groundwater quality protection, and that further community education on groundwater protection is warranted. The data also provide a benchmark to allow future assessment of the community's stewardship of this resource.

1 INTRODUCTION

In the Adelaide metropolitan area more than 1,200 domestic bores penetrate the upper Quaternary aquifer. However in 1993 the effects of up to 157 years of urbanisation on groundwater quality in the shallowest aquifer had not been determined, and the adequacy of existing groundwater protection measures was unknown.

The *Groundwater Watch* summer program of 1993/94 sprang from the need to assess the impacts of urbanisation, provide a benchmark to gauge the impacts of future developments (including aquifer storage and recovery of stormwater), and the recognition that the key to preventing diffuse source pollution is education not regulation. The Centre for Groundwater Studies (CGS) also has an agenda to raise the public profile of groundwater, especially with youth.

The idea of having a number of high-school students go out and sample groundwater, while maintaining quality control on sampling and analysis, was developed in cooperation with several organisations.

2 GROUNDWATER WATCH PROGRAM

CSIRO Double Helix Club, a science club for primary and secondary school students, was consulted on the tasks which high school students could be assigned, and on the design of a training program. Double Helix also

helped with recruitment of students by advertising in their magazine. The South Australian and National Water Watch Program coordinators were also consulted on the program structure, and provided encouragement.

In sympathy with the high-school science curriculum it was decided to call for year 9 and 10 student volunteers over the summer vacation.

CGS appointed three undergraduate scholars, each of whom had completed the third year of a science degree, to run the sampling program. They had responsibility for selection of bores for sampling, arrangement of sampling schedules with bore owners, helping with the training of students, organising and leading student parties in sampling bores, taking custody of samples, performing the microbial and heavy metal analyses on samples, and documenting the methodology.

High school students were responsible, under supervision, for sampling of bores using standard procedures, and for field analysis of samples.

Offers of support came from a number of laboratories (see acknowledgments). Grundfos Australia Pty Ltd loaned an MP1 sampling pump and covered the costs of their media and public relations consultants (Turnbull Fox Phillips) in promoting the program, and providing 'Groundwater Watch' T-shirts and groundwater information kits for all students at the training day.

Letters were written to owners of bores inviting their participation in the program. Each household whose bore was sampled was asked to complete a questionnaire covering the purposes for which they used water from the bore, their use of fertilisers and pesticides, and where the stormwater from their property was discharged.

Results of water quality analyses were forwarded to Grundfos Australia and, via Turnbull Fox Philips, to participating bore owners. Newspaper articles before, during and after the field effort, and a television news report on the evening of the training day served to heighten public awareness of the study and Adelaide's groundwater resources.

A one day training session was held on 5 January, 1994 , attended by 57 students from 32 city and country schools. Subsequently each student worked for one day that month on the groundwater sampling project. The training session included talks and videos on basic topics such as: *what is groundwater?, how does it get there?, how can it get polluted?,* and *what can we do to protect it?* Demonstrations were given on groundwater sampling, field and laboratory analyses, groundwater microbiology, and data processing. Students also rostered themselves into sampling parties.

Two station wagons were hired for four weeks and for four days a week two summer scholars would each take a group of three students sampling. Generally each group sampled 3 bores a day performing field analyses, interviewing the bore owner and returning to the lab to observe and assist in sample preparation for the various analyses, to enter the field data into spread-sheets and check them, to observe groundwater microbiota under a microscope, and to help the scholars prepare the equipment and organise sampling sites for the next day.

Four of the students elected to undertake one week of work experience at CGS during the April or July school holidays to compile the data then available from the various analytical laboratories, perform basic statistical analyses, and plot graphs and maps.

3 METHODOLOGY

3.1 *Selection of study areas*

The study methodology was based on the hypothesis that groundwater quality reflects a myriad of unknown local point sources of contamination as well as factors which are more regional in character. These could include time since European settlement, time of sewage scheme establishment, historical land use, soil type, and depth to water table.

Given that funds were limited, the impossibility of detecting all the local influences on groundwater quality, and our need to draw conclusions on the quality of groundwater at a scale relevant to planners and water resource managers, the study was designed to serve as a pilot which could determine the need for wider investigations. Therefore a focussed investigation, collecting a minimum of thirty samples in each of three

small areas with contrasting features was considered to be of greater value than a dispersed broader scale reconnaissance. The study was also intended to give guidance on the sampling requirements for subsequent studies, and identify physiographic, historical land use, and land management features which predicate increased risk of aquifer pollution.

Three areas were selected for investigation on the following grounds; (i) each area was reasonably homogeneous, but there were differences in hydrogeology and historical landuse between areas, (ii) they each contained a sufficiently large number and density of bores to characterise the groundwater quality in each area, and; (iii) their hydrogeological characteristics indicated suitability for aquifer storage and recovery (ASR) of stormwater. The three areas selected were:

· Torrens River valley, west of the city
· Sturt River area, and
· LeFevre Peninsula.

These areas are located within the boxes shown in Fig. 1 and are referred to in this paper as Torrens, Sturt and LeFevre respectively. The shaded areas shown in Fig. 1 have a depth to watertable greater than 2 metres, total dissolved solids content less than 2,000 mg L^{-1}, and bore yield in excess of 0.5 L s^{-1} and are considered suitable for domestic-scale ASR (Pavelic *et al.*, 1992). The physiographic features of each area are shown by Table 1.

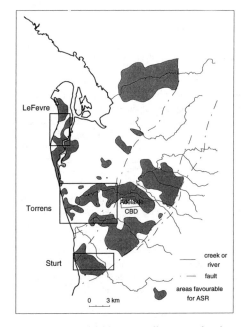

Figure 1. The Adelaide metropolitan area, showing the three investigation areas. *Areas favourable for ASR are shaded (from Pavelic et al., 1992).*

Table 1. Physiographic features of the three study areas.

	Torrens	Sturt	LeFevre
Area (km^2)	30	7	13
Number of sampled bores	30	33	36
Depth to watertable (m)	1.0 - 11.9	2.6 - 9.5	1.4 - 6.3
Conductivity of groundwater (µS cm^{-1})	2,200 - 7,900	1,400 - 4,600	800 - 3,800
Bore yield (Ls^{-1})	<0.5->4	0.5->4	<0.5 - 4
Elevation of watertable (m AHD)	0 - 20	0 - 30	0 - 2
Dominant soil type	Alluvial	Red Brown Earths	Aeolian
Current land use beside residential	market gardens, industrial	market gardens	comm-ercial
Period of residential development	>1880 - 1959	>1939 - >1959	<1880 - >1959
Period when sewerage was installed	1920-70	1931-53	1921-25
% bores receiving stormwater flows	27	21	6

3.2 Selection of sampling sites

All of the sampled bores were completed in the uppermost Quaternary aquifer. This is a thin sand and gravel unconfined to semi-confined aquifer generally only 1 to 5 m thick, within the Hindmarsh Clay Formation. Therefore the location of the slotted interval was always within a few metres of the water table. There was a preference for relatively new bores (post 1990), which are more likely to be operational for sampling in any future study.

3.3 Sampling and analytical methods

Depth to standing water level (below ground surface) was measured prior to pumping if there was sufficient space in the bore casing to insert a water level probe.

Generally bores were already equipped with a pump and this was used for sampling. A small submersible sampling pump was used for a few unequipped wells. Sampling was carried out after at least three casing volumes had been pumped, and the electrical conductivity and temperature readings had stabilised.

Field measurements for EC, temperature, pH, dissolved oxygen and redox potential were made with either the YSI 3500 or the TPS 90-FLMV field water quality meters. Alkalinity titrations using a HACH field titrator were also performed on site. There were problems with the stability of the oxygen probe in some instances, and so unstable values were not reported.

All pumps, taps and fittings were disinfected by rinsing in hypochlorite solution. Where an equipped bore was sampled, any extraneous hoses were removed, and samples taken as close to the headworks as possible.

Sample containers were cleaned and dried appropriately, and rinsed with groundwater prior to being filled. Glass containers were used for trace organic analysis. All samples were stored in ice during transport, filtered if required, and then refrigerated until analysed.

Sampling was repeated at three bores in each area, and on the second sampling visit split samples were taken from a single bulk sample. This served to test the repeatability of the analyses and the sources of variance.

The suite of parameters monitored is given in Table 2. A summary of the analytical methods is given in Dillon et al., (1995).

4 HYDROGEOLOGY AND LAND USE

Rainfall is 400 to 450 mm p.a. and is winter dominant, with 50% occurring between May and August. Peak groundwater use occurs during the drier summer months of December to February.

West of Adelaide the upper Quaternary aquifer typically occurs at a depth of less than 10 m, and consists of sands and gravels, between 1 and 5 metres thick, within more clayey formations. Dune sands occur along the coast. Groundwater salinities range from less than 1,000 mg L^{-1} near streams and other main recharge sources, to greater than 5,000 mg L^{-1} in some low-lying areas near the coast, with most groundwater less than 2,000 mg L^{-1}. Bore yields are low to moderate, ie. 0.2 to 4 Ls^{-1}. The direction of groundwater flow is predominantly to the north-west on the Plain, and towards the east on LeFevre Peninsula (Miles, 1952; Gerges, 1986; Martin & Gerges, 1994).

The upper Quaternary aquifer is used almost exclusively for domestic scale applications, mainly irrigation. A conservative estimate of extraction is 300

ML yr^{-1}. The questionnaire showed that a small percentage of users (<5%) drink their bore water. In a small proportion of higher yielding areas, such as in Sturt, this aquifer is also used by municipalities for larger scale irrigation.

Table 2. Suite of analytes.

Field:
electrical conductivity, pH, temperature,
dissolved oxygen, redox potential
  Inorganic:
sodium, calcium, magnesium, potassium,
strontium, chloride, sulphate, alkalinity
(bicarbonate)
  Metals:
copper, lead
  Nutrients:
nitrate, total Kjeldahl nitrogen
  Gross organic:
total organic carbon
  Trace organic:
benzene, toluene, m- and p-xylene, o-xylene, ethyl
benzene, 1,3,5- trimethyl benzene,
trichloroethene (TCE), perchlorobenzene,
napthalene, 1-methyl naphthalene,
2-methyl naphthalene
  Microbiological:
heterotrophic plate count,
total coliform bacteria, aeromonas spp.

In their present state the areas are extensively developed, with residential dwellings, typically on 0.1 Ha allotments, being the dominant land use. Interspersed in the eastern part of Torrens is a range of industrial activities. Groundwater sampling sites were located within residential allotments, although these sites were susceptible to the influence of surrounding landuses, as well as historical practices.

Disposal of road runoff via surface ponding is common around LeFevre. In the Torrens and Sturt areas disposal of runoff via bores was not identified, but probably occurs.

European settlement of the Adelaide Plains began in 1836. Until that time the Plains were the traditional home of the Kaurna Aborigines. This was then native woodlands, consisting mainly of Eucalyptus spp.

Apart from some urban development by 1880 on LeFevre Peninsula and by 1919 in the eastern part of Torrens, most of the three areas became urbanised between 1939 and 1959. Previously these areas were used for a variety of agricultural land uses, including pasture and cereals, market gardens, vineyards and orchards. The predominant rural land uses in 1957

comprised of market gardens for Torrens, and market gardens, vineyards and orchards for Sturt.

Initially septic tanks were the dominant form of sewage management, and sewerage was established concurrently with the expansion of urban development. Some parts of all areas were urbanised for a significant period prior to the installation of mains sewerage.

5 RESULTS AND DISCUSSION

The following is a brief summary of detailed results and discussion presented in Dillon *et al.,* (1995). The electrical conductivities are generally within broad guidelines for irrigation water for many plant species (ANZECC, 1992), but fall outside the limit for drinking water of 1,000 mg L^{-1} TDS (EC ~1,600 mS cm^{-1}) (NHMRC and ARMCANZ, 1994).

Table 3. Groundwater quality in the study areas.

	Torrens	Sturt	LeFevre
mean EC (μS cm^{-1})	3,100	2,500	1,800
%wells <1600 (μS cm^{-1})	0	6	44
mean NO$_3$-N (mgL^{-1})	20.2	9.6	4.7
% wells > 10 mgL^{-1} NO$_3$-N	43	39	11
TOC (mgL^{-1})	4.4	0.9	5.5
TCE detections	2	2	0
benzene detections	0	1	0
aeromonas detections	13	6	8
coliform detections	3	4	2

Nitrate is a commonly used indicator of agricultural and sewage contamination of groundwater, and the concentrations observed clearly show Adelaide's impact on groundwater quality (Fig. 2). The highest concentrations are in areas of former market gardens, and residential areas which were unsewered for a long period. Where groundwater is anoxic in the presence of organic carbon, nitrate is reduced. Some low nitrate and oxygen levels in LeFevre are related to buried decomposing seagrass beds, which have a high organic carbon content, and hydrogen sulphide was detected by the samplers. Denitrification was also detected in a study of the unconfined aquifer beneath Perth (Gerritse et al., 1990).

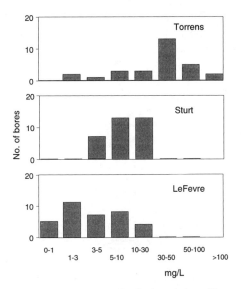

Figure 2. Frequency distribution of nitrate-N concentrations for each area. *Guideline values for drinking and livestock are 10 and 30 mg L^{-1} respectively.*

Copper and lead levels in groundwater were at trace concentrations, and significantly lower than the drinking water guidelines.

Of the 10 species of volatile organics and polyaromatic hydrocarbons for which analyses were performed on all samples, only trichloroethene (TCE) and benzene were detected in four wells and one well respectively. The maximum concentration of TCE, which is used in industrial solvents, was 120 µg L^{-1} and for benzene, a component of petrol, was 50 µg L^{-1}. In each case specific sources were not identified.

Coliform bacteria were used as indicators of recent faecal contamination. Groundwaters are unsuitable for drinking where coliforms are detected, as the drinking water guideline for coliforms is 0 cfu per 100 mL. The maximum concentration of coliforms (200 cfu per 100 mL) was less than the irrigation guideline of 1,000 cfu per 100 mL. The occurrence of coliform bacteria did not correspond with increased levels of heterotrophic bacteria, the occurrence of aeromonas bacteria, or disposal of household stormwater in bores. However, the number of detections of aeromonas was approximately twice that of coliforms, and concentrations were up to 2,000 cfu per 100 mL.

Aeromonas were of interest because they may also indicate faecal contamination, and have been associated with human gastroenteritis (Winkler, 1993). There are presently no Australian guidelines for levels of aeromonas in groundwater. Pathogenic microorganisms were however only a very small component of the microbial population in groundwater. Heterotrophic plate counts indicated microbial populations of up to 72,000 cfu per mL.

6 CONCLUSIONS

Groundwater Watch demonstrated that high-school students, with appropriate supervision, are capable of undertaking scientific investigations of groundwater quality, and through this gain an appreciation of groundwater protection. This has been a long-term investment in student, bore owner, and community education on groundwater quality.

The cost of sampling with a large number of high-school students and providing a sound level of supervision, exceeded the cost of performing the same sampling by technical staff. That is, there is a cost attached in turning a sampling project into a science educational experience for a number of students. It may be possible to contain costs by taking on fewer students, giving them more comprehensive training, and paying them a wage. However the educational outcomes would be different to those achieved in the *Groundwater Watch* program.

The sampling program showed that, in general, there is a low to moderate level of nitrate contamination in the groundwaters of the upper Quaternary aquifer. Of the bores which were sufficiently fresh to drink two were polluted by coliforms and therefore rendered non-potable. Two bores were unfit for livestock watering due to pollution by benzene and TCE. The level of contamination is also a concern for future groundwater quality protection if the factors responsible for contamination continue. Some of the contamination appears to reflect historical practices (such as high nitrate due to septic tanks).

With an absence of historic water quality data the long term trends in groundwater quality cannot be ascertained. Public education and monitoring will be necessary elements of effective policies to protect future groundwater quality.

Public education on the presence of groundwater, and impacts of land and waste management on its quality, will become increasingly important in protecting groundwater in the upper Quaternary aquifer in the Adelaide metropolitan area. A monitoring program, involving a number of bores sampled every 5 to 10 years (during summer), would provide evidence on the effectiveness of groundwater protection policies.

ACKNOWLEDGEMENTS

The authors thank the 57 high school students who volunteered part of their holidays to work on *Groundwater Watch*, and our summer scholars; Karen Rattray, Madeleine Schultz and Ingrid Winkler. The project relied on the support of: Mines and Energy, SA Dept. of Housing and Urban Development, SA Water, Dept. of Natural Resources and Environment, Dept. of Road Transport, CSIRO Div. Water Resources, Australian Centre for Water Quality Research, Grundfos Australia Pty. Ltd., Turnbull Fox Phillips, CSIRO Science Education Centre and the CSIRO Double Helix Club. We are particularly grateful to the late Mr Harrold Fennell formerly of Grundfos, without whose help *Groundwater Watch* would not have been possible.

REFERENCES

ANZECC, (1992) Australian water quality guidelines for fresh and marine waters. Australian and New Zealand Environment and Conservation Council.

Dillon, P.J., Pavelic, P., Rattray, K.J., Schultz, M., Winkler, I.G., Ragusa, S.R., Stanger, G. and Armstrong, D. (1995) The quality of water in the upper Quaternary aquifer at three selected sites in the Adelaide metropolitan area - GROUNDWATER WATCH: A study involving South Australian high school students. Centre for Groundwater Studies Report No. 60. (ISBN No. 1 875753 13 3).

Gerges, N.Z. (1986) Underground Water Resources of the Adelaide Metropolitan Area with the Latest Understanding of Recharge Mechanism. AWRC Conf., Groundwater Systems Under Stress, Brisbane, 1986. pp.141-151.

Gerritse, R.G., Barber, C. and Adeney, J.A. (1990) The impact of residential urban areas on groundwater quality: Swan Coastal Plain, Western Australia. CSIRO Water Resources Series No. 3.

Martin, R.R. and Gerges, N.Z. (1994) Replenishment of an urban dune system by stormwater recharge. *Proc. XXV IAH Congress, Water Down Under '94*, Adelaide, November, 1994. Inst. Engin. Aust. Publication NCP 94/14,Vol. 2, pp.21-25.

Miles, K.R. (1952) Geology and underground water resources of the Adelaide Plains area. Bull. 27, Geol. Surv. of South Australia.

NHMRC and ARMCANZ, (1994) Australian drinking water guidelines (draft). National Health and Medical Research Council and the Agricultural and Resource Management Council of Australia and New Zealand.

Pavelic, P., Gerges, N.Z., Dillon, P.J. and Armstrong, D. (1992) The potential for storage and reuse of Adelaide's stormwater runoff using the upper Quaternary groundwater system. Centre for Groundwater Studies Report No. 40.

Winkler, I.G. (1993) An investigation of Aeromonas in groundwaters. Honours Thesis, School of Pharmacy and Medical Science, University of South Australia.

Groundwater in the Urban Environment: Problems, Processes and Management, Chilton et al. (eds)
© 1997 Balkema, Rotterdam, ISBN 90 5410 837 1

Evaluation of groundwater vulnerability in an urbanizing area

Timothy T. Eaton & Alexander Zaporozec
Wisconsin Geological and Natural History Survey, Madison, Wis., USA

ABSTRACT: Evaluation of groundwater vulnerability in urbanizing areas is important for prevention of groundwater contamination as part of land-use planning. A wide range of data types complicates analysis in urban and suburban areas. This paper presents a new GIS-based approach to groundwater vulnerability mapping, which was developed for a regional groundwater inventory study in southeastern Wisconsin, USA.

1 INTRODUCTION

It is particularly important to evaluate groundwater vulnerability in urbanizing settings because of the concentration of potential contamination sources that accompany economic development. In addition to the numerous contamination sources, the process of urban development often results in infrastructure that increases groundwater vulnerability (such as improperly sealed old wells) or affects groundwater recharge (Foster et al. 1994; Zaporozec & Eaton 1996). Since it is often impossible or prohibitively costly to   clean up contaminated groundwater effectively (OTA 1984), a better approach for ensuring groundwater quality is to map groundwater contamination potential as part of land-use planning.

In a cooperative groundwater resource inventory project with the Southeastern Wisconsin Regional Planning Commission (SEWRPC), the Wisconsin Geological and Natural History Survey (WGNHS) has developed a method, using geographic information system (GIS) analysis, for assessing the contamination potential of shallow aquifers based on soils, geologic, and hydrogeologic factors. This method has been used in several urbanizing counties near the city of Milwaukee, in southeastern Wisconsin, U.S.A. (Figure 1).

The geologic setting of southeastern Wisconsin is a thick wedge of Paleozoic sedimentary rocks that overlie Precambrian crystalline basement rocks. The upper part of this bedrock sequence is overlain unconformably by Pleistocene deposits ranging·from 0 to 125m thick, which consist of sand and gravel or sandy, clayey silts dating from the late Wisconsin

Figure 1. Site location.

glaciation. The water-table aquifer is contained within these sediments and in the upper bedrock.

2 METHODS

One of the challenges of assessing groundwater vulnerability in urbanizing areas is the difference in geologic and hydrogeologic data available in rural compared to urban settings. Analysis of these data needs to be reasonably uniform ·in order to classify areas of differing contamination potential.

Most commonly used methods of mapping contamination potential recognize the major factors considered most significant to groundwater vulnerability assessment. These factors include soil characteristics, depth to the water table or aquifer unit, and geologic characteristics, specifically the permeability of surficial deposits. Some methods also

Table 1. Differences in data availability between suburban/rural and urban settings (adapted from Zaporozec and Eaton, 1996)

Data	Suburban/Rural	Urban
Sources	* Well Constructor's Reports * Geologic logs * Quarries/pits * Outcrops * Wetlands/ponds * Lakes/streams * Field work	* Piezometers & boring logs at spills, hazardous waste sites, landfills * Piezometers & boring logs at large construction sites * Geologic logs * Limited outcrops
Quality	* Regionally abundant * Wide distribution at low densities * Limited precision * Representative over long periods	* Locally abundant * Concentrated at specific sites * High precision and detail * Time-specific, subject to local influences

take into account groundwater recharge or soil percolation estimates as another factor. DRASTIC (Aller et al. 1987) is an example of a widely used system for evaluating groundwater contamination potential.

2.1 Data assessment for groundwater vulnerability

Differences in types of data available in suburban/ rural versus urban settings are summarized in Table 1. Areas in southeastern Wisconsin that remain predominantly rural are characterized by static, relatively invariant hydrologic systems, where water-table elevations are closely linked to abundant surface water features. Numerous private domestic wells provide ample data for groundwater resource inventory mapping.

In contrast, in more urban areas, drinking water is supplied from deep community wells or municipal water systems. Buildings, streets, and parking lots create impervious surfaces, which increase surface water runoff and inhibit direct infiltration. However, recharge to shallow groundwater may be increased by water main leakage (Foster et al. 1994). Surface water features are suppressed or channelled and no longer adequately represent regional hydrology. Urban development brings other sources of data because of the increase in economic activity and population, which involves use, storage, and transportation of additional potential contaminants to groundwater. Accidental spills of these substances and their disposal result in increased local groundwater monitoring and remediation by engineering consulting firms.

Construction of major underground facilities also involves hydrogeologic data collection. Piezometric data from these studies are generally of high precision but tend to be concentrated at specific sites. They are therefore not as representative for the purpose of regional study as data available in rural areas.

High-density data in suburban or urban areas require computerized database management techniques to sort, verify, and map geologic or hydrologic parameters. This was the case for the city of Milwaukee, where hundreds of water levels measured over different times were available from numerous piezometers installed for a deep stormwater tunnel project, but little reliable data from private domestic wells exists. In adjacent Waukesha County, data from nearly 7000 computerized domestic well records were used to map the water table and bedrock surface in an area of 1492 km^2.

Information from Pleistocene geology maps and soil classification maps is also important for the assessment of groundwater vulnerability. These types of maps have been compiled in digital form for most of the study area. However, conventional methods of producing such maps rely on field work and analysis of aerial photographs, neither of which is feasible in highly urbanized areas, such as the city of Milwaukee.

In the absence of modern conventional maps, detailed subsurface data from engineering consulting reports on the deep stormwater tunnel project were used in combination with an old, predevelopment Pleistocene map and local stratigraphic studies, to compile a surficial geology map of Milwaukee County. Soil percolation was estimated from soil classification and land-use maps, and was assumed to be low in impervious downtown urban areas.

2.2 Evaluation of groundwater vulnerability

One of the difficulties in using existing geologic and soil classification maps to assess groundwater vulnerability is their complexity. It is relatively straightforward in a digital environment to create simpler derivative maps illustrating the factors of concern in groundwater vulnerability assessment. Resulting maps can then be used in combination, by means of a GIS, to study groundwater vulnerability by mapping areas of differing contamination potential.

Existing methods for assessing groundwater vulnerability, such as DRASTIC (Aller et al. 1987), are not necessarily digitally based, but often rely on a numerical rating system to integrate the importance of different factors in an overall evaluation of sensitivity of groundwater to contamination. Numerical values with different weighting coefficients for different factors are assigned according to local conditions, and the values are summed by area to determine a final numerical index or measure of vulnerability.

A major limitation of these methods is that once different areas have been evaluated and mapped, often using a gradation of different colors, it is not evident from the map why any particular area received the rating it did. In addition, the use of subjectively assigned weighting coefficients is reminiscent of a "black box" approach, which is somewhat arbitrary. The method outlined in this paper seeks to overcome some of these limitations.

2.3 Component maps for contamination potential mapping

Vulnerability of shallow groundwater in any given area is essentially dependent on three parameters: the distance from the ground surface to the aquifer, the properties of the materials which contaminants have to penetrate to reach the aquifer, and the rates at which such contaminants can travel. The uppermost bedrock aquifer in southeastern Wisconsin is uniformly dolomite, so differences in the type of bedrock are not a factor in this analysis.

The first parameter, distance from ground surface to the shallow aquifer, is defined in this study by the position of the water table. If the water table is below the top of a bedrock or sand and gravel aquifer, then the most vulnerable areas are considered to be those where the top of the bedrock or sand and gravel is closest to land surface. Otherwise, distance to the aquifer is depth to the water table.

The first parameter is commonly represented by maps of the depth to bedrock and depth to the water table. The second (properties of materials) can be assessed by estimating vertical permeability of the materials in the unsaturated zone. The third (travel time) is the most difficult to assess, and in the case of soluble contaminants, is best represented by groundwater recharge, which is a complex process. However, for contamination potential mapping, the most important aspect of recharge is direct infiltration or soil percolation, which can be estimated or mapped based on soil classification.

Maps used in the mapping of contamination potential are listed in Table 2. These maps are either directly contoured, such as the depth to bedrock and depth to the water table, or derived from existing maps such as Pleistocene geology maps or soil classification

Table 2. Component maps for contaminant potential assessment.

* Depth to bedrock (contoured)
* Depth to the water table (contoured)
* Permeability of the unsaturated zone (derived)
* Soil percolation (derived)

Table 3. Vertical permeability of Pleistocene map units.

Class	Material	Estimated Permeability
High	sand and gravel/ outwash	>= 1E-03 cm s^{-1}
Moderate	sandy silt till/ glaciolacustrine	>= 1E-05 cm s^{-1}, < 1E-03 cm s^{-1}
Low	silt and clayey silt till	< 1E-05 cm s^{-1}

maps. The production of derivative maps is essentially a simplification of existing maps according to factors considered most important to groundwater vulnerability, as described below.

Permeability of the unsaturated zone was estimated from Pleistocene geology maps, cross sections, and water-table elevations. Existing field data on hydraulic conductivity of Pleistocene materials in Wisconsin were analyzed. Materials were assigned estimated hydraulic conductivities by type over a range of 1E-7 cm s^{-1} to 1E-2 cm s^{-1}. Pleistocene cross sections were then used to estimate overall vertical permeability of each Pleistocene map unit above the water table by weighting the conductivity of each material type by its thickness in profile (Freeze & Cherry 1979). Finally, Pleistocene geology map units were classified into three categories of estimated vertical permeability, as shown in Table 3.

Annual soil percolation rates were estimated by analyzing water budgets for different soil textures in several subwatersheds with different land uses, using a modified U.S. EPA method of calculating leachate generation from landfills (Eaton 1995). The results were generalized to three classes of soil percolation, and applied on a regional basis using the Hydrologic Soil Group (HSG) classification (USDA-Soil Conservation Service 1986), and a similar soil classification for attenuation of contaminants developed at WGNHS (Cates & Madison 1991). Urban areas were assigned a Low percolation rating regardless of soil, due to the extent of impervious surfaces. Estimated values of annual soil percolation are presented in Table 4, and represent approximately 10% and 19% of annual precipitation, which is 810 mm yr^{-1} in southeastern Wisconsin.

2.4 Contamination potential mapping

To assess groundwater vulnerability, the four maps mentioned in Table 2 were combined using a GIS analysis to evaluate contamination potential for different areas. The digital intersection of these maps results in a new network of polygons, each having four attributes corresponding to the classes of the component maps.

Subsets of these polygons can then be selected using Boolean logic to evaluate the contamination potential of different areas. Because each map has only three classes, this GIS operation can be more readily understood as a conceptual two-step procedure using 3x3 matrices. The first matrix (Table 5) combines ranges of estimated permeability of the unsaturated zone with the depth to aquifer parameter.

Depth to aquifer consists of mapped ranges of depth to either the water table, or bedrock, or sand and gravel aquifers. Three classes are considered: 0-7.5 m, 7.5-15 m, and >15 m. In assessing the depth to aquifer parameter, the most vulnerable situation (i.e. shallowest depth) is selected, depending on the position of the water table. Since in practice it is difficult to map areas of buried sand and gravel aquifers, the assumption was made that any area classified as highly permeable may contain a sand and gravel aquifer less than 7.5 m below the surface, and moderate to low permeability areas do not.

A qualitative rating of High (H), Moderate (M), or Low (L) is symmetrically distributed in the body of the matrix such that cross-referencing permeability (left column) and depth to aquifer (top row) gives a High (H), Moderate (M), or Low (L) initial vulnerability of the shallow aquifer. This allows an initial vulnerability rating to be assigned to any area on the basis of aquifer depth and estimated permeability.

The second step uses the initial vulnerability ratings of High, Moderate, or Low, as the left column of another matrix (Table 6), which combines this initial vulnerability rating with the final factor, estimated soil percolation. Three classes of soil percolation constitute the top row of the second matrix. Cross-referencing the columns and rows of this matrix gives the final contamination potential ranking of High (H), Moderate (M), or Low (L) in the body of the matrix, for each area under consideration.

The two-step matrix procedure is designed to

Table 4. Estimated values of annual soil percolation.

Percolation Class	HSG	Soil Texture	Estimated Percolation
High	A	fine sand/ sandy loam	>150 mm yr^{-1}
Moderate	B	silty loam/ loam	80-150 mm yr^{-1}
Low	C,D	clay loam/ clay	< 80 mm yr^{-1}

Table 5. Initial vulnerability matrix.

Estimated Permeability of Unsaturated Zone	Depth to Aquifer: water table or bedrock or sand & gravel aquifers		
	< 7.5m	7.5-15m	> 15m
High Permeability	H	H	M
Moderate Permeability	H	M	L
Low Permeability	M	L	L

Table 6. Contamination potential matrix.

Initial Vulnerability (from Table 5)	Estimated Soil Percolation Rate		
	< 80 mm yr^{-1}	80-150 mm yr^{-1}	> 150 mm yr^{-1}
High	M	H	H
Moderate	L	M	H
Low	L	L	M

conceptually illustrate the Boolean logic operations that are actually used to select the final contamination potential rankings using the GIS. The GIS procedures perform the operations globally on all the polygons in the mapped area at the same time, rather than individually as the matrices assume.

Since there are three classes for each of the three parameters considered in this procedure, there is a total of 27 possible different combinations of these classes, as shown in Table 7. One of the three final contamination potential rankings: High, Moderate, or

Low, is assigned to each combination on the basis of the two-step procedure using the matrices in Tables 5 and 6. This results in an "averaging" of the vulnerability factors associated with each parameter.

For instance, in the case of depth to aquifer greater than 15 m, low permeability, and low soil percolation, the logic operation would take the form:
"Select all polygons such that depth to water table >15 m *or* depth to bedrock >15 m *or* permeability <> H; then select from that subset all polygons such that permeability = L *and* soil percolation = L."

Because of the "or" operators in the first part of the Boolean logic queries and in Table 5, the resulting sets of polygons meeting each combination of vulnerability criteria are not always mutually exclusive. Therefore, the GIS procedure of selecting each of these subsets causes some reclassification, and the order of selection for contamination potential ranking is important. All cases corresponding to a Low ranking must be selected first, then all cases corresponding to a Moderate ranking, and finally all cases corresponding to a High ranking, in the same order as presented in Table 7.

3 DISCUSSION

Each of the possible combinations of vulnerability parameters may or may not occur in the area being mapped. Once ranked, the resulting sets of polygons (map areas) can be represented in different colors, such as red for High, yellow for Moderate, and green for Low, to indicate areas of differing vulnerability of the shallow aquifer. Labels corresponding to the letter-number designation of each final contamination potential ranking should be used to identify the different areas on the map.

Labeling each polygon enables the user of the map to identify the reasons for which any area was ranked, by referring to Table 7. All final rankings are understandable in terms of the three original groundwater vulnerability factors previously identified. As with any GIS polygon intersection operation, small meaningless "sliver" polygons are generated for this assessment, and polygons smaller than 0.65 km^2 were deleted for the final publishing scale of 1:96,000.

A simplified contamination potential map for Waukesha County is shown in Figure 2. Areas mapped with a High contamination potential ranking coincide with the distribution of highly permeable outwash deposits, shallow bedrock or water table, and areas that have sandy soils. Conversely, areas that have a Low contamination potential are primarily where low-permeability, silty till has been mapped, or where there

Table 7. Combinations of parameters for contamination potential mapping.

Depth to Aquifer	Estimated Permeability	Est. Soil Percolation	Final Ranking
> 15 m	Low	Low	L9: Low
> 15 m	Low	Moderate	L8: Low
> 15 m	Moderate	Low	L7: Low
> 15 m	Moderate	Moderate	L6: Low
> 15 m	High	Low	L5: Low
7.5-15 m	Low	Low	L4: Low
7.5-15 m	Low	Moderate	L3: Low
7.5-15 m	Moderate	Low	L2: Low
< 7.5 m	Low	Low	L1: Low
> 15 m	Low	High	M9: Moderate
> 15 m	Moderate	High	M8: Moderate
> 15 m	High	Moderate	M7: Moderate
7.5-15 m	Low	High	M6: Moderate
7.5-15 m	Moderate	Moderate	M5: Moderate
7.5-15 m	High	Low	M4: Moderate
< 7.5 m	Low	Moderate	M3: Moderate
< 7.5 m	Moderate	Low	M2: Moderate
< 7.5 m	High	Low	M1: Moderate
> 15 m	High	High	H9: High
7.5-15 m	Moderate	High	H8: High
7.5-15 m	High	Moderate	H7: High
7.5-15 m	High	High	H6: High
< 7.5 m	Low	High	H5: High
< 7.5 m	Moderate	Moderate	H4: High
< 7.5 m	Moderate	High	H3: High
< 7.5 m	High	Moderate	H2: High
< 7.5 m	High	High	H1: High

are extensive urban impervious areas. Mapping is currently in progress for the remaining counties in southeastern Wisconsin.

Any method for assessing and mapping of groundwater contamination potential should be evaluated. However, developing a conclusive verification procedure is not evident. The distribution of groundwater contamination is more a consequence of various land-use activities or spill events than any geologic or hydrogeologic factors. Furthermore, available data on groundwater quality tend to be concentrated at contamination sites and would not be representative of groundwater quality on a regional basis. For these reasons, correlative analyses would be misleading. Conclusive verification of the method or collection of data on regional groundwater quality was beyond the scope of this study.

Nevertheless, the correspondence of high contamination potential areas with local geologic, hydrogeologic, and soil characteristics conducive to groundwater vulnerability, and vice versa, provide a level of confidence in the internal consistency of the method. We stress, however, that this method is not designed as a replacement for site-specific field studies,

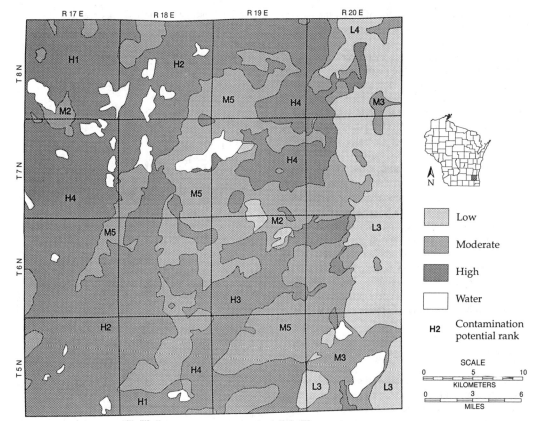

Figure 2. Simplified Contamination Potential for Waukesha County, Wisconsin

but rather as guidance for land-use planning. As such, it can be a tool for preventing shallow groundwater contamination. Groundwater contamination potential maps can be used in conjunction with an inventory of possible contamination sources for successful land-use and water-quality planning to protect groundwater.

REFERENCES

Aller, L., T. Bennett, J.H. Lehr, R.J. Petty & G. Hackett 1987. *DRASTIC: A standardized system for evaluating ground water pollution potential using hydrogeologic settings.* Ada, Oklahoma: U.S. EPA-600/2-87-035.

Cates, K. & F. Madison 1991. *Worksheet #11:Site evaluation.* Farm-A-Syst, G3536-11W, Madison, Wisconsin: University of Wisconsin-Extension.

Eaton, T. 1995. Estimating groundwater recharge using a modified soil-water budget method. *40th Midwest Groundwater Conference Program and abstracts,* Columbia, Missouri: Missouri Department of Natural Resources.

Foster, S.S.D., B.L. Morris & A.R. Lawrence 1994. Effects of urbanization on groundwater recharge. In W.B.Wilkinson (ed), *Groundwater problems in urban areas, ICE Conference Proc.* London: Institute of Civil Engineers.

Freeze, R.A. & J.A. Cherry 1979. *Groundwater.* Englewood Cliffs, New Jersey: Prentice-Hall.

OTA 1984. *Protecting the nation's groundwater from contamination.* OTA-O-233. Washington, D.C.: U.S. Congress Office of Technology Assessment.

U.S.D.A.-Soil Conservation Service 1986. *Urban Hydrology for Small Watersheds,* Technical Release 55, second edition.

Zaporozec, A. & T.T. Eaton 1996. Ground-water resource inventory in urbanized areas. *Hydrology and hydrogeology of urban and urbanizing areas, AIH Annual Meeting Proc.,* St. Paul, Minnesota: American Institute of Hydrology.

Scoping the impact of highway drainage on groundwater quality

Elizabeth Fellman & John A. Barker
Jackson Environment Institute & Department of Geological Sciences, University College London, UK

ABSTRACT: Pollution from road drainage is a potential source of groundwater contamination but fluxes to soakaways, and the chemical nature and concentrations of contaminants are largely unknown. Pollutants may arise from diffuse sources such as fuel additives deposited to the road surface, or from point sources such as accidental spillages. A comprehensive and balanced evaluation of the threat to groundwater quality is needed to aid improvements in the protection of groundwater; for example, improving policy formulation and the design and placement of highway drainage. This paper reviews work on potential highway-derived pollutants and explains the need for the development of a risk assessment methodology which is widely accepted by interested parties in the UK.

1 INTRODUCTION

Pollution from highway drainage is a widely recognized problem yet there is a lack of research investigating the risk of its potential impacts on groundwater. Current predictions of increasing drought frequency and public water supply problems in the UK indicate that groundwater will become an increasingly valuable resource which needs to be preserved. The paper gives a broad view of the work carried out to date, provides perspectives on what is needed and begins to indicate a way forward for research in this area. The perspectives have been drawn from numerous discussions with interested parties in the UK, and to some extent are viewpoints of individuals, rather than specific statements of policy.

Current projects within University College London (UCL) are beginning to investigate some of the problems associated with highway drainage, using the Chalk as a case study. The Chalk aquifer is the most important source of groundwater in southern England, providing 75% of the public water supply. It is particularly vulnerable to contamination from a variety of sources because of the potential for rapid flow through fissures.

2 CONSTITUENTS OF HIGHWAY DRAINAGE

Highway drainage constituents may be derived from point sources, or from diffuse sources (both vehicle and non-vehicle derived). Some of the most common constituents are discussed below.

Sediment is usually filtered out before discharge reaches the groundwater, but may continue to leach pollutants. Sediment and suspended solids are mainly derived from corrosion and wear of vehicles (including tyres), roads and bridges and may include metal particles or organic material. There may also be grit derived from de-icing salts.

Several metals are found in highway drainage, such as lead (from petrol and paint), zinc and cadmium (derived from brake and tyre wear and from corrosion of exhaust pipes), and iron (from vehicle corrosion).

De-icers and anti-skid compounds are a major source of dissolved and suspended solids in winter months. Sodium and chloride ions dominate, but road salt also contains small quantities of iron, bromide, nickel, lead, zinc, chromium and cyanide. Road salt can also cause the release of other substances by increasing corrosion rates of vehicles, road surfaces and structures. Alternatives to sodium chloride have also been tried. Urea and ethylene glycol have been used; urea hydrolyses to ammonia which can oxidise to nitrate. Calcium magnesium acetate (CMA) is a de-icer which has been tested extensively in the USA; it was found that it could leach to groundwater (Amrhein *et al.*, 1994), and that it may mobilize lead and zinc.

Hydrocarbons are a major category of potential pollutants derived from highways. Polycyclic aromatic hydrocarbons (PAHs) are a component of engine oil, other lubricants and exhaust emissions, but are also derived from rubber products and the erosion of asphalt or concrete binders. Other hydrocarbons may be those released from tyre wear and which include styrene, butadiene, isoprene and vinylcyclic hexane.

Methly tertiary butyl ether (MTBE) is another hydrocarbon of interest. MTBE is a fuel oxygenate replacement for lead in 'unleaded' fuel. MTBE is a potentially important groundwater contaminant because of its mobility and persistence.

Other potential pollutants may be organic phosphate (from engine parts), humic acids (washing onto the road and into the drainage system after an intense storm), and herbicides and fertilizers (from maintenance of roadside verges).

Accidental spillages may be minor in terms of total pollutant loading on highways, but when they occur they may pose the greatest risk to water resources. Accidental spillage can occur from any substance being transported by road and may include petrol, diesel, oils and other hydrocarbons, hazardous chemicals, toxic wastes, sewage sludge and foodstuffs.

3 FACTORS CONTROLLING POLLUTANT LOADING

The concentration of a potential pollutant entering the highway drainage system is controlled by a combination of factors. Rainfall amount and intensity are the main factors controlling pollutant fluxes. A feature of pollutants in highway runoff is the 'first-flush effect' which has been discussed extensively in the literature (e.g. Colwill et al., 1984). This effect describes a peak in the concentration of pollutants in runoff at the beginning of a storm, and the subsequent decrease in concentration throughout the storm duration. The process is not simple, and factors affecting it include both storm characteristics and physico-chemical properties. Pollutants may accumulate on the road surface during dry periods and are then washed off when rainfall occurs.

The character of the rainfall-runoff event is the major factor affecting the first-flush process. A critical flow velocity or rainfall intensity has to be reached for the phenomenon to occur, (Colwill et al., 1984). There is, however, a balance between rainfall causing a first-flush effect (producing runoff with high pollutant concentrations), and the point where the amount of rainfall is sufficiently high to dilute pollutant concentrations in drainage. Predictions for future rainfall patterns should also be considered. If there is the likelihood of more intense summer rainfall, this would increase the number of events where a first-flush effect occurs, and so increase the total pollutant loading in the highway drainage.

The ambient temperature may affect solubility and mobility of certain pollutants. When the ambient temperature drops below a certain point, then gritting and de-icing of the road will occur.

The type of traffic, traffic volume and the type of road will influence pollutant loadings. For example, trunk roads have higher accident risks than motorways. On motorways there is often a build-up of fine particles between wheel tracks in the inside lane from continuous use by heavy vehicles. The topography of the road will determine whether runoff will drain to a particular soakaway and in which direction runoff will occur. Air turbulence can mobilise and transport particles.

Locality may have a bearing on pollutant loading when comparing areas near industrial sites with those further away. There may be a larger volume of heavy lorries or a higher number of vehicles carrying hazardous loads. Different localities may be the responsibility of authorities with differing policies; for example, this may affect the type and frequency of de-icing. Locality should also be taken into consideration when assessing the proximity of the road drainage features to vulnerable aquifers, boreholes, and features likely to increase aquifer susceptibility. In the UK these would include karstic features in the Chalk.

Drainage design and maintenance have been reviewed elsewhere (Luker and Montague, 1994). Failure to maintain oil interceptors, for example, results in a decrease in efficiency and may even increase the pollution risk as a particularly heavy storm may wash out a build-up of pollutants.

4 PERSPECTIVES

Within the UK regulatory authorities there is a perception that the threat to surface waters from highway runoff is greater than that to groundwater. There has been a lack of monitoring of groundwater compared to surface water which may be one reason for the perceived view. It should also be remembered that remediation procedures to deal with contaminated groundwater are much more complex than those dealing with a contaminated surface water and the effects are potentially far more long-lasting. The problems of groundwater contamination are of two types: (a) those associated with existing roads and drainage schemes, and (b) how best to design drainage schemes for new roads, given current knowledge. Given the failings of many existing schemes and the seriousness of the potential hazards, it is important to formulate assessment procedures to improve the protection of groundwater resources in any future schemes.

England and Wales, via the regulatory body of the Environment Agency (EA), were innovative in

584

the development and implementation of the Policy and Practice for the Protection of Groundwater (NRA, 1992). The Policy has a stated position for each groundwater protection zone regarding drainage from roads. All groundwater protection policies are bound to evolve due to increases in understanding and techniques, increasing data availability and due to experience gained from encountering difficulties in policy implementation. It is recognized that difficulties can occur when applying groundwater protection policies to site-specific cases. Research at UCL aims to develop methodologies to aid decision-making which could prove useful in the further development for England and Wales of the Groundwater Protection Policy, particularly in its application to highway drainage across the unconfined Chalk aquifer.

There is growing interest within regulatory bodies and the water supply industry in the development of systems to aid decision making. Decision Support Systems (DSSs) are (normally computer-based) tools which utilize data and models in the solution of unstructured problems (Barker et al., 1995). In the long term it seems inevitable that such tools will become routinely used, therefore, it is important to start gathering the information and developing the understanding and models that will be necessary in their construction.

The lack of a DSS or risk assessment methodology which is accepted as a consistent national tool is of concern. For example, it appears that in the area of drainage design, although there are guidelines and 'best industry practice', the lack of formal standards means that, often, designs may not be the most appropriate for a particular situation.

Due to conflicts of interest in the decision-making process, it will prove difficult to develop decision-making mechanisms (e.g., DSSs). Such conflicts are most commonly between the proposers of a new scheme and the regulators; for example, when there are increased costs due to measures which are deemed to be necessary by the regulators. Conflicts of interest may also arise within the regulatory bodies themselves; for example, views on water quality and water quantity need to be balanced. One viewpoint from within the UK Highways Agency is that rather than soakaway drainage to an aquifer being a problem, it is the lack of soakaway drainage that may be the real problem. It has been argued that, if soakaway infiltration is reduced, and the country continues to have prolonged periods of low rainfall, potentially valuable aquifer recharge via soakaways will be lost. Any DSS must be able to help balance the views of those responsible for the highways and those responsible for the protection of the groundwater resources (both quantity and quality).

An agreed DSS would help overcome a current form of difficulty where a risk is found to be more serious than was previously thought, then measures to tackle the problem add an extra cost. A further, possibly linked, problem is that of responsibility. In particular, if it can be shown that a risk does exist and this risk is unacceptable, then which organization should take on the responsibility? Should the costs of lowering the risks to groundwater be borne by government agencies or should the cost be recovered from the users of the highways? For example, should tighter regulation be introduced regarding the carriage of hazardous substances and should the cost of installing tighter pollution prevention measures be borne by the operators (i.e. the haulage companies)?

It can be shown that the risk to groundwater from schemes currently in operation is greater than that perceived by many. This applies to the risk from accidental spillages, and the risks from diffuse sources, both vehicle-related and road maintenance-related.

Existing soakaway systems in the UK were often excavated to provide a rapid route to the water table for road drainage. For example, along the M40 motorway, some soakaways reach a depth of 30m into the Chalk. In some cases, karstic features have themselves been used for drainage. One such case was at the M1/M25 motorway interchange where untreated drainage was directed into a swallow hole in the Chalk. Price et al. (1989) showed, using tracer tests and modelling, that a pollutant entering a soakaway at this site could reach a nearby public water supply in a few days. Many drainage systems were built before the introduction of compulsory environmental impact assessments improved the situation; those systems pose a significant threat to groundwater quality.

There are existing UK guidelines for risk assessments; for example, within the Highways Agency's Design Manual for Roads and Bridges. Such guidelines tend to focus on risks to surface waters, although risks to groundwater are considered. Quantitative risk assessment methodology is discussed with respect to the risk of an accidental spillage only. It should also be borne in mind that, even if the calculated return period of an accidental spillage is deemed 'acceptable' (such that certain pollution control measures need not be considered), any one accidental spillage can have a devastating effect on a vulnerable aquifer such as the Chalk.

5 DISCUSSION: THE WAY FORWARD

It has been clear from discussions with those concerned with highway drainage and groundwater quality (including the Highways Agency, the water supply industry, highway drainage design engineers and the Environment Agency) that there is a need to develop the current Groundwater Protection Policy in the area of quantifiable risk assessment and, in particular, in the consideration of fractured aquifers such as the Chalk, and for these developments of the policy to be interpreted into legislation.

There is a need to integrate various types of data, for example, on events and processes of importance to the overall assessment of risks to groundwater. This would provide a more balanced and rational framework for decision making than is currently available. A Decision Support System would be an achievable goal, a valuable tool and would provide this framework. A sufficiently well-founded DSS might be accepted by a wide range of interested parties and thus help avoid many of the current problems and conflicts outlined in this paper. Such a system must recognize the value of a vulnerable groundwater resource, and the longevity of groundwater pollution, and must attempt to balance the issues.

In order to develop a DSS, research is required in the following areas (many of which are covered within current research projects at UCL): collection of data on potential pollutants (including their loading, toxicity and properties affecting attenuation processes), development of a groundwater transport model for which transport parameters can be obtained experimentally, and the identification of indicator chemicals (the monitoring of which will aid pollutant pathway modelling and help characterise highway pollutant sources).

Currently at UCL three monitoring sites are being established on the M25 London Orbital motorway, in areas which cross the unconfined Chalk aquifer. At these sites, highway runoff is being collected and analysed for many inorganic and organic constituents. The monitoring is being undertaken in conjunction with tracer testing and the modelling of attenuation and transport processes in the Chalk. Ongoing work is also developing (via a GIS) a risk assessment for M25 drainage, from available traffic statistics (including traffic flows and pollution incidents), and from a study of land use and groundwater quality. The data, models and knowledge collected and collated will provide input to a DSS which should be developed in conjunction with all interested parties.

REFERENCES

Amrhein, C., P.A. Mosher, J.E. Strong & P.G. Pacheco. 1994. Heavy metals in the environment: trace metal solubility in soils and waters receiving deicing salts. *J. Environ. Quality*, 23: 219-227.

Barker, J.A., D.G. Kinniburgh & D.M.J. Macdonald. 1995. Groundwater modelling and modelling methodology: a review. NRA R&D Project Report 295/20/A.

Brenner, M.V. & R. Horner. 1992. Effects of calcium magnesium acetate on dissolved oxygen in natural waters. *Resources, Conservation and Recycling*, 7: 239-265.

Colwill, D.M., C.J. Peters & R. Perry. 1984. Water quality of motorway runoff. Transport and Road Research Laboratory Supplementary Report 823.

Luker, M. & K. Montague. 1994. Control of pollution from highway drainage discharges. CIRIA Report No. 142.

NRA, 1992. Policy and Practice for the Protection of Groundwater.

Price, M., T.C. Atkinson, D. Wheeler, J.A. Barker, & R.A. Monkhouse. 1989. Highway drainage to the Chalk aquifer: the movement of groundwater in the Chalk near Bricket Wood, Hertfordshire, and its possible pollution by drainage from the M25 motorway. British Geological Survey Technical Report WD/89/3 Hydrogeology Series.

Groundwater in the Urban Environment: Problems, Processes and Management, Chilton et al. (eds)
© 1997 Balkema, Rotterdam, ISBN 90 5410 837 1

Economic and land-use planning tools for groundwater quality protection in Perth, Western Australia

Jeanette Gomboso
CSIRO, Land and Water, Perth Laboratory, W.A., Australia

ABSTRACT: Effective groundwater management is essential for the continued long term sustainable development of land uses over Perth's principal groundwater resource - the Gnangara Mound. A range of traditional and innovative groundwater protection policy instruments are available to provide planners and water resource managers with practical, implementable approaches for groundwater pollution control in the Gnangara Mound area. These include: land use planning and regulatory processes; exclusionary zoning policies; levies and charges on production inputs and pollution emissions; and tradeable pollution entitlements. The application of these instruments to the agricultural, horticultural, residential, industrial and transportation land uses in this area, is discussed. The effectiveness of each instrument is gauged in terms of its likely economic, environmental and landuse outcome.

1 BACKGROUND

This paper is a first in the series of papers to be published by CSIRO[1] on groundwater management in the Gnangara Mound area. The aims of the CSIRO Gnangara Mound project are to assess a range of economic instruments and land use planning tools that may be applied to agricultural, horticultural, residential, industrial and transportation land uses to manage groundwater pollution. The effectiveness of each instrument will be gauged in terms of its likely economic, environmental and land use impacts. The project will assess both traditional and innovative approaches aimed at bringing environmental values into decision-making. The objectives in this paper are to provide an overview of the Gnangara Mound: its location, climate, geology, hydrology and groundwater characteristics; and to discuss the existing and potential sources of groundwater pollution; current regulatory mechanisms for protection; and some complementary and alternative economic incentives that may be applied to this area.

---

[1]Commonwealth Scientific & Industrial Research Organisation

2 LOCATION AND GENERAL DESCRIPTION

2.1 *Location*

The Gnangara Mound is a large shallow groundwater aquifer which extends from Gingin Brook (in the north) to the Swan River (in the south); and from the Darling Scarp and Ellen Brook to the Indian Ocean (Figure 1). The Mound covers an area of approximately 2200 km^2 and is the largest and most important source of fresh groundwater for Perth (Moore *et al.* 1996).

2.2 *Climate*

The region has a Mediterranean climate, with hot dry summers and mild wet winters. Average annual rainfall over the Mound is 800 mm, with approximately 90 per cent occurring between April and October. Rainfall decreases northwards across the Mound and increases slightly eastwards from the coast to about midway to the Darling scarp, before declining. Total annual rainfall varies significantly from year to year.

Average maximum and minimum temperatures range from 34°C in February to 18°C in August. Annual average pan evaporation for Perth is 1819 mm, considerably higher than annual rainfall. Rainfall exceeds potential evaporation only in the

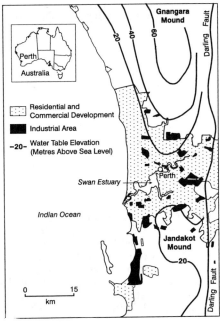

Source: Legislative Assembly Western Australia (1994).
Figure 1. Location map of the Gnangara Mound.

coldest and wettest months, between May and August, and it is this period which provides the greatest opportunity for rainfall to recharge the shallow aquifer (Water Authority 1995).

2.3 Geology and Hydrogeology

Most of the Perth region is situated on the Swan Coastal Plain, a sub-region of the Perth Basin. This Basin comprises deep layers of sand, clay and minor limestone sediments, up to 15 km thick and up to 286 million years old. The younger formations within the Basin vary between 10 and 100 m in thickness, and are less than 25 million years old (late Tertiary and Quaternary). These are known as the superficial formations, and consist of sand and limestone with discrete beds of silt and clay. Their porosity enables the storage and movement of significant volumes of groundwater (Water Authority 1995).

The geology and hydrogeology of the region is summarised in Figure 2. The Osborne Formation underlies the Superficial Formations and generally restricts the downward movement of groundwater, although some groundwater leaks downward through sandy, porous patches within the

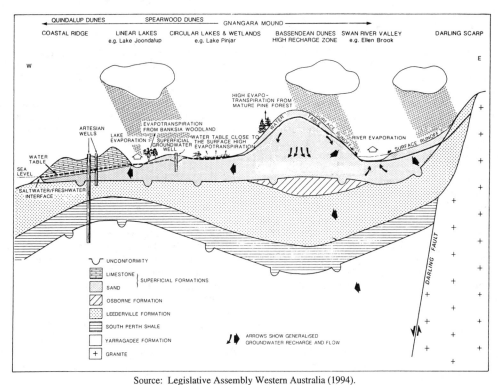

Source: Legislative Assembly Western Australia (1994).
Figure 2. Schematic hydrological cross section of the Gnangara Mound.

Formation). The Leederville Formation (Figure 2) is a major source of groundwater located immediately below the confining Osborne Formation, which is recharged by leakage through the Osborne Formation or directly where the Formation is in contact with the superficial aquifer. The South Perth Shale is a confining layer located beneath the Leederville Formation and the underlying Yaragadee Formation is also a major source of groundwater (Dames and Moore 1986).

The Gnangara Mound exists as a result of groundwater contained within the superficial sediments of the Swan Coastal Plain. Surface runoff within the area is minimal, due to the porous nature of the soils. Total storage of the Gnangara Mound is estimated to be $19,500 \times 10^6$ m^3.

The crest of the Mound is located between Muchea and Lake Pinjar, where the water level is as high as 75 m above sea level. The majority of groundwater flow is westerly from the top of the Mound, although there is some groundwater flow to each of the north, south and eastern boundaries. The rate of groundwater flow varies from 0.01 to 100 m yr^{-1}. Beneath the Bassendean Dunes, groundwater flows in a southerly direction at a rate of approximately 30 m yr^{-1}, and in the limestone sediments near the coast (refer Figure 2), groundwater flow is 90 m yr^{-1} in a westerly direction (Legislative Assembly of Western Australia 1994; Water Authority 1995).

2.4 Groundwater quality

In general, Gnangara Mound water is of excellent quality, although there are instances of groundwater pollution which have impacted upon public availability of potable supplies, and given rise to environmental concerns, as described below.

Salinity varies from about 130 to 12,000 mg l^{-1} TDS and average salinity within the Mound is 500 mg l^{-1}. Lower salinity groundwater occurs near the crest of the Mound, with plumes of higher salinity groundwater occurring near discharge areas, particularly down gradient of wetlands (Water Authority 1995; Dames and Moore 1986).

Groundwater pH ranges from 4.5 to 6.5, at the centre of the Mound where organic acids leached from wetland areas and reactions involving dissolved iron occur, to 6.5 to 8.0 in the limestone coastal areas. Limestone near the coast also causes water to be very hard, compared to the middle of the Mound where hardness varies from soft to slightly hard. Dissolved iron varies from <1 to 10 mg l^{-1}, with higher concentrations occurring in groundwater discharge areas around the coast and stream boundaries. Nitrate concentrations are generally low, but can exceed 5 mg l^{-1} -N in groundwater below urban areas and 10 mg l^{-1} -N below horticultural areas. Total phosphorus concentrations

are generally less than 0.1 mg l^{-1} except for a few isolated locations, and slightly higher concentrations occur along the eastern edge of the Mound. Heavy metal concentrations are low, except at several localised point source contamination sites. (Water Authority 1995; Dames and Moore 1986).

2.5 Land use

Most of the wetlands on the Swan Coastal Plain are part of the groundwater system, although since European settlement many (80 per cent) have been lost through landfills, industrial waste disposal, stormwater sumps, road construction and urban development. The importance of protecting wetlands, not only against further landfill and drainage establishment, but also from groundwater polluting activities, is becoming a major environmental issue (Godfrey 1989; Legislative Assembly, Western Australia 1994).

A range of land uses occupy the Gnangara Mound area. Most urban zoning is confined to the northwest corridor and comprises an area of 240 km^2. Several areas have been designated for industrial uses, and mining licenses are applied to most lakes. Rural land uses common to the Mound include: poultry farming, market gardening, viticulture, orchards, nurseries, fodder cropping, sheep, cattle and pig husbandry. Specialist rural activities include flower, mushroom and strawberry growing and gourmet pheasant production. Large areas of the Mound are State forest, comprising large areas of pine plantation and natural bushland. Nature reserves and conservation parks also exist (Water Authority 1995).

3 GROUNDWATER POLLUTION

Groundwater in the Gnangara Mound is vulnerable to contamination from a number of sources. In 1991, for example, there were 1112 known and inferred *point* sources of groundwater contamination in the Perth Basin, 700 of which were located in the Perth Metropolitan area (Legislative Assembly, Western Australia 1994; Hirschberg 1991). The major categories of contaminants included: landfills, liquid disposal sites, animal-based wastes; industrial waste; chemical-based wastes; food industry waste; cemeteries; and animal disposal sites. In addition, leaking underground storage tanks, particularly petroleum fuels from service stations, as well as associated pipelines and above-ground storage tanks, and *non-point* sources including fertiliser and pesticide applications in agriculture, road spraying, and septic tank areas, were also acknowledged as major contributors to groundwater pollution in Perth.

Over a six-year period ending 1993, accidental spills throughout the Gnangara Mound area included:

1. the overturning of a pesticide contractor's vehicle, spilling 700 L of 5 per cent Heptachlor and a small quantity of 40 per cent Heptachlor;

2. system failure of a bulk acid tank at a swimming pool chemical firm, resulting in the loss of 3,000 L of 30 per cent hydrochloric acid;

3. a fire in a warehouse containing automotive paints, thinners, lacquers and toluene, resulting in the loss of about 5,000 L of chemical substances;

4. the overturning of a fuel delivery tanker, spilling 6,800 L of diesel;

5. the discovery of a 1.5 km plume of the dense non-aqueous phase liquid (DNAPL), trichloroethylene (TCE), and other chemicals caused by an industrial company which used TCE for cleaning out and degreasing tanks; and

6. the discovery the herbicide atrazine and the pesticide fenamiphos, caused by a pesticide company which washed down its trucks into an unlined sump. (Legislative Assembly of Western Australia 1994).

As a result, a range of activities have been identified as high risk for the Gnangara Mound (Cadee 1996). These include:

1. microbiological contamination, due to on-site wastewater disposal systems;

2. petroleum hydrocarbons, from underground storage tank failure, particularly in older, poorly installed tanks;

3. the manufacture and formulation of pesticides;

4. industrial chemicals, ranging from organic solvents, petroleum-based products to inorganic toxins, such as heavy metals; and

5. broadscale use of pesticides and nitrogen-based fertilisers in agriculture and silviculture.

More recently, the risk of contamination from a garden supplies company that transports manure, green waste and sewage sludge to a site located on the Mound, has been identified. Finding an alternative suitable location for the company is proving difficult. Closure however, would result in the manure, sludge and wastes being diverted to landfill (West Australian 1997).

4 GROUNDWATER PROTECTION MEASURES

The continued availability of good quality, affordable supplies of water is essential for Perth's future. As Perth's needs for water supplies increase and its suburbs and industrial areas expand, it is vital to ensure groundwater resources are protected from overuse and pollution (Moore et al. 1996). Private bores, for example, currently supply about 50 per cent of Perth's total water needs. They are used to irrigate domestic gardens, market gardens, public open spaces, and by industry. Contamination of groundwater would have significant impacts on the availability and supply of water to the Perth region.

Groundwater sources account for 40 per cent of total public drinking water supply to the Perth region, and is likely to increase to 46 per cent over the next 15 years (Moore et al. 1996). Most of the groundwater comes from the Gnangara, with lesser contributions from the Jandakot Mound (Figure 1) and other resources to the north and south of the Perth region. Overall, about 70 per cent of all water use in Perth is supplied by groundwater (Moore et al. 1996; Stokes et al. 1996). Consequently, a range of water protection, land planning and environmental strategies are in place to protect the quality, and prevent the overuse and degradation of Gnangara Mound groundwater resources.

4.1 Water protection practices

The Water and Rivers Commission (formerly a part of the Water Authority of Western Australia), has responsibility for protecting the quality of water sources used for public water supply and to manage the use of groundwater to ensure adequate, safe supplies of drinking water. The Commission has established three categories within the Underground Water Pollution Control Areas (UWPCA) called Priority Source Protection Areas, aimed at protecting the quality of groundwater sources:

1. Priority 1 Source Protection Area - which is the most important for public water supplies, and where water protection must have the highest priority in land planning and management. Within this Area, strict land use limitations exist to avoid potential risk of groundwater pollution;

2. Priority 2 Source Protection Area - where some development has already occurred, but restrictions have been imposed to ensure that risk is minimised and the amount of pollution does not increase; and

3. Priority 3 Source Protection Area - where other land values are greater than water protection. However, as groundwater is still used for both public and private supplies in this Area, risks of pollution, should be minimised (Carew-Hopkins 1995).

4.2 Environmental strategies

The Environmental Protection (Gnangara Mound Crown Land) Policy (EPP), was prepared by the Western Australian Environmental Protection Authority (EPA) in 1992 to protect the quality and quantity of groundwater resources underlying Crown Land on the Gnangara Mound, and associated environmental systems that are dependent on groundwater. The Policy defines beneficial uses of the area; identifies activities which can degrade groundwater, native vegetation and wetlands; and specifies environmental quality objectives; and their means for achievement (Legislative Assembly, Western Australia 1994).

The Environmental Protection (Swan Coastal Plain Lakes) Policy is designed to protect the environmental values of nominated wetlands on the Swan Coastal Plain. This EPP defines the beneficial uses of the lakes as a basis for protection and identifies activities that can cause degradation or destruction of the lakes. This Policy prohibits any unauthorised filling, mining or excavation, construction or alteration of drainage systems, and discharge and disposal of effluent (Moore 1997).

A range of legislation pertaining to environmental management is relevant to the overall management of groundwater resources of the Gnangara Mound. These include the: Metropolitan Water Supply, Sewerage and Drainage Act (1909), Water Authority Act (1984), Metropolitan Water Authority Act (1982); Conservation and Land Management Act (1984); Wildlife Conservation Act (1984); Aboriginal Heritage Act (1972); and Rights in Water and Irrigation Act (1914) (Dames & Moore 1986).

4.3 Land planning

A range of policies and planning frameworks exist concerning land development over the Mound. These include the Metropolitan Region Scheme (MRS), Metroplan, Urban Expansion Policy (1990), North West Corridor Plan (1992), North East Corridor Plan (1994), Central Coast Regional Strategy (1994), Central Australian Planning Commission's Water Policy, Planning Control Area 29 - Lake Pinjar, Metropolitan Rural Policy, System Six areas, Conservation and Land Management Act, Local Authority Town Planning Schemes (for the City of Wanneroo, Shire of Swan, and Shire of Gingin) and Local Authority Rural Strategies.

Of particular importance is the Gnangara Statement of Planning Policy (SPP), which was prepared by the Ministry for Planning to support and extend objectives of the Gnangara Mound Crown Land EPP. The main purpose of the Gnangara SPP is to prevent development which could prejudice long term groundwater use. Acceptable land uses are those which are compatible with sustainable use of the groundwater resource and the retention of environmental values (Legislative Assembly, Western Australia, 1994; Moore 1997).

The objectives of the Gnangara SPP are four-fold. They are:

1. to protect the quality and quantity of groundwater resources for public supply;
2. to promote sustainable groundwater use;
3. to protect wetlands and natural vegetation; and
4. to encourage recharge to groundwater resources (Legislative Assembly, Western Australia 1994).

5 ECONOMIC INCENTIVES FOR PROTECTION

A range of economic, policy and community-based incentives are available to manage groundwater pollution. These comprise self-regulation, direct regulation and market-based control measures.

5.1 Self-regulation

'Self-regulation', as the name suggests, requires that land and water use practices causing groundwater contamination are restricted, and that these restrictions be imposed by the polluter, rather than through legislative or government regulatory measures. The most common instrument is a code of practice developed by water-users. Self-regulation can be encouraged by community awareness programs, including education and extension, advice and recommendations on existing land and water management practices. Examples of self-regulation for groundwater protection, particularly at a household level, include: proper disposal of paints, oils, fuels and thinners; adoption of more appropriate garden practices, such as avoiding over-watering and over-fertilising in public places and private premises.

Self-regulation practices also exist for the urban, industrial, commercial and agricultural activities. Only when the private incentives to manage groundwater fail to provide a socially optimum level of groundwater protection, may regulatory methods such as command-and-control mechanisms be considered as a more economically equitable and efficient option.

5.2 Direct regulation

Direct regulation is often the preferred strategy when environmental costs are difficult to determine or are infinite. This has generally been the Australian Governments preferred strategy in environmental management (Zarsky 1990).

Direct regulation refers to institutional measures aimed at directly influencing the environmental performance of polluters by regulating processes or products, limiting or abandoning groundwater polluting activities, and/or restricting activities to certain times and areas (OECD 1994, 1989). Regulatory approaches include standards, bans, permits, zoning, quotas, and use restrictions. They represent 'command-and-control' measures, where controls are implemented, compliance is monitored and non-compliance is penalised (Weimer & Vining 1992). Direct regulation includes controls which restrict activities ('at-source' controls), levels of production ('end result' controls) and processes of production ('methods-based' controls).

The establishment of the Priority 1, 2 and 3 Source Protection Areas, EPPs and SPPs are current examples of the use of direct regulatory measures for the Mound. Other controls that may be used to achieve groundwater quality objectives include:

1. institutional controls - such as litter/dumping regulations (which prohibit littering and prevent unwanted materials or the by-product of unwanted material, from entering the groundwater); pollution controls, (which prohibit practices that cause hazardous and harmful chemicals, oils, grease, solids, microorganisms and metals from entering groundwater); operating and maintenance regulations (including the inspection and maintenance of feedlots, poultry and piggery establishments, fertiliser and pesticide practices); and industrial and urban practices; and

2. design controls, - such as fuel storage tank design, vegetation maintenance, and the restriction of paving and the use of non-porous cover material in recharge areas.

On the Mound, the regulatory package is a 'mixed' one with some extension and advisory programs. The Government has also leant towards direct regulation because of: gaps in current knowledge of complex hydrogeological processes and principles; the existence of uncertainties regarding the advancements in abatement technologies; and uncertain future social values. Direct regulation may also be more efficient that other available tools, as some market approaches require new legislation and weather political powers.

In line with these uncertainties, a *precautionary principle* has been adopted in some instances which gives preference to risk-averse decisions and restricts investment that might irreversibly change ecosystems (Young, 1993). In this context, the precautionary principle represents an 'at-source' and direct institutional control. It also represents a form of the Polluter-Pays Principle (PPP), where the ground-water polluter is forced to pay *prior* to instigating the *possible* pollution. 'Payment' in this instance, represents the cost of foregone production resulting from the denied access to the resources in question, whether they be used as an input, or disposal source (Thomas & Gomboso 1996). The Priority 1 Source Protection Area represents an example.

The main features of these types of regulatory processes is that specific water quality targets or

pollution abatement standards are set, and the polluter must either comply with the regulation or face penalties. Regulatory controls are advantageous in their directness of impact (as they allow immediate protection of sensitive groundwater resources), and are relatively simple to implement administratively. They are also subject to a number of disadvantages:

1. If efficiency is the prime objective, substantial information is needed on the relative efficiency of all potential alternative land use practices and associated groundwater pollution levels. Difficulties in determining the exact extent of pollution caused by each polluter (especially in the case of non-point sources) make it difficult to determine the appropriate size and distribution of these regulations within the community;

2. Regulations are difficult and slow to adjust to rapid changes in consumer and producer tastes, demands and preferences; and

3. The incentive for users to achieve better than prescribed standards is reduced (Young et al. 1994, 1993; Rose and Cox 1991; Gomboso 1995).

5.3 Market-based approaches

Due to the various problems associated with direct regulation (described above), there is growing interest in the use of market-based incentives to manage environmental resources as both a complement and alternative to rule-based regulatory approaches (Pigram 1993; Howe et al. 1986; and others).

Several government and non-government market-based approaches to managing groundwater pollution exist. These include privately negotiated solutions (such as 'bribes', voluntary compensation, legal action and mergers) and government-initiated market solutions. This paper will focus only on government initiated solutions.

Two types of government-initiated, market-based solutions exist:

1. price mechanisms (such as levies or charges, and subsidies); and

2. rights markets (such as transferable pollution entitlements). These are discussed below.

Price Mechanisms: Pricing controls force operators to bear the costs that their activities impose on others. Two commonly used price-based mechanisms used by policy-makers include levies and charges, and subsidies.

Levies and charges may be considered as a 'price' to be paid for pollution, which may act as an incentive to reduce pollution or as a revenue source which may be redirected towards collective treatment, research on new abatement technologies or subsidising new investments. An *effluent charge* is a fee paid by groundwater polluters based on the quantity or concentration of pollutant discharged to the aquifer. By increasing the total cost of discharge, pollution charges provide an incentive to reduce the quantity discharged (James 1994).

Effluent charges (and other forms of levies) are based on the PPP, whereby the cost of groundwater pollution is borne directly by the polluter, rather than being imposed on society. Other levies or charges that may be applied for groundwater include levies on: the *inputs* used in the production process (fertilisers, chemicals, detergents, pesticides); the polluting activity (methods of production); or the outputs (or end-product).

A range of subsidies are also available to manage groundwater. Like levies, they may be applied on polluting activities, on inputs and on the end-product. Examples of subsidies include: government subsidies (cost-sharing) for pollution-reducing groundwater management practices; cost-sharing of Best Management Practices; the provision of low interest credit to finance the adoption of pollution-reducing technologies; income tax concessions on pollution-reducing expenditures, subsidies for inputs (including technologies) which reduce pollution; and subsidised technical assistance in the implementation of conservation practices (Dumsday 1983; Gomboso & Morrison 1996).

In comparison to direct regulation, levies and subsidy based systems exhibit a number of advantages. Levies on pollution emission, for example, allow producers to seek and use the most economical input and output combinations, thus enabling producers to decide on their optimal trade-offs between production, groundwater pollution, consequent payment of the levy, alternative costs of lowering production, or changing the means of production (Bureau of Industry Economics 1992; Rose and Cox 1991; Gomboso & Morrison 1996). The main advantages of a subsidy approach is its administrative feasibility, and its acceptance by producers (Oram & Dumsday 1986).

A number of disadvantages of levy and subsidy market-based instruments exist: authorities are less familiar with market-based approaches; they are considered too indirect; revenue and costs are too uncertain; they may have negative distribution effects, particularly where bad management practices are rewarded in favour of good; effects on environmental quality are uncertain; implementation may be time-consuming because of negotiations; they may be seen as a right to degrade; subsidies for conservation works usually treat symptoms rather than cause, and are likely to be remedial rather than preventative. Significant time lags between polluting landuse practices and actual signs of contamination may force subsidies to remain long-term, and there may be no incentive to change landuse practices in the future.

Rights Markets: An alternative to traditional price-based mechanisms is the establishment of a market in tradeable discharge permits. Rights markets are based on the principle of assigning property rights to natural resources and environmental goods that are normally regarded as common property (including water use and pollution discharges). By making these rights tradeable, the potential exists for these rights to be channelled into the hands of the most efficient operators (Rose & Cox 1991). The underlying characteristic of this system is that water managers (and other permit holders) can trade the right to emit a quantity of groundwater pollution. Polluters who find it expensive to reduce discharges will seek to *buy* pollution credits. Polluters who can reduce their pollution loads cheaply will find it more profitable to reduce their discharges and sell their credits. The objective of such a system is to ensure that total limits on loads are maintained, at least cost.

Young and Evans (1997), identify four types of rights markets that may be applied to manage diffuse sources of groundwater pollution. These are:

1. Tradeable emission-rights markets - where producers can sell their emission credits to others (as defined above). Sometimes surrogate indicators are used, such as a limit of the area of land that may be cropped in a vulnerable area;

2. Off-set systems - where any new developer must pay already-established enterprises to reduce their emissions;

3. Treater-pays systems - where a person who incurs the cost of cleaning up pollution pays someone else to stop polluting. For example, a drinking water treatment plant may find it cheaper to remove nutrients by paying for source control equipment/ management, rather than upgrading expensive treatment equipment at the plant; and

4. Conditional-rights markets - where restrictions are placed on the type of trading allowed. For example, trading may occur from high protection areas (such as Priority 1 Source Protection areas) to less vulnerable areas (such as Zones 2 and 3), but not the other way around.

In Australia, there has been an increasing use of tradeable permit schemes, including water entitlements (Murray-Darling Basin) and salt permits (Hunter River, New South Wales; and Murray-Darling Basin). The use, advantages and disadvantages of such schemes are presented in Morrison and Izmir (1994). A review of these schemes and other resource management policies are presented in Gomboso (1995). An extensive scoping study on the use of tradeable discharge permits for groundwater management in Australia is currently being undertaken by the CSIRO and Sinclair, Knight, Mertz (Young and Evans 1997).

6 CONCLUSION

Effective groundwater pollution management is essential for the long-term sustainability of groundwater resources within the Gnangara Mound. As the Perth population grows, and the demand for high quality groundwater resources continues to rise, the role of regulatory and economic instruments in managing groundwater resources will become increasingly important.

The challenge for groundwater managers is to integrate the multiple objectives of environmental preservation, social equity and economic efficiency into groundwater management decisions for the future.

7 REFERENCES

Bureau of Industry Economics 1992. *Environmental regulation: The economics of tradeable permits - a survey of theory and practice*. Research Report 42. Canberra: Australian Government Publishing Service (AGPS).

Cadee, K. 1996. Managing groundwater impacts in an expanding urban area. *Inaugural conference on groundwater and land-use planning*: 77-86. Centre for Groundwater Studies. 16-18 September. Western Australia: Fremantle.

Carew-Hopkins, D. 1995. Protection of groundwater. *Water resources - law and management in Western Australia*: 1-11. Perth, The Centre For Commercial and Resources Law. The University of Western Australia and Murdoch University. Western Australian Water Resources Council. Water Authority of Western Australia.

Dames and Moore. 1986. *Gnangara Mound groundwater resources: environmental review and management programme*. Water Authority of Western Australia.

Dumsday, R.G. 1983. Policy options for salinity management. in Taylor M.J (Ed) *Salinity in Victoria*: 69-86. Occasional Publication 6. Australian Institute of Agricultural Science: Melbourne.

Godfrey, N. 1989. Why wetlands matter. in Lowe, G. (Ed) *Swan Coastal Plain groundwater management conference*: 97-104. Water Resources Council. Western Australian: Perth

Gomboso, J. 1995. *A hydrogeological-economic modelling approach to dryland salinity in the North Stirling Land Conservation District, Western Australia*, PhD Thesis, Australian National University, Canberra, 2 Vols.

Gomboso, J. & M. Morrison 1996. Integrating the water cycle: economic and environmental benefits. in *WaterTech*: 225-32. Australian Water & Wastewater Association Inc. 27-28 May. The Centre, Darling Harbour, Sydney.

Hirschberg, K.-J. 1991. *Inventory of known and inferred point sources of groundwater contamination in the Perth Basin, W.A. Perth.*, Geological Survey of Western Australia. Department of Mines. Western Australia.

Howe, C.W., D.R. Schurmeier & W.D.Jr Shaw 1986. Innovative approaches to water allocation: the potential of water markets., *Water Resources Research* 22(4): 439-445.

James, D 1994. *Using economic instruments to control pollution in the Hawkesbury Nepean*, Environmental Economic Series 94/19, NSW Environment Protection Authority: Chatswood.

Legislative Assembly of Western Australia 1994. *The Select Committee on metropolitan development and groundwater supplies*. Legislative Assembly of the Parliament of Western Australia.

Moore, L. 1997 (in prep). *Draft Gnangara Land use and water management strategy: Section 6 - Planning, policies and controls*. Perth., Ministry for Planning, Western Australia.

Moore, L., R. McGowan, J. Dixon 1996. Land use planning over the Gnangara Mound. *Inaugural conference on groundwater and land-use planning*: 169-180. Centre for Groundwater Studies. 16-18 September. Western Australia: Fremantle.

Moore, L., R. McGowan & J. Dixon 1996. *Land use planning over the Gnangara Mound. Inaugural conference on groundwater and land-use planning*: 169-180. Centre for Groundwater Studies. 16-18 September. Western Australia: Fremantle.

Morrison, M & G. Izmir 1994. *Point/nonpoint source trading to reduce phosphorus discharges: literature review*. Environmental Economic Series 94/115. Environment Protection Authority. Chatswood: NSW.

OECD 1989. *Economic instruments for environmental protection*. Organisation for Economic Co-operation and Development: France.

Oram, D. A., & R. Dumsday 1986. *Reducing the risk of salting in dryland farming areas: Models, management strategies and policy options*. CRES Working Paper 1986/1, Australian National University, Canberra.

Pigram, J.J., 1993. Property rights and water markets in Australia: an evolutionary process toward institutional reform. *Water Resources Research* 29(4) 1313-1319.

Rose, R. & A. Cox 1991. *Australia's natural resources: Optimising present and future use.* ABARE Discussion Paper 91.5. Canberra: AGPS.

Stokes, R. A., A. S. Martens & Y.H. Ng 1996. The importance of groundwater to Perth's water consumer. *Inaugural conference on groundwater and land-use planning*: 23-31. Centre for Groundwater Studies. 16-18 September. Western Australia: Fremantle.

Thomas, J.F. & J. Gomboso 1996. The precautionary principle versus economic rationalism as a determinant of land use over groundwater. *Inaugural conference on groundwater and land-use planning*: 193-204. Centre for Groundwater Studies. 16-18 September. Western Australia: Fremantle.

Water Authority 1995. *Review of proposed changes to environmental conditions.* Water Authority, Western Australia.

Weimer, D. L. & A.R. Vining 1992. *Policy analysis: Concepts and practice.* New Jersey: Prentice Hall.

West Australian 1997. Firm Brought Down to Earth., Article in *West Australian Newspaper.* 14 March 1997. p.25.

Young, M.D. 1993. *Four our children's children: Some practical implications of inter-generational equity and the precautionary principle.* AGPS, Canberra.

Young, M.D. 1992. *Sustainable investment and resource use - equity, environmental integrity and economic efficiency.*, Man and the Biosphere Series, Volume 9., Published in association with Melbourne, Australia: CSIRO and Paris: Parthenon Publishing Group.

Young, M.D. & R. Evans. 1997 (in prep). *Managing groundwater pollution: when, where and how rights markets might help.* First report to the LWRRDC Steering Committee. Joint report prepared by CSIRO, Division of Wildlife and Ecology, Canberra., and Sinclair Knight Mertz, Armadale, Victoria.

Young, D., J. Gomboso, D. Collins & T. Howes. 1994. An economic perspective on the management of the occurrences of blue-green algae. *Outlook 93 Conference*, Canberra., 2 - 4 February, 1993, ABARE.

Young, D., J. Gomboso, D. Collins & T. Howes. 1993. Feedlots and water quality: a comparison of regulatory and market-based approaches. *Australian Journal of Environmental Management* 1(1): 42-55.

Zarsky, L. 1990. Sustainable development: Challenges for Australia. *The Commission for the Future*. Occasional Paper 9.

Managing the impact of urban groundwater rise

J.A. Heathcote
Entec UK Ltd, Shrewsbury, UK

D.M. Crompton
Cardiff Bay Development Corporation, Cardiff, UK

ABSTRACT: A number of cities worldwide are experiencing, or can be expected to experience, a rise in the level of groundwater beneath them. These rises are resulting from reduced groundwater abstraction and/or increased recharge, or will result from sea-level rise, either climatically-induced or from barrage construction. Rising groundwater levels have the potential to adversely affect buildings and the people who live in them.

Where rising water levels are a result of deliberate activity, the response can be planned. Cardiff Bay Barrage is an example of this, where the management approach has been prescribed in legislation. Elements of the work leading to the Cardiff Bay Barrage Act, intended to protect more than 100 000 people, are discussed.

Aspects of the approach used in Cardiff are relevant even where there is no clear association of groundwater level rise with a specific development. A pre-requisite is developing sufficient hydrogeological understanding to make proper commercial decisions before impact occurs.

1 INTRODUCTION

Rising groundwater levels affect a number of major cities around the world. Rising levels of urban groundwater originate from several processes:
- Reduction in groundwater abstraction: Birmingham (Knipe *et al.*, 1993), London (Simpson *et al.*, 1989)
- Increase in urban recharge: Doha (Qatar), Riyadh (Saudi Arabia) (Rushton and Al-Othman, 1994)
- Relative change in surface water elevation: Dhaka (Bangladesh), Bangkok (Thailand), Cardiff (UK).

A rise in groundwater levels within the urban environment has the potential to produce a number of deleterious effects:
- Flooding of streets
- Reduction of foundation bearing capacity
- Flooding of underground infrastructure (sewers, utility ducts, transport tunnels)
- Flooding of basements
- Rising damp
- Impact on amenity open space (dying trees, water-logged sports fields).

The particular effects seen and the extent of their deleterious impact will vary depending on the hydrogeological regime and climate of the area affected. However, all of these effects have an associated loss of monetary value and some also involve a loss of social value. It is thus desirable to avoid their occurrence, and should they occur, the issue of compensation for the loss of value is likely to be raised.

The various processes resulting in rising groundwater are often associated with multiple causes, e.g. reduction in overall abstraction as the result of the closure of several abstractors. In such cases, proving liability is very difficult. It is also difficult to organise an effective response, because in the absence of responsibility there is no focus for joint action. The difficulty of tackling this problem in London is discussed by Simpson *et al.* (1989).

The Cardiff Bay Barrage scheme is an example of an expected rise in groundwater levels as a result of a base level change which will be caused by an impoundment. The impoundment is part of a larger redevelopment scheme promoted by the Cardiff Bay Development Corporation (CBDC), an agency of the UK government. This is thus an example of groundwater rise where responsibility is clear, where the possibility of management and/or compensation is tenable. This paper documents the steps taken to reduce the monetary and social costs of the groundwater changes expected to be caused by the Cardiff Bay Barrage, and then examines the relevance of these steps to other rising groundwater situations.

2 THE CARDIFF BAY BARRAGE SCHEME

At low tide, Cardiff Bay is presently (1997) a large area of mud-flats, with limited visual appeal. Because of this Cardiff, the capital city of Wales, developed away from the waterfront, which was dominated by docks. Use of the docks has declined and the waterfront area has become run down. As part of a plan to develop the Cardiff waterfront and turn it into an asset to the city, a freshwater lake is being created by the construction of a tidal exclusion barrage across the bay, Figure 1. The lake will have a final water level of 4.5 mAOD, 4.2 m above the present mean tide level (mean spring tidal range is +6.0 mAOD to -5.1 mAOD). The possibility of this rise in local base level affecting groundwater levels was recognised at an early stage.

3 ISSUES

3.1 Legal Background

The Cardiff Bay Barrage, when constructed, will obstruct a tidal waterway. In 1993, such a construction required an Act of Parliament to grant consent. Other similar constructions require consent under the Town and Country Planning Act, 1990. Both procedures permit extensive public consultation in an adversarial framework, which can result in a thorough test of proposals (Crompton and Heathcote, 1994; Rushton, 1994).

In English Law, groundwater is only partly covered by primary legislation. The Water Resources Act 1989 covers the issues of abstraction of groundwater for use, discharge of water into the ground, and pollution of groundwater. Abstraction of water to permit excavations, and changes in the level of groundwater as a result of construction, are not covered directly by legislation. In these areas, the relevant law is common law, determined by precedents set by previous decisions. Adverse effects alleged to be caused by a rise in the level of groundwater caused by impoundment would have to be demonstrated to be a Nuisance. This would require actual damage to have been caused, and a direct link to be demonstrated between the damage and the impoundment. Unforseeability of the effect on the part of the defendant, and remoteness of the alleged cause and effect would be valid defences, but attempts by the defendant to mitigate the damage would not reduce the liability. Damages would be limited to the difference in value, plus consequential losses, and would not necessarily equal the cost of repair.

Thus for an individual to claim damages against CBDC in these circumstances would be onerous, and there is no incentive for CBDC to attempt to mitigate impact prior to its occurrence. The general difficulty of obtaining legal remedy where rising groundwater results from the combined effect of several independent causes can be appreciated. The passing of the Cardiff Bay Barrage Act 1993 allowed the specific case of groundwater impact from the barrage to be dealt with in a more suitable way, as discussed below.

3.2 Nature of affected area

Butetown developed in the early nineteenth century as an industrial area, associated with the adjacent docks. Large buildings had deep basements, which were often wet. The docks are now largely closed, and the area is being redeveloped as part of the Cardiff Bay scheme.

The area which is now Grangetown was tidal salt-flats until around 1850, with an elevation of 5.5-6.0 mAOD. It was thus inundated during spring high tides. In the latter part of the nineteenth century, the ground level was raised using material ranging from crushed stone, through colliery waste, to domestic refuse, and high density terraced housing was built. Many of these houses do not have deep foundations, though there are areas where under-floor voids of up to a metre exist. Damp-proof courses were not installed. Over a hundred years later, some of this housing is now in poor condition, with problems of settlement and dampness.

Until the latter part of this century, Leckwith was still low lying land, drained by open channels terminating in tidal sluices. This land has now also been reclaimed and is being developed for light industrial use. Such buildings have shallow pad foundations.

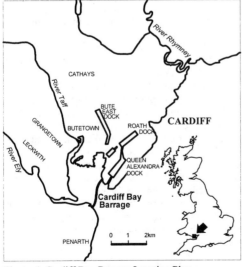

Figure 1 Cardiff Bay Barrage Location Plan

Table 1 Simplified Geological Succession in the Cardiff Area

Age	Formation	Description
Recent	Made ground	Fill materials of very variable composition
	Alluvium	Estuarine muds - grey muds with interbedded peats and gravels
	River gravel	Medium to very coarse gravels
Pleistocene	Upper till	Brown sandy clay
	Fluvio-glacial sands	Dense gravely sands
	Lower till	Degraded bedrock with sands
Triassic	Mercia Mudstone	Brown mudstones and siltstones with sandstones and evaporite nodules. In part weathered with solution cavities

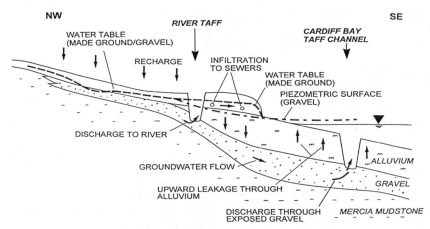

Figure 2 Conceptual cross section (NW-SE) of Cardiff groundwater system

4 GEOLOGY AND HYDROGEOLOGY

The geology of Cardiff is summarised in Table 1. This can be further simplified into three hydrogeological units. The uppermost layer, the Made Ground, is very variable but generally permeable, typically around 1 m thick, but locally several metres thick filling depressions in the underlying alluvium. The Made Ground generally contains water at its base, but there is no integrated water table present. The Alluvium is a soft to firm silty clay, generally of low permeability. Measured values of hydraulic conductivity lie in the range 4.2×10^{-6} - 2.5×10^{-3} m/d. Beneath this, the Gravel forms an aquifer 5-10 m thick, with a hydraulic conductivity of the order of 50 m/d, determined by a number of pumping tests (Hydrotechnica, 1991; Heathcote *et al.*, 1997).

Water levels in the Gravel are confined by the overlying Alluvium, and are lower than those in the Made Ground. The Gravel is in hydraulic continuity with the River Taff and with the sea in Cardiff Bay. The overall system is illustrated in schematic cross-section in Figure 2.

5 IMPACT ASSESSMENT

Initial consideration of the scheme by CBDC as the developer identified that change in groundwater level in the Gravel was probable, and that there may be an associated impact on housing constructed on the Made Ground. Given this, it was necessary to evaluate the likely rise more precisely and to assess the probable consequences. Key decisions needed to be taken.

i) Was there a probability of impact? (If not, the scheme could proceed with no hindrance)

ii) If yes, could the impact be tolerated? (If yes, the scheme could proceed, possibly at higher cost because of compensation payments)

iii) If not, mitigation was needed. Was mitigation possible and affordable? (If yes, the scheme could proceed at higher cost)

iv) If the effect could not be tolerated or mitigated at acceptable cost, the scheme could not proceed as envisaged.

The nature of these decisions, which affects the viability of the scheme, determined the detail of the impact assessment. This possibility of impact was also appreciated by residents organisations representing the owners of the potentially affected housing, who organised opposition during the public consultation process. All of the potential impacts listed in the Introduction were identified as of concern.

Impact assessment involved two stages: calculation of the expected changes in groundwater level as a consequence of impoundment, and assessment of the effect of this rise on property. Simple calculations of the expected rise in groundwater level, consequent on a 4.2 m rise in base level, suggest that the rise will be no greater than the base level rise. With existing groundwater levels less than 0.5 m below ground surface in some areas of southern Cardiff, a 4.2 m rise was clearly unacceptable and would prevent the scheme from proceeding. A more sophisticated approach was necessary, which led to the construction of numerical models of the urban groundwater system of Cardiff.

These models are described more fully by Heathcote *et al.* (1992). In summary, a regional layered model was constructed, with a 200 m grid, to investigate the overall groundwater system and to describe how groundwater recharge in Cardiff eventually discharges to the rivers and to the bay. Recharge needed to take into account both meteoric input and the input from leaking water mains, which was estimated as being ~45% of the total of 320 mm/a. The sewer system was identified as a key part of the groundwater discharge system. The sewers are large diameter, brick-lined with little or no mortar, and are below the water table in the Made Ground. In addition to the sewers, there are a large number of other service trenches which cross the urban area, connecting with the sewer trenches, producing an informal network of french drains with a linear density of >1/10 m. Detailed vertical section models were used to assess the effect of the sewers. These models demonstrated that most of the water entering the Made Ground leaves via the sewers. Once the regional model had been calibrated, it could be used to investigate the change in groundwater levels directly. Extensive sensitivity analysis was used to identify the likely range of final water levels, given irreducible uncertainties in the input data for the models, and an approximate cost of impact of £20 000/mm rise. The overall approach is discussed by Heathcote and Crompton (1996).

The effect of water level rise on property was estimated by relating present groundwater levels to the elevation of property, especially the inverts of basements. This allowed a semi-quantitative description of impact *versus* water level, with some impact in terms of dampness occurring when groundwater level approached within 1 m of underfloor voids. This analysis, using existing depths to water, indicates that dampness is a widespread existing problem in south Cardiff.

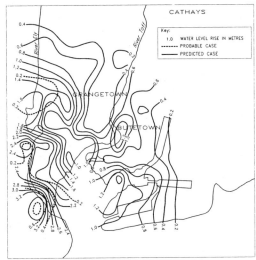

Figure 3 Predicted response of Made Ground water levels to impoundment, probable and extreme cases

The impact assessment showed that rise in water level in the Made Ground was expected to be generally small (<0.1 m), (see Figure 3 probable case), but substantial rises would occur in the Gravels, exceeding 3 m locally near the bay, where Gravel water levels are presently low but tidal. With these small rises, little or no impact would be expected on most houses founded on the Made Ground; occasional impacts would require only small scale remedial work. More extensive work, such as the waterproof lining of basements, would be needed where these penetrate the gravel.

However, the sensitivity analysis showed that there was a small probability of larger rises in the Made Ground, which could not be excluded by the available data, (see Figure 3 extreme case). The impact produced by these rises would require remedial work to a very large number of houses. Regional groundwater level control, preventing the rise in water level, was likely to be a cost-effective alternative remedial strategy. Outline costings indicated that remedial costs for this extreme case would be of the order of £10 million at 1991 prices, to cover the liabilities over the next 20 years. This compares with a then anticipated construction cost for the barrage itself of over £100 million.

6 REMEDIES

Given that the risk of impact could not be demonstrated to be completely negligible, and the relatively difficult remedy for any damage available through the courts, from an early stage it was deemed appropriate that the Cardiff Bay Barrage Act should provide additional remedies. This is an extremely unusual and important precedent, in that CBDC is accepting liability where under common law liability may have been otherwise difficult to prove. The desirability of such a provision was reinforced during the public consultation process, given the high public profile achieved by the groundwater issue.

The provision of adequate legal remedy must consider the existing poor condition of the housing stock, so that a requirement for remedial works is triggered only by problems caused by the barrage, and not pre-existing problems.

The Cardiff Bay Barrage Act thus contains the following provisions:

i) A very conservative Protected Property area is defined, outside which no groundwater level change is expected (this area includes all the area below 10 m AOD, compared with a top water level of 4.5 m AOD in the impoundment).

ii) All existing buildings (~17 000 houses) within the Protected Property area will be surveyed to assess their condition, especially any dampness, free of charge to the occupants

iii) All buildings will be re-surveyed after impoundment, to assess impact, free of charge to the occupants

iv) Any damage will be made good or compensated

v) Any building shown to be affected is entitled to further survey, and if necessary further remedy, up to 20 years after the last effects

vi) The same provisions are applicable for the remainder of the Cardiff area outside the Protected Property area, for a nominal fee of £40, refundable if impact is demonstrated. The same protection extends to the rest of England and Wales, but there may be a liability for the full survey cost if impact is not demonstrated

vii) Similar provisions are applicable to gardens, although in this case the provision of evidence is the responsibility of the householder

viii) There is an independent assessor

ix) An extensive groundwater monitoring network has been put in place, to provide data on changes in groundwater level (Mitchell and Exley, 1997)

x) These obligations last for a minimum of twenty years after the date of impoundment.

This legal remedy does not prevent CBDC from taking active measures to avoid groundwater impact, and provides a possible commercial incentive to execute preventive measures on a regional scale, rather than house by house. Regional groundwater control is under consideration. Studies have indicated that control by a small number of horizontal boreholes is feasible at an acceptable price.

The provisions of the Cardiff Bay Barrage Act apply only to houses and commercial property whose construction predates the start of construction of the barrage. New property is not covered. However, the fact that a property or parcel of land is within the Protected Property area under the Cardiff Bay Barrage Act, or has been surveyed under it, is recorded as a charge on the property and will be revealed by the statutory search which is performed whenever there is a change of ownership. Thus the issue of groundwater is brought to the attention of developers.

The obligations of CBDC for monitoring, surveys, remedial works and any groundwater control measures can be passed on to a successor only with agreement, otherwise they remain with CBDC, which is an agency of the UK government.

7 LESSONS FROM CARDIFF

7.1 Anticipation

Possible impact from rising urban groundwater has been appreciated *before* it occurred. This has allowed costing of the impact and its remediation, so that an informed decision on whether to proceed could be made. It has allowed legal protection to be given to those at risk. This legal protection covers both those at risk from the development, and the developer.

7.2 Responsibility

There is now a precedent for making the deliberate causer of a groundwater level rise responsible for the consequences, without an onerous burden of proof on the affected party. However, the Cardiff Bay Barrage Act does lay down a clear framework, intended to be fair, to protect CBDC against spurious claims, and limits the liability to making good, either by repair or compensation for loss of value. The concept of penal damages is excluded in this case. The Act lays down a clear requirement for monitoring to collect the data needed to assess liability, with an assessor independent of CBDC. There is effectively a government guarantee for at least 20 years into the future.

7.3 Planning

CBDC has no further liability towards future buildings, but there is an existing statutory mechanism in place to draw attention to the groundwater issue in Cardiff.

7.4 Other cases

In this case, the process leading to expected

groundwater rise was deliberate, consequences were foreseen, and a range of management options was available to produce a solution, which could be accepted through a public consultation process. Can the same concepts be applied where groundwater level rise is caused by cessation of abstraction, or by climate change?

If water levels in an urban area are depressed by groundwater abstraction, hydrogeological expertise is sufficient in most cases to predict the water level in the absence of abstraction, and therefore the consequences of its cessation can be estimated. This knowledge can be used to control new development, so that it will not be impacted by a possible future rise in water level. However, there may be costs in doing so (Simpson et al., 1989). Developers are faced with either accepting the known cost now of building for possible future water level rise, or facing an unknown cost of possible future water level control. This is a commercial decision, which will tend to favour doing nothing now. However, since a financial benefit accrues to the owner from this decision, it could be argued as unreasonable to expect government to pay for future remedial work when the water level does rise.

There is a problem with existing development impacted by water level rise, which was possibly not foreseeable given a previous level of knowledge, and under English Law at the moment no-one is directly responsible. An action for nuisance will not succeed in most cases since there is no single cause. However, the principle established by the Cardiff Bay Barrage Act could be extended to require abstractors to contribute to remedial work on cessation - this would require new laws.

In the case of climate change, planning and engineering options are still available, if the consequences are foreseen. However, in this case, the expense may be substantial, and is not related to the benefits derived from processes which cause climate change. An international legal remedy is still far off, but the matter is now being discussed (ENDS, 1996).

It is clear that the problem of urban groundwater rise is manageable if foreseen sufficiently early, albeit at a cost. The challenge is to foresee the rise. Urban groundwater systems are complex and often very dynamic. Changes to the water supply to, and drainage from, the groundwater system require careful consideration. As a by-product of the investigation for the barrage, the hydrogeological significance of the old brick-lined sewers in Cardiff is now appreciated. Extensive repairs to these with modern impermeable linings are likely to disrupt the groundwater drainage system, and would have more effect than the barrage. However, there is no formal mechanism in place in England and Wales to evaluate and control such possible impacts.

The study illustrates the essential rôle for hydrogeology in urban planning.

8 ACKNOWLEDGEMENT

The work described here was performed under contract to Cardiff Bay Development Corporation, whose permission to publish is gratefully acknowledged.

9 REFERENCES

Crompton, D.M. & J.A. Heathcote 1994. Discussion on quantification of processes. In Wilkinson, W. B. (ed.) *Groundwater problems in urban areas.* Thomas Telford, London.

ENDS, 1996. Policy machine moves up a gear to meet global warming challenge. *ENDS Report,* 258: 13-18.

Heathcote, J.A. & D.M. Crompton 1996. Risk of groundwater impact caused by the Cardiff Bay Barrage. In Burt, N. & J. Watts (eds.) *Barrages: Engineering design and environmental impact.* J Wiley & Sons, Chichester.

Heathcote, J.A., R.T. Lewis, D.I. Russell & R.W.N.S. Soley 1997. Cardiff bay barrage - investigating groundwater control in a tidal aquifer. *Q. J. Eng. Geol.* 30, in press.

Heathcote, J.A., R.T. Lewis & W.K. Sze 1992. Mathematical modelling of the impact of Cardiff Bay Barrage. In Blair, W.R. & E. Cabrera (eds.) *Fluid flow modelling.* Elsevier, Amsterdam

Hydrotechnica, 1991. *Cardiff Bay Barrage: final report on groundwater modelling.* Report 12057/R3.

Knipe, C.V., J.W. Lloyd, D.N. Lerner & R.B. Greswell 1993. *Rising groundwater levels in Birmingham and the engineering implications.* Spec. publ. 92, CIRIA, London.

Mitchell, R.C.S. & R. Exley 1997. Hydrometric monitoring in Cardiff. This volume.

Rushton, K.R., 1994. Discussion on quantification of processes. In Wilkinson, W. B. (ed.) *Groundwater problems in urban areas.* Thomas Telford, London.

Rushton, K.R. & A.A.R Al-Othman 1994. Control of rising groundwater levels in Riyadh, Saudi Arabia. In Wilkinson, W. B. (ed.) *Groundwater problems in urban areas.* Thomas Telford, London.

Simpson, B., T. Blower, R.N. Craig, & W.B. Wilkinson 1989. *The engineering implications of rising groundwater levels in the deep aquifer beneath London.* Special publ. 69, CIRIA, London.

Landfill leachate: Managing a valuable irrigation resource in the urban environment

M.J.Knight & D.B.Yates
National Centre for Groundwater Management, University of Technology, Sydney, N.S.W., Australia

B.G.Sutton
Department of Crop Sciences, University of Sydney, N.S.W., Australia

ABSTRACT: Domestic solid waste landfills, commonly found in urban areas, often produce leachate which can be used for irrigating recreational areas after fill completion. Hydraulic modelling of leachate outflow and irrigation scenarios is critical to managing this process. This paper describes a new, coupled predictive model which overcomes the problems of conventional water balance methods. Validation to within 10% of measured flow has been achieved at a landfill in Lucas Heights, Sydney, Australia where some 79 Ml y^{-1} (79000 m^3 y^{-1}) of leachate is derived from 58 hectares of fills. The leachate resource, as a substitute for mains water, is valued at $55,000 (AUD) per year. It is planned for use on a golf course and playing fields that are urgently needed in the urban area. Some stimulation of the gas field that currently produces 3MW (electrical power equivalent) is expected as a result of the irrigation.

1 INTRODUCTION

Domestic solid waste landfills are commonly found in urban areas of Australia, and often produce leachate. The leachate from fills at an advanced stage of stabilisation may still have valuable nutrients (nitrogen compounds, especially NH_4-N), and can be substituted for high quality, costly mains water for irrigating recreational land in urban areas. Health risks are minimal, especially with subsurface drip pipe delivery. A key problem is predicting and managing the leachate flow where gravity drainage is employed as the principal collection system.

In Sydney, Australia, the climate is seasonally very variable, and it is not uncommon for very intense rainfall (e.g. 214 mm in 2 days in 1978) to provide significant departures from base flow. Peak flows can vary from two to six times base flow in such free draining fill systems that are tabular and sloping. Thus, any predictive model needs robust and coupled transient and steady state elements.

The free draining tabular and sloping landfill design is considered to be optimal for stabilisation, (Knight 1990) which in turn is critical to a fill's later long-term sustainability in resource management, environmental, economic and socio-political senses (Knight 1997).

This paper describes the successful modelling and planned management of leachate at one of Australia's largest landfills at Lucas Heights, an outer, newly urbanised Sydney suburb which is in urgent need of recreational facilities. Plans for the construction of such facilities (playing fields, a golf course and passive vegetated areas) on top of the landfill are under discussion by local authorities in 1997.

2 MODELLING LEACHATE HYDRAULIC BEHAVIOUR

2.1 *Past strategies*

Leachate is generated from a combination of waste decomposition processes and their interaction with water derived from rainfall or groundwater infiltrating a landfill. When groundwater ingress is not present and where gravity drainage operates, the dominant hydraulic processes are vertical infiltration through the cover soil and waste to a leachate water table, and then, potentially, lateral flow under a hydraulic gradient that is either engineered or natural.

Modelling strategies began with the use of the water balance approach (Input = Output ± change in storage) of Fenn et al (1975) and its later extension to more sophisticated variants such as the HELP model (Schroeder et al, 1984). The water balance approach has been extensively reviewed, by Knox (1991), Lisk (1991) and Parsons (1994). The methodology has been practised widely including Knight et al. (1978). However, later research in 1980 at Lucas Heights, Sydney, suggested that there were problems when actual flow measurements were compared with predictions (Knight 1982). Alternative predictors were sought and established to some degree (Knight 1983). Others have also had doubts about the adequacy of the water balance approach (Parsons 1995).

2.2 Defining the problem

The key strategies in leachate prediction are to utilise the transient climatic variables (e.g. rainfall) which can have long records together with coversoil and waste hydraulic characteristics to predict water table response, which in turn causes changes to leachate outflow from the base flow condition. Water balances, and approaches involving rainfall, runoff and soil moisture in the cover soil have had some success but have failed in the waste zone. Addressing this issue, Knight (1983) indicated that a model which appeared to match observed outflows was a function of the fill's prior outflow state together with a new component. The new component was linked to the changes in water table elevation as a proportion of the total head loss for the fill, the transmissivity of the fill and the width of the drained outflow. The resulting algorithm was named the "Modified Darcian Model".

An important shortcoming of the model in a predictive sense is that it requires an input of water table elevation change, which in the case studied was measured in boreholes. The key now is to predict water table response arising from climatically variable events with a stochastic history, on and in the cover soil of a landfill.

These model components need to be coupled so as to produce a time series of leachate outflows. Other minor complications such as pumped boreholes can also be added. The successful coupling of these model elements has been validated at Lucas Heights, southwest of Sydney.

3 LUCAS HEIGHTS LANDFILL

3.1 Location and fill form

Lucas Heights is a relatively new southern suburb of Sydney. There are two major landfills located some

27 to 30 km south-west of Sydney City Centre; Lucas Heights No. 1 (an older fill now being rehabilitated, converted to playing field use and having gas extracted) and Lucas Heights No. 2 (currently an active fill). This paper relates to Lucas Heights Fill No. 1 (Figure 1). There are five main hydraulically distinct sloping tabular fills which were placed over the fifteen years 1972-1986. Land construction methods were used; successive 2 m layers of waste were covered with 30 cm of coversoil. Total waste mass exceeds 1 million tonnes and fill thickness varies from 5 m to 20 m.

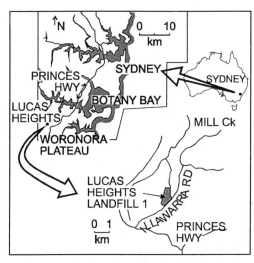

Figure 1. Location of Lucas Heights No. 1 Landfill in the outer suburbs of Sydney. Modified from Knight (1990).

Fill zones are defined as: A - Central; B - Southern; C and D - Northern; and E - Southwest; (Figure 2).

3.2 Hydrogeology

The hydrogeology of this site has been described previously by Knight et al. (1978) and revised by later more complete data (Knight 1983). The fills have been excavated into weathered Hawkesbury Sandstone of Triassic age and extend out from the margin of the Woronora Plateau. The "Sandstone" formation often contains lenticular shale lenses. Zones A, C and D have been drilled for gas extraction and a current drilling program is underway to establish further leachate monitoring bores. The Southern fill section is typical of the site's hydrogeology (Figure 3).

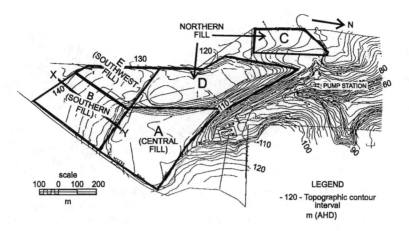

Figure 2. Topography of the five tabular fill zones as completed in 1986 at Lucas Heights No. 1 Landfill. Data modified from Waste Services et al (1996).

A range of studies have demonstrated that the fills are hydraulically isolated from each other due to drain locations and the impermeable nature of the rocks below. The sandstone has clay in the matrix and the joints are tight, restricting matrix and fracture flow respectively. Liners below the waste are unnecessary and have not been used.

3.3 Leachate management

Leachate management has varied over the years, including drainage to lagoons and pH controlled treatment linked to spray irrigation (1970s, early 1980s). By the mid 1980s irrigation had been replaced by pumping to sewer from a pump station to the north of the site (Figure 2). The pump station is fed by drains which surround the margins of each fill. Irrigation is about to recommence based on the modelling described in this paper.

4 MODEL STRUCTURE

4.1 Conceptual Picture

A conceptual picture of the physical model used to describe leachate hydraulic behaviour and its recycling by irrigation from a collection sump and pump station is illustrated in Figure 4.

4.2 Water balance model component

This component is an accounting format (Input = Output ± change in soil moisture storage) with output at the base of the root zone and cover soil of

Figure 3. Section X-Y (SW-NE) through the southern fill zone. After Knight (1983). See Figure 2 for location of section X-Y.

volumes of water/unit time step (days). Inputs and outputs include rainfall (alone or with irrigation), evapotranspiration (Ea) and runoff. Irrigation does not occur if sufficient rain is falling to generate runoff. To allow for denitrification, the irrigation areas can be brought to saturation for a specified period and then permitted to drain to field capacity.

Evapotranspiration was computed from the methodology of Doorenbos and Pruitt (1977), which utilises pan evaporation and crop coefficients. Computations of outflow were not very sensitive to the use of alternative estimates of Ea, for example Ea calculated using mean daily temperature data alone (Linacre 1977).

Runoff was computed using the EPIC formula of Littleboy et al. (1993) . This method requires knowledge of the soil type and its water holding capacity, which was obtained from field investigations.

Verification of the methodology has been achieved by comparing predicted runoff coefficients with those measured in 1980 (Southern Fill Zone, Knight (1982). The results were:

605

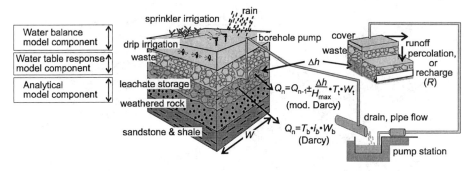

i_b : hydraulic gradient of the water table $\qquad$ Δh : change in water table elevation

T_b : transmissivity under baseflow conditions $\qquad$ T_t : transmissivity when water table rises

W : Width of seepage face normal to lateral flow at the lowest elevation where pipe flow operates

H_{max} : maximum head loss, from highest fill elevation $\qquad$ Q_b : baseflow discharge

Q_{n-1} : discharge in week previous to week of interest $\qquad$ Q_n : discharge in week of calculation

Figure 4. Conceptual picture of the physical models used to describe leachate drainage, collection and irrigation recycling. Data after Waste Services et al (1996).

Predicted runoff 8.0% of rainfall
Observed runoff 8.1% of rainfall

Some field testing of coversoil hydraulic conductivity was also available from the 1980 and later studies. The final outflow model was found to produce similar outcomes for both predicted and measured runoff coefficients.

The water balance model component provides output as percolation (recharge R, mm day^{-1}), which potentially infiltrates vertically from the coversoil to the leachate watertable causing a rise Δh.

4.3 Water table response model component

At the margins of each fill at Lucas Heights No. 1 landfill, 100 mm diameter porous plastic pipes act as the main drains for the leachate. During a recharge event, the water table fluctuations in a porous medium layer that is flat, but undergoing drainage with parallel drains, may be illustrated by Figure 5.

The fill is sufficiently flat (for example approximately 2.3% slope in zone B) to allow modelling by this theory. The model is symmetrical at the ($L/2$) position (Figure 5), which allows the application of the theory to the Lucas Heights situation. At Lucas Heights, each fill zone can be considered to be one half of the model described above (the distance $L/2$, Figure 5), since there is only a single major marginal drain. The result of the analysis, the change in water table height (Δh, Figure 5) therefore becomes the water table rise occurring in

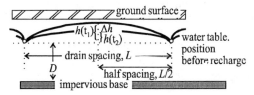

Figure 5. Changing water table [$\Delta h = h(t_1) - h(t_2)$] conditions during drainage (non steady state) by two parallel drains resulting from intermittent recharge events. Average saturation thickness is D (m). Data modified from Dieleman (1974).

the relevant fill zone as a result of some recharge event.

From a series of iterative computations, it has been found that $L/2 = 50$ m is optimal. This is physically sensible from a knowledge of drain positions. At this scale, the flat slope assumption is also reasonable. Furthermore the issue of a large scale sloping (i.e. not flat) porous medium is taken into account by the hydraulic gradient component of both the Darcy and modified Darcy flow equations described in the next section.

The drainage theory applicable to Lucas Heights has been described by Wesseling (1973) and Dieleman (1974). Non-steady state flow is governed by a partial differential equation that is based on the Dupuit-Forcheimer assumption (Wesseling 1973). Both Kraijenhoff Van De Leur (1958) and Maasland (1959) derived solutions for non-steady state groundwater flow to drains. The solution is based on steady recharge (R) over any time t (days or weeks) and is shown in Equation (1).

$$h_t = \frac{4}{\pi} \frac{R}{\mu} j \sum_{n=1,-3,5}^{\infty} \frac{1}{n^3} \left(1 - e^{-\frac{n^2 t}{j}} \right) \qquad 1$$

where h = the height of the water table midway between parallel drains at $x=L/2$, where x is the horizontal distance from a reference point at any time t; n = a summation index; and

$$j = \frac{\mu L^2}{\pi^2 KD} \quad \text{and is called the rerservoir coefficient} \qquad 2$$

where μ = drainable pore space, KD = transmissivity of the medium, and L = drain spacing.

Equation (1) is a sumation series which converges rapidly to produce water table heights (h_t) for times (t) following recharge events as illustrated by Dieleman (1974). The computation methodology is described in detail by Wesseling (1973) and utilises tabulations for the summation series.

The watertable response algorithms described above have been used to compute the predicted watertable changes (Δh) produced by recharge (percolation) derived from the water balance model for 1980/81 Southern Landfill data. These are compared with the observed average change in watertable for six bores in the same fill over the same period (Figure 6).

As can be seen most errors (predicted and observed) are less than ± 5% and for the very heavy rain event in week 26 the prediction was the same as observed.

4.4 *Analytical Model Component*

In research reported by Knight (1983) for the Southern Landfill Zone, it was found that two algorithms could be used to describe the lateral porous media flow in a sloping bed below a landfill on weathered Hawkesbury Sandstone (Figure 4). These have been named (Knight 1983) the Darcy (base flow) component and modified Darcian model component (water table changes).

Good validation was achieved by Knight (1983) based on observed leachate outflows for 1980/81, which were predicted to within 6% using measured watertable changes.

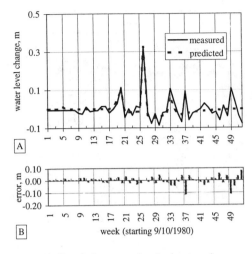

Figure 6. Borehole water level changes (measured and predicted), Southern Fill Zone, 1980/81 (A), and error between measured and predicted values (B). Data after Waste Services et al (1996)

4.5 *Irrigation Scenarios*

A range of irrigation scenarios utilising Fills A, B, C and D have been included in the overall model of the site. The scenarios include various combinations of irrigation style, as described in Figure 7, and variable irrigation plot size. The various irrigation scenarios provide inputs to the cover soil/rootzone water balance component of the model, by way of soil moisture parameters and rainfall equivalents.

The aim of the irrigation scenario modelling was to find the minimum irrigated area that satisfied two criteria. First, a proposed storage dam which is the source of the irrigation water should not be overtopped with unacceptable frequency. Second, in the long term, plant evapotranspiration should exceed that proportion of the rainfall which becomes groundwater accession.

4.6 *Validation of the coupled leachate drainage model and pumping bores for the entire landfill*

The various components of the model were linked into a program on an IBM compatible personal computer (Pascal programming language), allowing rapid model runs for verification and component testing.

The conceptual layout of the fills, pumping bores and their relationship with the irrigation scenarios for leachate recycling is illustrated in Figure 7.

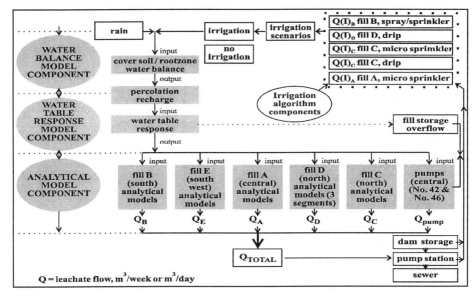

Figure 7. Conceptual layout of the proposed leachate modelling / recycling scheme at Lucas Heights No. 1 Landfill. Data after Waste Service et al (1996).

The algorithms described above have been coupled, and allow comparison of the predicted total leachate flow to the pump station with measured values (Figure 8). For the 49 weeks for which measurements were available the comparison is ; measured 58634 kl (58634 m³), predicted 56384 kl (56384 m³) representing an error of -3.8% which is acceptable in the light of measurement and other errors.

5. LEACHATE MANAGEMENT

5.1 *Irrigation*

Modelling results showed that leachate flows were governed by the approximately annual storms that are intense enough to generate groundwater recharge. Recycling of leachate via irrigation added about 25% to leachate flow during peaks of outflow, decaying to less than 5% during times of leachate baseflow. The scenarios that met the design criteria adequately (see section 4.5) were either 5 ha of irrigation in B or 8 ha of irrigation in D, with 0.5 ha in each of A and C.

5.2 *Dam Storage*

All leachate generated on the site is to be contained,

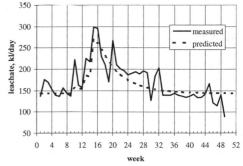

Figure 8. Total weekly leachate output from the fill site at the pump station, measured and predicted data for 1994. Data after Waste Services et al (1996).

evaporated, or stored temporarily in a detention basin. Modelling studies utilising past climatic data showed that for the period examined (1974 - 1994) a 3 Ml (3000 m³) dam could cope with 98% of the rainfall events for a range of irrigation scenarios combining drip, microjet and monsoon spray delivery modes. These scenarios will be used prior to and during the construction of the recreational facilities (playing fields, golf course, and passive vegetated areas).

Ultimately, the irrigation delivery method will probably be buried drip pipes in fills B, C and D.

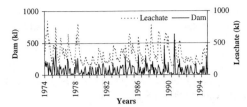

Figure 9. Leachate generated and dam storage requirements with fills B (5Ha), C (2Ha) and D (8Ha) irrigated. Data after Wastes Services et al (1996)

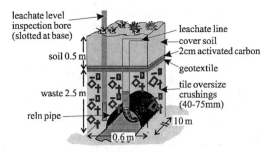

Figure 10. Cross section of an injection trench capable of injecting leachate into a fill for temporary leachate storage. Data after Waste Services et al (1996).

The dam storage requirement for the period 1974-1994 from the model for this scenario is illustrated in Figure 9.

With this irrigation strategy, there will only be need for 200 kl (200 m^3) storage of leachate, or less most of the time.

5.3 *Injection Trench*

When extreme events do occur, excess leachate will be managed by injection into fill D via a 600 m long trench at a groundwater divide position , (Figure 10).

A leachate mound will build up below the trench but would be delayed in its eventual discharge to drains until well after the extreme rainfall event. This would operate similarly to a stormwater detention basin.

5.4 *Irrigation and gas production*

Some 3 MW of power is generated currently from gas wells located in Fill areas A, C and D. Preliminary tests indicate a positive gas response to leachate ·addition. Irrigation could provide a way of extending the life of the gas/electrical generation system.

6. DISCUSSION

Leachate management and associated modelling tools are critical to the long term constructive use of a landfill surface. At Lucas Heights No. 1 fill, the leachate for irrigation of recreational areas is in fact a resource and will substitute for mains water valued at $55,000 per year (AUD) which is likely to exceed operational costs. Lucas Heights No. 1 fill is now entering the "Resource Optimisation Phase" of the three phase "Sustainable Landfill" defined by Knight (1997). The preceding phases are; establishment/

construction, and stabilisation. Sustainability is defined in terms of long-term resource use, environmental impact, economics, socio-political factors and intergenerational equity.

7. CONCLUSIONS

Landfills and their leachate can be positive features in an urban environment. Modelling tools and appropriate fill design are now available to enable use of the resource to be optimised.

8. REFERENCES

Dieleman, P.J. 1974. *Deriving soil hydrological constaints from field drainage tests.* In N.A. Ridder chief Ed.: Drainage Principles and Applications. ILRI 26(3):329 - 354

Doorenbos J. and W.O. Pruitt. 1977. *Crop Water Requirements Irrigation and Drainage*, Paper 24, Rome, FAO

Fenn D.G, K.J. Hanley and T.V. De Geare. 1975. Use of the water balance method for predicting leachate generation from solid waste disposal sites. *Rept EPA/SW-168 USEPA, Washington DC*

Knight M.J. 1982. *Disposal of selected liquid wastes in the Lucas Heights Regional Waste Disposal Depot.* Final Report to Metropolitan Waste Disposal Authority (unpub), Sydney.

Knight M.J. 1983. Modelling leachate discharged from a domestic solid waste landfill at Lucas Heights, Sydney, Australia. *Proc Internat. Conf. Groundwater and Man., AWRC Conf. Ser. 8, 2: 475-490: Canberra, AGPS.*

Knight M.J. 1990. Appropriate waste disposal and

evaluation of contaminated sites; Some keys to managed protection of groundwater and land. *Proc 6th International IAEG Congress Symposia: 325 - 336.*

Knight M.J. 1997. Sustainable landfills - making environmental and economic sense of land based waste management systems. *Proc. Int. Symp. Eng. Geol and the Environment, Athens Greece 23-27 June, Athens IAEG (in press)*

Knight M.J, J.G Leonard, and R.J. Whiteley. 1978. Lucas Heights solid waste landfill and downstream leachate transport - a case study in Environmental Geology. *Bull. Internatl. Assoc. Eng. Geol. 18:45-64*

Knox K. 1991. *A review of the water balance methods and their application to landfill in the UK.* Rept CWM 031/91 DOE, UK

Kraijenhoff van De Leur D.A. 1958. A study of non-steady groundwater flow with special reference to a reservoir - coefficient. *De Ingenieur 70:87.94*

Linacre E.T. 1977. A simple formula for calculating evaporation rates in various climates using temperature data alone *Agricultural Meteorology, 18, 409-424*

Lisk D.J. 1991. Environmental effects of landfills; *Science of the Total Environment 100; 415-468*

Littleboy M., D.M. Silburn, D.M. Freebairn, D.R Woodrull, and G.L. Hammer. 1993. *PERFECT: A Computer Simulation Model of Productivity, Erosion, Runoff Functions to Evaluate Conservation Techniques.* Queensland Department of Primary Industry

Maasland M. 1959. Watertable fluctuations induced by intermittent recharge. *J. Geophys. Res. 64:549-559*

Parsons R. 1994. *A review of approaches and methodologies for determining leachate generation at waste disposal sites and groundwater recharge.* WRC Rept No. 564/1/94. Water Research Commission, Pretoria, South Africa

Parsons R. 1995. The validity of the water balance method to predict leachate generation at waste disposal sites in light of geohydrological experiences. *Proc. 5th Internat. Landfill Symp. Oct. Sardinia 1:275-284*

Schroeder P.R, J.M. Morgan, T.M. Walski and A.C. Gibson. 1984. The Hydrogeologic Evaluation of Landfill Performance (HELP) model. Vol. 1 and 2, EPA/530-SW-010, U.S. Environmental Protection Agency, Office of Solid Waste and Emergency Response, Washington D.C.

Waste Service NSW, M.J. Knight, and B.G. Sutton. 1996. *Proposal for leachate management at Lucas Heights No. 1 landfill.* Waste Service of New South Wales, Rept. (*unpublished*)

Wesseling J. 1973. *Subsurface flow into drains.* In N.A. Ridder chief Ed.: Drainage Principles and Applications. ILRI 8(2):1 - 56

9. ACKNOWLEDGEMENTS

The Waste Service of New South Wales is gratefully acknowledge for their support of research at Lucas Heights No. 1 landfill over the 20 year period 1977 to 1997. Anand Thakur and Garry Legget are especially recognised.

610

Management of the environmental impacts of landfilling on the Sherwood Sandstone

Kathy Lewin, Chris Young & Nick Blakey
WRc plc, Medmenham, Marlow, UK

ABSTRACT: Two landfills which have accepted commercial and household waste from urban areas within Nottinghamshire have been studied in detail for nearly twenty years. The sites are non-contained and therefore investigations have focused on the migration and attenuation of liquid and gaseous contaminants within the unsaturated and saturated zones of the Sherwood Sandstone aquifer. The key factors controlling these processes have been established and can be used to identify other non-contained or contained landfills on the Sherwood Sandstone which could pose a risk to the quality of groundwater. By highlighting the higher risk landfills a revised management and monitoring plan for these sites can be introduced.

1 BACKGROUND

The Sherwood Sandstone is the second most important aquifer in the United Kingdom and is the main source of groundwater supplies and of base-flow to rivers in the Midlands and much of the North of England. In some places the groundwater is vulnerable to pollution by leachate derived from non-contained landfills and, potentially, by leakage from contained landfills.

Research initiated by Severn Trent Water in the late 1970s was continued with funding from the UK Department of the Environment and latterly with cofunding from the Severn Trent Region of the former National Rivers Authority. Two sites in Nottinghamshire have been investigated in order to gain information on the processes in the Sherwood Sandstone which may attenuate leachate. Both landfills are non-contained, infilled primarily with household waste, one with a thick (>50 m) unsaturated zone (Burntstump) and the other with a thin (<20 m) unsaturated zone (Gorsethorpe). The locations of both sites in relation to the outcrop of the Sherwood Sandstone and to Nottingham are shown in Figure 1. Data relating to the disposal histories have been presented elsewhere (DoE 1996). In summary, filling with Nottingham's waste commenced in shallow valleys at Burntstump in the early 1970s. In the early 1980s operations transferred to an adjacent sandpit, with phased sand

Figure 1. Location of the landfill sites on the Sherwood Sandstone.

extraction followed by waste backfill to a depth of up to 30 m. The current operator proposes that the final phase should be contained by an engineered lining system. Filling of the sandpit at Gorsethorpe began in 1969. The third phase was completed by 1983, when the whole site was capped with colliery shale. Both sites contain domestic and industrial

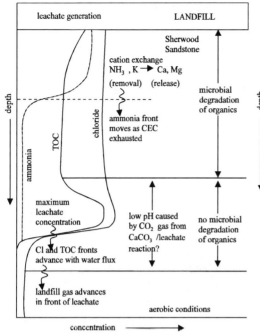

Figure 2. Schematic of attenuation processes occurring in the unsaturated zone of the Sherwood Sandstone (from DoE 1996).

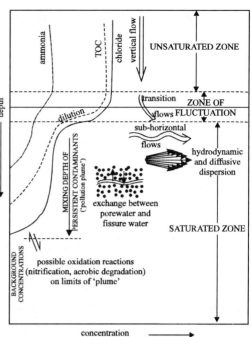

Figure 3. Schematic of attenuation processes occurring in the saturated zone of the Sherwood Sandstone (from DoE 1996).

waste from Nottingham, Mansfield and the surrounding areas.

Over the past 18 years it has been possible to study the products of waste degradation, both gases and liquids, and their migration through the Sherwood Sandstone. The investigations provide sufficient information to undertake a waste management facility risk assessment, including:

1. *source* - the landfilled wastes and processes generating leachate and gas (waste assay, biochemical methane potential, chemical analysis, leachability trials and porewater composition (analogous to migrating leachate));
2. *pathways* - the migration (and attenuation) of liquid and gaseous contaminants within the unsaturated and saturated zones;
3. *targets/receptors* - the impact of potential contaminants on groundwater quality.

2 MAIN FINDINGS

The primary processes which the research suggests operate within the unsaturated and saturated zones of the Sherwood Sandstone are presented in Figures

2 and 3. The key factors which have led to the selection of criteria for identifying high-risk sites can be summarised as follows:

Capping efficiency: The absence of consistent, low-permeability final capping of relatively shallow waste deposits (Gorsethorpe and the earlier phases of Burntstump) allowed continuous leachate generation to become established within a few years of initial waste emplacement. In contrast, field capacity in more recent, deeper and better compacted fill with low permeability capping had not been achieved five years after completion of filling, with leachate migration from the wastes being due to the effects of compression of the lower layers of waste.

Flow mechanism: Investigations indicate that recharge through the unsaturated zone of the Sherwood Sandstone is dominated by intergranular flow, with the consequence that the rate of vertical penetration of mobile and persistent dissolved contaminants is slow (generally <2 m y^{-1}), and directly proportional to the flux of leachate.

Geochemistry of the unsaturated zone: The Sherwood Sandstone has a low buffering capacity, due to a low calcite ($<1\%$) content and a limited cation exchange capacity (CEC of 2 meq $100g^{-1}$). Acidic conditions resulting from acetogenic leachate persist and inhibit methanogenic microbial activity. Consequently, leachate has passed through the shallow unsaturated zone with limited attenuation at Gorsethorpe and entered the groundwater. However, the deep unsaturated zone at Burntstump has allowed the establishment of conditions conducive to methanogenesis and a progressive and significant reduction in the organic strength of the leachate front (as shown by the total organic carbon (TOC) front in Figure 2). Acclimation of the sandstone to leachate attenuation is confirmed by the presence of viable bacterial populations beneath waste deposits which are some two orders of magnitude greater than in the unsaturated zone beneath adjacent farmland.

Age of wastes: Groundwater beneath the Gorsethorpe landfill is contaminated by leachate, but this is now decreasing as a result of the progressive reduction in strength of leachate generated by the ageing wastes. No firm evidence of groundwater pollution by leachate has been recorded at Burntstump, either immediately beneath the landfill area, or in the direction of groundwater flow.

3 QUALITY IMPLICATIONS FOR SHERWOOD SANDSTONE GROUNDWATER

The results of the initial investigations at the two sites were interpreted to indicate that the natural attenuating capacity of the formation was low, particularly with respect to potential organic contaminants (Harris & Lowe 1984).

However, subsequent studies have demonstrated that whilst the Sandstone possesses a significantly lower buffering capacity than limestone aquifers, and a lower exchange capacity than formations such as the Lower Greensand, it may still attenuate leachate. In aquifers in which intergranular flow is dominant, the vertical movement of water and dissolved substances through the unsaturated zone is slow. Therefore recognition of the beneficial effects of attenuation in the Sherwood Sandstone only became fully apparent with prolonged monitoring. The delay in reaching an understanding of the processes demonstrates the need to take account of the dynamics of contaminant transport and attenuation systems when designing investigations, and when reaching conclusions regarding long-term effects.

The identification of active attenuating processes in the unsaturated zone of the Sherwood Sandstone

has important implications for management of both existing landfills (contained and non-contained) and with respect to the planning and authorisation of future sites. This is a consequence of the incorporation into UK legislation of EC Directive 80/68/EEC (Protection of Groundwater against Pollution caused by Certain Dangerous Substances) as Regulation 15 of The Waste Management Licensing Regulations 1994. This makes it clear, that for the purposes of the regulation, the term groundwater should include only the water in the saturated zone.

The prolonged monitoring also suggests that a systematic decline in anaerobic degradation, as indicated by landfill gas production, began some fifteen to twenty years after disposal took place. A decrease in the strength of leachate forming in the wastes appears to have occurred within a similar time span. Nevertheless, the leachate (and gas) remain a potential environmental threat after about half the length of time for waste stabilisation ("generation" of 30 - 35 years, DoE 1995) which is proposed for sustainable landfilling, with the implication that production of leachate with significant organic components may continue for several tens of years, and ammoniacal nitrogen may remain a potential problem for even longer.

Outcrops of the Sandstone have been, and remain, extensively worked for building stone and aggregate with the result that there are large numbers of finished and operational landfills which may contribute actual or potential adverse effects on the quality of the groundwater resource. In addition, there is continued pressure for the development of new sites.

4 IMPLICATIONS FOR THE FUTURE MANAGEMENT OF LANDFILLS ON THE SHERWOOD SANDSTONE

4.1 *Existing non-contained landfills*

The operational histories of the sites at Burntstump and Gorsethorpe suggest that they provide good analogues for other non-contained sites on the Sandstone. In both cases, the majority of the observations have been made in areas where restoration has, until recently, been with relatively permeable materials, so that leachate generation and migration rates are likely to have been close to the maximum values for the local meteorological conditions. In the case of sites with thin (< c. 20 m) unsaturated zones, exemplified by Gorsethorpe, the attenuating capacity of the formation has proved insufficient to prevent significant local groundwater contamination by leachate, although extensive off-site groundwater pollution has not been found.

By contrast, there is evidence that a thick (> c. 30 m) unsaturated zone can provide significant attenuation of organic leachate components, with an important reduction in ammoniacal nitrogen flux due to the retarding effects of cation exchange. No persistent increases in groundwater concentrations below the old part of the Burntstump site, nor in the groundwater flow direction have been noted. The estimated rate of invasion of the unsaturated zone by leachate (c. $2 \, m \, y^{-1}$) suggests that significant contributions to groundwater contamination will not be made before about 2005. Further attenuation of the leachate by the formation is expected to take place and the strength of leachate being generated by the wastes in the non-contained areas of fill should continue to decline, with the result that the introduction of high-strength leachate to the groundwater may be short-lived. Water balance models have been employed to simulate and predict leachate generation rates at both Burntstump and Gorsethorpe and the significant reduction in generation rate that would accompany improved restoration/capping has been demonstrated. A reduction in leachate production would be expected to reduce proportionally the flux of contaminants to the water table, with a consequent increase in apparent attenuation by dilution. A negative effect of reducing the moisture flux may be to increase the time over which stabilisation (biodegradation of organic substrates and flushing of persistent compounds) of the wastes takes place.

However, it is considered unlikely that practical, controlled means of accelerating the flushing of wastes in non-contained landfills will be developed and it is suggested that the future management of non-contained landfills on the Sherwood Sandstone should be prioritised by categorising sites on the basis of Table 1.

Within any given area, sites scoring the greatest proportion of 'High' ratings would take top priority for the development of revised management programmes. Such programmes may include the need for additional site investigations and the establishment of a different groundwater monitoring schedule. The most probable effective remedial measure would be to improve the restoration surface to reduce the rate of potential infiltration.

Table 1. Identifying priority non-contained landfills on the Sherwood Sandstone.

Criterion	Priority level		
	High	Inter-mediate	Low
Waste type	Putre-scible	Mixed MSW[1]	Demo-lition, inert
Mean waste age (yrs)	<15	<30	>30
Proportion of fissure flow in sandstone (%)	>50	15-50	<15
CEC (meq $100g^{-1}$)	<2	2-5	>5
Mean infiltration relative to effective rainfall (%)	70-100	20-70	<20

[1] Municipal solid waste

4.2 Existing contained landfills

Existing, engineered containment landfills on the Sherwood Sandstone, as on other UK aquifers, have been designed to operate with a restricted leachate head above the basal lining, and to be progressively restored with low permeability caps to minimise infiltration and leachate production. The lining systems employed may be composite (e.g. synthetic membrane laid directly onto clay or bentonite-enhanced soil) or single (membrane, bitumen, concrete or clay layer) and may include multiple liners with intermediate drainage/leak detection layers. Lined landfills require leachate collection and control systems from which leachate may be pumped. In early containment sites the systems often consisted simply of shafts extending to the base of the wastes, from which leachate could be pumped, but more recent examples may be expected to incorporate perforated drains laid in a porous drainage blanket leading to one or more abstraction sumps.

In reviewing knowledge of the performance of membrane liners, Giroud & Bonaparte (1989) have suggested that membranes laid under appropriate quality assurance procedures would not be expected to have less than 5 defects per hectare, and that for small defects (<2 mm diameter) a head of 1 m would give rise to leakage rate per hole of about

100 l d^{-1}, which amounts, potentially, to 500 l d^{-1} ha^{-1}. However, this estimate assumes that the membrane is laid over a very free draining material (gravel) and it was stated that the leakage rate "would be significantly reduced if the pervious medium in contact with the geomembrane on one or both sides is sand or a less permeable material", which is the situation likely to be present at landfills located on the Sherwood Sandstone.

Shortly after the review by Giroud & Bonaparte (1989), the American Society of Civil Engineers (1990) recommended that, for design purposes a leakage rate of 200 l d^{-1} ha^{-1} should be assumed for a membrane-lined landfill, with not more than 1 m head of leachate, constructed to modern standards, under appropriate quality assurance. Describing experience gained from the operation of electric geomembrane leak location equipment, Colucci & Lavagnolo (1995) suggested that, from a sample of 25 landfills examined, only one had no liner defects, and that at the remainder there was an average of 15 defects per hectare. Leakage of 200 l d^{-1} ha^{-1} is equivalent to only about 3% of the potential drainage at a site such as Burntstump, before improvement of the restoration layers. Leakage of leachate at that rate would have less effect on groundwater quality than that observed at Gorsethorpe and management strategies with a basis similar to that for non-contained landfills would be appropriate. However, it is possible that greater localised groundwater impacts could develop with time in response to progressive deterioration in performance of the leachate drainage/control system. In particular this could be through the enlargement of existing defects, or due to reductions in porosity and permeability by chemical encrustations enlargement of existing defects, or due to reductions and biological slime build-up (Brune et al. 1991), or from progressive reduction in the storativity and permeability of the lower layers of waste with ageing and settlement (Beaven & Powrie 1995) making the control of leachate levels within the fill more difficult. One or a combination of these factors could lead to greater point leakage rates (greater head and/or enlarged leak). This could overwhelm the local attenuation capacity of the Sandstone, and possibly initiate rapid, fissure flow transfer of contaminants to groundwater.

It is suggested that in addition to the criteria proposed for prioritisation of non-contained landfills, the additional factors listed in Table 2 should be included for prioritising contained landfills.

Although it may be possible to restore the capacity of some leachate drain systems by jetting or rodding, practical methods for repairing leaks in liners are generally not available. In those cases where the drainage/liner system appears to be performing to specification and is less than 15 years old, consideration may be given to accelerating the stabilisation of waste by enhancing the moisture content of the wastes by recirculation, but possibly without attempting to achieve the flushing rates which are considered necessary for the flushing bioreactor approach to landfill (i.e. the removal of principal inorganic contaminants following the organics stabilisation phase). Where that option does not exist, it is suggested that improved capping and a suitable performance monitoring programme should be instigated.

Table 2. Identifying priority contained landfills on the Sherwood Sandstone.

Criterion	High	Intermediate	Low
		Priority level	
Liner construction	Single liner, membrane or clay/bentonite enhanced soil <0.3m	Single liner, clay/bentonite enhanced soil >0.3m	Composite liner
Leachate control system	Sumps only	Sumps and drains	Sumps, drains and continuous drainage blanket
Age of liner or leachate drainage system (yrs)	>30	15-30	<15
Depth of leachate over liner (m)	>10	1-10	<1

5 THE DEVELOPMENT OF SUSTAINABLE 'BIOREACTOR' LANDFILLS ON THE SHERWOOD SANDSTONE

Conclusions drawn from field and laboratory trials suggest that a high moisture content is required to optimise the rate of degradation of labile waste constituents. In addition/and, in order to remove persistent contaminants, such as ammoniacal nitrogen, it will be necessary to flush seven or eight bed volumes of liquid through the waste mass (Knox, 1990).

The decrease in permeability which accompanies waste maturation would be expected to lead to an increase in the difficulty of ensuring uniform distribution of flushing liquids and an extension of the time needed to pass a bed-volume through the wastes. A possible solution to this problem would be to restrict the depth of such fills to 10-20 m, to limit the self-weight compaction that would affect the basal layers of waste. Alternatively, maintenance of saturated conditions within the main body of the wastes would be expected to maintain high permeability, with a reduction only being noted when the wastes are drained following stabilisation. There would be a high potential for serious environmental damage in the event of a leak developing in a flooded system. Effective hydraulic barrier systems will need to be developed if such an approach were to be acceptable to the waste regulator. In view of the potential vulnerability of the Sherwood Sandstone to sudden contaminant loadings, it would be expected that detailed emergency response plans and very significant assurances would be needed before such sites could be developed on the aquifer.

6 CONCLUSIONS

The long-term monitoring of two non-contained landfills has identified key processes that control the migration and attenuation of leachate in the Sherwood Sandstone. This has enabled a set of criteria to be identified which can be used to highlight those sites which may have the greatest impact on the quality of groundwater within this major aquifer. The sites could be identified by querying the national landfill geographic system currently being developed for the UK Environment Agency. Those landfill sites which may require a revision to their management and monitoring programmes can therefore be readily prioritised.

ACKNOWLEDGEMENTS

The authors acknowledge the support of the UK Department of the Environment and the former Severn Trent Region of the National Rivers Authority through Dr Janet Gronow and Mr Bob Harris, both now in the Environment Agency for England and Wales. Their assistance with this long-term project is acknowledged. The views expressed by the authors do not necessarily represent those of the former funding agencies.

REFERENCES

American Society of Civil Engineers (1990) Waste containment systems: construction, regulation and performance. Geotechnical Special Publication. No. 26. Bonaparte, R. (Ed). ASCE, New York.

Beaven & Powrie (1995) Hydrogeological and geotechnical properties of refuse using a large scale compression cell. In: *Proc. Sardinia '95 Fifth Int. Landfill Symposium. Cagliari, Sardinia*

Brune, M., Ramke, H.G., Collins, H.J. & Hanert, H.H. (1991) Incrustation processes in drainage systems of sanitary landfills. *Proc. Third International Landfill Symposium, Cagliari, Sardinia.* 1. 999-1035.

Colucci, P. & Lavagnolo, M.C. (1995) Three years field experience in electrical control of synthetic landfill liners. 437-452. In: *Proc. Sardinia '95 Fifth Int. Landfill Symposium. Cagliari, Sardinia*

DoE (1995) Waste Management Paper 26B: Landfill design, construction and operational practice. HMSO, London.

DoE (1996) Long-term monitoring of non-contained landfills: Burntstump and Gorsethorpe on the Sherwood Sandstone (Lewin, K., Young, C.P., Blakey, N.C., Sims, P. & Reynolds, P) Published DoE Report - CWM 139/96.

Giroud, J.P. & Bonaparte, R. (1989) Leakage through liners constructed with geomembranes - Part 1. Geomembrane Liners. *Geotextiles and Geomembranes*, 8(2), 27-67.

Harris, R.C. & Lowe, D.R. (1984) Changes in the organic fraction of leachate from two domestic refuse sites on the Sherwood Sandstone, Nottinghamshire. *Q. J. Eng. Geol.*, 17(1), 57-69.

Knox, K (1990) The relationship between leachate and gas. 367-402 In: Richards, G.E. and Alston. Y.R (Eds) *Proc. Int. Conf. on Landfill Gas. Energy and Environment '90.* Harwell Laboratory, Oxon.

The role and limitations of groundwater vulnerability maps in evaluating groundwater pollution hazard beneath contaminated land

Melinda A. Lewis, Marianne E. Stuart & Nick S. Robins
Hydrogeology Group, British Geological Survey, Wallingford, UK

Ian R. Davey
Environment Agency, Thames Region, Reading, UK

ABSTRACT: Groundwater vulnerability maps are currently being produced for the UK as a tool to aid decision making regarding land use. The maps classify the hazard to groundwater in an underlying aquifer posed by a contaminant load on the ground surface. Their role in assessing the potential impact of contaminated land on groundwater is reviewed.

1 INTRODUCTION

Contaminated land is a legacy from past anthropogenic activity. Although most such land is located in urban industrial areas, activities such as mining or military use have taken place in otherwise rural areas.

The groundwater vulnerability maps which are currently being prepared for large parts of England, Scotland and Wales can be used to assess the potential impact of contaminated land on nearby groundwater resources as well as for the resiting of potentially polluting activities. To date, small scale maps have been prepared for England and Wales (NRA, 1992), Scotland (BGS, 1995) and Northern Ireland (DoENI, 1994). In addition a series of larger scale maps, at 1: 100 000 scale maps are being prepared for the whole of England and Wales and for parts of Scotland. The maps zone the soil and geological horizons of the unsaturated zone to assess the vulnerability of groundwater to pollution from the land surface.

Where contaminated land overlies low permeability strata, groundwater is unlikely to be contaminated due to the low transmissive potential of the strata but runoff provides a route to surface water. However, some contaminants may pollute even low permeability strata given sufficient time. Where aquifers occur at or near the surface, the effect of contaminated land on groundwater quality is a function of the type of contaminant, whether the contamination occurred at or below the surface, the soil type, the superficial and underlying geology (eg a carbonate aquifer may respond differently from a quartzose aquifer) and the nature and thickness of the unsaturated zone. In

particular the degree of fracturing will have a profound impact on groundwater vulnerability.

2 THE VULNERABILITY MAPS

Vrba and Zaporozec (1994) defined groundwater vulnerability as an intrinsic property of a groundwater system that depends on the sensitivity of that system to human and/or natural impacts. They further subdivided it into intrinsic/natural vulnerability which is solely a hydrogeological function, and specific/integrated vulnerability which also takes account of land use and type of contaminant. Groundwater vulnerability maps are used to indicate the spatial variability of groundwater vulnerability assessments.

The UK vulnerability maps are based solely on the properties of the soil and underlying rock. They classify the risk posed by a contaminant load applied at the ground surface, but they are intrinsic maps that do not show the location of contaminant sources. The maps can easily be used by non-specialists such as planners and the insurance industry. The classification provides an assessment of the physical and chemical characteristics of the soil, which is overlain on the geology and which is itself divided up according to lithology and permeability. In this way, seven classes of groundwater vulnerability have been defined (Palmer et al, 1995). The maps for England and Wales form a component part of the Environment Agency's Policy and Practice for the Protection of Groundwater (NRA, 1992), which defines the potentially polluting practices which are admissible on land of each class, although this cannot be specified retrospectively.

3 VULNERABILITY CLASSIFICATION

The soil zone is important due to its ability to adsorb and attenuate surface derived pollutants (Palmer and Lewis, in press). The soil zone, in which plants may root, is generally 1.5 to 2 m thick and is derived from the interaction of climate, soil organisms, vegetation and geology. It is the most chemically and biologically active part of the unsaturated zone. Organic material and clay-organo complexes can attenuate heavy metals and organic compounds percolating downwards. Soil may also contain physical inhibitors to vertical transport such as hard pans and dense, clay-rich layers.

The distribution of soil classes in the UK is based on soil texture, depth and duration of water logging, and the underlying rock type. The many soil series so derived (SSE&W, 1983) can be grouped according to their leaching potential (which in turn is a function of their texture, organic content, presence of raw peaty topsoils and low permeability layers, wetness and stoniness) which describes the relative rate of pollutant migration through the soil as high, intermediate or low. Built-up areas and mineral workings where the soil zone may have been removed or disturbed are classified as having high leaching potential, until site investigation shows otherwise.

The geological characteristics beneath the soil zone enable a classification to be made between highly permeable, moderately permeable and weakly permeable formations, equivalent to major, minor and non-aquifers on the Environment Agency maps. The highly permeable formations may have significant secondary permeability and include the Chalk and the Permo-Triassic aquifers. Moderately permeable formations may also be fractured but with a lower primary permeability, eg the Millstone Grit, they also include variably permeable formations, eg the Crag and some unconsolidated Quaternary strata. The weakly permeable formations include the Jurassic clays, the Mercia Mudstone Group and most Lower Palaeozoic strata.

The lithology and integrity of superficial strata may vary over short distances. Low permeability cover, such as till, is generally depicted by a stipple on the maps wherever it occurs over highly or moderately permeable aquifers (elsewhere it is not shown). The stipple indicates that the groundwater in the formation below the till may be protected if the cover is intact, and of adequate thickness, normally taken as greater than 5 m. In a few areas where detailed information is available (eg parts of Yorkshire and Lancashire), the thickness of the low permeability cover is taken into consideration when zoning the bedrock aquifer.

4 POLLUTANT CHARACTERISTICS

Land and underlying groundwater may become contaminated by accidental spillage such as leaking oil tanks, deliberate disposal as in landfill (particularly old unlined sites) as well as everyday activities such as disposal of run-off to soakaways. Contamination may arise at a range of sites, from animal processing through chemical and engineering works, to mines, landfills, Ministry of Defence property and hospitals as well as from the urban or agricultural use of pesticides.

Contamination becomes of concern where substances, either naturally occurring or alien to the environment, are present in concentrations which could be harmful to human or animal health or the built or natural environment. Very low concentrations of toxic or hazardous substances may be all that is required to pose risks. Where risks are significant and there is a pathway for contaminants to reach receptors, it will be possible to designate sites formally as contaminated, after the Environment Act (DoE, 1995) is implemented. Receptors may include important aquifers, such as those classified as highly permeable on vulnerability maps, as well as specific boreholes and springs.

The impact of contaminants can be moderated in the sub-surface environment by a variety of mechanisms: physico-chemical processes such as sorption onto natural organic materials or clays, chemical precipitation, oxidation/reduction reactions; and degradation, chemically or biologically mediated, to simple non-toxic compounds. These processes are most active in the soil zone where, for example, concentrations of organic material and micro-organisms are high and where sufficient oxygen and water are likely to be available. Below the soil zone the rates at which these processes take place are much reduced.

Table 1 summarises the physico-chemical characteristics of key groups of contaminants as well as .chloride and nitrate. The relative acceptable concentrations of the contaminants in potable water supply, the prime use of groundwater, is shown for comparison.

At various engineering and chemical manufacturing sites, spillage or disposal of liquids may have taken place to the ground surface, when the need for care was less understood than it is now.

In the past, volatile organic solvents were disposed of by spreading over land to evaporate. However, much was often lost to the ground and underlying groundwater, depending on the nature of the soils and underlying strata. At former gas works, iron oxides, used to remove cyanide, once spent, would often be

Table 1.   Physico-chemical characteristics of potential subsurface pollutants.

Pollutant	Aqueous solubility	Potential for NAPL* formation	Controlled by pH/Eh	Attenuated/ sorbed in soil zone	Persistent in subsurface	Acceptable concentrations in potable water
chloride	high	no	no	no	yes	low-moderate
nitrate	high	no	no	consumed by plants	yes where aerobic	low-moderate
heavy metals	low	no	yes	yes	yes	very low
hydrocarbons	low	yes	no	yes	varies	trace
chlorinated solvents	low	yes	no	yes	yes	trace-very low
pesticides	low	no	no	yes	varies	trace
pathogens	-	no	-	yes	varies	none
radionuclides	varies	no	yes	yes	yes	trace

*NAPL   non-aqueous phase liquids

spread out to "rejuvenate" before reuse or be disposed of to ground. In some cases liquors containing ammoniacal nitrogen, sulphate, phenols and tars were also discharged on site. Although the organic fraction may be susceptible to biological degradation and ammoniacal nitrogen may be sorbed on soils, often the natural attenuation capacity of the soils may have been exceeded.

Industry was commonly developed in low-lying floodplains, as is the case along the River Lee in north London. Here, the site level was often built up with wastes such as ash. The potential exists to leach out contaminants including metals, but clayey alluvial soils can reduce the contamination hazard to underlying groundwater.

5 DISCUSSION

The British groundwater vulnerability maps are designed primarily as a tool to help planners to identify areas where groundwater is likely to be at risk.

Local authorities will find them useful in considering their strategy for classifying contaminated land, as required under the Environment Act (DoE, 1995). In areas such as around Luton, where there is only a thin soil cover over the Chalk aquifer, the maps show a high vulnerability and it is likely that any contaminants present will have permeated deep into the ground.

The maps indicate the vulnerability of groundwater from diffuse contaminants in areas where the soil is intact and are therefore of most use in assessing the potential impact from contaminants spread on the ground. These include the use of nitrate fertilizers or pesticides in agriculture and farm and sewage sludges or other wastes for agricultural or ecological benefit.

The maps can also be used to consider the impact of more discrete or point sources which may give rise to contaminated land. However their value is more limited in these situations, particularly if the soil has been removed or disturbed, if contamination occurs beneath the soil layer or there is no unsaturated zone.

For example where leakage occurs from underground installations, such as storage tanks and associated pipework beneath the soil, the contaminants bypass the most active attenuation zone. It is believed that around 30% of underground storage facilities, such as petrol filling stations, leak.

In quarries the soil zone and possibly much of the unsaturated zone have been removed. The remaining strata may afford little attenuation to leachate which seeps out. This is the case in the Vale of St Albans sand and gravel belt, in Hertfordshire to the north of London, where the soils and near surface glacial drift provide considerable protection to the underlying Chalk aquifer, except where this is exposed through quarrying. Nevertheless, the maps still indicate the importance of the underlying aquifer in terms of permeability.

The maps need to be used in conjunction with other information, such as the depth to groundwater and the presence nearby of groundwater abstraction boreholes. Although they are helpful in preliminary assessment/ planning, for detailed evaluation, site investigations will be required in all contaminated land studies.

6 CONCLUSION

Groundwater vulnerability maps are therefore of most use:-
- for the broad scale classification of risk for planning purposes
- where the soil is intact
- where the contaminant load is a diffuse pollutant.

They are of limited use:-
- in urban areas, where no in-situ soil is present
- where the loss or discharge of contaminants takes place beneath the soil
- where landfilling is to quarries.

ACKNOWLEDGEMENTS: The authors are grateful for discussions with their respective colleagues, particularly Adrian Lawrence. The paper is published by permission of the Director, British Geological Survey (NERC). The views expressed in this paper are those of the authors and do not necessarily represent those of the Environment Agency.

REFERENCES

BGS 1995. *Groundwater Vulnerability Map of Scotland*, 1: 625 000 scale. Edinburgh, British Geological Survey.

DoE 1995. *The Environment Act* 1995. London, Department of the Environment.

DoENI 1994. *Groundwater Vulnerability Map of Northern Ireland*. Belfast, Department of the Environment for Northern Ireland.

NRA 1992. *Policy and Practice for the Protection of Groundwater*. Bristol, National Rivers Authority.

Palmer, R.C. & M.A. Lewis in press. Groundwater vulnerability: the UK perspective. In: *Groundwater pollution, aquifer recharge and vulnerability*, Geological Society Special Publication.

Palmer, R.C., I.P. Holman, N.S. Robins, & M.A. Lewis 1995. *Guide to groundwater vulnerability mapping in England and Wales*. London, HMSO for NRA.

SSE&W 1983. *Legend for the 1:250 000 scale soil map of England and Wales*. Silsoe, Soil Survey of England and Wales.

Vrba, J. & A. Zaporozec (Eds) 1994. Guidebook on mapping groundwater vulnerability. *International Contributions to Hydrogeology*, 16.

The role of Indian hydrogeologists in providing drinking water for the urban poor

S. D. Limaye
Groundwater Institute, Sadashiv Peth, Poona-Pune, India

ABSTRACT: Urban residents in India usually receive their drinking water supply from municipal water supply network. However, influx of the rural population into urban areas in search of employment·has resulted in rapid and unplanned growth of peri-urban settlements and slums, which are not connected to the water supply network. Surface water sources are polluted and cannot be used for drinking. Groundwater is also polluted to some degree due to seepage from septic tanks, peri-urban industrial effluents and irrigated farms. Hydrogeologists cannot exercise control over urban planning or the growth of slums. However, they can still help the urban poor and slum dwellers by locating proper sites for drinking water bore wells or dug wells, which would yield an adequate quantity of drinking water of acceptable quality.

1 INTRODUCTION

According to the 1991 census, 25.7 percent of India's population lived in the urban and peri-urban areas, producing about 60 percent of national wealth. By the year 2015, about 50 percent of India's population could be living in cities. Such rapid and unplanned urbanization brings with it the problems of water supply and sanitation, waste disposal, housing, traffic congestion, pollution of air, water and land, and an unsafe social and cultural environment. These problems virtually bring the cities to the verge of 'unsustainability'. Development policies have so far focussed on 'economic' growth without much regard to the urban environment.

The current populations of seven major cities in India are shown in Table 1. About 50 per cent of this population lives in hutments or slums. A slum may be defined as a predominantly residential area where the dwellings are dilapidated, overcrowded, unsafe, and without proper ventilation, light, water supply and sanitation facilities; resulting in living conditions which are detrimental to the safety, health and morals of the dwellers. Hydrogeologists are able to tackle just one of the problems: safe water supply for drinking.

The source of water supply to urban areas is often a perennial river, a lake, a reservoir or a canal. Raw water from such a surface source is taken to a water

Table 1. Current populations of major Indian cities

City	Population (millions)
Bombay	12.5
Calcutta	1 1.0
New Delhi	8.4
Madras	5.4
Hyderabad	4.3
Bangalore	4. 1
Poona (Pune)	2.5

treatment plant and then distributed to various sectors through the municipal network. As the quality of raw water deteriorates, water treatment becomes more and more expensive. There is no separate network for drinking water supply. The quality of 5 to 10 litres or so of drinking water per person per day is thus the same as the quality of about 100 litres of water supplied for non-potable uses, in the same pipeline. The quality of drinking water, therefore, can only reach a standard that is manageable and affordable to the municipal authorities and acceptable to the citizens, who in turn are reluctant to pay higher water rates.

In most Indian cities, water supply is available for 2 to 4 hours in the morning and 2 to 4 hours in the evening. In the summer season, the hours of supply can be even less than this. The quality of raw water is also poorer in summer because there is less fresh water in the river or canal to dilute pollutants. It is a common practice in buildings, houses and apartment complexes to provide water storage facilities at ground level, on the roof or terrace and even in the lofts in kitchens and toilets. As the water pressure is low, water has to be pumped from ground level storage to the tank on the roof or terrace. In some houses and apartments, the municipal supply is augmented by drilling a bore. Groundwater is pumped into the ground level storage tank, where it mixes with the municipal water, because the plumbing in the house or apartment does not provide a separate line for groundwater. Many apartment dwellers therefore, boil a few litres of water every day for drinking purpose or install filters and small ultraviolet (u-v) disinfection units. Even where the groundwater is not mixed with municipal supply, many people who do not trust the quality of municipal tap water prefer to boil their drinking water or use a u-v unit. If this is the situation for the middle class, one may imagine the conditions of water supply for the urban poor, who have no access or remote access to water from the municipal system and who depend upon raw surface water or groundwater for their domestic water use.

2 URBAN PLANNING AND PROBLEMS

The town planning department of the government prepares long term master plans or schemes of growth of towns and cities by zoning the urban and peri-urban lands into residential areas, industrial areas, green belts, and agricultural areas. Based on this zoning, the municipal authorities or the civic bodies prepare development plans for the areas within the extended city limits. The city limits themselves expand every few years due to the growth of population and industries. The development plan takes into consideration the required civic amenities for residential and industrial zones, such as the water supply, drainage, electricity, roads, schools, hospitals, parks, markets, open spaces, playgrounds, and cinema halls. Activities like acquisition of land for public purposes, reservation of land for specific use, restricting industrial growth in some areas, development of new industrial zones, monitoring the quality of industrial effluent water, and putting a ceiling on the maximum holding of residential land per family, are initiated as a part of the urban planning process.

In practice, however, this idealised development planning scenario is marred by several factors such as, (a) the uncontrolled growth of the urban population as a result of the exodus of job seekers from rural areas to urban and peri-urban areas; (b) a lack of coordination between the various departments involved; (c) a lack of funds for providing the planned civic amenities; (d) the low educational status of the majority of the elected representatives on the civic bodies and their inability to foresee and tackle civic problems; and most importantly (e) corruption at all levels. The greater the number of rules and regulations, the greater is the corruption.

Many decisions taken by the officers of government and civic bodies have a direct bearing on the quality of urban life. These decisions regarding, for example, laying of new water supply and drainage lines, reservation and dereservation of lands for public use, change of land use from agriculture to residential or industrial use, monitoring the quality of effluent water from certain industries, giving exemption from the provisions of the urban land ceiling act to certain parties having large vacant plots in urban areas, allowing uncontrolled growth of slums on government lands and later on undertaking slum clearance activities, and many such topics are subject to corrupt practices. Considering that urban land prices have increased 50 to 500 times within the last 20 years, these decisions affect transactions involving millions of rupees and are often controlled by nontechnical, external influences. The technical opinions of geoscientists, engineers and architects do not play any significant role in such decision making (Limaye 1993).

As a result of this, the planned growth of cities becomes a distant dream. In real life, cities, especially the big cities, are suffocating from polluted air and water, crowded streets, packed buses and trains, traffic jams, and shrinking open spaces due to encroachments. Hydrogeologists from government departments, universities, private firms and non-governmental organizations (NGOs), have to work in this environment and use their skills to provide safe drinking water to millions of urban poor; the most neglected and unfortunate sector of the urban population, who often live in precarious conditions on degraded, low priority lands on hill slopes or flood plains.

3 WATER SOURCES AND THE HYDRO-GEOLOGIST

Surface water sources near urban areas are usually polluted to some extent. Water intakes of many cities are located on rivers, streams or canals, on the upstream side of the urban area. After treatment, the water is supplied to residents and industries through the municipal distribution network. This in turn generates a large volume of industrial and domestic waste water which is sometimes treated at the effluent or sewage treatment plants and returned to the lower reaches of the valley of the same river or stream. For several kilometres downstream from the urban area, the river water is highly polluted because the level of treatment at the sewage or effluent treatment plants in the urban area depends on the technical, managerial and financial capability of the civic body and the industries and also on their tendency to bypass environmental regulations. In addition, storm water runoff from urban areas can also add highly polluted water to the river.

When a surface water source such as river, a stream or a canal flows close to a slum area, the slum dwellers use that water for bathing, washing clothes and for animals; and sometimes even for drinking, if the slum has not been provided with community taps from the municipal water system. When such slums are located on the upstream side of the city, the water becomes highly polluted even before it reaches the municipal water pumping station. For example, the city of Poona (Pune) in western India, with a population of about 2.5 million, pumps its raw water from a canal, which brings water from a major dam 10 km away. Slums have developed at many places along this canal. This has often resulted in an increase in E-Coli per 100 ml, from about 5 M.P.N. at the head of the canal near the dam, to about 2500 M.P.N. at the raw water pumping station. It is obvious that slums should be removed from the vicinity of the canal or that the city should bring its raw water in a pipeline from the dam. However, this has not been possible for the reasons stated in the previous section.

Industries located on the upstream side of the pumping station also affect the quality of raw water. An increase in dissolved organic compounds in raw water leads to the formation of carcinogenic halogenated organics after the pre and post-filter chlorination at the city's water treatment plant. Such technical considerations, however, do not affect decisions such as the location of the industrial zone, which are often more strongly influenced by vested commercial interests. As widely reported in this volume, groundwater in urban areas receives pollution from leakages in sewers, waste water and effluent lines, septic tanks, underground storage of chemicals and petroleum products, from leachates from solid waste deposits and landfills, and from percolation from chemical spills, storm water drains and streams. It is bad policy to locate industries, landfills or dwellings with septic tanks in the recharge area of the aquifer.

In order to minimize the effects of shallow percolation on borewell water in hard rock areas, steel or PVC casing is provided for the first 6 m depth or up to 3 m below the top of hard rock, whichever is deeper. Borewells are also located in the upgradient direction from nearby sources of pollution i.e. on a higher level than the slum areas, wherever possible. One borewell of 150 mm diameter and of about 60 to 100 m depth, with a hand pump installed on it, is usually provided for 200 to 250 dwellers. The foot valve, piston and cylinder assembly of the hand pump are usually placed at a depth of about 40 m below the ground level.

Hydrogeologists, working with government departments, universities, consulting firms and NGOs, can help to solve the drinking water problem of slum dwellers or the urban poor in the following ways:

(a) In slum areas where groundwater is likely to be available, borewells should be drilled with adequate length of casing pipe and a hand pump should be installed. The borewell should be about a hundred metres away from the slum area, in the upgradient direction of groundwater flow.

(b) In some cases, groundwater is not likely to be available in adequate quantity, as the hard and massive nature of the underlying rock provides neither adequate porosity or permeability. In this case, if there is a surface stream nearby, a dug well located in the sandy alluvium on the stream bank usually gives filtered water from the polluted surface water in the stream. The well can be regularly dosed with bleaching powder.

(c) In a few cases where groundwater and surface water are both absent, the only feasible solution is to connect the municipal water system to the slum area and provide a few public water taps. Funds which otherwise might be wasted on dry drilling or digging, can fruitfully be used, on the hydrogeologist's recommendation, for laying a pipeline.

4 CONCLUSIONS

(a) Geoscientists/hydrogeologists have virtually no control over urban land use planning or the extensive growth of slums in urban and peri-urban areas. However, they should always submit technical opinions and reports when required by the planners, politicians and policy makers, hoping that some day the planning process will be modified, learning from earlier mistakes.

(b) At local level, they are certainly in a position to help the urban poor or slum dwellers by digging or drilling drinking water wells or borewells for them at proper locations.

(c) For the long term benefits, hydrogeologists with the help of active NGOs, can educate slum dwellers about water and health; write articles in local newspapers on water pollution; and give lectures in schools about improving the urban environment.

(d) Although the paper is based on the experience in hard rock terrain in India, hydrogeologists from other developing countries may also have similar experience.

REFERENCES

Limaye, S.D. (1993) Changes in land use pattern and the role of geoscientists in developing countries. *Proc. Int. Symp. on Ecology and Landscape Management in Sri Lanka.* 443-446. Margraf Scientific Books, Weikersheim, Germany.

A groundwater information system as a tool for environmental management in Rotterdam

A. Molenaar & A. B. Roeloffzen
City of Rotterdam, Department of Environmental Policy, Netherlands

A. H. M. Pepels
City of Rotterdam, Environmental Engineering Division, Netherlands

J. M. A. Streng
City of Rotterdam, Geotechnical Engineering Division, Netherlands

H. Uil
TNO, Institute of Applied Geoscience, Delft, Netherlands

ABSTRACT: In the urban area of Rotterdam, situated in the western part of the Netherlands, it is unclear to what degree the phreatic and deep aquifers are contaminated and which groundwater flow patterns control the transport of contaminants. More insight into patterns and rates of contamination and transportation is desired to support several environmental management issues. The main issue is prioritization of contaminated sites for research and treatment. Therefore a computer-based Groundwater Information system for Rotterdam (GIRO) using the REGIS[PRO] system will be made operational to support the decision making process for environmental policy and groundwater management in the Rotterdam area. Based on a regional groundwater survey, the existing digitized information has been assessed and entered into a database in 1996. During this first phase a conceptual model has been developed. In the second phase (1997), additional non-digitized data and measurements will be added to the database and further area-specific detailing and modelling will be developed. The managerial interest in urban groundwater information is increasing rapidly in the Netherlands. In particular, the complicating anthropogenic influences are a challenging new aspect in the modelling process. In this framework, GIRO is seen as an important tool for more integral environmental management policy in the Rotterdam area.

1 INTRODUCTION

1.1 *The first programme in 1990-1994*

In 1990 a first study was initiated to describe the quality of the fresh groundwater in the Pleistocene aquifer (Pepels & van Leeuwen, 1994). The aim was to obtain a general idea of the degree of pollution in this "first" aquifer, the main contaminating sources (river, contaminated sites), and its suitability for drinking water in emergency situations. As funding was limited, it was decided to sample 30 existing wells which were in use for different purposes: fire and process water supply and emergency drinking water wells. As several wells were drilled more then 50 years ago, the presence of oils and PAHs in the groundwater samples indicated the use of creosoted casings, as no other source of pollution appeared to give a reasonable explanation. Also the well sampling network was not dense enough, so conclusive results were not obtainable. A more detailed study, based on modelling of groundwater flow patterns and more data-input, was considered necessary, and forms the background requirement of the present work.

1.2 *Redefinition of management needs*

In 1994 the Soil Protection Act was revised and updated with a Soil Remediaton paragraph. As severe shortages in finance for decontamination works had become obvious, the multifunctional approach was considered of secondary importance to prioritization of sites for treatment. Priority will not only be based on soil use, but also on spreading rates of contaminants by groundwater flow. For treated contaminated sites, aftercare may require monitoring of the local groundwater quality. Subsequently, a pre-assessment of the groundwater quality evolution in the area is necessary.

In the second Rotterdam Environmental Policy Plan of 1995 more emphasis was placed on prevention of soil pollution. Avoiding the spread of contaminants in the soil is a key issue in the framework of the sustainable use of urban groundwater. This applies especially to the deeper aquifers, which should be kept as clean as possible, so that they can fulfil all their actual and potential functions.

These include drinking water in case of emergency, fire and process water and ecological functions in the

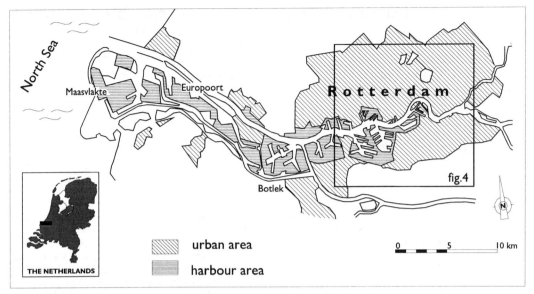

Figure 1. Location of the study area in the Netherlands (also showing the section for Figure 4.)

ecosystems in the polders which depend on groundwater. Nature protection and avoidance of desiccation of the soil becomes more urgent, as the urbanization process in the region progresses. Before 2010 another 53,000 houses need to be built, partially in new urban areas.

It is estimated that in the industrial, harbour and old urban areas more than 20,000 potential point sources of pollution are present. Of particular concern are those point-source sites contaminating the deeper aquifers, such as gasworks sites, waste disposal sites, galvanizing and creosote plants and petrochemical industries. It is suspected that the soil remediation process in the urban area of Rotterdam does not measure up to the speed with which the pollution is spread by groundwater flow. Thus there is an urgent need for linking prioritization of soil remediation to the nature and speed of contaminated groundwater flow. Essential for prioritization are issues of: a) whether or not sites are situated in "vulnerable" areas, b) where infiltration is combined with high groundwater flow rates, c) the location of sandy permeable Holocene cover and d) abstraction wells or seepage areas.

It is clear that these developments in soil policy have stimulated the implementation of a Groundwater Information System (GIRO), based on the REGIS[PRO]-software. The resulting regional groundwater survey should support the decision making process of environmental and groundwater management in the Rotterdam area (Diependaal & Molenaar, 1995).

The main objective of the survey is to gain more insight into spreading rates of contaminants in the deeper (especially "first") aquifer(s), e.g. contamination sources and effects on "vulnerable targets", which can be related to the spreading process. This knowledge should form the basis for area-specific prioritization for treatment and aftercare of contaminated sites and development of other strategic policy management tools.

Thus a flexible and multi-purpose Groundwater Information System is needed.

1.3 *Participants in the project*

This study can only be conducted by close cooperation between several interested parties from the field of groundwater policy. Groundwater modelling must be done by specialists. Collection of data relies on existing databases of the Engineering Departments of Public Works itself and other Institutes collecting data nation-wide (TNO Delft, Dutch Geologic Service). The following participants are working on the project:

- Public Works of Rotterdam (Department of Environmental Policy as well as the Environmental and Geotechnical Engineering Offices);
- The Provincial Government of Zuid-Holland (Department for Water and Environment);
- The Regional Drinking Water Company (Waterbedrijf Europoort);
- TNO Delft, Institute of Applied Geoscience.
- To be invited: Foundation of Companies in the Europoort-Botlek harbour area (Stichting EBB).

2 STUDY AREA AND METHODOLOGY

2.1 *Study area*

The study area includes the city of Rotterdam, its harbour area and surrounding urban and industrial areas in nearby towns along the mouths of the Rivers Maas and Rhine (Figure 1). The area has a population of more than one million people, and includes the largest port in the world. It is situated in the transition zone of marine and fluvial deposits, combined with peat formation. A coastal dune landscape borders the marine clay polders, which subsequently changes gradually into a peat landscape north-east of Rotterdam. As most of the peat has been excavated and the resulting lakes reclaimed, deep clay/peat polders have great impact on the groundwater flow pattern of the region.

The subsurface of the Rotterdam area can be described roughly as a sandy matrix with clayey intercalations (Figure 2). As the region is strongly urbanized, in general an anthropogenic sandy layer of 0 to 10 m (phreatic aquifer) is overlaying a Holocene cover of mostly peats and clays, being 10 to 25 m thick. Along the river banks and in the coastal dune areas the Holocene cover is much more sandy, so the phreatic aquifer may be up to 30 m thick. Under the Holocene cover a Pleistocene sandy aquifer of 10 to 20 m is present. The fresh to brackish groundwater in this "first" aquifer is the main subject of the study. Under loamy deposits (5 to 40 m thick) a second saline aquifer is present of 50 to 100 m thickness.

2.2 *Project management*

For management reasons, the project is to be carried out in three parts, schematically presented in Figure 3.

Phase I deals with the adaptation of REGIS[PRO] for the Rotterdam region (REGIS[Rotterdam]) and the importation of digitized data, being available in different information systems such as OLGA (On-Line Groundwater-Archive), and those of Public Works Rotterdam (Streng et al, 1996).

HYDROLOGICAL SPECIFICATIONS	LITHOLOGY	THICKNESS in meters
phreatic layer	sandy anthropogenic	0 - 10
aquitard (poorly permeable)	Holocene peat/clay (along coast more sandy)	10 - 25
"FIRST" AQUIFER	Pleistocene sandy deposits	10 - 20
aquitard (poorly permeable)	Pleistocene loamy deposits	5 - 40
"SECOND" AQUIFER	Pleistocene sandy deposits	50 - 100

Figure 2. General hydrogeological cross-section of the Rotterdam area.

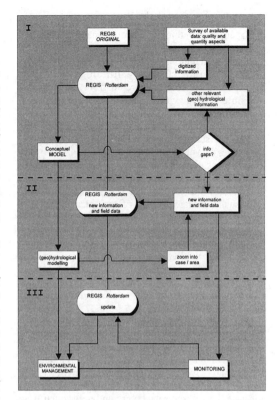

Figure 3. Project management scheme.

Based on this adapted model and the imported data a first attempt was made to model the regional groundwater system, to produce different information layers, and to make a list of information gaps. Then additional non-digitized information, needed to develop the conceptual model in more detail, will be fed into the database. It will be crucial to determine which information gaps should be closed as priority; less cost-effective gaps will not be closed.

In phase II additional data from new drilled sampling wells will be collected. The need for this information will be assessed from the results of phase I on the basis of cost-effectiveness. Also further area-orientated detailing and modelling will occur. This phase should be concluded by formulation of management recommendations and area-specific prioritization for soil sanitation projects.

In phase III a network of sampling wells may be installed, if considered necessary to support monitoring and policy management decisions.

2.3 *Information system design and modelling*

The REGIS model is the central part of the information system. REGIS is an interactive REgional

(Geo)hydrological Information System for water management, containing essential manipulative and interpretative features for evaluating (geo)hydrological situations on a regional scale (TNO, 1996). The model can be generated from the lithology and other hydrogeological data interpreted from investigation boreholes. Also within REGIS the geographical Information System ARC/INFO is implemented. All relevant data are imported into the system. These include the subsurface model for the study area and time series data of groundwater levels and groundwater quality measurements.

By means of interpolation, a threedimensional model of the subsoil was constructed. The information system can visualize the lateral extent of geological formations, including contour plots of layer thickness. Vertical cross-sections in any direction can also be constructed. Measuring points for groundwater levels and groundwater quality can be selected by means of indicating them on the display screen or by means of database queries, using Structured Query Language (SQL-statements) and by absolute depth or geohydrological layer.

One of the ultimate goals of the study, that of determining the priority sequence for remediation of polluted sites, will be determined at a sub-regional scale by means of overlay techniques available as a standard analytical tool within the GIS-environment of REGIS. Several basic thematic layers (maps) will be used to construct new composite layers and subsequently to produce the final (target) layer in the system (Table 1). Most of the basic information layers were generated within the system using the input data. Some others were derived from available national data-banks, such as the surface elevation map and the surface water level map.

The multi-layer-model is based on the principle: *"source (of soil contamination) - pathway (by groundwater flow) - effect on target (e.g. vulnerable object)"*.
Tentative definitions have been developed for:
- the vulnerability of the aquifer underlying the Holocene aquitard;
- the threat posed to the quality of the water in the aquifer by polluted sites.

3 PRELIMINARY RESULTS

3.1 *Hydrogeology*

The general groundwater flow pattern in the study area shows infiltration through the base of the river Nieuwe Maas and through the Holocene aquitard in areas where this layer appears to be relatively permeable. Also in some higher parts of the inner city little infiltration occurs. Caused by an artificial low groundwater level, upward seepage occurs in the deep polder areas in the north and south (Figure 4). Additionally in the city of Delft, northwest of Rotterdam, an industrial process water abstraction from the first aquifer has a considerable but decreasing impact on the flow pattern. Horizontal flow through the aquifer is the link between the infiltration areas and the seepage/abstraction areas.

The Holocene aquitard, overlying the phreatic aquifer plays an important role in determining the vulnerability of the groundwater in the 'first' aquifer. As this aquitard consists mainly of clay and peat layers, it has a high hydraulic resistance and thus tends to inhibit the downward movement of contaminated groundwater. Above this, both peat and clay have a high adsorption capacity, causing additional retardation for most contaminants.

Table 1. Structure of the multi-layer-model.

BASIC INFORMATION LAYERS	COMPOSITE LAYERS	TARGET LAYER
◆ thickness of sand layers ◆ thickness of peat layers ◆ thickness of clay layers ◆ anthropogenic activities (e.g. vertical drainage)	◆ hydraulic resistance of anthropogenic and holocene cover	
◆ surface elevation ◆ surface water levels in hydrological polder units ◆ groundwater level contour pattern ◆ groundwater quality	◆ map of seepage-infiltration areas ◆ groundwater flow pattern ◆ contamination of the aquifers	◆ prioritization on geographical basis
◆ actual point-sources of contamination ◆ potential point-sources of contamination ◆ occupational history of urban areas	◆ geographical pattern of point-sources of contamination	
◆ vulnerable objects (e.g. nature reserves) ◆ strategic groundwater reserves	◆ typology of vulnerability to soil contamination	

3.2 *Other results*

Preliminary analysis of these data shows that, within the municipal boundaries of Rotterdam, there is abundant information available about the groundwater system. However, most of this information has been collected as part of soil pollution surveys. Using data for a limited number of contaminants (with a sufficiently even distribution over the study area), the current "background quality" of groundwater in the study area has been provisionally characterized. The available infor-mation provides a sound basis for the construction of a simulation model for the research area, allowing a more detailed analysis of flow systems. Several information layers have been produced to determine the spatial prioritization of remediation sites (Table 1). Other relevant products are:

- cross-sections of geologic formations;
- maps with average contour levels of the first aquifer in different periods in the years 1984-1997, see Figure 4.
- maps with groundwater salinity contours in the first and second aquifer;
- a distribution map of point sources;
- distribution maps of measuring points for most relevant contaminants: heavy metals, PAHs, aromatics and ammonia;
- distribution maps of abstraction wells for process water, classified by abstraction volume per annum.

The contour maps of groundwater head have been constructed for the first aquifer by interpolation between the available observation points. From this map, combined with the surface water level maps and the subsurface model, the general groundwater flow pattern in the study area can be derived, both horizontally in the first aquifer and vertically in the Holocene aquitard.

3.3 *Preliminary conclusions and information gaps*

The preliminary report provides insight into the following interesting aspects:

- The REGIS[Rotterdam] system provides a useful tool for storage, manipulation, assessment and visualisation of groundwater data. Thus it is able to support strategic management decisions regarding environmental policy, e.g. soil pollution, based on assessment of groundwater characteristics.
- Sufficient quantitative data are available for the study area. However groundwater quality data are insufficient and not evenly distributed over the study area. Additional information is required to optimize the assessment of pollution levels and transport rates. Most available information has been collected as part of soil contamination surveys.

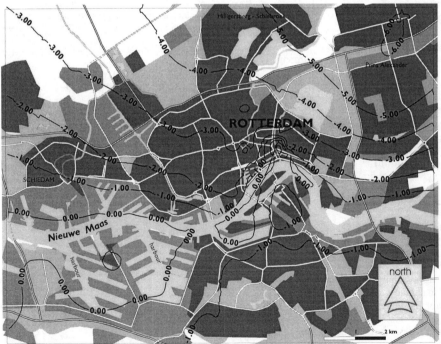

Figure 4. Pattern of groundwater level contours in meters related to mean sea level in winter 1995-1996 (the location of this part of Rotterdam is visualized in Figure 1.)

- From the results so far, it is known that the 'first' aquifer in the urban areas of Rotterdam is slightly to moderately polluted on a local scale with oils, PAHs and heavy metals.
- One of the main information gaps concerns the modifying effects of human activities in the urban area, such as:
  - manipulation of the natural groundwater levels, independent from surface water levels, by drain age systems, e.g. draining sewer systems;
  - the influence of vertical drainage systems (especially sand piles) and digging through the holocene cover (construction of tunnels etc.) on hydrogeological properties of the soil;
  - reduction of the precipitation surplus, because of the (semi-)impermeable cover by buildings and pavements.
- The inventory of point sources, potentially or actually contaminating the deep aquifer, is far from complete. In fact, most of it may be unknown, as only a few percent of all potential sources has been investigated so far. Additionally a groundwater quality map of the phreatic aquifer should be created so that its influence on the first aquifer may be better assessed.
- The available information is a sound basis for the construction of a simulation model of the research area, which will allow a more detailed analysis of groundwater flow systems in phase II of the study.

4 MANAGEMENT APPLICATIONS

Groundwater assessment in the urban area is a key factor for strategic developments in environmental policy, as Rotterdam is required to enforce the Soil Protection Act within her municipal boundaries. In the urban landscape, especially the multifunctionality of groundwater in aquifers is threatened. Only an integral approach may lead to correct prioritization of sites and appropriate preventative measures.

The Groundwater Information System provides a decision tool for both curative and preventative management strategies. The following objectives are to be addressed:
- prioritizing sites for exploratory soil survey or clean-up works;
- aftercare of landfill and remediated sites;
- planning of future land use (new urban areas);
- protection and restoration of ecosystems depending on groundwater;
- development of a preventative environmental policy and a monitoring strategy.

Dependent on available information, at first only an area-based management assessment is planned. Later, a more site-specific assessment can be performed to assist in prioritization.

In the Rotterdam region drinking water is produced from surface water, being extracted from the river Maas. However if a major emergency occurs, the groundwater in the first aquifer under the urban area may be a potential alternative source. Although an emergency drinking water supply is the responsibility of the city government, it is not clear who is responsible for the protection of the groundwater in the first aquifer. To address this issue, an integral approach and close cooperation with the Regional Drinking Water Company and Provincial Government is essential. Only then sustainable management, both qualitative and quantitative, of the urban groundwater reserves in the first aquifer can be achieved.

ACKNOWLEDGEMENTS

Thanks are offered to Joost Lankester and Govert van Gilst for their help with drawing figures and manipulation of the REGIS software.

REFERENCES

Diependaal, M.J. and A. Molenaar, 1995, *Integrale grondwater-verkenning stedelijk gebied regio Rotterdam; een strategisch beleidsvoorbereidend onderzoek*, Plan van Aanpak, Gemeentewerken Rotterdam, afdeling Milieubeleid, Rotterdam (in dutch).

Pepels, A. and J. van Leeuwen, 1994, *De kwaliteit van het diepe grondwater in Rotterdam*; eindrapportage, Gemeentewerken Rotterdam, Ingenieursbureau Geotechniek en Milieu, Rotterdam (in dutch).

Public Works Rotterdam, 1995, *Rotterdam Enivironmental* Policy *Plan II*

Streng, J., A.H.M. Pepels and H. Uil, 1996, *Integrale grondwater-verkenning stadsregio Rotterdam; fase Ia: Inventarisatie en karakterisatie, Gemeentewerken Rotterdam*, Ingenieursbureaus Geotechniek en Milieu / TNO Delft, Grondwater en Geo-Energie, Rotterdam/Delft (in dutch).

TNO, 1996, REGIS, Regional *Geohydrological Information System*, TNO, Institute of Applied Geo-science, Delft.

Groundwater management in Middle Valdarno urban area, Italy

C. Morosi & F. Landini
CONSIAG, Consorzio Intercomunale Acqua Gas e Pubblici Servizi, Prato, Italy

ABSTRACT: Progressive depletion and pollution of the groundwater supplying many of the Middle Valdarno aqueducts resulted from the lack of correct groundwater management during the development of civil and industrial settlements which took place in this area between 1960 and 1990. Laws issued in recent years will raise the quality of the Italian water service to the standards of other European countries enabling the planning and construction of plants for the recovery and optimization of the aqueduct and sewer networks as well as the recovery in quality and quantity of groundwater resources. Two significant case histories concerning particularly relevant areas are described here.

1 ITALIAN WATER REGULATIONS

1.1 *National laws*

In recent years Italy has developed a number of regulations concerning water resources (D.P.R. 236/88, Legge 183/89 and 36/94) for the achievement of reliable quality in the service and correct management criteria in this field. At the same time the law aims at pursuing economic efficiency through a progressive adjustment of fares. Presently in Italy the water service is still managed by thousands of local government and private undertakings while large areas of the country still lack effective treatment plants. The new laws are inspired by the reforms carried out in England that include the Water Act (1973 and 1989), the Water Industry Act (1991) and the Utilities Act (1992). They introduce the concepts of "urban water system" (drinking water pipelines, sewer network and waste water treatment) and "Ambito Territoriale Ottimale - A.T.O." (Optimum Territorial Range - large area facility). These concepts will become an important part of land planning since they will be taken into account in the Piani Territoriali di Coordinamento (territorial development plans) which are being undertaken by the Provinces.

1.2 *Regional laws*

The Regione Toscana has issued a specific regulation (L.R. 81/95) dividing the regional territory into six A.T.Os. The Integrated Water Service of each A.T.O. should - in the future - be managed by a single company under the supervision of a specific Authority (similar to the English "OFWAT", Office of Water Services). The accomplishments provided by the above listed laws will enable the adjustment of infrastructures through the investment of large capital, including private finance, and the rationalization of the management of the water and treatment services.

2 MIDDLE VALDARNO URBAN AREA

The Middle Valdarno Urban Area - contained in the A.T.O. n° 3, Middle Valdarno (50 Municipalities, 3,727 km^2, 1,300,000 inhabitants) - is located in the center of Tuscany and includes the cities of Firenze, Prato, Pistoia and other smaller municipalities.

In the Middle Valdarno Urban Area a total of about 1 million inhabitants live and work in an area of about 1,000 km^2. Estimated water consumptions in the area are as follows:

potable water:	100 Mm^{3}yr^{-1}
industrial water:	50 Mm^{3}yr^{-1}
irrigation:	30 Mm^{3}yr^{-1}

2.1 *Present conditions of water resources and plants*

Some important aquifers connected to the main streams are located in the Middle Valdarno: the fans of Ombrone Turrent (Pistoia) and of the Bisenzio River (Prato), the alluvial deposits of the Arno River

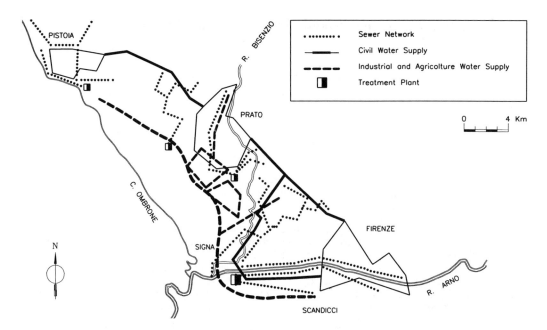

Figure 1. Large area infrastructural networks.

(Firenze and surrounding areas). These groundwaters are used to supply the many civil aqueducts as well as industrial plants and irrigation. At the same time the area of the Middle Valdarno is also entirely exploited and subjected to human activities (existing, planned or ongoing) mainly for residential and manufacturing purposes, transport infrastructure and agricultural activities.

Territorial exploitation has developed in the years between 1960 and 1990 either in the absence of territorial and urban development plans or in compliance with plans which took no account of the value of groundwater. As a result, water-consuming activities were located in areas with limited water resources and polluting plants were built above aquifers lacking natural protection. This is particularly obvious in the Prato area, where over-exploitation and contamination with nitrate and organochlorine compounds is found (Landini & Pranzini 1996). In the industrial area west of Firenze, over-exploitation and pollution with organochlorine compounds occurs. East of Pistoia where intensive agriculture (nursery-gardening) is carried out the presence of nitrate is observed (Bencini et al.).

The arrangement of water supplies still shows fragmentation both in treatment plants and transport infrastructure with a poorly interconnected network. Due to this vulnerability in the case of pollution or depletion of water resources, emergency actions have been necessarily undertaken at high, though unavoidable, economic and social costs. Treatment of waste waters is carried out only in a few areas of the Middle Valdarno (Pistoia and Prato), covering less than half of the resident population.

2.2 Large area infrastructural and managment projects

CONSIAG, a consortium of over 20 municipalities, is a management structure which is already operative within the area of A.T.O. n° 3. Thanks to its unusually large size, and its technical and financial resources, CONSIAG has been able to carry out, in cooperation with other local government and private undertakings, the planning and implementation of structural measures concerning the following fields: drinking water supplies, aqueducts for industrial use and sewerage collection and treatment.

The actions planned in the field of drinking water include the creation of a pipe line (DN 1000) connecting Firenze and Prato, to be expanded later in order to reach Pistoia, running lengthwise in Middle Valdarno. This pipeline will connect the existing aqueducts of the single municipalities through a system of tanks (Figure 1). The available resources (surface and groundwaters) will be shared on the basis of criteria of integration and substitution in the event of pollution or depletion of the water resource. The pipeline between Firenze and Prato is now under construction.

In the municipality of Prato an industrial aqueduct currently supplies mainly the industrial area named

Macrolotto I and part of the industries located south of the city. In the future, further development of the infrastructure will produce an industrial-water distribution axis running from east to west through the Middle Valdarno (Figure 1).

Measures in the field of treatment are focused on the southern part of the Middle Valdarno (Figure 1), with the construction of the San Colombano (Scandicci) treatment plant and related waste water collection systems. The San Colombano plant will serve the Firenze district, treating the waste water from 600,000 inhabitants. This facility will dramatically improve the quality of surface water bodies and groundwaters.

3 CASE HISTORIES

The planned measures concerning two important aquifers of the Middle Valdarno - the fan of the Bisenzio River in Prato and the alluvial deposit of the Arno in Renai (Signa) - are described in more detail below.

3.1 *The aquifer of Prato: savings of groundwater and artificial recharge*

The existing industrial aqueduct takes the water from the treatment plant of Baciacavallo mixed with surface water from the Bisenzio River. Work is now being carried out to increase the capacity of this industrial aqueduct (up to 15 Mm^3yr^{-1}), involving the construction of a well field close to the Bisenzio, the expansion of the water treatment plant and the creation of a new distribution network to supply the industrial area Macrolotto II located to the east of Prato.

The completion of the Industrial Aqueduct of Prato (Figure 2) will enable a considerable reduction in the amount of groundwater consumed by textile industries. The aim of completely ending industrial pumping from wells cannot be pursued for technical and economic reasons. In fact specific operations in wool processing and industrial sites located far from the industrial water distribution network will still depend on groundwater.

A 7-8 Mm^3yr^{-1} saving of groundwater will ensue from supplying recycled and surface waters to water consuming industrial plants, particularly the textile manufacturers of the Prato area. It is important to reverse the trend of groundwater levels which have been declining since 1960 by several meters per year and only recovering in years of heavy rainfall (1976/77 and 1991/93) rebalancing the groundwater budget. In 1988 the budget showed a deficit of about 3 Mm^3. The rebalancing may easily be achieved since the expected yearly saving in the pumping from the industrial wells is at least twice this deficit (Gambac-

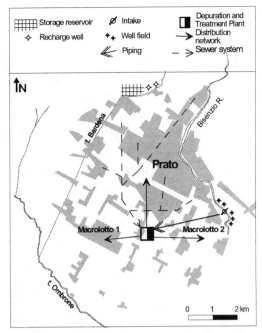

Figure 2. Scheme of Industrial Aqueduct and artificial recharge site.

ciani & Morosi 1996). Besides the existing intake of surface water and the recycling of treated waste waters, the industrial aqueduct will be supplied by 10 wells to be drilled on the left side of the Bisenzio River at Gonfienti. These wells will drain the gravels of the Bisenzio bed in an area where the river is no longer directly connected to the main aquifer. In this manner the impact of pumping on groundwater recharge will be minimized. The possibility of drawing water with wells ensures the continuity in the supply of the industrial aqueduct even in the event of low water or high turbidity of the river.

In the industrial areas closure of the wells which are often lacking the required sanitary measures to avoid the pollution of groundwater, will reduce the risk of contamination of the aquifers. The widespread presence of organochlorine compounds in groundwater shows the tangibility of this risk. Since the area of Gonfienti is some kilometers away from the drinking water wells, while the industrial wells of single establishments are often in the vicinity of those of the public water supply, competitiveness in the exploitation of groundwater resources will be diminished.

An artificial recharge site, in course of study, will provide a further contribution to the rebalancing of the groundwater budget. The recharge could take place in an area north of Prato (Figure 2) appointed to become a storage reservoir for the Bardena Creek. A relatively thick unsatured aquifer with high per-

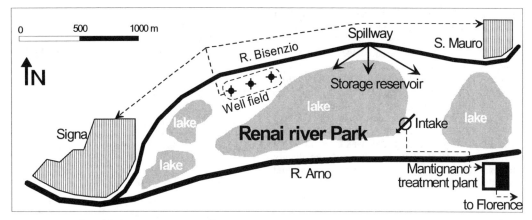

Figure 3. The Renai Lakes storage reservoir.

meability in this area is suitable for artificial recharge. The creek water will permit recharge during flood periods and the presence of the storage reservoir will allow the exploitation of high flow peaks after the settling of turbidity. The topographic drop and groundwater gradient will ensure that the subsurface flow is towards the potable water well fields. At present it is not possible to evaluate the yearly amount of water that this recharge will provide to the aquifer. The effect of the two measures described above on the groundwater will be evaluated through a subsurface water flow simulation model.

3.2 *The Renai Lakes*

In an area of about 3 km^2 to the north-east of Signa, in the southern part of Middle Valdarno (Figure 1), between the Rivers Bisenzio and Arno, several sand and gravel quarries, which were operative between 1950 and 1980, have exposed large parts of the aquifer. The gravels and sands present in the subsoil, though suitable for building purposes, represent a good aquifer well recharged by surface waters. In this area there are wells belonging to the public aqueduct of Signa. The area shows heavy signs of environmental degradation with disused factories and unauthorized dumps of urban waste.

The Basin Plan for the Arno River has chosen this area as a storage reservoir for the Bisenzio River with a capacity of about 15 Mm^3. A project for the environmental recovery of the Renai area is now under study. The project requires further excavation of the gravels in order to transform the many small lakes into a single large basin. The area will then be turned into a river park for recreation and sport purposes. Since the area must also function as a storage reservoir, the project considers the event of its being exceptionally flooded by the waters of the Bisenzio.

The Renai groundwater will be normally used by the aqueducts of Signa and S. Mauro. A newly constructed well field will be pumping the water at a rate of about 0,05 m^3/sec. In the event of low water or pollution of the waters of the Arno River an emergency supply can be obtained from the lakes through an intake with a capacity of 0,3 m^3/sec . The intake would supply the water treatment plant of Mantignano and hence the city of Firenze (Figure 3).

4 CONCLUSIONS

Thanks to the most recent Italian laws concerning urban water system services, this field will rise to the levels of efficiency of the other European countries.

Thus actions will be undertaken to improve the management and preservation of groundwaters for drinking use. The use of alternative water resources, preferably recycled waste waters, for industrial and irrigation purposes will enable the saving of groundwater and allow the rebalancing of the budget.

REFERENCES

Bencini, A., G. Cazzaroli, A. Gargini & G. Pranzini (In press). Qualité des eaux souterranines en relation au degré de protection contre la pollution des aquiferes. Un example en Toscane: la plaine de Florence. *Hydrogeologie*.

Gambacciani, A., & C. Morosi 1996. Industrial water supply of Prato: recycled water for industries and groundwater for residents. *Proc. 1st I.C. The impact of industry on groundwater resources*: 157-164. Cernobbio (Como).

Landini, F. & G. Pranzini 1996. The wool industry in Prato and the groundwater. *Proc. 1st I.C. The impact of industry on groundwater resources*: 157-164. Cernobbio (Como).

Evaluation of the risk of contamination of groundwater in Copiapo, Chile

J. F. Muñoz, E. Abujatum & P. Rengifo
Departamento Ingenieria Hidráulica y Ambiental, Pontificia Universidad Católica de Chile, Santiago, Chile

ABSTRACT: A methodology is presented for performing groundwater pollution risk evaluations upon sources used for potable water supplies. The scheme consists of estimating and comparing the vulnerability of aquifers, the potential contaminant loads that may reach the water table, and the capture zones for potable water sources. The methodology has been applied to the aquifer of the Copiapo river valley located 800 km north of Santiago, Chile. The principal results obtained regarding the general aquifer pollution risk are summarized.

1 INTRODUCTION

Groundwater is an attractive resource for potable water supplies and has been widely used in Chile, especially in the central and northern parts of the country. Although groundwater is generally of better quality than surface water, it has the drawback of being complicated and costly to treat once it becomes contaminated. Contamination of groundwater is a slow process due to the low flow velocities and the presence of strata overlying the saturated zone which in many cases prevent infiltration to the water table or, attenuate contaminants. Groundwater contamination problems have been identified in recent times in important aquifers of several countries. This fact, combined with the enormous dependence of many cities in Latin America on groundwater, e.g., Mexico City, Lima, Havana and others, has awakened the interest of researchers in developing methodologies which enable the groundwater pollution risk to be evaluated.

Copiapo, the capital city of Region 3, Chile, located in the northern part of the country, whose principal source of supply is groundwater, has experienced a steady increase in demand for potable water due to the growth of the city and the significant expansion of agricultural and mining activities. Agriculture and mining, along with the in-situ disposal of household wastewater and sewage in areas not covered by the sewage system, comprise the three major sources of potential groundwater pollution in the general area.

This paper presents a methodology for the evaluation of the pollution risk for groundwater as a source of potable water supply and applies this methodology to the Copiapo, Chile area. The proposed scheme is based on determining and comparing the vulnerability of aquifers, potential contaminant loads that may reach the water table, and capture zones or areas of influence for potable water supply sources.

2 METHODOLOGY

Groundwater pollution risk is understood as being the interaction between the vulnerability or natural susceptibility of an aquifer to contamination and the contaminant load applied or potentially to be applied to the underground environment as a result of human activities (Vrba & Zaporozec, 1994). Vulnerability depends on the inaccessibility of the aquifer from the hydraulic standpoint and the attenuation capacity of the medium (Foster & Hirata, 1991).

Pollution risk analysis for a groundwater supply source requires consideration of three variables: the intrinsic vulnerability of the aquifer, the potential contaminant load that may enter the aquifer, and the capture zone of the source.

2.1 *Intrinsic vulnerability*

The purpose of evaluating aquifer vulnerability is to

determine zones which are more vulnerable to contamination than others. The ultimate end pursued is therefore to represent graphically the surface, subdivided in accordance with its vulnerability classes, for the purpose of prescribing allowable uses. The vulnerability of groundwater is a relative, non-measurable property without dimension. The precision of vulnerability estimates depends on the quantity and quality of available data to represent the study area.

Two widely utilized vulnerability evaluation methods are those named GOD (Foster & Hirata, 1991) and DRASTIC (Aller et al., 1985). Both belong to the group of parametric methods and have advantages and disadvantages related to the quantity of available information and the selection criteria used for parameters and weights representing vulnerability.

The GOD method has a simple, pragmatic structure which makes it superior to DRASTIC for interpreting results. The number of variables and their weighting in the DRASTIC method allows relevant variables such as type of soil lithology to become obscured by other less relevant factors such as the mobility of the contaminant in the saturated zone. Foster and Skinner (1995) argue that the vulnerability index arrived at through use of the DRASTIC method is the result of the interaction of many parameters, the weightings for which are debatable and in certain cases are not independent but quite strongly correlated. The GOD method has associated with it a well-defined method for evaluating the pollution risk (Foster & Hirata, 1991), based on indexing and systematizing the contaminant load in order to obtain a numerical value. Vrba and Zaporozec (1994) consider that the greatest weakness of the DRASTIC method is its lack of flexibility for adaptation to specific needs. Based on the above arguments, the GOD method was chosen for use in this study to evaluate aquifer vulnerability in the Copiapo, Chile area.

The GOD method estimates vulnerability of an aquifer through multiplying three discrete phases representing three sets of spatial information: a) type of groundwater occurrence (G); b) lithology overlying the aquifer (O); and c) depth to the phreatic level or top of a confined aquifer (D).

The first phase corresponds to the identification of the type of groundwater occurrence (G), which is indexed in a range of from 0 to 1. Type of occurrence varies from the nonexistence of any aquifer, at one extreme, up through artesian, confined, semi-confined and unconfined overlain to open aquifers.

The second phase corresponds to the characterization of the strata overlying the saturated zone of the aquifer (O). This is performed in terms of two characteristics: (i) fracturing; and (ii) lithological characteristics - and hence, indirectly, in terms of relative porosity, permeability and moisture content or specific retention in the unsaturated zone. This information is used to obtain indices in the range 0.4 to 1.0.

The third phase consists of determining the depth to the phreatic surface, in the case of an unconfined aquifer, or the depth to the top of the aquifer in the case of a confined aquifer. According to the depth (D) found, this third component of the method may take on values of between 0.4 and 1.0.

The product of these three spatial components provides a spatial representation of the vulnerability index, which may vary between 0 and 1 to indicate negligible to extreme vulnerability.

2.2 Contaminant load

The only method which has a well prepared and well defined structure for systematically evaluating contaminant load is that described by Foster & Hirata (1991). This method was developed to evaluate pollution risk in combination with aquifer vulnerability estimated by the GOD method. The method is based on the identification of a set of characteristics for the different components of the contaminant load, viz.: type of source (point or k diffuse), type of contaminant (classification) and interaction characteristics with the transport medium (attenuation, degradation, persistence, mobility, etc.), intensity, location and manner in which the contaminant is deposited, and duration of the time during which the contaminant is applied.

When viewed from a theoretical standpoint, and assuming optimum availability of information, this methodology makes it possible to perform quantitative evaluations of the contaminant load. However, in the majority of cases the information available is not complete enough to obtain truly reliable indices.

The application of this approach for the area studied involved a number of practical restrictions which precluded all possibilities of arriving at a reliable quantification through use of indexation. Among such restrictions is the difficulty which is involved in obtaining detailed knowledge regarding the mode of disposal used for industrial effluents. Another difficulty arises in connection with the variability in behaviour exhibited by contaminants depending on the nature of the soil as well as the organic or acid loads present in the unsaturated zone.

For the purposes of applying this method to the Copiapo area, a proposal was made to compile information on the several, varied activities which are potentially contaminating in nature, particularly agricultural and mining activities, and thereafter enter this information on a series of maps.

2.3 *Pollution risk*

Pollution risk, as defined above, is the interaction between the contaminant load that is, will or could be applied to the subsoil and the vulnerability of the aquifer.

The method proposed by Foster and Hirata (1991) conceptualises groundwater pollution risk as the interaction between the vulnerability index (assigned a value of between 0 and 1), calculated by using the GOD scheme, and the contaminant load index (rated between 0 and 1).

Certain types of contaminant loads, such as those containing highly mobile, persistent contaminants or those released beneath the phreatic surface, give rise to high pollution risks for the aquifer almost regardless of the degree of vulnerability involved. Under all other circumstances, the interaction between the components of the contaminant load and vulnerability determines the pollution risk.

However, in practice, such as in the case of the city of Copiapo, Chile, and its surroundings, no possibilities exist for obtaining sufficient information for determining the contaminant load within any margin of safety. Such was true of this study, in which direct use of this methodology was not considered practicable. As an alternative, pollution risk was determined qualitatively. The proposed scheme involved treating separately all potentially contaminating sources considered significant, in order to obtain results derived from a set of spatial coverages plotted on graphs (i.e., maps on transparent overlay sheets) which are representative of each and every contaminant category considered and which are then superimposed separately (whether as the graphs themselves or as digital data) on the basic mapping of vulnerability to examine the spatial distribution of pollution risk for the aquifer for each specific contaminant.

In addition, consideration was given to the importance of being able to verify or validate the results obtained from the analysis as described above. For such purpose, data on spatial distribution of pollution indicators in the study area were compiled for comparison with the changes in pollution risk as determined on a spatial basis by the analysis.

The scheme for evaluating the pollution risk for groundwater sources used for potable water supplies consisted of determining by hydrogeologic modelling the capture zones corresponding to the groundwater abstraction points, and subsequent comparison of this information (graphed or expressed by digital means) with the maps of intrinsic vulnerability of the aquifer and the various categories of potential contaminants considered in the study.

To prepare estimates of the capture zones, use was made of the VISUAL MODFLOW model, developed by Franz and Guiguer (1995).

3 RESULTS

3.1 *Study area*

The study area covers approximately 500 km^2 of land (in the shape of a rectangle measuring 28 km long by 18 km wide) and was graphically represented on a 1:25,000-scale working map. It should be noted that out of the total area studied, only around 130 km^2 of land is associated with an aquifer as such. The rest of the study area was composed primarily of impermeable zones.

3.2 *Aquifer Vulnerability*

The vulnerability of the aquifer in the study area portion of Copiapo river valley varies from low to extreme. No area was found to have negligible vulnerability.

The areas of extreme vulnerability account for a land surface amounting to approximately 3 km^2, of which the major area is located to the north of the small locality of Nantoco in the southern portion of the study area. The areas of high vulnerability make up a land surface totalling approximately 31 km^2, accounted for in large part by six large areas, four of which are located on the valley floor while the other two are located to the side of the valley across the river from Copiapo. Units of moderate aquifer vulnerability are the type most commonly found in the study area and account for a total land surface of slightly less than 90 km^2. Finally, two areas of low vulnerability were identified inside the study area. Both combined account for a land surface of slightly less than 7 km^2.

The major sources of potential groundwater pollution identified in the Copiapo area are: a) in-situ wastewater and sewage disposal; b) agricultural crops; c) industrial activities; d) mine tailings disposal; e) solid waste disposal; and f potentially contaminated surface streams.

Concerning the contaminant load generated by in-situ wastewater and sewage disposal, the assumption was made that all areas located outside the areas covered by sewerage lines are potential polluters due to the possible or probable existence of septic pits, which may allow contaminants to infiltrate to the water table. In the study, wide coverage by sewerage lines was apparent inside town and city limits, thus implying that few urban areas currently exist where in-situ wastewater and sewage disposal is used. Nonetheless, it was also apparent that rural areas have not been provided with sewerage line coverage, and it is therefore assumed that they are potentially polluters, but to a minor extent only on account of a low existing rural population density.

Agricultural crops are a potential source of contamination due to the possible infiltration of fertilizers and pesticides into the ground, which may therefore reach the water table. Crops of one kind or another were noted throughout almost the entire extent of the Copiapo river valley in the study area. The principal agricultural crops identified in the area were: a) vineyards; b) orchards and other fruit; c) garden vegetables; and d) miscellaneous crops. Out of all of these crops, identification was made of those which entail the greatest risks of pollution of the aquifer by taking into account the use of agricultural chemicals, types of irrigation systems employed and associated efficiencies, and frequency of plowing practice~. The intensive vegetable crops turned out to be the main source of contamination from tilling. Vineyards and fruit orchards, nevertheless, were generally found to be significant source, of contamination as well.

Mine tailings disposal is a major source of groundwater pollution due to infiltrations occurring from tailings material during both transport and final disposal by impoundment in tailings ponds. In the

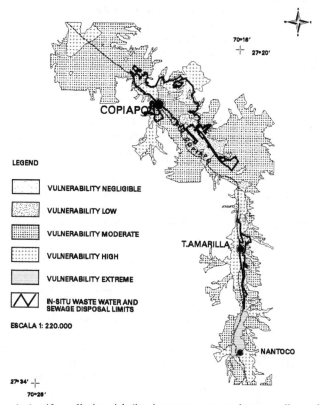

LEGEND

⬜ VULNERABILITY NEGLIGIBLE

▨ VULNERABILITY LOW

▦ VULNERABILITY MODERATE

▨ VULNERABILITY HIGH

▦ VULNERABILITY EXTREME

⬜ IN-SITU WASTE WATER AND SEWAGE DISPOSAL LIMITS

ESCALA 1: 220.000

Figure 1. Aquifer pollution risk (in-situ waste water and sewage disposal)

study area, a considerable number of mine tailings ponds belonging to small-medium- and large-scale mining operations were identified. Of these, a selection of the most important was made; these totalled more than 25 tailings ponds containing a combined amount of more than 95% of all tailings material deposited in the area.

In general, no large-scale industrial activities were noted, with the exception of the ore processing plants associated with mining.

In the study area, three operating solid waste disposal sites and one abandoned site were identified.

In the study area, one surface stream of any importance only is to be found in the Copiapo river! Stream water in this river can infiltrate down to the water table in certain areas.

3.4 Aquifer pollution risk

A brief qualitative analysis is presented for the aquifer pollution risk in the study area of the Copiapo river valley based on a digital superimposition of the

mapping of vulnerability and overlays of information associated with the three major sources of potential groundwater pollution in the general area. Generally speaking, the aquifer areas identified in this presentation are limited to those involving the greatest amount of pollution risk, and often corresponding to those areas rated as being of extreme or high vulnerability and having nearby potential pollution sources.

The analysis of the superimposition of aquifer vulnerably coverage mapping and the sewerage utility lines in the study area made it possible to identify an area located in the valley to the north of the small locality of Nantoco in the southern portion of the study area as that which has the greatest amount of pollution risk from wastewater and sewage, on account of this identified area having been classified as of extreme vulnerability and being an area in which wastewater and sewage is disposed of entirely by in-situ methods.

The area of greatest groundwater pollution risk from agricultural chemicals is that corresponding to a small land surface located south of Nantoco near the southern end of the study area. The high risk was due

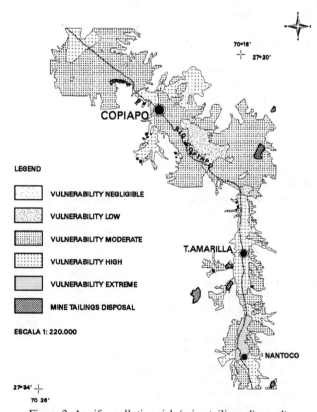

Figure 2. Aquifer pollution risk (mine tailings disposal).

to the fact that this is a Type 3 (garden vegetable) crop area located on land overlying high vulnerability aquifer areas.

In addition, in this entire area, only one tailings disposal facility of a large-scale mining operation was found to be located on impermeable ground on a site situated at a considerable distance from the aquifer. In comparison, the majority of the 15 tailings ponds classified as belonging to medium-sized mining operations were located predominantly in areas of moderate vulnerability, thus involving a significant groundwater pollution risk. The tailings ponds classified as belonging to small-scale mining operations are located in various areas rated as of moderate or high vulnerability.

The results for the aquifer pollution risk are shown in Figure 1 (in-situ wastewater and sewage disposal) and Figure 2 (mine tailings disposal).

4 CONCLUSIONS

1. A methodology is proposed for the evaluation of pollution risk for groundwater sources used for potable water supplies, based on techniques of recent development, presented and discussed herein, which are adaptable to the reality of a country on the road to development.

2. The aquifer of the Copiapo river valley, Chile, was found to be of variable vulnerabilities between low and extreme in the study area. The most commonly found class of vulnerability was moderate.

3. The potential contaminant loads recognized in the area originate from a variety of sources, noteworthy among these being septic pits, agricultural crops and mine tailings ponds.

4. Several areas of significant groundwater pollution risk were identified for each of the groupings of pollution sources studied.

ACKNOWLEDGEMENTS

The authors wish to thank all those who in one way or another aided or participated in the development of this project. Our sincere appreciation is also due to the following persons and organizations:

The British Geological Survey, with special thanks to Messrs. Stephen Foster and Brian Morris for their valuable comments and methodological suggestions.
EMSSAT S.A., and particularly Messrs. Nicolas Alvares and Rodrigo Veliz, for the cooperation they provided towards the performance of this study and for making possible the publication of this paper.
CPR&SIG of P.U.C. de Chile, and especially Ms. Jessica Acevedo, for their generous contributions and support in the area of digital and graphic geography and cartography.

REFERENCES

Aller, L., T. Bennett, J.H. Lehr & R. Petty, 1985. DRASTIC: A Standarized System for Evaluating Ground Water Pollution Potential Using Hydrogeologic Settings. US-EPA Report 600/2-85/018.

Foster, S.S.D. & R.C.A. Hirata, 1991. Determinacion del Riesgo de Contaminacion de Aguas Subterraneas. CEPIS, Lima, Peru.

Foster, S.S.D. & A.C. Skinner, 1995. Groundwater Protection: the science and
practice of land surface zoning. IAHS Publ. no. 225.

Franz, T. & N. Guiguer, 1995. User's Manual for Visual MODFLOW. Waterloo Hydrogeologic Inc., Ontario, Canada.

Vrba, J. & A. Zaporozec, 1994. Guidebook on Mapping Groundwater Vulnerability. IAH, vol 16.

Valuation of groundwater: Future trend in vulnerability mapping

B. Paczyński
Polish Geological Institute, Warsaw, Poland

ABSTRACT: An attempt to value both aquifers and groundwater systems is reported in this paper. This attempt would in future make it possible to arrange them in a ranking order. Valuation on a general scale has been applied in hydrogeological atlases of Poland. They are discussed here as illustrative examples of valuation criteria and procedure.

1 INTRODUCTION

A concept of groundwater valuation (Paczyński 1988) emerged in the course of preparation of the 1:500 000 Map of the 180 most important reservoirs of fresh groundwater in Poland (Kleczkowski 1990). The concept was utilized in the Hydrogeological Atlas of Poland on the scale 1:500 000 (Paczyński 1995) and in the valuation of fresh groundwater systems atlas of Poland (in print). The idea has also been adopted in Russia (Kuzmicka et al.1994). Vulnerability of groundwater (Robins et al. 1994; Vrba & Zaporozec 1994) constitutes an important link in the valuation procedure. Some studies conducted so far have exclusively dealt with fresh ground waters; however, an initial attempt was also made to evaluate therapeutic groundwater in Poland (Paczyński & Płochniewski 1996). Following further methodological improvement, valuation of groundwater may and should be applied to detailed mapping. This would make it possible to utilize these maps in planning of groundwater management, also on a local level.

2 CONCEPT OF GROUNDWATER VALUATION

The concept of valuation, being applied to the assessment of environmental impact exerted by planned investments, including those which are water-related (Dee et al. 1973), has not yet been utilized in hydrogeology in full. Hydrogeological assessment has been mainly limited to the determination of groundwater resources and evaluation of groundwater quality as compared with drinking water standards. Such important and well known criteria as vulnerability of groundwater systems to anthropogenic pressure, distinguishing of good and very good waters with respect to their quality and the role of groundwater in water supply - increasing in water-scarce areas and in areas where no alternative sources are available - have not been taken into account. Valuation is essential for rational groundwater management, particularly for (among others): price fixing for water use, delineation of protection zones, and decision-making on control of water use or on imposing a ban on abstraction of groundwater.

The valuation procedure requires that periodical verification be made as some valuation criteria are changeable. Different aquifers, even those of the same category of water quality can be given different values - a lower one in areas with considerable reserves of groundwater resources and a higher one in areas which are short of water, where import of water from distant sources or expensive treatment of poor-quality waters provides the only alternative. Cases of relaxed drinking water standards (up to 3000-5000 or even 10000 mg l^{-1} TDS) in arid areas or making use of poorly mineralized water (less than 100 mg l^{-1} TDS) are given here as examples of such practices that have been continued for years.

Areal value characterisation of groundwater may in future affect the price of land, and give preference to particularly protective measures related to high-potential but shallow groundwater of high vulnerability that constitute water supply sources in large well fields. Planned afforestation in such areas is the exemplary case of protective measures.

When concern deals with definition of valuation, then it stands for : - valuation of an aquifer/ground water system or groundwater regions or drainage basin or any area - conducted on the basis of accepted criteria of assessment, with those criteria and hierarchy being influenced mostly by the aim of evaluation and by valuation scale.

3 CRITERIA OF VALUATION

There are serious differences between the principles of valuation for fresh, therapeutic and thermal waters (Table 1). The following section of this paper focuses on fresh waters for which such criteria as water quality and vulnerability of groundwater to anthropogenic pressure have been deemed basic (Table 2). This is because both criteria mentioned here are decisive for determination of the initial point characteristics. The human pressure factor expresses itself by both the potential vulnerability of the system to pollution and by the water quality classes. Water was valued not only from the standpoint of chemical composition and susceptibility to treatment processes, but also through proven anthropogenic effects. Water of poor quality, with Total Dissolved Solids (TDS) in excess of 1000 mg l^{-1} or with concentration of constituents requiring expensive non-economic treatment have been excluded from valuation (0 points).

The resilience of a groundwater system has been evaluated mainly on the basis of isolation and can be expressed by time of migration of potential pollutants (Kleczkowski 1990). Accordingly, it is evaluated as:

- poor - up to 25 years and to a depth of 50 m,
- medium - 25-100 years, to a depth of 50-150 m,
- high - more than 100 years, to a depth >150 m.

This simplified evaluation results from the neglect of other parameters such as type of aquifer and of soil, and hydrodynamic position of the system. In the literature, the vulnerability of an aquifer is, in general, qualified in a more tolerant way, for instance: travel times of : - a week, a year, 20 years, more than 20 years (Robins et al. 1994), which is more appropriate for valuation of short-duration catastrophic events than those of permanent sources of pollution. In the group of important supplementary criteria (Table 2), the state of reserves in groundwater resources takes a prominent position since it expresses potential water-shortage in an area and is reflected by a computational index (α). Proper interpretation of the water-balance in an area is essential for valuation of this parameter. The area may also contain abundant but over-exploited aquifers (due to water supply and/or abstraction of mine waters) or an area affected by deteriorated water quality.

Table 1. Valuation criteria as related to groundwater types.

Water type	Water	Groundwater system
Fresh	Total Dissolved Solids (TDS), cost of treatment, age, taste values, chemical composition	Availability, vulnerability, state of reserves of groundwater resources
Therapeutic	Therapeutic properties, chemical composition, gas factor, temperature	Availability, abstraction conditions, climatic values, landscape amenities, recreational assets, potential receivers
Thermal	Temperature, artesian outflow, chemical composition, TDS, gas factor	Potential receivers, availability, abstraction conditions, recreational assets, climatic values, landscape amenities, resources

Table 2. Criteria for valuation of fresh waters.

Class	Criteria
1. Most important - basic	Water quality, vulnerability of groundwater system
2. Important -supplementary	State of reserves of groundwater resources/water shortage in the area, recharge, role of groundwaters in water supply, availability
3. Essential -valuation in detail	Economic aspects of water use (depth, transmissivity, distance to users), possibility of subsurface use of surface waters, potential/ availability of surface waters, possibility of protection of shallow ground waters (afforestation of protection zones)

Recharge of groundwater is another parameter closely connected with the previous one. It is assigned a recharge in mm yr^{-1} or $m^3 d^{1} km^{2}$. The lower its value, the higher the computational index (β). This group of criteria is completed by those dealing with the role of groundwater in water supply. Thus the more important the water supply infrastructure in the given area, the higher the value (γ). Availability of aquifers also belongs to this group. In areas with dense urban development, where the possibility of abstraction or of protection of shallow groundwater of high vulnerability is lacking - the value of deep isolated aquifers that can be subject to utilisation is raised.

The last group (3) of criteria (Table 2), particularly essential for detailed valuation, has not been employed to value aquifers and groundwater systems so far. An exception is the resource potential for availability of surface waters. In the Hydrogeological Atlas of Poland (Paczyński 1995) this criterion yielded a parameter which is related to surface water runoff. The groundwater rank (x), defined as an alternative source of water supply increases due to decreasing value of surface-water runoff modulus q (for instance: q=10 $m^3s^{-1}km^{-2}$ corresponds to x=1.0, but if q=3 $m^3s^{-1}km^{-2}$ - then x=1.25).

However, as a result of poor quality of water this parameter has not been applied in the value characterisation atlas. The economic aspect of groundwater use, though without detailed computational proposals, was tested in studies conducted at St. Petersburg University (Kuzmicka et al.1994).

Despite the fact that subsurface management of surface waters (infiltration wells on river banks) has not been tested so far and that it deals, in part, with surface waters, it should be taken into consideration when valuation assessment is concerned.

Afforestation of shallow vulnerable aquifers should be considered in any new proposals for valuation though it has not yet been discussed in full. This factor increases the value of those aquifers that normally are qualified relatively low.

4 RESULTS

The value-characterisation atlas of Poland is considered here as an example. The basic criteria compiled in Table 3 in a scoring order mark the starting point for valuation. Then, the basic criteria are multiplied by indices, according to supplementary criteria given in Table 4. The final result (the score W) was produced by the equation

$$W = w_1 . \alpha . \beta . \gamma$$

where w_1 - basic valuation criteria (water quality, degree of isolation); α - state of reserves of ground-water resources / water-shortage of an area; β – recharge of groundwater; γ - the main or the only water supply system in a town.
This was represented on three sets of maps:

MAP I   Shallow (to a depth of 100 m),

Table 3. Basic valuation criteria (1) and their basic score (w_1).

Water quality	Degree of isolation or depth (m)				
	v. high	high	average		low
	>150	100-150	50-100	15-50	<15
I Very good- without human impact	50	40	30	25	20
II Very good- with slight human impact	45	35	28	22	18
III Good-without human impact	40	30	25	20	15
IV Good-with slight human impact	30	25	20	15	10
V Average-with slight human impact	20	15	10	8	5
VI Average-with clear human impact	10	8	5	3	1
VII Poor	0	0	0	0	0

Table 4. Supplementary criteria (2) α, β, γ.

Criteria	Valuation parameter		Index
α - State of reserves of groundwater resources /water-shortage of an area	up to 25% of max		1,5
	25 - 75% of max		1,25
	more than 75% of max		1,0
β - Recharge of groundwater	up to 20	$m.^3 d^{-1} km^{-2}$	1,5
	20 -50	,,	1,3
	50 -100	,,	1,2
	100 -200	,,	1,1
	more than 200	,,	1,0
γ - Groundwater system constituting the main or the only water supply system in a town			1.5-1.1

predominantly porous groundwater systems
A Aquifers in Quaternary formation
B Aquifers in Tertiary, Lower Cretaceous, Lower and Middle Jurassic formations

MAP II   Shallow (to a depth of 100 m), predominantly fissured groundwater systems
C Aquifers in Tertiary, Mesozoic, and Palaeozoic formations

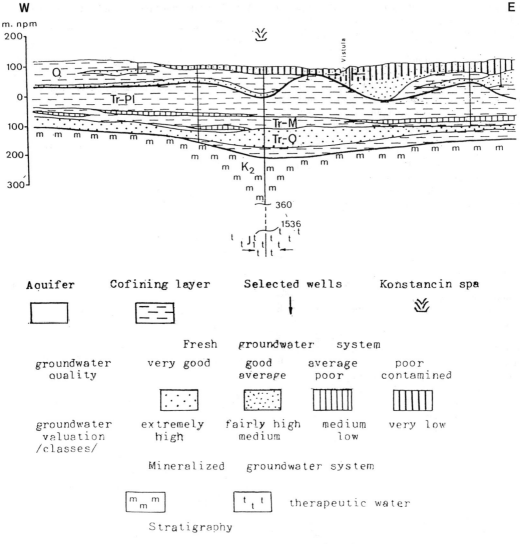

Figure 1. Groundwater valuation of the southern part of the Warsaw City complex.

W   E

m. npm

Aquifer   **Confining layer**   **Selected wells**   **Konstancin spa**

Fresh groundwater system

groundwater quality	very good	good average	average poor	poor contamined

groundwater valuation /classes/	extremely high	fairly high medium	medium low	very low

Mineralized groundwater system

therapeutic water

Stratigraphy

Q - Quarternary, Tr-Pl - Pliocene, Tr-M - Miocene, Tr-O - Oligocene

K_2 - Upper Cretaceous, J_1 - Lower Jurassic

MAP III   Deep (at a depth greater than 100 m), with porous and fissured groundwater systems

D₁   Aquifers in Tertiary formation
D₂   Aquifers in Mesozoic formations

30 - 49 points - high
20 - 29 points - fairly high
10 - 19 points - medium
5 - 9 points - low
< 5 points - very low.

The following value-characterisation classes were presented on the maps:

> 50 points - extremely high

5 CONCLUSIONS

1. The valuation procedure for aquifers followed the

methodology which gave priority to groundwater quality, degree of isolation of aquifers, state of water supply deficiency and state of environmental degradation.

2. The valuation of groundwater systems on a regional scale (1:100 000 - 1: 500 000) should be helpful in:
   - formulation of national and regional groundwater management plans,
   - establishing protection measures (such as strict abstraction control, water pricing, and areas of regional protection),
   -focusing on rational resource development, tailored to specific environmental circumstances.

3. Further elements that should be included in the valuation study on a more detailed scale (1:10 000 - 1:50 000) may be related to supposed climatic changes and to issues of ecology of urbanized areas.

4. Within urban areas (towns), the valuation criteria for groundwater can be limited to water quality and degree of isolation and recharge to aquifers as well. With respect to valuation assessment and the programme of groundwater use, waters of poor quality will be made available without limitation (industry), waters of high quality will be subject to limitation, and a ban may be imposed on use of waters of top quality, for instance until they are replenished in full. The degree of restriction imposed on valuable waters will define the allowable limits of their use, starting from municipal water wells made available to the population to piped water systems in selected quarters or developed zones in towns. An example of this is the permissible abstraction of water from sandy Oligocene horizon in Warsaw (Figure 1).

REFERENCES

Dee, N., J. Baker, N. Drobny, I. Whitman & D. Fahringer 1973. An Environmental Evaluation System for Water Resource Planning. *Water Resources Research* 1, 9.

Kleczkowski, A.S. (ed.).*1990.The Map of the critical protection areas (CPA) of the major groundwater basins (MGWB) in Poland* 1:500000.Academy of Mining and Metallurgy, Krakow.

Kuzmicka, O., A.S. Siennow & I.W. Chernyshewa 1994. Method of comparative of aquifers evaluation. St. Petersburg Univ.

Paczyński, B. 1988. Valuation of aquifers with respect to their protection. *Proc. Modern Issues in Hydrogeology*. Part III: 66-73. Gdańsk.

Paczyński, B. 1992. Screening of aquifers for the needs of efficient management and conservation of water. In V. Juodkazis (ed.).*Hydrogeological mapping and ground water monitoring in the Baltic states:* 25-30. Palanga: Lithuania

Paczyński, B. (ed.). 1995. *Hydrogeological Atlas of Poland* 1:500000. Polish Geol. Inst.

Paczyński, B. 1996. Valuation - a new direction of groundwater evaluation. *Prz Geol.* vol. 44, 1: 81-86.

Paczyński, B. & Z. Płochniewski 1996. *Mineral and therapeutic groundwater in Poland.* Polish Geol. Inst.

Robins, N. S., B. Adams, S.S.D. Foster & R. Palmer 1994. Groundwater vulnerability mapping: the British perspective. *Hydrogeologie* 1: 35-42.

Vrba, J. & A. Zaporozec 1994. *Guidebook on Groundwater Vulnerability.* IAH, Contributions to Hydrogeology, vol. 16.

Storm water management in urban areas: Risks and case studies

F. Remmler & U. Hütter
Institute for Water Research, Schwerte, Germany

ABSTRACT: Nowadays, in many cases, managed infiltration of runoff is practised as an alternative approach to storm water drainage. This practice supports the natural water cycle by the immediate reintroduction to the cycle of runoff components from different drainage areas. This increasingly widely used procedure has to be strictly assessed and controlled with the aim of soil and water protection. This paper presents some results of investigations with respect to the quality of topsoil in several infiltration troughs. A significant aspect to consider is whether long-term operation of the drainage systems could exhaust the buffer and filtration capacity of the soil. Investigations within specific infiltration projects showed that there is a high accumulation of substances in most materials used to construct roof drainage systems in the topsoil of the infiltration areas. Long-term operation can significantly reduce the cleaning effects of passage through the soil. Operational stability and reliable functioning of infiltration systems has to be guaranteed in the long-term. Therefore, the location, structure and operation of alternative storm water drainage systems have to meet some specific criteria.

1 INTRODUCTION

Nowadays, the natural water cycle is fundamentally influenced by anthropogenic factors. In recent years increasing urban settlement in drainage areas has led to intensified surface paving and consequently to an enormous increase in the water to be collected and transported from urban areas. Therefore current approaches to wastewater collection have caused different economic and environmental problems in urban hydrology. The main problems are the:

♦ overloading of sewage treatment plants,
♦ increasing number of flood events,
♦ reduced groundwater recharge,
♦ adverse impact on the quality of receiving water by, for example, combined sewer overflows,
♦ increasing investment and running costs for the sewage treatment facilities.

For this reason water management engineers have been searching for an alternative to the current approach to urban drainage systems via separate and combined sewers. A possible solution is the infiltration of runoff as an alternative storm water drainage system. This procedure uses the main principles of drainage, retention and infiltration, both separate and in various combinations depending on the porosity of the soil and the availability of open land. In many projects the infiltration of storm water runoff is already practised. This kind of infiltration management increases the input of water per infiltration area unit (m^2) as well as the volume and the spectrum of substances. With the aim of achieving soil and water protection, it is therefore necessary to question whether, and in which cases, storm water infiltration is sustainable and environmentally sound.

The Institute for Water Research is undergoing extensive investigations into the impact of storm water infiltration on the quality of soil and seepage water. In several research projects at different locations, the effect on environmental components is monitored over a period of 2 to 5 years. This paper presents selected results of investigations of the topsoil in different infiltration troughs.

2 POTENTIAL POLLUTION OF STORM WATER RUNOFF

By passing through the atmosphere, precipitation accumulates many chemical substances. The spectrum of polluting and dangerous substances normally increases further during the flowpath from the catchment area to the drainage system. The pollution of precipitation and storm water runoff results in the ubiquitous distribution of pollutants in the environment and the deposition of pollutants on all elements of the drainage area.

For more than 30 years many research projects have investigated the quality of precipitation and the different kinds of surface runoff (for example roof runoff, street runoff). The extensive results give evidence for varying pollution depending both on the local conditions and on the analytical conditions of the specific investigation. Therefore, these isolated cases are not universally applicable and cannot be transfered to other kinds of catchment areas.

At the moment the different kinds of surface runoff components can only be classified with a simplistic approach. Some typical surfaces are generally arranged in quality categories according to their expected potential degree of pollution. This categorisation distinguishes storm water runoff quality between harmless (=A), tolerable (=B) and not tolerable (=C) (Table 1).

Table 1. Classification of storm water runoff in different quality categories.

Quality Category		Origin of surface runoff
A = harm- less	A1	- roof surfaces in residential areas
	A2	- bicycle paths - footpaths with small crowds of people and animals - yard surfaces in residential areas with restricted use (e.g. carwash forbidden)
B = tolerable		- streets in residential areas with parking spaces and a low traffic density - open air ground with large crowds of people (for example pedestrian precinct, markets, open air events) - roof surfaces, yards and streets in industrial estates and roof surfaces in industrial areas if their pollution is demonstrably comparable to residential areas - runways of airports without winter operation (de-icing systems)
C = not tolerable		- main roads and major roads with a high traffic density and car parks with frequent inflow and outflow of traffic - railway systems - runways of airports with winter operation (de-icing systems) and surfaces where planes are refueled and/or washed - surfaces with storage and handling of water-endangering substances as well as liquid manure - roof surfaces, yards and streets in industrial areas - open air ground with large crowds of animals (for example fur farms, slaughterhouses, riding stables) - waste plants and composting facilities

The granting of permission to infiltrate depends on the quality of the storm water runoff and the kind of treatment facilities. The unpolluted and less polluted fractions can be reintroduced immediately into the natural water cycle, if some requirements related to the location, the structure and the operation of the infiltration system are fulfilled. As a rule, the runoff of categories A and B can be infiltrated by procedures which use passage through the topsoil. An infiltration system which does not use passage through the topsoil is only permissible in special cases (e.g. lack of open ground) for runoff of category A1 if the connected surfaces are outside areas with high atmospheric emission. In general - with only a few exceptions - surface runoff of category C is not allowed to be infiltrated.

The investigations which have been carried out to date have identified many chemical substances as components of storm water runoff. The following micropollutants deserve particular attention, due to their toxicity, persistence and accumulation in biological systems:

❑ organic micropollutants (e.g. polycyclic aromatic hydrocarbons, PAHs)
❑ inorganic micropollutants (e.g. heavy metals)

PAHs and some heavy metals are transported predominantly through their association with suspended solids. An assessment of the quality of storm water runoff is difficult because there are as yet no special quality standards.

During infiltration different processes cause a significant reduction in some pollutants. However, this physical or chemical adsorption and biological processes lead to increased concentrations in the soil of such infiltration systems. Biological degradation of some kinds of pollutants (e.g. heavy metals) in natural systems is negligible or does not occur at all. Therefore an accumulation of chemical substances in the topsoil can exhaust the buffer and filtration ability of the soil. The next section deals with some results of the investigations concerning this aspect.

3 INVESTIGATIONS AT DIFFERENT INFILTRATION TROUGHS

For estimating potential accumulation effects of chemical substances in alternative drainage systems it was necessary to observe the topsoil in several infiltration troughs. Another significant research aspect was whether long-term operation of the trough-trench-system could exhaust the buffer and filtration capacity of the soil.

For these reasons different drainage systems in Germany have been investigated with respect to the quality of soil. Soil samples were taken from the infiltration troughs at several depths after different lengths of time. At new infiltration sites, these samples were compared with a control sample taken during the construction work. At older infiltration sites, soil samples next to the infiltration areas were taken to enable an estimation to be made of the accumulation effects.

The next sections present the results of investigations at two different systems for storm water runoff infiltration. Because zinc is the material used in most roof drainage systems, this metal was taken as an example to illustrate the accumulation effects in the topsoil.

3.1 *Study sites and background information*

The first investigation site is located in the grounds of a day care centre in the urban area of Dortmund in North-Rhine-Westphalia. In 1993 the owner of the building, the Dortmunder Stadtwerke AG, chose a trough-trench-system as the storm water drainage method for the building. An approach such as this allows for the decentralising retention of storm water and the infiltration of storm water through a system of infiltration troughs with a trench underneath. The outdoor grounds, including the trough-trench-system were finished in autumn 1994. The drainage design consists of three grass-surfaced troughs and a trench below filled with lava rock. The groundwater level can be found at about 15 m below the trench. The trough-trench-system receives runoff mainly from the roofs, the terraces and a small carpark. In total nearly 1,030 m^2 of drainage surface are connected to the drainage system (Stecker & Remmler 1996). For the investigated infiltration trough the ratio between the connected impervious surfaces (A_{red}) and the infiltration area (A_S) is 5.5 to 1 (A_{red}/A_S).

The second investigation site is located in the suburb of Frohnau in the city of Berlin. There is an old infiltration trough for storm water runoff with an estimated operation time of 80 years at the Fürstendamm street. Because the time of the last sludge clearance is uncertain, a maximum of 80 years time in operation is assumed. This central trough receives the runoff mainly from road areas with a low traffic frequency. In total nearly 22,600 m^2 of drainage surface are connected to the infiltration system. For the investigated infiltration trough a ratio between the connected impervious surfaces and the infiltration area of 18.8 to 1 (A_{red}/A_S) can be given.

3.2 *Investigation methods*

At site one, the day care centre in Dortmund, soil samples were taken near (and in one case distant) to the influx area at the following depths: 0 - 5 cm, 5 - 10 cm, 10 - 20 cm and 20 - 30 cm. The soil samples were taken and investigated at different times:

a) unloaded sample (taken during the construction work)
b) after 1 year in operation (November 1995)
c) after 1½ year in operation (May 1996)

At the second site, the old infiltration trough in Berlin, soil samples were taken in autumn 1996 in the middle of the trough at the following depths: 0 - 5 cm, 5 - 10 cm, 10 - 20 cm and 20 - 30 cm. A second set of soil samples was taken at different depths outside the infiltration area to obtain a comparative control.

In order to determine the total amount of substances (e.g. heavy metals) and their leachability by changing pH-conditions, different examination methods were used:

a) Determination of the acid soluble portion of metals (DIN 38414/7 S7)
b) Determination of leachability by water (DIN 38414/4 S4)
c) Determination of leachability by water with pH 4 (pH$_{stat}$ leaching test, Obermann & Cremer 1992)

Whereas the S4 - procedure (b) only represents the starting conditions of leaching processes in nature, the pH$_{stat}$ - procedure (c) takes greater consideration of the long-term development of the pH-value in nature. The pH$_{stat}$ - procedure also gives information about the neutralisation buffer capacity of the soil for acids and bases. These characteristic magnitudes that describe the long-term leaching behaviour, in connection with data about the respective soil (coefficient of hydraulic conductivity, stratum thickness), yield conclusions about the probability of the worst case of leaching occurring.

3.3 *Selected Results*

Figure 1 shows, for the day care centre, the proportion of zinc which can be mobilised by the pH$_{stat}$ leaching test with pH 4 in the topsoil of the infiltration trough after 12 and 18 months of operation (Hütter & Remmler 1996). The pH$_{stat}$ leaching test with pH 4 describes the worst case of leaching because this low pH probably facilitates the release of most soluble heavy metals from a soil. In addition, a sample comparison is presented between the topsoil in the influx and the margin area of the trough and the control sample that was taken during the construction work (Figure 1).

The investigations showed a high accumulation of zinc in the top 5 cm and of course a higher accumulation in the influx area, because there is more runoff water infiltrating even at small precipitation events. Similar results were detected for copper. The results

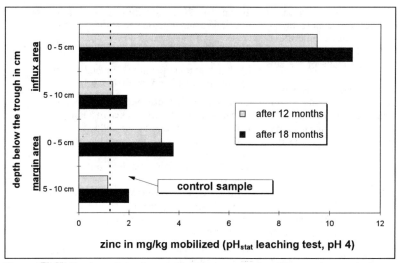

Figure 1. Mobilisation of zinc in an infiltration trough after different time periods.

also showed a slight decrease of the pH-value and the neutralisation buffer capacity of the soil for acids with time. These results can be explained by the fact that zinc and copper are a major part of the ma-materials that were used for the gutter and roof drain pipes.

Figure 2 shows the results for zinc in the topsoil of the old infiltration trough in Berlin. In addition the mobilised proportions of zinc from soil samples taken outside the trough are given. In contrast to the results at the day care centre in Dortmund the mobilised proportions of zinc are increasing with depth at a higher rate. At this site the first immobilised zinc in the topsoil is apparently moving deeper towards the groundwater. The almost exhausted neutralisation buffer capacity for acids and the very low pH of the soil (between 4.2 and 4.8) make long-term immobilisation in the upper centimetres of the topsoil impossible.

With regard to the protection of groundwater, such results provide important reasons for defining fundamental criteria for the operation of infiltration systems for storm water runoff.

4 REQUIREMENTS FOR THE INFILTRATION OF STORM WATER RUNOFF

In accordance with comprehensive soil and water protection, several requirements concerning the location, structure and operation of infiltration systems must be fulfilled. Many aspects of the following criteria are based on the planning, construction and operational experiences at several infiltration sites

within research projects in Germany in the last few years. Some of these practical aspects are already components of the German A 138 Standard and the additional report of the Abwassertechnische Vereinigung (ATV) -working group dealing with regulations for the infiltration of storm water runoff (ATV 1990, ATV 1995).

4.1 Location

A fundamental requirement for reducing the risks of pollution by storm water infiltration is a sufficient residence time for the seepage water in the unsaturated soil to ensure cleaning effects by biological, physical and chemical processes. Thus, the average hydraulic conductivity of the unsaturated zone below the infiltration system should range between 1×10^{-3} and 5×10^{-6} m s^{-1}.

Furthermore the groundwater level should be more than 1 m below the bottom of the infiltration system. This ensures that after passage through the topsoil to the unsaturated zone, concentration peaks can still be absorbed by filtration, sorption and ion-exchange processes.

To avoid the mobilisation of pollutants by seepage water it is also important that no residual pollution is present beneath the infiltration system.

4.2 Structure

The basic criterion for avoiding groundwater contamination is that infiltration of storm water runoff

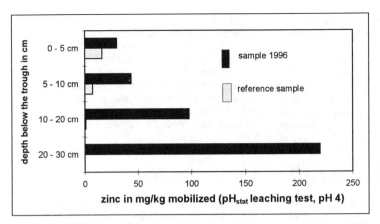

Figure 2. Mobilisation of zinc in an infiltration trough after a maximum of 80 years in operation.

should be via the topsoil. During natural groundwater replenishment and in the case of "natural" methods for artificial groundwater recharge, a well examined, intensive cleaning of the infiltration water occurs in the uppermost centimeters below the infiltration surface. To obtain comparable cleaning effects for the storm water infiltration systems there are specific requirements for the soil properties of the infiltration area:

a) A minimum thickness of 30 cm for the topsoil layer in the infiltration area is essential to allow for intensive cleaning effects.

b) For intensive biological degradation processes a sufficient residence time of the storm water in the topsoil is necessary. Therefore, a hydraulic conductivity of 1×10^{-5} m s^{-1} is indispensable for the first 30 cm of the soil.

c) To ensure a high buffer capacity there must be an adequate proportion of silt and clay in the topsoil. A high buffer capacity of the soil in the infiltration system is necessary, because a few groups of substances (e.g. heavy metals) are not degraded in the soil. They are exclusively fixed to the grain structure of the soil by sorption, precipitation or ionic exchange.

d) In addition to the immobilisation processes for heavy metals mentioned above, but also for their remobilisation by the percolating water, the pH of the soil solution in the oxidising soil area is of great importance. For the main heavy metals intensive adsorption in the soil is generally assumed to occur above a pH of 5.5. The remobilisation of some metals (e.g. copper and lead) can arise during alkaline soil reactions by the development of water soluble organic complexes. Therefore it is desirable, for the adsorption of pollutants, to maintain a pH between 5.5 and 8 for the topsoil (0-30 cm) of the infiltration systems. Taking into

consideration the natural soils available, this pH range can be reached by blending with carbonate rich soils or by liming the soils.

e) A further requirement must be taken into consideration during the construction of infiltration sites. Only materials should be allowed, which cause no detrimental changes to the quality of seepage water and groundwater in long term operation. This concerns all fill used for the filtration troughs and trenches.

f) During the construction of infiltration systems it is important that the basic principles of careful construction work and activity be kept for the protection of soil and groundwater. Sometimes considerable defects can be observed. Heavy construction equipment should not be used at the infiltration site to avoid soil compaction in the infiltration area. Thus, good supervision is important during the construction work to prevent the entry of pollutants and foreign substances like rubble or construction waste into the infiltration systems. Furthermore, the handling of water-endangering substances (e.g. gasoline used filling or cleaning of construction equipment) in the construction area of the infiltration system is strictly forbidden. Also the connection of the drainage surfaces to the infiltration site must be strictly inspected to avoid the connection of waste water pipes to the infiltration system.

4.3 Operation

There are two major aims for the operation of infiltration systems for storm water runoff. The cleaning potential of the infiltration system due to the adsorption of contaminants is of great importance as well as minimising the risk of remobilisation of these adsorbed pollutants and their release into the environment. Both aims must be guaranteed by appropriate maintenance and inspection activities.

In accordance with comprehensive water and soil protection there are several operating instructions which must be fulfilled to guarantee proper functioning of storm water infiltration systems. The maintenance must guarantee reliable functioning of the topsoil component. For this reason hydraulic weaknesses such as drying cracks or erosion damage of the soil must be avoided. If vegetation damage or decrease occurs the plants must be renewed. Furthermore, in the direct infiltration area no application of pesticides should be allowed.

During the operational period of an infiltration system, chemical substances accumulate in the soil. In order to ensure durable adsorption capacity of the topsoil these accumulated substances must be removed as the need arises or at regular intervals by suitable methods. The removed soil, contaminated with different kinds of substances, must be correctly disposed of and the soil and vegetation in the infiltration system must be renewed to guarantee proper functioning in future.

Storm water infiltration sites which are highly loaded have to be inspected at regular intervals (e.g. every 10 years). These inspections must assess whether the cleaning and adsorption capacity of the seepage area have become exhausted. Therefore suitable investigations of the topsoil and/or the seepage water and the groundwater must be carried out.

Furthermore the infiltration systems must be inspected if there are new unauthorised connections or a change of use of the connected areas, which could negatively influence the storm water quality. These maintenance and cleaning activities should be fixed in an established operational schedule.

5 CONCLUSIONS

Experiences with the planning and construction of several storm water infiltration systems and the soil investigations at some infiltration sites with lesser and longer times of operation showed that it is absolutely necessary to define specific criteria for storm water runoff infiltration as a form of storm water management. For long-term protection of soil and groundwater it is important to follow specific guidelines for the planning, construction and operation of storm water infiltration sites.

The risk of groundwater pollution can be minimised by using infiltration systems with low hydraulic surcharge, in which the storm water runoff percolates through the topsoil. An ecologically tenable storm water runoff infiltration system can only be achieved by exploitation of the cleaning and adsorption potential of existing and developing infiltration technologies and their combination. This will only function if, in addition, the requirements for the location, structure and operation are fulfilled.

Furthermore, there is a need to develop and use suitable instruments to monitor the long-term effectiveness of the infiltration systems. After long periods in operation, proper cleaning and disposal methods for the substances accumulated in the topsoil of infiltration systems must be used.

ACKNOWLEDGEMENT

We thank the German Environment Federal Foundation (DBU) and the Federal Ministry of Education, Science, Research and Technology (BMBF) for financial support of this work.

REFERENCES

ATV, 1990. Construction and dimensioning of facilities for decentralized percolation of non-harmful polluted surface water. Standard A 138, GFA, Hennef.

ATV, 1995. Hinweise zur Versickerung von Niederschlagsabflüssen. Arbeitsbericht der ATV-Arbeitsgruppe 1.4.1, Korrespondenz Abwasser, H. 5, 797 - 806.

DIN 38414/4. German standard methods for the examination of water, waste water and sludge; sludge and sediments (group S); determination of the leachability by water (S4).

DIN 38414/7. German standard methods for the examination of water, waste water and sludge; sludge and sediments (group S); digestion with aqua regia for subsequent determination of the acid soluble portion of metals (S7).

Hütter U. & F. Remmler, 1996. Storm water infiltration at a site with critical subsoil conditions: investigations of the potential pollution of soil, seeping water and groundwater. *Proceedings of the 7th International Conference on Urban Storm drainage*, Hannover, Vol. II, 713 - 718.

Obermann, P. & S. Cremer, 1992. Mobilisierung von Schwermetallen in Porenwässern von belasteten Böden und Deponien: Entwicklung eines aussagekräftigen Elutionsverfahrens. Landesamt für Wasser und Abfall (Hrsg.). Essen 1993. (=Materialien zur Ermittlung und Sanierung von Altlasten, Band 6).

Stecker, A. & F. Remmler, 1996. Alternative storm water drainage concept and design - a demonstration object -. *Proceedings of the 7th International Conference on Urban Storm drainage*, Hannover, Vol. III, 1831 - 1836.

Groundwater use management based on permanent-action models

Yu. F. Rudenko, V. M. Shestopalov, A. S. Boguslavsly & B. D. Stetsenko
Scientific-Engineering Centre for Radioecological Studies, National Academy of Sciences of Ukraine, Kyiv,
Ukraine

ABSTRACT The paper generalizes experience of stepwise investigations of urban territories for the purpose of increasing the reliability of assessment of exploitable groundwater reserves and estimating the impact of groundwater abstraction on the environment. A series of permanent-action hydrogeological models of different scales has been developed for the large urban agglomerations of Kyiv and Rivne in Ukraine. We consider the "permanent-action model" as a hydrogeological model which is permanently being adjusted and improved by obtaining new field data and corresponding model parameters. The methodology of groundwater resource assessment and the results of hydrodynamic and transport modelling are given and social and ecological problems are briefly discussed.

1 INTRODUCTION

As experience of hydrogeological investigations has shown, the resources of large-scale groundwater basins for the purposes of water supply to urban agglomerations based on mathematical models are periodically reassessed and models improved. This process is accompanied by development of model representations of water-exchange systems based on more complete description of the characteristics of groundwater in natural and exploited conditions.

The intensification of groundwater exploitation involves more precise definition of the problems concerning social and ecological impacts of water exchange between components of the aquifer complex as well as increasing requirements for reliable prediction of these impacts.

2 APPROACH TO STUDY

In retrospect this process could be divided into the following stages (Shestopalov et al. 1987):

1. Simplified schematic representation of hydrogeological conditions. The assessment of reserves in the exploited aquifer with the use of analytical methods, gives a so-called "strength of reserve indicator" by using worst case values for some parameters associated with sources of groundwater recharge.

2. Application of numerical modelling which allows for comprehensive representation of hydrogeological conditions. Even short-term pumping data can serve as a sufficient basis for nonsteady-state model calibration (solving of inverse problems) which provides more reliable evaluation of sources of groundwater recharge in exploited conditions and, hence, more comprehensive assessment of exploitable reserves.

3. Model development for more accurately defining the sources of exploitable reserves, evaluating the influence of groundwater exploitation on the environment and on water quality, and expanding the range of measures for the most rational environmental management scheme in conditions of intensive groundwater exploitation.

The comprehensive study of conditions and factors affecting groundwater resources through exploitation includes:

1) Detailed study and mapping of the main hydrogeological characteristics used for the development of models of filtration mechanisms.

2) Detailed study of boundary conditions directly influencing the formation of exploitable ground water reserves.

3) Study of the factors and conditions indirectly influencing the formation of exploitable groundwater reserves.

Using the given methodology the problems concerning water-supply to the largest regional centres of Ukraine (Kyiv and Rivne) have been studied in the Scientific-Engineering Centre for Radioecological Studies (SEC RES). The results of these studies are given below.

3 RESULTS

3. 1 *Kyiv*

The area of Kyiv Industrial Agglomeration (KIA) involves Kyiv City and the satellite towns of Vyshgorod, Boyarka, Brovary and Borispol, and adjoining territories within a radius of 60-70 km.

With regard to geological structure, aquifers of the Quaternary, Oligocene-Pliocene, Eocene, Cenomanian-Callovian and Middle Jurassic rocks can be distinguished within the KIA area. The hydrogeological section for Kyiv area is shown in Figure 1.

The major regional semi-permeable layers are composed of Neogene red and speckled clay, Upper Paleogene marl, Upper Cretaceous marl and chalk, Bathonian clay and siltstone, and Triassic clay. Their thickness ranges from 10 to 100 m. The Cenomanian-Callovian and underlying Upper Jurassic aquifers are the best prospects for intensive water supply and are widely exploited. The water quality of the deep aquifers is determined mainly by the state of the overlying aquifers through which groundwater recharge occurs.

A series of hydrogeological permanent action models of different scales has been developed. It includes a regional model at a scale of 1:200,000 covering the territory around Kyiv up to a radius of 70 km and a set of local models at a scale of 1:50,000 for the territory of Kyiv City proper and the eastern areas of Kyiv province which are a good prospect for groundwater utilization for the needs of centralized potable water supply.

The directions and velocities (both lateral and vertical) of groundwater flow in the heterogeneous multilayered aquifer system were determined. These characteristics were used in subsequent predictions of radionuclide migration through geological media. The impossibility of groundwater transfer to the KIA area from the contaminated exclusion zone of the Chernobyl Nuclear Power Plant was demonstrated. This is clear from the general flow direction pattern shown on Figure 2.

The model indicated the possibility of improvement of potable water supply with the use of groundwater exploitation in the eastern part of Kyiv province. The exploitable groundwater reserves were preliminarily evaluated to be 800,000 m^3/day.

The urgent problems concerning radionuclide behaviour in the geological environment were studied

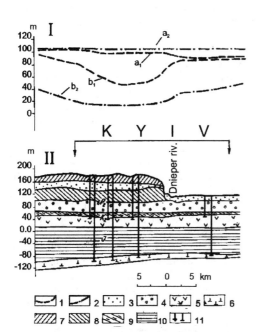

Explanation

I. Plot of the piezometric heads:
1- for the Cenomanian-Callovian aquifer (a_1-under natural conditions; b_1-under recent exploited conditions); 2-for the Middle Jurassic aquifer (a_2-under natural conditions; b_2-under recent exploited conditions).
II. Hydrogeological section.
Aquifers associated with:
3- Oligocene-Quaternary deposits (sand and sandy loam); 4- Eocene deposits (sand); 5- Cenomanian-Callovian deposits (limestone, chalk, sand, sandstone, gravel); 6-Upper Jurassic deposits (limestone).
Confining beds associated with:
7- Quaternary loam and clay; 8- Eocene marl; 9- Turonian marl; 10- Jurassic clay and clayey limestone; 11- wells of Kyiv water intake.

Figure 1. Hydrogeological section for Kyiv area with the plot of the piezometric heads of the main exploited aquifers.

by modelling their convection-dispersion transport processes in the unsaturated zone and in groundwater. The results showed contamination of all explored groundwater complexes with radionuclides, including the Upper Jurassic aquifer. But the level of contamination is small - a few orders of magnitude less than the maximum permissible concentration. The field data show that the real values of migration velocity between the unsaturated zone and groundwater must be higher than those obtained from modelling. This can be explained by the fact that the model representations do not account for some geological dislocations and breaks in continuity which serve as pathways for high-speed groundwater flow and radionuclide migration. In addition, the radionuclide penetration through drill annular space at the water-intake sites increases the level of groundwater contamination.

However, groundwater in the deeper aquifers still remains the most clean and reliable source for potable water supply of KIA, and its recovery for these purposes should be significantly increased (Bariakhtar 1995).

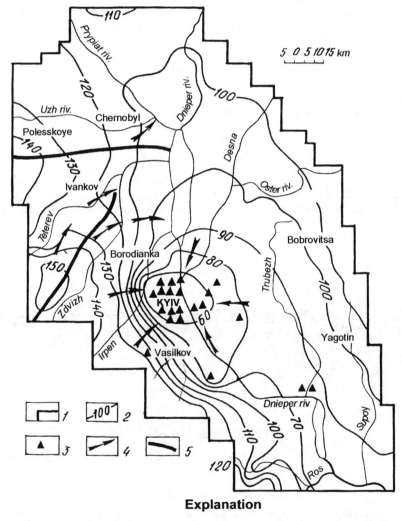

Explanation

1- boundary of the model; 2- contour of piezometric head (m); 3- working water intake;
4- the direction of groundwater flow; 5- groundwater divide

Figure 2. Map of the piezometric head contours for the Cenomanian-Callovian aquifer within the Kyiv Industrial Agglomeration (KIA), as measured in 1996.

The complexity of the hydrogeological permanent-action model is being gradually improved in the course of radio-hydrogeological monitoring. The model serves as a basis for accomplishing groundwater management in this area.

3.2 *Rivne*

The Rivne groundwater fields are situated within the marginal part of the Volynian-Podolian artesian basin on the western slope of the Ukrainian Shield. There, on the basement rocks descending westwards, monoclinally with tectonic breaks, lie the effusive and sedimentary deposits of Upper Proterozoic (Polessian, Volynian, Valdayian series), Lower Paleozoic (Cambrian, Silurian), and Mesozoic-Cenozoic (Upper Cretaceous, Neogene, and Quaternary) (Babinets 1980).

Of practical importance for water supply are the groundwater horizons and systems associated with marls and chalks of the Upper Cretaceous, Kanilovian and Nagoryanian suites of Valdayian series and Gorbashcvian deposits of the Volynian series of the Upper Proterozoic. The two last aquifers are separated by the low permeability deposits of the Berestovets tuffs (upper part of Volynian series) and the Yaryshev terrigenous bed (lower part of Valdayian series), as shown in a schematic hydrogeological section for the Rivne area (Figure 3).

The main factors of exploitable groundwater reserves formation in Rivne area are as follows:

1) the transmissivity of the aquifer around the well location and in the interfluvial area between the Ustye and Goryn Rivers being the zone of possible groundwater transport from recharge area to water intake;

2) vertical water exchange between the Gorbashevian aquifer and overlying aquifers, and surface water;

3) the total natural reserves for studied area, including those in the zone of Gorbashevian rocks underlying the Mesozoic-Cenozoic deposits.

Within the territory along Goryn River the conditions of exploitable groundwater reserves formation differ significantly from those previously described (Figure 3).

In the vicinity of exploration sites the thinning out of the low permeability layer of Berestovets tuffs occurs, hence the Gorbashevian aquifer immediately underlies the water-bearing Cretaceous and Quaternary deposits.

In natural conditions the discharge of the Gorbashevian aquifer proceeds mainly in this area, by the upward filtration through the layer of Berestovets tuffs into the watercourse of the Goryn River and its

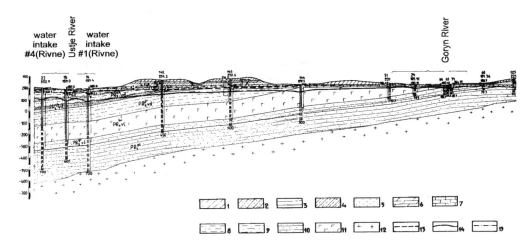

Explanation

1- loam; 2- sandy loam; 3- clay; 4- silt; 5- sand; 6- marl; 7- limestone; 8- claystone; 9- siltstone; 10- sandstone; 11- tuff; 12-granite, gneiss; 13-piezometric surface of the Upper Cretaceous aquifer under natural conditions; 14-piezometric surface of the Gorbashevian aquifer under exploited conditions; 15- piezometric surface of the Gorbashevian aquifer under natural conditions

Figure 3. Schematic hydrogeological section for Rivne area.

Table 1: Stages of assessment of groundwater resources for exploitation and solving of ecological and socio-economic problems during the permanent action model development for Rivne industrial complex

1(a):	Development of schematic representation of natural conditions in stages:
Stage I	The principal aquifers are isolated from each other. The upper aquifer is semibounded laterally, hydraulically connected with the river Ustye; the lower aquifer is unbounded laterally. Recharge of both aquifers takes place by lateral inflow.
Stage II	The principal aquifers interact with each other via aquitard and with rivers. Recharge of both aquifers takes place by lateral inflow.
Stage III	The Quaternary aquifer is separately defined. All aquifers are hydraulically connected via aquitards and with rivers. Feeding of aquifers occurs from the infiltration precipitation and by inflow from adjacent aquifers.
Stage IV	The model is complicated by the dependence of infiltration on time of travel through, and thickness of the unsaturated zone, and by accounting for annual variations of river levels. The geochemical information about distribution of water with various physicochemical properties and reactions are taken into account.
1(b):	Development of schematic representations of exploited conditions in stages:
Stage I	Exploitable reserves of groundwater in the upper aquifer are calculated on account of lateral groundwater inflow and by partial capture of the river Ustye underground flow during periods of low water level.
Stage II	Exploitable groundwater reserves of the upper principal aquifer are calculated on account of its own capacity and partial capturing of the river Ustye underground flow during periods of low water level. Formation of exploitable reserves in the deeper principal aquifers takes place on account of the natural resources and additional income from the upper aquifer.
Stage III	Exploitable groundwater reserves of principal aquifers are calculated on account of resources of the whole water-exchange system and partially by capturing of underground flow of the river Ustye.
Stage IV	Exploitable groundwater reserves of the upper productive aquifer are calculated on account of natural groundwater resources of the whole water-exchange system and the rivers Ustye and Goryn
2:	Development of model implementation in stages:
Stage I	Analytical calculations applying simplified formulas for groundwater dynamics.
Stage II	Analogue modelling applying the finite differences method.
Stage III	Digital modelling applying the method of finite differences.
Stage IV	Computer simulations on IBM PC using nonlinear finite difference schemes and graphic interface.
3:	Solving of environmental and socio-economic problems in stages:
Stage I	Not solved for the reason of absence of standard requirements to assessment of exploitable groundwater reserves.
Stage II	Assessment for the risk to wells from agricultural settlements adjacent to the river Goryn.
Stage III	Assessment of the influence of planned reservoir at Goryn river on the risk of possible flooding of adjacent territories. Assessment of this reservoir as a source of water supply, which proved its inefficiency by economic criteria. Recommendations given for additional water supply to small settlements in case of well dewatering, for rejection of the project providing the construction of drainage systems in the valley of Goryn river, and also for construction of buffer ponds for operative water supply.
Stage IV	Studying the influence of chemical composition of atmospheric deposits on chemical composition of groundwater taking into account the physico-chemical and biogeochemical processes in the aeration zone. Studying the changes in hydrochemical conditions which induce the release of earlier absorbed contaminants and secondary contamination of groundwater in aquifers. Revealing the sources of groundwater contamination and elaboration of recommendations on their localized effect along with socio-economic assessments. Determining the localities at the land surface which are subjected to the risk of landslides and karst subsidence after intensive groundwater exploitation.

valley, where numerous wetland areas are developed.

As follows from the available information, the watercourse of the river is separated from groundwater by fluvial deposits of low permeability (K=0. 1 m/day) that impede water exchange between surface and groundwater.

Since the 1960s, the problem of water supply to Rivne City and minimization of its impact on the environment has heightened the importance of assessing exploitable groundwater reserves. Urgency has arisen because of the increase of city demands for potable water; more precise information on the environmental characteristics and improvement of modelling techniques has been achieved.

The stages of development of the hydrogeological problems being solved during this period are described in Table 1.

4 CONCLUSIONS

Accumulated experience in the application of mathematical models in studying the groundwater management of large urban agglomerations subjected to intensive anthropogenic influences, indicates the expediency of further practical application of hydrogeological permanent-action models for solving analogous problems in other areas. Development of permanent-action models for the majority of industrial centres of Ukraine (as well as water supply optimization at the expense of groundwater exploitation), will enable not only the improvement of the potable water quality, but also the creation of a robust water-supply system in extreme situations.

REFERENCES

Shestopalov, V.M., Yu.F. Rudenko, & V.0. Baluta 1987. Stages of study of large hydrogeological units for rising entirety of assessment for groundwater exploitational resources and influence of their use on the environment. *International Symposium on Groundwater Quality Control and Resources Management.* Dresden, 1987.
Bariakhtar, V.G. (Editor) 1995. The Chernobyl Disaster. Kyiv, *Naukova Dumka* publisher. (In Russian).
Babinets, A.E. (Editor) 1980. Introduction into modelling of hydrogeological processes. Kiev, *Naukova Dumka* publisher. (In Russian).

Assigning a groundwater protection value: Methodology development

C. Scharp, T. Alveteg & P.-O. Johansson
Division of Land and Water Resources, Royal Institute of Technology (KTH), Stockholm, Sweden

M. Caldera
Nicaraguan Institute of Aqueducts and Sewage Systems (INAA), Managua, Nicaragua

ABSTRACT: A methodology for estimating groundwater protection value has been developed, aimed at identifying the groundwater resources which are most valuable for a society and therefore most important to protect. The methodology was applied in the Managua groundwater system in Nicaragua. A map indicating protection value was produced with the help of the geographical information system IDRISI. Through this method it was possible to identify the most valuable groundwater resources which need protection based on potential quantities one could extract or areas which are the most sensitive to changes in groundwater level. The results have served as input when constructing a general framework for groundwater protection.

1 INTRODUCTION

The importance of groundwater protection is increasing, particularly in countries highly dependent on groundwater for the water supply to their inhabitants. Contamination of groundwater resources can be seen as one of the most important factors endangering the long-term water supply in many regions in the world where water scarcity is already a major limitation to economic growth. The prevention of groundwater contamination by diminishing harmful fluxes to important groundwaters is a major challenge for decision makers and planners. Fundamental to effective groundwater protection is access to an extensive body of information about groundwater resources including geology, hydrogeology and potential contamination loads.

Not all groundwaters need protection to the same extent, and it is therefore important to initiate protective measures where the most important groundwater resources are located. By having a sound foundation in land-use planning, the location of potentially contaminating activities can be allocated to the least valuable or vulnerable areas thus producing less harm to the environment. Therefore assigning a certain value to different groundwater resources could be an effective instrument for defining the resources most needing protection.

1.1 *Groundwater protection value*

Groundwater resources can be said to possess a certain value based on the services the resource may provide to the society. This value may alter due to the society's degree of dependence on groundwater. The value of groundwaters constitutes the basic factor of interest for the society to protect the resource from becoming contaminated. The higher the value of the resource, the higher is the willingness to protect it.

By using economic terms, it is possible to single out three major characteristics of the groundwater resource which constitute sources for the value. These are; *use*, *option* and *existence* (O'Neil and Raucher 1990). The actual *use* of the resource for water supply is the major characteristic which determines the value of the resource and thereby the willingness to protect it from contamination. With a high dependence on groundwater for water supply follows a stronger willingness to take protective measures in a given society, than if the degree of dependence is low. The willingness to protect the resources are even higher if the availability of alternative sources in case of a damaged resource is limited.

In addition to this, a groundwater resource which is not in current use may have a value to the society due to its *potential* (*option*) to supply water. Based on the potential use there is a will to protect that resource. Finally groundwater can be valued according to its importance as a vital element for every ecosystem and every landscape and as forming distinctive environments of its own (*existence*).

The value of groundwater can be expressed in strict economic terms by, for example the cost of restoring contaminated groundwater to such a degree that it is able to provide the same services to the society as before. If this recovery of the groundwater is impossible, the value of the groundwater might be expressed as the cost of finding an alternative source of water supply. Methods by which water can be valued economically are reviewed by Winpenny (1996).

If these fundamental sources (*use, option and existence*) for the value of groundwater were transformed to general parameters it would be possible to define a *protection value* of the groundwater resource. This protection value would describe the importance of a particular resource to society in comparison to other groundwater resources. The protection value would indicate the need to consider protection measures to secure the long-term availability of a clean and safe resource for water supply.

This paper presents a study with the aim of developing a practical and general method to indicate the *protection value* of groundwater resources to be used as input in groundwater protection planning. This method is based on the evaluation of four key parameters corresponding to the factors influencing the sources for the value. To facilitate the implementation of the method the geographical information system (GIS) IDRISI (Eastman 1995) was used. The method developed was applied in the Eastern sub-basin of the Managua groundwater system in Nicaragua (Sustainable use of water resources project, 1996). Further experiences with application of the method are also presented in Scharp et al. (1997). The application in the Managua groundwater system was limited to the use of available data. Furthermore, the methodology has been used as an input to a general framework for groundwater protection adapted to developing countries which is based on groundwater vulnerability assessment and characterisation of contamination load (Johansson et al. 1997).

2 STUDY AREA DESCRIPTION

Managua, the capital city of Nicaragua is entirely

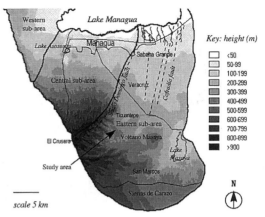

Figure 1. Managua groundwater system with study area indicated

dependent on groundwater for its water supply. The groundwater is extracted from the so called Managua groundwater system, which is to a large extent located beneath the city itself (Figure 1). Generally the groundwater is of very good quality, but in certain areas has some influence of geothermal water.

In the study area the pressure on the resource is high and this situation has been aggravated during the last few years. The rate of population increase of the area is high; from less than 0.5 million people in 1975 to more than 1.5 million in 1995, of which some 85 % live within the city. Managua also has the major industrial zones of the country. In addition, the area is important agriculturally for producing cash crops, and in the hilly region coffee is grown. Cotton used to be the major crop. These factors together constitute a threat to both the quality and the quantity of the available groundwater resource. Therefore guiding future land-use decisions to protect the groundwater is defined as an urgent issue.

The Managua groundwater system encompasses approximately 900 km^2 reaching from Lake Managua in the North (37 m.a.s.l) to the hilly region in the South (900 m.a.s.l). It can be divided into three sub-basins: Western- Central- and Eastern sub-basins. The rocks of the area are of volcanic origin, with a complex stratigraphic composition. Geological formations are mainly semi-consolidated pyroclastic deposits, pyroclastic flows with interbedded lavas and fossil soils. The groundwater system has three main water bearing formations: alluvial deposits with quaternary pyroclastic materials, the Masaya Group of volcanics (Pleistocene) and the Middle Las Sierras Group of volcanics (Plio-pleistocene). The saturated thickness varies between 100 and 400 m and the transmissivities measured in test wells are within the range 1 - 1000 m^2d^{-1}. The groundwater table is found at a depth of up to 300 m in the southern hilly region. The depth steadily decreases towards Lake Managua. Close to the lake groundwater is discharged through several springs (20 - 200 ls^{-1}) at the interface between the Masaya Group volcanics and the alluvial deposits.

The groundwater system is to be regarded as unconfined but perched water tables can be found locally. The average groundwater recharge is estimated to be 270 $mmyr^{-1}$ with large spatial variations (JICA/INAA 1993).

3 METHODOLOGY

With the purpose of estimating a protection value of the groundwater, a methodology was developed based on the evaluation of four key parameters: *available quantities, groundwater quality, present or planned use* and finally *sensitivity to changes in groundwater level*. The identified parameters are considered to correspond to the economic sources of the value.

The parameter *available quantities (Q_n)* estimates the possible quantities which can be extracted from a groundwater system without endangering the total groundwater balance. The evaluation of this parameter is based on transmissivity values (T m^2d^{-1}) and on groundwater recharge (R $mmyr^{-1}$). Depending on the location in the groundwater system the T and R factors have different significance for the quantity potential to abstract. At higher altitudes up-streams in a system groundwater recharge is relatively more important for the potential for abstraction than transmissivity. In lower parts of the system, down-streams, transmissivity is the dominating factor for the potential abstraction rather than recharge. Based on a hydrogeological conceptual model of the groundwater system it can be divided into three different zones: low, intermediate and high zone. Within each zone the T and R values respectively are multiplied with a "localisation factor" (T_f, T_r). Values for T, R, T_f and T_r can be seen in Table 1. The quantity parameter is calculated according to the following formula:

$$Q_n = TT_f + RR_f \qquad (1)$$

Any changes in the *groundwater quality (Q_l)* may have an impact on the environment and on human health. Primarily drinking water quality is to be assured but also the impacts of quality changes on ecosystems must be considered. The presence of a contaminant at a higher concentration than the so called baseline level would indicate penetration of a contaminant and is referred to as contamination. The parameter quality refers to the actual quality of the groundwater compared to accepted guidelines. It is suggested that comprehensive groundwater guidelines are used for example the list for groundwater quality monitoring in Denmark (Stockmarr, 1997). In this particular case the evaluation was based on WHO drinking water guidelines (WHO. 1984). The table for evaluation of the parameter *quality* is shown in Table 2.

Discharge areas with groundwater levels close to the ground surface form distinctive environments which may have very high protection values for the ecosystem (existence value). A change in the groundwater level would jeopardise the whole system. In addition to this a *change in groundwater level (G_{wl})* may have economic impacts by drying out wetlands used for pasture or causing land subsidence with effects on buildings and infrastructure. This parameter is evaluated relatively without any consideration of absolute measures of the decline of the groundwater level (Table 3).

When considering a protection value (V_a) for municipal water supply the terms (Q_n) and (Q_l) have additive values while the term (G_{wl}) will have a negative influence on the protection value for water supply since a decline of the water table is an effect caused by extraction for water supply. However it is still of great importance to indicate areas that are sensitive to changes in groundwater levels to a planner. Therefore this parameter is presented on a separate map. The final protection value index is calculated from the following formula:

$$V_a = 2V_{Qn} + 3 V_{Ql} - V_{Gwl} \qquad (2)$$

where V_a is the final protection value index, V_{Qn} is the evaluation of the potential quantity for extraction, V_{Ql} is the value index for groundwater quality and V_{Gwl} is the value index for areas sensitive to changes in groundwater level. Each of the parameters is assigned a weight, as shown in the formula, according to its importance for the overall value and are evaluated and given a rating taken from Tables 1 to 3. The final protection value is, by this process, given in qualitative relative terms, indicating increasing protection value in five classes. The

Table 1. Groundwater Quantity $(Q_n)^*$

Transmissivity T m²d⁻¹	Class	Recharge mm yr⁻¹	Class
< 10	1	< 50	1
10-99	3	50-99	3
100-1000	7	100-179	6
> 1000	10	180-250	8
		> 250	10

Zone	T factor (Tf)	R factor (Rf)
Low	0.7	0.3
Intermediate	0.5	0.5
High	0.3	0.7

* weighting 2 in equation 2

Table 2. Groundwater Quality $(Q_l)^*$

	Class
Water technically and economically very difficult or impossible to treat	1
Water fulfilling water quality standards after more complicated treatment	7
Water fulfilling quality standards after simple treatment (e.g. aeration, filtration)	9
Water fulfilling water quality standards without treatment	10

* weighting 3 in equation 2

Table 3. Changes in groundwater level $(G_{wl})^*$

	Class
Areas not sensitive to changes in groundwater levels	1
Areas which potentially are affected by changes in groundwater levels	6
Areas which are very sensitive to changes in groundwater levels	10

* weighting 1 in equation 2

Table 4. Groundwater use for municipal water supply

Abstraction ls⁻¹	Abstraction wells	Planned wells
2-20	•	•
20-100	●	○
> 100	●	○

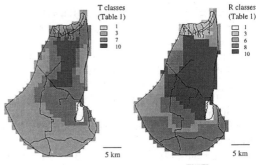

Figure 2. Transmissivity and recharge maps of study area.

The parameter *present and planned use* expresses the current and future demand for municipal water supply. This parameter is not included in the overlay procedure but is laid over the final map with symbols representing actual and planned extraction (Table 4).

4 RESULTS

For the evaluation of the parameter *quantity* available data from a well drilling project were used (JICA/INAA 1993). The map obtained gives a good picture of the potentially available quantities in the area. As shown in Figure 3, the area indicating large available quantities of groundwater, coincides well with areas of high recharge rate (>250 mm) and the two higher transmissivity ranges (100-1000 m²d⁻¹, >1000 m²d⁻¹ respectively) shown in Figure 2.

For the evaluation of groundwater *quality* existing data from a limited number of monitoring wells were used. Quality data were only obtainable from drinking water quality analyses. The water quality was assigned a value from Table 2. As the groundwater quality is uniformly good, only two classes (9 and 10) are reflected on the quality map. The lower class was assigned due to the influence of geothermal water which causes an increase of dissolved solids (TDS) to 150 - 400 mgl⁻¹, and a slightly elevated temperature (30-35° C) (Figure 4).

The major part of the groundwater system was assessed as not being sensitive to changes in groundwater level (Figure 5), with the exception of two areas adjacent to Lake Managua. In the area assigned to class 6, lowering of the water level causes drying up of springs and wetlands, which would have a negative impact on the local ecosystem and also negative economic effects for cattle-breeding farmers. In the area classed as 10, excessive pumping in wells close to the lake might cause

results derived from the evaluation of the parameters are presented as a map overlaid with the *use* parameter.

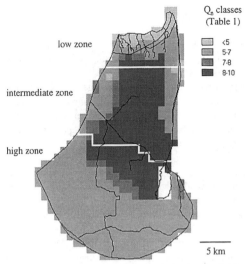

Figure 3. Parameter Quantity (Q_n) also indicating the division into zones with different altitudes significant to the T and R values.

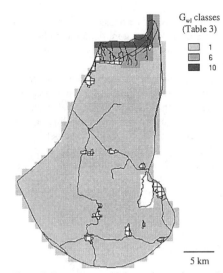

Figure 5. Parameter sensitivity to changes in groundwater level (G_{wl}).

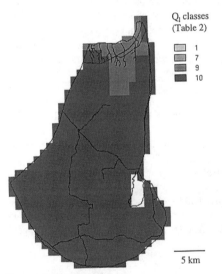

Figure 4. Parameter quality *(Q_l)*

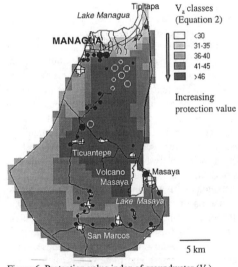

Figure 6. Protection value index of groundwater (V_a).

intrusion of polluted lake water.

The composite final protection value is presented in Figure 6. The map identifies the central area as the most valuable to protect. The overlaid *use* parameter (Table 4), also shows that most of the present and planned abstraction is located in this area, where both *T* and *R* values are relatively high. This area also includes the Volcano Masaya area which is considered to be of importance for groundwater recharge.

5 CONCLUSIONS

By the method described it has been possible to pinpoint those areas which have particular protection value and those that have less protection value for society's water supply. The overlay with present and future use enhances the visual impression of the map and facilitates the interpretation. It can be seen that all the points for planned abstraction are located within the area with high protection value. For a land-use planner it would be possible to extract from the map those areas where more detailed studies are needed and protection measures must be considered a priority.

In addition, through the parameter map *sensitivity to changes in groundwater level* it has been possible to identify areas with a high protection value due to effects that would be caused by a decline in the groundwater level. In the study, this parameter map has proved to have the most direct impact. It has been demonstrated that a lowering of the groundwater level would dry out wetlands and consequently be harmful to the economic activities in the area. In addition to this, valuable ecological environments would be destroyed in the area, as the natural spring zone would dry out. Because of this, protective measures must also be considered in this area.

The maps prepared have the advantage of being based on only a few parameters. They are, therefore transparent in the sense that the user can understand the contribution from the different parameters in the overlay procedure.

An important factor in society's willingness to protect a particular groundwater source is the availability for alternative sources of groundwater or surface water. In this study alternative sources have not been included as a parameter but have been discussed in the text accompanying the protection value maps. The Managua groundwater system is an enormous resource and any realistic alternative sources could not be found without tremendous financial investments. This should increase the society's willingness to protect the most valuable parts of the Managua groundwater system.

To conclude, this methodology contributes to the identification of areas with a high protection value, and through communicating this message to decision makers and land-use planners the willingness to protect the groundwater should increase, and protection measures should thereby be considered in future land-use planning.

It is hoped that after further development this methodology will become a valuable approach for improving the protection of the groundwater resources.

ACKNOWLEDGEMENT

The authors appreciate the support of the Swedish International Development Cooperation Agency to the Sustainable Use of Groundwater Resources project in Nicaragua within which this work has been incorporated.

REFERENCES

Eastman, J.R. 1995. IDRISI for windows, Clark University, Graduate school of Geography, Worcester, Massachusetts.

Japan international co-operation agency/ Nicaraguan institute of aqueducts and sewage systems (JICA/INAA). 1993. The study on water supply project in Managua - the main report, Kokusai kogyo Co., Tokyo.

Johansson, P.-O., C. Scharp, T. Alveteg, and A. Choza. 1997. A framework for groundwater protection adapted to developing countries - the Managua aquifer as an example, div. of Land and Water Resources, Royal Institute of Technology, Stockholm in preparation.

O'Neil, W. and R. Raucher. 1990. The cost of groundwater contamination, Journal of Soil and Water Conservation, Vol. 45, No. 2, pp 180-183.

Scharp, C., T. Alveteg, P.-O. Johansson and M. Caldera. 1997. Groundwater protection value - an input to groundwater protection planning, Div. of Land and Water Resources, Royal Institute of Technology, Stockholm in prepatation.

Stockmarr, J. 1997 Revised groundwater quality monitoring programme in Denmark 1998-2003. Geological Survey of Denmark and Greenland, DK-2200 Copenhagen, Denmark.

Sustainable use of water resources project. 1996. Estimation of the relative protection value in the Eastern sub-basin of the Managua aquifer. Nicaraguan Institute of Aqueducts and Sewage Systems, Managua, Nicaragua.

World Health Organisation (WHO). 1984 Guidelines for drinking water quality Vol.1, Geneva.

Winpenny, J.T. 1996. The value of water valuation. Water policy: Allocation and management in practice. (Ed Howsam and Crater) E&FN Spon, London.

Groundwater in the Urban Environment: Problems, Processes and Management, Chilton et al. (eds)
© 1997 Balkema, Rotterdam, ISBN 90 5410 837 1

Urban land-use study plan for the National Water-Quality Assessment Program, US Geological Survey

P.J. Squillace, J.S. Zogorski & C.V. Price
US Geological Survey, Rapid City, S. Dak., USA

ABSTRACT: A study plan for Urban Land-Use Studies has been initiated as part of the U.S. Geological Survey's National Water-Quality Assessment (NAWQA) Program. The two Urban Land-Use Study objectives are to define water quality in recharge areas of shallow aquifers underlying areas of new residential and commercial land in large metropolitan areas, and to determine which natural and human factors most strongly affect the occurrence of contaminants in these shallow aquifers.

To meet the first objective, each NAWQA Study Unit will install and collect water samples from at least 30 randomly located monitoring wells in a metropolitan area. To meet the second objective, aquifer characteristics and land-use information will be documented. These include particle-size analysis and percentage of organic carbon of each major lithologic unit in the unsaturated zone and in the aquifer near the water table. Geographic information system coverages will be created to document existing land use around the wells.

1 INTRODUCTION

The National Water-Quality Assessment (NAWQA) Program was implemented by the U.S. Geological Survey in 1991 as a systematic assessment of the quality of the Nation's water resources. The program will describe the status and trends in the quality of a large, representative part of the Nation's surface-water and ground-water resources and will define the primary natural and human factors affecting the quality of these resources. In meeting these goals, the NAWQA Program will produce information useful for policymakers, managers, and the general public at the National, State, and local levels. The building blocks of the NAWQA Program are 59 Study-Unit Investigations that include parts of most of the Nation's major river basins and aquifers (Figure 1). The proposed starting dates of the Study-Unit Investigations are staggered between 1991 and 1997. Gilliom et al. (1995) discuss the overall design of the NAWQA Program in more detail. Additional information on the NAWQA Program is available at "http://wwwrvares.er.usgs.gov/nawqa/nawqa_home.html."

The NAWQA study design for ground water focuses on assessing the water-quality conditions of major aquifers in each Study Unit (Study-Unit Surveys) with emphasis on the quality of recently recharged ground water associated targeted land use (Land-Use Studies). The general objective of the Land-Use Studies is to examine natural factors and human activities that affect the quality of recently recharged (generally less than 10 years old) shallow ground water that underlies key types of land use within each Study Unit. Land-Use Studies underlying urban and agricultural settings have been a primary focus in the NAWQA Program to date.

2 OBJECTIVES

There are two Urban Land-Use Study objectives: (1) Define the water quality in recharge areas of shallow aquifers underlying areas of new residential and commercial land use in large metropolitan areas, and (2) determine which natural and human factors most strongly affect the occurrence of contaminants in these shallow aquifers.

2.1 *Rationale for objective 1*

Residential and commercial areas compose the largest land use within metropolitan areas, and little is known about the associated effects of this land use on water quality. Because of the predominance of the residential and commercial land use, an understanding of the shallow ground-water quality beneath these areas is important for well-head protection of municipal and private supply wells. Also, residential areas are important because population density has been directly correlated to contamination in shallow ground water (Eckhardt & Stackelberg 1995).

The targeted residential and commercial areas contain "new" development constructed between

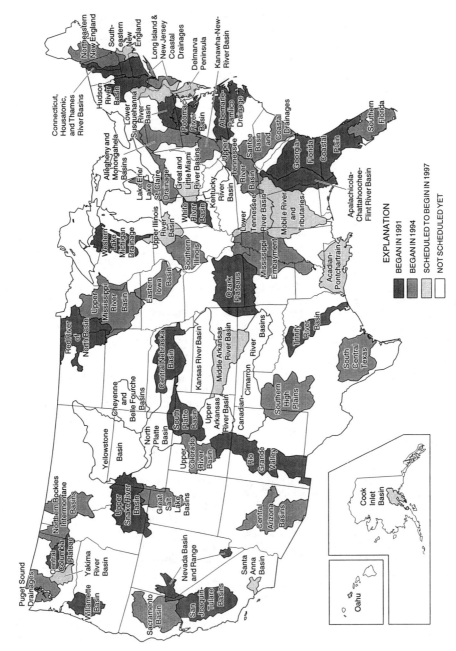

Figure 1. Location of National Water-Quality Assessment Program Study Units and their proposed implementation dates (from Gilliom et al. 1995).

666

about 1970 and 1990. Large industrial areas and the city centers are excluded from the NAWQA Urban Land-Use Studies. Industrial areas will not be investigated by NAWQA studies because data are already being collected in these areas by other Federal and State agencies. The city centers are excluded for three reasons: (1) ground water is generally not used in those areas, (2) urban land use in those areas are generally much older than 1970, and (3) land use in those areas are likely to have changed with time. If the land use has changed, the cause of contamination may be difficult to determine on the basis of current land use. The targeted residential and commercial land-use areas will be at least 5 years old because it takes some time for new development to affect shallow ground-water quality.

A study designed to investigate new residential and commercial areas is a forward-looking plan. Older residential and commercial areas may have ground-water contamination that resulted from practices that have already been banned, and studies carried out in these areas may be unable to distinguish between old and new contamination problems.

NAWQA study results should be helpful to resource managers and policymakers at Federal, State, and local levels in making sound decisions. There are probably three situations that most urban ground-water managers and suppliers face: (1) an existing well field lies within an established urban area, and there are proposals to expand the well field within the established urban area; (2) the existing municipal well field lies at the edge of the urban area, and new development is beginning to encroach on the recharge area; and (3) new residential developments at the edge of the urban area have their own wells and do not use the municipal water supply. Studying the new residential and commercial areas will provide the most valuable information to city planners and municipal water suppliers in the last two situations, although some information will be helpful to municipalities in the first situation also. The information derived from Urban Land-Use Studies of new areas will provide an understanding of water-quality issues and insights on how to better plan for new developments so as to minimize water-quality degradation.

Recharge zones in the Urban Land-Use Study areas are selected for study so that a relation between land use and shallow ground-water quality can be established. Furthermore, knowledge of the shallow ground-water quality may provide an early warning of contaminants that are reaching the water table before the contaminant reaches the deeper ground water used for water supplies.

2.2 Rationale for objective 2

Once contaminants have been identified, defining the source of contamination is of critical interest. In past Urban Land-Use Studies, little has been done to define the source of contamination. Therefore, more detailed ancillary data will be collected for future Urban Land-Use Studies to help define the sources of contamination.

Natural and human factors affect the occurrence of contaminants in shallow aquifers. Natural factors, such as the organic carbon content of the aquifer material, may limit the amount of contamination detected in shallow ground water. Human factors, such as proximity to commercial areas and highways, may explain the presence or absence of contaminants at a particular location. Within the residential and commercial land-use area, there are many potential sources of contamination, but there may be certain land-use activities that are major contributors of contaminants to shallow ground water. For example, ground-water contamination in residential areas may be related to the use of pesticides by homeowners or the release of volatile organic chemicals (VOCs) by certain industries; industrial areas may contribute VOCs to other land-use areas via air emissions, stormwater runoff, and ground-water flow.

It is also important to determine how climate affects the shallow ground-water quality given the same land use and similar aquifers. This knowledge could help indicate if uniform Federal regulations for ground-water quality monitoring are appropriate for all parts of the United States or if such monitoring might be better tailored to climatic regions. Furthermore, the knowledge gained could help guide future land development in certain areas of the United States to protect the water quality of shallow aquifers that contribute to drinking-water supplies.

3 SELECTION OF URBAN LAND-USE STUDY AREAS

Study Unit managers will locate Urban Land-Use Studies in areas where shallow ground water is most vulnerable to contamination due to anthropogenic and hydrogeologic factors. Anthropogenic factors such as pesticide and nutrient use, toxic chemical use and release, and population density may contribute to the presence of contamination in shallow ground water. Large metropolitan areas with underlying shallow unconfined bedrock or sand and gravel aquifers are best suited for Urban Land-Use Studies.

Study Units will locate their Urban Land-Use Study in a single metropolitan area. By limiting each Urban Land-Use Study to a single metropolitan area, there is a better chance that there will be similar climate, hydrogeology, and chemical use within the study area. The effects of selected natural and anthropogenic factors on the water quality of these shallow aquifers can then be investigated. Although metropolitan areas can be very large and in some cases are adjacent to other metropolitan areas, limiting the size of the actual study area is also necessary so that it will be easier to collect ancillary information and to create geographic information system (GIS) coverages of the study area.

Large metropolitan areas are being emphasized because population density has been related to contamination of shallow ground-water quality (Eckhardt & Stackelberg, 1995). Furthermore, 89 percent of the urban population of the United States lives in metropolitan areas of greater than 250,000 persons (U.S. Bureau of the Census, 1992). Areas with air pollution problems—that is, metropolitan areas classified by the U.S. Environmental Protection Agency as ozone or carbon-monoxide nonattainment areas—are preferred for study. Metropolitan areas with shallow ground water and permeable unsaturated zones are preferred for study. If the depth to water is great, then recharge probably would be smaller, and one would expect to see less contamination from land-use activities. There will also be some Urban Land-Use Studies initiated where the unsaturated zone is not as permeable and the depth to water is variable.

The results of the Urban Land-Use Studies will be more directly relevant if the water in the shallow aquifer investigated in metropolitan areas is used for drinking. Therefore, it is preferred that the shallow aquifer in the selected metropolitan areas be (1) used as a source of drinking water, (2) considered a potential source of drinking water, or (3) hydraulically connected to surface water or deeper ground water used as a source of drinking water. If the shallow ground water does not meet the preceding criteria, then it is preferred that the aquifer be similar to aquifers that are used as a water supply in other parts of the Study Unit or region. For example, an Urban Land-Use Study designed to look at natural and human effects on an alluvial aquifer in one part of the country may have transfer value to other similar areas of the country even if ground water is not used in that particular metropolitan area.

4 MAJOR WORK ELEMENTS

The major work elements necessary to accomplish an Urban Land-Use Study are discussed below.

4.1 *Define study area*

The study area is defined as the intersection of two GIS coverages: (1) the areal extent of the surficial aquifer and (2) the areal extent of the new residential and commercial land-use areas in the single metropolitan area targeted for study.

Residential and commercial land, golf courses, parks, roadways, and business highways are considered part of residential and commercial land use. Agricultural land use will be avoided or minimized in the Urban Land-Use Study area.

Industrial areas, city centers, and wide transportation corridors such as railway yards and limited-access highways, will be carefully excluded from the study area. Sampled monitoring wells will be located at least 1 km from heavy industry. Light industry that is mixed with commercial areas may be very difficult to avoid and wioll be allowed. Railways and limited-access highways consisting of two or more lanes are excluded from the study area if they have not already been excluded by the land-use coding system.

After the study area is defined, a subarea will be created for use in selecting drilling sites for monitoring wells. The selection of a subarea is necessary to avoid well sites being near the edge of the study area and affected by features outside the study area. The residential and commercial land use, as defined previously, will make up more than 75 percent of the land use within a 500-m radius of the final drilling sites.

4.2 *Randomly locate 30 primary and alternate locations for monitoring wells and verify land-use criteria onsite*

Monitoring wells for the Urban Land-Use Study need to be distributed randomly throughout the land-use setting after the land-use areas have been delineated. The locations of the wells will not be skewed either toward or away from possible point sources of contamination. Primary and alternate locations will be randomly selected using a computer program written by Scott (1990).

If a drill site cannot be located within 250 m of the primary location, then it will be necessary to move to an alternate random location. Once the primary or alternate random locations have been identified onsite, the actual drill site will be located as close to the primary or alternate random locations as possible to avoid biasing the site either toward or away from known contamination; the final drill site will be within 250 m of the random location.

Drilling sites for monitoring wells will not be closer than 1 km from each other to avoid the overlap of buffer areas around the wells. Overlapping buffer areas may introduce spatial autocorrelation effects, which can invalidate statistical analysis of the water-quality data (Barringer et al. 1990). This minimum separation distance can be specified as input to the random site-selection program (Scott, 1990).

Drill sites will be located in areas where shallow ground water originates within the designated land-use area. Therefore, drill sites can be located immediately downgradient from the selected urban land-use area.

Thirty wells is considered the minimum number of monitoring wells; some Study Unit leaders may want to install additional wells if their study area is very large. However, large metropolitan areas may encompass several cities with different socioeconomic factors which may affect ground-water quality. Therefore, adjacent cities may look similar on a map, but there may be important differences which affect the occurrence and distribution of contaminants in the adjacent areas. Combining these adjacent areas into a single Urban Land-Use Study would make interpretation of the data very difficult.

4.3 *Drill and install the monitoring wells*

Urban Land-Use Studies will be conducted by drilling monitoring wells rather than using existing wells. Drilling the monitoring wells provides the best control for well construction, ensures the wells are under U.S. Geological Survey ownership can be sampled in the future for trends analysis, ensures a random distribution of wells, and probably saves time and money when compared to finding existing wells in urban areas. By drilling wells for Urban Land-Use Studies, NAWQA can minimize the possibility that monitoring well locations are biased toward known point-source contamination, or that the construction technique is inadequate.

In almost all cases, existing urban wells are not constructed according to NAWQA protocols and, therefore will not be sampled. Wells need to be randomly located, screened near to the top of the water table, have flush-threaded polyvinyl-chloride casings, and be sealed. Existing monitoring wells drilled to define the upgradient conditions at a point-source contamination site are not acceptable. Most domestic drinking-water wells are normally screened deeper in the aquifer rather than close to the top.

Each monitoring well installed for Urban Land-Uses Studies will have a short screened interval (ideally less than 3 m in length). Generally, the top of the screen will be 0.6 to 1.5 m below the lowest anticipated position of the water table to reduce the chances of the well being dry during parts of the year and to avoid problems with interpreting data from wells with partially saturated, open intervals.

The 5-cm monitoring wells installed for Urban Land-Use Studies will be drilled following the guidelines outlined by Lapham et al. (1995). Wells will be installed using a hollow-stem auger in unconsolidated material. Auger drilling is the most suitable drilling technique because no drilling fluids are introduced into the aquifer. Air-rotary drilling is not advisable because air compressors use oils that may be introduced into the aquifer. Mud-rotary drilling introduces mud into the aquifer.

4.4 *Define aquifer characteristics*

Aquifer characteristics, such as percentage of organic carbon, type of aquifer, particle size, and soil pH, will be documented for each monitoring well. When drilling the wells, all drill cuttings will be logged, and split-spoon samples will be collected from all major lithologic units and the screened interval for analysis of grain size, organic carbon content, and soil pH. It is expected that about three split-spoon samples per well will be collected.

Dry-sieve analysis is recommended. About 200 to 300 g of sediment will be collected. Lithologic-unit samples can be stored in a freezer while a subsample is sent for analysis of percentage of organic carbon.

Analysis of organic carbon, to a reporting level of 0.01 percent is recommended (Powell et al. 1989). These analyses will be meaningful only if the sample has not been contaminated by drilling fluids. The sample will be chilled or frozen until analysis.

Soil pH is obtained by mixing 5 g of soil with 5 mL of distilled water for 10 minutes and measuring the pH. This measurement is important because the degradation of methyl *tert*-butyl ether (commonly detected in shallow ground-water in urban areas) and ethyl *tert*-butyl ether occurs only in soil with small organic matter content and with a pH of about 5.5 (Yeh & Novak, 1994).

It is strongly suggested that borehole-geophysical logging (such as gamma and electromagnetic logging) be performed on all monitoring wells. This information will improve understanding of the geology at the well site.

Other information, such as depth to the water table, depth of screen below land surface, estimated annual recharge, and presence of confining units also will be documented for each well. If available, a water-table map showing equal water-level contours will be provided in a GIS coverage for a 500-m radius around the well. A polygon coverage showing surficial geology, soil map, and bedrock geology will also be obtained.

4.5 Sample wells

Study Unit personnel will collect standard quality-assurance samples and standard ground-water quality samples. However, it is recommended that a total of six field-blank samples be collected (20 percent of the 30 ground-water samples collected in an Urban Land-Use Study). To quantify the type and potential magnitude of contamination bias, the six field-blank samples will be collected beginning with the 1st, then 6th, 12th, 18th, 24th, and 30th ground-water sample. To relate contamination bias to possible site conditions, the order of sampling sites will be arranged so that the field blanks are collected at diverse site conditions.

Chemical analyses include, but are not limited to, major ions, nutrients, pesticides, 87 volatile organic chemicals, and tritium. Sampling procedures have been described by Koterba et al. (1995).

4.6 Define age of water sampled

Water samples for age dating, based on concentrations of tritium, will be collected from all monitoring wells, but the samples will be stored until the concentrations of contaminants have been determined. This analysis will define the age of the water relative to 1953—that is, pre or post 1953. Tritium analyses will verify that the water is recently recharged water and not old water where one would not expect to find contamination. There are other methods of age dating that may be preferable, such as using concentrations of tritium/helium and Freon®, that have been recommended by Lapham et al. (1995). These other methods have the potential to date the water to a specific year.

4.7 Document land-use information around each well

Land-use information covering the Urban Land-Use Study area will be documented by creating GIS coverages from a variety of sources. Because the monitoring wells will not be spread across large areas, a single coverage will be applicable for all urban wells. Locations can be determined onsite using global positioning systems and aerial photography. The following coverages will be created:

Point coverage showing possible contaminant-release areas—for example, gas stations, dry cleaners, underground storage tanks, chemical plants, aboveground storage facilities.

Point coverage showing locations of known contaminant-release areas—for example, leaking underground storage tanks, waste-disposal ponds, landfills, oil wells, injection wells.

Line coverages of pipelines, roadways, topography, sewers, septic fields, hydrography (perennial and ephemeral streams, rivers, creeks, lined and unlined drainage ditches, ground-water drains, lined and unlined irrigation canals, natural and man-made lakes, lined and unlined reservoirs, bays or estuaries, springs, dry or wet playas).

Polygon coverages showing golf courses, lakes, airports, military bases, mines, and population density. Polygon coverage showing industrial, commercial, residential, and highway land-use areas around each monitoring well.

REFERENCES

Barringer, T., D. Dunn, W.A. Battaglin, & E.F. Vowinkel 1990. Problems and methods involved in relating land use to ground-water quality: *Water Resources Bulletin* 26 (1): 1-9.

Eckhardt, D.A.V. & P.E. Stackelberg 1995. Relation of ground-water quality to land use on Long Island, New York. *Ground Water* 33(6):1019-1033.

Gilliom, R.J., W.M. Alley & M.E. Gurtz 1995. *Design of the National Water-Quality Assessment Program--Occurrence and distribution of water-quality conditions.* U. S. Geological Survey Circular 1112.

Koterba, M.T., F.D. Wilde & W.W. Lapham 1995. *Ground-water data-collection protocols and procedures for the National Water-Quality Assessment Program--Collection and documentation of water-quality samples and data.* U.S. Geological Survey Open-File Report 95-399.

Lapham, W.W., F.D. Wilde & M.T. Koterba 1995. *Ground-water data-collection protocols and procedures for the National Water-Quality Assessment Program--Selection, installation, and documentation of wells, and collection of related data*: U.S. Geological Survey Open-File Report 95-398.

Powell, R.M., B.E. Bledsoe, G.P. Curtis & R.L. Johnson 1989. Interlaboratory methods comparison for the total organic carbon analysis of aquifer materials: *Environmental Science and Technology* 23 (10): 1246-1249.

Scott, J.C. 1990. *Computerized stratified random site-selection approaches for design of ground-water-quality sampling network*: U.S. Geological Survey Water-Resources Investigations Report 90-4101.

U.S. Bureau of the Census 1992. *Statistical abstract of the United States* (112th ed.). Washington, D.C.

Yeh, C.K. & J.T. Novak 1994. Anaerobic biodegradation of gasoline oxygenates in soils: *Water Environment Research* 66(5): 744-752.

A multi-functional surface water source control project: Groundwater implications

J.H.C.Thomas & V.K.Robinson
Environment Agency, Thames Region, Reading, UK

ABSTRACT: As a result of urbanisation, rainfall infiltration into soils is replaced by run-off from roofs and paving. 'Source control' encompasses a range of techniques designed to dispose of surface water from impermeable surfaces in a way which emulates natural processes as far as possible. Infiltration methods play a major role but it is important that these are only promoted in appropriate areas and a high standard of pollution prevention measures are incorporated to protect groundwater quality. Thames Region of the Environment Agency is promoting source control through a multi-functional task group which is developing maps to enable non-technical staff to make initial decisions on appropriate infiltration methods.

1 INTRODUCTION

'Surface water source control' is a methodology for controlling surface water run-off from the urban environment at its point of origin or source, such that the water is discharged gradually back into the receiving watercourse or aquifer in a manner which emulates natural processes. Methods of source control can be divided into two main categories: infiltration and retention systems. Infiltration includes a variety of techniques ranging from porous pavements to soakaways extending several metres below ground level.

The source control approach has a number of advantages: infiltration and groundwater recharge helps to maintain groundwater resources; rapid, high volume discharge into watercourses with resultant poor water quality is avoided; and a means of controlling flooding is provided.

However, there are potential areas of conflict between the different water-related functions of the Environment Agency in the promotion of source control and for this reason a multi-functional task group involving all the relevant skills has been set up within Thames Region of the Agency. The Agency was established in 1996, by the amalgamation of a number of existing statutory authorities, to cover a range of environmental responsibilities in England and Wales. The task group allows concerns to be discussed and the right balance of interests to be

achieved in the approach adopted. A significant area of concern is the potential conflict between promotion of infiltration and protection of groundwater quality. Since the quantity and quality aspects of water resources are inextricably linked, it is of paramount importance that groundwater quality is not compromised. A high standard of pollution prevention must be built into any source control technique which incorporates infiltration and natural attenuation is to be utilised to the full.

2 DRAINAGE DESIGN

Traditionally, the desire to avoid on-site flooding has led to design specifications requiring transfer of surface water as quickly as possible to a public sewer or watercourse. This is often the simplest and cheapest solution for developers, and avoids the risk of polluting groundwater. However, such discharge tends to overload the capacity of the receiving and downstream watercourses and prevents natural groundwater recharge. Where soakaways have been used there has been a desire to 'over-engineer' so that minimum maintenance is required. They have often penetrated permeable strata, frequently an aquifer, by several metres. As a result the Agency and its predecessors may have opposed their use or at least looked for a reduction in depth to protect groundwater quality. Discharge to the soil zone was rarely considered even though this is the natural route taken by rainfall.

Consequently, infiltration into the ground leading to slow seepage into watercourses via the soil zone and recharge of aquifers has been severely reduced in urban areas where paving and roofs predominate.

2.1 *Future policy*

Strategic guidance is seeking to limit future run-off to that which occurs from the pre-development green-field site, provided this can be done without risk to groundwater quality. A surface water control policy is required to sustain natural run-off processes within catchments. However, these need to be considered against cost to the developer and the best practicable environmental option sought. The policy needs to be consistently applied and promoted in collaboration with local authorities and the private water utilities.

Developers have been reluctant to use source control techniques for the following reasons:

(a) lack of strategic and technical guidance;
(b) unknown costs, particularly maintenance;
(c) land-take required;
(d) problems of adoption.

2.2 *Source control guidance*

With respect to (a) above, a great deal of guidance has been produced in recent years by, for example, the Construction Industry Research and Information Association (CIRIA 1994); the Standing Conference on Source Control chaired by Chris Pratt; Scottish Environment Protection Agency (1996); and Pratt (1995, 1996). However the importance of protecting groundwater quality is sometimes given low priority; it is important not to solve one set of problems but create another by inappropriate discharges to ground.

3 IMPACT ON GROUNDWATER

Groundwater forms an invaluable resource within the UK. It forms 35% (over 40% in Thames Region) of total supply of which 75% is abstracted for public supply. In addition, groundwater makes a major contribution to the flow in rivers, providing a stable base-flow of high quality water. This is particularly important in the case of Chalk streams which are largely groundwater-fed especially during the summer months.

A large proportion, about 70%, of the Thames catchment comprises aquifer outcrop and therefore is both vulnerable to pollution and, under natural conditions, receives recharge from infiltration.

3.1 *Attenuation*

Susceptibility of groundwater to pollution is dependent upon the hydrogeology and soil conditions. The soil zone can provide a high degree of attenuation as a result of physical, biological and chemical processes, for example, most pesticides are designed to be retained and broken down within the soil layer. The depth of the unsaturated zone can be crucial in further attenuating pollutants and by acting as a delay mechanism.

A conventional soakaway penetrating the aquifer by-passes or prevents many of the important attenuating processes and this effect is even more pronounced in the case of deep borehole soakaways (Thomas 1995). The loss of the upper part of the unsaturated zone is particularly important in a relatively soluble calcium carbonate, fissured aquifer such as the Chalk since permeability often increases in the zone of current or historic water-table fluctuation.

The discharge rate to the aquifer from a few soakaways will be high compared with natural infiltration and the effect of this in fissured aquifers must not be underestimated. Once infiltration exceeds the hydraulic conductivity of the matrix, within a Chalk aquifer, flow will occur directly down the fissures (Price 1987). It may therefore be appropriate to design infiltration systems which maintain flow rates below a critical level in sensitive fissured aquifer areas.

For essentially non-degradable, persistent pollutants, any delay in contaminants reaching the water table will not improve attenuation but will provide a greater opportunity for intervention and removal of the pollutant. If pollutants do enter strata via a deep soakaway, direct remedial action to prevent impact on groundwater is virtually impossible. In the case of a shallow soakaway it is feasible to excavate out the soakaway and the surrounding contaminated strata.

3.2 *Pollution*

Examples of groundwater pollution which can be attributed to soakaways are rare, possibly as a result of few investigations. However, there are many cases of historic contamination of soakaways in the Chalk where oily residues have been found on

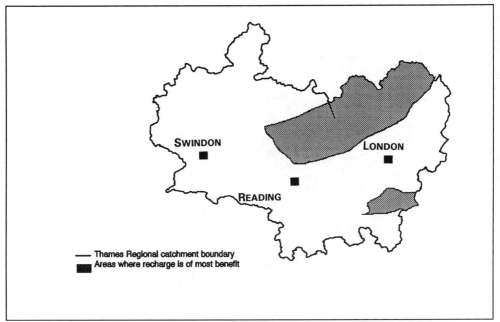

Figure 1. Areas where recharge is of most benefit to water resources.

excavation. Also, low level groundwater contamination with herbicides used for non-agricultural purposes, such as atrazine, is widespread and it is likely that a proportion has reached the groundwater, for example, via highway soakaways. Monitoring of discharges to soakaway along the M4 motorway following application of pesticides has identified significant concentrations of diuron. This pesticide has not been detected in the limited number of groundwater monitoring points in the vicinity although diuron contamination is known to be widespread, having been found in almost 20% of all Agency groundwater samples analysed for the herbicide in Thames Region.

Many cases of contaminated groundwater beneath major conurbations have come to light, and the study described by Tellam (1995) is typical. This, together with other work, indicates that virtually all heavy industrial sites pollute. Whilst the precise mechanisms are not always known, it is likely that at least a proportion of the pollutants have been transmitted via soakaways.

Policy Statement F of the Policy and Practice for the Protection of Groundwater (PPPG) (National Rivers Authority 1992) adopted by the Agency deals with discharges of surface water to soakaway in relation to both groundwater resource and abstraction or 'groundwater protection zones' (GPZs). Resource protection is based on aquifer vulnerability,

additional protection is required for abstractions used for human consumption. GPZ (Inner) is the estimated area within 50 day's travel time of the supply, based on saturated zone flow rates. GPZ (Outer) extends to the similarly modelled 400-day travel time boundary.

3.3 *Recharge considerations*

Soakaways generally provide groundwater recharge but the greatest attention to their acceptability, on quality grounds, should be focused on areas where recharge is most beneficial. These are identified as the major Chalk areas in the higher parts of the Thames catchment. In particular, the unconfined Chalk of the Chilterns and Colne Valley, parts of the upper Lee catchment and the North Downs between Leatherhead and Croydon (Figure 1). These areas are generally the most intensively abstracted for public water supply. In lower-lying areas the benefit is minimal since additional groundwater will generally discharge to a nearby river.

Deeper soakaways can have a deleterious effect on quantity when compared with natural surface infiltration. By-passing the soil zone may cause near-surface drought conditions leading to loss of trees and other vegetation. Also, artificially rapid movement to the water-table may induce losses from the aquifer by altering the natural seasonal regime.

SOURCE CONTROL - DISCHARGE MATRIX

Discharge of surface water from:	Discharge to ground						Discharge to watercourse
	Inside Groundwater Protection Zone			Other areas of aquifer outcrop		Non-aquifer	
	Inner Zone	Outer Zone		Shallow water table	Deep water table	Impermeable strata	
		Shallow water table	Deep water table				
Roof drainage							
Public amenity area							Interceptor required
Large car park		Interceptor required	Interceptor required	Interceptor likely	Interceptor likely	Interceptor likely	Interceptor required
Small car park							Interceptor required
Lorry park				Interceptor required	Interceptor required	Interceptor required	Interceptor required
Garage forecourt				Interceptor required	Interceptor required	Interceptor required	Interceptor required
Major road				Interceptor required	Interceptor required	Interceptor required	Interceptor required
Industrial site				Interceptor required	Interceptor required	Interceptor required	Interceptor required
Surface Water Sewer						Interceptor required	

Option	Description
1	No discharge to ground, by soakaway or seepage. Surface water disposal by other means.
2	Discharge to lined swales/ponds with either overflow to separate soakaway or surface water infiltration through vegetation, or surface water disposal by other means.
3	Discharge to conventional shallow soakaway or as in option 2.
4	Discharge to borehole soakaway or as in option 2 or 3.

Figure 2. Source control - discharge matrix

Deep soakaways encourage run-off to reach the water table more rapidly, leading to high groundwater levels in winter instead of more beneficially, at the start of the summer. Essentially deep soakaways lead to a "flashy" response in the same way as poorly designed discharges to watercourses. Shallow infiltration imitating the natural condition as closely as possible avoids this problem and can be regarded as a more sustainable approach.

4 SOURCE CONTROL TASK GROUP, ENVIRONMENT AGENCY, THAMES REGION

As a result of the findings and recommendations produced by the research and development initiatives referred to in section 2.2, a multi-functional group has been formed in Thames Region of the Environment Agency to review the subject and promote best working practices. Policies and design standards for the control of surface water run-off are required that meet the potentially conflicting requirements of the various internal departments.

This paper highlights the work carried out to ensure that groundwater is protected. The overall aim is to promote shallow infiltration methods in preference to conventional deeper soakaways as this approach is the most acceptable to all functions. A methodology based on decisions made in conjunction with simplified hydrogeological maps is currently being tested within the Region. It is designed to enable non-specialists to make initial assessments of the suitability of infiltration for a given development proposal in clear-cut cases. This releases groundwater specialists' time to carry out tasks which require greater technical expertise. Also, at present, many developments proceed without the views of the Agency being sought. If the Agency is to promote source control, it is essential that there is close dialogue with developers and others to ensure that groundwater is protected with respect to specific site proposals and through strategic planning documents.

4.1 Source control trial maps

The maps are used with an acceptability matrix which accords with the PPPG, providing a first 'filter' to enable early pro-active dialogue with developers (Figure 2).

A hierarchy of types of infiltration/soakaway system is summarised on the acceptability matrix as Options 2 to 4. Methods of shallow infiltration are at the top of the hierarchy, ie. the most favoured.

The hierarchy has a cut-off point below which design-types are unacceptable, this point is dependent upon sensitivity of groundwater at the given location and may mean that infiltration is unacceptable. Some of the techniques are innovative and little is known about their effectiveness under conditions in the UK. Further research is required; a current example within the Region is flow and quality monitoring of water after passage through a porous pavement.

The infiltration capacity of the soil zone above impermeable strata should also not be overlooked.

Use of the maps is designed to assist in a consistent, defensible risk assessment approach throughout the Region contributing to the information available to planners to make decisions on the most suitable method of source control for proposed developments. The maps are to be used in conjunction with consideration of other methods of source control (storage, balancing etc.) and the sensitivity of the area to discharges direct to river. Groundwater quality specialists still need to provide advice on anything other than straightforward proposals.

4.2 Map content

The maps contain the following hydrogeological information.

(i) A simple sub-division into aquifer and non-aquifer is taken from the Environment Agency's Groundwater Vulnerability Maps (1:100,000 scale). Soil leachability classes from the Vulnerability Maps are not included since even with shallow infiltration systems such as permeable pavements or swales, the natural soil profile will have been disturbed or removed.

(ii) Unsaturated zone thickness, sub-divided into shallow and deep water table. A fairly arbitrary 8m thickness forms the boundary between the two classes. Groundwater levels are not routinely monitored in minor aquifers therefore, as an important simplification, minor aquifer areas have been shown as shallow water table on the more recently constructed maps. Opportunities for soakaway are more restricted in shallow water table areas for the twin reasons that groundwater is more vulnerable to pollution and the benefits of infiltration as aquifer recharge are limited.

(iii) Major aquifer groundwater level contours are shown, mainly to provide an indication of groundwater flow direction.

(iv) Public water supply abstraction points and their GPZs are shown. Only the Outer Zones, are delineated on the maps. The maps are intentionally at a small scale so that a false accuracy is not assumed by users and it was felt that the Inner Zone boundary is too critical to be read off the maps. However a means of estimating a highly conservative Inner Zone is provided. If a site is within this conservative zone, groundwater specialists are required to advise.

The maps are printed on an Ordnance Survey topographical base map to assist in location of points on the map. Since the river system forms an integral part of source control, it is included in the overlaid information to give it greater prominence.

Maps are currently only in draft form and it is anticipated that they will be refined following the trial period. Emphasis has been placed on the production of good digital information which can be combined in a variety of ways to provide the most useful working maps for surface water drainage decisions and other purposes within the Agency. The widespread use of geographical information systems (GIS) throughout the Agency will enhance the benefit and flexibility of the methodology.

SUMMARY

As a contribution towards achieving sustainable development, the Environment Agency wishes to promote strategies and procedures which will encourage and facilitate source control techniques. One of the aims of the Thames Region task group is to ensure that groundwater issues are given full consideration. Shallow infiltration methods provide the best opportunity for satisfying conflicting requirements. These methods are being promoted through a hierarchical system which allows for a flexible, non-prescriptive approach based on the principles of risk assessment to ensure groundwater is given adequate protection.

REFERENCES

Construction Industry Research and Information Association. 1994. Control of pollution from highway drainage discharges. Report 142, CIRIA. London.

Environment Agency. Groundwater vulnerability maps, 1:100,000 scale. The Stationary Office. London.

National Rivers Authority 1992 Policy and practice for the protection of groundwater. National Rivers Authority, Bristol.

Pratt, C.J. 1995. A review of source control of

urban stormwater runoff. J. CIWEM, 9 132-139.

Pratt, C.J. 1996. Research and development in methods of soakaway design. J. CIWEM, 10 47-51.

Price, M. 1987. Fluid flow in the Chalk of England: In: Goff, J.C. & B.P.J. Williams (eds.) *Fluid Flow in Sedimentary Basins and Aquifers.* Geological Society, London, Special Publication, 34, 141-156.

Thomas, J. 1995. The use and design of deep soakaways - An NRA groundwater quality view. *Proceedings of the Standing Conference on Stormwater Source Control.* Coventry University. Quantity and Quality Vol XI.

Tellam, J.H. 1995 Urban Groundwater Pollution in the Birmingham Triassic Sandstone Aquifer. *Fourth Annual Conference on Groundwater Pollution.* IBC Technical Services Ltd.

Scottish Environment Protection Agency. 1996. Protecting the Quality of Scotland's Environment. A guide to Surface Water Best Management Practices.

ACKNOWLEDGEMENTS

The authors wish to thank the Environment Agency for permission to publish this paper. The views expressed are those of the authors and not necessarily those of the Agency.

Groundwater in the Urban Environment: Problems, Processes and Management, Chilton et al. (eds)
© *1997 Balkema, Rotterdam, ISBN 90 5410 837 1*

Albuquerque, New Mexico, USA: A sunbelt city rapidly outgrowing its aquifer

H.J.Turin – *Los Alamos National Laboratory, N.Mex., USA*

A.N.Gaume – *New Mexico Interstate Stream Commission, Santa Fe, N.Mex., USA*

M.J.Bitner – *CH2M Hill, Albuquerque, N.Mex., USA*

H.S.Hansen – *US Bureau of Reclamation, Albuquerque, N.Mex., USA*

F.B.Titus – *New Mexico State Engineer Office, Albuquerque, N.Mex., USA*

ABSTRACT: The Albuquerque metropolitan area is part of the rapidly growing "sunbelt" region of the southwestern United States and is undergoing rapid development. The municipal, industrial, and residential water needs of the entire population are currently met by groundwater, while agricultural needs within the basin are met by surface water diverted from the Rio Grande. While the city is blessed with an extremely productive aquifer, current metropolitan area groundwater extractions far exceed the sustainable yield of the aquifer. Continued drawdown will lead to greater pumping costs, ground subsidence, and eventual aquifer depletion. At the same time, industrial and non-point-source contamination and naturally occurring arsenic levels are raising concerns about groundwater quality. The City, in cooperation with local, state, and federal agencies, has explored a variety of conjunctive use proposals, all designed to permit the City to use its surface water more directly.

1 INTRODUCTION

Albuquerque was founded in 1706 along the Rio Grande in the Spanish province of New Mexico (Fig. 1). The city was part of the newly independent nation of Mexico from 1821 until 1848, when New Mexico was ceded to the United States as a result of the Mexican-American war. Albuquerque's emergence as a major city began with the arrival of the railroad in 1880. The town's population grew from 1,300 in 1880 to 12,000 by 1892 (Summers 1995). Steady growth continued into the 20th century, with the city population reaching 35,000 by 1940. World War II and the Cold War brought new federal installations (including an air force base and a nuclear weapons laboratory) to Albuquerque, and settlers began flocking to the area, both for the employment opportunities and for the increasingly well-publicized quality of life. Dramatic population growth since the 1940s continues today; the 1990 city population stood at 385,000, while the Albuquerque metropolitan area was home to 480,000 people, almost one third of the entire New Mexico state population. As Fig. 2 shows, this population growth is expected to continue well into the next century (Gregory 1996).

2 HYDROGEOLOGIC SETTING

The city is located in the middle Rio Grande Basin at an elevation of 1580 m, and extends from west of the river east to the Sandia Mountains. The basin, part of the Rio Grande Rift, is a major structural basin that has been subsiding and filling with sediments for about 30 million years (Thorn et al. 1993). These sediments, including both fluvial deposits laid down by the ancestral Rio Grande and locally derived material from the Sandia Mountains, comprise the Santa Fe Group, which today forms the aquifer supplying the entire metropolitan area. This is a highly productive aquifer, especially below the city where transmissivities as high as 7,400 m²/day have

Figure 1. Location of Albuquerque and the Rio Grande.

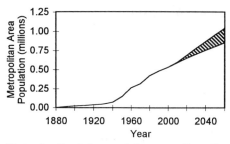

Figure 2. Population trend for metropolitan Albuquerque (CH2M HILL 1995; Summers 1995; Gregory 1996). Hatched area shows range in projections.

been measured (Thorn et al. 1993), and individual wells pump as much as 200 L/s. This world-class aquifer occurs in an arid region with an average annual precipitation of only 200 to 250 mm, with higher values in the adjacent mountains. The aquifer is recharged by the main-stem Rio Grande, which carries snowmelt from high mountains in southern Colorado and northern New Mexico, and local tributaries draining nearby ranges. Since 1972, an average of 1.2×10^8 m³/year of water has been imported to the basin through the San Juan - Chama project, a Bureau of Reclamation project that diverts water from streams feeding the San Juan River, a tributary of the Colorado River, into the Rio Chama, a tributary of the Rio Grande (Shupe & Folk-Williams 1988).

3 ALBUQUERQUE'S WATER SUPPLY

The first irrigators in the area were Pueblo people, who probably arrived sometime after the year 1100. Elaborate irrigation systems consisting of canals and acequias flourished during the Spanish period, and by 1880 over 50,000 ha were under irrigation (Thorn et al. 1993). Shallow wells met most of the growing city's municipal and industrial needs until the late 1940s, when an integrated system of large deep water-supply wells was developed (Summers 1995). Based on the contemporary hydrogeologic understanding and the pro-growth economic climate of the time, the aquifer was widely believed to be practically inexhaustible. In particular, it was believed that the Rio Grande was well-connected to the aquifer and recharge from the river rapidly replaced groundwater pumped from the aquifer. Through the 1970s, the aquifer system was being described as comparable to Lake Michigan in volume and capable of supporting a population of 1½ million (Reynolds 1980; Grant 1995).

In the mid-1980s, a number of disturbing developments began to cast doubt on this comfortable illusion. Heavy pumping caused some wells to experience unexpectedly large declines in water level, and

new wells drilled on the west side of the city did not encounter the expected highly productive zones. Under most of the city, present-day aquifer drawdown exceeds 30 m (Fig. 3); a drawdown of approximately 80 m is predicted to cause the widespread onset of irreversible surface subsidence. At the same time, a number of productive wells along the river have been removed from service due to industrial contamination and two wells have been shut down due to naturally occurring arsenic in excess of the current Environmental Protection Agency (EPA) standard of 50 ppb. The EPA is considering decreasing the arsenic standard to a range of 2 to 20 ppb; meeting a 5 ppb standard would require treatment of most of the City's groundwater at an estimated capital cost of $300 to $370 million (CH2M HILL 1995).

In response to these warning signs, the City of Albuquerque, in collaboration with private consulting firms and State and Federal agencies, began a major investigation of the geologic and hydrologic characteristics of the aquifer system. The two major findings to date are that the high-quality aquifer is far less extensive and the Rio Grande/aquifer connection is much weaker than previously thought. A three-dimensional numerical model (Kernodle et al. 1995) has demonstrated that if current trends in population and pumping rates continue, aquifer drawdown will accelerate, resulting in rapid aquifer depletion, increased pumping costs, major problems with ground subsidence, and increased water-quality problems as deeper, arsenic-rich water is drawn into wells. Fig. 3 shows that if current trends continue, large areas of the city will experience drawdown in excess of 80 m by the year 2060. Inaction will inevitably bring a major water resource crisis, but because of its existing unused surface-water resources, the City has a unique opportunity to address these issues. To understand the City's options, a brief introduction into the legal and regulatory structures built around water in the western states of the U.S. is required.

4 WATER LAW AND REGULATORY CONTEXT

Water resources in the western United States are subject to strict and sometimes conflicting regulatory controls at both the Federal and State level. The Federal government has jurisdiction over international and interstate affairs. On the Rio Grande, foremost is a 1906 treaty between the United States and Mexico, guaranteeing a certain amount of Rio Grande water to Mexico. In 1939, the U.S. Congress and President Franklin Roosevelt approved the Rio Grande Compact, allocating the river's water between the states of Colorado, New Mexico, and Texas (Shupe & Folk-Williams 1988). These two historic Federal regulations restricting use of the Rio Grande have

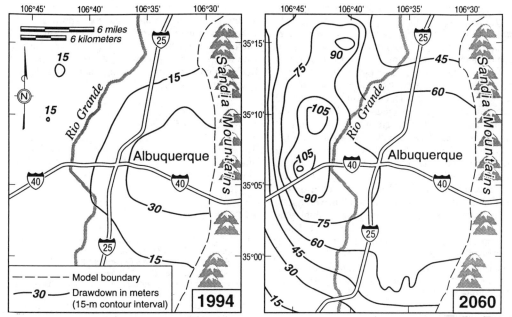

Figure 3. Simulated 1994 and predicted 2060 aquifer drawdown (m) beneath Albuquerque (CH2M HILL 1995; Kernodle et al. 1995). 2060 prediction assumes present population and water use trends continue.

been joined by a third, the Endangered Species Act. This Federal legislation prohibits any action that harms or disturbs an endangered species or reduces or destroys habitat. The U.S. Fish and Wildlife Service declared the Rio Grande Silvery Minnow an endangered species in 1993, and added the Southwestern Willow Flycatcher to the list in 1995. Much of the Rio Grande through central New Mexico may be declared critical habitat for these species. The full implications of this action are not yet clear but it is apparent that all future decisions pertaining to Rio Grande water resources will need to consider possible impacts on these species and their habitats.

Within the constraints of Federal regulation, the states are free to establish their own water laws. New Mexico's water law is based on the Doctrine of Prior Appropriation. Under this system, the right to use surface water is considered property, which can be bought and sold and transferred from one piece of land to another, regardless of proximity to a stream. Originally, a water right could be claimed by simply diverting water from a stream and putting it to beneficial use. By the early 1900s, the Rio Grande became "fully appropriated," with no unclaimed water available.

A consequence of the prior appropriation doctrine is that a water right does not guarantee actual delivery of water. The date of the original water claim is critical, because it is this appropriation date that determines the seniority of a water right. In the event of a water shortage, senior water rights have priority over junior water rights, and junior right owners may run dry.

This system was originally applied to surface water. Its extension to groundwater is based upon the concept of "keeping the river whole." Because most rivers in the state are fully appropriated and groundwater pumping will eventually decrease stream flow, that pumping will adversely affect older, senior water rights holders. Therefore, the groundwater developer must acquire sufficient surface water rights to offset the anticipated impacts of pumpage. The State Engineer has traditionally determined the necessary surface water rights using the Glover-Balmer equation (Glover & Balmer 1954).

Based on these calculations, the City of Albuquerque has acquired about 8.6×10^7 m³/yr of Rio Grande surface water, including both purchased rights and an allocation of 5.9×10^7 m³/yr of San Juan - Chama water. If the aquifer/river system behaved in accordance with the Glover-Balmer equation, this surface water combined with 7.4×10^7 m³/yr of reclaimed wastewater discharged to the river would recharge the aquifer, completely compensate for the City's current groundwater pumpage of 1.5×10^8 m³/yr, and maintain stable groundwater levels. This was a beautifully simple solution to Albuquerque's water supply: the aquifer would supply the City, the river would resupply the aquifer, and the City's purchased water rights would resupply the river. Unfortunately, it was based on an imperfect understanding of the aquifer/river system.

Since groundwater levels beneath Albuquerque are falling more rapidly than expected, something is clearly wrong. The problem lies with the Glover-Balmer equation. This method is based on an analytical approach involving numerous simplifying assumptions, including a homogeneous, isotropic, semi-infinite aquifer, a fully-penetrating stream and well, and perfect hydraulic connection between the stream and aquifer (Sophocleous et al. 1995). These assumptions all tend to overestimate the effect of pumping on streamflow, which, from a surface water rights point of view, is a conservative error that provides an·additional margin of protection to the water rights holder. However, it also greatly overestimates recharge to the aquifer. Recent three-dimensional numerical modeling of the aquifer/river system which eliminates many of these simplifying assumptions confirms that less than half of the City's pumping is being replaced by recharge. So, rather than resupplying the aquifer, the City's Rio Grande water is simply flowing downstream or being stored in upstream reservoirs for future use. Here lies Albuquerque's hope for the future.

5 FUTURE PLANS - A SOLUTION IN SIGHT

Based on the findings and recommendations of recent interagency water resource investigations, the City has proposed an ambitious new approach to water resources development and management (City of Albuquerque 1997; Hansen & Gorbach 1997). The strategy is based on conjunctive use of surface water, groundwater, and impaired-quality waters to better distribute demand across a broader range of available supplies. Key provisions include:

• Direct use of surface water. This will require construction of infiltration galleries along the Rio Grande, a water treatment plant, and transmission pipelines.

• Establishment of a groundwater reserve for drought years. This will involve both active and passive groundwater recharge projects using surface water supplies.

• Appropriate use of a combination of reclaimed (recycled) water, surface water, shallow groundwater, and deep groundwater, in which the various qualities of water available are matched with the needs of different users. For example, lower-quality waters could be used for irrigation and some industrial supplies, while high-quality water from the deep aquifer should be reserved where possible for domestic use. This will require additional water recycling facilities and new transmission pipelines for recycled water.

• Continued emphasis on water conservation, with the ultimate goal of reducing gross community water use by 30% from the current 950 liters per capita per day to 660 liters per capita per day.

Most of these measures are expensive, and all require public support and regulatory approval. The City is committed to a major public involvement and public education program, and is working closely with the State Engineer Office, the federal Bureau of Reclamation, and other local, state, and federal agencies to make this plan a reality.

ACKNOWLEDGMENT

The senior author's work was funded by the Science and Technology Base Program Office, Los Alamos National Laboratory.

REFERENCES

CH2M HILL 1995. *Albuquerque water resources management strategy, San Juan-Chama diversion project options.* City of Albuquerque Public Works Department Report.

City of Albuquerque 1997. *Water resources management strategy.* City of Albuquerque Public Works Department Report.

Glover, R.E. & G.G. Balmer 1954. River depletion resulting from pumping a well near a river. *Trans. Am. Geophys. Union* 35(3), 468-470.

Grant, P.R., Jr. 1995. Albuquerque's water -- gripping reality. In *The water future of Albuquerque and Middle Rio Grande Basin:* 59-60. New Mexico Water Resources Research Institute Report 290.

Gregory, J. 1996. Environmental topic: population growth. In H. Rosner & J. Rosner (eds), *Albuquerque's environmental story: toward a sustainable community.* Albuquerque, NM: Albuquerque Conservation Association.

Hansen, H.S. & C.A. Gorbach 1997. *Middle Rio Grande water assessment.* U.S. Bureau of Reclamation General Investigations Program Report.

Kernodle, J.M., D.P. McAda & C.R. Thorn 1995. *Simulation of ground-water flow in the Albuquerque Basin, central New Mexico, 1901-1994, with projections to 2020.* U.S. Geological Survey Water-Resources Investigations Report 94-4251.

Reynolds, S.E. 1980. Albuquerque's water supply probably best in Southwest. *Albuquerque Tribune.* Sept. 11, p. A-5.

Shupe, S.J. & J. Folk-Williams 1988. *The Upper Rio Grande: a guide to decision-making.* Santa Fe, NM: Western Network.

Sophocleous, M., A. Koussis, J.L. Martin & S.P. Perkins 1995. Evaluation of simplified stream aquifer depletion models for water rights administration. *Ground Water* 33(4), 579-588.

Summers, W.K. 1995. *Land-use trends and their effect on water use and the hydrologic budget in the Albuquerque Basin, New Mexico.* Ground-Water Science, Inc. Report.

Thorn, C.R., D.P. McAda & J.M. Kernodle 1993. *Geohydrologic framework and hydrologic conditions in the Albuquerque Basin, central New Mexico.* U.S. Geological Survey Water-Resources Investigations Report 93-4149.

Author index